A Dictionary of American Idioms

Second Edition
Revised and thoroughly updated by
ADAM MAKKAI, Ph.D.
Professor of Linguistics
University of Illinois at Chicago

Based on the earlier edition by
M. T. Boatner, J. E. Gates, and Adam Makkai

BARRON'S
New York • London • Toronto • Sydney

All inquiries should be addressed to:
Barron's Educational Series, Inc.
250 Wireless Boulevard
Hauppauge, NY 11788

International Standard Book No. 0-8120-3899-1

Library of Congress Catalog Card No. 84-9247

Library of Congress Cataloging-in-Publication Data

Main entry under title:

A Dictionary of American idioms.

   1. English language—United States—Dictionaries.
2. Americanisms—Dictionaries.   3. English language—
Terms and phrases—Dictionaries.   I. Makkai, Adam.
PE2839.D5   1987   423'.1   84-9247
ISBN 0-8120-3899-1

PRINTED IN THE UNITED STATES OF AMERICA

123   410   987

Contents

Acknowledgments

This dictionary is the result of the work of many hands. It was first published in 1966 in West Hartford, Connecticut, and later republished in 1969, copyrighted by the American School of the Deaf under the title *A Dictionary of Idioms for the Deaf,* edited by Maxine Tull Boatner, project director, aided by chief linguistic advisor, J. Edward Gates. The consulting committee consisted of Dr. Edmund E. Boatner, Dr. William J. McClure, Dr. Clarence D. O'Connor, Dr. George T. Pratt, Jack Brady, M.A., Richard K. Lane, and Professor H. A. Gleason, Jr., of the Hartford Seminary Foundation. Special editors for various subcategories, such as usage, sport terms, etc., were Elizabeth Meltzer, and E. Ward Gilman; Loy E. Golladay helped as language consultant with reviewing and editing. Definers were Edmund Casetti, Philip H. Cummings, Anne M. Driscoll, Harold J. Flavin, Dr. Frank Fletcher, E. Ward Gilman, Loy E. Golladay, Dr. Philip H. Goepp, Dr. Beatrice Hart, Dr. Benjamin Keen, Kendall Litchfield, Harold E. Niergarth, Ruth Gill Price, Thomas H. B. Robertson, Jess Smith, Rhea Talley Stewart, Harriet Smith, Elizabeth D. Spellman, John F. Spellman, and George M. Swanson, Barbara Ann Kipfer, and Justyn Moulds. The following have cooperated as simplifiers: Linda Braun, Dr. G. C. Farquhar, Carey S. Lane, Wesley Lauritsen, Nellie MacDonald, Ruth S. McQueen, and Donald Moores. In 1975 an edition was prepared for Barron's Educational Series, by the well-known expert on idioms Professor Adam Makkai of the University of Illinois at Chicago Circle.

For this new edition, Professor Makkai has deleted obsolete material, updated old entries, and added hundreds of modern idiomatic phrases to the collection. Many of these new entries are of the slang character, originating within recent cultural movements; others reflect the popular usage of specialized areas of endeavor, including computer technology. Professor Robert A. Hall, Jr. of Cornell reviewed the manuscript of the revision and made invaluable suggestions.

Preface to the Second Edition

Idioms are the lifeblood of evolving, changing languages indicating that the society using them is a dynamic one. The present *Dictionary of American Idioms* is in its 17th printing since it first was published by Barron's Educational Series in 1975. The demand for it, both in the United States and abroad, has been so great that it has been translated into Japanese and Chinese. Many other translations are currently in preparation. We have, therefore, decided to update it in keeping with the usage of the late seventies and eighties.

As a result, several dozen expressions no longer in popular use were dropped, and many new ones have been added to the main body of this dictionary. These include citizen's band radio jargon, drug culture expressions that have found their way into general usage, hippie slang, and other current phrases not found in dictionaries a decade ago, e.g., *that's a ten-four, good buddy, Joe's all strung out,* and *this is the pits*.

We encourage our readers to send their remarks and observations to the Update Editor, care of Barron's Educational Series, Inc.

Adam Makkai
September, 1987

Introduction

WHAT IS AN IDIOM?

If you understand every word in a text and still fail to grasp what the text is all about, chances are you are having trouble with the idioms. For example, suppose you read (or hear) the following:

Sam is a real cool cat. He never blows his stack and hardly ever flies off the handle. What's more, he knows how to get away with things . . . Well, of course, he is getting on, too. His hair is pepper and salt, but he knows how to make up for lost time by taking it easy. He gets up early, works out, and turns in early. He takes care of the hot dog stand like a breeze until he gets time off. Sam's got it made; this is it for him.

Needless to say, this is not great literary style, but most Americans, especially when they converse among themselves, will use expressions of this sort. Now if you are a foreigner in this country and have learned the words *cool* 'not very warm,' *cat* 'the familiar domestic animal,' *blow* 'exhale air with force,' *stack* 'a pile of something, or material heaped up,' *fly* 'propel oneself in the air by means of wings,' *handle* 'the part of an object designed to hold by hand'—and so forth, you will still not understand the above sample of conversational American English, because this basic dictionary information alone will not give you the meaning of the forms involved. An idiom—as it follows from these observations—is the assigning of a new meaning to a group of words which already have their own meaning. Below you will find a 'translation' of this highly idiomatic, colloquial American English text, into a more formal, and relatively idiom free variety of English:

Sam is really a calm person. He never loses control of himself and hardly ever becomes too angry. Furthermore, he knows how to manage his business financially by using a few tricks . . . Needless to say, he, too, is getting older. His hair is beginning to turn gray, but he knows how to compensate for wasted time by relaxing. He rises early, exercises, and goes to bed early. He manages his frankfurter stand without visible effort, until it is someone else's turn to work there. Sam is successful; he has reached his life's goal.

Now if you were to explain how the units are organized in this text, you would have to make a little idiom dictionary. It would look like this:

to be a (real) cool cat	to be a really calm person
to blow one's stack	to lose control over oneself, to become mad
to fly off the handle	to become excessively angry
what's more	furthermore, besides, additionally
to get away with something	to perpetrate an illegitimate or tricky act without repercussion or harm
of course	naturally
to be getting on	to age, to get older
pepper and salt	black or dark hair mixed with streaks of gray
to make up for something	to compensate for something
lost time	times wasted, time spent at fruitless labor
to take it easy	to relax, to rest, not to worry
to get up	to rise from bed in the morning or at other times
to work out	to exercise, to do gymnastics
to turn in	to go to bed at night
like a breeze	without effort, elegantly, easily
time off	period in one's job or place of employment during which one is not performing one's services
to have got it made	to be successful, to have arrived
this is it	to be in a position or in a place, or to have possession of an object, beyond which more of the same is unnecessary

Many of the idioms in this little sample list can be found in this dictionary itself. The interesting fact about most of these idioms is that they can easily be identified with the familiar parts of speech. Thus some idioms are clearly verbal in nature, such as *get away with, get up, work out,* and *turn in.* An equally large number are nominal in nature. Thus *hot dog* and *cool cat* are nouns. Many are adjectives, as in our example *pepper and salt* meaning 'black hair mixed with gray.' Many are adverbial, as the examples *like the breeze* 'easily, without effort,' *hammer and tongs* 'violently' (as in *she ran after him hammer and tongs*), and so forth.

These idioms which correlate with the familiar parts of speech can be called *lexemic idioms*.

The other most important group of idioms are of larger size. Often they are an entire clause in length, as our examples *to fly off the handle*, 'lose control over oneself,' and *to blow one's stack*, 'to become very angry.' There are a great many of these in American English. Some of the most famous ones are: *to kick the bucket* 'die,' *to be up the creek* 'to be in a predicament or a dangerous position,' *to be caught between the devil and deep blue sea* 'to have to choose between two equally unpleasant alternatives,' *to seize the bull by the horns* 'to face a problem and deal with it squarely,' and so on. Idioms of this sort have been called *tournures* (from the French), meaning 'turns of phrase,' or simply *phraseological idioms*. What they have in common is that they do not readily correlate with a given grammatical part of speech and require a paraphrase longer than a word.

Their form is set and only a limited number of them can be said or written in any other way without destroying the meaning of the idiom. Many of them are completely rigid and cannot show up in any other form whatever. Consider the idiom *kick the bucket*, for example. In the passive voice, you get an unacceptable form such as *the bucket has been kicked by the cowboy*, which no longer means that the 'cowboy died.' Rather it means that he struck a pail with his foot. Idioms of this type are regarded as *completely frozen forms*. Notice, however, that even this idiom can be inflected for tense, e.g., it is all right to say *the cowboy kicked the bucket, the cowboy will kick the bucket, he has kicked the bucket*, etc. Speakers disagree as much as do grammarians whether or not, for example, it is all right to use this idiom in the gerund form (a gerund being a noun derived from a verb by adding -*ing* to it, e.g., *singing* from *sing*, *eating* from *eat*, etc.) in *His kicking the bucket surprised us all*. It is best to avoid this form.

The next largest class of idioms is that of well established sayings and proverbs. These include the famous types of *don't count your chickens before they're hatched* (meaning 'do not celebrate the outcome of an undertaking prematurely because it is possible that you will fail in which case you will look ridiculous'); *don't wash your dirty linen in public* (meaning 'do not complain of your domestic affairs before strangers as it is none of their business'), and so forth. Many of these originate from some well known literary source or come to us from the earliest English speakers of the North American Continent.

Lack of predictability of meaning (or precise meaning) is not the only criterion of idiomaticity. Set phrases or phraseological units are also idiomatic, even though their meanings may be transparent. What is idiomatic (unpredictable) about them is their construction. Examples include *How about a drink? What do you say, Joe?* (as a greeting); *as a matter of fact, just in case; just to be on the safe side*, and many more.

Another important case of idiomaticity is the one-word idiom that occurs when a word is used in a surprisingly different meaning from the original one. Examples include *lemon*, said of bad watches, cars, or machines; and *dog*, said of a bad date or a bad exam. (*My car is a lemon; my math exam was a dog.*)

Why is English, and especially American English, so heavily idiomatic? The most probable reason is that as we develop new concepts, we need new expressions for them, but instead of creating a brand new word from the sounds of the language, we use some already existent words and put them together in a new sense. This, however, appears to be true of all known languages. There are, in fact, no known languages that do not have some idioms. Consider the Chinese expression for 'quickly,' for example. It is *mǎ shàng*, and translated literally it means 'horseback.' Why should the concept of 'quick' be associated with the back of a horse? The answer reveals itself upon a moment's speculation. In the old days, before the train, the automobile, and the airplane, the fastest way of getting from one place to the other was by riding a horse, i.e., on horseback. Thus Chinese *ma shang* is as if we said in English *hurry up! We must go 'on horseback,'* i.e., 'Hurry up! We must go quickly.' Such a form would not be unintelligible in English at all, though the speaker would have to realize that it is an idiom, and the foreigner would have to learn it. However, in learning idioms a person may make an incorrect guess. Consider the English idiom *Oh well, the die is cast!* What would you guess this means—in case you don't know it? Perhaps you may guess that the speaker you heard is acquiescing in something because of the *Oh well* part. The expression means 'I made an irreversible decision and must live with it.' You can now try to reconstruct how this idiom came into being: The image of the die that was cast in gambling cannot be thrown again; that would be illegal; whether you have a one, a three, or a six, you must face the consequences of your throw, that is, win or lose, as the case may be. (Some people may know that the phrase was used by Caesar when he crossed the Rubicon, an event that led to war.)

How, then, having just learned it, will you use this idiom correctly? First of all, wait until you hear it from a native speaker in a natural context; do not experiment yourself with using an idiom until you have mastered the basics of English grammar. Once you have heard the idiom being used more than once, and fully understand its meaning, you can try using it yourself. Imagine that you have two job offers, one sure, but lower paying, and one that pays more, but is only tentative. Because of nervousness and fear of having no job at all, you accept the lower paying job, at which moment the better offer comes through and naturally you feel frustrated. You can then say *Oh well, the die is cast . . .* If you try this on a native speaker and he looks at you with sympathy and does not ask 'what do you mean?' — you have achieved your first successful placement of a newly learned idiom in an appropriate context. This can be a rewarding experience. Native Americans usually react to foreigners more politely than do people of other nations, but they can definitely tell how fluent you are. If a person always uses a bookish, stilted expression and never uses an idiom in the right place, he might develop the reputation of being a dry, unimaginative speaker, or one who is trying to be too serious and too official. *The use of idioms is, therefore, extremely important. It can strike a chord of solidarity with the listener.* The more idioms you use in the right context, the more at ease native Americans will feel with you and the more they will think to themselves 'this is a nice and friendly person—look at how well he expresses himself!'

We will now take a look at some practical considerations regarding the use of *A Dictionary of American Idioms*.

HOW TO USE THIS DICTIONARY

This dictionary can be used successfully by nonnative speakers of English, students, workers, immigrants—in short, anybody who wants to make his English more fluent, more idiomatic. It contains phrases of the types mentioned above, lexemic idioms, phrase idioms, and proverbial idioms, that have a special meaning. When a phrase has a special meaning that you cannot decode properly by looking up and understanding the individual words of which it is composed, then you know you are dealing with an idiom. You may already know some of these idioms or may be able to imagine what they mean. Look in the book for any of the following idioms that you may already know well, this will help you to understand how you should use this book: *boy friend, girl friend, outer space, piggy bank, get even, give up, going to, keep on, keep your mouth shut, lead somebody by the nose, look after, show off, throw away, all over, in love, mixed-up, out of this world, throw away, I'll say, both X and Y.*

A dictionary is like any other tool: You must familiarize yourself with it and learn how to use it before it begins to work well for you. Study the directions carefully several times, and practice looking up idioms. That way, searching for an idiom and finding it will become second nature to you. If you hear an idiomatic expression that is not in this book, after using it for a while, you will develop the ability to track down its meaning and write it down for yourself. Keep your own idiom list at home, right beside your regular dictionary. If you read a technical text, or a novel or a newspaper article and do not understand an expression, look it up in your reg-

ular school dictionary first; if you do not find it, try this one.

How do you find out if this dictionary can help you understand a hard sentence? Sometimes you can easily see what the phrase is, as with *puppy love, fun house, dog-eat-dog, mixed-up.* If not, pick out an important word from the most difficult part and look for that. If it is the first word in the idiom, you will find the whole phrase, followed by an explanation. Thus the expression *bats in the belfry* is listed in this dictionary under *b*, the word *bats*. If the word you picked is not the first word, you will find a list of idioms that contain that word. For example, the word *toe* will be found in entries such as *curl one's hair OR curl one's toes, on one's toes, step on the toes (of somebody).* You may, of course, find that the reason why you do not understand a particular sentence is not because of any idioms in it; in that case your regular dictionary will be of help to you. Also, there are more idioms than listed in this book; only the most frequently occurring in *American English* are included. British English, for example, or the English spoken in Australia, certainly has many idiomatic expressions that are not a part of American English.

TYPES OF ENTRY

This dictionary contains four kinds of entry: *main entries, run-on entries, cross reference entries,* and *index entries.* A main entry includes a full explanation of the idiom. A run-on entry is a phrase which is derived from another idiom but would be separated from it if it entered at its own alphabetical place. These derived idioms have been run on at the end of the main entry (e.g., *fence-sitter* at *sit on the fence*) with an illustration and a paraphrase; an extra explanation has been added when understanding the derivative from the main explanation seemed difficult. When an idiom has come to be used as more than one part of speech, a separate entry has been made for each usage.

A cross-reference entry guides you to a definition in another place. Suppose you want to look up *cast in one's lot with.* You can look under *cast,* and under *lot;* but the cross-reference entry will send you to *throw* in the phrase *throw in one's lot with.* The reason for this is that *cast* is a much rarer word nowadays and so the usual, more frequent form of this idiom starts with the verb *throw.*

An index entry directs you to all other entries containing the index word. Thus the word *chin* is followed by the phrases of which it is a part, e.g., *keep one's chin up, stick one's chin (or neck) out, take it on the chin, up to the chin in.*

PARTS OF SPEECH LABELS

Those idioms that correlate with a well-defined grammatical form class carry a part of speech label. Sometimes, as with many prepositional phrases, a double label had to be assigned because the given phrase has two grammatical uses, e.g., *in commission* can be either adverbial or adjectival. Many prepositional phrases are adverbial in their literal sense, but adjectival in their nonpredictable, idiomatic sense. *v.* stands for verb; it was assigned to phrases containing a verb and an adverb; verb and preposition; or verb, preposition, and adverb.

v.phr. stands for 'verbal phrase'; these include verbs with an object, verbs with subject complement, and verbs with prepositional phrase.

RESTRICTIVE USAGE LABELS

You must pay particular attention to whether it is appropriate for you to use a certain idiom in a certain setting. The label *slang* shows that the idiom is used only among very close friends who are quite familiar with one another. *Informal* indicates that the form is used in conversation but should be avoided in formal composition. *Formal* indicates the opposite; this is a form that people usually do not say, but they will write it in an essay or will state it in a speech or a university lecture. *Literary* alerts you to the fact that people are usually aware that the form is a quotation; it would be inappropriate for you to use these too often. *Vulgar* indicates that you should altogether avoid the form; recognizing it may, of course, be important to you as you can judge a person by the language he uses. *Substandard* labels a form as chiefly used by less educated people; *nonstandard* means that a phrase is felt to be awkward. *Archaic* (rarely used in this book) means that the form is heavily restricted to Biblical or Shakespearean English, *Dialect* means that the form is restricted to its geographical source; e.g., *chiefly British* means that Americans seldom use it, *Southern* means that the form is of much higher currency in the South of the United States than in the North.

Adam Makkai, Ph.D.
Professor of Linguistics
University of Illinois at Chicago
Executive Director and Director of
Publications, Linguistic Association of
Canada and the United States (LACUS). Inc.

Guide to the Parts of an Entry

The following are complete entries as given in this book, for *throw out* or *toss out, out of this world, give up, hot water, get lost, feather in one's cap,* and *polish the apple—apple polishing.* A guide to the different parts of these entries is given at the left. The order in the outline shows how the different information about the words is presented in this dictionary.

Guide

1. ENTRY FORM

The idiom in a basic dictionary form, with a, an, or the or a possessive cut off the beginning, and any words that change left out of the middle.

2. VARIANT

Additional wordings of the same idiom, differing in one or a few words.

3. PART-OF-SPEECH LABEL

Tells you how the phrase is used—like a noun, verb, adjective, adverb, preposition, conjunction, interjection. Some idioms are not used like a single word, but like two or more different parts of speech, or like sentences; these have no part-of-speech label.

4. STYLE LABEL

Tells you whether the phrase is *vulgar* (best avoided), *slang* (used only in very informal situations), *informal* (used only in familiar speaking and writing, not in English compositions, except in dialogue), *formal* (used only in formal writing and speaking, not in friendly talk and letters to familiar friends and relatives), *literary* (used only in stories and poems, for special effects.)

5. SENSE NUMBER

Marks the beginning of one of two or more meanings of an idiom. Each different sense begins with a new number. Closely related senses have letters added to the numbers (e.g., 1a, 1b.).

6. DEFINITION

Tells you the meaning of the idiom. There may be two or more definitions, but they nearly always mean the same thing. They just say the same thing in different words. A different meaning will be marked by a different sense number.

Parts of an Entry

[**throw out**][1] *or* [toss out][2] [*v.*][3] [**1**][5] [To put somewhere to be destroyed because not wanted.][6] [*He didn't need the brush any more so he threw it out*][8] [(He junked the brush when it was no longer useful.)][9] [Syn. THROW AWAY.][11] [**2**][5] [To refuse to accept.][6] [*The inspector tossed out all the parts that didn't work.*][8] [(The inspector refused to accept any parts that were no good.)][9] [**3**][5] [To force to leave; dismiss.][6] [*When the baseball manager complained too loudly, the umpires threw him out.*][8] [(The umpires ordered the manager to leave the game when he complained too loudly.)][9] [Syn. KICK OUT, TURN OUT.][11] [**4**][5] [To cause to be out in baseball by throwing the ball.][6] [*The shortstop tossed the runner out.*][8]

[**out of this world**][1] [*adj. phr.*,][3] [slang][4] [Wonderfully good or satisfying; terrific; super.][6]—[A cliché.][7] [*The dress in the store window was out of this world!*][8] [(The dress was very beautiful.)][9] [*Mother was on TV last night. Isn't that out of this world?*][8] [(Isn't that thrilling?)][9]

[**give up**][1] [*v.*][3] [**1a**][5] [To stop trying to keep; surrender; yield.][6] [*The dog had the ball in his mouth and wouldn't give it up.*][8] [(He wouldn't drop the ball from his mouth.)][9] [*Jimmy is giving up his job as a newsboy when he goes back to school.*][8] [(He won't keep the job when he goes back to school.)][9] [Compare GIVE ONESELF UP, HAND OVER, LET GO.][10] [**1a**][5] [Contrast HOLD ON TO.][12] [**1b**][5] [To allow, permit.][6] [*Ford gave up two walks in the first inning.*][8] [(Ford allowed two men to walk in the first inning.)][9] [**2**][5] [To stop doing or having; abandon; quit.][6] [*The doctor told Mr. Harris to give up smoking.*][8] [(He told him to stop smoking.)][9] [*Jane hated to give up her friends when she moved away.*][8] [(She didn't want to stop having them for friends.)][9] [Compare LEAVE OFF, PART WITH.][10] [**3**][5] [To stop hoping for, waiting for, or trying to do.][6] [*Johnny was given up by the doctors after the accident, but he lived just the same.*][8] [(He was hurt so badly that the doctors stopped hoping he would live.)][9] [*When Mary didn't come by* nine o'clock, we gave her up.]⁸ [(We stopped waiting.)]⁹ [*I couldn't do the puzzle so I gave it up.*]⁸ [(I quit trying.)]⁹ **[4]**⁵ [To stop trying; quit; surrender.]⁶ [*The war will be over when one of the countries gives up.*]⁸ [(When one country stops fighting the war will be finished.)]⁹ [*The other team gave up after we scored three touchdowns.*]⁸ [(They didn't try to win after we were ahead.)]⁹ [Compare GIVE IN, RESIGN ONESELF, THROW IN THE SPONGE.]¹⁰

7. USAGE NOTE

Gives you additional information about the way the idiom is used.

[hot water]¹ [*n.*]³ [*informal*]⁴ [Trouble.]⁶— [Used with *in, into, out of*.]⁷ [*John's thoughtless remark got him into a lot of hot water.*]⁸ [(His remark got him into a lot of trouble.)]⁹ [*It was the kind of trouble where it takes a friend to get you out of hot water.*]⁸ [(It was a jam of the kind in which a friend is the best means of getting out of trouble.)]⁹

8. ILLUSTRATIVE SENTENCES

Shows one or more ways the idiom is used in sentences.

9. PARAPHRASE

Gives the meaning of the sentence, or the part of the sentence in which the idiom is; explains the illustrative sentence.

[get lost]¹ [*v. phr.,*]³ [*slang*]⁴—Go away!]⁶ [Usually used as a command.]⁷ [*Get lost! I want to study.*]⁸ [(Go away; I want to study.)]⁹ [*John told Bert to get lost.*]⁸ [(John told Bert to go away.)]⁹ [Compare DROP DEAD.]¹⁰

10. CROSS REFERENCE

Directs you to another idiom defined in this book, which is similar or opposite in meaning.

11. SYNONYM

Means the two entries are the same in meaning, but differ in form, or in some way.

[feather in one's cap]¹ [*n. phr.*]³ [Something to be proud of; an honor.]⁶ [*It was a feather in his cap to win first prize.*]⁸ [(It was an honor for him to win first prize.)]⁹ [From the medieval practice of placing a feather in the helmet of one who won honors in battle.]¹³

12. CONTRAST

Means the entries are opposite in meaning.

13. ETYMOLOGY

Explains the origin of the expression.

14. RUN-ON ENTRY

An idiom that comes from another idiom but has a different first letter has been put into this book at the main entry, so that you can study them together.

[polish the apple]¹ [*v. phr.,*]³ [*slang*]⁴ [To try to make someone like you; to try to win favor by flattery.]⁶ **[apple polisher]**¹ [*n.,*]³ [*slang*]⁴ [A person who is nice to the one in charge in order to be liked or treated better; a person who does favors for a superior. *Jane is an apple polisher. She is always helping the teacher and talking to him.* (Jane wants the teacher to like her better than he likes the other boys and girls.)]¹⁴

Key to Abbreviations:

adj.—adjective
adv.—adverb
cl.—clause
conj.—conjunction
interj.—interjection
interrog.—interrogative

n.—noun
phr.—phrase
prep.—preposition
syn.—synonym
v.—verb

A

abide by *v.* To accept and obey; be willing to follow. *A basketball player may know he did not foul, but he must abide by the referee's decision.* (The player must be willing to follow the referee's decision; he must do as the referee says or he cannot play.) *The members agree to abide by the rules of the club.* (They promise to obey its rules.)

a bit *n., informal* A small amount; some. *There's no sugar in the sugar bowl, but you may find a bit in the bag.* (You may find some sugar in the bag.) *If the ball had hit the window a bit harder, it would have broken it.* (The ball nearly broke the window.)—Often used like an adverb. *This sweater scratches a bit.* (This sweater is a little scratchy.)—Also used like an adjective before *less, more.* *Janet thought she could lose weight by eating a bit less.* (She did not eat as much as usual.) *"Have some more cake?" "Thanks. A bit more won't hurt me."*—Often used adverbially after verbs in negative, interrogative, and conditional sentences, sometimes in the form *one bit.* *"Won't your father be angry?" "No, he won't care a bit."* (He will not be even a little angry; it will make no difference to him.) *Helen feels like crying, but I'll be surprised if she shows it one bit.* (I do not think she will show how she feels.)—Sometimes used with *little* for emphasis, also in the emphatic form *the least bit.* *"Wasn't Bob even a little bit sorry he forgot his date?"* (Wasn't Bob sorry some?) *"No, Bob wasn't the least bit sorry."* (Bob didn't care.) Syn. A LITTLE. Compare A FEW. Contrast A LOT.

about one's ears *or* **around one's ears** *adv. phr.* To or into complete collapse, defeat, or ruin; to the destruction of a person's plans, hopes, or happiness.—A cliché. *They planned to have factories all over the world but the war brought their plans down about their ears.* (The war ruined their big plans.) *John hoped to go to college and become a great scientist some day, but when his father died he had to get a job, and John's dreams came crashing around his ears.* (John's dream of becoming a great scientist was spoiled when he had to leave school.) Compare ON ONE'S HEAD.

about time *n. phr.* Finally, but later than it should have been; at last. *Mother said, "It's about time you got up, Mary."* (Mary got up late, and Mother told her she should have gotten up earlier.) *"The basketball team won last night. About time."* (It has been a long time since the team won a game.)

about to **1** Close to; ready to.—Used with an infinitive. *We were about to leave when the snow began.* (We were ready to leave when snow began to fall.) *I haven't gone yet, but I'm about to.* (I'm almost ready to go.) Com-pare GOING TO, ON THE POINT OF. **2** *informal* Having a wish or plan to.—Used with an infinitive in negative sentences. *Freddy wasn't about to give me any of his ice-cream cone.* (He had no plan to give me any.) *"Will she come with us?" asked Bill. "She's not about to," answered Mary.* (She certainly won't come; she doesn't want to come with us.)

above all *adv. phr.* Of first or highest importance; most especially. *Children need many things, but above all they need love.* (They need love the most.) Syn. FIRST AND LAST.

above suspicion *adj. phr.* Too good to be suspected; not likely to do wrong. *The umpire in the game must be above suspicion of supporting one side over the other.* (The umpire must be a fair man who would not help one side against the other.)

absentia See IN ABSENTIA.

Acapulco gold *n., slang, drug culture* Marijuana of an exceptionally high quality. *Jack doesn't just smoke pot, he smokes Acapulco gold.* (Jack doesn't smoke ordinary marijuana, he uses the highest quality stuff there is.)

accord See OF ONE'S OWN ACCORD *or* OF ONE'S OWN FREE WILL.

according as *conj.* **1** Depending on which; whichever. *You may take an oral or written exam according as you prefer.* (Which do you like better, an oral exam or a written exam? You may take the one you like better.) **2** Depending on whether; if. *We will play golf or stay home according as the weather is good or bad.* (If the weather is good, we will play golf, if it rains we will stay home.)

according to *prep.* **1** So as to match or agree with; so as to be alike in. *Many words are pronounced according to the spelling but some are not.* (Many words are pronounced in a way that agrees with their spelling.) *The boys were placed in three groups according to height.* (The boys were divided by height into three groups. The boys in each group were similar in height.) **2** On the word or authority of. *According to the Bible, Adam was the first man.* (The Bible says that Adam was the first man.)

according to Hoyle *adv. or adj. phr., informal* By the rules; in the usual and correct way; regular.—A cliché. *It's not according to Hoyle to hit a man when he's down.* (It's not fair to hit a man when he's down.) *In quitting without notice, he didn't act according to Hoyle.* (In quitting without first telling the boss, he didn't act by the rules.)

account See CALL TO ACCOUNT, CHARGE ACCOUNT, LEAVE OUT OF ACCOUNT, ON ACCOUNT, ON ACCOUNT OF, ON ONE'S ACCOUNT, ON ONE'S OWN ACCOUNT, SAVINGS ACCOUNT, TAKE INTO ACCOUNT.

ace See WITHIN AN ACE OF.

ace in the hole *n. phr.* **1** An ace given to a player face down so that other players in a card game cannot see it. *When the cowboy* *bet all his money in the poker game he did not know that the gambler had an ace in the hole and would win it from him.* (He did not know that the gambler had a hidden high card which would win the game and the money he bet.) **2** *informal* Someone or something important that is kept as a surprise until the right time so as to bring victory or success.—A cliché. *The football team has a new play that they are keeping as an ace in the hole for the big game.* (They are keeping the play as a surprise to win the game.) *The lawyer's ace in the hole was a secret witness who saw the accident.* (No one knew that the lawyer had a witness who had seen the accident.) Compare CARD UP ONE'S SLEEVE.

acid head *n., slang, drug culture* A regular user of LSD on whom the hallucinogenic drug has left a visible effect. *The reason John acts so funny is that he is a regular acid head.* (The reason why he acts funny is that he is a regular user of LSD which has left a detrimental effect on him.)

acid rock *n., slang, drug culture* A characteristic kind of modern jazz in which loudness and beat predominate over melody; especially such music as influenced by drug experiences. *John is a regular acid rock freak.* (John is unusually and excessively fond of hallucinogenic modern jazz in which beat predominates over melody.)

acorn See GREAT OAKS FROM LITTLE ACORNS GROW.

acoustic perfume *n., slang* Sound for covering up unwanted noise, such as music over loudspeakers in a noisy construction area. *Let's get out of here—this acoustic perfume is too much for my ears.* (The music covering up the basic noise is hard to endure.)

across the board *adv. phr.* **1** So that equal amounts of money are bet on the same horse to win a race, to place second, or third. *I bet $6 on the white horse across the board.* (I bet $2 that the white horse would win, $2 that he would be second, and $2 that he would be third in the race.)—Often used with hyphens as an adjective. *I made an across-the-board bet on the white horse.* (Equal amounts were bet that the horse would either win or place second or third.) **2** *informal* Including everyone or all; so that all are included. *The President wanted taxes lowered across the board.* (He wanted the taxes of everyone, rich and poor,, to be lowered.)—Often used with hyphens as an adjective. *The workers at the store got an across-the-board pay raise.* (Everyone got more pay.)

across the tracks See THE TRACKS.

act See READ THE RIOT ACT.

actions speak louder than words What you do shows your character better and is more important than what you say.—A proverb. *John promised to help me, but he didn't. Actions speak louder than words.* (It is more important for John to help than just to promise to help.) *Joe is very quiet, but actions speak louder than words. He is the best player on the team.* (We judge Joe by the way he plays, not by what he does or doesn't say about it.)

act one's age *or* **be one's age** *v. phr.* To do the things that people expect someone of your age to do; not act as if you were much younger than you are. *Bobby cried when he broke his kite. Mother said, "You're a big boy now. Act your age."* (Mother told Bobby to act like a big boy, not cry like a baby.) *Mr. O'Brien was playing tag with the children at the party. Then Mrs. O'Brien said, "Henry! Act your age!" and he stopped.*

actor See BAD ACTOR.

act out *v.* **1** To show an idea, story, or happening by your looks, talk, and movements. *He tried to act out a story that he had read.* (He tried to tell the story by acting and talking like each person in it.) **2** To put into action. *All his life he tried to act out his beliefs.* (He tried to do what he believed.) Syn. CARRY OUT.

act up *v., informal* **1** To behave badly; act rudely or impolitely. *The dog acted up as the postman came to the door.* (The dog barked and jumped when the mailman came.) **2** To work or run poorly (as a machine); skip; miss. *The car acted up because the spark plugs were dirty.* (The car ran in a jerky way because the spark plugs needed cleaning.)

add fuel to the flame *v. phr.* To make a bad matter worse by adding to its cause; spread trouble; increase anger or other strong feelings by talk or action. *By criticizing his son's girl, the father added fuel to the flame of his son's love.* (The father made his son love the girl more when he criticized her.) *Bob was angry with Ted and Ted added fuel to the flame by laughing at him.* (Ted laughed at Bob and Bob became angrier.)

add insult to injury *v. phr.* **1** To hurt someone's feelings after doing him harm.—A cliché. *He added insult to injury when he called the man a rat after he had already beaten him up.* (He fought the man and also called him bad names.) **2** To make bad trouble worse. *We started on a picnic, and first it rained; then, to add insult to injury, the car broke down.* (On the way to the picnic we were caught in rain, and then, to make things worse, the car broke down.)

addition See IN ADDITION.

address See PUBLIC-ADDRESS SYSTEM.

add up *v.* **1** To come to the correct amount. *The numbers wouldn't add up.* (He couldn't add the numbers so as to get the right total.) **2** *informal* To make sense; be understandable. *His story didn't add up.* (His story didn't make sense.)

add up to *v.* **1** To make a total of; amount to. *The bill added up to $12.95.* (The bill amounted to $12.95.) **2** *informal* To mean;

result in. *The rain, the mosquitoes, and the crowded cabin all added up to a spoiled vacation.* (It meant a spoiled vacation.)

advance See IN ADVANCE *or* IN ADVANCE OF.

advantage See TAKE ADVANTAGE OF, TO ADVANTAGE.

a few *n. or adj.* A small number (of people or things); some. *The dry weather killed most of Mother's flowers, but a few are left.* (A small number of flowers are still alive.) *In the store, Mary saw many pretty rings and bracelets, and she wanted to buy a few of them.* (Mary wanted to buy some of the jewelry.) *After the party, we thought that no one would help clean up, but a few couples did.* (Not many boys and girls stayed to help, but some did.) *Alice wanted to read a few pages more before she stopped.* (Alice wanted to read several pages more.)—Usually *a few* is different in meaning from *few*, which emphasizes the negative; *a few* means "some," but *few* means "not many." *We thought no one would come to lunch, but a few came.* (Some came.) *We thought many people would come to lunch, but few came.* (Not many came.) But sometimes *a few* is used with *only*, and then it is negative. *We thought many people would come to lunch, but only a few came.* (Not many came.)—Sometimes used like an adverb. *Three students have no seats; we need a few more chairs.* (We need some more chairs.) *If we can set up chairs faster than people come and sit in them, we will soon be a few ahead.* (We will have a small number of chairs ready before they are needed.)—Sometimes used with *very* for emphasis. *Uncle Ralph gave away almost all of his sea shells, but he still had a very few left.* (He still had a very small number of shells.) Compare A LITTLE. Contrast A LOT, QUITE A FEW.

affair See LOVE AFFAIR.

afoul of *prep.* **1** In collision with. *The boat ran afoul of a buoy.* (The boat struck a buoy.) **2** In or into trouble with. *The thief ran afoul of the night watchman.* (The thief was seen and caught by the night watchman.) *Speeders can expect to fall afoul of the law sometimes.* (People who drive too fast can expect to get in trouble with the law.)

afraid of one's shadow *adj. phr., informal* Scared of small or imaginary things; very easily frightened; jumpy; nervous.—A cliché. *Mrs. London won't stay alone in her house at night; she is afraid of her own shadow.* (She is afraid of all sorts of little things.) *Johnny cries whenever he must say hello to an adult; he is afraid of his own shadow.* (He is so shy that he is afraid to say "hello.")

after a fashion *adv. phr.* Not very well or properly; poorly. *He played tennis after a fashion.* (He knew how to play tennis, but he did not play well.) *The roof kept the rain out after a fashion.* (The roof leaked in places.) Compare IN A WAY.

after all *adv. phr.* **1** As a change in plans;

anyway.—Used with emphasis on *after*. *Bob thought he couldn't go to the party because he had too much homework, but he went after all.* (At first Bob thought he couldn't go to the party, but he changed his plan and went to it; he went anyhow.) **2** For a good reason that you should remember.—Used with emphasis on *all*. *Why shouldn't Betsy eat the cake? After all, she baked it.* (Betsy should eat some cake because she baked it. Don't say Betsy can't have any cake; remember, she baked it.)

after a while *informal or* **in a while** *adv. phr.* Later, at some time in the future; after a time that is not short and not long. *"Dad, will you help me make this model plane?" "After a while, son, when I finish reading the newspaper."* (I will help you later, not now.) *The boys gathered some wood, and in a while, a hot fire was burning.* (The boys made a fire and soon had it burning well.) Syn. BY AND BY. Contrast RIGHT AWAY.

after hours *adv. or adj. phr.* Not during the regular, correct, or usual time; going on or open after the usual hours. *The store was cleaned and swept out after hours.* (The store was cleaned after the regular closing time.) *The children had a secret after hours party when they were supposed to be in bed.* (The children had a party secretly after the time they should have been in bed.)

after one's own heart *adj. phr., informal* Well liked because of agreeing with your own feelings, interests, and ideas; to your liking; agreeable.—A cliché. Used after *man* or some similar word. *He likes baseball and good food; he is a man after my own heart.* (I like him because he likes the same things that I like.) *Thanks for agreeing with me about the class party; you're a girl after my own heart.* (You pleased me by agreeing with me about the party.) Compare SEE EYE TO EYE.

again See COME AGAIN, EVERY NOW AND THEN *or* EVERY NOW AND AGAIN, NOW AND THEN *or* NOW AND AGAIN, OFF AGAIN, ON AGAIN *or* ON AGAIN, OFF AGAIN, SOMETHING ELSE AGAIN, THEN AGAIN, TIME AND AGAIN, YOU SAID IT *or* YOU CAN SAY THAT AGAIN.

against it See UP AGAINST IT.

against the clock See AGAINST TIME.

against the current *or* **against the stream** See SWIM AGAINST THE CURRENT.

against the grain *adv. phr.* **1** Across rather than with the direction of the fibers (as of wood or meat). *He sandpapered the wood against the grain.* (He sandpapered the wood the wrong way.) **2** So as to annoy or trouble, or to cause anger or dislike.—Usually follows *go*. *His coarse and rude ways went against the grain with me.* (His rudeness irritated me.) *It went against the grain with him to have to listen to her gossip.* (He hated to listen to her mean talk.) Compare RUB THE WRONG WAY.

against time *or* **against the clock** *adv. phr.*
1 As a test of speed or time; in order to beat
a speed record or time limit. *John ran around
the track against time, because there was no
one else to race against.* (John timed himself
with a watch to see how fast he could run
around the track.) **2** As fast as possible; so
as to do or finish something before a certain
time. *It was a race against the clock whether
the doctor would get to the accident soon
enough to save the injured man.* (The doctor
had to get there as quickly as possible or the
injured man might die.) **3** So as to cause delay by using up time. *The outlaw talked
against time with the sheriff, hoping that his
gang would come and rescue him.* (The outlaw kept talking so his friends would have
more time to come and save him before the
sheriff could put him in jail.)

age See ACT ONE'S AGE *or* BE ONE'S AGE,
DOG'S AGE *or* COON'S AGE, LEGAL AGE *or* LAW-
FUL AGE, OF AGE, OVER AGE, UNDER AGE.

agent See FREE AGENT.

Agent Orange *n.* An herbicide used as a de-
foliant during the Vietnam War, considered by
some to cause birth defects and cancer, hence,
by extension, an instance of 'technological
progress pollution.' *If things continue as they
have, we'll all be eating some Agent Orange
with our meals.* (We will all be poisoned by
chemical by-products.)

ago See WHILE AGO.

agree with *v.* To have a good effect on; suit.
The meat loaf did not agree with him. (The
meat loaf made him sick.) *The warm, sunny
climate agreed with him, and he soon grew
strong and healthy.* (It had a good effect on
his health.)

ahead See DEAD AHEAD, GET AHEAD.

ahead of *prep.* **1** In a position of advantage
or power over. *He studies all the time, because he wants to stay ahead of his classmates.* (He studies hard, because he wants to
have the best marks in his class.) **2** In front
of; before. *The troop leader walked a few feet
ahead of the boys.* (The boys followed a
few feet behind the leader.) **3** Earlier than;
previous to; before. *Betty finished her test
ahead of the others.* (Betty finished writing
the test before the other students.)

ahead of the game *adv. or adj. phr., informal*
1 In a position of advantage; winning (as in
a game or contest); ahead (as by making
money or profit); making it easier to win or
succeed.—A cliché. *The time you spend studying when you are in school will put you
ahead of the game in college.* (You will get
along better in college than others who have
studied less.) *After Tom sold his papers, he
was $5 ahead of the game.* (He made a $5
profit.) **2** Early; too soon; beforehand. *When
Ralph came to school an hour early, the
janitor said, "You're ahead of the game."*
(The janitor said, "You are early.") *John
studies his lessons only one day early; if he*

*gets too far ahead of the game, he forgets
what he read.* (When John reads his lesson
very early, he forgets what he read.)

ahead of time *adv. phr.* Before the expected
time; early. *The bus came ahead of time, and
Mary was not ready.* (The bus came early.)
The new building was finished ahead of time.
(It was finished before the day on which the
builder had promised to be done.) Contrast
BEHIND TIME.

a hell of a *or* **one hell of a** *adj., or adv. phr.
informal* Extraordinary, very. *He made a
hell of a shot during the basketball game.* (He
made a fantastic shot.) *Max said seven months
was a hell of a time to have to wait for a simple
visa.* (Max said seven months was too long to
wait.) *The fall Max took left one hell of a bruise
on his knee.* (It left a very severe bruise.)

aim See *take aim.*

air See BUILD CASTLES IN THE AIR, CLEAR THE
AIR, GIVE ONESELF AIRS, GET THE AIR at GET
THE BOUNCE 1., GIVE THE AIR at GIVE THE
BOUNCE 1., IN THE AIR, INTO THIN AIR,
LEAVE HANGING *or* LEAVE HANGING IN THE
AIR, ON THE AIR, OUT OF THIN AIR, UP IN
THE AIR, WALK ON AIR.

airbus *n.* A trade name, also used informally
for a wide-bodied airplane used chiefly as a
domestic passenger carrier. *Airbuses don't fly
overseas, but mainly from coast to coast.*

airquake *n.* An explosive noise of undeter-
mined origin usually heard in coastal com-
munities and appearing to come from some
higher point in elevation. *What was that awful
noise just now?—I guess it must have been an
airquake.*

air one's dirty linen in public *or* **wash one's
dirty linen in public** *v. phr.* To talk about
your private quarrels or disgraces where
others can hear; make public something embarrassing that should be kept secret.—A
cliché. *Everyone in the school knew that the
superintendent and the principal were angry
with each other because they aired their dirty
linen in public.* (They quarreled where anyone could hear.) *No one knew that the boys'
mother was a drug addict, because the family
did not wash its dirty linen in public.* (The
family did not talk to other people about its
secrets.)

air shuttle *n., informal* Air service for regular commuters operating between major
cities at not too far a distance, e.g., between
Boston and New York City; such flights
operate without reservation on a frequent
schedule. *My dad takes the air shuttle from
Boston to New York once a week.* (He uses
the unscheduled air service between the two
cities.)

a la *prep.* In the same way as; like. *Billy
played ball like a champion today, a la the
professional ball players.* (He played so well
that people might have thought he was really
a professional player.) *Joe wanted to shoot
an apple off my head a la William Tell.* (He

wanted to shoot the apple from my head in the same way that William Tell shot one from his son's head.) [From French *à la*, in the manner of.]

albatross around one's neck *n. phr., literary* Guilt, the haunting past, an unforgettable problem. *Even though it was an accident, John's father's death has been an albatross around John's neck.* (He has felt guilty and responsible for it.) Compare MONKEY ON ONE'S BACK.

alert See ON THE ALERT.

a little *n. or adj.* A small amount (of); some.—Usually *a little* is different in meaning from *little*, which emphasizes the negative; *a little* means "some"; but *little* means "not much." We say *"We thought that the paper was all gone, but a little was left."* (Some was left.) But we say, *"We thought we still had a bag of flour, but little was left."* (Not much was left.) Also, we say, *"Bob was sick yesterday, but he is a little better today."* (He is better today; he is getting well.) But we say, *"Bob was sick yesterday, and he is little better today."* (He is nearly as sick today as he was yesterday.) Sometimes *a little* is used with *only*, and then it is negative: *We thought we had a whole bag of flour, but only a little was left.* (Not much was left.) *We have used most of the sugar; but a little is left.* (A small amount of sugar is left.) *We did not eat all the cake; we saved a little of it for you.* (We saved some cake for you.) *I'm tired; I need a little time to rest.* (I need some time to rest.) *Where is the paper? I need a little more.* (I need two or three more pieces of paper.)—Often used like an adverb. *Usually the teacher just watched the dancing class, but sometimes she danced a little to show them how.* (Sometimes the teacher danced for a minute to show the students the right way.) *The children wanted to play a little longer.* (They wanted to play several minutes longer.)—Sometimes used with *very* for emphasis. *The sick girl could not eat anything, but she could drink a very little tea.* (She could take a swallow of tea.) Syn. A BIT. Compare A FEW. Contrast A LOT, QUITE A LITTLE.

a little knowledge is a dangerous thing *literary* A person who knows a little about something may think he knows it all and make bad mistakes.—A proverb. *John has read a book on driving a car and now he thinks he can drive. A little knowledge is a dangerous thing.* (It would be dangerous for John to try to drive just because he has read about it.)

alive See COME ALIVE, KNOW ——— IS ALIVE, LOOK ALIVE, SKIN ALIVE.

alive with *prep., informal* Crowded with; filled with. *The lake was alive with fish.* (The lake was filled with fish.) *The stores were alive with people the Saturday before Christmas.* (There were crowds of people in the stores.)

all See AFTER ALL, AND ALL, AT ALL, BEAT ALL *or* BEAT THE DUTCH, FOR ALL, FOR ALL ONE IS WORTH, FOR ALL ONE KNOWS, FOR ALL THE WORLD, FOR GOOD *also* FOR GOOD AND ALL, FROM THE BOTTOM OF ONE'S HEART *or* WITH ALL ONE'S HEART, HAVE ALL ONE'S BUTTONS *or* HAVE ALL ONE'S MARBLES, IN ALL, JUMP ON *or* JUMP ALL OVER *or* LAND ALL OVER, KNOW-IT-ALL, ON ALL FOURS, ONCE AND FOR ALL, PUT ALL ONE'S EGGS IN ONE BASKET, STRIKE ALL OF A HEAP, WALK OVER *or* WALK ALL OVER *or* STEP ALL OVER.

all along *or (informal)* **right along** *adv. phr.* All the time; during the whole time. *I knew all along that we would win.* (I knew it all the time.) *I knew right along that Jane would come.* (I believed during the whole time she would come.)

all at once *adv. phr.* **1** At the same time; together. *The teacher told the children to talk one at a time; if they all talked at one time, she could not understand them.* (The teacher could not listen to all the children at once; they should speak one at a time, in turn.) *Bill can play the piano, sing, and lead his orchestra all at once.* (He can do three things at the same time.) **2** *or* **all of a sudden** Without warning; abruptly; suddenly; unexpectedly. *All at once we heard a shot and the soldier fell to the ground.* (Suddenly we heard a shot and the soldier fell to the ground.) *All of a sudden the ship struck a rock.* (Without warning the ship. struck a rock.) Compare AT ONCE.

all better *adj. phr.* Fully recovered; all well again; no longer painful.—Usually used to or by children. *"All better now,"* he kept repeating to the little girl.* (He kept telling the little girl that the pain was all gone away.)

all but *adv. phr.* Very nearly; almost. *Crows all but destroyed a farmer's field of corn.* (They ate nearly all the corn.) *The hikers were exhausted and all but frozen when they were found.* (The hikers were almost frozen.)

all ears *adj. phr., informal* Very eager to hear; very attentive.—Used in the predicate. *Go ahead with your story; we are all ears.* (We are very eager to hear your story.) *When John told about the circus, the boys were all ears.* (They heard nothing else.)

alley See BLIND ALLEY, DOWN ONE'S ALLEY *or* UP ONE'S ALLEY.

alley cat *n., slang* **1** A stray cat. **2** A person (usually a female) of rather easygoing, or actually loose sexual morals; a promiscuous person. *You'll have no problem dating her; she's a regular alley cat.* (She will offer you no resistance; she is easy to seduce.)

all eyes *adj. phr., informal* Wide-eyed with surprise or curiosity; watching very closely.—Used in the predicate. *At the circus the children were all eyes.* (The children were interested in the circus and watched closely.)

all here See ALL THERE.

all hours *n. phr., informal* Late or irregular

times. *The boy's mother said he must stop coming home for meals at all hours.* (She told him to stop coming early or late to meals instead of at the regular time.) *He stayed up till all hours of the night to finish his school work.* (He worked until very late at night.)

all in *adj. phr., informal* Very tired; exhausted. *The players were all in after their first afternoon of practice.* (They were very tired.) Syn. PLAYED OUT, WORN OUT.

all in a day's work *or* **all in the day's work** *adj. phr., informal* Unpleasant or bad but to be expected; not harder than usual; not unusual. *Keeping ants away from a picnic lunch is all in the day's work.* (The ants are a usual nuisance at picnics.) *When the car had a flat tire, Father said that it was all in a day's work.* (Flat tires are common, they must be expected.) Compare PAR FOR THE COURSE, PUT UP WITH.

all in all¹ *n. phr., literary* The person or thing that you love most. *She was all in all to him.* (He loved her more than anything else in the world.) *Music was his all in all.* (Music was the most important thing in his life.)

all in all² *or* **in all** *adv. phr.* When everything is thought about; in summary; altogether. *All in all, it was a pleasant day's cruise.* (A few things went wrong, but mostly the day on the boat was pleasant.) *All in all, the pilot of an airplane must have many abilities and years of experience before he can be appointed.* (An airplane pilot needs many skills and many years of experience in order to get the job.) Compare ON THE WHOLE 1. *Counting the balls on the green, we have six golf balls in all.* (With the four balls here, we have six counting the two on the green.)

all kinds of *adj. phr., informal* Plenty of. *People say that Mr. Fox has all kinds of money.* (People say he has plenty of money.) *When Kathy was sick, she had all kinds of company.* (Many people came to visit her.) Compare GREAT DEAL.

all manner of *adj. phr., formal* Many different kinds of; all sorts of. *In a five-and-ten-cent store you can buy all manner of things.* (You can buy many kinds of things.)

all of *adj. phr., informal* **1** At least the amount or number of; fully; no less than. *It was all of ten o'clock before they finally started.* (It was at least ten o'clock, if not later.) *She must have paid all of $50 for that hat.* (It looks like a very expensive hat.) **2** Showing all the signs of; completely in.—Used with *a.* *The girls were all of a twitter before the dance.* (They were greatly excited.) *Mother is all of a flutter because of the thunder and lightning.* (She is frightened and nervous.) *The dog was all of a tremble with cold.* (The dog was trembling all over with cold.)

all of a sudden See ALL AT ONCE 2.

all out *adv. phr., informal* With all your strength, power, or determination; to the best of your ability; without holding back.—Usually used in the phrase *go all out. We went all out to win the game.* (We tried our hardest to win.) *John went all out to finish the job and was very tired afterwards.* (John used up a lot of energy and was tired out.) Compare ALL THE WAY 2, FULL TILT, GO THE WHOLE HOG, GO TO ANY LENGTH, LEAVE A STONE UNTURNED, WITH MIGHT AND MAIN.

all over *adv. phr.* **1** In every part; everywhere. *He has a fever and aches all over.* (All parts of his body ache.) *I have looked all over for my glasses.* (I have looked everywhere.) Compare FAR AND WIDE. **2** *informal* In every way; completely. *She is her mother all over.* (She is just like her mother.) **3** *informal* Coming into very close physical contact, as during a violent fight, wrestling. *Before I noticed what happened, he was all over me.* (Before I noticed what happened, he was wrestling and tangling with me.)

all over but the shouting *adv. phr., informal* Finally decided or won; brought to an end; not able to be changed.—A cliché. *After Bill's touchdown, the game was all over but the shouting.* (Bill's touchdown decided the winner of the game.) *John and Tom both tried to win Jane, but after John's promotion it was all over but the shouting.* (John's promotion made Jane decide to marry him instead of Tom.)

all over someone See FALL ALL OVER SOMEONE.

allowance See MAKE ALLOWANCE.

allow for *v.* To provide for; leave room for; give a chance to; permit. *She cut the skirt four inches longer to allow for a wide hem.* (She cut the skirt four inches long to leave material for a wide hem.) *Democracy allows for many differences of opinion.* (Democracy gives people the opportunity to tell their own opinions.)

all right¹ *adv. phr.* **1** Well enough. *The new machine is running all right.* (The new machine is doing satisfactorily.) **2** *informal* I am willing; yes. *"Shall we watch television?" "All right."* ("Shall we watch television?" "Yes.") Compare VERY WELL. **3** *informal* Beyond question; certainly.—Used for emphasis and placed after the word it modifies. *It's time to leave, all right, but the bus hasn't come.* (It is certainly time to go, but the bus has not come.)

all right² *adj. phr.* **1** Good enough; correct; suitable. *His work is always all right.* (His work is always satisfactory.) **2** In good health or spirits; well. *"How are you?" "I'm all right."* (How do you feel? I feel fine.) **3** *slang* Good. *He's an all right guy.* (He's a good fellow.)

all right for you *interj.* I'm finished with you! That ends it between you and me!—Used by children. *All right for you! I'm not playing with you any more!* (I'm angry with you and I won't play with you any more.)

all roads lead to Rome *literary* The same end or goal may be reached by many different ways.—A proverb. *"I don't care how you get the answer," said the teacher, "All roads lead to Rome."* (If you get the right answer to the question, it makes no difference how you figure it.)

all set *adj., informal* Ready, completed. *"How are you doing fixing my tire?"—Joe asked. "All set,"—the man answered.* (He says he is ready with the tire.)

all shook up *also* **shook up** *adj., slang* In a state of great emotional upheaval, disturbed, agitated. *What are you so shook up about?* (What is it that disturbs you so?)

all systems go *Originally from space English, now general colloquial usage* Everything is complete and ready for action; it is now all right to proceed. *After they wrote out the invitations, it was all systems go for the wedding.* (After they wrote the invitations, everything was in order to proceed with the wedding ceremony.)

all the[1] *adj. phr., dial.* The only. *A hut was all the home he ever had.* (A hut was the only home he had in his whole life.)

all the[2] *adv. phr.* Than otherwise; even.— Used to emphasize comparative adjectives, adverbs, and nouns. *Opening the windows made it all the hotter.* (Opening the windows made it even hotter than it was before.) *Take a bus instead of walking and get home all the sooner.* (If you take a bus, you will get home sooner than you would walking.) *If you don't eat your dessert, all the more for us.* (We will have even more than we would if you didn't leave yours.)

all the better See ALL THE.[2]

all the ———er *substandard* The ———est; as . . . as.—Used with a comparative adjective or adverb and subordinate clause in place of a superlative adjective or adverb. *That was all the bigger he grew.* (That was as big as he grew. He didn't grow any bigger.) *Is that all the faster you can go?* (Is that the fastest you can go? Can't you go faster than that?)

all there *or* **all here** *adj. phr., informal* Understanding well; thinking clearly; not crazy. —Usually used in negative sentences. *Joe acted queerly and talked wildly, so we thought he was not all there.* (He showed that he was somewhat crazy.)

all the same[1] *or* **all one** *n. phr.* Something that makes no difference; a choice that you don't care about. *If it's all the same to you, I would like to be waited on first.* (If it doesn't make any difference to you, I would like the clerk to wait on me before you.) *You can get there by car or by bus—it's all one.* (It makes no difference if you go by car or if you go by bus; you can get there at the same time.)

all the same[2] *or* **just the same** *adv. phr., informal* As if the opposite were so; nevertheless; anyhow; still. *Everyone opposed it, but Sally and Bob got married all the same.* (Although everyone was against their getting married, Sally and Bob did so.) *Mary is deaf, but she takes tap dancing lessons just the same.* (Although Mary can not hear, she is learning to tap dance as if she could hear.) Compare AT THAT 3, IN SPITE OF.

all the thing *or* **all the rage, the in thing** *n. phr.,* The fashionable or popular thing to do, the fashionable or most popular artist or form of art at a given time. *After "The Graduate" Dustin Hoffman was all the rage in the movies.* (He was one of the most popular actors.) *It was all the thing in the late sixties to smoke pot and demonstrate against the war in Viet Nam.* (It was fashionable to indulge in marijuana and criticize the foreign policy of the Johnson administration.)

all the time *adv. phr.* **1** *or* **all the while** During the whole period; through the whole time. *Mary went to college in her home town, and lived at home all the while.* (Mary always lived at home while she was going to college.) *Most of us were surprised to hear that Mary and Tom had been engaged all year, but Sue said she knew it all the time.* (Sue knew it all year.) **2** Without stopping; continuously. *Most traffic lights work all the time.* (The lights that tell the cars when to stop and go work all day and all night.) **3** Very often; many times. *Ruth talks about her trip to Europe all the time, and her friends are tired of it.* (Ruth talks too often about her trip to Europe.)

all the way *or* **the whole way** *adv. phr.* **1** From start to finish; during the whole distance or time. *Jack climbed all the way to the top of the tree.* (He climbed as high as he could go.) *Joe has played the whole way in the football game and it's almost over.* (He has played the whole game till now.) **2** In complete agreement; with complete willingness to satisfy.—Often used in the phrase *go all the way with. I go all the way with what George says about Bill.* (I agree completely.) *Mary said she was willing to kiss Bill, but that did not mean she was willing to go all the way with him.* (Mary wasn't willing to do anything that Bill wanted.) *The bank was willing to lend Mr. Jones money to enlarge his factory, but it wasn't willing to go all the way with his plans to build another in the next town.* (The bank wasn't willing to satisfy Mr. Jones by building a factory in another town.) Compare ALL OUT, GO THE WHOLE HOG.

all the worse See ALL THE.[2]

all thumbs *adj., informal* Awkward, especially with your hands; clumsy. *Harry tried to fix the chair, but he was all thumbs.* (Harry had trouble fixing the chair, because his hands were clumsy.)

all told   *adv. phr., informal* Counting or including everything. *Including candy sale profits, we have collected $300 all told.* (We have collected a total of $300, including profits from candy sales.)

all to the good   See TO THE GOOD.

all up   *adj. phr., informal* Near to certain death or defeat; without any more chance or hope. *With their ammunition gone the patrol knew that it was all up with them.* (They knew that defeat and capture were now certain.)

all very well   *adj.* All right; very good and correct; very true.—Usually followed by a *but* clause. *It's all very well for you to complain but can you do any better?* It's all right to complain, but can you do better yourself?) *It's all very well if Jane comes with us, but how will she get back home?* (Jane can come with us, but how will she get home again?) Compare WELL AND GOOD.

all wet   *adj., slang* Entirely confused or wrong; mistaken. *When the Wright brothers said they could build a flying machine, people thought they were all wet.* (When the Wright brothers told of their plans for a flying machine, people thought they were imagining something impossible.) *If you think I like baseball, you're all wet.* (You are all wrong, if you think I like baseball.) Compare OFF ONE'S ROCKER.

all wool and a yard wide   *adj. phr.* Of fine character; *especially,* very generous and kindhearted.—A cliché. *He's a wonderful brother —all wool and a yard wide.* (He's a very good brother—so generous and helpful.)

all work and no play makes Jack a dull boy Too much hard work without time out for play or enjoyment is not good for anyone.— A proverb. *Bill's mother told him to stop studying and to go out and play, because all work and no play makes Jack a dull boy.* (Bill's mother did not want him to work too hard or make himself sick.)

alone   See LET ALONE *or* LEAVE ALONE, LET WELL ENOUGH ALONE *or* LEAVE WELL ENOUGH ALONE.

along   See ALL ALONG *or* RIGHT ALONG, COME ALONG, GET ALONG, GO ALONG, RUN ALONG, STRING ALONG.

along for the ride   *adv. phr., informal* Being in a group for the fun or the credit without doing any of the work.—A cliché. *He wants no members in his political party who are just along for the ride.* (He wants no members who will not work for the party.)

along in years *or* **on in years**   *adj. phr.* Elderly; growing old. *As Grandfather got on in years, he became quiet and thoughtful.* (As Grandfather became elderly, he became quiet and thoughtful.) *Our dog isn't very playful because it is getting on in years.* (Our dog isn't very playful because it is growing old.)

alongside of   *prep.* 1 At or along the side of. *We walked alongside of the river.* (We walked near the edge of the river.) 2 Together with. *I played alongside of Tom on the same team.* (Tom and I played together on the team.) Compare SHOULDER TO SHOULDER, SIDE BY SIDE. 3 *informal* Compared with or to; measured next to. *His money doesn't look like much alongside of a millionaire's.* (The amount of money he has is small compared to a millionaire's.)

a lot   *n., informal* A large number or amount; very many or very much; lots. *I learned a lot in Mr. Smith's class.* (I learned much in Mr. Smith's class.) *A lot of our friends are going to the beach this summer.* (Many of our friends are going to the beach.) —Often used like an adverb. *Ella is a jolly girl; she laughs a lot.* (Ella often laughs.) *Grandfather was very sick last week, but he's a lot better now.* (Grandfather is much better now.) *You'll have to study a lot harder if you want to pass.* (You must study much harder to pass.)—Also used as an adjective with *more, less,* and *fewer. There was a good crowd at the game today, but a lot more will come next week.* (Many more people will come to the game next week.)—Often used with *whole* for emphasis. *John has a whole lot of marbles.* (John has a very large number of marbles.) *Jerry is a whole lot taller than he was a year ago.* (Jerry is much taller.) Compare GOOD DEAL, GOOD MANY, A NUMBER. Contrast A FEW, A LITTLE.

aloud   See THINK ALOUD *or* THINK OUT LOUD.

alpha wave   *n.* A brain wave, 8–12 cycles per second, associated with a state of relaxation and meditation and, hence, free of anxieties. *Try to produce some alpha waves; you will instantly feel a lot better.* (Put yourself into a mental state of relaxation.)

alter   See CIRCUMSTANCES ALTER CASES.

always   See GRASS IS ALWAYS GREENER ON THE OTHER SIDE OF THE FENCE.

ambulance chaser   *n.* An attorney who specializes in representing victims of traffic accidents. By extension, a lawyer of inferior ranks or talent. *Don't hire Murgatroid; he's just another ambulance chaser.* (There are better lawyers available.)

anchor   See AT ANCHOR.

——— **and** ———   1 —*And* is used between repeated words to show continuation or emphasis. *When the children saw the beautiful Christmas tree, they looked and looked.* (The children looked for a long time at the Christmas tree.) *Old Mr. Bryan has known Grandfather for years and years, since they were boys.* (Mr. Bryan has known Grandfather for many years.) *Billy dived to the bottom of the lake again and again, looking for the lost watch.* (Billy dived many times.) *Everyone wished the speaker would stop, but he talked on and on.* (The man talked longer than he should have talked; he did not stop.) Compare THROUGH AND THROUGH. 2 —When *and* is used between words with opposite meaning, it often emphasizes how much you mean. *Mr. Jones worked early and late to earn enough to live.* (Mr. Jones worked from early morning till late in the evening.) *The parents hunted high and low for the lost child.* (The parents looked everywhere for the lost child.) Compare DAY AND NIGHT, FROM —————— TO, INSIDE AND OUT.

and all *informal* And whatever goes with it; and all that that means. *We don't go out much nowadays, with the new baby and all.* (We stay home because the new baby needs many things done for him.) *Jack's employer provided the tools and all.* (His employer provided everything he needed to do the job.)

and how! *interj. informal* Yes, that is certainly right!—Used for emphatic agreement. *"Did you see the game?" "And how!"* (I surely did!) *"Isn't Mary pretty?" "And how she is!"* (She is very pretty!) Syn. YOU BET, YOU SAID IT. Compare BUT GOOD.

and so forth *or* **and so on** And more of the same kind; and further amounts or things like the ones already mentioned. *The costumes were red, pink, blue, purple, yellow, and so forth.* (The costumes seemed to include every color—red, pink, blue, purple, yellow and all the others.) Compare WHAT HAVE YOU.

and then some And a lot more; and more too. *It would cost all the money he had and then some.* (It would cost all the money he had, and more too.) *Talking his way out of this trouble was going to take all his wits and then some.* (It was going to need more cleverness than he had to explain his way out of this trouble.)

and what not See WHAT NOT.

angel dust *n., slang, drug culture* Phencyclidine, an addictive hallucinatory narcotic drug extremely dangerous to the users' health, also called PCP. *Algernon has gone from grass to angel dust; he will end up in the morgue.* (He started using much more potent and dangerous PCP and is likely to die.)

another See DANCE TO ANOTHER TUNE.

answer back See TALK BACK.

answer for *v.* **1** To take responsibility for; assume charge or supervision of. *The secret service has to answer for the safety of the President and his family.* (The secret service is responsible for the safety of the President and his family.) **2** To say you are sure that (someone) has good character or ability; guarantee; sponsor. *When people thought Ray had stolen the money, the principal said, "Ray is no thief. I'll answer for him."* (When people thought Ray might have stolen the cash, the principal spoke for his honesty.) **3** Take the blame or punishment for. *When Mother found out who ate the cake, Tom had to answer for his mischief.* (Tom was punished.)

ante up *v., informal* To produce the required amount of money in order to close a transaction; to pay what one owes. *"I guess I'd better ante up if I want to stay an active member of*

the Association," Max said. (He realizes that he has to pay his membership dues in order to remain a member.)

ants in one's pants *n. phr., slang* Nervous over-activity; restlessness.—A cliché. *Jane can not sit still; she has ants in her pants.* (Jane is a very restless girl. She always likes to do something.) *You have ants in your pants today. Is something wrong?* (You are very nervous today. Are you worried about something?)

a number *n.* A rather large number; numbers.—Used when there are more than several and fewer than many. *The parents were invited to see the program, and a number came.* (A small crowd of parents came.) *We knew the Smiths rather well; we had visited them a number of times.* (We had visited them fairly often.)—Used like an adjective before *less, more. We have not set up enough folding chairs; we need a number more.* (We need to set up about a dozen more.) Compare QUITE A FEW.

any See HARDLY ANY *or* SCARCELY ANY.

any number *n., informal* A large number; many. *There are any number of reasons for eating good food.* (There are many reasons for eating good food.) *Don't ask George what his excuse is. He can invent any number.* (George can think of many excuses.) Compare A LOT, A NUMBER, GOOD MANY.

anything See HAVE NOTHING ON *or* NOT HAVE ANYTHING ON, IF ANYTHING.

anything but *adv. phr.* Quite the opposite of; far from being. *I don't mean he's lazy— anything but!* (Whatever he is, he is not lazy.) *The boys knew they had broken the rules, and they were anything but happy when they were called to the office.* (They were unhappy and afraid.)

anything like *or* **anywhere near** *adv.* Nearly. —Used in negative, interrogative, and conditional sentences, often in the negative forms *nothing like or nowhere near. It's not anything like as hot today as it was yesterday.* (It is not nearly as hot today.) *Do you think that gold ring is worth anywhere near a hundred dollars?* (Is that ring worth as much as $100?) *Today's game was nowhere near as exciting as yesterday's game.* (Today's game was much less exciting.) *Studying that lesson should take nothing like two hours.* (Studying that lesson should not take two hours; it should take much less.)

anywhere near See ANYTHING LIKE *or* ANYWHERE NEAR.

any which way See EVERY WHICH WAY.

apart See JOKING ASIDE *or* JOKING APART, POLES APART, TELL APART.

apart from *or* **aside from** *prep. phr.* Beside or besides; in addition to. *The children hardly see anyone, apart from their parents.* (The children hardly see anyone other than their parents.) *Aside from being fun and good exercise, swimming is a very useful skill.* (Besides being fun and good exercise, swimming is a useful skill.) Syn. EXCEPT FOR, OUTSIDE OF.

ape See GO APE.

appear See SPEAK OF THE DEVIL AND HE AP-PEARS.

appearance See PUT IN AN APPEARANCE *also* MAKE AN APPEARANCE.

apple See POLISH THE APPLE.

applecart See UPSET THE APPLECART *or* UP-SET ONE'S APPLECART.

apple of one's eye *n. phr.* Something or someone that is adored; a cherished person or object.—A cliché. *Charles is the apple of his mother's eye.* (Charles's mother loves him more than anything else. She adores him.) *John's first car was the apple of his eye. He was always polishing it.* (John was very proud of his first car.)

apple-pie order *n. phr., informal* Exact orderly arrangement; neatness; tidy arrangement. *The house was in apple-pie order.* (The house was neat and tidy.) *Like a good secretary, she kept the boss's desk in apple-pie order.* (The secretary kept her boss's desk orderly and neat.)

apple polisher; apple polishing See POLISH THE APPLE.

approval See ON APPROVAL.

apron See TIED TO ONE'S MOTHER'S APRON STRINGS.

apropos of *prep., formal* In connection with; on the subject of; about; concerning. *Apropos of higher tuition, Mr. Black told the boy about the educational loans that banks are offering.* (In connection with higher tuition, Mr. Black told the boy that banks now lend money to students to help them pay for their college education.) *Mr. White went to see Mr. Richards apropos of buying a car.* (He went to see Mr. White about buying a car.)

arm See GIVE ONE'S RIGHT ARM, IN THE ARMS OF MORPHEUS, KEEP AT A DISTANCE *or* KEEP AT ARM'S LENGTH, SHOT IN THE ARM, TAKE UP ARMS, TWIST ONE'S ARM, UP IN ARMS, WITH OPEN ARMS.

arm and a leg *n., slang* An exorbitantly high price that must be paid for something that isn't really worth it. *To get a decent apartment these days in New York you have to pay an arm and a leg.* (You have to pay an exorbitant amount to get a decent apartment.)

armed to the teeth *adj. phr.* Having all needed weapons; fully armed.—A cliché. *The paratroopers were armed to the teeth.* (They had many things to fight with.)

arm in arm *adv. phr.* With your arm under or around another person's arm, especially in close comradeship or friendship. *Sally and Joan were laughing and joking together as they walked arm in arm down the street.* (The two girls' arms were joined together because they felt close and friendly.) *When they arrived at the party, the partners walked arm in arm to meet the hosts.* (Each girl's arm was linked around the arm of her boyfriend as they walked together.) Compare HAND IN HAND.

around one's ears See ABOUT ONE'S EARS.

around the clock *also* **the clock around** *adv. phr.* For 24 hours a day continuously; all day and all night. *The factory operated around the clock until the order was filled.* (The factory ran for 24 hours a day until it had filled the order.) *He studied around the clock for his history exam.* (He studied all day and all night for his history exam.)—**round-the-clock** *adj.* *That filling station has round-the-clock service.* (You can go there or telephone for help all day and all night.)

around the corner *adv. phr.* Soon to come or happen; close by; near at hand.—A trite expression. *The fortune teller told Jane that there was an adventure for her just around the corner.* (The adventure would soon happen.)

arrest See UNDER ARREST.

as See FOR AS MUCH AS, INASMUCH AS.

as an old shoe See COMFORTABLE AS AN OLD SHOE.

as an old shoe See COMMON AS AN OLD SHOE.

as ——— as —Used with an adjective or adverb in a comparison or with the effect of a superlative. *John is as tall as his father now.* (John's height is the same as his father's height.) *I didn't do as badly today as I did yesterday.* (Today I did better than yesterday.) *John's father gave him a hard job and told him to do as well as possible.* (Father gave John more than he could do, but told him to do the best he could.) *The sick girl was not hungry, but her mother told her to eat as much as she could.* (Her mother told her to eat the most she could eat.)—Also used in the form *so ——— as* in some sentences, especially negative sentences. *This hill isn't nearly so high as the last one we climbed.* (This hill is lower than the last one.)—Often used in similes (comparisons that are figures of speech). *The baby mouse looked as big as a minute.* (The baby mouse looked very tiny.) *Jim's face was red as a beet after he made the foolish mistake.* (Jim's face became very red from embarrassment.)—Most similes in conventional use are clichés, avoided by careful speakers and writers.

as best one can *adv. phr.* As well as you can; by whatever means are available; in the best way you can. *The car broke down in the middle of the night, and he had to get home as best he could.* (When the car broke down late at night, he had to get home in any way he could find.) *George's foot hurt, but he played the game as best he could.* (Although his foot hurt, George played the game as well as he could.) *The girl's mother was sick, so the girl got dinner as best she could.* (The girl tried hard to fix a good dinner, but it was not as good as her mother's dinner.)

as catch can *See* CATCH AS CATCH CAN.

as far as *or* **so far as** *adv. phr.* **1** To the degree or amount that; according to what, how much, or how far. *John did a good job as far as he went, but he did not finish it.* (He did a good job at first, but did not finish.) *So far as the weather is concerned, I do not think it matters.* (I do not care what the weather is.) *As far as he was concerned, things were going well.* (He was satisfied with affairs.) **2** To the extent that; within the limit that. *He has no brothers so far as I know.* (Within the limits of my knowledge, he has no brothers.) Compare FOR ALL 2.

as far as that goes *or* **as far as that is concerned** *or* **so far as that is concerned** *also* **so far as that goes** *adv. phr.* While we are talking about it; also; actually. *You don't have to worry about the girls. Mary can take care of herself, and as far as that goes, Susan is pretty independent, too.* (Mary can take care of herself and, actually, Susan can too.) *I didn't enjoy the movie, and so far as that is concerned, I never like horror movies.* (I didn't like this particular movie, and in fact, I don't like any horror movie.) Syn. FOR THAT MATTER, IN FACT. Compare COME TO THINK OF IT.

as follows A list of things that come next; what is listed next.—Followed by a colon. *My grocery list is as follows: bread, butter, meat, eggs, sugar.* (My grocery list is written next.) *The names of the members are as follows: John Smith, Mary Webb, Linda Long, Ralph Harper.* (The names of the members are those that come next.) *The route is as follows: From City Hall go south on Main Street to Elm Street, east on Elm to 5th Street, and south on 5th two blocks to the school.*

as for *prep.* **1** In regard to; speaking of; concerning. *We have plenty of bread, and as for butter, we have more than enough.* (Speaking of butter, we have plenty.) **2** Speaking for. *Most people like the summer, but as for me, I like winter much better.* (I prefer the winter.) Compare FOR ONE'S PART.

as good as *adv. phr.* Nearly the same as; almost. *She claimed that he as good as promised to marry her.* (She claimed that he talked about marrying her and she got the idea that he would marry her.) *He as good as called me a liar.* (He almost called me a liar, but not exactly.) *We'll get to school on time; we're as good as there now.* (We're almost to the school now.) *The man who had been shot was as good as dead.* (The man was almost dead.) —Often used without the first *as* before adjectives. *When the car was repaired, it looked good as new.* (When the car was repaired it looked like a new car.)

as good as a mile See MISS IS AS GOOD AS A MILE.

as good as one gets See GIVE AS GOOD AS ONE GETS.

as good as one's promise See AS GOOD AS ONE'S WORD.

as good as one's word *or* **good as one's word** *adj. phr.* Trustworthy; sure to keep your promise.—A cliché. *The coach said he would give the players a day off if they won, and he was as good as his word.* (The coach said he would give the players a day off if they won, and he kept his promise.) *We knew she was always good as her word, so we trusted her.* (We knew she was perfectly dependable.)

aside See JOKING ASIDE, SET ASIDE.

aside from See APART FROM.

aside of *prep., dialect* Beside; by the side of. *Mary sits aside of her sister on the bus.* (Mary sits beside her sister.)

as if *or* **as though** *conj.* **1** As (he, she, it) would if; in the same way one would if; seeming to show. *The baby laughed as if he understood what Mother said.* (The baby laughed in the way he would if he understood her.) *The book looked as though it had been out in the rain.* (The book looked spotted and wrinkled; maybe it got wet because someone left it in the rain.) *The waves dashed on the rocks as if in anger.* (The waves hit the rocks hard, the way a person would when he was angry.) **2** That. *It seems as if you are the first one here.* (It seems that you are the first one here.)

as if one has come out of a bandbox See LOOK AS IF ONE HAS COME OUT OF A BANDBOX.

as is *adv.* Without changes or improvements; with no guarantee or promise of good condition.—Used after the word it modifies. *They agree to buy the house as is.* (They agree to buy it just as it is, with no repairs or changes.) *He bought an old car as is.* (He bought it without any repairs, just as it was.) Compare AT THAT 1.

as it were *adv. phr.* As it might be said to be; as if it really were; seemingly.—Used with a statement that might seem silly or unreasonable, to show that it is just a way of saying it. *In many ways children live, as it were, in a different world from adults.* (Children and adults seem to live in different worlds, but it's just because their interests are so different.) *The sunlight on the icy branches made, as it were, delicate lacy cobwebs from tree to tree.* (The ice on the trees seemed to be lacy cobwebs.) Compare SO TO SPEAK.

ask See FOR THE ASKING.

ask for *v., informal* To make (something bad) likely to happen to you; bring (something bad) upon yourself. *Charles drives fast on worn-out tires; he is asking for trouble.* (He is likely to have a blowout and wreck the car.) *The workman lost his job, but he asked for it by coming to work drunk several times.* (The workman brought the loss of his job upon himself, because he came to work drunk.) Compare HAVE IT COMING, SERVE RIGHT, SIGN ONE'S OWN DEATH WARRANT.

ask for the moon *or* **cry for the moon** *v. phr.* To want something that you cannot reach or have; try for the impossible.—A cliché. *John asked his mother for a hundred dollars today. He's always asking for the moon.* (John has as little chance of getting $100 from his mother as he has of getting the moon if he asked for that.) Compare PROMISE THE MOON.

asleep at the switch *adj. phr.* **1** Asleep when it is one's duty to move a railroad switch for cars to go on the right track. *The new man was asleep at the switch and the two trains crashed.* (He did not move the switch as he should have.) **2** *informal* Failing to act promptly as expected; not alert to an opportunity.—A cliché. *When the ducks flew over, the boy was asleep at the switch and missed his shot.* (He was not watchful and did not shoot in time.)

as long as *or* **so long as** *conj.* **1** Since; because; considering that. *As long as you are going to town anyway, you can do something for me.* (Since you are going to town, you can do something for me.) **2** Provided that; if. *You may use the room as you like, so long as you clean it up afterward.* (You may use the room if you clean it up afterward.)

as luck would have it *adv. clause* As it happened; by chance; luckily or unluckily. *As luck would have it, no one was in the building when the explosion occurred.* (Luckily, no one was in the building to be hurt.) *As luck would have it, there was rain on the day of the picnic.* (As it happened, it rained on the day of the picnic.)

as much *n.* The same; exactly that. *Don't thank me; I would do as much for anyone.* (Don't thank me; I would do the same for anyone.) *Did you lose your way? I thought as much when you were late in coming.* (Did you lose your way? I thought you did.)

as much as *adv. phr.* **1** *or* **much as** Even though; although. *As much as I hate to do it, I must stay home and study tonight.* (Though I hate to do it, I must stay home and study.) **2** *or* **so much as.** Just the same as; almost; practically; really. *By running away he as much as admitted that he had taken the money.* (His running away showed that he had probably taken the money.) *You as much as promised you would help us.* (You did not quite say so, but we understood that you would help us.) *The clerk as much as told me that I was a fool.* (The clerk the same as called me a fool; he said things that meant I was foolish.) Compare AS GOOD AS. **3** See FOR AS MUCH AS.

as of *prep.* At or until (a certain time). *I know that as of last week he was still unmarried.* (I know that up to last week he was not married.) *As of now we don't know much about Mars.* (At present we don't know much about Mars.)

as one goes See PAY AS ONE GOES.

as regards *prep.* Regarding; concerning; about. *You needn't worry as regards the cost of the operation.* (You need not worry about the cost.) *He was always secretive as regards his family.* (He was always secretive concerning his family.)

as soon as *conj.* Just after; when; immediately after. *As soon as the temperature falls to 70, the furnace is turned on.* (When the temperature falls, the furnace goes on.) *As soon as you finish your job let me know.* (Tell me when you finish.) *He will see you as soon as he can.* (He is busy now; he will see you when he is free.)

as the crow flies *adv. clause* By the most direct way; along a straight line between two places.—A cliché. *It is seven miles to the next town as the crow flies, but it is ten miles by the road, which goes around the mountain.* (It is seven miles in a perfectly straight line to the next town, but it is ten miles by the road, which curves around the bottom of the mountain.)

as though See AS IF.

as to *prep.* **1** In connection with; about; regarding. *There is no doubt as to his honesty.* (There is no doubt about his honesty.) *As to your final grade, that depends on your final examination.* (About your final grade, it depends on your examination.) Syn. WITH RESPECT TO. **2** According to; following; going by. *They sorted the eggs as to size and color.* (They classed the eggs according to size and color.)

as usual *adv. phr.* In the usual way; as you usually do or as it usually does. *As usual, Tommy forgot to make his bed before he went out to play.* (Tommy usually forgets to make his bed, and he forgot it this time, too.) *Only a week after the fire in the store, it was doing business as usual.* (Fire burned many things in the store, but only a week later it was open for business in the same way it had always been.)

as well *adv. phr.* **1** In addition; also; too; besides. *The book tells about Mark Twain's writings and about his life as well.* (It tells about his writings and about his life.) *Tom is captain of the football team and is on the baseball team as well.* (Tom is on the baseball team, too.) **2** Without loss and possibly with gain. *After the dog ran away, Father thought he might as well sell the dog house.* (Father thought he might sell the dog house without losing anything useful and might get money for it.) *Since he can't win the race, he may as well quit.* (Because Peter can't win the race, he has nothing to lose if he gives up.) *It's just as well you didn't come yesterday, because we were away.* (It's good you didn't come; we were not here.)

as well as *conj.* In addition to; and also; besides. *Hiking is good exercise as well as fun.* (Hiking is good exercise and also fun.) *He was my friend as well as my doctor.* (Besides being my doctor, he was my friend.) *The book tells about the author's life as well as about his writings.* (It tells about his life in addition to his writings.)

as yet *adv. phr.* Up to the present time; so far; yet. *We know little as yet about the moon's surface.* (We do not know much yet about the moon's surface.) *She has not come as yet.* (She has not come yet.)

as you please 1 As you like; whatever you like or prefer; as you choose. *You may do as you please.* (You may do what you want.) 2 *informal* Very.—Used after an adjective or adverb often preceded by *as. There was Tinker, sitting there, cheerful as you please.* (There was Tinker, sitting there very cheerfully.) *She was dressed for the dance, and she looked as pretty as you please.* (She was dressed for the dance, and she looked very pretty.)

at a blow *or* **at a stroke** *or* **at one stroke** *adv. phr.* Immediately; suddenly; with one quick or forceful action. *The pirates captured the ship and captured a ton of gold at a blow.* (They captured a ton of gold at one time.) *A thousand men lost their jobs at a stroke when the factory closed.* (They all lost their jobs together and right away.) *All the prisoners escaped at one stroke.* (They all ran away suddenly at the same time.) Compare AT ONCE, AT ONE TIME.

at all *adv. phr.* At any time or place, for any reason, or in any degree or manner.—Used for emphasis with certain kinds of words or sentences. 1 Negative *It's not at all likely he will come.* (There is very little chance of it.) 2 Limited *I can hardly hear you at all.* (Your voice is very faint.) 3 Interrogative *Can it be done at all?* (Is there any way to do it?) 4 Conditional *She will walk with a limp, if she walks at all.* (She may never walk again.) Syn. IN THE LEAST.

at all costs *adv. phr.* At any expense of time, effort, or money. Regardless of the results. *Mr. Jackson intended to save his son's eyesight at all costs.* (He wanted to save his son's eyesight, it did not matter how much time and money he might have to spend.) *Carl is determined to succeed in his new job at all costs.* (He is determined to be successful; he doesn't care how hard he has to work.)

at all events See IN ANY CASE.

at all hazards *adv. phr.* With no regard for danger; at any risk; regardless of the chances you must take. *The racer meant to win the 500-mile race at all hazards.* (He meant to win the 500-mile race even though it was dangerous.)

at a loss *adj. phr.* In a state of uncertainty; without any idea; puzzled. *A good salesman is never at a loss for words.* (He can always think of something to say.) *When Don missed the last bus, he was at a loss to know what to do.* (He did not know how he would get home.)

at anchor *adj. phr.* Held by an anchor from floating away; anchored. *The ship rode at anchor in the harbor.* (The ship was held by an anchor and chain in the harbor.)

at any rate *adv. phr.* In any case; anyhow. *It isn't much of a car, but at any rate it was not expensive.* (It isn't much of a car, but at least he didn't pay a high price for it.) Compare AT LEAST 2, IN ANY CASE.

at arm's length See KEEP AT A DISTANCE *or* KEEP AT ARM'S LENGTH.

at a snail's pace See SNAIL'S PACE.

at a straw See GRASP AT STRAWS.

at a stroke See AT A BLOW *or* AT A STROKE.

at a time *adv. phr.* At once; at one time; in one group or unit, together. *He checked them off one at a time as they came in.* (He checked them off one after another as they came in.) *He ran up the steps two at a time.* (He ran up the steps, stepping over two steps each time.) See EVERY OTHER. *They showed up for class three and four at a time.* (They arrived at class in groups of three and four.)

at bay *adv. or adj. phr.* In a place where you can no longer run away; unable to go back farther; forced to stand and fight, or face an enemy; cornered. *The dog ran the rat into a corner, and there the rat turned at bay.* (Cornered, the rat turned to fight the dog.) *The police chased the thief to a roof, where they held him at bay until more policemen came to help.* (The police chased the thief to a roof, and held him there at gunpoint until more policemen arrived.) Compare BRING TO BAY.

at best *or* **at the best** *adv. phr.* 1 Under the best conditions; as the best possibility. *A coal miner's job is dirty and dangerous at best.* (Even under the best conditions, a coal miner's job is dirty and dangerous.) *We can't get to New York before ten o'clock at best.* (The earliest possible time we can get to New York is ten o'clock.) Compare AT MOST. Contrast AT WORST. 2 In the most favorable way of looking at something; even saying the best about the thing. *The treasurer had at best been careless with the club's money, but most people thought he had been dishonest.* (The kindest explanation was that the treasurer had been careless with the money, but most people thought he had stolen it.)

at both ends See BURN THE CANDLE AT BOTH ENDS.

at call *adj. or adv. phr.* 1 Ready or nearby for use, help, or service; on request. *Thousands of auto insurance agents all over the country are at the insured person's call, wherever he may travel.* (Thousands of agents will give service anywhere in the country where the auto insurance policy holder may want to call him.) 2 At the word of command; at an order or signal. *The dog was trained to come at call.* (The dog was trained to come when he was ordered to come.)

at cross purposes *adv. phr.* With opposing meanings or aims; with opposing effect or result; with aims which hinder or get in each other's way. *Tom's parents acted at cross purposes in advising him; his father wanted him to become a doctor; but his mother wanted him to become a minister.* (Tom's father and mother gave him opposing advice; his father wanted him to become a doctor but his mother wanted him to become a minister.)

at death's door *adj. or adv. phr.* Very near death; dying.—A cliché. *He seemed to be at death's door from his illness.* (He seemed to be dying from his illness.)

at ease *or* **at one's ease** *adj. or adv. phr.* **1** In comfort; without pain or bother. *You can't feel at ease with a toothache.* (You can't feel comfortable or free of pain.) **2** *or* **at one's ease** Comfortable in one's mind; relaxed, not troubled.—Often used in the phrase *put at ease* or *put at one's ease. We put Mary at her ease during the thunderstorm by reading her stories.* (We made Mary forget about the storm and relax.) Compare AT HOME 2. Contrast ILL AT EASE, ON EDGE. **3** Standing with your right foot in place and without talking in military ranks. *The sergeant gave his men the command "At ease!"* (The men did not have to stand stiffly but could relax when they stood in line.) Compare PARADE REST.

at every turn *adv. phr.* Every time; all the time; continually; without exception. *Because of his drinking, the man was refused a job at every turn.* (People knew that the man drank too much, and every time he asked for a job, they refused.)

at fault *adj. phr.* Responsible for an error or failure; to blame. *The driver who didn't stop at the red light was at fault in the accident.* (The driver who went through the red light was to blame for the accident.) *When the engine would not start, the mechanic looked at all the parts to find what was at fault.* (He looked to see which part was keeping the engine from working.) Syn. IN THE WRONG.

at first *adv. phr.* In the beginning; at the start. *The driver didn't see the danger at first.* (He didn't see the danger when he began.) *At first the job looked good to Bob, but later it became tiresome.* (In the beginning Bob thought he had a wonderful job, but after a time he grew tired of doing the same thing again and again.) *There was a little trouble at first, but things soon were quiet.* (He had a little trouble at the start, but things were soon all right.)

at first blush *adv. phr.* When first seen; without careful study. *At first blush the offer looked good, but when we studied it, we found things we could not accept.* (At first, the offer seemed good, but after careful study we found things we could not accept.)

at first glance *or* **at first sight** *adv. or adj. phr.* After a first quick look. *At first sight, his guess was that the whole trouble between the two men resulted from personalities that did not*

agree. (His first guess was that the two men just couldn't get along.) *Tom met Mary at a party, and it was love at first sight.* (He loved her as soon as he saw her.)

at hand *also* **at close hand** *or* **near at hand** *adv. phr.* **1** Easy to reach; nearby. *When he writes, he always keeps a dictionary at hand.* (When he writes, he keeps a dictionary where he can reach it easily when he needs it.) **2** *formal* Coming soon; almost here. *Examinations are past and Commencement Day is at hand.* (It is almost Commencement Day.)

at heart *adv. phr.* **1** In spite of appearances; at bottom; in reality. *His manners are rough, but he is a kind man at heart.* (He is really a kind man in spite of his rough manners.) **2** As a serious interest or concern; as an important aim or goal. *He has the welfare of the poor at heart.* (He thinks the health and happiness of the poor are important.)

at home *adv. or adj. phr.* **1** In the place where you live or come from. *I went to his house, but he was not at home.* (He was not in his house.) *Americans abroad are protected by the government like Americans at home.* (Americans outside their country are protected by the U.S. government in the same way as Americans in their own country.) **2** Knowing what to do or say; familiar; comfortable. *Charles and John enjoy working together because they feel at home with each other.* (They feel familiar and relaxed with each other.) *The politician was at home among poor farmers and among rich factory owners.* (The politician knew how to act with both the rich and poor people.) *Make the new student feel at home in your school.* (Make the new student feel that he belongs in the school and everyone is his friend.) *Would you be at home driving a truck?* (Would you know what to do, and feel comfortable, driving a truck?) *Jim always lived by a lake, and he is at home in the water.* (Jim knows how to swim well and feels comfortable in the water.) *Tom has read many books about missiles and is at home in that subject.* (He knows many things about missiles and can easily talk about them.) Syn. AT EASE 2. Compare IN ONE'S ELEMENT, MAKE ONESELF AT HOME. Contrast AT A LOSS.

at issue *adj. phr.* **1** In dispute; to be settled by debate, by vote, by battle, or by some other contest. *His good name was at issue in the trial.* (His good name depended on how the trial came out.) *The independence of the United States from England was at issue in the Revolutionary War.* (The freedom of the United States was being won or lost in the Revolutionary War.) Compare IN QUESTION. **2** Not in agreement; in conflict; opposing. *His work as a doctor was at issue with other doctors' practice.* (He did things as a doctor that most physicians disapprove of.) Syn. AT ODDS.

15

at it *adj. phr.* Busily doing something; active. *His rule for success was to keep always at it.* (His rule for success was to work hard.) *The couple who owned the little cleaning shop were at it early and late.* (They were on the job at all hours.) *Mr. Curtis heard a loud crash in the next apartment—the neighbors were at it again.* (The neighbors were fighting again.)

at large *adv. or adj. phr.* **1** Not kept within walls, fences, or boundaries; free. *The killer remained at large for weeks.* (The killer succeeded in not being caught for weeks.) Compare AT LIBERTY. *Cattle and sheep roamed at large on the big ranch.* (Cattle and sheep roamed freely over the big, unfenced ranch.) **2** In a broad, general way; at length; fully. *The superintendent talked at large for an hour about his hopes for a new school building.* (He talked all about a new building, not only about getting the money, not only about why it was needed, not only about where it would be built.) **3** As a group rather than as individuals; as a whole; taken together. *The junior class at large was not interested in a senior yearbook.* (Almost no one in the junior class was interested in a senior yearbook.) **4** As a representative of a whole political unit or area rather than one of its parts; from a city rather than one of its wards, or a state rather than one of its districts. *He was elected congressman at large.* (He was elected congressman by the vote of the whole state, rather than by the vote of only one congressional district.) *Aldermen are voted for at large.* (Aldermen are voted for in all wards of the city instead of one alderman from each ward.)

at last *also* **at long last** *adv. phr.* After a long time; finally. *The war had been long and hard, but now there was peace at last.* (The war had been long and hard, but now, finally, there was peace.) *The boy saved his money until at last he had enough for a bicycle.* (He saved his money and after a long time he was able to buy a bicycle.)

at least *adv. phr.* **1** *or* **at the least** At the smallest guess; no fewer than; no less than. *You should brush your teeth at least twice a day.* (It is necessary for you to brush your teeth two times every day and no less.) *At least three students are failing in mathematics.* (Three or more students are failing mathematics.) *Mr. Johnson must weigh 200 pounds, at least.* (Mr. Johnson appears to weigh 200 pounds, and probably weighs more.) Compare ALL OF. **2** Whatever else you may say; anyhow; anyway. *It was a clumsy move, but at least it saved her from getting hit.* (It was awkward, but it saved her from getting hit, anyway.) *She broke her arm, but at least it wasn't the arm she writes with.* (Luckily, she writes with the arm that is not broken.) *The Mortons had fun at their picnic yesterday— at least the children did—they played while their parents cooked the food.* (Maybe the

parents didn't have fun, but the children had fun, anyhow.) *He's not coming—at least that's what he said.* (Maybe he will come, but he said he would not come.) Compare AT ANY RATE, IN ANY CASE.

at leisure *adj. or adv. phr.* **1** Not at work; not busy; with free time; at rest. *Come and visit us some evening when you're at leisure.* (Come and visit us when you have free time.) **2** *or* **at one's leisure** When and how you wish at your convenience; without hurry. *John made the model plane at his leisure.* (He worked on the plane whenever he felt like working.) *You may read the book at your leisure.* (You may read it slowly without rushing.)

at length *adv. phr.* **1** In detail; fully. *You must study the subject at length to understand it.* (You must study the subject fully to understand it.) *The teacher explained the new lesson at length to the students.* (He explained everything about the new lesson to the students.) **2** In the end; at last; finally. *The movie became more and more exciting, until at length people were sitting on the edge of their chairs.* (The movie made people sit excitedly on the edge of their chairs.)

at liberty *adv. or adj. phr.* Free to go somewhere or do something; not shut in or stopped. *The police promised to set the man at liberty if he told the names of the other robbers.* (The police promised to let the man go free.) *I am sorry, but I am not at liberty to come to your party.* (I can not come to your party because I have something else I must do at that time.) Compare AT LARGE 1.

at loggerheads *adj. or adv. phr.* In a quarrel; in a fight; opposing each other. *The two senators had long been at loggerheads on foreign aid.* (The two senators had long been enemies about foreign aid.) *Because of their barking dog, the Morrises lived at loggerheads with their neighbors.* (The Morrises were not friends with their neighbors; they quarreled about the noisy dog.) Compare AT ODDS.

at long last See AT LAST.

at loose ends *adj. phr.* Without a regular job or settled habits; uncertain what to do next; having nothing to do for a while; undecided; unsettled; restless. *Feeling at loose ends, I went for a long walk.* (I didn't know what to do next, so I took a long walk.) *He had finished college but hadn't found a job yet, so he was at loose ends.* (He had finished college but was still looking for work, so he was unsure what he would be doing next.)

at most *or* **at the most** *adv. phr.* By the largest or most generous guess; at the upper limit; by the maximum account; not more than; at best; at worst. *It was a minor offense at most.* (At worst, it was not a serious wrongdoing.) *He had been gone 15 minutes at the most.* (He had been gone not more than 15 minutes.) *Their new house lot is a quarter* *acre at most.* (By the most liberal measurement, their lot is still only a quarter acre.)

at odds *adj. phr.* In conflict or disagreement; opposed. *The boy and girl were married a week after they met and soon found themselves at odds about religion.* (They married too soon after they met, and quickly found that they were in serious disagreement about religion.) Compare AT LOGGERHEADS.

at once *adv. phr.* 1 Without delay; right now or right then; immediately. *Put a burning match next to a piece of paper, and it will begin burning at once.* (Right then the paper will begin to burn; in a second it will be hot enough to burn.) *Mother called the children to lunch, and Paul came at once, but Brenda stayed in the sandpile a little longer.* (Paul did not stay in the sandpile after his mother called him; he came when Mother called.) Syn. RIGHT AWAY *or* RIGHT OFF. Compare ALL AT ONCE 2.

at one *adj. phr.* 1 In union or harmony; in agreement or sympathy. Not usually used informally. *He felt at one with all the poets who have sung of love.* (He was in close agreement with all the poets of love.) 2 Of the same opinion; in agreement. *Husband and wife were at one on everything but money.* (Husband and wife agreed about everything but money.) Contrast AT ODDS.

at one fell swoop See IN ONE FELL SWOOP.

at one's beck and call *or* **at the beck and call of** *adj. phr.* Ready and willing to do whatever someone asks; ready to serve at a moment's notice. *A good parent isn't necessarily always at the child's beck and call.* (One can be a good parent without always jumping to the child's demands.)

at one's door *or* **at one's doorstep** *adv. phr.* 1 Very close; very near where you live or work. *Johnny is very lucky because there's a swimming pool right at his doorstep.* (The swimming pool is very close to Johnny's house.) *Mr. Green can get to work in only a few minutes because the subway is at his door.* (The subway is near where Mr. Green lives.) 2 See LAY AT ONE'S DOOR.

at one's ease See AT EASE 2.

at one's elbow *adv. phr.* Close beside you; nearby. *The President rode in an open car with his wife at his elbow.* (The President rode in an open car with his wife close beside him.) *Mary practiced for several years to become a champion swimmer, and her mother was always at her elbow to help her.* (Mary's mother stayed near her while she practiced, to help her.) Contrast BREATHE DOWN ONE'S NECK.

at one's feet *adv. phr.* Under your influence or power. *She had a dozen men at her feet.* (A dozen men were courting her.) *Her voice kept audiences at her feet for years.* (Her singing impressed audiences for years.) Compare THROW ONESELF AT SOMEONE'S FEET.

at one's fingertips *adv. phr.* 1 Within easy reach; quickly touched; nearby. *Seated in the cockpit, the pilot of a plane has many controls at his fingertips.* (As he sits in the cockpit, an airplane pilot has many controls where he can touch them easily.) 2 Readily usable as knowledge or skill; familiar. *He had several languages at his fingertips.* (He could speak and write several languages easily.) *He had the whole design of the machine at his fingertips.* (He was thoroughly familiar with the plan of the machine.)

at one's heels *adv. phr.* Close behind; as a constant follower or companion. *The boy got tired of having his little brother at his heels all day.* (He didn't like having his little brother follow him around all the time.) *John ran by the finish line with Ned at his heels.* (John passed by the finish line and was close behind him.) *Bad luck followed at his heels all his life.* (He had bad luck all his life.)

at one's leisure See AT LEISURE 2.

at one's service *adv. phr.* 1 Ready to serve or help you; prepared to obey your wish or command; subject to your orders. *He placed himself completely at the President's service.* (He offered to serve the President in any way possible.) *"Now I am at your service,"* the dentist told the next patient. ("Now I am ready to take care of you," the dentist told the next patient.) 2 Available for your use; at your disposal. *He put a car and chauffeur at the visitor's service.* (He made a car and chauffeur ready for the visitor's use. He told the visitor that he could use the car and chauffeur.)

at one stroke See AT A BLOW *or* AT ONE STROKE.

at one's wit's end *or* **at wits end** *adj. phr.* Having no ideas as to how to meet a difficulty or solve a problem; feeling puzzled after having used up all of your ideas or resources; not knowing what to do; puzzled. *He had approached every friend and acquaintance for help in vain, and now he was at his wit's end.* (He had asked everyone he could think of for help, and now he was unable to think what to do next.) *The designer was at his wit's end: he had tried out wings of many different kinds, but none would fly.* (The designer could think of no more ideas; he had tried many different kinds of wings without finding a wing that would fly on the new airplane.) Compare AT A LOSS, END OF ONE'S ROPE.

at one's word See TAKE AT ONE'S WORD.

at one time *adv. phr.* 1 In the same moment; together. *Let's start the dance again, all at one time.* (Let's start all together.) *Mr. Reed's bills came all at one time, and he could not pay them.* (The bills came on the same day.) Syn. AT THE SAME TIME 1. 2 At a certain time in the past; years ago. *At one time people thought that Minnesota was not a good place to live in.* (Many years ago people thought that Minnesota was not a good

17

at the drop of a hatat the drop of a hat

place to live in.) *At one time most school teachers were men, but today there are more women than men.* (In the past, most school teachers were men.)

at pains *adj. phr.* Making a special effort. *At pains to make a good impression, she was prompt for her appointment.* (She made a special effort to make a good impression by being punctual.)

at present *adv. phr.* At this time; now. *It took a long time to get started, but at present the road is half finished.* (They were slow in starting to build the road, but it is half finished now.) *At present the house is empty, but next week a family will move in.* (The house is empty now; next week people will come to live in it.)

at random *adv. phr.* With no order, plan, or purpose; in a mixed-up, or thoughtless way. *He opened the letters at random.* (He opened the letters in no regular order. *His clothes were scattered about the room at random.* (His clothes were thrown about the room.)

at sea[1] *adv. or adj. phr.* **1** On an ocean voyage; on a journey by ship. *They had first met at sea.* (They met for the first time on an ocean voyage.) **2** Out on the ocean; away from land. *By the second day the ship was well out at sea.* (By the second day the ship was far from land.) *Charles had visited a ship in dock, but he had never been on a ship at sea.* (Charles had not been on a ship when it was away from land.)

at sea[2] *adj. phr.* Not knowing what to do; bewildered; confused; lost. *The job was new to him, and for a few days he was at sea.* (The job was strange at first, and it took him a few days before he knew how to do it.) *When his friends talked about chemistry, Don was at sea, because he did not study chemistry.* (Don did not understand what his friends were talking about.) Compare AT A LOSS.

at sight *or* **on sight** *adv. phr.* **1** The first time the person or thing is seen; as soon as the person or thing is seen. *First graders learn to read many words on sight.* (First graders learn to read and know many words the minute that they see them.) *Mary had seen many pictures of Grandfather, so she knew him on sight.* (As soon as Mary saw her grandfather, she knew him from having seen pictures of him.) Compare AT ONCE 1. **2** On demand; on asking the first time. *The money order was payable at sight.* (The money order was to be paid immediately when presented.)

at sixes and sevens *adj. phr.* Not in order; in confusion; in a mess. *He apologized because his wife was away and the house was at sixes and sevens.* (He explained that his wife was away and so the house was in a mess.) *Our teacher had just moved to a new classroom, and she was still at sixes and sevens.* (She was still not organized; she did not know on which shelves her things were.) *After the captain of the team broke his leg, the other*

players were at sixes and sevens. (They were troubled and did not know what to do without a leader.)

at ——— stage of the game *adv. phr.* At (some) time during an activity; at (some) point. *At that stage of the game, our team was doing so poorly that we were ready to give up.* (At that time during the game, we were ready to give up.) *It's hard to know what will happen at this stage of the game.* (It's hard to guess what will happen at this point.) *At what stage of the game did the man leave?* (What was happening when the man left?)

at stake *adj. phr.* Depending, like a bet, on the outcome of something uncertain; in a position to be lost or gained. *The team played hard because the championship of the state was at stake.* (The team could win or lose the state championship. It depended on the outcome of the game.) *The farmers were more anxious for rain than the people in the city because they had more at stake.* (The farmers would lose more than the city people if there were no rain.) Compare HANG IN THE BALANCE.

at straws See GRASP AT STRAWS.

at swords' points *adj. phr.* Ready to start fighting; very much opposed to each other; hostile; quarreling. *The dog's barking kept the Browns at swords' points with their neighbors for months.* (The Browns had been quarreling with the neighbors for months because of the dog.) *The mayor and the reporter were always at swords' points.* (The mayor and the reporter were always opposed and ready for a quarrel.)

at table See AT THE TABLE; WAIT AT TABLE.

at that *adv. phr., informal* **1** As it is; at that point; without more talk or waiting. *Ted was not quite satisfied with his haircut but let it go at that.* (Ted thought his haircut was good enough for now.) **2** In addition; also. *Bill's seatmate on the plane was a girl and a pretty one at that.* (His companion was a girl and a pretty one, too.) **3** After all; in spite of all; anyway. *The book was hard to understand, but at that Jack enjoyed it.* (The book wasn't easy reading, but Jack liked it and could understand it.) Syn. ALL THE SAME.

at the best See AT BEST.

at the bit See CHAMP AT THE BIT.

at the drop of a hat *adv. phr., informal* **1** Without waiting; immediately; promptly.—A cliché. *If you need a babysitter quickly, call Mary, because she can come at the drop of a hat.* (She needs almost no time to get ready.) Compare ON THE SPUR OF THE MOMENT. **2** Whenever you have a chance; with very little cause or urging.—A cliché. *At the drop of a hat, he would tell the story of the canal he wanted to build.* (At any time, he would tell the story of the canal he wanted to build.) *He was quarrelsome and ready to fight at the drop of a hat.* (He was quarrelsome and always ready for a fight.)

at the end of one's rope See END OF ONE'S ROPE.

at the kill See IN AT THE KILL.

at the least See AT LEAST.

at the mercy of *or* **at one's mercy** *adj. phr.* In the power of; subject to the will and wishes of; without defense against. *The champion had the other boxer at his mercy.* (The other boxer could not fight well any more against him. The champion could hurt him if he wished to.) *The picnic was at the mercy of the weather.* (The picnic would be canceled if it rained.) *The small grocer was at the mercy of people he owed money to.* (The small grocer owed people so much money that his business could be closed up if they wished.

at the most See AT MOST.

at the point of *prep.* Very near to; almost at or in. *When Mary broke her favorite bracelet, she was at the point of tears.* (Mary was almost crying.) *The boy hurt in the accident lay at the point of death for a week; then he got well.* (The boy was near death for a week.) Compare ABOUT TO 1, ON THE POINT OF.

at the ready *adj. phr.* Ready for use. *The sailor stood at the bow, harpoon at the ready, as the boat neared the whale.* (He was prepared to use the weapon at any moment.)

at the same time *adv. phr.* **1** In the same moment; together. *The two runners reached the finish line at the same time.* (The two runners reached the finish line together.) Syn. AT ONCE, AT ONE TIME. **2** In spite of that fact; even though; however; but; nevertheless. *John did pass the test; at the same time, he didn't know the subject very well.* (John did pass the test, even though he didn't know the subject well.)

at the seams See BURST AT THE SEAMS.

at the table *or* **at table** *adv. phr.* At a meal; at the dinner table. *The telephone call came while they were all at table.* (They were at dinner when the telephone rang.)

at the tip of one's tongue *or* **on the tip of one's tongue** *adv. phr., informal* **1** Almost spoken; at the point of being said.—A cliché. *It was at the tip of my tongue to tell him, when the phone rang.* (I was just starting to tell him, when the telephone interrupted me.) *John had a rude answer on the tip of his tongue, but he remembered his manners just in time.* (John almost gave a rude answer.) **2** Almost remembered; at the point where one can almost say it but cannot because it is forgotten. *I have his name on the tip of my tongue.* (I can almost remember his name.)

at the top of one's voice *or* **at the top of one's lungs** *adv. phr.* As loud as you can; with the greatest possible sound; very loudly. *He was singing at the top of his voice.* (He was singing as loudly as he could.) *He shouted at the top of his lungs.* (He shouted with all his strength.)

at this rate *or* **at that rate** *adv. phr.* At a speed like this or that; with progress like this or that. *John's father said that if John kept going at that rate he would never finish cutting the grass.* (If John cut the grass as slowly as he was, it would take him a very long time to finish.) *So Johnny has a whole dollar! At this rate he'll be a millionaire.* (He will soon be a millionaire.) *"Three 100's in the last four tests! At this rate you'll soon be teaching the subject," Tom said to Mary.* (He said that Mary was learning so much that soon she would know as much about the subject as the teacher knew.)

at times *adv. phr.* Not often; not regularly; not every day; not every week, occasionally; sometimes. *At times Tom's mother lets him hold the baby.* (Sometimes Tom's mother lets him hold the baby.) *You can certainly be exasperating at times!* (Sometimes you are very annoying.) *We have pie for dinner at times.* (We have pie for dinner occasionally, but not every day.) Syn. FROM TIME TO TIME, NOW AND THEN, ONCE IN A WHILE.

at will *adv. phr.* As you like; as you please or choose freely. *Little Bobby is allowed to wander at will in the neighborhood.* (He is permitted to go where he pleases in his own neighborhood.) *With an air conditioner you can enjoy comfortable temperatures at will.* (You can be cool if you have an air conditioner.)

at wits end See AT ONE'S WIT'S END.

at work *adj. phr.* Busy at a job; doing work. *The teacher was soon hard at work correcting that day's test.* (The teacher was soon busy correcting the day's tests.) *Jim is at work on his car.* (Jim is fixing his car.)

at worst *or* **at the worst** *adv. phr.* **1** Under the worst conditions; as the worst possibility. *When Don was caught cheating in the examination, he thought that at worst he would get a scolding.* (Don thought that a scolding was the worst thing that would happen to him.) Compare AT MOST. Contrast AT BEST. **2** In the least favorable view; to say the worst about a thing. *The treasurer had certainly not stolen any of the club's money; at worst, he had forgotten to write down some of the things he had spent money for.* (The worst you could say about the treasurer was that he did not keep careful records.)

aught See FOR AUGHT at FOR ALL 2, FOR ALL ONE KNOWS.

Aunt Tom *n., slang, originally from Black English* A successful professional or business woman who, due to her success in a masculine profession, doesn't care about the women's liberation movement or the passing of the Equal Rights Amendment to the U.S. Constitution. *Hermione is a regular Aunt Tom, she'll never vote for the ERA.* (Since she is successful in a man's world, she will not promote women's rights.)

avail See TO NO AVAIL *or* OF NO AVAIL.

average See ON AN AVERAGE *or* ON THE AV-
ERAGE, LAW OF AVERAGES.

awe See STAND IN AWE OF.

ax to grind *n. phr., informal* Something to
gain for yourself; a selfish reason.—A cliché.
*In praising movies for classroom use, he has
an ax to grind; he sells motion picture equipment.* (In urging movies for school use, he
wanted his own profit, since his business is
motion picture equipment.) *When Charles
told the teacher that he saw Arthur copying
his homework from Jim, he had an ax to
grind; Arthur would not let Charles copy from
him.* (Charles told the teacher about Arthur's
cheating because Arthur made him angry;
Charles had a selfish reason for doing it.)

B

babe in the woods *n. phr.* A person who is inexperienced or innocent in certain things. *He is a good driver, but as a mechanic he is just a babe in the woods.* (He can drive, but he knows so little about the car that he can't fix it if anything goes wrong.) Compare OVER ONE'S HEAD, BEYOND ONE'S DEPTH.

baby See WAR BABY.

baby kisser *n., slang* A person campaigning for votes in his quest for elected political office; such persons often kiss little children in public. *Nixon was a baby kisser when he ran for Vice President with Eisenhower.* (He indulged in emotion-rousing campaign tactics such as the kissing of little children in public.)

back See BACK OF *or* IN BACK OF, BEHIND ONE'S BACK, BRUSH BACK, COME BACK, CUT BACK, DOUBLE BACK, DRAW BACK, DROP BACK, EYES IN THE BACK OF ONE'S HEAD, FADE BACK, FALL BACK, FALL BACK ON, FLANKER BACK, FROM WAY BACK, GET BACK AT, GET ONE'S BACK UP, GIVE THE SHIRT OFF ONE'S BACK, GO BACK ON, HANG BACK, HARK BACK, HOLD BACK, LIKE WATER OFF A DUCK'S BACK, LOOK BACK, OFF ONE'S BACK, ON ONE'S BACK, PAT ON THE BACK, PIGGY-BACK, PIN ONE'S EARS BACK, PUT BACK THE CLOCK *or* TURN BACK THE CLOCK, PUT ONE'S BACK TO IT, SCRATCH ONE'S BACK, SET BACK, SET BACK ON ONE'S HEELS, SIT BACK, STAB IN THE BACK, TAKE A BACK SEAT, TAKE BACK, TALK BACK *also* ANSWER BACK, TURN ONE'S BACK ON, WEIGHT OF THE WORLD ON ONE'S SHOULDERS *or* WORLD ON ONE'S BACK, WHILE BACK.

back and forth *adv.* Backwards and forwards. *The chair is rocking back and forth.* (The chair rocks backward and then forward. *The tiger is pacing back and forth in his cage.* (The tiger keeps walking from one end of his cage to the other and back again.) Compare TO AND FRO.

back away *v.* To act to avoid or lessen one's involvement in something; draw or turn back; retreat. *The townspeople backed away from the building plan when they found out how much it would cost.* (They no longer supported the plan.)

back door *n., slang, citizen's band radio jargon* Rear of vehicle. *I am watching your back door.* (I am watching the rear of your vehicle to prevent you from being overtaken unawares by the police.)

back down *or* **back off** *v., informal* To give up a claim; not follow up a threat. *Bill said he could beat Ted, but when Ted put up his fists Bill backed down.* (Bill was not brave enough to fight.) *Harry claimed Joe had taken his book, but backed down when the teacher talked with him.* (Harry gave up and confessed that Joe had not taken his book.) Syn. BEAT A RETREAT. Compare BACK OUT, GIVE IN, GO BACK ON 1.

back of *or* **in back of** *prep.* 1 In or at the rear of; to the back of; behind. *The garage is back of the house.* (The garage stands behind the house.) *Our car was in back of theirs at the traffic light.* (Our car was behind their car.) 2 *informal* Being a cause or reason for; causing. *Hard work was back of his success.* (Hard work was the reason he succeeded.) *The principal tried to find out what was back of the trouble on the bus.* (The principal wanted to learn the cause of the trouble.) 3 *informal* In support or encouragement of; helping. *Jones will be elected, because many powerful men are back of him.* (Powerful men support Jones.) *Get in back of your team by cheering them at the game.* (Encourage the team by cheering.)

back out *v., informal* To fail to keep a promise; get out of an agreement. *She backed out of her engagement.* (She had promised to marry him, but broke her promise.) *He agreed to help him with a loan, but backed out.* (He agreed to lend him money, but changed his mind.) Compare BEG OFF, GO BACK ON.

back seat See TAKE A BACK SEAT.

backseat driver *n., informal* A bossy person in a car who always tells the driver what to do. *The man who drove the car became angry with the back seat driver.* (The driver became angry with the bossy passenger.)

back street *n.* A street not near the main streets or from which it is hard to get to a main street. *We got lost in the back streets going through the city and it took us a half hour to find our way again.* (We got lost and far away from the main street we wanted.) Compare SIDE STREET.

back to the salt mines *informal* Back to the job; back to work; back to work that is as hard or as unpleasant as working in a salt mine would be.—An overworked phrase, used humorously. *The lunch hour is over, boys. Back to the salt mines!* (The lunch hour is over. Let's get back to work!) *"Vacation is over," said Billy. "Back to the salt mines."* (After being on vacation, going back to school will be hard work.)

back to the wall *or* **back against the wall** *adv. phr.* In a trap; with no way to escape; in bad trouble. *The soldiers had their backs to the wall.* (The soldiers were trapped and had to fight or give up.) *He was in debt and could not get any help; his back was against the wall.* (He owed money and could not get help; he was in bad trouble.) *The team had their backs to the wall in the second half.* (The team was in trouble and might be beaten.) Compare BETWEEN THE DEVIL AND THE DEEP BLUE SEA, LAST DITCH, ON THE SPOT, UP AGAINST IT.

back up *v.* 1 To move backwards. *The train was backing up.* (It was moving back.) 2 To help or be ready to help; stay behind to help; agree with and speak in support of. *Jim has joined the Boy Scouts and his father is back-*

ing him up. (His father is helping him to be a good Scout.) *In football the linebacker backs up the linemen.* (The linebacker is behind, ready to help the linemen.) *The principal backs up the faculty.* (He supports and agrees with the teachers.) *Jim told us what had happened and Bob backed him up.* (Bob agreed that Jim's account was correct.) Compare BACK OF 3, STAND BY 4. **3** To move behind (another fielder) in order to catch the ball if he misses it. *The shortstop backed up the second baseman on the throw.* (The shortstop ran behind the second baseman so he could catch the throw if the second baseman missed it.)

backward See BEND OVER BACKWARD *or* LEAN OVER BACKWARD; FALL OVER BACKWARDS *or* FALL OVER ONESELF.

backward and forward *or* **backwards and forwards** *adv. phr.* To the full extent; in all details; thoroughly; completely. *He understood automobile engines backwards and forwards.* (He knew everything about automobile mechanics.) *He knew basketball rules backwards and forwards.* (He knew all the basketball rules thoroughly.) *I explained matters to him so that he understood backwards and forwards how it was.* (I explained everything so he fully understood the trouble.)

bacon See BRING HOME THE BACON.

bad See GO FROM BAD TO WORSE, IN A BAD WAY, IN BAD, IN ONE'S BAD GRACES, LEAVE A BAD TASTE IN ONE'S MOUTH, NOT BAD *or* NOT SO BAD *or* NOT HALF BAD, ON ONE'S BAD SIDE, TOO BAD, WITH BAD GRACE.

bad actor *n., informal* A person or animal that is always fighting, quarreling, or doing bad things. *The boy was a bad actor and nobody liked him.* (He was always fighting or doing bad things.)

bad blood *n., informal* Anger or misgivings due to bad relations in the past between individuals or groups. *There's a lot of bad blood between Max and Jack; I bet they'll never talk to each other again.* (They won't be able to overcome their past differences.) Compare BAD SHIT.

bad egg *n., slang* A ne'er-do-well; good-for-nothing; a habitual offender. *The judge sent the bad egg to prison at last.* (He often broke the law and the judge sent him to prison.) Contrast GOOD EGG.

bad mouth (someone) *v., slang* To say uncomplimentary or libelous things about someone; deliberately to damage another's reputation. *It's not nice to badmouth people.* (It isn't nice to make disparaging remarks about others.)

bad news *n., slang* An event, thing, or person which is disagreeable or an unpleasant surprise. *What's the new professor like? — He's all bad news to me.* (I don't like him at all; he seems unpleasant and is best avoided.)

bad paper *n., slang* **1** A check for which there are no funds in the bank. **2** Coun-

terfeit paper money. *Why are you so mad? —I was paid with some bad paper.* (I was given a check that bounced, or a counterfeit banknote.)

bad shit *n., vulgar, avoidable* An unpleasant event or situation, such as a long lasting and unsettled quarrel or recurring acts of vengeance preventing two people or two groups from reaching any kind of reconciliation. *There is so much bad shit between the two gangs that I bet there will be more killings this year.* (The two gangs have been feuding for so long that chances are more people will be killed.) Compare BAD BLOOD.

bad trip *n., slang, drug culture; also used colloquially* A disturbing or frightening experience, such as terrifying hallucinations, while under the influence of drugs; hence, by colloquial extension any bad experience in general. *Why's John's face so distorted?—He had a bad trip.* (He had a frightening hallucinogenic experience.) *How was your math exam?—Don't mention it; it was a bad trip.* (I had a terrible time while I took it; I think I flunked.)

bag See GRAB BAG, IN THE BAG, LEAVE HOLDING THE BAG, LET THE CAT OUT OF THE BAG.

bag and baggage *adv., informal* With all your clothes and other personal belongings, especially movable possessions; completely. *If they don't pay their hotel bill they will be put out bag and baggage.* (They will be put out with everything they own.)

baggage See BAG AND BAGGAGE.

bail See JUMP BAIL *or* SKIP BAIL.

bail out¹ *v.* **1** To secure release from prison until trial by leaving or promising money or property for a while. *When college students got into trouble with the police, the college president would always bail them out.* (He would promise to have them return for trial or pay money himself.) **2** *informal* To free from trouble by giving or lending money. *He started a small business, which prospered after his father had to bail him out a couple of times.* (He started a small business, which succeeded after his father helped him out of some troubles with money.)

bail out² *v.* To jump from an airplane and drop with a parachute. *When the second engine failed, the pilot told everyone to bail out.* (When the second engine failed, the pilot told everyone to leave the plane.)

bail out³ *v.* To dip water from a filling or leaking boat; throw water out of a boat to prevent its sinking. *Both men were kept busy bailing out the rowboat after it began to leak.* (Both men were kept busy dipping out the water from the leaking rowboat.)

bait See FISH OR CUT BAIT.

bake See HALF-BAKED.

baker's dozen *n., informal* Thirteen. "How many of the jelly doughnuts, Sir? the salesclerk asked. "Oh, make it a baker's dozen." (*Make it thirteen.*)

balance See HANG IN THE BALANCE, OFF BALANCE.

ball See BASE ON BALLS, CARRY THE BALL, FLY BALL, FOUL BALL, GET THE BALL ROLLING, SET THE BALL ROLLING, START THE BALL ROLLING, GOPHER BALL, GROUND BALL, HAVE A BALL, HAVE SOMETHING ON THE BALL, JUMP BALL, KEEP THE BALL ROLLING, LONG BALL, ON THE BALL, PASSED BALL, PLAY BALL.

ball game *n., slang, also informal* The entire matter at hand; the whole situation; the entire contest. *You said we can get a second mortgage for the house?! Wow! That's a whole new ball game.* (Getting the loan changes the situation entirely in our favor.)

ball of fire *n., informal* A person with great energy and ability; a person who can do something very well. *He did poorly in school but as a salesman he is a ball of fire.* (He is a very successful salesman.) *The new shortstop is a good fielder but certainly no ball of fire in batting.* (He is not a very good batter.) Compare HOT NUMBER, HOT ONE.

balloon See TRIAL BALLOON.

ballot-stuffing See STUFF THE BALLOT BOX.

ball up *v., slang* To make a mess of; confuse. *Don't ball me up.* (Don't get me all confused.) *Hal balled up the business with his errors.* (Hal made a mess of the business.) —Often used in the passive. *He was so balled up that he did not know if he was coming or going.* (He was all confused.) Compare MIXED UP.

baloney *n., informal* Nonsense, unbelievable, trite, or trivial. *Max brags that he's won the $10 million lottery, and I think it's just a lot of baloney.* (I believe that Max is talking nonsense.) *"Will you marry Joe?" mother asked. "Baloney," Hermione answered with a disgusted look.* (She denies and downplays the likelihood of marrying Joe.) *Do you still believe all that baloney about socialism excluding free enterprise? Look at China and Hungary.* (China and Hungary show that it is possible to have free enterprise in a socialist country.)

banana oil *n., slang* Flattery that is an obvious exaggeration; statements that are obviously made with an ulterior motive. *Cut out the banana oil; flattery will get you nowhere!* (Stop flattering me so exaggeratedly; it has no effect on me.)

band See BEAT THE BAND.

bandbox See LOOK AS IF ONE HAS COME OUT OF A BANDBOX.

bandwagon See JUMP ON THE BANDWAGON.

bang-up *adj., informal* Very successful; very good; splendid; excellent. *The football coach has done a bang-up job this season.* (The coach led the team through a fine season of games.) *John did a bang-up job painting the house.* (John did a very good painting job.) Syn. FIRST-CLASS.

bank See PIGGY BANK.

bank on *v., informal* To depend on; put one's trust in; rely on. *He knew he could bank on public indignation to change things, if he could once prove the dirty work.* (He knew he could rely on public anger to clean up the mess, if he could get them started by showing the dishonesty.) *The students were banking on the team to do its best in the championship game.* (The students expected the team to do its best.) Syn. COUNT ON.

bar See BEHIND BARS, PARALLEL BARS.

bargain See DRIVE A BARGAIN, IN THE BARGAIN *or* INTO THE BARGAIN.

bargain for *or* **bargain on** *v.* To be ready for; expect. *When John started a fight with the smaller boy he got more than he bargained for.* (The smaller boy surprised John by giving him a good fight.) *The final cost of building the house was much more than they had bargained on.* (It cost more than they had expected to pay when they began.) Compare COUNT ON.

barge in *v. phr., informal* To appear uninvited at someone's house or apartment, or to interrupt a conversation. *I'm sorry for barging in like that, Sir, but my car died on me and there is no pay phone anywhere.* (Apologizes for coming in as a total stranger and wants to use the phone.) *I'm sorry for barging in while you two are having a discussion, but could you please tell me where the nearest exit is?* (Offers apology for interrupting conversation and seeks information on how to leave the building.)

bark up the wrong tree *v. phr., informal* To choose the wrong person to deal with or the wrong course of action; mistake an aim.—A cliché. *If he thinks he can fool me, he is barking up the wrong tree.* (He can not fool me; I know him too well.) *He is barking up the wrong tree when he blames his troubles on bad luck.* (His troubles come from his own mistakes, not luck.) *The police were looking for a tall thin man, but were barking up the wrong tree; the thief was short and fat.* (The police were hunting the wrong man.)

bark worse than one's bite *informal* Sound or speech more frightening or worse than your actions.—A cliché. *The small dog barks savagely, but his bark is worse than his bite.* (The small dog sounds mean, but he really is not.) *The boss sometimes talks roughly to the men, but they know that his bark is worse than his bite.* (The boss sounds very angry, but does not attack or fire the men.) *She was always scolding her children, but they knew her bark was worse than her bite.* (She scolded them but did not punish them very much.)

barn See LOCK THE BARN DOOR AFTER THE HORSE IS STOLEN.

barrel See OVER A BARREL *also* OVER THE BARREL, SCRAPE THE BOTTOM OF THE BARREL.

barrelhead See CASH ON THE BARRELHEAD.

bar the door See CLOSE THE DOOR.

base See FIRST BASE, GET TO FIRST BASE or REACH FIRST BASE, LOAD THE BASES, OFF BASE, SECOND BASE, STOLEN BASE, THIRD BASE.

base on balls *n.* First base given to a baseball batter who is pitched four balls outside of the strike zone. *He was a good judge of pitchers and often received bases on balls.* (He was good at telling strikes from balls and often got to first base by not swinging at bad pitches.)

basket See PUT ALL ONE'S EGGS IN ONE BASKET.

basket case *n., slang, also informal* **1** A person who has had both arms and both legs cut off as a result of war or other misfortune. **2** A helpless person who is unable to take care of himself, as if carried around in a basket by others. *Stop drinking, or else you'll wind up a basket case!* (If you don't stop drinking you will become entirely helpless as if suffering from a terminal disease.)

bat See AT BAT, GO TO BAT FOR, RIGHT AWAY or RIGHT OFF also RIGHT OFF THE BAT.

bat an eye *or* **bat an eyelash** *v. phr., informal* To show surprise, fear, or interest; show your feelings.—Used in negative sentences. *When I told him the price of the car he never batted an eye.* (He was not surprised or upset at the price.) *Bill told his story without batting an eyelash, although not a word of it was true.* (He told his story which he knew was not true, but he was calm and did not show any embarrassment.) Compare STRAIGHT FACE.

bath See SPONGE BATH, THROW THE BABY OUT WITH THE BATH.

bats in one's belfry *or* **bats in the belfry** *n. phr., slang* Wild ideas in his mind; disordered senses; great mental confusion. *When he talked about going to the moon he was thought to have bats in his belfry.* (His friends thought he had wild ideas and talked foolishly.)

bat the breeze See SHOOT THE BREEZE.

battle See HALF THE BATTLE.

bawl out *v., informal* To reprove in a loud or rough voice; rebuke sharply; scold. *The teacher bawled us out for not handing in our homework.* (The teacher gave us a loud scolding.) Compare HAUL OVER THE COALS, LIGHT INTO, TELL A THING OR TWO.

bay See AT BAY, BRING TO BAY.

be See LET BE, TO-BE.

beach See NOT THE ONLY PEBBLE ON THE BEACH.

beach bunny *n., slang* An attractive girl seen on beaches—mostly to show off her figure; one who doesn't get into the water and swim. *What kind of a girl is Susie?—She's a beach bunny; she always comes to the Queen's Surf on Waikiki but I've never seen her swim.* (She never enters the water just parades in her bikini to get attention.)

bead See DRAW A BEAD ON.

beam See OFF THE BEAM, ON THE BEAM.

bean See FULL OF BEANS, SPILL THE BEANS, USE ONE'S HEAD or USE ONE'S BEAN.

bear See GRIN AND BEAR IT, LOADED FOR BEAR.

bear a hand See LEND A HAND.

beard See LAUGH UP ONE'S SLEEVE or LAUGH IN ONE'S SLEEVE or LAUGH IN ONE'S BEARD.

bear down *v.* **1** To press or push harder; work hard; give full strength and attention. *She is bearing down in her studies to win a scholarship.* (She is working harder on her studies.) *The baseball pitcher is bearing down.* (He is trying to keep the other team from scoring.) *The pitcher bore down on the star batter.* (He pitched harder and more carefully to the star batter.) *Teachers of the deaf bear down on English.* (They give much attention to teaching English.) *The sergeant bears down on lazy soldiers.* (He scolds them and tries to make them do better.) Contrast LET UP 2B. **2** To move toward in an impressive or threatening way.—Often used with on. *While he was crossing the street a big truck bore down on him.* (A big truck was coming toward him and might hit him.) *The little ship tried to escape when the big pirate ship bore down.* (The little ship saw the big pirate ship coming and tried to escape.) *After the boys threw the snowballs they saw a large lady bearing down upon them from across the street.* (She was coming towards them perhaps to scold them.)

bear in mind See IN MIND.

bear in the air *or* **bear in the sky** *n. phr., slang, citizen's band jargon* A police helicopter flying overhead watching for speeders. *Slow down, good buddy, there's a bear in the air.* (You are being observed by a police helicopter.)

bear off the palm See CARRY OFF THE PALM.

bear one's cross See CARRY ONE'S CROSS.

bear out *v.* To show to be right; prove; support. *Modern findings do not bear out the old belief that the earth is flat.* (New facts do not support the old belief that the earth is flat.) *Fulton's faith in his steamboat was borne out, even though it was once called "Fulton's Folly."* (Fulton's faith in his invention was shown to be correct, even though he was once laughed at.)

bear trap *n., slang, citizen's band radio jargon* A police radar unit designed to catch speeders. *Watch the bear trap at exit 101.* (At exit 101 there is police radar speed control, so slow down.)

bear up *v.* **1** To hold up; carry; support; encourage. *The old bridge can hardly bear up its own weight any more.* (The old bridge is hardly strong enough to hold itself up any more.) *He was borne up by love of country.* (Love of country kept up his courage and eagerness.) **2** To keep up one's courage or strength; last.—Often used with under. *This boat will bear up under hurricane winds.* (This boat will stay afloat even in a storm.) *She bore up well at the funeral.* (She was brave and calm at the funeral.) Syn. STAND UP. Compare CARRY ON.

bear watching *v. phr.* **1** To be worth watching or paying attention to; have a promising future. *That young ball player will bear watching.* (That young player may have a great career ahead.) **2** To be dangerous or untrustworthy. (*Those tires look badly worn; they will bear watching.*) (Those tires are dangerous and may blow out at any time.) Compare KEEP AN EYE ON.

bear with *v., formal* To have patience with; not get angry with. *Your little sister is sick. Try to bear with her when she cries.* (Try to have patience with her when she cries.) *It is hard to bear with criticism.* (It is hard to be patient when others criticize you.) Syn. PUT UP WITH. Compare CARRY ONE'S CROSS.

beat See HEART SKIP A BEAT, OFF THE BEATEN TRACK.

beat about the bush *or* **beat around the bush** *v. phr., slang* To talk about things without giving a clear answer; avoid the question or the point. *He would not answer yes or no, but beat about the bush.* (He talked about other things but did not really answer.) *He beat about the bush for a half hour without coming to the point.* (He talked around the question, missing the point.) Compare BESIDE THE POINT. Contrast COME TO THE POINT.

beat all *or* **beat the Dutch** *v. phr., informal* To be strange or surprising. *John found a box full of money buried in his garage. Doesn't that beat all!* (Isn't that strange!) *It beats the Dutch how Tom always makes a basket.* (It is surprising that Tom always throws the ball through the basket.)

beat all hollow *also* **beat hollow** *v. phr., slang* To do much better than; to beat very badly. *We beat their team all hollow.* (We beat their team very badly.) *As a speaker, he beats us all hollow.* (He is a far better speaker than any of us.)

beat a retreat *v. phr.* **1** To give a signal, esp. by beating a drum, to go back. *The Redcoats' drums were beating a retreat.* (The drums were beating a signal for the Redcoats to turn back.) **2** To run away. *They beat a retreat when they saw that they were too few.* (They gave up the idea of fighting and ran off.) *The cat beat a hasty retreat when he saw the dog coming.* (The cat left quickly when he saw the dog.) Compare BACK DOWN, FALL BACK.

beat around the bush See BEAT ABOUT THE BUSH.

beat down *v.* **1** To crush or break the spirit of; win over; conquer. *All their defenses were beaten down by the tanks.* (Their defenses were completely crushed by the tanks.) **2** *informal* **a** To try to get reduced; force down by discussing. *Can we beat down the price?* (Can we get a lower price and save money?) **b** To persuade or force (someone) to accept a lower price or easier payments. *He tried to beat us down, so we did not sell the house.* (He tried to make us lower our price, and we refused to sell.) **3** To shine brightly or hotly. *At noon the sun beat down on our heads as we walked home.* (The sun felt hot on our heads.)

beat hollow See BEAT ALL HOLLOW.

beat into one's head *v. phr., informal* To teach by telling again and again; repeat often; drill; also, to be cross and punish often. *Tom is lazy and stubborn and his lessons have to be beaten into his head.* (His teacher has to be cross and tell him often.) *I cannot beat it into his head that he should take off his hat in the house.* (I have told him often and punished him, but he still wears his hat in the house.)

beat it *v., slang* To go away in a hurry; get out quickly. *When he heard the crash he beat it as fast as he could.* (He ran away as fast as he could.)—Often used as a command. *The big boy said, "Beat it, kid. We don't want you with us."* (The big boy told the little boy to go away.) Compare CLEAR OUT 2, LIGHT OUT, HEAD FOR THE HILLS.

beat one's brains out *or* **beat one's brains** *v. phr., slang* To try very hard to understand or think out something difficult; tire yourself out by thinking. *It was too hard for him and he beat his brains out trying to get the answer.* (He tried very hard to understand.) *Some students are lazy, but others beat their brains and succeed.* (Some try much harder than others.)

beat one's gums *v. phr., slang* To engage in idle talk, or meaningless chatter; generally to talk too much. *"Stop beating your gums, Max," Joe cried. "I am falling asleep."* (Joe says that Max's idle chatter is soporific.) Compare CHEW THE FAT *or* CHEW THE RAG, SHOOT THE BREEZE *or* BAT THE BREEZE *or* FAN THE BREEZE *or* SHOOT THE BULL.

beat one's head against a wall *v. phr.* To struggle uselessly against something that can't be beaten or helped; not succeed after trying very hard.—A cliché. *Trying to make him change his mind is just beating your head against a wall.* (He is so stubborn that it is hopeless to try to persuade him.)

beat the band *adv. phr., informal* At great speed; with much noise or commotion.—A cliché;—Used after *to. The fire engines were going down the road to beat the band.* (They were going full speed.) *The audience cheered and stamped and clapped to beat the band.* (The audience clapped as loudly as they could.)

beat the bushes *also* **beat the brush** *v. phr., informal* To try very hard to find or get something. *The mayor was beating the bushes for* *funds to build the playground.* (He went to every possible source for money.) Contrast BEAT ABOUT THE BUSH *or* BEAT AROUND THE BUSH.

beat the gun See JUMP THE GUN.

beat the ——— out of *or* **lick the ——— out of** *or* **whale the ——— out of** *v. phr., informal* To beat hard; give a bad beating to. —Used with several words after *the,* as *daylights, living daylights, tar. The big kid told Charlie that he would beat the daylights out of him if Charlie came in his yard again.* (The big boy told Charlie not to come there again or he would give him a bad beating.)

beat the meat *v. phr., vulgar, avoidable* To masturbate (said primarily of men). *"So what did you do for sex in prison for seven years?"* Joe asked. *"Well, unless you want to become gay, you can beat the meat and that's about it,"* Max answered. (Max says that masturbation is the only available sexual outlet unless one becomes a homosexual.)

beat to *v., informal* To do something before someone else does it. *I was waiting to buy a ticket but only one ticket was left, and another man beat me to it.* (He bought the ticket just before I had a chance to buy it.) *We were planning to send a rocket into space but the Russians beat us to it.* (They sent out a space rocket before we were ready.) Compare GET THE JUMP ON.

beat to the punch *or* **beat to the draw** *v. phr., slang* To do something before another person has a chance to do it.—A cliché. *John was going to apply for the job, but Ted beat him to the draw.* (Ted applied and got the job before John applied.) *Lois bought the dress before Mary could beat her to the punch.* (Lois bought the dress before Mary could buy it.)

beat up *v., informal* To give a hard beating to; hit hard and much; thrash; whip. *When the new boy first came, he had to beat up several neighborhood bullies before they would leave him alone.* (When he first came, he had to fight and beat several tough boys in the neighborhood to gain their respect.)—Used with *on* in substandard speech. *The tough boy said to Bill, "If you come around here again, I'll beat up on you."* (The boy warned Bill not to come there again or he would beat him.)

beauty sleep *n.* A nap or rest taken to improve the appearance. A trite expression. *She took her beauty sleep before the party.* (She took a nap before the party, so that she would look fresh and not tired.) *Many famous beauties take a beauty sleep every day.* (Many famous beauties take a nap every day.)

beaver *n., slang, citizen's band radio jargon* A female, especially one driving along the highway and operating a CB radio. *I didn't know there was a beaver aboard that eighteen-wheeler.* (I didn't know there was a woman in that truck and trailer.)

because of *prep.* On account of; by reason of; as a result of. *The train arrived late because of the snowstorm.* (The snowstorm caused the train to be late.)

beck See AT ONE'S BECK AND CALL.

bed See GET UP ON THE WRONG SIDE OF THE BED, GO TO BED WITH THE CHICKENS, MAKE ONE'S BED AND LIE IN IT, PUT TO BED.

bed of roses *or* **bowl of cherries** *n. phr.* A pleasant easy place, job, or position; an easy life.—A cliché. *A coal miner's job is not a bed of roses.* (A coal miner's work is very hard and unpleasant.) *After nine months of school, summer camp seemed a bowl of cherries.* (School was a time of hard study, but summer camp was easy.) Compare IN CLOVER, LIFE OF RILEY.

bee See BIRDS AND THE BEES.

beef up *v., informal* To make stronger by adding men or equipment; make more powerful; reinforce. *The general beefed up his army with more big guns and tanks.* (He got more guns and tanks to strengthen his army.) *The university beefed up the football coaching staff by adding several good men.* (The university made their coaching staff better by getting several new men.)

bee in one's bonnet *n. phr., informal* A fixed idea that seems fanciful, odd, or crazy.—A cliché. *Robert Fulton had a bee in his bonnet about a steamboat.* (He was stubborn in his idea and people thought it was foolish.) *Grandmother has some bee in her bonnet about going to the dance.* (She has a foolish idea about going to the dance, but she is too old.)

beeline See MAKE A BEELINE FOR.

before long *adv. phr.* In a short time; without much delay; in a little while; soon. *Class will be over before long.* (Class will be over soon.) *We were tired of waiting and hoped the bus would come before long.* (We hoped the bus would come in a short time.)

before one can say Jack Robinson *adv. cl., informal* Very quickly; suddenly.—An overused phrase. *Before I could say Jack Robinson, the boy was gone.* (The boy ran away suddenly.) Compare IN A FLASH, RIGHT AWAY.

before swine See CAST PEARLS BEFORE SWINE *or* CAST ONE'S PEARLS BEFORE SWINE.

beg See GO BEGGING.

beggars can't be choosers People who can not choose what they will have, must accept what they get; if you are not in control, you must take what you can get.—A cliché. *We wanted to leave on the train in the morning but it doesn't go until afternoon, so we must go then. Beggars can't be choosers.* (We can't choose the time we want to leave on the train. We must go in the afternoon.) *Mary got a red dress from her sister, although she didn't like red. She kept it because she said beggars should not be choosers.* Mary thought she shouldn't be fussy because her sister gave her a red dress.) Compare LOOK A GIFT HORSE IN THE MOUTH.

beg off v. To ask to be excused. *Father told Tom to rake the yard, but Tom tried to beg off.* (Tom tried to get his father to excuse him.) *Mrs. Crane accepted an invitation to a luncheon, but a headache made her beg off.* (She asked to be excused from the luncheon.) Compare BACK OUT.

beg the question v. phr., literary To accept as true something that is still being argued about, before it is proved true; avoid or not answer a question or problem. *The girls asked Miss Smith, if they should wear formal dresses to the party; Miss Smith said they were begging the question because they didn't know yet if they could get permission for a party.* (The girls were trying to plan for a party before the question of permission for a party was decided.) *Laura told Tom that he must believe her argument because she was right; Father laughed and told Laura she was begging the question.* (Father told Laura she thought she had won the argument; but really she had not yet proved she was right.) Compare TAKE FOR GRANTED.

behalf See IN BEHALF OF or ON BEHALF OF, IN ONE'S BEHALF or ON ONE'S BEHALF.

behavior See ON ONE'S GOOD BEHAVIOR.

behind See DRY BEHIND THE EARS, FALL BEHIND, GET BEHIND, HANG BACK or HANG BEHIND.

behind bars adv. phr. In jail; in prison. *He was a pickpocket and had spent many years behind bars.* (He had spent many years in prison.) *That boy is always in trouble and will end up behind bars.* (He may get in bad trouble and be put in jail.)

behind one's back adv. phr. When one is absent; without one's knowledge or consent; in a dishonest way; secretly; sneakily. *Say it to his face, not behind his back.* (Say it openly. Do not say one thing when he is here, and another when he is gone.) *It is not right to criticize a person behind his back.* (It is better to tell him what he does wrong.) Contrast TO ONE'S FACE.

behind the eight-ball adj. phr., slang In a difficult position; in trouble.—A cliché. *Mr. Thompson is an older man, and when he lost his job, he found he was behind the eight-ball.* (He found it hard to get another job at his age.) *Bill can't dance and has no car, so he is behind the eight-ball with the girls.* (He is in a difficult position with the girls because he can't dance and has no car.) Compare HAVE TWO STRIKES AGAINST ONE 2, IN A HOLE.

behind the scenes adv. phr. Out of sight; unknown to most people; privately. *Much of the banquet committee's work was done behind the scenes.* (Most people did not know what the committee did.) *John was president of the club, but behind the scenes Lee told*

him what to do. (People thought John made the decisions, but really Lee did.)

behind the times adj. phr. Using things not in style; still following old ways; old-fashioned. *Johnson's store is behind the times.* (The store is old-fashioned; it looks as stores looked 40 years ago.) *The science books of 30 years ago are behind the times now.* (The old science books do not explain new discoveries.) *Mary thinks her parents are behind the times because they still do the fox-trot and don't know any new dances.* (Mary's parents are old-fashioned in their dancing.)

behind time adv. or adj. phr. **1a** Behind the correct time; slow. *That clock is behind time.* (That clock is wrong. It is slow.) **1b** behind schedule; late. *The train is running behind time today.* (The train is not on time today.) **2** Not keeping up; not at the proper time; overdue. *Your lessons are good, but why are you behind time?* (Why were your lessons not ready on time?) *We are behind time in paying the rent.* (We are paying the rent later than usual, or later than we should.) Contrast AHEAD OF TIME, IN TIME, ON TIME.

be-in n., slang, hippie and drug culture usage spreading to other areas A gathering or social occasion with or without a discernible purpose, often held in a public place like a park or under a large circus tent. *The youngsters really enjoyed the great springtime jazz be-in at the park.* (They enjoyed themselves at the jazz festival.) *"What's going on?" Jim asked. "Nothing much," Sylvia answered. "We're just having an after-holiday family be-in."* (She says that nothing special or planned is going on, people just sit around having informal conversations.) *"Why are the riot police out in force?" Jack asked. "Well, the be-in turned into a drug orgy and two people died," Fred answered.* (He says that the apparently purposeless gathering turned out to be an occasion for illegal drug use that killed two people, so the police had to come.)

being See FOR THE TIME BEING.

be into something v. phr., informal To have taken something up partly as a hobby, partly as a serious interest of sorts (basically resulting from the new consciousness and self-realization movement that originated in the late Sixties). *Roger's wife is into women's liberation and women's consciousness.* (Roger's wife has taken up the cause of women's liberation and women's consciousness.) *Did you know that Syd is seriously into transcendental meditation?* (Did you know that Syd practices transcendental meditation seriously?) *Jack found out that his teenage son is into pot smoking and gave him a serious scolding.* (Jack learned that his son had started to smoke marijuana and took corrective measures.)

be it so See SO BE IT.

belfry See BATS IN ONE'S BELFRY or BATS IN THE BELFRY.

believe See MAKE BELIEVE, SEEING IS BELIEVING.

believe one's ears *v. phr.* **1** To believe what one hears; trust one's hearing.—Used with a negative or limiter, or in an interrogative or conditional sentence. *He thought he heard a horn blowing in the distance, but he could not believe his ears.* (He thought his ears were fooling him.) **2** To be made sure of (something). *Is he really coming? I can hardly believe my ears.* (Are you sure he is coming? It is surprising!)

believe one's eyes *v. phr.* **1** To believe what one sees; trust one's eyesight.—Used with a negative or limiter or in an interrogative or conditional sentence. *Is that a plane? Can I believe my eyes?* (Are my eyes deceiving me? Is it really a plane?) **2** To be made sure of seeing something. *She saw him there but she could hardly believe her eyes.* (She saw him, but she could hardly believe that it was true.)

bell See RING A BELL, WITH BELLS ON.

belly up *adj., informal* Dead, bankrupt, or financially ruined. *Tom and Dick struggled on for months with their tiny computer shop, but last year they went belly up.* (They survived for a while but soon went bankrupt.)

belly up *v., informal* To go bankrupt, become afunctional; to die. *Uncompetitive small businesses must eventually all belly up.* (Small businesses eventually die, they go bankrupt.)

below the belt *adv. phr.* **1** In the stomach; lower than is fair in boxing. *He struck the other boy below the belt.* (He struck the other boy a foul blow.) **2** *informal* In an unfair or cowardly way; against the rules of sportsmanship or justice; unsportingly; wrongly. *It was hitting below the belt for Mr. Jones's rival to tell people about a crime that Mr. Jones committed when he was a young boy.* (It was unfair for the man to tell about something past that makes no difference now.) *Pete told the students to vote against Harry because Harry was crippled and couldn't be a good class president, but the students thought Pete was hitting below the belt.* (They thought Pete was breaking the rules of sportsmanship.)

belt See BELOW THE BELT, SEAT BELT, TIGHTEN ONE'S BELT, UNDER ONE'S BELT.

belt out *v., slang* To sing with rough rhythm and strength; shout out. *She belted out ballads and hillbilly songs one after another all evening.* (She shouted out simple rhythmic songs all evening.) *Young people enjoy belting out songs.* (They like to sing loudly.)

be my guest *v. phr.* Feel free to use what I have; help yourself. *When Suzie asked if she could borrow John's bicycle, John said, "Be my guest."* (He encouraged her to feel free to use it.)

bench See ON THE BENCH, WARM THE BENCH.

bench warmer See WARM THE BENCH.

bend over backward *or* **lean over backward** *v. phr., informal* To try so hard to avoid a mistake that you make the opposite mistake instead; do the opposite of something that you know you should not do; do too much to avoid doing the wrong thing; *also,* make a great effort; try very hard.—A cliché. *Instead of punishing the boys for breaking a new rule, the principal bent over backward to explain why the rule was important.* (The principal probably wanted to punish the boys for breaking the new rule, but instead he explained pleasantly why the new rule would really help the boys.) *Mary was afraid the girls at her new school would be stuck up, but they leaned over backward to make her feel at home.* (The girls at the new school tried to make Mary happy instead of leaving her alone.) Compare GO OUT OF ONE'S WAY.

benefit See GIVE THE BENEFIT OF THE DOUBT.

bent on *or* **bent upon** Very decided, determined, or set. *The sailors were bent on having a good time.* (They had only one purpose, to have a good time.) *The policeman saw some boys near the school after dark and thought they were bent on mischief.* (The policeman thought the boys planned to do something bad.) *The bus was late, and the driver was bent upon reaching the school on time.* (The driver was determined to go fast and get to the school before classes started.)

be one's age See ACT ONE'S AGE.

berth See GIVE A WIDE BERTH.

beside oneself *adj. phr.* Very much excited; somewhat crazy. *She was beside herself with fear.* (She was so afraid that she did not know what to do.) *He was beside himself, he was so angry.* (He was terribly angry.) *When his wife heard of his death, she was beside herself.* (The news of her husband's death shocked and almost crazed her.)

beside the point *or* **beside the question** *adj. or adv. phr.* Off the subject; about something different. *What you meant to do is beside the point; the fact is you didn't do it.* (What you meant to do doesn't matter now.) *The judge told the witness that his remarks were beside the point.* (His remarks had nothing to do with the case.) Compare BEAT AROUND THE BUSH, NEITHER HERE NOR THERE.

best See AS BEST ONE CAN, AT BEST, FOR THE BEST, GET THE BETTER OF *or* GET THE BEST OF, HAD BETTER *or* HAD BEST, HE LAUGHS BEST WHO LAUGHS LAST, MAKE THE BEST OF, PUT ONE'S BEST FOOT FORWARD, SECOND BEST, TO THE BEST OF ONE'S KNOWLEDGE, WITH THE BEST *or* WITH THE BEST OF THEM.

best bib and tucker *or* **Sunday best** *or* **Sunday-go-to-meeting clothes** *n. phr., informal* Best clothes or outfit of clothing.—A cliché. *The cowboy got all dressed up in his best bib and tucker to go to the dance.* (He wore the best clothes he had.) *Mary went to the party* *in her Sunday best and made a hit with the boys.* (She wore her best clothes.) Compare GLAD RAGS.

bet See YOU BET *or* YOU BET YOUR BOOTS *or* YOU BET YOUR LIFE.

bet one's boots *or* **bet one's bottom dollar** *or* **bet one's shirt** *v. phr., informal* **1** To bet all you have. *This horse will win. I would bet my bottom dollar on it.* (I am so sure he will win, I would bet my only dollar on it.) **2** *or* **bet one's life.** To feel very sure; have no doubt. *Jim said he would bet his boots that he would pass the examination.* (Jim was very sure he would pass.) *Was I scared when I saw the bull running at me? You bet your life I was!* (You can be sure that I was scared.)

bet on the wrong horse *v. phr., informal* To base your plans on a wrong guess about the result of something; misread the future; misjudge a coming event. *To count on the small family farm as an important thing in the American future now looks like betting on the wrong horse.* (To depend heavily on the future of the U.S. small family farm now looks like misreading the future.) *He expected Stevenson to be elected President in 1952 but as it happened, he bet on the wrong horse.* (He thought Stevenson would be elected in 1952, but that was a bad guess.)

better See ALL BETTER, DISCRETION IS THE BETTER PART OF VALOR, FOR BETTER OR WORSE, FOR THE BETTER, GET THE BETTER OF, GO ——— ONE BETTER, HAD BETTER, HALF A LOAF IS BETTER THAN NONE *or* HALF A LOAF IS BETTER THAN NO BREAD, SEE BETTER DAYS, THINK BETTER OF.

better half *n., informal* One's marriage partner (mostly said by men about their wives.) *"This is my better half, Mary,"* said Joe. (He is introducing his wife.)

better late than never It is better to come or do something late than never.—A cliché. *The firemen didn't arrive at the house until it was half burned, but it was better late than never.* (If the firemen did not come at all, the fire would have burned all of the house.) *Grandfather is learning to drive a car. "Better late than never,"* he says. (It is better to learn to drive when you are old than never to learn.) Compare HALF A LOAF IS BETTER THAN NONE.

better than *prep. phr.* More than; greater than; at a greater rate than. *The car was doing better than eighty miles an hour.* (The car was going faster than eighty miles an hour.) *It is better than three miles to the station.* (It is a distance of more than three miles to the station.)

between See BETWIXT AND BETWEEN, COME BETWEEN, FEW AND FAR BETWEN.

between life and death *adv. phr.* In danger of dying or being killed; with life or death possible. *He held on to the mountainside between life and death while his friends went to get help.* (He was in danger of falling to his

death.) *The little sick girl lay all night between life and death until her fever was gone.* (She almost died, but her fever went down.)

between the devil and the deep blue sea *or literary* **between two fires** *or literary* **between Scylla and Charybdis** *adv. phr.* Between two dangers or difficulties, not knowing what to do. *The pirates had to fight and be killed or give up and be hanged; they were between the devil and the deep blue sea.* (Either way, they faced danger.) *The boy was between the devil and the deep blue sea; he had to go home and be whipped or stay in town all night and be picked up by the police.* (He didn't know which to choose, a whipping or arrest.) *When the man's wife and her mother got together, he was between two fires.* (He was scolded by both.) Compare COMING AND GOING 2, IN A BIND.

between the eyes See HIT BETWEEN THE EYES.

between the lines See READ BETWEEN THE LINES.

between two fires See BETWEEN THE DEVIL AND THE DEEP BLUE SEA.

be up to no good *v. phr., informal* To be plotting and conniving to commit some illegal act or crime. *"Let's hurry!" Susan said to her husband. "It's dark here and those hoodlums obviously are up to no good."* (She urges that they leave because she believes the hoodlums are up to attack and rob them.)

be up to something *v. phr., informal* **1** To feel strong enough or knowledgeable enough to accomplish a certain task. *Are you up to climbing all the way to the 37th floor?* (Do you have the strength to climb that high?) *Are we up to meeting the delegation from Moscow and speaking Russian to them?* (Is our knowledge of Russian adequate to talking to the delegation?) **2** Tendency to do something mischievous. *I'm afraid Jack is up to one of his old tricks again.* (He's about to pull off one of his old tricks.)

beyond measure *adj. or adv. phr., formal* So much that it can not be measured or figured; without any limits. *With her parents reunited and present at her graduation, she had happiness beyond measure.* (She was very happy.) *No one envied him, for he was popular beyond measure.* (He was liked by everyone.)

beyond one's depth *adj. or adv. phr.* **1** Over your head in water; in water too deep to touch bottom. *Jack wasn't a good swimmer, and nearly drowned when he drifted out beyond his depth.* (Jack got too far out to touch bottom.) **2** In or into something too difficult for you; beyond your understanding or ability. *Bill decided that his big brother's geometry book was beyond his depth.* (It was too hard for Bill.) *Sam's father started to explain the atom bomb to Sam, but he soon got beyond his depth.* (Sam's father soon told all he knew and could not explain any more.) *When Bill played checkers against the city champion, Bill was beyond his depth.* (Playing against an expert was beyond Bill's ability.) Compare OVER ONE'S HEAD 1.

beyond one's nose See SEE BEYOND ONE'S NOSE.

beyond question[1] *adj. phr.* Not in doubt; certain; sure.—Used in the predicate. *People always believe anything that Mark says; his honesty is beyond question.* (Everyone believes Mark; they know that he is honest; no one doubts that he is honest.) Contrast IN QUESTION.

beyond question[2] *or* **without question** *adv. phr.* Without doubt or argument; surely; unquestionably. *Beyond question, it was the coldest day of the winter.* (It was certainly the coldest day.) *John's drawing is without question the best in the class.* (John's drawing is undoubtedly the best in the class.)

beyond reasonable doubt *adv. phr., formal and legal* Virtually certain; essentially convincing. *The judge instructed the jurors to come up with a verdict of guilty only if they were convinced beyond a reasonable doubt that Algernon was the perpetrator.* (The judge told the jurors to find Algernon guilty only if they found the case against him sufficiently convincing.)

beyond the pale *adv. or adj. phr.* In disgrace; with no chance of being accepted or respected by others; not approved by the members of a group.—A cliché. *After the outlaw killed a man he was beyond the pale and not even his old friends would talk to him.* (The outlaw lost all his friends.) *Tom's swearing is beyond the pale; no one invites him to dinner any more.* (Polite people don't invite Tom because he uses bad words.)

beyond the shadow of a doubt *adv. phr., formal and legal* Absolutely certain; totally convincing. *Max burglarized Mrs. Brown's apartment, beyond the shadow of a doubt.* (It's absolutely certain that Max is the burglar.)

bib See BEST BIB AND TUCKER.

bide one's time *v. phr.* To await an opportunity; wait patiently until your chance comes. *Refused work as an actor, Tom turned to other work and bided his time.* (When Tom couldn't get work as an actor, he supported himself in other ways, and waited for his chance.) *Jack was hurt deeply, and he bided his time for revenge.* (Jack was hurt deeply, and he waited for an opportunity to get even.)

bid fair *v., literary* To seem likely; promise. *He bids fair to be a popular author.* (He is likely to be generally liked.) *The day bids fair to be warm.* (The day seems likely to be warm.)

big See IN A BIG WAY, LITTLE FROG IN A BIG POND, LITTLE PITCHERS HAVE BIG EARS, TALK BIG, TOO BIG FOR ONE'S BREECHES, WHAT'S THE BIG IDEA.

big as life *or* **large as life** *adj. phr.* **1** *or* **life-size** The same size as the living person or thing. *The statue of Jefferson was big as life.* (It was the same size as Jefferson himself was.) *The characters on the screen were life-size.* (The screen was so big that the actors were full size.) **2** *or* **big as life and twice as natural** *informal* In person; real and living. *I had not seen him for years, but there he was, big as life and twice as natural.* (He looked the same as ever.)

big cheese *or* **big gun** *or* **big shot** *or* **big wheel** *or* **big wig** *n., slang* An important person; a leader; a high official; a person of high rank. *Bill had been a big shot in high school.* (Bill had been a leader in student affairs.) *John wanted to be the big cheese in his club.* (John wanted to be the most important member of his club.) Compare WHOLE CHEESE.

big daddy *n., slang, informal* The most important, largest thing, person or animal in a congregation of similar persons, animals, or objects. *The whale is the big daddy of everything that swims in the ocean.* (It is the biggest water creature.) *The H-bomb is the big daddy of all modern weapons.* (It is the deadliest of all modern weapons.) *Al Capone was the big daddy of organized crime in Chicago during Prohibition.* (He was the leader of the criminals.)

big deal *interj., slang; informal* (loud stress on the word *deal*) Trifles; an unimportant, unimpressive thing or matter. *So you became college president—big deal!* (I am not impressed with the fact that you became a college president.)

big frog in a small pond *n. phr., informal* An important person in a small place or position; someone who is respected and honored in a small company, school, or city; a leader in a small group. *As company president, he had been a big frog in a small pond, but he was not so important as a new congressman in Washington.* (As company president in a small company he was respected and honored, but in Washington the other congressmen did not know or honor him.) Contrast LITTLE FROG IN A BIG POND.

bigger than one's stomach See EYES BIGGER THAN ONE'S STOMACH.

big head *n., informal* Too high an opinion of your own ability or importance; conceit. *When Jack was elected captain of the team, it gave him a big head.* (He became conceited. He was full of his own importance.) Compare SWELLED HEAD.

big lie, the *n., informal* A major, deliberate misrepresentation of some important issue made on the assumption that a bold, gross lie is psychologically more believable than a timid, minor one. *We all heard the big lie during the Watergate months.* (We were fed major misrepresentations of the facts.) *The pretense of democracy by a totalitarian regime is part* *of the big lie about its government.* (The "people's government" gives the people no political choices.)

big mouth *or* **big-mouthed** See LOUD MOUTH, LOUD-MOUTHED.

big stink *n., slang* A major scandal; a big upheaval. *I'll raise a big stink if they fire me.* (If they fire me, I will cause a major scandal or commotion by complaining to the right people.)

big time *n., informal* **1** A very enjoyable time at a party or other pleasurable gathering. *I certainly had a big time at the club last night.* (I certainly enjoyed myself at the club.) **2** The top group; the leading class; the best or most important company. *After his graduation from college, he soon made the big time in baseball.* (He was a fine player and soon was in the big leagues.) *Many young actors go to Hollywood, but few of them reach the big time.* (It is hard to succeed in becoming a movie star.)

big-time *adj.* Belonging to the top group; of the leading class; important. *Jean won a talent contest in her home town, and only a year later she began dancing on big-time television.* (Jean danced in programs on the big television networks.) *Bob practices boxing in the gym every day; he wants to become a big-time boxer.* (Bob wants to become a famous fighter in boxing.)—Often used in the phrase *big-time* operator. *Just because Bill has a new football uniform he thinks he is a big-time operator.* (Bill exaggerates his importance.) Compare SHOW OFF. Contrast SMALL-TIME.

big top *n.* The main tent under which a circus gives its show; the circus and circus life. *Lillian Leitzel was one of the great stars of the big top.* (She was one of the great circus performers.) *The book tells of life under the big top.* (It tells of circus life.)

big wheel *n., informal* An influential or important person who has the power to do things and has connections in high places. *Uncle Ferdinand is a big wheel in Washington, maybe he can help you with your problem.* (He works for the government and has good connections.)

bill See CLEAN BILL OF HEALTH, FILL THE BILL.

bind See DUTY BOUND, IN A BIND, MUSCLE-BOUND, ROOT-BOUND.

bingo card *n., slang* A response card, bound into a periodical, containing numbers keyed to editorial or advertising matter, giving the reader the opportunity to send for further information by marking the numbers of the items he is interested in; such a card can be mailed free of charge. *Jack thinks he is saving time by filling out bingo cards instead of writing a letter.* (He believes that this form of advertising saves him time.)

bird See EARLY BIRD CATCHES THE WORM *or* EARLY BIRD GETS THE WORM, EAT LIKE A BIRD, FINE FEATHERS DO NOT MAKE FINE BIRDS, FOR THE BIRDS, KILL TWO BIRDS WITH ONE STONE.

bird has flown *slang* The prisoner has escaped; the captive has got away. *When the sheriff returned to the jail, he discovered that the bird had flown.* (When the sheriff returned to the jail, he found that his prisoner had escaped.)

bird in the hand is worth two in the bush Something we have, or can easily get, is more valuable than something we want that we may not be able to get; we shouldn't risk losing something sure by trying to get something that is not sure.—A proverb. *Johnny has a job as a paperboy, but he wants a job in a gas station. His father says that a bird in the hand is worth two in the bush.* (Keep the job you have until you are sure of a better one.)

birds and the bees *n. phr., informal* The facts we should know about our birth. *At various ages, in response to questions, a child can be told about the birds and the bees.* (A child can be told the facts of sex and birth to fit each stage of maturity.)

birds of a feather flock together People who are alike often become friends or are together; if you are often with certain people, you may be their friends or like them.—A proverb. *Don't be friends with bad boys. People think that birds of a feather flock together.* (If you are friends with bad boys and people see you with them often, they will think that you are bad, too.)

bird watcher *n.* A person whose hobby is to study birds close-up in their out-door home. *A bird watcher looks for the first robin to appear in the spring.* (A person whose hobby is birds looks for the first robin to appear in the spring.)

birthday suit *n.* The skin with no clothes on; complete nakedness.—A cliché. *The little boys were swimming in their birthday suits.* (They were swimming without any clothes on.)

bit See A BIT, CHAMP AT THE BIT, FOUR BITS, QUITE A LITTLE *or* QUITE A BIT, SIX BITS, TAKE THE BIT IN ONE'S MOUTH, TWO BITS.

bitch See SON OF A BITCH.

bite See BARK WORSE THAN ONE'S BITE, PUT THE BITE ON, ONCE BITTEN, TWICE SHY at BURNT CHILD DREADS THE FIRE.

bite off more than one can chew *v. phr., informal* To try to do more than you can; be too confident of your ability. *He bit off more than he could chew when he agreed to edit the paper alone.* (He took on a job that was too hard for him when he agreed to edit the paper without help.) *He started to repair his car himself, but realized that he had bitten off more than he could chew.* (He started to repair his car himself, but soon realized that he didn't know enough to do it.)

bite the dust *v. phr., informal* **1** To be killed

in battle. *Captain Jones discharged his gun, and another guerilla bit the dust.* (Captain Jones fired his gun, and another guerilla dropped dead.) **2** To fall in defeat; go down before enemies; be overthrown; lose. *Our team bit the dust today.* (Our team lost.)

bite the hand that feeds one *v. phr.* To turn against or hurt a helper or supporter; repay kindness with wrong. *He bit the hand that fed him when he complained against his employer.* (He was injuring the man he was dependent on when he made the complaint.)

bitter See TO THE BITTER END.

bitter pill *n.* Something hard to accept; disappointment. *Jack was not invited to the party and it was a bitter pill for him.* (He felt bad about not being invited.)

black See BLACK AND WHITE, IN THE BLACK, LOOK BLACK, POT CALLS THE KETTLE BLACK.

black and white *n. phr.* **1** Print or writing; words on paper, not spoken; exact written or printed form. *He insisted on having the agreement down in black and white.* (He wanted the agreement written, not just spoken.) *Mrs. Jones would not believe the news, so Mr. Jones showed her the article in the newspaper and said, "There it is in black and white."* (He showed her that the news was printed in the paper.) **2** The different shades of black and white of a simple picture, rather than other colors. *He showed us snapshots in black and white.* (He showed us pictures that were black, grey, and white, not colored.)

black-and-white *adj.* Divided into only two sides that are either right or wrong or good or bad, with nothing in between; thinking or judging everything as either good or bad. *Everything is black-and-white to Bill; if you're not his friend, you are his enemy.* (You can't be anything in between or different from his friend or enemy.) *The old man's religion shows his black-and-white thinking; everything is either completely good or completely bad.* (The old man judges everything as very good or very bad.)

black out *v.* **1** To darken by putting out or dimming lights. *In some plays the stage is blacked out for a short time and the actors speak in darkness.* (In some plays the lights are turned off for a while.) *In wartime, cities are blacked out to protect against bombing from planes.* (The lights are turned off so bombers cannot find them.) **2** To prevent or silence information or communication; refuse to give out truthful news. *In wartime, governments often black out all news or give out false news.* (In wartime, governments conceal much news.) *Dictators usually black out all criticism of the government.* (Dictators do not let the people know the facts.) *Some big games are blacked out on television to people who live nearby.* (People can not get the games on their television sets.) **3** *informal* To lose

consciousness; faint. *It had been a hard and tiring day, and she suddenly blacked out.* (She had had a bad day, and suddenly she fainted.)

blame See TO BLAME.

blank check *n.* **1** A bank check written to a person who can then write in how much money he wants. *John's father sent him a blank check to pay his school bills.* (His father signed it and John could write the amount himself.) **2** *informal* Permission to another person to do anything he decides to do. *The teacher gave the pupils a blank check to plan the picnic.* (He told them they were free to plan the picnic themselves.)

blanket See WET BLANKET.

blast off *v.* **1** To begin a rocket flight. *The astronaut will blast off into orbit at six o'clock.* (He will begin a rocket flight.) **2** *Also* **blast away** *informal* To scold or protest violently. *The coach blasted off at the team for poor playing.* (He gave the team a violent scolding.)

blaze a trail *v. phr.* **1** To cut marks in trees in order to guide other people along a path or trail, especially through a wilderness. *Daniel Boone blazed a trail for other hunters to follow in Kentucky.* (He made marks with an axe and left a path through the woods so others could follow it and not get lost.) **2** To lead the way; make a discovery; start something new.—A cliché. *Henry Ford blazed a trail in manufacturing automobiles.* (Henry Ford led the way in building automobiles.) *The building of rockets blazed a trail to outer space.* (Rockets have started something new in space travel.)—**trail-blazer** *n.* A person who finds or tries something new; pioneer; discoverer. *Scientists are trail-blazers in finding cures for disease.* (Scientists are discoverers of new cures for diseases.)

bleep out See BLIP OUT.

blessing See MIXED BLESSING.

blind See FLY BLIND.

blind alley *n.* **1** A narrow street that has only one entrance and no exit. *The blind alley ended in a brick wall.* (The alley stopped at a brick wall.) **2** A way of acting that leads to no good results. *John did not take the job because it was a blind alley.* (The job would not lead to a better job.) *Tom thought of a way to do the algebra problem, but he found it was a blind alley.* (Tom's figures did not give the right answer.)

blind leading the blind One or more people who do not know or understand something trying to explain it to others who do not know or understand.—A cliché. *Jimmy is trying to show Bill how to skate. The blind are leading the blind.* (Jimmy does not know how to skate himself, but he is trying to teach Bill.)

blink See ON THE BLINK.

blip out *or* **bleep out** *v. phr., informal* To delete electronically a word on television or on radio either because it mentions the name of an established firm in a commercial or because it is a censored word not allowed for television audiences, resulting in a sound resembling the word "bleep." *What was the old product they compared Spic-n-Span to?— I don't know; they've bleeped it out.* (I can't tell you what they compared the new detergent to; its name was deleted electronically.)

blitz See SAFETY BLITZ.

block See CHIP OFF THE OLD BLOCK, KNOCK ONE'S BLOCK OFF, ON THE BLOCK.

blockhead *n., informal* An unusually dense, or stupid person whose head is therefore exaggeratedly compared to a solid block of wood. *Joe is such a blockhead that he flunked every course as a freshman.* (He is so stupid that he couldn't even get through his freshman year.)

blood See DRAW BLOOD, FLESH AND BLOOD, IN COLD BLOOD, IN ONE'S BLOOD *or* INTO ONE'S BLOOD, MAKE ONE'S BLOOD BOIL *or* MAKE THE BLOOD BOIL, NEW BLOOD, OUT OF ONE'S BLOOD, RUN IN THE BLOOD *or* RUN IN THE FAMILY, SPORTING BLOOD, SWEAT BLOOD, WARM ONE'S BLOOD.

blood and thunder *n. phr.* The violence and bloodshed of stories that present fast action rather than understanding of character. *Crime movies and westerns usually have lots of blood and thunder.* (Crime movies and westerns usually have much violence and killing.) —Often used like an adjective. *John likes to watch blood-and-thunder stories on television.* (He likes to watch stories with plenty of violent action.)

blood freezes See BLOOD RUNS COLD.

blood is thicker than water Persons of the same family are closer to one another than to others; relatives are favored or chosen over outsiders.—A cliché. *Mr. Jones hires his relatives to work in his store. Blood is thicker than water.* (Mr. Jones trusts his relatives and likes to have them working for him.)

blood runs cold *also* **blood freezes** *or* **blood turns to ice** You are chilled or shivering from great fright or horror; you are terrified or horrified.—A cliché, usually used with a possessive. *The horror movie made the children's blood run cold.* (The movie frightened the children badly.) *Mary's blood froze when she had to walk through the cemetery at night.* (Mary was very much scared.) *Oscar's blood turned to ice when he saw the shadow pass by outside the window.* (Oscar was very surprised and frightened.) Compare HAIR STAND ON END, THE CREEPS.

blood turns to ice See BLOOD RUNS COLD.

bloody See SCREAM BLOODY MURDER.

blow See AT A BLOW, BODY BLOW, COME TO BLOWS, IT'S AN ILL WIND THAT BLOWS NOBODY GOOD, WAY THE WIND BLOWS *or* HOW THE WIND BLOWS.

blow a fuse *or* **blow a gasket** *or* **blow one's top**

or **blow one's stack** *v. phr., slang* To become extremely angry; express rage in hot words. *When Mr. McCarthy's son got married against his wishes, he blew a fuse.* (Mr. McCarthy got very angry when his son married against his wishes.) *When the umpire called Joe out at first, Joe blew his top and was sent to the showers.* (Joe used hot words toward the umpire, who put him out of the game.) Syn. BLOW UP 1b, FLIP ONE'S LID, LOSE ONE'S TEMPER. Compare BLOW OFF STEAM 2.

blow great guns See GREAT GUNS.

blow hot and cold *v. phr.* To change your ways or likes often; be fickle or changeable. *Tom blows hot and cold about coming out for the baseball team; he cannot decide.* (Tom changes his mind about joining the team.) *Mary blew hot and cold about going to college; every day she changed her mind.* (She could not make up her mind to go or not.) *The boys will get tired of Ann's blowing hot and cold.* (She likes one and then another.)

blow in *v., slang* To arrive unexpectedly or in a carefree way. *The house was already full of guests when Bill blew in.* (Bill arrived unexpectedly.) Compare SHOW UP 3.

blow into *v., slang* To arrive at (a place) unexpectedly or in a carefree way. *Bill blows into college at the last minute after every vacation.* (Bill arrives late in a carefree way.) *Why Tom, when did you blow into town?* (Why Tom, when did you arrive in town?)

blow off steam See LET OFF STEAM.

blow one's brains out *v. phr.* **1** To shoot yourself in the head. *Mr. Jones lost all his wealth, so he blew his brains out.* (Mr. Jones killed himself by shooting himself in the head.) **2** *slang* To work very hard; overwork yourself.—A cliché. *The boys blew their brains out to get the stage ready for the play.* (The boys worked very hard to get the stage ready.) *Mary is not one to blow her brains out.* (Mary does not work very hard.) Compare BREAK ONE'S NECK.

blow one's cool *v. phr., slang, informal* To lose your composure or self-control. *Whatever you say to the judge in court, make sure that you don't blow your cool.* (Make an effort to preserve your composure and self-restraint.)

blow one's lines *or* **fluff one's lines** *v. phr., informal* To forget the words you are supposed to speak while acting in a play. *The noise backstage scared Mary and she blew her lines.* (Mary forgot what she was supposed to say because of the noise behind the stage.)

blow one's mind *v. phr., slang, informal; originally from the drug culture* **1** To become wildly enthusiastic over something as if understanding it for the first time in an entirely new light. *Read Lyall Watson's book* Supernature; *it will simply blow your mind!* (It will make you see things suddenly in an entirely new light.) **2** To lose one's ability to function, as if due to an overdose of drugs. *Joe is entirely incoherent — he seems to have blown his mind.* (He seems to have overdosed on drugs; he cannot talk coherently.) Contrast BLOW ONE'S COOL.

blow one's own horn *or* **toot one's own horn** *v. phr., slang* To praise yourself; call attention to your own skill, intelligence, or successes; boast. *People get tired of a man who is always blowing his own horn.* (They don't like to hear him boasting.) *A person who does things well does not have to toot his own horn; his abilities will be noticed by others.* (People will notice his successes and praise him to others.)

blow over *v.* To come to an end; pass away with little or no bad effects. *The sky was black, as if a bad storm were coming, but it blew over and the sun came out.* (We expected a storm, but the wind blew the clouds away and there was no storm.) *They were bitter enemies for a while, but the quarrel blew over.* (They were bitter enemies, but later became friends again.) *He was much criticized for the divorce, but it all blew over after a few years.* (People blamed him, but later forgot about it.)

blow the lid off *v. phr., informal* Suddenly to reveal the truth about a matter that has been kept as a secret either by private persons or by some governmental agency. *The clever journalists blew the lid off the Watergate cover-up.* (They found and revealed the fact that there has been a governmental cover-up about the Watergate robbery.)

blow the whistle on *v. phr., slang* **1** To inform against; betray. *The police caught one of the bank robbers, and he blew the whistle on two more.* (They caught one man, and he named two others.) **2** To act against, stop, or tell people the secrets of (crime or lawlessness). *The mayor blew the whistle on gambling.* (The mayor started arresting gamblers.) *The police blew the whistle on hot rodding.* (The police became strict about reckless driving by youngsters.)

blow up *v.* **1a** To break or destroy or to be destroyed by explosion. *He blew up the plane by means of a concealed bomb.* (He destroyed the airplane with a hidden bomb.) *The fireworks factory blew up when something went wrong in an electric switch.* (The factory exploded when an electric switch went wrong.) **1b** *informal* To explode with anger or strong feeling; lose control of yourself. *When Father bent the nail for the third time, he blew up.* (He became very angry.) Compare BLOW A FUSE. **1c** To stop playing well in a game or contest, usually because you are in danger of losing or are tired; *especially:* To lose skill or control in pitching baseball. *The champion blew up and lost the tennis match.* (He stopped playing well.) *Our*

team was behind but the pitcher on the other team blew up and we got the winning runs. (The pitcher did not pitch as well as he had been pitching.) **2** *informal* To be ruined as if by explosion; be ended suddenly. *The whole scheme for a big party suddenly blew up.* (The plan suddenly collapsed; there was no party.) **3a** To pump full of air; inflate. *He blew his tires up at a filling station.* (He put air in his tires at a filling station.) **3b** To make (something) seem bigger or important. *It was a small thing to happen but the newspapers had blown it up until it seemed important.* (It was not important, but the newspapers had made it seem so.) **4** To bring on bad weather; also, to come on as bad weather. *The wind had blown up a storm.* (The wind had brought a storm.) *A storm had blown up.* (A storm had come.) **5** To copy in bigger form; enlarge. *He blew up the snapshot to a larger size.* (He made a large copy of the snapshot.)

blow up in one's face *v. phr., informal* To fail completely and with unexpected force. *The thief's plan to rob the bank blew up in his face when a policeman stopped him.* (His plan was unexpectedly frustrated.)

blue See BETWEEN THE DEVIL AND THE DEEP BLUE SEA, BOLT FROM THE BLUE, ONCE IN A BLUE MOON, OUT OF THE BLUE *or* OUT OF A CLEAR BLUE SKY.

blue around the gills See GREEN AROUND THE GILLS.

blue in the face *adj. phr., informal* Very angry or upset; excited and very emotional.—A hackneyed phrase. *Tom argued with Bill until he was blue in the face.* (Tom argued until he was so angry he couldn't talk any more.) *Mary scolded Jane until she was blue in the face, but Jane kept on using Mary's paints.* (Mary talked until she was very much upset.)

blue Monday *n.* A Monday when you have to work after a happy weekend.—A trite expression. *It was blue Monday and John nodded sleepily over his books.* (John didn't feel like school.) *Housewives sometimes wish they could sleep through blue Monday.* (They don't want to work on Monday.)

bluff See CALL ONE'S BLUFF.

blush See AT FIRST BLUSH.

board See ACROSS THE BOARD, COLLEGE BOARDS, GO BY THE BOARD *or* PASS BY THE BOARD, ON BOARD, SANDWICH BOARD.

boarding house reach *n. phr., informal* Skill at quickly reaching for food that is a long distance away on the table.—A trite expression. *John developed a boarding house reach while he was away at camp.* (John learned to reach for things at the far end of the table.)

boat See BURN ONE'S BRIDGES *also* BURN ONE'S BOATS, IN THE SAME BOAT, MISS THE BOAT, ROCK THE BOAT.

bob up See POP UP 1.

body See KEEP BODY AND SOUL TOGETHER.

body blow *n., informal* A great disappointment; a bitter failure. *When he failed to get on the team it came as a body blow to him.* (When he was not chosen for the team he felt much disappointed.)

body English *n., informal* The wishful attempt to make a ball move in the right direction after it has been hit or let go, by twisting the body in the desired direction. *He tried to help the putt fall by using body English.* (He twisted in the direction of the hole in hopes his putt would fall into it.)

bog down, to get bogged down *v. phr., mostly intransitive or passive* **1** To stop progressing; to slow to a halt. *Work on the new building bogged down, because the contractor didn't deliver the needed concrete blocks.* (Progress on the building stopped.) **2** To become entangled with a variety of obstacles making your efforts unproductive or unsatisfying. *The novelist wrote little last summer because she got bogged down in housework.* (Her housework kept her from writing.)

boggle the mind *v. phr., informal* To stop the rational thinking process by virtue of being too fantastic or incredible. *It boggles the mind that John should have been inside a flying saucer!* (The story that John has been inside a flying saucer is so fantastic that it is intellectually undigestible.)

boil See MAKE ONE'S BLOOD BOIL *or* MAKE THE BLOOD BOIL.

boil down *v.* **1** To boil away some of the water from; make less by boiling. *She boiled down the maple sap to a thick syrup.* (She boiled off enough of the water so that the thin sap became a thick syrup.) *The fruit juice boiled down until it was almost not good for jelly.* (The juice boiled away almost too much.) **2** To reduce the length of; cut down; shorten. *The reporter boiled the story down to half the original length.* (He cut the story down to half the first length.) **3** To reduce itself to; come down to; be briefly or basically. *The whole discussion boils down to the question of whether the government should fix prices.* (The question simply is whether the government should fix prices.)

boiling point *n.* **1** The temperature at which a liquid boils. *The boiling point of water is 212° Fahrenheit.* (Water turns to steam when it reaches 212° Fahrenheit.) **2** The time when you become very angry. *He has a low boiling point.* (He gets angry very easily.) *After being teased for a long time, John reached the boiling point.* (John became angry.) *When John made the same mistake for the fourth time, his teacher reached the boiling point.* (John's teacher lost his temper because John kept making the same mistake.) Compare BLOW UP, 1b, MAKE ONE'S BLOOD BOIL.

bolt from the blue *n. phr.* Something sudden and unexpected; an event that you did not see coming; a great and usually unpleasant surprise; shock. *We had been sure she was in Chicago, so her sudden appearance was a bolt from the blue.* (We had been sure that she was far away, so her sudden appearance was most unexpected.) *His decision to resign was a bolt from the blue.* (His decision was sudden and a surprise to us.) Compare OUT OF THE BLUE.

bombshell See EXPLODE A BOMBSHELL.

bond See SAVINGS BOND.

bone See BRED IN THE BONE, FEEL IN ONE'S BONES *or* KNOW IN ONE'S BONES, FUNNY BONE, MAKE NO BONES, SKIN AND BONES, T-BONE STEAK, WORK ONE'S FINGERS TO THE BONE.

bonehead *n., slang* An unusually dense or stupid person. *John is such a bonehead—small wonder he flunks all of his courses.* (It's no surprise that he fails, he is so dumb.)

bone of contention *n. phr.* Something to fight over; a reason for quarrels; the subject of a fight. *The boundary line between the farms was a bone of contention between the two farmers.* (The line was something the two farmers had always fought over.) *The use of the car was a bone of contention between Joe and his wife.* (They quarreled about using the car.)

bone to pick *or* **crow to pick** *n. phr., informal* A reason for dispute; something to complain of or argue about.—Often used jokingly. *"I have a bone to pick with you," he said.* ("I have a quarrel with you," he said.) *There was always a crow to pick about which one would shave first in the morning.* (Which one was to shave first always caused a fuss.) Compare BONE OF CONTENTION.

bone up *v., informal* To fill with information; try to learn a lot about something in a short time; study quickly. *Carl was boning up for an examination.* (He was preparing very hard for an examination.) *Jim had to make a class report the next day on juvenile delinquency, and he was in the library boning up on how the courts handle it.* (He was trying to get quickly all the information he could about the handling of juvenile delinquency by the courts.)

bonnet See BEE IN ONE'S BONNET.

book See CLOSED BOOK, CLOSE THE BOOKS, HIT THE BOOKS, KEEP BOOKS, NOSE IN A BOOK, ONE FOR THE BOOKS, READ ONE LIKE A BOOK, TALKING BOOK, THROW THE BOOK AT.

boom See LOWER THE BOOM.

boot See DIE IN ONE'S BOOTS, IN ONE'S SHOES *also* IN ONE'S BOOTS, LICK ONE'S BOOTS, SHAKE IN ONE'S SHOES *or* SHAKE IN ONE'S BOOTS, TO BOOT, TOO BIG FOR ONE'S BREECHES *or* TOO BIG FOR ONE'S BOOTS, YOU BET *or* YOU BET YOUR BOOTS.

boot out See KICK OUT.

boot strap See PULL ONESELF UP BY THE BOOTSTRAPS.

bore to death See TO DEATH.

bore to tears *v. phr.* To fill with tired dislike; tire by dullness or the same old thing; bore.—A cliché. *The party was dull, and Roger showed plainly that he was bored to tears.* (Anyone could see that Roger was tired of the party.) *Mary loved cooking, but sewing bores her to tears.* (Mary is not at all interested in sewing.)

born See NATURAL-BORN, TO THE MANNER BORN.

born out of wedlock *adj. phr.* Born to parents who are not married to each other; without legal parents. *Sometimes when a married couple can't have children, they adopt a child who was born out of wedlock.* (Some married couples adopt children with no legal parents.) *Today we no longer make fun of children born out of wedlock.* (We don't blame the child because his parents were not married when he was born.)

born with a silver spoon in one's mouth *adj. phr.* Born to wealth and comfort; provided from birth with everything wanted; born rich. —A cliché. *The stranger's conduct was that of a man who had been born with a silver spoon in his mouth.* (He acted like a man who has always had everything.) Compare WELL-HEELED.

born yesterday *adj. phr.* Inexperienced and easily fooled; not alert to trickery; easily deceived or cheated.—A trite expression. Usually used in negative sentences. *When Bill started the new job, the other workers teased him a little, but he soon proved to everyone that he wasn't born yesterday.* (He showed that he was no fool.) *I won't give you the money till I see the bicycle you want to sell me. Do you think I was born yesterday?* (Do you think you can fool me?) Compare NOBODY'S FOOL.

borrow See LIVE ON BORROWED TIME.

borrow trouble *v. phr.* To worry for nothing about trouble that may not come; make trouble for yourself needlessly. *Don't borrow trouble by worrying about next year. It's too far away.* (Don't worry about what may never happen.) *You are borrowing trouble if you try to tell John what to do.* (You are making trouble for yourself.) Compare ASK FOR, CROSS ONE'S BRIDGES BEFORE ONE COMES TO THEM, CRY BEFORE ONE IS HURT.

boss See STRAW BOSS.

both See CUT BOTH WAYS, PLAGUE ON BOTH YOUR HOUSES.

both —— and *coord. conj.* Used to emphasize that two or more things are talked about. *Both Frank and Mary were at the party.* (Frank was at the party and Mary was at the party.) *Millie is both a good swimmer and a good cook.* (Millie swims and cooks well.) *In the program tonight Mary will both sing and dance.* (Mary will not just sing; she will also dance.) *The frog can move quickly both on land and in the water.* (The frog can move fast on the land and also in the water.) Compare AS WELL AS. Contrast EITHER —— OR.

bothered See HOT AND BOTHERED.

bottle blond *n., slang* A person who is obviously not a natural blond but whose hair is artificially colored. *I doubt that Leonora's hair color is natural; she strikes me as a bottle blond.* (She gives me the impression that her hair is artificially colored.)

bottle up *v.* **1** To hide or hold back; control. *There was no understanding person to talk to, so Fred bottled up his unhappy feeling.* (He found no friend, so he hid his unhappiness without telling anyone about it.) **2** To hold in a place from which there is no escape; trap. *Our warships bottled up the enemy fleet in the harbor.* (They trapped the enemy ships in the harbor.)

bottom See BET ONE'S BOOTS *or* BET ONE'S BOTTOM DOLLAR, FROM THE BOTTOM OF ONE'S HEART, FROM —— TO ——, GET TO THE BOTTOM OF, HIT BOTTOM *or* TOUCH BOTTOM, ROCK BOTTOM, SCRAPE THE BOTTOM OF THE BARREL.

bottom dollar *n., v. phr., informal* One's last penny, one's last dollar. *He was down to his bottom dollar when he suddenly got the job offer.* (He had no more money to live on when the new job offer came and rescued him.)

bottom drop out *or* **bottom fall out** *v. phr., informal* **1** To fall below an earlier lowest price. *The bottom dropped out of the price of peaches.* (The price of peaches went much lower than it had gone before.) **2** To lose all cheerful qualities; become very unhappy, cheerless, or unpleasant. *The bottom dropped out of the day for John when he saw his report card.* (John became very unhappy when he saw his report card.) *The bottom fell out for us when the game ended with our team on the two-yard line and six points behind.* (Everybody was hoping for a touchdown to tie the score but the game ended too soon, and our hopes were lost.)

bottom line *n., informal* (stress on *line*) **1** The last word on a controversial issue, a final decision. *"Give me the bottom line on the proposed merger,"* said John. (He wants to know what is the final decision.) **2** The naked truth without embellishments. *Look, the bottom line is that poor Max is an alcoholic.* (After everything is said, one must admit that Max is an alcoholic.) **3** The final dollar amount; for example, the lowest price two parties reach in bargaining about a sale. *"Five-hundred,"* said the used car dealer, *"is the bottom line. Take it or leave it."* (He states that he will not sell the used car for less than $500.)

bottom line *v., informal* (stress on *bottom*) To finish; to bring to a conclusion. *Okay, you guys, let's bottom line this project and break for coffee.* (It is suggested that the project be brought to a conclusion.)

bounce See GET THE BOUNCE, GIVE THE BOUNCE.

bound See BIND, BY LEAPS AND BOUNDS, OUT OF BOUNDS, WITHIN BOUNDS.

bound for *adj. phr.* On the way to; going to. *I am bound for the country club.* (I am on my way to the country club.) *The ship is bound for Liverpool.* (The ship is going to Liverpool.)

bow See TAKE A BOW.

bow and scrape *v.* To be too polite or obedient from fear or hope of gain; act like a slave.—A trite expression. *The old servant bowed and scraped before them, too obedient and eager to please.* (He made a great show of obedience and courtesy; he bowed low and swept the ground with his cap.)

bowl of cherries See BED OF ROSES.

bowl over *v., informal* 1 To knock down as if with a bowled ball. *The taxi hit him a glancing blow and bowled him over.* (The taxi hit him a side blow and knocked him down.) 2 To astonish with success or shock with misfortune; upset; stun. *He was bowled over by his wife's sudden death.* (He was badly shocked by the loss of his wife.) *The young actress bowled over everybody in her first movie.* (She surprised them with her fine acting.)

bow out *v., informal* To give up taking part; excuse yourself from doing any more; quit. *Mr. Black often quarreled with his partners, so finally he bowed out of the company.* (Mr. Black was not happy with his partners, so he quit the business.) *While the movie was being filmed, the star got sick and had to bow out.* (Before the movie was finished the star got sick and had to leave the group.) 2 To stop working after a long service; retire. *He bowed out as train engineer after forty years of railroading.* (He retired as engineer after forty years' service.)

box See IN A BIND *or* IN A BOX, PENALTY BOX, PRESS BOX, STUFF THE BALLOT BOX, VOICE BOX.

box office *n., informal* 1 The place at movies and theaters where tickets may be purchased just before the performance instead of having ordered it through the telephone or having bought it at a ticket agency. *No need to reserve the seats; we can pick them up at the box office.* 2 A best selling movie, musical, or drama (where the tickets are all always sold out and people line up in front of the box office). *John Wayne's last movie was a regular box office.* (It was an instant sell-out.) 3 Anything successful or well liked. *Betsie is no longer box office with me.* (I don't like her any more.)

boy See ALL WORK AND NO PLAY MAKES JACK A DULL BOY, FAIR-HAIRED BOY, MAMA'S BOY, OLD BOY, SEPARATE THE MEN FROM THE BOYS.

boy friend *n., informal* 1 A male friend or companion. *"John and his boy friends have gone to the ball game," said his mother.* (John and his friends have gone.) 2 A girl's steady date; a woman's favorite man friend; a male lover or sweetheart. *Jane's new boy friend is a senior in high school.* (The boy that is Jane's favorite date is a senior.) Contrast GIRL FRIEND.

boys will be boys Boys are only children and must sometimes get into mischief or trouble or behave too roughly.—A cliché. *Boys will be boys and make a lot of noise, so John's mother told him and his friends to play in the park instead of the back yard.* (John's mother knew that boys playing together would make a lot of noise.)

brain See BEAT ONE'S BRAINS OUT, BLOW ONE'S BRAINS OUT, ON THE BRAIN, RACK ONE'S BRAIN, GET ONE'S BRAINS FRIED.

brain bucket *n., slang* A motorcycle helmet. *If you want to share a ride with me, you've got to wear a brain bucket.* (I won't take you on a motorcycle ride unless you wear a motorcycle helmet.)

brain drain *n., informal* 1 The loss of the leading intellectuals and researchers of a country due to excessive emigration to other countries where conditions are better. *Britain suffered a considerable brain drain to the United States after World War II.* (Many outstanding British intellectuals moved to the U.S. after W.W. II.) 2 An activity requiring great mental concentration resulting in fatigue and exhaustion. *That math exam I took was a regular brain drain.* (The math exam exhausted me greatly.)

brake See RIDE THE BRAKE.

branch off *v.* To go from something big or important to something smaller or less important; turn aside. *At the bridge a little road branches off from the highway and follows the river.* (A smaller road leaves the highway and goes along the river.) *Martin was trying to study his lesson, but his mind kept branching off onto what girl he should ask to go with him to the dance.* (His mind left the lesson and turned to the dance.)

branch out *v.* To add new interests or activities; begin doing other things also. *First Jane collected stamps; then she branched out and collected coins, too.* (Jane collected both stamps and coins; she added a hobby to the one she had.) *John started a television repair shop; when he did well, he branched out and began selling television sets too.* (John made his business larger by selling TV sets too.)

brand-new *also* **bran-new** *adj.* As new or fresh as when just made and sold by the manufacturer; showing no use or wear. *He had taken a brand-new car from the dealer's floor and wrecked it.* (He had wrecked a new car.) *In Uncle Tom's trunk, we found a wedding ring, still in its little satin-lined box, still brand-new.* (In the trunk, we found a wedding ring still in the first box and never worn.)

brass See DOUBLE IN BRASS, GET DOWN TO BRASS TACKS.

brass hat *n., slang* **1** A high officer in the army, navy, or air force. *The brass hats in Washington often discuss important secrets.* (High officers in Washington often discuss secret matters.) **2** Any person who has a high position in business, politics, or other work. *Mr. Woods, the rich oil man, is a political brass hat.* (He is a leader in politics.)

brave it out *v. phr.* To endure something difficult or dangerous through to the end; keep on through trouble or danger. *It was a dangerous ocean crossing in wartime, but captain and crew braved it out.* (They took the ship across the ocean although they knew the ship might be sunk.)

brazen it out *v. phr.* To pretend you did nothing wrong; be suspected, accused, or scolded without admitting you did wrong; act as if not guilty. *The teacher found a stolen pen that the girl had in her desk, but the girl brazened it out; she said someone else must have put it there.* (When the teacher accused the girl of stealing the pen, the girl did not admit it; she pretended to have done nothing wrong.)

bread See HALF A LOAF IS BETTER THAN NONE, KNOW WHICH SIDE ONE'S BREAD IS BUTTERED ON, TAKE THE BREAD OUT OF ONE'S MOUTH.

bread and butter[1] *n. phr.* The usual needs of life; food, shelter, and clothing.—A cliché. *Ed earned his bread and butter as a bookkeeper, but added a little jam by working with a dance band on weekends.* (He earned his living as a bookkeeper, but got some extra money by working with a dance band on weekends.)

bread and butter[2] *adj.* Thanking someone for entertainment or a nice visit; thank-you. *After spending the weekend as a guest in the Jones' home, Alice wrote the Joneses the usual bread-and-butter letter.* (When she got home after the weekend, she sent the Joneses a thank-you note.)

bread and butter[3] *interj., informal* Spoken to prevent bad luck that you think might result from some action. *We'd say "Bread and butter!" when we had passed on opposite sides of a tree.* (We thought the tree would divide our friendship if we did not say that.)

breadbasket *n., slang* The stomach. *John is stuffing his breadbasket again.* (He is eating again.)

break See COFFEE BREAK.

break camp *v. phr.* To take down and pack tents and camping things; take your things from a camping place. *The scouts broke camp at dawn.* (The scouts took down their tents and left at dawn.)

breakdown See NERVOUS BREAKDOWN.

break down *v.* **1** To smash or hit (something) so that it falls; cause to fall by force. *The firemen broke down the door.* (They smashed the door so that it fell down.) **2** To reduce or destroy the strength or effect of; weaken; win over. *By helpful kindness the teacher broke down the new boy's shyness.* (She lessened his shyness by helpfulness and kindness.) *Advertising breaks down a lot of stubbornness against change.* (Advertising removes much opposition to change.) **3** To separate into elements or parts; decay. *Water is readily broken down into hydrogen and oxygen.* (Water is readily changed into hydrogen and oxygen.) *After many years, rocks break down into dirt.* (Rocks break into smaller and smaller pieces until they become dirt.) **4** To become unusable because of breakage or other failure; lose power to work or go. *The car broke down after half an hour's driving.* (Mechanical failure made it impossible to drive the car after half an hour.) *His health broke down.* (His health failed.) *When the coach was sick in bed, the training rules of the team broke down.* (The training rules were not obeyed by the team.) Compare GO BACK ON 2.

breaker See JAW-BREAKER.

break even *v. phr., informal* To end a series of gains and losses having the same amount you started with; have expenses equal to profits; have equal gain and loss. *The storekeeper made many sales, but his expenses were so high that he just broke even.* (The storekeeper's profits were balanced by his expenses, so he didn't make any money.) *If you gamble you are lucky when you break even.* (Most people who gamble lose money, so you are lucky if you win enough to balance your losses.)

break ground *v. phr.* **1** To begin a construction project by digging for the foundation; especially, to turn the formal first spadeful of dirt. *City officials and industrial leaders were there as the company broke ground for its new building.* (City officials and industrial leaders watched the program as the company president turned the first spadeful of earth for its new building.) **2** To begin something never done before. *The school broke new ground with reading lessons that taught students to guess the meaning of new words.* (The school began giving a new kind of reading lesson.)

break in *v.* **1a** To break from outside. *The firemen broke in the door of the burning house.* (The firemen forced the door from the outside.) **1b** To enter by force or unlawfully. *Thieves broke in while the family was away.* (Thieves forced their way in while the family was away.) **2** To enter suddenly or interrupt. *A stranger broke in on the meeting without knocking.* (A stranger rushed into the room without waiting to get permission.) *The secretary broke in to say that a telegram had arrived.* (The secretary interrupted to say that a telegram had come.) Compare CUT IN 2. **3** To make a start in a line of work or with a company or association; begin a new job. *He* *broke in as a baseball player with a minor league.* (He got his start in baseball with a minor league team.) **4** To teach the skills of a new job or activity to. *An assistant foreman broke in the new man as a machine operator.* (An assistant foreman taught the new man to operate a machine.) **5** To lessen the stiffness or newness of by use. *He broke in a new pair of shoes.* (He wore the new shoes until they were soft and comfortable.) *Breaking in a new car requires careful driving at moderate speeds.* (To lessen the stiffness of a new car means driving it carefully at moderate speeds for the first few hundred miles.)

break into *v.* **1** To force an entrance into; make a rough or unlawful entrance into. *Thieves broke into the store at night.* (Thieves forced their way into the store by breaking open a rear door.) **2** *informal* To succeed in beginning (a career, business, or a social life). *He broke into television as an actor.* (He got a start as a TV actor.) **3** To interrupt. *He broke into the discussion with a shout of warning.* (He interrupted the talk to shout a warning.) **4** To begin suddenly. *He broke into a sweat.* (He suddenly began to sweat.) *She broke into tears.* (She suddenly began to cry.) *The dog heard his master's whistle and broke into a run.* (The dog began to run.)

break off *v.* **1** To stop suddenly. *The speaker was interrupted so often that he broke off and sat down.* (His hearers bothered him with shouts and noise until he stopped speaking and sat down.) *When Bob came in, Jean broke off her talk with Linda and talked to Bob.* (Jean suddenly stopped talking to Linda and started talking to Bob.) **2** *informal* To end a friendship or love. *I hear that Tom and Alice have broken off.* (I hear they have stopped dating each other.) *She broke off with her best friend.* (She ended the friendship with her.)

break one's balls *v. phr., slang, vulgar, avoidable* To do something with maximum effort; to do something very difficult or taxing. *I've been breaking my balls to buy you this new color TV set and you aren't the least bit appreciative!* (It took me a great effort to buy it for you and you don't appreciate it.) Compare BREAK ONE'S NECK.

break one's heart *v. phr.* To discourage greatly; make very sad or hopeless.—A cliché. *His son's disgrace broke his heart.* (His son's disgrace made him very sad.) *When Mr. White lost everything he had worked so hard for, it broke his heart.* (Losing his money and his property made Mr. White feel that life was not worth living.)

break one's neck *v. phr., slang* To do all you possibly can; try your hardest.—Usually used with a limiting adverb or negative. *John nearly broke his neck trying not to be late to school.* (John tried very hard to get to school on time.) *Mother asked Mary to go to the*

store when she was free, but not to break her neck over it. (It was not very important that Mary go to the store. She could do it when she felt like it.)

break out *v.* **1** To begin showing a rash or other skin disorder.—Often used with *with.* *He broke out with scarlet fever.* (His skin showed a rash from scarlet fever.) **2** To speak or act suddenly and violently. *He broke out laughing.* (He began to laugh loudly.) *She broke out, "That is not so!"* (She suddenly shouted, "That is not so!") **3** To begin and become noticeable. *Fire broke out after the earthquake.* (Fires began and grew worse.) *War broke out in 1812.* (War began in 1812.) Compare FLARE UP. **4** *informal* To bring out; open and show. *When word of the victory came, people began breaking out their flags.* (People got out their flags and hung them up to be seen.) *When Mr. Carson's first son was born, he broke out the cigars he had been saving.* (He opened a box of cigars and gave them to his friends to celebrate.)

break the ice *v. phr., informal* **1** To conquer the first difficulties in starting a conversation, getting a party going, or making an acquaintance.—A cliché. *To break the ice, Ted spoke of his interest in mountain climbing, and they soon had a conversation going.* (Mountain climbing proved to be an interest of both, and soon they were talking eagerly.) *Some people use an unusual thing, such as an unusual piece of jewelry, to break the ice.* (Sometimes an unusual piece of jewelry makes it easier to get a conversation going.) **2** To be the first person or team to score in a game. *The Wolves broke the ice with a touchdown.* (The Wolves were the first team to score, making a touchdown.)

break through *v.* To be successful after overcoming a difficulty or bar to success. *Dr. Salk failed many times but he finally broke through to find a successful polio vaccine.* (He had a hard time, but he finally found it.) *Jim studied very hard this semester in college, and he finally broke through onto the Dean's List for the first time.* (Jim's name was on the Dean's List of best students at last.)

break up *v.* **1** To break into pieces. *The workmen broke up the pavement to dig up the pipes under it.* (The workmen broke the pavement into pieces.) *River ice breaks up in the spring.* (The ice in rivers that have been frozen over melts in the spring and separates into pieces that float away.) **2** *informal* To lose or destroy spirit or self-control.—Usually used in the passive. *Mrs. Lawrence was all broken up after her daughter's death, and did not go out of the house for two months.* (Mrs. Lawrence lost her wish to live; she could not control her sadness.) Compare CRACK UP, GO TO PIECES. **3** To come or to put to an end, especially by separation; separate. *Some men kept interrupting the speakers, and finally broke up the meeting.* (People kept booing the speakers until it was impossible to go on with the meeting.) *The party broke up at midnight.* (The party ended at midnight.)—Often used in the informal phrase *break it up. The boys were fighting, and a passing policeman ordered them to break it up.* (The policeman ordered them to stop fighting.) Compare CUT OUT 1. **4** *informal* To stop being friends. *Mary and June were good friends and did everything together, but then they had a quarrel and broke up.* (Mary and June quarreled and stopped being friends.) Compare BREAK OFF.

break with *v.* To separate yourself from; end membership in; stop friendly association with. *He broke with the Democratic party on the question of civil rights.* (He left the Democratic party.) *He had broken with some friends who had changed in their ideas.* (Because some of his friends had changed their ideas, he ended his friendship with them.)

breast See MAKE A CLEAN BREAST OF.

breath See CATCH ONE'S BREATH, DRAW A LONG BREATH *or* TAKE A LONG BREATH, HOLD ONE'S BREATH, IN THE SAME BREATH, OUT OF BREATH, SAVE ONE'S BREATH, SECOND WIND *also* SECOND BREATH, TAKE ONE'S BREATH AWAY, UNDER ONE'S BREATH, WASTE ONE'S BREATH.

breathe down one's neck *v. phr., informal* To follow closely; threaten from behind; watch every action.—A cliché. *Too many creditors were breathing down his neck.* (He owed money to many people and they were asking him to pay them.) *The carpenter didn't like to work for Mr. Jones, who was always breathing down his neck.* (Mr. Jones followed him around and watched his work.)

breathe easily *or* **breathe freely** *v.* To have relief from difficulty or worry; relax; feel that trouble is gone; stop worrying. *Now that the big bills were paid, he breathed more easily.* (When he had paid the big bills, he was less worried.) *His mother didn't breathe easily until he got home that night.* (She was uneasy until he returned.)

breathe one's last *v. phr.* To die.—A cliché. *The wounded soldier fell back on the ground and breathed his last.* (The wounded soldier fell back and died.)

bred in the bone *adj. phr.* Belonging to your nature or character, especially from early teaching or long habit; natural from belief or habit; believing deeply. *The Willett children's cleanness is bred in the bone.* (They have been taught to be clean so that it is natural to them.) Often used, with hyphens, before the noun. *Joe is a bred-in-the-bone horseman; he has been riding since he was six.* (Joe learned about horses very early and from long practice.) Contrast SKIN-DEEP.

breeches See TOO BIG FOR ONE'S BREECHES.

breeze See SHOOT THE BREEZE *or* BAT THE BREEZE *or* FAN THE BREEZE, WIN IN A WALK *or* WIN IN A BREEZE.

breeze in *v. phr., slang, informal* To walk into a place casually (like a soft blowing wind). *Betsie breezed in and sat down at the bar.* (She sauntered in casually and sat down at the bar.)

brew See HOME BREW.

brick See MAKE BRICKS WITHOUT STRAW.

brick wall See STONE WALL.

bridge See BURN ONE'S BRIDGES, CROSS A BRIDGE BEFORE ONE COMES TO IT, WATER OVER THE DAM *or* WATER UNDER THE BRIDGE.

brief See HOLD A BRIEF FOR, IN BRIEF *or* IN SHORT *or* IN A WORD.

bright and early *adj. phr.* Prompt and alert; on time and ready; cheerful and on time or before time.—A trite phrase. *He came down bright and early to breakfast.* (He came to breakfast in good spirits and on time.) *She arrived bright and early for the appointment.* (She got to the appointment cheerful and a little before the hour.)

bring about *v.* To cause; produce; lead to. *The war had brought about great changes in living.* (The war had made great changes in the way people behaved to each other.) *Drink brought about his downfall.* (Drink caused his failure in life.)

bring around *or* **bring round** *v.* **1** *informal* To restore to health or consciousness; cure. *He was quite ill, but good nursing brought him around.* (Good nursing helped to make him well.) Compare BRING TO 1. **2** To cause a change in thinking; persuade; convince; make willing. *After a good deal of discussion he brought her round to his way of thinking.* (He got her to agree with him.)

bringdown *n., slang, informal* **1** (from *bring down,* past *brought down*). A critical or cutting remark said sarcastically in order to deflate a braggard's ego. *John always utters the right bringdown when he encounters a braggard.* (He knows how to deflate a braggard's ego.) **2** A person who depresses and saddens others by being a chronic complainer. *John is a regular bringdown.* (He is a person in whose company one gets depressed.)

bring down *v. phr., slang, informal* **1** To deflate (someone's ego). *John brought Ted down very cleverly with his remarks.* (He deflated his ego cleverly.) **2** To depress (someone). *The funeral brought me down completely.* (It depressed me very much.)

bring down about one's ears *or* **bring down around one's ears** See ABOUT ONE'S EARS.

bring down the house *v. phr., informal* To start an audience laughing or clapping enthusiastically.—A cliché. *The principal's story was funny in itself and also touched their loyalties, so it brought down the house.* (The story made them all laugh.) *The President made a fine speech which brought down the house.* (His speech made them all clap their hands long and hard.)

bring home *v.* To show clearly; emphasize; make (someone) realize; demonstrate. *The* *accident caused a death in his family, and it brought home to him the evil of drinking while driving.* (The accident showed him that it is dangerous to drink and drive.) *A parent or teacher should bring home to children the value and pleasure of reading.* (Parents or teachers should make children realize the value of reading.)

bring home the bacon *v. phr., informal* **1** To support your family; earn the family living.—A cliché. *He was a steady fellow, who always brought home the bacon.* (He was a dependable person, and always took good care of his family.) **2** To win a game or prize. *The football team brought home the bacon.* (The team won the game.)

bring in *v. In baseball:* To enable men on base to score; score. *Dick's hit brought in both base runners.* (Dick's hit helped both men on base to score.) *A walk and a triple brought in a run in the third inning.* (A walk and a triple scored a run in the third inning.)

bring off *v.* To do (something difficult); perform successfully (an act of skill); accomplish (something requiring unusual ability). *By skillful discussion, Mr. White had brought off an agreement that had seemed impossible to get.* (He had got the groups to agree when it didn't seem possible.) *He tried several times to break the high jump record, and finally he brought it off.* (He finally succeeded in breaking the record.) Compare PUT OVER 2.

bring on *v.* To result in; cause; produce. *The murder of an Austrian nobleman in the summer of 1914 brought on the First World War.* (The murder of an Austrian nobleman started the First World War.) *Spinal meningitis brought on John's deafness when he was six years old.* (Spinal meningitis at the age of six caused John's deafness.) *Reading in a poor light may bring on a headache.* (Reading in a poor light may result in a headache.)

bring out *v.* **1** To cause to appear; make clear. *His report brought out the foolishness of the plan.* (His report made the foolishness of the plan clear.) *Brushing will bring out the beauty of your hair.* (Brushing your hair will make its beauty appear.) **2** To help (an ability or skill) grow or develop. *The teacher's coaching brought out a wonderful singing voice of great power and warmth.* (He developed the singer's fine voice.) **3** To offer to the public by producing, publishing, or selling. *He brought out a new play.* (He produced a new play.) *The company brought out a line of light personal airplanes.* (The company began to make small private airplanes for sale.)

bring round See BRING AROUND.

bring to *v.* **1** To restore to consciousness; wake from sleep, anesthesia, hypnosis, or fainting. *Smelling salts will often bring a fainting person to.* (A special salt with a strong smell will often wake up a person who

has fainted.) Compare BRING AROUND 1. **2** To bring a ship or boat to a stop. *Reaching the pier, he brought the boat smartly to.* (He stopped the boat expertly at the pier.)

bring to bay *v. phr.* To chase or force into a place where escape is impossible without a fight; trap; corner. *The police brought the robber to bay on the roof and he gave up.* (The police followed him up on the roof where he could not escape, so he gave up.) *The fox was brought to bay in a hollow tree and the dogs stood around it barking.* (The dogs chased the fox until it hid in a hollow tree where it could not escape.) Compare AT BAY.

bring to heel See TO HEEL.

bring to light *v. phr.* To discover (something hidden); find out about; expose. *Many things left by the ancient Egyptians in tombs have been brought to light by scientists and explorers.* (Many things have been found in the tombs.) *His enemies brought to light some foolish things he had done while young, but he was elected anyway because people trusted him.* (His enemies found out some foolish things he had done and told people.) Compare COME TO LIGHT.

bring to one's knees *v. phr.* To seriously weaken the power or impair the function of. *The fuel shortage brought the automobile industry to its knees.* (Because there was not much gas, the industry nearly failed.)

bring to pass *v. phr., formal* To make (something) happen; succeed in causing. *By much planning, the mother brought the marriage to pass.* (By much planning, she succeeded in getting the two married.) *The change in the law was slow in coming, and it took a disaster to bring it to pass.* (The change was slow in coming, and required a terrible event to get people to accept it.) Compare BRING ABOUT, COME TO PASS.

bring to terms *v. phr.* To make (someone) agree or do; make surrender. *The two brothers were brought to terms by their father for riding the bicycle.* (Their father made them agree about using the same bicycle.) *The war won't end until we bring the enemy to terms.* (We must make the enemy surrender.) Contrast COME TO TERMS.

bring up *v.* **1** To take care of (a child); raise; train; educate. *He gave much attention and thought to bringing up his children.* (He tried to raise them well.) *Joe was born in Texas but brought up in Oklahoma.* (He was born in Texas but raised in Oklahoma.) **2** *informal* To stop; halt.—Usually used with short. *He brought the car up short when the light changed to red.* (He stopped the car suddenly.) *Bill started to complain, I brought him up short.* (I quickly told him to stop complaining.) **3** To begin a discussion of; speak of; mention. *At the class meeting Bob brought up the idea of a picnic.* (He started talking about a future picnic.)

bring up the rear *v. phr.* **1** To come last in a march, parade, or procession; end a line. *The fire truck with Santa on it brought up the rear of the Christmas parade.* (Santa on the fire truck was at the end of the parade.) *The governor and his staff brought up the rear of the parade.* (The governor and his officers marched at the end of the parade.) **2** *informal* To do least well; do the most poorly of a group; be last. *In the race, John brought up the rear.* (John came in last.) *In the basketball tournament, our team brought up the rear.* (All the other teams won more games.)

broke See GO BROKE, GO FOR BROKE, STONE-BROKE *or* DEAD BROKE *or* FLAT BROKE, STRAW THAT BROKE THE CAMEL'S BACK.

Bronx cheer *n. phr., slang* A loud sound made with tongue and lips to show opposition or scorn. *When he began to show anti-union feelings, 'he was greeted with Bronx cheers all around.* (The audience answered his criticism of unions with loud, rude noises.)

broom See NEW BROOM SWEEPS CLEAN.

broth See SCOTCH BROTH.

brow See BY THE SWEAT OF ONE'S BROW.

brown See DO UP BROWN.

brown bagger *n., slang, informal* A person who does not go to the cafeteria or to a restaurant for lunch at work, but who brings his homemade lunch to work in order to save money. *John became a brown-bagger not because he can't afford the restaurant, but because he is too busy to go there.* (He just wants to get lunch finished quickly so he can return to work.)

brown-nose *v., slang, avoidable, though gaining in acceptance* To curry favor in a subservient way, as by obviously exaggerated flattery. *Max brown-noses his teachers, that's why he gets all A's in his courses.* (His flattery helps him get the good grades.) Compare POL-ISH THE APPLE.

brown paper bag *n., slang, citizen's band radio jargon* An unmarked police car. *The beaver got a Christmas card because she didn't notice the brown paper bag at her back door.* (The woman driver got a speeding ticket because she failed to notice the unmarked police car that was following her.) See PLAIN WHITE WRAPPER.

brown study *n. phr.* A time of deep thought about something; a deep thoughtful mood. *When his wife found him, he had pushed away his books and was in a brown study.* (He was thinking and forgot where he was.)

brush See BEAT THE BUSHES *or* BEAT THE BRUSH.

brush back *v.* To throw a baseball pitch close to. *The pitcher threw a high inside pitch to brush the batter back.* (The pitcher threw a pitch close to the batter's head to make him nervous and not able to hit so well.) Syn. DUST OFF.

brushoff See GET THE BRUSHOFF, BRUSH OFF *or* GIVE THE BRUSHOFF.

brush off *or* **give the brush off** *v. phr.* **1** To refuse to hear or believe, quickly and impatiently; not take seriously or think important. *John brushed off Bill's warning that he might fall from the tree.* (John paid no attention.) *I said that it might rain and to take the bus, but Joe gave my idea the brushoff.* (He didn't believe it would rain.) *Father cut his finger but he brushed it off as not important and kept working.* (He didn't think the cut was serious.) **2** *informal* To be unfriendly to; not talk or pay attention to (someone); get rid of. *Mary brushed off Bill at the dance.* (She wouldn't pay attention to Bill or dance with him.) *I said hello to Mr. Smith, but he gave me the brushoff.* (He didn't talk to me.) Compare COLD SHOULDER, HIGH-HAT. Contrast GET THE BRUSH OFF.

brush up *or* **brush up on** *v.* To refresh one's memory of or skill at by practice or review; improve; make perfect. *She spent the summer brushing up on her American History as she was to teach that in the fall.* (She gave the summer to reviewing American History as she was to teach that in the fall.) *He brushed up his target shooting.* (He practiced target shooting.)

bubble gum music *n., slang* The kind of rock'n'roll that appeals to young teen-agers. *When will you learn to appreciate Mozart instead of that bubble gum music?* (When will you graduate to the classics from the teen-age jazz?)

bubble trouble *n, slang, citizen's band radio jargon* Tire trouble, flat tire. *The eighteen-wheeler ahead of me seems to have bubble trouble.* (The truck and trailer ahead seems to have a flat tire.)

buck See FAST BUCK *or* QUICK BUCK, PASS THE BUCK.

bucket See KICK THE BUCKET, RAIN CATS AND DOGS *or* RAIN BUCKETS.

bucket of bolts *n., slang* A very old and shaky car that barely goes. *When are you going to get rid of that old bucket of bolts?* (When are you going to sell that no good, old car?)

buckle See BUCKLE DOWN *or* KNUCKLE DOWN.

buckle down *or* **knuckle down** *v.* To give complete attention (to an effort or job); attend. *They chatted idly for a few moments then each buckled down to work.* (They talked for a little while, and then started to work.) *Jim was fooling instead of studying; so his father told him to buckle down.* (His father told him to get serious and study.)

buck passer, buck-passing See PASS THE BUCK.

buck up *v. phr., informal* To make or become more cheerful; make or become free from discouragement; become more hopeful.

After the heavy rain, the scoutmaster bucked up the boys by leading them in a song. (The scoutmaster cheered up the boys by getting them to sing.) *Tom was disappointed that he didn't make the team; but he soon bucked up.* (Tom soon got over his disappointment.)

bud See NIP IN THE BUD.

bug-eyed *adj., slang* Wide-eyed with surprise. *He stood there bug-eyed when told that he had won the award.* (He was wide-eyed with surprise when told of the prize.)

buggy-whip *n., slang* An unusually long, thin radio antenna on a car that bends back like a whip when the car moves fast. *He's very impressed with himself ever since he got a buggy whip.* (He thinks he is something special because he owns a long, thin antenna on his car.)

bughouse¹ *n., slang* An insane asylum. *They took Joe to the bughouse.* (They took him to the insane asylum.)

bughouse² *adj., slang* Crazy, insane. *Joe's gone bughouse.* (Joe has gone mad.)

bug in one's ear *n. phr., informal* A hint; secret information given to someone to make him act; idea. *I saw Mary at the jeweler's admiring the diamond pin; I'll put a bug in Henry's ear.* (I know Mary likes the pin, so I'll tell Henry secretly so he can buy it as a present for Mary.)

build See JERRY-BUILT.

build a fire under *v. phr.* To urge or force (a slow or unwilling person) to action; get (someone) moving; arouse.—A cliché. *The health department built a fire under the restaurant owner and got him to clean the place up by threatening to cancel his license.* (The health department got action by saying they would take away his license.)

build castles in the air *or* **build castles in Spain** *v. phr.* To make impossible or imaginary plans; dream about future successes that are unlikely.—A cliché. *He liked to build castles in the air, but never succeeded in anything.* (He liked to dream about the future, but never was a success.) *To build castles in Spain is natural for young people and they may work hard enough to get part of their wishes.* (Young people dream and plan great things, some of which may come true.)

build up *v.* **1** To make out of separate pieces or layers; construct from parts. *Johnny built up a fort out of large balls of snow.* (Johnny made a snow fort.) *Lois built up a cake of three layers.* (Lois made a cake three layers high.) **2** To cover over or fill up with buildings. *The fields where Tom's father played as a boy are all built up now.* (The town has spread out and now the fields are covered with streets and houses.) *A driver should slow down when he comes to an area that is built up.* (A driver should slow down where there are many houses.) **3a** To increase slowly or by small amounts; grow. *John built*

up a bank account by saving regularly. (John gradually made his bank account larger.) *The noise built up until Mary couldn't stand it any longer.* (The noise grew louder and louder until Mary couldn't stand it.) **3b** To make stronger or better or more effective. *Fred exercised to build up his muscles.* (Fred exercised to make his muscles big and strong.) *Joanne was studying to build up her algebra.* (Joanne was studying so that she could solve algebra problems more easily.) **3c** *informal* To advertise quickly and publicize so as to make famous. *The press agent built up the young actress.* (The news writer succeeded in making the young actress famous.) *The movie company spent much money building up its new picture.* (The movie company spent much money advertising its new picture.)

bull See HIT THE BULL'S-EYE, SHOOT THE BREEZE *or* SHOOT THE BULL, TAKE THE BULL BY THE HORNS.

bullet lane *n., slang, citizen's band radio jargon* The passing lane. *Move over into the bullet lane, this eighteen wheeler is moving too slow.* (Get into the passing lane.)

bull in a china shop *n. phr.* A rough or clumsy person who says or does something to anger others or upset plans; a tactless person. —A cliché. *We were talking politely and carefully with the teacher about a class party, but John came in like a bull in a china shop and his rough talk made the teacher say no.* (John upset the teacher with his rough talk.)

bull session *n., slang* A long informal talk about something by a group of persons. *After the game the boys in the dormitory had a bull session until the lights went out.* (After the game the boys had a long talk until the lights went out.)

bullshit *n., vulgar, but gaining in acceptance by some* Exaggerated or insincere talk meant to impress others. *Max, this is a lot of bullshit!* (This is a lot of exaggerated, insincere talk.)

bullshit *v., vulgar to informal, gaining in social acceptance by some* To exaggerate or talk insincerely in an effort to make yourself seem impressive. *Stop bullshitting me, Max, I can't believe a word of what you're saying.* (Stop this exaggerated and unbelievable talk.)

bullshit artist *n., slang, vulgar, but gaining in social acceptance* A person who habitually makes exaggerated or insincerely flattering speeches designed to impress others. *Max is a regular bullshit artist; small wonder he keeps getting promoted ahead of everyone else.* (His success is due to his exaggerated and insincerely flattering speeches.)

bump See GOOSE BUMPS.

bump into *v., informal* To meet without expecting to; happen to meet; come upon by accident. *Mary was walking down the street, when she suddenly bumped into Joan.* (Mary met Joan coming the other way.) *Ed was sur-*

prised to bump into John at the football game. (Ed was surprised to see John at the football game.) Syn. RUN INTO.

bump off *v., slang* To kill in a violent way; murder in gangster fashion. *Hoodlums in a speeding car bumped him off with tommy guns.* (Gangsters speeding by in a car shot him to death with machine guns.)

bum's rush *n. phr., slang* Throwing or pushing someone out from where he is not wanted. *When John tried to go to the party where he was not invited, Bill and Fred gave him the bum's rush.* (Bill and Fred carried John out of the house and dropped him outside.) *Tom became too noisy, and he got the bum's rush.* (Tom became too noisy, and he was thrown out.) **2** To hurry or rush (someone). *The salesman tried to give me the bum's rush.* (The salesman tried to pressure me into buying something fast.)

bundle up See WRAP UP 1.

burn See EARS BURN, KEEP THE HOME FIRES BURNING, MONEY TO BURN.

burn a hole in one's pocket *v. phr.* To make you want to buy something; be likely to be quickly spent.—A cliché. *Money burns a hole in Linda's pocket.* (Linda can't save money; she spends it almost as soon as she gets it.) *The silver dollar that Don got for his birthday was burning a hole in his pocket, and Don hurried to a dime store.* (Don was impatient to spend the money he had gotten.)

burn in effigy See HANG IN EFFIGY.

burn one's bridges *also* **burn one's boats** *v. phr.* To make a decision that you cannot change; remove or destroy all the ways you can get back out of a place you have got into on purpose; leave yourself no way to escape a position.—A cliché. *The coach burned his bridges in the ninth inning by putting in a pinch hitter for his best pitcher.* (The coach could not put the pitcher back in the game if he needed him again.) *Bob was a good wrestler but a poor boxer. He burned his boats by letting Mickey choose how they would fight.* (If Mickey chose to box, Bob could not then ask to wrestle instead.) *When Dorothy became a nun, she burned her bridges behind her.* (After she promised to be a member of a religious order, she could not later decide to do something else instead.)

burn one's fingers *v. phr., informal* To get in trouble doing something and fear to do it again; learn caution through an unpleasant experience. *He had burned his fingers in the stock market once, and didn't want to try again.* (He had lost money in stocks once, and didn't want to try trading again.) *Some people can't be told; they have to burn their fingers to learn.* (Some people can't accept advice; they have to learn from unhappy experience.)

burn out *v. phr.* **1** To destroy by fire or by overheating. *Mr. Jones burned out the clutch on his car.* (Mr. Jones let the clutch get too hot and it had to be fixed.) **2** To destroy someone's house or business by fire so that they have to move out. *The Christmas tree caught fire, and the family was burned out.* (The family had to leave their home because it caught fire and was badly damaged.) **3a** To make or become no good because of long use or overheating. *The light bulb in the bathroom burned out, and Father put in a new one.* (The bathroom light bulb stopped making light, and Father put in a new bulb.) *The electric motor was too powerful, and it burned out a fuse.* (The motor needed more electric current than the wires could safely carry. A special small wire in the fuse got hot very quickly and broke.) **3b** To break, tire, or wear out by using up all the power, energy, or strength of. *Bill burned himself out in the first part of the race and could not finish.* (Bill tired himself out by running too fast in the early part of the race.) *The farmer burned out his field by planting the same crop every year for many years.* (The field was no longer good for raising crops because all of the plant foods in the soil were used up.)

burn rubber *v. phr., slang* (stress on *rubber*), **1** To start up a car or a motorcycle from dead stop so fast that the tires (made of rubber) leave a mark on the road. *The neighborhood drag racers burned a lot of rubber — look at the marks on the road!* (They started up very fast many times.) **2** To leave in a hurry. *I guess I am going to have to burn rubber.* (I will have to leave in a hurry.)

burnt child dreads the fire *or* **once bitten, twice shy** (*proverb*) A person who has suffered from doing something has learned to avoid doing it again. *Once Mary had got lost when her mother took her downtown. But a burnt child dreads the fire, so now Mary stays close to her mother when they are downtown.* (Mary was frightened when she was lost and has learned not to get lost again.)

burn the candle at both ends *v. phr.* To work or play too hard without enough rest; get too tired.—A cliché. *He worked hard every day as a lawyer and went to parties and dances every night; he was burning the candle at both ends.* (He worked all day and was up late at parties, not getting enough rest.)

burn the midnight oil *v. phr.* To study late at night.—A cliché. *Exam time was near, and more and more pupils were burning the midnight oil.* (Examinations were getting close, and pupils were studying late.)

burn to a crisp *v. phr.* To burn black; burn past saving or using especially as food. *While getting breakfast, Mother was called to the telephone, and when she got back, the bacon had been burned to a crisp.* (While Mother was telephoning, the bacon was burned too badly to eat.)

burn up v. **1** To burn completely; destroy or be destroyed by fire. *Mr. Scott was burning up old letters.* (He was burning them to ashes.) *The house burned up before the firemen got there.* (When the firemen got there, the house was destroyed.) **2** *informal* To irritate; anger; annoy. *The boy's laziness and rudeness burned up his teacher.* (His laziness and rudeness made the teacher angry.) *The breakdown of his new car burned Mr. Jones up.* (It made Mr. Jones cross.)

burn up the road v. phr., informal To drive a car very fast. *In his eagerness to see his girl again, he burned up the road on his way to see her.* (He drove at high speeds because he was impatient to get to his girl.) *Speed demons burning up the road often cause accidents.* (Motorists driving too fast often cause accidents.)

burst at the seams v. phr., informal To be too full or too crowded. *John ate so much he was bursting at the seams.* (John ate too much, and felt uncomfortably full.) *Mary's album was so full of pictures it was bursting at the seams.* (Mary's album was too full, and pictures were falling out of it.)

bury one's head in the sand See HIDE ONE'S HEAD IN THE SAND.

bury the hatchet v. phr., informal To settle a quarrel or end a war; make peace.—A cliché. *The two men had been enemies a long time, but after the flood they buried the hatchet.* (They ended a long bitterness after the flood showed them their need of each other.) Compare MAKE UP 5.

bus See MISS THE BOAT *or* MISS THE BUS.

bush See BEAT ABOUT THE BUSH, BIRD IN THE HAND IS WORTH TWO IN THE BUSH.

bushel See HIDE ONE'S LIGHT UNDER A BUSHEL.

bushes See BEAT THE BUSHES.

business See DO THE BUSINESS, HAVE NO BUSINESS, LAND-OFFICE BUSINESS, MEAN BUSINESS, MONKEY BUSINESS, THE BUSINESS.

busy work n. Work that is done not to do or finish anything important, but just to keep busy. *When the teacher finished all she had to say it was still a half hour before school was over. So she gave the class a test for busy work.* (She wasn't really testing the children. She was just keeping them busy.)

but for See EXCEPT FOR.

but good adv. phr., informal Very much so; thoroughly; completely; forcefully.—Used for emphasis. *Jack called Charles a bad name, and Charles hit Jack, but good.* (Charles hit Jack very hard.) *Tom fell and broke his leg. That taught him but good not to fool around in high trees.* (Tom's fall was a very good lesson not to fool around in high trees.) Compare AND HOW.

but not least See LAST BUT NOT LEAST.

butter See BREAD AND BUTTER.

butterflies in one's stomach n. phr. A queer feeling in the stomach caused by nervous fear or uncertainty; a feeling of fear or anxiety in the stomach.—A cliché. *When Bob walked into the factory office to ask for a job, he had butterflies in his stomach.* (He was excited and nervous.)

butter up v., informal To try to get the favor or friendship of (a person) by flattery or pleasantness. *He began to butter up the boss in hope of being given a better job.* (He tried to gain the boss's favor saying and doing nice things to him.) Compare POLISH THE APPLE.

butter wouldn't melt in one's mouth informal You act very polite and friendly but do not really care; you are very nice to people but are not sincere. *The new secretary was rude to the other workers, but when she talked to the boss, butter wouldn't melt in her mouth.* (She was polite and respectful to the boss to make him like her.)

butt in v., slang To join in with what other people are doing without asking or being asked; interfere in other people's business; meddle. *Mary was explaining to Jane how to knit a sweater when Barbara butted in.* (Barbara started to explain to Jane without being asked.) Often used with *on. John butted in on Bill and Tom's fight, and got hurt.* (John tried to help, but they didn't want any help. So both of them started fighting John.) Compare HORN IN.

button See HAVE ALL ONE'S BUTTONS, ON THE BUTTON, PUSH THE PANIC BUTTON.

button down v., slang (stress on *down*) To state precisely, to ascertain, to pin down, to peg down. *First let's get the facts buttoned down, then we can plan ahead.* (First let us ascertain the facts and then we can proceed with the plans.)

button-down attrib. adj., slang (stress on *button*) Well-groomed, conservatively dressed. *Joe is a regular button-down type.* (He wears business clothes.)

button one's lip also **zip one's lip** v. phr., slang To stop talking; keep a secret; shut your mouth; be quiet. *The man was getting loud and insulting and the cop told him to button his lip.* (The man was shouting offensive language, and the cop ordered him to shut up.) *John wanted to talk, but Dan told him to keep his lip buttoned.* (Dan told him not to say anything.) Syn. KEEP ONE'S MOUTH SHUT, SHUT UP.

buy off v. To turn from duty or purpose by a gift. *When the police threatened to stop the gambling business, the owner bought them off.* (The gambler paid the police to let him continue his gambling business.) *The Indians were going to burn the cabins, but the men bought them off with gifts.* (The settlers gave the Indians gifts so they would leave the cabins alone.) Compare PAY OFF.

buy out v. **1** To buy the ownership or a

share of; purchase the stock of. *He bought out several small stockholders.* (He bought the stock of several small owners.) **2** To buy all the goods of; purchase the merchandise of. *Mr. Harper bought out a nearby hardware store.* (He bought all the store's goods.) Contrast SELL OUT.

buzz See GIVE A RING *also* GIVE A BUZZ.

by See TOO —— BY HALF.

by a hair See HANG BY A THREAD *or* HANG BY A HAIR.

by all means *also* **by all manner of means** *adv. phr.* Certainly; without fail. *He felt that he should by all means warn Jones.* (He felt that he certainly ought to caution Jones.) Contrast BY NO MEANS.

by all odds *adv. phr.* Without question; certainly. *He was by all odds the strongest candidate.* (He was the strongest candidate no matter how you looked at it.) *By all odds we should win the game, because the other team is so weak.* (We should certainly win.) Compare FAR AND AWAY.

by a long shot *adv. phr., informal* By a big difference; by far.—Used to add emphasis. *Bert was the best swimmer in the race, by a long shot.* (Bert was certainly the best swimmer.) Often used with a negative. *Tom isn't the kind who would be fresh to a teacher, by a long shot.* (Tom would never be fresh.) *Our team didn't win—not by a long shot.* (Our team didn't come near winning; they were badly beaten.) Compare MISS BY A MILE.

by a mile See MISS BY A MILE.

by and by *adv.* After a while; at some time in the future; later. *Roger said he would do his homework by and by.* (He said he would do it later.) *The mother knew her baby would be a man by and by and do a man's work.* (Her baby would be a man in the future.) Syn. AFTER A WHILE.

by and large *adv. phr.* As it most often happens; more often than not; usually; mostly. *There were bad days, but it was a pleasant summer, by and large.* (There were unpleasant happenings, but most of the time it was a good summer.) *By and large, women can bear pain better than men.* (Usually women can bear pain better.) Syn. FOR THE MOST PART, ON THE WHOLE 2.

by any means See BY NO MEANS.

by a thread See HANG BY A THREAD.

by chance *adv. phr.* Without any cause or reason; by accident; accidentally. *Tom met Bill by chance.* (Tom met Bill without planning to meet him and not knowing Bill was near.) *The apple fell by chance on Bobby's head.* (Bobby happened to be passing underneath when the apple dropped and hit him.)

by choice *adv. phr.* As a result of choosing; because of wanting to; freely. *John helped his father by choice.* (John didn't have to help his father. He did it because he wanted to.) *Mary ate a plum, but not by choice. Her*

mother told her she must eat it.* (Mary did not eat the plum because she wanted to eat it.)

by dint of *prep.* By the exertion of; by the use of; through. *By dint of sheer toughness and real courage, he lived through the jungle difficulties and dangers.* (By firmness and courage, he came through alive.) *His success in college was largely by dint of hard study.* (He succeeded because he studied.)

bye See BY THE WAY *also* BY THE BYE.

by far *adv. phr.* By a large difference; much. *His work was better by far than that of any other printer in the city.* (His work was much better than that of any other printer in the city.) *The old road is prettier, but it is by far the longer way.* (It is a much longer way.) Compare FAR AND AWAY.

by fits and starts *adv. phr.* With many stops and starts; a little now and a little more later; not all the time; irregularly. *He had worked on the invention by fits and starts for several years.* (He had worked irregularly on his invention for years.) *You will never get anywhere if you study just by fits and starts.* (If you keep studying and stopping you will not learn much.) Compare FROM TIME TO TIME, OFF AND ON.

bygone See LET BYGONES BE BYGONES.

by heart *adv. phr.* By exact memorizing; so well that you remember it; by memory. *The pupils learned many poems by heart.* (The pupils memorized many poems.) *He knew the records of the major league teams by heart.* (He knew perfectly the records of the major league teams.)

by hook or by crook *adv. phr.* By honest ways or dishonest; in any way necessary.—A cliché. *The wolf tried to get the little pigs by hook or by crook.* (He tried any way he could.) *The team was determined to win that last game by hook or by crook, and three players were put out of the game for fouling.* (The players wanted to win very badly, and they used both fair and unfair ways.)

by inches *adv. phr.* By small or slow degrees; little by little; gradually. *The river was rising by inches.* (The river was rising very slowly.) *They got a heavy wooden beam under the barn for a lever, and managed to move it by inches.* (They got a beam under it and succeeded in moving it a little at a time.) *He was dying by inches.* (He was slowly dying.)

by leaps and bounds *adv. phr.* With long steps; very rapidly.—A cliché. *Production in the factory was increasing by leaps and bounds.* (Production was rising very rapidly.) *The school enrollment was going up by leaps and bounds.* (The school enrollment was increasing very fast.)

by means of *prep.* By the use of; with the help of. *The fisherman saved himself by means of a floating log.* (He saved himself with a floating log.) *By means of monthly payments, people can buy more than in the past.* (By use of monthly payments, people can buy more than they could many years ago.)

by mistake *adv. phr.* As the result of a mistake; through error. *He picked up the wrong hat by mistake.* (He picked up the wrong hat through error.)

by no means *or* **not by any means** *also* **by no manner of means** *or* **not by any manner of means** *adv. phr.* Not even a little; certainly not. *He is by no means bright.* (He is really not bright.) *"May I stay home from school?" "By no means."* (Certainly not.) *Dick worked on his project Saturday, but he is not finished yet, by any means.* (He is far from being finished.) Contrast BY ALL MEANS.

B.Y.O. *(Abbreviation) informal* Bring Your Own. Said of a kind of party where the host or hostess does not provide the drinks or food but people bring their own.

B.Y.O.B. Bring Your Own Bottle. Frequently written on invitations for the kind of party where people bring their own liquor.

by oneself *adv. phr.* **1** Without any others around; separate from others; alone. *The house stood by itself on a hill.* (There were no other houses near it on the hill.) *Tom liked to go walking by himself.* (Tom liked to go walking alone.) *Betty felt very sad and lonely by herself.* (Betty felt very sad when there was no one else around.) **2** Without the help of anyone else; by your own work only. *John built a flying model airplane by himself.* (John built a model airplane without any help.) *Lois cleaned the house all by herself.* (Lois cleaned the house without any help from anyone.)

by one's own bootstraps See PULL ONESELF UP BY THE BOOTSTRAPS.

by storm See TAKE BY STORM.

by surprise See TAKE BY SURPRISE.

by the board See GO BY THE BOARD *also* PASS BY THE BOARD.

by the bootstraps See PULL ONESELF UP BY THE BOOTSTRAPS.

by the bye See BY THE WAY

by the dozen *or* **by the hundred** *or* **by the thousand** *adv. phr.* Very many at one time; in great numbers. *Tommy ate cookies by the dozen.* (Tommy ate a great many cookies.) Often used in the plural, meaning even larger numbers. *The ants arrived at the picnic by the hundreds.* (Very many ants came to the picnic.) *The enemy attacked the fort by the thousands.* (The enemy attacked the fort with thousands of soldiers.)

by the horns See TAKE THE BULL BY THE HORNS.

by the hundred See BY THE DOZEN.

by the nose See LEAD BY THE NOSE.

by the piece *adv. phr.* Counted one piece at a time; separately for each single piece. *John bought boxes full of bags of potato chips and sold them by the piece.* (John sold one bag of potato chips at a time.) *Mary made pothold-ers and got paid by the piece.* (Mary was paid for each potholder she made, and not for the hours she worked.)

by the seat of one's pants See FLY BY THE SEAT OF ONE'S PANTS.

by the skin of one's teeth *adv. phr.* By a narrow margin; with no room to spare; barely. —A cliché. *The drowning man struggled, and I got him to land by the skin of my teeth.* (The drowning man fought me and I was just able to bring him to land.) *She passed English by the skin of her teeth.* (She barely passed English.) Compare SQUEAK THROUGH, WITHIN AN ACE OF *or* WITHIN AN INCH OF.

by the sweat of one's brow *adv. phr.* By hard work; by tiring effort; laboriously.—A cliché. *Even with modern labor-saving machinery, the farmer makes his living by the sweat of his brow.* (In spite of modern machinery, farming is still hard work.)

by the thousand See BY THE DOZEN.

by the way *also* **by the bye** *adv. phr.* Just as some added fact or news; as something else that I think of.—Used to introduce something related to the general subject, or brought to mind by it. *We shall expect you; by the way, dinner will be at eight.* (Also, dinner will be at eight.) *I was reading when the earthquake occurred, and, by the way, it was* The Last Days of Pompeii *that I was reading.* (Just as a small matter of interest, I was reading about a volcano when the earthquake happened.)

by the wayside See FALL BY THE WAYSIDE.

by turns *adv. phr.* First one and then another in a regular way; one substituting for or following another according to a repeated plan. *On the drive to Chicago, the three men took the wheel by turns.* (On the drive to Chicago, the three men drove the car one by one.) *The teachers were on duty by turns.* (They are on duty one after another in a regular plan.) *When John had a fever, he felt cold and hot by turns.* (First he felt cold, then hot, then cold again, and so on.) Syn. IN TURN. Compare TAKE TURNS.

by virtue of *also* **in virtue of** *prep.* On the strength of; because of; by reason of. *By virtue of his high rank and position, the President takes social leadership over almost everyone else.* (Because of his high office, the President is above nearly everyone else at dinners and parties.) *Plastic bags are useful for holding many kinds of food, by virtue of their clearness, toughness, and low cost.* (Plastic bags are good packages for foods, because they are clear, tough, and cheap.) Compare BY DINT OF.

by way of *prep.* **1** For the sake or purpose of; as. *By way of example, he described his own experience.* (As an example, he described his own experience.) **2** Through; by a route including; via. *He went from New York to San Francisco by way of Chicago.* (He went from New York to San Francisco by a route that passed through Chicago.)

by word of mouth *adv. phr.* From person to person by the spoken word; orally. *The news got around by word of mouth.* (The news was passed from person to person orally.) *The message reached him quietly by word of mouth.* (Someone came up and told him the message quietly.)

C

cahoots See IN LEAGUE WITH *or* IN CAHOOTS WITH.

Cain See RAISE CAIN.

cake See EAT 'ONE'S CAKE AND HAVE IT TOO, PAT-A-CAKE, TAKE THE CAKE.

calculated risk *n.* An action that may fail but is judged more likely to succeed. *The sending of troops to the rebellious island was a calculated risk.* (The sending of troops to the island might have started a war, but the country that sent them thought the troops would end the rebellion without a war starting.)

calf love See PUPPY LOVE.

call See AT CALL, AT ONE'S BECK AND CALL, CLOSE CALL, ON CALL, PORT OF CALL, POT CALLS THE KETTLE BLACK, WITHIN CALL.

call a halt *v. phr.* To give a command to stop. *The scouts were tired during the hike, and the scoutmaster called a halt.* (The scouts were tired, and the scoutmaster let the boys rest from their hike.) *When the children's play got too noisy, their mother called a halt.* (When the children got too noisy, their mother made them quiet down.)

call a spade a spade *v. phr.* To call a person or thing a name that is true but not polite; speak bluntly; use the plainest language.—A Cliché. *A boy took some money from Dick's desk and said he borrowed it, but I told him he stole it; I believe in calling a spade a spade.* (I believe in calling things by their true names, and taking money without permission is stealing.)

call down *also* **dress down** *v., informal* To scold. *Jim was called down by his teacher for being late to class.* (The teacher scolded Jim for coming to class late.) *Mother called Bob down for walking into the kitchen with muddy boots.* (Mother told Bob he did something bad.) Compare CALL ON THE CARPET, CHEW OUT, BAWL OUT, READ THE RIOT ACT.

called strike *n.* A pitch in baseball that the batter does not swing at but that the umpire calls a strike because it was a good pitch. *The batter was fooled by the pitch and let it go past for a called strike.* (The batter thought the pitch would be bad and didn't swing at it, but the umpire called it a strike.)

call for *v.* **1** To come or go to get (someone or something). *John called for Mary to take her to the dance.* (John came to Mary's house to get her.) Syn. PICK UP. **2** To need; require. *The cake recipe calls for two cups of flour* (The recipe needs two cups of flour to be successful.) *Success in school calls for much hard study.* (To succeed in school, you need to study hard.)

call girl *n., slang* A prostitute catering to wealthy clientele, especially one who is contacted by telephone for an appointment. *Rush Street is full of call girls.* (There are many prostitutes on Rush Street.)

calling down *also* **dressing down** *n. phr., informal* A scolding; reprimand. *The judge gave the boy a calling down for speeding.* (The judge gave the boy a scolding for speeding.)

call in question *or* **call into question** *or* **call in doubt** *v. phr.* To say (something) may be a mistake; express doubt about; question. *Bill called in question Ed's remark that basketball is safer than football.* (Ed said "Basketball is safer than football," and Bill said, "I don't believe that. Can you prove it?")

call it a day *v. phr., informal* To stop for the day; quit. *Bob studied hard till 10 P.M., and then decided to call it a day and went to bed.* (He decided he had done enough work for one day and quit.) *Mr. Johnson painted his house all morning; then he called it a day and went to the ball game.* (After lunch Mr. Johnson quit work for the day.) *It was nearly midnight, so Mrs. Byron decided to call it a day, and left the party, and went home.* (Mrs. Byron decided she had done enough for that day; it was time to stop.) *The four golfers played nine holes and then called it a day.* (They quit and went home.) Compare CLOSE UP SHOP.

call it quits *v. phr., informal* **1** To decide to stop what you are doing; quit. *When Tom had painted half the garage, he called it quits.* (Tom decided to stop painting when he was half-finished.) **2** To agree that each side in a fight is satisfied; stop fighting because a wrong has been paid back; say things are even. *Pete called Tom a bad name, and they fought till Tom gave Pete a bloody nose; then they called it quits.* (They agreed that Tom had paid Pete back for calling him a bad name; they said they were even again.)

call names *v. phr.,* To use ugly or unkind words when speaking to someone or when talking about someone.—Usually used by or to children. *Bill got so mad he started calling Frank names.* (Bill spoke to Frank in ugly, nasty, and unkind words.)

call off *v.* To stop (something planned); quit; cancel. *When the ice became soft and sloppy, we had to call off the ice-skating party.* (We had to stop skating because of the danger of soft, weak ice.) *The baseball game was called off because of rain.* (It was cancelled.)

call on *or* **call upon** *v.* **1** To make a call upon; visit. *Mr. Brown called on an old friend while he was in the city.* (He went to visit an old friend while he was in the city.) **2** To ask for help. *He called on a friend to give him money for the busfare to his home.* (He asked his friend to help him when he didn't have enough money.)

call one's bluff *v. phr., informal* To ask someone to prove what he says he can or will do. *Tom said he could jump twenty feet and* *so Dick called his bluff and said "Let's see you do it!"* (Dick knew Tom was bragging and could not jump that far, so he asked him to try and prove it.)

call one's shot *v. phr.* **1** To tell before firing where a bullet will hit. *An expert rifleman can call his shot regularly.* (An expert is able to say where on the target his shots will hit.) *The wind was strong and John couldn't call his shots.* (A strong wind was pushing the bullet to the side so John couldn't be sure where it would land.) **2** *or* **call the turn** To tell in advance the result of something before you do it. *Mary won three games in a row, just as she said she would. She called her shots well.* (Mary predicted well when she said she would win three games in a row.) *Nothing ever happens as Tom says it will. He is very poor at calling his shots.* (Tom is very poor at predicting what will happen.)

call on the carpet *v. phr., informal* To call (a person) before an authority (as a boss or teacher) for a scolding or reprimand. *The worker was called on the carpet by the boss for sleeping on the job.* (The worker was asked to come into the boss's office and was scolded for sleeping on the job.) *The principal called Tom on the carpet and warned him to stop coming to school late.* (The principal called Tom into his office and warned him against coming to school late.)

call the shots *v. phr., informal* To give orders; be in charge; direct; control. *Bob is a first-rate leader who knows how to call the shots.* (Bob knows how to give orders and control people.) *The quarterback called the shots well, and the team gained twenty yards in five plays.* (The quarterback gave good directions, and the team made quick gains.) Syn. CALL THE TUNE.

call the tune *v. phr., informal* To be in control; give orders or directions; command. *Bill was president of the club, but Jim was secretary and called the tune.* (Jim was the one who really was in charge of the club.) *The people supported the mayor, so he could call the tune in city matters.* (He could decide and give orders.) Syn. CALL THE SHOTS.

call the turn See CALL ONE'S SHOT 2.

call to account *v. phr.* **1** To ask (someone) to explain why he did something wrong (as breaking a rule). *The principal called Jim to account after Jim left school early without permission.* (The principal asked Jim to tell why he left early.) **2** To scold (as for wrong conduct); reprimand. *The father called his son to account for disobeying him.* (The father scolded his son for disobedience.)

call to order *v. phr.* **1** To open (a meeting) formally. *The chairman called the committee to order.* (The chairman said that the committee must be quiet and do business.) *The president pounded with his gavel to call the convention to order.* (The chairman pounded the table to get the attention of the convention and open its meeting.) **2** To warn not to break the rules of a meeting. *The judge called the people in the court room to order when they talked too loud.* (The judge ordered them to be quiet.)

call up *v.* **1** To make someone think of; bring to mind; remind. *The picture of the Capitol called up memories of our class trip.* (The picture brought memories of our class trip; it made us think of things that happened on the trip.) **2** To tell to come (as before a court). *The district attorney called up three witnesses.* (He told them to come to court and tell what they saw.) **3** To bring together for a purpose; bring into action. *Jim called up all his strength, pushed past the players blocking him, and ran for a touchdown.* (Jim collected all his strength so that he had enough to make a touchdown.) *The army called up its reserves when war seemed near.* (The army called all the men on its lists to active service.) **4** To call on the telephone. *She called up a friend just for a chat.* (She called a friend on the telephone just to talk.)

call upon See CALL ON.

camel See STRAW THAT BROKE THE CAMEL'S BACK *at* LAST STRAW.

camp See BREAK CAMP.

campaign See WHISPERING CAMPAIGN.

camp follower *n.* **1** A man or woman who goes with an army, not to fight but to sell something. *Nowadays camp followers are not allowed as they were long ago.* (Nowadays men and women are not allowed to go with an army and sell things as they were long ago.) **2** A person who goes with a famous or powerful person or group in hope of profit. *A man who runs for president has many camp followers.* (A man who runs for president has many people with him who hope to profit if he is elected.)

camp out *v.* To live, cook, and sleep out of doors (as in a tent). *We camped out near the river for a week.* (We lived and slept out of doors near the river for a week.)

can See AS BEST ONE CAN, CATCH AS CATCH CAN.

canary See LOOK LIKE THE CAT THAT ATE THE CANARY *or* LOOK LIKE THE CAT THAT SWALLOWED THE CANARY.

cancel out *v.* To destroy the effect of; balance or make useless. *The boy got an "A" in history to cancel out the "C" he got in arithmetic.* (The boy got an "A" in history to balance the "C" he got in arithmetic.) *Our track team won the mile relay to cancel out the other team's advantage in winning the half-mile relay.* (Our track team won the mile relay to make the score even after the other team won the half-mile relay.) *Tom's hot temper cancels out his skill as a player.* (Tom's hot temper makes his skill as a player useless.)

cancer stick *n., slang* A cigarette. *Throw away that cancer stick! Smoking is bad for you!* (Throw away that cigarette.)

candle BURN THE CANDLE AT BOTH ENDS, GAME IS NOT WORTH THE CANDLE, HOLD A CANDLE.

canned heat *n.* Chemicals in a can which burn with a hot, smokeless flame. *Some people use canned heat to keep food warm.* (Some people use chemicals that burn in a can to keep food warm.) *The mountain climbers used canned heat for cooking.* (The mountain climbers used canned fuel for cooking.)

canned laughter *n., informal* The sounds of laughter heard on certain television programs that were obviously not recorded in front of a live audience and are played for the benefit of the audience from a stereo track to underscore the funny points. *How can there be an audience in this show when it is taking place in the jungle? — Why, it's canned laughter you're hearing.* (It is not a real audience laughing; you hear the laughter from a sound track.)

canoe See PADDLE ONE'S OWN CANOE.

can of worms *n., slang, informal* **1** A complex problem, or complicated situation. *Let's not get into big city politics—that's a different can of worms.* (Let us avoid the subject of big city politics—that is a different messy problem.) **2** A very restless, jittery person. *Joe can't sit still for a minute—he is a can of worms.* (He is so jittery—as if he were a can of worms that wiggle all the time.)

can't help but (*informal*) ALSO (*formal*) **cannot but** *v. phr.* To be forced to; can only; must. *When the streets are full of melting snow, you can't help but get your shoes wet.* (With melting snow on the ground, you are sure to get your shoes wet.) *When a friend gave Jim a ticket to the game, he couldn't help but go.* (When a friend gave Jim a ticket, he just had to go.) *When your country calls you for help, you cannot but go.* (When your country calls you to help, you must go; you feel that is your duty.) *When a close friend dies, you cannot but feel sad.* (The death of your friend makes you feel sad.) Compare CAN HELP, HAVE TO.

can't see the wood for the trees *or* **can't see the woods for the trees** *or* **can't see the forest for the trees** *v. phr.* To be unable to judge or understand the whole because of attention to the parts; criticize small things and not see the value or the aim of the future achievement. *Teachers sometimes notice language errors and do not see the good ideas in a composition; they cannot see the woods for the trees.* (They see small errors and miss big ideas.) *The voters defeated a bond issue for the new school because they couldn't see the forest for the trees; they thought of their taxes rather than of their children's education.* (They paid more attention to the cost of the new school than to the need for it.) *We should think of children's growth in character and understanding more than of their little faults and misdeeds; some of us can't see the wood for the trees.* (We do not understand what is most important.)

cap See FEATHER IN ONE'S CAP, SET ONE'S CAP FOR, PUT ON ONE'S THINKING CAP.

card See CREDIT CARD, FLASH CARD, HOUSE OF CARDS, IN THE CARDS *or* ON THE CARDS, LAY ONE'S CARDS ON THE TABLE, PLAY ONE'S CARDS RIGHT, PUT ONE'S CARDS ON THE TABLE, STACK THE CARDS, TRUMP CARD.

cards stacked against one See STACK THE CARDS.

card up one's sleeve *n. phr., informal* Another help, plan, or argument kept back and produced if needed; another way to do something.—A cliché. *John knew his mother would lend him money if necessary, but he kept that card up his sleeve.* (He didn't borrow it, but waited until it was necessary.) *Bill always has a card up his sleeve, so when his first plan failed he tried another.* (He was smart enough to have thought of another plan.) Compare ACE IN THE HOLE 2.

care See COULDN'T CARE LESS, HAVE A CARE, GIVE A HANG *or* CARE A HANG, TAKE CARE.

carpet See CALL ON THE CARPET, MAGIC CARPET, ROLL OUT THE RED CARPET.

car pool *n.* A group of people who own cars and take turns driving each other to work or on some other regular trip. *It was John's father's week to drive his own car in the car pool.* (It was John's father's turn to drive his friends to work in his car.)

carriage trade *n., literary* Rich or upper class people. *The hotel is so expensive that only the carriage trade stays there.* (The hotel is so expensive that only rich or upper class people stay there.) *The carriage trade buys its clothes at the best stores.* (Rich or upper class people buy their clothes at the best stores.)

carrot and stick *n. phr.* The promise of reward and threat of punishment, both at the same time. *John's father used the carrot and stick when he talked about his low grades.* (John's father promised to reward him if he would get better grades and to punish him if he didn't.)

carry See CASH-AND-CARRY.

carry a torch *or* **carry the torch** *v. phr.* **1** To show great and unchanging loyalty to a cause or a person. *Although the others gave up fighting for their rights, John continued to carry the torch.* (Although the others gave up fighting for their rights, John continued to be faithful to the cause by fighting on.) **2** *informal* To be in love, usually without success or return. *He is carrying a torch for Anna, even though she is in love with someone else.* (He loves Anna, even though she loves someone else.)

carry away *v.* To cause very strong feeling; excite or delight to the loss of cool judgment. *The music carried her away.* (The music pleased her so much that she couldn't do anything but listen.) *He let his anger carry him away.* (He was so angry that he lost all judgment.)—Often used in the passive. *She was carried away by the man's charm.* (She was very much attracted by him and saw nothing against him.) *He was carried away by the sight of the flag.* (Seeing the flag greatly impressed him.)

carry coals to Newcastle *v. phr.* To do something unnecessary; bring or furnish something of which there is plenty.—A cliché. *The man who waters his grass after a good rain is carrying coals to Newcastle.* (The watering is not needed; the grass is soaked.) *Joe was carrying coals to Newcastle when he told the doctor how to cure a cold.* (The doctor knew more about it than Joe.) [Newcastle is an English city near many coal mines, and coal is sent out from there to other places.]

carrying charge *n.* An extra cost added to the price of something bought on weekly or monthly payments. *The price of the bicycle was $50. Jim bought it for $5.00 a month for ten months plus a carrying charge of $1 a month.* (Jim paid $50 for the bicycle, plus $10 extra so that he would not have to pay for it all at once.)

carry off *v.* **1** To cause death of; kill. *Years ago smallpox carried off hundreds of Indians of the Sioux tribe.* (Many Sioux Indians died of smallpox.) Compare WIPE OUT. **2** To succeed in winning. *Bob carried off honors in science.* (Bob led in science.) *Jim carried off two gold medals in the track meet.* (Jim won two gold medals.) **3** To succeed somewhat unexpectedly in. *The spy planned to deceive the enemy soldiers and carried it off very well.* (He succeeded in doing what he had planned.) *In the class play, Lloyd carried off his part surprisingly well.* (He performed his part in the play very well.)

carry —— off one's feet See KNOCK OFF ONE'S FEET, SWEEP OFF ONE'S FEET.

carry off the palm *or* **bear off the palm** *v. phr., literary* To gain the victory; win. *John carried off the palm in the tennis championship match.* (John won the tennis match.) *Our army bore off the palm in the battle.* (Our army won the battle.) [From the fact that long ago a palm leaf was given to the winner in a game as a sign of victory.]

carry on *v.* **1** To work at; be busy with; manage. *Bill and his father carried on a hardware business.* (They managed and worked in a hardware store.) *Mr. Jones and Mr. Smith carried on a long correspondence with each other.* (They wrote many letters to each other.) **2** To keep doing as before; continue. *After his father died, Bill carried on with the business.* (He kept on running the store.) *The colonel told the soldiers to carry on while he was gone.* (He told them to keep on doing their duties.) *Though tired and hungry, the Scouts carried on until they reached camp.* (They kept on walking to the camp.) Compare BEAR UP 2, GO ON 1a. **informal** To behave in a noisy, foolish, and troublesome manner. *The boys carried on in the swimming pool until the lifeguard ordered them out.* (The boys were so rough and disorderly that the lifeguard got them out.) **3b** *informal* To make too great a show of feeling, such as anger, grief, and pain. *John carried on for ten minutes after he hit his thumb with the hammer.* (He yelled and cried for ten minutes.) Compare TAKE ON 4. **4** *informal* To act in an immoral or scandalous way; act disgracefully. *The townspeople said that he was carrying on with a neighbor girl.* (They were acting shamefully.)

carry one's cross *or* (*literary*) **bear one's cross** *v. phr.* To live with pain or trouble; keep on even though you suffer or have trouble.—A cliché. *Weak ankles are a cross Joe carries while the other boys play basketball.* (Weak ankles are a trouble Joe has to live with while the other boys play basketball.) *We didn't know the cheerful woman was bearing her cross, a son in prison.* (We didn't know the cheerful woman was keeping on, even though she had trouble, a son in prison.)

carry out *v.* To put into action; follow; execute. *The generals were determined to carry out their plans to defeat the enemy.* (The generals wanted to try their plans to defeat the enemy.) *John listened carefully and carried out the teacher's instructions.* (John followed the teacher's instructions.)

carry over *v.* **1** To save for another time. *The store had some bathing suits it had carried over from last year.* (The store had some bathing suits kept from last year.) *What you learn in school should carry over into adult life.* (You should remember the things you learn in school and use them in adult life.) **2** To transfer (as a figure) from one column, page, or book to another. *When he added up the figures, he carried over the total into the next year's account book.* (He transferred the total from one account book to the next year's book.) **3** To continue in another place. *The story was carried over to the next page.* (The story was continued on the next page.)

carry the ball *v. phr., informal* To take the most important or difficult part in an action or business.—A cliché. *None of the other boys would tell the principal about their breaking the window, and John had to carry the ball.* (When the other boys wouldn't tell the principal, John had to.) *When the going is rough, Fred can always be depended on to carry the ball.* (When things are difficult, you can be sure that Fred will lead in fixing the trouble.)

carry the day *v. phr., informal* To win completely; to succeed in getting one's aim accomplished. *The defense attorney's summary before the jury helped him carry the day.* (His summary helped him win the case.)

carry the torch See CARRY A TORCH.

carry the weight of the world on one's shoulders See WEIGHT OF THE WORLD ON ONE'S SHOULDERS.

carry through. *v.* **1a** To put into action. *Mr. Green was not able to carry through his plans for a hike because he broke his leg.* (He could not put his plans into action; he could not go on the hike.) **1b** To do something you have planned; put a plan into action. *Jean makes good plans but she cannot carry through with any of them.* (Jean cannot finish what she starts to do.) Compare GO THROUGH WITH, CARRY OUT. **2** To keep (someone) from failing or stopping; bring through; help. *When the tire blew out, the rules Jim had learned in driving class carried him through safely.* (What Jim learned in driving class helped him stop the car safely.)

cart before the horse *n. phr., informal* Things in wrong order; something backwards or mixed up.—An overused expression. Usually used with *put* but sometimes with *get* or *have. When the salesman wanted money for goods he hadn't delivered, I told him he was putting the cart before the horse.* (When he wanted to be paid first, and deliver the things later, I told him he was going at things the wrong way around.) *To get married first and then get a job is getting the cart before the horse.* (You should get a job first before thinking of marriage.)

cart off *or* **cart away** *v., informal* To take away, often with force or with rough handling or behavior. *The police carted the rioters off to jail.* (The police hauled the members of the mob away to jail.) *When Bobby wouldn't eat his supper, his mother carted him away to bed.* (When Bobby wouldn't eat his supper, his mother carried him to bed.)

case See BASKET CASE, CIRCUMSTANCES ALTER CASES, COUCH CASE, GET DOWN TO BRASS TACKS *also* GET DOWN TO CASES, IN ANY CASE, IN CASE *or* IN THE EVENT, IN CASE OF *also* IN THE EVENT OF, VANITY CASE.

case in point *n. phr.* An example that proves something or helps to make something clearer. *An American can rise from the humblest beginnings to become President. Abraham Lincoln is a case in point.* (His life shows that a man from the humblest beginning can become President.)

cash See COLD CASH.

cash-and-carry[1] *adj.* Selling things for cash money only and letting the customer carry them home, not having the store deliver them; *also* sold in this way. *This is a cash-and-carry store only.* (This store only sells for cash, and does not deliver.) *You can save money at a cash-and-carry sale.* (You can save money at a sale of things to be bought for cash and carried away.)

cash-and-carry[2] *adv.* With no credit, no time payments, and no deliveries. *Some stores sell cash-and-carry only.* (They do not allow time payments and do not deliver.) *It is cheaper to buy cash-and-carry.* (It is cheaper to pay cash and to carry home your purchases.)

cash crop *n.* A crop grown to be sold. *Cotton is a cash crop in the South.* (Cotton is grown in the South to be sold.) *They raise potatoes to eat, but tobacco is their cash crop.* (They raise potatoes to eat, but tobacco is grown to be sold.)

cash in *v.* **1** To exchange (as poker chips or bonds) for the value in money. *He paid the bill by cashing in some bonds.* (He paid the bill by first selling some bonds.) *When the card game ended, the players cashed in their chips and went home.* (They traded their chips for real money.) **2** *or* **cash in one's chips** *slang* To die.—A cliché. *When the outlaw cashed in his chips, he was buried with his boots on.* (When he died, he was buried with his boots on.) *He was shot through the body and knew he was going to cash in.* (He knew he was going to die.)

cash in on *v., informal* To see (a chance) and profit by it; take advantage of (an opportunity or happening). *Mr. Brown cashed in on people's great interest in camping and sold three hundred tents.* (He noticed people were interested in camping and sold many tents.)

cash on the barrelhead *n. phr., informal* Money paid at once; money paid when something is bought.—A cliché. *Father paid cash on the barrelhead for a new car.* (He paid money at once for a new car.) *Some lawyers want cash on the barrelhead.* (Some lawyers want to be paid at once.) Compare COLD CASH.

cast about *also* **cast around** *v., literary* **1** To look everywhere; search. *The committee was casting about for an experienced teacher to take the retiring principal's place.* (They were looking everywhere to find a new principal.) **2** To search your mind; try to remember something; try to think of something. *The teacher cast about for an easy way to explain the lesson.* (The teacher tried to think of an easy way to explain the lesson.) *Jane cast around for a good subject for her report.* (She thought hard trying to find a good subject.)

cast down *adj.* Discouraged; sad; unhappy. —Used less often than the reverse form, *downcast. Mary was cast down at the news of her uncle's death.* (Mary felt saddened.) *Charles felt cast down when he lost the race.* (He felt discouraged.)

cast in one's lot with *formal* See THROW IN ONE'S LOT WITH.

castle in the air See BUILD CASTLES IN THE AIR.

cast off *v.* **1a** *or* **cast loose** To unfasten; untie; let loose (as a rope holding a boat).

*The captain of the boat cast off the line and
we were soon out in open water.* (The captain untied the rope holding the boat and we
were soon out in open water.) **1b** To untie a rope holding a boat or something suggesting a boat. *We cast off and set sail at 6
A.M.* (We untied the boat and set sail at 6
A.M.) **2** To knit the last row of stitches.
*When she had knitted the twentieth row of
stitches she cast off.* (When she had finished
knitting the twentieth row of stitches she knit
one more row, which was the last.) **3** To say
that you do not know (someone) any more;
not accept as a relative or friend. *Mr. Jones
cast off his daughter when she married
against his wishes.* (He said she could not be
his daughter after that.)

cast one's lot with See THROW IN ONE'S LOT
WITH.

cast out *v., formal* To force (someone) to
go out or away; banish; expel. *After the
scandal, he was cast out of the best society.*
(After his shameful action he was banished
from the best society; he was not a friend of
good people after that.) Compare CAST OFF 3.

cast pearls before swine *or* **cast one's pearls
before swine** *n. phr., literary* To waste
good acts or valuable things on someone who
won't understand or be thankful for them, just
as pigs won't appreciate pearls.—A cliché;
often used in negative sentences. *I won't waste
good advice on John any more because he
never listens to it. I won't cast pearls before
swine.* (Why should I throw away good advice on John if he never follows it?)

cast the first stone *v. phr., literary* To be
the first to blame someone; lead accusers
against a wrongdoer.—A cliché. *Jesus said
that a person who was without sin could cast
the first stone.* (Jesus said that a person should
not criticize unless he was perfect himself.)
*Although Ben saw the girl cheating, he did
not want to cast the first stone.* (He did not
want to be the first to accuse her.)

cast up *v.* **1** *literary* To turn or direct upward; raise. *The dying missionary cast up his
eyes to heaven and prayed.* (The missionary
looked upward to the sky and prayed.) **2**
archaic To do sums; do a problem in addition; add. *Cast up 15, 43, 27, and 18.* (Add
15, 43, 27, and 18.) *When John had all the
figures, he cast them up.* (When John had all
the figures, he added them together.)

cat See COPY CAT, CURIOSITY KILLED THE CAT,
FRAIDY-CAT *or* FRAID-CAT *or* SCAREDY CAT *or*
SCARED-CAT, HOLY CATS, LET THE CAT OUT OF
THE BAG, LOOK LIKE THE CAT THAT ATE THE
CANARY, PLAY CAT AND MOUSE WITH, RAIN
CATS AND DOGS.

catch See EARLY BIRD CATCHES THE WORM,
FAIR CATCH, SHOESTRING CATCH.

catch-as-catch-can[1] *adv. phr.* In a free manner; in any way possible; in the best way you
can. *On moving day everything is packed and
we eat meals catch-as-catch-can.* (We eat
whatever we can find and sit almost anywhere.)

catch-as-catch-can[2] *adj. phr.* Using any
means or method; unplanned; free. *He was
an expert at catch-as-catch-can wrestling.* (He
was an expert at a kind of free and unlimited
wrestling.) *Rip van Winkle seems to have led
a catch-as-catch-can life.* (He lived freely
without much care for his future.) *Politics is
rather a catch-as-catch-can business.* (In politics one has to meet many unexpected emergencies.) Compare HIT-OR-MISS.

catch at *v.* **1** To try to catch suddenly; grab
for. *The boy on the merry-go-round caught
at the brass ring, but did not get it.* (He tried
to grab the brass ring.) **2** To seize quickly;
accept mentally or physically. *The hungry
man caught at the sandwich and began to
eat.* (He quickly seized the sandwich when it
was offered.) *Joe caught at Bill's offer to help.*
(Bill offered to help and Joe quickly accepted.)

catch at a straw See GRASP AT STRAWS.

catch cold *v. phr.* **1** *or* **take cold** To get
a common cold-weather sickness that causes
a running nose, sneezing, and sometimes sore
throat and fever or other symptoms. *Don't
get your feet wet or you'll catch cold.* (Wear
your rubbers in wet, cold weather or you may
become sick.) **2** *informal* To catch unprepared or not ready for a question or unexpected happening. *I had not studied my lesson
carefully, and the teacher's question caught
me cold.* (I was not ready for the question
and could not answer it.) *The opposing team
was big and sure of winning, and they were
caught cold by the fast, hard playing of our
smaller players.* (The big team was surprised
and upset by our small, fast players.)

catch dead *v. phr., informal* To see or hear
(someone) in an embarrassing act or place at
any time; ever catch.—Used in the negative,
usually in the passive. *You won't catch Bill
dead taking his sister to the movies.* (Bill
wouldn't take his sister to the movies. If he
were made to, he wouldn't let anyone see him.
That would be embarrassing.) *John wouldn't
be caught dead in the necktie he got for
Christmas.* (John wouldn't ever want to be
seen wearing it. He is ashamed of it.)

catch fire *v. phr.* **1** To begin to burn. *When
he dropped a match in the leaves, they caught
fire.* (When he dropped the match in the
leaves they began to burn.) **2** To become excited. *The audience caught fire at the speaker's words and began to cheer.* (The audience
became wildly excited at the speaker's words
and began to cheer.) *His imagination caught
fire as he read.* (His imagination was excited to great activity as he read.)

catch flat-footed See FLAT-FOOTED 2.

catch forty winks See FORTY WINKS.

catch it *or* **get it** *v. phr., informal* To be
scolded or punished.—Usually used of chil-

dren. *John knew he would catch it when he came home late for supper.* (He knew he would get a scolding when he arrived late for supper.) *Wow, Johnny! When your mother sees those torn pants, you're going to get it.* (Your mother will scold or punish you.) Compare GET WHAT'S COMING TO ONE. Contrast GIVE IT TO 2.

catch it in the neck *or* **get it in the neck** *v. phr., slang* To be blamed or punished. *Tom got it in the neck because he forgot to close the windows when it rained.* (Tom was punished because of the damage caused by the water.) *Students get it in the neck when they lose library books.* (They are scolded for their carelessness.) Compare CATCH IT, GET WHAT'S COMING TO ONE.

catch on *v., informal* **1** To understand; learn about.—Often used with *to. You'll catch on to the job after you've been here awhile.* (You'll get the idea of how to do the job.) *Don't play any tricks on Joe. When he catches on, he will beat you.* (When Joe sees that you are playing a trick on him, he will beat you.) **2** To become popular; be done or used by many people. *The song caught on and was sung and played everywhere.* (The song was liked by many people.) **3** To be hired; get a job. *The ball player caught on with a big league team last year.* (He was hired to play for the team.)

catch one's breath *v. phr.* **1** To breathe in suddenly with fear or surprise. *The beauty of the scene made him catch his breath.* (The beauty of the scene surprised him and he took a quick breath.) Compare TAKE ONE'S BREATH AWAY. **2a** To rest and get back your normal breathing, as after running. *After running to the bus stop, we sat down to catch our breath.* (We stopped until our hard breathing had slowed down to normal.) **2b** To relax for a moment after any work. *After the day's work we sat down over coffee to catch our breath.* (We relaxed over coffee after the day's work.)

catch one's death of *or* **take one's death of** *v. phr., informal* To become very ill with (a cold, pneumonia, flu). *Johnny fell in the icy water and almost took his death of cold.* (Johnny got wet and caught a very bad cold.) Sometimes used in the short form *"catch your death." Johnny! Come right in here and put your coat and hat on. You'll catch your death!* (You will get a bad cold.)

catch one's eye *v. phr.* To attract your attention. *I caught his eye as he moved through the crowd, and waved at him to come over.* (I attracted his attention as he moved through the crowd.) *The dress in the window caught her eye when she passed the store.* (The dress in the window attracted her attention when she passed the store.)—**eye-catcher** *n.* That new girl in our class is a real eye-catcher. (That new girl is very attractive.)

catch sight of *v. phr.* To see suddenly or unexpectedly. *Allan caught sight of a kingbird in a maple tree.* (Allan suddenly saw a kingbird in a maple tree.) Contrast LOSE SIGHT OF.

catch some rays *v. phr., slang, informal* To get tanned while sunbathing. *Tomorrow I'll go to the beach and try to catch some rays.* (I'll try to get a sun tan on the beach.)

catch some Z's *v. phr., slang, informal* To take a nap, to go to sleep. (Because of the *z* sound resembling snoring.) *I want to hit the sack and catch some Z's.* (I want to go to bed and get some sleep.)

catch-22 *n., informal* From Joseph Heller's novel *Catch-22*, set in World War II. A regulation or situation that is self-contradictory or that conflicts with another regulation. In Heller's book it referred to the regulation that flight crews must report for duty unless excused for reasons of insanity, but that any one claiming such an excuse must, by definition, be sane. *Government rules require workers to expose any wrongdoing in their office, but the Catch-22 prevents them from their doing so, because they are not allowed to disclose any information about their work.* (The rule about secrecy denies the possibility of reporting, so the workers are unable to comply.) **2** A paradoxical situation. *The Catch-22 of job-hunting was that the factory wanted to hire only workers who had experience making cigars, but the only way to get the experience was by working at the cigar factory.* (Those conditions seemed to make getting a job impossible.)

catch up *v.* **1** To take or pick up suddenly; grab (something). *She caught up the book from the table and ran out of the room.* (She grabbed the book and ran away.) **2** To capture or trap (someone) in a situation; concern or interest very much.—Usually used in the passive with *in. The Smith family was caught up in the war in Europe and we did not see them again till it was over.* (They were in Europe while the war was going on and couldn't leave till it was over.) *We were so caught up in the movie we forgot what time it was.* (We got so interested in the movie we forgot the time.) Compare MIX UP. **3** To go fast enough or do enough so as not to be behind; overtake; come even.—Often used with *to* or *with. Johnny ran hard and tried to catch up to his friends.* (He ran so that he could be with them.) *Mary missed two weeks of school; she must work hard to catch up with her class.* (She is behind in her studies.) Compare UP TO. **4** To find out about or get proof to punish or arrest.—Usually used with *with. Billy is always fooling in class but the teacher will catch up with him someday.* (The teacher will find out and punish him.) *A man told the police where the robbers were hiding, so the police finally caught up with them.* (The police finally arrested them.) **5** To result in something bad; bring punishment.—Usually used with *with*. *The boy's fighting caught up with him and he was expelled from school.* (The boy was finally punished for his fighting.) *Smoking will catch up with you.* (Something bad will happen to you because you smoke.) Compare CHICKENS COME HOME TO ROOST. **6** To finish; not lose or be behind.—Used with *on* and often in the phrase *get caught up on*. *Frank stayed up late to get caught up on his homework.* (He studied late to finish his homework.) *I have to catch up on my sleep.* (I did not get enough sleep. I must go to bed early to get enough sleep.) *We caught up on all the latest news when we got back to school and saw our friends again.* (We found out what had happened and what our friends had done.) Syn. KEEP UP.

catch with one's pants down *v. phr., slang* To surprise someone in an embarrassing position or guilty act. *They thought they could succeed in the robbery, but they got caught with their pants down.* (They thought they could succeed in the robbery, but the police caught them when they broke into the store.) *When the weather turned hot in May, the drive-in restaurant was caught with its pants down, and ran out of ice cream before noon.* (The drive-in was caught unprepared for hot weather.)

cat get ones' tongue You are not able or willing to talk because of shyness.—A cliché. Usually used about children or as a question to children. *Tommy's father asked Tommy if the cat had got his tongue.* (His father asked if he could not speak.) *The little girl had a poem to recite, but the cat got her tongue.* (She became too shy and nervous to speak her piece.) Compare LOSE ONE'S TONGUE.

cat has nine lives A cat can move so fast and jump so well that he seems to escape being killed many times.—A cliché. *We thought our cat would be killed when he fell from the roof of the house. He was not, but he used up one of his nine lives.* (The cat was very lucky not to be killed as we thought he would be.)

cathouse *n., slang* A house of ill repute, a house of prostitution. *Massage parlors are frequently cathouses in disguise.* (Massage parlors are really houses of prostitution.)

cat's meow *or* **cat's pajamas** *n. slang* Something very wonderful, special, or good. *John's new bike is really the cat's meow.* (John's new bike is a very, very good one.) *Mary's party is going to be the cat's pajamas.* (Mary's party is going to be a very special one.)

caught short *adj. phr., informal* Not having enough of something when you need it. *Mrs. Ford was caught short when the newspaper boy came for his money a day early.* (Mrs. Ford did not have enough change when the newspaper boy came for his money a day early.) *The man was caught short of clothes when he had to go on a trip.* (The man did not have enough clothes when he had to go on a trip.)

cause tongues to wag See TONGUES TO WAG.

caution See THROW CAUTION TO THE WINDS.

cave in *v.* **1** To fall or collapse inward. *The mine caved in and crushed three miners.* (The roof of the mine fell down and covered the miners.) *Don't climb on that old roof. It might cave in.* (The roof might break and fall in if you walk on it.) **2** *informal* To weaken and be forced to give up. *The children begged their father to take them to the circus until he caved in.* (He weakened and took them.) *After the atomic bomb, Japan caved in and the war ceased.* (Japan gave up fighting.)

ceiling See HIT THE CEILING *or* HIT THE ROOF.

cent See TWO CENTS, WORTH A CENT.

center See FRONT AND CENTER, OFF-CENTER, SHOPPING CENTER.

center field *n.* The part of a baseball outfield behind second base and between left and right fields. *The ball went over the pitcher's head and into center field for a single.* (The ball went over the pitcher's head and into the middle part of the field for a hit.) Compare LEFT FIELD, RIGHT FIELD.—**center fielder** *n.* The outfielder in baseball who plays in center field. *The center fielder was playing very far back in the outfield on a straight line back from home plate and second base.* (The center fielder was playing very far back in his position.)

century See TURN OF THE CENTURY.

ceremony See STAND ON CEREMONY.

certain See FOR SURE *or* FOR CERTAIN.

chain letter *n.* A letter which each person receiving it is asked to copy and send to several others. *Most chain letters die out quickly.* (Most letters which each person is asked to copy and send to several others soon stop because people just throw them away.)

chain-smoke *v.* To smoke cigarettes or cigars one after another without stopping. *Mr. Jones is very nervous. He chain-smokes cigars.* (Mr. Jones smokes cigars one after another.) —**chain smoker** *n. Mr. Jones is a chain smoker.* (Mr. Jones smokes cigars one after another.) **chain-smoking** *adj. or n. Chain-smoking is very dangerous to health.* (Smoking cigarettes continuously is very unhealthy.)

chair See MUSICAL CHAIRS.

chalk See WALK THE CHALK.

chalk up *v., informal* **1** To write down as part of a score; record. *The scorekeeper chalked up one more point for the home team.* (The scorekeeper added another point to the home team's score.) **2** To make (a score or part of a score); score. *The team chalked up another victory.* (The team won another victory.) *Bob chalked up a home run and two base hits in the game.* (Bob made a home run and two base hits.) *Mary chalked up good* *grades this term.* (Mary got good grades this term.)

champ at the bit *v. phr.* To be eager to begin; be tired of being held back; want to start. —A cliché. *The horses were champing at the bit, anxious to start racing.* (The horses were very anxious for the race to begin and were chewing at the steel bits.) *As punishment John was kept after school for two hours. He was champing at the bit to go out.* (After two hours of staying after school, John was restless and anxious to go outdoors.)

chance See BY CHANCE, FAT CHANCE, STAND A CHANCE, TAKE A CHANCE.

chance on *also* **chance upon** *v.* To happen to find or meet; find or meet by accident. *On our vacation we chanced upon an interesting antique store.* (We happened to find an interesting antique store.) *Mary dropped her ring in the yard, and Mother chanced on it as she was raking.* (Mother found it by accident.) Syn. HAPPEN ON. Compare RUN INTO.

change See RING THE CHANGES.

change color *v. phr.* **1** To become pale. *The sight was so horrible that Mary changed color from fear.* (Mary turned pale from fear of the horrible sight.) *Bill lost so much blood from the cut that he changed color.* (Bill became pale from loss of blood.) **2** To become pink or red in the face; become flushed; blush. *Mary changed color when the teacher praised her drawing.* (Mary blushed when the teacher praised her drawing.) *Tom got angry at the remark and changed color.* (Tom became angry and red in the face at the remark.)

change horses in the middle of a stream *or* **change horses in midstream** *v. phr.* To make new plans or choose a new leader in the middle of an important activity.—A cliché. *When a new President is to be elected during a war, the people may decide not to change horses in the middle of a stream.* (They may decide to keep the same President until the war is over.)

change off *v., informal* To take turns doing something; alternate. *John and Bill changed off at riding the bicycle.* (John and Bill took turns riding the bicycle.) *Bob painted one patch of wall and then he changed off with Tom.* (Bob painted a part and then Tom painted one.)

change of heart *n. phr.* A change in the way one feels or thinks about a given task, idea or problem to be solved. *Joan had a change of heart and suddenly broke off her engagement to Tim.* (She decided not to marry him despite an earlier commitment.) *Fred got admitted to medical school, but he had a change of heart and decided to go into the Foreign Service instead.* (Although admitted to study medicine, he opted for a diplomatic career.)

change of pace *n. phr.* **1** A quick change in what you are doing. *John studied for three hours and then read a comic book for a change of pace.* (John studied for three hours

and then read a comic book as a change from the hard book he had been reading.) *The doctor told the man he needed a change of pace.* (The doctor told the man he needed a change in the way he had been living; he should stop hurrying and take a vacation.) **2** A slow pitch in baseball when the batter is expecting a fast ball. *The batter struck out on a change of pace.* (The batter struck out when a slow pitch was thrown when he was expecting a fast ball.) *A good pitcher has a change of pace.* (A good pitcher has a slow pitch to throw when the batter is expecting a fast ball.) Compare LET UP 4.

change one's tune *v. phr., informal* To make a change in your story, statement, or claim; change your way of acting. *The man said he was innocent, but when they found the stolen money in his pocket he changed his tune.* (He admitted that he was guilty.) *Bob was rude to his teacher, but she threatened to tell the principal and he changed his tune.* (He apologized and was polite.) Syn. SING A DIFFERENT TUNE.

change up See LET UP 4.

character See IN CHARACTER.

charge See CARRYING CHARGE, CHARGE OFF 2, IN CHARGE, IN CHARGE OF, TAKE CHARGE.

charge account *n.* An agreement with a store through which you can buy things and pay for them later. *Mother bought a new dress on her charge account.* (She bought a new dress, to be paid for later.) *Mr. Jones has a charge account at the garage on the corner.* (Mr. Jones can buy gasoline and other things at the garage and pay for them later.)

charge off *v.* **1** To consider or record as a loss, especially in an account book. *The store owner charged off all of the last season's stock of suits.* (The store owner recorded the cost of the suits left from the last season as a loss in his account books.) Syn. WRITE OFF 1. **2** *or* **charge up** *informal* To accept or remember (something) as a mistake and not worry about it any more.—Often used with *to experience. He charged off his mistakes to experience.* (He accepted his mistakes because they were made from lack of experience, and he did not worry about them or make them again.) Syn. CHALK UP. Compare CHARGE TO.

charge to *v.* **1** To place the blame on; make responsible for. *John failed to win a prize, but he charged it to his lack of experience.* (John placed the blame for his failure on his lack of experience.) *The coach charged the loss of the game to the team's disobeying his orders.* (The coach blamed the team for disobeying his orders.) **2** To buy something on the credit of. *Mrs. Smith bought a new pocketbook and charged it to her husband.* (Mrs. Smith bought a new pocketbook, and had the bill sent to her husband.) *Mr. White ordered a box of cigars and had it charged to his account.* (Mr. White bought the cigars and had the cost added to his bill, which is sent to him every month for payment.)

charmed life *n.* A life often saved from danger; a life full of lucky escapes. *He was in two airplane accidents, but he had a charmed life.* (He was in two airplane accidents but was never hurt.) *During the war a bullet knocked the gun out of his hand, but he had a charmed life.* (During the war a bullet knocked the gun out of his hand but he had a lucky escape from death.)

Charybdis See BETWEEN THE DEVIL AND THE DEEP BLUE SEA *or* BETWEEN SCYLLA AND CHARYBDIS.

chase See GIVE CHASE, GO CHASE ONESELF, LEAD A MERRY CHASE.

chase after See RUN AFTER.

chase around See RUN AROUND.

cheap skate *n., informal* A selfish or stingy person; a person who will not spend much.— An insulting term. *None of the girls like to go out on a date with him because he is a cheap skate.* (Nobody likes to go out with him because he will not spend much.)

cheat on *v. phr., informal* To be unfaithful (to one's wife or husband, or to one's sweetheart or fiancé). *It is rumored that Joe cheats on his wife.* (It is rumored that Joe is having an affair with another woman.)

check See BLANK CHECK, CLAIM CHECK, DOUBLE CHECK, IN CHECK, RAIN CHECK, RUBBER CHECK, SALES CHECK.

check in *v.* **1a** To sign your name (as at a hotel or convention). *The last guests to reach the hotel checked in at 12 o'clock.* (The last guests at the hotel signed their names in the hotel book at 12 o'clock.) Contrast CHECK OUT. **1b** *informal* To arrive. *The friends we had invited did not check in until Saturday.* (The friends we had invited did not arrive until Saturday.) **2** To receive (something) back and make a record of it. *The coach checked in the football uniforms at the end of the school year.* (The coach took back the uniforms and noted that each one had been returned.) *The students put their books on the library desk, and the librarian checked them in.* (The librarian made a record of their return.)

check off *v.* To put a mark beside (the name of a person or thing on a list) to show that it has been counted. *The teacher checked off each pupil as he got on the bus.* (The teacher counted each pupil and put a check beside his name when he got on the bus.) *Bill wrote down the names of all the states he could remember, and then he checked them off against the list in his book.* (Bill compared his list with the list in his book to see which he had forgotten.) Compare TICK OFF.

check on *or* **check up on** *v.* To try to find out the truth or rightness of; make sure of; examine; inspect; investigate. *We checked on Dan's age by getting his birth record.* (We found out how old he really was.) *Mrs. Brown*

said she heard someone downstairs and Mr. Brown went down to check up on it. (He went down to find out.) *You can check on your answers at the back of the book.* (You can find out if you have the right answers.) *The police are checking up on the man to see if he has a police record.* (They are investigating the man's past.) *Grandfather went to have the doctor check on his health.* (The doctor examined grandfather to see if he was healthy.) Compare LOOK INTO, LOOK OVER.

check out *v.* **1a** To pay your hotel bill and leave. *The last guests checked out of their rooms in the morning.* (The last guests paid their accounts and moved out of the hotel in the morning.) Contrast CHECK IN. **1b** *informal* To go away; leave. *I hoped our guest would stay but he had to check out before Monday.* (I hoped our guest would stay but he had to leave before Monday.) Compare CHECK IN. **2a** To make a list or record of. *They checked out all the goods in the store.* (They made a list of the goods in the store.) **2b** To give or lend (something) and make a record of it. *The boss checked out the tools to the workmen as they came to work.* (The boss gave the tools to the men and wrote down what he gave them.) **2c** To get (something) after a record has been made of it. *I checked out a book from the library.* (I went and got a book from the library; the librarian wrote down what I took.) **3** *informal* To test (something, like a part of a motor). *The mechanic checked out the car battery.* (He tested the car battery.) **4** *slang* To die. *He seemed too young to check out.* (He seemed too young to die.)

check up *v.* To find out or try to find out the truth or correctness of something; make sure of something; investigate. *Mrs. Brown thought she had heard a burglar in the house, so Mr. Brown checked up, but found nobody.* (Mr. Brown went to find out if Mrs. Brown was right.) *Bill thought he had a date with Janie, but phoned her to check up.* (He tried to find out if he really had a date.)

cheek See TURN THE OTHER CHEEK.

cheer See BRONX CHEER.

cheer up *v.* **1** To feel happy; stop being sad or discouraged; become hopeful, joyous, or glad. *Jones was sad at losing the business, but he cheered up at the sight of his daughter.* (Jones was sad when he lost the business, but just the sight of his daughter made him feel better.) *Cheer up! The worst is over.* (Be hopeful! The worst is past.) **2** To make cheerful or happy. *The support of the students cheered up the losing team and they played harder and won.* (The students' support made the team feel better.) *We went to the hospital to cheer up a sick friend.* (We went to the hospital to make our sick friend happier.) *Flowers cheer up a room.* (Flowers make a room more cheerful.)

cheese See BIG CHEESE, WHOLE CHEESE.

cheesebox *n., slang* A small, suburban house built by a land developer available at low cost and resembling the other houses around it. *They moved to a suburb, but their house is just a cheesebox.* (It is not a fancy or well built house at all.)

cheesecake *n., slang, informal* A showing of the legs of an attractive woman or a display of her breasts as in certain magazines, known as cheesecake magazines. *Photographer to model: Give us some cheesecake in that pose!* (I am about to take your picture for an advertisement, show more of your legs.)

cherry farm *n., slang* A correctional institution of minimal security where the inmates, mostly first offenders, work as farm hands. *Joe got a light sentence and was sent to a cherry farm for six months.* (He has to work as a farm hand at the penal institution for first offenders for half a year.)

chest See OFF ONE'S CHEST, ON ONE'S CHEST.

chew See BITE OFF MORE THAN ONE CAN CHEW.

chew out *v., slang* To scold roughly. *The boy's father chewed him out for staying up late.* (The boy's father scolded him for staying up late.) *The coach chews out lazy players.* (The coach scolds lazy players roughly.) Syn. BAWL OUT, CALL ON THE CARPET, HAUL OVER THE COALS.

chew the fat *or* **chew the rag** *v. phr., slang* To talk together in an idle, friendly fashion; chat. *We used to meet after work, and chew the fat over coffee and doughnuts.* (We used to talk together over coffee and doughnuts after work.) *The old man would chew the rag for hours with anyone who would join him.* (He would talk about various things with anyone.)

chew the scenery *v. phr., slang* To act over-emotionally in a situation where it is inappropriate, to engage in histrionics. *I don't know if Joe was sincere about our house, but he sure chewed up the scenery!* (He certainly acted very exaggeratedly.)

chicken See COUNT ONE'S CHICKENS BEFORE THEY ARE HATCHED, GO TO BED WITH THE CHICKENS, SPRING CHICKEN.

chicken feed *n., slang* A very small sum of money. *John and Bill worked very hard, but they were only paid chicken feed.* (John and Bill were paid very little money for the work they did.) *Mr. Jones is so rich he thinks a thousand dollars is chicken feed.* (Mr. Jones is so rich he doesn't think a thousand dollars is very much money.)

chicken-livered *adj., slang, colloquial* Easily scared, cowardly. *Joe sure is a chicken-livered guy.* (He certainly is a cowardly person.)

chicken out *v. phr., informal* To stop doing something because of fear, to decide not to do something after all even though previously having decided to try it. *I used to ride a motorcycle on the highway, but I've chickened out.* (I stopped riding it because I lost my nerve, I got scarred.) *I decided to take flying lessons but just before they started I chickened out.* (I changed my mind in the last minute because of fear.)

chickens come home to roost *informal* Words or acts come back to cause trouble for a person; something bad you said or did receives punishment; you get the punishment that you deserve. *Fred's chickens finally came home to roost today. He was late so often that the teacher made him go to the principal.* (He had to go to the principal for a scolding or punishment.)—Often used in a short form. *Mary's selfishness will come home to roost some day.* (She will get what she deserves.)

chicken switch *n., slang, Space English* **1** The emergency eject button used by test pilots in fast and high flying aircraft by means of which they can parachute to safety if the engine fails; later adopted by astronauts in space capsules. *Don't pull the chicken switch, unless absolutely necessary.* (Don't use the eject button unless you are in real danger.) **2** The panic button; a panicky reaction to an unforeseen situation, such as unreasonable or hysterical telephone calls to friends for help. *Joe pulled the chicken switch on his neighbor when the grease started burning in the kitchen.* (Joe telephoned his neighbor for help when he burned the grease instead of putting the fire out himself.)

child See BURNT CHILD DREADS THE FIRE, WITH CHILD.

children and fools speak the truth Children and fools say things without thinking; they say what they think or know when grown-ups might not think it was polite or wise to do so. —A proverb. *"Uncle Willie is too fat," said little Agnes. "Children and fools speak the truth," said her father.* (A grown-up might be afraid to say that Uncle Willie was too fat.)

chill See SPINE-CHILLING.

chime in *v.* **1** *informal* To join in. *The whole group chimed in on the chorus.* (The whole group joined in singing the chorus.) *When the argument got hot, John chimed in.* (When the argument got hot, John joined in it.) **2** To agree; go well together.—Usually used with *with*. *Dick was happy, and the holiday music chimed in with his feelings.* (The holiday music agreed with Dick's happiness.) *When Father suggested going to the shore for the vacation, the whole family chimed in with the plan.* (When Father suggested a shore vacation, the whole family agreed readily.)

chin See KEEP ONE'S CHIN UP, STICK ONE'S NECK OUT *or* STICK ONE'S CHIN OUT, TAKE IT ON THE CHIN, UP TO THE CHIN IN.

china shop See BULL IN A CHINA SHOP.

china syndrome *n., informal* From the title

of the movie with Jane Fonda and Jack Lemmon. The possibility that an industrial nuclear reactor might explode, literally affecting the other side of the planet (as if by eating a hole through the earth all the way to China.) *Antinuclear demonstrators are greatly worried about the China syndrome.* (They are afraid that nuclear reactors are unsafe.)

chip See CASH IN ONE'S CHIPS *at* CASH-IN, IN THE CHIPS. LET THE CHIPS FALL WHERE THEY MAY, FISH-AND-CHIPS, WHEN THE CHIPS ARE DOWN.

chip in *or* **kick in** *v., informal* To give together with others; contribute. *The pupils chipped in a dime apiece for the teacher's Christmas present.* (They gave a dime apiece toward the teacher's Christmas present.) *All the neighbors kicked in to help after the fire.* (All the neighbors contributed to help the people who had a fire.) *Lee chipped in ten points in the basketball game.* (Lee scored ten of his team's points.) *Joe didn't say much but chipped in a few words.* (Joe talked a little.)

chip off the old block *n. phr., informal* A son who looks or acts like his father.—A cliché. *From both his looks and his acts, you could see that he was a chip off the old block.* (You could see that he was his father's son.)

chip on one's shoulder *n. phr., informal* A quarrelsome nature; readiness to be angered. —A cliché. *He went through life with a chip on his shoulder.* (All his life he was too sensitive and ready to get upset and angry.) *Charles often gets into fights because he goes around with a chip on his shoulder.* (He thinks everyone is trying to boss or cheat or insult him.)

chips See WHEN THE CHIPS ARE DOWN.

choice See BY CHOICE, FIELDER'S CHOICE.

choke off *v.* To put a sudden end to; stop abruptly or forcefully. *It was almost time for the meeting to end, and the presiding officer had to move to choke off debate.* (The presiding officer had to act quickly to stop debate completely.) *The war choked off diamond shipments from overseas.* (The war stopped diamond shipments from other countries.)

choke up *v.* **1a** To come near losing calmness or self-control from strong feeling; be upset by your feelings. *When one speaker after another praised John, he choked up and couldn't thank them.* (The praise was almost too much, and John's feelings nearly upset him.) *When Father tried to tell me how glad he was to see me safe after the accident, he choked up and was unable to speak.* (Father was upset by his joy and couldn't say a word.) **1b** *informal* To be unable to do well because of excitement or nervousness. *Bill was a good batter, but in the championship game he choked up and did poorly.* (He was nervous and did not bat well.) **2** To fill up; become clogged or blocked; become hard to pass through. *The channel had choked up with*

sand so that boats couldn't use it. (The channel had got so full of sand that boats found it useless.)

choose See PICK AND CHOOSE.

chooser See BEGGARS CAN'T BE CHOOSERS.

choose up sides *v. phr.* To form two teams with two captains taking turns choosing players. *The boys chose up sides for a game of softball.* (The boys divided into two teams to play softball. Each captain chose the boys he wanted for his team.) *Tom and Joe were the captains. They chose up sides.* (Tom and Joe took turns choosing the boys they wanted to play on their teams.)

chop See LICK ONE'S CHOPS.

chow line *n., slang* A line of people waiting for food. *The chow line was already long when John got to the dining hall.* (The line of people waiting for food was already long when John got to the dining hall.) *The soldiers picked up trays and got into the chow line.* (The soldiers picked up trays and got into the line waiting for food.)

Christmas See FATHER CHRISTMAS.

Christmas card *n., slang, citizen's band radio jargon* A speeding ticket. *Smokey just gave a Christmas card to the eighteen wheeler we passed.* (The tractor-trailer we passed got a speeding ticket.)

Christmas club *n.* A plan for putting money in the bank to be saved for Christmas shopping. *John deposits $10 each week in the Christmas club.* (John deposits $10 each week in the bank to be saved for Christmas shopping.) *The woman will get her Christmas club money on December 10.* (The woman will get the money she put in the bank to be saved for Christmas shopping on December 10.)

cigar-store Indian *n. phr.* A wooden statue of an Indian which in the past was placed in front of a cigar store. *A cigar store Indian used to mean a cigar store in the same way a barber pole still means a barber shop.* (A wooden Indian was used to attract customers to a cigar store as a barber pole attracts customers to a barber shop.)

circle See COME FULL CIRCLE, IN A CIRCLE *or* IN CIRCLES, RUN CIRCLES AROUND *also* RUN RINGS AROUND.

circulation See IN CIRCULATION, OUT OF CIRCULATION.

circumstance See UNDER THE CIRCUMSTANCES *also* IN THE CIRCUMSTANCES.

circumstances alter cases *formal* The way things are, or happen, may change the way you are expected to act. *John's father told him never to touch his gun, but one day when Father was away, John used it to shoot a poisonous snake that came into the yard. Circumstances alter cases.* (John was right to disobey his father—perhaps the snake might have bitten one of the family.)

circus See THREE-RING CIRCUS.

citizen See SENIOR CITIZEN.

civil See KEEP A CIVIL TONGUE IN ONE'S HEAD.

claim See STAKE A CLAIM.

claim check *n.* A ticket needed to get back something. *The man at the parking lot gave Mrs. Collins a claim check.* (The man at the parking lot gave Mrs. Collins a ticket needed to get her car back.) *The boy put the dry cleaning claim check in his billfold.* (The boy put the ticket needed to get his dry cleaning back in his billfold.) *The man told Mary the pictures would be ready Friday and gave her a claim check.* (The man told Mary the pictures would be ready Friday and gave her a ticket to get them back.)

clamp down *v., informal* To put on strict controls; enforce rules or laws. *After the explosion, police clamped down and let no more visitors inside the monument.* (After the explosion, police enforced strict rules on visitors.) *The school clamped down on smoking.* (The school limited smoking strictly.) *When the crowds became bigger and wilder, the police clamped down on them and made everyone go home.* (The police became stricter and told everybody to go home.)

clam up *v., slang* To refuse to say anything more; stop talking. *The suspect clammed up, and the police could get no more information out of him.* (The suspect would not give the police any more information.)

class See HIGH-CLASS, SECOND CLASS.

clay See FEET OF CLAY.

clay pigeon *n., slang, informal* **1** A popular target at practice shooting made of clay and roughly resembling a pigeon; an easy target that doesn't move. *All he can shoot is a clay pigeon.* (He is not good enough a marksman to shoot at a moving target.) **2** A person who, like a clay pigeon in target practice, is immobilized or is in a sensitive position and is therefore easily criticized or otherwise victimized. *Poor Joe is a clay pigeon.* (He is easily victimized or criticized because of his situation.) **3** A task easily accomplished like shooting an immobile clay pigeon. *The math exam was a clay pigeon.* (It presented no real challenge.)

clean See COME CLEAN, KEEP ONE'S NOSE CLEAN, MAKE A CLEAN BREAST OF, NEW BROOM SWEEPS CLEAN, TAKE TO ONE'S HEELS, *also* SHOW A CLEAN PAIR OF HEELS.

clean bill of health *n. phr.* **1** A certificate that a person or animal has no infectious disease. *The government doctor gave Jones a clean bill of health when he entered the country.* (He wrote that Jones had no infectious disease.) **2** *informal* A report that a person is free of guilt or fault. *The stranger was suspected in the bank robbery, but the police gave him a clean bill of health.* (People thought the stranger might have been the bank robber, but the police said he didn't have anything to do with it.)

cleaners See TO TAKE TO THE CLEANERS.

clean hands *n. phr., slang* Freedom from guilt or dishonesty; innocence. *John grew up in a bad neighborhood, but he grew up with clean hands.* (John grew up in a bad neighborhood, but he grew up without doing anything wrong.) *There was much proof against Bill, but he swore he had clean hands.* (It looked as if Bill had done wrong, but he swore that he had not done anything wrong.)

clean out *v.* **1** *slang* To take everything from; empty; strip. *George's friends cleaned him out when they were playing cards last night.* (George's friends won all his money playing cards.) *The sudden demand for paper plates soon cleaned out the stores.* (Everyone wanted paper plates and soon there were none left in the stores.) **2** *informal* To get rid of; remove; dismiss. *The new mayor promised to clean the crooks out of the city government.* (The new mayor promised to get rid of the crooks in the city government.)

clean slate *n. phr.* A record of nothing but good conduct, without any errors or bad deeds; past acts that are all good without any bad ones. *Johnny was sent to the principal for whispering. He had a clean slate so the principal did not punish him.* (This was Johnny's first bad mark, so the principal did not punish him.) *Mary stayed after school for a week, and after that the teacher let her off with a clean slate.* (After Mary finished her punishment, the teacher let her begin again and try for a perfect record.) Compare TURN OVER A NEW LEAF.

clean up *v.* **1** To clean everything; put in order. *She cleaned up the house for her party.* (She cleaned everything in the house for her party.) *After the dirty job he cleaned up for supper.* (He washed himself well and put on clean clothes for supper.) **2** *informal* To finish doing. *John kept at the job until he had cleaned it up.* (John worked until he had finished doing the job.) **3** *slang* To make a lot of money; make a big profit. *Dick cleaned up in the stock market.* (Dick made a lot of money buying and selling stocks.) *The company cleaned up in real estate.* (The company made large profits in land and buildings.) *Jim cleaned up in a crap game.* (Jim won much money in a dice game.)

clear See COAST IS CLEAR, IN THE CLEAR, OUT OF THE BLUE *or* OUT OF A CLEAR SKY *or* OUT OF A CLEAR BLUE SKY, SEE ONE'S WAY CLEAR, STEER CLEAR OF.

clear-eyed *adj.* Understanding problems or events clearly; being able to tell very well the results of a way of acting. *Tom is very clear-eyed. He knows he doesn't have much chance of winning the race, but he will try his best.* (Tom knows that he doesn't have much chance of winning the race.) *He is a clear-eyed and independent commentator on the news.* (He is a very wise and understanding news speaker.)

clear out *v.* **1** To take everything out of; empty. *When Bill was moved to another class he cleared out his desk.* (He took everything out and left the desk empty.) **2** *informal* To leave suddenly; go away; depart. *The cop told the boys to clear out.* (The policeman told the boys to leave at once.) *Bob cleared out without paying his room rent.* (He went away without paying his room rent.) *Clear out of here! You're bothering me.* (Go away! You are disturbing me.) Compare BEAT IT.

clear the air *v. phr.* To remove angry feelings, misunderstanding, or confusion. *The President's statement that he would run for office again cleared the air of rumors and guessing.* (The President's statement ended rumors and guessing about the situation.) *When Bill was angry at Bob, Bob made a joke, and it cleared the air between them.* (They laughed and relaxed and didn't feel angry any more.)

clear up *v.* **1** To make plain or clear; explain; solve. *The teacher cleared up the harder parts of the story.* (The teacher made the harder parts of the story understandable.) *Maybe we can clear up your problem.* (Maybe we can solve your problem.) **2** To become clear. *The weather cleared up after the storm.* (The sun came out after the storm.) **3** To cure. *The pills cleared up his stomach trouble.* (The pills cured his stomach trouble.) **4** To put back into a normal, proper, or healthy state. *The doctor can give you something to clear up your skin.* (The doctor can give you something to bring your skin back to its normal healthy condition.) *Susan cleared up the room.* (She put the room back into a neat and orderly condition.) **5** To become cured. *This skin trouble will clear up in a day or two.* (This trouble will go away in a day or two.)

clerk See ROOM CLERK *or* DESK CLERK.

cliffdweller *n., slang, informal* A city person who lives on a very high floor in an apartment building. *Joe and Nancy have become cliffdwellers—they moved up to the 30th floor.* (They moved up very high in a high-rise apartment building.)

cliffhanger *n., informal* A sports event or a movie in which the outcome is uncertain to the very end keeping the spectators in great suspense and excitement. *Did you see the Guns of Navarrone? It's a regular cliffhanger.* (It is a very exciting and suspenseful movie.)

climb See SOCIAL CLIMBER.

climb on the bandwagon See ON THE BAND-WAGON.

climb the wall *v. phr., slang. informal* **1** To react to a challenging situation with too great an emotional response, frustration, tension, and anxiety. *By the time I got the letter that I was hired, I was ready to climb the wall.* (I almost went crazy with frustration). **2** To be so disinterested or bored as to be most anxious to get away at any cost. *If the chairman doesn't stop talking, I'll climb the wall.* (If he doesn't stop talking, I'll be ready to escape no matter how.)

clinging vine *n.* A very dependent woman; a woman who needs much love and encouragement from a man.—A trite phrase. *Mary is a clinging vine; she cannot do anything without her husband.* (Mary depends on her husband more than is normal.)

cling to one's mother's apron strings See TIED TO ONE'S MOTHER'S APRON STRINGS.

clip joint *n. slang* A low-class night club or other business where people are cheated. *The man got drunk and lost all his money in a clip joint.* (The man got drunk and was cheated of all his money in a low-class night club.) *The angry woman said the store was a clip joint.* (The angry woman said the store was a business where people were cheated.)

clip one's wings *v. phr.* To limit or hold you back; bring you under control; prevent your success. *When the new president tried to become dictator, the generals soon clipped his wings.* (When the new president tried to become a dictator, his generals kept him from doing it by limiting his power.) *Jim was spending too much time on dates when he needed to study so his father stopped his allowance; that clipped his wings.* (Stopping Jim's allowance stopped him from spending too much time with girls.)

cloak-and-dagger *adj.* Of or about spies and secret agents. *It was a cloak-and-dagger story about some spies who tried to steal atomic secrets.* (It was a story about spies and secret activity.) *The book was written by a retired colonel who used to take part in cloak-and-dagger plots.* (The book was written by a retired colonel who used to work with spies and undercover men in laying traps for enemy agents.) [From the wearing of cloaks and daggers by people in old adventure stories.] Compare BLOOD AND THUNDER.

clock See AGAINST TIME *or* AGAINST THE CLOCK, AROUND THE CLOCK *or* THE CLOCK AROUND, PUT BACK THE CLOCK *or* TURN BACK THE CLOCK, GO LIKE CLOCKWORK *or* GO OFF LIKE CLOCKWORK, TURN THE CLOCK BACK.

clock watcher *n. phr., informal* A worker who always quits at once when it is time; a man who is in a hurry to leave his job. *When Ted got his first job, his father told him to work hard and not be a clock watcher.* (His father told him to not think too much about time to quit.)

closed book *n.* A secret; something not known or understood.—A cliché. *The man's early life is a closed book.* (The man's early life is a secret.) *For Mary, science is a closed book.* (For Mary, science is something not understood.) *The history of the town is a closed book.* (The history of the town is not known.)

closed-door *adj.* Away from the public; in

private or in secret; limited to a few. *The officers of the club held a closed-door meeting.* (The officers of the club held a secret meeting.) *The committee decided on a closed-door rule for the investigation.* (The committee decided not to allow the public in during the investigation.) Compare IN PRIVATE.

close down *or* **shut down** *v.* To stop all working, as in a factory; stop work entirely; *also:* to stop operations in. *The factory closed down for Christmas.* (The factory stopped all working until after Christmas.) *The company shut down the factory for Christmas* (The company stopped work in the factory until after Christmas.)

close in *v.* To come in nearer from all sides. *We wanted the boat to reach shore before the fog closed in.* (We wanted to get to shore before we were surrounded by fog.)—Often used with *on. The troops were closing in on the enemy.* (The troops were coming in towards the enemy from all sides.)

close its doors *v. phr.* **1** To keep someone or something from entering or joining; become closed. *The club has closed its doors to new members.* (The club has stopped taking in new members.) **2** To fail as a business; go bankrupt. *The fire was so damaging that the store had to close its doors.* (The fire was so damaging, the store went out of business.) *Business was so poor that we had to close our doors after six months.* (Business was so poor that we had to go out of business in six months.) Compare CLOSE THE DOOR. Contrast OPEN ITS DOORS.

close-knit *adj.* Closely joined together by ties of love, friendship, or common interest; close. *The Joneses are a close-knit family.* (The Joneses are held closely to one another by family love.) *The three boys are always together. They form a very close-knit group.* (The three boys have many interests in common and do things together.)

close one's eyes *or* **shut one's eyes** *v. phr.* To refuse to see or think about. *The park is beautiful if you shut your eyes to the litter.* (The park is beautiful if you refuse to notice the litter.) *The ice was very thin, but the boys shut their eyes to the danger and went skating.* (The boys refused to see or think about the danger of skating on thin ice.) Compare OPEN ONE'S EYES.

close out *v.* To sell the whole of; end (a business or a business operation) by selling all the goods; *also,* to sell your stock and stop doing business. *The store closed out its stock of garden supplies.* (The store sold all its garden supplies and stopped selling goods of that kind.) *Mr. Jones closed out his grocery.* (Mr. Jones sold all his grocery stock and went out of business.) *Mr. Randall was losing money in his shoe store, so he decided to close out.* (He decided to sell all the shoes and end the business.)

close ranks *v. phr.* **1** To come close together in a line especially for fighting. *The soldiers closed ranks and kept the enemy away from the bridge.* (They moved close together in lines and did not let the enemy soldiers come through.) **2** To stop quarreling and work together; unite and fight together. *The Democrats and Republicans closed ranks to win the war.* (The Democrats and Republicans stopped quarreling to work together to win the war.) *The leader asked the people to close ranks and plan a new school.* (The leader asked the people to stop quarreling and work together and plan a new school.)

closet See SKELETON IN THE CLOSET.

close the books *v. phr.* To stop taking orders; end a bookkeeping period. *The tickets were all sold, so the manager said to close the books.* (The tickets were all sold, so the manager said to stop taking orders.) *The department store closes its books on the 25th of each month.* (The department store ends its bookkeeping period on the 25th of each month.)

close the door *or* **bar the door** *or* **shut the door** *v. phr.* To prevent any more action or talk about a subject. *The President's veto closed the door to any new attempt to pass the bill.* (The President's refusal to approve the bill stopped any more action on or talk about it.) *Joan was much hurt by what Mary said, and she closed the door on Mary's attempt to apologize.* (Joan would not listen to Mary's explanation.) *After John makes up his mind, he closes the door to any more arguments.* (When John makes up his mind, he will not listen to any more argument.) Contrast OPEN THE DOOR.

close to home *adv. phr.* Too near to someone's personal feelings, wishes, or interests. —A cliché. *When John made fun of Bob's way of walking, he struck close to home.* (John was talking about something very personal to Bob and Bob didn't like it.) *When the preacher spoke about prejudice, some people felt he had come too close to home.* (They were against some people and things and didn't like to be criticized.)

close up shop *v. phr.* **1** To shut a store at the end of a day's business; *also,* to end a business. *The grocer closes up shop at 5 o'clock.* (The grocer closes his shop for the day at 5 o'clock.) *After 15 years in business at the same spot, the garage closed up shop.* (The garage went out of business after 15 years at the same spot.) **2** *informal* To stop some activity; finish what you are doing. *After camping out for two weeks, the scouts took down their tents and closed up shop.* (The scouts took down their tents and finished their camping trip.) *The committee finished its business and closed up shop.* (The committee finished its business and stopped their meeting.) Compare CALL IT A DAY.

clothes See BEST BIB AND TUCKER *or* SUNDAY-GO-TO-MEETING CLOTHES.

clothing See WOLF IN SHEEP'S CLOTHING.

cloud See EVERY CLOUD HAS A SILVER LINING, IN THE CLOUDS, ON CLOUD NINE, UNDER A CLOUD.

clover See FOUR-LEAF CLOVER, IN CLOVER *or* IN THE CLOVER.

club See CHRISTMAS CLUB.

cluck and grunt *n., slang, avoid it in restaurants* The familiar restaurant dish of ham and eggs; since ham is made of pork (and pigs grunt) and eggs come from hens (which cluck.) *I am sorry I can't fix you an elaborate meal, but I can give you a quick cluck and grunt.* (No time for anything else except a quick ham and eggs.)

clutch See RIDE THE BRAKE.

coal See CARRY COALS TO NEWCASTLE, HAUL OVER THE COALS *or* RAKE OVER THE COALS, HEAP COALS OF FIRE ON ONE'S HEAD.

coast is clear No enemy or danger is in sight; there is no one to see you.—A trite expression. *When the teacher had disappeared around the corner, John said, "Come on, the coast is clear."* (When the teacher was out of sight, John said, "Come on, no one will see us now.") *The men knew when the night watchman would pass. When he had gone, and the coast was clear, they robbed the safe.* (When the watchman had passed and no one else was in sight, the men robbed the safe.) *When Father stopped the car at the stop sign, Mother said, "The coast is clear on this side."* (Mother told Father that no car was coming from the side on which she was sitting.)

coat tail See ON ONE'S COAT TAILS.

cock See GO OFF HALF-COCKED *also* GO OFF AT HALF COCK.

coffee break *n.* A short recess or time out from work in which to rest and drink coffee. *The girls in the office take a coffee break in the middle of the morning and the afternoon.* (The girls in the office are given a short recess from work in the middle of each morning and afternoon to drink coffee and talk with their friends.)

coffee hour *n.* A time for coffee or other refreshments after a meeting; a time to meet people and have refreshments. *After the business meeting we had a coffee hour.* (After the business meeting we had a period for coffee and other refreshments.) *The Joneses had a coffee hour so their visitor could meet their neighbors.* (The Joneses had a time for coffee and other refreshments so their visitor could meet their neighbors.)

coffee table *n.* A low table used in a living room. *There were several magazines on the coffee table.* (There were several magazines on the low table in the living room.)

cog See SLIP A COG *or* SLIP A GEAR.

coin money *or* **mint money** *v. phr., informal* To make a lot of money quickly; profit heavily; gain big profit. *Fred coined money with many cigarette vending machines and juke boxes.* (Fred made a lot of money by owning many machines that sell cigarettes or play records when money is put in them.)

cold See BLOOD RUNS COLD, BLOW HOT AND COLD, CATCH COLD *or* TAKE COLD, IN COLD BLOOD, OUT COLD, OUT IN THE COLD, PASS OUT 2, STONE-COLD, STOP COLD, THROW COLD WATER ON.

cold cash *or* **hard cash** *n.* Money that is paid at the time of purchase; real money; silver and bills. *Mr. Jones bought a new car and paid cold cash for it.* (Mr. Jones bought a new car. He paid for it with paper money out of his billfold.) *Some stores sell things only for cold cash.* (Some stores sell only for money. They do not sell on credit.) Compare CASH ON THE BARRELHEAD.

cold comfort *n.* Something that makes a person in trouble feel very little better or even worse. *When Tim lost the race, it was cold comfort to him to hear that he could try again in two weeks.* (It did not make him feel much better to know he could try again in two weeks.) *Mary spent her vacation sick in bed and Jane's letter about her trip was cold comfort.* (Jane's letter did not cheer Mary up; it made her more unhappy.)

cold feet *n. phr., informal* A loss of courage or nerve; a failure or loss of confidence in yourself.—A cliché. *Ralph was going to ask Mary to dance with him but he got cold feet and didn't.* (He lost his nerve and didn't ask Mary to dance with him.)

cold fish *n., informal* A queer person; a person who is unfriendly or does not mix with others. *No one knows the new doctor; he is a cold fish.* (The new doctor is unfriendly and does not mix with others.) *Nobody invites Eric to parties because he is a cold fish.* (Nobody invites him because he does not mix with others.)

cold-shoulder *v., informal* To act towards a person with dislike or scorn; be unfriendly to. *Fred cold-shouldered his old friend when they passed on the street.* (Fred pretended not to see his old friend.) *It is impolite and unkind to cold-shoulder people.* (It is impolite and unkind to act too proudly toward other people.) Compare BRUSH OFF 2, HIGH-HAT, LOOK DOWN ONE'S NOSE AT.

cold shoulder *n., informal* Unfriendly treatment of a person; a showing of dislike for a person or of looking down on a person.—Used in the clichés *give the cold shoulder* or *turn a cold shoulder to* or *get the cold shoulder*. *When Bob asked Mary for a date she gave him the cold shoulder.* (When Bob asked Mary for a date she didn't even answer him and turned her back on him.) *The membership committee turned a cold shoulder to Jim's request to join the club.* (The committee wouldn't even think about Jim's request to join the club.)

cold snap *n.* A short time of quick change from warm weather to cold. *The cold snap killed everything in the garden.* (It was cold enough to kill the vegetables and flowers.)

cold turkey *adv., slang, informal* **1** Abruptly and without medical aid to withdraw from the use of an addictive drug or from a serious drinking problem. *Joe is a very brave guy; he kicked the habit cold turkey.* (He gave up his addictive habit on his own and without medical help.) **2** *n.* An instance of withdrawal from drugs, alcohol, or cigarette smoking. *Joe did a cold turkey.* (Joe withdrew from his addictive habit without help.)

cold war *n.* A struggle that is carried on by other means and not by actual fighting; a war without shooting or bombing. *After World War II, a cold war began between Russia and the United States.* (Russia and the United States worked against each other in many ways, but they did not fight with guns and bombs.)

collar See HOT UNDER THE COLLAR, ROMAN COLLAR, SAILOR COLLAR.

collective farm *n.* A large government-run farm made by combining many small farms. *The Russian farmers live on collective farms.* (Russian farmers live on large farms run by the government.)

collector's item *n.* Something rare or valuable enough to collect or save. *Jimmy's mother found an old wooden doll in the attic that turned out to be a collector's item.* (She found an old doll of a rare kind that doll collectors wanted.)

College Boards *n.* A set of examinations given to test a student's readiness and ability for college. *John got a high score on his College Boards.* (John got a high score on his examinations for college.) *College Boards test both what a student has learned and his ability to learn.* (Tests for college are given to find out a student's achievement in school and his ability to learn.)

color See CHANGE COLOR, GIVE COLOR TO *or* LEND COLOR TO, HAUL DOWN ONE'S COLORS, HORSE OF A DIFFERENT COLOR, NAIL ONE'S COLORS TO THE MAST, OFF-COLOR *or* OFF-COLORED, SAIL UNDER FALSE COLORS, SEE THE COLOR OF ONE'S MONEY, SHOW ONE'S COLORS, WITH FLYING COLORS.

color guard *n.* A military guard of honor for the flag of a country; *also:* a guard of honor to carry and protect a flag or banner (as of a club). *There were four Marines in the color guard in the parade.* (The Marines carried the flag to protect and honor it.) *Bob was picked to be a color guard and to carry the banner of the drum corps at the football game.* (Bob was chosen to carry the drum corps flag when they marched at the football game.)

color scheme *n.* A plan for colors used together as decoration. *The color scheme for the dance was blue and silver.* (The combination of colors used to decorate the gym for the dance was blue and silver.) *Mary decided on a pink and white color scheme for her*

room. (She chose white wallpaper with little pink roses all over it, and matching pink curtains and bedspread.)

comb See FINE-TOOTH COMB.

come See CHICKENS COME HOME TO ROOST, CROSS A BRIDGE BEFORE ONE COMES TO IT, EASY COME—EASY GO, FIRST COME—FIRST SERVED, GET WHAT'S COMING TO ONE, HAVE IT COMING, HOW COME *also* HOW'S COME, IF WORST COMES TO WORST, JOHNNY-COME-LATELY, KNOW ENOUGH TO COME IN OUT OF THE RAIN, KNOW IF ONE IS COMING OR GOING, LOOK AS IF ONE HAS COME OUT OF A BANDBOX, SHIP COME IN.

come about *v.* To take place; happen; occur. *Sometimes it is hard to tell how a quarrel comes about.* (You can't always be sure what causes a quarrel.) *When John woke up he was in the hospital, but he didn't know how that had come about.* (John wasn't sure what had happened to put him in the hospital.)

come a cropper **1** To fall off your horse. *John's horse stumbled, and John came a cropper.* (John's horse stumbled and John fell off.) **2** To fail. *Mr. Brown did not have enough money to put into his business and it soon came a cropper.* (It soon failed.) Compare RIDING FOR A FALL.

come across *v.* **1** *or* **run across** To find or meet by chance. *He came across a dollar bill in the suit he was sending to the cleaner.* (He found a dollar bill that he had forgotten in a suit that he was sending to the cleaner.) *The other day I ran across a book that you might like.* (I happened to find a book that you might like.) *I came across George at a party last week; it was the first time I had seen him in months.* (I happened to meet George.) Compare COME ON 3, RUN INTO 3b. **2** To give or do what is asked. *The robber told the woman to come across with her purse.* (He told the woman to give him her purse.) *For hours the police questioned the man suspected of kidnapping the child, and finally he came across with the story.* (Finally the man told the police about his stealing the child.)

come again *v., informal* Please repeat; please say that again.—Usually used as a command. *"Harry has just come into a fortune," my wife said. "Come again?" I asked her,* not believing it. (I asked her to repeat, because I didn't believe her at first.) *"Come again,"* said the hard-of-hearing man. (He asked his friend to say it again; he had not heard it.)

come alive *or* **come to life** *v.* **1** *informal* To become alert or attentive; wake up and look alive; become active. *When Mr. Simmons mentioned money, the boys came alive.* (When Mr. Simmons mentioned money, the boys showed interest.) *Bob pushed the starter button, and the engine came alive with a roar.* (The engine started.) **2** To look real; take on a bright, natural look. *Under skillful lighting, the scene came alive.* (The scene looked real when the lighting had been arranged.) *The President came alive in the picture as the artist worked.* (The painting made it seem that the President was right there.)

come along *v.* To make progress; improve; succeed. *He was coming along well after the operation.* (He was doing well after the operation.) *Rose is coming right along on the piano.* (Rose is getting better at playing the piano.)

come a long way *v. phr.* To show much improvement; make great progress. *The school has come a long way since its beginnings.* (It has made great progress. It has more buildings, more students, and better teaching.) *Little Jane has come a long way since she broke her leg.* (Jane can almost walk again.)

come apart at the seams *v. phr., slang, informal* To become upset to the point where one loses self-control and composure as if having suffered a sudden nervous breakdown. *After his divorce Joe seemed to be coming apart at the seams.* (His divorce upset him so much that he was no longer in control of himself.)

come around See COME ROUND.

come at *v.* **1** To approach; come to or against; advance toward. *The young boxer came at the champion cautiously.* (The challenger moved cautiously toward the champion.) **2** To understand (a word or idea) or master (a skill); succeed with. *The sense of an unfamiliar word is hard to come at.* (The meaning of a new word is often hard to understand.)

come back *v., informal* **1** To reply; answer. *The lawyer came back sharply in defense of his client.* (The lawyer answered sharply in defense of the man that he was acting for.) *No matter how the audience heckled him, the comedian always had an answer to come back with.* (No matter how hard people in the audience tried to upset him, the comedian always had a quick, sharp reply.) **2** To get a former place or position back; reach again a place which you have lost. *After a year off to have her baby, the singer came back to even greater fame.* (She returned to the stage and gained even greater honors.) *It is hard for a retired prize fighter to come back and beat a younger man.* (Age and lack of practice make it hard for him to win against a younger man.)

comeback *n., v. phr., slang, citizen's band radio jargon* A return call. *Thanks for your comeback.* (Thank you for your return call.)

come back to earth *or* **come down to earth** *v. phr.* To return to the real world; stop imagining or dreaming; think and behave as usual. —A hackneyed expression. *After Jane met the movie star it was hard for her to come back to earth.* (Jane was thrilled and excited to meet the movie star and it was hard to stop thinking about it.) *Bill was sitting and daydreaming so his mother told him to come down*

to earth and to do his homework. (Bill's mother wanted him to think about his homework and not be dreaming about something else.) Compare COME TO ONE'S SENSES, DOWN-TO-EARTH. Contrast IN THE CLOUDS.

come between *v.* To part; divide; separate. *John's mother-in-law came to live in his home, and as time passed she came between him and his wife.* (John's mother-in-law caused trouble between him and his wife that broke up his marriage.) *Bill's hot rod came between him and his studies, and his grades went down.* (Bill spent too much time on his car.)

come by *v.* To get; obtain; acquire. *A good job like that is hard to come by.* (A good job like that is hard to get.) *Money easily come by is often easily spent.* (Money obtained easily is likely to be easily spent.) *How did she come by that money?* (How did she get that money?)

come by honestly *v. phr., informal* To inherit (a characteristic) from your parents. *Joe comes by his hot temper honestly; his father is the same way.* (Joe gets his hot temper from his father.)

come clean *v. phr., slang* To tell all; tell the whole story; confess. *The boy suspected of stealing the watch came clean after long questioning.* (He confessed everything after long questioning.)

come down *v.* **1** To reduce itself; amount to no more than.—Followed by *to*. *The quarrel finally came down to a question of which boy would do the dishes.* (The quarrel finally became no more than a question of which boy had to do the dishes.) Syn. BOIL DOWN 3. **2** To be handed down or passed along; descend from parent to child; pass from older generation to younger ones. *Mary's necklace had come down to her from her grandmother.* (Mary's necklace had been passed along to her by her grandmother.)

come down hard on *v., informal* **1** To scold or punish strongly. *The principal came down hard on the boys for breaking the window.* (He scolded them hard.) **2** To oppose strongly. *The minister in his sermon came down hard on drinking.* (He was very much against drinking liquor.)

come down in the world *v. phr.* To lose a place of respect or honor; become lower (as in rank or fortune). *The stranger plainly had come down a long way in the world.* (He had once been wealthy and respected, but he had lost wealth and honor.) Compare DOWN ON ONE'S LUCK.

come down with *v., informal* To become sick with; catch. *We all came down with the mumps.* (We all got the mumps.) *After being out in the rain, George came down with a cold.* (George caught a cold.)

come full circle *v. phr., informal* **1** To become totally opposed to one's own earlier conviction on a given subject. *Today's conser-*

vative businessperson has come full circle from former radical student days. (His philosophy is totally different from what it used to be.) **2** To change and develop, only to end up where one started. *From modern permissiveness, ideas about child raising have come full circle to the views of our grandparents.* (The newest idea is much the same as the old ones were before.)

come hell or high water *adv. phr., informal* No matter what happens; whatever may come. *Grandfather said he would go to the fair, come hell or high water.* (Grandfather said that nothing would stop him from going to the fair.) Compare COME WHAT MAY, THROUGH THE MILL.

come home to roost See CHICKENS COME HOME TO ROOST.

come in *v.* **1** To finish in a sports contest or other competition. *He came in second in the hundred-yard dash.* (He took second place in the hundred-yard run.) **2** To become the fashion; begin to be used. *Swimming trunks for men came in after World War I; before that men used full swim suits.* (Men began to use trunks for swimming after World War I.)

come in for *v.* To receive. *He came in for a small fortune when his uncle died.* (He got a lot of money when his uncle died.) *His conduct came in for much criticism.* (Many people said bad things about the way he acted.)

come in handy *v. phr., informal* To prove useful. *Robinson Crusoe found tools in the ship which came in handy when he built a house.* (The tools were useful in building his house.) *The French he learned in high school came in handy when he was in the army in France.* (He found his knowledge of French a useful thing.)

come into *v.* To receive, especially after another's death; get possession of. *He came into a lot of money when his father died.* (He inherited a lot of money when his father died.) *He came into possession of the farm after his uncle died.* (His uncle left the farm to him.)

come into one's own *v. phr.* To receive the wealth or respect that you should have. *John's grandfather died and left him a million dollars; when John is 21, he will come into his own.* (When John is 21, he will receive his money.) *With the success of the Model T Ford, the automobile industry came into its own.* (It received the respect that it deserved. People began to see its worth.)

come of age See OF AGE.

come off *v.* **1** To take place; happen. *The picnic came off at last, after being twice postponed.* (The picnic was finally held, after being put off twice.) **2** *informal* To do well; succeed. *The attempt to bring the quarreling couple together again came off, to people's astonishment.* (The effort to settle the quarrel of the two succeeded, although people had not expected it would.)

come off it *also* **get off it** *v. phr., slang* Stop pretending; bragging, or kidding; stop being silly.—Used as a command. *"So I said to the duchess. . ." Jimmy began. "Oh, come off it," the other boys sneered.* (Jimmy pretended to have known a duchess personally, but the other boys told him to quit boasting.) *Fritz said he had a car of his own. "Oh, come off it," said John. "You can't even drive."* (Fritz said he owned his own car, but John told him to stop trying to fool him.)

come on *v.* **1** To begin; appear. *Rain came on toward morning.* (Rain began just before morning.) *He felt a cold coming on.* (He felt he was catching a cold.) **2** To grow or do well; thrive. *The wheat was coming on.* (The wheat was growing well.) *His business came on splendidly.* (His business succeeded.) **3** *or* **come upon.** To meet accidentally; encounter; find. *He came on an old friend that day when he visited his club.* (He met an old friend that day when he called at his club.) *He came upon an interesting idea in reading about the French Revolution.* (He found an interesting idea in reading about the French Revolution.) Syn. COME ACROSS, HAPPEN ON. **4** *informal* Let's get started; let's get going; don't delay; don't wait.—Used as a command. *"Come on, or we'll be late," said Joe, but Lou still waited.* ("Let's get started, or we'll be late." said Joe.) **5** *informal* Please do it!—Used in begging someone to do something. *Sing us just one song, Jane, come on!* (Please sing us just one song.) *Come on, Laura, you can tell me. I won't tell anybody.* (Please tell me the secret.)

come-on *n., slang* An attractive offer made to a naive person under false pretenses in order to gain monetary or other advantage. *Joe uses a highly successful come-on when he sells vacant lots on Grand Bahama Island.* (He uses promises that cannot be kept when he sells the lots.)

come one's way *v. phr.* To be experienced by someone; happen to you. *Tom said that if the chance to become a sailor ever came his way, he would take it.* (If it ever happened that Tom had a chance to become a sailor, he would do so.) *I hope bad luck isn't coming our way.* (I hope we are not going to experience bad luck.) *Luck came Bill's way today and he hit a home run.* (Bill was lucky today.) Compare GO ONE'S WAY, IN ONE'S FAVOR.

come on strong *v. phr., slang* To overwhelm a weaker person with excessively strong language, personality, or mannerisms; to insist extremely strongly and claim something with unusual vigor. *Joe came on very strong last night about the War in Indochina; most of us felt embarrassed.* (He made his points so vigorously that it was embarrassing.)

come out *v.* **1** *Of a girl:* To be formally introduced to polite society at about age eighteen, usually at a party; begin to go to big parties. *In society, girls come out when they reach the age of about eighteen, and usually it is at a big party in their honor; after that they are looked on as adults.* (Girls are formally introduced to polite society in a big party in their honor when they are about eighteen.) *Mary came out with her cousin at a joint party.* (Mary went to her first big party, which was in honor of both her cousin and herself.) **2** To be published. *The book came out two weeks ago.* (The book was published two weeks ago.) **3** To become publicly known. *The truth finally came out at his trial.* (The truth at last became known at his trial.) **4** To end; result; finish. *How did the story come out?* (How did the story end?) *The game came out as we had hoped.* (The game ended in victory for our team.) *The snapshots came out well.* (The pictures were good.) **5** To announce support or opposition; declare yourself (for or against a person or thing). *The party leaders came out for an acceptable candidate.* (They gave their support to a candidate they thought everyone would vote for.) *Many Congressmen came out against the bill.* (Many Congressmen announced they were against the proposed law. **6** See GO OUT FOR.—**coming-out** *adj.* Introducing a girl to polite society. *Mary's parents gave her a coming-out party when she was 17.* (Mary's parents had a party introducing her to polite society when she was 17.)

come out with *v. phr.* **1** To make a public announcement; make known. *He came out with a clear declaration of his principles.* (He made known his ideas and beliefs.) **2** To say. *He comes out with the funniest remarks you can imagine.* (He says the funniest things you can imagine.)

come over *v.* To take control of; cause sudden strong feeling in; happen to. *A sudden fit of anger came over him.* (A sudden feeling of anger seized him.) *A great tenderness came over her.* (A great tenderness affected her.) *What has come over him?* (What is causing him to act this way?)

come round or **come around** *v.* **1** To happen or appear again and again in regular order. *And so Saturday night came around again.* (It was Saturday night again in the passing of the week.) *I will tell him when he comes round again.* (I will tell him when he appears again.) **2** *informal* To get back health or knowledge of things; get well from sickness or a faint. *Someone brought out smelling salts and Mary soon came round.* (Mary woke from her faint when someone let her smell a strong chemical.) *Jim has come around after having had stomach ulcers.* (Jim has recovered his health after trouble with ulcers.) **3** To change direction. *The wind has come round to the south.* (The wind has changed to the south.) **4** *informal* To change your opinion or purpose to agree with another's. *Tom came round when Dick told him the whole*

story. (Tom changed his idea and agreed with the others instead of opposing them.)

come through *v., informal* To be equal to a demand; meet trouble or a sudden need with success; satisfy a need. *When the baseball team needed a hit, Willie came through with a double.* (When the baseball team needed a hit badly, Willie was able to do it and hit a double.) *John needed money for college and his father came through.* (John needed help and his father got the money for college.)

come to *v.* (stress on *to*) **1** To wake up after losing consciousness; get the use of your senses back again after fainting or being knocked out. *She fainted in the store and found herself in the first aid room when she came to.* (She was in the first aid room when she woke up from her faint.) *The boxer who was knocked out did not come to for five minutes.* (The boxer did not regain his senses for five minutes after having been knocked unconscious.) *The doctor gave her a pill and after she took it she didn't come to for two days.* (The pill put her to sleep for two days.) Compare BRING TO. **2** (stress on *come*) To get enough familiarity or understanding to; learn to; grow to.—Used with an infinitive. *John was selfish at first, but he came to realize that other people counted, too.* (John began to realize that other people were important, too.) *During her years at the school, Mary came to know that road well.* (After she became familiar with the school, she knew that road well.) **3** To result in or change to; reach the point of; arrive at. *Mr. Smith lived to see his invention come to success.* (He lived long enough to see his invention become successful.) *Grandfather doesn't like the way young people act today; he says, "I don't know what the world is coming to."* (Grandfather thinks the world is getting worse and is afraid something terrible will happen.) **4** To have something to do with; be in the field of; be about.—Usually used in the phrase *when it comes to. Joe is not good in sports, but when it comes to arithmetic he's the best in the class.* (Joe is not an athlete, but he is very good at arithmetic.) *The school has very good teachers, but when it comes to buildings, the school is poor.* (The school has very good teachers but poor buildings.)

come to blows *v. phr.* To begin to fight. *The two quarreling boys came to blows after school.* (The boys' quarrel led to a fight between them after school.) *The two countries came to blows because one wanted to be independent from the other.* (The countries went to war.)

come to grief *v. phr.* To have a bad accident or disappointment; meet trouble or ruin; end badly; wreck; fail. *Bill came to grief learning to drive a car.* (Bill had a bad accident while he was trying to learn to drive a car.)

Nick's hopes for a new house came to grief when the house he was building burned down. (Nick's hopes for a new house were ruined when the one he was building burned down.) *The whaling ship came to grief off Cape Hatteras.* (The ship was wrecked off Cape Hatteras.)

come to grips with *v. phr.* **1** To get hold of (another wrestler) in close fighting. *After circling around for a minute, the two wrestlers came to grips with each other.* (They began to fight seriously.) **2** To struggle seriously with (an idea or problem). *Mr. Blake's teaching helps students come to grips with the important ideas in the history lesson.* (He helps boys and girls think seriously about the big ideas.) *Harry cannot be a leader, because he never quite comes to grips with a problem.* (Harry never completely understands and solves a problem.) Compare COME TO TERMS 2.

come to hand *v. phr.* To be received or obtained. *Father's letter was mailed from Florida last week and came to hand today.* (Father's letter was received today.) *The new books came to hand today.* (The new books arrived today.) *New information about the boy's disappearance came to hand yesterday.* (New information was discovered.)

come to heel See TO HEEL.

come to life See COME ALIVE.

come to light *v. phr.* To be discovered; become known; appear. *John's thefts from the bank where he worked came to light when the bank examiners made an inspection.* (John's thefts from the bank were discovered by the bank examiners.) *When the old woman died, it came to light that she was actually rich.* (It was discovered when the old woman died that she was rich.) *New facts about ancient Egypt have recently come to light.* (New facts about ancient Egypt have recently been discovered.) Compare BRING TO LIGHT.

come to nothing *also formal* **come to naught** *v. phr.* To end in failure; fail; be in vain. *The dog's attempts to climb the tree after the cat came to nothing.* (The dog could only jump up. He could not climb the tree like a cat.)

come to one's senses *v. phr.* **1** Become conscious again; wake up. *The boxer was knocked out and did not come to his senses for several minutes.* (The boxer did not wake up for several minutes.) *The doctors gave Tom an anesthetic before his operation; then the doctor took out Tom's appendix before he came to his senses.* (The doctors gave Tom something to make him sleep through the operation. Later he woke up again.) Compare COME TO 1. **2** To think clearly; behave as usual or as you should; act sensibly. *A boy threw a snowball at me and before I could come to my senses he ran away.* (I was surprised and before I could think what to do the boy ran away.) *Don't act so foolishly. Come to your senses!* (Behave yourself properly.) Contrast OUT OF ONE'S HEAD.

come to pass *v. phr., literary* To happen; occur. *Strange things come to pass in troubled times.* (Strange things happen in times of trouble.) *It came to pass that the jailer visited him by night.* (It happened that the jailer went to see him at night.) *His hopes of success did not come to pass.* (He hoped to succeed, but failed.) Compare BRING TO PASS, COME ABOUT.

come to terms *v. phr.* To reach an agreement. *Management and the labor union came to terms about a new arrangement and a strike was prevented.* (They reached a negotiated settlement and so there was no strike.)

come to the point *or* **get to the point** *v. phr.* To talk about the important thing; reach the important facts of the matter; reach the central question or fact. *Henry was giving a lot of history and explanation, but his father asked him to come to the point.* (Henry was telling about everything that led to his trouble, but his father asked him to just tell what the matter was.) *A good newspaper story must come right to the point and save the details for later.* (A good newspaper story must begin with the most important things and give the rest of the details later.) Contrast BEAT ABOUT THE BUSH.

come to think of it *v. phr., informal* As I think again; indeed; really. *Come to think of it, he has already been given what he needs.* (He really has already been given what he needs.) *Come to think of it, I should write my daughter today.* (I had forgotten, but really I should write her.)

come true *v.* To really happen; change from a dream or a plan into a fact. *It took years of planning and saving, but their seagoing vacation came true at last.* (After years of saving, their sea trip became a reality.) *It was a dream come true when he met the President.* (Meeting the President made his dream become true.) *His hope of living to 100 did not come true.* (He died before he was 100.)

come up *v.* **1** To become a subject for discussion or decision to talk about or decide about. *"He was a good salesman, and price never came up until the very last,"* Mary said. (Mary said they did not talk about price until the very last.) *The question of wage increases came up at the board meeting.* (Pay raises were among the things the board members talked about.) *Mayor Jones comes up for re-election this fall.* (Mayor Jones will run for re-election this fall.) **2** To be equal; match in value.—Used with *to*. *The new model car comes up to last year's.* (The new car is fully as good as last year's model.) **3** To approach; come close. *We saw a big black bear coming up on us from the woods.* (The bear was getting near us.) *Christmas is coming up soon.* (It will soon be here.) *The team was out practising for the big game coming up.* (The team was practising for the game they would soon play.) **4** To provide; supply; furnish.—Used with *with*. *For years Jones kept coming up with new and good ideas.* (He gave us many new ideas which proved good.) *The teacher asked a difficult question, but finally Ted came up with a good answer.* (Ted gave a good answer.)

come up in the world *or* **rise in the world** *v. phr.* To gain success, wealth, or importance in life; rise to a position of greater wealth or importance.—A trite expression. *He had come up in the world since he peddled his wife's baked goods from a pushcart.* (He had won more honor and importance in business and social life.) Compare GET AHEAD. Contrast COME DOWN IN THE WORLD.

come upon See COME ON 3.

come what may *adv. phr.* Even if troubles come; no matter what happens; in spite of opposition or mischance. *Charles has decided to get a college education, come what may.* (He says he will get a college education, no matter what happens.) *The editor says we will publish the school paper this week, come what may.* (We will print the paper this week even if we have all kinds of trouble.)

comfort See COLD COMFORT.

comfortable as an old shoe *adj. phr., informal* Pleasant and relaxed; not stiff, strict or too polite; easy to talk and work with. *The stranger was as comfortable as an old shoe, and we soon were talking like old friends.* (The stranger was easy to talk with; he made me feel comfortable.)

coming and going *or* **going and coming** *adv. phr.* **1** Both ways; in both directions. *The truck driver stops at the same cafe coming and going.* (The truck driver stops at the same cafe both ways.) *John was late. He got punished both going and coming; his teacher punished him and his parents punished him.* (John got punished both ways; his teacher punished him and his parents punished him.) **2** Caught or helpless; in your power; left with no way out of a difficulty.—Used after *have*. *If Beth stayed in the house, Mother would make her help with the cleaning; if she went outside, Father would make her help wash the car—they had her coming and going.* (Whichever Beth did, she would have to work; she was caught.) *Uncle Mike is a good checker player, and he soon had me beat coming and going.* (Uncle Mike soon had me beaten at checkers.) Compare BETWEEN THE DEVIL AND THE DEEP BLUE SEA.

coming out See COME OUT 1.

comings and goings *n. pl., informal* **1** Times of arriving and going away; movements. *I can't keep up with the children's comings and goings.* (I can't keep up with the children as they go in and out of the house.) **2** Activities; doings; business. *Mary knows all the comings and goings in the neighborhood.* (She knows everything that is happening.)

command module *n., Space English* **1** One of the three main sections of the basic Apollo spacecraft. It weighs six tons and is cone shaped. It contains crew compartments and from it the astronauts can operate the lunar module (LM), the docking systems, etc. **2** *Informal transferred sense.* The cockpit, the chief place where a person does his most important work. *My desk is my command module.* (I do most of my really important work at my desk.)

commission See IN COMMISSION *or* INTO COMMISSION, OUT OF COMMISSION.

common See IN COMMON.

common as an old shoe *adj. phr., informal* Not showing off; not vain; modest; friendly to all.—A cliché. *Although Mr. Jones ran a large business, he was common as an old shoe.* (He was friendly, modest, and equally kind to everyone.) *The most famous people are sometimes as common as an old shoe.* (They are friendly to all and do not show off.)

common ground *n.* Shared beliefs, interests, or ways of understanding; ways in which people are alike. *Bob and Frank don't like each other because they have no common ground.* (Bob and Frank don't like or believe the same things.) *The only common ground between us is that we went to the same school.* (The only thing we know about each other and talk about is the school we both went to.) Compare IN COMMON.

common touch *n.* The ability to be a friend of the people; friendly manner with everyone. *Voters like a candidate who has the common touch.* (People like a man who is a friend of the people.)

company See KEEP COMPANY, PART COMPANY.

company man *n., informal* A worker who always agrees with management rather than labor.—Usually used to express dislike or disapproval. *Joe was a company man and refused to take a part in the strike.* (He agreed with management rather than labor and stayed on the job when his fellow workers walked out.) Compare YES-MAN.

compare notes *v. phr., informal* To exchange thoughts or ideas about something; discuss together. *Mother and Mrs. Barker like to compare notes about cooking.* (They talk about the ways they cook and how they are the same or different.)

compliment See RETURN THE COMPLIMENT.

conclusion See JUMP TO A CONCLUSION.

condition See IN SHAPE *or* IN CONDITION, IN THE PINK *or* IN THE PINK OF CONDITION, ON CONDITION THAT, OUT OF SHAPE *or* OUT OF CONDITION.

conference See PRESS CONFERENCE.

congregate housing *n., informal* A form of housing for elderly persons in which dining facilities and services are shared in multiple dwelling units. *Jerry put Grandma in a place where they have congregate housing.* (He put her in a place for senior citizens where she has her own apartment but doesn't have to cook for herself as they have a common kitchen.)

conk out *v. phr., slang, informal* To fall asleep suddenly with great fatigue or after having drunk too much. *We conked out right after the guests had left.* (We fell asleep immediately after they left.)

consent See SILENCE GIVES CONSENT.

consequence See IN CONSEQUENCE, IN CONSEQUENCE OF.

consideration See IN CONSIDERATION OF.

consumer goods *or* **consumer items** *n.* Food and manufactured things that people buy for their own use. *In time of war, the supply of consumer goods is greatly reduced.* (In wartime the supply of food and manufactured articles that people want for their own use is cut.)

content See TO ONE'S HEART'S CONTENT.

contention See BONE OF CONTENTION.

contrary See ON THE CONTRARY, TO THE CONTRARY.

control room *n.* A room containing the panels and switches used to control something (like a TV broadcast). *While a television program is on the air, engineers are at their places in the control room.* (While the TV program is being broadcast, engineers are sitting in front of the panels and switches in a room controlling the amount of light and sound needed.)

control tower *n.* A tower with large windows and a good view of an airport so that the traffic of airplanes can be seen and controlled, usually by radio. *We could see the lights at the control tower as our plane landed during the night.* (We could see the tower at the edge of the landing field.)

conversation See MAKE CONVERSATION.

conversation piece *n.* Something that interests people and makes them talk about it; something that looks unusual, comical, or strange. *Uncle Fred has a glass monkey on top of his piano that he keeps for a conversation piece.* (Uncle Fred keeps the glass monkey where people can see it and will laugh and talk about it.)

conviction See HAVE THE COURAGE OF ONE'S CONVICTIONS.

cook See SHORT-ORDER COOK, WHAT'S UP *or* WHAT'S COOKING.

cook one's goose *v. phr., slang* To ruin someone hopelessly; destroy one's future expectations or good name. *The bank treasurer cooked his own goose when he stole the bank's funds.* (He ruined himself for life when he stole the bank's money.) *She cooked John's goose by reporting what she knew to the police.* (She ruined John completely by telling the police what she knew.) *The dishonest official knew his goose was cooked when the*

newspapers printed the story about him. (He knew that he was discovered when the newspapers printed the story.)

cook up *v., informal* To plan and put together; make up; invent. *The boys cooked up an excuse to explain their absence from school.* (The boys made up an excuse to explain why they were absent from school.)

cool See BLOW ONE'S COOL.

cool as a cucumber *adj. phr., informal* Very calm and brave; not nervous, worried, or anxious; not excited; composed.—A cliché. *Bill is a good football quarterback, always cool as a cucumber.* (He never gets nervous or excited.)

cool down *or* **cool off** *v.* **1** To lose or cause to lose the heat of any deep feeling (as love, enthusiasm, or anger); make or become calm, cooled or indifferent; lose interest. *A heated argument can be settled better if both sides cool down first.* (If two angry people let their feelings quiet down, they can usually settle their quarrel better.) *John was deeply in love with Sally before he left for college, but he cooled off before he got back.* (John lost interest in Sally while he was away.) *Their friendship cooled off when Jack gave up football.* (Their friendship became less warm when Jack gave up football.) *The neighbor's complaint about the noise cooled the argument down.* (When the neighbor complained about the noise, they had to stop arguing.)

cool one's heels *v. phr., slang* To be kept waiting by another's pride or rudeness; be forced to wait by someone in power or authority; wait.—A cliché. *He cooled his heels for an hour in another room before the great man would see him.* (He had to wait for an hour for the great man, who seemed to want to show his importance and power.) *I was left to cool my heels outside while the others went into the office.* (I had to wait outside while the others went into the office.)

coon's age See DOG'S AGE.

coop See FLY THE COOP.

cop a feel *v. phr., vulgar, avoidable* To attempt to arouse sexually by manual contact, usually by surprise. *John talks big for a 16 year old, but all he's ever done is cop a feel in a dark movie theater.* (He never had intercourse.) Compare FEEL UP. Contrast COP A PLEA.

cop a plea *v. phr., slang, colloquial* To plead guilty during a trial in the hope of getting a lighter sentence as a result. *The murderer of Dr. Martin Luther King, Jr., copped a plea of guilty, and got away with a life sentence instead of the death penalty.* (He pleaded guilty to the murder and as a result he drew the lighter sentence of a life term instead of the electric chair.)

cop out *v. phr., slang, informal* To avoid committing oneself in a situation where doing so would result in difficulties. *Nixon copped*

out on the American people with Watergate.
(In order to avoid the consequences, Nixon
didn't commit himself to revealing the truth
about Watergate to the American people.)

cop-out *n. phr., slang, informal* (stress on
cop) An irresponsible excuse made to avoid
something one has to do, a flimsy pretext.
*Come on, Max, that's a cheap cop-out, and I
don't believe a word of it!* (Max is told that his
excuse sounds flimsy, irresponsible, and unbelievable.)

copy cat *n.* Someone who copies another
person's work or manner.—Usually used by
children or when speaking to children. *He
called me a copy cat just because my new
shoes look like his.* (He said I was copying
him because my shoes look like his.)

corn ball *n., slang, informal* **1** A superficially sentimental movie or musical in which
the word *love* is mentioned too often; a theatrical performance that is trivially sentimental. *That movie last night was a corn
ball.* (It was superficially and boringly sentimental.) **2** A person who behaves in a
superficially sentimental manner or likes
performances portraying such behavior. *Suzie
can't stand Joe; she thinks he's a corn ball.*
(She thinks of him as a sappy, sentimental
fellow.)

corner See AROUND THE CORNER, CUT COR-
NERS, FOUR CORNERS, OUT OF THE CORNER OF
ONE'S EYE.

cotton See ON TOP OF THE WORLD *also* SIT-
TING ON HIGH COTTON.

cotton picking, cotton-pickin' *adj., slang, colloquial* Worthless, crude, common, messy.
*Keep your cotton picking hands off my flow-
ers!* (Keep your crude hands away from my
flowers!) *You've gotta clean up your room,
son, this is a cotton-pickin' mess!* (You must
clean your room; it is in great disorder.)

couch case *n., slang, informal* A person
judged emotionally so disturbed that people
think he ought to see a psychiatrist (who,
habitually, make their patients lie down on
a couch). *Joe's divorce messed him up so
badly that he became a couch case.* (He became so disturbed that he had to see a
psychiatrist.)

couch doctor *n., slang, colloquial* A psychoanalyst who puts his patients on a couch
following the practice established by Sigmund
Freud. *I didn't know your husband was a
couch doctor, I thought he was a gynecol-
ogist!* (I didn't know he was a psychiatrist.)

cough up *v., slang* **1** To give (money) unwillingly; pay with an effort. *Her husband
coughed up the money for the party with a
good deal of grumbling.* (He paid for the
party unwillingly.) **2** To tell what was secret;
make known. *He coughed up the whole story
for the police.* (He told the whole story to the
police.)

couldn't care less *v. phr., informal* To be indifferent; not care at all. *The students couldn't
care less about the band; they talk all through
the concert.* (The students are not interested
in listening to the band.) Also heard increas-
ingly as *could care less* (substandard in this
form.)

counsel See KEEP ONE'S OWN COUNSEL.

count See STAND UP AND BE COUNTED.

countdown *n., Space English, informal* **1**
A step-by-step process which leads to the
launching of a rocket. *Countdown starts at
23:00 hours tomorrow night and continues for
24 hours.* **2** Process of counting inversely
during the acts leading to a launch; liftoff
occurs at zero. **3** The time immediately
preceding an important undertaking, borrowed from Space English. *We're leaving for
Hawaii tomorrow afternoon; this is countdown time for us.* (We are feverishly preparing for our imminent departure.)

counter See UNDER THE COUNTER.

count heads *or* **count noses** *v. phr., informal*
To count the number of people in a group. *On
the class picnic, we counted heads before we
left and when we arrived to be sure that no
one got lost.* (We counted the number in the
group to make sure we were keeping together.) *The usher was told to look out into
the audience and count noses.* (The usher was
told to count the number of people in the
audience.)

count off *v.* **1** To count aloud from one end
of a line of men to the other, each man
counting in turn. *The soldiers counted off
from right to left.* (The first soldier shouted
"one," the second "two," and so on to the end
of the line.) **2** To place into a separate group
or groups by counting. *The coach counted
off three boys to carry in the equipment.* (The
coach chose three boys from the team to bring
in the equipment.) *Tom counted off enough
newspapers for his route.* (Tom took newspapers one at a time from a pile, counting until he had the number of papers he needed.)

count on *v.* **1** To depend on; rely on; trust.
The team was counting on Joe to win the race.
(The team expected Joe to win the race.) *I'll
do it; you know you can count on me.* (I'll
do it; you know you can depend on me.) *The
company was counting on Brown's making
the right decision.* (They trusted Brown to decide right.) Syn. BANK ON. **2** See FIGURE ON 2.

count one's chickens before they're hatched *v.
phr., informal* To depend on getting a profit
or gain before you have it; make plans that
suppose something will happen; be too sure
that something will happen.—A cliché; usually
used in negative sentences. *When Jim said
that he would be made captain of the team,
John told him not to count his chickens before
they were hatched.* (John told Jim not to be
so sure that he would be made captain.)
Maybe some of your customers won't pay,

and then where will you be? Don't count your chickens before they're hatched. (You may not be able to collect all your bills, so don't expect to have the money.)

count out *v.* **1** To leave (someone) out of a plan; not expect (someone) to share in an activity; exclude. *"Will this party cost anything? If it does, count me out, because I'm broke."* (If the party will cost something, leave me out, because I have no money.) *When the coach was planning who would play in the big game, he counted Paul out, because Paul had a hurt leg.* (The coach did not expect that Paul could play.) **2** To count out loud to ten to show that (a boxer who has been knocked down in a fight) is beaten or knocked out if he does not get up before ten is counted. *The champion was counted out in the third round.* (The referee counted to ten while the champion was knocked down and the champion was beaten.) **3a** To add up; count again to be sure of the amount. *Mary counted out the number of pennies she had.* (She counted them to find out the number.) **3b** To count out loud, (especially the beats in a measure of music). *The music teacher counted out the beats "one-two-three-four," so the class would sing in time.* (The music teacher counted the beats of the music.)

count to ten *v. phr., informal* To count from one to ten so you will have time to calm down or get control of yourself; put off action when angry or excited so as not to do anything wrong. *Father always told us to count to ten before doing anything when we got angry.* (Father meant for us to wait a little while and calm down so we would not do anything foolish.) Compare KEEP ONE'S HEAD. Contrast BLOW A FUSE, FLY OFF THE HANDLE.

county mounty *n., slang, citizen's band radio jargon* Sheriff's deputy. *The county mounties are parked under the bridge.* (The sheriff's deputies are waiting for speeders under the bridge; slow down.)

courage See HAVE THE COURAGE OF ONE'S CONVICTIONS, SCREW UP ONE'S COURAGE.

course See IN DUE COURSE, MATTER OF COURSE, OF COURSE, PAR FOR THE COURSE.

court See DAY IN COURT, FRONT COURT, HOLD COURT, KANGAROO COURT.

cousin See FIRST COUSIN, SECOND COUSIN.

cover See FROM COVER TO COVER *at* FROM —— TO 3, UNDER COVER.

covered-dish supper *or* **potluck supper** A meal to which each guest brings a share of the food. *Dolly made a chicken casserole for the covered-dish supper.* (She made a chicken casserole to take with her as her part to the party.)

cover girl *n.* A pretty girl or woman whose picture is put on the cover of a magazine. *Ann is not a cover girl, but she is pretty enough to be.* (Even though Ann's picture is not on magazine covers, she is very pretty.)

cover ground *or* **cover the ground** *v. phr.* **1** To go a distance; travel. *Mr. Rogers likes to travel in planes, because they cover ground so quickly.* (Mr. Rogers likes air travel, because he can go a distance more quickly.) **2** *informal* To move over an area at a speed that is pleasing; move quickly over a lot of ground. *The new infielder really covers the ground at second base.* (The team's new player can go quickly a long way to catch batted balls.) *Herby's new car really covers ground!* (Herby's new car goes very fast.) **3** To give or receive the important facts and details about a subject. *If you're thinking about a trip to Europe, the airline has a booklet that covers the ground pretty well.* (The airline has a booklet that will tell you most of the important things about a trip to Europe.) *The class spent two days studying the Revolutionary War, because they couldn't cover that much ground in one day.* (They couldn't learn all the important facts about the Revolutionary War in one day.)

cover one's tracks *or* **cover up one's tracks** *v. phr.* **1** To hide and not leave anything, especially foot marks, to show where you have been, so that no one can follow you. *The deer covered his tracks by running in a stream.* (The deer knew that the hunter was following him and ran in the water so there would be no marks to follow.) **2** *informal* To hide or not say where you have been or what you have done; not tell why you do something or what you plan to do. *The boys covered their tracks when they went swimming by saying that they were going for a walk.* (The boys did not tell where they were really going because they did not want anyone to know.) Compare COVER UP 1.

cover the waterfront *v. phr.* To talk or write all about something; talk about something all possible ways.—A cliché. *The principal pretty well covered the waterfront on student behavior.* (The principal talked all about what students should do and should not do. He didn't forget anything.)

cover up *v., informal* **1** To hide something wrong or bad from attention. *The spy covered up his picture-taking by pretending to be just a tourist.* (The spy took pictures of secret places and things while pretending to be taking tourist pictures.) *A crooked banker tried to cover up his stealing some of the bank's money by starting a fire to destroy the records.* (He tried to hide his stealing by burning the papers that proved some money was gone.) Compare COVER ONE'S TRACKS 2. **2** *In boxing:* To guard your head and body with your gloves, arms, and shoulders. *Jimmy's father told him to cover up and protect his chin when he boxed.* (Jimmy's father told him to guard his chin from behing hit by keeping his gloves in front of it.) **3** To protect someone else from blame or punishment; protect someone with a lie or alibi.—Often used with *for*. *The teacher wanted to know who* *broke the window and told the boys not to try to cover up for anyone.* (The teacher told the boys not to try to protect the one who did it.) *The burglar's friend covered up for him by saying that he was at his home when the robbery occurred.* (The burglar's friend said that the burglar was somewhere else and did not commit the robbery.)

cover-up *n., slang* A plan or excuse to escape blame or punishment; lie, alibi. *When the men robbed the bank, their cover-up was to dress like policemen.* (The robbers dressed like policemen so that no one would think they were robbers.) *Joe's cover-up to his mother after he had been fighting was that he fell down.* (Joe used the excuse to his mother that he fell down.)

cow See HOLY CATS *or* HOLY COW, SACRED COW.

cowboy *n., slang, informal* A person who drives his car carelessly and at too great a speed in order to show off his courage. *Joe's going to be arrested some day—he is a cowboy on the highway.* (He drives much faster than the speed limit.)

cow college *n., slang* **1** An agricultural college; a school where farming is studied. *A new, bigger kind of apple is being grown at the cow college.* (The apple is being studied at the college and they are trying to grow big apples.) **2** A new or rural college not thought to be as good as older or city colleges. *John wanted to go to a big college in New York City, not to a cow college.* (John didn't want to go to a small school in a farm area.)

cow's tail *n., dialect* A person who is behind others. *John was the cow's tail at the exam.* (John was the last student to finish the tests.) *Fred was always the old cow's tail for football practice.* (He was slow in getting to the field for practice.)

cozy up *v., slang* To try to be close or friendly; try to be liked.—Usually used with *to*. *John is cozying up to Henry so he can join the club.* (John is trying to become friends with Henry so he can join the club too.)

crack See HARD NUT TO CRACK *or* TOUGH NUT TO CRACK.

crack a book *v. phr., slang* To open a book in order to study.—Usually used with a negative. *John did not crack a book until the night before the exam.* (John did not study until the night before the exam.) *Many students think they can pass without cracking a book.* (They think they can pass without reading their lessons.)

crack a joke *v. phr., informal* To make a joke; tell a joke. *The men sat around the stove, smoking and cracking jokes.* (The men sat around the stove, smoking and telling jokes.)

crack a smile *v. phr., informal* To let a smile show on one's face; permit a smile to appear. *Bob told the whole silly story without even cracking a smile.* (Bob told the silly story and didn't smile once.) *Scrooge was a gloomy*

man, who never cracked a smile. (Scrooge never let a smile appear on his face.) *When we gave the shy little boy an ice cream cone, he finally cracked a smile.* (He finally smiled.)

crack down *v. phr., informal* To enforce laws or rules strictly; require full obedience to a rule. *After a speeding driver hit a child, the police cracked down.* (They got strict about speeding.)—Often used with *on*. *Police suddenly cracked down on the selling of liquors to minors.* (Police suddenly began making arrests for selling liquor to teenagers.) *The coach cracked down on the players when he found they had not been obeying the training rules.* (The coach began to enforce the rules strictly.)

cracked up *adj. phr., informal* Favorably described or presented; praised.—Usually used in the expression *not—it's cracked up to be. The independent writer's life isn't always everything it's cracked up to be.* (The life of the self-employed writer doesn't always come up to its praises.) *In bad weather, a sailing cruise isn't what it's cracked up to be.* (In bad weather, a sailing trip on a sailboat isn't much fun.)

cracking See GET CRACKING—at GET GOING 2.

crackpot *n., attrib. adj., informal* **1** *n.* An eccentric person with ideas that don't make sense to most other people. *Don't believe what uncle Noam tells you—he is a crackpot.* (His ideas are weird or absurd; pay no attention to him.) **2** *attrib. adj.* *That's a crackpot idea.* (That is a stupid, unrealistic idea.)

crack the whip *v. phr., informal* To get obedience or cooperation by threats of punishment. *If the children won't behave when I reason with them, I have to crack the whip.* (When the children won't behave even when they know they should, I have to threaten to punish them.)

crack up *v.* **1** To wreck or be wrecked; smash up. *The airplane cracked up in landing.* (The airplane was wrecked in landing.) *He cracked up his car.* (He wrecked his car.) **2** *informal* To become mentally ill under physical or mental overwork or worry. *He had kept too busy for years, and when failures came, he cracked up.* (He broke down when his business got into difficulties.) *It seemed to be family problems that made him crack up.* (He broke down under the worry of problems at home.) **3** burst into laughter *or* cause to burst into laughter. *That comedian cracks me up.* (That comedian makes me burst out laughing.)

cradle See ROB THE CRADLE.

cradle robber, cradle robbing See ROB THE CRADLE.

cramp See WRITER'S CRAMP.

cramp one's style *v. phr., informal* To limit your natural freedom; prevent your usual behavior; limit your actions or talk. *It cramped his style a good deal when he lost his money.*

(Being poor kept him from doing many things us used to do.) *Army rules cramped George's style.* (Army rules kept George from living as he had been used to doing.)

crash dive *n.* A sudden dive made by a submarine to escape an enemy; a dive made to get deep under water as quickly as possible. *The captain of the submarine told his crew to prepare for a crash dive when he saw the enemy battleship approaching.* (The captain wanted the submarine to go deep in the water suddenly so it could not be seen or reached by enemy bombs.)

crash-dive *v.* **1** To dive deep underwater in a submarine as quickly as possible. *We shall crash-dive if we see enemy planes coming.* (We shall dive our submarine quickly underwater if we see enemy planes.) **2** To dive into (something) in an airplane. *When the plane's motor was hit by the guns of the enemy battleship, the pilot aimed the plane at the ship and crash-dived into it.* (The pilot crashed his plane into the battleship.)

crash the gate *v. phr., slang* To enter without a ticket or without paying; attend without an invitation or permission. *Bob got into the circus without paying. He crashed the gate.* (Bob sneaked into the circus without paying.) *Three boys tried to crash the gate at our party but we didn't let them in.* (Three boys who weren't invited tried to get in.)

craw See STICK IN ONE'S CRAW.

crawl up See RIDE UP.

cream See VANISHING CREAM.

cream of the crop *n. phr.* The best of a group; the top choice.—An overused expression. *May Queen candidates were lovely, but Betsy and Nancy were the cream of the crop.* (They were the top choice. It was hard to decide which one was prettier.) *The students had drawn many good pictures and the teacher chose the cream of the crop to hang up when the parents came to visit.* (The teacher chose the best pictures to hang up.)

credibility gap *n., Hackneyed phrase, politics* An apparent discrepancy between what the government says and what one can observe for oneself. *There was a tremendous credibility gap in the USA during the Watergate years.* (During the Watergate years one couldn't believe the government.)

credit See DO CREDIT.

creek See UP THE CREEK *or* UP THE CREEK WITHOUT A PADDLE.

creep See THE CREEPS.

creep up on *v.* **1** To crawl towards; move along near the ground; steal cautiously towards so as not to be seen or noticed. *The mouse did not see the snake creeping up on it over the rocks.* (The snake crawled quietly so that the mouse didn't see it.) *Indians were creeping up on the house through the bushes.* (The Indians moved softly, hiding themselves in the bushes.) **2** *or* **sneak up on** To come

little by little; arrive slowly and unnoticed. *The woman's hair was turning gray as age crept up on her.* (Her hair turned gray gradually as she became older.) *Winter is creeping up on us little by little.* (Winter is coming a little more every day.) *The boys didn't notice the darkness creeping up on them while they were playing.* (The boys were so interested in their play, they didn't notice the dark.) Compare COME OVER.

crepe hanger *n., slang* A person who always talks about the troubles and sadness of life; a gloomy person. *John is a crepe hanger. He never expects the team to win.* (John always talks about our team losing, before a game is played.) Compare WET BLANKET.

crepe paper *n.* A thin, crinkled paper made to look like crepe cloth and often used for decoration. *Crepe paper of many bright colors was hung across the ceilings for the party.* (Special paper was used to decorate the room for the party.)

crew See SECTION GANG *or* SECTION CREW.

crew cut *or* **crew haircut** *n.* A boy's or man's hair style, cut so that the hair stands up in short, stiff bristle. *Many boys like to get crew cuts during the summer to keep cooler.* (Many boys get their hair cut short during summer because it keeps them cooler.)

crisp See BURN TO A CRISP.

crocodile tears *n.* Pretended grief; a show of sorrow that is not really felt.—A hackneyed expression. *When his rich uncle died, leaving him his money, John shed crocodile tears.* (John pretended to be sorry when his uncle died, but he was really glad to have his money.) [From the old legend that crocodiles make weeping sounds to attract victims and then shed tears while eating them.]

crook See BY HOOK OR BY CROOK.

crop See CASH CROP, CREAM OF THE CROP, STICK IN ONE'S CRAW *or* STICK IN ONE'S CROP.

crop out *v.* To appear at the surface; come through or show through from hiding or concealment. *Rocks often crop out in New England pasture land.* (Rocks often push through the soil in New England pastures.) *A hidden hate cropped out in his words.* (His words showed hate that he had hidden before.)

cropper See COME A CROPPER.

crop up *v.* To come without warning; appear or happen unexpectedly. *Problems cropped up almost every day when Mr. Reed was building his TV station.* (He kept meeting difficulties when he was building his TV station.) *Serious trouble cropped up just when Martin thought the problem of his college education was solved.* (A big difficulty appeared just when he thought his college education was sure.) Compare TURN UP.

cross See AT CROSS PURPOSES, CARRY ONE'S CROSS, DOUBLE CROSS, KEEP ONE'S FINGERS CROSSED *at* CROSS ONE'S FINGERS 1b.

cross a bridge before one comes to it *v. phr.* To worry about future events or trouble before they happen—Usually used in negative sentences, often as a proverb. *"Can I be a soldier when I grow up, Mother?" asked Johnny. "Don't cross that bridge until you come to it," said his mother.* (It is time enough to worry about being a soldier when you grow up.) Compare BORROW TROUBLE.

cross-check[1] *v.* To test the truth of by examining in different ways or by seeing different reports about. *If you see something in a book that may not be true, be sure to cross-check it in other books.* (See if other books say that it is true too.)

cross-check[2] *n.* The testing of the truth of by checking one report against another or others. *A cross-check with other books will show us if this story is true.* (An examination of other books about this story will tell us if it is told accurately in this book.)

cross fire *n.* 1 Firing in a fight or battle from two or more places at once so that the lines of fire cross. *The soldiers on the bridge were caught in the cross fire coming from both sides of the bridge.* (There was shooting from both ends of the bridge and the soldiers were caught in between.) 2 Fast or angry talking back and forth between two or more people; *also*, a dispute; a quarrel. *There was a cross fire of excited questions and answers between the parents and the children who had been lost in the woods.* (The parents and children fired questions and answers back and forth at each other.) *The principal and the graduates quarreled about the football team, and the coach was caught in the cross fire and lost his job.* (The coach did not enter the fight between the principal and the graduates, but lost his job because of it.)

cross one's fingers *v. phr.* **1a** To cross two fingers of one hand for good luck. *Mary crossed her fingers during the race so that Tom would win.* (Mary crossed her two fingers to bring Tom good luck.) **1b** *or* **keep one's fingers crossed** *informal* To wish for good luck.—A cliché. *Keep your fingers crossed while I take the test.* (Hope that I am lucky and that I pass the test.) 2 To cross two fingers of one hand to excuse an untruth that you are telling. *Johnny crossed his fingers when he told his mother the lie.* (Johnny put one finger over the other because he believed it was all right to lie if he did that.)

cross one's heart *or* **cross one's heart and hope to die** *v. phr., informal* To say that what you have said is surely true; promise seriously that it is true.—Often used by children in the longer form. *Children often make a sign of a cross over the heart as they say it, for emphasis. "Cross my heart, I didn't hide your bicycle," Harry told Tom.* (Harry told him that it was surely true that he had not hidden his bicycle.) *"I didn't tell the teacher what you said. Cross my heart and hope to die," Mary said to Lucy.* (Mary promised Lucy seriously that she did not tell the teacher.)

cross one's mind *or* **pass through one's mind** *v. phr.* To be a sudden or passing thought; be thought of by someone; come to your mind; occur to you. *At first Bob was puzzled by Virginia's waving, but then it crossed his mind that she was trying to tell him something.* (The idea came to him that Virginia was trying to tell him something.) *When Jane did not come home by midnight, many terrible fears passed through Mother's mind.* (Mother thought of many things that might have happened to Jane.)

cross street *n.* A street that crosses a main street and runs on both sides of it. *Elm Street is a cross street on Main Street and there is a traffic light there.* (Elm Street crosses Main Street.) Compare THROUGH STREET.

cross swords *v. phr., literary* To have an argument with; fight.—Often used with *with*. *Don't argue with the teacher; you're not old enough to cross swords with her.* (You don't know enough to beat the teacher in an argument.)

cross the wire *v. phr.* To finish a race. *The Russian crossed the wire just behind the American.* (The Russian runner finished the race, just behind the American.)

cross up *v., informal* 1 To block or upset; throw into confusion or disorder. *We were going to catch him at the gate, but he crossed us up by going in the back way.* (He upset our plan by going in the back door.) *Father crossed up the surprise party we had planned for him by not getting back in time.* (Father upset the surprise party by not getting back in time for it.) 2 To deceive or be false to. *George crossed up his partner by selling a lot of things secretly.* (George cheated his partner by selling a lot of things without telling him.)

crow See EAT CROW.

crow before one is out of the woods *v.phr.* To be glad or brag before you are safe from danger or trouble.—Usually used in negative sentences, often as a proverb, "Don't crow before you are out of the woods." *John thought his team would win because the game was almost over, but he didn't want to crow before they were out of the woods.* (John's team had not won yet and could still lose, so he didn't want to brag too soon.) Often used in a short form, *out of the woods. Mary nearly died during the operation, and she is not out of the woods yet.* (She is not out of danger yet.)

crown jewels *n. pl.* The crown, staff, and jewels used for the crowning of a king or queen; the crown and jewels representing royal power and authority. *The crown jewels are handed down from one king to the next when the new king is crowned.* (When the old king dies the new king receives the crown jewels, which means that he now has the power of the king.)

crow to pick See BONE TO PICK *or* CROW TO PICK.

crust See UPPER CRUST.

cry See FAR CRY, FOR CRYING OUT LOUD, HUE AND CRY.

cry before one is hurt *or* **holler before one is hurt** *v. phr., informal* To complain when there is no reason for it; become upset because you are worried or afraid—Used in negative sentences. *When Billy went to the barber, he began to cry before the barber cut his hair and his father told him not to cry before he was hurt.* (Billy was afraid the barber would hurt him and began to cry before the barber touched him.) Often used as a proverb. *John was worried because he would soon have a new boss. His mother said, "Don't cry before you're hurt!"* (His mother told John not to be afraid of the new boss before he met him.) Syn. BORROW TROUBLE.

cry for *or* **cry out for** *v., informal* To need badly; be lacking in. *It has not rained for two weeks and the garden is crying for it.* (The garden is very dry and needs rain.) *The school is crying out for good teachers.* (The school needs good teachers.)

cry out *v.* **1** To call out loudly; shout; scream. *The woman in the water cried out "Help!"* (The woman shouted for help.) **2** To complain loudly; protest strongly.—Used with *against. Many people are crying out against the new rule.* (Many people don't like the new rule and are complaining about it.)

cry out for See CRY FOR.

cry over spilled milk *or* **cry over spilt milk** *v. phr., informal* To cry or complain about something that has already happened; be unhappy about something that cannot be helped. *After the baby tore up Sue's picture book, Sue's mother told her there was no use crying over spilled milk.* (Sue's mother told her not to cry because the book was already torn up.) *You have lost the game but don't cry over spilt milk.* (Don't feel sorry about the game. It is already lost.) Compare MAKE ONE'S BED AND LIE IN IT, WATER OVER THE DAM *or* WATER UNDER THE BRIDGE.

crystal ball *n.* A ball, usually made of quartz crystal (glass) that is used by fortune-tellers. *The fortune-teller at the fair looked into her crystal ball and told me that I would take a long trip next year.* (The fortune-teller told me what might happen next year by looking into her big glass ball.) **2** Any means of predicting the future. *My crystal ball tells me you'll be making the honor roll.* (I have a feeling you'll make the honor roll.)

crystal gazing *n.* The attempt to predict future events. *The magician's specialty was crystal gazing.* (He was noted for his skill in predicting future events by looking into a glass ball.)

cry uncle See SAY UNCLE.

cry wolf *v. phr.* To give a false alarm; warn of a danger that you know is not there.—A cliché. *The general said that the candidate was just crying wolf when he said that the army was too weak to fight for the country.* (The general said that the candidate's warnings of the army's weakness were false and made up to frighten people so they would vote for him.) [From an old story about a shepherd boy who falsely claimed a wolf was killing his sheep, just to start some excitement.]

cub scout *n.* A member of the Cub Scouts, the junior branch of the Boy Scouts for boys 8–10 years of age. *Jimmie is only seven, too young to be a Cub Scout.* (Jimmie must be eight years old to be a Cub Scout.)

cucumber See COOL AS A CUCUMBER.

cudgel See TAKE UP THE CUDGELS FOR.

cudgel one's brains See BEAT ONE'S BRAINS OUT.

cue in *v. phr., informal* To add new information to that which is already known. *Let's not forget to cue in Joe on what has been happening.* (Let us not forget to tell him what has been happening.)

cuff See OFF-THE-CUFF, ON THE CUFF.

culture vulture *n., slang, informal* A person who is an avid cultural sightseer, one who seeks out cultural opportunities ostentatiously, such as going to the opera or seeing every museum in a town visited, and brags about it. *My aunt Mathilda is a regular culture vulture; she spends every summer in a different European capital going to museums and operas.* (She is a culturally snobbish tourist.)

cup See IN ONE'S CUPS.

cup of tea *also* **dish of tea** *n. phr., informal* **1** Something you enjoy or do well at; a special interest, or favorite occupation.—A cliché. Used with a possessive. *You could always get him to go for a walk: hiking was just his cup of tea.* (Hiking was his favorite occupation.) Compare DOWN ONE'S ALLEY. **2** Something to think about; thing; matter.—A cliché. *That's another cup of tea.* (That's a different matter entirely.) Compare KETTLE OF FISH.

curb service *n.* Waiting on customers while they sit in their cars. *Families with small children often look for hamburger stands that offer curb service.* (They look for places that sell cooked food where they can get waited on without getting out of the car.)

curiosity killed the cat *informal* Getting too nosy may lead a person into trouble.—A proverb. *"Curiosity killed the cat." Fred's father said, when he found Fred hunting around in closets just before Christmas.* (Fred's father warned him about being nosy.)

curl See PIN CURL.

curl one's hair *v. phr., slang* To shock; frighten; horrify; amaze.—A hackneyed expression. *Wait till you read what it says about you—this'll curl your hair.* (You'll be shocked by what it says about you.) *The movie about monsters from another planet curled his hair.* (The movie monsters frightened him.)

curl up *v.* **1a** To become curly or wavy. *Bacon curls up when it is cooked.* (Bacon becomes wrinkled when it is cooked.) **1b** To roll oneself into a ball. *Tim curled up in bed and was asleep in five minutes.* (Tim rolled himself up like a ball and went to sleep.) **2** See FOLD UP.

current See SWIM AGAINST THE CURRENT.

curry favor *v.* To flatter or serve someone to get his help or friendship. *Joe tried to curry favor with the new teacher by doing little services that she didn't really want.* (Joe hoped to improve his marks by doing things for the teacher; he was seeking profit and not trying to be kind.) *Jim tried to curry favor with the new girl by telling her she was the prettiest girl in the class.* (He tried to make her like him.) Compare POLISH THE APPLE.

curve See THROW A CURVE.

cut See FISH OR CUT BAIT.

cut across *v.* **1** To cross or go through instead of going around; go a short way. *John didn't want to walk to the corner and turn, so he cut across the yard to the next street.* (John walked across the yard instead of going around the corner.) **2** To go beyond to include; stretch over to act on; affect. *The love for reading cuts across all classes of people, rich and poor.* (Love of reading is experienced by people of all classes, rich and poor alike.)

cut-and-dried *adj. phr.* Decided or expected beforehand; following the same old line; doing the usual thing. *The decision of the judge was cut-and-dried.* (His decision was what everyone expected.) *The ways of the king's court were cut-and-dried.* (The court always followed the old customs.) *People at the convention heard many cut-and-dried speeches.* (They heard many dull and boring speeches.)

cut and run *v., informal* To abandon an unfavorable situation. *When the price of coffee dropped sharply many investors wanted to cut and run.* (They hoped to save what they had left by selling their stock.)

cut a swathe *v. phr.* **1a** To mow a path through a field. *The farmer cut a swathe through the high grass with his scythe.* (He cut down the grass and made a path through the field.) **1b** To cut down as if by mowing. *The machine gun cut a swathe in the lines of enemy soldiers.* (The gun hit the lines of soldiers and seemed to mow them down like grass.) **2** *informal* To attract notice; make an impression; seem important.—A cliché. *The movie star cut a wide swathe when he walked down the street.* (He attracted a lot of attention.) *John tries to show off and cut a big swathe with the girls.* (He tries to make the girls think that he is important.) Compare GO OVER 6, MAKE A HIT.

cut back *v.* **1** To change direction suddenly while going at full speed. *The halfback started to his left, cut back to his right, and ran for a touchdown.* (The halfback turned suddenly and ran to his right after starting to his left, and made a touchdown.) **2** To use fewer or use less. *After the big job was finished, the builder cut back the number of men working for him.* (The builder fired many of his workers.) *The school employed forty teachers until a lower budget forced it to cut back.* (After the school received less money, it had to let some teachers go.)

cut both ways *or* **cut two ways** *v. phr.* To have two effects; cause injury to both sides. *People who gossip find it cuts both ways.* (They find that gossip may cause people to think less of the person they talk about, but it also causes people to think less of the gossiper.)

cut corners *v. phr.* **1** To take a short way; not go to each corner. *He cut corners going home in a hurry.* (He went the shortest way, across lots and through fields.) **2** To save cost or effort; manage in a thrifty way; be saving. *John's father asked him to cut corners all he could in college.* (John's father asked him to be as saving as he could in college.) **3** To do less than a very good job; do only what you must do on a job. *He had cut corners in building his house, and it didn't stand up well.* (He had done a poor job in building his house, and the house soon showed the poor materials and workmanship.)

cut down *v.* To lessen; reduce; limit. *Tom had to cut down expenses.* (Tom had to reduce his spending.) *The doctor told Mr. Jones to cut down on smoking.* (The doctor told Mr. Jones to do less smoking.)

cut down to size *v. phr., informal* To prove that someone is not as good as he thinks.—A cliché. *The big boy told John he could beat him, but John was a good boxer and soon cut him down to size.* (John beat the big boy proving that he was not as good as he said.) Syn. PUT IN ONE'S PLACE.

cut ice *v. phr., informal* To make a difference; make an impression; be accepted as important.—Usually used in negative, interrogative, or conditional sentences. *When Frank had found a movie he liked, what others said cut no ice with him.* (He did not care what they said.) *Jones is democratic; a man's money or importance never cuts any ice with him.* (Rich or poor, it was all the same to him.) *Does comfort cut any ice with you?* (Do you want to be comfortable?) *I don't know if beauty in a woman cuts any ice with him.* (I don't know if he thinks beauty important.)

cut in *v.* **1** To force your way into a place between others in a line of cars, people, etc.; push in. *After passing several cars, Fred cut in too soon and nearly caused an accident.* (Fred

got back in line too close to the car behind.)
—Often used with *on*. *A car passed Jean and cut in on her too close; she had to brake quickly or she would have hit it.* (The other car turned back into line too close to Jean.) *The teacher beside the lunch line saw Pete cut in, and she sent him back to wait his turn.* (She saw Pete force himself into the line ahead of other students.) **2** To stop a talk or program for a time; interrupt. *While Mary and Jim were talking on the porch, Mary's little brother cut in on them and began to tell about his fishing trip.* (Her little brother began to speak while they were talking to each other, and they had to stop.) *While we were watching the late show, an announcer cut in to tell who won the election.* (The announcer stopped the program to tell who was elected.) Syn. BREAK IN 2. **3** *informal* To tap a dancer on the shoulder and claim the partner. *Mary was a good dancer and a boy could seldom finish a dance with her; someone always cut in.* (When Mary was dancing, another boy was always there to take her away from her partner.)—Often used with *on*. *At the leap year dance, Jane cut in on Sally because she wanted to dance with Sally's handsome date.* (She tapped Sally on the shoulder, and Sally had to let Jane dance with her date.) **4** To connect to an electrical circuit or to a machine. *Harry threw the switch and cut in the motor.* (Harry turned on the electric power and set the motor going.) *The airplane pilot cut in a spare gas tank.* (The pilot connected a spare gas tank to his motors.) **5** *informal* To take in; include. *When John's friends got a big contract, they cut John in.* (When they got a big·contract, John's friends gave him part of the business and profits.)

cut into *v.* **1** To make less; reduce. *The union made the company pay higher wages, which cut into the profits.* (The higher wages to the workers made the profits for the owners smaller.) *The other houses got old and shabby, and that cut into the value of his house.* (His house was worth less.) *At first Smith led in votes, but more votes came in and cut into his lead.* (The late votes lessened his lead.) **2** To get into by cutting in. *She heard the other women gossiping and cut into the talk.* (She joined in the conversation.) *While Bill was passing another car, a truck came around a curve heading for him, and Bill cut back into line quickly.* (Bill quickly turned back into line.)

cut loose *v.* **1** To free from ties or connections; cut the fastenings of. *The thief hastily cut the boat loose from its anchor.* (He was in a hurry, and cut the anchor rope instead of hauling up the anchor.) Compare LET LOOSE 1a. **2** *informal* To break away from control; get away and be free. *The boy left home and cut loose from his parents' control.* (He didn't follow the rules of his home.) **3** *informal* To behave freely or wildly. *The men had come to*

the convention to have a good time, and they really cut loose.* (They behaved wildly.) *When he got the news of his job promotion, Jack cut loose with a loud "Yippee!"* (He yelled loudly "Yippee!") Compare LET GO 6.

cut off *v.* **1** To separate or block. *The flood cut the townspeople off from the rest of the world.* (The flood separated the townspeople from the rest of the world.) *The woods cut off the view.* (The woods block the view.) *His rudeness cuts him off from friends he might have.* (His rudeness shuts him off from making friends he might have.) **2** To interrupt or stop. *The television show was cut off by a special news report.* (The television show was interrupted by a special news report.) *We were told to pay the bill or the water would be cut off.* (We had to pay the bill or the water coming to the house would be stopped.) **3** To end the life of; cause the death of. *Disease cut Smith off in the best part of life.* (Disease ended Smith's life while he was still in his best years.) **4** To give nothing to at death; leave out of a will. *Jane married a man her father hated, and her father cut her off.* (He wrote in his will that when he died, she would get nothing.) *Frank's uncle cut him off without a penny.* (Frank's uncle left him out of his will; he did not leave him even one penny.) **5** To stop from operating; turn a switch to stop. *The ship cut off its engines as it neared the dock.* (The ship stopped its engines as it neared the dock.) Syn. SHUT OFF, TURN OFF.

cut off one's nose to spite one's face *v. phr.* To make things worse for yourself because you are angry, usually at someone else.—A cliché. *When Ted's father wouldn't let him go to the ball game, Ted cut off his nose to spite his face. He wouldn't eat his frankfurters for dinner, even though he liked them very much.* (Ted hurt himself, not anyone else, by not eating.)

cut-offs *n.*, *colloquial* Pants cut to the length of shorts and usually left unhemmed so as to look old and worn, e.g., considered cool and elegant. *Jack always wears cut-offs during the summer.* (He wears short-length unhemmed pants.)

cut one's eyeteeth on See CUT TEETH 2.

cut one's teeth on See CUT TEETH 2.

cut one's throat *v. phr.*, *informal* To spoil one's chances; ruin a person. *He cut his own throat by his carelessness.* (He lost his chances by seeming not to care about his job.) *The younger men in the company were cutting each other's throats in their eagerness to win success.* (Each was spoiling the others' chances in his effort to advance.) *John cut Freddie's throat with Mary by telling her lies.* (John made Mary dislike Freddie by telling her lies.)

cut out¹ *v.*, *slang* **1** To stop; quit. *All right, now—let's cut out the talking.* (Please stop the talking.) *He was teasing the dog and Joe told* *him to cut it out.* (Joe told him to stop teasing the dog.) Compare BREAK UP 3. **2** To displace in favor. *Tony cut Ed out with Mary.* (Tony got Mary to like him better than Ed.) *John cut out two or three other men in trying for a better job.* (John was promoted over two or three other men.)

cut out² *adj.* **1** Made ready; given for action; facing. *Mary agreed to stay with her teacher's children all day; she did not know what was cut out for her.* (Mary did not know all the work and problems of the job.)—Often used in the phrase *have one's work cut out for one. If Mr. Perkins wants to become a senator, he has his work cut out for him.* (Perkins has a big job ahead of him to get elected to the Senate.) **2** Suited to; fitted for. *Warren seemed to be cut out for the law.* (He seemed to be naturally fitted to be a lawyer.) *It was clear very early that Fred was cut out to be a doctor.* (Fred early showed his fitness to be a doctor.)

cut rate¹ *n.* A lower price; a price less than usual. *Toys are on sale at the store for cut rates.* (The prices of the toys are low.)

cut-rate² *adj.* Sold for a price lower than usual; selling cheap things. *If you buy cut-rate things, be sure they are good quality first.* (Be sure you aren't buying things that are not very good for a low price.) *John's brother bought a cut-rate bicycle at the second-hand store.* (He bought the bicycle at a low price.) *There is a cut-rate drugstore on the corner.* (The drugstore sells its goods cheap.)

cut short *v.* To stop or interrupt suddenly; end suddenly or too soon. *Rain cut short the ball game.* (Rain stopped the ball game in the middle.) *An auto accident cut short the man's life.* (An auto accident killed the man.) *When Dick began to tell about his summer vacation, the teacher cut him short, saying "Tell us about that another time."* (The teacher stopped Dick and did not let him finish his story.)

cut teeth *v. phr.* **1** To have teeth grow out through the gums. *The baby was cross because he was cutting teeth.* (The baby was cross because his teeth were just coming through the gums and hurting him.) **2** *or* **cut eye teeth** *informal* To learn something very early in life; gain experience; start by learning or doing.—Used with a possessive, usually used with *on. The professional ball player cut his teeth on a baseball bat in the sandlots.* (He learned to bat and play as a boy in sandlot leagues.) *Mr. Jones's company is building the new Post Office in town but Mr.*

Jones cut his eye teeth as a carpenter. (Mr. Jones started by learning to be a carpenter.)

cut the ground from under *v. phr. informal* To make (someone) fail; upset the plans of; spoil the argument for (a person) in advance. *Paul wanted to be captain but we cut the ground from under him by saying that Henry was the best player on the team.* (We spoiled Paul's plans to be captain by saying that the best player should be captain.) *Several workers applied for the retiring foreman's job, but the owner cut the ground from under them by hiring a foreman from another company.* (The owner spoiled their hopes and arguments by choosing an outsider.)

cut the mustard *v. phr., slang* To do well enough in what needs to be done; to succeed. *His older brothers and sisters helped Max through high school, but he couldn't cut the mustard in college.* (He flunked his college courses once he was on his own.)

cut to pieces *v. phr.* **1** To divide into small parts with something sharp; cut badly or completely. *Baby has cut the newspaper to pieces with scissors.* (Baby has cut the paper all apart.) **2** To destroy or defeat completely. *The soldiers were cut to pieces by the Indians.* (The soldiers were badly beaten.) *When Dick showed his book report to his big sister for correction, she cut it to pieces.* (She found many mistakes.)

cut to the bone *v. phr.* To make (something) the least or smallest possible amount; reduce severely; leave out everything extra or unnecessary from. *Father cut Jane's allowance to the bone for disobeying him.* (Father gives Jane only money that she really must have.) *When father lost his job, our living expenses had to be cut to the bone.* (We spent only enough money to stay alive.)

cut to the quick *v. phr.* To hurt someone's feelings deeply.—A cliché. *The children's teasing cut Mary to the quick.* (The children were unkind and made Mary feel very unhappy.)

cut two ways See CUT BOTH WAYS.

cut up *v.* **1** *informal* To hurt the feelings of; wound.—Usually used in the passive. *John was badly cut up when Susie gave him back his ring.* (John's feelings were hurt.) **2** *slang* To act funny or rough; clown. *Joe would always cut up if there were any girls watching.* (Joe would always act the clown if he had an audience of girls.) *At the party Jim and Ron were cutting up and broke a chair.* (They were playing in a rough way and broke a chair.) Compare FOOL AROUND.

D

dab See SMACK-DAB *or* SMACK-TO DAB.

dagger See CLOAK-AND-DAGGER, LOOK DAGGERS.

daily dozen *n., informal* Gymnastic exercises; *especially,* several different exercises done daily. *The boys did their daily dozen early each morning.* (The boys did their regular exercises early every day.)

daisy See PUSH UP DAISIES.

dam See WATER OVER THE DAM.

damn See GIVE A HANG, NOT WORTH A TINKER'S DAMN.

dance See SONG AND DANCE.

dance to another tune *v. phr.* To talk or act differently, usually better because things have changed; be more polite or obedient because you are forced to do it. *Johnny refused to do his homework but punishment made him dance to another tune.* (The teacher punished him, and he did what she wanted.) Compare CHANGE ONE'S TUNE, SING A DIFFERENT TUNE.

dander See GET ONE'S BACK UP, GET ONE'S DANDER UP *or* GET ONE'S IRISH UP.

dandy See JIM-DANDY.

dangerous See A LITTLE KNOWLEDGE IS A DANGEROUS THING.

dare say *v. phr.* To think probable; suppose; believe.—Used in first person. *Mary is unhappy now but I dare say she will be laughing about this tomorrow.* (I think that Mary will be happy again tomorrow.) *There is no more ice cream on the table, but I dare say we can find some in the kitchen.* (I think there is ice cream in the kitchen.)

dark See IN THE DARK, SHOT IN THE DARK, WHISTLE IN THE DARK.

darken one's door *or* **darken the door** To appear, as in a doorway; enter someone's home or establishment.—A cliché—Used in negative imperative sentences especially with *never* and *again. If you leave this house now, never darken my door again.* (If you leave this house now, never enter it again.) *After a son shamed his father by having to go to prison, the father told him never to darken his door again.* (The father told him never to enter his house again, or to stay away.)

dark horse *n., informal* A political candidate little known to the general voting public; a candidate who was not expected to run. *Every once in a while a dark horse candidate gets elected President.* (Every once in a while a candidate is elected who is relatively unknown.)

dark of the moon *n. phr., literary* A time when the moon is not shining or cannot be seen. *It was the dark of the moon when the scouts reached camp, and they had to use flashlights to find their tents.* (It was so dark without any moonlight that the scouts had to use flashlights to find their tents.) Contrast FULL OF THE MOON.

dash cold water on See THROW COLD WATER ON.

dash light *n.* A light on the front inside of a car or vehicle. *Henry stopped the car and turned on the dash lights to read the road map.* (Henry put on a light near the steering wheel.)

dash off *v.* To make, do, or finish quickly; especially, to draw, paint, or write hurriedly. *Ann took out her drawing pad and pencil and dashed off a sketch of the Indians.* (Ann drew a picture of the Indians quickly.) *John can dash off several letters while Mary writes only one.* (John can write two or three letters while Mary is writing one.) *Charles had forgotten to write his English report and dashed it off just before class.* (Charles wrote it hurriedly in a few minutes.)

date See DOUBLE-DATE, TO DATE.

dawn on *v.* To become clear to. *It dawned on Fred that he would fail the course if he did not study harder.* (Fred began to understand that he must study harder.)

day See ALL IN A DAY'S WORK, CALL IT A DAY, CARRY THE DAY, EVERY DOG HAS HIS DAY, FATHER'S DAY, FOREVER AND A DAY, GOOD DAY, MAKE A DAY OF IT, NAME DAY, NIGHT AND DAY, ONE OF THESE DAYS, *or* SOME OF THESE DAYS, PASS THE TIME OF DAY, RAINY DAY, SAVE THE DAY, SEE BETTER DAYS, THAT'LL BE THE DAY.

day and night *or* **night and day** *adv.* **1** For days without stopping; continually. Syn. AROUND THE CLOCK. *Some filling stations on great highways are open day and night 365 days a year.* (Some filling stations never close.) *The three men took turns driving the truck, and they drove night and day for three days.* (They drove for three days without stopping to sleep.) **2** Every day and every evening. *The girl knitted day and night to finish the sweater before her mother's birthday.* (The girl worked every day and every evening.)

day in and day out *or* **day in, day out** *adv. phr.* Regularly; consistently; all the time; always. *He plays good tennis day in and day out.* (He always plays good tennis.)—Also used with several other time words in place of *day: week, month, year. Every summer, year in, year out, the ice cream man comes back to the park.* (The ice cream man comes back every summer to sell ice cream.)

day in court *n. phr.* A chance to be heard; an impartial hearing; a chance to explain what one has done. *The letters from the faculty members to the dean gave Professor Smith his day in court.* (The faculty members wrote to the dean explaining Professor Smith's side of the story.)

daylight See SCARE OUT OF ONE'S WITS *or* SCARE THE DAYLIGHTS OUT OF, SEE DAYLIGHT.

daylight saving time *also* **daylight saving** *or* **daylight time** *or* **fast time** *n.* A way of keeping time in summer that is one or two hours ahead of standard time.—Abbreviation DST. *Many places in the United States keep their clocks on daylight saving time in the summer; in this way people get up earlier and have more free time in the afternoon and evening while it is still daylight.* (People in many places agree to set their clocks ahead, to have more free time while it is still daylight.) *Father said that next week it will get dark later because we will change to daylight saving time.* (Darkness will come an hour later because the clocks are an hour later than usual.) *We go off daylight saving in the fall.* (The clocks are put back to the usual time in the fall.) Compare CENTRAL TIME. Contrast STANDARD TIME.

days are numbered (Someone or something) does not have long to live or stay.—A cliché. *The days of the old school building are numbered.* (The old building will soon be torn down.) *When a man becomes ninety years old, his days are numbered.* (He will not live many more years.)

dazzle See RAZZLE-DAZZLE.

dead See CATCH DEAD, DROP DEAD, STONE-DEAD.

dead ahead *adv., informal* Exactly in front; before. *The school is dead ahead about two miles from here.* (The school is straight on, in the direction you are going, from here.) *Father was driving in a fog, and suddenly he saw another car dead ahead of him.* (He saw another car very close in front of him.)

deadbeat *n., slang* A person who never pays his debts and who has a way of getting things free that others have to pay for. *You'll never collect from Joe—he's a deadbeat.* (Joe will never pay you, that's the way he is.)

dead broke See STONE-BROKE.

dead center *n.* The exact middle. *The treasure was buried in the dead center of the island.* (The treasure was buried exactly in the middle of the island.) Often used like an adverb. *The arrow hit the circle dead center.* (The arrow hit the exact middle of the circle.)

dead duck *n., slang* A person or thing in a hopeless situation or condition; one to whom something bad is sure to happen. *When the pianist broke her arm, she was a dead duck.* (She couldn't perform her recital.)

deadhead *n., slang* An excessively dull or boring person. *You'll never get John to tell a joke—he's a deadhead.* (He is unable to function in a witty manner.)

dead on one's feet *adv. phr., informal* Very tired but still standing or walking; too tired to do more; exhausted. *Jimmy never leaves a job unfinished. He continues to work even when he's dead on his feet.* (Jimmy keeps on working though he is very tired.) *After the soldiers march all night, they are dead on their feet.* (They are very tired and can go no farther.) Compare DEAD TIRED, WEAR OUT 2.

deadpan *adj., adv., slang* With an expressionless or emotionless face; without betraying any hint of emotion. *She received the news of her husband's death deadpan.* (She betrayed no emotion when she received the news of his death.)

dead pedal *n., slang, citizen's band radio jargon* A slow moving vehicle. *Better pass that eighteen wheeler, Jack; it's a dead pedal.* (We had better pass that truck and trailer, it's too slow.)

dead tired *adj. phr., informal* Very tired; exhausted; worn out. *She was dead tired at the end of the day's work.* (She had no energy left at the end of the day's work.) Compare DEAD ON ONE'S FEET.

dead to rights *adv. phr., informal* Without a chance of escaping blame; proven wrong. *Mother had Bob dead to rights, because she caught him with his hand in the cooky jar.* (Bob could not say that he had not been taking cookies without permission.) *The police caught the man dead to rights.* (The police saw him doing wrong and he could not say he had not done it.)

dead to the world *adj. phr., informal* **1** Fast asleep.—A cliché. *Tim went to bed very late and was still dead to the world at 10 o'clock this morning.* (Tim was still fast asleep.) **2** As if dead; unconscious. *Tom was hit on the head by a baseball and was dead to the world for two hours.* (Tom was knocked unconscious by the baseball.)

deaf See TURN A DEAF EAR TO.

deal See GOOD DEAL or GREAT DEAL, NEW DEAL, NO DEAL, THINK A GREAT DEAL OF, WHEEL AND DEAL.

dealer See WHEELER-DEALER at WHEEL AND DEAL.

dear See FOR DEAR LIFE.

dear me *interj.* —Used to show surprise, fear, or some other strong feeling. *Dear me! My purse is lost; what shall I do now?* (The lady is unhappy over the loss of her purse.)

death See AT DEATH'S DOOR, BETWEEN LIFE AND DEATH, CATCH ONE'S DEATH OF or TAKE ONE'S DEATH OF, SIGN ONE'S OWN DEATH WARRANT, TO DEATH.

death knell *n. formal* **1** The ringing of a bell at a death or funeral. *The people mourned at the death knell of their friend.* (They were sad when they heard the bell ringing to honor him when he died.) **2** *literary* Something which shows a future failure. *Bill's poor grade on his final examination sounded the death knell of his hope to be a doctor.* (His failure in examinations meant he could not become a doctor.) *His sudden deafness was the death knell of his hope to become President.* (When he lost his hearing, he knew he could never be President.)

death on *adj. phr., informal* **1** Very successful in meeting or dealing with. *Joe is death on fast balls. He usually knocks them out of* *the park.* (Joe is very good at hitting fast balls.) **2** Disliking or strongly against; very strict about. *The new teacher is death on students who come late to class.* (The new teacher is hard on students who come late.) *The twins' grandmother is death on smoking.* (She is very much against smoking.)

deck See HIT THE DECK, ON DECK.

decked out *adj. phr., informal* Dressed in fancy clothes; specially decorated for some festive occasion. *The school band was decked out in bright red uniforms with brass buttons.* (They wore fancy uniforms.) *Main Street was decked with flags for the Fourth of July.* (Main Street was adorned with flags for Independence Day.)

declare See I DECLARE.

deep See BETWEEN THE DEVIL AND THE DEEP BLUE SEA, GO OFF THE DEEP END, IN DEEP, KNEE-DEEP.

deep-six *v., slang* To throw away; dispose of. *As the police boat came near, the drug smugglers deep-sixed their cargo.* (They threw the illegal drugs out of their boat.) (An expression originally used by sailors, suggesting throwing something into water six fathoms deep.)

deep water *n.* Serious trouble or difficulty. —A trite expression. *When Dad tried to take Mom's place for a day, he found himself in deep water.* (He found the housework and children too much for him to manage.)

defense See ZONE DEFENSE.

defiance See IN DEFIANCE OF.

degree See TO A DEGREE, TO THE NTH DEGREE.

deliver the goods *v. phr.* **1** To carry things and give them to the person who wants them. *Lee delivered the goods to the right house.* (He carried them to the right person.) **2** *slang* To succeed in doing well what is expected. *The new pitcher delivered the goods by striking out 20 men in his first game.* (He pitched very well and won his game.) *This power saw surely delivers the goods.* (It works very satisfactorily.) Compare BRING HOME THE BACON.

delta wave *n., informal, semi-technical* A brain wave 1-3 cycles per second, associated with very deep sleep. *Good night, honey, I'm off to produce some delta waves.* (I am turning in for the night to get some sleep.) Compare CATCH SOME Z'S, HIT THE HAY *or* HIT THE SACK.

demand See IN DEMAND.

dent See MAKE A DENT IN.

deposit See ON DEPOSIT.

depth See BEYOND ONE'S DEPTH.

desk clerk See ROOM CLERK.

detective See HOUSE DETECTIVE.

devil See BETWEEN THE DEVIL AND THE DEEP BLUE SEA, FULL OF THE OLD NICK *or* FULL OF THE DEVIL, GIVE THE DEVIL HIS DUE, GO TO THE DEVIL, PLAY THE DEVIL WITH, RAISE THE DEVIL, SPEAK OF THE DEVIL AND HE APPEARS.

devil-may-care *adj.* Not caring what happens; unworried. *Johnny has a devil-may-care*

feeling about his school work. (Johnny doesn't care about how well he does in school.) *Alfred was a devil-may-care youth but became more serious as he grew older.* (Alfred was foolish and careless but learned to be wise and careful.)

devil of it *or* **heck of it** *n. phr.* **1** The worst or most unlucky thing about a trouble or accident; the part that is most regrettable. *Andy lost his notebook, and the devil of it was that the notebook contained all his homework for the coming week.* (He lost his notebook, and worse still, it had all his homework inside.) *When I had a flat tire, the devil of it was that my spare tire was flat too.* (I had a flat and worse—the spare tire was flat too.) **2** Fun from doing mischief.—Used after *for*. *The boys carried away Miss White's front gate just for the devil of it.* (The boys took Miss White's gate just because they thought that mischief would be fun; they did not take it because they hated her.)

devil to pay *n. phr.* Great trouble.—Used after *the*. *There'll be the devil to pay when the teacher finds out who broke the window.* (There will be much trouble or punishment for the person who broke the window.) *When Jim wrecked his father's car, there was the devil to pay.* (Jim was in bad trouble; his father would be very angry with him.)

dewey-eyed See MISTY-EYED.

diamond in the rough *or* **rough diamond** *n. phr.* A good person who seems rough or impolite; a person of ability who can become better with training or experience.—A cliché. *The boss looks grouchy, but he is a diamond in the rough.* (The boss is better-natured than he looks.) *John looks awkward for a ball player, but he is a rough diamond.* (John has the ability to become a very good ball player.)

dibs See TO HAVE DIBS ON *or* TO PUT DIBS ON.

dice See NO DEAL *or* NO DICE.

Dick See TOM, DICK AND HARRY.

die See CROSS ONE'S HEART *or* CROSS ONE'S HEART AND HOPE TO DIE, DO-OR-DIE, NEVER SAY DIE.

die away *or* **die down** *v.* To come slowly to an end; grow slowly less or weaker. *The wind died down.* (The wind stopped blowing.) *The music died away.* (The music slowly came to an end.) *He waited until the excitement had died down.* (He waited until they were no longer excited.) *His mother's anger died away.* (Her anger lessened and was gone.)

die in one's boots *or* **die with one's boots on** *v. phr., informal* To be killed or hanged rather than die in bed.—A hackneyed phrase. *The badmen of the Old West usually died in their boots.* (They were often killed by other outlaws or by law officers.) *The robber said he wanted to die with his boots on.* (He did not want to get sick and die in bed, but to be killed in a gun fight.)

die off *v.* To die one at a time. *The flowers*

are dying off because there has been no rain. (When no rain falls to bring water, flowers and plants die one after the other.)

die on the vine *or* **wither on the vine** *v. phr.* To fail or collapse in the planning stages.—A cliché. *The program for rebuilding the city died on the vine.* (The program was partly planned but never done.)

die out *v.* To die or disappear slowly until all gone *This kind of bird is dying out.* (The birds of this kind are dying, and someday all will be dead; there will be none of this kind.) *If you pour salt water on grass, it dies out.* (Salt water slowly kills grass.) *The American colonists started colleges so that learning would not die out.* (The colonists knew that the young people must be educated or someday there would be no educated people left.)

difference See MAKE A DIFFERENCE, SPLIT THE DIFFERENCE.

different See SING A DIFFERENT TUNE *or* WHISTLE A DIFFERENT TUNE.

dig down *v., slang* To spend your own money. *The school let the club use the bus and driver free for their trip, but they had to dig down to pay for gas and meals.* (The bus was free but the club members had to pay their own money for gas and meals.) *"So you broke Mrs. Brown's window?" Tom's father said, "You'll have to dig down and pay for it."* (Tom's father said Tom would have to use his own money to pay for the window he broke.)

dig in *v., informal* **1** To dig ditches for protection against an enemy attack. *The soldiers dug in and waited for the enemy to come.* (The soldiers dug ditches and hid in them for protection.) **2a** To go seriously to work; work hard. *John dug in and finished his homework very quickly.* (John began to work hard.) **2b** To begin eating. *Mother set the food on the table and told the children to dig in.* (She told them to start eating.)

dig out *v.* **1** To find by searching; bring out (something) that was put away. *Jack dug his sled out of the cellar.* (He brought the sled from where it was stored away.) *The newspaper printed an old story dug out of their records.* (The news men searched their records for the story.) Compare DIG UP. **2** *informal* To escape.—Usually used with *of.* Often used in the phrase *dig oneself out of a hole. The pitcher dug himself out of a hole by striking the batter out.* (He got out of difficulty.)

dig up *v., informal* To find or get (something) with some effort. *Sue dug up some useful material for her English composition.* (Sue found this information in books and magazine articles.) *Jim asked each boy to dig up twenty-five cents to pay for the hot dogs and soda.* (Jim asked each boy to get twenty-five cents somehow.) Compare DIG OUT.

dilemma See HORNS OF A DILEMMA.

dim See TAKE A DIM VIEW OF.

dime a dozen *adj. phr., informal* Easy to get and so of little value; being an everyday thing because there are many of them; common.—A cliché. *Mr. Jones gives A's to only one or two students, but in Mr. Smith's class, A's are a dime a dozen.* (Mr. Jones gives few A's and they are a special honor; but Mr. Smith gives many A's, and they are an everyday grade.)

dime store *or* **five-and-dime** *or* **five-and-ten** *n. phr.* A store that sells things that cost little. *Charles bought a pencil at the five-and-dime.* (He bought the pencil at the store where he could buy it cheap.)

dint See BY DINT OF.

dirt See EAT DIRT, HIT THE DIRT, PAY DIRT.

dirty See AIR ONE'S DIRTY LINEN IN PUBLIC *or* WASH ONE'S DIRTY LINEN IN PUBLIC.

dirty look *n., informal* A look that shows dislike. *Miss Parker sent Joe to the principal's office for giving her a dirty look.* (Joe's face showed anger because of something that Miss Parker had done or said.)

dirty one's hands *or* **soil one's hands** *v. phr.* To lower or hurt one's character or good name; do a bad or shameful thing *The teacher warned the children not to dirty their hands by cheating in the examination.* (The teacher told the children not to cheat in the examination because it would give them a bad name.) *I would not soil my hands by going with bad people and doing bad things.* (I would not hurt my good name by being bad.)

discretion See THROW CAUTION TO THE WINDS *also* THROW DISCRETION TO THE WINDS.

discretion is the better part of valor *literary* When you are in danger or trouble, good sense helps more than foolish risks; it is better to be careful than to be foolishly brave.—A proverb. *When you are riding a bicycle, discretion is the better part of valor.* (It is better for you to be careful than to take foolish chances on your bicycle.)

dish See COVERED-DISH SUPPER.

dish of tea See CUP OF TEA.

dish out *v.* **1** To serve (food) from a large bowl or plate. *Ann's mother asked her to dish out the beans.* (Mother asked Ann to take beans from the serving bowl and put some on each person's plate.) **2** *informal* To give in large quantities. *That teacher dished out so much homework that her pupils complained to their parents.* (The teacher gave the students much homework.) **3** *slang* To scold; treat or criticize roughly. *Jim likes to dish it out, but he hates to take it.* (Jim likes to scold or criticize other people, but he does not like to have other people scold him.) Compare HAND OUT.

dish the dirt *v. phr., slang* To gossip, to spread rumors about others. *Stop dishing the dirt, Sally, it's really quite unbecoming!* (Stop gossiping, the role doesn't fit you.)

dispose of *v.* **1** To throw away; give away,

or sell; get rid of. *John's father wants to dispose of their old house and buy a new one.* (John's father wants to sell the old house.) *Jim's mother asked him to dispose of the garbage.* (She asked him to throw out the garbage.) **2** To finish with; settle; complete. *The boys were hungry, and quickly disposed of their dinner.* (They quickly finished their dinner.) *The committee soon disposed of all its business.* (The committee soon decided what to do about its business.) **3** To destroy or defeat. *The champion disposed of the other fighter by knocking him out in the second round.* (The champion defeated the other fighter.) *Our planes disposed of two enemy planes.* (Our planes destroyed two enemy planes.)

dispute See IN DISPUTE.

distance See KEEP AT A DISTANCE, KEEP ONE'S DISTANCE.

ditch See LAST DITCH.

dive See GO INTO A TAIL SPIN *or* GO INTO A NOSE DIVE.

do See HAVE DONE, HAVE DONE WITH, HAVE TO DO WITH, LET GEORGE DO IT, LET ONE'S RIGHT HAND KNOW WHAT ONE'S LEFT HAND IS DOING, LET'S DON'T, MAKE DO, WELL-TO-DO, WHAT'S UP *or* WHAT'S DOING.

do a double take *v. phr., informal* To look again in surprise; suddenly understand what is seen or said. *John did a double take when he saw Bill in girls' clothes.* (He was surprised and looked again at Bill.) *When Evvie said she was quitting school, I did a double take.* (I did not understand at first but suddenly I caught her meaning.)

do a job on *v. phr., slang* To damage badly; do harm to; make ugly or useless. *The baby did a job on Mary's book.* (The baby tore the pages and chewed on the cover of Mary's book.) *Jane cut her hair and really did a job on herself.* (Jane cut her own hair and made it look very bad.)

Doakes See JOE DOAKES.

do away with *v.* **1** To put an end to; stop. *The teachers want to do away with cheating in their school.* (The teachers want the cheating to stop.) *The city has decided to do away with overhead wires.* (The city has decided to put all the wires underground; there will be no overhead wires.) Compare RID OF. **2** To kill; murder. *The robbers did away with their victims.* (The robbers killed their victims.)

do by *v.* To deal with; treat.—Used with a qualifying adverb between *do* and *by*. *Andy's employer always does very well by him.* (The man Andy works for acts kindly towards him.

do credit *or* **do credit to** *also* (*informal*) **do proud** To add to or improve the reputation, good name, honor, or esteem of; show (you) deserve praise. *Your neat appearance does you credit.* (Your neat appearance adds to your good name.) *Mary's painting would do credit to a real artist.* (Mary's painting is so good that a real artist could be proud of it.)

doctor See JUST WHAT THE DOCTOR ORDERED.

do duty for *v. phr.* To substitute for; act in place of. *The bench often does duty for a table.* (The bench is often used as a table.)

Doe See JOHN DOE.

do for *v., informal* To cause the death or ruin of; cause to fail.—Used usually in the form *done for*. *The poor fellow is done for and will die before morning.* (He has had such a serious accident that he must die soon.) *Andy's employer always does very well by him.* (The man Andy works for acts kindly towards him.) *If Jim fails that test, he is done for.* (If Jim fails that test, he cannot pass his grade.)

dog See EVERY DOG HAS HIS DAY, GO TO THE DOGS, HOT DOG, LEAD A DOG'S LIFE, LET SLEEPING DOGS LIE, RAIN CATS AND DOGS.

dog-eat-dog[1] *n.* A way of living in which every person tries to get what he wants for himself no matter how badly or cruelly he must treat others to get it; readines to do anything to get what you want.—A cliché. *In some early frontier towns it was dog-eat-dog.* (Everyone was tough to everyone else in order to get what he wanted for himself.)

dog-eat-dog[2] *adj.* Ready or willing to fight and hurt others to get what you want. *During the California gold rush, men had a dog-eat-dog life.* (They had a life in which every man tries to get what he wants for himself without thinking of other people.)

doghouse See IN THE DOGHOUSE.

dog's age *or* **coon's age** *n., informal* A very long time.—A cliché. Usually used after *for* or *in* with a negative. *Charlie Brown! I haven't seen you for a coon's age.* (I have not seen you for a long time.) *Father hasn't had a night out with the boys in a dog's age.* (It has been a long time since Father had a night out with the boys.) *I waited for him for a dog's age, but he didn't come.* (I waited a long time, but he didn't come.) Syn. MONTH OF SUNDAYS.

do in *v., slang* **1** To ruin; destroy. *Mr. Smith's business was done in by a fire that burned down his store.* (Mr. Smith had to go out of business because of the fire.) **2a** To kill; murder. *The poor man was done in by two gangsters who ran away after the crime.* (The man was killed by two gangsters.) **2b** To make tired; exhaust. *The boys were done in after their long hike.* (The long hike made the boys very tired.) Syn. WEAR OUT **2**. **3** To cheat; swindle. *Mr. Jones was done in by two men who claimed to be collecting money for orphans and widows.* (Mr. Jones gave money to two swindlers who were not what they claimed to be. The men fooled him and took his money.)

doing See NOTHING DOING.

do justice to *v. phr.* **1** To do (something) as well as you should; do properly. *Barbara had so many things to do that she could not do justice to her lessons.* (Barbara tried to do too much, and did not do her lessons well.) *The newspaper man did not do justice to the* *story*. (He did not write the story as well as he might have.) **2** To eat or drink with enthusiasm or enjoyment. *The boy did justice to the meal*. (He ate as though he really enjoyed it.)

dollar See BET ONE'S BOTTOM DOLLAR *at* BET ONE'S BOOTS, FEEL LIKE A MILLION *or* FEEL LIKE A MILLION DOLLARS, LOOK LIKE A MILLION DOLLARS.

doll up *v., slang* **1** To dress in fine or fancy clothes. *The girls dolled up for the big school dance of the year*. (They put on their best clothes for the dance.) *The girls were all dolled up for the Christmas party*. (They dressed up nicely.) **2** To make more pretty or attractive. *The classrooms were all dolled up with Christmas decorations*. (The classrooms were decorated for Christmas.) Compare DECKED OUT.

done to a turn See TO A T *or* TO A TURN.

don't cross your bridges until you come to them See CROSS A BRIDGE BEFORE ONE COMES TO IT.

don't cry before you're hurt See CRY BEFORE ONE IS HURT.

don't let's See LET'S DON'T.

don't look a gift horse in the mouth See LOOK A GIFT HORSE IN THE MOUTH.

do one good *or* **do one's heart good** *v. phr.* To give satisfaction; please; gratify. *It does my heart good to see those children play*. (Seeing the children play makes me happy.)

do one's thing *or* **do one's own thing** *v. phr., informal* **1** To do what one does well and actually enjoys doing. *Two thousand fans paid $15 each to hear the rock group do their thing*. (They were paying a high sum to hear the musicians perform.) **2** To follow one's bent; for example, to be engaged in left-wing politics, some sort of meditation, or use of drugs (particularly in the sixties). *The hippies were doing their own thing when the cops came and busted them*. (They were engaged in some apparently peaceful but actually illegal activity, so they got arrested.) **3** To be engaged in an unusual activity that strikes others as odd. *Leave Max alone, he's just doing his own thing when he's standing on his head*. (Standing on his head is Max's way of relaxation; leave him alone.)

door See AT DEATH'S DOOR, AT ONE'S DOOR, CLOSED-DOOR, CLOSE ITS DOORS, CLOSE THE DOOR *or* BAR THE DOOR *or* SHUT THE DOOR, DARKEN ONE'S DOOR, *or* DARKEN THE DOOR, FOOT IN THE DOOR, KEEP THE WOLF FROM THE DOOR, LAY AT ONE'S DOOR, LOCK THE BARN DOOR AFTER THE HORSE IS STOLEN, NEXT DOOR, OPEN ITS DOORS, OPEN THE DOOR, SHOW THE DOOR, SLAM THE DOOR IN ONE'S FACE *at* IN ONE'S FACE².

do-or-die *adj.* Strongly decided; very eager and determined. *With a real do-or-die spirit, the team scored two touchdowns in the last five minutes of the game*. (The team tried very hard to win the game.) *The other army was larger but our men showed a do-or-die determination and won the battle*. (Our soldiers fought stubbornly and did not give up before they had won.)

doorstep See AT ONE'S DOOR *or* AT ONE'S DOORSTEP.

do out of *v., informal* To cause to lose by trickery or cheating. *The clerk in the store did me out of $2.00 by overcharging me*. (The clerk cheated me out of $2.00 by charging me more than the article really cost.)

dope out *v., slang* To think of something that explains. *The detectives tried to dope out why the man was murdered*. (The detectives tried to discover by putting the facts together in their minds why the man had been killed.) Syn. FIGURE OUT.

do proud See DO CREDIT.

dose of one's own medicine *or* **taste of one's own medicine** *n. phr.* Being treated in the same way you treat others; something bad done to you as you have done bad to other people. *Jim was always playing tricks on other boys. Finally they decided to give him a dose of his own medicine*. (They decided to play a trick on Jim.)

dot See ON THE DOT *also* ON THE BUTTON.

do tell *interj., informal* —An inelegant expression used to show that you are a little surprised by what you hear. *"You say George is going to get married after all these years? Do tell! said Mrs. Green*. (Mrs. Green was a little surprised at the news.) Syn. YOU DON'T SAY.

do the business *v. phr., informal* To do what is needed or wanted; get the job done; take proper action. *The boys had trouble in rolling the stone, but four of them did the business*. (Four of the boys did what they wanted to do and rolled the stone.) *When the little boy cut his finger a bandage did the business*. (Putting a bandage on the cut finger was the right thing to do.)

do the honors *v. phr.* To act as host or hostess (as in introducing guests, carving, or paying other attentions to guests.)—A trite phrase. *The president of the club will do the honors at the banquet*. (The club president will be the host at the dinner; he will introduce speakers and be sure the guests enjoy themselves.)

do the trick *v. phr., informal* To bring success in doing something; have a desired result. *Jim was not passing in English, but he studied harder and that did the trick*. (Jim studied harder and succeeded in improving.) *The car wheels slipped on the ice, so Tom put sand under them, which did the trick*. (The sand kept the wheels from slipping and the car went on.) Compare TURN THE TRICK.

double back *v.* **1** To turn back on one's way or course. *The escaped prisoner doubled back on his tracks*. (He went back the same way that he came.) **2** To fold over, usually in the middle. *The teacher told Johnny to double back the sheet of paper and tear it in half.* (The teacher told Johnny to fold the sheet of paper in the middle.)

double check *n.* A careful second check to be sure that something is right; a careful look for errors. *The policeman made a double check on the doors in the shopping area.* (He tried them all carefully to be sure that they were locked.)

double-check *v.* 1 To do a double check on; look at again very carefully. *When the last typing of his book was finished, the author double-checked it.* (He read it very carefully again to be sure that it had no mistakes.) 2 To make a double check; look carefully at something. *The proofreader double-checks against errors.* (The proofreader looks again very carefully to be sure there are no mistakes.)

double-cross *v.* To promise one thing and deliver another; to deceive. *The lawyer double-crossed the inventor by manufacturing the gadget instead of fulfilling his promise to arrange a patent for his client.* (The lawyer betrayed his client's trust.) Compare SELL DOWN THE RIVER, TWO-TIME.

double date *n., informal* A date on which two couples go together. *John and Nancy went with Mary and Bill on a double date.* (All four went out on a date together.)

double-date *v., informal* To go on a double date; date with another couple. *John and Nancy and Mary and Bill double-date.* (They go out on dates together.)

double duty *n.* Two uses or jobs; two purposes or duties. *Matthew does double duty. He's the janitor in the morning and gardener in the afternoon.* (He does the two jobs of janitor and gardener.) *Our new washer does double duty; it washes the clothes and also dries them.* (The machine is both a washer and a drier.)

double-header *n.* Two games or contests played one right after the other, between the same two teams or two different pairs of teams. *The Yankees and Senators played a double-header Sunday afternoon.* (The Yankees and Senators played two successive games Sunday afternoon.) *We went to a basketball double-header at Madison Square Garden and saw Seton Hall play St. Johns and N.Y.U. play Notre Dame.* (We saw two basketball games between two pairs of teams.)

double in brass *v. phr., informal* To do two different things; be useful for two purposes. —An overused expression. *This heavy weight doubles in brass as a doorstop and as a nutcracker.* (It is used to hold a door open and also to crack nuts.) *He doubles in brass as a porter and doorman.* (He carries things and attends to the door.)

double nickel *adv., slang, citizen's band radio jargon* The nationally enforced speed limit on some highways—55 MPH. *We'd better go double nickel on this stretch, partner; there's a bear in the air.* (Keep the 55 MPH speed limit as there is a police helicopter watching us.)

double-park *v.* To park a car beside another car which is at the curb. *Jimmy's father double-parked his car and the police gave him a ticket.* (Jimmy's father left his car in the street beside a parked car and the police gave him a ticket.) *If you double-park, you block other cars from passing.* (If you park beside another car it makes trouble for other drivers.)

double play *n.* A play in baseball in which two players are put out. *The Tigers had a man on first base with one out, but the next batter hit into a double play.* (The Tiger batter hit the ball and the other team got two outs by getting the ball to second base before the runner and then throwing it to first base before the batter got there.)

double reverse *n.* A football play that changes direction twice. *The team scored its first touchdown on a double reverse.* (The team scored its first touchdown on a play that started to the left, then went to the right, then back to the left again.)

double-talk *n.* 1 Something said that is worded, either on purpose or by accident, so that it may be understood in two or more different ways. *The politician avoided the question with double talk.* (He escaped giving a real answer by saying something that could be understood two different ways.) 2 Something said that does not make sense; mixed up talk or writing; nonsense. *The man's explanation of the new tax bill was just a lot of double-talk.* (It was mixed up; it meant nothing.)

double up *v.* 1 To bend far over forward. *Jim was hit by the baseball and doubled up with pain.* (He fell down holding his stomach, with his knees up to his chest.) 2 To share a room, bed, or home with another. *When relatives came for a visit, Ann had to double up with her sister.* (Ann had to give up her room and share her sister's room.)

doubt See GIVE THE BENEFIT OF THE DOUBT, NO DOUBT.

do up *v.* 1a To clean and prepare for use or wear; launder. *Ann asked her mother to do up her dress.* (Ann asked her mother to clean and iron the dress.) 1b To put in order; straighten up; clean. *At camp the girls have to do up their own cabins.* (The girls clean their own cabins.) 2 To tie up or wrap. *Joan asked the clerk to do up her purchases.* (Joan asked the clerk to wrap the things she had bought.) 3a To set and fasten (hair) in place. *Grace helped her sister to do up her hair.* (Grace helped her sister make her hair look pretty.) Compare PUT UP. 3b *informal* To dress or clothe. *Suzie was done up in her fine new skirt and blouse.* (Suzie was prettily dressed.)

do up brown *v. phr., slang* To do in a thorough or complete way.—An overworked phrase. *When Jim does a job, he does it up* *brown.* (Jim does what he has to do in a very satisfactory way.)

do with *v.* **1** To find enough for one's needs; manage.—Usually follows *can. Some children can do with very little spending money.* (Some children can buy what they need for only a little money.) Compare GET ALONG, MAKE-DO. **2** To make use of; find useful or helpful. —Follows *can* or *could. After a hard day's work, a man can do with a good, hot meal.* (A man needs or wants a good hot meal.) *After cleaning out the basement, the boy could do with a bath.* (He needs a bath.)

do without *or* **go without** *v.* **1** To live or work without (something you want); manage without. *Ann said that she likes candy, but can do without it.* (Ann likes candy, but it does not make her unhappy to be without it.) *We had to go without hot food because the stove was broken.* (We lived without having hot food.) **2** To live or work without something you want; manage. *If George cannot earn money for a bicycle, he will have to do without.* (George must live without a bicycle.) Compare GET ALONG, GET BY.

down-at-heel *or* **down-at-the-heel** *or* **down-at-the-heels** *adj.* Poorly kept up or dressed; shabby; not neat; sloppy. *John is always down-at-the-heels, but his sister is always very neat.* (John always is poorly or carelessly dressed.) *Old houses sometimes look down-at-the-heel.* (They sometimes are unpainted and need repairs.)

down east *or* **Down East** *n.* The northeast coastal part of the United States and part of Canada; *especially:* the coastal parts of Maine. *Many people in Boston like to go down east for their summer vacation.* (Many Boston people like to visit the coast of Maine during their summer vacation.)

down in the dumps *or* **down in the mouth** *adj. phr., informal* Sad or discouraged; gloomy; dejected.—A cliché. *The boys were certainly down in the dumps when they heard that their team had lost.* (The boys felt very unhappy because their team lost the game.)

down in the mouth See DOWN IN THE DUMPS.

down on *adj. phr., informal* Having a grudge against; angry at. *John is down on his teacher because she gave him a low grade.* (John is angry at his teacher.)

down one's alley *or* **up one's alley** *adj. phr., slang* Suited to your tastes and abilities; what you like or like to do. *Baseball is right down Jim's alley.* (Jim likes to play baseball and does well at it.) Compare CUP OF TEA.

down one's neck See BREATHE DOWN ONE'S NECK.

down one's nose See LOOK DOWN ONE'S NOSE AT.

down one's throat See JUMP DOWN ONE'S THROAT, SHOVE DOWN ONE'S THROAT *or* RAM DOWN ONE'S THROAT.

down on one's luck *adj., informal* Having bad luck; having much trouble; not successful in life. *Harry asked me to lend him ten dol-*

lars, because he was down on his luck. (He was having a hard time.) *The teacher is easy on Jane because Jane has been down on her luck lately.* (She has had several accidents and losses.) Compare HARD ROW TO HOE, HARD SLEDDING, ON ONE'S UPPERS.

down the drain *adj. or adv. phr., informal* Wasted; lost. *It is money down the drain if you spend it all on candy.* (The money is wasted because it is all eaten up.) *Our plans to go swimming went down the drain when it rained.* (The rain spoiled our plans.) Compare GO BY THE BOARD.

down the line *adv. phr., informal* **1** Down the road or street; straight ahead. *The church is down the line a few blocks.* (The church is along the street several blocks.) **2** All the way; completely; thoroughly. *Bob always follows the teacher's directions right down the line.* (Bob follows the directions completely.)

down-to-earth *adj.* Showing good sense; practical. *The committee's first plan for the party was too fancy, but the second was more down-to-earth.* (The second plan could be used.) *Mr. Jenkins never seems to know what is happening around him, but his wife is friendly and down-to-earth.* (Mrs. Jenkins sees and likes the people and things around her.) Compare COME BACK TO EARTH.

down to the wire *adj., slang* **1** Running out of time, nearing a deadline. *Bob is down to the wire on his project.* (He is nearing the deadline for completion of his project.) **2** Being financially almost broke, being very low on cash or other funds. *We can't afford going to a restaurant tonight—we're really down to the wire!* (We cannot afford to go out, we are so low on funds.)

dozen See BY THE DOZEN, DAILY DOZEN, DIME A DOZEN, SIX OF ONE AND HALF-A-DOZEN OF THE OTHER.

drag in *v.* To insist on bringing (another subject) into a discussion; begin talking about (something different.) *No matter what we talk about, Jim drags in politics.* (No matter what we talk about, Jim brings politics into the discussion.) *Whenever anyone mentions travel, Grace has to drag in the trip to Mexico she took ten years ago.* (Whenever anyone speaks about travel, Grace insists on talking about her trip to Mexico.)

drag on *or* **drag out** *v.* **1** To pass very slowly. *The cold winter months dragged on until we thought spring would never come.* (The cold winter months passed so slowly that we thought spring would never come.) **2** To prolong; make longer. *The meeting would have been over quickly if the members had not dragged out the argument about dues.* (The meeting would have been shorter if the members had not made the argument about longer dues.)

drag oneself up by one's boot straps See PULL ONESELF UP BY THE BOOT STRAPS.

drag one's feet *or* **drag one's heels** *v. phr.*
To act slowly or reluctantly. *The children
wanted to watch television, and dragged their
feet when their mother told them to go to bed.*
(The children wanted to watch television, and
acted very slowly when their mother told them
to go to bed.) *The city employees said the
mayor had promised to raise their pay, but
was now dragging his feet.* (They said he was
too slow about keeping his promises.)

drag out See DRAG ON.

drag race *n., slang* An automobile race in
which the drivers try to cover a certain distance (usually one quarter mile) in the shortest possible time. *Drag races are often held on
airport landing strips.* (Races in which the
drivers try to cover some distance in the shortest possible time are often held on airport
landing strips.) *Holding drag races is a good
way to stop teenage hot rod racing on public
highways.* (Holding races in which the drivers
race with time is a good way to stop teenage
hot rod racing on public highways.) Compare
DRAG STRIP.

drag strip *n., slang* A place where drag races
are held. *Before the race Paul loaded his racer
onto the trailer to take it out of town to the
drag strip for the race.* (Paul took his racer
to the place out of town where the drag races
were held.) Compare DRAG RACE.

drain See DOWN THE DRAIN.

draw See BEAT TO THE PUNCH *or* BEAT TO
THE DRAW.

draw a bead on *v. phr. informal* **1** To aim
at; sight (with a gun). *The deer bounded into
the forest before the hunters could draw a
bead on them.* (The deer ran into the forest
before the hunters could aim their guns at
them.) *John drew a bead on the elk, but
didn't have the heart to pull the trigger.* (John
sighted at the elk with his gun, but could not
bring himself to shoot it.) **2** To take (something) as an aim or goal. *"I'm drawing a bead
on the Literary Society president's office,"
said Tom.* (Tom was aiming to be elected
president of the Literary Society.) **3** To use
as a target of attack; criticize. *Whenever a politician makes a mistake, his opponents are
ready to draw a bead on him.* (His opponents
are always ready to complain and criticize
him.)

draw a blank *v. phr., informal* **1** To obtain nothing in return for an effort made or
to get a negative result. *I looked up all the
Joneses in the telephone book but I drew a
blank every time I asked for Archibald Jones.*
(I was unable to locate Archibald Jones.)
2 To fail to remember something. *I am trying to think of the name but I keep drawing
a blank.* (The name just won't come to me.)
3 To be consistently unsuccessful at doing
something. *I keep trying to pass that math
exam but each time I try it I draw a blank.*
(Each time I try it, I fail it.)

draw a line *or* **draw the line** *v. phr.* **1** To
think of as different. *The law in this country
draws a line between murder and manslaughter.* (The law in this country makes
murder and manslaughter different.) *Can you
draw the line between a lie and a fib?* (Can
you tell the difference between a lie and a fib?)
2 To set a limit to what will be done; say
something cannot be done. *We would like to
invite everybody to our party, but we have to
draw a line somewhere.* (We would like to
invite everybody, but we must set a limit
somewhere.)—Often used with *at. Mrs. Jones
draws the line at permitting the children to
play in their father's den.* (Mrs. Jones does
not let the children play in their father's study
room.) *People fighting for their freedom often
do not draw the line at murder.* (They will kill
a man if he is against them.)

draw a long breath *or* **take a long breath** *v.
phr.* To breathe deeply when getting ready
to speak or act.—A hackneyed phrase. *Father
asked who broke the window. Jim drew a
long breath and admitted that he had done it.*
(Jim breathed deeply before saying that he
had broken the window.) *The salesman took
a long breath and started his talk.* (The salesman breathed deeply and began his sales
talk.)

draw back *v.* To move back; back away;
step backward. *When the man spotted the
rattlesnake, he drew back and aimed his shotgun.* (When the man saw the rattlesnake, he
stepped backward and aimed his shotgun at
it.) *The children drew back from the dog
when it barked at them.* (The children backed
away from the dog when it barked at them.)
*When the pitcher drew back his arm to pitch
the ball, Tom ran as fast as he could to steal
second base.* (Tom waited until the pitcher
started to throw to the batter, then he ran towards second base.) *Some juice from the
grapefruit that Father was eating squirted in
his eye and he drew back in surprise.* (Father
was surprised and leaned back in his chair.)
Compare DROP BACK.

draw blood *v. phr., informal* To make
someone feel hurt or angry. *If you want to
draw blood, ask Jim about his last money-
making scheme.* (If you want to hurt Jim's
feelings, ask him about his last plan to make
money.) *Her sarcastic comments drew blood.*
(Her mean talk caused hurt and angry feelings.)

drawer See TOP-DRAWER.

draw fire *v. phr.* **1** To attract or provoke
shooting; be a target. *The general's white
horse drew the enemy's fire.* (The white horse
was a good target for the enemy.) **2** To bring
criticism or argument; make people say bad
things about you. *Having the newest car in
your group is sure to draw fire.* (Having the
newest car may cause some remarks about
whether you need it or can pay for it.)

draw in one's horns See PULL IN ONE'S HORNS.

draw out *v. phr.* **1** To take out; remove. *Johnny drew a dollar out of the bank to buy his mother a present.* (Johnny went to the bank and took a dollar out that he had put there.) *The hunter drew out his gun and shot the snake.* (He took the gun from its holder.) **2** To make (a person) talk or tell something. *Jimmy was bashful but Mrs. Wilson drew him out by asking him about baseball.* (Mrs. Wilson made Jimmy talk because he liked to talk about baseball.) **3** To make come out; bring out. *The bell of the ice-cream truck drew the children out of the houses.* (The bell brought the children out to buy ice cream or to see the truck.) *Mary was drawn out of her silence by Billy's jokes.* (Billy made Mary laugh and talk.) **4** To make longer or too long; stretch. *The Smiths drew out their vacation at the beach an extra week.* (They stayed an extra week.) *It was a long drawn out meeting because everybody tried to talk at once.* (The meeting was too long because no one would listen while others talked.) *Mary and her mother drew out their goodbyes so long at the bus station that Mary almost missed the bus.* (They didn't want to leave and Mary almost missed the bus.)

draw the line See DRAW A LINE.

draw up *v.* **1** To write (something) in its correct form; put in writing. *The rich man had his lawyers draw up his will so that each of his children would receive part of his money when he died.* (The lawyers wrote the man's will in the proper way.) **2** To plan or prepare; begin to write out. *The two countries drew up a peace treaty after the war ended.* (The countries agreed to plan how they would live in peace.) *Plans are being drawn up for a new school next year.* (Plans are being made ready.) Compare WRITE UP. **3** To hold yourself straight or stiffly, especially because you are proud or angry. *When we said that Mary was getting fat, she drew herself up angrily and walked out of the room.* (Mary held herself stiff and straight because she was angry.) **4** To stop or come to a stop. *The cowboy drew up his horse at the top of the hill.* (The cowboy made his horse stop at the top of the hill.) *A big black car drew up in front of the house.* (A big car stopped in front of the house.) Syn. PULL UP.

dread See BURNT CHILD DREADS THE FIRE.

dream of *v.* To think about seriously; think about with the idea of really doing; consider seriously.—A cliché; usually used with a negative. *I wouldn't dream of wearing shorts to church.* (I would never think of doing such a thing.)

dressing down *n., informal* A scolding. *The sergeant gave the soldier a good dressing down because his shoes were not shined.* (The sergeant scolded the soldier.)

dress up *v.* **1a** To put on best or special clothes. *Billy hated being dressed up and took off his best suit as soon as he got home from church.* (Billy didn't like to wear his best clothes.) **1b** To put on a costume for fun or clothes for a part in a play. *Mary was dressed up to play Cinderella in her school play.* (Mary wore a costume to look like Cinderella.) **2** To make (something) look different; make (something) seem better or more important. *A fresh coat of paint will dress up the old bicycle very much.* (The paint will make the old bicycle look newer and better.) *Tommy dressed up the story of what he did on vacation and made it seem twice as interesting as it was.* (The stories Tommy told about his vacation were not exactly true but they were interesting.)

drive See LINE DRIVE.

drive a bargain *v. phr.* **1** To buy or sell at a good price; succeed in a trade or deal. *Tom's collie is a champion; it should be easy for Tom to drive a bargain when he sells her puppies.* (It should be easy for Tom to get a good price for the puppies.) *Father drove a hard bargain with the real estate agent when we bought our new house.* (Father bought the house for a very low price.) **2** To make an agreement that is better for you than for the other person; make an agreement to your advantage. *The French drove a hard bargain in demanding that Germany pay fully for World War I damages.* (The French said firmly that Germany must pay for all the damage it did to France.)

drive a hard bargain See DRIVE A BARGAIN.

drive at *v.* To try or want to say; mean.—Used in the present participle. *John did not understand what the coach was driving at.* (John did not understand what the coach was trying to tell him.) *He had been talking for half an hour before anyone realized what he was driving at.* (No one understood what he meant until he had been explaining for half an hour.)

drive like Jehu *v. phr., informal* To drive very fast, carelessly, or recklessly.—A cliché. *When Joe is late for work, he drives like Jehu.* (When Joe is late for work, he drives very fast and recklessly.)

driver See BACKSEAT DRIVER.

drive to the wall See TO THE WALL.

drop See AT THE DROP OF A HAT, BOTTOM DROP OUT, JAW DROP or JAW DROP A MILE.

drive someone bananas or **drive someone nuts** or **drive someone ape** *v. phr., slang, informal* To excite someone to the point that he or she goes out of his or her mind; to drive someone crazy. *You're driving me bananas/nuts with that kind of talk!* (That kind of talk disorients me; it thoroughly confuses me; it drives me wild!)

drop a line *v. phr., informal* To write and mail a note or letter. *Judy's friend asked her* *to drop her a line while she was away on vacation.* (Her friend wanted Judy to write to her.) *Please drop a line to me when you get to Québec.* (Please write to me when you arrive.)

drop back *v.* To move or step backwards; retreat. *The soldiers dropped back before the enemy's attack.* (The soldiers retreated when the enemy attacked.) *The quarterback dropped back to pass the football.* (The quarterback stepped backwards to pass.) Compare DRAW BACK, FADE BACK, FALL BACK.

drop by *or* **stop by** *v.* **1** *or* **drop around** To make a short or unplanned visit; go on a call or errand; stop at someone's home. *Drop by any time you're in town.* (Pay a visit any time you come.) *My sister dropped around last night.* (My sister came on a short visit.) *Don't forget to stop by at the gas station.* (Don't forget to go to the gas station to get what is needed.) Syn. DROP IN. **2** *or* **drop into** To stop (somewhere) for a short visit or a short time. *We dropped by the club to see if Bill was there, but he wasn't.* (We stopped for a short time at the club to see if Bill was there.) *I dropped into the drugstore for some toothpaste and a magazine.* (I stopped at the drugstore to get some toothpaste and a newspaper.)

drop by the wayside See FALL BY THE WAYSIDE.

drop dead *v., slang* To go away or be quiet; stop bothering someone.—Usually used as a command. *"Drop dead!" Bill told his little sister when she kept begging to help him build his model airplane.* (Bill didn't want his little sister's help, and when she kept asking he told her to go away.) *When Sally bumped into Kate's desk and spilled ink for the fifth time, Kate told her to drop dead.* (Kate was angry and told Sally to go away and stop bothering her.) Compare BEAT IT, GET LOST.

drop in *v.* To make a short or unplanned visit; pay a call.—Often used with *on. We were just sitting down to dinner when Uncle Willie dropped in.* (Uncle Willie paid a visit at dinner time.) *The Smiths dropped in on some old friends on their vacation trip to New York.* (The Smiths visited their friends in New York, but their friends were not expecting them.) Syn. DROP BY, RUN IN 2.

drop off *v.* **1** To take (someone or something) part of the way you are going. *Joe asked Mrs. Jones to drop him off at the library on her way downtown.* (Joe asked Mrs. Jones to give him a ride to the library on her way downtown.) **2** To go to sleep. *Jimmy was thinking of his birthday party as he dropped off to sleep.* (He was thinking of his party as he went to sleep.) **3** To die. *The patient dropped off in his sleep.* (The patient died in his sleep.) **4** *or* **fall off** To become less. *Business picked up in the stores during December, but dropped off again after Christmas.* (Business became less after Christmas.) Contrast PICK UP 14.

drop out *v.* To stop attending; quit; stop; leave. *In the middle of the race, Joe got a blister on his foot and had to drop out.* (He got a blister on his foot and had to leave the race.) *Teenagers who drop out of high school have trouble finding jobs.* (Teenagers who leave high school have trouble finding jobs.)

drown one's sorrows *or* **drown one's troubles** *v. phr., informal* To drink liquor to try to forget something unhappy.—A cliché. *When his wife was killed in an auto accident, Mr. Green tried to drown his sorrows in whiskey.* (Mr. Green tried to forget his unhappiness about his wife's death by often drinking whiskey.) *When Fred lost his job and had to give up his new car, he tried to drown his troubles at the nearest beer tavern.* (When Fred had so much trouble, he tried to forget it by drinking a lot.)

drown one's troubles See DROWN ONE'S SORROWS.

drown out *v.* To make so much noise that it is impossible to hear (some other sound). *The children's shouts drowned out the music.* (The children made so much noise shouting that no one could hear the music.) *The actor's words were drowned out by applause.* (The audience made so much noise clapping that people could not hear the actor's voice.)

drum up *v.* **1** To get by trying or asking again and again; attract or encourage by continued effort. *The car dealer tried to drum up business by advertising low prices.* (The car dealer tried to get customers by advertising low prices.) **2** To invent. *I will drum up an excuse for coming to see you next week.* (I will make up an excuse for coming to see you next week.) Syn. MAKE UP 2, THINK UP.

dry See CUT AND DRIED, HIGH AND DRY.

dry behind the ears *adj. phr., informal* Experienced; knowing how to do something.—A cliché, usually used in the negative. *John had just started working for the company, and was not dry behind the ears yet.* (John was not yet experienced and did not yet know how to do the work.) Compare KNOW ONE'S WAY AROUND. Contrast WET BEHIND THE EARS.

dry up *v.* **1** To become dry. *The reservoir dried up during the four-month drought.* (The reservoir became dry during the time of no rain.) **2** To disappear or vanish as if by evaporating. *The Senator's influence dried up when he was voted out of office.* (The Senator's power disappeared when he was not elected again.) **3** *slang* To stop talking.—Often used as a command. *"Dry up!" Tony said angrily when his friend told him for the third time that he had made a mistake in his theme.* (Tony told his friend to shut up when he had repeated his criticism three times.) Syn. SHUT UP 1.

dual highway See DIVIDED HIGHWAY.

duck See DEAD DUCK, KNEE HIGH TO A GRASSHOPPER *or* KNEE HIGH TO A DUCK, LAME DUCK, LIKE WATER OFF A DUCK'S BACK.

duckling See UGLY DUCKLING.

duck soup *n., slang* **1** A task easily accomplished or one that does not require much effort. *That history test was duck soup.* (That history test was very easy to pass.) **2** A person who offers no resistance; a pushover. *How's the new history teacher?—He's duck soup.* (He is easy to handle, he offers no serious challenge.)

duddy See FUDDY-DUDDY.

due See GIVE ONE'S DUE, GIVE THE DEVIL HIS DUE, IN DUE COURSE *at* IN GOOD TIME.

due to *prep.* Because of; owing to; by reason of. *His injury was due to his careless use of the shot gun.* (He was hurt because he handled the gun carelessly.) *Joe's application to the University was not accepted due to his failing English.* (Joe was not accepted at the University because he had failed English.)

dull See ALL WORK AND NO PLAY MAKES JACK A DULL BOY.

dumb bunny *n., slang, informal* Any person who is gullible and stupid. *Jack is a regular dumb bunny.* (He is a naive person lacking in brains and common sense.)

dumps See DOWN IN THE DUMPS *or* DOWN IN THE MOUTH.

dust See BITE THE DUST, KICK UP A FUSS *or* KICK UP A DUST, WATCH ONE'S DUST.

dust off *v., informal* **1** To get ready to use again. *Four years after he graduated from school, Tom decided to dust off his algebra book.* (He decided to review algebra.) **2** To throw a baseball pitch close to. *The pitcher dusted off the other team's best hitter.* (The pitcher threw the ball close to the other team's best hitter and made him nervous and unable to hit very well.) Syn. BRUSH BACK.

Dutch See BEAT ALL *or* BEAT THE DUTCH, GO DUTCH, IN DUTCH.

dutch treat *n., informal* A meal in a restaurant or an outing at the movies, concert, or theater where each party pays his or her own way. *"I am willing to accept your invitation,"* Mary said, *"but it will have to be Dutch treat."* (She is accepting the invitation on the condition that she will pay her own way.)

duty See DO DUTY FOR, DOUBLE DUTY, HEAVY-DUTY, OFF DUTY, ON DUTY.

duty bound *adj. phr.* Forced to act by what you believe is right. *Abraham Lincoln walked miles once to return a few pennies that he had overcharged a woman because he felt duty bound to do it.* (Lincoln went out of his way to do what he felt he should do.) *John felt duty bound to report that he had broken the window.* (John felt that it would be wrong to keep it secret, so he said that he broke it.)

dwell on *or* **dwell upon** *v.* To stay on a subject; not leave something or want to leave; not stop talking or writing about. *Joe dwelt on his mistake long after the test was over.* (He thought and talked too long about his mistakes.) *Our eyes dwelled on the beautiful sunset.* (We looked at the sky and sun for a long time because we liked it.) *The principal dwelled on traffic safety in his talk.* (He paid most attention to safey in his talk.) Compare HARP ON. Contrast TOUCH ON.

E

each and every *adj. phr.* Every.—Used for emphasis. *The captain wants each and every man to be here at eight o'clock.* (The captain wants every man to be here at eight o'clock.) *The teacher must learn the name of each and every pupil.* (The teacher must learn every pupil's name.) Syn. EVERY SINGLE.

each other *or* **one another** *pron.* Each one the other; one the other. *That man and his wife love each other.* (The man loves his wife and his wife loves him.) *Bill and Mary gave one another Christmas presents last year.* (Each gave the other a present.) *All the children at the party were looking at one another trying to recognize one another in their masks and costumes.* (Each child looked at the others trying to recognize them.) *The birds fought each other over the bread.* (Every bird fought the others.)

eager beaver *n. phr., slang* A person who is always eager to work or do anything extra, perhaps to win the favor of his leader or boss. *Jack likes his teacher and works hard for her, but his classmates call him an eager beaver.* (The other pupils think he tries to please the teacher.) *The man who was promoted to be manager was an eager beaver who got to work early and left late and was always offering to do extra work.* (He worked harder than other employees.)

ear See ABOUT ONE'S EARS *or* AROUND ONE'S EARS, BELIEVE ONE'S EARS, DRY BEHIND THE EARS, FLEA IN ONE'S EAR, GIVE AN EAR TO *or* LEND AN EAR TO, GO IN ONE EAR AND OUT THE OTHER, JUG-EARED, LITTLE PITCHERS HAVE BIG EARS, MUSIC TO ONE'S EARS, PIN ONE'S EARS BACK, PLAY BY EAR, PRICK UP ONE'S EARS, ROASTING EAR, TURN A DEAF EAR, UP TO THE CHIN IN *or* UP TO THE EARS IN, WET BEHIND THE EARS.

early See BRIGHT AND EARLY.

early bird catches the worm *or* **early bird gets the worm** A person who gets up early in the morning has the best chance of succeeding; if you arrive early or are quicker, you get ahead of others.—A proverb. *When Billy's father woke him up for school he said, "The early bird catches the worm."* (Children who get to school early will be more successful than pupils who are late.) *Charles began looking for a summer job in January; he knows that the early bird gets the worm.* (Charles knew that if you get ahead of others, you have a better chance for success.) Compare FIRST COME, FIRST SERVED.

earnest See IN EARNEST.

ears burn *informal* To feel embarrassment or shame at hearing others talk about you. *Joan overheard the girls criticizing her and it made her ears burn.* (She was ashamed because they criticized her.) *Joe's ears burned when he heard his classmates praising him*

to each other. (Joe was embarrassed when he heard his classmates praise him.)

earth See COME BACK TO EARTH *or* COME DOWN TO EARTH, DOWN-TO-EARTH, IN THE WORLD *or* ON EARTH, MOVE HEAVEN AND EARTH.

ear to the ground *n. phr., informal* Attention directed to the way things are going, or seem likely to go, or to the way people feel and think. *The city manager kept an ear to the ground for a while before deciding to raise the city employees' pay.* (The mayor found out how people felt before he raised the pay of city employees.) *Reporters keep an ear to the ground so as to know as soon as possible what will happen.* (Reporters watch closely for news to write about.)

ease See AT EASE *or* AT ONE'S EASE, ILL AT EASE.

ease off *or* **ease up** *v.* To make or become less nervous; relax; work easier. *When the boss realized that John had been overworking, he eased off his load.* (The boss gave John less work.) *With success and prosperity, Mr. Smith was able to ease off.* (When success came, Mr. Smith did not work so hard.) Compare LET UP 3.

easily See BREATHE EASILY *or* BREATHE FREELY.

east See DOWN EAST *or* DOWN EAST.

easy See FREE AND EASY, GET OFF EASY, ON EASY STREET, TAKE IT EASY *or* GO EASY *or* TAKE THINGS EASY.

easy come, easy go *truncated sent, informal* Something you get quickly and easily may be lost or spent just as easily.—A cliché. *Grandfather thought Billy should have to work for the money Father gave him, saying "Easy come, easy go."* (Grandfather thought that if Billy got the money too easily, he would spend it quickly and foolishly.)

easy does it *informal* Let's do it carefully, without sudden movements and without forcing too hard or too fast; let's try to just hard enough but not too hard. *"Easy does it," said the boss as they moved the piano through the narrow doorway.* ("Let's do it slowly and carefully," the boss said.) Compare TAKE IT EASY.

easy money *n. informal* Money gained without hard work; money that requires little or no effort. *The movie rights to a successful play mean easy money to the writer of the play.* (The money from the movie rights often requires no more work.) *Young people who look for easy money are usually disappointed.* (It's hard to get money without work.)

eat See DOG-EAT-DOG, LIVE HIGH OFF THE HOG *or* EAT HIGH ON THE HOG, LOOK LIKE THE CAT THAT ATE THE CANARY.

eat away *v.* To rot, rust, or destroy. *Rust was eating away the pipe.* (Rust was destroying the pipe.) *Cancer ate away the healthy flesh.* (Cancer turned healthy flesh into diseased and unhealthy tissue.) See EAT OUT 2.

eat crow *v. phr.* To admit you are mistaken or defeated; take back a mistaken statement.

John had boasted that he would play on the first team; but when the coach did not choose him, he had to eat crow. (He had to admit that he was not good enough.) *Fred said he could beat the new man in boxing, but he lost and had to eat crow.* (He had to admit he had talked too much.) Compare BACK DOWN, EAT HUMBLE PIE, EAT ONE'S WORDS.

eat dirt *v. phr., informal* To act humble; accept another's insult or bad treatment. *Mr. Johnson was so much afraid of losing his job that he would eat dirt whenever the boss got mean.* (He would let the boss treat him badly.)

eat (live) high on the hog *or* **eat (live) high off the hog** *v. phr.* To eat or live well or elegantly. *For the first few days after the check arrived, they ate high on the hog.* (For the first few days after money came, they ate very well.) Compare IN CLOVER *or* IN THE CLOVER, ON EASY STREET.

eat humble pie *v. phr.* To be humbled; to accept insult or shame; admit your error and apologize. *Tom told a lie about George, and when he was found out, he had to eat humble pie.* (Tom had to confess that he had lied and to ask George's pardon.) *In some old stories a boy with a stepfather has to eat humble pie.* (He is dependent upon his stepfather and accepts insults from him.)

eat like a bird *v. phr.* To eat very little; have little appetitie.—An overused expression. *Mrs. Benson is on a diet and she eats like a bird.* (She eats very little.) *Alice's mother is worried about her; she eats like a bird and is very thin.* (She eats little and is too thin.) Contrast EAT LIKE A HORSE.

eat like a horse *v. phr.* To eat a lot; eat hungrily.—An overused expression. *The harvesters worked into the evening, and then came in and ate like horses.* (The harvesters put in a long day, and then came in and ate a great deal as they were very hungry.) Contrast EAT LIKE A BIRD.

eat one's cake and have it too *v. phr.* To use or spend something and still keep it; have both when you must choose one of two things. —A cliché. Often used in negative sentences. *Roger can't make up his mind whether to go to college or get a job. You can't eat your cake and have it too.* (Roger can't do both; he must choose one.) *Mary wants to buy a beautiful dress she saw at the store, but she also wants to save her birthday money for camp. She wants to eat her cake and have it too.* (She really wants to buy the dress and still have money for camp.)

eat one's heart out *v. phr.* To grieve long and hopelessly; to become thin and weak from sorrow. *For months after her husband's death, Joanne simply ate her heart out.* (She grieved hopelessly, and lost her usual interest in life.) *We sometimes hear of a dog eating its heart out for a dead owner.* (The dog is so unhappy that it will not eat.)

eat one's words *also* **swallow one's words** *v. phr.* To take back something you have said; admit something is not true. *John had called Harry a coward, but the boys made him eat his words after Harry bravely fought a big bully.* (The boys made John admit that Harry was no coward.) Compare EAT CROW.

eat out *v.* **1** To eat in a restaurant; eat away from home. *Fred ate out often even when he wasn't out of town.* (Fred ate in restaurants often even when he wasn't travelling.) **2** To rust, rot, or be destroyed in time. *Rust had eaten out the gun barrel.* (Rust had ruined the inside of the gun barrel and made it useless.) See EAT AWAY.

eat out of one's hand *v. phr., informal* To trust someone fully; believe or obey someone without question. *The governor has the reporters eating out of his hand.* (The governor has the reporters so well fooled that they don't doubt what he says; they just accept his word.) *Helen is so pretty and popular that all the boys eat out of her hand.* (They follow her around and do anything she tells them.)

eat up *v.* **1** To eat all of. *After hiking all afternoon, they quickly ate up all of the dinner.* (They finished their dinners hungrily.) **2** To use all of. *Idle talk had eaten up the hour before they knew it.* (Idle talk had used up all the hour.) **3** *slang* To accept eagerly; welcome. *The girls told John he was a hero because he made the winning touchdown, and he ate up their praise.* (John received their praise greedily.) *Jim told Martha that she was as smart as she was beautiful and Martha ate it up.* (Martha liked very much to hear his praise.)

edge *See* HAVE AN EDGE ON, ON EDGE, SET ONE'S TEETH ON EDGE, TAKE THE EDGE OFF, THE EDGE.

edge in *v.* To move slowly; get in quietly, especially with some difficulty, by force or without a big enough opening. *People had crowded around the senator, but Don succeeded in edging in.* (Don moved slowly and quietly through to meet the senator.) *Harry edged the book in on the shelf.* (Harry forced the book into a tight place on the shelf.)

edge on *adv. phr.* Edgewise; with the narrow side forward. *The board struck him edge on.* (The board hit him with its edge.)

edge out *v.* To defeat in competition or rivalry; take the place of; force out. *Harry edged out Tom for a place in Mary's affections.* (Harry won out over Tom so that Mary liked Harry better.) *Signal lights on cars have gradually edged out hand signals.* (Signal lights on cars have more and more taken the place of hand signals.)

edgeways *See* GET A WORD IN *or* GET A WORD IN EDGEWISE, *also* GET A WORD IN EDGEWAYS.

edgewise *See* GET A WORD IN *or* GET A WORD IN EDGEWAYS.

education *See* HIGHER EDUCATION.

effect *See* IN EFFECT, INTO EFFECT, SOUND

EFFECTS, TAKE EFFECT, TO THAT EFFECT, TO THE EFECT THAT.

effigy See HANG IN EFFIGY or BURN IN EF-FIGY.

egg See BAD EGG, GOOD EGG, KILL THE GOOSE THAT LAID THE GOLDEN EGG, LAY AN EGG, PUT ALL ONE'S EGGS IN ONE BASKET, ROTTEN EGG.

egg on v. To urge on; excite; lead to action. *Joe's wife egged him on to spend money to show off.* (Joe's wife encouraged him to spend just to show off.) *The big boys egged on the two little boys to fight.* (The big boys talked and persuaded and shamed the two younger ones into fighting.) Compare PUT UP 6.

either a feast or a famine See FEAST OR A FAMINE.

either hide or hair See HIDE OR HAIR.

eke out v. **1** To fill out or add a little to; increase a little. *Mr. Jones eked out a country teacher's small salary by hunting and trapping in the winter.* (Mr. Jones added a little to his small salary by hunting and trapping in the winter.) *The modest meal was eked out with bread and milk.* (There was not much to eat but the family filled up on bread and milk.) **2** To get (little) by hard work; to earn with difficulty. *Fred eked out a bare living by farming on a rocky hillside.* (With hard work he managed to earn a poor living trying to grow food on a rocky hillside.)

elbow See AT ONE'S ELBOW, RUB ELBOWS, UP TO THE CHIN IN or UP TO THE ELBOWS IN.

element See IN ONE'S ELEMENT, OUT OF ONE'S ELEMENT.

else See SOMETHING ELSE AGAIN.

end See AT LOOSE ENDS, AT ONE'S WITS' END, BURN THE CANDLE AT BOTH ENDS, GO OFF THE DEEP END, HAIR STAND ON END, HOLD ONE'S END UP or HOLD UP ONE'S END or KEEP ONE'S END UP or KEEP UP ONE'S END, LIVING END, LOOSE ENDS, MAKE AN END OF, MAKE ENDS MEET, NO END, NO END TO or NO END OF, ON END, PUT AN END TO, REAR END, SHORT END, SPLIT END, TAG END or TAIL END, TIGHT END, TO THE BITTER END, WORLD WITH-OUT END.

end for end adv. phr. In a reversed or op-posite position (as upside down or back-wards); the other way around; over. *The box turned end for end as it fell, and everything spilled out.* (The box turned over with the bottom up.) *The wind caught the canoe and turned it end for end.* (The wind swung the canoe around so that it pointed in the oppo-site direction.)

end in itself n. phr. Something wanted for its own sake; a purpose, aim, or goal we want for itself alone and not as a way to something else. *The miser never spent his gold because for him it was an end in itself.* (The miser didn't want the gold so he could buy things with it, he wanted to keep the gold.)

end of one's rope or **end of one's tether** n. phr., informal The end of your trying or

imagining; the last of your ability, or ideas of how to do more. *Frank was out of work and broke, and he was at the end of his rope.* (Frank couldn't think what to do next.) *The doctor saw that Mother had reached the end of her tether, and told us to send her away for a holiday.* (The doctor saw that Mother was at the end of her strength and patience.) Compare AT ONE'S WIT'S END, FED UP, UP AGAINST IT, UP A TREE.

end of the road or **end of the line** n. phr. The final result or end (as of a way of action or behavior); the condition that comes when you can do no more. *He had left a trail of forgery and dishonesty across seven states; he had got out of each trouble with a new trick. Now the police had caught up with him, and it was the end of the road.* (He was in jail, and there was nothing more he could do.) *"When I get to the end of the line," Jones thought, "I'd like my children to like and respect me still."* (He thought it would be good to keep his children still fond of him and still respecting him to the end of his life.)

end run n. A football play in which a back tries to run around one end of the opponent's line. *Smith's end run scored the winning touchdown.* (Smith ran around one side of the opponent's team and scored a touchdown.)

end up v. **1** To come to an end; be ended or finished; stop. *How does the story end up?* (Tell the end of the story.) **2** To finally reach or arrive; land. *I hope you don't end up in jail.* (I hope the things you do won't get you arrested.) **3** informal To die, be killed. *The gangster ended up in the electric chair.* (He was put to death.) **4** or **finish up.** To put an end to; finish; stop. *The politician finally ended up his speech.* (He finally finished his speech.) Syn. WIND UP.

end zone n. Either of the marked areas be-hind the goal line. *He caught a pass in the end zone for a touchdown.* (He caught the pass back of the goal line and inside the marked area and it counted for a touchdown.)

English See BODY ENGLISH.

enjoy oneself v. phr. To have a good time; be happy; feel pleasure. *Mary enjoyed herself at the party.* (Mary had a good time at the party.) *"Enjoy yourselves, children,"* Mother urged the guests at our party. (As the chil-dren arrived, Mother told them she wanted them to have a good time.)

enlarge on or **enlarge upon** or **expand on** or **expand upon** v. To talk or write more about; say or explain more completely or at greater length. *The teacher enlarged on the uses of atomic power.* (The teacher told more about the future uses of atomic power.)

en masse adv. phr. As a group; in one big mass or group.—Used after the word it modi-fies. *The school turned out en masse to cheer the returning astronaut.* (The school turned out as one big group.)

enough See GIVE ONE ENOUGH ROPE, AND HE WILL HANG HIMSELF, KNOW ENOUGH TO COME IN OUT OF THE RAIN, LET WELL ENOUGH ALONE, SURE-ENOUGH.

enough is enough That's enough, let's not have any more; that will do, let's cut it short; that's the limit, let's stop there. *"I don't mind good clean fun, but enough is enough," the principal said.* ("I don't mind good clean fun, but this fooling around has gone far enough," the principal said.)

enterprise See FREE ENTERPRISE.

entry See PORT OF ENTRY.

envy See GREEN WITH ENVY.

equal to *adj. phr.* Able to meet, do, or control; able to do something about. *The situation took quick thinking, but John was equal to it.* (John was able to do it successfully.) *When a guest upset the coffee pot, Mrs. Smith's tact and quickness of mind were equal to the occasion.* (Mrs. Smith said or did something so that almost no one noticed it, and the guest was not embarrassed.)

error See TRIAL AND ERROR.

eve See ON THE EVE OF.

even See BREAK EVEN, GET EVEN, ON AN EVEN KEEL.

evening See GOOD EVENING.

even so *adv.* Although that is true; nevertheless; still. *The fire was out, but even so, the smell of smoke was strong.* (The fire was out, but the smell was still there.)

event See IN ANY CASE *or* AT ALL EVENTS, IN ANY CASE *also* IN ANY EVENT *or* AT ALL EVENTS, IN CASE *or* IN THE EVENT, IN CASE OF *also* IN THE EVENT OF.

ever See FOREVER AND EVER, HARDLY EVER *or* SCARCELY EVER.

every See AT EVERY TURN, EACH AND EVERY.

every cloud has a silver lining Every trouble has something hopeful that you can see in it, like the bright edge around a dark cloud.—A proverb. *The doctor told Tommy to cheer up when he had measles. "Every cloud has a silver lining," he said.* (The doctor told Tommy that he would soon be better again.) Compare IT'S AN ILL WIND THAT BLOWS NOBODY GOOD.

every dog has his day Everyone will have his chance or turn; everyone is lucky or popular at some time.—A proverb. *Mary will be able to go to dances like her sister when she grows up. Every dog has his day.* (Mary's chance to go to dances will come.)

every inch *adv. phr.* To the last part, in every way; completely. *He was every inch a man.* (He was a man in all ways.) *Henry looked every inch a soldier.* (Henry had a completely soldierly appearance.)

every last See EVERY SINGLE.

every last man *also* **every man jack** *n. phr.* Every single man; each man without exception. *I want every last man to be here on time tomorrow morning.* (Not one of you is excused from being on time tomorrow.) *Every man jack of you must do his duty.* (All of you must do your duty.)

every man jack See EVERY LAST MAN.

every now and then *or* **every now and again** *or* **every so often** *or* **every once in a while** *adv. phr.* At fairly regular intervals; fairly often; repeatedly. *John comes to visit me every now and then.* (John comes to visit me pretty often.) *It was hot work, but every so often Susan would bring us something cold to drink.* (It was hot work, but Susan brought us out cold drinks fairly often.) Compare NOW AND THEN.

every other *adj. phr.* Every second; every alternate. *The milkman comes every other day.* (The milkman comes every second day; he comes one day and skips one.) *On St. Patrick's day, it seems as if every other man you meet is wearing a shamrock.* (Half the men you meet seem to be Irish.)

every single *or* **every last** *adj. phr.* Every.—Used for emphasis. *She dropped the box, and when she opened it, every single glass was broken.* (When she opened the box she had dropped she found that all the glasses were broken.) *When she got home she found every last tomato in the box was rotten.* (When she got home she found every tomato was rotten.) Syn. EACH AND EVERY.

every so often See EVERY NOW AND THEN.

everything See HOLD IT *or* HOLD EVERYTHING.

every time one turns around *adv. phr., informal.* Very often.—A hackneyed phrase. *Mr. Winston must be rich. He buys a new suit every time he turns around.* (He buys new suits often.) *No, Charles—I can't drive you to the park every time I turn around.* (You want me to drive you to the park too often.)

every which way *also* **any which way** In all directions. *Bricks and boards were scattered in confusion on the ground every which way, just as they had fallen after the tornado.* (Bricks and boards were scattered everywhere.) Compare HELTER-SKELTER.

evidence See IN EVIDENCE.

example See FOR EXAMPLE, MAKE AN EXAMPLE OF.

except for *or formal* **but for** *prep.* **1** With the exception of; if (a certain person or thing) were left out; omitting. *Except for John, the whole class passed the test.* (John was the one exception; John was the only one to fail.) **2** Without. *I'd have been lost but for you.* (I'd have been lost without your help; you were the one person who saved me.)

exception See TAKE EXCEPTION TO.

exception proves the rule Something unusual that does not follow a rule tests that rule to see if it is true; if there are too many exceptions, the rule is no good.—A proverb. *Frank is very short but is a good basketball player. He is the exception that proves the rule.*

(Frank is an unusual basketball player because they are usually tall.)

excuse oneself *v. phr.* **1** To think of reasons for not being to blame; think yourself not at fault. *John excused himself for his low grades on the ground that the teacher didn't like him.* (He told himself he wasn't to blame, because he thought the teacher wouldn't give him good grades no matter how good his work was.) **2** To ask to be excused after doing something impolite. *John excused himself for his tardiness, saying his watch was wrong.* (John asked to be excused for being late.) **3** To ask permission to leave a group or place. *The committee meeting lasted so long that Mr. Wilkins excused himself to keep an appointment.* (Mr. Wilkins asked permission to leave.) *John had to go to the dentist's, so he excused himself and left the classroom.* (John asked the teacher to excuse him and left the room.)

exert oneself *v. phr.* To make an effort; try hard; work hard. *Susan exerted herself all year to earn good marks.* (Susan worked hard all year to earn good marks.) *Jerry exerted himself to please the new girl.* (Jerry tried hard to please the new girl.)

expand on *or* **expand upon** See ENLARGE ON *or* ENLARGE UPON.

explain away *v.* To explain (something) so that it does not seem true or important. *John explained away his unfinished homework by showing the teacher his broken arm in a cast.* (John showed his broken arm, and that explained why he couldn't write his homework.) *It is hard to explain away Abraham Lincoln's dream about being dead, which he had a few days before he was shot.* (We cannot explain why Lincoln had such a strange dream, which came true.) *The man could not explain away the gun and the marked money from the bank robbery that the police found in his car.* (The man was caught with a gun and some of the stolen money, and he couldn't give a good reason for having them.)

explain oneself *v. phr.* **1** To make your meaning plainer; make your first statement clear. *When we didn't understand Fritz, he went on to explain himself.* (Fritz explained his meaning in simpler words.) **2** To give a good reason for something you did or failed to do which seems wrong. *When Jack brought Mary home at three o'clock in the morning, her father asked him to explain himself.* (He asked Jack why they were so late.)

explode a bombshell *v. phr., informal* To say something startling; suggest or show something astonishing or shocking. *The police exploded a bombshell when they arrested the kindly old banker for stealing money from the bank.* (The police surprised everyone by naming the banker as a thief.) *The principal exploded a bombshell by cancelling the dance as a penalty.* (Calling off the dance came as a shock to the pupils.) *Politi-cal leaders exploded a bombshell when they picked the young lawyer to run for mayor.* (No one expected the young lawer to be the candidate.)

express oneself *v. phr.* To say what you think or feel; put your thoughts or feelings into words by speaking or writing. *The boy expressed himself well in debate.* (The boy spoke his thoughts well in debate.) *The mayor expressed himself as opposed to any borrowing.* (The mayor said he was against any more borrowing.)

extra point *n.* **1** A point scored after a touchdown in football by kicking the ball over the bar between the goalposts. *Our team lost 7 to 6 because we missed the extra point.* (Our team lost 7 to 6 because the kick to score the seventh point was outside the goal posts.) **2** [plural] Two points scored after a touchdown in football by passing or carrying the ball over the goal line. *Our team won 8 to 7 by scoring the extra points on a pass.* (We won 8 to 7 by completing a pass for two points after the touchdown.)

eye See APPLE OF ONE'S EYE, BAT AN EYE *or* BAT AN EYELASH, BELIEVE ONE'S EYES, CATCH ONE'S EYE, CLEAR-EYED, CLOSE ONE'S EYES *or* SHUT ONE'S EYES, EYES OPEN, EYE OUT, EYE TO, FEAST ONE'S EYES ON, FOUR-EYES, GET THE EYE, GIVE THE EYE, GREEN-EYED MONSTER, HALF AN EYE, HAVE AN EYE ON, HAVE EYES ONLY FOR, HIT BETWEEN THE EYES, IN ONE'S MIND'S EYE, IN THE PUBLIC EYE, KEEP AN EYE ON *or* KEEP ONE'S EYE ON, KEEP ONE'S EYES PEELED *or* KEEP ONE'S EYES SKINNED, LAY EYES ON *or* SET EYES ON, LOOK IN THE EYE, MAKE EYES AT, MEET ONE'S EYE, MISTY-EYED *or* DEWEY-EYED, ONE EYE ON, OPEN ONE'S EYES *or* OPEN UP ONE'S EYES, OUT OF THE CORNER OF ONE'S EYE, PULL THE WOOL OVER ONE'S EYES, SEE EYE TO EYE, SHUT-EYE, SIGHT FOR SORE EYES, STARS IN ONE'S EYES, ROUND-EYED *or* WIDE-EYED *also* LARGE-EYED, PRIVATE EYE, TO THE EYE, UP TO THE CHIN IN *or* UP TO THE EYES IN, WEATHER EYE.

eyebrow See RAISE EYEBROWS.

eye-catching See CATCH ONE'S EYE.

eye-filling *adj., literary* Attractive to the eye; beautiful; especially grand; splendid; majestic. *The mountains in the distance were an eye-filling sight.* (The mountains in the distance thrilled you with their beauty.)

eye for an eye and a tooth for a tooth A blow or injury should be given back as hard as each one that is received; every crime or injury should be punished or paid back. *In ancient times if a man's eye was put out by his enemy, he might get revenge by putting his enemy's eye out. This was the rule of an eye for an eye and a tooth for a tooth.* (In old times it was common to punish crimes and enemies severely.) Sometimes used in a short form. *Churches today teach that we should forgive people who hurt us, not follow the rule of an* *eye for an eye.* (We should forgive people who hurt us, not try to hurt them back.) [From the old command in the Bible meaning when you pay back a person, you should not hurt him more than he hurt you.] Compare DOG EAT DOG, GIVE AS GOOD AS ONE GETS, TIT FOR TAT.

eye-opener See OPEN ONE'S EYES.

eye out Careful watch or attention; guard. —Used after *keep, have* or *with. Keep an eye out. We're close to Joe's house.* (Be ready to see Joe's house.) Usually used with *for. Mary has her eye out for bargains.* (She watches carefully for bargains.) *They went through the woods very quietly, with an eye out for Indians.* (They were guarding against Indians.) Compare LOOK OUT 2, ON GUARD, ON THE ALERT, ON THE WATCH.

eyes are bigger than one's stomach *informal* You want more food than you can eat. *Annie took a second big helping of pudding, but her eyes were bigger than her stomach.* (Annie took a second big helping of pudding, but she couldn't eat it all.) *"Your eyes are bigger than your stomach," mother told little Tommy when he piled up food on his plate.* (Mother told Tommy that he had a wish for more food than he could eat, and it would be wasted.)

eye shadow *n. phr.* A cream used to darken the eyelids in order to make the eyes more noticeable. *Jane's mother told her that girls in the ninth grade shouldn't be using eye shadow.* (Jane's mother told her she was too young to use eye cosmetics.)

eyes in the back of one's head *n. phr., informal* Ability to know what happens when your back is turned.—A cliché. *Mother must have eyes in the back of her head, because she always knows when I do something wrong.* (Even though Mother is not looking, she knows I've done something wrong.)

eyes open 1 Careful watch or attention; readiness to see—Usually used with *for. Keep your eyes open for a boy in a red cap and sweater.* (Watch out and try to see the boy.) *The hunter had his eyes open for rabbits.* (He was hunting for rabbits.) *They drove on with their eyes open for a gas station.* (They looked for a gas station as they drove.) Syn. EYE OUT, KEEP ONE'S EYES PEELED. 2 Full knowledge; especially of consequences; understanding of what will or might result.— Used with *have* or *with. Automobile racing is dangerous. Bob went into it with his eyes open.* (Bob knew what might happen when he began to race in automobiles.) *Betty had her eyes open when she got married.* (She knew what it meant to get married.) Contrast close ONE'S EYES.

eyes pop out *informal* (You) are very much surprised.—Used with a possessive noun or pronoun. *Mary's eyes popped out when her mother entered her classroom.* (Mary was very much surprised to see her mother come into the classroom.) *When Joan found a clock radio under the Christmas tree, her eyes popped out.* (She was much surprised.)

eye teeth See CUT ONE'S EYE TEETH ON *at* CUT TEETH 2.

eye to 1 Attention to.—Usually used with *have* or *with. Have an eye to spelling in these test papers.* (Pay attention to your spelling in these papers.) 2 Plan for, purpose of.—Usually used with *have* or *with. Save your money now with an eye to the future.* (Save your money to have some in the future.) *John is going to college with an eye to becoming a lawyer.* (He plans to become a lawyer.)

F

face See BLUE IN THE FACE, CUT OFF ONE'S NOSE TO SPITE ONE'S FACE, FLY IN THE FACE OF, HATCHET FACE, HIDE ONE'S FACE, IN ONE'S FACE, IN THE FACE OF, LONG FACE, LOOK IN THE EYE *or* LOOK IN THE FACE, MAKE A FACE, ON THE FACE OF IT, SAVE FACE, SET ONE'S FACE AGAINST, SHOOT OFF ONE'S MOUTH *or* SHOOT OFF ONE'S FACE, SHOW ONE'S FACE, SLAP IN THE FACE, STARE IN THE FACE, STRAIGHT FACE, THROW IN ONE'S FACE, TO ONE'S FACE.

face down *v. phr.,* To confront boldly and win; to defy. *The President faced down the heckler who interrupted his speech.* (The President boldly opposed the man interrupting him; after this the heckler shut up.) *Max told the robbers in the alley that he was a black-belt in karate; they felt faced down and fled.* (Max scares the robbers by telling them that he is a trained fighter.)

face-saver, face-saving See SAVE FACE.

face the music *v. phr., informal* To go through trouble or danger, especially because of something you did; accept your punishment.—A cliché. *The boy was caught cheating in an examination and had to face the music.* (He could not escape being punished.) *The official who had been taking bribes was exposed by a newspaper, and had to face the music.* (He had to accept being put on trial and sent to prison.) *George knew his mother would cry when he told her, but he decided to go home and face the music.* (He did not want to make his mother cry, but he decided that he must tell her.) Compare MAKE ONE'S BED AND LIE IN IT, PAY THE PIPER, TAKE ONE'S MEDICINE.

face-to-face *adv. phr.* 1 With your face looking toward the face of another person; each facing the other. *Turning a corner, he found himself face-to-face with a policeman.* (When he turned a corner, he nearly bumped into a policeman coming toward him.) *The two teams for the spelling bee stood face-to-face on opposite sides of the classroom.* (They stood on opposite sides of the room, facing each other.) *The church and the school stand face-to-face across the street.* (The church is just across the street from the school.) 2 In the presence of another or others. *She was thrilled to meet the President face-to-face.* (She was thrilled to actually meet and speak to the President.) *I have heard about him, but I never met him face-to-face.* (I have heard about him, but I have never met him in person.) Compare IN PERSON. 3 To the point where you must do something.—Used with *with. The solution of the first problem brought him face-to-face with a second problem.* (He solved the first problem but this brought him to another that he had to solve.) Compare UP AGAINST.

face-to-face *adj.* Being in the presence of a person; being right with someone. *The British prime minister came to Washington for a face-to-face meeting with the President.* (The Prime Minister came to see and talk with the President, not just write letters or talk on the telephone.)

face up to *v.* To accept (something hard or unpleasant.) *The boy knew he should tell his neighbor that he broke the window, but he couldn't face up to it.* (He couldn't make himself do it.) *We must face up to our responsibilities and not try to get out of them.* (We must accept our responsibilities.) Compare FACE THE MUSIC.

face value *n.* 1 The worth or price printed on a stamp, bond, note, piece of paper money, etc. *The savings bond had a face value of $25.* (The bond would be worth $25 at the right time in the future.) 2 The seeming worth or truth of something. *She took his stories at face value and did not know he was joking.* (She believed his stories, but they were not true, only jokes.)

fact See IN FACT, MATTER-OF-FACT.

facts of life *n. phr.* 1 The truth which we should know about sex, marriage, and births. *His father told him the facts of life when he was old enough.* (His father told him the truth about sex and marriage when he was a little older.) 2 The truths one learns about people and their good and bad habits of life, work, or play.—A trite expression. *As a cub reporter he would learn the facts of life in the newspaper world.* (Beginning a job as a newspaper writer, he would learn how people work on a newspaper.)

fade back *v.* To back away from the line before passing in football. *The quarterback is fading back to pass.* (He is backing away from the line and looking for someone to pass to.) Compare DROP BACK.

fail See WITHOUT FAIL.

fair See BID FAIR, PLAY FAIR.

fair and square *adv. phr., informal* Without cheating; honestly. *He won the game fair and square.* (He won the game honestly.)

fair catch *n.* A catch of a kicked football by a player after he holds up his hand to show that he will not run with the ball. *He saw that he would not be able to run with the ball, so he signalled for a fair catch.* (He knew that the other players would catch him; he held up his hand first and they let him alone.)

fair-haired boy *n., informal* A person that gets special favors; favorite; pet. *If he wins the election by a large majority, he will become his party's fair-haired boy.* (He will be the most favored member of his party if he wins the election by a large majority.) *The local boy playing first base could do no wrong; he was the fair-haired boy of the fans.* (The local boy was a great favorite with the fans and everything he did was all right with them.)

Charles was a good student and behaved very well; he became the teacher's fair-haired boy. (She liked him and let him do things others could not.)

fair play *n.* Equal and right action (to another person); justice. *The visiting team did not get fair play in the game.* (The home team did wrong to the visiting team.) *The judges decided against Bob, but he said that he had gotten fair play.* (The judges decided against him, but he said they were honest and right to him.) *Sally's sense of fair play made her a favorite with her classmates.* (Sally's classmates liked her because she treated them fairly.)

fair sex *n., informal* Women in general; the female sex. *"Better not use four-letter words in front of a member of the fair sex," Joe said.* (He warns against the use of vulgarities before women.)

fair shake *n., informal* Honest treatment. *Joe has always given me a fair shake.* (He has never cheated me, he has always treated me honestly.)

fair-weather friend *n.* A person who is a friend only when you are successful.—A cliché. *Everyone knows that John's only a fair-weather friend.* (Everyone knows that John is friendly only with people who are successful. He does not stay friendly if a person has bad luck.)

fairy godmother *n.* **1** A fairy believed to help and take care of a baby as it grows up. **2** A person who helps and does much for another. *The rich man played fairy godmother to the boys and had a baseball field made for them.* (He got a field and gave it to them, as if he had magic powers.) *Jane was a fairy godmother to her poorer friends.* (She had money and was always giving her friends things.)

faith See GOOD FAITH, ON FAITH.

fall See BOTTOM DROP OUT OR BOTTOM FALL OUT, RIDING FOR A FALL.

fall all over *v. phr., informal* To show too much love or thanks toward (someone). *She must love him. Every time you see them, she's falling all over him.* (She shows her love for him by hugging and petting him.) *When Bob found the lady's ring and returned it, she fell all over him.* (The woman was excited and thanked Bob again and again.)

fall back *v.* To move back; go back.—Usually used with a group as subject. *The army fell back before their stubborn enemies.* (The army stopped fighting and went back.) *The crowd around the hurt boy fell back when someone shouted "Give him air!"* (The crowd moved back away from the boy.) Compare DROP BACK, GIVE WAY.

fall back on *or* **fall back upon** *v.* **1** To retreat to. *The enemy made a strong attack, and the soldiers fell back on the fort.* (The soldiers retreated to the fort.) **2** To go for help to; turn to in time of need. *When the big bills for*

Mother's hospital care came, Father was glad he had money in the bank to fall back on. (Father was glad he had money saved to use in a time of special need.) *If Mr. Jones can't find a job as a teacher, he can fall back on his skill as a printer.* (Mr. Jones can find a job as a printer instead of working as a teacher, though he would rather teach.)

fall behind *v.* To go slower than others and be far behind them. *When the campers took a hike in the woods, two boys fell behind and got lost.* (Two boys walked slowly and let the others go very far ahead of them; then they could not find them.) *Frank's lessons were too hard for him, and he soon fell behind the rest of the class.* (The work was too hard for him and his classmates learned more than he did.) *Mary was not promoted because she dreamed too much and fell behind in her lessons.* (She dreamed too much and didn't know her lessons.)

fall by the wayside *also* **drop by the wayside** *v. phr.* To give up or fail before the finish.—A cliché. *The boys tried to make a 50-mile hike, but most of them fell by the wayside.* (The boys tried to walk 50 miles, but most of them gave up before the finish.) *George, Harry, and John entered college to become teachers, but Harry and John fell by the wayside, and only George graduated.* (Harry and John could not finish college and become teachers.)

fall down on the job *v. phr., informal* To fail to work well. *The boss was disappointed when his workers fell down on the job.* (The boss was disappointed when his workers failed to work well.)

fall flat *v., informal* To be a failure; fail. *The party fell flat because of the rain.* (The party was a failure because of the rain.) *His joke fell flat because no one understood it.* (His joke failed because no one understood it.)

fall for *v., slang* **1** To begin to like very much. *Dick fell for baseball when he was a little boy.* (He began to play baseball and liked it from the first.) **2** To begin to love (a boy or a girl.) *Helen was a very pretty girl and people were not surprised that Bill fell for her.* (People were not surprised that he loved her.) **3** To believe (something told to fool you.) *Nell did not fall for Joe's story about being a jet pilot.* (Nell did not believe he was a jet pilot.)

fall from grace *v. phr.* To go back to a bad way of behaving; do something bad again.—A trite expression. *The boys behaved well during dinner until they fell from grace by eating their dessert with their fingers instead of their forks.* (The boys behaved well until they went back to their old bad manners by eating dessert with their fingers instead of their forks.) *The boy fell from grace when he lied.* (The boy did something bad when he lied.)

fall in v. To go and stand properly in a row like soldiers. *The captain told his men to fall in.* (He told them to stand right in line.) Contrast FALL OUT 3.

fall in for v. To receive; get. *The boy fell in for some sympathy when he broke his leg.* (The boy received sympathy.) *The team manager fell in for most of the blame when his team lost the playoffs.* (The manager got most of the blame for his team's failure in the playoffs.)

falling-out n. Argument; disagreement; quarrel. *Mary and Jane had a falling-out about who owned the book.* (Mary and Jane had an argument about who owned the book.) *The boys had a falling-out when each said that the other had broken the rules.* (They disagreed about the rules, became angry with each other, and were not friends after that.)

fall in line or **fall into line** See IN LINE, INTO LINE.

fall in love See IN LOVE.

fall in with v., informal 1 To meet by accident. *Mary fell in with some of her friends downtown.* (Mary met some of her friends by accident downtown.) 2 To agree to help with; support. *I fell in with Jack's plan to play a trick on his father.* (I agreed to help Jack with his plan.) 3 To become associated with a group detrimental to the newcomer. *John fell in with a wild bunch; small wonder he flunked all of his courses.* (He became associated with a harmful group.) Compare PLAY ALONG.

fall off See DROP OFF 4.

fall off the wagon v. phr., slang alcoholism and drug culture To return to the consumption of an addictive, such as alcohol or drugs, after a period of abstinence. *Poor Joe has fallen off the wagon again—he is completely incoherent today.* (Joe returned to drinking and is drunk again.)

fall on or **fall upon** v. 1 To go and fight with; attack. *The robbers fell on him from behind trees.* (The robbers hid and attacked him.) 2 formal To meet (troubles). *The famous poet fell upon unhappy days.* (The poet was famous at first but became poor and unhappy.)

fallout n. 1 Result of nuclear explosion; harmful radioactive particles. *Some experts consider fallout as dangerous as the bomb itself.* 2 Undesirable aftereffects in general. *As a fallout of Watergate, many people lost their faith in the government.* (They lost their faith as a result of Watergate.)

fall out v. 1 To happen. *As it fell out, the Harpers were able to sell their old car.* (They did not know if they could sell the car, but at last they did sell it.) Compare TURN OUT 6. 2 To quarrel; fight; fuss; disagree. *The thieves fell out over the division of the loot.* (The thieves quarreled about dividing the stolen goods.) 3 To leave a military formation. *You men are dismissed. Fall out!* (You men may

leave now.) Contrast FALL IN. 4 To leave a building to go and line up. *The soldiers fell out of the barracks for inspection.* (The men came out of the barracks to stand in line for inspection.)

fall over backwards or **fall over oneself** v. phr. To do everything you can to please someone; try very hard to satisfy someone. *The hotel manager fell over backwards to give the movie star everything she wanted.* (The manager gave the movie star many services that ordinary people at the hotel would not get.) *The boys fell over themselves trying to get the new girl's attention.* (The boys tried very hard to make the new girl notice them.)

fall over yourself See FALL OVER BACKWARDS.

fall short v. To fail to reach (some aim); not succeed. *His jump fell three inches short of the world record.* (His jump was three inches less than the best in the world.) *The movie fell short of expectations.* (The movie was not as good as we thought it would be.) Contrast MEASURE UP.

fall through v., informal To fail; be ruined; not happen or be done. *Jim's plans to go to college fell through at the last moment.* (His plans did not succeed.) *Mr. Jones' deal to sell his house fell through.* (The deal was not completed.) Contrast COME OFF.

fall to v. 1 To begin to work. *The boys fell to and quickly cut the grass.* (They began to work and quickly cut the grass.) Syn. TURN TO. 2 To begin to fight. *They took out their swords and fell to.* (They took out their swords and began to fight.) 3 To begin to eat. *The hungry boys fell to before everyone sat down.* (The boys began to eat before everyone sat down.) 4 Begin; start. *The old friends met and fell to talking about their school days.* (They began to talk about things they did in school.)

false See PLAY ——— FALSE, SAIL UNDER FALSE COLORS.

family See RUN IN THE BLOOD or RUN IN THE FAMILY, IN A FAMILY WAY.

famine See FEAST OR A FAMINE.

fancy pants n., slang A man or boy who wears clothes that are too nice or acts like a woman or girl; sissy. *The first time they saw him in his new band uniform, they yelled "Hey, fancy pants, what are you doing in your sister's slacks?"* (They thought his new band uniform looked like girls' clothing, and called him a fancy pants.)

fan See HIT THE FAN.

fan the breeze See SHOOT THE BREEZE.

fan the breeze v. phr. 1 See SHOOT THE BREEZE. 2 slang To swing and miss the ball in baseball. *The batter tried to hit a home run, but he fanned the breeze.* (The batter tried to hit a home run but he swung and missed the ball.)

far See AS FAR AS or SO FAR AS, SO FAR also THUS FAR, BY FAR, FEW AND FAR BETWEEN, SO FAR, SO GOOD.

far and away *adv. phr.* Very much. *The fish was far and away the biggest ever caught on the lake.* (It was much bigger than any other fish ever caught on the lake.) Compare BY FAR, HEAD AND SHOULDERS 2.

far and near *n. phr.* Far places and near places; everywhere. *People came from far and near to hear him speak.* (People came from many different places to hear the speaker.)

far and wide *adv. phr.* Everywhere, in all directions. *The wind blew the papers far and wide.* (The wind blew the papers away in all directions.) *My old school friends are scattered far and wide now.* (My friends have separated far away from each other.) *The movie company looked far and wide for a boy to act the hero in the new movie.* (The movie people looked everywhere for a boy who could act the important part in the new movie.) Compare ALL OVER.

far cry *n.* Something very different. *His last statement was a far cry from his first story.* (He changed his first story and said something different.) *The first automobile could run, but it was a far cry from a modern car.* (It would run but it did not look like our cars now.)

farm See COLLECTIVE FARM.

farm out *v.* **1** To have another person do (something) for you; send away to be done. *Our teacher had too many test papers to read, so she farmed out half of them to a friend.* (The teacher gave half of the papers to a friend to read for her.) **2** To send away to be taken care of. *While Mother was sick, the children were farmed out to relatives.* (Father sent the children to relatives to be taken care of.) **3** To send a player to a league where the quality of play is lower. *The player was farmed out to Rochester to gain experience.* (The player was sent to Rochester to gain experience in a league where the competition is not so hard.)

far-out *adj.* **1** Very far away; distant. *Scientists are planning rocket trips to the moon and far-out planets.* (Scientists are planning to send men in rockets to the moon and to distant planets.) **2** *informal* Very different from others; queer; odd, unusual. *He enjoyed being with beatniks and other far-out people.* (He liked to be with queer people.) *Susan did not like some of the paintings at the art show because they were too far-out for her.* (Susan did not like some of the pictures at the show because they were odd and did not look like anything real.)

fashion See AFTER A FASHION, HIGH FASHION or HIGH STYLE.

fast See HARD-AND-FAST, PLAY FAST AND LOOSE.

fast and furious *adj. or adv. phr.* Very fast; with much speed and energy. *He was mowing the grass at a fast and furious rate.* (He was mowing the law with great speed.) *When I last saw her she was driving fast and furious down the street.* (The last time I saw her she was driving very fast down the street.) Compare GREAT GUNS.

fast buck *or* **quick buck** *slang* Money earned quickly and easily, and sometimes dishonestly. *You can make a fast buck at the golf course by fishing balls out of the water trap.* (You can easily earn money at the golf course by finding golf balls in the pond.) *He isn't interested in a career; he's just looking for a quick buck.* (He is just looking for a way to get money without working hard.)

fast talker *n., slang, informal* A con artist or a swindler, one who is particularly apt to get away with illegitimate transactions because of the clever way he talks. *I wouldn't trust uncle Noam if I were you,—he is a fast talker.* (I wouldn't trust him in your position because he is a swindler.)

fast time See DAYLIGHT SAVING TIME.

fat See CHEW THE FAT.

fat chance *n. phr., slang* Little or no possibility; almost no chance. *A high school team would have a fat chance of beating a strong college team.* (I do not think the high school team would win.) *Jane is pretty and popular; you will have a fat chance of getting a date with her.* (She has many friends; I don't think she would go with you.) Compare GHOST OF A.

fat city *n., slang* A state of contentment due to wealth and position. *Bully for the Smiths; they have arrived in Fat City.* (Good for them; they have reached a state of financial and social satisfaction.)

fate See TEMPT FATE or TEMPT THE FATES.

father See LIKE FATHER, LIKE SON.

Father Christmas *n., British* The joyful spirit of Christmas; Santa Claus. *English children look forward to the visit of Father Christmas.* (English children happily expect Santa Claus to visit them.)

Father's Day *n.* The third Sunday in June set aside especially to honor fathers whether living or dead. *The children gave nice presents to their father on Father's Day.* (On the Sunday set aside especially to honor all fathers, the children gave their father presents.)

fat is in the fire Something has happened that will cause trouble or make a bad situation worse.—A cliché. *He found out you took it? Well, the fat's in the fire now.* (You're going to have trouble now that he knows that you took it.)

fat of the land *n. phr.* The best and richest food, clothes, everything.—An overused phrase. *When I'm rich I'll retire and live off the fat of the land.* (When I become rich, I'll stop working and have the best of everything.)

fault See AT FAULT, FIND FAULT, TO A FAULT.

favor See CURRY FAVOR, IN FAVOR OF.

favorite son *n.* A man supported by his home state for President. *At a national con-*

vention, states often vote for their favorite sons first; then they change and vote for another man. (They vote first for men from their own states to honor them.)

fear See FOR FEAR.

fear and trembling or **fear and trepedation** *n. phr.* Great fear. *He came in fear and trembling to tell his father he had a bad report card.* (He was very much afraid when he told his father he had a bad report card.)

feast one's eyes on *v. phr.* To look at and enjoy very much.—A cliché. *He feasted his eyes on the beautiful painting.* (He enjoyed looking at the beautiful painting very much.)

feast or a famine *n. phr.* Plenty or very little; big success or bad failure. *In this business it's either a feast or a famine.* (This line of business is successful or a failure.) *He is very careless with his money; it is always a feast or a famine with him.* (When he has money, he lives high; when he is broke, he starves.)

feather See BIRDS OF A FEATHER FLOCK TOGETHER, TAR AND FEATHER, FINE FEATHERS DO NOT MAKE FINE BIRDS, FUSS AND FEATHERS, MAKE THE FEATHERS FLY, RUFFLE FEATHERS.

feather in one's cap *n. phr.* Something to be proud of; an honor. *It was a feather in his cap to win first prize.* (It was an honor for him to win first prize.) [From the medieval practice of placing a feather in the helmet of one who won honors in battle.]

feather one's nest *v. phr., informal* **1** To use for yourself money and power, especially from a public office or job in which you are trusted to help other people. *The rich man told his lawyer to use his money after he died to build a hospital for poor people, but the lawyer feathered his own nest with the money instead.* (The lawyer used the money for himself and did not build a hospital.) *The man feathered his nest in politics by getting money from contractors who built roads.* (He made the contractors pay him money before he gave them jobs to build the roads.) Syn. LINE ONE'S POCKETS. **2** To make your home pleasant and comfortable; furnish and decorate your house. *Furniture stores welcome young couples who want to feather their nests.* (Furniture stores are happy to sell things to young couples who are furnishing their new home.)

fed up (*informal*) ALSO (*slang*) **fed to the gills** or **fed to the teeth** *adj. phr.* Having had too much of something; at the end of your patience; disgusted; bored; tired. *People get fed up with anyone who brags all the time.* (People become bored and disgusted with anyone who is always talking about how wonderful he is.) *I've had enough of his complaints. I'm fed up.* (I have heard all of the complaints I can stand.) *He was fed to the teeth with television and sold his set to a cousin.* (He sold his television set to his cousin because he lost patience with the programs.)

John quit football because he was fed to the gills with practice. (He stopped playing because he was tired of it.) Compare SICK AND TIRED.

feed See BITE THE HAND THAT FEEDS ONE, CHICKEN FEED, OFF FEED or OFF ONE'S FEED, SPOON FEED.

feel See GET THE FEEL OF, HARD FEELING.

feel a draft *v. phr., slang* To have the sensation that one is not welcome in a place; that one has gotten a cold reception. *Let's go, Suzie, I feel a draft.* (Let us go away from here, I have the impression that we aren't exactly welcome.)

feel for someone *v. phr., informal* To be able to sympathize with someone's problems. *I can really feel for you, John, for losing your job.* (I sympathize with you and understand how you feel.)

feel in one's bones or **know in one's bones** *v. phr.* To have an idea or feeling but not know why. *I feel in my bones that tomorrow will be a sunny day.* (I didn't read the weather report but I have an idea that tomorrow will be sunny.) *I know in my bones that God will protect us.* (I am sure that God will protect us.)

feel like *v., informal* To want to do or have. *I don't feel like running today.* (I do not want to run today.) *I just don't feel like pancakes this morning.* (I don't want pancakes this morning.)

feel like a million or **feel like a million dollars** *v. phr., informal* To be in the best of health and spirits.—A cliché. *I feel like a million this morning.* (I feel fine this morning.) *He had a headache yesterday but feels like a million dollars today.* (He feels wonderful today.) Compare LOOK LIKE A MILLION.

feel like two cents See TWO CENTS.

feel no pain *v. phr., slang* To be drunk. *After a few drinks, the man felt no pain and began to act foolishly.* (The man was drunk and began to act foolishly.)

feel one's oats *v. phr., slang* **1** To feel frisky or playful; be eager and excited. (*The horses were feeling their oats.* (The horses felt good and wanted to run.) *When they first got to camp, the boys were feeling their oats.* (They were playful and ran around the yard.) **2** To act in a proud or important way. *The new gardener was feeing his oats and started to boss the other men.* (He was proud of his new job and acted bossy.)

feel out *v.* To talk or act carefully with someone and find what he thinks or can do. *The pupils felt out the principal about a party after the game.* (They talked with him to see if he would agree about a party.) *John felt out his father about letting him have the car that evening.* (John talked carefully to see if his father would let him use the car.) *At first the boxers felt each other out.* (Each fighter fought carefully at first to find out how good the other was.) Compare SOUND OUT.

feel up *v. phr., vulgar, avoidable* To arouse sexually by manual contact. *You mean to tell me that you've been going out for six months and he hasn't ever tried to feel you up?* (Are you saying that he hasn't made any advances with his hands?) Contrast COP A FEEL.

feel up to something *v. phr., informal* To feel adequately knowledgeable, strong, or equipped to handle a given task. *Do you feel up to jogging a mile a day with me?* (Do you think you're strong enough to do it?) Contrast BE UP TO SOMETHING.

feet See FOOT.

feet of clay *n. phr.* A hidden fault or weakness in a person which is discovered or shown. —A cliché. *The famous general showed he had feet of clay when he began to drink liquor.* (People thought the general was a fine man but he began to drink liquor.) *The banker seemed to be honest, but he had feet of clay and was arrested for stealing.* (People found he was dishonest.)

feet on the ground *n. phr.* An understanding of what can be done; sensible ideas.—A cliché, used with a possessive. *John has his feet on the ground; he knows he cannot learn everything at once.* (He understands that it will take time to get an education.) *Ted dreams of sudden riches, but Henry keeps his feet on the ground and expects to work for his money.* (Ted is in a dream world, but Henry knows he must get a job.) *Mrs. Smith was a dreamer, but her husband was a man with his feet on the ground.* (Mr. Smith was very practical.) Contrast IN THE CLOUDS.

fell See AT ONE FELL SWOOP.

fellow See HAIL-FELLOW-WELL-MET, REGULAR GUY *or* REGULAR FELLOW.

fence See GRASS IS ALWAYS GREENER ON THE OTHER SIDE OF THE FENCE, MEND ONE'S FENCES, ON THE FENCE.

fence in *or* **hedge in** *or* **hem in** *v.* To keep (someone) from doing what he or she would like to do.—Usually used in the passive. *Mary felt fenced in because her father would not let her drive a car or have dates with boys.* (Mary felt that she could not do as she liked.) *John didn't like his job because he had to do the same kind of work all the time. He felt that he was hemmed in.* (He did not feel free to do as he liked.)

fence-sitter See ON THE FENCE.

fence-sitting See ON THE FENCE.

fence with *or* **spar with** *v.* To talk with (someone) as if you were fighting like a swordsman or boxer; to give skillful answers or arguments against (someone). *The governor was an expert at fencing with reporters at press conferences.* (The governor was very good at answering questions and at avoiding questions he didn't want to answer during press conferences.)

ferret out *literary or* **smell out** *or* **sniff out** *v.* To hunt or drive from hiding; to bring out into the open; search for and find. *John ferreted out the answer to the question in the library.* (He looked hard and found the answer in the library.) *Jane smelled out the boys' secret hiding-place in the woods.* (Jane discovered their hiding-place.)

few See MAN OF FEW WORDS, NOT A FEW, QUITE A FEW.

few and far between *adj. phr.* Not many; few and scattered; not often met or found; rare.—Used in the predicate. *People who will work as hard as Thomas A. Edison are few and far between.* (Not many people will work as hard as Thomas A. Edison.) *Places where you can get water are few and far between in the desert.* (There are very few places to find water in the desert.) *Really exciting games are few and far between.* (You seldom see such an exciting game.)

fiddle See PLAY SECOND FIDDLE.

fiddle around See FOOL AROUND 3.

fiddler See PAY THE PIPER *or* PAY THE FIDDLER.

field See CENTER FIELD, LEFT FIELD, OUT IN LEFT FIELD, PLAY THE FIELD, RIGHT FIELD.

fielder's choice *n.* A try by a baseball fielder to put out a man on base rather than the batter. *Jones was out at third on a fielder's choice.* (Jones was out at third base by the fielder who decided to throw the ball to third instead of throwing to first base to put out the batter.)

field goal *n.* **1** A score in football made by kicking the ball over the bar between the goal posts. *The Giants were not able to make a touchdown but they kicked two field goals.* (The Giants scored twice by kicking the ball between the goal posts although they did not score a touchdown.) Compare EXTRA POINT. **2** A score in basketball made by a successful shot through the basket not made on a free throw. *A field goal counts two points.* (A successful shot through the basket during play counts two points.) Compare FOUL SHOT, FREE THROW.

fifth See TAKE THE FIFTH.

fifty-fifty[1] *adv., informal* Equally; evenly. *The two boys divided the marbles they won fifty-fifty.* (Each boy gave the other boy half the marbles he won.) *When Dick and Sam bought an old car, they divided the cost fifty-fifty.* (Each paid half the cost.)

fifty-fifty[2] *adj., informal* **1** Divided or shared equally. *It will be a fifty-fifty arrangement; half the money for me and half for you.* (The agreement is to divide the money equally.) **2** Half for and half against; half good and half bad. *There is only a fifty-fifty chance that we will the game.* (The chances of winning or losing are the same.) Compare HALF AND HALF.

fight fire with fire *v. phr. slightly formal, of Biblical origin* To fight back in the same way one was attacked; make a defense similar to the attack. *The candidate was determined to fight fire with fire in the debate.* (The candidate was determined to answer his opponent with the same kind of attack.)

fight tooth and nail See TOOTH AND NAIL.

figure in *v.* **1** *informal* To add to a total; remember to put down in figures. *We figured in the travel expenses but forgot the cost of meals.* (When we added together the money needed for our trip, we added in the cost of traveling but forgot the cost of meals.) **2** To have a part in; be partly responsible for. *Joe figured in all our touchdowns.* (Joe helped to make all the touchdowns we scored.) *Mary's good grades figured in her choice as class president.* (Her class named her as president partly because she has good grades.)

figure on *v.* **1** To expect and think about while making plans. *We did not figure on having so many people at the picnic.* (We did not think so many people would come.) *He figured on going to town the next day.* (He planned to go to town the next day.) Syn. PLAN ON. **2** To depend on; be sure about. *You can figure on him to be on time.* (You can be sure he will be on time.) Syn. COUNT ON.

figure out *v.* **1** To find an answer by thinking about (some problem or difficulty); solve. *Tom couldn't figure out the last problem on the arithmetic test.* (Tom could not find the answer; he did not know how to work the problem.) *Sam couldn't figure out how to print a program until the teacher showed him how.* (Sam tried to think of the things the teacher would do to print a program, but he could not.) *Mary couldn't figure out why her cake tasted so funny until she found salt mixed in the sugar bag.* (She couldn't understand why her cake tasted so strange.) Compare FIND OUT 1. **2** To learn how to explain; understand. *Laurence is an odd boy; I can't figure him out.* (I can't explain why Laurence acts as he does; I don't understand him.) Compare MAKE OUT 2.

fill in *v.* **1** To write words needed in blanks; put in; fill. *You should fill in all the blanks on an application for a job.* (You should write your name, age, and other things asked.) **2** *informal* To tell what you should know. *The new boy didn't know the rules so Bob filled him in.* (Bob told the new boy what the rules were.) *The teacher filled in Mary about classwork done while she was sick.* (The teacher explained what lessons Mary had missed.) **3** To take another's place; substitute. *The teacher was sick and Miss Jones filled in for her.* (Miss Jones taught the sick teacher's class.)

fill one's shoes *v. phr.* To take the place of another and do as well; to substitute satisfactorily for.—A cliché. *When Jack got hurt, the coach had nobody to fill his shoes.* (Jack was a fine player and nobody could do as well.) *Joe hopes to fill his father's shoes.* (Joe hopes

to have his father's job when he grows up and to do the work as well.) See IN ONE'S SHOES.

fill out *v.* **1** To put in what is missing; complete; finish; *especially,* to complete (a printed application blank or other form) by writing the missing facts in the blank spaces; to write down facts which are asked for in (a report or application.) *After Tom passed his driving test he filled out an application for his driver's license.* (He wrote his name and other facts on a printed paper to get his driver's license.) *The policeman filled out a report of the accident.* (The policeman wrote down the facts about the accident.) **2** To become heavier and fatter; gain weight. *When Bill was nineteen he began to fill out.* (At the age of nineteen Bill gained weight and looked heavier.) *The girl was pale and thin after her sickness, but in a few months she filled out.* (After getting well and resting a few months, she gained back her lost weight.)

fill the bases See LOAD THE BASES.

fill the bill *v. phr., informal* To be just what is needed; be good enough for something; be just right. *The boss was worried about hiring a deaf boy, but after he tried Tom out for a few weeks, he said that Tom filled the bill.* (He found that Tom did good work.) *I thought I would need a special tool, but this wrench fills the bill.* (This wrench seems to work in place of a special tool.)

filthy lucre *n., informal* Money, especially when thought of as bad or shameful. *When the rich gambler tried to make Sarah marry him, she said, "Keep your filthy lucre—I shall marry the man I love."* (Sarah told him she did not want him or the money he got by gambling.)—Sometimes used in a joking way. *Come and let's get rid of some filthy lucre.* (Let's spend our money.)

finders keepers *or* **finders keepers, losers weepers** *informal* Those who find lost things can keep them.—Used usually by children to claim the right to keep something they have found. *I don't have to give it back; it's finders keepers.* (I don't have to give it back because I found it and can keep it.) *Finders keepers, losers weepers! It's my knife now!* (I found the knife and I'm going to keep it.)

find fault *v. phr.* To find something wrong; complain; criticize. *She tries to please him, but he always finds fault.* (He finds something wrong with everything she does.) *They found fault with every box I made.* (They found something wrong or something they didn't like in every box I made.) Compare JUMP ON, PICK AT 3.

find it in one's heart *v. phr.* To be able or willing because of your nature.—A somewhat formal cliché used mainly in negative or interrogative sentences. *He could not find it in his heart to tell her about her mother's death.* (He was not hard-hearted enough to tell her that her mother was dead.) *Can you find it* *in your heart to forgive me?* (Are you kind enough to forgive me?) *He could never find it in his heart to be mean to a dog.* (He was too kind to be mean to a dog.)

find one's —— *v. phr.* To become able to use (some power of the body or mind.) *In the program for the parents, John was nervous and could not speak at first; then he found his tongue.* (First he could not speak; then he was able again to speak.) *The young bird had just found its wings.* (The young bird had just learned how to fly.) *The baby was just beginning to find its feet.* (The baby was just beginning to learn how to walk.) *The question surprised him, and it was a minute before he found his tongue.* (He was so surprised by the question that he couldn't say anything for a minute.)

find oneself *v. phr.* To find out what one is fitted for and succeed in that. *Mary tried several lines of work, but at last found herself as a teacher.* (She had other jobs but liked teaching best and succeeded in it.) *Sometimes young people move around a long time from job to job before they find themselves.* (They try many jobs and at last find the job they like and do well.)

find out *v.* **1** To learn or discover (something you did not know before.) *One morning the baby found out for the first time that she could walk.* (She discovered by trying that she could walk.) *I don't know how this car works, but I'll soon find out.* (I don't know how the car works, but I'll learn by trying it.) *He watched the birds to find out where they go.* (He hoped to learn where birds go by watching them.) *Mary was angry when Jane found out her secret.* (Mary was angry when Jane learned something that Mary wanted to keep secret.) **2** To get facts; to get facts about. *He wrote to find out about a job in Alaska.* (He wrote for information on a job in Alaska.) *She found out how much the house would cost.* (She got the facts on how much the house would cost.) **3** To discover (someone) doing wrong; catch. *Some children are bad when no one is watching them, but they are usually found out.* (Some children are bad when no one is watching them, but their parents usually catch them or learn about it later.) *The boy knew that if he cheated on the test the teacher would find him out.* (He knew the teacher would discover that he cheated.)

find out the hard way See HARD WAY.

fine feathers do not make fine birds *literary* A person who wears fine clothes may not be as good as he looks.—A proverb. *Mary is pretty and she wears pretty clothes, but she is very mean. Fine feathers do not make fine birds.* (Although Mary looks very nice, she is really not nice at all.) Compare HANDSOME IS AS HANDSOME DOES.

fine kettle of fish See KETTLE OF FISH.

fine-tooth comb *n. phr.* Great care; careful attention so as not to miss anything. *The police searched the scene of the crime with a fine-tooth comb for clues.* (The police searched very carefully for clues.) *My room is so clean you couldn't find dirt if you went over it with a fine-tooth comb.* (You won't find any dirt in my room no matter how hard you look.) Compare LEAVE NO STONE UNTURNED.

finger See BURN ONE'S FINGERS, CROSS ONE'S FINGERS, *or* KEEP ONE'S FINGERS CROSSED, LAY A FINGER ON, LIFT A FINGER, PUT ONE'S FINGER ON *also* LAY ONE'S FINGER ON, SLIP THROUGH ONE'S FINGERS, SNAP ONE'S FINGERS AT, STICKY FINGERS, TWIST AROUND ONE'S LITTLE FINGER, WORK ONE'S FINGERS TO THE BONE.

finger in the pie *n. phr., informal* Something to do with what happens; part interest or responsibility.—A cliché. *When the girls got up a Christmas party, I felt sure Alice had a finger in the pie.* (I was sure Alice was one of the girls who planned the party.) *The Jones Company was chosen to build the new hospital and we knew Mr. Smith had a finger in the pie.* (We knew Mr. Smith had helped the Jones Company to get the job of building the new hospital.) *Jack is a boy with a finger in every pie at school, from dramatics to football.* (Jack is active in very many activities at school.) Compare HAVE A HAND IN, TOO MANY IRONS IN THE FIRE.

fingertip See AT ONE'S FINGERTIPS.

finish up See END UP 4.

fire See BALL OF FIRE, BETWEEN THE DEVIL AND THE DEEP BLUE SEA *or* BETWEEN TWO FIRES, BUILD A FIRE UNDER, BURNT CHILD DREADS THE FIRE, CATCH FIRE, DRAW FIRE, FAT'S IN THE FIRE, FIGHT FIRE WITH FIRE, HANG FIRE, HEAP COALS OF FIRE ON ONE'S HEAD, HOLD ONE'S FIRE *or* HOLD FIRE, IRON IN THE FIRE, KEEP THE HOME FIRES BURNING, LINE OF FIRE, ON FIRE, OPEN FIRE, OUT OF THE FRYING PAN INTO THE FIRE, PLAY WITH FIRE, PULL ONE'S CHESTNUTS OUT OF THE FIRE, SET FIRE TO, SET THE WORLD ON FIRE, TILL THE LAST GUN IS FIRED *or* UNTIL THE LAST GUN IS FIRED, UNDER FIRE.

firing squad *n.* A group of soldiers chosen to shoot a prisoner to death or to fire shots over a grave as a tribute. *A dictator often sends his enemies before a firing squad.* (A man who seizes power often has his enemies shot.) *The dead general was honored by a firing squad.* (Some soldiers fired shots over the grave to honor him.)

first See AT FIRST BLUSH, AT FIRST SIGHT, CAST THE FIRST STONE, GET TO FIRST BASE *or* REACH FIRST BASE, IN THE FIRST PLACE, OF THE FIRST WATER.

first and foremost *adv. phr.* As the most important thing; first. *First and foremost they needed food.* (Food was the very first thing they needed.) *I want you to remember to pay that bill first and foremost.* (I want you to pay that bill before you do anything else.)

First and foremost, we must keep America free. (The most important thing is to keep America free.)

first and last *adv. phr.* Most noticeably; all the time; chiefly. *He was first and last a school teacher.* (He loved teaching better than anything else.) *Steven joined the army because first and last he wanted to help his country.* (Steven's chief wish was to help his country so he joined the army.) Syn. ABOVE ALL.

first base *n. phr.* **1** The base that must be touched first by a baseball player after batting. *He got to first base on four balls.* (The pitcher made four bad pitches and the batter went to first base.) **2** See GET TO FIRST BASE.

first class *n.* **1** The first rank; the highest class; the best group. *The pianist was quite good but he was not in the first class.* (He was not good enough to compare to the very best pianists.) **2** The most expensive or comfortable class of travel; the best or one of the best groups in which to travel, especially by ship, train, or airplane. *Most people can't afford the first class when they take a long journey by ship.* (The first class is too expensive for most people.) **3** The way of sending all mail that includes letters and post cards, anything written by hand or typewriter, and anything sealed so that it cannot be inspected, and that is the most expensive class of mail but receives the best treatment. *The usual way to send a letter is by first class.* (First class is the regular way of sending a letter.) Compare SECOND CLASS, THIRD CLASS.

first-class¹ *adj.* **1** Of the highest class or best kind; excellent; first-rate. *Jane did a first-class job of repairing the coat.* (She did a very good job.) *It was a first-class TV program.* (It was a very good program.) Compare TOP-NOTCH. **2** Of the best or most expensive class of travelling. *Mr. Jones bought a first-class plane ticket to Chicago.* (He bought the most expensive ticket for the best kind of seat on the plane.) **3** Belonging to the class of mail for sending letters, post cards, and handwritten or typewritten mail that is sealed. *It is expensive to send a heavy letter by first-class mail.* (The heavier the letter the more the first-class mailing costs.)

first-class² *adv.* With the best material; in the best or most expensive way. *When Mr. Van Smith goes anywhere he always travels first-class.* (He pays enough to travel in the most comfortable way.) *How did you send the package? First-class.* (The package was sent by first-class mail.)

first come, first served *truncated sent, informal* If you arrive first, you will be served first; people will be waited on in the order they come; the person who comes first will have his turn first. *Get in line for your ice cream, boys. First come, first served.* (You will get ice cream in your turn in the line.) *The rule in the restaurant is first come, first served.*

(People who come to the restaurant first get their food first.) *The team's owners announced that tickets for the World Series would be sold on a first come, first served basis only.* (The team's owners announced that tickets would be sold first to those who applied first.) *There are only a few seats left so it's first come, first served.* (The few seats left will be given to those first ones who come and sit in them.) Compare EARLY BIRD CATCHES THE WORM.

first cousin *n.* The child of your aunt or uncle. *Tom's only first cousin was Ralph, the son of his Uncle John.* (Ralph is the only child of Tom's uncles or aunts, so he is Tom's only first cousin.)

first off *adv. phr., informal* Before anything else; first. *First off, I want you to mow the lawn.* (The first thing I want you to do is cut the grass.)

first-run *adj. phr.* Shown for the first time; new. *The local theater showed only first-run movies.* (The local theater showed only new movies which had not been seen there before and did not show old films.)

first stone See CAST THE FIRST STONE.

first string¹ *n., informal* **1** The best group of players on a team; first team; A team. *Dick loved basketball and practiced hard until he was put on the first string.* (He was put on the first team, to play against other schools.) **2** The best group of workers. *Tom learned his trade so well that his boss soon called him one of his first string.* (The boss called him one of his best workers.)

first-string *adj., informal* **1** On the starting team or A team. *He was the first-string quarterback.* (He was the quarterback who started the game, not a B player.) **2** Of the best quality; foremost. *He was the least expensive of the city's first-string lawyers.* (He charged lower fees than all the other fine lawyers.)

first things first Other things must wait until the most important and necessary things are done. *Study your lessons before you go out to play. First things first.* (Your lessons are more important and must be done before play.)

fish See COLD FISH, KETTLE OF FISH, NEITHER FISH NOR FOWL, NOT THE ONLY FISH IN THE SEA, OTHER FISH TO FRY.

fish-and-chips *n. phr.* Fried fish and french-fried potatoes. *The family went to a drive-in restaurant and had fish-and-chips.* (They ate fried fish and french-fried potatoes.)

fish for *v., informal* To try to get or to find out (something), by hinting or by a roundabout way to try to lead someone else to give or tell you what you want by hinting. *Jerry was always fishing for an invitation to Bob's house.* (He was always saying something to show he would like to be invited to Bob's house.) *Near examination time, some of the students fish for information.* (They try to make the teacher give them a hint about what will be in the examination.)

fish fry *n.* An outdoor party or picnic at which fish are fried and eaten. *The guests at the fish fry caught and cooked their own fish.* (At the outdoor fish party the guests caught and cooked their own fish.)

fish or cut bait *v. phr., informal* **1** Decide what you want to do and stop wasting time; either act now or give someone else a chance or turn. *Jack couldn't decide whether to go to college or get a job, so his father told him to fish or cut bait.* (He told Jack to make his choice.) *Buy the kind of ice cream you want or give someone else in line a chance. Fish or cut bait!* (Don't take all day to decide because there is a line of people.) Compare MAKE UP ONE'S MIND. **2** Either try hard and do your best, or quit. *Frank missed football practice so often that the coach told him to fish or cut bait.* (Come to every practice or quit.)

fish out of water *n. phr.* A person who is out of his proper place in life; someone who does not fit in.—A cliché. *Because Ed could not swim, he felt like a fish out of water at the beach.* (Ed did not know how to swim and felt uncomfortable at the beach where everyone else was swimming.) *She was the only girl at the party not in a formal dress and she felt like a fish out of water.* (All the other girls were in formal dresses and she was embarrassed.) Compare OUT OF ONE'S ELEMENT, OUT OF PLACE.

fist See HARD-FISTED.

fit See BY FITS AND STARTS, GIVE FITS, HAVE A FIT *or* HAVE FITS, IF THE SHOE FITS, WEAR IT, SEE FIT *also* THINK FIT, SURVIVAL OF THE FITTEST.

fit as a fiddle *adj. phr.* In very good health.—A cliché. *The man was almost 90 years old but fit as a fiddle.* (He was almost 90 but in very good health.) *Mary rested at home for a few weeks after her operation; then she felt fit as a fiddle.* (She felt very well after her rest.)

fit like a glove *v. phr.* To fit perfectly.—A cliché. *Her new dress fits her like a glove.* (Her new dress fits perfectly.)

fit out *or* **fit up** *v.* To give things needed; furnish. *The soldiers were fitted out with guns and clothing.* (The soldiers were given the guns and clothing needed.) *The government fitted out warships and got sailors for them.* (The government put everything needed in the ships.) *The house was fitted out very nicely.* (The house had nice furniture and other things in it.) *He fitted his room up as a photographic laboratory.* (He made his room into a photographic laboratory.)

fit the bill See FILL THE BILL.

fit to a T See TO A T.

fit to be tied[1] *adj. phr., informal* Very angry or upset.—A cliché. *She was fit to be tied when she saw the broken glass.* (She was very angry and upset at seeing the glass broken.)

fit to be tied[2] *adv. phr., substandard* Very hard.—Used for emphasis. *Uncle Willie was laughing fit to be tied at the surprised look on Mother's face.* (Uncle Willie was laughing very hard.)

fix See GET A FIX *or* GIVE SOMEONE A FIX, GET A FIX ON.

fix someone's wagon *or* **fix someone's little red wagon** *v. phr., informal* **1** (Said to a child as a threat) to administer a spanking. *Stop that right away or I'll fix your (little red) wagon!* (Stop that or I'll spank you.) **2** (Said of an adult) to thwart or frustrate another, to engineer his failure. *If he sues me for slander, I will counter-sue him for malicious prosecution. That will fix his wagon!* (I will counter his moves against him thereby engineering his downfall.)

fix someone up with *v. phr., informal* To help another get a date with a woman or man by arranging a meeting for the two. *Say Joe, can you possibly fix me up with someone this weekend? I am so terribly lonesome!* (Can you possibly get me a date with a girl, I have no one to go out with.)

fizzle out *v., informal* **1** To stop burning; die out. *The fuse fizzled out before exploding the firecracker.* (The fuse didn't stay lit long enough to blow up the firecracker.) **2** To fail after a good start; end in failure. *The power mower worked fine for a while but then it fizzled out.* (The mower ran fine for a short time but then sputtered and stopped.) *The party fizzled out when everyone went home early.* (The party ended in failure when the people went home early.)

flag down *v., informal* To stop by waving a signal flag or as if waving a signal flag. *The signalman flagged down the freight train.* (The signalman stopped the train by waving a signal flag.) *A policeman flagged down the car with his flashlight.* (A policeman stopped the car by waving at it.)

flakeball *or* **flake** *n., slang, drug culture* A disjointed, or "flaky" person, who is forgetful and incoherent, as if under the influence of narcotics. *Hermione is a regular flakeball.* (She is as disjointed as if she were under the influence of drugs.) Compare SPACED OUT.

flame See ADD FUEL TO THE FLAME, GO UP IN FLAMES.

flanker back *n.* A football back who can play far to the outside of his regular place. *The coach is still looking for a speedy boy to play flanker back.*) The coach is still looking for a boy who is fast enough to play the wide backfield position and catch passes.)

flare up *v.* **1** To burn brightly for a short time especially after having died down. *The fire flared up again and then died.* (The fire burned brightly for a short time and then died.) **2** To become suddenly angry. *The mayor flared up at the reporter's remark.*

(The mayor suddenly got angry at what the reporter said.) *The mother flared up at her children.* (Suddenly the mother showed great anger toward her children.) **3** To begin again suddenly, especially for a short time after a quiet time. *Mr. Gray's arthritis flared up sometimes.* (He sometimes had attacks of arthritis.) *Even after they had conquered the country, revolts sometimes flared up.* (New fighting sometimes started suddenly.)

flash See IN A FLASH.

flash card *n.* A card with numbers or words on it that is used in teaching a class. *The teacher used flash cards to drill the class in addition.* (The teacher used cards with problems on one side and answers on the other to drill the class in addition.)

flash in the pan *n. phr., slang* A person or thing that starts out well but does not continue. *The new quarterback was a flash in the pan.* (The new quarterback started out well but after a while he did not do very well.) *Mary got 100 on the first test in arithmetic but it was just a flash in the pan because she failed in arithmetic.* (Mary did very well in the beginning but didn't continue her good work.)

flat See FALL FLAT, IN NO TIME *or* IN NOTHING FLAT, LEAVE FLAT.

flat broke See STONE-BROKE.

flatfoot *n., slang, derogatory* A policeman. *What does Joe do for a living?—He's a flatfoot.* (He is a policeman.)

flat-footed *adj., informal* **1** Straightforward; forthright; direct; outright. *The governor issued a flat-footed denial of the accusation.* (The governor said the accusation was false.) *He came out flat-footed against the idea.* (He spoke right out against the idea.) **2** Not ready; not prepared;—usually used with *catch. The teacher's question caught Tim flat-footed.* (Tim was not prepared to answer the teacher's question.) *Unexpected company at lunch time caught Mrs. Green flat-footed.* (Unexpected company for lunch caught Mrs. Green unprepared to feed them.)

flat-out *adv. phr., informal* **1** Without hiding anything; plainly; openly. *The student told his teacher flat-out that he was not listening to her.* (The student told his teacher honestly that he was not listening to her.) **2** At top speed; as fast as possible. *He saw two men running flat-out from the wild rhinoceros.* (He saw the men running as fast as they could from the angry rhinoceros.)

flatter oneself To be sure of your own talent or skill; highly confident. *I flatter myself that I am a better swimmer than he is.* (I am very sure that I am a better swimmer than he is.)

flea in one's ear *n. phr., informal* An idea or answer that is not welcome; an annoying or surprisingly sharp reply or hint.—A cliché. *I'll put a flea in his ear if he bothers me once more.* (I'll give him a sharp hint not to bother me if he comes to see me again.)

flea market *n. phr.* A place where antiques, second-hand things, and cheap articles are sold, and especially one in the open air. *The local antique dealers held a flea market and fair on the high-school athletic field.* (The local antique dealers set up an open-air market on the high-school field for the sale of antiques and other items.) *There are many outdoor flea markets in Europe.* (There are many places in Europe where cheap and used things are sold outdoors.)

flesh See IN PERSON *also* IN THE FLESH, NEITHER FISH NOR FOWL *also* NEITHER FISH, FLESH, NOR FOWL, PRESS THE FLESH, THORN IN THE FLESH.

flesh and blood *n.* **1** A close relative (as a father, daughter, brother); close relatives.—A cliché; used in the phrase *one's own flesh and blood. Such an answer from her—and she's my own flesh and blood, too!* (I am shocked at such an answer from a near relation.) **2** The appearance of being real or alive.—A cliché. *The author doesn't give his characters any flesh and blood.* (The characters in his book do not seem real.) **3** The human body. *Before child labor laws, small children often had to work 50 or 60 hours a week in factories. It was more than flesh and blood could bear.* (It was too hard for children, and many became sick or had their health ruined for life.)

flesh out *v., informal* **1** To add to; make fuller, bigger, or longer. *The author fleshed out his story by adding more about his war experiences.* (He made his story longer by adding more.) **2** *also* **flesh up** To become heavier, put on weight, or flesh. *He lost weight after his illness but is beginning to flesh out again.* (He's regaining lost weight.) See FILL OUT.²

flesh up See FLESH OUT 2.

fling oneself at See THROW ONESELF AT.

fling oneself at someone's head See THROW ONESELF AT SOMEONE'S HEAD.

flip-flop¹ *v., informal* To alternate the positions of; exchange the places of; switch. *The football coach had one play in which he flip-flopped his left halfback and fullback.* (In one of the coach's plays, the left halfback and the fullback exchanged places.)

flip-flop² *n., informal* A complete change; a switch from one thing to an entirely different one. *John wanted to be a carpenter like his father, but when he saw the print shop he did a flip-flop and now he's learning printing.* (He made a complete change in his plans for the future.)

flip-flop³ *adj. phr., informal* Involving or using a change from one of two places, positions, or alternatives to the other. *The machine was controlled by a flip-flop switch.* (The machine was controlled by a switch that was either off or on.) *The football coach hoped to surprise his opponents by using a flip-flop* *offense.* (The coach hoped to surprise his opponents by using an offense in which players exchange positions.)

flip one's lid *also* **flip one's wig** *slang* **1** To lose one's temper. *When that pushy salesman came back Mom really flipped her lid.* (Mother grew very angry when the stubborn salesman came back.) Compare BLOW A FUSE. **2** To lose your mind; become insane. *When he offered me three times the pay I was getting, I thought he had flipped his lid.* (I thought he must be crazy when he offered me three times as much money.) **3** To become unreasonably enthusiastic. *She flipped her lid over a hat she saw in the store window.* (She just had to have that new hat.) *He's flipped his lid over that new actress.* (He has become crazy about a movie actress.)

flip out *v. phr., slang, informal* To go insane, to go out of one's mind. *It is impossible to talk to Joe today—he must have flipped out.* (It is impossible to talk to him—he must have gone mad.)

flock See BIRDS OF A FEATHER FLOCK TOGETHER.

floor See GROUND FLOOR, MOP THE FLOOR WITH, WALK THE FLOOR.

flop See FLIP-FLOP.

flower child *n., slang, informal* **1** A young person who believes in nonviolence and carries flowers around to symbolize his peace-loving nature. *Flower children are supposed to be nonviolent, but they sure make a lot of noise when they demonstrate!* (These young people are supposedly peace-loving but they can be noisy and violent.) **2** Any person who cannot cope with reality. *Face facts, Suzie, stop being such a flower child!* (Stop being so naively idealistic.)

flower power *n., slang* The supposed power of love and nonviolence as intended to be used by members of the anti-culture to change American society. *The young people were marching for flower-power.* (They marched in order to demonstrate on behalf of changing American society by nonviolent means.)

fluff one's lines See BLOW ONE'S LINES.

fluff stuff *n., slang, citizen's band radio jargon* Snow. *We can expect some fluff stuff this afternoon.* (It will be snowing.)

flush it *v., slang* **1** To fail (something). *I really flushed it in my math course.* (I failed my math course.) **2** *Interj., used imperatively* Expression registering refusal to believe something considered stupid or false. *You expect me to buy that story? Flush it!* (You expect me to believe that? Nonsense!)

fly See BIRD HAS FLOWN, GO FLY A KITE, MAKE THE FEATHERS FLY, MAKE THE FUR FLY, ON THE FLY, POP FLY, SACRIFICE FLY.

fly at one's throat *v. phr.* To attack you suddenly with great anger. *When Tom called Dick a bad name, Dick flew at his throat.* (Dick attacked Tom suddenly.)

fly ball *n.* A baseball hit high into the air. *He hit an easy fly ball to center field.* (He hit a ball in the air to center field that was not hard to catch.)

fly blind *v. phr.* **1** To fly an airplane by instruments alone. *In the heavy fog he had to fly blind.* (He couldn't see in the fog so he had to use his instruments to fly.) **2** *informal* To do something without understanding what you are doing. *I'm glad the car runs now; I was flying blind when I fixed it.* (I'm glad the car runs now because I was only guessing when I fixed it.) *He's flying blind when he talks about philosophy.* (He doesn't understand what he's talking about when he talks about philosophy.)

fly-by-night[1] *adj.* Set up to make a lot of money in a hurry, then disappear so people can't find you to complain about poor work, etc.; not trustworthy; not reliable. *Mrs. Blank bought her vacuum cleaner from a new company; when she tried to have it fixed, she found it was a fly-by-night business.* (She found that the company had closed its business and no one could be found there.)

fly-by-night[2] *n., informal* **1** A company that sells many cheap things for a big profit and then disappears. *A dependable company honors its guarantees, but a fly-by-night only wants your money.* (A dependable company does what it promises to do, but a fly-by-night company doesn't.) **2** A person who does not pay his bills, but sneaks away (as at night.) *Hotels are bothered by fly-by-nights.* (Hotels are bothered by people who sneak away at night and don't pay their bills.)

fly by the seat of one's pants *v. phr., slang* To fly an airplane by feel and instinct rather than with the help of the instruments. *Many pilots in World War I had to fly by the seat of their pants.* (Many pilots in World War I flew with few or no instruments, by touch or feeling.)

flying See WITH FLYING COLORS.

flying high *adj., slang* Very happy; joyful. *Jack was flying high after his team won the game.* (He was very happy when his team won.) Compare IN THE CLOUDS, ON TOP OF THE WORLD.

flying tackle *n., informal* A tackle made by jumping through the air at the person to be tackled. *Most football coaches don't want their players to make flying tackles.* (Most coaches don't want their players to make tackles by jumping through the air.) *The policeman stopped the burglar with a flying tackle.* (The policeman jumped through the air to knock down the burglar.)

flying wedge *n., informal* **1** An offensive formation in football in which players link arms and line up to form a "V" with the ball carrier in the middle. *The flying wedge was so* *dangerous and hurt so many players that rules have forbidden it for over 50 years.* (This "V" formation was so dangerous in football that it had to be stopped by rules.) **2** A group (as of guards or policemen) who use a "V" formation to help someone get through a crowd. *Police had to form a flying wedge to get the movie star through the crowd of autograph hunters.* (The police linked arms in two lines like an upside-down "V" and pushed the crowd aside.)

fly in the face of *or* **fly in the teeth of** *v. phr.* To ignore; go against; show disrespect or disregard for. *You can't fly in the face of good business rules and expect to be successful.* (You can't expect to be successful if you refuse to follow good business rules.) *Floyd's friends tried to help him, but he flew in the teeth of their advice and soon became a drunkard.* (He refused to accept their advice and kept on drinking too much.)

fly in the ointment *n. phr., informal* An unpleasant part of a pleasant thing; something small that spoils your fun.—A cliché. *We had a lot of fun at the beach; the only fly in the ointment was George's cutting his foot on a piece of glass.* (The only thing that spoiled our fun was the cut on George's foot.) *Your new job sounds too good to be true—interesting work, high pay, short hours. Isn't there any fly in the ointment?* (Isn't there something about the job that you don't like?)

fly off the handle *v. phr., informal* To become very angry.—A cliché. *John flew off the handle whenever Mary made a mistake.* (Every time Mary made a mistake, John became very angry.) *The children's noise made the man next door fly off the handle.* (The neighbor became angry when the children made too much noise.) Syn. LOSE ONE'S TEMPER.

fly the coop *v. phr., slang* To leave suddenly and secretly; run away. *The robbers flew the coop before the police arrived.* (The robbers ran away before the police arrived.) *His partner flew the coop with all the money.* (His partner ran away with all the money.)

foam at the mouth *v. phr., slang* To be very angry, like a mad dog. *By the time Uncle Henry had the third flat tire he was really foaming at the mouth.* (He was as angry as he could be when he had the third flat tire.)

fob off *v., informal* **1** To get something false accepted as good or real. *The peddler fobbed off pieces of glass as diamonds.* (The peddler said the pieces of glass were diamonds and fooled the people.) Syn. PALM OFF, PASS OFF. **2** To put aside; not really answer but get rid of. *Her little brother asked where she was going, but she fobbed him off with an excuse.* (She didn't answer but said something else to quiet him.)

fog See IN A FOG.

foggy bottom *n., slang* An area in downtown Washington, D.C. where many offices of the Department of State are located; hence figuratively, the U.S. Department of State. *The press secretary gave us a lot of foggy bottom double-talk about the hostage crisis in the Near East.* (The report on the hostage crisis was shrouded in ambiguous State Department jargon.)

fold up *v., informal* To collapse; fail. *The team folded up in the last part of the season.* (The team did well in the beginning but failed later in the season.) *The new restaurant folded up in less than a year.* (The new restaurant went out of business in less than a year.) Compare FALL APART.

folk See WEE FOLK.

follow See AS FOLLOWS.

follower See CAMP FOLLOWER.

follow in one's footsteps *also* **follow in one's tracks** *v. phr.* To follow someone's example; follow someone exactly.—A cliché. *He followed in his father's footsteps and became a doctor.* (He followed his father's example and became a doctor.) Compare LIKE FATHER, LIKE SON.

follow one's nose *v. phr., informal* **1** To go straight ahead; continue in the same direction. *Just follow your nose and you'll get there.* (Just continue in the same way and you'll get there.) **2** To go any way you happen to think of. *Oh, I don't know just where I want to go. I'll just follow my nose and see what happens.* (I'll just go where I feel like going; I don't have any plans.)

follow out *v .phr., informal* **1** To do fully; finish (what you are told to do.) *The boy followed out the instructions and made a fine model plane.* (He did what the instructions told him to do.) Compare FOLLOW THROUGH. **2** To keep working at (something) until it is finished; give (something) your attention until it comes to an end or conclusion. *The student followed out all the index references in the encyclopedia until he found what he wanted to know.* (He looked up all the words that he thought might help, and finally found an article telling him what he wanted to know.) Compare FOLLOW UP.

follow suit *v. phr.* **1** To play a card of the same color and kind that another player has put down. *When diamonds were led, I had to follow suit.* (When a diamond card was put down, I had to play another diamond.) **2** To do as someone else has done; follow someone's example. *When the others went swimming, I followed suit.* (When the others went swimming, I went too.)

follow through *v. phr.* **1** To finish a movement that you have started; continue an action to its natural ending. *A football passer should follow through after he throws the ball.* (He shouldn't stop the motion of his arm after the ball has left his hand.) **2** To finish an action that you have started. *Bob drew plans for a* *table for his mother, but he did not follow through by making it.* (Bob made good plans but did not finish the job; he did not make the table.)

follow up *v. phr., informal* **1** To chase or follow closely and without giving up. *The Indians followed up the wounded buffalo until it fell dead.* (They did not let it get away from them.) **2** Make (one action) more successful by doing something more. *After Mary sent a letter to apply for a job; she followed it up by going to talk to the personnel manager.* (She showed she was interested in the job by going to see the man who hired new workers for the company.) *The doctor followed up Billy's operation with x-rays and special exercises to make his foot stronger.* (The doctor kept caring for his foot until it was all right again.) Compare FOLLOW OUT, FOLLOW THROUGH 2. **3a** To hunt for (more news about something that has already been in the newspapers, radio or TV news); find more about. *The day after news of the fire at Brown's store, the newspaper sent a reporter to follow up Mr. Brown's future plans.* (The newspaper sent a reporter to ask for more news.) **3b** To print or broadcast (more news about some happening that has been in the news before). *The fire story was printed Monday, and Tuesday's paper followed it up by saying that Mr. Brown planned to build a bigger and better store at the same place.* (The newspaper told more about the fire story on Tuesday.)

follow-up *n.* Additional work or research by means of which an earlier undertaking's chances of success are increased. *I hope you'll be willing to do a bit of follow-up.* (I hope you will continue to pursue the work you have been doing.)

fond of Having a liking for; attracted to by strong liking. *Alan is fond of candy.* (He likes candy.) *Uncle Bill was the children's favorite, and he was fond of them too.* (Uncle Bill had a strong liking for the children, too.)

food for thought *n. phr.* Something to think about or worth thinking about; something that makes you think.—A hackneyed phrase. *The teacher told John that she wanted to talk to his father, and that gave John food for thought.* (It made John wonder what she wanted to talk to his father about.) *There is much food for thought in this book.* (The book is interesting and makes you think.)

fool See CHILDREN AND FOOLS SPEAK THE TRUTH, MAKE A FOOL OF.

fool and his money are soon parted A foolish person soon wastes his money.—A proverb. *Jimmy spends all his pennies for candy. A fool and his money are soon parted.* (Jimmy wastes his pennies on candy and doesn't save them.)

fool around *or* **mess around** *or* **play around** *or* **monkey around** *v., informal* **1** To spend time playing, fooling, or joking instead of be-

ing serious or working; waste time. *If you go to college, you must work, not fool around.* (You must study seriously, not waste your time.) *The boys fooled around all afternoon in the park.* (They played lazily.) Compare CUT UP 2. To treat or handle carelessly. *Bob cut himself by fooling around with a sharp knife.* (Bob didn't handle the dangerous knife carefully.) *Mother says she wishes John would quit playing around with the girls and get married.* (She says he should be serious about one girl and marry her.) **3** *or* **fiddle around** To work or do something in an irregular or unplanned way; tinker. *Jimmy likes to monkey around with automobile engines.* (He likes to tinker and try out the engines and learn about them.) *Alice is fooling around with the piano in her spare time.* (She plays the piano sometimes but not too seriously.)

fool away *or* **fritter away** *v., informal* To waste foolishly. *Paul failed history because he fooled away his time instead of studying.* (Paul wasted his time idly instead of studying, so he failed.) *The man won a lot of money, but he soon frittered it away and was poor again.* (He wasted the money he won and was soon poor again.)

foolish See PENNY WISE AND POUND FOOLISH.

foot See AT ONE'S FEET, COLD FEET, DEAD ON ONE'S FEET, DRAG ONE'S FEET, FROM HEAD TO FOOT, GET OFF ON THE WRONG FOOT, GET ONE'S FEET WET, HAND AND FOOT, KEEP ONE'S FEET, KNOCK OFF ONE'S FEET, LAND ON ONE'S FEET, LET GRASS GROW UNDER ONE'S FEET, ONE FOOT IN THE GRAVE, ON FOOT, ON ONE'S FEET, PLAY FOOTSIE, PUT ONE'S BEST FOOT FORWARD, PUT ONE'S FOOT DOWN, PUT ONE'S FOOT IN IT, SET FOOT, SHOE ON THE OTHER FOOT, STAND ON ONE'S OWN FEET, SWEEP OFF ONE'S FEET, THINK ON ONE'S FEET, THROW ONESELF AT SOMEONE'S FEET.

footed See FLAT FOOTED.

foot in the door *n. phr., informal* The first step toward getting or doing something; a start toward success; opening. *Don't let Jane get her foot in the door by joining the club or soon she'll want to be president.* (If you give Jane a chance she'll want to run the club.)

footstep See FOLLOW IN ONE'S FOOTSTEPS.

for a fall See RIDING FOR A FALL.

for all **1** In spite of; even with.—Used for contrast. *For all his city ways, he is a country boy at heart.* (He has city ways, but he is still a country boy.) *There may be mistakes occasionally, but for all that, it is the best book on the subject.* (It is the best book on the subject, even though it has a few mistakes; it is best, anyhow.) *For all his money, he was very unhappy.* (He was sad, even though he was rich.) **2** *also* **for aught** To the extent that;—Used like a negative with *care* and *know*. *For all I care, you can throw it away.* (I don't care if you throw it away.) *For all he knows, we might be in Boston.* (He doesn't know where we are. We might be in Boston, but he wouldn't know.) Compare AS FAR AS 2, ONCE AND FOR ALL.

for all one is worth With all of your strength; as hard as you can. *Roger ran for all he was worth to catch the bus.* (He ran as fast as he could to catch the bus.)

for all one knows *adv. phr.* Possibly—one has no way to know whether or not it is true; maybe. *For all I know, the moon is made of green cheese.* (I certainly can't tell what the moon is made of.)

for all the world *adv. phr.* 1 For anything; for any price.—A cliché; used with a negative. *I would not change places with him for all the world.* (I wouldn't change places with him for anything.) Compare FOR LOVE OR MONEY. 2 Just exactly. *When he came through that door he looked for all the world like his father when he was a boy.* (When he came through the door he looked exactly like his father when his father was a boy.)

for a loop See KNOCK FOR A LOOP *or* THROW FOR A LOOP.

for a loss See THROW FOR A LOSS.

for a ride See TAKE FOR A RIDE.

for as much as *conj., formal* Because; since. *For as much as the senator is eighty years old, we feel he should not run for reelection.* (Since the senator is eighty, we feel he should not run again.) Syn. INASMUCH AS.

for a song *adv. phr., informal* At a low price; for a bargain price; cheaply. *He sold the invention for a song and its buyers were the ones who got rich.* (He sold his invention for very little money and the people who bought it got rich.) *They bought the house for a song and sold it a few years later at a good profit.* (They bought the house cheaply and sold it for a good profit.)

for aught See FOR ALL 2.

for bear See LOADED FOR BEAR.

for better or worse *or* **for better or for worse** *adv. phr.* With good or bad effect, depending on how one looks at the matter. *The historian did justice, for better or worse, to the careers of several famous men.* (He wrote the truth about them whether they were good or bad.) 2 *(Archaic, restricted to marriage vows)* Forever, for as long as one may live. *With this ring I thee wed, for richer or poorer, in sickness and in health, for better or worse, til death do us part.* (The marriage vow says that they are marrying one another no matter what may happen in the future, under all conditions and eventualities.)

forbid See GOD FORBID.

for broke See GO FOR BROKE.

force See IN FORCE, JOIN FORCES.

force one's hand *v. phr.* To make you do something or tell what you will do sooner than planned. *Ben did not want to tell where he was going, but his friend forced his hand.*

(He did not want to tell where he was going, but his friend made him tell.) *Mr. Smith planned to keep his land until prices went up, but he had so many doctor bills that it forced his hand.* (He had to sell his land before he was ready, because he needed money.)

force play *or* **force-out** *n.* A play in baseball in which a runner is out because he does not run to the next base before the fielder with the ball touches the base. *Bob was out at second base when Joe hit into a force play.* (Bob was out at second base because the fielder got the ball that Joe hit and touched the base before Bob did.)

for certain See FOR SURE.

for crying out loud *informal* —Used as an exclamation to show that you feel surprised or cross. *For crying out loud, look who's here!* (Well! I am surprised to see you.) *For crying out loud! that's the third time you've done it wrong.* (I am getting quite cross; that's the third time you've done it wrong.) Compare FOR ——— SAKE.

for dear life. *adv. phr.* As though afraid of losing your life—A trite expression. *He was running for dear life toward town.* (He was running toward town as if he thought his life was in danger.) *When the horse began to run, she held on for dear life.* (When the horse began to run, she held on as tightly as she could.)

fore See TO THE FORE.

foremost See FIRST AND FOREMOST.

forest See CAN'T SEE THE WOOD FOR THE TREES *or* CAN'T SEE THE FOREST FOR THE TREES.

forever and a day *adv. phr., informal* For a seemingly endless time; forever; always.—A cliché used for emphasis. *We waited forever and a day to find out who won the contest.* (We waited for what seemed like a very long time to find out who won.) *They promised to remain friends forever and a day.* (They promised to be friends always.)

forever and ever *adv. phr.* Forever; always. —Used for emphasis, usually about spiritual things. *God will live forever and ever.* (God will live forever.)

for example *or* **for instance** *adv. phr.* As an example; as proof; to give an example or illustration. *Not only rich men become President. For example, Lincoln was born poor.* (Not only rich men become President. As one example or proof, Lincoln was a poor man.) *There are jobs more dangerous than truck driving; for instance, training lions.* (There are jobs more dangerous than truck driving; as an example, training lions is more dangerous.) Compare FOR ONE THING.

for fear Because of fear. *He left an hour early for fear of missing his train.* (He was afraid he would miss his train, so he left one hour early.) *She worried for fear that the child would be hurt.* (She was afraid that the child would be hurt.)

for free *adj. phr. substandard* Without having to pay; free. *Hey you guys, look at this balloon! They're for free down at the new store.* (These balloons are free at the new store.)

forget See FORGIVE AND FORGET.

forget oneself *v. phr.* To do something one should have remembered not to do; do something below one's usual conduct although one knows better; let one's self-control slip. *He forgot himself only once at dinner—when he belched.* (He had bad manners at dinner only when he belched.) *He knew he should hold his temper, but because of the trouble he forgot himself and began to shout.* (He lost his temper even though he knew he shouldn't.)

forgive and forget *v.* To have no bad feelings about what happened in the past.—A cliché. *After the argument the boys decided to forgive and forget.* (The boys decided to have no bad feelings about the argument.) Syn. LET BYGONES BE BYGONES, LIVE AND LET LIVE.

for good *also* **for good and all** Permanently, forever, for always. *The lost money was gone for good.* (They never found the lost money.) *He hoped that the repairs would stop the leak for good.* (He hoped that the repairs would keep the pipe from leaking any more.) *When John graduated from school, he decided that he was done with study for good and all.* (John decided that he would never go to school again.) Syn. FOR KEEPS 2.

for good measure *adv. phr.* As something more added to what is expected or needed; as an extra. *He sold me the car at a cheap price and included the radio for good measure.* (He sold me the car cheaply and gave the radio as an extra at no more cost.) *She puts in the spices the recipe calls for and then adds an extra pinch for good measure.* (She puts in a little more spice than the recipe calls for.) Compare IN THE BARGAIN, TO BOOT.

for granted See TAKE FOR GRANTED.

for instance See FOR EXAMPLE.

for it See RUN FOR IT.

for keeps *adv. phr.* **1** For the winner to keep. *They played marbles for keeps* (The winner could keep the marbles.) **2** *informal* For always; forever. *He left town for keeps.* (He went away from town and stayed away.) Syn. FOR GOOD. **3** Seriously, not just for fun. *This is not a joke, it's for keeps.* (It is meant seriously not as a joke.)—Often used in the phrase *play for keeps. The policeman knew that the robber was trying to shoot him. He was playing for keeps.* (The robber wasn't trying to scare him, he was trying to shoot him.)

fork over *or* **fork out** *also* **fork up** *v.* To pay; pay out. *He had to fork over fifty dollars to have the car repaired.* (He had to pay fifty dollars to have the car fixed.) Compare HAND OVER.

for love or money *adv. phr.* For anything;

for any price.—A cliché; used in negative sentences. *I wouldn't give him my dog for love or money.* (I wouldn't give him my dog no matter what he offered.) Compare FOR ALL THE WORLD 1.

form See RAN TRUE TO FORM.

for no man See TIME AND TIDE WAIT FOR NO MAN.

for one As the first of several possible examples; as one example. *Many people do not like certain foods. I for one do not like cabbage.* (As an example, I do not like cabbage.)—Also used with similar words instead of *one. Several materials can be used to make the box: plywood, for one; masonite, for another; sheet metal, for a third.* (Several materials are good for making the box, as first, plywood; second, masonite; third, sheet metal.)

for one's part *also* **on one's part** *adv. phr.* As far as you are concerned; the way you feel or think. *I don't know about you, but for my part I don't want to go to that place.* (The way I feel, I don't want to go to that place.) Compare AS FOR.

for one thing *adv. phr.* As one thing of several; as one in a list of things. *The teacher said, "You get a low mark, for one thing, because you did not do your homework."* (The teacher told the boy one reason why he got a low mark.) *The house was poorly built; for one thing, the roof leaked.* (One thing wrong with the house was a leaky roof.) Compare FOR EXAMPLE, IN THE FIRST PLACE.

for real[1] *adj. phr., informal* Not practice or play; earnest, real, serious. *The war games were over now. This battle was for real.* (This battle was a real battle, not a practice war game.)

for real[2] *adv. pnr., substandard* Not for practice; really; seriously. *Let's do our work for real.* (Let's do our work seriously.)

for —— sake *adv. phr., informal* Used with different possessive nouns to show surprise, crossness, or impatience. *For heaven's sake, where did you come from?* (You surprised me; I didn't see you coming.) *For Pete's sake, look who's here!* (I am pleased and surprised to see you.) *Well, for pity's sake, I wish you'd told me sooner.* (I am cross that you didn't tell me before.) *Oh, for gosh sake, let me do it.* (I am impatient with your trying to do it; I'll do it myself.)

for shame *interj.* Shame on you; you should be ashamed of yourself.—An exclamation no longer in common use, having been largely replaced by *shame on you. For shame, John, taking the toy from your baby brother!* (Shame on you, John, for taking the toy away from your baby brother.)

for short *adv. phr.* So as to make shorter; as an abbreviation or nickname. *The boy's name was Humperdink, or "Dink" for short.* (We call the boy Dink because it is shorter and easier.) *The National Broadcasting Company is called NBC for short.* (When we are in a hurry, NBC is shorter to say.)

for sure *or* **for certain** *adv. phr.* **1** Without doubt; certainly; surely. *He couldn't tell for sure from a distance whether it was George or Tom.* (He was too far away to be sure if the person he saw was George or Tom.) *He didn't know for certain which bus to take.* (He was not sure which bus he should get on.) *I know for certain that he has a car.* (Without doubt he has a car.) **2** *slang* Certain. *"That car is smashed so badly it's no good any more." "That's for sure!"* (It's certain that the smashed car will never be fixed again.) Compare SURE THING.

fort See HOLD THE FORT.

forth See AND SO FORTH, BACK AND FORTH, CALL FORTH, HOLD FORTH, SET FORTH.

for that matter *adv. phr.* With regard to that; about that. *I don't know, and for that matter, I don't care.* (I don't care about that either.) *Alice didn't come, and for that matter, she didn't even telephone.* (Alice didn't even telephone about not coming.) Compare MATTER OF FACT.

for the asking *adv. phr.* By asking; by asking for it; on request. *John said I could borrow his bike any time. It was mine for the asking.* (All I had to do was to ask if I wanted to borrow it.) *Teacher said her advice was free for the asking.* (If the pupils wanted advice, they just had to ask.)

for the best *adj. or adv. phr.* good or best; not bad as thought; lucky; well, happily. *Maybe it's for the best that your team lost; now you know how the other boys felt.* (Maybe it isn't so bad that you lost if you understand now how the other boys felt when they lost.) *John's parents thought it would be for the best if he stayed out of school for the rest of the year.* (They thought that it would do the most good for John to stay out of school.) Often used in the phrase *turn out for the best. You feel unhappy now because you got sick and couldn't go with your friends, but it will all turn out for the best.* (It will end happily, even if you are sad now and don't think so.) Compare TURN OUT 6. Contrast FOR THE WORSE.

for the better *adj. or adv. phr.* With a better result; for something that is better. *The doctor felt that moving Father to a dry climate would be for the better.* (The doctor felt that the change would make Father more healthy.) *The new large print in the book is a change for the better.* (The new book has larger letters. This is better for reading.) Compare TAKE A TURN. Contrast FOR THE WORSE.

for the birds *adj. phr., slang* Not interesting; dull; silly, foolish; stupid. *I think history is for the birds.* (I think history is dull and boring.) *I saw that movie. It's for the birds.* (I saw the movie and I did not like it.)

for the books See ONE FOR THE BOOKS.

for the devil of it See DEVIL OF IT.

for the hills See HEAD FOR THE HILLS.

for the life of one *adv., informal* No mat-ter how hard you try.—Used for emphasis with negative statements. *I can't for the life of me remember his name.* (I can't remember his name no matter how hard I try.)

for the moon See ASK FOR THE MOON *or* CRY FOR THE MOON.

for the most part *adv. phr.* In general; mostly; most of the time; commonly; gener-ally. *European countries are, for the most part, tired of war.* (Most of them are tired of war.) Syn. BY AND LARGE, ON THE WHOLE.

for the nonce See FOR THE TIME BEING.

for the ride See ALONG FOR THE RIDE.

for the time being *also* *literary* **for the nonce** *adv. phr.* For now; for a while; temporarily. *I haven't any note paper, but this envelope will do for the time being.* (I haven't any note paper, but this envelope will do for now.) *She hasn't found an apartment yet; she's staying with her aunt for the time being.* (She hasn't found an apartment yet and is staying with her aunt until she does.)

for the world See NOT FOR THE WORLD.

for the worse *adj. phr. or adv. phr.* For something that is worse or not as good, with a worse result. *He bought a new car but it turned out to be for the worse.* (His new car wasn't as good as his old one.) *The sick man's condition changed for the worse.* (The sick man's condition got worse.) Compare TAKE A TURN. Contrast FOR THE BETTER.

for to *prep. phr., dialect* So that you can; to. *Simple Simon went a-fishing for to catch a whale.* (Simple Simon went fishing in order to catch a whale.) Syn. IN ORDER TO.

forty winks *n. phr., informal* A short period of sleep; a nap. *When the truck driver felt sleepy, he stopped by the side of the road to catch forty winks.* (The truck driver stopped by the side of the road to take a short nap.) Compare SHUT-EYE.

forward See BACKWARD AND FORWARD, LOOK FORWARD TO, PUT ONE'S BEST FOOT FORWARD.

forward wall *n.* The line of a football team. *Princeton's line outplayed the Rutgers for-ward wall.* (The Princeton line played better than the Rutgers line.)

for you See THAT'S ———— FOR YOU.

foul ball *n.* A batted baseball that lands out-side the foul line. *Mickey hit a long foul ball that landed on the roof.* (Mickey's hit looked like a home run but it landed outside the foul line.)

foul line *n.* **1** Either of two lines separating fair from foul ground in baseball. *Willie hit the ball just inside the foul line for a double.* (The ball that Willie hit was on the fair side of the line and he went for a double.) **2** A line across the upper end of a bowling alley across which a bowler must not step. *John bowled a strike but it didn't count because he stepped over the foul line.* (John's strike did not count because he stepped past the line he was sup-posed to stay behind.) **3** A line on the floor in front of the basket in basketball, from which foul shots are made. *Tony scored eight points from the foul line.* (Tony scored 8 points on foul shots.)

foul out *v.* **1** To make an out in baseball by hitting a foul fly ball that is caught. *He fouled out to the catcher.* (He was out when the catcher caught his fly ball in foul territory.) **2** To be forced to leave a basketball game because of getting more than the limit number of personal fouls. *A professional basketball player is allowed six personal fouls before fouling out.* (A professional basketball player can have six personal fouls called against him, but if he has a seventh he must leave the game.)

foul shot *n.* A free throw given in basketball to a player who has been fouled. *Tony was given two foul shots when he was fouled while trying to shoot.* (Tony was given two free shots at the basket because he was fouled.) Compare FIELD GOAL 2, FREE THROW.

foul up *v., informal* **1** To make dirty. *The birds fouled up his newly washed car.* (Birds dirtied his car shortly after he had washed it.) **2** To tangle up. *He tried to throw a lasso but he got the rope all fouled up.* (He tried to throw a cowboy rope but the rope got all tangled.) **3** To ruin or spoil by stupid mistakes; botch. *He fouled the whole play up by forgetting his part.* (He spoiled the whole play by forgetting his part.) **4** To make a mistake; to blunder. *Blue suit and brown socks! He had fouled up again.* (He had made a mistake in wearing brown socks with his blue suit.) **5** To go wrong. *Why do some people foul up and become criminals?* (Why do some people go wrong and become criminals?)

foul-up *n.* (stress on *foul*) **1** *informal* A confused situation; confusion; mistake. *The luncheon was handled with only one or two foul-ups.* (There were very few mistakes or confusions in plans for the luncheon.) **2** *informal* A breakdown. *There was a foul-up in his car's steering mechanism.* (Something broke in the car's steering mechanism.) **3** *slang* A person who fouls up or mixes things. *He had gotten a reputation as a foul-up.* (He had become known as a person who mixes things up.)

foundation garment *n.* A close-fitting garment designed for women to wear underneath their clothes to make them look slim; a piece of woman's underwear. *Jane wears a foundation garment under her evening dress.* (To look slim, Jane wears a close-fitting garment under her evening dress.)

four See HIT ON ALL FOUR, ON ALL FOURS.

four bits *n., slang* Fifty cents. *"Tickets to the play are four bits," said Bill.* (Tickets cost fifty cents.) Compare TWO BITS.

four corners *n.* All parts of a place. *People came from the four corners of the world to see him.* (People came from many places in the world to see him.) *He has been to the four corners of the country.* (He has been in all parts of the country.) Compare ALL OVER.

four-eyes *n., slang* A person who wears glasses.—A rude expression. *Hey, four-eyes, come over here.* (Hey, you with the glasses, come over here.)

four-leaf clover *n.* A small green plant with four leaves which many people think means good luck because clover plants usually have three leaves. *John has a four-leaf clover in his pocket. He thinks he will have good luck now.*

fourth class *n.* A class of mail that is not sealed and weighs a pound or more, that includes things that are bought and sold and sent in the mail, and printed things that are not second or third class mail. *Bill sent away 98 cereal box tops and a dollar and got back a sheriff's badge and gun in the mail by fourth class.* (The package in which Billy's badge and gun came was in the fourth class mail because it weighed more than a pound.)

fourth-class[1] *adj.* Belonging to the fourth class of mail. *The package weighed a pound and a half, so it had to be sent by fourth-class mail.* (The package had to be sent fourth-class because it weighed over a pound.)

fourth-class[2] *adv.* By fourth-class mail. *How did the company mail the package? Fourth-class.* (They paid the price to send it by the fourth-class of mail.)

fourth world *n., informal* The poor nations of the world, as distinguished from the oil-rich nations of the third world. *Sri Lanka will never join OPEC, since it is a fourth world nation.* (It will never become a member of the Oil Producers' Economic Cartel as it is a poor nation without oil.)

fowl See NEITHER FISH NOR FOWL.

fox and geese *n. phr.* A tag game in which the player representing the fox tries to catch one of the players representing geese as they run around the outside of a circle.

fraidy-cat or **fraid-cat** or **scaredy-cat** or **scared-cat** *n., informal* A shy person; someone who is easily frightened.—Usually used by or to children. *Tom was a fraidy-cat and wouldn't go in the water.* (Tom was afraid to go into the water.)

freak *n., slang* **1** A good, or well-liked person, the opposite of a square, someone with long hair and who is likely (or known) to be a marijuana smoker or a drug user. Also said of homosexuals. *Is Joe a square, establishment type?—Oh no, he's a regular freak.* (Oh no, he is a good guy, he is one of us.) **2** ——— **freak** An enthusiast, a person who does or cultivates something in excess. *Ellen is a film-freak.* (She avidly enjoys seeing films.)

freak-out[1] *n., slang* An act of losing control; a situation that is bizarre or unusual. *The party last night was a regular freak-out.* (It was a bizarre experience.)

freak out[2] *v. phr., slang* To lose control over one's conscious self due to the influence of hallucinogenic drugs. *Joe freaked out last night.* (He was out of his mind.)

free See FOR FREE, MAKE FREE, MAKE FREE WITH, OF ONE'S OWN ACCORD *or* OF ONE'S OWN FREE WILL.

free agent *n.* A professional player who does not have a contract with a team. *The Giants signed two free agents who had been released by the Cardinals.* (The Giants signed two men to contracts who had been released from their contracts by the Cardinals.)

free and easy *adj.* Not strict; relaxed or careless. *The teacher was free and easy with his students.* (The teacher was not strict.) *He had a free and easy way of acting that attracted many friends.* (He attracted many friends by his relaxed pleasant manner.) *They were free and easy with their money and it was soon gone.* (They soon used up all their money by spending it carelessly.)

free ball *n.* A ball in football that is in play, that is not in the possession of anyone, that is not a legally thrown forward pass, and that belongs to the first team which can grab it. *A Notre Dame player fell on a free ball and recovered it for his team.* (A Notre Dame player fell on the ball which belonged to neither side and got it for his team.)

free enterprise *n. phr.* A system in which private business is controlled by as few government rules as possible. *The United States is proud of its free enterprise.* (The U.S. is proud that the government does not control business in America. Private businesses are free.)

free hand *n.* Great freedom. *The teacher had a free hand in her classroom.* (The teacher had great freedom. She could do almost anything she wanted in her classroom.) *Bob put paint on the fence with a free hand.* (He put a large amount of paint on the fence.) Compare FREE REIN.

freeload *v.* To have oneself supported in terms of food and housing at someone else's expense. *When are you guys going to stop freeloading and do some work?* (When will you stop sponging off others and do some work?)

free rein *n.* Freedom to do what you want. *The king had free rein in his country.* (The king could do anything he wanted.) *Father is strict with the children, but Mother gives them free rein.* (Mother lets the children do as they please.) Compare FREE HAND.

free throw *n.* A shot at the basket in basketball without interference from opponents. *Mike scored the winning point on a free throw.* (Mike won the game when he scored on a shot his opponents were not allowed to try to block.) Compare FIELD GOAL 2, FOUL SHOT.

freeze See BLOOD RUNS COLD *or* BLOOD FREEZES.

freeze one's blood See BLOOD RUNS COLD.

freeze out *v., informal* To force out or keep from a share or part in something by unfriendly or dishonest treatment. *The other boys froze John out of the club.* (The others were so unfriendly that John left the club.)

freeze over *v.* To become covered with ice. *The children wanted the lake to freeze over so they could ice-skate.* (The children wanted the lake to become covered with ice so they could skate.)

French fried potato *or* **French fry** *n.* A narrow strip of potato fried in deep fat.—Usually used in the plural. *Sue ordered a hamburger and french fries.* (She ordered fried potatoes.)

friction tape *n.* Black cloth tape with one sticky side used around electric wires. *The boy fixed his cracked baseball bat with some friction tape.* (He put heavy black tape around his cracked bat.)

Friday See GIRL FRIDAY.

friend See BOY FRIEND, FAIR-WEATHER FRIEND, GIRL FRIEND, LADY FRIEND, MAKE FRIENDS.

friends with Friendly to; a friend of. *Alice found several girls to be friends with on the first day of school.* (She made several friends on the first day of school.) *At first I didn't like John, but now I am friends with him.* (I am a friend of his.)

frightened out of one's wits See OUT OF ONE'S WITS.

frightened to death See TO DEATH.

fritter away See FOOL AWAY.

fro See TO AND FRO.

frog See BIG FROG IN A SMALL POND, LITTLE FROG IN A BIG POND.

from bad to worse See GO FROM BAD TO WORSE.

from grace See FALL FROM GRACE.

from hand to hand *adv. phr.* From one person to another and another. *The box of candy was passed from hand to hand.* (The candy was passed from one person to another.) *Jane brought her engagement ring, and it passed from hand to hand until all the girls had admired it.* (Each girl in turn looked at the ring and passed it on to another.)

from hand to mouth See LIVE FROM HAND TO MOUTH.

from little acorns See GREAT OAKS FROM LITTLE ACORNS GROW.

from Missouri *adj. phr., slang* Doubtful; suspicious. *Don't try to fool me. I'm from Missouri.* (Don't try to fool me. I am suspicious and don't believe what you tell me.)

from pillar to post *adv. phr.* From one place to another many times.—A cliché. *Sarah's father changed jobs several times a year, and the family was moved from pillar to post.* (The family had to move to a new home again and again.)

from scratch *adv. phr., informal* With no help from anything done before; from the beginning; from nothing. *Dick built a radio from scratch.* (Dick bought the parts and put them together himself.) *In sewing class, Mary already knew how to sew a little, but Jane had to start from scratch.* (Jane had to learn sewing from the beginning.) Compare FROM THE GROUND UP.

from the bottom of one's heart *or* **with all one's heart** *adv. phr.* With great feeling; sincerely.—A cliché. *A mother loves a baby from the bottom of her heart.* (A mother loves a baby sincerely and with great feeling.) *John thanked his rescuer from the bottom of his heart.* (John very warmly thanked the man who had saved him.) *The people welcomed the returning soldiers from the bottom of their hearts.* (The people were sincerely happy to have the soldiers come back home.)

from the door See KEEP THE WOLF FROM THE DOOR.

from the ground up *adv. phr.* From the beginning; entirely; completely. *After the fire they had to rebuild their cabin from the ground up.* (After their cabin burned down they had to build the whole thing over again.) *Sam knows about baseball from the ground up.* (He knows all about baseball. He knows it completely.) *The new cars have been changed from the ground up.* (The new cars have been changed completely. Everything in the new cars has been changed.)

from the heart *adv.* Sincerely; honestly. *John always speaks from the heart.* (John always speaks sincerely.)

from time to time *adv. phr.* Not often; not regularly; sometimes; occasionally; at one time and then again at another time. *Even though the Smiths have moved, we still see them from time to time.* (We still see the Smiths sometimes.) *Mother tries new recipes from time to time, but the children never like them.* (The children don't like the new foods their mother occasionally cooks.) Syn. NOW AND THEN, AT TIMES, ONCE IN A WHILE. Compare BY FITS AND STARTS, OFF AND ON.

from —— to —— **1** Used with a repeated word to show that something keeps on. Without ending. *The world grows wiser from age to age.* (The world is always growing wiser.) *He goes from day to day without changing his necktie.* (He never seems to change his necktie.)—Also used in a short form like an adjective. *The superintendent spends more time on plans for the future, and the principal handles the day-to-day problems of the school.* (The principal manages the everyday business of the school.) **2** Used with a repeated word to show that something happens again and again. *She sells face cream from door to door.* (She goes to each house in a neighborhood to sell face cream.) *The artist goes from place to place painting pictures.* (The artist paints pictures of different places.) —Also used in a short form like an adjective.

Mr. Roberts began as a door-to-door salesman, and now is president of the company. (Mr. Roberts started his career as a salesman going to all the houses in an area.) **3**—Used with words showing opposite or extreme limits, often to emphasize that something is very large or complete. *The eagle's wings measured six feet from tip to tip.* (The wings were six feet wide.) *Sarah read the book from cover to cover.* (She read the whole book.) *Mrs. Miller's dinner included everything from soup to nuts.* (She served everything that could be expected at a dinner.) *That book is a best-seller from Maine to California.* (The book is selling well across the whole country.) *The captain looked the boy over from head to foot.* (The captain looked him over carefully.) *The dog sniffed the yard from end to end in search of a bone.* (The dog sniffed all over the yard to find a bone.) *This new car has been redesigned from top to bottom.* (The new car has been changed all over.) *That book store has books on everything from archery to zoology.* (That book stores has books about many different things.) *The television show was broadcast from coast to coast.* (The television show was seen all across the country.) *He knows mathematics from A to Z* (He knows everything there is to know about mathematics.)—Sometimes used in a short form like an adjective. *The airplane made a non-stop coast-to-coast flight.* (The plane flew from one coast to the coast on the other side of the country without stopping.)

from under See OUT FROM UNDER, PULL THE RUG OUT FROM UNDER.

from way back *adv. or adj. phr., informal* Since a long time ago; for a long time. *Mr. Jones said he knew my father from way back.* (Mr. Jones knew my father when he was young.)

front See IN FRONT OF.

front and center *adv., slang.* Used as a command to a person to go to someone who wants him. *Front and center, Smith. The boss wants to see you.* (Smith, go to see the boss now.)

front court *n.* The half of a basketball court that is a basketball team's offensive zone. *The guard brought the ball up to the front court.* (The guard brought the ball into the offensive zone, ready to make a score.)

front office *n., informal* The group of persons who manage a business; the officers. *The front office decides how much the workers are paid.* (The managers decide the pay of the staff.)

fruitcake See NUTTY AS A FRUITCAKE.

fry See OTHER FISH TO FRY, OUT OF THE FRYING PAN INTO THE FIRE, SMALL FRY.

fuck around *v. phr., vulgar, avoidable* **1** To be promiscuous. *John fucks around with the secretaries.* (He engages in sex with them.) **2** To play at something without purpose, to mess around. *He doesn't accomplish anything, because he fucks around so much.* (His purposeless waste of time is his downfall.)

fuck off *v. phr., vulgar, avoidable* **1** Go away! *Can't you see you're bothering me? Fuck off!* (Go away, said very rudely.) **2** To be lazy. *John said "I don't feel like working, so I'll fuck off today."* (He said he feels lazy.) Compare BEAT IT, GOOF OFF.

fuck up *v. phr., vulgar, avoidable* To make a mess of something or oneself. *Because he was totally unprepared, he fucked up his exam.* (He made a mess of it.) *He is so fucked up he doesn't know whether he is coming or going.* (His confusion is so great he has no idea what he is doing.)

fuddy-duddy *n.* A person whose ideas and habits are old-fashioned. *His students think Professor Jones is an old fuddy-duddy.* (His students think him old fashioned, not modern in his ideas.)

fuel See ADD FUEL TO THE FLAME.

full See HAVE ONE'S HANDS FULL, IN FULL SWING, TO THE FULL.

full-fledged *adj.* Having everything that is needed to be something; complete. *A girl needs three years of training to be a full-fledged nurse.* (The rules say that a girl must have three years of training before she can become a regular nurse.) *The book was a full-fledged study of American history.* (The book was a complete study of American history.)

full of beans *adj. phr., slang* **1** Full of pep; feeling good; in high spirits. *The football team was full of beans after winning the tournament.* (After winning the last game, the students were very happy.) *The children were full of beans as they got ready for a picnic.* (The idea of going on a picnic put the children in high spirits.) **2** *also* **full of prunes.** Being foolish and talking nonsense. *You are full of prunes; that man's not 120 years old.* (You are being foolish; he is not 120 years old.)

full of it See FULL OF THE OLD NICK.

full of oneself *adj. phr., informal* Interested only in yourself. *Joe would be a nice boy if he would stop being so full of himself.* (He would be nice if he would stop being interested only in himself.) Compare BIG HEAD.

full of prunes See FULL OF BEANS 2.

full of the moon *n. phr., literary* The moon when it is seen as a full circle; the time of a full moon. *The robbers waited for a dark night when the full of the moon was past.* (The robbers waited until the full moon was gone, so they could not be seen.) Contrast DARK OF THE MOON.

full of the Old Nick *or* **full of the devil** *or* **full of it** *adj. phr., informal* Always making trouble; naughty; bad. *That boy is full of the Old Nick.* (That boy is always making trouble.)

full tilt *adv.* At full speed; at high speed. *He ran full tilt into the door and broke his arm.* (He ran into the door at full speed and broke his arm.)

fun See MAKE FUN OF.

fun and games *n., slang, informal* **1** A party or other entertaining event. **2** Something trivially easy. **3** Petting, or sexual intercourse. **4** (Ironically) An extraordinary difficult task. *How was your math exam? —(With a dismayed expression):—Yeah, 't was all fun and games, man.* (It was extraordinarily difficult.)

fun house *n.* A place where people see many funny things and have tricks played on them to make them laugh or have a good time. *The boys and girls had a good time looking at themselves in mirrors in the fun house.* (The mirrors made them look thin, fat, or tall.)

funny bone *n.* **1** The place at the back of the elbow that hurts like electricity when accidentally hit. *He hit his funny bone on the arm of the chair.* **2** *or informal* **crazy bone** Sense of humor; understanding jokes. *Her way of telling the story tickled his funny bone.* (He thought the way she told the story was funny.)

fur See MAKE THE FUR FLY.

furious See FAST AND FURIOUS.

fuse See BLOW A FUSE.

fuss See KICK UP A FUSS.

fuss and feathers *n., informal* Unnecessary bother and excitement. *She is full of fuss and feathers this morning.* (She is full of excitement and worried about unnecessary things.)

G

gab See GIFT OF GAB or GIFT OF THE GAB.
gaff See STAND THE GAFF.
gain ground *v. phr.* **1** To go forward; move ahead. *The soldiers fought hard and began to gain ground.* (The soldiers began to move ahead; they began to seize land from the enemy.) **2** To become stronger; make progress; improve. *The sick man gained ground after being near death.* (The sick man became stronger after almost dying.) *Under Lincoln, the Republican party gained ground.* (The party became stronger by gaining more members and power.) Contrast LOSE GROUND.
gallery See PLAY TO THE GALLERY.
gallon See TEN-GALLON HAT.
game See AHEAD OF THE GAME, LOVE GAME, NAME OF THE GAME, PLAY THE GAME, AT ———— STAGE OF THE GAME.
game at which two can play *n. phr.* A plan, trick, or way of acting that both sides may use. *Rough football is a game two can play.* (If the other team is rough, we can be too.) *Politics is a game at which two can play.* (If one candidate says bad things about his opponent, he will have bad things said about himself.)
game is not worth the candle *literary* What is being done is not worth the trouble or cost; the gain is not worth the effort.—A cliché. *I don't want to walk so far on such a hot day. The game is not worth the candle.* (It is not worth it to walk so far.)
game is up or *slang* **jig is up** The secret or plan won't work; we are caught or discovered. *The game is up; the teacher knows who took her keys.* (It's no use to pretend any longer; the teacher has found out who took her keys.) *The jig's up; the principal knows the boys have been smoking in the basement.* (The principal has found out that the boys have been smoking in the basement and will stop them.) Compare FAT IS IN THE FIRE.
gang See ROAD GANG, SECTION GANG.
gang up on or **gang up against** *v., informal* To attack in a group; get together to do a harm to. *The older boys ganged up on the boy who beat up a younger boy.* (The older boys got together to beat up the boy who was mean to a weaker boy.) *A group of people ganged up against the man who beat his dog.* (The people got together and stopped the man.) Compare LINE UP 4b.
garbage down *v. phr., slang* To eat eagerly and at great speed without much regard for manners or social convention. *The children garbaged down their food.* (They devoured their food in great haste.)
garden apartment *n.* An apartment with a garden near it. *The couple live in a garden apartment.* (They live in an apartment which has grass, plants, and trees in the rear.)

garment See FOUNDATION GARMENT.
gas See STEP ON IT or STEP ON THE GAS.
gasket See BLOW A FUSE or BLOW A GASKET.
gas up *v., informal* **1** To fill the gasoline tank of. *The mechanics gassed up the planes for their long trip.* (The mechanics filled up the gasoline tanks of the planes for their long trip.) **2** To fill the tank with gasoline. *The big truck stopped at the filling station and gassed up.* (The man at the filling station filled the tank with gas.)
gate See GET THE BOUNCE or GET THE GATE, GIVE THE BOUNCE or GIVE THE GATE.
gate crasher See CRASH THE GATE.
gather See ROLLING STONE GATHERS NO MOSS.
gather in *v. informal* To catch. *The end gathered in the pass and went over for a touchdown.* (The end caught the pass and scored a touchdown.)
gauntlet See RUN THE GAUNTLET, THROW DOWN THE GAUNTLET.
gay nineties *n.* The years between 1890 and 1900; remembered as a happy exciting time. *Ladies wore large hats in the gay nineties.* (Large hats were in style between 1890 and 1900.) *Picnics were popular in the gay nineties.* (People enjoyed picnics very much between 1890 and 1900.)
gaze See CRYSTAL GAZING.
gear See HIGH GEAR, SLIP A COG or SLIP A GEAR, THROW OUT OF GEAR.
geese See FOX AND GEESE.
gee whiz *interj., informal* Used as an exclamation to show surprise or other strong feeling. Rare in written English. *Gee whiz! I am late again.* (Oh! I am late again.)
general See IN GENERAL.
generation gap *n., informal, hackneyed phrase* The difference in social values, philosophies, and manners between children and their parents, teachers and relatives which causes a lack of understanding between them and frequently leads to violent confrontations. *My daughter is twenty and I am forty, but we have no generation gap in our family.* (We get along fine with each other.)
George See LET GEORGE DO IT.
get See GIVE AS GOOD AS ONE GETS, EARLY BIRD CATCHES THE WORM or EARLY BIRD GETS THE WORM, GO-GETTER, TELL ———— WHERE TO GET OFF.
get about See GET AROUND at 1b.
get across *v.* **1** To explain clearly, make (something) clear; to make clear the meaning of. *Mr. Brown is a good coach because he can get across the plays.* (He is a good coach because he makes the plays easy to understand.) Syn. PUT ACROSS. **2** To become clear. *The teacher tried to explain the problem, but the explanation did not get across to the class.* (The teacher tried to explain the problem, but the explanation was not clearly understood by the class.)

get after *v., informal* **1** To try or try again to make someone do what he is supposed to do. *Ann's mother gets after her to hang up her clothes.* (Ann's mother keeps trying to make her hang up her clothes.) **2** To scold or make an attack on. *Bob's mother got after him for tracking mud into the house.* (Bob's mother scolded him for tracking mud into the house.) *The police are getting after the crooks in the city.* (They are arresting or chasing them out.)

get ahead *v.* **1** *informal* To become successful. *Mr. Brown was a good lawyer and soon began to get ahead.* (Mr. Brown was a good lawyer and soon began to be successful.) *The person with a good education finds it easier to get ahead.* (A good education helps a person to become successful.) **2** To be able to save money; get out of debt. *In a few more years he will be able to get ahead.* (He will be earning more money than he spends.) *After Father pays all the doctor bills, maybe we can get a little money ahead and buy a car.* (When we don't owe any more money, maybe we can buy a car.)

get a load of *v. phr., slang* **1** To take a good look at; see (something unusual or interesting.)—Often used to show surprise or admiration. *Get a load of that pretty girl!* (See how pretty that girl is!) *Get a load of Dick's new car!* (Look at that fine new car!) Compare LOOK OVER. **2** To listen to carefully or with interest, especially exciting news.—Often used as a command. *Get a load of this: Alice got married yesterday!* (Listen to this. Alice got married!)

get along *also* **get on** *v.* **1** To go or move away; move on. *The policeman told the boys on the street corner to get along.* (He told them to get away from the corner.) **2** To go forward; make progress; advance. *John is getting along well in school. He is learning more every day.* (John is doing well.) Syn. GET AHEAD. **3** To advance; become old or late. *It is getting along towards sundown.* (It is getting dark.) *Grandmother is 68 and getting along.* (She looks quite old.) **4** To get or make what you need; manage. *It isn't easy to get along in the jungle.* (It isn't easy to get what you need and stay alive.) *We can live on $100 a week.* (We can live on it.) Compare DO WITHOUT 2, GET BY, MAKE DO. **5** To live or work together in a friendly way; agree, cooperate; not fight or argue. *We don't get along with the Jones family.* (We disagree with them.) *Jim and Jane get along fine together.* (They are friendly.) *Don't be hard to get along with.* (Don't be disagreeable.)

get a fix *or* **give a fix** *v. phr., slang, drug culture* To provide (someone) with an injection of narcotics. *The neighborhood pusher gave Joe a fix.* (The local dealer in illegal narcotics supplied Joe with a shot of heroine or some other drug.) Contrast GET A FIX ON.

get a fix on *v. phr., informal* Receive a reading of a distant object by electronic means, as by radar or sonar. *Can you get a fix on the submarine?* (Can you locate the submarine electronically?) Contrast GET A FIX.

get a move on *informal or slang* **get a wiggle on** *v. phr.* To hurry up; get going.—Often used as a command. *Get a move on, or you will be late.* (Hurry up, or you will be late.)

get a rise out of *v. phr., slang* To have some fun with (a person) by making (him) angry; tease. *The boys get a rise out of Joe by teasing him about his girl friend.* (The boys make Joe angry by teasing him about his girl friend.)

get around *v.* **1a** To go to different places; move about. *Mary's father really gets around; Monday he was in Washington; Wednesday he was in Chicago; and today he is in New York.* (Mary's father often travels from one place to another.) *Fred broke his leg, but he is able to get about on crutches.* (Fred is able to walk on crutches.) **1b** *or* **get about** To become widely known especially by being talked about. *Bad news gets around quickly.* (Bad news spreads fast.) **2a** *informal* To get by a trick or flattery what you want from (someone). *Mary knows how to get around her father.* (Mary knows how to talk or act to get what she wants from her father.) **2b** *informal* To find a way of not obeying or doing; escape from. *Some people try to get around the tax laws.* (Some people try to find ways of not paying their taxes.) *John did not weigh enough to join the Navy, but he got around that; he drank a lot of water before his physical examination.* (John found a way to get into the Navy, even though the rule said he didn't weigh enough.)

get around to *v.* To do (something) after putting it off; find time for. *Mr. Lee hopes to get around to washing his car next Saturday.* (Mr. Lee hopes to find time to wash his car next Saturday.)

get at *v.* **1** To reach an understanding of; find out the meaning. *This book is very hard to get at.* (It is hard to understand it.) **2** To do harm to. *The cat is on the chair trying to get at the canary.* (The cat is trying to reach him and eat him.) Compare GET BACK AT. **3** To have a chance to do; attend to. *I hope I have time to get at my homework tonight.* (I hope I have time to take care of it.) Compare GET TO 2. **4** To mean; aim at; hint at *What was Betty getting at when she said she knew our secret?* (What secret did she mean?) *What the teacher was getting at in this lesson was that it is important to speak correctly.* (What he was trying to explain was the importance of talking right.) Syn. DRIVE AT. Compare GET ACROSS.

get away *v.* **1** To get loose or get free; become free from being held or controlled; succeed in leaving; escape. *As Jim was trying the* *bat, it got away from him and hit Tom.* (The bat flew out of Jim's hands and hit Tom.) *Someone left the door open, and the puppy got away.* (The puppy escaped from the house.) *Mary tried to catch a butterfly, but it got away from her.* (The butterfly succeeded in going away free; it was not caught.) *The bank robbers used a stolen car to get away.* (The bank robbers used a stolen car to run off with the money.) *If Mr. Graham can get away from his store this afternoon, he will take Johnny fishing.* (If he isn't too busy at work, he will go fishing.) **2** To begin; start. *We got away early in the morning on the first day of our vacation.* (We started early.) *The race got away to a fast start.* (The racers started fast.) Compare GET OFF 3, START IN, START OUT.

get away with *v., informal* To do (something bad or wrong) without being caught or punished. *Some students get away without doing their homework.* (They leave their work undone without being caught or punished.) See GET BY 3.

get away with murder *v. phr., informal* To do something very bad without being caught or punished.—An overused expression. *John is scolded if he is late with his homework, but Robert gets away with murder.* (Robert is very late with his homework or doesn't do it at all, but he is not caught or punished.) *Mrs. Smith lets her children get away with murder.* (She doesn't punish them even when they are very bad.)

get a wiggle on See GET A MOVE ON.

get a word in *or* **get a word in edgewise** *also* **get a word in edgeways** *v. phr.* To find a chance to say something when others are talking. *The little boy listened to the older students and finally got in a word.* (The little boy found a chance to say something at last.) *Mary talked so much that Jack couldn't get a word in edgewise.* (He hardly had a chance to talk.)

get back at *v., informal* To do something bad to (someone who has done something bad to you); hurt in return. *John played a joke on Henry, and next day Henry got back at him.* (John played a joke on Henry, and then Henry did the same thing to John.) *The elephant waited many years to get back at the man who fed him red pepper.* (The elephant waited many years to get even with the man who fed him red pepper.) Syn. PAY BACK, SETTLE A SCORE, TIT FOR TAT. Compare GET AT 2, GET EVEN.

get behind *v.* **1** To go too slowly; be late; do something too slowly. *The post office got behind in delivering Christmas mail.* (They are late because there is so much mail.) Syn. FALL BEHIND. Contrast KEEP UP. **2** *informal* To support; help. *A club is much better if members get behind their leaders.* (If members help their leaders as much as they can, the club is better.) *We got behind Mary to be*

class president. (We gave her our support.) Compare BACK OF 3. **3** *informal* To explain; find out the reason for. *The police are questioning many people to try and get behind the bank robbery.* (They are asking questions to find out who did it.) Syn. GET TO THE BOTTOM OF.

get by *v., informal* **1** To be able to go past; pass. *The cars moved to the curb so that the fire engine could get by.* (The cars moved to the side of the street so that the fire engine could pass.) **2** To satisfy the need or demand. *Mary can get by with her old coat this winter.* (She does not need a new coat.) *The janitor does just enough work to get by.* (He does only the work his employer demands and no more.) Syn. GET ALONG 4. **3** Not to be caught and scolded or punished. *The soldier thought he could get by with his dirty rifle.* (He thought the officer would not see the dirt on his rifle and punish him.) *The boy got by without answering the teacher's question because a visitor came in.* (The boy was not scolded for failing to answer the question.) Compare GET AWAY WITH.

get couthed up *v. phr., slang* To get oneself dressed up neatly and look elegant and presentable. *What are you getting all couthed up for?* (What is the occasion for your getting dressed up?) (This derives from *uncouth* 'outlandish, ill-mannered' by leaving off the prefix *un-*.)

get cracking *v. phr., slang, informal* To hurry up, to start moving fast. (Used mostly as an imperative). *Come on, you guys, let's get cracking!* (Let's hurry up!) Compare GET GOING 2.

get ———— down *v. phr., informal* To make (someone) unhappy; cause low spirits; cause discouragement. *Low grades are getting Helen down.* (Low grades are causing Helen to be unhappy.) *Three straight losses got the team down.* (Three straight losses caused the team to be discouraged.)

get down off your high horse See OFF ONE'S HIGH HORSE.

get down to *v., informal* To get started on, being on. *Joe wasted a lot of time before he got down to work.* (He wasted a lot of time before he got started on his work.) *Let's get down to work.* (Let's get started on our work.) Compare GET AT 3, GET GOING, GET TO.

get down to brass tacks *also* **get down to cases** *v. phr., informal* To begin the most important work or business; get started on the most important things to talk about or know.—A cliché. *The men talked about little things and then got down to brass tacks.* (They talked about little things and then talked about important business.) *A busy doctor wants his patients to get down to brass tacks.* (He wants his patients to tell him what is wrong with them instead of talking a long time about other things.)

get even *v., informal* **1** To owe nothing. *Mr. Johnson has a lot of debts, but in a few years he will get even.* (He owes a lot of money now, but in a few years he will be able to pay all he owes.) **2** To do something bad to pay someone back for something bad; get revenge; hurt back. *Jack is waiting to get even with Bill for tearing up his notebook.* (Jack is waiting to pay Bill back by doing something to hurt him.) *Last April First Mr. Harris got fooled by Joe, and this year he will get even.* (This year Mr. Harris will fool Joe.) Compare GET BACK AT.

get going *v., informal* **1** To excite; stir up and make angry. *The boys' teasing gets John going.* (The teasing excites him and makes him angry.) *Talking about her freckles gets Mary going.* (Talking about her freckles stirs up Mary and makes her angry.) **2** *or chiefly British* **get cracking** To begin to move; get started. *The teacher told Walter to get going on his history lesson.* (The teacher told Walter to get started on the lesson.) *The foreman told the workmen to get cracking.* (He told them to start work.) *Let's get going. It's almost supper time.* (Let's go. Supper will be soon.) Compare GET DOWN TO, STEP LIVELY.

get gray hair *or* **get gray** *v. phr., informal* To become old or gray from worrying; become very anxious or worried.—A trite expression; often used with *over*. *"If John doesn't join the team, I won't get gray hair over it,"* the coach said. ("I won't worry, because John isn't that important.") *Naughty children are why mothers get gray.* (Mothers with naughty children get old faster because of the trouble they cause.) Compare GIVE GRAY HAIR.

get hold of *v.* **1** To get possession of. *Little children sometimes get hold of sharp knives and cut themselves.* (They find sharp knives and cut themselves.) **2** To find a person so you can speak with him. *Mr. Thompson spent several hours trying to get hold of his lawyer.* (Mr. Thompson spent several hours trying to find his lawyer so that he could talk with him.)

get in one's hair See IN ONE'S HAIR.

get in one's way See IN ONE'S WAY.

get it See CATCH IT.

get it all together *v. phr.* **1** To be in full possession and control of one's mental faculties; have a clear purpose well pursued. *You've sure got it all together, haven't you?* (You certainly are a cool and level-headed person who knows what he is doing.) **2** Retaining one's self-composure under pressure. *A few minutes after the burglars left he got it all together and called the police.* (He regained his self-composure and made the call.) **3** To be well built, stacked (said of girls and women.) *Sue's sure got it all together, hasn't she?* (She is a well-built girl, isn't she?)

get it in the neck See CATCH IT IN THE NECK.

get lost *v. phr., slang* Go away!—Used as a command. *Get lost! I want to study.* (Go away; I want to study.) *John told Bert to get lost.* (John told Bert to go away.) Compare DROP DEAD.

get off *v.* **1** To come down from or out of. *The ladder fell, and Tom couldn't get off the roof.* (The ladder fell, and Tom couldn't get down from the roof.) *The bus stopped, the door opened, and Father got off.* (Father stepped out of the bus.) **2** To take off. *Joe's mother told him to get his wet clothes off.* (She told him to take off his wet clothes.) **3** To get away; leave. *Mr. Johnson goes fishing whenever he can get off from work.* (He goes fishing whenever he can get away from work.) *William got off early in the morning.* (He left early in the morning.) **4** To go free. *Mr. Andrews got off with a $5 fine when he was caught passing a stop sign.* (He was allowed to go free after paying a $5 fine.) **5** To make (something) go. *The halfback got off a long pass.* (He threw a long pass.) *John got a letter off to his grandmother.* (He sent a letter to his grandmother.) **6** To tell. *The governor got off several jokes at the beginning of his speech.* (He told several jokes first.)

get off easy *v. phr., informal* To have only a little trouble; escape something worse. *The children who missed school to go to the fair got off easy.* (They were not punished much for missing school.) *John got off easy because it was the first time he had taken his father's car without permission.* (He was not punished much because he had never done that before.)

get off it See COME OFF IT.

get off one's back *v. phr., slang, colloquial* To stop criticizing or nagging someone. *Get off my back! Can't you see how busy I am?* (Stop bothering, nagging and criticizing me, don't you see how busy I am?)

get off one's chest See OFF ONE'S CHEST.

get off one's tail *v. phr., slang* To get busy, to start working. *OK you guys! Get off your tails and get cracking!* (All right boys, let's get busy and do the job!)

get off on the wrong foot *v. phr.* To make a bad start; begin with a mistake. *Peggy got off on the wrong foot with her new teacher; she chewed gum in class and the teacher didn't like it.* (Peggy made a bad start with the teacher. She made the teacher angry by chewing gum.)

get off the ground *v. phr., informal* To make a successful beginning; get a good start; go ahead; make progress. *Our plans for a party didn't get off the ground because no one could come.* (We couldn't even begin to make plans for the party because no one could come.)

get off the hook See OFF THE HOOK.

get on *or* **get onto** *v., informal* **1** To speak to (someone) roughly about something he did wrong; blame; scold. *Mrs. Thompson got on the girls for not keeping their rooms clean.*

(Mrs. Thompson scolded the girls.) *The fans got on the new shortstop after he made several errors.* (The fans began to boo and yell insults at the new shortstop for making errors.) Syn. JUMP ON. **2** See GET ALONG. **3** To grow older. *Work seems harder these days; I'm getting on, you know.* (I am getting older.)

get one's See GET WHAT'S COMING TO ONE.

get one's back up *v. phr., informal* To become or make angry or stubborn. *Fred got his back up when I said he was wrong.* (He became angry when I said he was wrong.) *Our criticisms of his actions just got his back up.* (When we criticized his actions, it made him stubborn.)

get one's brains fried *v. phr., slang also used colloquially* **1** To sit in the sun and sunbathe for an excessive length of time. *Newcomers to Hawaii should be warned not to sit in the sun too long—they'll get their brains fried.* (They'll get a sunstroke.) **2** To get high on drugs. *He can't make a coherent sentence anymore—he's got his brains fried.* (He is so high on drugs that he cannot talk coherently.)

get one's dander up *or* **get one's Irish up** *v. phr.* To become or make angry. *The boy got his dander up because he couldn't go to the store.* (He became angry because he couldn't go to the store.) *The children get the teacher's dander up when they make a lot of noise.* (The children make the teacher angry.) Compare BLOW A FUSE.

get one's ducks in a row *v. phr., informal* To get everything ready. *The scoutmaster told the boys to get their ducks in a row before they went to camp.* (He told them to get everything ready before they went to camp.) *Mr. Brown got his ducks in a row for his trip.* (Mr. Brown packed his bag, bought train tickets, made hotel reservations, and did everything necessary to be ready.) Compare LINE UP.

get one's feet wet *v. phr., informal* To begin; do something for the first time.—A cliché, often used as a command. *The party was at Bill's house and when Ruth and I got there the party had already started. "Jump right in and don't be afraid to get your feet wet," said Bill.* (Join the other boys and girls in the party.) *"It's not hard to dance once you get your feet wet," said the teacher.* (It's not hard to dance after you've begun and stopped being bashful.)

get one's goat *v. phr., informal* To make a person disgusted or angry. *The boy's laziness all summer got his father's goat.* (The boy's laziness made his father angry.) *The slow service at the cafe got Mr. Robinson's goat.* (The slow service made him disgusted.)

get one's hands on See LAY ONE'S HANDS ON.

get one's number *or* **have one's number** *v. phr., informal* To find out or know what kind of person somebody is. *The boys soon had the new student's number.* (In a short time they knew what kind of student he was.) *The girls got their new roommate's number the first week of school.* (They found out what kind of girl their new roommate was.)

get one's rear in gear *v. phr., slang* To hurry up, to get going. *I'm gonna have to get my rear in gear.* (I will have to hurry up.)

get one's teeth into *or* **sink one's teeth into** *v. phr., informal* To have something real or solid to think about; go to work on seriously; struggle with.—A cliché. *After dinner, John got his teeth into the algebra lesson.* (John went to work in earnest on his algebra.) *Frank chose a subject for his report that he could sink his teeth into.* (It was a hard subject to struggle with; it needed a lot of thought.)

get one's tongue See CAT GET ONE'S TONGUE.

get on one's nerves *v. phr.* To make you nervous. *John's noisy eating habits get on your nerves.* (His noisy eating habits make you nervous.) *Children get on their parents' nerves by asking so many questions.* (Children make their parents nervous by asking so many questions.)

get on the ball See ON THE BALL.

get on the bandwagon See JUMP ON THE BANDWAGON.

get on the good side of See ON THE GOOD SIDE OF.

get on the stick *v. phr., slang, informal* To get moving; to stop being idle and to start working vigorously. *All right, man, let's get on the stick!* (Let's get going, and do something worthwhile!) Compare ON THE BALL, GET OFF ONE'S TAIL.

get out of the way See OUT OF THE WAY.

get over *v.* **1** To finish. *Tom worked fast to get his lesson over.* (He worked fast to finish his lesson.) **2** To pass over. *It was hard to get over the muddy road.* (It was hard to travel over the muddy road.) **3** To get well from; recover from. *The man returned to work after he got over his illness.* **4** To accept or forget (a sorrow or surprise.) *It is hard to get over the death of a member of your family.* (It is hard to forget your sorrow when a member of the family dies.) *We could not get over the speed of Mary's recovery from pneumonia.* (We were surprised for a long time because Mary got well so fast.)

get set *v. phr.* To get ready to start. *The runners got set.* (They bent down ready to start.) *The seniors are getting set for the commencement.* (They are getting ready to be in the commencement program.)

get short shrift See SHORT SHRIFT.

get the air See GET THE BOUNCE 1.

get the ax *v. phr., slang* **1** To be fired from a job. *Poor Joe got the ax at the office yesterday.* (He was fired from his job.) **2** To be dismissed from school for improper conduct, such as cheating. *Joe got caught cheating on his final exam and he got the ax.*

(He was dismissed from school.) **3** To have a quarrel with one's sweetheart or steady ending in a termination of the relationship. *Joe got the ax from Betsie—they won't see each other again.* (She told him that she doesn't want to see him any more.)

get the ball rolling *or* **set the ball rolling** *or* **start the ball rolling** *informal* To start an activity or action; make a beginning; begin. *George started the ball rolling at the party by telling a new joke.* (George began the fun by telling a joke.) Compare KEEP THE BALL ROLLING.

get the better of *or* **get the best of** *v. phr.* **1** To win over, beat; defeat. *Our team got the best of the visitors in the last quarter.* (Our team won in the last quarter.) *George got the better of Robert in a game of checkers.* (George beat Robert.) *When the opposing player fouled John, John let his anger get the better of his good sense and hit the boy back.* (John let his anger win out over his good sense.) *Dave wanted to study till midnight, but sleepiness got the best of him.* (Dave fell asleep.) Compare RUN AWAY WITH 1. **2** *or* **have the best of** *or* **have the better of** To win or be ahead in (something); gain most from (something.) *Bill traded an old bicycle tire for a horn; he got the best of that deal.* (Bill won in the trade.) *Our team had the best of it today, but they may lose the game tomorrow.* (Our team won the game today.) *The champion had all the better of it in the last part of the fight.* (The champion was far better in the last part.) Contrast GET THE WORST OF.

get the bounce *or* **get the gate** *v. phr., slang* **1** *or* **get the air** To lose one's sweetheart; not be kept for a friend or lover. *Joe is sad because he just got the gate from his girl.* (Joe lost his girl.) *Shirley was afraid she might get the air from her boy friend if she went out with other boys while he was away.* (Shirley was afraid her boy friend would stop seeing her.) **2** *or* **get the sack** *also* **get the hook** To be fired; lose a job. *Uncle Willie can't keep a job; he got the sack today for sleeping on the job.* (Uncle Willie got fired again.) *You're likely to get the bounce if you are absent from work too much.* (If you don't come to work very often, you may lose your job.) Contrast GIVE THE BOUNCE.

get the brush-off *v. phr., slang* **1** To be paid no attention; not be listened to or thought important. *My idea for a party got the brush-off from the other children.* (They did not like or accept the idea.) **2** To be treated in an unkind or unfriendly way; be ignored. *Frank and Jane had an argument, so the next time he telephoned her, he got the brush-off.* (Jane would not talk to him.) Compare COLD SHOULDER, HIGH-HAT. Contrast BRUSH OFF.

get the cart before the horse See CART BEFORE THE HORSE.

get the eye *v. phr., informal* **1** To be looked at, especially with interest and liking. *The pretty girl got the eye as she walked past the boys on the street corner.* (The boys looked at her because she was pretty.) **2** To be looked at or stared at, especially in a cold, unfriendly way. *When Mary asked if she could take home the fur coat and pay later, she got the eye from the clerk.* (The clerk did not know Mary, and gave her an unfriendly look when she asked to take the coat without paying.) Contrast GIVE THE EYE.

get the feel of *v. phr.* To become used to or learn about, especially by feeling or handling; get used to the experience or feeling of; get skill in. *John had never driven a big car, and it took a while for him to get the feel of it.* (It took him time to get used to driving and handling the big car.) *You'll get the feel of the job after you've been there a few weeks.* (You'll become experienced and more skillful after a few weeks.)

get the goods on *or* **have the goods on** *v. phr., slang* To find out true and, often, bad information about; discover what is wrong with; be able to prove the guilt of. *Tell the truth, Johnny. We know who your girl is because we've got the goods on you.* (We know who your girl is.) *The police had the goods on the burglar before he came to trial.* (They could prove he was guilty before his trial.) Compare HAVE SOMETHING ON.

get the hook See GET THE BOUNCE 2.

get the jump on *or* **have the jump on** *v. phr., slang* To get ahead of; start before (others); have an advantage over. *Don't let the other boys get the jump on you at the beginning of the race.* (Don't let them start quicker than you at the beginning.) *Our team got the jump on their rivals in the first minutes of play, and held the lead to win.* (Our team scored first and stayed ahead of the other team to the end, so we won.)

get the last laugh See HAVE THE LAST LAUGH.

get the lead out of one's pants *v. phr., slang* To get busy; work faster.—A cliché; often considered rude. *The captain told the sailors to get the lead out of their pants.* (He told them to get busy.) *The coach told the players to get the lead out of their pants.* (He told them to work harder and run faster.)

get the message *or* **get the word** *v. phr., slang* To understand clearly what is meant. *The principal talked to the students about being on time, and most of them got the message.* (Most of the students understood.) *Mary hinted to her boy friend that she wanted to break up, but he didn't get the message.* (He didn't understand that Mary wanted to break up their romance.) Compare THE PICTURE.

get the picture See THE PICTURE.

get the runaround See THE RUNAROUND.

get the sack *v. phr., slang* **1** To be fired or dismissed from work. *John got the sack* *at the factory last week.* (He was dismissed from his job.) **2** To be told by one's lover that the relationship is over. *Joanna gave Sam the sack.* (She told him that she doesn't want to see him any more.) See GET THE AX *and* GET THE BOUNCE 2.

get the show on the road   *v. phr., informal* To start a program; get work started.—A cliché. *It was several years before the rocket scientists got the show on the road.* (It was several years before they got the rocket program started.) Compare GET THE BALL ROLLING.

get the word   See GET THE MESSAGE.

get the works   See THE WORKS.

get the worst of *also* **have the worst of**   *v. phr.* To lose; be defeated or beaten in; suffer most. *Joe got the worst of the argument with Molly.* (Joe lost the argument.)—Often used in the phrase *the worst of it. If you start a fight with Jim, you may get the worst. of it.* (You may be beaten.) *Bill had the worst of it in his race with Al.* (Bill lost the race.) *Jack traded his knife for a few marbles; he got the worst of it in that trade.* (Jack lost most in the trade.) *The driver of the car got the worst of it in the accident.* (The driver was hurt worst in the accident.) Contrast GET THE BETTER OF 2.

get through one's head   *v. phr.* **1** To understand or believe. *Jack couldn't get it through his head that his father wouldn't let him go to camp if his grades didn't improve.* (Jack couldn't believe that his father wouldn't let him go if his grades weren't better.) *At last Mary got it through her head that she had failed to pass the test.* (At last she understood that she had failed.) **2** To make someone understand or believe. *I'll get it through his head if it takes all night.* (I'll make him understand it.)

get through to   *v.* To be understood by; make (someone) understand. *The little boy could not get through to his housemother.* (He could not make himself understood.) *Deaf people sometimes find it hard to get through to strangers.* (Deaf people sometimes find it hard to make themselves understood by strangers.) *When the rich boy's father lost his money, it took a long time for the idea to get through to him that he'd have to work and support himself.* (He couldn't understand or believe that he'd have to go to work.)

get to   *v. phr., informal* **1** To begin by chance; begin to.—Used with a verbal noun or an infinitive. *George meant to save his dime, but he got to thinking how good an ice cream cone would taste, and he spent it.* (George began to think about ice cream, and spent his dime.) *On a rainy day, Sally got to looking around in the attic and found some old pictures of Father.* (Sally happened to look around in the attic and found some old pictures.) *I got to know Mary at the party.* (I began to know Mary.) *I was just getting to*

know John when he moved away. (I was beginning to know John well.) Compare TAKE TO 2. **2** To have a chance to; be able to. *The Taylors wanted to go to the beach Saturday, but it rained and they didn't get to.* (The Taylors could not go to the beach because it rained.) *Did you get to see the king?* (Did you succeed in seeing him?) Compare GET AT 3. **3** See HAVE TO.

get to first base *or* **reach first base**   *v. phr.* To make a good start; really begin; succeed.—A cliché, usually in negative, interrogative, or conditional sentences. *Joe had a long paper to write for history class, but when the teacher asked for it, Joe hadn't got to first base yet.* (Joe had not begun writing the report.) *Suppose Sam falls in love with Betty. Can he even get to first base with her?* (Would Betty even give Sam a date?) *George wants to go to college and become a teacher, but I'll be surprised if he even reaches first base.* (I'll be surprised if he even gets into college.) *If you don't dress neatly, you won't get to first base when you look for a job.* (If you don't dress neatly, you won't even be tried out.) Compare FIRST BASE.

get together   *v.* To come to an agreement; agree. *Mother says I should finish my arithmetic lesson, and Father says I should mow the lawn. Why don't you two get together?* (Why don't you agree on one thing you want me to do?)

get to the bottom of   *v. phr.* To find out the real cause of.—A cliché. *The superintendent talked with several students to get to the bottom of the trouble.* (The superintendent talked with several students to find out the real cause of the trouble.) *The doctor made several tests to get to the bottom of the man's headaches.* (The doctor made several tests to find out the real cause of the man's headaches.) Compare GET TO THE HEART OF.

get to the heart of   *v. phr.* To find the most important facts about or the central meaning of; understand the most important thing about.—A cliché. *You can often get to the heart of someone's unhappiness by letting him talk.* (You can often learn the main thing making a person unhappy by letting him talk.) *"If you can find a topic sentence, often it will help you get to the heart of the paragraph," said the teacher.* (The teacher said that the topic sentence will often give you the most important facts of the paragraph.)

get to the point   See COME TO THE POINT.

get under one's skin   *v. phr.* To bother; upset.—A cliché. *The students get under Mary's skin by talking about her freckles.* (They bother Mary by talking about her freckles.) *Children who talk too much in class get under the teacher's skin.* (Children who talk too much upset the teacher.)

get up   *v.* **1** To get out of bed. *John's mother told him that it was time to get up.* (She told him that it was time to get out of bed.) **2** To stand up; get to your feet. *A man should get up when a woman comes into the room.* (He should stand up when a woman comes into the room.) **3** To prepare; get ready. *Mary got up a picnic for her visitor.* (Mary planned a picnic for her visitor.) *The students got up a special number of the newspaper to celebrate the school's 50th birthday.* (The students made a special issue of the newspaper when their school had its 50th birthday.) **4** To dress up. *One of the girls got herself up as a witch for the Halloween party.* (One of the girls dressed as a witch for the Halloween party.) **5** To go ahead. *The wagon driver shouted, "Get up!" to his horses.* (He told them to go ahead.)

get-up *n.* (stress on *get*) Fancy dress or costume. *Some get-up you're wearing!* (That's an unusual outfit you have on.)

get-up-and-go *also* **get-up-and-get** *n. phr., informal* Energetic enthusiasm; ambitious determination; pep; drive; push. *Joe has a lot of get-up-and-go and is working his way through school.* (Joe has a lot of ambition and works to pay his own way through school.)

get up on the wrong side of the bed *v. phr., informal* To awake with a bad temper.—A cliché. *Henry got up on the wrong side of the bed and wouldn't eat breakfast.* (He woke up in a bad mood and wouldn't eat breakfast.) *The man went to bed very late and got up on the wrong side of the bed.* (He went to bed very late and awoke feeling cross.)

get up the nerve *v. phr.* To build up your courage until you are brave enough; become brave enough. *Jack got up the nerve to ask Ruth to dance with him.* (He became brave enough to ask her to dance with him.) *The hungry little boy got up nerve to ask for another piece of cake.* (He built up enough courage to ask for another piece of cake.)

get what's coming to one *or slang* **get one's** *v. phr.* To receive the good or bad that you deserve; get what is due to you; get your share. —A cliché. *At the end of the movie the villain got what was coming to him and was put in jail.* (He was a bad man and was put in jail as he deserved.) *John didn't think he was getting what was coming to him, so he quit the job.* (John didn't think he was being paid enough or treated right.) *Mother told Mary that she'd get hers if she kept on being naughty.* (Mary would be punished.) Compare CATCH IT, HAVE IT COMING, SERVE RIGHT.

get wind of *v. phr.* To get news of; hear rumors about; find out about. *The police got wind of the plans to rob the bank.* (The police in some way found out about the plans to rob the bank.) *The captain didn't want the sailors to get wind of where the ship was going.* (He didn't want the sailors to find out about where the ship was going.)

get wise *v. phr., slang* To learn about something kept secret from you; become alert.

One girl pretended to be sick on gym days when she had athletics, until the teacher got wise and made her go anyway. (The teacher finally saw the girl's trick.) Often used with *to. The boys got wise to Jack's fondness for bubble gum.* (They found out about his liking bubble gum.) *If you don't get wise to yourself and start studying, you will fail the course.* (If you don't become alert to your laziness, you will fail.) Compare CATCH ON, SEE THROUGH. Contrast IN THE DARK.

get with it *v. phr., slang* To pay attention; be alive or alert; get busy. *The students get with it just before examinations.* (The students become busy just before examinations.) *The coach told the team to get with it.* (The coach told the team to pay attention to him.) Compare ON THE BALL.

ghost See GIVE UP THE GHOST.

ghost of a Least trace of; slightest resemblance to; smallest bit even of; a very little.— A cliché; usually used with *chance* or *idea* in negative sentences, or with *smile. There wasn't a ghost of a chance that Jack would win.* (There was no chance he would win.) *We didn't have the ghost of an idea where to look for John.* (We had no idea where to look for John.) *The teacher scolded Harold for drawing a funny picture on the chalkboard, but she had a ghost of a smile.* (She couldn't help smiling a little.) Compare FAT CHANCE.

gift of gab *or* **gift of the gab** *n. phr., informal* Skill in talking; ability to make interesting talk that makes people believe you. *Many men get elected because of their gift of gab.* (They get elected because of their skill in talking.) *Mr. Taylor's gift of gab helped him get a good job.* (His skill in talking helped him get a good job.)

gild the lily *also* **paint the lily** *v. phr.* To add unnecessarily to something already beautiful or good enough.—A cliché. *To talk about a beautiful sunset is to gild the lily.* (To talk about a beautiful sunset is unnecessary because it is already beautiful enough.) *For the beautiful girl to use makeup would be to gild the lily.* (She is so beautiful already that she doesn't need makeup.) *Frank's father is a millionaire, but Frank gilds the lily by saying he is a billionaire.* (Frank tries to say his father is even richer.)

gill See FED TO THE GILLS *at* FED UP, GREEN AROUND THE GILLS *or* PALE AROUND THE GILLS.

gird one's loins *v. phr., literary* To prepare for action; get ready for a struggle or hard work. *David girded up his loins and went out to meet the giant Goliath.* (David got ready and went out to fight the giant Goliath.) *Seniors must gird their loins for the battles of life.* (Seniors must get ready for the battles of life.)

girl Friday *n.* A very dependable and helpful female office worker; *especially* a secretary. *Miss Johnson is the manager's girl Friday.*

(She is the person upon whom the manager depends greatly.) *There was an advertisement in the newspaper for a girl Friday.* (There was an advertisement for a dependable female office worker.)

girl friend *n., informal* **1** A female friend or companion. *Jane is spending the night at her girl friend's house.* (Jane is staying at her friend's house.) **2** A boy's steady girl; the girl or woman partner in a love affair; girl; sweetheart. *John is taking his girl friend to the dance.* (John is taking his steady girl to the dance.) Contrast BOY FRIEND.

give See SILENCE GIVES CONSENT.

give a buzz See GIVE A RING.

give a cold shoulder See COLD SHOULDER.

give ———— a free hand See FREE HAND.

give a hand See LEND A HAND.

give a hang *or* **care a hang** *v. phr., informal* To have any interest or liking; care.—Used also with other words in the place of *hang,* such as *damn, rap, straw;* usually used in the negative. *You can quit helping me if you want to.* I *don't give a hang.* (I don't care; it makes no difference to me.) *Some people don't care a rap about sports.* (Some people are not interested in sports.) *Bruce never goes to the dances; he does not care a straw about dancing.* (He does not like to dance.)

give a hard time *v. phr., informal* **1** To give trouble by what you do or say; complain.—A cliché. *Jane gave her mother a hard time on the bus by fighting with her sister and screaming.* (Jane was very troublesome for her mother.) *Don't give me a hard time, George. I'm doing my best on this job.* (Don't scold or criticize too much.) Compare GIVE FITS. **2** To get in the way by teasing or playing; kid.—A cliché. *Don't give me a hard time, boys. I'm trying to study.* (Don't play or tease me while I'm studying.) Compare ACT UP, IN ONE'S HAIR.

give-and-take *n. phr.* **1** A sharing; giving and receiving back and forth between people; a giving up by people on different sides of part of what each one wants so that they can agree. *Jimmy is too selfish. He has no notion of give-and-take with the other children but wants everything for himself.* (Jimmy won't give anything to others. He wants to keep everything.) *There has to be give-and-take between two countries before they can be friends.* (Each must be willing to give up something to the other.) Compare LIVE AND LET LIVE. **2** Friendly talking or argument back and forth. Friendly sharing of ideas which may not agree; also: an exchange of teasing remarks. *After the meeting there was a lot of give-and-take about plans for the dance.* (Some of us argued for one idea and some for another, but we all learned something from the others and no one became angry.)

give an ear to *or* **lend an ear to** *v. phr., literary* To listen to. *Children should give an ear to their parents' advice.* (Children should listen to their parents' advice.) *The king lent an ear to the complaints of his people.* (The king listened to his people.)

give a pain *v. phr., slang* To make (you) disgusted; annoy. *Ann's laziness gives her mother a pain.* (Ann's laziness disgusts her mother.) *John's bad manners give his teacher a pain.* (John's bad manners are not liked by his teacher.) Compare PAIN IN THE NECK.

give ———— a piece of one's mind *v. phr., informal* To scold angrily; say what you really think to (someone).—A cliché. *Mr. Allen gave the other driver a piece of his mind.* (Mr. Allen spoke angrily to the other driver.) *The sergeant gave the soldier a piece of his mind for not cleaning his boots.* (The officer angrily scolded the soldier whose boots were dirty.) Syn. TELL OFF. Compare BAWL OUT, DRESS DOWN, GIVE IT TO, TONGUE LASHING.

give ———— a ring *also informal* **give a buzz** To call on the telephone. *Mrs. Jacobs promised to give her husband a ring in the afternoon.* (Mrs. Jacobs promised to telephone her husband in the afternoon.) *Alice will give her friend a buzz tonight.* (Alice will telephone her friend tonight.)

give as good as one gets *v. phr.* To be able to give back blow for blow; defend yourself well in a fight or argument.—A cliché. *The Americans gave as good as they got in the war with the English.* (The Americans were able to pay back the English in the fighting.) *George gave as good as he got in his fight with the older boy.* (George was able to hit as often and as hard as the older boy hit him.) Compare EYE FOR AN EYE, GAME AT WHICH TWO CAN PLAY.

giveaway *or* **dead giveaway** *n.* (stress on *give*) **1** An open secret. *By mid-afternoon, it was a dead giveaway who the new boss would be.* (Everyone knew who the new boss would be, although there was no official announcement.) **2** A forced or sacrifice sale at which items are sold for much less than their market value. *The Simpson's garage sale was actually a big giveaway.* (They were selling their things for much less than they were worth.)

give away *v.* **1** To give as a present. *Mrs. Jones has several kittens to give away.* (She has several kittens to give away as presents.) **2** To hand over (a bride) to her husband at the wedding. *Mr. Jackson gave away his daughter.* (He handed his daughter over to the groom at the wedding.) **3** To let (a secret) become known; tell the secret of. *The little boy gave away his hiding place when he coughed.* (He let others know where he was hiding when he coughed.) *Mary said she didn't care anything about John, but her blushing face gave her away.* (Her blushing face showed she was not telling the truth; it showed her real feelings.) Compare SPILL THE BEANS, LET THE CAT OUT OF THE BAG. **4** See GIVE ONESELF AWAY.

give a wide berth *v. phr.* To keep away from; keep a safe distance from.—A cliché.

Mary gave the barking dog a wide berth. (She kept a safe distance from the dog.) *Jack gave a wide berth to the fallen electric wires.* (He kept a safe distance from the fallen electric wires.) *After Tom got Bob into trouble, Bob gave him a wide berth.* (He stayed away from him.)

give chase *v. phr.* To chase or run after someone or something. *The dog saw a rabbit and gave chase.* (The dog ran after the rabbit.) *The policeman gave chase to the man who robbed the bank.* (The policeman ran after the man who robbed the bank.)

give color to *or* **lend color to** *v. phr.* To make (something) seem true or likely. *The boy's torn clothes gave color to his story of a fight.* (The boy's torn clothes made his story of a fight seem true.) *The way the man ate lent color to his story of near starvation.* (The hungry way the man ate made his story that he was almost starved to death seem probably true.)

give fits *v. phr., informal* To upset; bother very much. *Paul's higher grades give John fits.* (Paul's higher grades upset John.) *The short guard gave his tall opponent fits.* (The short guard bothered his tall opponent very much.) Compare GIVE A HARD TIME.

give free rein to See GIVE REIN TO.

give gray hair *v. phr., informal* To make (someone) anxious, confused, or worried.— A trite expression. *The traffic problem is enough to give a policeman gray hairs.* (The traffic can make a policeman worry and work very hard. Compare GET GRAY HAIR.

give ground *v. phr.* To go backward under attack; move back; retreat. *After fighting for a while the troops slowly began to give ground.* (The troops began to move backward.) *Although they were outnumbered by the enemy, the men refused to give ground.* (The men held their position firmly.) Compare DRAW BACK, DROP BACK, LOSE GROUND. Contrast HOLD ONE'S GROUND, STAND OFF, STAND ONE'S GROUND, STAND PAT, STAVE OFF.

give her the gun See GIVE IT THE GUN.

give in *v.* To stop fighting or arguing and do as the other person wants; give someone his own way; stop opposing someone. *Mother kept inviting Mrs. Smith to stay for lunch, and finally she gave in.* (Finally Mrs. Smith agreed to stay for lunch.) *After Billy proved that he could ride a bicycle safely, his father gave in to him and bought him one.* (Billy's father did not want him to have a bicycle, but he let him have one after he showed that he was a good rider.) Compare GIVE UP, SAY UNCLE.

give it the gun *or* **give her the gun** *v. phr., slang* To gun or speed up a motor; make a car, airplane, or something driven by a motor go faster. *The race driver gave it the gun.* (He speeded up his engine.) *The speedboat pilot gave her the gun.* (He ran the boat faster.) Compare STEP ON IT.

give it to *v. phr., informal* **1** To give pun-ishment to; beat. *The crowd yelled for the wrestler to give it to his opponent.* (The crowd yelled for the wrestler to beat his opponent.) Syn. LET HAVE IT. **2** To scold. *Jerry's mother gave it to him for coming home late.* (Jerry's mother scolded him for coming home late.) Compare GIVE A PIECE OF ONE'S MIND, LACE INTO. Contrast CATCH IT.

give off *v.* To send out; let out; put forth. *Rotten eggs give off a bad smell.* (Rotten eggs send out a bad smell.) *Burning leaves give off thick smoke.* (Burning leaves let out thick smoke.) Syn. GIVE OUT 2.

give of oneself *v. phr., literary* To give your time and effort to help others. *You should give of yourself sometimes.* (You should help others sometimes.) *During World War II, Governor Baldwin gave of himself by sweeping the halls of a hospital every afternoon.* (Because of the need for workers, even Governor Baldwin gave some of his time to help.)

give one an inch, and he will take a mile If you give some people a little or yield anything, they will want more and more; some people are never satisfied.—A cliché. *I gave Billy a bite of candy and he wanted more and more. If you give him an inch, he'll take a mile.* (Billy is never satisfied. He always wants more.) *The counselor said to Jack, "No, I can't let you get a haircut until Saturday. It's against the rules, and if I give an inch, someone will take a mile."* (If the counselor made one rule weaker by breaking it, Jack and other boys might think the other rules could be broken.)

give one enough rope and he will hang himself *informal* Give a bad person enough time and freedom to do as he pleases, and he may make a bad mistake or get into trouble and be caught.—A proverb. *Johnny is always stealing and hasn't been caught. But give him enough rope and he'll hang himself.* (If he keeps on stealing he will be caught someday.) —Often used in a short form, *give one enough rope. Mother didn't know who robbed the cookie jar, but she thought she could catch him if she gave him enough rope.* (Mother thought that if she pretended not to notice the cookies were gone, he would try again and be caught.)

give one's due *v. phr.* To be fair to (a person); give credit that (a person) deserves. *The boxer who lost gave the new champion his due.* (The boxer who lost was fair and gave credit to the man who beat him.) *We should give a good worker his due.* (We should be fair and praise a good worker.) Compare GIVE THE DEVIL HIS DUE.

give oneself airs *v. phr.* To act proud; act vain.—A cliché. *Mary gave herself airs when she wore her new dress.* (Mary acted proud when she wore her new dress.) *John gave himself airs when he won first prize.* (John acted vain when he won first prize.)

give oneself away *v. phr.* To show guilt;

show you have done wrong. *The thief gave himself away by spending so much money.* (The thief showed he had done wrong by spending so much money.) *Carl played a joke on Bob and gave himself away by laughing.* (Carl played a joke on Bob and showed his guilt by laughing.) Compare GIVE AWAY.

give oneself up *v.* To stop hiding or running away; surrender. *The thief gave himself up to the police.* (He went to the police and surrendered.) *Mr. Thompson hit another car, and his wife told him to give himself up.* (Mr. Thompson's wife told him to go to the police and confess.) Compare TURN IN.

give oneself up to *v. phr.* Not to hold yourself back from; let yourself enjoy. *Uncle Willie gave himself up to a life of wandering.* (He spent his life travelling.) *John came inside from the cold and gave himself up to the pleasure of being in a warm room.* (He enjoyed the warm room very much.) Compare ENJOY ONESELF, LET ONESELF GO.

give one's right arm *v. phr.* To give something of great value.—A cliché. *Mr. Thomas would give his right arm to be able to travel in Europe.* (He would give a great deal to be able to go to Europe.) *After it is too late, some people would give their right arm for a better education.* (After it is too late, some people would give a lot for a better education.)

give or take *v. phr.* To add or subtract. Used with a round number or date to show how approximate it is. *The house was built in 1900, give or take five years.* (The house was built around 1900, possibly five years earlier or later.)

give out *v.* **1** To make known; let it be known; publish. *Mary gave out that she and Bob were going to be married.* (She told people.) **2** To let escape; give. *The cowboy gave out a yell.* (He gave a shout.) Syn. GIVE OFF, LET GO. **3** to give to people; distribute. *The barber gives out free lollipops to all the children.* (He gives them away.) Compare HAND OUT, PASS OUT. **4** To fail; collapse. *Tom's legs gave out and he couldn't run any farther.* (His legs were too tired to run any more.) *The chair gave out under the fat man.* (The chair broke.) Compare WEAR OUT. **5** To be finished or gone. *When the food at the party gave out, they bought more.* (After the food was all eaten they bought more.) *The teacher's patience gave out.* (The teacher's patience was gone and he got angry.) Syn. RUN OUT, RUN SHORT. Compare USE UP, WEAR OUT. **6** *slang* Not to hold back; act freely; let yourself go.—Often used in the imperative. *You're not working hard, Charley. Give out!* (Don't hold back; be lazy.) **7** *informal* To show how you feel. *When Jane saw the mouse, she gave out with a scream.* (She let people know that she was scared.) *Give out with a little smile.* (Give us a smile.) Compare LET GO.

give pause *v. phr.* To cause you to stop and think; make you doubt or worry. *The heavy monthly payments gave Mr. Smith pause in his plans to buy a new car.* (The heavy monthly payments caused Mr. Smith to stop and think about his plans to buy a new car.) *The bad weather gave Miss Carter pause about driving to New York City.* (The bad weather caused Miss Carter to stop and think about driving to New York City.)

give rein to *or* **give free rein to** *v. phr.* To allow to move or to do with freedom. *Some parents give rein to their children.* (Some parents let their children do what they want to do.) *The principal gives free rein to the students who are honor students.* (The principal lets the students who are honor students do things with more freedom than the others.) *Sitting alone in the house at night, Mary gave free rein to her imagination, and was soon badly frightened by every noise and shadow.* (Mary let her imagination work freely; she thought the house was full of things that would hurt her.)

give rise to *v. phr.* To be the reason for; cause. *A branch floating in the water gave rise to Columbus' hopes that land was near.* (A branch floating in the water started Columbus' hopes that land was near.) *John's black eye gave rise to rumors that he had been in a fight.* (John's black eye made people think he had been in a fight.)

give ——— short shift See SHORT SHRIFT.

give someone his rights *or* **read someone his rights** *v. phr., informal* **1** The act of advising arrested criminals that they have the right to remain silent and that everything they say can be held against them in a court of law; that they have the right to the presence of an attorney during questioning and that if they can't afford one and request it, an attorney will be appointed for them by the State. *The cops gave Smith his rights immediately after the arrest.* (The police advised Smith of his legal defenses.) **2** To sever a relationship by telling someone that he or she can go and see a divorce lawyer or the like. *Sue gave Mike his rights before she slammed the door in his face.* (Sue told Mike he could go to a lawyer if he wished to do so.) Compare READ THE RIOT ACT.

give the air See GIVE THE BOUNCE 1.

give the ax *v. phr., colloquial* **1** Abruptly to finish a relationship. *She gave me the ax last night.* (Our romantic engagement came to an abrupt end.) **2** To fire an employee in a curt manner. *His boss gave John the ax last Friday.* (He fired him curtly.)

give the benefit of the doubt *v. phr.* To believe (a person) is innocent rather than guilty when you are not sure. *The money was stolen and John was the only boy who had known where it was, but the teacher gave him the benefit of the doubt.* (The teacher believed John was innocent rather than guilty of stealing the money because it was not sure that he did.) *George's grade was higher than usual* *and he might have cheated, but his teacher gave him the benefit of the doubt.* (George's teacher had no proof he had cheated, so he did not doubt his grade.)

give the bounce *or* **give the gate** *v. phr., slang* **1** *or* **give the air** To stop being a friend or lover to (a person); separate from.—A cliché. *Mary gave John the bounce after she saw him dating another girl.* (Mary was angry and didn't want to be John's girl any more.) *Bill and Jane had an argument and Bill is giving her the gate.* (Bill doesn't want to be her friend any more.) **2** *or* **give the sack** *also* **give the hook** To fire from a job; dismiss. *The ball team gave Joe the gate because he never came to practice.* Contrast GET THE BOUNCE.

give the creeps See THE CREEPS.

give the devil his due *v. phr.* To be fair, even to someone who is bad; tell the truth about a person even though you don't like him.—A cliché. *I don't like Mr. Jones, but to give the devil his due, I must admit that he is a good teacher.* (To be fair to Mr. Jones, he is a good teacher.)

give ——— the eye *v. phr., slang* **1** To look at, especially with interest and liking. *A pretty girl went by and all the boys gave her the eye.* (They all looked because she was pretty.) **2** To look or stare at, especially in a cold or unfriendly way. *Mrs. Jones didn't like Mary and didn't speak. She just gave her the eye when they met on the street.* (She stared at Mary in an unfriendly way.)

give the gate See GIVE THE BOUNCE

give the glad eye *v. phr., slang* To give (someone) a welcoming look as if saying "come over here, I want to talk to you." *I was surprised when Joe gave me the glad eye.* (I was surprised by his looking at me so invitingly and welcomingly.)

give the go-by *v. phr.* To pay no attention to a person; avoid. *John fell in love with Mary, but she gave him the go-by.* (John fell in love with Mary, but she avoided him.) *The boy raised his hand to answer the question, but the teacher gave him the go-by.* (The boy raised his hand to answer the question, but the teacher paid no attention to him.) Compare THE RUNAROUND.

give the high sign See HIGH SIGN.

give the hook See GIVE THE BOUNCE 2.

give the lie to *v. phr., literary* **1** To call (someone) a liar. *The police gave the lie to the man who said that he had been at home during the robbery.* (The police told the man he was lying.) **2** To show (something) to be false; prove untrue. *The boy's dirty face gave the lie to his answer that he had washed.* (The boy's dirty face showed that his answer was false.)

give the sack See GIVE THE BOUNCE 2.

give the shirt off one's back *v. phr., informal* To give away something or everything that you own.—A cliché. *He'd give you the shirt off his back.* (He is very generous and will give you anything he has.)

give the slip *v.* To escape from (someone); run away from unexpectedly; sneak away from. *An Indian was following, but Boone gave him the slip by running down a hill.* (Boone escaped the Indian by unexpectedly running down a hill.) *Some boys were waiting outside the school to beat up Jack, but he gave them the slip.* (Jack got out of the school and away, and the boys did not see him.)

give ——— the works See THE WORKS.

give to understand *v. phr., informal* **1** To make a person think that something is true but not tell him; suggest; hint. *Mr. Johnson gave Billy to understand that he would pay him if he helped him clean the yard.* (Mr. Johnson did not say so, but Billy thought he meant it.) **2** To make a person understand by telling him very plainly or boldly. *Frank was given to understand in a short note from the boss that he was fired.* (He was told very clearly.)

give up *v.* **1a** To stop trying to keep; surrender; yield. *The dog had the ball in his mouth and wouldn't give it up.* (He wouldn't drop the ball from his mouth.) *Jimmy is giving up his job as a newsboy when he goes back to school.* (He won't keep the job when he goes back to school.) Compare GIVE ONESELF UP, HAND OVER, LET GO 1a. Contrast HOLD ON TO. **1b** To allow; permit. *Ford gave up two walks in the first inning.* (Ford allowed two men to walk in the first inning.) **2** To stop doing or having; abandon; quit. *The doctor told Mr. Harris to give up smoking.* (He told him to stop smoking.) *Jane hated to give up her friends when she moved away.* (She didn't want to stop having them for friends.) Compare LEAVE OFF, PART WITH. **3** To stop hoping for, waiting for, or trying to do. *Johnny was given up by the doctors after the accident, but he lived just the same.* (He was hurt so badly that we gave her up. (We stopped waiting.) *I couldn't do the puzzle so I gave it up.* (I quit trying.) **4** To stop trying; quit; surrender. *The war will be over when one of the countries gives up.* (When one country stops fighting the war will be finished.) *The other team gave up after we scored three touchdowns.* (They didn't try to win after we were far ahead.) Compare GIVE IN 2, RESIGN ONESELF, THROW IN THE SPONGE.

give up the ghost *v. phr.* To die; stop going. —A cliché. *After a long illness, the old woman gave up the ghost.* (After a long illness, the old woman died.) *The motor turned over a few times and gave up the ghost.* (The motor turned over a few times and stopped.)

give up the ship *v. phr.* To stop fighting and surrender; stop trying or hoping to do something.—A cliché usually used in negative sentences. *"Don't give up the ship, John" said his* *father when John failed a test.* (He told him not to quit trying because he failed one test.)

give voice *v. phr., formal* To tell what you feel or think, especially when you are angry or want to object.—Used with *to. The students gave voice to their pleasure over the new building.* (The students spoke up about their pleasure over the new building.) *Little Willie gave voice to his pain when the dog bit him by crying loudly.* (He cried because he was hurt.) Compare CRY OUT, SPEAK OUT.

give way *v.* **1** To go back; retreat. *The enemy army is giving way before the cannon fire.* (They are going back.) Compare FALL BACK. **2** To make room; get out of the way. *The children gave way and let their mother through the door.* (They stepped aside to make room for their mother to get through the door.) Compare MAKE WAY. **3** To lose control of yourself; lose your courage or hope; yield. *Mrs. Jones didn't give way during the flood, but she was very frightened.* (She didn't become too upset.) Compare GIVE UP, LOSE ONE'S HEAD. **4** To collapse; fail. *The river was so high that the dam gave way.* (There was so much water that it broke the dam.) *Mary's legs gave way and she fainted.* (Her legs would not hold her up.) Compare GIVE OUT 4, LET GO 1a. **5** To let yourself be persuaded; give permission. *Billy kept asking his mother if he could go to the movies and she finally gave way.* (His mother finally let him go to the movies.) Compare GIVE IN.

give way to *v. phr.* **1a** To make room for; allow to go or pass; yield to. *John gave way to the old lady and let her pass.* (John gave room to her to pass.) **1b** To allow to decide. *Mrs. Rogers gave way to her husband in buying the car.* (She let him pick the car.) **1c** To lose control of (your feelings), not hold back. *Timmy gave way to his feelings when his dog died.* (Timmy cried when his dog died.) **2** or **give place to**. To be replaced by. *Radio has given way to television in popularity.* (Television has taken the place of radio in popularity.) *When she saw the clowns, the little girl's tears gave way to laughter.* (The girl was crying, but when she saw the clowns, she began laughing.)

glad hand *n., informal* A friendly handshake; a warm greeting. *Father went to the front door to give Uncle Fred the glad hand when he arrived.* (Father welcomed him by shaking hands and saying hello.) *The politician went down the street on election day giving everyone the glad hand.* (He shook hands with everyone, hoping people would vote for him.)

glad rags *n., slang* Clothes worn to parties or on special occasions; best clothes. *Mrs. Owens put on her glad rags for the party.* (Mrs. Owens put on her fine clothes for the party.) Compare BEST BIB AND TUCKER.

glance See AT FIRST GLANCE *or* AT FIRST SIGHT.

glass See PEOPLE WHO LIVE IN GLASS HOUSES SHOULD NOT THROW STONES, SAFETY GLASS.

glasses See LOOK AT THE WORLD THROUGH ROSE-COLORED GLASSES.

glass jaw *n., slang* The inability of a boxer to get a hard punch on the jaw without being knocked out; a tendency to be knocked out easily. *He would have been champion except for his glass jaw.* (He was good enough to be champion, but he never got that far because he got knocked out easily.)

glory See IN ONE'S GLORY.

gloss over *v.* To try to make what is wrong or bad seem right or not important; try to make a thing look easy; pretend about; hide. *Billy broke a window and Mother tried to gloss it over by saying it wouldn't cost much to have it fixed, but Father spanked Billy anyway.* (Mother tried to make the broken window seem unimportant so that Father wouldn't spank Billy.) *John glossed over his mistake by saying that everybody did the same thing.* (He tried to make it seem not so bad as it was.)

glove See FIT LIKE A GLOVE, HAND IN GLOVE *or* HAND AND GLOVE, HANDLE WITH GLOVES.

go See HERE GOES, HERE GOES NOTHING, BEST BIB AND TUCKER *or* SUNDAY-GO-TO-MEETING CLOTHES, COMINGS AND GOINGS, EASY COME EASY GO, GET GOING, GET-UP-AND-GO, HAVE A GO AT, HEART GOES OUT TO, KNOW WHETHER ONE IS COMING OR GOING, LET GO, MAKE A GO OF, NO DEAL *or* NO GO, ON THE GO, PAY AS ONE GOES, TOUCH AND GO.

go about *v.* **1** To be busy with; keep busy at or working on; start working on; do. *Bobby is going about his homework very seriously tonight.* (He is working hard at his homework.) *Just go about your business and don't keep looking out of the window.* (Just keep on doing your work.) *How will you go about building the bird house?* (How will you start it?) Syn. GO AT 2. **2a** To move from one place or person to another. *Some people go about telling untrue stories.* (They tell stories to one person after another wherever they are.) **2b** To go together.—Usually used with *with. Mother doesn't want me to go about with Jane and her friends any more.* (She doesn't want me to go with them where they go any more.) Syn. GO AROUND 1b.

go after *v.* To try to get. *"First find out what job you want and then go after it," said Jim's father.* (Try to get the job that you want.)

go against the grain See AGAINST THE GRAIN 2.

go ahead *v.* To begin to do something; not wait. *The teacher told the students not to write on the paper yet, but John went ahead and wrote his name.* (John did not wait until the teacher told him to write his name.) *"May I ask you a question?" "Go ahead."* (Ask the question.) Compare GO ON 1.

goal See FIELD GOAL.

goal line *n.* A line that marks the goal in a

game (as football.) *The fullback went over the goal line from five yards out.* (The fullback ran five yards over the line marking the goal to score a touchdown.)

goal line stand *n.* A strong defensive effort right in front of the goal line. *A goal line stand by the home team held the visitors on the two-yard line.* (The home team kept the visitors from scoring even though they were only two yards away from a touchdown.)

go all the way with See ALL THE WAY.

go along *v.* **1** To move along; continue. *Uncle Bill made up the story as he went along.* (He made up the story while he was telling it.) Compare GO ON 1. **2** To go together or as company; go for fun.—Often used with *with*. *Mary went along with us to Jane's house.* (Mary kept us company.) *John just went along for the ride to the ball game. He didn't want to play.* (He just went for fun or company.) *When one filling station cuts gasoline prices, the others usually go along.* (When one filling station cuts gasoline prices, the others usually follow.) **3** To agree; cooperate.—Often. used with *with*. *"Jane is a nice girl." "I'll go along with that," said Bill.* (I agree that she is a nice girl.) *Just because the other boys do something bad, you don't have to go along with it.* (You don't have to do it too.)

go ape *v. phr., slang* To become highly excited or behave in a crazy way. *Amy went ape over the hotel and beautiful beaches.* (Amy was very excited and enthusiastic about the hotel and beaches.) *The electric door opener malfunctioned and caused the garage door to go ape.* (Something went wrong in the electric door opener, and the garage door went up and down crazily.)

go around *v.* **1a** To go from one place or person to another. *Mr. Smith is going around looking for work.* (He is going to different places looking for a job.) *Don't go around telling lies like that.* (Don't go to different people and tell such lies.) *Chicken pox is going around the neighborhood.* (Chicken pox is passing from one person to another.) *A rumor is going around school that we will get the afternoon off.* (Everyone says there will be no school this afternoon.) **1b** To go together; keep company.—Usually used with *with*. *Bill goes around with boys older than he is because he is big for his age.* (He has big boys for friends and is often with them.) Syn. GO ABOUT 2b. **2** To be enough to give to everyone; be enough for all. *There are not enough desks to go around in the classroom.* (There are more children than there are desks.)

go around in circles See IN A CIRCLE.

goat See GET ONE'S GOAT.

go at *v.* **1** To start to fight with; attack. *The dog and the cat are going at each other again.* (They are fighting.) **2** To make a beginning on; approach; tackle. *How are you going to go at the job of fixing the roof?* (How are you going to begin and do it?) Compare START IN. Syn. GO ABOUT 1.

go at it hammer and tongs *v. phr., informal* **1** To attack or fight with great strength or energy; have a bad argument.—A hackneyed phrase. *Bill slapped George's face and now they're going at it hammer and tongs in back of the house.* (They are fighting as hard as they can.) *Helen and Mary have been arguing all day, and now they are going at it hammer and tongs again.* (They are having another argument.) **2** To start or do something with much strength, energy, or enthusiasm. —A hackneyed phrase. *The farmer had to chop down a tree and he went at it hammer and tongs.* (He began to chop it down with a lot of energy.) *Charles had a lot of homework to do and he went at it hammer and tongs till bedtime.* (He studied hard and seriously.) Compare IN EARNEST, WITH MIGHT AND MAIN.

go back on *v. phr.* **1** To turn against; not be faithful or loyal to. *Many of the man's friends went back on him when he was sent to prison.* (Many of the man's friends turned against him when he was sent to prison.) *The boy's father told him not to go back on his promise.* (The boy's father told him not to break his promise or be unfaithful.) Compare BACK DOWN, TURN ONE'S BACK. **2** To fail to do necessary work; not work. *Grandfather's eyes are going back on him.* (His eyes are getting poor.) Compare BREAK DOWN 4, GIVE OUT.

go begging *v. phr.* To be not needed or wanted. *Many old homes in the city go begging.* (Many old homes in the city are not wanted.) *Most of the apples on the market went begging.* (Most of the apples on the market were not wanted and could not be sold.)

go broke *v. phr., slang* To lose all one's money; especially by taking a chance; owe more than you can pay. *The inventor went broke because nobody would buy his machine.* (The inventor owed more than he could pay because nobody would buy his machine.) *Dan had a quarter but he went broke matching pennies with Fred.* (He lost the money he had.)

go-by See GIVE THE GO-BY.

go by *v.* **1** To go or move past; pass. *Bob had to go by the post office on his way to school, so he mailed the letter.* (He had to pass the post office.) **2** To follow; copy; obey. *Mother goes by a pattern when she makes a dress.* (She copies an example of a dress.) *You will find Main Street without trouble if you go by Father's directions.* (If you go the way Father tells you to, you will find it.) *If you ride a bicycle, you must go by the rules of the road.* (You must obey the rules of travelling on the streets.) **3** To be known by; be called. *Many actors do not go by their real* names. (Many actors use other names, not their real names.) *Fred goes by the nickname of Chubby.* (Fred is called Chubby.) **4** To pass; be over; end. *Time goes by quickly on vacation.* (Time passes quickly.) *The horse and buggy days have gone by.* (They are ended.) *The flowers have all gone by. What will I do for a bouquet?* (The flowers are not pretty any more.) **5** To stop for a short visit; go to someone's house for a short while. *"Have you seen Bill lately?" "Yes, I went by his house last week."* (I visited him for a little while.) Compare STOP BY.

go by the board *also* **pass by the board**   *v. phr.* To go away or disappear forever; be forgotten or not used. *Tom had several chances to go to college, but he let them go by the board.* (Tom let the chances to by; he did not take them.) *Grandfather said he was too old to go to the beach. "Those days have passed by the board," he said.* (The days when he was young enough to go to the beach were over.) Compare DOWN THE DRAIN.

go chase oneself   *v. phr., slang* Go away and stop being a nuisance. *John's father was busy and told him to go chase himself.* (John's father was busy and told him to go away.) *The owner of the store told the boys in front to go chase themselves.* (The owner of the store told the boys in front to go away.) Compare BEAT IT, GO JUMP IN THE LAKE.

God   See IN THE LAP OF THE GODS *also* ON THE KNEES OF THE GODS, MY GOD *or* MY GOODNESS, WOULD THAT *or* WOULD GOD.

God forbid   *interj.* May God prevent (something from happening); I hope that will not happen or is not true. *Someone told the worried mother that her son might have drowned. She said, "God forbid!"* (She asked God not to let her son be drowned.) *God forbid that the dam break and flood the valley!* (Let us hope the dam does not break and flood the valley!) Compare PERISH THE THOUGHT.

Godfrey   See GREAT GODFREY.

God knows *or* **goodness knows** *or* **heaven knows**   *informal* **1** Maybe God knows but I don't know and no one else knows.—Often used with *only. Do you know where Susan is? God only knows!* (I have no idea. Maybe God knows, but I don't.) **2** Surely; certainly. *Goodness knows, the poor man needs the money.* (The man surely needs the money.) *Heaven only knows, I have tried hard enough.* (I really have tried hard.)

Godmother   See FAIRY GODMOTHER.

go down in history *or* **go down in the records**   *v. phr.* To be remembered or recorded for always. *The lives of great men go down in history.* (The lives of great men are remembered.) *Babe Ruth went down in history as a home run hitter.* (Babe Ruth is remembered as a home run hitter.) *The boy's straight A's for four years of college went down in the records.* (The boy's straight A's for four years

of college were recorded for always.) *The President said that the day the war ended would go down in history.* (The day would be historic.)

God tempers the wind to the shorn lamb   *literary* A person who is already helpless will not have more trouble; you will not have more trouble than you can bear. *After Mr. Smith lost his job, the Smith's house caught fire, but the fire was put out before much harm was done. Mr. Smith said, "God tempers the wind to the shorn lamb."* (If the house had burned down, the Smiths would not have known what to do, but that did not happen.) Contrast IT NEVER RAINS BUT IT POURS.

go Dutch   *v. phr., informal* To go out for fun together but have each person pay for himself. *High school students often go Dutch to basketball games.* (High school students often go together to basketball games and have each one pay for himself.) *Sometimes boys and girls go Dutch on dates.* (Sometimes boys and girls each pay their own expenses on dates.) *The girl knew her boy friend had little money, so she offered to go Dutch.* (The girl knew her boy friend had little money, so she offered to pay her way while he paid his.) Compare DUTCH TREAT.

go easy   See TAKE IT EASY 1.

go fly a kite   *v. phr., slang* To go away; leave.—Usually used as a command, to show that you do not accept someone's ideas. *Harry was tired of John's advice and told him to go fly a kite.* (Harry was tired of John's advice and told him to go away.) *After Mary stood around telling Sue what was wrong with her dress, Sue told her to go fly a kite.* (After Mary stood around telling Sue what was wrong with her dress, Sue told her to go away.) Compare DROP DEAD, GO JUMP IN THE LAKE.

go for   *v. phr., informal* **1** To try to get; aim for; try for. *Our team is going for the championship in the game tonight.* (They will try to win the championship.) *The dog went for Bob's leg.* (He aimed at Bob's leg to bite it.) **2** To favor; support; like. *Little Susie really goes for ice cream.* (Little Susie likes ice cream very much.) *Bob goes for Jane in a big way.* (He likes her very much.) **3** To attack; begin to fight or argue with. *The Indian jumped out of the bush and went for Daniel.* (He attacked Daniel.) *Molly went for James about being late as soon as he got home.* (She scolded James.)

go for broke   *v. phr., slang* To risk everything on one big effort; use all your energy and skill; try as hard as possible.—A cliché. *The racing car driver decided to go for broke in the biggest race of the year.* (The driver decided he would have to go as hard and as fast as he could with no thought for later if he wanted to win the big race.) Compare ALL-OUT.

go for nothing *also* *formal* **go for naught** *v. phr.* To count for nothing; be useless; be wasted. *What the teacher said went for nothing because the pupils did not pay attention.* (The teacher's talk did not help because the pupils didn't listen.) *I hope that all your good work doesn't go for naught.* (I hope you will be successful.) Compare IN VAIN.

go from bad to worse *adv. phr.* To change from a bad position or condition to a worse one; become worse. *Dick's typing went from bad to worse when he was tired.* (His poor typing became worse because he was tired and careless.) *Jack's conduct in school has gone from bad to worse.* (He was a bad boy at first and became worse.) Compare OUT OF THE FRYING PAN INTO THE FIRE.

go-getter *n.* A person who works hard to become successful; an active, ambitious person who usually gets what he wants. *The governor of the state has always been a go-getter.* (The governor of the state has always been a person who works hard and fast to become successful.) *The best salesmen are the go-getters.* (The best salesmen are the persons who work hard.)

go-go *adj., slang, informal* **1** vigorous youthful, unusually active. *Joe is a go-go kind of guy.* (He is extremely vigorous, and unusually active.) **2** Of a discotheque or the music or dances performed there **3a** unrestrained **3b** very up-to-date, hip. *Mary wore handsome go-go boots to the discotheque last night.* (She had on the type of good looking boots worn during dancing at clubs.)

go great guns See GREAT GUNS.

go halfway *or* **go halfway to meet one** *or* **meet one halfway** *v. phr.* To give up part of what you want or to do your share in reaching an agreement with someone. *Our neighbors are willing to go halfway to meet us and pay their share for a fence between our houses.* (They agree to pay half and we will pay half.) *Bob wants to make up after your fight and you should meet him halfway.* (You should agree to be friends with him too.) *If you're willing to go halfway with us, we'll be friends again.* (If you'll do your share, we can be friends.) *Bill met Mary halfway after their argument.* (Bill wasn't stubborn by wanting all of his own way.)

go halves *v. phr., informal* To share half or equally become partners. *The boys went halves in raising pigs.* (The boys shared equally in raising pigs.) *The men are going halves in a new business.* (The men are going to become partners in a new business.) *The girl bought a box of candy and went halves with her roommate.* (The girl bought a box of candy and gave her roommate half of it.)

go hang *v. phr., slang* **1** To stop being of interest or importance; be forgotten.—Usually used with *let*. *Mr. Johnson let his business go hang after his wife died.* (Mr. Johnson let his business stop being of importance after his

wife died.) **2** To leave you alone; not bother. *When the neighbor told Father how to manage his children, Father told him to go hang.* (Father told the neighbor to stop telling him what to do.) Compare TELL WHERE TO GET OFF.

go hard with *v. phr.* To be painful, troublesome, or hard for; happen or result badly for. —Used after *it*. *It will go hard with you if I catch you smoking.* (You will be punished severely if I catch you.)

go haywire *v. phr., informal* Mixed-up, out of order, not in regular working condition. *My electric typewriter has gone all haywire; I have to call the repair man.* (Something went wrong with the machine and it won't work properly.)

go in a circle *or* **go in circles** See IN A CIRCLE.

go in for *v. phr., informal* To try to do; take part in; take pleasure in. *Most girls do not go in for rough games.* (Most girls do not take part in rough games.) *Mrs. Henry goes in for simple meals.* (Mrs. Henry tries to cook simple meals.) Compare GO INTO 3, TAKE UP 5b.

going and coming See COMING AND GOING.

going for one *adj. phr.* Working to help; in one's favor. *The young woman surely will get the job; she has everything going for her.* (Everything is working to help her get the job.)

going on *adv. phr.* Almost; nearly. *Joe is going on six years old.* (Joe is almost six years old.) *It is going on six o'clock.* (It is almost six o'clock.)

going through changes *v. phr., slang, informal* To be in trouble, to have difficulties, to be trapped in unfavorable circumstances. *What's the matter with Joe?—He's going through changes.* (He is caught up in unfavorable circumstances and has a hard time extricating himself from them.)

going to Can be expected to; planning to.— Used after *is* (or *was*, etc.), with an infinitive, in the same way *will* is used, to show future. *Some day that big tree is going to rot and fall.* (Someday the tree will become rotten and fall.) *Look at those dark clouds. It's going to rain.* (We can expect rain to come soon.) *The boys are going to practice football this afternoon.* (The boys are planning to have football practice this afternoon.) *For a minute Ben thought the car was going to hit him.* (Ben thought the car would hit him.) *I was going to attend the meeting, but after supper I forgot about it.* (I planned to go to the meeting, but then I forgot it.)—Sometimes used without the infinitive. *That worn rope hasn't broken yet, but it's going to.* (The rope is sure to break sometime.) *Put some more wood on the fire. "I'm going to."* (I will; I plan to do it.) Compare ABOUT TO 1.

go in one ear and out the other *v. phr., informal* To be not really listened to or understood; be paid no attention.—A cliché. *The teacher's directions to the boy went in* *one ear and out the other.* (The boy did not really listen to the directions.) *Mother scolded Martha, but it went in one ear and out the other.* (Martha did not pay any attention when her mother scolded her.)

go into *v.* **1a** To go or fit inside of; able to be put in. *The table is too big to go into the closet.* (The table won't fit.) **1b** To be able to be divided into; be divisible into. *Two goes into four two times.* (Two can be divided into four twice.) **2** To enter a state or condition of; pass into. *John went into a fit of temper when he didn't get his own way.* (John got angry.) *The sick man went into a coma.* (He became unconscious for a long time.) *The country went into mourning when the king died.* (The country missed their king and showed their sorrow.) **3** To be busy in or take part in; enter as a job or profession. *The mayor went into politics as a very young man.* (He was young when he got interested and began to take part in politics.) *Mr. Johnson is going into business for himself.* (He will open his own business.) *Bill wants to go into law when he gets out of school.* (He wants to be a lawyer.) Compare GO IN FOR, TAKE UP 5b. **4** To start to talk about; bring up the subject of; examine. *We'll talk about the dead mouse after dinner, Billy. Let's not go into it now.* (Let's not talk about the dead mouse until we have eaten our dinner.) *The teacher went into the subject of newspapers today.* (He talked about newspapers.) Compare LOOK INTO.

go into a huddle *v. phr.* **1** To gather close together as a team in a football game, usually to find out your team's next play. *The football team which has the ball goes into a huddle before every play to get orders on what play they will use.* (They find out what the play will be without letting the other team know.) **2** *informal* To talk together privately about something; discuss something where others cannot hear.—A hackneyed phrase. *The man went into a huddle with his lawyers before answering the question.* (The man discussed the question privately with his lawyers before he answered.) *The doctors went into a huddle and decided to operate.* (The doctors had a private talk and decided to operate.)

go into a nose dive See GO INTO A TAIL SPIN.

go into a tailspin *or* **go into a nose dive** *v. phr., informal* To fall or go down badly; collapse; give up trying.—A cliché. *The team went into a tailspin after their captain was hurt, and they were badly beaten.* (The team played very badly.) **2** *informal* To become very anxious, confused, or mentally sick; give up hope. —A cliché. *The man went into a tailspin after his wife died and he never got over it.* (The man lost interest in life after his wife died.)

go into orbit *v. phr., slang* **1** To become very happy or successful. *Our team has gone into orbit.* (Our team has become successful.) Compare FLY HIGH. **2** To lose one's temper or control completely; become very angry. *John*

was afraid his father would go into orbit when he found out about the car accident. (John was afraid his father would go into a rage.) Compare HIT THE CEILING.

go it *v. phr., informal* **1** To go fast; run hard; not to spare yourself.—Often used as a command. *The coach yelled to the runner to go it.* (The coach yelled to the runner to go fast.) *At the party the girls cheered for their partners to go it.* (At the party the girls cheered for their partners to go fast.) *The boys called, "Go it!" to the dog chasing the cat.* (The boys called, "Go fast!" to the dog chasing the cat.) **2** To live; continue to do or work. *John wants to leave home and go it alone.* (He wants to try to live away from home and support himself.) Compare ON ONE'S OWN.

go jump in the lake *v. phr., informal* To go away and quit being a bother. *George was tired of Tom's advice and told him to go jump in the lake.* (George was tired of Tom's advice and told him to go away and quit bothering him.) Compare GO CHASE YOURSELF, GO FLY A KITE.

gold See HEART OF GOLD.

golden See KILL THE GOOSE THAT LAID THE GOLDEN EGG.

goldfish bowl *n., slang, informal* **1** A situation in which it is not possible to keep things secret for any length of time. *Washington Society is a goldfish bowl.* (It is not possible to keep secrets in Washington Society.) **2** An apartment or place that provides no privacy for its occupant, e.g., an office that has too many windows. *Joe's office is a goldfish bowl, that's why I didn't let him kiss me there.* (I didn't let him kiss me there, because anybody can see in from the street.)

golf widow *n., informal* A woman whose husband is often away from home playing golf. *Mrs. Thompson didn't like being a golf widow.* (Mrs. Thompson didn't like being a woman whose husband was away a lot, playing golf.)

go like clockwork *or* **go off like clockwork** *v. phr., informal* To run smoothly and regularly like the workings of a clock; go smoothly and without difficulty; go on time or as planned.—A hackneyed phrase. *The car's motor went like clockwork after Bob fixed it.* (The motor ran well again.) *The birthday party went off like clockwork and everyone had a good time.* (There was no trouble or delay and it was a good party.)

gone goose *also* **gone gosling** *n., slang* A person for whom there is no hope. *Herbert's grades have been so low that he is a gone goose for the year.* (Herbert's grades have been so low that there is no hope for him to pass.) *The man was a gone gosling when a policeman caught him breaking the store window.* (There was no hope for the man when a policeman caught him breaking the store window.)

gone with the wind *adj. phr.* Gone forever; past; vanished.—A cliché. *All the Indians who used to live here are gone with the wind.* (They are gone and won't come back.) *Joe knew that his chance to get an "A" was gone with the wind when he saw how hard the test was.* (He knew that he had no chance.) Compare DOWN THE DRAIN.

good See AS GOOD AS, AS GOOD AS ONE GETS, BUT GOOD, DO ONE GOOD, FOR GOOD, FOR GOOD MEASURE, GET THE GOODS ON, HOLD GOOD, IN GOOD, IN GOOD FAITH, IN GOOD TIME, IN ONE'S GOOD GRACES, IT'S AN ILL WIND THAT BLOWS NOBODY GOOD, MAKE GOOD, MISS IS AS GOOD AS A MILE, NO GOOD, ON ONE'S GOOD BEHAVIOR, ON ONE'S GOOD SIDE, SO FAR, SO GOOD, STAND IN GOOD STEAD, TO THE GOOD, WELL AND GOOD, WITH GOOD GRACE.

good and ——— *adv., informal* Very; completely. *John's father was good and mad when John came home late.* (John's father was very mad when John came home late.) *Jack knew good and well that Tom had thrown the snowball at him.* (Jack knew very well that Tom had thrown the snowball at him.) *I pushed Bill good and hard.* (I gave him a hard push.) *Susan wouldn't come out till she was good and ready.* (She came when she wanted to come.) *I beat Joe good and proper in the game of marbles.* (I beat him badly.)

good as See AS GOOD AS.

good as one's promise See AS GOOD AS ONE'S WORD.

good as one's word See AS GOOD AS ONE'S WORD.

good buddy *n., slang, citizen's band radio jargon* Salutation used by truckers and automobile drivers who have CB radios. *What's the Smokey situation, good buddy?* (Hi, what's the police report?)

good day *interj.* Hello or goodbye.—Used as a formal greeting or salute when you meet or leave someone during the day. *Miss Rogers said, "Good day!" when she met her friend on the street.* (Miss Rogers said, "Hello!" when she met her friend on the street.) *Mr. Lee said "Good day!" and left the office.* (Mr. Lee said, "Good bye!" and left the office.)

good deal *or* **great deal** *n., informal* A large amount; much.—Used with *a. Mrs. Walker's long illness cost her a good deal.* (Mrs. Walker's long sickness cost her much money.) *George spends a great deal of his time watching television.* (George spends much of his time watching television.)—Often used like an adverb. *Cleaning up after the party took a great deal more work than the girls expected.* (Cleaning up took much more work than the girls thought it would take.) *Usually it takes Father half an hour to drive to work, but in bad weather it takes a good deal longer.* (In bad weather it may take three-quarters of an

hour.) *Mother likes the gloves Mary gave her, and she uses them a good deal.* (She uses them often.) *George is a good deal like his father; they both love to eat.* (George is much like his father.) Syn. A LOT, QUITE A LITTLE. Compare ALL KINDS OF, GOOD MANY. Contrast A LITTLE.

good egg *slang or informal* **good scout** *n. phr.* A friendly, kind or good-natured person; a nice fellow. *Tommy is such a good egg that everybody wants to be his friend.* (Tommy is very friendly and nice to people.) Syn. REGULAR GUY. Contrast BAD EGG.

good evening *interj.* Hello or goodbye.— Used as a formal greeting or salute when you meet or leave someone in the evening. *When the TV program began, an announcer appeared and said, "Good evening, everyone."* (The announcer welcomed people to the program.) *Finally Aunt May stood up and said, "I will not sell the house. Good evening, Mr. Flynn."* (Aunt May said goodbye to the man; she wanted him to go.)

good faith *n.* **1** Belief in another person's honesty; trust. *Uncle Dick let me have the keys to his candy store to show his good faith.* (He gave me the keys to show that he trusted me not to steal candy.)—Often used in the phrase *in good faith. The teacher accepted Bob's excuse for being late in good faith.* (The teacher accepted the excuse without proof because he believed Bob.) **2** Honesty of purpose; trustworthiness. *John agreed to buy Ted's bicycle for $20, and he paid him $5 right away to show his good faith.* (He paid Ted $5 to show that he was honest and would do as he had agreed.)

good for *or* **hurrah for** ——Used with a name or pronoun to praise someone. *Good for George! He won the 100-yard dash.* (Praise George! He won the 100-yard dash.) *You got 100 on the test? Hurrah for you.* (You got 100 on the test? Fine!)

good grief! *interj., informal* Wow! Indication of surprise, good or bad. *"Good grief," Joe cried out loud. "Is this all you will pay me for my hard work?"* (He is dismayed and surprised at how little they want to pay him.) *What a figure Melanie has, good grief! I wonder if she would be willing to go out with me.* (The speaker wonders if Melanie, who has such a striking figure, would date him.) Compare GOODNESS GRACIOUS!, HEAVENLY DAYS!, HOLY CATS *or* HOLY COW *or* HOLY MACKEREL *or* HOLY MOSES. See GOODNIGHT 2.

good head on one's shoulders *n. phr.* Good sense; good judgment. *Jack has a good head on his shoulders; he never drives too fast.* (Jack is careful; he never drives too fast.) *Alice is a girl with a good head on her shoulders; she always keeps good company.* (Alice has good judgment; she always chooses carefully the people she goes with.) *George showed he had a good head on his shoulders* *by refusing to cheat.* (George showed he had good judgment by refusing to cheat.)

good many *or* **great many** *n. or adj.* A large number (of); very many. Used with *a*. *We found some fall flowers, but the frost had already killed a good many.* (Frost had killed many flowers.) *A great many of the houses were knocked down by the earthquake.* (Very many houses were knocked down.) *Tom has a good many friends at school.* (Tom has many friends at school.) *Mary has a great many ideas for interesting programs.* (Mary has a lot of ideas for interesting programs.) Syn. QUITE A FEW. Compare A LOT; ANY NUMBER; GOOD DEAL. Contrast A FEW.

good nature *n.* Readiness to please others and to be pleased. Cheerfulness; pleasantness. *Everybody likes Mr. Crowe because of his good nature.* (Everybody likes Mr. Crowe because of his cheerfulness.) *Miss Reynolds was remembered by her students for her good nature.* (Miss Reynolds was remembered by her students because she was always pleasant.)

goodness See HONEST-TO-GOODNESS, MY GOD *or* MY GOODNESS.

goodness gracious *interj., slightly archaic* Exclamation of surprise and a certain degree of disapproval. *"Can my boyfriend stay overnight, Dad?" Melanie asked. "Goodness gracious, most certainly not!" her father replied. "What would the neighbors think?"* (Her father emphatically denies permission for her boyfriend to sleep over.)

goodness knows See GOD KNOWS.

good night *interj.* **1**—Used as a polite phrase when you leave someone at night. *"Good night! said Bob as he left Dick's house after the party. "I'll see you in the morning."* (Bob said goodbye to Dick and left.) *Bill said good night to his parents and went upstairs to bed.* (Bill said goodbye politely to his parents.) **2** *or* **good grief**—Used to show surprise and often some fear or anger. *Mr. Johnson's eyes opened wide when he saw the fish his little boy had caught, and said, "Good night!"* (Mr. Johnson's eyes opened wide when he saw the fish his little boy had caught, and he voiced his surprise.) *Mother was angry and said to Mary, "Good grief! Haven't you started the dishes yet?"* ("Haven't you begun yet? Why not?")

good riddance *n.* A loss that you are glad about. Often used as an exclamation, and in the sentence *good riddance to bad rubbish.* To show that you are glad that something or somebody has been taken or sent away. *The boys thought it was good riddance when the troublemaker was sent home.* (The boys were glad when the troublemaker was sent home.) *When Mr. Roberts' old car was stolen he thought it was good riddance.* (When Mr. Roberts' old car was stolen, he was glad because the car was no good anyhow.) *Betty thought it was good riddance when her little*

brother broke his toy drum. (Betty was glad when her little brother broke his toy drum.) *"I'm going and won't come back," said John. "Good riddance to bad rubbish!" said Mary.* ("I'm angry and I'm glad you're leaving," said Mary.)

goods See DELIVER THE GOODS, CONSUMER GOODS.

good scout See GOOD EGG.

go off *v.* **1** To leave; to depart. *Helen's mother told her not to go off without telling her.* (Helen's mother told her not to leave without telling her.) **2a** To be fired; explode. *The firecracker went off and scared Jack's dog.* (The firecracker was exploded and scared Jack's dog.) **2b** To begin to ring or buzz. *The alarm clock went off at six o'clock and woke Father.* (The alarm clock began to buzz at six o'clock.) **3** To happen. *The party went off without any trouble.* (The party happened without any trouble.) *The parade went off without rain.* (The parade was held without rain.)

go off half-cocked *also* **go off at half cock** *v. phr., informal* To act or speak before getting ready; to do something too soon. *Bill often goes off half cocked.* (Bill often acts or speaks before getting ready.) *Mr. Jones was thinking about quitting his job, but his wife told him not to go at half cock.* (Mr. Jones was thinking about quitting his job, but his wife told him not to quit before he had thought carefully about it and was ready.)

go off like clockwork See GO LIKE CLOCKWORK.

go off the deep end *or* **go overboard** *v. phr., informal* To act excitedly and without careful thinking.—A cliché. *John has gone off the deep end about owning a motorcycle.* (John has become excited about motorcycles and decided to buy one without first thinking about it carefully.) *Mike warned his roommate not to go off the deep end and get married.* (Mike warned his roommate not to get married without careful thinking.) *Some girls go overboard for handsome movie and television actors.* (Some girls act excited about handsome movie and television actors.)

goof off *v., slang* To loaf or be lazy; not want to work or be serious; fool around. *Tom didn't get promoted because he goofed off all the time and never did his homework.* (Tom didn't want to work or be serious.) *If you goof off on the job too much, you'll be fired.* (If you don't work hard enough, you'll be fired.)

go on *v.* **1a** To continue; not stop. *After he was hit by the ball, Billy quit pitching and went home, but the game went on.* (The game did not stop when Billy quit.) *The TV picture began to jump, and it went on like that until Father turned a knob.* (The picture did not stop jumping till Father turned a knob.) *I asked Jane a question but she went on read-*

ing and didn't answer. (She didn't stop reading.) *Mother told Jim to stop, but he went on hitting Susan.* (Jim did not stop.) Syn. KEEP ON. **1b** To continue after a pause; begin with the next thing. *"Go on! I'm listening,"* *said Mother.* (Mother said to continue talking.) *The teacher pointed to the map, and went on, "But the land that Columbus came to was not India."* (After he pointed to the map, the teacher continued with the next idea.)—Often used before an infinitive. *Father said Mother had gone to the hospital, and went on to say that Grandmother was coming to take care of us.* (Next he said Grandmother was coming.) **1c** *Of time:* To pass. *As time went on, Mary began to wonder if John had forgotten their date.* (As time passed and it became very late, Mary thought John might have forgotten their date.) *The years went on, and Betty's classmates became grey-haired men and woman.* (Years passed, and the boys and girls who graduated with Betty became middle-aged and old.) **2** To happen. *Mr. Scott heard the noise and went to see what was going on in the hall.* (Mr. Scott heard the noise and went to see what was happening in the hall.) *The teacher knows what goes on when she leaves the room.* (The teacher knows what happens when she leaves the room.) Syn. TAKE PLACE. **3** To talk for too long, often angrily. *We thought Jane would never finish going on about the amount of homework she had.* (We thought Jane would never stop complaining about her homework.) **4** To fit on; be able to be worn. *My little brother's coat wouldn't go on me. It was too small.* (I couldn't wear his coat.) **5** Stop trying to fool me; I don't believe you.—Used as a command, sometimes with *with*. *When Father told Mother she was the prettiest girl in the world, Mother just said, "Oh, go on, Charles."* (Mother told father to stop trying to fool her.) *"Aunt May, your picture is in the paper." "Go on with you, boy!"* (I don't believe you.)

go _____ one better *v. phr., informal* To do something better than (someone else); do more or better than; beat. *Bill's mother gave the boys in Bill's club hot dogs for refreshments, so Tom's mother said that she would go her one better next time by giving them hot dogs and ice cream.* (Tom's mother said that she would do more than Bill's mother did.) *John made a good dive into the water, but Bob went him one better by diving in backwards.* John did well, but Bob beat him by doing something harder.)

go one's way *v. phr.* **1** To start again or continue to where you are going. *The milkman left the milk and went his way.* (He left and continued his milk route.) *The man stopped and asked me for a match, then went his way.* (He went on to where he was going.) Compare GO ALONG, GO ON. **2** To go or act the way you want to or usually do. *Joe just wants to go his way and mind his own busi-*

ness. (He just does what he wants and doesn't want trouble.) *Don't tell me how to do my job. You go your way and I'll go mine.* (You do your job the way you want and I'll do my job the way I want.) *George was not a good sport; when the game did not go his way, he became angry and quit.* (When the game did not go the way George wanted, George got angry and quit playing.)

goose See COOK ONE'S GOOSE, FOX AND GEESE, KILL THE GOOSE THAT LAID THE GOLDEN EGG, GONE GOOSE.

goose bumps *or* **goose pimples** *n. plural, informal* Small bumps that come on a person's skin when he gets cold or afraid. *Nancy gets goose bumps when she sees a snake.* (Nancy gets little bumps on her skin when she sees a snake because she is scared.) *Ann, put on your sweater; you're so cold you have goose pimples on your arms.* (Your skin is rough with little bumps because you are cold.)

go out for *or* **come out for** *v. phr.* To try for a place on (an athletic team). *Ten boys went out for track that spring.* (Ten boys tried to be members of the track team.) *The coach asked Tom why he didn't come out for basketball.* (The coach suggested to Tom that he try to get on the basketball team.)

go out of one's way *v. phr.* To make an extra effort; do more than usual. *Jane went out of her way to be nice to the new girl.* (Jane tried especially to be friendly to the new girl.) *Don did not like Charles, and he went out of his way to say bad things about Charles.* (Don did not need to say bad things about Charles, but he did it anyway.) Compare BEND OVER BACKWARD, KNOCK ONESELF OUT.

go out the window *v. phr., informal* To go out of effect; be abandoned. *During the war, the school dress code went out the window.* (Conditions caused the rules about what students could wear to be forgotten or disregarded.)

go over *v.* **1** To examine; think about or look at carefully. *The teacher went over the list and picked John's name.* (He looked at the list in order to decide which name to pick.) *The police went over the gun for fingerprints.* (They examined the gun closely to find fingerprints.) **2** To repeat; do again. *Don't make me go all over it again.* (Don't make me say it all again.) *We painted the house once, then we went over it again.* (We painted the house again.) **3** To read again; study. *After you finish the test, go over it again to look for mistakes.* (Read it again carefully.) *They went over their lessons together at night.* (They studied and read their lessons together at night.) **4** To cross; go to stop or visit; travel. *We went over to the other side of the street.* (We crossed the street.) *I'm going over to Mary's house.* (I'm going to visit Mary.) *We went over to the next town to the game.* (We travelled to the next town.) **5** To change what you believe. *Father is a Democrat, but he says that he is going over to the Republicans in the* *next election.* (He will change from one political party to the other.) *Many of the natives on the island went over to Christianity after the white men came.* (They changed their religion.) **6** To be liked; succeed.—Often used in the informal phrase go over big. *Bill's joke went over big with the other boys and girls.* (They liked Bill's joke.) *Your idea went over well with the boss.* (The boss liked the idea.)

go over like a lead balloon *v. phr., informal* To fail to generate a positive response or enthusiasm; to meet with boredom or disapproval. *The president's suggested budget cuts went over like a lead balloon.* (His budget cut proposal was received with great displeasure.) *Jack's off-color jokes went over like a lead balloon.* (His ill-mannered jokes evoked only frowns.)

go over with a fine-tooth comb See FINE-TOOTH COMB.

gopher ball *n., slang* A baseball pitch that is hit for a home run. *The pitcher's only weakness this year is the gopher ball.* (The only trouble with the pitcher this year is that he is allowing too many home runs.)

go places See GO TO TOWN 2.

go sit on a tack *v. slang* Shut up and go away; stop bothering.—Usually used as a command and considered rude. *Henry told Bill to go sit on a tack.* (Henry told Bill to shut up and go away.) Compare GO JUMP IN THE LAKE.

gosling See GONE GOOSE *also* GONE GOSLING.

go steady *v. phr.* To go on dates with the same person all the time; date just one person. *At first Tom and Martha were not serious about each other, but now they are going steady.* (Now they go to all the dances and parties together; Tom does not date other girls and Martha does not date other boys.) *Jean went steady with Bob for a year; then they had a quarrel and stopped dating each other.* (Jean dated no one except Bob for a year.) Syn. KEEP COMPANY. Contrast PLAY THE FIELD.

go straight *v. phr., slang* To become an honest person; lead an honest life. *After the man got out of prison, he went straight.* (After the man got out of prison, he led an honest life.) *Mr. Wright promised to go straight if the judge would let him go free.* (Mr. Wright promised to lead an honest life if the judge would let him go free.)

got a thing going *v. phr., slang, informal* To be engaged in a pleasurable or profitable activity with someone else as a partner either in romance or in mutually profitable business. *You two seem to've got a thing going, haven't you?* (You two are having an affair, haven't you?) *You've got a good thing going with your travel bureau, why quit now?* (You are successful with your travel bureau, don't give it up.)

go the rounds *v. phr.* To pass or be told from one person to another; spread among many people. *There is a rumor going the rounds that Mr. Norton will be the new superintendent.* (There is a rumor being told by many people, from one person to another, that Mr. Norton will be the new superintendent.) *The story about Mr. Cox's falling into the lake is making the rounds.* (The story about Mr. Cox's falling into the lake is being told by many people, from one person to another.) Syn. GO AROUND.

go the whole hog *or* **go whole hog** *v. phr., informal* To do something completely or thoroughly; to give all your strength or attention to something. *When Bob became interested in model airplanes, he went the whole hog.* (When Bob became interested in model airplanes, he gave them all his time.) *The family went whole hog at the fair, and spent a lot of money.* (The family saw and did everything at the fair.) Compare ALL OUT, ALL THE WAY, SHOOT THE WORKS.

go through *v.* **1** To examine or think about carefully; search. *I went through the papers looking for Jane's letter.* (I looked at each paper to see if it was the letter.) *Mother went through the drawer looking for the sweater.* (She searched in the drawer.) Syn. GO OVER. **2** To experience; suffer; live through. *Frank went through many dangers during the war.* (He was in danger many times.) **3** To do what you are supposed to do; do what you promised. *I went through my part of the bargain, but you didn't go through your part.* (I did my part of the bargain.) Syn. CARRY OUT. **4** To go or continue to the end of; do or use all of. *Jack went through the magazine quickly.* (He read it quickly.) *We went through all our money at the circus.* (We used all of our money.) Syn. RUN THROUGH. **5** To be allowed; pass; be agreed on. *I hope the new law we want goes through Congress.* (I hope that Congress allows the law.) *The sale of the store went through quickly.* (The sale was quickly agreed on.)

go through hell and high water *v. phr., informal* To go through danger, or trouble. —A cliché. *John is ready to go through hell and high water to help his chum.* (John is ready to go through a lot of danger or trouble to help his chum.) *The soldiers went through hell and high water to capture the fort.* (The soldiers went through a lot of danger to capture the fort.) Compare COME HELL OR HIGH WATER, THROUGH THE MILL.

go through the motions *v. phr.* To pretend to do something by moving or acting as if you were really doing it; do something without really trying hard or caring. *Jane was angry because she couldn't go out, and when her mother said to dust her room she just went through the motions.* (She dusted without working hard.) *The team was so far behind in the game that they just went through the motions of playing at the end.* (When the game was almost finished they were behind and played without any enthusiasm.)

go through with *v. phr.* To finish; do as planned or agreed; not stop or fail to do. *The boys don't think Bob will go through with his plans to spend the summer at a camp.* (The boys don't think Bob will carry out his plans to spend the summer at a camp.) *Mr. Trent hopes the city won't go through with its plans to widen the street.* (Mr. Trent hopes the city won't finish its plans to widen the street.) Syn. CARRY OUT. Compare CARRY THROUGH, LIVE UP TO

go to *v.* To be ready to do; start doing something. *When Jack went to write down the telephone number, he had forgotten it.* (By the time he was ready to write the number on paper, he forgot it.)

go to any length *v. phr.* To do everything you can. *Bill will go to any length to keep Dick from getting a date with Mary.* (Bill does not want Dick to have a date with Mary, and he will do anything to stop him.) Compare ALL OUT.

go to bat for *v. phr., informal* To help out in trouble or need; give aid to. *Everybody else thought Billy had broken the window, but Tom went to bat for him.* (Tom helped Billy prove he did not break the window.) *Mary went to bat for the new club program.* (Mary tried to get the other club members to vote for the program.) Syn. STAND UP FOR.

go to bed with the chickens *v. phr., informal* To go to bed early at night.—A cliché. *On the farm John worked hard and went to bed with the chickens.* (On the farm John worked hard and went to bed early.) *Mr. Barnes goes to bed with the chickens because he has to get up at 5 A.M.* (Mr. Barnes goes to bed early at night because he has to get up at 5 A.M.)

go together *v.* **1** To go with the same boy or girl all the time; date just one person. Herbert and Thelma go together. (Herbert and Thelma go with each other all the time as lovers.) Compare GO STEADY, GO WITH 2, KEEP COMPANY. **2** To be suitable or agreeable with each other; match. *Roast turkey and cranberries go together.* (Roast turkey and cranberries are suitable for each other.) *Ice cream and cake go together.* (Ice cream and cake are suitable with each other.) *Green and yellow go together.* (The two colors match well.)

go to one's head *v. phr.* **1** To make one dizzy. *Beer and wine go to a person's head.* (Beer and wine make a person dizzy.) *Looking out the high window went to the woman's head.* (Looking out the high window made the woman dizzy.) **2** To make someone too proud; make a person think he is too important. *Being the star player went to John's head.* (Being the star player made John bigheaded.) *The girl's fame as a movie actress went to her head.* (The girl's fame as a movie actress made her big-headed.)

go to pieces *v. phr.* To become very nervous or sick from nervousness; become wild. *Mrs. Vance went to pieces when she heard her daughter was in the hospital.* (Mrs. Vance became very nervous when she heard her daughter was in the hospital.) *The man went to pieces when the judge said he would have to go to prison for life.* (The man became wild when the judge said he would have to go to prison for life.) *Mary goes to pieces when she can't have her own way.* (Mary becomes wild when she can't have her own way.)

go to pot *v. phr., informal* To be ruined; become bad; be destroyed. *Mr. Jones' health has gone to pot.* (Mr. Jones' health has become weak.) *The motel business went to pot when the new highway was built.* (The motel business began to lose money when the new highway was built.) Compare GO TO WRACK AND RUIN, GO TO THE DOGS.

go to prove See GO TO SHOW.

go to seed *or* **run to seed** *v. phr.* **1** To grow seeds. *Onions go to seed in hot weather.* (Onions make seeds in hot weather.) **2** To lose skill or strength; stop being good or useful. *Sometimes a good athlete runs to seed when he gets too old for sports.* (He gets fat or lazy.) *Mr. Allen was a good carpenter until he became rich and went to seed.* (Mr. Allen was spoiled by the money and did not work any more.)

go to show *or* **go to prove** *v. phr., informal* To seem to prove; act or serve to show (a fact); demonstrate.—Often used after *it*. *Our team beat a bigger team, and it just goes to show you can win if you play hard enough.* (Our team played so hard that they proved they could beat a bigger team.) *The hard winter at Valley Forge goes to show that our soldiers suffered a great deal to win the Revolution.* (The soldiers' suffering proved that they had a hard time.)

go to the devil *v. phr., informal* **1** To go away; mind your own business.—Used as a command; considered rude. *George told Bob to go to the devil.* (George told Bob to go away.) *"Go to the devil!" said Jack, when his sister tried to tell him what to do.* (Go away and don't bother me!) **2** To become bad or ruined; become useless.—A trite expression. *The boy got mixed up with bad company and began to steal and rob his friends. He went to the devil.* (He became a bad boy.) *Mr. Jones went to the devil after he lost his business.* (He lost hope or became very discouraged.)

go to the dogs *v. phr., informal* To go to ruin; to be ruined or destroyed.—A trite expression. *The man went to the dogs after he started drinking.* (The man went to ruin after he started drinking.) *After the death of the owner, the business went to the dogs.* (After the death of the owner, the business went to ruin.) *The team went to the dogs when its best players got hurt.* (The team lost all its games after several best players got hurt.) Compare GO TO POT.

go to the trouble *or* **take the trouble** *v. phr.* To make trouble or extra work for yourself; bother. *John told Mr. Brown not to go to the trouble of driving him home.* (He told Mr. Brown not to bother.) *Since your aunt took the trouble to get you a nice birthday present, the least you can do is to thank her.* (If your aunt was nice enough to get you the present, you should thank her.) Compare PUT OUT 5.

go to town *v. phr., slang* **1** To do something quickly or with great force or energy; work fast or hard. *The boys went to town on the old garage, and had it torn down before Father came home from work.* (The boys quickly tore down the old garage.) *While Sally was slowly washing the dishes, she remembered she had a date with Pete that evening; then she really went to town.* (Then Sally finished the dishes very quickly.) Compare IN NO TIME, MAKE TIME. Contrast TAKE ONE'S TIME. **2** *or* **go places.** To do a good job; succeed. *Our team is going to town this year. We have won all five games that we played.* (Our team is doing very well this year.) *Dan was a good student and a good athlete; we expect him to go places in business.* (We expect Dan to succeed in business.)

go to waste *v. phr.* To be wasted or lost; not used. *The strawberries went to waste because there was nobody to pick them.* (The strawberries were not used because there was nobody to pick them.) *Joe's work on the model automobile went to waste when he dropped it.* (Joe's work on the model automobile was lost when he dropped it.) Compare IN VAIN.

go to wrack and ruin *v. phr.* To fall apart and be ruined; to become useless.—A cliché. *The barn went to wrack and ruin after the farmer moved.* (The barn became useless from being neglected.) *The car will soon go to wrack and ruin standing out in all kinds of weather.* (The car will soon be ruined standing out in all kinds of weather.)

go under *v.* **1** To be sunk. *The ship hit an iceberg and went under.* (The ship hit an iceberg and was sunk.) **2** To fail; be defeated. *The filling station went under because there were too many others on the street.* (The filling station failed because there were too many other filling stations nearby.)

go up *v.* **1** To go or move higher; rise. *Many people came to watch the weather balloon go up.* (They came to watch the balloon rise up into the sky.) *The path goes up the hill.* (The path leads up the hill.) **2** To be able to become heard; become loud or louder. *A shout went up from the crowd at the game.* (The crowd shouted.) **3** Grow in height while being built; to be built. *The new church is going up on the corner.* (It is getting higher as it is built.) **4** To increase. *Prices of fruit and vegetables have gone up.* (Prices of fruit and vegetables have increased.)

go up in smoke *or* **go up in flames** *v. phr.* To burn; be destroyed by fire. **1** *The house went up in flames.* (The house burned.) *The barn full of hay went up in smoke.* (The barn full of hay was destroyed by fire.) **2** Disappear; fail; not come true. *Jane's hopes of going to college went up in smoke when her father lost his job.* (Jane lost any chance to go to college.) *The team's chances to win went up in smoke when their captain was hurt.* (They lost their chance to win.)

gourd See SAW WOOD *or* SAW GOURDS.

go with *v.* **1** To match; to look good with. *A yellow blouse goes with her blonde hair.* (A yellow blouse looks good with her blonde hair.) *The woman bought a purse to go with her new shoes.* (The woman bought a purse to match her new shoes.) **2** To go out in the company of. *Tom goes with the girl who lives across the street.* (Tom goes out with the girl who lives across the street.)

go without See DO WITHOUT.

go without saying *v. phr.* To be too plain to need talking about; not be necessary to say or mention. *It goes without saying that children should not be given knives to play with.* (It is clear that children should not be given knives to play with.) *A person with weak eyes should wear glasses. That goes without saying.* (It is not necessary to say that a person with weak eyes should wear glasses.)

gown See TOWN AND GOWN.

grab bag *n.* **1** A bag from which surprise packages are chosen; a bag in which there are many unknown things. *The woman paid a quarter for a chance at the grab bag.* (The woman paid a quarter for a chance to choose a surprise package.) *The children brought packages to be sold from the grab bag at the school carnival.* (The children brought packages to be sold from the bag of surprise things at the school carnival.) **2** A group of many different things from which to choose; a variety. *The TV program was a grab bag for young and old alike.* (It had something for people of all ages.)

grab off *v., informal* To take quickly; take or grab before anybody else can; choose for yourself. *The people who got to the show first grabbed off the best seats.* (The people who got to the show first took the best seats quickly.) *The women hurried to the store to grab off the things on sale.* (The women hurried to the store to take the things on sale before anybody else could.) *The prettiest girls at the dance were grabbed off for partners first.* (The prettiest girls were picked first.) Compare SNAP UP.

grabs See UP FOR GRABS.

grace See FALL FROM GRACE, IN ONE'S BAD GRACES, IN ONE'S GOOD GRACES, WITH BAD GRACE, WITH GOOD GRACE.

grace period *or* **period of grace** *n.* The time or extra time allowed in which to do something. *Most insurance companies have a grace period of one month for payments.* (Most insurance companies have a period of one month allowed for payments.) *The teacher gave the class a week's period of grace to finish workbooks.* (The teacher gave the class a week to finish workbooks.)

grade See MAKE THE GRADE.

grain See AGAINST THE GRAIN, TAKE WITH A GRAIN OF SALT.

grand slam *n.* A home run hit when there are three men on the bases. *Tony's grand slam won the game for the Yankees, 4–0.* (The home run with the bases loaded scored runs for the Yankees.)

grandstand *v., slang, informal* To show off, to perform histrionics needlessly. *Stop grandstanding and get down to honest work!* (Stop showing off and start working.)

grandstander *n., slang, informal* A show-off, a person who likes to engage in histrionics. *Many people think that Evel Knievel is a grandstander.* (Many people think he is a show-off.)

granted See TAKE FOR GRANTED.

grasp at straws *or* **clutch at straws** *v. phr.* To depend on something that is useless or unable to help in a time of trouble or danger; try something with little hope of succeeding. —A trite phrase. *To depend on your memory without studying for a test is to grasp at straws.* (You can't depend on your memory alone; you must study.) *The robber clutched at straws to make excuses. He said he wasn't in the country when the robbery happened.* (He tried to lie and excuse himself even though everyone knew he was lying.)

grass See LET GRASS GROW UNDER ONE'S FEET, SNAKE IN THE GRASS.

grasshopper See KNEE-HIGH TO A GRASSHOPPER.

grass is always greener on the other side of the fence *or* **grass is always greener on the other side of the hill** We are often not satisfied and want to be somewhere else; a place that is far away or different seems better than where we are.—A cliché. *John is always changing his job because the grass always looks greener to him on the other side of the fence.* (Other jobs always seem better to him than the one he has.)

grave See ONE FOOT IN THE GRAVE, TURN IN ONE'S GRAVE *or* TURN OVER IN ONE'S GRAVE.

gravy See PAN GRAVY.

gravy train *n., slang, informal* The kind of job that brings in a much higher income than the services rendered would warrant. *Jack's job at the Athletic Club as Social Director is a regular gravy train.* (He gets a high salary at the Athletic Club as Social Director and works little for it.)

gray See GET GRAY HAIR *or* GET GRAY, GIVE GRAY HAIR.

grease-ball *n., slang, derogatory* (avoid) An immigrant from a southern country, such as Mexico, Italy, or Spain; a person with oily looking black hair. *Mr. White is a racist; he calls Mr. Lopez from Tijuana a grease-ball, because he has has dark hair.* (White uses derogatory language toward immigrants of Latin-American descent.)

grease monkey *n., slang* **1** A person who greases or works on machinery; a mechanic or worker in a garage or gasoline station. *Hey, grease monkey, fill up my gas tank!* (Hey, garage worker, fill up the tank.) *The grease monkey was all dirty when he came out from under the car.* (He was greasy and oily.) **2** Airplane mechanic. *Jack was a grease monkey in the Air Force.* (Jack was a man who worked on airplane motors in the Air Force.)

grease one's palm *or* **grease the palm** *slang* **1** To pay a person for something done or given, especially dishonestly; bribe.—A cliché. *Some politicians will help you if you grease their palms.* (They will do what you ask if you pay them dishonestly without telling anybody.) **2** To give a tip; pay for a special favor or extra help.—A cliché. *We had to grease the palm of the waiter to get a table in the crowded restaurant.* (We had to pay him to find a table for us.)

grease the wheels *v. phr., informal* To do something or act to make something go smoothly or happen in the way that is wanted. —A cliché. *Mr. Davis asked a friend to grease the wheels so he could borrow money from the bank.* (Mr. Davis asked a friend to speak for him so it would be easy for him to borrow money from the bank.) *William's father tried to grease the wheels for him to get a new job.* (William's father tried to arrange for William to get a new job.)

greasy spoon *n., informal* Any small, inexpensive restaurant patronized by workers or people in a hurry; a place not noted for its excellence of cuisine or its decor. *I won't have time to eat lunch at the club today; I'll just grab a sandwich at the local greasy spoon.* (I'll just go to the little neighborhood restaurant around the corner where service is fast and cheap.)

great See THINK A GREAT DEAL OF.

great deal See GOOD DEAL.

great Godfrey *or* **great guns** *or* **great Scott** *interj., informal* A saying usually used to show surprise or anger. *Great Godfrey! Uncle Willie is sitting on top of the flagpole!* (What can he be doing up there?) *Great guns! The lion is out of his cage.* (How did he get out?) *Great Scott! Who stole my watch?* (Who could have taken my watch?)

great guns *adv. phr., informal* **1** Very fast or very hard.—Usually used in the phrases *blow great guns, go great guns. The wind was blowing great guns, and big waves beat the shore.* (The wind was blowing very hard.) *The men were going great guns to finish the job.* (The men were working very hard.) Compare FAST AND FURIOUS. **2** Very well; successfully. *Smith's new store opened last week* *and it's going great guns.* (The new store has many customers.)

great many See GOOD MANY.

great oaks from little acorns grow As great oak trees grow from tiny acorns, so many great people or things grew from a small and unimportant beginning, so be patient.—A proverb. *Many great men were once poor, unimportant boys. Great oaks from little acorns grow.* (We cannot expect to grow great or important in a short time.)

Great Scott See GREAT GODFREY.

green See GRASS IS ALWAYS GREENER ON THE OTHER SIDE OF THE FENCE *or* GRASS IS ALWAYS GREENER ON THE OTHER SIDE OF THE HILL.

green around the gills *or* **pale around the gills** *adj. phr., slang* Pale-faced from fear or sickness; sickly; nauseated.—A cliché. *Bill's father took him for a ride in his boat while the waves were rough, and when he came back he was green around the gills.* (He was pale from being seasick.) *The car almost hit Mary crossing the street, and she was pale around the gills because it came so close.* (Mary was frightened and pale.)—Also used with other prepositions besides *around,* as *about, at, under,* and with other colors, as *blue, pink, yellow, white.*

green-eyed monster *n. phr.* Jealousy; envy. —A cliché. *When John's brother got the new bicycle, the green-eyed monster made John fight with him.* (John became so jealous of his brother that it made him very angry.)

green power *n., slang, informal* The social prestige or power money can buy one. *In American political elections the candidates that win are usually the ones who have green power backing them.* (The winning candidates are usually the ones who are backed by the financial power of big business.)

green thumb *n., informal* A talent for gardening; ability to make things grow.—Considered trite by many. *Mr. Wilson's neighbors say his flowers grow because he has a green thumb.* (The neighbors say flowers grow better for Mr. Wilson because he has a talent for gardening.)

green with envy *adj. phr.* Very jealous; full of envy.—A cliché. *Alice's girl friends were green with envy when they saw her new dress.* (Alice's classmates were very jealous when they saw her new dress.) *The other boys were green with envy when Joe bought a second-hand car.* (The other boys were full of envy when Joe bought a second-hand car.) Compare GREEN-EYED MONSTER.

grief See COME TO GRIEF, GOOD GRIEF, GOOD NIGHT 2 *or* GOOD GRIEF.

grin and bear it *v. phr., informal* To be as cheerful as possible in pain or trouble; do something without complaining.—A trite expression. *The doctor told Mrs. Howard that she had to stop eating sweets if she wanted to lose weight, and she tried to grin and bear*

it. (She didn't like to stop eating sweets but tried to do it without complaining.) *If you must have a tooth drilled, all you can do is grin and bear it.* (If the work on the tooth is painful, you have to stand it because it is necessary.) Compare MAKE THE BEST OF, PUT UP WITH.

grind See AX TO GRIND.

grindstone See KEEP ONE'S NOSE TO THE GRINDSTONE.

grind to a halt *v. phr., informal* To slow down and stop like a machine does when turned off.—A cliché. *The old car ground to a halt in front of the house.* (The old car slowed down and stopped in front of the house.) *The Cardinals' offense ground to a halt before the stubborn Steeler defense.* (The Cardinals' attack was unsuccessful against the Steeler defense.)

grip See COME TO GRIPS WITH, LOSE ONE'S GRIP.

groove See IN THE GROOVE.

gross out *v., slang* To commit a vulgar act; to repel someone by saying a disgusting or vulgar thing. *You are going to gross out people if you continue talking like that.* (You will repel people if you don't change your manners.)

gross-out session *n., slang, avoidable* A verbal contest between teen-agers in which the object of the game is to see who can be more disgusting or vulgar than anybody else. *When Jim got home he found his two teen-age sons engaged in a gross-out session; he bawled them out and cut their weekly allowance.* (He found them engaged in a duel of verbal obscenities and punished them accordingly.)

ground See BREAK GROUND, COMMON GROUND, COVER GROUND *or* COVER THE GROUND, CUT THE GROUND FROM UNDER, EAR TO THE GROUND, FEET ON THE GROUND, GAIN GROUND, GET OFF THE GROUND, GIVE GROUND, HAPPY HUNTING GROUND, HOLD ONE'S GROUND, LOSE GROUND, MIDDLE GROUND, RUN INTO THE GROUND, STAMPING GROUND, STAND ONE'S GROUND, FROM THE GROUND UP.

ground ball *n.* A ball batted onto the ground in baseball; a grounder. *Taylor hit a ground ball to the shortstop.* (Taylor hit the ball on the ground toward the shortstop.)

ground floor *n.* **1** First floor of a house or building. *Mrs. Turner has an apartment on the ground floor.* (Mrs. Turner has an apartment on the first floor.) **2** *informal* The first or best chance, especially in a business. *That man got rich because he got in on the ground floor of the television business.* (That man got rich because he was one of the first in the television business.)

ground rule *n.* **1** A rule in sports that is made especially for the grounds or place where a game is played.—Usually used in the plural. *There was such a big crowd at the* *baseball game, that the ground rules of the field were changed in case a ball went into the crowd.* (The rules were made to cover what would happen if a ball went into the crowd.) **2** A rule, usually not written, of what to do or how to act in case certain things happen.—Usually used in the plural. *When you go to a new school, you don't know the ground rules of how you are supposed to behave.* (You don't know how the teachers and children expect you to behave.)

grow See GREAT OAKS FROM LITTLE ACORNS GROW, LET GRASS GROW UNDER ONE'S FEET.

growing pains *n.* **1** Pains in children's legs supposed to be caused by changes in their bodies and feelings as they grow. *The little girl's legs hurt, and her mother told her she had growing pains.* (The little girl's legs hurt, and her mother told her she had pains caused by growing.) **2** *informal* Troubles when something new is beginning or growing. *The factory has growing pains.* (The factory has troubles while it is growing.) *The new high school had growing pains for several years.* (The new high school had troubles for several years while it was growing.)

grow on *or* **grow upon** *v.* **1** To become stronger in; increase as a habit of. *The habit of eating before going to bed grew upon John.* (The habit of eating before going to bed became more and more a habit with John.) *The wish to go to California grew upon Miss Lee.* (The wish to go to California became more and more important to Miss Lee.) **2** To become more interesting to or liked by. *The more Jack saw Mary, the more she grew on him.* (Jack liked Mary better the more he saw her.) *Football grew on Billy as he grew older.* (He got more interested in football every year.)

grow up *v.* To increase in size or height; become taller or older; reach full height. **1** *Johnny is growing up; his shoes are too small for him.* (He is getting bigger.) *I grew up on a farm.* (I lived on a farm while I was young.) *The city has grown up since I was young.*

(The city has become much bigger.) **2** To become adult in mind or judgment; become old enough to think or decide in important matters. *Tom wants to be a coach when he grows up.* (He wants to be a coach when he is a man.) *Grow up, you're not a baby any more!* (Don't behave like a baby.)

grudge See NURSE A GRUDGE.

guard See COLOR GUARD, OFF GUARD, ON GUARD.

guest See BE MY GUEST.

gum up *v., slang* To cause not to work or ruin; spoil; make something go wrong.—Often used in the phrase *gum up the works. Jimmy has gummed up the typewriter.* (He has made the typewriter stop working or work wrong.) *Don't gum up the works by telling Mother what we are going to do.* (Don't spoil the plans.) Syn. THROW A MONKEY WRENCH.

gun See BIG CHEESE *or* BIG GUN, GIVE IT THE GUN *or* GIVE HER THE GUN, GREAT GODFREY *or* GREAT GUNS, JUMP THE GUN, SON OF A GUN, STICK TO ONE'S GUNS *or* STAND BY ONE'S GUNS, TILL THE LAST GUN IS FIRED *or* UNTIL THE LAST GUN IS FIRED.

gun for *v., informal* **1** To hunt for with a gun; look hard for a chance to harm or defeat. *The cowboy is gunning for the man who stole his horse.* (The cowboy wanted to punish the man.) *Bob is gunning for me because I got a higher mark than he did.* (He is jealous and wants to hurt me.) **2** To try very hard to get. *The man is gunning for first prize in the golf tournament.* (The man is trying to get the first prize in the golf tournament.) *Roy is gunning for an "A" in science.* (Roy is trying to get an "A" in science.)

gung-ho *adj., colloquial* Enthusiastic, full of eagerness in an uncritical or unsophisticated manner. *Suzie is all gung-ho on equal rights for women, but fails to see the consequences.* (She is uncritically over-enthusiastic on equal rights for women.)

guts See HATE ONE'S GUTS, HAVE THE GUTS TO DO SOMETHING.

guy See REGULAR GUY, WISE GUY.

H

hackle See RAISE HACKLES *or* RAISE ONE'S HACKLES.

had as soon *or* **had as lief** See AS SOON.

had better *or* **had best** *informal* Should, must. *I had better leave now, or I'll be late.* (I must leave now, or I'll be late.) *If you want to stay out of trouble, you had best not make any mistakes.* (You must not make any mistakes.) *Jim decided he had better do his home work instead of playing ball.* (Jim decided that his homework was the best thing to do instead of the other things he might do.)

had rather *or* **had sooner** *v.* To choose to (do one thing instead of another thing); like better to; would prefer to.—Used with an infinitive without *to. My aunt invited me to the movies, but I said I had rather go on a picnic with the girls.* (I chose to go on the picnic.) *I had sooner live in the city than on a farm.* (I would prefer to live in the city rather than on a farm.)

hail See WITHIN CALL *or* WITHIN HAIL.

hail-fellow-well-met[1] *adj. phr.* Talking easily and in a friendly way to everyone you meet.—A cliché. *John won the election as class president because he was hail-fellow-well-met.* (John won the election because he was friendly to everyone and easy to know.)

hail-fellow-well-met[2] *n. phr.* A good friend and companion; buddy; pal. *John just moved to town but he and the boys in the neighborhood are already hail-fellows-well-met.* (John hasn't been here long but he is friends with the boys already.)

hail from *v., informal* To have your home in; come from; be from; *especially*, to have been born and raised in. *Mrs. Gardner hails from Mississippi.* (Mrs. Gardner was born and raised in the state of Mississippi.) *Mr. Brown and Mr. White are old friends because they both hail from the same town.* (Mr. Brown and Mr. White were born and raised in the same town.)

hair See CURL ONE'S HAIR, GET GRAY HAIR *or* GET GRAY, GIVE GRAY HAIR, HANG BY A THREAD *or* HANG BY A HAIR, HIDE OR HAIR *or* HIDE NOR HAIR, IN ONE'S HAIR, LET ONE'S HAIR DOWN, OUT OF ONE'S HAIR, SPLIT HAIRS, TEAR ONE'S HAIR.

haircut place *n., slang, citizen's band radio jargon* Bridge or overpass with tight clearance. *Are we going to make it in that haircut place?* (Is our truck going to be able to go through that very low clearance?)

hair stand on end *informal* The hair of your head rises stiffly upwards as a sign or result of great fright or horror.—A cliché. *When he heard the strange cry, his hair stood on end.* (He was very much frightened.) *The sight of the dead man made his hair stand on end.* (Seeing the dead man horrified him and his hair rose.) Compare BLOOD RUN COLD, HEART IN ONE'S MOUTH, HEART STAND STILL, JUMP OUT OF ONE'S SKIN, SPINE-CHILLING.

hale and hearty *adj. phr.* In very good health; well and strong.—A cliché. *Grandfather will be 80 years old tomorrow, but he is hale and hearty.* (Grandfather is in good health though he is quite old.) *That little boy looks hale and hearty, as if he is never sick.* (The little boy is strong and well.)

half See GO HALVES, GO OFF HALF-COCKED *also* GO OFF AT HALF COCK, IN HALF, SIX OF ONE AND HALF-A-DOZEN OF THE OTHER, TIME AND A HALF, TOO—BY HALF.

half a loaf is better than none *or* **half a loaf is better than no bread** Part of what we want or need is better than nothing.—A proverb. *Albert wanted two dollars for shoveling snow from the sidewalk but the lady would only give him a dollar. And he said that half a loaf is better than none.* (Albert did the work for a dollar because that was better than nothing.) Compare BETTER LATE THAN NEVER.

half a mind *also* **half a notion** *n. phr., informal* A wish or plan that you have not yet decided to act on; a thought of possibly doing something.—Used after *have* or *with* and before *to* and an infinitive. *I have half a mind to stop studying and walk over to the brook.* (I am somewhat tempted to do it.) *Jerry went home with half a mind to telephone Betty.* (Jerry was thinking of telephoning Betty, but he had not fully decided.)

half-and-half[1] *adj.* As much one thing as the other. *We asked the coach if more boys than girls were interested in debating, and he said it was about half-and-half.* (The coach said that as many girls as boys were interested in debating.) *The show last night was neither very good nor very poor—just half-and-half.* (It was partly good and partly poor.) Compare FIFTY-FIFTY.

half-and-half[2] *n.* A mixture of milk and cream in equal parts, used with cereal or coffee. *John uses half-and-half with his cereal, but his wife, who is dieting, uses milk.* (John uses thin cream; his wife uses plain milk.)

half an eye *n. phr.* A slight glance; a quick look. *The substitute teacher could see with half an eye that she was going to have trouble with the class.* (She knew at a glance that she would have trouble.) *While Mary was cooking she kept half an eye on the baby to see that he didn't get into mischief.* (Mary glanced at the baby sometimes while she was cooking.)

half bad See NOT BAD.

half-baked *adj., informal* Not thought out or studied thoroughly; not worth considering or accepting. *We wish Tom would not take our time at meetings to offer his half-baked ideas.* (His ideas are not good; he does not study them well.) *We cannot afford to put the government in the hands of people with half-baked plans.* (We should vote for men who have reasonable ideas.)

half-holiday *n.* A day on which you get out of school or work in the afternoon. *The principal said that Tuesday would be a half-holiday.* (After we left for lunch on Tuesday, we would not have to return to school.)

half the battle *n. phr.* A large part of the work.—A cliché. *When you write an essay for class, making the outline is half the battle.* (When you finish the outline for your essay, you have done much of the work.) *To see your faults and decide to change is half the battle of self-improvement.* (Understanding and decision are a good beginning.)

half-time *n.* A rest period in the middle of certain games. *I saw Henry at the football game and I went over and talked to him at half-time.* (I talked to Henry while the football players were resting in the middle of the game.) *The pep squad put on a drill at half-time when we played basketball with our old rivals.* (The pep squad entertained the crowd while the players rested between halves.)

halfway See GO HALFWAY *or* MEET ONE HALFWAY *or* GO HALFWAY TO MEET ONE.

halt See CALL A HALT, GRIND TO A HALT.

ham-handed *adj., slang* 1 Having very large hands. *Pete is a big, ham-handed man who used to be a football player.* (Pete has very big hands.) 2 See HEAVY-HANDED.

ham it up *v. phr., slang* To do more than looks natural in acting a part; pretend too much; exaggerate. *When Tom told the teacher he was too sick to do homework, he really hammed it up.* (Tom acted as if he were very sick, more than he really was.) *The old-fashioned movies are funny to us because the players hammed it up.* (The early movies look funny to us because the actors and actresses acted too much.) Compare LAY IT ON.

hammer See GO AT IT HAMMER AND TONGS, UNDER THE HAMMER.

hammer at *or* **hammer away at** *v.* 1 To work steadily at; keep at. *That lesson is not easy, but hammer away at it and you will get it right.* (If you work steadily at the lesson, you will get it.) 2 To talk about again and again; emphasize. *The speaker hammered at his opponent's ideas.* (The speaker talked again and again against the other man's ideas.)

hammer out *v.* 1 To write or produce by hard work. *The President sat at his desk till midnight hammering out his speech for the next day.* (He worked hard writing his speech.) 2 To remove, change, or work out by discussion and debate; debate and agree on (something). *Mrs. Brown and Mrs. Green have hammered out their difference of opinion.* (They have discussed the matter and come to an agreement.) *The club members have hammered out an agreement between the two groups.* (They have discussed their differences and come to an agreement.) Compare IRON OUT.

Hancock See JOHN HANCOCK *or* JOHN HENRY.

hand See AT HAND, BIRD IN THE HAND IS WORTH TWO IN THE BUSH, BITE THE HAND THAT FEEDS ONE, CLEAN HANDS, DIRTY ONE'S HANDS, EAT OUT OF ONE'S HAND, FORCE ONE'S HAND, FREE HAND, FROM HAND TO HAND, GLAD HAND, HAM-HANDED, HANG HEAVY *or* HANG HEAVY ON ONE'S HANDS, HAT IN HAND, HAVE A HAND IN, HAVE ONE'S HANDS FULL, HEAVY-HANDED, IN HAND, JOIN FORCES *or* JOIN HANDS, KEEP ONE'S HAND IN, LAY HANDS ON, LAY ONE'S HANDS ON *or* GET ONE'S HAND ON *or* PUT ONE'S HAND ON, LEND A HAND *or* GIVE A HAND *or* BEAR A HAND, LET ONE'S LEFT HAND KNOW WHAT ONE'S RIGHT HAND IS DOING, LIFT A FINGER *or* LIFT A HAND *also* RAISE A HAND, LIVE FROM HAND TO MOUTH, MANY HANDS MAKE LIGHT WORK, OFF ONE'S HANDS, ON HAND, ON ONE'S HANDS, ON THE OTHER HAND, OUT OF HAND, PLAY INTO ONE'S HANDS, PUT ONE'S HAND TO *or* SET ONE'S HAND TO *or* TURN ONE'S HAND TO, PUT ONE'S HAND TO THE PLOW, ROB THE TILL *or* HAVE ONE'S HAND IN THE TILL, SECTION HAND, SIT ON ONE'S HANDS, TAKE ONE'S LIFE IN ONE'S HANDS, TAKE THE LAW INTO ONE'S OWN HANDS, THROW UP ONE'S HANDS, THROW UP ONE'S HANDS IN HORROR, TIE ONE'S HANDS, TRY ONE'S HAND, UPPER HAND *or* WHIP HAND, WASH ONE'S HANDS OF.

hand and foot *adv. phr.* 1 So that the hands and feet cannot be used.—Used with *bind* or a synonym. *The robbers bound him hand and foot and left him on the floor.* (They tied his hands and feet so he could not use them.) 2 So that no free action is possible.—Used with *bind* or a synonym. *If Mr. Jones signs that paper, he will be bound hand and foot in the matter.* (He will not be able to act freely in the matter.) 3 See WAIT ON HAND AND FOOT.

hand and glove See HAND IN GLOVE.

hand down *v.* To arrange to give or leave after death. *Joe will have his father's gold watch because it is handed down in the family.* (The watch passes to one in the family and is never sold.) *In old times, property was usually handed down to the oldest son at his father's death.* (The oldest son was given all or almost all of the property.) Compare PASS ON.

hand in See TURN IN 1.

hand in glove *or* **hand and glove** *adj. or adv. phr.* Very close or friendly; working together; in very close agreement or cooperation, especially for bad purposes. *The Navy and the Coast Guard work hand and glove, especially in war time.* (They cooperate with each other to win the war.) *Judges and others in high office sometimes are hand in glove with gangsters to cheat and steal.* (They help each other to do bad things.)

hand in hand *adv. phr.* 1 Holding hands. *Bob and Mary walked along hand in hand in the park.* (They walked along holding hands with each other.) Compare ARM IN ARM. 2 Accompanying each other; together; closely connected.—Used with *go*. *Ignorance and* *poverty often go hand in hand.* (People who are uneducated are often poor too.) *Selfishness and unhappiness often go hand in hand.* (Selfish people are often unhappy.)

hand it to *v. phr., informal* To admit the excellence of; give credit or praise to. *You have to hand it to Jim; he is very careful and hard-working in all he does.* (Everyone must admit that Jim always does his work well.) *The teacher said, "I hand it to Jane for the way she managed the Music Club."* (Jane deserves praise for the fine way in which she led the Music Club.) Syn. TAKE OFF ONE'S HAT TO.

handle See FLY OFF THE HANDLE.

handle to one's name *n. phr., slang* A special title used before your name. *Jim's father has a handle to his name. He is Major Watson.* (Jim's father is called Major Watson, not plain Mr. Watson.) *Bob came back from the University with a handle to his name and was called Dr. Jones.* (Bob took graduate work and received a doctor's degree.)

handle with gloves *or* **handle with kid gloves** *v. phr., informal* To treat very gently and carefully.—A cliché. *Sally is such a baby that she cries if the teacher does not handle her with gloves.* (Sally cries if the teacher is not very gentle and careful with her.) *An atomic bomb is handled with kid gloves.* (The men carry it very carefully.)

hand-me-down *n., informal* Something given away after another person has no more use for it; especially, used clothing. *Alice had four older sisters, so all her clothes were hand-me-downs.* (Alice's sisters gave her the clothes that they were too big for.)

hand off *v.* To hand the football to another back. *The quarterback faked to the fullback and handed off to the halfback.* (The quarterback pretended to give the ball to the fullback but gave it to the halfback.)

hand on *v.* To pass along to the next person who should have it. *Everyone in class should read this, so when you have finished, please hand it on.* (Please give the paper to the next person in the class.) *In the early days, news was handed on from one person to another.* (News was told from person to person, again and again.)

hand out *v., informal* To give (things of the same kind) to several people. *The teacher handed out the examination papers.* (The teacher gave each pupil an examination paper.) *At the Christmas party Santa Claus handed out the presents under the tree.* (Santa Claus gave each person one of the presents.) *Handing out free advice to all your friends will not make them like you.* (Your friends do not want you always telling them what to do. Compare GIVE OUT 3.

hand over *v.* To give control or possession of; give (something) to another person. *When the teacher saw Johnny reading a comic book in study period, she made him hand over the*

book. (Johnny had to give the teacher the comic book.) *When Mr. Jones gets old, he will hand over his business to his son.* (It will be the son's turn to run the business so Mr. Jones will give it to him.) Syn. FORK OVER, GIVE UP 1, TURN OVER 3.

hand over fist *adv. phr., informal* Fast and in large amounts.—A cliché. *Fred may get a pony for Christmas because his father is making money hand over fist.* (Fred's father is making a lot of money very fast.) *Business is so bad that the store on the corner is losing money hand over fist.* (The store is losing a lot of money fast.)

hand over hand *adv. phr.* By taking hold with one hand over the other alternately. *The only way to climb a rope is hand over hand.* (The only way to go up a rope is by putting one hand over the other, one after the other, again and again, and pulling yourself up.)

hand-pick *v., informal* To choose very carefully. *This debating team should win because its members are all hand-picked.* (The members of the debating team were chosen with great care and therefore are the very best ones.) *The political bosses hand-picked a man for mayor who would agree with them.* (The bosses chose a man who would help them.)

hands-down *adj., informal* **1** Easy. *The Rangers won a hands-down victory in the tournament.* (It was easy for the Rangers to win the tournament.) **2** Unopposed; first; clear. *Johnny was the hands-down favorite for president of the class.* (Everybody wanted Johnny for president of the class.)

hands down *adv. informal* **1** Without working hard; easily. *The Rangers won the game hands down.* (They won easily.) **2** Without question or doubt; without any opposition; plainly. *Johnny was hands down the best player on the team.* (Johnny was clearly the best player.)

hands off *informal* Keep your hands off or do not interfere; leave that alone.—Used as a command. *I was going to touch the machine, but the man cried, "Hands off!" and I let it alone.* (The man warned me not to touch the machine, and I did not.)

hands-off *adj., informal* Leaving alone, not interfering; inactive. *The United States told the European governments to follow a hands-off policy toward Latin America.* (The United States told the European governments not to interfere in Latin America.) *I did not approve of his actions, but I have a hands-off rule in personal matters, so I said nothing.* (I do not believe in personal criticism, so I did not say anything.)

handsome is as handsome does *informal* A person must act well and generously so that he will be truly worth respecting.—A proverb. *Everyone thinks that Bob is a very handsome boy, but he is very mean too. Handsome is as handsome does.* (Bob is not as good as he looks.) Compare FINE FEATHERS DO NOT MAKE FINE BIRDS.

hands up *informal* Hold up your hands! Put your hands up high and keep them there!— Used as a command. *The sheriff pointed his gun at the outlaws and called out, "Hands up!"* (The sheriff ordered the outlaws to hold their hands up high in the air.) Syn. REACH FOR THE SKY.

hand something to someone on a silver platter *v. phr.* To give a person a reward that has not been earned. *The lazy student expected his diploma to be handed to him on a silver platter.* (He thought he should get it without having to study.)

hand to hand *adv. phr.* Close together, near enough to hit each other. *The two soldiers fought hand to hand until one fell badly wounded.* (They stood near each other and fought.) *In modern naval warfare, men seldom fight hand to hand.* (They do not often get near to each other—they fight with big guns.) Compare FACE TO FACE.

hand-to-hand *adj.* Close to each other; near enough to hit each other. *The result of the battle was decided in hand-to-hand combat.* (The soldiers got near each other and fought that way.) *When the police tried to break up the riot, there was hand-to-hand fighting with fists, stones, and clubs.* (The police and the rioters fought close to each other.) Compare FACE-TO-FACE.

hand-to-mouth See LIVE FROM HAND TO MOUTH.

handwriting on the wall *n. phr.* A sign that something bad will happen.—A cliché; usually used with *see* or *read*. *When Bill's team lost four games in a row, he saw the handwriting on the wall.* (Bill could see that his team would have a very bad season.) *John's employer had less and less work for him; John could read the handwriting on the wall and looked for another job.* (John knew that he would soon be fired.)

hang See GO HANG, GIVE A HANG *or* CARE A HANG, GIVE ONE ENOUGH ROPE, AND HE WILL HANG HIMSELF, LEAVE HANGING *or* LEAVE HANGING IN THE AIR.

hang around *v., informal* **1** To pass time or stay near without any real purpose or aim; loaf near or in. *The principal warned the students not to hang around the corner drugstore after school.* (He told them not to gather in or near the drugstore after school.) Compare HANG OUT 1. **2** To spend time or associate. *Jim hangs around with some boys who live in his neighborhood.* (Jim spends much of his time with some boys who live near him.)

hang back *or* **hang off** *or* **hang behind** **1** To stay some distance behind or away; be unwilling to move forward. *Mary offered the little girl candy, but she was shy and hung back.* (The little girl did not come forward and take

the candy.) **2** To hesitate or be unwilling to do something. *Lou wanted Fred to join the club, but Fred hung off.* (Fred hesitated to join the club.)

hang behind See HANG BACK 1.

hang by a thread *or* **hang by a hair** *v. phr.* To depend on a very small thing; be in doubt. —A cliché. *For three days Tom was so sick that his life hung by a thread.* (It was hard to tell if he would live or die.) *As Joe got ready to kick a field goal, the result of the game hung by a hair.* (The field goal would win the game.) Compare HANG IN THE BALANCE.

hanger See CREPE HANGER.

hang fire *v. phr.* **1** To fail or be slow in shooting or firing. *Smith pulled the trigger, but the gun hung fire and the deer escaped.* (The gun did not fire.) **2** To be slow in beginning; to be delayed; to wait. *The boys' plans for organizing a scout troop hung fire because they could not find a man to be scoutmaster.* (Their plans were delayed; they had no scoutmaster.)

hang heavy *or* **hang heavy on one's hands** *v. phr.* To pass slowly or uninterestingly; be boring with little to do.—A cliché. *The vacation time hung heavy on Dick's hands because all his friends were away at camp.* (The time seemed to pass slowly; he was bored.) Compare ON ONE'S HANDS.

hang in effigy *or* **burn in effigy** *v. phr.* To hang or burn a figure, usually a stuffed dummy, representing a person who is disliked or scorned. *When the high school team lost the championship game, the coach was hung in effigy by the townspeople.* (The people hung a stuffed dummy with the coach's name on it.) *During World War II, Hitler was sometimes burned in effigy in the United States.* (Americans sometimes burned a figure made to look like Hitler.)

hang in the balance *v. phr.* To have two equally possible results; to be in doubt; be uncertain. *Until Jim scored the winning touchdown, the outcome of the game hung in the balance.* (Either team might win.) *She was very sick and her life hung in the balance for several days.* (The doctor did not know if she would live or die.) Compare HANG BY A THREAD.

hang in (there) *v. phr., slang, informal* To persevere; not to give up; to stick to a project and not lose faith or courage. *Hang in there old buddy; the worst is yet to come.* (Don't give up, old friend, harder times are yet ahead.)

hang it *interj., informal* An exclamation used to express annoyance or disappointment. *Oh, hang it! I forgot to bring the book I wanted to show you.* (I am annoyed because I forgot the book.) *Hang it all, why don't you watch where you're going?* (I am displeased by your carelessness in bumping into me.)

hang off See HANG BACK.

hang on *v.* **1** To hold on to something, usually tightly. *Jack almost fell off the cliff, but managed to hang on until help came.* (Jack held tightly to the cliff until help came.) Syn. HOLD ON 1. **2a** To continue doing something; persist. *The grocer was losing money every day, but he hung on, hoping that business would improve.* (He continued to do business although things were very difficult.) Compare HOLD OUT, STICK OUT **2b** To hold a lead in a race or other contest while one's opponents try to rally. *The favorite horse opened an early lead and hung on to win as two other horses almost passed him in the final stretch.* (The favorite horse got way ahead in the early part of the race and won even though two others almost passed him near the end.) *Bunning, staked to a 6–0 lead in the first inning, hung on to beat the Dodgers 6–4.* (Bunning kept ahead and won even though the Dodgers rallied for four runs.) **3** To continue to give trouble or cause suffering. *Lou's cold hung on from January to April.* (Lou's cold continued from January to April.) **4** To continue listening on the telephone. *Jerry, asked John, who had called him on the phone, to hang on while he ran for a pencil and a sheet of paper.* (Jerry asked John to stay at the phone until he could get pencil and paper.) Compare HOLD ON 3.

hang one on *v. phr., slang* **1** To give a heavy blow to; hit hard. *The champion hung one on his challenger in the second round and knocked him out of the ring.* (The champion hit the other man very hard and knocked him out of the ring.) **2** To get very drunk. *After Smith lost his job, he went to a bar and hung one on.* (Smith went to an eating place where liquor is sold and got very drunk.)

hang one's head *v. phr.* To bend your head forward in shame. *Johnny hung his head when the teacher asked him if he broke the window.* (Johnny turned his face toward the floor because he was ashamed of what he had done.) Compare HIDE ONE'S HEAD.

hang on the words of *also* **hang on the lips of** *v. phr.* To listen very attentively to.—A cliché. *Ann hangs on every word of her history teacher and takes very careful notes.* (She listens attentively to him.) *As he went on with his speech, his auditors, deeply interested, hung on his lips.* (They paid close attention to the speaker.)

hang on to *v.* To hold tightly; keep firmly. *The child hung on to its mother's apron, and would not let go.* (The child held its mother's apron firmly.) *John did not like his job, but decided to hang on to it until he found a better one.* (He decided to keep his job until he found a better one.)

hang on to one's mother's apron strings See TIED TO ONE'S MOTHER'S APRON STRINGS.

hang on to your hat *or* **hold on to your hat** *or* **hold your hat** *v. phr., informal* **1** Watch out; be prepared.—Used as a command, usually to warn of an unexpected action. *"Hold on to your hat," said Jim as he stepped on the gas and the car shot forward.* ("Watch out," said Jim, "I'm really going fast now.") **2** Get ready for a surprise.—Used as a command, usually to warn of unexpected news. *"Hold on to your hat," said Mary. "Jim asked me to marry him."* (Mary said, "Listen to this surprising news—Jim asked me to marry him.")

hang out *v.* **1** *slang* To spend your time idly or lounging about. *The teacher complained that Joe was hanging out in poolrooms instead of doing his homework.* (Joe was spending his time idling in poolrooms.) Compare HANG AROUND 1. **2** *slang* To live; reside. *Two policemen stopped the stranger and asked him where he hung out.* (They wanted to know where the stranger lived.) **3** To reach out farther than the part below. *The branches of the trees hung out over the road.* (The trunks of the trees were beside the road, but the branches went out over the road.) *The upper floor of that house hangs out above the first.* (The second floor is wider than the first; its floor and wall go out farther than the wall of the first floor.)

hang out one's shingle *v. phr., informal* To give public notice of the opening of an office, especially a doctor's or lawyer's office, by putting up a small signboard.—A cliché. *The young doctor hung out his shingle and soon had a large practice.* (He put up a small sign to tell people he was a doctor.)

hang over *v.* **1** To be going to happen to; threaten. *Great trouble hangs over the little town because its only factory has closed down.* (The closing of the factory will make many people unemployed and will cause much unhappiness.) **2** To remain to be finished or settled. *The committee took up the business that hung over from its last meeting.* (The committee discussed the unfinished business of the last meeting.)

hang over one's head *v. phr.* To be a danger or threat to you.—An overused phrase. *Over Jimmy's head hung the teacher's suspicion that Jimmy had cheated in the final examination.* (The suspicion that Jimmy had cheated in the examination was a danger to his good standing in school.) *Death hangs over a bullfighter's head every time he performs.* (He may be killed any time he fights a bull.)

hang round See HANG AROUND.

hang ten *v., slang* **1** To be an outstanding performer on a surfboard or on a skateboard (referring to the user's ten toes). *I bet I am going to be able to hang ten if you let me practice on your skate board.* (I will be as good on the skate board as you are.) **2** To be a survivor despite great odds. *Don't worry about Jack, he can hang ten anywhere!* (He can survive and make it under unfavorable conditions.)

hang together *v.* **1** To stay united; help and defend one another. *The club members always hung together when one of them was in trouble.*) Syn. STICK TOGETHER. Compare STAND BY, STAND UP FOR. **2** *informal* To form a satisfactory whole; fit together. *Jack's story of why he was absent from school seems to hang together.* (The parts of Jack's story seem to agree with each other; his explanation is satisfactory.)

hang up *v.* **1** To place on a hook, peg, or hanger. *When the children come to school, they hang up their coats in the cloakroom.* (They put their coats on hooks in the cloakroom.) **2a** To place a telephone receiver back on its hook and break the connection. *Carol's mother told her she had talked long enough on the phone and made her hang up.* (Her mother made her stop talking and put the receiver back in place.) **2b** To put a phone receiver back on its hook while the other person is still talking.—Used with *on*. *I said something that made Joe angry, and he hung up on me.* (Joe put the receiver back on its hook so I could not talk to him any more.) **3a** *informal* To cause to be stuck or held so as to be immovable.—Usually used in the passive. *Ann's car was hung up in a snowdrift and she had to call a garageman to get it out.* (The car was stuck in the snowdrift and she could not get out.) **3b** *informal* To stick or get held so as to be immovable. *A big passenger ship hung up on a sandbar for several hours.* (It ran on a sandbar and was stuck.) **4** *informal* To cause a wait; delay. *Rehearsals for the school play were hung up by the illness of some of the actors.* (Some of the actors got sick and caused practice not to be held until later.) **5** *informal* To set (a record.) *Bob hung up a school record for long-distance swimming.* (Bob did better in long-distance swimming than any one else in that school had done.)

hang-up *n., informal* (stress on *hang*) **1** A delay in some process. *The mail has been late for several days; there must be some hang-up with the trucks somewhere.* (There has to be some trouble and/or some delay with the mail trucks.) **2** A neurotic reaction to some life-situation probably stemming from a traumatic shock which has gone unconscious. *Doctor Simpson believes that Suzie's frigidity is due to some hang-up about men.* (He thinks her frigidity is due to a traumatic shock settled in her unconscious.)

happen on *or* **happen upon** *v. literary* To meet or find accidentally or by chance. *The Girl Scouts happened on a charming little brook not far from the camp.* (They found a pretty little brook near the camp.) *At the convention I happened upon an old friend I had not seen for years.* (I met an old friend

by chance.) Syn. CHANCE ON, COME ACROSS 1, 3. Compare HIT ON.

happy See STRIKE A HAPPY MEDIUM, TRIGGER HAPPY *at* QUICK ON THE TRIGGER.

happy hour *n., informal* A time in bars or restaurants when cocktails are served at a reduced rate, usually one hour before they start serving dinner. *Happy hour is between 6 and 7 PM at Celestial Gardens.* (They serve cocktails at reduced rate between 6 and 7 PM.)

happy hunting ground *n. phr.* **1** The place where, in American Indian belief, a person goes after death; heaven. *The Indians believed that at death they went to the happy hunting ground.* (They believed that dead Indians went to a place where hunting was good.) **2** *informal* A place or area where you can find a rich variety of what you want, and plenty of it. *The forest is a happy hunting ground for scouts who are interested in plants and flowers.* (In the forest scouts can find many different plants and flowers.) *Shell collectors find the ocean beaches happy hunting grounds.* (They will find many different shells on the ocean beaches.)

hard See GIVE A HARD TIME, GO HARD WITH, SCHOOL OF HARD KNOCKS.

hard-and-fast *adj.* Not to be broken or changed; fixed; strict. *The teacher said that there was a hard-and-fast rule against smoking in the school.* (The rule could not be broken for any reason.)

hard as nails *adj. phr., informal* **1** Not flabby or soft; physically very fit; tough and strong.—A cliché. *After a summer of work in the country, Jack was as hard as nails, without a pound of extra weight.* (Jack was strong and tough.) **2** Not gentle or mild; rough; stern.—A cliché. *Johnny works for a boss who is as hard as nails and scolds Johnny roughly whenever he does something wrong.* (His boss is very rough and strict.)

hard cash See COLD CASH.

hard feeling *n.* Angry or bitter feeling; enmity.—Usually used in the plural. *Jim asked Andy to shake hands with him, just to show that there were no hard feelings.* (Jim wanted Andy to show that he was not angry at Jim.) *Bob and George once quarreled over a girl, and there are still hard feelings between them.* (The boys are still not friendly to each other.)

hard-fisted *adj.* **1** Able to do hard physical labor; strong. *Jack's uncle was a hard-fisted truckdriver with muscles of steel.* (He was strong and tough.) **2** Not gentle or easy-going; tough; stern. *The new teacher was a hard-fisted woman who would allow no nonsense.* (She was stern and strict in enforcing rules.) **3** Stingy or mean; not generous with money. *The hard-fisted banker refused to lend Mr. Jones more money for his business.*

hard-hitting *adj.* Working hard to get things done; strong and active; stubbornly eager. *The boys put on a hard-hitting drive to raise money for uniforms for the football team.* (The boys worked very hard to raise the money.) *He is a hard-hitting and successful football coach.* (He trains his boys hard.)

hardly any *or* **scarcely any** Almost no or almost none; very few. *Hardly any of the students did well on the test, so the teacher explained the lesson again.* (Few of the students knew the answers to the test.) *Charles and his friends each had three cookies, and when they went out, hardly any cookies were left.* (Almost no cookies were left.)

hardly ever *or* **scarcely ever** *adv. phr.* Very rarely; almost never; seldom. *It hardly ever snows in Florida.* (It almost never snows in Florida.) *Johnny hardly ever reads a book.* (Johnny rarely reads.)

hard-nosed *adj., slang* Tough or rugged; very strict; not weak or soft; stubborn, especially in a fight or contest. *Joe's father was a hard-nosed army officer who had seen service in two wars.* (Joe's father was strict and tough.) *Pete is a good boy; he plays hard-nosed football.* (He is a rough and tough player.)

hard nut to crack *also* **tough nut to crack** *n. phr., informal* Something difficult to understand or to do. *Tom's algebra lesson was a hard nut to crack.* (Tom had trouble understanding his algebra lesson.) *Mary found knitting a hard nut to crack.* (It was difficult for Mary to learn how to knit.) Compare HARD ROW TO HOE.

hard put *or* **hard put to it** *adj.* In a difficult position; faced with difficulty; barely able. *John was hard put to find a good excuse for his lateness in coming to school.* (John had trouble in thinking up a good excuse for coming late.) *The scouts found themselves hard put to it to find the way home.* (They had trouble finding the way home.)

hard row to hoe *or* **tough row to hoe** *n. phr.* A hard life to live; a very hard job to do.—A cliché. *She has a hard row to hoe with six children and her husband dead.* (She has a hard time with her husband dead and six children to care for.) *Young people without enough education will have a tough row to hoe when they have to support themselves.* (They will have trouble getting good jobs and keeping them.) Syn. HARD SLEDDING. Compare DOWN ON ONE'S LUCK, HARD NUT TO CRACK.

hard sell *n., informal* A kind of salesmanship characterized by great vigor, aggressive persuasion, and great eagerness on the part of the person selling something; opposed to 'soft sell'. *Your hard sell turns off a lot of people; try the soft sell for a change, won't you?* (A lot of people resent your energetic persuasions and will not buy from you; if you try less hard, you might do better.)

hard sledding *or* **rough sledding** *or* **tough sled-** **ding** *n., informal* Difficulty in succeeding or making progress. *Jane had hard sledding in her math course because she was poorly prepared.* (Jane had a hard or difficult time passing the course.) *When Mr. Smith started his new business, he had tough sledding for a while but things got better.* (His new store wasn't successful at first.)

hard-top *n.* **1** A car that has a metal roof; a car that is not a convertible. *Every spring Mr. Jones sells his hard-top and buys a convertible.* (In the spring Mr. Jones likes to own a car with a top that comes down.) **2** *or* **hard-top convertible** A car with windows that can be completely lowered with no partitions left standing, and with a top that may or may not be lowered. *Mr. Brown's new car is a hard-top convertible.* (Mr. Brown's car has a metal top but the windows can be completely open.)

hard up *adj., informal* Without enough money or some other needed thing. *Dick was hard up and asked Lou to lend him a dollar.* (Dick had no money or almost no money.) *The campers were hard up for water because their well had run dry.* (They had very little water or had to get it from a distance.) Compare UP AGAINST IT.

hard way *n.* The harder or more punishing of two or more ways to solve a problem, do something, or learn something.—Used with *the*. *The mayor refused the help of the crooks and won the election the hard way by going out to meet the people.* (The mayor might have won the election easily with the help of crooks, but he chose to do it by himself with much effort.) *The challenger found out the hard way that the champion's left hand had to be avoided.* (Although his trainers warned him to look out for the champion's left hand, the challenger ignored their advice and was knocked out.)

hare See MAD AS A HATTER *or* MAD AS A MARCH HARE, RUN WITH THE HARE AND HUNT (RIDE) WITH THE HOUNDS.

hark back *v. literary* **1** To recall or turn back to an earlier time or happening. *Judy is always harking back to the good times she had at camp.* (Judy likes to recall the good times she had at camp.) **2** To go back to something as a beginning or origin. *The cars of today hark back to the first automobiles made about 1900.* (Those early automobiles led to the making of the cars of today.) *The slit in the back of a man's coat harks back to the days when men rode horseback.* (The slit was needed long ago when riding horseback.)

harp on *v.* To mention again and again. *In his campaign speeches, Jones harps on his rival's wealth and powerful friends.* (He continually draws attention to those things.)

Harry See TOM, DICK, AND HARRY.

harum-scarum[1] *adv., informal* In a careless, disorderly or reckless way. *Jim does his homework harum-scarum, and that is why his* *schoolwork is so poor.* (Jim does his homework in a very careless or sloppy way.)

harum-scarum² *adj., informal* Careless, wild, or disorderly in one's acts or performance; reckless. *Jack is such a harum-scarum boy that you can never depend on him to do anything right.* (Jack is not reliable because he does not do things in a careful, planned way.)

hash See SETTLE ONE'S HASH, SLING HASH.

hash house *n., slang* An eating place where cheap meals are served. *Joe and his friends went to a hash house around the corner after the game.* (They went to a cheap restaurant.)

hash out *v., informal* To talk all about and try to agree on; discuss thoroughly. *The teacher asked Susan and Jane to sit down together and hash out their differences.* (She asked the girls to talk about their differences and try to agree.) *The students hashed out the matter and decided to drop it.* (They discussed the 'trouble and decided to drop it all.)

hash up *v., slang* **1** To make a mess of; do badly. *Bob really hashed up that exam and failed the course.* (Bob got all mixed up in the exam.) **2** To bring to life; remember and talk about. *The teacher advised Sue not to hash up old bitterness against her schoolmates.* (She advised Sue not to bring up or recall old bitterness.)

haste See MAKE HASTE.

hat See AT THE DROP OF A HAT, BRASS HAT, HANG ON TO YOUR HAT *or* HOLD ON TO YOUR HAT *or* HOLD YOUR HAT, HIGH-HAT, KEEP UNDER ONE'S HAT, OLD HAT, PULL OUT OF A HAT, TAKE OFF ONE'S HAT TO, TALK THROUGH ONE'S HAT, TEN-GALLON HAT, THROW ONE'S HAT IN THE RING.

hat in hand *adv. phr., informal* In a humble and respectful manner. *They went hat in hand to the old woman to ask for her secret recipe.* (They asked her politely and respectfully.)

hatch See COUNT ONE'S CHICKENS BEFORE THEY ARE HATCHED.

hatchet See BURY THE HATCHET.

hatchet face *n.* A long narrow face with sharp parts; also, a person with such a face. *Johnny was sent to the principal's office because he called his teacher old hatchet face.* (Johnny called the teacher a rude name.) *He was hatchet-faced and not at all handsome.* (He had a thin sharp face.)

hatchet man *n., colloquial* **1** A politician or newspaper columnist whose job is to write and say unfavorable things about the opposition. *Bill Lerner is the hatchet man for the Mayor's Party; he smears all the other candidates regularly.* (It is Lerner's job to write derogatory pieces on members of the opposition.) **2** An executive officer in a firm whose job it is to fire superfluous personnel, cut back on the budget, etc., in short, to do the necessary but unpleasant things. *The firm hired Cranhart to be hatchet man; his title is that of Executive Vice President.* (Cran-

hart has to do the unpopular but necessary things for the firm.)

hate one's guts *v. phr., slang* To feel a very strong dislike for someone. *Dick said that he hated Fred's guts because Fred had been very mean to him.* (Dick said he hated Fred.)

hats off to *or* **one's hat is off to** *truncated phr., informal* Used to recognize and praise a job well-done. *Hats off to anyone who runs the twenty-six mile race.* (That person is to be congratulated.) *My hat is off to the chef who created this delicious meal.* (I admire the fine cooking.) Compare TAKE OFF ONE'S HAT TO.

hatter See MAD AS A HATTER.

haul See LONG HAUL.

haul down *v., informal* **1** To catch (as a ball) usually after a long run. *Willie hauled down a long fly to center field for the third out.* (After a long run, Willie caught the long fly ball in center field.) *The star halfback hauled down the pass for a touchdown.* (He caught it for a touchdown.) **2** To tackle in football. *Ted was hauled down from behind when he tried to run with the ball.* (When Ted tried to run with the ball, a player on the other team tackled him from behind.)

haul down one's colors *or* **strike one's colors** *v. phr* **1** To pull down a flag, showing you are beaten and want to stop fighting. *After a long battle, the pirate captain hauled down his colors.* (He pulled down his flag to show he was ready to quit fighting.) **2** To admit you are beaten; say you want to quit. *After losing two sets of tennis, Tom hauled down his colors.* (Tom lost two sets and decided not to try anymore.)

haul in *or* **haul up** *or* **pull in** *v. slang* To bring before someone in charge for punishment or questioning; arrest. *John was hauled in to court for speeding.* (The police arrested John for speeding.) *The tramp was hauled up for sleeping on the sidewalk.* (He was arrested.) Compare CALL ON THE CARPET.

haul in one's horns See PULL IN ONE'S HORNS.

haul off *v.* To move suddenly.—Used with *and* usually before a verb like *hit* or *kick*. *Ed hauled off and hit the other boy in the nose.* (Ed suddenly hit the other boy.) *Lee hauled off and threw a touchdown pass.* (No one thought Lee would pass, but he did.)

haul over the coals *or* **rake over the coals** *v. phr.* To criticize sharply; rebuke; scold.—A cliché. *The sergeant raked the soldier over the coals for being late for roll call.* (The sergeant scolded him severely for being late.) Syn. DRESS DOWN.

have See CAT HAS NINE LIVES, ONE'S CAKE AND HAVE IT TOO, EVERY CLOUD HAS A SILVER LINING, EVERY DOG HAS HIS DAY, HAVE NOTHING ON *or* HAVE ANYTHING ON, LITTLE PITCHERS HAVE BIG EARS, *or* an important word after this in the sentence.

have a ball *v. phr., slang* Enjoy yourself very much; have a wonderful time. *Johnny* *had a ball at camp.* (Johnny enjoyed himself at camp.) *Mary and Tom had a ball exploring the town.* (Mary and Tom had a wonderful time.) *After their parents left, the children had a ball.* (The children had a lot of fun.) Syn. HAVE A TIME 2.

have a bone to pick See BONE TO PICK.

have a care *v. phr., formal* To be careful what you do. *Jane, have a care what you're doing with that valuable glass.* (Jane, be careful with that glass—it's worth money.) *The judge told him to have a care what he said in court.* (The judge told him to be careful what he said in court.)

have a finger in the pie See FINGER IN THE PIE.

have a fit *or* **have fits** *or* **throw a fit** *v. phr.* 1 To have a sudden illness with stiffness or jerking of the body. *Our dog had a fit yesterday.* (He was suddenly sick and his body jerked about.) 2 *informal* To become angry or upset. *Father will throw a fit when he sees the dent in the car.* (Father will be angry at us for damaging his car.) *Howard will have a fit when he learns that he lost the election.* (He will be upset.) *When John decided to drop out of college, his parents had fits.* (John's parents were very angry.)

have a go at *v. phr., informal* To try, especially after others have tried. *Bob asked Dick to let him have a go at shooting at the target with Dick's rifle.* (Bob asked Dick to let him try the gun.) *She had a go at archery, but did not do very well.* (She tried archery, at which she was not expert.)

have a hand in *v. phr.* To have a part in or influence over; to be partly responsible for. *Sue's schoolmates respect her and she has a hand in every important decision made by the Student Council.* (She has a leading part in decisions.) *Ben had a hand in getting ready the Senior play.* (He did some of the work on it.) Compare FINGER IN THE PIE.

have a heart *v. phr., informal* To stop being mean; be kind, generous, or sympathetic. *Have a heart, Bob, and lend me two dollars.* (Be generous and lend me the money.) *Have a heart, Mary, and help me with this lesson.* (Be kind and help me.) *He didn't know if the teacher would have a heart and pass him.* (He didn't know if she would be sorry for him and let him pass.)

have all one's buttons *or* **have all one's marbles** *v. phr., slang* To have all your understanding; be reasonable.—Usually used in the negative or conditionally. *Mike acts sometimes as if he didn't have all his buttons.* (Mike acts at times in a strange or senseless way.) *He would not go to town barefooted if he had all his marbles.* (He acts queerly; he would not do so if his mind were clear.)

have an ear to the ground See EAR TO THE GROUND.

have an edge on *v. phr., informal* 1 To have an advantage (over someone). *I can't beat you at tennis, but I have an edge on you in ping-pong.* (When it comes to ping-pong, I am slightly better than you are.) 2 To be mildly intoxicated; to have had a few drinks. *Joe sure had an edge on when I saw him last night.* (He was slightly drunk when I saw him.) Compare EDGE ON.

have an eye for *v. phr.* To be able to judge correctly of; have good taste in. *She has an eye for color and style in clothes.* (She can choose colors and styles correctly.) *He has an eye for good English usage.* (He can tell what English is right.)

have an eye on *or* **have one's eye on** *v. phr., informal* 1 To look at or think about (something wanted); have a wish for; have as an aim. *I bought ice cream, but Jimmy had his eye on some candy.* (Jimmy wanted to buy candy.) *John has his eye on a scholarship so he can go to college.* (John would like to get a scholarship.) Compare IN MIND. 2 See KEEP AN EYE ON 1.

have an eye out See EYE OUT.

have an eye to See EYE TO.

have a screw loose *v. phr., slang* To act in a strange way; to be foolish.—A cliché. *Now I know he has a screw loose—he stole a police car this time.* (Now I know he is crazy; he stole a police car.) *He was a smart man but had a screw loose and people thought him odd.* (He was not crazy but somewhat peculiar.)

have a time *v. phr., informal* 1 To have trouble; have a hard time. *Poor Susan had a time trying to get the children to go to bed.* (Susan had trouble putting the children to bed.) *John had a time passing his math course.* (John had a hard time with math.) 2 To have a good time; to have fun.—Used with a reflexive pronoun. *Bob had himself a time going to every night club in town.* (John had a good time.) *Mary had herself a time dancing at the party.* (Mary enjoyed herself at the party.) Syn. HAVE A BALL.

have a way with *v. phr.* To be able to lead, persuade, or influence. *Dave has such a way with the campers that they do everything he tells them to do.* (Dave knows how to make the campers like and agree with him.) *Ted will be a good veterinarian, because he has a way with animals.* (He is able to manage them and make friends with them.)

have been around *v. phr., informal* Have been to many places and done many things; know people; have experience and be able to take care of yourself.—A cliché. *Uncle Willie is an old sailor and has really been around.* (He knows the world and people.) *Betty likes to go out with Jerry, because he has been around.* (Jerry has had a lot of experience and knows places to go and things to do that are fun.) *It's not easy to fool him; he's been around.* (He has learned by experience.) Compare GET AROUND, KNOW ONE'S WAY AROUND.

have dibs on *or* **put dibs on** *v. phr., slang* To demand a share of something or to be in line for the use of an object usable by more than one person. *Don't throw your magazine away! I put (my) dibs on it, remember?* (Don't put the magazine away, it is my turn to read it after you have finished with it.)

have done *v., formal* To stop; finish. *When the teacher had done, she asked for questions from the class.* (After she finished, she asked for questions.) *If you have done, I will explain the matter.* (If you are through talking, I'll explain.)

have done with *v.* To stop doing or using something. *When you have done with that paintbrush, Barbara, I would like to use it.* (When you have finished with the paintbrush, let me use it.) *I wish you would have done with your criticisms.* (I am tired of your criticisms.)

have eyes only for *v. phr.* To see or want nothing else but; give all your attention to; be interested only in.—A cliché. *Of all the horses in the show, John had eyes only for the big white one.* (The only horse that John cared about was the white one.) *All the girls liked Fred, but he had eyes only for Helen.* (Helen was the only girl Fred was interested in.)

have fits See HAVE A FIT.

have had it *v. phr., slang* To have experienced or suffered all you can; to have come to the end of your patience or life. *"I've had it,"* said Lou, *"I'm resigning from the job of chairman right now."* (Lou has been patient with the job as long as he can, and that is why he is resigning.) *When the doctor examined the man who had been shot, he said, "He's had it."* (The doctor thought the man would die.)

have hair *v. ph., slang* To possess courage, fortitude, guts, sex-appeal. *I like him, he's got a lot of hair.* (He has a lot of courage and sex-appeal.)

have in one's hair See IN ONE'S HAIR.

have it *v. phr.* **1** To hear or get news; understand. *I have it on the best authority that we will be paid for our work next week.* (I have the news from someone that I believe.) **2** To do something in a certain way. *Make up your mind because you can't have it both ways. You must either stay home or come with us.* (You can't do both things.) *Bobby must have it his way and play the game by his rules.* (He wants to play the way he understands the game, not the way anyone else does.) **3** To claim; say. *Rumor has it that the school burned down.* (There is a story that the school burned down.) *Gossip has it that Mary is getting married.* (People are saying that Mary will be married.) *The man is very smart the way his family has it, but I think he's silly.* (His family says that he is smart.) **4** To allow it—Usually used with *will* or *would* in negative sentences. *Mary wanted to give the party at her house, but her mother*

wouldn't have it. (She wouldn't let Mary.) Syn. HEAR OF, STAND FOR. **5** To win. *When the senators vote, the ayes will have it.* (The senators who vote "Aye" or "Yes" will win.) **6** To get or find the answer; think of how to do something. *"I have it!" said John to Mary. "We can buy Mother a nice comb for her birthday."* (I have thought of the right present to buy for Mother.) **7** *informal* To have an (easy, good, rough, soft) time; have (certain kinds of) things happen to you; be treated in a (certain) way by luck or life. *Everyone liked Joe and he had it good until he got sick.* (Joe was always lucky until he got sick.) *Mary has it easy; she doesn't have to work.* (Mary has an easy time. She is lucky.) **8** See AS LUCK WOULD HAVE IT.

have it all over See HAVE IT OVER.

have it coming *v. phr.* To deserve the good or bad things that happen to you. *I feel sorry about Jack's failing that course, but he had it coming to him.* (Jack deserved to fail, because he did not study hard enough.) *Everybody said that Eve had it coming when she won the scholarship.* (They knew she had worked hard and deserved to win.) Compare ASK FOR, GET WHAT'S COMING TO ONE, SERVE RIGHT.

have it in for *v. phr., informal* To wish or mean to harm; have a bitter feeling against. *George has it in for Bob because Bob told the teacher that George cheated in the examination.* (George hates Bob and wants to hurt him.) *After John beat Ted in a fight, Ted always had it in for John.* (After John beat Ted, Ted wanted to get even.)

have it made *v. phr., slang* To be sure of success; have everything you need. *With her fine grades Alice has it made and can enter any college in the country.* (Alice is a very successful student and can get into the college of her choice.) *The other seniors think Joe has it made because his father owns a big factory.* (They think Joe's father will give him a good job.)

have it out *v. phr.* To settle a difference by a free discussion or by a fight. *Joe called Bob a bad name, so they went back of the school and had it out. Joe got a bloody nose and Bob got a black eye.* (Joe insulted Bob, and they had a fight.) *The former friends finally decided to have it out in a free argument and they became friends again.* (They discussed their trouble and finished with it.)

have it over *or* **have it all over** *v. phr.* To be better than; be superior to. *Anne has it all over Jane in looks and charm.* (Anne is prettier and more charming than Jane.) *A professional golfer usually has it all over an amateur.* A golfer who plays for money is usually better than a golfer who plays for fun.) *A jeep has it over a regular car on rough mountain trails.* (A jeep goes better on rough mountain trails than a regular car.) Compare BEAT ALL HOLLOW.

have kittens v. phr., slang To become very much worried or upset. Mrs. Jones was having kittens because it was very late and Susan wasn't home yet. (Mrs. Jones was very upset.) Compare HAVE A FIT.

have lots (everything) going for one v. phr. To have abilities or qualities that help in achieving one's goal; assets working in one's favor. The young woman will surely get the job; she has everything going for her. (Everything is helping her get the job.)

have money to burn See MONEY TO BURN.

have no business v. phr. To have no right or reason. Jack had no business saying those nasty things about Dick. (Jack had no cause or need to say those things.) Vern's mother told him he had no business going swimming that day. (She told him he should not have gone swimming.)

have none of v. phr. To refuse to approve or allow. The teacher said she would have none of Mike's arguing. (The teacher said that she would not allow Mike to argue with her.) When the fullback refused to obey the captain, the captain said he would have none of that. (The captain said he would not allow disobedience.)

have nothing on or **not have anything on** v. phr. Not to be any better than; to have no advantage over. Susan is a wonderful athlete, but when it comes to dancing she has nothing on Mary. (Susan is not any better at dancing than Mary.) Even though he is older, John has nothing on Peter in School. (Peter is just as good as John in school.) Although the Smiths have a Rolls Royce, they have nothing on the Jones' who have a Cadillac and a Jaguar. (The Smiths are not better than the Jones'.) 2 To have no information or proof that someone broke the law. Mr. James was not worried when he was arrested because he was sure they had nothing on him. (Mr. James was sure they had no proof that he had done anything wrong.) Mr. Brown was an honest politician and they had nothing on him. (No one could show that Mr. Brown had done anything wrong.)

have no use for See NO USE.

have on v. 1 To be dressed in; wear. Mary had on her new dress. (Mary was wearing her new dress.) 2 To have (something) planned; have an appointment; plan to do. Harry has a big weekend on. (Harry has plans for a big weekend.) I'm sorry I can't attend your party, but I have a meeting on for that night. (I have a meeting to attend on that night.) 3 See HAVE NOTHING ON, HAVE SOMETHING ON.

have one's ass in a sling v. phr., slang, vulgar, avoidable To be in an uncomfortable predicament; to be in the doghouse; to be at a disadvantage. Al sure had his ass in a sling when the boss found out about his juggling the account. (He was in serious trouble when he was found to be an embezzler.)

have one's ears on v. phr., slang, citizen's band radio jargon To have one's CB radio in receiving condition. Good buddy in the eighteen wheeler southbound, got your ears on? (Hello there in the truck and trailer moving south, can you hear me?)

have oneself v. phr., nonstandard To enjoy. —Sometimes used in very informal speech to provide emphasis. As soon as their parents left, the boys had themselves some fun. (The boys had a good time.) After working hard all day, John had himself a good night's sleep. (John enjoyed a good night's sleep.)

have someone by the balls v. phr., slang, vulgar, avoidable To have someone at a disadvantage or in one's power. The kidnappers had the company by the balls for six long weeks. (They had the company at a great disadvantage.)

have one's hand in the till See ROB THE TILL.

have one's hands full v. phr. To have as much work as you can do; be very busy. The plumber said that he had his hands full and could not take another job for two weeks. (The plumber had as much work as he could do and so could not take any more jobs.) With three small children to take care of, Susie's mother has her hands full. (The care of three small children keeps Susie's mother very busy.)

have one's hands tied See TIED ONE'S HANDS.

have one's head in the sand See HIDE ONE'S HEAD IN THE SAND.

have one's heart in the right place See HEART IS IN THE RIGHT PLACE.

have one's hide v. phr., informal To punish severely. John's mother said she would have his hide if he was late to school again. (She said that she would punish him hard.)

have one's nose to the grindstone See KEEP ONE'S NOSE TO THE GRINDSTONE.

have one's number See GET ONE'S NUMBER.

have one's work cut out for See CUT OUT 1.

have on the ball See ON THE BALL.

have rocks in one's head v. phr., informal To be stupid; not have good judgment. When Mr. James quit his good job with the coal company to begin teaching school, some people thought he had rocks in his head. (They thought he showed bad judgment in giving up his good job.)

have something going for one v. phr., slang, informal To have ability, talent, or good looks; to have influence in important places helping one to be successful. Well now, Pat Jones, that's another story—she's got something going for her. (Unlike others, Pat Jones has talent, intelligence, good looks, and influence in important places.)

have something on v. phr., informal To have information or proof that someone did something wrong. Mr. Jones didn't want to run for office because he knew the opponents had something on him. (Mr. Jones knew that his opponents could prove that he had done something wrong.) *Mr. Smith keeps paying black mail to a man who has something on him.* (Mr. Smith pays a man not to tell what he knows about him.) *Although Miss Brown is not a good worker, her boss does not fire her because she has something on him.* (Miss Brown knows something about her boss which she might tell if he fires her.) Compare GET THE GOODS ON. Contrast HAVE NOTHING ON.

have something on the ball *v. phr., slang, colloquial* To be smart, clever; to be skilled and have the necessary know-how. *You can trust Syd; he's got a lot on the ball* OR *he's got something on the ball.* (You can trust Syd because he knows what he is doing.)

have the best of *or* **have the better of** See GET THE BETTER OF 2.

have the better of *or* **have the best of** See GET THE BETTER OF.

have the cart before the horse See CART BEFORE THE HORSE.

have the courage of one's convictions *v. phr.* To be brave enough to act according to your beliefs. *Steve showed that he had the courage of his convictions by refusing to help another student cheat in the exam.* (Steve acted according to his belief that cheating was wrong.) *Owen knew that Pete had started the fight, but he was afraid to say so; he did not have the courage of his convictions.* (He was afraid to be honest and blame Pete.)

have the goods on See GET THE GOODS ON.

have the guts to do something *v. phr., informal* To be brave enough to do something difficult or dangerous. *Jack wants to marry Jill, but he doesn't have the guts to pop the question.* (He is afraid to propose to her.)

have the jump on See GET THE JUMP ON.

have the last laugh *or* **get the last laugh** *v. phr.* To make someone seem foolish for having laughed at you. *Other schools laughed at us when our little team entered the state championship, but we had the last laugh when we won it.* (We got to laugh at them for being wrong about us.) Compare HE LAUGHS BEST WHO LAUGHS LAST, TURN THE TABLES.

have the worst of See GET THE WORST OF.

have to *or* **have got to** *v., informal* To be obliged or forced to; need to; must. *Do you have to go now?* (Is it really necessary for you to go now?) *He had to come. His parents made him.* (His parents forced him to come.) *I have got to go to the doctor.* (I need to go. It is necessary for me to go.) *I have to go to Church.* (It is my duty to go.)

have to do with *v. phr.* **1** To be about; be on the subject of or connected with. *The book has to do with airplanes.* (The book is about airplanes.) **2** To know or be a friend of; work or have business with.—Usually used in negative sentence. *Tom said he didn't want to have anything to do with the new boy.* (Tom didn't want to know the boy or be his friend.)

I had nothing to do with the party; I was home that night. (I wasn't at the party and wasn't connected with it in any way.)

have too many irons in the fire See TOO MANY IRONS IN THE FIRE.

have two strikes against one *or* **have two strikes on one** *v. phr., informal* To have things working against you; be hindered in several ways; be in a difficult situation; be unlikely to succeed.—A cliché. *Children from the poorest parts of a city often have two strikes against them before they enter school.* (Children from poor neighborhoods often are not prepared for school work and do poorly.) *George has two strikes against him already. Everybody is against what he wants to do.* (He will have a hard time doing what he wants to do because everybody is against it.) Compare BEHIND THE EIGHT BALL. [In baseball, three strikes are out. If the umpire calls two strikes against the batter, he has only one strike left and will be out if he gets one more strike.]

haw See HEM AND HAW.

hay See HIT THE HAY.

haystack See NEEDLE IN A HAYSTACK.

haywire See GO HAYWIRE.

hazard See AT ALL HAZARDS.

haze See IN A FOG *or* IN A HAZE.

head See ACID HEAD, BEAT INTO ONE'S HEAD, BEAT ONE'S HEAD AGAINST A WALL, BIG HEAD, COUNT HEADS, EYES IN THE BACK OF ONE'S HEAD, FROM HEAD TO FOOT, GET THROUGH ONE'S HEAD, GOOD HEAD ON ONE'S SHOULDERS, GO TO ONE'S HEAD, HANG ONE'S HEAD, HAVE ONE'S HEAD IN THE SAND, HAVE ROCKS IN ONE'S HEAD, HEAP COALS OF FIRE ON ONE'S HEAD, HIT THE NAIL ON THE HEAD, HANG OVER ONE'S HEAD, HIDE ONE'S FACE OR HIDE ONE'S HEAD, HOLD ONE'S HEAD UP, KEEP A CIVIL TONGUE IN ONE'S HEAD, KEEP ONE'S HEAD, LOSE ONE'S HEAD, MAKE HEAD OR TAIL OF, OFF THE TOP OF ONE'S HEAD, ON ONE'S HEAD, OUT OF ONE'S HEAD, *also* OFF ONE'S HEAD, OVER ONE'S HEAD, PRICE ON ONE'S HEAD, PUT THEIR HEADS TOGETHER *or* LAY THEIR HEADS TOGETHER, SWELLED HEAD, TAKE INTO ONE'S HEAD, TELL —— WHERE TO GET OFF *or* TELL —— WHERE TO HEAD IN, THROW ONESELF AT SOMEONE'S HEAD *or* FLING ONESELF AT SOMEONE'S HEAD, TURN ONE'S HEAD, USE ONE'S HEAD.

head above water *n. phr.* out of difficulty; clear of trouble.—A cliché. *How are your marks at school? Are you keeping your head above water?* (Are you getting passing grades?) *Business at the store is bad. They can't keep their heads above water.* (The store does not make enough money. They can't make a living from it.)

head and shoulders *adv. phr.* **1** By the measure of the head and shoulders. *The basketball player is head and shoulders taller than the other boys.* (His head and shoulders are above the other boys' heads.) **2** By far; by a great deal; very much.—An overused phrase. *She is head and shoulders above the rest of the class in singing.* (She is a much better singer than anyone else in the class.) See FAR AND AWAY.

header See DOUBLE-HEADER.

head for the hills *v. phr., informal* To get far away in a hurry; run away and hide.— Often used imperatively. *Head for the hills. The Indians are coming.* (Get out of here fast. The Indians are coming.) *He saw the crowd chasing him, so he headed for the hills.* (He ran away from the crowd and hid.) *When they saw the mean boy coming, they all headed for the hills.* (They all ran away when they saw the mean boy coming.) Compare BEAT IT, LIGHT OUT, TAKE TO THE WOODS.

head-hunting *n., slang, informal* **1** The custom of seeking out, decapitating, and preserving the heads of enemies as trophies **2** A search for qualified individuals to fill certain positions. *The president sent a committee to the colleges and universities to do some head hunting; we hope he finds some young talent.* (A committee was sent to recruit young people for special jobs.) **3** A systematic destruction of opponents, especially in politics. *Billings was hired by the party to do some head hunting among members of the opposition.* (He was hired to destroy some prominent members of the opposition.)

head in the clouds See IN THE CLOUDS.

head in the sand See HIDE ONE'S HEAD IN THE SAND.

head off *v.* **1** To get in front of and stop, turn back, or turn aside. *The sheriff said to head the cattle thieves off at the pass.* (The sheriff said to take the shortest way to the pass and catch the thieves there.) **2** To block; stop; prevent. *He will get into trouble if someone doesn't head him off.* (If someone doesn't stop him before he does what he wants to do, he will be in trouble.)

head-on *adj. or adv. phr.* **1** With the head or front pointing at; with the front facing; front end to front end. *Our car skidded into a head-on crash with the truck.* (The front of the car hit the front of the truck.) *In the fog the boat ran head-on into a log.* (The front of the boat hit the log.) *There is a head-on view of the parade from our house.* (Our house faces the front of the parade.) Compare FACE-TO-FACE. Contrast REAR-END. **2** In a way that is exactly opposite; against or opposed to in argument. *If you think a rule should be changed, a head-on attack against it is best.* (It is best to attack the rule by arguing the exact opposite.) *Tom did not want to argue head-on what the teacher said, so he said nothing.* (He didn't want to say the opposite of what the teacher said.)

head out *v.* **1** To go or point away. *The*

ship left port and headed out to sea.* (The ship sailed out towards the sea.) *The car was parked beside the house. It was headed out towards the street.* (The car faced towards the street.) **2** *informal* Leave; start out. *I have a long way to go before dark. I'm going to head out.* (I have a long way to go. I'm going to start now.)

head over heels *also* **heels over head** **1a** In a somersault; upside down; head first. *It was so dark Bob fell head over heels into a big hole in the ground.* (Bob fell head first into the hole.) Compare UPSIDE DOWN. **1b** In great confusion or disorder; hastily. *The children all tried to come in the door at once, head over heels.* (The children all tried to come in at the same time, so there was great confusion.) Compare TOPSY-TURVY. **2** *informal* Completely; deeply. *He was head over heels in debt.* (He was very much in debt.) *She was head over heels in love.* (She was deeply in love.)

head shrinker *n., slang, informal* A psychoanalyst, also called a *shrink. Forrester is falling apart; his family physician sent him to a head shrinker (to a shrink).* (He was sent to a psychiatrist to be psychoanalyzed.)

head start *n.* **1** A beginning before someone; lead or advantage at the beginning. *The other racers knew they couldn't catch Don if he got too big a head start.* (They knew they couldn't catch him if they let him get too far ahead.) *Joe has a head start. He began to study earlier than we did.* (Joe is ahead of us. He has an advantage because he started to study earlier than we did.) **2** A good beginning. *Let's get a head start in painting the house by getting up early.* (If we get up early, we will be able to start sooner and get more done.) *The teacher gave the class a head start on the exercise by telling them the answers to the first two problems.* (The teacher gave them answers that put them ahead and helped them.) Compare RUNNING START.

heads up *interj., informal* Keep your head up and be careful or ready.—Used as a warning to prepare for something or clear the way. *"Heads up!" said the waiter carrying the hot food.* ("Be careful and let me through!" said the waiter.) *Heads up, boys! A train is coming.* (Get ready for the train and stay off the tracks.) *Heads up, now! You can do better than that.* (Be more careful. Stay alert, and you can do better.) Syn. LOOK ALIVE, LOOK OUT.

heads-up *adj., informal* Wide-awake; alert; watchful; intelligent. *You must play hard, heads-up baseball to win this game.* (You must not only play hard, you must be smart and alert to win this game.) Compare ON ONE'S TOES, ON THE BALL.

head up *v., informal* **1** To be at the head or front of. *The elephants headed up the whole parade.* (The elephants walked in front of everyone else.) **2** To be the leader or boss of. *Mr. Jones will head up the new business.* (Mr. Jones will be in charge of the new business.) *The class planned a candy sale, and they elected Mary to head it up.* (They elected Mary to be chairman of the committee working on the candy sale.)

health See CLEAN BILL OF HEALTH.

heap See STRIKE ALL OF A HEAP.

heap coals of fire on one's head *v. phr., literary* To be kind or helpful to someone who has done wrong to you, so that he is ashamed. *Alice heaped coals of fire on Mary's head by inviting her to a party after Mary had gossiped about her.* (Mary gossiped about Alice, but Alice invited her to a party and made her ashamed.) *Jean Valjean stole the Bishop's silver, but the Bishop heaped coals of fire on his head by giving the silver to him.* (The Bishop returned good for bad and shamed Jean.)

hear See WILL NOT HEAR OF.

heart See AFTER ONE'S OWN HEART, AT HEART, EAT ONE'S HEART OUT, BREAK ONE'S HEART, BY HEART, CHANGE OF HEART, CROSS ONE'S HEART, DO ONE GOOD *or* DO ONE'S HEART GOOD, FIND IT IN ONE'S HEART, FROM THE BOTTOM OF ONE'S HEART *or* WITH ALL ONE'S HEART, FROM THE HEART, GET TO THE HEART OF, HAVE A HEART, HEAVY HEART, LOSE HEART, LOSE ONE'S HEART, OPEN HEART, OPEN ONE'S HEART, SEARCH ONE'S HEART, SET ONE'S HEART ON, TAKE HEART, TAKE TO HEART, TO ONE'S HEART'S CONTENT, WEAR ONE'S HEART ON ONE'S SLEEVE.

heart and soul¹ *n.* Eager love; strong feeling; great enthusiasm.—A cliché. Often used with a singular verb. *When Mr. Pitt plays the piano, his heart and soul is in it.* (He plays with all his mind and energy.) *John plays tennis badly, but with heart and soul.* (John plays with full interest and joy.) *Mary wanted a puppy with all her heart and soul.* (Mary wanted a puppy very much.)

heart and soul² *adv.* Wholly and eagerly; with all one's interest and strength; completely.—A cliché. *Will you try to make our city a better place? Then we are with you heart and soul.* (We agree with you and will gladly help you; we support you completely.) *Mike was heart and soul against the new rules.* (He hated them.) Compare BODY AND SOUL.

heart goes out to *formal* You feel very sorry for; you feel pity or sympathy for.—Used with a possessive. *Frank's heart went out to the poor children playing in the slum street.* (He felt pity for them.) *Our hearts went out to the young mother whose child had died.* (We were sorry for her.)

hear the beat *or* **see the beat** *v. phr., dialect* To hear of or to see someone or something better or surpassing.—Usually used in negative or interrogative sentences and often followed by of. *I never heard the beat! John swam all the way across the river. Did you ever hear the beat of it?* (I never heard of anyone who could swim better or further than John. Did you ever hear of anyone?) *The juggler spun a table around on the tip of his finger. I never saw the beat of that.* (I never saw anything done better.)

heart in one's mouth *or* **heart in one's boots** A feeling of great fear or nervousness.—Often considered trite. *Charles got up to make his first speech with his heart in his mouth.* (Charles was nervous before his first speech.) *My heart was in my mouth as I went into the haunted house.* (My heart was beating hard from fright when I went into the ghostly house.) *When the bear came out of the woods towards us, our hearts were in our mouths.* (We were so startled, our hearts seemed to jump up into our mouths.) Compare HAIR STAND ON END.

heart is in the right place *or* **have one's heart in the right place.** To be kind-hearted, sympathetic or well-meaning; have good intentions.—A cliché. *All the tramps and stray dogs in the neighborhood knew that Mrs. Brown's heart was in the right place.* (They knew that she was kind and friendly and would give them food.) *Tom looks very rough but his heart is in the right place.* (Tom means well and is good, even though he doesn't look it.)

heart miss a beat See HEART SKIP A BEAT.

heart of gold *n. phr.* A kind, generous, or forgiving nature.—A cliché. *John has a heart of gold. I never saw him angry at anyone.* (John is very kind to people. He never gets angry at them.) *Mrs. Brown is a rich woman with a heart of gold.* (She is rich, but she is not stingy. She is very generous with her money.) Compare GOOD AS GOLD, HEART IN THE RIGHT PLACE.

heart of stone *n. phr.* A nature without pity. —A cliché. *Mr. Smith has a heart of stone. He whipped his horse until it fell down.* (Mr. Smith has no mercy or pity. He beat the horse so badly that it fell down.)

heart-searching See SEARCH ONE'S HEART.

heart set See SET ONE'S HEART ON.

heart sink To lose hope, courage, or eagerness; be very disappointed. *The soldiers' hearts sank when they saw that they were surrounded by Indians.* (They were afraid that they would be killed by the Indians.) *The children were happy because they were going to the beach to swim, but their hearts sank when it began to rain.* (They were very disappointed when they saw that it would rain and they would not be able to go.)

heart skip a beat *or* **heart miss a beat** **1** The heart leaves out or seems to leave out a beat; the heart beats hard or leaps from excitement or strong feeling.—Often considered trite. *When Paul saw the bear standing in front of him, his heart skipped a beat.* (When he saw the bear, his heart seemed to stop for a moment from fright.) **2** To be startled or excited from surprise, joy, or fright. *When Linda was told that she had won, her heart missed a beat.* (She was very surprised and happy that she had won.)

heart stand still *v. phr.* To be very frightened or worried.—A cliché. *Johnny's heart stood still when he saw his dog run into the street in front of a car.* (Johnny was very frightened.) *Everybody's heart stood still when the President announced that war was declared.* (Everybody was worried.) Compare HAIR STAND ON END.

heart-to-heart *adj.* Speaking freely and seriously about something private. *The father decided to have a heart-to-heart talk with his son about smoking.* (He decided to have an honest talk with him and ask him if it was true that he smoked.) *She waited until they were alone so she could have a heart-to-heart talk with him.* (She wanted to talk to him in private about something serious.) Compare MAN-TO-MAN.

hearty See HALE AND HEARTY.

heat See CANNED HEAT.

heave in sight *v. phr.* To seem to rise above the horizon at sea and come into sight; come into view; become visible.—Usually used of ships. *A ship hove in sight many miles away on the horizon.* (From many miles away a ship seemed to rise up from below the horizon.)

heaven See MOVE HEAVEN AND EARTH, WOULD THAT *or* WOULD HEAVEN.

heaven knows *or* **heaven only knows** See GOD KNOWS.

heavenly days! *interj., informal* Exclamation of amazement and disbelief with negative coloring. *Heavenly days! Look what happened! The dog did it again on the Persian carpet!* (Speaker exclaims in disgust over the fact that the dog is still not properly housebroken.) Compare GOOD GRIEF!

heave to *v.* To bring a ship to a stop; bring a sailing ship to a standstill by setting the sails in a certain way. *"Heave to!" the captain shouted to his crew.* (Each man carry out his duty to bring the ship to a stop!) *We fired a warning shot across the front of the pirate ship to make her heave to.* (We gave the pirates warning to stop their ship.)

heave up See THROW UP.

heavy See HANG HEAVY *or* HANG HEAVY ON ONE'S HANDS, HOT AND HEAVY.

heavy-duty *adj.* Made for long or hard use; very strong. *The lumbermen used heavy-duty trucks for hauling logs down the mountains.* (The trucks were well-built and strong.) *The workers in the steel mill have heavy-duty gloves for handling hot steel.* (The gloves are very thick to protect the workers' hands.) *Mrs. Carlson bought a heavy-duty cleanser to clean her greasy oven.* (The cleanser is unusually strong.)

heavy-footed *adj.* **1** Slow and clumsy in walking or movement; awkward in using your feet. *The fat man tried to dance, but he was too heavy-footed.* (He was too heavy on his feet. He couldn't move quickly enough.) *Martha is not fat, but she is heavy-footed and walks noisily.* (Martha puts her feet down too hard when she walks; she is not graceful.) **2** Awkward in choice and order of words; not smooth and graceful; clumsy. *In Mary's compositions, the words seem to dance, but John's compositions are always heavy-footed.* (John's compositions are written awkwardly; the words do not go smoothly.) **3** *or* **lead-footed** *informal* Likely to drive an automobile fast. *Jerry is a bad driver because he is too heavy-footed.* (Jerry drives too fast.) Compare STEP ON IT.

heavy-handed *adj.* **1** Not skillful or graceful; clumsy. *George is heavy-handed and seldom catches the ball.* (George moves his hands slowly and awkwardly, and he cannot catch the ball.) *My sister plays the piano badly; she is too heavy-handed.* (Her hands are not skillful enough.) *Tim told a heavy-handed joke about the principal's baldness that embarrassed everyone.* (The joke was more insulting than funny.) **2** Likely to hit or punish hard; harsh or cruel in making (someone) obey. *Years ago many fathers were heavy-handed bosses in their homes.* (Years ago many fathers made children obey them by punishing them hard and often.) *Many American colonists believed that the English tax collectors were too heavy-handed.* (Many men in the English colonies in America thought that the English were pushing them too hard to pay taxes.) **3** See HAM-HANDED.

heavy heart *n. phr.* A feeling of being weighed down with sorrow; unhappiness. *They had very heavy hearts as they went to the funeral.* (They felt very sad and unhappy as they went to the funeral.)

heck See RAISE THE DEVIL *or* RAISE HECK *or* RAISE HOB *or* RAISE NED.

heck of it See DEVIL OF IT.

hedge about *or* **hedge in** **1** To surround with a hedge or barrier; protect or separate by closing in. *The house is hedged about with bushes and trees.* (The house has bushes and trees all around it.) *The little garden is hedged in to keep the chickens out.* (The garden has bushes around it to keep out the chickens.) **2** To keep from getting out or moving freely; keep from acting freely; block in. *The boys are hedged in today. They can only play in the backyard.* (They are kept from going outside the backyard.) *The king said he could not make new laws if he was so hedged in by old ones.* (The king could not make new laws because old laws kept him from doing so. He was not free to make new laws.) Syn. FENCE IN.

hedged in See FENCED IN.

heed See TAKE HEED.

heel See AT ONE'S HEELS, COOL ONE'S HEELS,

DOWN AT-THE-HEEL *or* DOWN-AT-HEEL, DRAG ONE'S FEET *or* DRAG ONE'S HEELS, HEAD OVER HEELS, KICK UP ONE'S HEELS, ON ONE'S HEELS *or* ON THE HEELS OF, SET BACK ON ONE'S HEELS *or* KNOCK BACK ON ONE'S HEELS, TAKE TO ONE'S HEELS *also* SHOW A CLEAN PAIR OF HEELS, TO HEEL, TURN ON ONE'S HEEL, WELL-HEELED.

heels over head See HEAD OVER HEELS.

he laughs best who laughs last A person should go ahead with what he is doing and not worry when others laugh at him. When he succeeds he will enjoy laughing at them for being wrong more than they enjoyed laughing at him.—A proverb. *Everyone laughed at Mary when she was learning to ski. She kept falling down. Now she is the state champion. He laughs best who laughs last.* (Mary looked silly falling down all the time, but now she can enjoy being a champion skier when the people who laughed at her can't ski at all.) Compare CHANGE ONE'S TUNE, LAST LAUGH, LAUGH ON THE OTHER SIDE OF ONE'S MOUTH, SHOE ON THE OTHER FOOT.

hell See COME HELL OR HIGH WATER, GO THROUGH HELL AND HIGH WATER, HELL-ON-WHEELS, LIKE HELL, TO HELL WITH, UNTIL HELL FREEZES OVER, WHEN HELL FREEZES OVER.

hell and high water *n. phr.* Troubles or difficulties of any kind.—A cliché. *After John's father died he went through hell and high water, but he managed to keep the family together.* (John had lots of difficulties.) Compare COME HELL OR HIGH WATER.

hell-on-wheels *n., slang* A short-tempered, nagging, or crabby person especially one who makes another unhappy by constantly criticizing him even when he has done nothing wrong. *Finnegan complains that his wife is hell on wheels; he is considering getting a divorce.* (He complains that she is unduly nagging and critical and wants to divorce her.)

help See CAN HELP, CAN'T HELP BUT *or* CANNOT BUT, SO HELP ME.

help oneself *v. phr.* To take what you want; take rather than ask or wait to be given. *Help yourself to another piece of pie.* (Take another piece of pie without someone's giving it to you.) *John helped himself to some candy without asking.* (John took some candy without asking if it was all right if he took some.)

help out *v.* **1** To be helpful or useful; help sometimes or somewhat. *Mr. Smith helps out with the milking on the farm.* (He helps by milking the cows.) *Tom helps out in the store after school.* (Tom does some work in the store.) **2** To help (someone) especially in a time of need; aid; assist. *Jane is helping out Mother by minding the baby.* (Jane is helping Mother.) *When John couldn't add the numbers, the teacher helped him out.* (The teacher gave John help.)

helter-skelter *adv.* **1** At a fast speed, but in confusion. *The batted ball broke Mr. Jones's window, and the boys ran away helter-skelter.* (The boys ran away in every direction.) *When the bell rang, the pupils ran helter-skelter out of the door.* (Each of the pupils tried to get out of the room first, and they all got in each other's way.) **2** In a confusing group; in disorder. *The movers piled the furniture helter-skelter in the living room of the new house.* (The movers piled the furniture all together in one mixed pile.) *Mary fell down, and her books, papers, and lunch landed helter-skelter over the sidewalk.* (Mary's papers and books fell mixed-up all over the sidewalk.) Compare EVERY WHICH WAY.

he-man *n., informal* A man who is very strong, brave, and healthy. *Larry was a real he-man when he returned from service with the Marines.* (Larry was strong, brave and healthy when he came home from the service.)

hem and haw *v. phr.* **1** To pause or hesitate while speaking, often with little throat noises. *The man was a poor lecturer because he hemmed and hawed too much.* (He paused and made little noises.) **2** To avoid giving a clear answer; be evasive in speech. *The principal asked Bob why he was late to school, and Bob only hemmed and hawed.* (Bob didn't have a good reason and he said only a few words, avoiding a clear answer.) Compare BEAT AROUND THE BUSH.

hem in *or* **hem around** *or* **hem about** *v.* **1** To put something around, or to be placed around; surround. *Mountains hemmed the town in on all sides.* (There were mountains on all sides of the town.) *As soon as Tom and Bob started to fight, they were hemmed around by other boys.* (Other boys were watching on all sides.) **2** See FENCE IN.

hen See MAD AS A HORNET, *or* MAD AS HOPS *or* MAD AS A WET HEN.

hen party *n. phr., informal* A party to which only women or girls are invited. *The sorority gave a hen party for its members.* (The sorority had a party for its members, without any dates.)

Henry See JOHN HANCOCK *or* JOHN HENRY.

her See GIVE IT THE GUN *or* GIVE HER THE GUN.

herd See RIDE HERD ON.

here See ALL THERE *or* ALL HERE, NEITHER HERE NOR THERE, SAME HERE.

here and now[1] *adv. phr.* At this very time and place; right now; immediately. *I want my dime back, and I want it here and now.* (I want my dime back, and I want it right now, not later.) Compare THEN AND THERE.

here and now[2] *n.* The present time and place; today. *He enjoys the pleasures of the here and now and never worries about the future.* (He enjoys today's pleasures and never worries about tomorrow.)

here and there *adv. phr.* **1** In one place

and then in another. *I looked here and there for my pen, but I didn't look everywhere.* (I looked in a few places for my pen, but not in every place:) *Here and there in the yard little yellow flowers had sprung up.* (In various places among the grass little yellow flowers were growing.) **2** In various directions. *We went here and there looking for berries.* (We went in this direction and then in that direction looking for berries.) Compare HITHER AND THITHER.

here goes *interj., informal* I am ready to begin; I am now ready and willing to take the chance; I am hoping for the best.—Said especially before beginning something that takes skill, luck, or courage. *"Here goes!" said Charley, as he jumped off the high diving board.* (I am jumping and I hope nothing goes wrong.) *"Here goes!" said Mary as she started the test.* (I hope I'm lucky and know the answers.)

here goes nothing *interj., informal* I am ready to begin, but this will be a waste of time; this will not be anything great; this will probably fail.—Used especially before beginning something that takes skill, luck or courage. *"Here goes nothing," said Bill at the beginning of the race.* (I don't think I'll win but wish me luck anyway.)

hide See HAVE ONE'S HIDE, TAN ONE'S HIDE.

hide one's face *or* **hide one's head** *v. phr.* **1** To lower your head or turn your face away because of shame or embarrassment. *The teacher found out that Tom had cheated, and Tom hid his head.* (Tom could not let the teacher look at his face after the teacher found out.) *When Bob said how pretty Mary was, she blushed and hid her face.* (Mary blushed and turned her face away in embarrassment.) **2** To feel embarrassed or ashamed. —A cliché. *We will beat the other team so badly that they will hide their heads in shame.* (The other team will be ashamed because we beat them so badly.)

hide one's head in the sand *or* **bury one's head in the sand** *or* **have one's head in the sand** To keep from seeing, knowing, or understanding something dangerous or unpleasant; to refuse to see or face something.—A cliché. *If there is a war, you cannot just bury your head in the sand.* (If there is war, you can't act as if there were not, as if nothing had happened.) [Some people think that the ostrich buries its head in the sand when danger comes, believing that it will not be seen and harmed.]

hide one's light under a bushel *v. phr.* To be very shy and modest and not show your abilities or talents; be too modest in letting others see what you can do.—A cliché. *When Joan is with her close friends she has a wonderful sense of humor, but usually she hides her light under a bushel.* (When Joan is with people that she doesn't know, she is too shy to show her sense of humor.) *Mr. Smith is an expert in many fields, but most people think he is not very smart because he hides his light under a bushel.* (Mr. Smith is too modest to show how much he knows.) *All year long Tommy hid his light under a bushel and the teacher was surprised to see how much he knew when she read his exam paper.* (Tommy did not show his abilities until the exam.)

hide or hair *or* **hide nor hair** *n. phr., informal* A sign or trace of someone that is gone or lost; any sign at all of something missing.—A cliché. Usually used in negative or interrogative sentence. *Tommy left the house this morning and I haven't seen hide or hair of him since.* (I haven't seen anything of Tommy since he left.) *A button fell off my coat and I could find neither hide nor hair of it.* (I couldn't find the button anywhere.)

high See COME HELL OR HIGH WATER, FLYING HIGH, GO THROUGH HELL AND HIGH WATER, HELL AND HIGH WATER, HIT THE HIGH SPOTS, LIVE HIGH OFF THE HOG *or* EAT HIGH ON THE HOG, OFF ONE'S HIGH HORSE, ON TOP OF THE WORLD *or* SITTING ON TOP OF THE WORLD *also* (*Southern*) SITTING ON HIGH COTTON, RIDING HIGH.

high and dry *adv. or adj. phr.* **1** Up above the water; beyond the reach of splashing or waves. *Mary was afraid she had left her towel where the tide would reach it, but she found it high and dry.* (Mary found her towel higher up the beach than the tide reached.) *When the tide went out the boat was high and dry.* (The boat was left out of the water and lying on the beach.) **2** Without anyone to help; alone and with no help. *When the time came to put up the decorations, Mary was left high and dry.* (Mary was left to do the work all by herself.) *At first the other boys helped, but when the work got hard, Bob found himself high and dry.* (The other boys left, and Bob had to do the hard work without any help.) Compare LEAVE IN THE LURCH, OUT IN THE COLD.

high-and-mighty *adj., informal* Feeling more important or superior to someone else; too proud of yourself. *John wasn't invited to the party, because he acted too high-and-mighty.* (John wasn't invited because the other children did not like his proud acting.) *Mary became high-and-mighty when she won the prize, and Joan would not go around with her any more.* (Mary's new pride lost her Joan's friendship.) Compare STUCK-UP.

high camp *n., slang, show business* **1** Kitsch, or pretentious material in bad taste that is still liked by higher class audiences. *The Potsdam Quartet is a play full of high camp.* (The play, about homosexual musicians who played chamber music to Churchill, Stalin, and Roosevelt in Potsdam was judged by critics to be high class kitsch.) **2** An exaggerated movie or theater scene that loses believability. *Scarecrow and Mrs King and Sledge Hammer* are so full of high camp that no sensible people watch them anymore. (The two television shows mentioned are full of exaggerated scenes which has led to a drop in their popularity rating.) **middle camp** and **low camp** refer to theatrical kitsch preferred by middle class and low class audiences, respectively.

high-class adj. Of the best quality; very good; superior.—Avoided by many careful speakers. When Mr. Brown got a raise in pay, Mrs. Brown started to look for a high-class apartment. (Mrs. Brown wanted a better apartment.) Mrs. Smith always gets her clothing at high-class shops. (Mrs. Smith shops in the better stores.) Mr. Jones always gets his office workers from Burns Agency because they have high-class help. (The Burns Agency has superior workers.) Compare FIRST-CLASS.

higher education n. Schooling after graduation from high school, especially in a college or university. Tom plans to get his higher education at the state university. (Tom is going to the state university when he graduates from high school.)

higher-up n., informal One of the people who has one of the more important positions in an organization; an important official. The teacher's problem was discussed by the higher-ups. (The teacher's problem was discussed by the principal and the superintendent.) The local officers of the scout group approved the plan, but the state higher-ups did not accept it. (The people in charge of the scout group in the whole state did not agree with the people in charge of only one city.)

high fashion or **high style** n. phr. The new style in women's dress set each season by designers in Paris or other fashion centers and accepted by fashionable women. The high styles designed in Paris are often quickly copied by makers of cheap clothing. (Makers of cheap dresses often copy the expensive styles of fashion leaders.)

high gear n. phr., informal Top speed; full activity. Production got into high gear after the vacation. (The factory began to work at full speed after the vacation.) An advertising campaign for the new toothpaste promptly moved into high gear. (Advertising for the new toothpaste showed up everywhere in all ways.)

high-handed adj. Depending on force rather than right; bossy; dictatorial. With high-handed daring, John helped himself to the best food on the table. (John took the best there was simply because he was big and strong and no one dared stop him.) Mr. Smith was a high-handed tyrant in his office. (Mr. Smith managed his office as he pleased without considering the feelings or wishes of others.)

high-hat[1] adj., slang Treating others as inferior; acting above others. It was an expensive place to eat, and the customers were likely to be a little high-hat. (It was a res-taurant where prices were high and customers looked down on others who were not able to eat there.) Jones acted high-hat toward anyone poorer than he. (Jones treated people with less money as inferior.)

high-hat[2] v., slang To treat others as inferior; look down on. After she had married a rich man, Mary high-hatted her former friends. (Mary made her former friends feel that she was looking down on them.) "Don't high-hat me," Fred warned, when Harry began to walk away as if he didn't know him. (Fred warned Harry not to act as if he were better than Fred.) Compare BRUSH OFF.

high jinks n. phr., informal Noisy or rough gaiety; wild play; tricks. The sailors were on shore leave, and high jinks were to be expected. (Rough play was usual with a lot of men on shore from a Navy ship.) The high school seniors engaged in high jinks after commencement. (They took part in rough and noisy play.)

high off the hog See LIVE HIGH OFF THE HOG.

high place n. phr. A position of responsibility, honor, and power. Jones had reached a high place in the government at Washington. (Jones had risen to a position of responsibility in the government in Washington.)

high seas n. phr. The open ocean, not the waters near the coast. It was a big powerful liner built to sail on the high seas. (It was a ship built to sail the open ocean.) The ships of every country have the right to sail on the high seas. (All ships have the right to sail freely on the ocean far from shore.)

high sign n. phr., informal A silent signal of recognition, greeting, or warning; an open or secret signal between two persons.—Used with get or give. The Joneses saw us across the hotel dining room and gave us the high sign. (They waved to us in greeting.) John could see that Grace wanted to tell him something, but he got her attention and frowned. She got the high sign and waited until the teacher had moved on before speaking. (John frowned as a warning signal.)

high-sounding adj. Sounding important; said for showing off; too fancy. The politician's speech was full of high-sounding words. (His speech was very fancy.) Mr. Brown filled his son with many high-sounding ideas about life. (Mr. Brown made life sound better than it really is.)

high style See HIGH FASHION.

hightail it v. phr., slang To travel fast; move rapidly. After school, Frank would hightail it home. (Frank would go straight home as fast as he could.) The two men who held up the bank hightailed it out of town. (They drove rapidly away.)

high time adj. phr., used predicatively (stress on time) Dire, necessary, and sufficient circumstances prompting action. It is high time we sold the old house; it will fall apart within *a year.* (Selling the old house is long overdue, we should have done it earlier.)

highway See DIVIDED HIGHWAY *or* DUAL HIGHWAY.

highway robbery *n. phr.* **1** A hold-up of or theft from a person committed on an open road or street usually by an armed man. *Highway robbery was common in England in Shakespeare's day.* (People were often robbed in the streets and roads of England in Shakespeare's day.) **2** An extremely high price or charge; a profiteer's excessive charge. *To someone from a small town, the prices of meals and theater tickets in New York often seem to be highway robbery.* (The prices seem very high.)

hill See GRASS IS ALWAYS GREENER ON THE OTHER SIDE OF THE FENCE *or* GRASS IS ALWAYS GREENER ON THE OTHER SIDE OF THE HILL, HEAD FOR THE HILLS.

hilt See TO THE HILT *or* UP TO THE HILT.

hinge on *or* **hinge upon** *v.* To depend on as decisive; be decided by. *In a dictatorship, everything hinges on one man.* (In a dictatorship, everything is decided by one man.) *A tobacco grower's income for the year may hinge on what the weather is like in a few summer weeks.* (His income may depend on the early summer's weather.)

hired man *n. phr.* A man employed to do jobs every day about a house or farm. *The hired man was sick, and a lot of the daily chores were not done.* (Work that needed to be done each day was neglected because of the illness of the man whose job it was.)

hire out *v., informal* **1** To accept a job; take employment. *Frank hired out as a saxophonist with a dance band.* (Frank got a job as a saxophonist with a dance band.) **2** To rent (as owner). *John used to hire out his tractor sometimes when he didn't need it himself.* (John used to rent his tractor to people sometimes when he didn't need it.)

history See GO DOWN IN HISTORY *or* GO DOWN IN THE RECORDS.

hit See HARD-HITTING, MAKE A HIT, SMASH HIT.

hit and miss See HIT OR MISS.

hit-and-run *adj.* **1** Of or about an accident after which a motorist drives away without giving his name and offering help. *Judges are stern with hit-and-run drivers.* (Judges are stern with drivers who leave the scene of an accident without giving their names.) **2** Striking suddenly and leaving quickly. *The Indians often made hit-and-run attacks on wagon trains.* (They attacked wagon trains and then quickly rode away.)

hit and run *n.* A play in baseball in which a runner on base starts to run as the ball is pitched and the batter must try to hit the ball. *As the pitcher started to pitch to the batter, Jack ran toward second base as if he were going to steal the base, but the batter hit the ball, so Jack scored from first base on the hit and run.* (Jack began to run sooner than he usually would, so he could run farther if the ball was hit.) *Nelson went from first to third base when Richardson made a perfect hit and run.* (Nelson started for second base with the pitch and when Richardson singled, he was able to get to third base before the ball was fielded.)

hit below the belt See BELOW THE BELT.

hit between the eyes *v. phr., informal* To make a strong impression on; surprise greatly. *Helen hit Joe right between the eyes the moment he saw her.* (Helen greatly impressed Joe at first sight.) *It was a wonderfully life-like picture, and it hit Sol right between the eyes.* (It made a strong impression on Sol.) *To learn that his parents had endured poverty for his sake hit John between the eyes.* (When he learned of his parents' sacrifice for him, John was greatly surprised and grateful.)

hit bottom *or* **touch bottom** *v. phr., informal* **1** To be at the very lowest. *In August there was a big supply of corn and the price hit bottom.* (In August the price of corn was lower than it had ever been.) *When Johnny failed the exam his spirits hit bottom.* (Johnny felt worse than he had ever felt before.) **2** To live through the worst; not to be able to go any lower. *After all their troubles, they thought they had hit bottom and then something else happened.* (They thought nothing worse could happen to them, but it did.) *When they lost all their money they thought they had touched bottom and things would have to get better.* (They thought that they had lived through the worst.)

hitch one's wagon to a star *v. phr.* To aim high; follow a great ambition or purpose.—A cliché. *In trying to be a famous pianist, Mary had hitched her wagon to a star.* (She had aimed high; it would have taken less effort just to sing in the church choir.) *John hitched his wagon to a star and decided to try to become President.* (He was very ambitious and aimed for the Presidency.)

hither and thither *or* **hither and yon** *adv. phr., literary* In one direction and then in another. *Bob wandered hither and thither looking for a playmate.* (Bob wandered around looking for a playmate.) Compare HERE AND THERE.

hither and yon See HITHER AND THITHER.

hit it off *v. phr., informal* To enjoy one another's company; be happy and comfortable in each other's presence. *Tom and Fred hit it off well with each other.* (Tom and Fred get along well together.) *Mary and Jane hit it off from the first.* (Mary and Jane liked each other from the time they first met.) Syn. GET ALONG.

hit on *or* **hit upon** *v.* To happen to meet, find, or reach; to choose or think by chance. *John hit on a business that was just starting* *to grow rapidly.* (John happened to choose a business that was soon to grow fast.) *There seemed to be several explanations of the crime, but the detectives hit on the right one the first time.* (The detectives thought of the right explanation the first time.) Compare HAPPEN ON.

hit on all cylinders *v. phr.* **1** To run smoothly or at full power without any missing or skipping.—Said of a motor. *The mechanic tuned the car engine until it was hitting on all cylinders.* (He adjusted it to run perfectly.) **2** *informal* To think or work well; to use all your ability. *The football team was hitting on all cylinders and scored a big victory.* (The team played very well with all the boys doing their best.) *Bob began to write his examination, and found himself hitting on all cylinders.* (He was thinking clearly and words were coming as he wanted them.)

hit one's stride *v. phr.* **1** To walk or run at your best speed; reach your top speed or game. *After walking the first mile, Jim was just hitting his stride.* (Jim was beginning to walk at the speed he liked best.) *The horse began to hit his stride and moved ahead of the other horses in the race.* (The horse began to run at his fastest speed.) **2** To do your best work; do the best job you are able to. *Mary didn't begin to hit her stride in school until the fifth grade.* (Mary began to learn much faster and get better marks.)

hit-or-miss *also* **hit-and-miss** *adj.* Unplanned; uncontrolled; aimless; careless. *John did a lot of hit-or-miss reading, some of it about taxes.* (He didn't pick out just the things that had to do with taxes; he read a lot, and once in a while some of it would be about taxes.) *Mary packed her bag in hurried, hit-or-miss fashion.* (She threw things in without selecting what she knew she would need; she packed things she would have no use for, and forgot some that she would want.)

hit or miss *also* **hit and miss** *adv.* In an unplanned or uncontrolled way; aimlessly; carelessly. *George didn't know which house on the street was Jane's, so he began ringing doorbells hit or miss.* (George rang the doorbell of one house and then another in no order, just any way.)

hit parade *n.* **1** A list of songs or tunes arranged in order of popularity. *Tom was overjoyed when his new song was named on the hit parade on the local radio station.* (It was chosen as one of the best liked new songs.) **2** *slang* A list of favorites in order of popularity. *Jack is no longer number one on Elsie's hit parade.* (Jack is not her best boy friend now.)

hitter See PINCH HIT, PINCH HITTER, PULL HITTER.

hit the books *v. phr., informal* To study your school assignments; prepare for classes. *Jack broke away from his friends, saying, "I've got to hit the books."* (Jack told his friends he had to study.)

hit the bull's-eye *v. phr., informal* To go to the important part of the matter; reach the main question.—A cliché. *John hit the bull's-eye when he said the big question was one of simple honesty.* (John named the important question as that of simple honesty. John was exactly right.)

hit the ceiling *or* **hit the roof** *v. phr., slang* To become violently angry; go into a rage. *When Elaine came home at three in the morning, her father hit the ceiling.* (Her father became very angry.) *Bob hit the roof when Joe teased him.* (Bob became very angry.) Syn. BLOW A FUSE.

hit the deck *v. phr.* To get up from bed, to start working. (From sailor's language as in *"All hands on the deck!"*) *OK boys, it's time to hit the deck!* (It is time to get up and start working.)

hit the dirt *v. phr., slang, military* To take cover under gunfire by falling on the ground. *We hit the dirt the moment we heard the machine gun fire.* (The moment we heard the machine guns, we threw ourselves down on the ground to avoid being hit.)

hit the fan *v. phr., informal* To become a big public problem or controversy. *The whole mess hit the fan when the judge was arrested for drunken driving for the second time.* (The result was a scandal involving many people.)

hit the hay *or* **hit the sack** *v. phr., slang* To go to bed. *The men hit the hay early, in order to be out hunting at dawn.* (The men went to bed early.) *Louis was so tired that he hit the sack soon after supper.* (He went to bed soon after supper.)

hit the high spots *v. phr.* To consider, mention, or see only the more important parts of something such as a book, war, or school course. *In his lecture, the speaker hit the high spots of his subject.* (He mentioned the more important parts.) *The first course in general science hits only the high spots of the physical sciences.* (It considers the chief topics of the physical sciences.) *The Bakers went to the fair for one day, and only hit the high spots.* (They saw only the things that were most important to them.)

hit the jackpot *v. phr., slang* To be very lucky or successful.—A cliché. *Mr. Brown invented a new gadget which hit the jackpot.* (Mr. Brown's gadget was very successful.) *Mrs. Smith hit the jackpot when she got Lula for a maid.* (Mrs. Smith was very lucky to get such a good maid as Lula.)

hit the nail on the head *v. phr.* To get something exactly right; speak or act in the most fitting or effective way.—A cliché. *The mayor's talk on race relations hit the nail on the head.* (He said the right thing; exactly what should be said.)

hit the road *v. phr., slang* **1** To become a wanderer; to live an idle life; become a tramp or hobo. *When Jack's wife left him, he felt a desire to travel, so he hit the road.* (He became a tramp and wandered about the country.) **2** To leave, especially in a car. *It is getting late, so I guess we will hit the road for home.* (We will start off in the car.) *He packed his car and hit the road for California.* (He loaded his car and left for California.)

hit the roof   See HIT THE CEILING.

hit the sack   See HIT THE HAY.

hit the sauce   *v. phr., slang*   To drink alcoholic beverages—especially heavily and habitually. *When Sue left him, Joe begin to hit the sauce.* (She left him and he became a habitual drinker.)

hit the spot   *v. phr., informal*   To refresh fully or satisfy you; bring back your spirits or strength—used especially of food or drink. *A cup of tea always hits the spot when you are tired.* (A cup of tea is very refreshing when you are tired.) *Mother's apple pie always hits the spot with the boys.* (The boys think Mother's pies are delicious.)

hit upon   See HIT ON.

hob   See PLAY THE DEVIL WITH *or* PLAY HOB WITH.

hoe   See HARD ROW TO HOE *or* TOUGH ROW TO HOE.

hoe one's own row   *v. phr.*   To make your way in life by your own efforts; get along without help.—A cliché. *David's father died when he was little, and he has always had to hoe his own row.* (He has had to earn his own living without help.)   Syn. PADDLE ONE'S OWN CANOE, STAND ON ONE'S OWN FEET.

hog   See EAT (LIVE) HIGH ON THE HOG *or* EAT (LIVE) HIGH OFF THE HOG, GO THE WHOLE HOG *or* GO WHOLE HOG, ROAD HOG.

hog-tie   *v., informal*   **1** To tie (an animal) so it is unable to move or escape. *The Cowboy caught a calf and hog-tied it.* (He tied the calf with rope so it could not get up.)   **2** To make someone unable to act freely; limit. *The welfare worker wanted to help at once, but rules and regulations hog-tied her, so she could only report the case.* (The welfare worker had to follow the rules and wait for action by her superiors.)

hoist with one's own petard   *adj. phr.*   Caught in your own trap or trick.—A cliché. *Jack carried office gossip to the boss until he was hoisted by his own petard.* (The boss became disgusted with Jack for gossiping about others and fired him.)   [From Shakespeare; literally, blown up with one's own bomb.]

hold   See GET HOLD OF, LAY HOLD OF, LEAVE HOLDING THE BAG *or* LEAVE HOLDING THE SACK.

hold a brief for   *v. phr.*   To argue in support of; defend.—Usually used with a negative. *I hold no brief for John, but I do not think he was responsible for the accident.* (I am not supporting John, but I think he was not responsible.) *The lawyer said he held no brief for thievery, but he considered the man should*

be given another chance. (The lawyer said he was not defending thievery, but thought the man deserved mercy.)

hold a candle to *also* **hold a stick to**   *v. phr.*   To be fit to be compared with; be in the same class with.—A trite phrase used in negative, interrogative, and conditional sentences. *Henry thought that no modern ball club could hold a candle to those of 50 years ago.* (Henry thought that no modern ball club was as good as those of 50 years ago.)

hold all the trumps   *v. phr.*   To have the best chance of winning; have all the advantages; have full control.—A cliché. *Most of the team wants John for captain and he is the best player. He will be elected captain because he holds all the trumps.* (Everything is in John's favor.) *Freddy has a quarter and I have no money, so he holds all the trumps and can buy whatever he wants with it.* (He has charge of the money and he can decide what to buy.)

hold back   *v.*   **1** To stay back or away; show unwillingness. *The visitor tried to get the child to come to her, but he held back.* (The child stayed away from the visitor.) *John held back from social activity because he felt embarrassed with people.* (John did not take part in social activities because he was shy.)   **2** To keep someone in place; prevent from acting. *The police held back the crowd.* (The police prevented the crowd from acting.)

hold court   *v. phr.*   **1** To hold a formal meeting of a royal court or a court of law. *Judge Stephens allowed no foolishness when he held court.* (Judge Stephens enforced strict order at meetings of his court.)   **2** *informal*   To act like a king or queen among subjects. *Even at sixteen, Judy was holding court for numbers of charmed boys.* (She was acting like a queen over boys who admired her.)

hold down   *v.*   **1** To keep in obedience; keep control of; continue authority or rule over. *Kings used to know very well how to hold down the people.* (Kings understood how to make the people obey.)   **2** *informal*   To work satisfactorily at. *John had held down a tough job for a long time.* (He had worked satisfactorily at the job.)

hold everything   See HOLD IT.

hold fire   See HOLD ONE'S FIRE.

hold forth   *v.*   **1** To offer; propose. *As a candidate, Jones held forth the promise of a bright future.* (He offered the promise of a bright future.)   **2** To speak in public; preach. —Usually used with little respect. *Senator Smith was holding forth on free trade.* (He was giving a speech on free trade.)

hold good   *v.*   **1** To continue to be good; last. *The coupon on the cereal box offered a free toy, but the offer held good only till the end of the year.* (After the end of the year you could not send in the coupon and get the toy; the offer was not good after that.) *Attend-*

ance at the basketball games held good all winter. (Crowds of people kept coming to the games all winter.) **2** To continue; endure; last. *The demand for new houses held good all that year.* (The need for new houses continued all year.) *The agreement between the schools held good for three years.* (The agreement lasted three years.) See HOLD TRUE.

hold it *or* **hold everything** *v. phr., informal* To stop something one is doing or getting ready to do.—Usually used as a command. *The pilot was starting to take off, when the control tower ordered "Hold it!"* (The control tower ordered the pilot to wait.)

hold off *v.* **1a** To refuse to let (someone) become friendly. *The president's high rank and chilly manner held people off.* (His rank and manner kept people from being friendly.) Compare KEEP AT A DISTANCE. **1b** To be rather shy or unfriendly. *Perkins was a scholarly man who held off from people.* (He kept away from people; he wasn't very friendly.) Compare KEEP AT A DISTANCE. **2** To keep away by fighting; oppose by force. *The man locked himself in the house and held off the police for an hour.* (He fought back the police and was not captured for an hour.) **3** To wait before (doing something); postpone; delay. *Jack held off paying for the television set until the dealer fixed it.* (He postponed paying for it until it was satisfactory.) *Mr. Smith held off from building while interest rates were high.* (He chose not to build until interest rates were lower.)

hold on *v.* **1** To keep holding tightly; continue to hold strongly. *As Ted was pulling on the rope, it began to slip and Earl cried, "Hold on, Ted!"* (Earl told Ted to hold tightly.) Syn. HANG ON. **2** To wait and not hang up a telephone; keep a phone for later use. *Mr. Jones asked me to hold on while he spoke to his secretary.* (Mr. Jones asked me to wait on the phone while he spoke to his secretary.) **3** To keep on with a business or job in spite of difficulties. *It was hard to keep the store going during the depression, but Max held on and at last met with success.* (He did not give up; he worked hard and kept the business going.) **4** *informal* To wait a minute; stop.—Usually used as a command. *"Hold on!" John's father said, "I want the car tonight."* (John's father told him to stop, not to take the car.)

hold one's breath *v. phr.* **1** To stop breathing for a moment when you are excited or nervous.—A cliché. *The race was so close that everyone was holding his breath at the finish.* (At the end people were not breathing normally for a moment, they were so excited.) **2** To endure great nervousness, anxiety, or excitement. *John held his breath for days before he got word that the college he chose had accepted him.* (He was nervous and worried until he knew that he had been accepted.)

hold one's end up *or* **hold up one's end** *or*

keep one's end up *or* **keep up one's end** *v. phr., informal* To do your share of work; do your part. *Mary washed the dishes so fast that Ann, who was drying them, couldn't keep her end up.* (Ann could not do her part of the job because she was slower than Mary.) *Susan kept up her end of the conversation, but Bill did not talk very much.* (Susan did her share of talking, but Bill didn't.) *Bob said he would lend me his bicycle if I repaired the flat tire, but he didn't keep up his end of the bargain.* (Bob didn't do as he agreed.)

hold one's fire *or* **hold fire** *v. phr.* To keep back arguments or facts; keep from telling something. *Tom could have hurt Fred by telling what he knew, but he held his fire.* (Tom didn't tell the bad thing he knew about Fred.) *Mary held fire until she had enough information to convince the other club members.* (Mary waited until she could explain all the facts at once.)

hold one's head up *v. phr.* To show self-respect; not be ashamed; be proud. *When Mr. Murray had paid off his debts, he felt that he could hold his head up again.* (He felt that he could be proud of himself again.)

hold one's horses *v. phr., informal* To stop; wait; be patient.—Usually used as a command. May be considered rude. *"Hold your horses!" Mr. Jones said to David when David wanted to call the police.* (Mr. Jones told David to wait when David wanted to call the police.)

hold one's nose to the grindstone See KEEP ONE'S NOSE TO THE GRINDSTONE.

hold one's own *v. phr.* To keep your position; avoid losing ground; keep your advantage, wealth, or condition without loss. *Mr. Smith could not build up his business, but he held his own.* (He kept his business from getting smaller, although he could not expand it.) *The team held its own after the first quarter.* (The team did as well as the opponents after the first quarter, even if they couldn't win.) *Mary had a hard time after the operation, but soon she was holding her own.* (After the first difficult days, Mary did not get worse, although she didn't begin to get better.)

hold one's peace *v. phr., formal* To be silent and not speak against something; be still; keep quiet. *I did not agree with the teacher, but held my peace as he was rather angry.* (I did not say anything against the teacher's idea.) Compare HOLD ONE'S TONGUE.

hold one's temper *or* **keep one's temper** *v. phr.* To make yourself be quiet and peaceful; not become angry. *The meeting will go smoothly if the president keeps his temper.* (The meeting will go smoothly if the president does not become angry.) *Dave can't keep his temper when he drives in heavy traffic.* (Dave becomes angry when he drives in heavy traffic.) Contrast LOSE ONE'S TEMPER, BLOW ONE'S STACK.

hold one's tongue *v. phr.* To be silent; keep still; not talk.—May be considered rude. *The teacher told Fred to hold his tongue.* (The teacher told Fred to keep still.) *If people would hold their tongues from unkind speech, fewer people would be hurt.* (If people would keep still rather than say unkind things, fewer people would be hurt.)

hold on to *v. phr.* **1a** *or* **hold to** To continue to hold or keep; hold tightly. *When Jane played horse with her father, she held on to him tightly.* (Jane sat on her father's back and held tightly.) *The teacher said that if we believed something was true and good we should hold on to it.* (We should continue to believe it.) *The old man held on to his job stubbornly and would not retire.* (He continued to work and would not retire.) **1b** To stay in control of. *Ann was so frightened that she had to hold on to herself not to scream.* (She had to try hard and control her feelings so she would not scream.) Contrast LET GO. **2** To continue to sing or sound. *The singer held on to the last note of the song for a long time.* (She continued singing the last note a long time.)

hold on to your hat See HANG ON TO YOUR HAT.

hold out *v.* **1** To put forward; reach out; extend; offer. *Mr. Ryan held out his hand in welcome.* (He offered his hand in greeting; he offered to shake hands.) *The clerk held out a dress for Martha to try on.* (The clerk offered a dress to Martha to try on.) *The Company held out many fine promises to Jack in order to get him to work for them.* (The company made many promises to persuade Jack to work for them.) **2** To keep resisting; not yield; refuse to give up. *The city held out for six months under siege.* (The city did not surrender while surrounded for six months.) Compare HANG ON, HOLD ON. **3** To refuse to agree or settle until one's wishes have been agreed to. *The strikers held out for a raise of five cents an hour.* (The strikers would not return to work until they got a raise of five cents an hour.) **4** *slang* To keep something from; refuse information or belongings to which someone has a right. *Mr. Porter's partner held out on him when the big payment came in.* (He didn't tell Mr. Porter about the payment or share it fairly with him.) *Mother gave Bobby cookies for all the children in the yard, but he held out on them and ate the cookies himself.* (He did not give them the cookies that Mother sent to them.) *John knew that the family would go to the beach Saturday, but he held out on his brother.* (He didn't tell his brother.)

hold over *v.* **1** To remain or keep in office past the end of the term. *The city treasurer held over for six months when the new treasurer died suddenly.* (The old treasurer kept the job for six months when the newly elected treasurer died.) *The new President held the*

members of the Cabinet over for some time before appointing new members.* (He kept the old Cabinet members in office for a while. **2** To extend the engagement of; keep longer. *The theater held over the feature film for another two weeks.* (The theater showed the film for two weeks more.) **3** To delay action on; to postpone; to defer. *The directors held over their decision until they could get more information.* (They waited to make their decision until they had more information.)

hold the fort *v. phr.* **1** To defend a fort successfully; fight off attackers. *The little group held the fort for days until help came.* (The group fought off the enemy until more troops came to help them.) **2** *informal* To keep a position against opposing forces. *Friends of civil liberties held the fort during a long debate.* (Congressmen supporting civil liberties did not weaken even during a long debate.) **3** *informal* **to keep service or operations going** *It was Christmas Eve, and a few workers held the fort in the office.* (Just a few people were keeping the office open.) *Mother and Father went out and told the children to hold the fort.* (The children should take care of the house while their parents were gone.)

hold the line *v. phr.* To keep a situation or trouble from getting worse; hold steady; prevent a setback or loss. *The mayor held the line on taxes.* (The mayor did not allow an increase in taxes.) *The company held the line on employment.* (The company did not let its workers go.)

hold the stage *v. phr.* **1** To continue to be produced and to attract audiences. *"Peter Pan" holds the stage year after year at its annual Christmas showing in London.* ("Peter Pan" attracts audiences year after year at its annual Christmas showing in London.) **2** To be active in a group; attract attention. *We had only an hour to discuss the question and Mr. Jones held the stage for most of it.* (Mr. Jones talked so much that the others could say little in the time left.) *Jane likes to hold the stage at any party or meeting, so she does and says anything.* (She does and says anything to attract attention.)

hold to See HOLD ON TO.

hold true *or* **hold good** *v. phr.* To remain true. *It has always held true that man cannot live without laws.* (It has always proved true that man cannot live without laws.) *Bob is a good boy and that holds true of Jim.* (Jim is a good boy also.)

hold up *v.* **1** To raise; lift. *John held up his hand.* (John raised his hand.) **2** To support; bear; carry. *The chair was too weak to hold up Mrs. Smith.* (The chair was not strong enough to support Mrs. Smith's weight.) **3** To show; call attention to; exhibit. *The teacher held up excellent models of composition for her class to imitate.* (The teacher

showed her class examples of good writing.)
4 To check; stop; delay. *The wreck held up traffic on the railroad's main line tracks.* (The wreck blocked traffic on the main line.) **5** *informal* To rob at gunpoint. *Masked men held up the bank.* (Masked men robbed the bank with guns.) **6** To keep one's courage or spirits up; remain calm; keep control of oneself. *The grieving mother held up for her children's sake.* (The grieving mother kept control of herself so that her children might not be worried.) **7** To remain good; not get worse; *Sales held up well.* (Selling continued at a steady rate.) *Our team's luck held up, and they won the game.* (The team continued lucky.) *The weather held up and the game was played.* (The weather stayed fair and the game was played.) **8** To prove true. *The police were doubtful at first, but Tony's story held up.* (His story proved true.) **9** To delay action; defer; postpone. Often used with *on*. *The college held up on plans for the building until more money came in.* (The college put off plans for the building.) *The President held up on the news until he was sure of it.* (The President did not announce the news until he was sure of it.)

hold up one's end See HOLD ONE'S END UP.

hold water *v. phr.* **1** To keep water without leaking. *That pail still holds water.* (That pail doesn't leak.) **2** *informal* To prove true; stand testing; bear examination.—Usually used in negative, interrogative, or conditional sentences. *Ernest told the police a story that wouldn't hold water.* (His story turned out to be false.)

hold your hat See HANG ON TO YOUR HAT.

hole See ACE IN THE HOLE, BURN A HOLE IN ONE'S POCKET, IN A HOLE *or* IN A SPOT, IN THE HOLE, OUT OF THE HOLE, SQUARE PEG IN A ROUND HOLE.

hole in See HOLE UP.

hole in one *n. phr.* A shot in golf that is hit from the tee and goes right into the cup. *Many golfers play for years before they get a hole in one.* (It is very hard to get a shot in golf that goes right into the cup.)

hole-in-the-wall *n. phr.* A small place to live, stay in, or work in; a small, hidden, or inferior place. *The jewelry store occupied a tiny hole-in-the-wall.* (The jewelry store occupied a tiny, narrow store.) *When Mr. and Mrs. Green were first married, they lived in a little hole-in-the-wall in a cheap apartment building.* (They had a very small, cheap apartment.) **2** *slang, citizen's band radio jargon* A tunnel. *Let's get through this hole in the wall, then we'll change seats.* (We'll change seats after passing the tunnel.)

hole out *v.* To finish play in golf by hitting the ball into the cup. *The other players waited for Palmer to hole out before they putted.* (They waited for Palmer to hit his ball into the cup before they took their turn.)

hole up *also* **hole in** *v., slang* To take refuge or shelter; put up; lodge. *After a day's motoring, Harry found a room for rent and holed up for the night.* (He put up for the night in a rented room.) *The thief holed up at an abandoned farm.* (The thief hid for safety at a deserted farm.) *"Let's hole in," said Father as we came to a motel that looked good.* ("Let's stay here," said Father.)

holiday See HALF-HOLIDAY.

holier-than-thou *adj.* Acting as if you are better than others in goodness, character, or reverence for God; acting as if morally better than other people. *Most people find holier-than-thou actions in others hard to accept.* (A show of superior goodness annoys most people.) *After Mr. Howard stopped smoking, he had a holier-than-thou manner toward his friends who still smoked.* (Mr. Howard seemed to think he was a better man than his friends who still smoked.)

holistic health *n., informal, semi-technical* The maintenance of health and the avoidance of disease through such psychogenic practices and procedures as biofeedback, meditation, alternative methods of childbirth, and avoidance of drugs. *The Murgatroyds are regular holistic health freaks—why, they won't even take aspirin when they have a headache.* (They refuse to take a pain killer; they'd rather meditate to get rid of a headache.)

holler before one is hurt See CRY BEFORE ONE IS HURT.

hollow See BEAT ALL HOLLOW *also* BEAT HOLLOW.

hollow out *v.* To cut or dig out or to cut or dig a hole in; make a cut or cave in; excavate. *The soldier hollowed out a foxhole in the ground to lie in.* (He dug out a hole in the ground to lie in.) *The Indians used to hollow out a log to make a canoe.* (The Indians would cut, burn, or dig out the inside of a log to make a canoe.) *Joe's father hollowed out a pumpkin to make a jack-o'-lantern.* (He cut out the inside of the pumpkin.)

holy cats *or* **holy cow** *or* **holy mackerel** *or* **holy Moses** *interj., informal* —Used to express strong feeling (as astonishment, pleasure, or anger); used in speech or when writing conversation. *"Holy cats! That's good pie!" said Dick.* (The pie pleased Dick very much.) *"Holy cow! They can't do that!" Mary said when she saw the boys hurting a much smaller boy.* (Mary was astonished and angry to see the little boy being hurt.)

holy terror *n., informal* A very disobedient or unruly child; brat. *All the children are afraid of Johnny because he's a holy terror.* (Johnny always causes trouble.)

home See AT HOME, BRING HOME, BRING HOME THE BACON, CHICKENS COME HOME TO ROOST, CLOSE TO HOME, CONVALESCENT HOME *or* NURSING HOME *or* REST HOME, KEEP THE HOME FIRES BURNING, MAKE ONESELF AT

HOME, NOBODY HOME, WRITE HOME ABOUT.

home brew *n. phr.* A beer or other malt liquor made at home, not in a brewery. *Home brew reached its greatest popularity in America during national prohibition.* (Beer was often made at home during prohibition when making and selling beer was against the law.)

home on *or* **home in on** *v.* To move toward a certain place by following a signal or marker. *The airplane homed in on the radio beacon.* (The airplane followed the radio beacon home to the airport.) *The ship homed on the lights of New York harbor.* (The ship steered for the lights of New York harbor.)

home plate *n.* The base in baseball where the batter stands and that a runner must touch to score. *The runner slid across home plate ahead of the tag to score a run.* (The runner slid across the last base before the catcher could tag him with the ball.)

home run *n.* A hit in baseball that allows the batter to run around all the bases and score a run. *Frank hit a home run over the left field wall in the second inning.* (Frank was able to run around all the bases and score a run because his hit went over the wall.)

honestly See COME BY HONESTLY.

honest to goodness *or* **honest to God** *adj. phr., informal* Really; truly; honestly.—Used to emphasize something said. *When we were in Washington, we saw the President, honest to goodness.* (We saw the president—I'm telling you the truth.) *"Honest to goodness, Jane, I think you are the messiest girl in the world," said Mother.* (Mother showed that she was much annoyed with Jane.)

honest-to-goodness *or* **honest-to-God** *adj. phr., informal* Real; genuine.—Used for emphasis. *She served him honest-to-goodness deep dish apple pie.* (She served him real deep dish apple pie.) *It was the first honest-to-goodness baseball game he'd seen since going abroad.* (It was the first real baseball game he'd seen since going abroad.)

honeymoon is over The first happy period of friendship and cooperation between two persons or groups is over.—A cliché. *A few months after a new President is elected, the honeymoon is over and Congress and the President begin to criticize each other.* (At first they are very friendly and cooperative, but after a while they begin to blame each other.) *The honeymoon was soon over for the new foreman and the men under him.* (At first they got along well, but soon they began to criticize each other.)

honky-tonk *n.* A cheap night club or dance hall. *There were a number of honky-tonks near the army camp.* (Many cheap dance halls and taverns were near the camp.)

honor See DO THE HONORS, IN HONOR OF, ON ONE'S HONOR.

hook See BY HOOK OR BY CROOK, GET THE HOOK *at* GET THE BOUNCE 2, GIVE THE HOOK *at* GIVE THE BOUNCE 2, OFF THE HOOK.

hookey See PLAY HOOKEY.

hook, line and sinker *adv. phr., informal* Without question or doubt; completely.—A cliché. *Johnny was so easily fooled that he fell for Joe's story hook, line and sinker.* (Johnny accepted Joe's story without question.) *Mary was such a romantic girl that she swallowed the story Alice told her about her date, hook, line and sinker.* (Mary believed Alice's story completely.) *Bobby trusted Jim so he was taken in by his hard-luck story hook, line and sinker.* (Jim fooled Bobby completely.)

hook up *v.* To connect or fit together. *The company sent a man to hook up the telephone.* (The company sent a man to connect the telephone.) *They could not use the gas stove because it had not been hooked up.* (The company had not connected the stove to the gas pipe.)

hoop See JUMP THROUGH A HOOP.

hop See MAD AS A HORNET *or* MAD AS HOPS.

hope See CROSS ONE'S HEART *or* CROSS ONE'S HEART AND HOPE TO DIE, IN HOPES.

hope against hope *v. phr.* To try to hope when things look black; hold to hope in bad trouble. *The mother continued to hope against hope although the plane was hours late.* (The mother clung to hope for hours after the plane should have arrived.) *Jane hoped against hope that Joe would call her.* (She thought he would not, but anyway she hoped.)

hop to it *v. phr., slang* To get started; start a job; get going. *"There's a lot to do today, so let's hop to it," the boss said.* ("Let's get started," the boss said.)

hopped up *adj., slang* **1** Doped with a narcotic drug. *Police found Jones hiding in an opium den, among other men all hopped up with the drug.* (Police found him in an opium den, where everyone else was under the influence of the drug.) **2** Full of eagerness; excited. *Fred was all hopped up about going over the ocean.* (Fred was excited by the expectation of a trip on a ship.)

horn See BLOW ONE'S OWN HORN *or* TOOT ONE'S OWN HORN, PULL IN ONE'S HORNS *or* DRAW IN ONE'S HORNS, TAKE THE BULL BY THE HORNS.

hornet See MAD AS A HORNET *or* MAD AS HOPS *or* MAD AS A WET HEN, STIR UP A HORNET'S NEST.

horn in *v., slang* To come in without invitation or welcome; interfere. Often used with *on.* *Jack would often horn in on conversations discussing things he knew nothing about.* (Jack often was stubborn about getting into talk even when he was ignorant of the subject being discussed.) *Lee horned in on Ray and Annie and wanted to dance with Annie.* (Lee went in where he was not wanted.) Compare BUTT IN.

horns of a dilemma *n. phr.* Two choices possible in a situation in which neither is wanted.—A cliché, usually used after *on. Joe found himself on the horns of a dilemma; if he went to work, he'd miss seeing Mary; if he stayed out, he'd be too broke to take her anywhere.* (Joe had two choices, neither of which satisfied him.)

horror See THROW UP ONE'S HANDS IN HORROR.

horse See BET ON THE WRONG HORSE, CART BEFORE THE HORSE, CHANGE HORSES IN THE MIDDLE OF THE STREAM *or* CHANGE HORSES IN MIDSTREAM, EAT LIKE A HORSE, HOLD ONE'S HORSES, IRON HORSE, LOCK THE BARN DOOR AFTER THE HORSE IS STOLEN, LOOK A GIFT HORSE IN THE MOUTH, OFF ONE'S HIGH HORSE, ON ONE'S HIGH HORSE, PUT ONE'S MONEY ON A SCRATCHED HORSE, STRAIGHT FROM THE HORSE'S MOUTH.

horse around *v., slang* To join in rough teasing; play around. *They were a bunch of sailors on shore leave, horsing around where there were girls and drinks.* (The sailors were playing a bit rough; they were being noisy and teasing.) *John horsed around with the dog for a while when he came in from school.* (He played with the dog.)

horse of a different color *or* **horse of another color** *n. phr., informal* Something altogether separate and different.—A cliché. *Anyone can be broke, but to steal is a horse of a different color.* (To be broke is one thing, but to steal is different.) *Do you mean that the boy with that pretty girl is her brother? I thought he was her boy friend. Well, that's a horse of another color.* (That is something different from what I thought.)

horse sense *n., informal* A good understanding about what to do in life; good judgment; wisdom in making decisions. *Bill had never been to college, but he had plenty of horse sense.* (He was not foolish.) *Some people are well educated and read many books, but still do not have much horse sense.* (They have poor judgment and make mistakes.)

horse trade *n.* **1** The sale of a horse or the exchange of two horses. *It was a horse trade in which the owner of the worse animal gave a rifle to make the trade equal.* (He swapped a horse and rifle for the other man's horse.) **2** *informal* A business agreement or bargain arrived at after hard and skillful discussion. *Party leaders went around for months making horse trades to get support for their candidate.* (They made bargains and promises in return for support.) *The horse trade finally called for a new car for the radio station in exchange for several weeks of advertising for the car dealer.* (The dealer traded a new car for some radio advertising.)

hot See BLOW HOT AND COLD, MAKE IT HOT.

hot air *n., informal* Nonsense exaggerated talk, wasted words characterized by emotion rather than intellectual content. *That was just a lot of hot air what Joe said.* (What he said was just exaggerated nonsense.)

hot and bothered *adj., informal* Excited and worried, displeased, or puzzled.—A hackneyed phrase. *Fritz got all hot and bothered when he failed in the test.* (He was excited and disappointed.) *Leona was all hot and bothered when her escort was late in coming for her.* (She was nervous and worried.) *Jerry was hot and bothered about his invention when he couldn't get it to work.* (He was excited and puzzled.) *It is a small matter; don't get so hot and bothered.* (Don't worry so much.)

hot and heavy *adv. phr., informal* Strongly; vigorously; emphatically. *Fred got it hot and heavy when his wife found out how much he had lost at cards.* (Fred got a hard scolding.) *The partners had a hot and heavy argument before deciding to enlarge their store.* (The partners argued excitedly for a long time before they decided to make their store bigger.)

hot dog *n. phr., informal* A frankfurter or wiener in a roll. *The boys stopped on the way home for hot dogs and coffee.* (They had frankfurters and rolls with coffee.)

hot dog *interj., informal* Hurrah!—A cry used to show pleasure or enthusiasm. *"Hot dog!" Frank exclaimed when he unwrapped a birthday gift of a small record player.* ("Hurrah!" "Isn't that something!" he exclaimed.)

hot dog roast See WIENER ROAST.

hot number *n., informal* A person or thing noticed as newer, better, or more popular than others. *The boys and girls thought that song was a hot number.* (They thought it was new and fine.) *The new car that Bob is driving is a real hot number.* (It is fast and fancy.) *John invented a new can opener that was a hot number in the stores.* (It sold fast in the stores.)

hot one *n., slang, informal* Something out of the ordinary; something exceptional, such as a joke, a person whether in terms of looks or intelligence. *Joe's joke sure was a hot one.* (It was extraordinary.) *Sue is a hot one, isn't she?* (She is an extraordinary, striking girl.)

hot potato *n., informal* A question that causes strong argument and is difficult to settle. *Many school boards found segregation a hot potato in the early '60s.* (They found it a question that was hard to handle without stirring up strong feelings.)

hot rod *n., informal* An older automobile changed so that it can gain speed quickly and go very fast. *Hot rods are used by young people especially in drag racing.* (Cars with speed and pickup are used by young men especially in races in which quick increase in speed is important.)

hot seat *n., slang* The electric chair used to cause death by electrocution in legal executions. *Many a man has controlled a murder-*

ous rage when he thought of the hot seat. (Many a man has checked the wish to kill when he thought of the electric chair.) **2** *informal* A position in which you can easily get into trouble. *A judge in a beauty contest is on the hot seat. If he chooses one girl, the other girls will be angry with him.* (A judge in a beauty contest is in a position likely to get him into trouble; he must choose one girl, and then the others will be angry.)

hot stuff *n., slang, citizen's band radio jargon* Coffee. *Let's stop and get some hot stuff.* (Let's stop for some coffee.)

hot under the collar *adj. phr., informal* Angry—A cliché. *Mary gets hot under the collar if you joke about women drivers.* (Mary does not like it said that women are poor drivers.) *Tom got hot under the collar when his teacher punished him.* (Tom got angry when he was punished.)

hot water *n., informal* Trouble.—Used with in, into, out of. *John's thoughtless remark about religion got him into a lot of hot water.* (His remark got him into a lot of trouble.) *It was the kind of trouble where it takes a friend to get you out of hot water.* (It was a jam of the kind in which a friend is the best means of getting out of trouble.)

hound See ROCK HOUND, RUN WITH THE HARE AND HUNT (RIDE) WITH THE HOUNDS.

hour See AFTER HOURS, ALL HOURS, COFFEE HOUR, ON THE HOUR, ZERO HOUR.

house See BOARDING HOUSE REACH, BRING DOWN THE HOUSE, FUN HOUSE, HASH HOUSE, KEEP HOUSE, ON THE HOUSE, PARISH HOUSE, PEOPLE WHO LIVE IN GLASS HOUSES SHOULD NOT THROW STONES, PLAGUE ON BOTH YOUR HOUSES or PLAGUE O' BOTH YOUR HOUSES, PUT ONE'S HOUSE IN ORDER or SET ONE'S HOUSE IN ORDER.

house detective *n.* A detective employed by a hotel, store, or other business to watch for any trouble. *The one-armed man sweeping the bank floor was really the house detective.* (The one-armed sweeper was secretly a detective paid by the bank.)

house of cards *n. phr.* Something badly put together and easily knocked down; a poorly founded plan, hope, or action.—A hackneyed expression. *John's business fell apart like a house of cards.* (John's business failed like a house built of playing cards.) *Their plan for a trip to Europe proved to be just a house of cards.* (The trip to Europe proved to have no chance, and it never came true.)

housetop See SHOUT FROM THE HOUSETOPS or SHOUT FROM THE ROOFTOPS.

how See AND HOW!

how about or **what about** *interrog.*—Used to ask for a decision, action, opinion, or explanation. **1** Will you have or agree on? *How about another piece of pie?* (Will you have another piece of pie?) *What about a game of tennis?* (Would you like to play tennis?)

How about going to the dance with me Saturday? (Will you go to the dance with me Saturday?) **2** Will you lend or give me? *How about five dollars until Friday?* (Will you lend me five dollars?) *What about a little help with these dishes?* (Will you help me wash these dishes?) **3** What is to be done about? *What about the windows? Shall we close them before we go?* (What is to be done about the windows before we go?) **4** How do you feel about? What do you think about? What is to be thought or said? *What about women in politics?* (What do you think about women in politics?) *How about this button on the front of the typewriter?* (What does this button on the typewriter do?)

how about that or **what about that** *informal* An expression of surprise, congratulation, or praise. *When Jack heard of his brother's promotion, he exclaimed, "How about that!"* (Jack meant that it was wonderful.) *Bill won the scholarship! What about that!* (What a wonderful thing for him!)

how come *informal also nonstandard* **how's come** *interrog.* How does it happen that? Why? *How come you are late?* (Why are you late?) *You're wearing your best clothes today. How come?* (You are wearing your best clothes. Why?) Compare WHAT FOR.

how do you do *formal* How are you?— Usually as a reply to an introduction; it is in the form of a question but no answer is expected. *"Mary, I want you to meet my friend Fred. Fred, this is my wife, Mary." "How do you do, Mary?" "How do you do, Fred?"*

howling success *n., informal* A great success; something that is much praised; something that causes wide enthusiasm.—A cliché. *The party was a howling success.* (Everybody was enthusiastic about the party.) *The book was a howling success.* (The reviewers praised it, and people bought many copies.)

how's come See HOW COME.

how so *interrog.* How is that so? Why is it so? How? Why? *I said the party was a failure and she asked, "How so?"* (She asked in what way it was a failure.) *He said his brother was not a good dancer and I asked him, "How so?"* (I asked why or in what way he was not a good dancer.)

how's that *informal* What did you say? Will you please repeat that? *"I've just been up in a balloon for a day and a half." "How's that?"* ("What did you say?") *"The courthouse is on fire." "How's that again?"* ("Please say that again. I didn't hear you or can't believe it.")

how the land lies See LAY OF THE LAND.

how the wind blows See WAY THE WIND BLOWS.

Hoyle See ACCORDING TO HOYLE.

huddle See GO INTO A HUDDLE.

hue and cry *n.* **1** An alarm and chase after a supposed wrongdoer; a pursuit usually by shouting men. *"Stop, thief," cried John as he* *ran. Others joined him, and soon there was a hue and cry.* (Soon many men were chasing the thief and shouting.) **2** An excited mass protest, alarm, or outcry of any kind. *The explosion was so terrible that people at a distance raised a great hue and cry about an earthquake.* (They spread the alarm that there had been an earthquake.) *Someone said the bank had failed, and soon there was a hue and cry as people shouted for their money.* (Many depositors were soon shouting for their money.)

hug the road *v. phr.* To stay firmly on the road; ride smoothly without swinging. *A heavy car with a low center of gravity will hug the road.* (It will ride smoothly without swinging or threatening to turn over.) *At high speeds a car will not hug the road well.* (It will not stay on the road very well.)

huh-uh *or* **hum-um** *or* **uh-uh** *adv., informal* No.—Used only in speech or to record dialogue. *Did Mary come? Huh-uh.* (No, Mary didn't come.) *Is it raining out? Uh-uh.* (No, it isn't raining.) Contrast UH-UH.

humble See EAT HUMBLE PIE.

hump See OVER THE HUMP.

hundred See BY THE DOZEN *or* BY THE HUNDRED *or* BY THE THOUSAND.

hunt See RUN WITH THE HARE AND HUNT (RIDE) WITH THE HOUNDS.

hunt and peck *n. phr., informal* Picking out typewriter keys by sight, usually with one or two fingers; not memorizing the keys. *Many newspaper reporters do their typing by hunt and peck.* (They type by sight, often with only one or two fingers.)—Often used, with hyphens, as an adjective. *Mr. Barr taught himself to type, and he uses the hunt-and-peck system.* (Mr. Barr has to look at the keys when he types.)

hunt down *v.* **1** To pursue and capture; look hard for an animal or person until found and caught. *The police hunted down the escaped prisoner.* (The police kept hunting until they found the escaped prisoner and cap-

tured him.) Compare TRACK DOWN. **2** To search for (something) until one finds it. *Professor Jones hunted down the written manuscript in the library of Congress.* (Professor Jones searched for the manuscript in the library of Congress and finally found it.) Syn. TRACK DOWN.

hunting See HAPPY HUNTING GROUND.

hunt up *v.* To find or locate by search. *When John was in Chicago, he hunted up some old friends.* (He searched for some old friends he knew were there, although he hadn't their addresses, and he finally found them.) *The first thing Fred had to do was to hunt up a hotel room.* (The hotels were crowded, and it took searching to find one that he could rent.) *To show the doubting children, their mother hunted up some old photographs in the attic.* (She searched the attic until she found the old pictures that proved her story.)

hurt See CRY BEFORE ONE IS HURT *or* HOLLER BEFORE ONE IS HURT.

hush-hush *adj., informal* Kept secret or hidden; kept from public knowledge; hushed up; concealed. *The company had a new automobile engine that it was developing, but kept it a hush-hush project until they knew it was successful.* (They let no news of it leak out until they had succeeded in making the engine successfully.)

hush up *v.* **1** To keep news of (something) from getting out; prevent people from knowing about. *It isn't always easy to hush up a scandal.* (You can't always keep word of a disgraceful story from spreading.) **2** *informal* To be or make quiet; stop talking, crying, or making some other noise.—Often used as a command. *"Hush up," Mother said, when we began to repeat ugly gossip.* (Mother told us to be quiet when we began to repeat gossip.) *The little girl was noisy in church but her mother hushed her up.* (Her mother made her stop talking.)

I

ice See BLOOD RUNS COLD *or* BLOOD TURNS TO ICE, BREAK THE ICE, CUT ICE, ON ICE, SKATE ON THIN ICE.

iceberg See COOL AS AN ICEBERG.

idea See THE IDEA, WHAT'S THE BIG IDEA *or* WHAT'S THE IDEA.

I declare *interj., dialect* Well; oh my; truly. —Used for emphasis. *I declare, it has been a very warm day!* (The day was hot.) *Mother said, "I declare, John, you have grown a foot."* (Mother thought that John had grown much taller.)

idiot box *n., slang* A television set. *Phil has been staring at the idiot box all afternoon.* (He has been watching television all afternoon.)

if See WHAT IF.

if anything *adv. phr.* More likely; instead; rather. *The weather forecast is not for cooler weather; if anything, it is expected to be warmer.* (The weather is not expected to change. But if it does change, it will become warmer.) *Joe isn't a bad boy. If anything, he's a pretty good one.* (If we say what Joe is, he is a pretty good boy instead of a bad one.) Compare MATTER OF FACT.

if only I wish. *If only it would stop raining!* (I wish it would stop raining.) *If only Mother could be here.* (I wish Mother could be here.) Syn. WOULD THAT.

if the hill will not come to Mahomet, Mahomet will go to the hill If one person will not go to the other, then the other must go to him. —A proverb. *Grandfather won't come to visit us, so we must go and visit him. If the hill won't come to Mahomet, then Mahomet will go to the hill.* (Because Grandfather won't come to us, we must go to him.)

if the shoe fits, wear it If what is said describes you, you are meant.—A proverb. *I won't say who, but some children are always late. If the shoe fits, wear it.* (If you are always late, you are one that I mean.)

if worst comes to worst If the worst thing happens that be imagined; if the worst possible thing happens; if troubles grow worse. *If worst comes to worst and Mr. Jones loses the house, he will send his family to his mother's farm.* (If the worst thing we can think of happens to Mr. Jones, which is to lose his house, he will send his family to his mother.) *If worst comes to worst, we shall close the school for a few days.* (If the worst things happen that can happen, we shall have to close school.)

ill See IT'S AN ILL WIND THAT BLOWS NO-BODY GOOD, TAKE ILL.

ill at ease *adj. phr.* Not feeling at ease or comfortable; anxious; worried; unhappy. *Donald had never been to a big party before and he was ill at ease.* (He was embarrassed and nervous at the party.) *When Joe first went to dancing school, he was ill at ease, not knowing how to act.* (He didn't enjoy it.) Contrast AT EASE 2.

I'll bet you my bottom dollar *interj., informal* An exaggerated assertion of assurance. *I bet you my bottom dollar that the Cubs will win this year.* (I am willing to bet any amount that they will win, I am very sure.)

I'll say *or* **I tell you** *interj., informal* I agree with this completely.—Used for emphasis. *Did the children all enjoy Aunt Sally's pecan pie? I'll say!* (Yes, all the children certainly did enjoy the pie!) *I'll say this is a good movie!* (This certainly is a good movie and I want everyone to know I think so.)

I'll tell you what *or* **tell you what** *informal* Here is an idea. *The hamburger stand is closed, but I'll tell you what, let's go to my house and cook some hot dogs.* (Here is an idea that I just thought of: let's go to my house.)

image See SPITTING IMAGE *or* SPIT AND IMAGE.

impose on *v.* To try to get more from (a person who is helping you) than he intended to give. *Don't you think you are imposing on your neighbor when you use his telephone for half an hour?* (Your neighbor was kind and let you use his telephone, but when you talked so long, you were trying to get more from him than he intended to give.) *You may swim in the Allens' pool so long as you do not impose on them by bringing all your friends.* (The Allens permit you to swim in their pool but they do not expect you to bring all your friends.) Compare TAKE ADVANTAGE.

improve on *or* **improve upon** *v.* To make or get one that is better than (another). *Dick made good marks the first year, but he thought he could improve on them.* (Dick thought he could make better marks.) *Charles built a new model racer for the derby race, because he knew he could improve upon his old one.* Charles knew he could build a faster racer.)

I'm telling you *informal* It is important to listen to what I am saying. *Marian is a smart girl but I'm telling you, she doesn't always do what she promises.* (You should listen when I tell you that Marian doesn't always do what she promises.)

in a bad way *adv. phr., informal* In trouble or likely to have trouble. *If you have only those two girls to help you, you are in a bad way.* (You will probably have trouble if you have only those two girls helping.) *Jerry has written only one sentence of his term paper that is due tomorrow, and he knows he is in a bad way.* (Jerry knows he is likely to have trouble because he has not written more of his paper.) *Mrs. Jones has cancer and is in a bad way.* (She is very sick with cancer.) *A new supermarket opened across the street, and the*

Peters' grocery business was soon in a bad way. (The Peters soon lost most of their business.)

in a big way *adv. phr., informal* As fully as possible; with much ceremony.—A hackneyed expression. *Our family celebrates birthdays in a big way.* (We have big parties for all birthdays in our family.) *John likes to entertain his dates in a big way.* (John takes his dates to expensive or famous restaurants and theaters.)

in a bind *or* **in a box** *adv. phr., informal* Likely to have trouble whether you do one thing or another. *Sam is in a bind because if he carries home his aunt's groceries, his teacher will be angry because he is late, and if he doesn't, his aunt will complain.* (Sam is likely to have trouble whether he does something to please his aunt or something to please his teacher.) Compare BETWEEN THE DEVIL AND THE DEEP BLUE SEA, HORNS OF A DILEMMA.

in a breeze See WIN IN A WALK *or* WIN IN A BREEZE.

in absentia *adv. phr., formal* When the person is absent.—Used in graduation exercises when presenting diplomas to an absent student or during a court case. *On Commencement Day, Joe was sick in bed and the college gave him his bachelor's degree in absentia.* (The college gave Joe his B.A. degree although he was not present at the graduation program.) [Latin, meaning "in absence."]

in a circle *or* **in circles** *adv. phr.* Without any progress; without getting anywhere; uselessly. *The committee debated for two hours, just talking in circles.* (They talked uselessly, solving nothing.) *If you don't have a clear aim, you can work a long time and still be going in circles.* (Without an aim you will make no progress.) *He seemed to be working hard, but was just running around in circles.* (He was working aimlessly and making no progress.)

in addition *adv. phr.* As something extra; besides. *We saw a Mickey Mouse cartoon in addition to the cowboy movie.* (The cartoon was extra; we saw it and the movie.) *Aunt Mary gave us sandwiches for our picnic and a bag of cookies in addition.* (She gave us sandwiches and cookies besides.) *He has two cars and in addition a motorboat.* (He has two cars and also a motorboat.)

in advance *or* **in advance of** *adv. phr.* **1** In front; ahead (of the others); first. *In the parade, the band will march in advance of the football team.* (The band will march in front of the football team.) *The soldiers rode out of the fort with the scouts in advance.* (The scouts rode first and were followed by the soldiers.) **2** Before doing or getting something. *The motel man told Mr. Williams he would have to pay in advance.* (Mr. Williams had to pay before he could have the room.) *The paperhanger mixed his paste quite a while in advance so it would have time to cool.*

(He mixed his paste some time beforehand.) *It will be easier to decorate the snack bar if we cut the streamers in advance of the actual decorating.* (It will be easier to cut the streamers first and then hang them.)

in a family way *or* **in the family way** *adj. phr., informal* Going to have a baby.—A cliché; used as a euphemism. *Sue and Liz are happy because their mother is in the family way.* (Their mother is going to have a baby.) *The Ferguson children are promising kittens to everyone because their cat is in a family way.* (The Ferguson cat is going to have kittens.) Compare WITH CHILD.

in a flash *also* **in a trice** *adv. phr.* Very suddenly. *We were watching the bird eat the crumbs; then I sneezed, and he was gone in a flash.* (The bird flew away very suddenly.) *Bob was looking over his notes for English class and in a flash he knew what he would write his paper about.* (Very suddenly Bob knew what he wanted to write about.)

in a fog *or* **in a haze** *adv. phr.* Mentally confused; not sure what is happening. *I didn't vote for Alice because she always seems to be in a fog.* (Alice seems to be confused about things.) *I was so upset that for two days I went around in a haze, not even answering when people spoke to me.* (I was mentally confused and dreamy.) Contrast ALL THERE, HIT ON ALL CYLINDERS.

in a hole *or* **in a spot** *adj. phr., informal* In an embarrassing or difficult position; in some trouble. *When the restaurant cook left at the beginning of the busy season, it put the restaurant owner in a hole.* (It made trouble for the owner of the restaurant.) Compare BEHIND THE EIGHT BALL, IN THE HOLE.

in a kind of way See IN A WAY 1.

in a lather *adj., slang* In great excitement, all worked up; extremely agitated. *I couldn't get across to Joe, he was all in a lather.* (I wasn't able to communicate with him; he was in much too agitated a state.)

in all *adv. phr.* **1** All being counted; altogether. *You have four apples and I have three bananas, making seven pieces of fruit in all.* (We have a total of seven pieces of fruit.) *In all we did very well.* (Everything considered, we did very well.) **2** See ALL IN ALL 2.

in and out *adv. phr.* **1** Coming in and going out often. *He was very busy Saturday and was in and out all day.* (He had to go out on business many times and back to the office.) **2** See INSIDE OUT 2.

in another's place See PUT ONESELF IN ANOTHER'S PLACE.

in a nutshell *adv. phr., informal* In a few words; briefly, without telling all about it.—A cliché. *We are in a hurry, so I'll give you the story in a nutshell.* (I'll tell you quickly the main facts of the story without all details.) *In a nutshell, the car is no bargain.* (In a few words, the car is not worth the money.) Compare IN SHORT.

in any case *also* **in any event** *or* **at all events** *adv. phr.* **1** No matter what happens; surely; without fail; certainly; anyhow; anyway. *It may rain tomorrow, but we are going home in any case.* (We are going home tomorrow no matter whether it rains or not.) *I may not go to Europe, but in any event, I will visit you during the summer.* (I shall certainly visit you during the summer.) **2** Regardless of anything else; whatever else may be true; anyhow; anyway. *Tom was not handsome and he was not brilliant, but at all events he worked hard and was loyal to his boss.* (He wasn't very good looking and he wasn't very bright, but at least he worked hard and stayed with the job.) *I don't know if it is a white house or a brown house. At all events, it is a big house on Main Street.* (Anyhow, whatever color it is, it is a big house on Main Street.) Compare AT ANY RATE, AT LEAST 2.

in any event See IN ANY CASE.

in a pig's eye *adv., slang, informal* Hardly, unlikely, not so. *Would I marry him? In a pig's eye.* (Not very likely, hardly.)

in arms *adv. phr.* Having guns and being ready to fight; armed. *When our country is at war, we have many men in arms.* (In times of war we have men in the services.) Syn. UP IN ARMS!

in a row See GET ONE'S DUCKS IN A ROW.

in arrears *adv. phr.* Late or behind in payment of money or in finishing something.— Usually used of a legal debt or formal obligation. *Poor Mr. Brown! He is in arrears on his rent.* (Mr. Brown owes rent that he should have already paid.) *He is in arrears on the story he promised to write for the magazine.* (He is behind in his writing.)

in a sense *adv. phr.* In some ways but not in all; somewhat. *Mr. Smith said our school is the best in the state, and in a sense that is true.* (Our school is the best in some ways but not all.) *In a sense, arithmetic is a language.* (Arithmetic is somewhat like a language.)

inasmuch as *conj.* **1** See INSOFAR AS. **2** *also* **for as much as** *formal* Because; for the reason that; since. *Inasmuch as this is your team, you have the right to choose your own captain.* (For the reason that this is your team, you have the right to choose your own captain.) *Inasmuch as the waves are high, I shall not go out in the boat.* (Because the waves are high, I shall not go out in the boat.)

in a sort of way See IN A WAY 1.

in a spot See ON THE SPOT 2.

in a trice See IN A FLASH.

in at the kill *adj. phr., informal* Watching or taking part, usually with pleasure, at the end of a struggle; present at the finish.—A cliché. *Frank and John have been quarreling for a long time and tonight they are having a fight. Bill says he wants to be in at the kill, because he is Frank's friend.* (Bill wants to be there and hopes that Frank wins.)

in a walk See WIN IN A WALK.

in a way *adv. phr.* **1** *also informal* **in a kind of way** *or informal* **in a sort of way** To a certain extent; a little; somewhat. *I like Jane in a way, but she is very proud.* (I like Jane partly, even though she is proud.) Compare AFTER A FASHION, MORE OR LESS. **2** In one thing. *In a way, this book is easier; it is much shorter.* (This book is shorter. In this respect it is easier.)

in awe of See STAND IN AWE OF.

in a while See AFTER WHILE, EVERY NOW AND THEN *or* EVERY ONCE IN A WHILE.

in a whole skin See WITH A WHOLE SKIN.

in a word See IN BRIEF.

in a world of one's own *or* **in a world by oneself** **1** In the place where you belong; in your own personal surroundings; apart from other people. *They are in a little world of their own in their house on the mountain.* (Their house is alone and not near other people.) **2a** In deep thought or concentration. *Mary is in a world of her own when she is playing the piano.* (Mary pays no attention to anything else when she plays the piano.) Compare LOSE ONESELF. **2b** *slang* Not caring about or connected with other people in thoughts or actions.—Usually used sarcastically. *That boy is in a world all by himself. He never knows what is happening around him.* (He doesn't see or care about what is happening.)

in a zone *adv., slang, informal* In a daze; in a daydream; in a state of being unable to concentrate. *Professor Smith puts everyone in a zone.* (Professor Smith's lectures make the audience unable to concentrate; their minds start to wander as in a daydream.)

in back of See BACK OF.

in bad *adv. phr., substandard* Out of favor; unpopular; in difficulty; in trouble. *No, I can't go swimming today. Father told me to stay home, and I don't want to get in bad.* (I don't want to get in trouble.)—Usually used with *with*. *Mary is in bad with the teacher for cheating on the test.* (Mary is in trouble with her teacher.) *The boy is in bad with the police for breaking windows.* (The boy is in trouble with the police.) Contrast IN GOOD, IN ONE'S FAVOR.

in behalf of *or* **on behalf of** *prep., formal* **1** In place of; as a representative of; for. *John accepted the championship award on behalf of the team.* (John was given the award as the representative of the team; he received it for all of them.) **2** As a help to; for the good of. *The minister worked hard all his life in behalf of the poor.* (The minister worked to help poor people.) Compare IN ONE'S BEHALF, IN ONE'S FAVOR.

in black and white See BLACK AND WHITE.

in brief *or* **in short** *or* **in a word** *adv. phr.* Briefly; to give the meaning of what has been said or written in a word or in a few words; in summary. *The children could play as long as they liked, they had no work to do, and* *nobody scolded them; in short, they were happy.* (With all their freedoms, it added up to complete happiness.) *The speaker didn't know his subject, nor did he speak well; in brief, he was disappointing.* (He was a poor speaker in many ways.) *John is smart, polite, and well-behaved. In a word, he is admirable.* (John has so many good qualities that he must be admired.)

in cahoots with   See IN LEAGUE WITH.

in case[1] *or* **in the event**   *conj.* If it happens that; if it should happen that; if; lest. *Tom took his skates in case they found a place to skate.* (Tom wanted to have his skates with him to use if they found a place to skate.) *Let me know in case you're not coming.* (Let me know if you're not coming.) *The night watchman is in the store in case there is ever a fire.* (The watchman will see a fire if there should ever be one.) *Keep the window closed in case it rains.* (Keep the window closed lest the rain should come in.) *I stayed home in case you called.* (I stayed home so that if you called, I would be there.) *In the event that our team wins, there will be a big celebration.* (If our team wins, there will be a celebration.) *What shall we do in case it snows?* (What shall we do if that happens?)

in case[2]   *adv. phr., informal* In order to be prepared; as a precaution; if there is need.— Usually used in the phrase *just in case. The bus is usually on time, but start early, just in case.* (The bus is usually on time, but you should start early so that you will be there if it leaves early.) *The big dog was tied up, but John carried a stick, just in case.* (John carried the stick to protect himself if the dog got loose and tried to bite him.)

in case of *also* **in the event of**   *prep.* In order to meet the possibility of; lest there is; if there is; if there should be. *Take your umbrellas in case of rain.* (Take your umbrellas so that if there is rain you will be ready.) *The wall was built along the river in case of floods.* (The wall was built in order to guard against possible floods.)

inch   See BY INCHES, EVERY INCH, GIVE ONE AN INCH AND HE WILL TAKE A MILE, WITHIN AN ACE OF *or* WITHIN AN INCH OF, WITHIN AN INCH OF ONE'S LIFE.

in character   *adv. or adj. phr.* **1** In agreement with a person's character or personality; in the way that a person usually behaves or is supposed to behave; as usual; characteristic; typical; suitable. *John was very rude at the party, and that was not in character because he is usually very polite.* (John did not behave politely as he usually does.) *The way Judy comforted the little girl was in character. She did it gently and kindly.* (She comforted the little girl just as she always was kind to anyone in trouble.) **2** Suitable for the part or the kind of part being acted; natural to the way a character in a book or play is supposed to act. *The fat actor in the movie was in character because the character he played was supposed to be fat and jolly.* (The fat actor was just right for the part he played in the movie.) *It would not have been in character for Robin Hood to steal from a poor man.* (Robin Hood did not steal from the poor. He stole from the rich to give to the poor.) Contrast OUT OF CHARACTER.

in charge   *adv. or adj. phr.* **1** In authority or control; in a position to care for or supervise; responsible. *If you have any questions, ask the boss. He's in charge.* (The boss decides everything and will answer your questions.) **2** Under care or supervision. *The sick man was taken in charge by the doctor.* (The sick man was taken under the care of the doctor.) *During your visit to the library, you will be in the librarian's charge.* (The librarian will tell you what to do.) Compare TAKE CARE OF.

in charge of   *prep.* **1** Responsible for; having supervision or care of. *Marian is in charge of selling tickets.* (Marian takes care of the tickets and is responsible for selling them.) *The girl in charge of refreshments forgot to order the ice cream for the party.* (The girl who was supposed to get the refreshments forgot the ice cream.) *When our class had a play, the teacher put Harold in charge of the stage curtain.* (The teacher told Harold to pull open or shut the curtain at the right time.) **2** *or* **in the charge of** Under the care or supervision of. *Mother puts the baby in the charge of the baby-sitter while she is out.* (Mother put the baby under the baby-sitter's care.) *The money was given in charge of Mr. Jackson for safe-keeping.* (The money was given to Mr. Jackson and he will be responsible for it.)

in check   *adv. phr.* In a position where movement or action is not allowed or stopped; under control; kept quiet or back. *The boy was too small to keep the big dog in check, and the dog broke away from his leash.* (The boy was too small to hold the dog by his leash and the dog ran away.) *The soldiers tried to keep the attacking Indians in check until help came.* (They tried to keep away the Indians until help came.) *Mary couldn't hold her feelings in check any longer and began to cry.* (She could not stop her tears.)

in circles   See IN A CIRCLE.

in circulation *or* **into circulation**   *adj. phr., informal* Going around and doing things as usual; joining what others are doing. *John broke his leg and was out of school for several weeks, but now he is back in circulation again.* (Now he is able to go around and do things again.) *Mary's mother punished her by stopping her from dating for two weeks, but then she got back into circulation.* (After two weeks she could have dates again.) Contrast OUT OF CIRCULATION.

in clover *or* **in the clover**   *adv. or adj. phr.,*

informal In rich comfort; rich or successful; having a pleasant or easy life.—A cliché. *They live in clover because their father is rich.* (They are wealthy and have everything they need.) *When we finish the hard part we'll be in the clover.* (When we finish the hard part, we can do the easy and pleasant part.) Compare BED OF ROSES, LIFE OF RILEY, LIVE HIGH OFF THE HOG, ON EASY STREET.

in cold blood *adv. phr.* Without feeling or pity; in a purposely cruel way; coolly and deliberately.—A cliché. *The bank robbers planned to shoot in cold blood anyone who got in their way.* (They planned to shoot without pity anyone who got in their way.) *The soldiers planned to murder in cold blood all Indians in the camp by the river.* (The soldiers planned to kill without pity all Indians living by the river.)

in commission *or* **into commission** *adv. or adj. phr.* **1** On duty or ready to be put on duty by a naval or military service; in active service. *The old battleship has been in commission for twenty years.* (The battleship has been on duty in the Navy for twenty years.) *It took many months to build the new bomber, and now it is ready to be put into commission.* (The bomber is ready for service. It has guns and equipment and men to fly it.) **2** In proper condition; in use or ready for use; working; running. *The wheel of my bicycle was broken, but it is back in commission now.* (The wheel of my bicycle was broken but it has been fixed.) Compare IN ORDER 2. Contrast OUT OF COMMISSION 2.

in common *adv. phr.* Shared together or equally; in use or ownership by all. *Mr. and Mrs. Smith own the store in common.* (Mr. and Mrs. Smith own the store together.) *The four boys grew up together and have a lot in common.* (The boys shared many experiences together.) *The swimming pool is used in common by all the children in the neighborhood.* (All the children in the neighborhood may use the pool.) Compare COMMON GROUND.

in condition See IN SHAPE.

in consequence *adv. phr.* As a result; therefore; so. *Jennie got up late, and in consequence she missed the bus.* (Because she got up late, Jennie missed the bus.) *You studied hard, and in consequence you passed the test.* (You studied hard, so you passed the test.)

in consequence of *prep., formal* As a result of. *In consequence of the deep snow, school will not open today.* (Because the snow is so deep, there will be no school today.) *In consequence of his promise to pay for the broken window, Bill was not punished.* (He wasn't punished, because he promised to pay for it.) Compare BECAUSE OF, ON ACCOUNT OF.

in consideration of *adv. phr.* **1** After thinking about and weighing; because of. *In consideration of the boy's young age, the judge did not put him in jail for carrying a gun.*

(The judge thought about the boy's young age and decided not to jail him.) **2** In exchange for; because of; in payment for. *In consideration of the extra work Joe had done, his boss gave him an extra week's pay.* (He gave Joe more money to pay for the extra work.) Compare IN RETURN.

in deep *adj. phr.* Seriously mixed up in something, especially trouble. *George began borrowing small sums of money to bet on horses, and before he knew it he was in deep.* (George was in serious trouble; he lost the money and could not pay it back.) Compare DEEP WATER, UP TO THE CHIN IN.

in deep water See DEEP WATER.

in defiance of *prep.* Acting against; in disobedience to. *The girl chewed gum in defiance of the teacher's rule.* (It was against the rule to chew gum, but the girl did not obey.) *Bob stayed up late in defiance of the coach's orders.* (The coach told the boys to go to bed early, but Bob did not do it.)

in demand *adj. phr.* Needed; wanted. *Men to shovel snow were in demand after the snow storm.* (There was a need for men to help remove the snow.) *The book about dogs was much in demand in the library.* (Many children wanted to read the book about dogs that was in the library.)

Indian See CIGAR-STORE INDIAN.

Indian sign *n., informal* A magic spell that is thought to bring bad luck; curse; jinx; hoodoo.—Used with *the,* usually after *have* or *with;* and often used in a joking way. *Bill is a good player, but Ted has the Indian sign on him and always beats him.* (Bill is a good player but he is unlucky when he plays Ted.) *Father says that he always wins our checker games because he has put the Indian sign on me, but I think he is joking.* (He says that he has put a magic spell on me but he is joking.) Compare GET ONE'S NUMBER.

in dispute *adj. phr.* Disagreed about; being argued. *The penalty ordered by the referee was in dispute by one of the teams.* (One team did not agree with the punishment given by the referee.) *Everyone in the class wanted to say something about the subject in dispute.* (Each student wanted to give his belief about the thing being argued.)

in due course *or* **in due season** *or* **in due time** See IN GOOD TIME 2.

in due season *or* **in due time** See IN GOOD TIME.

industrial park *n., informal* A complex of industrial buildings and/or businesses usually located far from the center of a city in a setting especially landscaped to make such buildings look better. *The nearest supermarket that sells car tires is at the industrial park twenty miles from downtown.* (The store is within the group of buildings located 20 miles out of town.)

in Dutch *adj. phr., slang* In trouble. *George*

got in Dutch with his father when he broke a window. (George broke a window and got in trouble with his father.) John was in Dutch with his mother because he tore his new jacket. (John tore his new jacket, and his mother was angry.)

in earnest adv. or adj. phr. Seriously; in a determined way. The beaver was building his dam in earnest. (The beaver was working very hard on his dam.) Bill did his homework in earnest. (Bill was serious about his school work.)—Often used like a predicate adjective. Sometimes used with dead, for emphasis. Betty's friends thought she was joking when she said she wanted to be a doctor, but she was in dead earnest. (She really wanted to become a doctor.)

in effect adv. or adj. phr. 1 The same in meaning or result. The teacher gave the same assignment, in effect, that she gave yesterday. (The teacher gave almost the same thing to study today that she gave yesterday.) Helping your mother with the dishes is in effect earning your allowance. (If you wash and dry the dishes that is like earning the money which your parents give you.) 2 Necessary to obey; being enforced. The coach says that players must be in bed by midnight, and that rule is in effect tonight. (The rule must be obeyed tonight; the coach will punish players who break the rule.) Syn. IN FORCE.

in effigy See HANG IN EFFIGY or BURN IN EFFIGY.

in evidence adj. phr. Easily seen; noticeable. The little boy's measles were very much in evidence. (It was easy to see that the little boy had measles.) The tulips were blooming; spring was in evidence. (The tulips blooming were a sign of spring.)

in fact also **in point of fact** adv. phr. Really; truthfully.—Often used for emphasis. No one believed it but, in fact, Mary did get an A on her book report. (Mary really got an A on her book report.) It was a very hot day; in fact, it was 100 degrees. (It was 100 degrees and a very hot day.) Compare MATTER OF FACT.

in favor of prep. On the side of; in agreement with. Everyone in the class voted in favor of the party. (All of the children voted to have a party.) Most girls are in favor of wearing lipstick. (The girls agree with the idea of wearing lipstick.) Compare IN BACK OF 2.

in fear and trembling See FEAR AND TREMBLING.

in for prep., informal Unable to avoid; sure to get. The naughty puppy was in for a spanking. (The bad little puppy was sure to get spanked.) On Christmas morning we are in for some surprises. (We will certainly have some surprises on Christmas morning.) We saw Father looking angrily out of the broken window, and we knew we were in for it. (We knew that Father would punish us for break-

ing the window.) 2 See HAVE IT IN FOR.

in force adj. phr. 1 To be obeyed. New times for eating meals are now in force. (The schedule in the dining room has been changed.) Syn. IN EFFECT. 2 In a large group. People went to see the parade in force. (Nearly all of the people went together at the same time to see the parade.) Syn. EN MASSE.

in front of prep. Ahead of; before. The rabbit was running in front of the dog. (A dog was chasing a rabbit and the rabbit was ahead of the dog.) A big oak tree stood in front of the building. (The building had a large oak tree in the front yard.) Contrast IN BACK OF 1.

in full swing adj. phr. Actively going on; in full action. The Valentine party was in full swing. (The Valentine party was gay with games being played and ice cream being served.) All of the children were planting seeds; the gardening project was in full swing. (The children were all actively at work planting a garden.)

in general[1] adv. phr. Usually; very often. In general, mother makes good cookies. (Mother usually makes good cookies.) The weather in Florida is warm in general. (Weather in Florida is very often warm.) Compare ON THE WHOLE 2.

in general[2] adj. phr. Most; with few exceptions. Women in general like to shop for new clothes. (Most women like to look for and buy new clothes.) Boys in general like active sports more than girls do. (With few exceptions, boys like active sports more than girls do.) Contrast IN PARTICULAR.

in glass houses See PEOPLE WHO LIVE IN GLASS HOUSES SHOULD NOT THROW STONES.

in good adj. phr., informal Well liked; accepted.—Used with with. The boy washed the blackboards so that he would get in good with his teacher. (The boy felt that if he did an extra job, his teacher would like him more.) Although Tom was younger, he was in good with the older boys. (Tom was younger than the other boys but they liked him.) Compare ON ONE'S GOOD SIDE. Contrast IN BAD.

in good faith See GOOD FAITH.

in good season See IN GOOD TIME.

in good stead See STAND IN GOOD STEAD.

in good time or **in good season** adv. phr. 1 A little early; sooner than necessary. The school bus arrived in good time. (The bus came into the yard before the bell rang.) The students finished their school work in good time. (They finished it before the time when the teacher said they must stop.) We reached the station in good season to catch the 9:15 bus for New York. (We arrived at the station early enough to get on the 9:15 bus.) 2 or **in due course** or **in due season** or **in due time** In the usual amount of time; at the right time; in the end. Spring and summer will arrive in due course. (The seasons will come when the right amount of time has passed.) *Sally finished her spelling in due course.* (Sally got through with her spelling lesson at the right time.)

in half *adv. phr.* **1** Into two equal parts. *The ticket taker at the football game tore the tickets in half.* (The ticket taker tore the tickets into two pieces.) *Mother cut the apple in half so each child could have an equal share.* (Mother divided the apple in two equal parts.) Syn. IN TWO. **2** To half the size before; to one half as big. *As a punishment, Father cut Bob's allowance in half.* (Father gave Bob only one dollar a week instead of two dollars a week.)

in hand *adv. or adj. phr.* **1** Under control. *The principal was happy to find that the new teacher had her class in hand.* (The teacher had her class under control.) *The baby-sitter kept the children well in hand.* (The children were obeying the baby-sitter.) *Mabel was frightened when the barking dog ran at her, but she soon got herself in hand and walked on.* (Mabel soon controlled her fear and was able to go ahead.) Contrast OUT OF HAND. **2** In your possession; with you.—Often used in the phrase *cash in hand. Tom figured that his cash in hand with his weekly pay would be enough to buy a car.* (Tom thought that the money he already had added to the pay he would get was enough for a car.) Compare ON HAND. **3** Being worked on; with you to do. *We should finish the work we have in hand before we begin something new.* (We should first finish the work we have started.)

in honor of *prep.* As an honor to; for showing respect or thanks to. *We celebrate Mother's Day in honor of our mothers.* (One day of each year is set aside as a special day to show our thanks and respect to our mothers.) *The city dedicated a monument in honor of the general.* (The city put up a monument to show its respect for the general.)

in hopes *adj. phr.* Hopeful; hoping. *The Mayor was in hopes of having a good day for the parade.* (The Mayor was wishing for a good day for the parade.) *Mother was in hopes that the cake would be good to eat.* (Mother wanted the cake to be liked by all who ate it.)

in horror See THROW UP ONE'S HANDS IN HORROR.

in hot water See HOT WATER.

in itself See END IN ITSELF.

injury See ADD INSULT TO INJURY.

in keeping *adj. phr.* Going well together; agreeing; similar. *Mary's hair style was in keeping with the latest fashion.* (Mary's hair style was just right.) *Having an assembly on Friday morning was in keeping with the school program.* (The Friday assembly was the usual procedure of the school.) Contrast OUT OF KEEPING.

in kind *adv. phr.* In a similar way; with the same kind of thing. *My neighbor pays me in kind for walking her dog.* (My neighbor often walks my dog to repay me for walking hers.) *Lois returned Mary's insult in kind.* (Because Mary insulted Lois, Lois insulted Mary.)

in knots See TIE IN KNOTS.

in league with *or informal* **in cahoots with** *prep.* In secret agreement or partnership with (someone); working together secretly with, especially for harm. *People once believed that some women were witches in league with the devil.* (Long ago people believed that some women secretly helped the devil do harm.) *The mayor's enemies spread a rumor that he was in cahoots with gangsters.* (The mayor's enemies told people that the mayor secretly worked with gangsters.)

in left field See OUT IN LEFT FIELD.

in lieu of See INSTEAD OF.

in light of *also* **in the light of** *adj. phr.* **1** As a result of new information; by means of new ideas. *The teacher changed John's grade in the light of the extra work in the work book.* (When the teacher saw the extra work that John had done, he changed the grade.) **2** Because of. *In light of the muddy field, the football team wore their old uniforms.* (The field was muddy, so the team decided to wear old uniforms.) Syn. IN VIEW OF.

in line[1] *adv. phr.* In or into a straight line. *The boys stood in line to buy their tickets.* (The boys stood one behind the other at the ticket window.) *Tom set the chairs in line along the wall.* (Tom put the chairs one beside the other along the wall.) *The carpenter put the edges of the boards in line.* (The carpenter made the edge of one board lie along the edge of the other.)

in line[2] *adj. phr.* **1** In a position in a series or after someone else. *John is in line for the presidency of the club next year.* (John is likely to be the next president of the club.) *Mary is fourth in line to be admitted to the sorority.* (Mary will be admitted to the sorority after the three other girls are admitted.) **2** Obeying or agreeing with what is right or usual; doing or being what people expect or accept; within ordinary or proper limits. *The coach kept the excited team in line.* (The coach made the team do what was right; he kept them under control.) *When the teacher came back into the room, she quickly brought the ̖class back in line.* (The teacher made the class calm down and pay attention.) *The government passed a new law to keep prices in line.* (The law will keep prices from becoming too high.) Compare IN HAND. Contrast OUT OF LINE.

in line with *prep.* In agreement with. *Behavior at school parties must be in line with school rules.* (The things students do at parties in the school must follow the school rules.) *In line with the custom of the school, the students had a holiday between Christmas and New Years Day.* (The Christmas holiday agrees with school custom; it follows the usual practice.)

in love *adj. phr.* Liking very much; loving. *John is in love with Helen.* (John likes Helen very much.) *Tom and Ellen are in love.* (Tom and Ellen love each other.) *Mary is in love with her new wristwatch.* (Mary likes her new wristwatch very much.)

in luck *adj. phr.* Being lucky; having good luck; finding something good by chance. *Bill was in luck when he found the money on the street.* (Bill found some money that he did not expect to find.) *Mary dropped her glasses and they did not break. She was in luck.* (It was lucky that Mary's glasses did not break when she dropped them.)

in memory of *prep.* As something that makes people remember (a person or thing); as a reminder of; as a memorial to. *The building was named Ford Hall in memory of a man named James Ford.* (The people gave the building the name of a man that they wanted to remember.) *Many special ceremonies are in memory of famous men.* (People often have special programs to honor famous men.)

in midair See UP IN THE AIR 2.

in mind *adv. phr.* **1** In the center of your thought; in your close attention. *You have to be home by 11 o'clock. Keep that in mind, Bob.* (Don't forget that you have to be home by 11, Bob.) *Mary is studying hard with a good grade in mind.* (Mary is studying hard because she keeps thinking about the good grade she wants to get.) *Bear in mind the rules of safety when you swim.* (Keep remembering the safety rules when you swim.) *Bill's father told him to bear in mind that his allowance had to last all week.* (He told him not to forget that he must not spend his allowance all at once.) Compare ON ONE'S MIND. **2** See PUT IN MIND OF.

in name *adj. or adv. phr.* Having a title, but not really doing what someone with the title is expected to do. *The old man is a doctor in name only. He does not have patients now.* (The doctor has retired, but he still is called doctor.) *He was the captain of the team in name only.* (He was called the captain of the team, but he did not lead the other players.)

inner city *n., colloquial* Densely populated areas in large metropolitan areas inhabited by low income families usually of minority backgrounds, such as Mexicans, Puerto Ricans, or blacks; characterized by slums and government owned high rises. *Joe comes from the inner city—he may need help with his reading.* (He comes from a part of the city where students are educationally deprived; he may need help.)

in nothing flat See IN NO TIME.

in no time *or* **in nothing flat** *adv. phr., informal* In a very little time; soon; quickly. *When the entire class worked together they finished the project in no time.* (Working to-gether, the class finished the project quickly.) *The bus filled with students in nothing flat.* (The bus was quickly filled with students.)

in no uncertain terms See IN SO MANY WORDS 2.

in on *prep.* **1** Joining together for. *The children collected money from their classmates and went in on a present for their teacher.* (The children shared their money and bought a present for their teacher.) **2** Told about; having knowledge of. *Bob was in on the secret.* (Bob knew the secret.) *The other girls wouldn't let Mary in on what they knew.* (The other girls wouldn't tell Mary what they knew.)

in one fell swoop *or* **at one fell swoop** *adv. phr.* **1** *literary* In one attack or accident; in one bad blow. *The millionaire lost his money and his friends at one fell swoop.* (He lost money and friends in one unlucky happening.) **2** At one time; at the same time. *Three cars drove into the driveway, and Mrs. Crane's dinner guests all arrived at one fell swoop.* (They all came at the same time.)

in one ear and out the other See GO IN ONE EAR AND OUT THE OTHER.

in one's bad graces *adj. phr.* Not approved by; not liked by. *John was in his mother's bad graces because he spilled his milk on the tablecloth.* (His mother did not like him to spill the milk on the tablecloth.) *Don got in the bad graces of the teacher by laughing at her hat.* (John is not liked by the teacher because he laughed at her hat.) Compare DOWN ON, IN BAD, OUT OF FAVOR. Contrast IN ONE'S GOOD GRACES.

in one's behalf *or* **on one's behalf** *adv. phr., informal* **1** For someone else; in your place. *My husband could not be here tonight, but I want to thank you on his behalf.* (I want to thank you for him.) **2** For the good of another person or group; as a help to someone. *My teacher went to the factory and spoke in my behalf when I was looking for a job.* (My teacher talked to someone at the factory to help me get a job.) Compare IN BEHALF OF, ON ONE'S ACCOUNT.

in one's blood *or* **into one's blood** *adv. phr.* Agreeing perfectly with one's sympathies, feelings, and desires.—A cliché. *Living in a warm section of the country gets in your blood.* (You get to love deeply living in a warm section of the country.) *The woods got into Jim's blood.* (Jim got to love living in the woods.) Contrast OUT OF ONE'S BLOOD.

in one's bones See FEEL IN ONE'S BONES.

in one's boots See DIE IN ONE'S BOOTS *or* DIE WITH ONE'S BOOTS ON, IN ONE'S SHOES *also* IN ONE'S BOOTS.

in one's craw *or* **in one's crop** See STICK IN ONE'S CRAW *or* STICK IN ONE'S CROP.

in one's cups *adj. phr., literary* Drunk. *The man was in his cups and talking very loudly.*

(The man was drunk and talked in a loud voice.)

in one's element *adv. phr.* **1** In one's natural surroundings. *The deep-sea fish is in his element in deep ocean water.* (The deep-sea fish can live only in the deep ocean.) **2** Where you can do your best. *John is in his element working on the farm.* (John likes the farm and does his best work there.) Compare AT HOME 2. Contrast OUT OF ONE'S ELEMENT.

in one's face *adv. phr.* **1** Against your face. *The trick cigar blew up in the clown's face.* (It blew up next to his face while he was smoking it.) *A cold wind was in our faces as we walked to school.* (A cold wind blew against us.) **2** In front of you. *The maid slammed the door in the salesman's face.* (She slammed the door in front of him.) *I told the boys that they were wrong, but they laughed in my face.* (The boys laughed in front of me for saying they were wrong.) Compare IN THE FACE OF, THROW —— IN ONE'S FACE, TO ONE'S FACE, UNDER ONE'S NOSE.

in one's favor *adv. or adj. phr.* In a way that is good for you. *Both teams claimed the point, but the referee decided in our favor.* (The referee decided we were right; he gave us the point.) *Bob made good grades in high school, and that was in his favor when he looked for a job.* (Bob's good grades helped him get a job.) Compare COME ONE'S WAY.

in one's footsteps See FOLLOW IN ONE'S FOOTSTEPS.

in one's glory *adj. phr.* Pleased and contented with yourself. *When John won the race, he was in his glory.* (John was very proud of himself.) *Tom is very vain, and praise puts him in his glory.* (Tom likes to be praised.)

in one's good books See IN ONE'S GOOD GRACES.

in one's good graces *or* **in one's good books** *adv. phr.* Approved of by you; liked by someone. *Ruth is in her mother's good graces because she ate all her supper.* (Her mother likes her to eat all her supper.) *Bill is back in the good graces of his girl friend because he gave her a box of candy.* (Bill's girl friend is not angry with him any more because he gave her candy.) Compare IN GOOD. Contrast IN ONE'S BAD GRACES.

in one's grave See TURN IN ONE'S GRAVE *or* TURN OVER IN ONE'S GRAVE.

in one's hands See TAKE ONE'S LIFE IN ONE'S HANDS.

in one's hair *adj. phr., informal* Bothering you again and again; always annoying. *Johnny got in Father's hair when he was trying to read the paper by running and shouting.* (Johnny kept disturbing Father while he was reading.) *The grown-ups sent the children out to play so that the children wouldn't be in their hair while they were talking.* (The grown-ups didn't want to be annoyed by the children so they sent them outside.) Compare GIVE A HARD TIME, IN ONE'S WAY. Contrast OUT OF ONE'S HAIR.

in one's mind's eye *adv. phr.* In the memory; in the imagination. *In his mind's eye he saw again the house he had lived in when he was a child.* (In his memory, he was able to see the house he had lived in when he was a child.) *In his mind's eye, he could see just what the vacation was going to be like.* In his imagination he pictured the things he would do on his vacation.)

in one's mouth See BUTTER WOULDN'T MELT IN ONE'S MOUTH, MELT IN ONE'S MOUTH.

in one's own juice See STEW IN ONE'S OWN JUICE.

in one's shell *or* **into one's shell** *adv. or adj. phr., informal* In or into bashfulness; into silence; not sociable; unfriendly.—A cliché. *After Mary's mother scolded her, she went into her shell.* (Mary became very quiet after the scolding.) *The teacher tried to get Rose to talk to her, but she stayed in her shell.* (She was shy and silent.) Contrast OUT OF ONE'S SHELL.

in one's shoes *also* **in one's boots** *adv. phr.* In or into one's place or position. *How would you like to be in a lion tamer's boots?* (How would you like to be a lion tamer?) Compare PUT ONESELF IN ANOTHER'S PLACE, STEP INTO ONE'S SHOES.

in one's sleeve See UP ONE'S SLEEVE.

in one's tracks *adv. phr., informal* **1** Just where one is at the moment; abruptly; immediately. *The hunter's rifle cracked and the rabbit dropped in his tracks.* (At the sound of the rifle, the rabbit fell down right where he was.) *Mary stopped dead in her tracks, turned around, and ran back home.* (Mary stopped suddenly where she was and turned around.) Syn. ON THE SPOT 1, THEN AND THERE. **2** See FOLLOW IN ONE'S FOOTSTEPS.

in one's way *adv. or adj. phr.* **1** Within reach; likely to be met; before you. *The chance to work for a printer was put in my way.* (I was offered the chance.) Compare PUT IN THE WAY OF. **2** *or* **in the way** In your path as a hindrance; placed so as to block the way. *Fred tried to get to the door, but the table was in the way.* (The table stopped him from getting to the door.) *A tree had fallen across the street and was in Father's way as he drove.* (Father could not get past the fallen tree with his car.) *Mary tried to clean the house, but the baby was always in the way.* (The baby stopped Mary from getting the housework done.)

in order *adv. or adj. phr.* **1** In arrangement; in the proper way of following one another. *Come to my desk in alphabetical order as I call your names.* (Follow one another alphabetically.) *Line up and walk to the door in order.* (Walk to the door in your proper places in line.) *Name all the Presidents in* *order.* (Name the Presidents as they followed one another.) Compare IN TURN. **2** In proper condition. *The car was in good working order when I bought it.* (The car ran well and was in good condition.) *The club leader looked at the club treasurer's records of money collected and spent, and found them all in order.* (The records were all correct.) Compare IN COMMISSION 2, PUT ONE'S HOUSE IN ORDER. **3** Following the rules; proper, suitable. *Is it in order to ask the speaker questions at the meeting?* (Is it proper according to the rules to ask questions?) *At the end of a program, applause for the performers is in order.* (Applause is proper at the end of the program.) Compare IN PLACE. Contrast OUT OF ORDER. **3** See PUT ONE'S HOUSE IN ORDER *or* SET ONE'S HOUSE IN ORDER.

in order that See SO THAT 1.

in order to *or* **so as to** *conj.* For the purpose of; to.—Used with an infinitive. *In order to follow the buffalo, the Indians often had to move their camps.* (The reason that the Indians moved camp often was to follow the buffalo.) *We picked apples so as to make a pie.* (We picked apples for the purpose of making a pie.) Compare SO THAT.

in part *adv. phr.* To some extent; partly; not wholly.—Often used with *large* or *small. We planted the garden in part with flowers. But in large part we planted vegetables.* (We planted a part of the garden with flowers, but we planted mostly vegetables.) *Tom was only in small part responsible.* (Tom was responsible but only a little bit.)

in particular *adv. phr.* In a way apart from others; more than others; particularly; especially. *The speaker talked about sports in general and about football in particular.* (He said some things that are true about any sports and some things that are true only about football.) *All the boys played well and Bill in particular.* (Although all the boys played well, Bill was especially good.) *Margaret liked all her classes, but she liked sewing class in particular.* (Margaret liked sewing class best.) Contrast IN GENERAL.

in passing *adv. phr.* While talking about that subject; as extra information; also. *Our teacher showed us different kinds of flowers and told us in passing that those flowers came from her garden.* (Our teacher told us in addition that those flowers came from her garden.) *The writer of the story says he grew up in New York and mentions in passing that his parents came from Italy.* (While telling where he came from, the writer also tells where his parents came from.) Compare BY THE WAY.

in person *also* **in the flesh** *adv. phr.* Yourself; personally. *A TV actor appeared in person today in school.* (The TV actor, himself, appeared in school today.) *The governor cannot march in the parade in person today but his wife will march.* (The governor cannot personally march in the parade but his

wife will march.) Compare FACE-TO-FACE 2. Contrast INSTEAD OF.

in place[1] *adv. phr.* **1a** In the right or usual place or position. *Nothing is in place after the earthquake. Even trees and houses are turned over.* (Trees and houses are not where they have always been and should be after the earthquake.) *The picture is not in place on the wall. It is crooked.* (The picture is not hanging where it should on the wall.) **1b** In one place. *Our first exercise in gym class was running in place.* (Our first exercise was running in one spot, not moving ahead.) **2** In proper order. *Stay in place in line, children.* (Keep in order in line, children.) Compare IN ORDER. Contrast OUT OF PLACE.

in place[2] *adj. phr.* In the right place or at the right time; suitable; timely. *A dog is not in place in a church.* (A dog should not be brought into a church. He does not belong there.) *Linda wondered if it would be in place to wish the bride good luck after the wedding.* (Linda wondered if saying "Good luck" to the bride would be the right thing to do.) Compare IN ORDER 1. Contrast OUT OF PLACE.

in place of See INSTEAD OF.

in practice[1] *also* **into practice** *adv. phr.* In actual doing. *The idea sounds good but will it work in practice?* (Will it work when it is really tried?) *It is easy to say that we will be good. It is harder to put the saying into practice.* (It is easier to say that we will be good than to really do it.)

in practice[2] *adj. phr.* In proper condition to do something well through practice. *A pianist gets his fingers in practice by playing scales.* (A pianist exercises his fingers by playing scales.) *An ice-skater keeps in practice by skating every day.* (A skater remains able to skate well by practicing every day.) Compare IN SHAPE. Contrast OUT OF PRACTICE.

in print *adj. phr.* Obtainable in printed form from a printer or publisher; printed. *The author has finished writing his book but it is not yet in print.* (The book is not yet printed or on sale by the publisher.) *The story of the students' trip to Washington appeared in print in the newspaper.* (The students' trip was written about and printed in the paper.) *It is a very old book and no longer in print.* (The book is old and is no longer printed by the publisher.) Contrast OUT OF PRINT.

in private *adj. or adv. phr.* Not openly or in public; apart from others; confidentially; secretly. *Mr. Jones waited until they were home in private before he punished his son.* (Mr. Jones did not punish his son outside in public but waited until they were home.) *The teacher told Susan that she wanted to talk to her in private after class.* (The teacher wanted to talk to Susan alone, apart from the rest of the class.) Compare IN SECRET. Contrast IN PUBLIC.

in progress *adj. phr.* Going ahead; being made or done; happening. *Plans are in progress to build a new school next year.* (Plans are going ahead to build a new school.) *A dog ran out on the playing field while the game was in progress.* (A dog ran on the field while the game was being played.) Contrast IN CHECK.

in public *adv. phr.* **1** In a place open to the people; in such a way that the public may see, hear, or know; not secretly; openly. *Two boys down the street are dancing in public for pennies.* (The boys are dancing where anyone can come to see them.) *Actors are used to appearing in public.* (Actors are used to appearing and speaking before people.) *The mayor has told his friends that he is sick but will not admit it in public.* (The mayor will not admit that he is sick except to his friends.) Contrast IN PRIVATE. **2** See AIR ONE'S DIRTY LINEN IN PUBLIC, *or* WASH ONE'S DIRTY LINEN IN PUBLIC.

in question *adj. phr.* **1** In doubt; in dispute; being argued about or examined. *I know Bill would be a good captain for the team. That is not in question. But does he want to be captain?* (I do not doubt that Bill would be a good captain; but I wonder if he wants to be captain.) Contrast BEYOND QUESTION. **2** Under discussion; being talked or thought about. *The girls in question are not in school today.* (The girls we are talking about are not in school.) *On the Christmas day in question, we could not go to Grandmother's house, as we do every year.* (On the Christmas day of the year we are talking about, we could not go to Grandmother's house.)

in quest of See IN SEARCH OF.

in reason *adv. phr., formal* Following the rules of reasoning; sensibly; reasonably. *One cannot in reason doubt that freedom is better than slavery.* (It is only sensible that freedom is better than slavery.)

in reference to *or* **with reference to** *or* **in regard to** *or* **with regard to** *prep.* In connection with; from the standpoint of; concerning; regarding; about. *I am writing with reference to your last letter.* (I am writing about your last letter.) *He spoke in reference to the Boy Scouts.* (He talked about the Boy Scouts.) *I spoke to him with regard to his low marks.* (I talked to him about his low marks.) *In regard to the test tomorrow, it is postponed.* (Concerning the test, it is put off until later.) Compare IN RELATION TO, IN RESPECT TO.

in regard to See IN REFERENCE TO.

in relation to *or* **with relation to** *prep.* In connection with; in dealing with; as concerns; in comparison to, respecting; about. *Father spoke about school in relation to finding a job when we are older.* (Father talked about school and how important it is in finding a job later.) *What did you say in relation to what happened yesterday?* (What did you say

about what happened yesterday?) *With relation to his job, skill is very important.* (Skill and know-how are very important in this job.) *In relation to Texas, Rhode Island is quite a small state.* (In comparison to Texas, Rhode Island is small.) Compare IN REFERENCE TO, IN RESPECT TO.

in respect to or with respect to In connection with; related to; about; on. *The teacher told stories about Washington and Lincoln in respect to the importance of being honest.* (The teacher told stories of Washington and Lincoln's honesty to show honesty is important.) *In respect to your visit with us, we hope you can come before September.* (We hope you can make the visit you promised us before September.) *There was no shortage in respect to food.* (There was plenty of food.) Compare AS TO, IN REFERENCE TO, IN RELATION TO.

in return *adv. phr.* In order to give back something; as payment; in recognition or exchange.—Often used with *for*. *Bud gave me his knife and I gave him marbles in return.* (I gave Bud back marbles for his knife.) *The lady helped Mother when she was sick and in return Mother often invited her to dinner.* (Mother invited the lady to dinner to show thanks for her kindness.) *How much did John give you in return for your bicycle?* (How much did John pay you for the bicycle?) *I hit him in return for the time he hit me.* (I hit him because he hit me.) *I wrote Dad a letter and got a package in return.* (I got a package in answer to my letter.)

in reverse *adj. or adv. phr.* In a backward direction; backward. *John hit the tree behind him when he put the car in reverse without looking first.* (John moved the car backward without first looking and hit a tree.) *The first of the year Bob did well in school, but then he started moving in reverse.* (Bob's grades began to get worse.)

ins and outs *n. phr.* The special ways of going somewhere or doing something; the different parts. *The janitor knows all the ins and outs of the big school building.* (The janitor knows every part of the building.) *Jerry's father is a good life insurance salesman; he knows all the ins and outs of the business.* (Jerry's father knows all about life insurance.)

in search of *or literary* **in quest of** *prep.* Seeking or looking for; in pursuit of. *Many men went West in search of gold.* (Many men went out West to try to find gold.) *The hunter stayed in the woods all day in quest of game.* (The hunter stayed all day to hunt game.) *We looked everywhere in search of our dog.* (We tried to find our dog everywhere.)

in season *adv. or adj. phr.* **1** *literary* At the proper or best time. *Fred's father told him that he was not old enough yet but that he would learn to drive in season.* (Fred would learn to drive when he became old enough.)

2a At the right or lawful time for hunting or catching. *Deer will be in season next week.* (Hunting deer will be allowed by the law next week.) *In spring we'll go fishing when trout are in season.* (We will go fishing during the fishing season.) **2b** At the right time or condition for using, eating, or marketing; in a ripe or eatable condition. *Christmas trees will be sold at the store in season.* (They will be sold at the right time before Christmas.) *Native tomatoes will be in season soon.* (Tomatoes grown in the nearby countryside will soon be ripe and can be bought.) *Oysters are in season during the "R" months.* (We can buy and eat oysters in the months which have "R" in them—September to April, but not May to August.) Compare IN GOOD TIME. Contrast OUT OF SEASON.

in secret *adv. phr.* In a private or secret way; in a hidden place. *The miser buried his gold in secret and no one knows where it is.* (The miser buried it in a secret hiding place.) *The robbers went away in secret after dark.* (The robbers left secretly without telling anyone.) Compare IN PRIVATE.

in shape *or* **in condition** *adj. phr.* In good condition; able to perform well. *The football team will be in shape for the first game of the season.* (The boys on the football team will be ready to play when it is time for the first game.) *Mary was putting her French in shape for the test.* (Mary was studying her French so she would do well on the test.) Compare IN PRACTICE. Contrast OUT OF SHAPE.

in short See IN BRIEF.

in short order *adv. phr.* Without delay; quickly. *Johnny got ready in short order after his father said that he could come to the ball game if he was ready in time.* (Johnny got ready quickly after his father spoke.)

in short supply *adj. phr.* Not enough; in too small a quantity or amount; in less than the amount or number needed. *The cookies are in short supply, so don't eat them all up.* (There are not enough cookies.) *We have five people and only four beds, so the beds are in short supply.* (We have fewer than the number of beds we need.)

inside See STEP INSIDE.

inside and out See INS AND OUTS, INSIDE OUT 2.

inside of *prep.* In; within; on or in an inside part of; not beyond; before the end of. *There is a broom inside of the closet.* (There is a broom in the closet.) *There is a label on the inside of the box.* (The label is on the inner side of the box.) *Hand your papers in to me inside of three days.* (Hand them in before three days are over.) Contrast OUTSIDE OF.

inside out *adv.* **1** So that the inside is turned outside. *Mother turns the stockings inside out when she washes them.* (Mother pulls the inside of the stockings to the outside.) **2** *or* **inside and out** *also* **in and out** In every part; throughout; completely. *David knows the parts of his bicycle inside out.* (David knows

all the parts of the bicycle and how they work.) *We searched the house inside and out for the kitten.* (We hunted in every part of the house.) Compare BACKWARDS AND FORWARDS, INS AND OUTS, THROUGH AND THROUGH.

inside track *n. phr.* **1** The inside, shortest distance around a curved racetrack; the place that is closest to the inside fence. *A big white horse had the inside track at the start of the race.* (A big white horse had the inside place and the other horses were following him in outside places.) **2** *informal* A favored place; an advantage. *John has the inside track for the job because he had the best marks.* (John will probably get the job because he had the best marks in school.)

insofar as *conj.* To the extent that; to the point that; as much as. *You will learn your lessons only insofar as you are willing to keep studying them.* (How well you learn your lessons depends on how well you study them.)

in so many words *adv. phr.* **1** In those exact words. *He hinted that he thought we were foolish but did not say so in so many words.* (He thought that we were foolish but he did not say that we were foolish.) **2** *or* **in no uncertain terms** In an outspoken way; plainly; directly. *I told him in so many words that he was crazy.* (I spoke up and told him plainly that he was crazy.) *Bob was very late for their date, and Mary told Bob in no uncertain terms what she thought of him.* (Mary was angry and did not talk politely.) Compare WORDS OF ONE SYLLABLE.

in someone else's shoes See IN ONE'S SHOES.

insomuch as See INASMUCH AS.

in spite of *prep. phr.* Against the influence or effect of; in opposition to; defying the effect of; despite. *In spite of the bad storm John delivered his papers on time.* (John did not let the storm keep him from delivering his papers.) *In spite of all their differences, Joan and Ann remain friends.* (Joan and Ann remain friends even though they are different.)

instance See FOR EXAMPLE *or* FOR INSTANCE.

in state See LIE IN STATE.

instead of *or* **in place of** *also formal* **in lieu of** *prep.* In the place of; in substitution for; in preference to; rather than. *I wore mittens instead of gloves.* (I wore mittens, not gloves.) *The grown-ups had coffee but the children wanted milk in place of coffee.* (The children wanted milk rather than coffee.) *The boys went fishing instead of going to school.* (They went fishing and did not go to school.) *The Vice-President talked at the meeting in place of the President, because the President was sick.* (The Vice-President spoke, not the President; he took the President's place.) *The magician appeared on the program in lieu of a singer.* (The singer could not appear on the program, so a magician substituted for him.) Compare IN PERSON.

in step *adv. or adj. phr.* **1** With the left or right foot stepping at the same time as another's or to the beat of music; in matching strides with another person or persons. *The long line of soldiers marched all in step: Left, right! Left, right!* (The soldiers all stepped together and at the same time with their left or right foot.) *Johnny marched behind the band in step to the music.* (Johnny marched in time to the beat of the music.) **2** In agreement; abreast.—Often followed by *with. Mary wanted to stay in step with her friends and have a doll too.* (Mary wanted to be like her friends who had dolls.) Contrast OUT OF STEP.

in stitches *adj. phr., informal* Laughing so hard that the sides ache; in a fit of laughing hard. *The comedian was so funny that he had everyone who was watching him in stitches.* (Everyone laughed at the comedian until it hurt to laugh any more.)

in stock *adj. phr.* Having something ready to sell or use; in present possession or supply; to be sold. *The store had no more red shoes in stock, so Mary chose brown ones instead.* (There were no more red shoes in the store's supply of shoes.) Compare IN STORE, ON HAND. Contrast OUT OF STOCK.

in store *adj. or adv. phr.* **1** Saved up in case of need; ready for use or for some purpose. *If the electricity goes off, we have candles in store in the closet.* (We have candles put away if we need them for light.) *The squirrel has plenty of nuts in store for the winter.* (He has saved the nuts for winter.) Compare IN RESERVE, IN STOCK, ON HAND. **2** Ready to happen; waiting.—Often used in the phrase *hold* or *have in store. What does the future hold in store for the boy who ran away?* (What will happen to the boy? *There is a surprise in store for Helen when she gets home.* (A surprise is waiting for her.)

in stride See TAKE IN STRIDE.

in substance *adv. phr.* In important facts; in the main or basic parts; basically; really. *In substance the weather report said that it will be a nice day tomorrow.* (What the weather report really said was that tomorrow would be a nice day.) *The two cars are the same in substance, except one is red and the other is red and white.* (The main parts of the cars are the same but they are painted differently.)

insult See ADD INSULT TO INJURY.

intent See TO ALL INTENTS AND PURPOSES.

in terms of *prep.* **1** In the matter of; on the subject of; especially about; about. *He spoke about books in terms of their publication.* (He spoke about books and especially about their publication.) *What have you done in terms of fixing the house?* (What have you done about the matter of fixing the house?) *The children ate a great many hot dogs at the party. In terms of money, they ate $20 worth.* (They ate about $20 worth of hot dogs.) **2** As to the amount or number of. *We swam a great distance. In terms of miles, it was three.* (We swam about three miles.)

in that *conj.* For the reason that; because. *I like the city, but I like the country better in that I have more friends in the country.* (Because I have more friends in the country, I like it better than the city.)

in the air *adv. phr.* **1** In everyone's thoughts. *Christmas was in the air for weeks before.* (Everyone was thinking about Christmas and planning for it for weeks before.) *The war filled people's thoughts every day; it was in the air.* (People's minds were kept on the war in many ways.) Compare IN THE WIND. **2** Meeting the bodily senses; surrounding you so as to be smelled or felt. *Spring is in the air.* (You can smell the smells of spring, and see its signs, and feel it about you.) *Rain is in the air.* (It feels as if it is going to rain.) **3** See LEAVE HANGING, UP IN THE AIR.

in the arms of Morpheus *adj. phr.* Asleep. —A cliché. *I'll be in the arms of Morpheus about as soon as I turn out the light.* (I'll be asleep.) [Morpheus was the ancient Greek god of dreams.]

in the back See STAB IN THE BACK.

in the bag *adj. phr., informal* Sure to be won or gotten; certain.—A cliché. *Jones had the election in the bag after the shameful news about his opponent came out.* (He had the election won.) *We thought we had the game in the bag.* (We thought our team couldn't lose.) Compare SEWED UP.

in the balance See HANG IN THE BALANCE.

in the bargain *or* **into the bargain** *adv. phr.* In addition; besides; also. *Frank is a teacher, and an artist into the bargain.* (Frank is a teacher, and an artist also.) *The heat failed, and then the roof began to leak in the bargain.* (The heat failed, and then the roof began to leak, too.) Compare TO BOOT; FOR GOOD MEASURE.

in the black *adv. or adj. phr., informal* In a successful or profitable way; so as to make money. *The big store was running in the black.* (The big store was making a profit; it was in good business condition.) *A business must stay in the black to keep on.* (A business cannot last unless it makes money.) Contrast IN THE RED.

in the blood See RUN IN THE BLOOD *or* RUN IN THE FAMILY.

in the bud See NIP IN THE BUD.

in the can *adj., slang, movie jargon* Ready, finished, completed, about to be duplicated and distributed to exhibitors. *No sneak previews until it's all in the can!* (No one may see the film in advance before it is ready for duplicating and distribution.) *Once my book's in the can, I'll go for a vacation.* (I will take a rest when my book is entirely finished.)

in the cards *also* **on the cards** *adj. phr., informal* To be expected; likely to happen; foreseeable; predictable.—A cliché. *It was in the cards for the son to succeed his father as head of the business.* (It was in the natural order for the son to take charge.) *John finally decided that it wasn't in the cards for him to succeed with that company.* (John decided that it wasn't to be expected that he could rise in that company.)

in the charge of   See IN CHARGE OF 2.

in the chips *slang or informal* **in the money** *adj. phr.* Having plenty of money; prosperous; rich. *After his rich uncle died, Richard was in the chips.* (He became rich.) *After years of struggle and dependence, air transportation is in the money.* (Air transportation has become profitable business.) Compare ON EASY STREET, WELL-TO-DO.

in the circumstances See UNDER THE CIRCUMSTANCES.

in the clear *adj. phr.* **1** Free of anything that makes moving or seeing difficult; with nothing to limit action. *The plane climbed above the clouds and was flying in the clear.* (The plane was flying free of clouds that would make it hard to see where it was going.) *Jack passed the ball to Tim, who was in the clear and ran for a touchdown.* (There was no one around Tim to stop him.) **2** *informal* Free of blame or suspicion; not thought to be guilty. *After John told the principal that he broke the window, Martin was in the clear.* (At first the principal thought Martin broke the window, but John said he did, and the principal stopped suspecting Martin.) *Steve was the last to leave the locker room, and the boys suspected him of stealing Tom's watch, but the coach found the watch and put Steve in the clear.* (The coach freed Steve of blame.) **3** Free of debt; not owing money to anyone. *Bob borrowed a thousand dollars from his father to start his business, but at the end of the first year he was in the clear.* (He earned enough to pay his father the money and was not in debt any more.) Syn. IN THE BLACK.

in the clouds *adj. phr.* Far from real life; in dreams; in fancy; in thought.—A cliché. *When Alice agreed to marry Jim, Jim went home in the clouds.* (Jim went home dreaming of their future happiness.)—Often used with *head, mind, thoughts. Mary is looking out the window, not at the chalkboard; her head is in the clouds again.* (Mary isn't paying attention to the lesson; she is dreaming again.) *A good teacher should have his head in the clouds sometimes, but his feet always on the ground.* (A good teacher should have imagination, but also be able to really do things.) Contrast COME BACK TO EARTH, FEET ON THE GROUND.

in the clover See IN CLOVER.

in the cold See OUT IN THE COLD.

in the dark *adj. phr.* In ignorance; without information. *John was in the dark about the job he was being sent to.* (He didn't know what he would find.) *If the government controls the news, it can keep people in the dark on any topic it chooses.* (It can keep them in ignorance.) *Mary had a letter from Sue yesterday, but she was left in the dark about Sue's plans to visit her.* (Sue did not tell Mary when she was coming or how long she would stay.) Contrast IN THE KNOW. **2** See WHISTLE IN THE DARK.

in the doghouse *adj. phr., slang* In disgrace or disfavor.—A cliché. *Our neighbor got in the doghouse with his wife by coming home drunk.* (Our neighbor's wife is angry with him for coming home drunk.) *Jerry is in the doghouse because he dropped the ball, and the other team won because of that.* (The other players are angry with Jerry.)Compare DOWN ON.

in the door See FOOT IN THE DOOR.

in the dumps See DOWN IN THE DUMPS.

in the event See IN CASE.[1]

in the event of See IN CASE OF.

in the eye See LOOK IN THE EYE.

in the face See BLUE IN THE FACE, LOOK IN THE EYE *or* LOOK IN THE FACE, SLAP IN THE FACE, STARE IN THE FACE.

in the face of *adv. phr.* **1** When met or in the presence of; threatened by. *He was brave in the face of danger.* (He was not afraid even though he might be injured or killed.) *She began to cry in the face of failure.* (When she realized she might fail, she began to cry.) **2** Although opposed by; without being stopped by. *Talking continued even in the face of the teacher's command to stop.* (They kept on talking even though the teacher commanded them to stop.) Syn. IN SPITE OF. Compare FLY IN THE FACE OF, IN ONE'S FACE. **3** See FLY IN THE FACE OF.

in the family See RUN IN THE BLOOD *or* RUN IN THE FAMILY.

in the first place *adv. phr.* **1** Before now; in the beginning; first. *You already ate breakfast! Why didn't you tell me that in the first place instead of saying you didn't want to eat?* (Why didn't you tell me you already ate breakfast when I first asked if you wanted some?) *Carl patched his old football but it soon leaked again. He should have bought a new one in the first place.* (Carl should have bought a new football when the old football first leaked.) **2** See IN THE PLACE.

in the flesh See IN PERSON.

in the groove *adj. phr., slang* Doing something very well; near perfection; at your best. *The band was right in the groove that night.* (The band was playing its best.) *It was an exciting football game; every player was really in the groove.* (Every player did his part perfectly.)

in the hole *adv. or adj. phr., informal* **1a** Having a score lower than zero in a game, especially a card game; to a score below zero. *John went three points in the hole on the first hand of the card game.* (John lost on the first play and his score was three below zero.) **1b** Behind an opponent; in difficulty in a sport or game. *We had their pitcher in the hole with the bases full and no one out.* (Their pitcher was in danger of losing the game.) Compare ON THE SPOT. **2** In debt; behind financially. *John went in the hole with his hot dog stand.* (He lost money on it.) *It's a lot easier to get in the hole than to get out again.* (It's easier to get in debt than to get out of it.) Compare IN A HOLE, IN THE RED. Contrast OUT OF THE HOLE.

in the know *adj. phr., informal* Knowing about things that most people do not know about; knowing secrets or understanding a special subject. *Tina helped Mother make some of the Christmas surprises, and she felt important to be in the know.* (Tina felt important because she knew about the Christmas secrets.) *In a print shop, Mr. Harvey is in the know, but in a kitchen he can't even cook an egg.* (Mr. Harvey understands printing, but not cooking.) Compare GET WISE. Contrast IN THE DARK.

in the lap of luxury *adv. phr.* Well supplied with luxuries; having most things that money can buy.—*A cliché. Mike grew up in the lap of luxury.* (Mike grew up with most things that money can buy.) Compare ON EASY STREET, WELL-TO-DO.

in the lap of the gods *also* **on the knees of the gods** *adv. phr., literary* Beyond human control; not to be decided by anyone.—*A cliché. Frank had worked hard as a candidate, and as election day came he felt that the result was in the lap of the gods.* (He felt that there was nothing more he could do to effect the result; he felt that many other things would help decide the election.) *The armies were evenly matched and the result of the battle seemed to be on the knees of the gods.* (It seemed that either side might win.)

in the least *adv. phr.* Even a little; in any degree or amount.—*Used in negative, interrogative, and conditional sentences. Sue did not understand baseball in the least.* (Sue didn't understand baseball even a little.) *Are you in the least interested in sewing?* (Are you interested in sewing even a little?) *Mother won't be upset if you come for supper; I'll be surprised if she cares in the least.* (I'll be surprised if it makes any difference to her.) *Mike was not upset in the least by the storm.* (Mike was not bothered in any way.) *It is no trouble to help you. Not in the least.* (It isn't any trouble at all.) Compare AT ALL.

in the line of duty *adj. phr.* Done or happening as part of a job. *The policeman was shot in the line of duty.* (The policeman was shot while he was working.) *The soldier had to clean his rifle in the line of duty.* (Cleaning his rifle is a part of a soldier's job.)

in the long run *adv. phr.* In the end; in the final result. *John knew that he could make a success of the little weekly paper in the long run.* (John knew that if he had enough time, he could make the paper profitable at last.) *You may make good grades by studying only before examinations, but you will succeed in the long run only by studying hard every day.* (By studying hard every day you will learn what you need to succeed in life.)

in the lurch See LEAVE IN THE LURCH.

in the main *adv. phr., formal* In most cases; generally; usually. *In the main, small boys and dogs are good friends.* (Boys and dogs are good friends most of the time.) *In the main, the pupils did well on the test.* (Most of the pupils did well on the test.)

in the market for *adj. phr.* Wishing to buy; ready to buy. *Mr. Jones is in the market for a new car.* (Mr. Jones is ready to buy a new car.) *People are always in the market for entertainment.* (People are always ready to pay to be entertained.)

in the middle *adv. or adj. phr.* In between two sides of an argument; caught between two dangers. *Mary found herself in the middle of the quarrel between Joyce and Ethel.* (Joyce and Ethel were quarrelling and Mary had to try to help both her friends.) *John promised Tom to go fishing, but his father wanted him to help at home. John was in the middle.* (John had a difficult choice between two duties.)

in the money See IN THE CHIPS.

in the mouth See LOOK A GIFT HORSE IN THE MOUTH.

in the neck See CATCH IT IN THE NECK *or* GET IT IN THE NECK.

in the nick of time *adv. phr.* Just at the right time; barely soon enough; almost too late.—*A cliché. The doctor arrived in the nick of time to save the child from choking to death.* (The doctor got there just in time to save the child from choking to death.) *Joe saw the other car in the nick of time.* (Joe saw the other car almost too late to prevent a crash.) Compare IN TIME.

in the pink *or* **in the pink of condition** *adj. phr., informal* In excellent health; strong and well; in fine shape.—*A cliché. Mr. Merrick had aged well; he was one of those old men who always seem in the pink of condition.* (He always seemed in fine health.) *After a practice and a rubdown, Joe felt in the pink.* (He felt very good.)

in the ——— place *adv. phr.* As the (first or second or third, etc.) thing in order or importance; first, second, or third, etc.—*Used with first, second, third,* and other ordinal numbers. *No, you cannot go swimming. In the first place, the water is too cold; and, in the second place, there is not time enough before dinner.* (The first reason is that the water is too cold; another reason is the lack of time.) *Stealing is wrong, in the first place, because it hurts others, and, in the second place, because it hurts you.* (Stealing hurts others and also yourself.) Compare FOR ONE THING.

in the public eye *adj. phr.* Widely known; often seen in public activity; much in the news.—A cliché. *The senator's activity kept him in the public eye.* (His political life made him well known.) *A big league ballplayer is naturally much in the public eye.* (People see him play and read about him.)

in the raw *adj. or adv. pnr.* **1** In the simplest or most natural way, with no frills. *Henry enjoyed going into the woods and living life in the raw.* (Henry liked to live in a simple way in the woods.) **2** *informal* Without any clothing; naked. *In the summer the boys slept in the raw.* (In summer the boys slept with no pajamas.)

in the red *adv. or adj. phr., informal* In an unprofitable way; so as to lose money. *A large number of American radio stations operate in the red.* (Many American radio stations lose money.) *A rich man who has a farm or ranch often runs it in the red, but makes his money with his factory or business.* (He runs his farm or ranch for pleasure, losing money.) Contrast IN THE BLACK. [From the fact that people who keep business records usually write in red ink how much money they lose and in black ink how much money they gain.]

in the right *adj. phr.* With moral or legal right or truth on your side; in agreement with justice, truth, or fact; correct. *When the cars collided, John was clearly in the right.* (John had the right of way and was obeying the rules of the road.) *In going before his wife down the stairs, Mr. Franklin was in the right.* (He was in agreement with the rule that a man should be where he can protect the woman.) *In many disputes, it is hard to say who is in the right.* (It is hard to prove that one side is all right and the other all wrong.) Contrast IN THE WRONG.

in the rough See DIAMOND IN THE ROUGH.

in the running *adj. or adv. phr.* Having a chance to win; not to be counted out; among those who might win. *At the beginning of the last lap of the race, only two horses were still in the running.* (Only two still had any chance to win the race.) *A month before Joyce married Hal, three of Joyce's boy friends seemed to be still in the running.* (She seemed to like three of them.) *Al was in the running for the trophy until the last hole of the golf tournament.* (He wasn't defeated until the last hole.) Contrast OUT OF THE RUNNING.

in the saddle *adv. or adj. phr.* In command; in control; in a position to order or boss others.—A cliché. *Mr. Park was in the saddle when he had over half the company's stock.* (He could have his way; he controlled the company.) *Getting appointed chief of police put Stevens in the saddle.* (When he became chief, he could give orders in the police department.)

in the same boat *adv. or adj. phr.* In the same trouble; in the same fix; in the same bad situation.—A cliché. *When the town's one factory closed and hundreds of people lost their jobs, all the storekeepers were in the same boat.* (Nobody had any money to pay any of them.) *Dick was disappointed when Fern refused to marry him, but he knew others were in the same boat.* (He knew she had refused several other men.)

in the same breath *adv. phr.* **1** At the same time; without waiting. *John would complain about hard times, and in the same breath boast of his prizewinning horses.* (He didn't realize that he left a strange impression when he said he was having money trouble and then boasted of his horses.) *Jane said Bill was selfish, but in the same breath she said she was sorry to see him leave.* (She criticized him but also praised him somewhat.) **2** In the same class; in as high a group.—A cliché usually used in the negative with *mention*, *speak*, or *talk*. *Mary is a good swimmer, but she should not be mentioned in the same breath with Joan.* (Mary is not nearly as good a swimmer as Joan.)

in the same place See LIGHTNING NEVER STRIKES TWICE IN THE SAME PLACE.

in the sand See HIDE ONE'S HEAD IN THE SAND.

in the second place See IN THE ——— PLACE.

in the soup *adj. phr., slang* In serious trouble; in confusion; in disorder. *When his wife overdrew their bank account without telling him, Mr. Phillips suddenly found himself really in the soup.* (He found himself in serious trouble.) *The police misunderstood Harry's night errand, and arrested him, which put him in the soup with the boss.* (His boss got the wrong idea, and lost faith in him.)

in the swim *adj. phr.* Doing the same things that other people are doing; following the fashion (as in business or social affairs) busy with what most people are doing. *Jim found some college friends at the lake that summer, and soon was in the swim of things.* (He was soon included in their activities.) *Mary went to New York with introductions to writers and artists, and that winter she was quite in the swim.* (She was included in their parties.) Contrast OUT OF THE SWIM.

in the third place See IN THE ——— PLACE.

in the till See ROB THE TILL or HAVE ONE'S HAND IN THE TILL.

in the wake of *prep., literary* As a result of; right after; following. *Many troubles follow in the wake of war.* (Much trouble follows war.) *There were heavy losses of property in the wake of the flood.* (The flood caused much loss of property.)

in the way See IN ONE'S WAY.

in the way of See PUT IN THE WAY OF.

in the wind *adj. phr.* Seeming probable; being planned; soon to happen. *Changes in top management of the company had been in the wind for weeks.* (It had been rumored for weeks that the directors were going to bring in a new president.) *Tom's close friends knew that marriage was in the wind.* (They knew

Tom planned to marry soon.) Compare IN THE AIR 1.

in the works *adv. or adj. phr.* In preparation; being planned or worked on; in progress. *John was told that the paving of his street was in the works.* (He was told that paving had been ordered and was being planned.) *It was reported that the playwright had a new play in the works.* (He was said to be working on a new play.) *The manager told the employees that a raise in wages was in the works.* (Higher pay was being arranged.) Compare UNDER WAY.

in the world *or* **on earth** *adv. phr., informal* Of all possible things; ever.—Usually used for emphasis after words that ask questions, as *who, why what,* etc. *Where in the world did you find that necktie?* (Where of all possible places did you find a tie like that?) *The boys wondered how on earth the mouse got out of the cage.* (The boys wondered how the mouse ever got out of the cage.) *Betty could not understand what on earth the teacher meant.* (Betty could not understand anything the teacher said.)

in the wrong *adj. phr.* With moral or legal right or truth against you; against justice, truth, or fact; wrong. *In attacking a smaller boy, Jack was plainly in the wrong.* (Jack showed himself a bully and a coward.) *Mary was in the wrong to drink from a finger bowl.* (That's not what it's for.) *Since he had put pennies behind the fuses, Bill was in the wrong when fire broke out.* (He had taken away the protection that the fuses are supposed to give.) Compare OUT OF THE WAY. Contrast IN THE RIGHT.

in time *adv. or adj. phr.* **1** Soon enough. *We got to Washington in time for the cherry blossoms.* (We visited Washington early enough to see the cherry blossoms.) *We got to the station just in time to catch the bus.* (We got there just before the bus left.) *John liked to get to work in good time and talk to the man who worked on his machine before him.* (He arrived early enough to find out how things were going; he didn't just rush in at the last minute.) **2** In the end; after a while; finally. *Fred and Jim did not like each other at first, but in time they became friends.* (After a long time, they became friends.) **3** In the right rhythm; in step. *The marchers kept in time with the band.* (They kept in step with the beat of the music.) *Johnny didn't play his piano piece in time.* (He didn't get the time right; he held some parts too long and others not long enough.)

into account See TAKE INTO ACCOUNT.

into a nose dive See GO INTO A TAIL SPIN or GO INTO A NOSE DIVE.

into a tail spin See GO INTO A TAIL SPIN.

into commission See IN COMMISSION.

into effect *adv. phr.* Into use or operation. *The new rule was put into effect at once.* (It was made to begin immediately.) *The judge*

ordered the old suspended penalty *into effect.* (He ordered the suspension stopped and the penalty begun.)

into hot water See HOT WATER.

into line *adv. phr.* **1** Into agreement. *The department's spending was brought into line with the budget.* (It was made to agree with the planned limits.) **2** Under control. *Independent congressmen were brought into line by warnings that jobs for their friends would be kept back.* (Rebels in Congress were brought to obedience by limits on jobs for their friends.) *The players who had broken training rules fell into line when the coach warned them that they would be put off the team.* (The players obeyed the coach's rules after that.)

into one's blood See IN ONE'S BLOOD.

into one's head See BEAT INTO ONE'S HEAD, TAKE INTO ONE'S HEAD.

into one's own See COME INTO ONE'S OWN.

into one's own hands See TAKE THE LAW INTO ONE'S OWN HANDS.

into one's shell See IN ONE'S SHELL.

into one's shoes See STEP INTO ONE'S SHOES.

into practice See IN PRACTICE.

into question *adv. phr.* Into doubt or argument.—Usually used with *call, bring* or *come. This soldier's courage has never been called into question.* (There has never been any doubt or argument that this soldier is not brave.) *If a boy steals, his parents' teaching comes into question.* (People will doubt that the boy was taught to do right.)

into the bargain See IN THE BARGAIN.

into the fire See OUT OF THE FRYING PAN INTO THE FIRE.

into the ground See RUN INTO THE GROUND.

into the hands of See PLAY INTO THE HANDS OF.

into thin air *adv. phr.* Without anything left; completely.—A cliché. *When Bob returned to the room, he was surprised to find that his books had vanished into thin air.* (Bob's books were not there and he could not understand why.) Compare OUT OF THIN AIR.

in toto *adv. phr.* As a whole; in its entirety; totally; altogether. *The store refused the advertising agency's suggestion in toto.* (They threw the whole thing out.) *They bought the newspaper business in toto.* (They bought the whole property.) *The paving job was accepted in toto.* (The city approved the whole job and accepted it.) [Latin, meaning "in the whole".]

in touch *adj. phr.* Talking or writing to each other; giving and getting news. *John kept in touch with his school friends during the summer.* (John and his school friends wrote letters to each other during the summer.) *Police anywhere in the U.S. can get in touch instantly with any other police department by teletype.* (They can send and receive messages instantly.) *The man claimed to be* *in touch with people on another planet.* (He claimed to get messages from another planet and answer them.) Compare KEEP TRACK. Contrast OUT OF TOUCH.

in tow *adj. phr.* **1** Being pulled. *The tugboat had the large ocean liner in tow as they came into the harbor.* (The tug pulled the liner into the harbor.) *An engine came with a long string of cars in tow.* (An engine came with a long string of cars being pulled by it.) **2** Being taken from place to place; along with someone. *Janet took the new girl in tow and showed her where to go.* (Janet told the new girl to follow her.) *Mrs. Hayes went to the supermarket with her four little children in tow.* (Mrs. Hayes took her children along with her to the supermarket.)

in trust *adv. or adj. phr.* In safe care for another. *The money was held by the bank in trust for the widow.* (The bank took care of the money for the widow and kept it safely.) *At his death Mr. Brown left a large sum in trust for his son until he was twenty-five.* (The money was kept safe for the son until he was twenty-five.)

in tune *adv. or adj. phr.* **1** At the proper musical pitch; high or low enough in sound. *The piano is in tune.* (Each string of the piano is adjusted to its proper sound.) **2** Going well together; in agreement; matching, agreeable.—Often used with *with*. *In his new job, John felt in tune with his surroundings and his associates.* (He liked the place where he worked and the people he worked with.) Contrast OUT OF TUNE.

in turn *adv. phr.* According to a settled order; each following another. *Each man in turn got up and spoke.* (Each man got up and spoke, one after another.) *Two teachers supervised the lunch hour in turn.* (One teacher was in charge one day, and the other the next day.) *Each of the three boys teases his younger brother—John, the biggest, teases Bob, the middle boy; and Bob in turn teases Tim, the youngest.* (Bob, as the next biggest, teases Tim.) Compare IN ORDER.

in two *adv. phr.* Into two parts or pieces; into two divisions. *John and Mary pulled on the wishbone until it came in two.* (It broke into two parts.) *There was only one piece of cake, but we cut it in two.* (We cut it into two pieces.) Syn. IN HALF.

in two shakes of a lamb's tail *adv., informal* Quickly, in no time at all. *I'll be back in two shakes of a lamb's tail.* (I'll be back right away.)

in —— up to the See UP TO THE —— IN.

in vain *adv. phr.* **1** Without effect; without getting the desired result; without success. *The drowning man called in vain for help.* (He called for help without getting it.) *To cry over spilled milk is to cry in vain.* (It does no good to cry over spilled milk.) Compare

GO FOR NOTHING, NO USE. **2** See TAKE ONE'S NAME IN VAIN.

in view *adv. or adj. phr.* **1** In sight; visible. *We came around a bend and there was the ocean in view.* (We could see the ocean.) **2** As a purpose, hope, or expectation. *John had his son's education in view when he began to save money.* (He saved for the purpose of educating his son.) *The end that we must keep always in view is peace with justice.* (The purpose that we must hold before us is peace with fairness.) Compare EYE TO.

in view of *prep.* After thinking about; because of. *Schools were closed for the day in view of the heavy snowstorm.* (Schools were closed for the day because of the heavy snowstorm.) *In view of rising labor costs, many companies have turned to automation.* (After studying rising labor costs, many companies have begun to use automatic methods.) Syn. IN THE LIGHT OF.

in virtue of See BY VIRTUE OF.

in wait See LIE IN WAIT.

in with *prep.* In friendship, favor, or closeness with; in the trust or liking of. *We trusted on Byrd's being in with the mayor, not knowing that the mayor no longer liked him.* (We depended on his being a friend of the mayor, but he no longer was.) *It took the new family some time to get in with their neighbors.* (It was a while before their new neighbors accepted them as friends.)

Irish See GET ONE'S DANDER UP *or* GET ONE'S IRISH UP.

iron horse *n., informal* A railroad locomotive; the engine of a railroad train. *In its first days, the iron horse frightened many people as it roared around country scattering sparks.* (Early railroad engines frightened many people.)

iron in the fire *n. phr.* Something you are doing; one of the projects with which a person is busy; job. *John had a number of irons in the fire, and he managed to keep all of them hot.* (He was working on several things at the same time, and doing them well.)—Usually used in the phrase *too many irons in the fire.* *"Ed has a dozen things going all the time, but none of them seem to work out." "No wonder. He has too many irons in the fire."* (It is not strange that most of his projects fail. He has too many going at one time to do any one of them properly.)

iron out *v., informal* To discuss and reach an agreement about (a difference); find a solution for (a problem); remove (a difficulty). *The company and its workers ironed out their differences over hours and pay.* (They talked over their disagreements and reached an agreement.) *The House and Senate ironed out the differences between their two different tax bills.* (They got together and agreed on a bill that both could pass.) Compare MAKE UP 5.

is See SUCH AS IT IS, THAT IS.

island See SAFETY ISLAND.

issue See AT ISSUE, TAKE ISSUE.

is that so *informal* **1** Oh, indeed? That's interesting.—Used in simple acceptance or reply. *"The Republicans have pulled a trick at City hall." "Is that so?"* (Oh, really?) **2** Surely not? Oh come now, not really? Oh, nonsense!—Used in disbelief or sarcasm. *"The moon is made of green cheese." "Is that so?"* (Oh, nonsense!) *"I'm going to take your girl friend to the dance," said Bob. "Oh, is that so!", said Dick. "Try it and you'll be sorry."* (Dick said, "Oh, no you won't.")

itching palm *n., slang* A wish for money; greed.—A cliché. *He was born with an itching palm.* (He always has wanted money.) *The bellboys in that hotel seem always to have itching palms.* (They seem very eager to get tips.)

I tell you See I'LL SAY.

I tell you what See I'LL TELL YOU WHAT.

item See COLLECTOR'S ITEM, CONSUMER ITEMS.

it is an ill wind that blows nobody good No matter how bad a happening is, someone can usually gain something from it.—A proverb. *When Fred got hurt in the game John got a chance to play. It's an ill wind that blows nobody good.* (It was a bad thing that Fred got hurt, but for John it was lucky.)

it never rains but it pours One good thing or bad thing is often followed by others of the same kind.—A proverb. *John got sick, then his brothers and sisters all got sick. It never rains but it pours.* (Not only John was sick in the family. There was a great deal of sickness.)

it's been —, it's been real *informal* Shortened form for "it has been real nice (being with you)"—used colloquially between very close friends.

itself See END IN ITSELF.

Ivy League *n.* A small group of the older and more famous eastern U.S. colleges and universities. *Several Ivy League teams play each other regularly each year.* (Teams of the top eastern colleges keep up regular athletic competition.) *Harvard, Yale, and Princeton were the original Ivy League.* (Harvard, Yale, and Princeton were the three eastern schools first called "Ivy League.")

J

Jack See ALL WORK AND NO PLAY MAKES JACK A DULL BOY.

jack See EVERY LAST MAN *also* EVERY MAN JACK.

jack of all trades *n., informal* (Often followed by the words "master of none.") A person who is knowledgeable in many areas. Can be used as praise, or as a derogatory remark depending on the context and the intonation. *Peter is a jack of all trades; he can survive anywhere!* (He is being complimented on his versatility.) *"How come Joe did such a sloppy job?" Mary asked. "He's a jack of all trades,"* *Sally answered.* (Sally explains his poor performance by blaming it on his overdiversification.)

jackpot See HIT THE JACKPOT.

jack-rabbit start *n., informal* A very sudden start from a still position; a very fast start from a stop. *Bob made a jack-rabbit start when the traffic light turned green.* (The car moved ahead so suddenly that it seemed to jump.)

Jack Robinson See BEFORE ONE CAN SAY JACK ROBINSON.

jack up *v.* **1** To lift with a jack. *The man jacked up his car to fix a flat tire.* (The man used a tool to raise his car off the ground.) **2** *informal* To make (a price) higher; raise. *Just before Christmas, some stores jack up their prices.* (Some stores raise the cost of things just before Christmas because they know that people will buy them.)

jailbait *n., slang* A girl below the legal age of consent for sex; one who tempts you to intimacy which is punishable by imprisonment. *Stay away from Arabella, she is a jailbait.* (Don't become intimate with Arabella, because she is a minor.)

jake flake *n., slang* A boring person whose company is usually not wanted. *Please don't invite Turner, he is a jake flake.* (He is a bore, don't invite him.)

jaw See GLASS JAW.

jaw-breaker *n.* **1** A large piece of hard candy or bubblegum. *Billy asked his mother for a quarter to buy some jawbreakers and a chocolate bar.* (Billy bought some hard candy and a chocolate bar.) **2** *informal* A word or name that is hard to pronounce. *His name, Nissequogue, is a real jaw-breaker.* (His name is very hard to say.)

jaw drop *or* **jaw drop a mile** *informal* Mouth fall wide open with surprise.—Used with a possessive. *Tom's jaw dropped a mile when he won the prize.* (Tom was so surprised, his mouth fell wide open.)

jaws tight *adj., slang, informal* Angry, uptight, tense. *Why are you getting your jaws so tight?* (Why are you getting so angry?)

jazz up *v., slang* To brighten up; add more noise, movement, or color; make more lively or exciting. *The party was very dull until Pete jazzed it up with his drums.* (When Pete played his drums, everyone at the party enjoyed it more.)

Jehu See DRIVE LIKE JEHU.

jerk *or* **jerker** See SODA JERK *or* SODA JERKER.

jerry-built *adj.* **1** Built poorly or carelessly of cheap materials; easily broken. *That jerry-built cabin will blow apart in a strong wind.* (A strong wind will blow down that poorly-made cabin.) **2** Done without careful preparation or thought; planned too quickly. *When the regular television program didn't come on, a jerry-built program was substituted at the last minute.* (The regular program had to be called off, and a poor program was put on at the last minute.)

Jesus boots *or* **Jesus shoes** *n., slang* Men's sandals, particularly as worn by hippies and very casually dressed people. *I dig your Jesus boots, man, they look cool.* (I like your sandals, friend, they look comfortable.)

jig's up See GAME'S UP.

jim-dandy *n., slang* Something wonderful; something very good. *Tommy's new boat is really a jim-dandy! I wish I had one like it.* (I wish I had a wonderful new boat like Tommy's.)

jink See HIGH JINKS.

job See DO A JOB ON, FALL DOWN ON THE JOB, LIE DOWN ON THE JOB, ON THE JOB.

Joe Doakes *n.* —A name used informally for the average man. *Let us say that Joe Doakes goes to the movies three times a year.* (Let's say that the average man goes three times a year.) Compare MAN IN THE STREET, SO-AND-SO.

John Doe *n.* —A name used for an unknown person, especially in police and law business. *The alarm went out for a John Doe who stole the diamonds from the store.* (The police are looking for an unknown person who stole the diamonds.)

John Hancock *or* **John Henry** *n., informal* Your signature; your name in writing. *The man said, "Put your John Hancock on this paper."* (He asked the person to sign his name on the paper.) *Joe felt proud when he put his John Henry on his very first driver's license.* (Joe was proud to sign his name on his first driver's license.)

Johnny-come-lately *n.* Someone new in a place or group; newcomer; *also:* a new person who takes an active part in group affairs before the group has accepted him; upstart. *Everybody was amazed when a Johnny-come-lately beat the old favorite in the race.* (A newcomer won the race.) *When it looked as though Mr. Brown had a good chance of winning, many Johnny-come-latelies began to support him.* (Many new people joined Mr. Brown's supporters as soon as they realized he might win.)

Johnny-on-the-spot *adj. phr.* At the right place when needed; present and ready to help; very prompt; on time. *A good waterboy is always Johnny-on-the-spot.* (A good waterboy is always ready when water is needed.) *The firemen were Johnny-on-the-spot and put out the fire in the house soon after it started.* (The firemen came quickly when they were needed.) Compare ON THE JOB.

John Q. Public *n.* —A name used informally for the average citizen. *It is John Q. Public's duty to vote at each election.* (It is every citizen's duty to vote.) Compare JOE DOAKES.

join forces *or* **join hands** *v. phr.* To get together for the same aim; group together for a purpose; unite. *The students and the graduates joined forces to raise money when the gym burned down.* (The students and the graduates worked together to raise money for a new gym.) *The American soldiers joined hands with the British in the war against Germany.* (The American and British soldiers fought together against the German army.) Compare JOIN HANDS, THROW IN ONE'S LOT WITH.

join hands See JOIN FORCES.

joint See CLIP JOINT, PUT ONE'S NOSE OUT OF JOINT.

joke See CRACK A JOKE.

joking apart See JOKING ASIDE.

joking aside *or* **joking apart** *v. phr., informal* No fooling; without exaggerating; seriously. *Joking aside, although the conditions were not very comfortable, we had a wonderful time.* (Speaking truthfully, we had a good time despite the uncomfortable conditions.) *Joking apart, there must have been over a hundred people in the room.* (Without exaggerating, there were more than a hundred people there.)

Jones See KEEP UP WITH THE JONESES.

judgment seat *n.* A place where you are judged; a place where justice and punishment are given out.—A cliché. *Mrs. Smith is so bossy, she always acts as though she is in the judgment seat.* (Mrs. Smith always tells everybody what's right and what's wrong.)

jug-eared *adj.* With ears that stick out like the handles of a jug. *Tommy was a red-headed, freckle-faced, jug-eared boy.* (Tommy had ears that stuck out like the handles of a jug.)

juice See STEW IN ONE'S OWN JUICE.

juice dealer *n., slang* An underworld money lender who charges exorbitant fees to his clientele and frequently collects payment by physical force. *No matter how broke you are, never go to a juice dealer.* (Never go to an underworld money lender.)

jump See GET THE JUMP ON *or* HAVE THE JUMP ON, GO JUMP IN THE LAKE, NOT KNOW WHICH WAY TO TURN *or* NOT KNOW WHICH WAY TO JUMP.

jump all over See JUMP ON.

jump at *v.* To take or accept quickly and gladly. *Johnny jumped at the invitation to go swimming with his brother.* (Johnny quickly accepted the invitation to go swimming with his brother.) Compare TAKE UP 7.

jump bail *or* **skip bail** *v. phr., informal* To run away and fail to come to trial, and so to give up a certain amount of money already given to a court of law to hold with the promise that you would come. *The robber paid $2000 bail so he wouldn't be put in jail before his trial. But he jumped bail and escaped to Mexico.* (When the robber did not come back for his trial, the court kept the bail money.) *The man skipped bail because he was afraid the court might put him in jail for a long time.* (He gave up his bail money to the court by running away.)

jump ball *n.* The starting of play in basketball by tossing the ball into the air between two opposing players, each of whom jumps and tries to hit the ball to a member of his own team. *Two players held onto the ball at the same time and the referee called a jump ball.* (The referee decided to put the ball in play by tossing it up between the two players who were both holding on to it.)

jump down one's throat *v. phr.* To suddenly become very angry at someone; scold severely or angrily.—A cliché. *The teacher jumped down Billy's throat when Billy said he did not do his homework.* (The teacher became very angry and scolded Billy because he did not do his homework.)

jump from the frying pan into the fire See OUT OF THE FRYING PAN INTO THE FIRE.

jumping-off place *n. phr.* **1** A place so far away that it seems to be the end of the world. *Columbus' sailors were afraid they would arrive at the jumping-off place if they sailed further west.* (They thought they would arrive at the end of the world and fall off.) *So you visited Little America? That sounds like the jumping-off place!* (Little America is so far south that it seems like the end of the world.) **2** The starting place of a long, hard trip or of something difficult or dangerous. *The jumping-off place for the explorer's trip through the jungle was a little village.* (The village was where the explorer started on his trip.)

jump on *or* **jump all over** *or* **land on** *or* **land all over** *v. phr., informal* To scold; criticize; blame. *Tom's boss jumped all over Tom because he made a careless mistake.* (His boss scolded him crossly for being careless.) *Janice landed on Robert for dressing carelessly for their date.* (Janice complained about the way Robert dressed.) *"I don't know why Bill is always jumping on me; I just don't understand him," said Bob.* (Bob didn't understand why Bill was always criticizing him.) Compare FIND FAULT, GET ON, LAY OUT 7

jump on the bandwagon *or* **get on the bandwagon** *v. phr., informal* To join a popular cause or movement. *At the last possible moment, the senator jumped on the winning candidate's bandwagon.* (He sided with the winner at the moment of victory.)

jump out of one's skin *v. phr., informal* To be badly frightened; be very much surprised. —A cliché. *The lightning struck so close to Bill that he almost jumped out of his skin.* (Bill was badly frightened when the lightning struck close to him.) Compare HAIR STAND ON END.

jump pass *n.* A pass (as in football or basketball) made by a player while jumping. *The Bruins scored when the quarterback tossed a jump pass to the left end.* (They scored when the quarterback jumped up and threw a short pass to the left end.)

jump the gun *also* **beat the gun** *v. phr.* **1** To start before the starter's gun in a race. *The runners were called back because one of them jumped the gun.* (One of them began to run before the starter shot off his gun.) **2** *informal* To start before you should; start before anyone else. *The new students were not supposed to come before noon, but one boy jumped the gun and came to school at eight in the morning.* (The new students were not supposed to come before noon, but one boy came at eight in the morning.) *The students planned to say happy birthday to the principal when the teacher raised her hand, but Sarah jumped the gun and said it when he came into the room.* (Sarah said happy birthday before she was supposed to.)

jump the traces See KICK OVER THE TRACES.

jump the track *v. phr.* **1** To go off rails; go or run the wrong way. *The train jumped the track and there was a terrible accident.* (The train wheels did not stay on the track where they belonged.) *The pulley of the clothesline jumped the track and Mother's washing fell down.* (The rope came loose from the pulley wheel.) **2** *informal* To change from one thought or idea to another without plan or reason; change the thought or idea you are talking about to something different. *Bob didn't finish his algebra homework because his mind kept jumping the track to think about the new girl in class.* (Bob couldn't keep his mind on his algebra work because he kept thinking about her.) Compare OFF THE TRACK.

jump through a hoop *v. phr., informal* To do whatever you are told to do; obey any order.—A cliché. *Bob would jump through a hoop for Mary.* (Bob would do anything Mary asked him to do.) Compare TWIST AROUND ONE'S LITTLE FINGER, *or* UNDER ONE'S THUMB.

jump to a conclusion *v. phr.* To decide too quickly or without thinking or finding the facts. *Jerry saw his dog limping on a bloody leg and jumped to the conclusion that it had been shot.* (When Jerry saw the blood and the lame leg, he decided without really knowing that his dog had been shot.) Contrast LOOK BEFORE YOU LEAP.

junked up *adj., v. phr., slang, drug culture* To be under the influence of drugs, especially heroine. *You can't talk to Billy, he's all junked up.* (You can't talk to him, he is under the influence of drugs.)

just about *adv., informal* Nearly; almost; practically. *Just about everyone in town came to hear the mayor speak.* (Almost everybody came.) *The dress came down to just about the middle of her knee.* (The dress was almost to the middle of her knee.) *Has Mary finished peeling the potatoes? Just about.* (Mary is nearly finished peeling the potatoes.)

justice See DO JUSTICE TO.

just in case See IN CASE².

just in time See IN TIME.

just now *adv. phr.* **1** Just at this moment; at this time. *Mr. Johnson isn't here just now. Will you phone back later?* (He is out for a little while.) **2** *informal* A very short time ago; only a moment ago; only a little while ago. *"Where could that boy have gone so quickly? He was here just now!"* (He was here only a minute ago.) Compare WHILE AGO.

just so¹ *adj.* Exact, exactly right. *Mrs. Robinson likes to keep her house just so, and she makes the children take off their shoes when they come in the house.* (Mrs. Robinson makes the children take their shoes off, so they won't get the house dirty.)

just so² *conj.* Provided, if. *Take as much food as you want, just so you don't waste any food.* (Take as much food as you want, but be sure to eat it all.) Syn. AS LONG AS 2.

just so *adv. phr.* With great care; very carefully. *In order to raise healthy African violets you must treat them just so.* (In order to raise healthy African violets you must treat them very carefully.)

just the same See ALL THE SAME.

just what the doctor ordered *n. phr., informal* Exactly what is needed or wanted.—A cliché. *"Ah! Just what the doctor ordered!"* exclaimed Joe when Mary brought him a cold soda. (Joe was so hot he was happy to get the cold soda, which was exactly what he wanted.)

K

kangaroo court *n.* A self-appointed group that decides what to do to someone who is supposed to have done wrong. *The Chicago mob held a kangaroo court and shot the gangster who competed with Al Capone.* (They murdered him after a mock trial.)

keel See ON AN EVEN KEEL.

keel over *v.* 1 To turn upside down; tip over; overturn.—Usually refers to a boat. *The strong wind made the sailboat keel over and the passengers fell into the water.* (The strong wind turned the boat over.) 2 *informal* To fall over in a faint; faint. *It was so hot during the assembly program that two girls who were standing on the stage keeled over.* (Two girls fainted because they were so hot.) *When the principal told the girl her father died, she keeled right over.* (The girl fainted when she heard that her father died.)

keep a civil tongue in one's head *v. phr.* To be polite in speaking.—A cliché. *He was very angry with his boss, but he kept a civil tongue in his head.* (He talked in a polite way, but he really felt like shouting.) *The bus driver began yelling at the woman and she told him to keep a civil tongue in his head.* (The woman told the driver not to be fresh.)

keep after *v., informal* To speak to (someone) about something again and again; remind over and over again. *Some pupils will do sloppy work unless the teacher keeps after them to write neatly.* (The pupils do sloppy work unless the teacher reminds them over and over again to write neatly.) *Sue's mother had to keep after her to clean her bedroom.* (Sue's mother had to keep reminding her to clean her bedroom.)

keep an ear to the ground See EAR TO THE GROUND.

keep an eye on *or* **keep one's eye on** *v. phr.* 1 *or* **have one's eye on** To watch carefully; not stop paying attention to. *Keep an eye on the stove in case the coffee boils.* (Watch the stove.) *You must keep your eye on the ball when you play tennis.* (You have to keep watching the ball.) *A good driver keeps his eye on the road.* (He doesn't stop paying attention.) *The teacher had her eye on me because she thought I was cheating.* (She tried to see me cheating and catch me.) *Billy keeps a jealous eye on his toys.* (Billy is jealous if anyone else uses his toys.) *The lion tamer keeps a sharp eye on the lions when he is in the cage.* (He doesn't stop watching them carefully.) Compare LOOK OUT, LOOK OVER. 2 To watch and do what is needed for; mind. *Mother told Jane to keep an eye on the baby while she was in the store.* Mother told Jane to take care of the baby.) *Mr. Brown told John to keep an eye on the store while he was out.* (Mr. Brown said to mind the store and to help customers.) Syn. TAKE CARE OF 1.

keep an eye out See EYE OUT.

keep a stiff upper lip *v. phr.* To be brave; face trouble bravely—A cliché. *He was very much worried about his sick daughter, but he kept a stiff upper lip.* (He didn't become discouraged.) *Although he was having some trouble with the engine, the pilot kept a stiff upper lip and landed the plane safely.* (The pilot did not show his fear.) Compare KEEP ONE'S CHIN UP.

keep at *v.* To continue to do; go on with. *Mary kept at her homework until she finished it.* (Mary continued doing her homework till she finished it. She did not stop to play or dream.) Compare KEEP ON 1, KEEP UP 1b.

keep —— at a distance *or* **keep —— at arms length** *v. phr.* To avoid (someone's) company; not become too friendly toward. *Mr. Smith is kind to the workers in his store, but after work he keeps them at a distance.* (Mr. Smith is not friendly to the workers after working hours. He stays away from them.) *Betty likes Bill and is trying to be friendly, but he keeps her at arms length.* (Bill does not want to become her friend.) Compare KEEP ONE'S DISTANCE, HOLD OFF 1a.

keep body and soul together *v. phr.* To keep alive; survive.—A cliché. *John was unemployed most of the year and hardly made enough money to keep body and soul together.* (John hardly earned enough money to keep alive.) Compare KEEP THE WOLF FROM THE DOOR.

keep books *v. phr.* To keep records of money gained and spent; do the work of a bookkeeper. *Miss Jones keeps the company's books.* (Miss Jones is the company's bookkeeper.)

keep company *v. phr.* 1 To stay or go along with (someone) so that he will not be lonely; to visit with (someone). *John kept Andy company while his parents went to the movies.* (John stayed with Andy until his parents came home from the movies.) *I'll go shopping with you just to keep you company.* (I'll go just to be a companion to you.) 2 To go places together as a couple; date just one person. *After keeping company for one year, Mary and John decided to marry.* (After going steady for one year, Mary and John decided to get married.) *Who is Bill keeping company with now?* (Who does Bill date regularly now?) Compare GO STEADY.

keep down *v.* Keep from progressing or growing; keep within limits; control. *The children could not keep their voices down.* (The children could not keep their voices from becoming too loud.) *We hoe the garden to keep down the weeds.* (We hoe the garden to stop the weeds from growing.) *You can't keep a good man down.* (You can't stop a good man from progressing.) Compare GET AHEAD.

keeper See FINDERS KEEPERS.

keep from *v., informal* To hold yourself back from; stop or prevent yourself from (doing something). *Can you keep from repeating gossip?* (Can you stop yourself from spreading unkind stories about people?) *Jill can't keep from talking about her trip.* (Jill can't hold herself back from talking about her trip.)—Usually used with *can* in the negative. *You can't keep from liking Jim.* (It is impossible not to like Jim.) Compare CAN HELP.

keep house *v. phr.* To do the necessary things in a household; do the cooking and cleaning. *Since their mother died, Mary and her brother keep house for their father.* (They do the housework.)

keep house² *also* **play house** *v. phr., informal* To live together without being married. *Bob and Nancy keep house these days.* (They are living together but aren't married.)

keeping See IN KEEPING, OUT OF KEEPING.

keep in mind See IN MIND.

keep on *v.* **1** To go ahead; not stop; continue. *The neighbors asked them to stop making a noise, but they kept right on.* (They refused to stop making a noise.) *Columbus kept on until he saw land.* (Columbus went ahead; he did not turn back.)—Often used before a present participle. *Columbus kept on sailing until he saw land.* (Columbus sailed on; he did not stop.) *The boy kept on talking even though the teacher had asked him to stop.* (The boy continued to talk; he did not quit.) Syn. GO ON. Compare KEEP AT, KEEP UP. **2** To allow to continue working for you. *The new owner kept Fred on as gardener.* (Fred continued to work as gardener; the new owner didn't fire him.)

keep one's chin up *v. phr.* To be brave; be determined; face trouble with courage.—A cliché. *He didn't think that he would ever get out of the jungle alive, but he kept his chin up.* (He went on bravely although he was afraid.) Compare KEEP A STIFF UPPER LIP.

keep one's distance *v. phr.* To be cool toward someone; avoid being friendly. *Mary did not like her co-worker, Betty, and kept her distance from her.* (Mary did not act friendly toward Betty.) Compare KEEP AT A DISTANCE.

keep one's end up See HOLD ONE'S END UP.

keep one's eye on See KEEP AN EYE ON.

keep one's eye on the ball *v. phr.* **1** To watch the ball at all times in a sport, usually in order to hit it or get it; not stop watching the ball. *Keep your eye on the baseball or you won't be able to hit it.* (If you stop watching it after it is thrown to you, you won't hit it with the baseball bat.) **2** *informal* To be watchful and ready; be wide-awake and ready to win or succeed; be smart.—A cliché. *Tom is just starting on the job but if he keeps his eye on the ball, he will be promoted.* (If he is smart and ready to take the opportunity, he will succeed.) Compare ON THE BALL.

keep one's eyes open See EYES OPEN.

keep one's eyes peeled *or* **keep one's eyes skinned** *v. phr., informal* To watch carefully; be always looking. *The bird watcher kept his eyes peeled for bluebirds.* (He watched carefully for bluebirds.) *When the boys walked through the roads, they kept their eyes skinned for snakes.* (The boys were watching for snakes.) Compare EYES OPEN 1, EYE OUT.

keep one's feet *v. phr.* To keep from falling or slipping down; keep your balance; remain standing. *The boy stumbled on the stairs but was able to keep his feet.* (He stumbled but did not fall.) Compare REGAIN ONE'S FEET.

keep one's feet on the ground See FEET ON THE GROUND.

keep one's fingers crossed See CROSS ONE'S FINGERS 1b.

keep one's hand in *v. phr.* To keep in practice; continue to take part. *After he retired from teaching, Mr. Brown kept his hand in by giving a lecture once in a while.* (Mr. Brown continued to teach once in a while.) *Mr. Smith left the planning of the trip to his wife, but he kept his hand in, too.* (Mr. Smith took some part in planning the trip.) Compare KEEP UP.

keep one's head *also* **keep one's wits about one** *v. phr.* To stay calm when there is trouble or danger. *When Tim heard the fire alarm he kept his head and looked for the nearest exit.* (Tim did not get too excited, he thought of the best way to get out.) Compare COUNT TO TEN. Contrast LOSE ONE'S HEAD.

keep one's mouth shut *v. phr., informal* To be or stay silent.—A rude expression when used as a command. *When the crooks were captured by the police, their leader warned them to keep their mouths shut.* (The leader of the gang warned the crooks not to tell the police anything.) *Charles began to tell Barry how to kick the ball, and Barry said angrily, "Keep your mouth shut!"* (Barry was angry and impolitely told Charles to be quiet.) Syn. SHUT UP 1.

keep one's nose clean *v. phr., slang* To stay out of trouble; do only what you should do. —A cliché. *The boss said Jim could have the job as long as he kept his nose clean and worked hard.* (The boss said Jim could have the job as long as he stayed out of trouble and worked hard.) *The policeman warned the boys to keep their noses clean unless they wanted to go to jail.* (The policeman warned the boys not to do anything wrong or they would go to jail.) Compare STEER CLEAR OF 2.

keep one's nose to the grindstone *or* **have one's nose to the grindstone** *or* **hold one's nose to the grindstone** *v. phr., informal* To work hard all the time; keep busy with boring or tiresome work. *Sarah keeps her nose to the grindstone and saves as much as possible to start her own business.* (She is willing to work very hard to achieve her ambition.)

keep one's own counsel *v. phr., formal* To keep your ideas and plans to yourself. *John listened to what everyone had to say in the discussion, but he kept his own counsel.* (John listened to the others, but he did not tell them his thoughts.) *Although everybody gave Mrs. O'Connor advice about what to do with her house, she kept her own counsel.* (Mrs. O'Connor didn't tell people what she decided to do.)

keep one's shirt on *v. phr., slang* To calm down; keep from losing your temper or getting impatient or excited. *Bob got very angry when John accidentally bumped into him, but John told him to keep his shirt on.* (John told Bob not to get excited.)—Usually used as a command; may be considered impolite. *John said to Bob, "Keep your shirt on."* (John said to Bob, "Don't get excited." (Contrast GET ONE'S DANDER UP.

keep one's temper See HOLD ONE'S TEMPER.

keep one's weather eye open See WEATHER EYE.

keep one's wits about one See KEEP ONE'S HEAD.

keep on the good side of See ON ONE'S GOOD SIDE.

keep pace *v. phr.* To go as fast; go at the same rate; not get behind. *When they go for a walk, Johnny has to take long steps to keep pace with his father.* (Johnny must take long steps or he will not go as fast as his father; his father will get ahead.) *When Billy was moved to a more advanced class, he had to work hard to keep pace.* (Billy had to work hard to do the same work that the other children did.) Compare KEEP UP 2a.

keeps See FOR KEEPS.

keep tab on *or* **keep tabs on** *v. phr., informal* **1** To keep a record of. *The government tries to keep tabs on all the animals in the park.* (The government tries to keep a record of how many animals are in the park, and what kinds.) **2** To keep a watch on; check. *The house mother kept tabs on the girls to be sure they were clean and neat.* (The house mother looked at the girls often.) Compare KEEP TRACK OF.

keep the ball rolling *v. phr., informal* To keep up an activity or action; not allow something that is happening to slow or stop. *Clyde kept the ball rolling at the party by dancing with a lamp shade on his head.* (Clyde kept the people laughing by acting silly.) Compare GET THE BALL ROLLING.

keep the home fires burning *v. phr.* To keep things going as usual while someone is away; wait at home to welcome someone back.—A cliché. *While John was in the army, Mary kept the home fires burning.* (Mary took care of'things at home until John came back from the army.)

keep the wolf from the door *v. phr.* To keep out hunger; not starve.—A cliché. *Mil-*

lions of poor people in China and India find it very hard to keep the wolf from the door. (Millions of poor people in China and India are always near starvation.) *John earned very little money and could hardly keep the wolf from the door.* (John barely made enough money to keep from starving.) Compare KEEP BODY AND SOUL TOGETHER.

keep time *v. phr.* **1** To show the right time. *My watch has not kept good time since I dropped it.* (My watch has not been running right since I dropped it.) **2** To keep the beat; keep the same rhythm; keep in step. *Many people are surprised at how well deaf people keep time with the music when they dance.* (They keep in step; they dance with the same rhythm as the music.)

keep to oneself See TO ONESELF *adv. phr.* 2.

keep track *v. phr.* To know about changes; stay informed or up-to-date; keep a count or record. *What day of the week is it? I can't keep track.* (I can't remember the days.)— Usually used with *of. Mr. Stevens kept track of his business by telephone when he was in the hospital.* (He found out what was going on by telephone.) *The farmer has so many chickens, he can hardly keep track of them all.* (He can hardly remember how many he has and where they all are.) Compare IN TOUCH, KEEP UP 3. Contrast LOSE TRACK.

keep under one's hat *v. phr., informal* To keep secret; not tell.—A cliché. *Mr. Jones knew who had won the contest, but he kept it under his hat until it was announced publicly.* (Mr. Jones did not tell who had won until everyone was told.)—Often used as a command. *Keep it under your hat.* (Don't tell anyone.) Syn. KEEP TO ONESELF.

keep up *v.* **1a** To go on; not stop; continue. *The rain kept up for two days and the roads were flooded.* (The rain went on for two days.) Compare KEEP ON. **1b** To go on with (something); continue steadily; never stop. *Mrs. Smith told John to keep up the good work.* (Mrs. Smith told John to go on with the good work, not to stop it.) *The teacher asked Dick to stop bothering Mary, but he kept it up.* (Dick did not stop bothering Mary; he went on doing it.) Compare KEEP AT. **2a** To go at the same rate as others. *John had to work hard to keep up.* (John had to work hard to keep from getting behind the others.) *Billy was the youngest boy on the hike, but he kept up with the others.* (He walked as fast as they did.) Compare CATCH UP, KEEP PACE. Contrast FALL BEHIND, GET BEHIND 1. **2b** To keep (something) at the same level or rate or in good condition. *The shortage of tomatoes kept the prices up.* (The prices stayed high because there weren't enough tomatoes.) *Grandfather was too poor to keep up his house.* (Grandfather was too poor to keep his house painted and repaired.) **3** To keep informed.—Usually used with *on* or *with. Mary is interested in politics and* *always keeps up with the news.* (Mary reads the newspapers and always knows what is happening in the world.) Compare KEEP TRACK.

keep up one's end   See HOLD ONE'S END UP.

keep up with the Joneses   *v. phr.* To follow the latest fashion; try to be equal with your neighbors.—A cliché. *Mrs. Smith kept buying every new thing that was advertised. Finally Mr. Smith told her to stop trying to keep up with the Joneses and to start thinking for herself.* (Mr. Smith told his wife to stop wanting to have everything the neighbors had.)

keep your fingers crossed   See CROSS ONE'S FINGERS.

kettle   See KETTLE OF FISH, POT CALLS THE KETTLE BLACK.

kettle of fish   *v. phr., informal* Something to be considered; how things are; a happening; business. *I thought he needed money, but it was another kettle of fish—his car had disappeared.* (He did not need a loan, but help in finding his car.)—Usually used with *pretty, fine, nice,* but meaning bad trouble. *He had two flat tires and no spare on a country road at night, which was certainly a pretty kettle of fish.* (He was in real trouble.) *This is a fine kettle of fish! I forgot my book.* (This is a bad thing to happen! I forgot my book.) Compare CUP OF TEA 2.

key   See LOW KEY, OFF-KEY.

keyed up   *adj., informal* Excited; nervous. *Mary was all keyed up about the exam.* (Mary was very nervous.) *Mother would not let Tom read a ghost story at bedtime; she said it would get him keyed up.* (A ghost story would make Tom too excited to sleep.)

kick about   See KICK AROUND 3.

kick against the pricks   *v. phr., literary.* To fight against rules or authority in a way that just hurts yourself.—A cliché. *Johnny kicked against the pricks in his foster home until he learned that he could trust his new family.* (Johnny kept rebelling against his foster parents until he learned to trust them.)

kick around   *v., informal* **1** To act roughly or badly to; treat badly; bully. *John likes to kick around the little boys.* (He likes to be mean to them.) *Mr. Jones is always kicking his dog around.* (He hurts the dog.) Syn. PUSH AROUND. **2** To lie around or in a place; be treated carelessly; be neglected. *This old coat has been kicking around the closet for years.* (The coat has not been used but has been left there carelessly.) *The letter kicked around on my desk for days.* (The letter was pushed around on the desk and neglected for days.) **3** *slang* To talk easily or carelessly back and forth about; examine in a careless or easygoing way. *Bob and I kicked around the idea of going swimming, but it was hot and we were too lazy.* (We talked it over carelessly.) Compare TRY OUT, TALK OVER. **4** To move about often; go from one job or place to another; become experienced. *Harry has kicked around all over the world as a merchant seaman.* (Harry has lived a rough life as a sailor and knows the world.) Compare HAS BEEN AROUND.

kick back   *v., slang, informal* To pay money illegally for favorable contract arrangements. *I will do it if you kick-back a few hundred for my firm.* (I will do it if you bribe me.)

kickback   *n., slang, informal* Money paid illegally for favorable treatment. *He was arrested for making kickback payments.* (They arrested him for making illegal bribes.)

kick down   *v. phr., slang* To shift an automobile, jeep, or truck into lower gear by hand-shifting. *Joe kicked the jeep down from third to second; and we slowed down.* (He shifted down from third to second gear).

kick in   See CHIP IN.

kick in the pants *or* **kick in the teeth**   *n. phr., informal* Unexpected scorn or insult when praise was expected; rejection.—A cliché. *Mary worked hard to clean up John's room, but all she got for her trouble was a kick in the teeth.* (John did not feel thankful for what Mary had done for him; all he did was insult her.) Compare SLAP IN THE FACE.

kick it   *v. phr., slang* To end a bad or unwanted habit such as drinking, smoking, or drug addiction. *Farnsworth finally kicked it; he's in good shape.* (He finally stopped his harmful habit, which is good for him.)

kick off   *v.* **1** To make the kick that begins a football game. *John kicked off and the football game started.* (John started the football game by kicking the ball.) **2** *informal* To begin; launch; start. *The candidate kicked off his campaign with a speech on television.* (The candidate started his campaign by making a speech on T.V.) *The fund raising drive was kicked off with a theater party.* (A theater party was the first event in the fund raising drive.) **3** *slang* To die. *Mr. Jones was almost ninety years old when he kicked off.* (Mr. Jones was almost ninety when he died.) Syn. KICK THE BUCKET.

kick oneself   *v. phr., informal* To be sorry or ashamed; regret. *When John missed the train, he kicked himself for not having left earlier.* (John felt sorry for not having left early enough to catch the train.) *Mary could have kicked herself for letting the secret out before it was announced officially.* (Mary was sorry that she told the secret before she should have.)

kick out *or* **boot out**   *v., informal* To make (someone) go or leave; get rid of; dismiss. *The boys made so much noise at the movie that the manager kicked them out.* (The manager made the boys leave the theater.) *The chief of police was booted out of office because he was a crook.* (He was forced to resign.) Syn. THROW OUT 3.

kick over v. 1 *Of a motor:* To begin to work. *He had not used his car for two months and when he tried to start it, the motor would not kick over.* (His car would not start after it had been left for so long.) 2 *slang* To pay; contribute. *The gang forced all the storekeepers on the block to kick over $5 a week.* (The storekeepers had to pay the gang every week.) 3 *slang* To die. *Mrs. O'Leary's cow kicked over this morning.* (The cow died.)

kick over the traces *also* **jump the traces** v. phr. To break the rules; behave badly.—A cliché. *When their teacher was absent and they had a substitute, the children kicked over the traces.* (The children disobeyed the substitute teacher and talked and played.) Compare ACT UP, CUT UP, LET LOOSE, OUT OF HAND, RAISE CAIN.

kick the bucket v. phr., slang To die. *Old Mr. Jones kicked the bucket just two days before his ninety-fourth birthday.* (Mr. Jones died.) Compare KICK OFF 3.

kick up v., informal To show signs of not working right. *John had had too much to eat and his stomach started to kick up.* (John had a stomach ache.) *After working well for a year the air conditioner suddenly started kicking up.* (The air conditioner was not working right.)

kick up a fuss or **kick up a row** or **raise a row** also **kick up a dust** v. phr., informal To make trouble; make a disturbance. *When the teacher gave the class five more hours of homework, the class kicked up a fuss.* (The class objected loudly.) *When the teacher left the room, two boys kicked up a row.* (Two boys began to fight.) Compare RAISE CAIN, RAISE THE ROOF.

kick up one's heels v. phr., informal To have a merry time; celebrate.—A cliché. *When exams were over the students went to town to kick up their heels.* (The students celebrated the end of exams by having a good time.) *Mary was usually very quiet but at the farewell party she kicked up her heels and had a wonderful time.* (Mary celebrated freely.)

kid See HANDLE WITH GLOVES or HANDLE WITH KID GLOVES, HANDLE WITHOUT GLOVES or HANDLE WITHOUT KID GLOVES.

kiddie car n., slang, citizen's band radio jargon A school bus. *Watch out for that kiddie car coming up behind you!* (The school bus is nearing from behind; be cautious.)

kill See CURIOSITY KILLED THE CAT, IN AT THE KILL.

kill off v. To kill or end completely; destroy. *The factory dumped poisonous wastes into the river and killed off the fish.* (The factory waste materials were poison and killed all the fish in the river.) *The President suggested a new law to Congress but many members of Congress were against the idea and they killed it off.* (Many Congressmen voted against the new law and it was defeated.) *Mother made Nancy practice her dancing an hour every day; Nancy got tired of dancing and that killed off her interest.* (Having to dance too long each day made Nancy lose interest in dancing.)

kill the goose that laid the golden egg To spoil something that is good or something that you have, by being greedy.—A proverb. *Mrs. Jones gives you an apple from her tree whenever you go by her house, but don't kill the goose that laid the golden egg by bothering her too much.* (Don't be too greedy or Mrs. Jones will stop giving you apples.)

kill two birds with one stone v. phr. To succeed in doing two things by only one action; get two results from one effort. *Mother stopped at the supermarket to buy bread and then went to get Jane at dancing class; she killed two birds with one stone.* (Mother bought bread and brought Jane home with only one trip in the car.) *The history teacher told us that making an outline kills two birds with one stone; it makes us study the lesson till we understand it, and it gives us notes to review before the test.* (Outlining has two results; it forces us to understand and it gives us notes for review.)

kilter See OUT OF KILTER.

kind See IN A WAY also IN A KIND OF WAY, IN KIND.

kindly See TAKE KINDLY TO.

kind of or **sort of** adv. phr., informal Almost but not quite; rather. *A guinea pig looks kind of like a rabbit, but it has short ears.* (A guinea pig looks much like a rabbit. It would look more like a rabbit if its ears were longer.) *Bob was kind of tired when he finished the job.* (Bob was somewhat tired after working.) *The teacher sort of frowned but then smiled.* (He frowned a little, then smiled.) *Mary wouldn't tell what she wanted to be when she grew up; it was sort of a secret.* (Mary's plan for her life was not really a secret, but she did not like to talk about it.)

kite See GO FLY A KITE.

kitten See HAVE KITTENS.

knee See BRING TO ONE'S KNEES, IN THE LAP OF THE GODS also ON THE KNEES OF THE GODS, ON ONE'S KNEES, UP TO THE CHIN IN or UP TO THE KNEE IN.

knee-deep or **neck-deep** adv. or adj. phr. 1 Very much, deeply; having a big part in. *Johnny was knee-deep in trouble.* (He was badly in trouble.) 2 Very busy, working hard at. *We were neck-deep in homework before the exams.* (We were very busy.) 3 Getting or having many or much. *The television station was knee-deep in phone calls.* (They received many phone calls.) Compare UP TO —————— IN.

knee-high to a grasshopper also **knee-high to a duck** adj. phr., informal As tall as a very small child; very young.—A hackneyed phrase. *Charles started reading when he was knee-high to a grasshopper.* (Charles began to read when he was very small.) *I've known Mary ever since she was knee-high to a duck.* (I've known her since she was a very small child.)

kneeling bus *n., informal* A bus equipped with a hydraulic device to enable it to drop almost to curb level for greater ease of boarding and leaving vehicle, as a convenience for elderly or handicapped passengers. *The man on crutches was pleased to see the kneeling bus.* (The injured man was relieved when he realized he could enter the bus easily.)

knell See DEATH KNELL.

knit See CLOSE-KNIT.

knitting See STICK TO ONE'S KNITTING *or* TEND TO ONE'S KNITTING.

knock See SCHOOL OF HARD KNOCKS.

knock about *or* **knock around** *v.* To travel without a plan; go where you please. *After he graduated from college, Joe knocked about for a year seeing the country before he went to work in his father's business.* (Joe traveled around the country, going where he pleased, before he went to work.) Compare KICK AROUND.

knock back on one's heels See SET BACK ON ONE'S HEELS.

knocked out *adj., slang* Intoxicated, drugged, out of one's mind. *Kinworthy sounds so incoherent, he must be knocked out.* (He must be drunk or high on drugs; he makes no sense.)

knock for a loop *or* **throw for a loop** *v. phr., slang* To surprise very much. *When I heard they were moving, I was really knocked for a loop.* (I was very much surprised when I heard they were moving.) *The news of their marriage threw me for a loop.* (Their marriage surprised me very much.)

knock it off *v. phr., slang, informal* **1** To stop talking about something considered not appropriate or nonsensical by the listener; used frequently as an imperative. *Come on, Joe, knock it off, you're not making any sense at all!* (Stop talking nonsense, you're not making sense.) **2** To cease doing something, to quit; heavily favored in the imperative. *Come on boys, knock it off, you're breaking the furniture in my room!* (The boys were fighting and breaking the furniture; their father tells them to stop it.)

knock off *v. phr., slang* **1** To burglarize someone. *They knocked off the Manning residence.* (They burglarized the Manning residence.) **2** To murder someone. *The gangsters knocked off Herman.* (They murdered Herman.)

knock off one's feet *v. phr.* To surprise (someone) so much that he does not know what to do. *Her husband's death knocked Mrs. Jones off her feet.* (Mr. Jones's death was such a surprise that Mrs. Jones couldn't think of anything else for a while.) *When Charlie was given the prize, it knocked him off his feet for a few minutes.* (Charlie was so surprised he didn't know what to think or say.) Compare BOWL OVER 2, SWEEP OFF ONE'S FEET.

knock one's block off *v. phr., slang* To hit someone very hard; beat someone up. *Stay out of my yard or I'll knock your block off.* (Keep out of my yard or I'll beat you up.) *Jim will knock your block off if he catches you riding his bike.* (Jim will hit you hard if he catches you riding his bike.)

knock oneself out *v. phr., informal* To work very hard; make a great effort. *Mrs. Ross knocked herself out planning her daughter's wedding.* (Mrs. Ross worked harder than necessary planning her daughter's wedding.) *Tom knocked himself out to give his guests a good time.* (Tom made a great effort to give his guests a good time.) Compare BREAK ONE'S NECK, FALL OVER BACKWARDS, OUT OF ONE'S WAY.

knock on wood *v. phr.* To knock on something made of wood to keep from having bad luck.—Many people believe that you will have bad luck if you talk about good luck or brag about something, unless you knock on wood; often used in a joking way. *Charles said, "I haven't been sick all winter." Grandfather said, "You'd better knock on wood when you say that."* (Grandfather pretended that Charles would get sick if he didn't knock on something made of wood, because he bragged about his good health.)

knockout *n., slang* Strikingly beautiful woman. *Sue is a regular knockout.* (She is a strikingly beautiful woman.)

knock out *v. phr.* To make helpless, unworkable, or unusable. *The champion knocked out the challenger in the third round.* (The champion defeated the challenger by hitting him until he was unconscious.) *The soldier knocked out two enemy tanks with his bazooka.* (The soldier destroyed two enemy tanks.)

knock the living daylights out of *v. phr., slang, informal* To render (someone) unconscious (said in exaggeration). *The news almost knocked the living daylights out of me.* (I almost fainted when I heard the news.)

knot See TIE IN KNOTS, TIE THE KNOT.

know See FOR ALL ONE KNOWS, GOD KNOWS *or* GOODNESS KNOWS *or* HEAVEN KNOWS, IN THE KNOW, NOT KNOW WHICH WAY TO TURN *or* NOT KNOW WHICH WAY TO JUMP.

know enough to come in out of the rain *v. phr.* To have good sense; know how to take care of yourself.—A cliché. Usually used in the negative. *Bob does so many foolish things that his mother says he doesn't know enough to come in out of the rain.* (Bob does so many foolish things that his mother says he can't take care of himself.) *Sally may look stupid, but she knows enough to come in out the rain.* (Although Sally looks stupid, she has a lot of good sense.)

know if one is coming or going *or* **know whether one is coming or going** *v. phr.* To feel able to think clearly; know what to do.— A cliché. Usually used in the negative or with limiters. *On Monday, the car broke down; on Tuesday, Mother broke her arm; on Wednesday, the children all became ill with the mumps; by Thursday, poor Father didn't know if he was coming or going.* (So many things happened that Father was upset and confused.) *My cousin is so much in love that she scarcely knows whether she's coming or going.* (She can't think clearly; she doesn't know what she is doing most of the time.) Compare IN A FOG.

know in one's bones See FEEL IN ONE'S BONES.

know ⸺ is alive *v. phr.* Not to notice a person.—Used with negative or limiting words and in questions. *She was a good-looking girl but she didn't know I was alive.* (She was a good-looking girl but she didn't notice me.) Compare GIVE A HANG.

know-it-all *n.* A person who acts as if he knows all about everything; someone who thinks no one can tell him anything new. *After George was elected as class president, he wouldn't take suggestions from anyone; he became a know-it-all.* (George became a person who thinks he knows all about a subject and won't let anyone tell him anything.) —Also used like an adjective. *The other students didn't like George's know-it-all attitude.* (The other students did not like the way George acted, thinking he knew more than anyone else.)

knowledge See A LITTLE KNOWLEDGE IS A DANGEROUS THING, TO THE BEST OF YOUR KNOWLEDGE.

know one's way around *or* **know one's way about** *v. phr.* **1** To understand how things happen in the world; be experienced in the ways of the world.—A cliché. *The sailor had been in the wildest ports in the world. He knew his way around.* (He knew what dangers to look out for anywhere.) Compare HAVE BEEN AROUND. **2** *or* *informal* **know one's onions** *or* **know one's stuff** To have experience and skill in an activity. *Before trying to make any pottery, it is better to get advice from someone who knows his way about in ceramics.* (You should get advice from someone experienced in making pottery before you try making your own.) Compare DRY BEHIND THE EARS.

know the ropes See THE ROPES.

know the score See THE SCORE.

know which side one's bread is buttered on *v. phr.* To know who can help you and try to please him; know what is for your own gain. *Dick was always polite to the boss; he knew which side his bread was buttered on.* (Dick knew that he would lose his job if he made the boss angry at him.)

know which way to turn See NOT KNOW WHICH WAY TO TURN.

knuckle See BUCKLE DOWN *or* KNUCKLE DOWN, RAP ONE'S KNUCKLES.

knuckle down See BUCKLE DOWN.

knuckle under *v. phr.* To do something because you are forced to do it. *Bobby refused to knuckle under to the bully.* (Bobby refused to do what the bully told him to do.) Compare GIVE IN.

L

labor movement *n.* Groups which form, strengthen, and increase membership in labor unions. *His father was connected with the labor movement in the 1920's.* (His father helped organize labor unions in the 1920's.)

labor of love *n. phr.* Something done for personal pleasure and not pay or profit.—A cliché. *Building the model railroad was a labor of love for the retired engineer.* (The retired engineer built the model railroad because he wanted to and enjoyed doing it, not because he could get money for it.)

lace into *or* **tie into** *v., informal* To attack physically or with words; begin to hit or criticize. *The boxer laced into his opponent.* (The boxer attacked his opponent with his fists.) *The critics laced into the new movie.* (The critics attacked the new movie with words.) Syn. LAY INTO, RIP INTO. Compare GIVE IT TO.

lady friend *n.* **1** A woman friend. *His aunt stays with a lady friend in Florida during the winter.* (His aunt stays with a woman friend in Florida during the winter.) **2** A woman who is the special friend of a man— used by people trying to appear more polite, but not often used by careful speakers. *The lawyer took his lady friend to dinner.* (The lawyer took the woman who is his special friend to dinner.) Syn. GIRL FRIEND.

lady killer *n., informal* **1** Any man who has strong sex appeal toward women. *Joe is a regular lady killer.* (He has strong sex appeal toward women.) **2** A man who relentlessly pursues amorous conquests, is successful at it, and then abandons his heartbroken victims. *The legendary Don Juan of Spain is the most famous lady killer of recorded history.* (Don Juan was the most famous conqueror of women whom he subsequently abandoned.) (See LADY'S MAN.)

lady's man *n.* A man or boy who likes to be with women or girls very much and is popular with them.—A trite expression. *Charlie is quite a lady's man now.* (Charlie is with the girls much of his time.)

lake See GO JUMP IN THE LAKE.

lam See ON THE LAM.

lamb See GOD TEMPERS THE WIND TO THE SHORN LAMB, IN TWO SHAKES OF A LAMB'S TAIL.

lame duck *n., informal* An elected public official who has been either defeated in a new election or whose term cannot be renewed, but who has a short period of time left in office during which he can still perform certain duties, though with somewhat diminished powers. *In the last year of their second terms, American presidents are lame ducks.* (They cannot be re-elected for a third term.)

land See FAT OF THE LAND, LAY OF THE LAND *also* HOW THE LAND LIES.

land all over See JUMP ON.

landing ship *n.* A ship built to land troops and army equipment on a beach for an invasion. *The landing ship came near the beach, doors in the bow opened, and marines ran out.* (The special ship built to carry soldiers near the beach came near it and let the soldiers go ashore.)

land-office business *n. informal* A great rush of business. *It was a hot day, and the drive-ins were doing a land-office business in ice cream and cold drinks.* (The refreshment stands were selling ice cream and cold drinks as fast as they could serve them.)

land of nod *n. phr.* Sleep. *The little girl went off to the land of nod.* (The little girl fell asleep.)

land on See JUMP ON.

land on one's feet *also* **land on both feet** *v. phr., informal* To get yourself out of trouble without damage or injury and sometimes with a gain; be successful no matter what happens. *No matter what trouble he gets into, he always seems to land on his feet.* (He often gets into trouble, but he never seems to lose.) *Mary lost her first job because she was always late to work, but she landed on her feet and soon had a better job.* (She was lucky, and her bad record did not hurt her.)

lane See LOVERS' LANE.

lap See IN THE LAP OF LUXURY, IN THE LAP OF THE GODS.

lap up *v.* **1** To eat or drink with the tip of the tongue. *The kitten laps up its milk.* (The kitten licks the milk up with its tongue.) **2** *informal* To take in eagerly. *She flatters him all the time and he just laps it up.* (She flatters him and he loves it.) *William is interested in rockets and space, and he laps up all he can read about them.* (He eagerly learns anything about space.) Syn. EAT UP 3.

lardhead *n., slang* A stupid or slow-witted person. *You'll never convince Donald; he's a lardhead.* (You'll never manage convincing him: he is so slow-witted.)

large See AT LARGE, BY AND LARGE.

large as life See BIG AS LIFE.

large-eyed See ROUND-EYED.

lash See TONGUE LASHING.

lash out *v.* **1** To kick. *The horse lashed out at the man behind him.* (The horse kicked at the man behind him.) **2** To try suddenly to hit. *The woman lashed out at the crowd with her umbrella.* (The woman swung her umbrella at the crowd.) **3** To attack with words. *The senator lashed out at the administration.* (The senator criticized the administration severely.) *The school newspaper lashed out at the unfriendly way some students treated the visiting team.* (The newspaper scolded the students.)

last See AT LAST, EVERY LAST MAN, EVERY SINGLE *or* EVERY LAST, FIRST AND LAST, HE LAUGHS BEST WHO LAUGHS LAST, HAVE THE LAST LAUGH, ON ONE'S LAST LEGS, TILL THE

LAST GUN IS FIRED *or* UNTIL THE LAST GUN IS FIRED.

last but not least *adv. phr.* In the last place but not the least important.—A cliché. *Billy will bring sandwiches, Alice will bring cake, Susan will bring cookies, John will bring potato chips, and last but not least, Sally will bring the lemonade.* (Sally is mentioned last, but her lemonade is as important to the picnic as the other things.)

last ditch *n.* The last place that can be defended; the last resort. *They will fight reform to the last ditch.* (They will fight reform as long as they can.)

last-ditch *adj.* Made or done as a last chance to keep from losing or failing. *He threw away his cigarettes in a last-ditch effort to stop smoking.* (He was afraid he would not be able to stop smoking so he threw his cigarettes away before he could start again.) Compare BACK TO THE WALL.

last laugh See HAVE THE LAST LAUGH.

last out *v.* **1** To be enough until the end of. *There is enough food in the house to last out the snowstorm.* (There will be enough of food until the storm is over.) *Our candles won't last out the night.* (The candles will burn and be gone before morning.) **2** To continue to the end of; continue to live after; live or go through. *The old man is dying; he won't last out the night.* (He won't live the rest of the night.) *This car will never last out the winter.* (The car is not good enough to keep running.) Compare HOLD OUT.

last straw *or* **straw that breaks the camel's back** *n. phr.* A small trouble which follows other troubles and makes one lose patience and be unable to bear them. *Bill had a bad day in school yesterday. He lost his knife on the way home, then he fell down, and when he broke a shoe lace, that was the last straw and he began to cry.* (He had too many troubles and began to cry.) *Mary didn't like it when the other girls said she was proud and lazy, but when they said she told fibs it was the straw that broke the camel's back and she told the teacher.* (The last thing they said, added to the others, was just too much to bear.)

last word *n.* **1** The last remark in an argument. *I never win an argument with her. She always has the last word.* (She always has one more thing to say than I do in an argument.) **2** The final say in deciding something. *The superintendent has the last word in ordering new desks.* (He is the one who decides when to order new desks.) **3** *informal* The most modern thing. *Mrs. Greens's stove is the last word in stoves.* (Her stove is the most modern stove there is.)

latch on *or* **latch onto** *v. informal* **1** To get hold of; grasp or grab; catch. *He looked for something to latch onto and keep from falling.* (He looked for something to get hold of to keep from falling.) *The football player*

latched *onto a pass.* (The football player caught a pass.) **2** *slang* To get into your possession. *The banker latched on to a thousand shares of stock.* (The banker bought a thousand shares of stock.) **3** *slang* To understand. *The teacher explained the idea of jet engines until the students latched onto it.* (The teacher explained jet engines until the students understood how they work.) Syn. CATCH ON. **4** *informal* To keep; to hold. *The poor woman latched on to the little money she had left.* (The poor woman kept the little money she had left.) **5** *slang* To stay with; not leave. *Marie and Dick wanted to go to the movies by themselves, but Marie's little brother latched onto them.* (Marie's little brother went with them, and would not leave them alone.)

latch string *n.* **1** A string that opens an old-fashioned door by lifting a small bar. *The early settlers kept the latch string outside the door when they were working around the house, but at night they pulled it to the inside.* (At night the settlers kept the string inside so that no one could get in.) **2** *informal* A warm welcome; a friendly greeting. —Used in such phrases as *the latch string is out. Mary has her latch string out for everyone who comes.* (Mary has a welcome ready for everyone who comes.) Syn. WELCOME MAT 2.

late See BETTER LATE THAN NEVER, OF LATE.

lately See JOHNNY-COME-LATELY.

later See SOONER OR LATER.

later on *adv.* Later; not now. *Finish your lessons. Later on, we may have a surprise.* (Later, we may have a surprise.) *Bill couldn't stand on his head when school started, but later on he learned how.* (Later Bill learned to stand on his head.)

lather See IN A LATHER.

laugh See HE LAUGHS BEST WHO LAUGHS LAST, HAVE THE LAST LAUGH.

laughing matter *n.* A funny happening; a silly situation.—Usually used with *no. John's failing the test is no laughing matter!* (This is not a funny happening.) *We were amused when our neighbor's cat had five kittens, but when our own cat had six kittens it was no laughing matter.* (When our cat had six kittens, it did not seem so funny.)

laugh in one's beard See LAUGH UP ONE'S SLEEVE.

laugh in one's sleeve See LAUGH UP ONE'S SLEEVE.

laugh off *v.* To dismiss with a laugh as not important or not serious; not take seriously. *He had a bad fall while ice skating but he laughed it off.* (He did not let the fall he had while skating bother him.) *You can't laugh off a ticket for speeding.* (You must take a ticket for speeding as a serious matter.) Compare MAKE LIGHT OF.

laugh on the wrong side of one's mouth *or* **laugh on the other side of one's mouth** *or*

laugh out of the other side of one's mouth *v. phr., informal* To be made sorry; to feel annoyance or disappointment; cry. *Paul boasted that he was a good skater, but after he fell, he laughed out of the other side of his mouth.* (After he fell, he was sorry that he had boasted that he was a good skater.)

laugh up one's sleeve *or* **laugh in one's sleeve** *or* **laugh in one's beard** To be amused but not show it; hide your laughter. Usually considered trite. *He was laughing up his sleeve when Joe answered the phone because he knew the call would be a joke.* (He was amused but didn't show it when Joe went to answer the joke telephone call.)

launch window *n., Space English; informal* **1** A period of time when the line-up of planets, Sun, and Moon are such as to make favorable conditions for a specific space launch. *The mission was cancelled until the next launch window which will be exactly six weeks from today.* (The next appropriate time for a launch will be six weeks from now.) **2** A favorable time for starting some kind of ambitious adventure. *My next launch window for a European trip isn't until school is over in June.* (My next chance to go to Europe is in June when school ends.)

laurel See LOOK TO ONE'S LAURELS, REST ON ONE'S LAURELS.

lavender See LAY OUT 7.

law See LAY DOWN THE LAW, PARLIAMENTARY LAW, TAKE THE LAW INTO ONE'S OWN HANDS.

lawful age See LEGAL AGE.

law of averages *n. phr.* The idea that you can't win all the time or lose all the time. *The Celtics have won 10 games in a row but the law of averages will catch up with them soon.* (The Celtics have won 10 games in a row but they are bound to lose a few soon.)

law unto oneself *n. phr., literary.* A person who does only what he wishes; a person who ignores or breaks the law when he doesn't like it. *Everybody in Germany feared Hitler because he was a law unto himself.* (Hitler made up his own laws.) *Mr. Brown told Johnny that he must stop trying to be a law unto himself.* (Johnny was acting as though he could do whatever he pleased.) Compare TAKE THE LAW INTO ONE'S OWN HANDS.

lay See KILL THE GOOSE THAT LAID THE GOLDEN EGG.

lay about one *v. phr.* To hit out in all directions.—Used with a reflexive object: *her, him,* or *them. The Indians surrounded Wetzel, but he laid about him so hard, with his gun used as a club, that they stepped back and let him escape.* (Wetzel hit out all around him until the Indians let him escape.) *Mrs. Franklin didn't kill the mouse, but she laid about her so hard with the broom that she scared it away.* (She didn't kill the mouse, but she hit out at it so hard with the broom that it ran away.)

lay a finger on *v. phr.* To touch or bother, even a little.—Used in negative, interrogative, and conditional sentences. *Don't you dare lay a finger on the vase!* (Don't you dare touch that vase!) *Suppose Billy takes his brother with him; will the mean, tough boy down the street dare lay a finger on him?* (If Billy takes big brother with him, will the mean boy down the street bother or tease him?) *If you so much as lay a finger on my boy, I'll call the police.* (If you even touch my boy, I will call the police.) Compare LAY HANDS ON, PUT ONE'S FINGER ON.

lay an egg *v. phr., slang* To fail to win the interest or favor of an audience.—A trite expression. *His joke laid an egg.* (No one laughed at his joke.) *Sometimes he is a successful speaker, but sometimes he lays an egg.* (Sometimes the audience does not like his speech.)

lay aside *v. phr.* **1** To put off until another time; interrupt an activity. *The president laid aside politics to turn to foreign affairs.* (He turned from politics to foreign affairs.) **2** To save. *They tried to lay aside a little money each week for their vacation.* (They tried to save a little each week for their vacation.)

lay at one's door *v. phr., literary* To blame (something) on a person. *The failure of the plan was laid at his door.* (The failure of the plan was blamed on him.) Compare LAY TO 1.

lay away *v.* **1** To save. *She laid a little of her pay away each week.* (She saved a little of her pay each week.) **2** To bury (a person). —Used to avoid the word *bury,* which some people think is unpleasant. *He was laid away in his favorite spot on the hill.* (He was buried in his favorite spot on the hill.)

lay-away plan *n.* A plan for buying something that you can't pay cash for; a plan in which you pay some money down and pay a little more when you can, and the store holds the article until you have paid the full price. *She could not afford to pay for the coat all at once, so she used the lay-away plan.* (She paid five dollars every month until her coat was paid for; then she could take the coat home.)

lay by *v.* To save, especially a little at a time. *The Martins laid a little money by every week till they had enough for a trip to Florida.* (They saved enough money to take a trip to Florida.) *The farmer laid by some of his best corn to use the next year for seed.* (The farmer saved some of his best corn to plant the next year.)

lay down *v.* **1** To let (something) be taken; give up or surrender (something). *The general told the troops to lay down their arms.* (The general told the soldiers to give up their guns.) *He was willing to lay down his life for his country.* (He was willing to die for his country.) Compare GIVE UP. **2** To ask people to follow; tell someone to obey; make (a rule or principle). *The committee laid down rules* *about the size of tennis courts.* (The committee made rules for the size of tennis courts.) **3** To declare; say positively; say surely; state. *She laid it down as always true that "a fool and his money are soon parted."* (She said without doubt that it is always true that a fool soon spends or loses his money.) **4** To store or save for future use, especially in a cellar. *They laid down several barrels of cider.* (They put away several barrels of cider for future use.)

lay down one's cards See LAY ONE'S CARDS ON THE TABLE.

lay down the law *v. phr.* **1** To give strict orders. *The teacher lays down the law about homework every afternoon.* (She gives strict orders to the students about their homework.) **2** To speak severely or seriously about a wrongdoing; scold. *The principal called in the students and laid down the law to them about skipping classes.* (The principal called in the students and scolded them for skipping classes.) Compare TELL ——— WHERE TO GET OFF.

lay eyes on *or* **set eyes on** *v. phr.* To see. *She knew he was different as soon as she laid eyes on him.* (She could tell he was different as soon as she saw him.) *I didn't know the man; in fact, I had never set eyes on him.* (I had never seen him before.)

lay for *v., informal* To hide and wait for in order to catch or attack; to lie in wait for. *The bandits laid for him along the road.* (The bandits hid along the road and waited for him to come by so they could attack him.) *I knew he had the marks for the exam, so I was laying for him outside his office.* (I was waiting to see him outside his office because I knew he had the exam marks with him.)

lay hands on *v. phr.* **1** To get hold of; find; catch. *The treasure hunters can keep any treasure they can lay hands on.* (The treasure hunters can keep any treasure they can get hold of.) *If the police can lay hands on him, they will put him in jail.* (If they can catch him, they will put him in jail.) Compare LAY ONE'S HAND ON 2. **2** To do violence to; harm; hurt. *They were afraid that if they left him alone in his disturbed condition he would lay hands on himself.* (They were afraid that he would harm himself if they left him alone because he was so upset.)

lay hold of *v. phr.* **1** To take hold of; grasp; grab. *He laid hold of the rope and pulled the boat ashore.* (He grabbed the rope and pulled the boat ashore.) **2** To get possession of. *He sold every washing machine he could lay hold of.* (He sold every washing machine he could get.) **3** *Chiefly British* To understand. *Some ideas in this science book are hard to lay hold of.* (Some of the ideas are hard to understand.)

lay in *v.* To store up a supply of; to get and keep for future use. *Mrs. Mason heard that* *the price of sugar might go up, so she laid in a hundred pounds of it.* (She bought one hundred pounds of sugar.) *Before school starts, the principal will lay in plenty of paper for the students' written work.* (The principal will get a big supply of paper ready.) Compare LAY UP.

lay into *or* **light into** *v., informal* **1** To attack physically; go at vigorously. *The two fighters laid into each other as soon as the bell rang.* (The two fighters began fighting hard as soon as the bout began.) *John loves Italian food and he really laid into the spaghetti.* (John loves Italian food and he really ate a lot of spaghetti.) Syn. PITCH INTO, SAIL INTO. **2** *slang* To attack with words. *The senator laid into the opponents of his bill.* (The senator spoke strongly against the men who were against his idea for a new law.) Syn. LACE INTO, RIP INTO. Compare BAWL OUT, TELL OFF.

lay it on *or* **lay it on thick** *also* **put it on thick** *or* **spread it on thick** *or* **lay it on with a trowel** *v. phr., informal* To persuade someone by using very much flattery; flatter. *Bob wanted to go to the movies. He layed it on thick to his mother.* (Bob tried to flatter his mother into letting him go to the movies.) *Mary was caught fibbing. She sure spread it on thick.* (Mary tried flattery to get people to forget that she had fibbed.) Compare PUT ON 2b.

lay it on the line See LAY ON THE LINE 2.

lay low *v.* **1** To knock down; to force into a lying position; to put out of action. *Many trees were laid low by the storm.* (Many trees were knocked down by the storm.) *Jane was laid low by the flu.* (Jane had to stay in bed with the flu.) **2** To kill. *The hunters laid low seven pheasants.* (The hunters shot seven pheasants.) **3** See LIE LOW.

lay off *v.* **1** To mark out the boundaries or limits. *He laid off a baseball diamond on the vacant lot.* (He measured the lines for a baseball diamond.) Compare LAY OUT 5. **2** To put out of work. *The company lost the contract for making the shoes and laid off half its workers.* (The company had to stop making the shoes and let half its workmen out of their jobs.) **3** *slang* To stop bothering; leave alone.—Usually used in the imperative. *Lay off me, will you? I have to study for a test.* (Leave me alone; I have to study.) **4** *slang* To stop using or taking. *His doctor told him to lay off cigarettes.* (His doctor told him to stop smoking cigarettes.)

lay of the land *also* **how the land lies** *n. phr.* **1** The natural features of a piece of land, such as hills and valleys. *The style of house the contractor builds depends partly on the lay of the land.* (The contractor builds one kind of house on a hill, and another kind on level land.) **2** The way something is arranged; the important facts about something; how things are. *The banker wanted to check the lay of the land before buying the stock.* (The banker wanted to check everything about the stock before buying any of it.) *Before the new boy will join our club, he wants to see how the land lies.* (The new boy first wants to know what clubs he could join and who belongs to them.)

lay on *v.* **1** To spread on or over a surface; apply. *He told us that we should lay on a second coat of paint for better protection against the weather.* (He told us to apply a second coat of paint for better protection against the weather.) **2** To beat; to strike. *Little John seized a staff and began to lay on with great energy.* (Little John seized a pole and began striking hard.) **3** See LAY IT ON.

lay one's cards on the table *or* **lay down one's cards** *or* **put one's cards on the table** *v. phr., informal* To let someone know your position and interest openly; deal honestly; act without trickery or secrets.—A cliché. *In talking about buying the property, Peterson laid his cards on the table about his plans for it.* (In trying to buy the property, he said honestly what he would use it for.) *Some of the graduates of the school were unfriendly toward the new superintendent, but he put his cards on the table and won their support.* (The group was against him, but he won their support by his honesty about school problems.)

lay oneself out *v. phr., informal* To make an extra hard effort; try very hard. *Larry wanted to win a medal for his school, so he really laid himself out in the race.* (Larry tried very hard in the race.)

lay one's finger on See PUT ONE'S FINGER ON.

lay one's hands on *or* **get one's hands on** *v. phr.* **1** To seize in order to punish or treat roughly. *If I ever lay my hands on that boy he'll be sorry.* (If I ever get hold of that boy to punish him, he'll be sorry.) Compare LAY A FINGER ON. **2** To get possession of. *He was unable to lay his hands on a Model T Ford for the school play.* (He couldn't get a Model T Ford for the school play.) Compare LAY HANDS ON 1. **3** *or* **lay one's hand on** *or* **put one's hand on** To find; locate. *He keeps a file of letters so he can lay his hands on one whenever he needs it.* (He keeps a file of letters so he can easily find one when he needs it.)

lay on the line *or* **put on the line** *v. phr., informal* **1** To pay or offer to pay. *The sponsors had to lay nearly a million dollars on the line to keep the show on TV.* (The sponsors had to give nearly a million dollars to keep the show on TV.) *The bank is putting $5,000 on the line as a reward to anyone who catches the robber.* (The bank is offering $5,000 as a reward.) Compare PUT UP. **2** To say plainly so that there can be no doubt; tell truthfully. *I'm going to lay it on the line for you, Paul. You must work harder if you want to pass.* (I'm going to make you understand, Paul, by

telling you clearly and truthfully.) **3** To take a chance of losing; risk. *The champion is laying his title on the line in the fight tonight.* (The champion is risking the loss of the championship in the fight.) *Frank decided to lay his job on the line and tell the boss that he thought he was wrong.* (He decided to risk making the boss angry and losing his job by saying that the boss was wrong.)

lay out *v.* **1** To prepare (a dead body) for burial. *The corpse was laid out by the undertaker.* (The corpse was readied for burial by the undertaker.) **2** *slang* To knock down flat; to hit unconscious. *A stiff right to the jaw laid the boxer out in the second round.* (A hard right to the jaw knocked him flat in the second round.) **3** To plan. *Come here, Fred, I have a job laid out for you.* (Come here, Fred, I have a job planned for you.) **4** To mark or show where work is to be done. *The foreman laid out the job for the new machinist.* (The foreman marked where he wanted the new machinist to work.) **5** To plan the building or arrangement of; design. *The architect laid out the interior of the building.* (The architect made a drawing showing how the inside of the building was to be built.) *The early colonists laid out towns in the wilderness.* (The early colonists planned and built towns in the wilderness.) Compare LAY OFF 1. **6** *slang* To spend; pay. *How much did you have to lay out for your new car?* (How much did you have to pay for your new car?) **7** *or* **lay out in lavender** *slang* To scold; lecture. *He was laid out in lavender for arriving an hour late for the dance.* (His girl gave him a severe scolding for arriving at the dance an hour late.) Compare JUMP ON, LAY INTO 2, LET HAVE IT 1c.

lay over *v.* **1** To put off until later; delay; postpone. *We voted to lay the question over to our next meeting for decision.* (We voted to wait until the next meeting to decide the matter.) **2** To arrive in one place and wait some time before continuing the journey. *We had to lay over in St. Louis for two hours waiting for a plane to Seattle.* (Arriving in St. Louis, we had to wait two hours for the plane to Seattle.)

lay rubber *or* **lay a patch** *v. phr., slang* To take off in a car or a motorcycle so fast that the tires (made of rubber) leave a mark on the pavement. *Look at those crazy drag racers; they laid rubber in front of my house /they laid a patch in front of my house.* (They accelerated so fast that they left skid marks in front of my house.)

lay their heads together See PUT THEIR HEADS TOGETHER.

lay to *v.* **1** To give the blame or credit to; to name as cause. *He was unpopular and when he made money, it was laid to his dishonesty, but when he lost money, it was laid to his stupidity.* (When he made money, the people said it was because he was dishonest; when he lost money, they said it was because he was stupid.) Compare LAY AT ONE'S DOOR. **2** To hold a ship or boat still against the wind. *The pirates decided to lay to that night and go ashore in the morning.* (The pirates decided to hold the ship there during the night and to go ashore in the morning.) Compare LIE TO. **3** To exert oneself; to work hard. *He picked up a shovel and laid to with the rest of the gang.* (He picked up a shovel and went to work with the rest of the men.)

lay to heart See TAKE TO HEART.

lay to rest *v. phr., informal* **1** To put a dead person into a grave or tomb; bury. *President Kennedy was laid to rest in Arlington National Cemetery.* (He was buried there.) **2** To get rid of; put away permanently; stop. *The Scoutmaster's fears that Tom had drowned were laid to rest when Tom came back and said he had gone for a boat ride.* (The Scoutmaster's worries about Tom were stopped when Tom returned.) *The rumor that the principal had accepted another job was laid to rest when he said it wasn't true.* (The rumor was gotten rid of when he said it wasn't true.)

lay up *v.* **1** To collect a supply of; save for future use; store. *Bees lay up honey for the winter.* (They collect a supply of it so that they will have enough to eat until the next spring, when they can make more.) **2** To keep in the house or in bed because of sickness or injury; disable. *Jack was laid up with a twisted knee and couldn't play in the final game.* (He was kept in his bed by the injury which stopped him from playing football.) **3** To take out of active service; put in a boat dock or a garage. *Bill had to lay up his boat when school started.* (He had to put it away until summer came again.) *If you lay up a car for the winter, you should take out the battery.* (If you let a car sit unused in a garage, you should remove the battery.)

lay waste *v. phr., literary* To cause wide and great damage to; destroy and leave in ruins, wreck. *Enemy soldiers laid waste the land.* (They caused much damage to it, wrecking buildings and destroying crops as they went on.)

lead See ALL ROADS LEAD TO ROME, BLIND LEADING THE BLIND.

lead See GET THE LEAD OUT OF ONE'S PANTS.

lead a dog's life *v. phr., informal* To live a hard life; work hard and be treated unkindly. —A cliché. *A new college student of long ago led a dog's life.* (He was treated roughly. Any upperclassman could order him to do things.)

lead a merry chase *v. phr.* To delay or escape capture by (someone) skillfully; make (a pursuer) work hard. *The deer led the hunter a merry chase.* (The deer was hard to catch; it ran and dodged and disappeared into bushes.) *Valerie is leading her boy friend a merry chase.* (She is making him work hard to get her to marry him.)

lead by the nose *v. phr., informal* To have full control of; make or persuade (someone) to do anything whatever.—A hackneyed phrase. *Many people are easily influenced and a smart politician can lead them by the nose.* (He can get them to follow him and do as he wishes.) *Don't let anyone lead you by the nose; use your own judgment and do the right thing.* (Don't let anyone tell you what to do unless it is right.)

leader See MAJORITY LEADER, MINORITY LEADER.

lead-footed See HEAVY-FOOTED.

lead off *v.* To begin, start, open. *Richardson led off the inning with a double.* (Richardson began the inning by hitting a double.) *We always let Henry lead off.* (We let Henry be our first batter.) *Mr. Jones led off with the jack of diamonds.* (He began the card game by playing the jack of diamonds.) *When the teacher asked if the film helped them to understand, Phil led off by saying that he learned a lot from it.* (Phil was the first pupil to say something about the film.)

lead on *v. phr.* To encourage you to believe something untrue or mistaken. *Tom led us on to believe that he was a world traveler, but we found out that he had never been outside our state.* (Tom made us believe that he had traveled all over the world, which was not true.) *We were led on to think that Jeanne and Jim were engaged to be married.* (We were given reasons to believe that Jeanne and Jim were engaged, when they were not.)

lead the way *v. phr.* To go before and show how to go somewhere; guide. *The boys need someone to lead the way on their hike.* (The boys need someone to go with them and guide them on their hike.) *The men hired an Indian to lead the way to the Pueblo ruins.* (The men hired an Indian to guide them to the Pueblo ruins.) *That school led the way in finding methods to teach reading.* (That school was the first to find a new way to teach reading and other schools learned from it.)

leaf See TURN OVER A NEW LEAF.

league See IN LEAGUE WITH, IVY LEAGUE.

leaguer See TEXAS LEAGUER.

lean on *v. phr., slang, informal* To pressure (someone) by blackmailing, threats, physical violence, or the withholding of some favor in order to make the person comply with a wish or request. *I would gladly do what you ask if you only stopped leaning on me so hard!* (I would do what you want if you only stopped pressuring me.)

lean over backward See BEND OVER BACKWARD.

leap See BY LEAPS AND BOUNDS.

learn See LIVE AND LEARN.

learn by heart See BY HEART.

learn one's way around See KNOW ONE'S WAY AROUND.

learn the ropes See THE ROPES.

least See AT LEAST, IN THE LEAST, LAST BUT NOT LEAST, LINE OF LEAST RESISTANCE.

leatherneck *n., slang, informal* A member of the United States Marine Corps. *I didn't know your son Joe became a leatherneck.* (I didn't know he joined the Marine Corps.)

leave See SHORE LEAVE, TAKE IT OR LEAVE IT, TAKE LEAVE OF, TAKE ONE'S LEAVE.

leave a bad taste in one's mouth *v. phr.* To feel a bad impression; make you feel disgusted.—A cliché. *Seeing a man beat his horse leaves a bad taste in your mouth.* (It makes you feel disgusted.) *His rudeness to the teacher left a bad taste in my mouth.* (I got a bad impression of him.)

leave alone See LET ALONE.

leave a stone unturned *v. phr.* To try in every way; miss no chance; do everything possible.—A cliché; usually used in the negative. *The police will leave no stone unturned in their search for the bank robbers.* (They will try every way they know to find the men who robbed the bank.) Compare ALL OUT, FINE-TOOTH COMB.

leave flat *v. phr., informal* To quit or leave suddenly without warning when wanted or needed; desert; forsake; abandon. *Sam found that being a member of the trail-clearing group was a lot of hard work, so he left them flat.* (Sam got tired of helping chop bushes so he walked away and quit helping.) *My car ran out of gas and left me flat, ten miles from town.* (My car quit running when I needed it to finish the trip to town.) Compare LEAVE IN THE LURCH; WALK OUT 2.

leave hanging *or* **leave hanging in the air** *v. phr.* To leave undecided or unsettled. *Because the committee could not decide on a time and place, the matter of the spring dance was left hanging.* (The committee did not make a final decision about the dance.) *Ted's mother didn't know what to do about the broken window, so his punishment was left hanging in the air until his father came home.* (She postponed the matter until his father came.) Compare UP IN THE AIR.

leave high and dry See HIGH AND DRY.

leave holding the bag *or* **leave holding the sack** *v. phr., informal* **1** To cause (someone) not to have something needed; leave without anything.—A cliché. *In the rush for seats, Joe was left holding the bag.* (There were not enough seats for everyone, and Joe's slowness left him without one.) **2** To force (someone) to take the whole responsibility or blame for something that others should share.—A cliché. *When the ball hit the glass, the team scattered and left George holding the bag.* (They ran away and left George to take all the blame for the broken window.) *After the*

party, the other girls on the clean-up committee went away with their dates, and left Mary holding the bag. (They left Mary with all the work of cleaning the room.)

leave in the lurch *v. phr.* To desert or leave alone in trouble; refuse to help or support.—A cliché. *The town bully caught Eddie, and Tom left him in the lurch.* (Tom refused to stay and help him. He left Eddie to fight his battle alone.) *Bill quit his job, leaving his boss in the lurch.* (His boss needed help but Bill left anyway.) Compare LEAVE FLAT, HIGH AND DRY 2, WALK OUT 2.

leave off *v.* To come or put to an end; stop. *There is a high fence where the school yard leaves off and the woods begin.* (The fence is where the school yard ends.) *Don told the boys to leave off teasing his little brother.* (He told them to stop teasing his little brother.) *Marion put a marker in her book so that she would know where she left off.* (Marian put a bookmark between the pages when she closed the book, so that she would know where she stopped reading.) Contrast TAKE UP.

leave out in the cold See OUT IN THE COLD.

leave out of account *v. phr.* To fail to consider; forget about. *The picnic planners left out of account that it might rain.* (They failed to consider the chance of rain and were not prepared for it.) Contrast TAKE INTO ACCOUNT.

leave-taking See TAKE ONE'S LEAVE.

leave well enough alone See LET WELL ENOUGH ALONE.

leave without a leg to stand on See LEG TO STAND ON.

left See OUT IN LEFT FIELD, RIGHT AND LEFT.

left field *n.* **1** The part of a baseball outfield to the batter's left. *Right-handed batters usually hit to left field.* (Right-handed batters usually hit toward the left.) Compare CENTER FIELD, RIGHT FIELD **2** See OUT IN LEFT FIELD—**left fielder** The player in baseball who plays in left field. *The scoreboard in the ball park is on the fence behind the left fielder.* (The scoreboard is in the outfield to the left of the batter, where the left fielder plays.)

left-handed *adj., informal* **1** Using the left hand habitually **2** Crooked, phoney, homosexual. *Morris is such a left-handed guy.* **3** Clumsy, untoward, awkward. *Grab that hammer and stop acting so left-handed.* (Stop acting so clumsily.)

left-handed compliment An ambiguous compliment which is interpretable as an offense. *I didn't know you could look so pretty! Is that a wig you're wearing?* (I find it unusual that you look so good, most often you don't measure up to my expectations.)

left-wing *adj.* That which is or belongs to a group of people in politics that favors radical change in the direction of socialism or communism. *The left-wing faction called for an immediate strike.* (The radical group wanted to go on strike immediately.)

leg See ON ONE'S LAST LEGS, SHAKE A LEG, PULL ONE'S LEG, TAIL BETWEEN YOUR LEGS.

legal age *or* **lawful age** The age at which a person is allowed to do a certain thing or is held responsible for an action. *In most states the legal age for voting is 21.* (In most states a person must be 21 before he can vote.) *He could not get a driver's license because he was not of lawful age.* (He was not old enough to get a license.)

leg man *n., informal* **1** An errand boy, one who performs messenger services, or the like. *Joe hired a leg man for the office.* (He hired an errand boy to do the running back and forth.) **2** *Slang, semi-vulgar, avoidable* A man who is particularly attracted to good looking female legs and pays less attention to other parts of the female anatomy. *Herb is a leg man.* (He doesn't care what a girl's face looks like as long as she has sexy legs.)

leg-pulling See PULL ONE'S LEG.

Legree See SIMON LEGREE.

leg to stand on *n. phr.* A firm foundation of facts; facts to support your claim.—A cliché. Usually used in the negative. *Jerry's answering speech left his opponent without a leg to stand on.* (Jerry's arguments were so good that they left his opponent with no good points for his side of the debate.) *Amos sued for damages, but did not have a leg to stand on.* (Amos had no facts to support his case and lost in court.)

leg work *n., informal* The physical end of a project, such as the typing of research reports; the physical investigating of a criminal affair; the carrying of books to and from libraries, etc. *Joe, my research assistant, does a lot of leg work for me.* (He does the physical part of the work for me.)

leisure See AT LEISURE *or* AT ONE'S LEISURE.

lend a hand *or* **give a hand** *also* **bear a hand** *v. phr.* To give help; make yourself useful; help. *The stage manager asked some of the boys to lend a hand with the scenery.* (He asked them to help move the stage backgrounds.) *Dick saw a woman with a flat tire and offered to give her a hand with it.* (He offered to change the tire.) Compare LIFT A FINGER.

lend an ear to See GIVE AN EAR TO.

lend color to See GIVE COLOR TO.

lend itself to *v. phr.* To give a chance for or be useful for; to be possible or right for. *Bob was sick and did not go to Jane's party, but his absence lent itself to misunderstanding.* (He could not go because he was sick, but some people thought he was angry with Mary. His absence was something they could misunderstand.) *The teacher's paperweight*

was a heavy piece of metal which sometimes lent itself to use as a hammer. (The metal paperweight was heavy and good for using as a hammer.) *This poem lends itself to our program very well.* (This poem is right to use in our program.) Compare LEND ONESELF TO.

lend oneself to *v. phr.* To give help or approval to; encourage, assist. *Alice wouldn't lend herself to the plot to hide the teacher's chalk.* (She refused to give help or approval to the idea.)

length See AT LENGTH, GO TO ANY LENGTH, KEEP AT A DISTANCE *or* KEEP AT ARM'S LENGTH.

less See MORE OR LESS, MUCH LESS.

lesson See TEACH A LESSON.

less than *adv.* Not; little. *We were busy and less than delighted to have company that day.* (We were busy that day and we were not pleased to have company.) *The boys were less than happy about having a party.* (The boys were unhappy about having a party.) Contrast MORE THAN.

less than no time *n. phr., informal.* Very quickly. *We can be ready to go in less than no time.* (We can be ready to go very quickly.) *It took Mother less than no time to get dinner ready.* (Mother prepared dinner very quickly.)

let See LIVE AND LET LIVE.

let alone *conj. phr.* Even less; certainly not. —Used after a negative clause. *I can't add two and two, let alone do fractions.* (I can't do simple arithmetic, certainly not fractions.) *Jim can't drive a car, let alone a truck.* (He can't drive a car and of course he cannot drive a truck.) Compare MUCH LESS, NOT TO MENTION.

let alone *or* **leave alone** *v.* To stay away from; keep hands off; avoid. *When Joel gets mad, just let him alone.* (Stay away from him until he feels better.) *Little Patsy was warned to leave the birthday cake alone.* (She was told to keep her hands off it and not spoil the frosting.) Compare LET BE.

let be *v.* To pay no attention to; disregard; forget. *Let her be; she has a headache.* (Do not bother her now.) Compare LET ALONE.

let bygones be bygones *v. phr.* To let the past be forgotten.—A cliché. *After a long, angry quarrel the two boys agreed to let bygones be bygones and made friends again.* (The boys agreed to forget their quarrel and to be friends again.) *We should let bygones be bygones and try to get along with each other.* (We should forget unpleasant things that happened in the past and try to be friends now.) Syn. FORGIVE AND FORGET. Compare BURY THE HATCHET, LIVE AND LET LIVE.

let down *v.* **1** To allow to descend; lower. *Harry let the chain saw down on a rope and then came down himself.* (He lowered the saw to the ground and then climbed down himself.) **2** To relax; stop trying so hard;

take it easy. *The horse let down near the end of the race and lost.* (He ran slower and the other horses beat him.) *The team let down in the fourth quarter because they were far ahead.* (The team had a much bigger score, so they did not play hard in the last quarter.) Compare LET GO. **3** To fail to do as well as (someone) expected; disappoint. *The team felt they had let the coach down.* (They felt they had disappointed him by not playing as well as he expected them to.)

let down easy *v. phr.* To refuse or say no to (someone) in a pleasant manner; to tell bad news about a refusal or disappointment in a kindly way. *The teacher had to tell George that he had failed his college examinations, but she tried to let him down easy.* (She tried to tell the bad news so it would not be a big shock.) *The boss tried to let Jim down easy when he had to tell him he was too young for the job.* (He told him that he was too young but perhaps when he was older he could work there.)

let down one's hair See LET ONE'S HAIR DOWN.

let George do it *v. phr., informal* To expect someone else to do the work or take the responsibility.—A cliché. *Many people expect to let George do it when they are on a committee.* (They do not work hard themselves and expect somebody else to do everything, but they still want to get credit later themselves.) Compare PASS THE BUCK.

let go *v.* **1a** To stop holding something; loosen your hold; release. *The boy grabbed Jack's coat and would not let go.* (The boy would not loosen his hold on Jack's coat.) Often used with *of. When the child let go of her mother's hand, she fell down.* (The child fell when she did not hold her mother's hand.) Compare GIVE UP 1a, LET LOOSE. **1b** To weaken and break under pressure. *The old water pipe suddenly let go and water poured out of it.* (The pipe broke and let water out.) Syn. GIVE WAY. Contrast HOLD ON TO. **2** To pay no attention to; neglect. *Robert let his teeth go when he was young and now he has to go to the dentist often.* (He did not take care of his teeth and now they are bad.) *After she was married, Jane let herself go and was not pretty any more.* (She neglected her looks and was not pretty.) **3** To allow something to pass; do nothing about. *When Charles was tardy, the teacher scolded him and let it go at that.* (She did not punish him much, but was satisfied to scold him.) *The children teased Frank, but he smiled and let it go.* (Frank did not mind the teasing.) Compare LET OFF 2, LET RIDE. **4** to discharge from a job; fire. *Mr. Wilson got into a quarrel with his boss and was let go.* (His boss fired him because they had an argument.) **5** To make (something) go out quickly; shoot; fire. *The soldiers let go a number of shots.* (The

soldiers fired their guns.) *Robin Hood let go an arrow at the deer.* (He sent an arrow toward the deer.) *Paul was so angry that he let go a blow at the boy.* (Paul tried to hit him with his fist.) *The truck driver saw the flat tire and let go a loud curse.* (The driver was angry and swore.) *The pitcher let go a fast ball and the batter swung and missed.* (The pitcher threw a fast ball.) Compare CUT LOOSE, LET OUT. **6** *or* **let oneself go** *informal* To be free in one's actions or talk; relax. *Judge Brown let go at the reunion of his old class and had a good time.* (Judge Brown enjoyed himself with his old schoolmates and did not have to be polite and dignified.) *The cowboys worked hard all week, but on Saturday night they went to town and let themselves go.* (They did as they pleased and had a good time.) Syn. CUT LOOSE, LET LOOSE 3, LET OFF STEAM 2.

let go hang See GO HANG.

let go of one's mother's apron strings See TIED TO ONE'S MOTHER'S APRON STRINGS.

let grass grow under one's feet *v. phr.* To be idle; be lazy; waste time.—A cliché. Used in negative, conditional, and interrogative sentences. *The new boy joined the football team, made the honor roll, and found a girl friend during the first month of school. He certainly did not let any grass grow under his feet.* (He did not waste any time, but worked hard and made use of every minute.)

let ——— have it *v. phr.* **1a** *slang* To hit hard. *He drew back his fist and let the man have it.* (He hit the man with his fist.) *Give him a kick in the pants; let him have it!* (Kick him from behind!) Syn. GIVE IT TO. **1b** *slang* To use a weapon on; shoot; knife. *The guard pulled his gun and let the robber have it in the leg.* (He shot the robber in the leg.) Compare OPEN UP. **1c** *or* **let ———**

have it with both barrels *slang* To attack with words; scold, criticize. *Mary kept talking in class until the teacher became angry and let her have it.* (The teacher gave Mary a hard scolding.) Syn. LIGHT INTO 2. **2** *informal* To tell about it.—Used in the imperative phrase, *let's have it. Now, Mary, let's have it from the beginning.* (Now, Mary tell us all about it.) *We will take turns reading; John, let's have it from page one.* (John, you begin reading from page one.)

let it all hang out *v. phr., slang, informal* Not to disguise anything; to let the truth be known. *Sue can't deceive anyone; she just lets it all hang out.* (She lets the truth be known.)

let it lay *v. phr., used imperatively, slang* Forget it; leave it alone; do not be concerned or involved. *Don't get involved with Max again—just let it lay.* (Stay away from him; leave the whole matter alone.)

let it rip *v. phr., used imperatively, slang* **1** Don't be concerned; pay no attention to what happens. *Why get involved? Forget* *about it and let it rip.* (Let the situation turn out as it will; be unconcerned.) **2** (Imperatively) Do become involved and make the most of it; get in there and really try to win. *Come on man, give it all you've got and let it rip!* (Try as hard as you can and win!) **let loose** *v.* **1a** *or* **set loose** *or* **turn loose.** To set free, loosen or give up your hold on. *The farmer opened the gate and let the bull loose in the pasture.* (The farmer let the bull go free.) *They turned the balloon loose to let it rise in the air.* (They dropped the rope of the balloon and let it rise in the air.) **1b** *or* **turn loose** To give freedom (to someone) to do something; to allow (someone) to do what he wants. *Mother let Jim loose on the apple pie.* (Mother let Jim have all the apple pie he wanted.) *The children were turned loose in the toy store to pick the toys they wanted.* (The children were allowed to go all over the toy store to pick the toys they wanted.) **1c** To stop holding something; loosen your hold. *Jim caught Ruth's arm and would not let loose.* (He would not let her get away.) Compare LET GO, LET OUT. **2a** *informal* To let or make (something) move fast or hard; release. *The fielder let loose a long throw to home plate after catching the ball.* (The fielder threw the ball through the air to home plate.) **2b** *informal* To release something held. *Those dark clouds are going to let loose any minute.* (It is going to rain hard.) Syn. CUT LOOSE, LET GO. **3** *informal* To speak or act freely; disregard ordinary limits. *The teacher told Jim that some day she was going to let loose and tell him what she thought of him.* (Some day she was going to scold him hard.) *Mother let loose on her shopping trip today and bought things for all of us.* (She didn't care what it cost; she just bought everything we wanted.) Syn. CUT LOOSE, LET GO. **let me see** *or* **let us see** *informal* **1** Let us find out by trying or performing an action. *Let me see if you can jump over the fence.* (Show me if you can jump over the fence.) **2** Give me time to think or remember. *I can't come today. Let me see. How about Friday?* (Let me have time to think. Is Friday all right?) *Let's see. Where did I put the key?* (Let me think and remember where I put the key.) **let off** *v.* **1** To discharge (a gun); explode; fire. *Willie accidentally let off his father's shotgun and made a hole in the wall.* (Willie touched the trigger of the shotgun accidentally and the gun fired.) Syn. GO OFF; LET LOOSE 2. **2** To permit to go or escape; excuse from a penalty, a duty, or a promise. *Two boys were caught smoking in school but the principal let them off with a warning.* (The principal did not punish the two boys. He only warned them.) *Mary's mother said that she would let Mary off from drying the supper*

dishes. (Mary's mother excused her from drying the supper dishes.) *The factory closed for a month in the summer and let the workers off.* (The factory gave the workers a month of vacation without pay.) Compare LET GO. **3** *or informal* **let off the hook** To miss a chance to defeat or score against, especially in sports or games. *We almost scored a touchdown in the first play against Tech but we let them off the hook by fumbling the ball.* (We lost a good chance to score by fumbling the ball.) *The boxer let his opponent off the hook many times.* (The boxer missed many opportunities to knock out his opponent.) **let off steam** *or* **blow off steam** *v. phr.* **1** To let or make steam escape; send out steam. *The janitor let off some steam because the pressure was too high.* (He opened a valve and let some of the steam go out of the furnace boiler so it would not burst.) **2** *informal* To get rid of physical energy or strong feeling through activity; talk or be very active physically after forced quiet. *After the long ride on the bus, the children let off steam with a race to the lake.* (They were tired of being quiet in the bus and enjoyed the run.) *When the rain stopped, the boys let off steam with a ball game.* (They had been kept inside and were full of energy so they used it in a ball game.) *Bill's mother was very angry when he was late in coming home, and let off steam by walking around and around.* (She held back her anger but showed it by impatient walking.) *Bill had to take his foreman's rough criticisms all day and he would blow off steam at home by scolding the children.* (Bill kept silent with his boss but scolded his children.) Compare BLOW ONE'S TOP, LET GO 6.

let off the hook See LET OFF 3.
let on *v. informal* **1** To tell or admit what you know.—Usually used in the negative. *Frank lost a quarter, but he didn't let on to his mother.* (Frank didn't want his mother to know that he lost the quarter. He didn't tell her.) **2** To try to make people believe; pretend. *The old man likes to let on that he is rich.* (The old man likes to make people believe that he is rich.)
let oneself go See LET GO 6.
let one's hair down *or* **let down one's hair** *v. phr., informal* Act freely and naturally; relax.—A cliché. *Kings and queens can seldom let their hair down.* (Their public duties give them very little chance to relax in private.) *After the dance, the college girls let their hair down and compared dates.* (They talked naturally and freely about the boys.) Compare LET GO 6.
let one's left hand know what one's right hand is doing *v. phr.* **1** To make a show of your kindness or help to others.—A cliché. Used in the negative. *The Bible tells us not*

to let the left hand know what the right hand is doing when we give to the poor. (We should give to the poor in secret, not boast about it.) **2** *informal* To let everyone taking part in something know what each is doing; encourage cooperation in working.—A cliché. *Tom told Fred and Bill to meet him in town, but he forgot to tell them where. Next time he'll let his left hand know what his right hand is doing.* (Next time he will tell his friends everything they need to know so they can meet.)—Often used in the negative. *Our team lost today because the coach and captain did not let the left hand know what the right was doing, and the players were all mixed up.* (The coach and captain did not tell each player what the others were to do.)

let out *v.* **1a** To allow to go out or escape. *The guard let the prisoners out of jail to work in the garden.* (The guard let the prisoners go outside of the jail to work in the garden.) *Mother won't let us out when it rains.* (We can't go outside the house when it rains. Mother won't let us.) Compare LET LOOSE. **1b** *informal* To make (a sound) come out of the mouth; utter. *A bee stung Charles. He let out a yell and ran home.* (Charles yelled when the bee stung him.) *Father told Betty to sit still and not let out a peep during Church.* (Betty must not make even a small sound.) **2** To allow to be known; tell. *I'll never tell you another secret if you let this one out.* (If you tell this secret to other people, I'll never tell you a secret again.) Compare LET THE CAT OUT OF THE BAG. **3** To make larger (as clothing) or looser; allow to slip out (as a rope). *Mary's mother had to let out her dress because Mary is growing so tall.* (Mary's mother had to make Mary's dress longer so it would fit.) *Father hooked a big fish on his line. He had to let the line out so the fish wouldn't break it.* (If Father didn't allow the line to slip out longer on his fishing pole, the big fish might break the line or the pole.) Compare PIECE OUT. Contrast TAKE IN. **4** *informal* To allow to move at higher speed. *The rider let out his horse to try to beat the horse ahead of him.* (The jockey let his horse run faster, or as fast as he could to try to win the race.) **5** *informal* To free from blame, responsibility, or duty.—Often used with *of*. *Last time I let you out of it when you were late. I'll have to punish you this time.* (I did not punish you the last time you were late. This time you will be punished.) *Frank has shoveled the snow from the sidewalk. That lets me out.* (I will not have to shovel the sidewalk because Frank has already done it.) Compare LET GO, LET OFF. **6** *informal* To discharge from a job; fire. *The shop closed down and all the men were let out.* (All the men who worked at the shop lost their jobs when the shop closed down.) **7** *informal* To dismiss or be dis-

missed. *The coach let us out from practice at 3 o'clock.* (The coach finished our practice at three o'clock and let us go.) *I'll meet you after school lets out.* (After school is over, I'll meet you.)

let ride *v. phr., informal* To allow to go on without change; accept (a situation or action) for the present. *The committee could not decide what to do about Bob's idea, so they let the matter ride for a month or so.* (They waited another month to see how things would be.) *The class was rather noisy but the teacher let it ride because it was near Christmas.* (She did not scold the children because she knew they were excited about Christmas.) *Ruth's paper was not very good, but the teacher let it ride because she knew Ruth had tried.* (The teacher accepted the paper because Ruth had done her best with it.) Compare LET GO 3, LET WELL ENOUGH ALONE.

let's don't *also* **don't let's** *substandard* Let's not; let us not; I suggest that we don't. *"Let's go out and play," said Fred. "Let's don't until the rain stops," said Mary.* ("Let's not go out until the rain stops," said Mary.) *Don't let's go now. Let's go tomorrow instead.* (Let's not go now. Let's wait until tomorrow.)

let's have it See LET HAVE IT.

let sleeping dogs lie Do not make (someone) angry and cause trouble or danger; do not make trouble if you do not have to.—A proverb. *Don't tell Father that you broke the window. Let sleeping dogs lie.* (You don't have to tell Father that you broke the window, he will be angry.)

letter See CHAIN LETTER, NIGHT LETTER, TO THE LETTER.

let the cat out of the bag *v. phr., informal* To tell about something that is supposed to be a secret.—A cliché. *We wanted to surprise Mary with a birthday gift, but Allen let the cat out of the bag by asking her what she would like.* (We planned a surprise for Mary, but Allen let her know about it.) Sometimes used in another form. *Well, the cat is out of the bag—everybody knows about their marriage.* (They were secretly married, but someone found out and told others.) Compare GIVE AWAY 3, LET OUT 2, SPILL THE BEANS.

let the chips fall where they may *v. phr.* To pay no attention to the displeasure caused others by your actions.—A cliché. *The Senator decided to vote against the bill and let the chips fall where they might.* (He decided to vote as he thought right, no matter who might be angry.) *The police chief told his men to give tickets to all speeders and let the chips fall where they might.* (He didn't care who might be angry about it.) Compare COME WHAT MAY.

let up *v., informal* **1** To become less or weaker; or quiet; become slower or stop. *It's raining as hard as ever. It's not letting up at all.* (It's still raining as hard as it has been, without changing.) *It snowed for three days before it let up and we could go out doors.* (The snow storm didn't stop for three days.) **2** To do less or go slower or stop; relax; stop working or working hard. *Grandfather has been working all his life. When is he going to let up?* (When is he going to stop working so hard?) *Let up for a minute. You can't work hard all day.* (You have to stop working and rest sometimes.) *Jim ran all the way hon e without letting up once.* (Jim did not slow down but ran all the way home.) Compare SLOW DOWN. Contrast BEAR DOWN. **3** To become easier, kinder, or less strict.—Usually used with *on. Let up on Jane. She is sick.* (Don't be so hard on her.) Syn. EASE UP. **4** or **change up** To pitch a ball at less than full speed in baseball.—Usually used with *on. John pitched a ball that was very fast and the batter missed it. Then he let up on the next pitch and the batter was badly fooled.* (John fooled the batter by pitching one ball very fast and the next much slower.)

let well enough alone or **leave well enough alone** *v. phr.* To be satisfied with what is good enough; not try to improve something because often that might cause more trouble. *John wanted to make his kite go higher, but his father told him to let well enough alone because it was too windy.* (His father told him to be satisfied; trying to get it higher might damage the kite.) *Ed polished up his car until his friends warned him to leave well enough alone.* (His friends told him he might damage the paint.) *Ethel made a lot of changes in her test paper after she finished. She should have let well enough alone, because she made several new mistaakes.* (She would not have made new mistakes if she had not changed her answers.) Compare LET RIDE.

level See ON THE LEVEL.

level off or **level out** *v.* **1** To make flat or level. *The steamroller leveled out the gravel roadbed and then the concrete was poured.* (The steam roller flattened the gravel road and then concrete was poured on top of the gravel.) **2** To move on an even level. *The airplane leveled out at 2,000 feet.* (The airplane flew upward until it was 2,000 feet above the ground and then it continued to fly at the same level.) *After going up for six months, the cost of living leveled off in September.* (The cost of living stopped going up and stayed at the same level in September.)

liberty See TAKE LIBERTIES.

lick and a promise *n. phr., informal* A careless, hasty job; an unsatisfactory piece of work.—A trite expression. *You didn't wash your hands. You just gave them a lick and a promise.* (Your hands are still dirty. You didn't do a good job of washing them.) *The boys didn't cut the grass properly. All it got*

was a lick and a promise. (They tried to cut the grass in a hurry and didn't do it well.)

lickety-split also **lickety-cut** *adv., informal* At full speed; with a rush. *As soon as school was out the boys ran lickety-split to the swimming pool.* (The boys ran as fast as they could to the swimming pool.)

lick one's boots *v. phr.* To flatter or act like a slave; do anything to please another.—A cliché. *She wanted her boy friend to lick her boots all the time.* (She wanted him to do anything she told him to and be her slave.) *A wise king would not want his friends and officials to lick his boots.* (A wise king would not want his helpers to flatter him too much or do everything he wanted.)

lick one's chops *v. phr., informal* To think about something pleasant; enjoy the thought of something.—A cliché. *John is licking his chops about the steak dinner tonight.* (John is looking forward to the steak dinner with a happy feeling.) *Tom is licking his chops about the lifeguard job he will have at the beach next summer.* (Tom likes to think about a job where he can swim often and get a suntan.) *Our team is licking its chops because we beat the champions last night.* (We are very happy because we beat the champions.) [From the fact that some animals lick their mouths when they expect to be fed or when they see food, and after eating.] Compare LOOK FORWARD TO, MAKE ONE'S MOUTH WATER.

lick the ——— out of See BEAT THE ——— OUT OF.

lid See FLIP ONE'S LID, THE LID.

lie See GIVE THE LIE TO, LET SLEEPING DOGS LIE, MAKE ONE'S BED AND LIE IN IT.

lie down on the job *v. phr., informal* To purposely fail to do your job; neglect a task; loaf.—A cliché. *Bill isn't trying to learn his lessons. He is lying down on the job.* (Bill doesn't study his lessons or pay attention in school.) *If you lie down on your job, you will lose it.* (If you don't try to do your job, you will be fired.)

lief See AS SOON also AS LIEF, HAD AS SOON also HAD AS LIEF.

lie in state *v. phr. Of a dead person:* To lie in a place of honor, usually in an open coffin and be seen by the public before burial. *When the President died, thousands of people saw his body lying in state.* (The President was seen in his coffin by thousands of people before he was buried.)

lie in wait *v. phr.* To watch from hiding in order to attack or surprise someone; hide and wait for someone. *The driver of the stagecoach knew that the thieves were lying in wait somewhere along the road.* (The thieves were hiding somewhere waiting for the stagecoach to come.)

lie low or *nonstandard* **lay low** *v., informal* **1** To stay quietly out of sight; try not to attract attention; hide. *After holding up the bank, the robbers lay low for a while.* (They lived quietly where not many would see them.) **2** To keep secret one's thoughts or plans. *I think he wants to be elected president, but he is lying low and not saying anything.* (He is keeping his plans secret now.)

lie to *v.* Of a ship: To stay in one place facing against the wind; stop. *Our ship will lie to outside the harbor until daylight.* (Our ship will stop outside the harbor until it is daylight.) Compare LAY TO 2.

lieu See INSTEAD OF *also* IN LIEU OF.

life See BETWEEN LIFE AND DEATH, BIG AS LIFE, CAT HAS NINE LIVES, CHARMED LIFE, COME ALIVE *or* COME TO LIFE, FACTS OF LIFE, FOR DEAR LIFE, FOR THE LIFE OF ONE, LEAD A DOG'S LIFE, NIGHT LIFE, NOT ON YOUR LIFE OR ONE'S LIFE, TAKE ONE'S LIFE IN ONE'S HANDS, TIME OF ONE'S LIFE, YOU BET *or* YOU BET YOUR LIFE, WALK OF LIFE, WITHIN AN INCH OF ONE'S LIFE.

life of Riley *n. phr., informal* A soft easy life; pleasant or rich way of living. *He's living the life of Riley. He doesn't have to work any more.* (He has an easy life because he doesn't have to work.) Compare BED OF ROSES, IN CLOVER, LIVE HIGH OFF THE HOG.

life of the party *n. phr.* A person who makes things enjoyable or interesting for a group of people.—A cliché. *Bill is the life of the party at school. He is always making us laugh.* (Bill keeps things lively for everyone at school by making us laugh.)

lift a finger *or* **lift a hand** *also* **raise a hand** *v. phr.* **1** To do something; do your share; to help.—Usually used in the negative. *We all worked hard except Joe. He wouldn't lift a finger.* (Joe wouldn't work at all. He did nothing.) *The king did not lift a hand when his people were hungry.* (The king did not help his people in any way when they were hungry.) Compare LEND A HAND.

light See BRING TO LIGHT, COME TO LIGHT, DASH LIGHT, HIDE ONE'S LIGHT UNDER A BUSHEL, IN THE LIGHT OF, MAKE LIGHT OF, MANY HANDS MAKE LIGHT WORK, OUT LIKE A LIGHT, SEE THE LIGHT, TRAVEL LIGHT.

light housekeeping *n., slang* An arrangement in which an unmarried couple live together. *Are Joe and Sue married?—Oh, no,—it's just a case of light housekeeping.* (They are not married; they just moved in with each other.) See SHACK UP WITH.

light into See LAY INTO.

lightly See ONCE OVER LIGHTLY *at* ONCE OVER 2.

lightning never strikes twice in the same place The same accident does not happen twice; the same person does not have the same luck again.—A proverb. *Billy won a pony in the contest last year, but lightning never strikes twice in the same place.* (Billy was lucky to win the contest once. It cannot happen again.)

light on *also* **light upon** *v.* To pick out by sight from among others; see; notice. *His eyes lighted on the cookies and he remembered how hungry he was.* (He saw the cookies and remembered that he was very hungry.) *Her eyes lighted upon the row of boxes, and she asked what was in them.* (She noticed the row of boxes and asked what they had in them.)

light out *v., slang* **1** To run as fast as you can. *The boy lit out for home with the bully chasing him.* (He ran home as fast as he could.) *On the next pitch the runner will light out for second.* (The runner will run for second base on the next pitch.) **2** To go away in a hurry; leave suddenly. Often used with *for. Jack won't be in town long. He wants to light out as soon as he has enough money saved.* (He will leave quickly when he has enough money.) *The robbers lit out for Mexico.* (The robbers got away as fast as they could and went to Mexico.) Syn. BEAT IT, TAKE OFF 1, HEAD FOR THE HILLS.

light up *v.* Suddenly to look pleased and happy. *Martha's face lit up when she saw her old friend.* (Martha suddenly looked pleased and happy when she saw her old friend.) *Tom will really light up when he sees his new bike!* (Tom will really look pleased and happy when he sees his new bike.)

like See EAT LIKE A BIRD, FEEL LIKE, LOOK LIKE THE CAT THAT ATE THE CANARY, NOTHING LIKE, THE LIKES OF *or* THE LIKE.

like a bird See EAT LIKE A BIRD.

like a book See READ ONE LIKE A BOOK.

like a fish out of water See FISH OUT OF WATER.

like a glove See FIT LIKE A GLOVE.

like a horse See EAT LIKE A HORSE.

like a light See OUT LIKE A LIGHT.

like a million See FEEL LIKE A MILLION.

like a million dollars See LOOK LIKE A MILLION DOLLARS.

like a steel trap See MIND LIKE A STEEL TRAP.

like clockwork See GO LIKE CLOCKWORK *or* GO OFF LIKE CLOCKWORK.

like father, like son A son is usually like his father in the way he acts.—A proverb. *Frank's father has been on the city council, he is now the mayor, and is running for governor. Frank is on the student council and is likely to be class president. Like father, like son.* (Frank is like his father. His father is in politics, and he is in student government.) *Mr. Jones and Tommy are both quiet and shy. Like father, like son.* (Mr. Jones and Tommy are the same in the way they act.) Compare SPITTING IMAGE, FOLLOW IN ONE'S FOOTSTEPS.

like hell *adv., slang, vulgar, avoidable* **1** With great vigor. *As soon as they saw the cops, they ran like hell.* (As soon as they noticed the police, they started running very fast.) **2** *interj.* Not so, untrue; indicates the speakers lack of belief in what he heard. *Like hell you're gonna bring me my dough!*

(I don't believe that you will bring me my money.)

like it is See TELL IT LIKE IT IS.

like looking for a needle in a haystack See NEEDLE IN A HAYSTACK.

like mad *or* **like crazy** *adv., slang, informal* With great enthusiasm and vigor; very fast. *We had to drive like mad (like crazy) to get there on time.* (We had to drive very fast to get there on time.) See LIKE HELL.

like water *adv. phr.* As something easily poured out or wasted; freely.—Usually used in the phrase *spend money like water. Sailors on shore leave often spend money like water.* (They spend money freely, without limit or care.) *During the World Wars, the United States spent money like water.* (We spent much money freely to win the wars.)

like water off a duck's back *adv. phr., informal* Without changing your feelings or opinion; without effect.—A cliché. *Advice and correction roll off him like water off a duck's back.* (He pays no attention to advice as a duck's back will not take in water.) *Many people showed him they didn't like what he was doing, but their disapproval passed off him like water off a duck's back.* (People's disapproval had no effect on him; he didn't care what they thought.)

lily See GILD THE LILY *also* PAINT THE LILY.

limb See OUT ON A LIMB.

line See DOWN THE LINE, DRAW A LINE *or* DRAW THE LINE, DROP A LINE, BLOW ONE'S LINES *or* FLUFF ONE'S LINES, CHOW LINE, END OF THE ROAD *or* END OF THE LINE, FOUL LINE, GOAL LINE, GOAL LINE STAND, HOLD THE LINE, HOOK, LINE AND SINKER, IN LINE, IN LINE WITH, INTO LINE, OUT OF LINE, LAY ON THE LINE, *or* PUT ON THE LINE, ON THE LINE, OUT OF LINE WITH, READ BETWEEN THE LINES, TOE THE LINE, WALK THE CHALK *or* WALK THE CHALK LINE.

line drive *n.* A batted baseball that is usually hit hard and travels in the air not far above the ground. *The batter hit a line drive to left field for a single.* (He hit the ball sharply but not high in the air to left field for a hit.)

linen See AIR ONE'S DIRTY LINEN IN PUBLIC *or* WASH ONE'S DIRTY LINEN IN PUBLIC.

line of fire *n. phr.* The path that something fired or thrown takes. *When the bandit and the police began to shoot, John was almost in their line of fire.* (John was almost in the path of the bullets and might have been hit.) Compare CROSS FIRE.

line of least resistance *or* **path of least resistance** *n. phr.* The easiest way; the way that takes least effort.—A cliché. *In becoming a doctor like his father John had really just followed the line of least resistance.* (John did the easiest thing; he had not gone against his father.) *Some parents take the path of least resistance with their children and let them do as they please.* (Some parents don't want

to be bothered to argue with their children or be strict with them; they are lazy.)

line of scrimmage *n. phr.* An imaginary line on a football field parallel to the goal lines where each play except the kickoff begins. *The play was stopped at the line of scrimmage.* (The play was stopped right where it began.)

line one's pockets *also* **line one's purse** *v. phr., informal* To get a lot of money unfairly; get rich by being dishonest.—A cliché. *The policeman lined his pockets by taking bribes.* (He accepted money for letting someone break the law.) *The inspector lined his pockets by permitting contractors to use poor building materials.* (He passed the poor materials as if they were good. Then contractors made more money, and rewarded him with money.) Compare FEATHER ONE'S NEST.

line up *v.* **1** To take places in a line or formation; stand side by side or one behind another; form a line or pattern. *The boys lined up and took turns diving off the springboard.* (They formed a line and dived one after another.) *The football team lined up in a "T" formation.* (Each member of the team placed himself in this particular formation after coming out of the huddle.) **2** To put in line. *John lined up the pool balls.* (He arranged them in a line.) **3** To adjust correctly. *The garage man lined up the car's wheels.* (He adjusted the wheels so that they would track correctly.) **4a** *informal* To make ready for action; complete a plan or agreement for; arrange. *Henry's friends lined up so many votes for him that he won the election.* (They persuaded many people to vote for him, and he won.) *Roger lined up a summer job before school was out.* (Before school closed, Roger had found a job for the summer.) *The superintendent lined up all the new teachers he needed before he went on vacation.* (He found enough teachers who agreed to teach.) **4b** *informal* To become ready for action; come together in preparation or agreement. *The football schedule is lining up well; the coach has arranged all games except one.* (Plans about what other teams our football team will play, and where, are coming well.) *Larry wanted to go to the seashore for the family vacation, but the rest of the family lined up against him.* (The others agreed that they did not want to go to the seashore.) Compare GANG UP, SHAPE UP, TAKE SIDES.

lining See EVERY CLOUD HAS A SILVER LINING.

link See MISSING LINK.

lip See BUTTON ONE'S LIP *or* ZIP ONE'S LIP, HANG ON THE WORDS OF *or* HANG ON THE LIPS OF, KEEP A STIFF UPPER LIP, SLIP OF THE TONGUE *also* SLIP OF THE LIP.

lip service *n.* Support shown by words only and not by actions; a show of loyalty that is not proven in action.—Usually used with *pay. By holding elections, Communism pays* *lip service to democracy, but it offers only one candidate per office.* (Communism pretends to be democratic, but it doesn't give people democratic choices.) *Some people pay lip service to education, but don't vote taxes for better schools.* (They say they support the schools, but do not want to pay taxes to improve them.)

liquor up *v. phr., slang* To drink an excessive amount of liquor before engaging in some activity as if comparing oneself to a car that needs to be filled before a journey. *Joe always liquors up before he takes Sue for a dance.* (He drinks heavily before taking her to a dance.)

list See SUCKER LIST, WAITING LIST.

listen in *v.* **1** To listen to a radio broadcast. *We found them listening in to the President's speech.* (We found them listening to the President's speech on radio.) **2** To listen to the talk of others, often to talk that is not intended for your ears; eavesdrop. *When Mary talked to her boy friend on the telephone, her little brother listened in.* (He listened to their private talk.)

listen to reason *v. phr.* To listen to and think about advice that you are given. *Joe was stubborn and would not listen to reason.* (Joe stubbornly refused to listen to or think about advice that he was given.) *It will save you a lot of trouble if you will just listen to reason.* (It will save you much trouble if you will listen to and think about advice that you are given.)

litterbug *n., slang, informal* A person who leaves garbage in a public place, such as a park or beach or a street, one who litters. *Don't be a litterbug; keep the city clean!* (Don't be a litterer.)

little See A LITTLE, A LITTLE KNOWLEDGE IS A DANGEROUS THING, GREAT OAKS FROM LITTLE ACORNS GROW, LITTLE FROG IN A BIG POND, MAKE LITTLE OF, NOT A LITTLE, QUITE A LITTLE *or* QUITE A LITTLE BIT, THINK LITTLE OF, TWIST AROUND ONE'S LITTLE FINGER.

little folk or little people See WEE FOLK.

little frog in a big pond *or* **small frog in a big pond** *n. phr.* An unimportant person in a large group or organization.—A cliché. *In a large company, even a fairly successful man is likely to feel like a little frog in a big pond.* (He will feel unimportant because the company is so big.) *When Bill transferred to a larger high school, he found himself a small frog in a big pond.* (There were so many students that he was not noticed.) Contrast BIG FROG IN A SMALL POND.

little pitchers have big ears Little children often overhear things they are not supposed to hear, or things adults do not expect they would notice.—A proverb. *Be especially careful not to swear in front of little children. Little pitchers have big ears.* (Do not swear in front of little children. They will be sure to notice the swear words and start using them.)

little theater *n.* A theater, usually with non-professional actors and actresses, which presents plays more for personal pleasure and practice than for profit. *Little theater groups are active in all parts of the United States.* (There are many groups in our country which put on plays for pleasure and practice.) *Many famous actors began in little theaters.* (Many noted actors first were in non-professional groups.)

live See PEOPLE WHO LIVE IN GLASS HOUSES SHOULD NOT THROW STONES.

live and learn You learn more new things the longer you live; you learn by experience. —A proverb. *"Live and learn," said Mother. "I never knew that the Indians once had a camp where our house is."* (The longer you live the more new things you learn.) *Janet made her new dress from cheap cloth, and when she washed it it shrank and was too little. Live and learn.* (Janet learned from experience that cheap cloth will shrink when washed.)

live and let live To live in the way you prefer and let others live as they wish without being bothered by you. *Father scolds Mother because she wears her hair in curlers and Mother scolds Father because he smokes a smelly pipe. Grandfather says it's her hair and his pipe; live and let live.* (They should each do as he wishes and not keep bothering each other.) Compare GIVE AND TAKE 1, LET BYGONES BE BYGONES, FORGIVE AND FORGET.

live down *v.* To remove (blame, distrust or unfriendly laughter) by good conduct; cause (a mistake of fault) to be forgiven or forgotten by not repeating it. *John's business failure hurt him for a long time, but in the end he lived it down.* (People gained new confidence in him when they saw that he always paid his debts.) *Frank was rather a bad boy, but he lived it down as he grew up.* (He was at heart a sensible boy and people forgot his early mischief.) *Sandra called her principal the wrong name at the banquet, in front of everyone, and she thought she would never live it down.* (Sandra thought people would never forget her mistake and stop laughing at her.)

live from hand to mouth *v. phr.* To live on little money and spend it as fast as it comes in; live without saving for the future; have just enough.—A cliché. *Mr. Johnson got very little pay, and the family lived from hand to mouth when he had no job.* (They lived with nothing extra. They were very poor.) *These Indians live from hand to mouth on berries, nuts, and roots.* (They make a bare living and eat what they find in the woods.)—**hand-to-mouth** *adj.* Not providing for the future; living from day to day; not saving for later. *Many native tribes lead a hand-to-mouth existence,* content to have food for one day at a time. (They do not or can not have enough food to save some for the next day.) *John is not a saving boy; he spends his money without thought for the future, and lives a hand-to-mouth life.* (He is not worried about the future.)

live high off the hog *or* **eat high on the hog** See EAT (LIVE) HIGH ON THE HOG *or* EAT (LIVE) HIGH OFF THE HOG.

live in *or* **room in.** *v., informal* To live in the school you attend or the place where you work. *Jack decided to live in during his freshman year at college.* (Jack decided to live in a dormitory room during his first year.) *Many women advertise for mother's helpers to room in with families and help take care of children.* (Many women advertise for girls to live in their homes in return for taking care of children.)

live it up *v. phr., informal* To pursue pleasure; enjoy games or night life very much; have fun at places of entertainment. *Joe had had a hard winter in lonesome places; now he was in town living it up.* (He was having fun in the restaurants and shows.) *The western cowboys usually went to town on Saturdays to live it up.* (They worked all week and enjoyed themselves on Saturdays.)

live off the fat of the land See FAT OF THE LAND.

live on borrowed time *v. phr.* To live or last longer than was expected.—A cliché. *Ever since his operation, Harvey felt he was living on borrowed time.* (He felt he was living longer than he had expected.) *Mr. Brown was living on borrowed time because a year ago the doctors had told him he would only live six months.* (The doctors expected Mr. Brown to die in six months, but he was still living one year later.)

live out *v.* **1** To finish (a period of time); spend. *Smith lived out the year in the North as he had agreed, but then moved South again.* (He stayed the full year, as he had promised.) *After retiring, John and his wife lived out their lives in Florida.* (They spent all the rest of their lives in Florida.) **2** To last through; endure to the end of. *We lived out the winter on short ration.* (We endured to the end of the winter with less food than we wanted.) *He lived out the earthquake, but his house was destroyed.* (He had a hard time, but lived.)

live up to *v.* To act according to; come up to; agree with; follow. *So far as he could, John had always tried to live up to the example he saw in Lincoln.* (John had tried to act according to Lincoln's example.) *Bob was a man who lived up to his promises.* (Bob did what he promised to do.) *The new house didn't live up to expectations.* (The new house was not as good as the buyer had thought it was.)

living daylights See BEAT THE _____ OUT OF,

KNOCK THE _____ OUT OF.

living end *adj., slang* Great, fantastic, the ultimate. *That show we saw last night was the living end.* (It was fantastically good.)

load See GET A LOAD OF.

loaded for bear *adj. phr., slang* Ready for action; prepared and eager.—A cliché. *Frank liked the new merchandise and as he set out on his rounds as a salesman, he felt really loaded for bear.* (He felt anxious and eager to sell.) *The football team arrived Friday noon, loaded for bear.* (They were ready to play and expected to win.)

load the bases *or* **fill the bases** *v. phr.* To get men on all three bases in baseball. *The Mets loaded the bases with two singles and a base on balls.* (The Mets got men on all three bases.) *Don hit a home run with the bases loaded.* (Don hit a home run after three men were on base.)

loaf See HALF A LOAF IS BETTER THAN NONE *or* HALF A LOAF IS BETTER THAN NO BREAD.

local yokel *n., slang, citizen's band radio jargon* City police officer, as opposed to state police or highway patrol. *There's a local yokel westbound on the move.* (A local police car is moving west.)

lock See SCALP LOCK.

lock the barn door after the horse is stolen To be careful or try to make something safe when it is too late.—A proverb. *After Mary failed the examination, she said she would study hard after that. She wanted to lock the barn door after the horse was stolen.* (Mary said she would study hard when it was already too late, because she had already failed.)

lock up *v. phr., slang* To be assured of success. *How did your math test go?—I locked it up, I think* (I think success is assured; I did well at it.)

loggerhead See AT LOGGERHEADS.

loin See GIRD UP ONE'S LOINS.

lone wolf *n.* A man who likes to work or live alone. *The man who paints a picture or establishes a business is often a lone wolf; so is the criminal outlaw.* (Men who like to work alone include some who do valuable things and some who are criminals.) *Jones is a good pitcher, but he is a lone wolf.* (He does not cooperate with the other players.)

long See AT LAST *or* AT LONG LAST, BEFORE LONG, COME A LONG WAY, IN THE LONG RUN, NO LONGER, SO LONG, THE LONG AND THE SHORT.

long ball *n.* A baseball hit far enough to be a home run. *The White Sox need a player who can hit the long ball.* (They need a player who can hit home runs.)

long face *n.* A sad look; disappointed look. *He told the story with a long face.* (John looked sad when he told the story.)—Often used in the phrase *pull a long face. Don't pull a long face when I tell you to go to bed.* (Don't look so hurt just because you have to go to bed.)

longhair[1] **1** *n., slang* A male hippie. *Who's that longhair?—It's Joe.* (Who's that male hippie? It's Joe.) **2** An intellectual who prefers classical music to jazz or rock acid. *Catwallender is a regular longhair; he never listens to modern jazz.*

longhair[2] *adj., slang* Pertaining to classical art forms; primarily in dancing and music. *Cut out that longhair Mozart Symphony and put on a decent pop record!* (Stop the classical music and put on a popular song.)

long haul *or* **long pull** *n., informal* **1** A long distance or trip. *It is a long haul to drive across the country.* (It is a long, hard distance to drive.) Contrast SHORT HAUL. **2** A long length of time during which work continues or something is done; a long time of trying. *A boy crippled by polio may learn to walk again, but it may be a long haul.* (It may take a long time.)—Often used in the phrase *over the long haul. Over the long haul, an expensive pair of shoes may save you money.* (During a long time, the expensive shoes may still be good when cheaper shoes would be worn out.) Contrast SHORT HAUL.

long pull See LONG HAUL.

long shot *n.* **1** A bet or other risk taken though not likely to succeed. *The horse was a long shot, but it came in and paid well.* (The horse was figured to have a poor chance, but it won, and people who had bet on it made a good profit.) *Jones was a long shot for mayor.* (Jones's election as mayor was regarded as unlikely.) *The business long shot that succeeds often pays extremely well.* (The business that seems to have a poor chance often turns out very profitable if it succeeds.) **2** See BY A LONG SHOT.

look See DIRTY LOOK.

look after *also* **see after** *v.* To watch over; attend to. *John's mother told him to look after his younger brother.* (John's mother told him to take care of his younger brother.) *When he went to Europe, Mr. Jenkins left his son to see after the business.* (He left his son to manage it.) Syn. TAKE CARE OF 1. Compare LOOK OUT 3.

look a gift horse in the mouth To complain if a gift is not perfect.—A proverb. Usually used with a negative. *John gave Joe a baseball but Joe complained that the ball was old. His father told him not to look a gift horse in the mouth.* (Joe should not complain, because he got the ball for nothing.)

look alive *v.* Act lively; be quick; wake up and work; be busy; hurry.—Often used as a command. *"Look alive there," the boss called.* (The boss told his men to work fast.)

look as if butter wouldn't melt in one's mouth See BUTTER WOULDN'T MELT IN ONE'S MOUTH.

look as if one has come out of a bandbox *v. phr., informal* To look very clean and fresh; look as if you had just had a bath and put on all-new clothing.—A trite phrase. *In spite of the long, hot train ride, Jody arrived looking as if she had come out of a bandbox.* (Jody had a long, hot ride on the train, but she looked very clean and fresh when she arrived.) *After a day at the rodeo we were all dusty and tired except for Hope, who looked as if she'd come out of a bandbox.* (Hope looked very clean and fresh.)

look at *v.* To have a way of thinking or feeling toward; think about something in a certain way. *Is he a hero or a villain? That depends on how you look at it.* (Is he a good man or a bad man? That depends on your way of feeling toward what happened.) *Depending on how you looked at it, the tea party could be called a pleasure or a bore.* (Depending on how you thought about it, the party could be called either fun or boring.)

look at the world through rose-colored glasses *or* **see with rose-colored glasses** *v. phr.* To see everything as good and pleasant; not see anything hard or bad.—A cliché. *When Jean graduated from high school, she looked at the world through rose-colored glasses.* (Jean expected everything in life to be easy and pleasant.) *If you see everything through rose-colored glasses, you will often be disappointed.* (If you are falsely cheerful, you may be disappointed.)

look back *v.* To review the past; think of what has happened. *As John looked back, his life seemed good to him.* (As John recalled it, he felt he had had a good life.) *Murphy looked back on his early struggles as having made him feel especially alive.* (Murphy remembered his youthful struggles as having been the brightest and most lively part of his life.) *When Ed applied for a job and asked the school to recommend him, the principal looked back over his records.* (The principal looked at Ed's school records to see if he had done good work and could be recommended for the job.)

look black *v.* To indicate misfortune; appear threatening or ruinous. *As prices dropped lower and lower, things looked black for Henry's company.* (Ruin faced Henry's company.) *Many witnesses gave testimony against Jerry and his case looked black.* (His case seemed lost.) *The future looked black when Father got hurt and could not work.* (The future was dark when Father got hurt and was unable to earn a living.)

look daggers *v. phr.* To show anger with a look; express hate or enmity by a look or stare; look fiercely. *The other driver looked daggers at Morris for turning in before him.* (The other driver looked angry when Morris turned in before him.) *Mary did not dare talk back to her father, but she looked daggers.* (She said nothing, but she gave an angry look.)

look down on also **look down upon** v. To think of (a person or thing) as less good or important; feel that (someone) is not as good as you are, or that (something) is not worth having or doing; consider inferior. *Mary looked down on her classmates because she was better dressed than they were.* (Mary thought she was better than her classmates. *Jack looked down on Al for his poor manners.* (He thought Al was inferior because of his rude behavior.) *Miss Tracy likes tennis but she looks down on football as too rough.* (She thinks football is not a good game.)

look down one's nose at v. phr., informal To think of as worthless; feel scorn for.—A cliché. *The banker's wife has beautiful china cups, and she looked down her nose at the plastic cups that Mrs. Brown used.* (She thought Mrs. Brown should be ashamed to serve coffee in plastic cups.) *Harry has never had to work, and he looks down his nose at people in business.* (He thinks he is much better than people who buy and sell for profit.) *Jerry was the athlete who looked down his nose at the weak student.* (He showed scorn for the student who wasn't physically strong.)

look for v. 1 To think likely; expect. *We look for John to arrive any day now.* (We expect that John will arrive any day now.) *The frost killed many oranges, and housewives can look for an increase in their price.* (Housewives can expect oranges will soon cost more.) *Bob wouldn't go for a ride with the boys because he was looking for a phone call from Julie.* (Bob thought that Julie might call him.) 2 To try to find; search for; hunt. *Fred spent all day looking for a job.* (Fred hunted for a job all day.) *Mary and Joe looked for the Smiths at the play.* (They looked all around through the crowd, hoping to find the Smiths.) 3 To do things that cause (your own trouble); make (trouble) for yourself; provoke. *Joe often gets into fights because he is always looking for trouble.* (Joe says and does things that make other boys angry.) *If you say the opposite of everything that others say, you are looking for a quarrel.* (If you always say other people are wrong, you make them quarrel with you.)

look for a needle in a haystack See NEEDLE IN A HAYSTACK.

look forward to v. 1 To expect. *At breakfast, John looked forward to a difficult day.* (He expected a tough day.) 2 To expect with hope or pleasure. *Frank was looking forward to that evening's date.* (He expected to enjoy the date.)

look-in n., informal A chance or hope.— Usually used with a negative. *It wasn't much of a look-in, but it was the only chance they let him have.* (It was a poor chance, but it was all he was allowed.) *Charlie didn't realize it, but he never had a look-in with Bonnie.*

(Charlie never had a chance to make Bonnie like him.)

look in on v. To go to see; make a short visit with; make a call on. *On his way downtown, Jim looked in on his aunt.* (Jim made a short call on his aunt.) *The doctor looked in on Mary each day when he went by.* (The doctor stopped to see Mary each day when he was passing.)

look in the eye or **look in the face** v. phr. To meet with a steady look; to face bravely or without shame.—A cliché. *Mary looked the gangster in the eye, and he turned away without hurting her.* (She showed no fear.) *John had looked death in the face many times.* (John had risked death many times without fear.) *We often believe a person who looks us in the eye, but it does not prove he is truthful.* (We are likely to believe a man who looks straight at us.) *I promised Harry to write to him while I was on vacation, and if I don't do it, I won't be able to look him in the eye.* (I will be ashamed to meet him again if I have not kept my promise.)

look into v. To find out the facts about; examine; study; inspect. *The mayor felt he should look into the decrease of income from parking meters.* (The mayor felt he should study the drop in parking meter income, and try to discover its cause.) *Mr. Jones said he was looking into the possibility of buying a house.* (Mr. Jones said he was studying the buying of a house to decide if he should do it.) Compare GO INTO 4, SEE ABOUT.

look like a million dollars v. phr., informal To look well and prosperous; appear healthy and happy and lucky; look pretty and attractive.—A cliché. *John came back from Florida driving a fine new car, tanned and glowing with health. He looked like a million dollars.* (He gave every evidence of health and prosperity.) *Dressed in the new formal and in a new hairdo, Betty looked like a million dollars.* (Betty looked very pretty in her new formal and new hairdo.) Compare FEEL LIKE A MILLION.

look like the cat that ate the canary or **look like the cat that swallowed the canary** v. phr. To seem very self-satisfied; look as if you had just had a great success.—A cliché. *Peter bet on the poorest horse in the race and when it won, he looked like the cat that ate the canary.* (He looked proud and pleased with himself.) *When she won the prize, she went home looking like the cat that swallowed the canary.* (She looked very self-satisfied.)

look on or **look upon** v. 1 To regard; consider; think of. *The stuff had always been looked on as a worthless factory waste.* (It had been thought of as a waste product of no value.) *Until the day Bob made the touchdown, the other boys had looked upon him as rather a sissy.* (They had thought Bob was a weak player.) 2 To be an observer; watch without taking part. *Fred had never been able to do more than look on at athletic sports.* (He had had to limit himself to watching—he could never take part.) *The children played in the park while their mother looked on.* (She watched but did not join them.) Compare SIT IN.

look oneself *v. phr.* To appear self-possessed and well; look or seem in full possession of your abilities and in good health; to appear all right or normal. *Mary had had a long illness, but now she looked quite herself again.* (She seemed to be all well again.) *It had been a big night, and Uncle John had been drinking freely, but he looked entirely himself after a night's sleep.* (He was fully in control of himself the next morning.) —Often used in the negative. *What's wrong with Larry? He doesn't look himself.* (He looks strange in a way that makes you think he's sick or upset.)

lookout See ON THE LOOKOUT.

look out *or* **watch out** *v.* 1 To take care; be careful; be on guard.—Usually used as a command or warning. *"Look out!" John called, as the car came toward me.* (John warned me to be careful not to be hit.) *"Look out for the train," the sign at the railroad crossing warns.* (The sign tells people to watch for trains that may be coming.) 2 To be alert or watchful; keep watching. *A collector of antique cars asked Frank to look out for a 1906 gas head lamp.* (He asked Frank to keep looking for a 1906 head lamp; he asked him to watch for one.) Compare EYE OUT, ON THE WATCH 3 *informal* To watch or keep (a person or thing) and do what is needed; provide protection and care. —Used with *for*. *Lillian looked out for her sister's children one afternoon a week.* (Mary cared for her sister's children one afternoon a week.) *Uncle Fred looked out for his brother's orphan son until the boy was through college.* (Uncle Fred supported his brother's son and cared for him until the boy had his education.) Compare LOOK AFTER.

look over *v.* To look at and try to learn something about; look at every part or piece of or at every one of; examine; inspect; study. *I looked hurriedly over the apples in the basket and took one that looked good.* (I looked quickly at all the apples and chose one.) *Mrs. Jones spent the evening looking over the month's bills and writing checks.* (She looked at the bills carefully and wrote checks to pay them.) *When a new boy comes to school, the others usually look him over rather carefully.* (They study him and make up their minds about him.) *We looked over several kinds of new cars before deciding.* (We inspected several kinds of new cars before choosing one to buy.) Compare ONCE-OVER, SIZE UP.

look sharp *v.* To be alert; be very attentive;

keep a close watch. *It pays to look sharp in traffic.* (It is worth while to stay alert in traffic.) *The guide told us to look sharp because there were rattlesnakes around.* (He told us to watch where we were going.)

look to *v.* 1 To attend to; get ready for; take care of. *Plans had been prepared that looked to every possibility.* (Plans had been arranged to take care of every possibility.) *The president assigned a man to look to our needs.* (The president chose a man to do necessary things for us.) 2 To go for help to; depend on. *The child looks to his mother to cure his hurts.* (He depends on his mother to help when he is hurt.) 3 See SEE TO.

look to one's laurels To make sure that your reputation is not spoiled; protect your good name; keep your record from being beaten by others.—A cliché. *Tom won the broad jump, but he had to look to his laurels.* (Tom won the broad jump, but other boys were ready to try again to beat him.) *Look to your laurels, Joan. Betty says she is going to run against you for head cheerleader.* (Practice your cheerleading or Betty will do better than you and take your place.)

look up *v.* 1 *informal* To improve in future chances; promise more success. *The first year was tough, but business looked up after that.* (Business improved after the first year.) 2 To search for; hunt for information about; find. *It is a good habit to look up new words in a dictionary.* (It is wise to find the meaning of new words in a dictionary.) 3 To seek and find. *While he was in Chicago, Henry looked up a friend of college days.* (He hunted for and found his friend.)

look upon See LOOK ON 1.

look up to *v.* To think of (someone) as a good example to copy; honor; respect. *Mr. Smith had taught for many years, and all the students looked up to him.* (All the students admired him and wanted to be like him.) *Young children look up to older ones, so older children should be good examples.* (Young children admire and copy the actions of older ones, so they should be good examples to them.)

loop See KNOCK FOR A LOOP *or* THROW FOR A LOOP.

loose See AT LOOSE ENDS, CAST OFF *or* CAST LOOSE, CUT LOOSE, FAST AND LOOSE, HAVE A SCREW LOOSE, LET LOOSE *or* SET LOOSE *or* TURN LOOSE, ON THE LOOSE.

loose ends *n.* 1 Parts or things that should be finished or put together. *Mary's composition had many loose ends.* (She did not fully explain her ideas.) *When George came home after a long trip, he started picking up the loose ends.* (He talked with his friends and learned what had happened and what was needed.) 2 See AT LOOSE ENDS.

lord it over *v. phr.* To act as the superior and master of; dominate; be bossy over; control. *John learned early to lord it over other children.* (He learned to boss them around.) *The office manager lorded it over the clerks and typists.* (He ruled in a bossy way over his department.)

Lord knows See GOD KNOWS.

lose See HEADS I WIN, TAILS YOU LOSE.

lose face *v.* To be embarrassed or shamed by an error of failure; lose dignity, influence, or reputation; lose self-respect or the confidence of others. *Many Japanese soldiers were killed in World War II because they believed that to give up or retreat would make them lose face.* (They would be shamed and lose their self-respect if they stopped fighting.) *John's careless work made him lose face with his employer.* (He lost his employer's confidence and influence.) *The banker lost face when people found out he bet on horse races.* (He lost his dignity and reputation because people would have no trust in him.)

lose ground 1 To go backward; retreat. *The soldiers began to lose ground when their leader was killed.* (After their leader was killed, the soldiers wouldn't fight so they retreated.) Compare GIVE GROUND. 2 To become weaker; get worse, not improve. *The sick man began to lose ground when his cough grew worse.* (The sick man became weaker when his cough grew worse.) *When the Democrats are in power, the Republicans lose ground.* (When the Democrats are in power the Republicans become weaker.) Contrast GAIN GROUND.

lose heart *v. phr.* To feel discouraged because of failure; to lose hope of success. *The team had won no games and it lost heart.* (They were beaten often and felt unable to win.) Contrast TAKE HEART.

lose oneself *v. phr.* 1 To go wrong; miss your way; become unable to find the right direction. *Fred lost himself in the confusion of downtown Boston streets.* (Fred became confused and lost his way.) 2 To conceal yourself; hide. *The pickpocket lost himself in the crowd and escaped the police.* (He hid from the police by mixing in the crowd.) 3 To become deeply interested and forget yourself; become absorbed. *Sometimes Harry would lose himself in a book for an afternoon at a time.* (He would become so interested in a book that he forgot where he was all afternoon.) Compare IN A WORLD OF ONE'S OWN.

lose one's grip *v. phr.* To fail in control or command; lose your strength, force, or ability to lead. *Mr. Jones began to lose his grip: he no longer wanted the hard jobs, and he left decisions to others.* (Mr. Jones was no longer fully able to do his work.) *When a locomotive engineer loses his grip, he is no longer trusted with express runs.* (When a locomotive engineer is no longer able to handle the fast trains, he is given easier jobs.)

lose one's head *v. phr.* To become upset, excited or confused; act wildly; lose control of yourself. *When Mary saw the train coming, she lost her head altogether and stepped on the gas.* (She got badly confused and did not stop but drove faster.) *When the fire broke out in the movies, the people lost their heads and ran in all directions.* (People were so frightened they could not think, and they acted wildly.) Contrast KEEP ONE'S HEAD.

lose one's heart *v. phr.* To fall in love; begin to love.—A trite phrase. *She lost her heart to the soldier with the broad shoulders and the deep voice.* (She fell in love with the soldier.) *Bill lost his heart to the puppy the first time he saw it.* (Bill began to love the puppy the first time he saw it.)

lose one's shirt *v. phr., slang* To lose all or most of your money.—A cliché. *Uncle Joe spent his life savings to buy a store, but it failed, and he lost his shirt.* (Uncle Joe lost all his savings.) *Mr. Matthews lost his shirt betting on the horses.* (Mr. Matthews bet a lot of money on horse races and lost it all.)

lose one's temper *v. phr.* To lose control over one's anger; to get angry. *He lost his temper when he broke the key in the lock.* (He got very angry when the key broke.) Compare BLOW A FUSE, FLY OFF THE HANDLE. Contrast HOLD ONE'S TEMPER.

lose one's tongue *v. phr., informal* To be so embarrassed or surprised that you cannot talk. *The man would always lose his tongue when he was introduced to new people.* (The man would always be unable to talk when he was introduced to new people.) Compare CAT GET ONE'S TONGUE.

lose out *v.* To fail to win; miss first place in a contest; lose to a rival. *John lost out in the rivalry for Mary's hand in marriage.* (Mary married someone else.) *Fred didn't want to lose out to the other salesman.* (He didn't want the other salesman to get the order.) Compare MISS OUT. Contrast WIN OUT.

loser See FINDERS KEEPERS *or* FINDERS KEEPERS LOSERS WEEPERS.

lose sight of *v. phr.* 1 Not to be able to see any longer. *I lost sight of Mary in the crowd.* (I couldn't see Mary in the crowd.) *I watched the plane go higher and higher until I lost sight of it.* (I watched the plane until I couldn't see it any more.) Contrast CATCH SIGHT OF. 2 To forget; overlook. *Johnny was so interested in the game he lost sight of the time.* (Johnny forgot the time.) *No matter how rich and famous he became, he never lost sight of the fact that he had been born in the slums.* (He never forgot that he was born in a very poor neighborhood.)

lose touch *v. phr., informal* To fail to keep in contact or communication. Usually used with *with. After she moved to another town, she lost touch with her childhood friends.* (They did not see each other or write letters.) Compare OUT OF TOUCH.

lose track *v. phr.* To forget about something; not stay informed; fail to keep a count or record. *What's the score now? I've lost track.* (I haven't been able to follow the score and know what it is.)—Usually used with *of. Mary lost track of her friends at camp after summer was over.* (She didn't see her friends or know what they were doing.) *John lost track of the money he spent at the circus.* (John didn't keep count of the money he spent.) Compare OUT OF TOUCH. Contrast KEEP TRACK.

loss See AT A LOSS, THROW FOR A LOSS.

lost See GET LOST, NO LOVE LOST.

lot See A LOT, CAST ONE'S LOT WITH, SAND LOT, THINK A GREAT DEAL OF *or* THINK A LOT OF, THROW IN ONE'S LOT WITH *or* CAST IN ONE'S LOT WITH.

loud See ACTIONS SPEAK LOUDER THAN WORDS, FOR CRYING OUT LOUD, OUT LOUD, THINK ALOUD *or* THINK OUT LOUD.

loud mouth *or* **big mouth** *n., slang* A noisy, boastful, or foolish talker. *Fritz is a loud mouth who cannot be trusted with secrets.* (He tells any secrets he finds out.) *When he has had a few drinks, Joe will make empty boasts like any other big mouth.* (He will talk foolishly and make boasts that he cannot prove.)

loud-mouthed *or* **big-mouthed** *adj., slang* Talking noisily, boastfully, or foolishly. *Fred was a loud-mouthed fellow, whose talk no one listened to.* (He was noisy, boastful, and foolish, and no one paid much attention to what he said.) *If I were you, I would not listen to that loud-mouthed boy.* (He talks too much and too foolishly.)

louse up *v., slang* To throw into confusion; make a mess of; spoil; ruin. *When the man who was considering John's house heard that the basement was wet, that was enough to louse up the sale.* (He was not willing to buy when he learned that the basement was wet.) *Fred's failure in business not only lost him his business but loused him up with his wife.* (He lost his business and his wife left him.) *The rain loused up the picnic.* (The rain spoiled the picnic.)

love See FOR LOVE OR MONEY, IN LOVE, LABOR OF LOVE, MAKE LOVE, NO LOVE LOST, PUPPY LOVE *also* CALF LOVE.

love affair *n.* A friendship between lovers; a romance or courtship. *The love affair of Bob and Jane went on for months.* (Bob courted Jane for months.) *Harry had many love affairs, but he never married.* (Harry was in love with many girls.)

love game *n.* A game of tennis which is won without the opponent scoring. *Britain took a love game on Sangster's service.* (The British team won a game when Sangster won without his American opponent scoring.)

love-in *n., slang, informal* A festival or occasion to celebrate life, human sensuality, the beauty of nature, human sexuality, and universal love; affairs so conceived by some frequently deteriorate into obscenity and drug using sessions in parody of their stated purpose. *The hippies gathered for a big love-in in the Haight-Ashbury district of San Francisco.* (They gathered for a festival celebrating universal love.)

lovers' lane *n.* A hidden road or walk where lovers walk or park in the evening. *A parked car in a lonely lovers' lane often is a chance for holdup men.* (Holdup men often rob lovers parked in a lonely place.)

low See LAY LOW, LIE LOW.

lowdown *n., slang, informal* The inside facts of a matter; the total truth. *Nixon has never given the American people the lowdown on Watergate.* (He never divulged the inside facts as he knew them.)

lower the boom *v. phr., informal* To punish strictly; check, or stop fully.—A cliché. *The mayor lowered the boom on outside jobs for city firemen.* (The mayor ordered city firemen not to hold outside jobs.) *Father lowered the boom on the girls for staying out after midnight.* (Father scolded the girls sternly for staying out after midnight.) Syn. CRACK DOWN. *The police lowered the boom on open gambling.* (The police put a stop to open gambling.)

low-key *adj.* Relaxed and easygoing. *Surprisingly, dinner with the governor was a low-key affair.* (The occasion was relaxed and informal.)

luck See DOWN ON ONE'S LUCK, LUCK OUT, PRESS ONE'S LUCK *or* PUSH ONE'S LUCK, IN LUCK, OUT OF LUCK.

luck out *v. phr., slang, informal* **1** Suddenly to get lucky when in fact the odds are against one's succeeding. *I was sure I was going to miss the train as I was three minutes late; but I lucked out; the train was five minutes late.* (I didn't miss the train because, luckily for me, it was later than I was.) **2** To be extraordinarily fortunate. *Catwallender really lucked out at Las Vegas last month; he came home with $10,000 in cash.* (He won a great deal of money in the gambling casinos in Las Vegas.) **3** (By sarcastic opposition) to be extremely unfortunate; to be killed. *Those poor marines sure lucked out in Saigon, didn't they?* (They were killed in Saigon.)

lucky See THANK ONE'S LUCKY STARS.

lucky star *n.* A certain star or planet which, by itself or with others, is seriously or jokingly thought to bring a person good luck and success in life. *John was born under a lucky star.* (He seems always to have good luck and success in life.) *Ted was unhurt in the car accident, for which he thanked his lucky stars.* (He thought he was lucky not to have been hurt.)

lump in one's throat   *n. phr.*   A feeling (as of grief or pride) so strong that you almost sob.—A cliché. *John's mother had a lump in her throat at his college graduation.* (John's mother was nearly crying with tender pride at his college graduation.) *All during her husband's funeral, Aunt May had a lump in her throat.* (At her husband's funeral, Aunt May could hardly control her grief.) *The bride's mother had a lump in her throat.* (The bride's mother felt like crying at the wedding.)

lunar module (L.M.) *or* **Lem**   *n., Space English*   That portion of the rocket assemblage on a flight to the Moon in which the astronauts descend to the Moon's surface. *Building the LM was one of the most expensive parts of the American space program.* (The vehicle in which astronauts descend to the Moon's surface is one of the most expensive items.)

lung   See AT THE TOP OF ONE'S VOICE *or* AT THE TOP OF ONE'S LUNGS.

lurch   See LEAVE IN THE LURCH.

luxury   See IN THE LAP OF LUXURY.

M

mackerel See HOLY CATS or HOLY MACKEREL.

mad as a hatter *or* **mad as a March hare** *adj. phr.* Not able to think right; crazy.—A cliché. *Anyone who thinks the moon is made of green cheese is mad as a hatter.* (The moon is a small planet, and anyone who thinks it is made of cheese is crazy.)

mad as a hornet *or* **mad as hops** *or* **mad as a wet hen** *adj. phr., informal* In a fighting mood; very angry. *When my father sees the dent in his fender, he'll be mad as a hornet.* (My father told me to be careful when he let me take the car and he's going to very angry when he sees I have dented the fender.) *Bill was mad as hops when the fellows went on without him.* (Bill expected his friends to wait for him and was angry when they didn't.) *Mrs. Harris was mad as a wet hen when the rabbits ate her tulips.* (She was very angry when the rabbits chewed off the tops of the sprouting tulip bulbs and kept them from blooming.)

mad as a March hare See MAD AS A HATTER.

mad as hops See MAD AS A HORNET.

made of money *adj. phr.* Very rich; wealthy.—A trite expression. *Mr. Jones buys his children everything they want. He must be made of money.* (Mrs. Jones must be very rich.) Compare MONEY TO BURN.

made-to-measure *or* **tailor-made** *adj.* Made to fit a special set of measurements or needs. *John has a new made-to-measure suit.* (John's new suit was made especially to fit him.) *The club is tailor-made for Jane.* (The activities of the club fit perfectly into Jane's interests.) Syn. MADE-TO-ORDER.

made to order *adj. phr.* **1** Made specially in the way the buyer wants instead of all the same in large amounts; made especially for the buyer. *Mr. Black's clothes were all made to order.* (Mr. Black's clothes were all specially made to his own measurements and wishes.) Compare MADE-TO-MEASURE. **2** just right. *The weather was made to order for the hike.* (The weather was just right for the hike.)

made up out of whole cloth See OUT OF WHOLE CLOTH.

magic carpet *n.* **1** A rug said to be able to transport a person through the air to any place he wishes. *The caliph of Bagdad flew on his magic carpet to Arabia.* (The caliph made his flying carpet carry him to Arabia.) **2** Any form of transportation that is comfortable and easy enough to seem magical. *Flying the Concord from Dallas to London seemed like boarding the magic carpet.* (It was swift and comfortable.) *Mr. Smith's new car drove so smoothly it seemed like a magic carpet.* (Mr. Smith's car seemed to fly through the air just by wishing and not by driving.)

Mahomet See IF THE HILL WON'T COME TO MAHOMET, THEN MAHOMET MUST COME TO THE HILL.

main See IN THE MAIN, WITH MIGHT AND MAIN.

main drag *n., colloquial* **1** The most important street or thoroughfare in a town. *Lincoln Avenue is the main drag of our town.* (Lincoln Avenue is the most important street in our town.) **2** The street where the dope pushers and the prostitutes are. *Wells Street is the main drag of Chicago, actionwise.* (Wells street, a part of Old Town, is where the pushers and the prostitutes hang out.)

main squeeze *n., slang* **1** The top ranking person in an organization or in a neighborhood; an important person, such as one's boss. *Mr. Bronchard is the main squeeze in this office.* (He is the top man, the boss here.) **2** The top person in charge of an illegal operation, such as drug sales, etc. *Before we can clean up this part of town, we must arrest the main squeeze.* (Before we can get rid of the petty criminals, we must catch their boss.) **3** One's principal romantic or sexual partner. *The singer's main squeeze is a member of the band.* (The singer is dating a band member.)

majority leader *n.* The leader of the political party with the most votes in a legislative house. *The majority leader of the House of Representatives tried to get the members of his party to support the bill.* (The leader tried to get his party to vote for the bill.) Compare MINORITY LEADER.

make See ALL WORK AND NO PLAY MAKES JACK A DULL BOY, HAVE IT MADE, MANY HANDS MAKE LIGHT WORK, ON THE MAKE.

make a beeline for *v. phr.* To go in a straight line toward.—A cliché. *The runner made a beeline for first base.* (The runner ran straight to first base.) *When the bell rang Ted made a beeline for the door of the classroom.* (Ted took the shortest, fastest route to the door.)

make a clean breast of *v. phr.* To admit (your guilt); tell all about (your wrong doing); confess everything.—A cliché. *The police caught the hit-and-run driver and he made a clean breast of his crime.* (The police found the driver who had run down the man, and the driver confessed he was guilty.) *Arthur worried because he cheated on the test, and finally he went to the teacher and made a clean breast of it.* (Arthur finally went to the teacher and told him he had cheated.) Compare OFF ONE'S CHEST.

make a day of it *v. phr., informal* To do something all day. *When they go to the beach they take a picnic lunch and make a day of it.* (When they go to the beach they take a picnic lunch and spend the whole day there.) Compare MAKE A NIGHT OF.

make a dent in *v. phr., informal* To make less by a very small amount; reduce slightly. —Usually used in the negative or with such qualifying words as *hardly* or *barely*. *John shoveled and shoveled, but he didn't seem to make a dent in the pile of sand.* (John shoveled and shoveled, but the pile didn't seem to get smaller.) *Mary studied all afternoon and only made a dent in her homework.* (Mary only finished a small part of her homework.)

make a difference *or* **make the difference** *v. phr.* To change the nature of something or a situation; be important; matter. *John's good score on the test made the difference between his passing or failing the course.* (By getting a good score on the test, John passed the course instead of failing it.) *It doesn't make a bit of difference if you are late to my party. I just want you to come.* (I want you to come to my party even if you have to be late.)

make a face *v. phr., informal* To twist your face; make an ugly expression on your face (as by sticking out your tongue.) *The boy made a face at his teacher when she turned her back.* (The boy stuck out his tongue at his teacher when she was not looking at him.) *The sick boy swallowed the medicine and made a face.* (After taking the medicine the boy showed on his face that he did not like the taste of the medicine.)

make a fool of *or* (*informal*) **make a monkey of** *v. phr.* To make (someone) look foolish. *The boy made a fool of himself.* (He acted foolishly.) *Mary's classmates made a fool of her by telling her the party was to be a masquerade.* (She came to the party in costume and people laughed at her, as it was not a masquerade party.)

make a go of *v. phr., informal* To cause to be a success; produce good results. *He was sure he could make a go of the filling station.* (He felt sure that he could run the filling station so that it would be a success.)

make a hit *v. phr., informal* To be successful; be well-liked; get along well. *Mary's new red dress made a hit at the party.* (Everybody liked Mary's new red dress.) *Alice was so happy that her boy friend made a hit with her parents.* (Alice's parents liked her boy friend.) Compare GO OVER 6.

make allowance *v. phr.* To judge results by the circumstances.—Often used in plural. *When a small boy is helping you, you must make allowances for his age.* (When you are being helped by a small boy, you must judge results by the circumstances. You can't expect the same kind of help from him as from a grown man.)

make a monkey of See MAKE A FOOL OF.

make a mountain out of a molehill To think a small problem is a big one; try to make something unimportant seem important.—A cliché. *You're not hurt badly, Johnny. Stop trying to make a mountain out of a molehill*

with crying. (I know you're not hurt badly, even though you are crying.) *Sarah laughed at a mistake Betty made in class, and Betty won't speak to her; Betty is making a mountain out of a molehill.* (Betty is taking Sarah's laughing much too seriously.)

make an appearance See PUT IN AN APPEARANCE.

make an end of *v. phr.* To make (something) end; put a stop to; stop. *To make an end of rumors that the house was haunted, a reporter spent the night there.* (To stop rumors that there were ghosts in the house, a reporter stayed overnight in it.)

make an example of *v. phr.* To punish (someone) publicly to show what happens when someone does wrong. *The teacher made an example of the boy who copied from another student during a test.* (Before all the students, the teacher punished the boy who copied another student's work as a warning.) *The Pilgrims made an example of a thief by putting him in the stocks.* (When the Pilgrims caught a thief they put him in an outdoor wooden frame as a warning to others not to steal.)

make a night of it *v. phr., informal* To spend the whole night at an activity. *The dog found the door unlatched and made a night of it.* (When the dog discovered that the door was open, he slipped out and spent the whole night roaming around the neighborhood.) *The boys and girls at the dance made a night of it.* (They danced all night.) Compare MAKE A DAY OF IT.

make a pass at *v. phr., slang, informal* Make advances toward a member of the opposite sex (usually man to a woman) with the goal of seducing the person. *We've been dating for four weeks but Joe has never even made a pass at me.* (Even though they have been dating for four weeks, Joe has never made advances toward her regarding sex.)

make a play for *v. phr., slang* To try to get the interest or liking of; flirt with; attract.— A cliché. *Bob made a play for the pretty new girl.* (Bob did his best to attract the new girl.) *John made a play for the other boys' votes for class president.* (John tried to get the other boys to vote for him for class president.)

make a point *v. phr.* To try hard; make a special effort.—Used with *of* and a verbal noun. *He made a point of remembering to get his glasses fixed.* (He tried hard to remember to take his glasses to be repaired.) *He made a point of thanking his hostess before he left the party.* (He made a special effort to thank her.)

make a practice of *v. phr.* To make a habit of; do regularly. *Make a practice of being on time for work.* (You should make it a habit to get to work on time.)

make a virtue of necessity *v. phr.* Make the

best of things as they are; do cheerfully what you do.—A cliché. *After Mr. Wilson lost all his money, he made a virtue of necessity and found a new and interesting life as a teacher.* (Mr. Wilson had to earn his own living, and found that he liked that even better than living on the money his father left him.) Compare MAKE THE BEST OF.

make away with *v., informal* Take; carry away; cause to disappear. *The lumber jack made away with a great stack of pancakes.* (The lumberjack ate a great stack of pancakes.) *Two masked men held up the clerk and made away with the payroll.* (Masked bandits stole the payroll.) Compare MAKE OFF.

make believe *v.* To act as if something is true while one knows it is not; pretend. *Let's make believe we have a million dollars.* (Let's pretend we're millionaires.) *Danny made believe he didn't hear his mother calling.* (Danny heard his mother calling but pretended he did not.)

make bricks without straw *v. phr.* To make something without the wherewithal; do something the hard way; do a job under hard conditions.—A cliché. *John could not go to a library, and writing the report was a job of making bricks without straw.* (He could not get to a library, and it was hard to write the report, because he didn't have all the information he needed.) *It was making bricks without straw to put on plays in that old barn.* (To put on plays in the old barn meant that the actors had to do without things they thought they needed.)

make conversation *v. phr.* To talk with someone just so that there will be talk. *John made conversation with the stranger so that he would not feel left out.* (John talked with the stranger to make him feel less awkward, even though they had nothing to talk about.) *Mary didn't really mean what she said about Joan. She was only making conversation.* (Mary said what she said without thinking and just to say something.)

make do *v. phr.* To use a poor substitute when one does not have the right thing. *John did not have a hammer, and he had to make do with a heavy rock.* (John had to use the rock for a hammer.) *This motel isn't what we wanted, but we must make do.* (This is not the kind of place we were looking for, but we must be satisfied with it.) *Many families manage to make do on very little income.* (Many families are able to live with a very small income.) Compare GET ALONG.

make ends meet *v. phr.* To have enough money to pay one's bills; earn what it costs to live.—A cliché. *Both husband and wife had to work to make ends meet.* (Living costs were so high that the salaries of husband and wife added together came to just enough money to pay the bills.)

make eyes at *v. phr., informal* To look at a girl or boy in a way that tries to attract him to you; flirt. *The other girls disliked her way of making eyes at their boy friends instead of finding one of her own.* (The other girls were disgusted at her flirting with their boy friends.)

make for *v.* To go toward; start in the direction of. *The children took their ice skates and made for the frozen pond.* (The pond was covered with ice. The children took their skates and went toward the pond.) *The bee got his load of pollen and made for the hive.* (The bee got pollen on his hairy legs and started in the direction of the hive.)

make free with *v.* **1** To take or use (things) without asking. *Bob makes free with his roommate's clothes.* (Bob wears his roommate's clothes but does not ask his permission.) *A student should not make free with his teacher's first name.* (A student should not call his teacher by his first name unless the teacher tells him to do it.) **2** To act toward (someone) in a rude or impolite way. *The girls don't like Ted because he makes free with them.* (Ted is rude and the girls don't like it.) Compare TAKE LIBERTIES.

make friends *v. phr.* To become friends; form a friendship. *Mrs. Jones invited Bobby to her home to play with Don. She hoped that they would make friends with each other.* (Mrs. Jones invited Bobby to her home. She hoped that Don and Bobby would become friends.) *You can make friends with an elephant by giving him peanuts.* (You can cause an elephant to be friendly by giving him peanuts.)

make fun of *or* **poke fun at** *v. phr., informal* To joke about; laugh at; tease; mock. *Men like to make fun of the trimmings on women's hats.* (Men like to joke about the fruit and flowers women wear on their hats.) *James poked fun at the new pupil because her speech was not like the other pupils.* (James teased the new pupil because her speech was not like the speech of the other children in the class.)

make good *v. phr.* **1** To do what one promised to do; make something come true. *Mr. Smith borrowed some money. He promised to pay it back on payday. He made good his promise.* (When he got his money he paid back what he borrowed. He did what he promised to do.) *Joe made good his boast to swim across the lake.* (Joe did what he bragged he would do.) *John's mother promised to take him and his friends to the zoo on Saturday. She made good her promise.* (John's mother took him and his friends to the zoo as she promised.) Compare CARRY OUT. **2** To compensate; pay for loss or damage. *The policeman told the boy's parents that the boy must make good the money he had stolen or go to jail.* (The policeman said that the boy had to give back the same amount of money as he had stolen.)—Often used in the phrase *make it good. The radio was broken while it was being delivered so the store had to make it good and send us a new radio.* (The store had to replace the damaged radio.) Compare MAKE UP. **3** To do good work at one's job; succeed. *Kate wanted to be a nurse. She studied and worked hard in school. Then she got a job in the hospital and made good as a nurse.* (Kate worked hard and learned to be a good nurse. She succeeded.)

make haste *v. phr.* To move fast; hurry.—Rarely used in speaking. *The dog wriggled into one end of the hollow log, and the rabbit made haste to get out the other end.* (The dog was trying to follow the rabbit into the log and the rabbit was moving fast to get out the other end of it.) *Mary saw that she had hurt Jane's feelings, and made haste to say she was sorry.* (Mary quickly said she was sorry.) Compare MAKE TRACKS.

make hay while the sun shines *v. phr.* To do something at the right time; not wait too long. *Dick had a free hour so he made hay while the sun shone and got his lesson for the next day.* (Dick did not waste time, but used a free hour to get his lesson.) Compare MAKE THE MOST OF.

make head or tail of *v. phr., informal* To see the why of; finding a meaning in; understand.—Used in negative, conditional, and interrogative sentences. *She could not make head or tail of the directions on the dress pattern.* (She could not understand the instructions telling how to make her dress.) *Can you make head or tail of the letter?* (Can you understand it?)

make it hot *v. phr., informal* To bring punishment; cause trouble. *Dick threatened to make it hot for anyone who tied knots in his pajama legs again.* (Dick threatened to cause trouble for anyone who tied knots in his pajamas again.)

make it snappy *v. phr., informal* To move quickly; be fast; hurry.—Usually used as a command. *"Make it snappy," Mother said, "or we'll be late for the movie."* ("Hurry," Mother said.) *The man hurried into the restaurant and told the waitress, "A cup of coffee, and make it snappy."* (The man told the waitress to give him a cup of coffee quickly.)

make it with *v. phr., slang, informal* **1** To be accepted by a group. *Joe finally made it with the in crowd in Hollywood.* (He was finally accepted by the in-group in Hollywood.) **2** *vulgar* To have sex with (someone). *I wonder if Joe has made it with Sue.* (I wonder if he had sex with her.)

make light of *v. phr.* To treat as of little importance; make as small as possible; minimize. *The soldier made light of his wound.* (He talked about it as not important; he said it was only a scratch.) *She made light of her disappointment at being too sick to go to the*

dance. (She made her disappointment seem very small at having to miss the dance; she said she would hurry and get well and be ready for the next one.) Compare LAUGH OFF. Contrast MAKE MUCH OF.

make little of *v. phr.* To make (something) seem unimportant; belittle. *Mary made little of Jane's new bicycle because she was jealous.* (Mary was jealous of Jane's new bicycle. She talked about it as if it were just a cheap toy.) *Tom made little of his saving the drowning boy.* (Tom acted as if his saving the drowning boy was something of no great importance.) Contrast MAKE MUCH OF.

make love *v. phr.* **1** To be warm, loving and tender toward someone of the opposite sex; try to get him or her to love you too. *There was moonlight on the roses and he made love to her in the porch swing.* (Moonlight on the roses made everything romantic. The boy was warm and loving to the girl as they sat in the porch swing.) **2** To have sexual relations with (someone). *It is rumored that Alfred makes love to every girl he hires as a secretary.* (It is rumored that he has sexual relations with every girl he hires.)

make merry *v. phr., literary* To have fun, laugh and be gay. *In Aesop's fable the grasshopper made merry while the ant worked and saved up food.* (The grasshopper had a good time and did not work.) *In the Bible story a rich man ate and drank and made merry.* (He laughed and joked and did not worry.)

make much of *v. phr.* To make something seem of more worth or importance than it really is; praise. *Visitors made much of the new collie.* (They praised him and said they had never seen such a fine dog.) *The boy made much of the hard things of his mountain climb.* (He made the hard things of his mountain climb seem big. He wanted to make himself look bigger and more important.) Contrast MAKE LIGHT OF, MAKE LITTLE OF.

make no bones *v. phr., informal* **1** To have no doubts; not to worry about right or wrong; not to be against.—Used with *about. Bill makes no bones about telling a lie to escape punishment.* (Bill is not ashamed to lie if it will save him from being punished.) *The boss made no bones about hiring extra help for the holidays.* (The boss was not against getting in extra clerks to handle the Christmas rush. He felt that extra clerks would sell more for him.) **2** To make no secret; not keep from talking; admit.—Used with *about* or *of the fact. John thinks being poor is no disgrace, and he makes no bones of the fact.* (John does not try to hide the fact that he is poor.) *Mary made no bones about her love of poetry even after some of her friends laughed at her.* (Mary did not keep secret her love of poetry.)

make off *v.* To go away, run away, leave. *When the deer saw the hunter, it made off at once.* (The deer saw the hunter and ran away.) *A thief stopped John on a dark street and made off with his wallet.* (The thief robbed John and ran away with his money.) Compare TAKE OFF.

make one's bed and lie in it To be responsible for what you have done and so to have to accept the bad results.—A cliché. *Billy smoked one of his father's cigars and now he he is sick. He made his bed, now let him lie in it.* (It is Billy's own fault that he is sick. He smoked, and now let him suffer for it.) Compare FACE THE MUSIC 2.

make one's blood boil *or* **make the blood boil** *v. phr., informal* To make someone very angry.—A cliché. *When someone calls me a liar it makes my blood boil.* (I get very angry if anyone calls me a liar.) *It made Mary's blood boil to see the children make fun of the crippled girl.* (Mary was furious because the children teased the crippled girl.) Compare BOILING POINT.

make one's blood run cold See BLOOD RUNS COLD.

make one's ears burn See EARS BURN.

make oneself at home *v. phr.* To feel comfortable; act as if you were in your own home. *If you get to my house before I do, help yourself to a drink and make yourself at home.* (Relax and make yourself comfortable in my house.) *John was an outdoor man and could make himself at home in the woods at night.* (He felt comfortable in the woods at night.) Compare AT EASE, AT HOME 2.

make oneself scarce *v. phr., slang* To leave quickly; go away. *The boys made themselves scarce when they saw the principal coming to stop their noise.* (The boys left quickly when the principal came to tell them to be quiet.) *A wise mouse makes himself scarce when a cat is near by.* (A wise mouse goes away when a cat comes near him.)

make one's hair stand on end See HAIR STAND ON END.

make one's mark *v. phr.* To become known to many people; do well the work you started to do; make a reputation. *Shakespeare made his mark as a playwright.* (Shakespeare became known to many people as a writer of plays for the stage.)

make one's mouth water *v. phr.* 1 To look or smell very good; make you want very much to eat or drink something you see or smell—A cliché. *The pies in the store window made Dan's mouth water.* (The pies in the store window looked so good he wanted to eat a piece of the pie.) *The picture of the ice cream soda made his mouth water.* (The picture of the ice cream soda made him hungry for one.) 2 To be attractive; make you want to have something very much. *Judy collects folk song records, and the records in the store window made her mouth water.* (Judy wanted

very much to get the records.) Compare LICK ONE'S CHOPS.—**mouth-watering** *adj.* Smelling or looking very good to eat. *It was a mouth-watering meal.* (It smelled and tasted good.)

make one's way *v. phr.* 1 To go forward with difficulty; find a path for yourself. *They made their way through the crowd.* (They went forward with difficulty through the crowd of people.) 2 To do many hard things to earn a living; make a life work for yourself. *He was anxious to finish school and make his own way in the world.* (He was anxious to finish college and start earning a living.) Compare SHIFT FOR ONESELF.

make out *v.* 1 To write the facts asked for (as in an application blank or a report form); fill out. *The teacher made out the report cards and gave them to the students to take home.* (The teacher wrote the students' grades on the report cards.) *Mrs. Smith gave the clerk in the store some money, and the clerk made out a receipt.* (The clerk took a printed form and wrote in the blanks telling what Mrs. Smith had bought and how much she had paid.) 2 To see, hear, or understand by trying hard. *It was dark, and we could not make out who was coming along the road.* (We could not see clearly who was coming.) *They could not make out what the child had drawn.* (They could not understand what the child had drawn.) *The book had many hard words, and Anne could not make out what the writer meant.* (Anne could not understand the book.) *Mr. White does many strange things. No one can make him out.* (No one can understand him; they do not know why he does those things.) Syn. FIGURE OUT. 3 *informal* To make someone believe; show; prove. *Charles and Bob had a fight, and Charles tried to make out that Bob started it.* (Charles tried to make people believe that John started the fight.) *The boy said he did not take the money, but the teacher found the money in the boy's desk and it made him out to be a liar.* (Finding the money in the boy's desk made the teacher think that he was lying.) 4 *informal* Do well enough; succeed. *John's father wanted John to do well in school, and asked the teacher how John was making out.* (John's father asked the teacher if John was doing well in school.) *The sick woman could not make out alone in her house, so her friend came and helped her.* (The sick woman could not do anything for herself, so her friend came and helped her.) 5 To kiss or pet. *What are Jack and Jill up to?—They're making out on the back porch.* (They're kissing and hugging.)

make over *v.* 1 To change by law something from one owner to another owner; change the name on the title (lawful paper) from one owner to another. *Mr. Brown made over the title to the car to Mr. Jones.* (Mr. Brown changed the owner of the car from himself to

Mr. Jones by writing a new legal paper saying Mr. Jones was the owner.) **2** To make something look different; change the style of. *He asked the tailor to make over his pants. The tailor cut off the cuffs and put a belt across the back.* (The tailor made the pants look different by making these changes.)

make rounds *v. phr.* To travel the same route, making several stops along the way. *The milkman makes his rounds every morning.* (He travels the same route, making several stops to deliver milk.) *The doctor makes the rounds of the hospital rooms.* (He goes through the hospital, and stops in the rooms to see the sick people.)

make sense *v. phr.* **1** To be something you can understand or explain; not be difficult or strange. *The explanation in the school book made no sense, because the words were hard.* (The explanation was difficult; the students could not understand it.) Compare MAKE HEAD OR TAIL OF. **2** To seem right to do; sound reasonable or practical. *Does it make sense to let little children play with matches?* (Does it seem right to give matches to little children to play with? They may accidentally set the house on fire with the matches.)

make short work of *v. phr.* To finish rapidly. *The cat made short work of the baby rabbit.* (The cat rapidly ate the baby rabbit.) *Tim was anxious to get to the movies, so he made short work of his homework.* (Tom did his homework quickly so he could go to the movies.)

make something of *v. phr.* **1** To make (something) seem important. *When girls see another girl with a boy, they often try to make something of it.* (Girls often guess that a girl and boy seen together are serious about each other.) **2** To start a fight over; use as an excuse to start a quarrel. *Bob accidentally shoved Bill in the corridor, and Bill made something of it.* (Bill started a fight over Bob's shoving him.) *Ann didn't like what Mary said about her. She tried to make something of what Mary said.* (Ann used what Mary said as a reason for being angry with her.) Compare START SOMETHING.

make sport of See MAKE FUN OF.

make sure *v. phr.* To see about something yourself; look at to be sure. *Father makes sure that all the lights are off before he goes to bed.* (He looks to be sure that no lights are left burning all night to waste electricity.) *Mary thought she had time to get to school, but she ran all the way just to make sure.* (Mary ran to school; she wanted to be sure that she got there before classes started.) *Before you write your report on the life of Washington, you should make sure of your facts.* (You should look at good books to be sure you have correct facts.)

make the best of *v. phr.* To do something you do not like to do and not complain; accept with good humor. *The girl did not like*

to wash dishes, but she made the best of it. (She hated to wash dishes, but she did it and was not cross about it. She did it without complaining.) Compare MAKE A VIRTUE OF NECESSITY.

make the blood boil See MAKE ONE'S BLOOD BOIL.

make the feathers fly *v. phr., informal* **1** To enjoy working; be strong and work hard. *When Mrs. Hale did her spring cleaning she made the feathers fly.* (When she cleaned the house in the spring, she washed and scrubbed hard and fast. She enjoyed seeing things clean.) **2** See MAKE THE FUR FLY.

make the fur fly *or* **make the feathers fly** *v. phr., informal* Say or write mean things about someone or to jump on and fight hard. —A cliché. *A man fooled Mr. Black and got his money. Mr. Black will really make the fur fly when he finds the man.* (Mr. Black will jump on him and beat him up.) *Mrs. Baker's dog dug holes in her neighbor's garden. The neighbor really made the fur fly when she saw Mrs. Baker.* (The neighbor talked strongly to Mrs. Baker and told her to keep the dog at home.)

make the grade *v. phr., informal* **1** To make good; succeed. *It was clear that Mr. Baker had made the grade in the insurance business.* (It was clear that he had succeeded in the insurance business.) *It takes hard study to make the grade in school.* (You need to study hard to succeed in school.) **2** To meet a standard; qualify. *That whole shipment of cattle made the grade as prime beef.* (All that shipment of cattle qualified as the best kind of beef.)

make the most of *v. phr.* To do the most you can with; get the most from; use to the greatest advantage. *She planned the weekend in town to make the most of it.* (She planned the weekend to do as many things as she could.) *George studied hard. He wanted to make the most of his chance to learn.* (George wanted to learn as much as he could while he had the chance.) *The teacher went out of the room for five minutes, and some bad boys made the most of it.* (They talked and played while they had a chance.) *Bill liked Mary; he would do anything for her, and Mary made the most of it.* (She made him do many things for her.) Compare MAKE HAY WHILE THE SUN SHINES.

make the scene *v. phr., slang* To be present; to arrive at a certain place or event. *I am too tired to make the scene; let's go home.* (I am too tired to be there, let's return home.)

make time *v. phr., slang* **1** To be successful in arriving at a designated place in short or good time. *We're supposed to be there at 6 PM, and it's only 5:30—we're making good time.* (They are not going to be late.) **2** To be successful in making sexual advances to someone. *Joe sure is making time with Sue, isn't he?* (He is successful in his advances toward her.)

make tongues wag See TONGUES TO WAG.

make tracks *v. phr., informal* To go fast; get a speedy start; hurry. *Man, it's time we made tracks!* (Man, we'd better hurry.) *The boys made tracks for home when it began to get dark.* (They hurried home.) Compare GET GOING, MAKE HASTE.

makeup *n.* (stress on *make*) **1** Cosmetics. *All the actors and actresses put on a lot of makeup.* (They lavishly adorned themselves with cosmetics.) **2** *Attributive auxiliary* in lieu of, or belated. *The professor gave a makeup to the sick students.* (He gave the students another chance to take a substitute examination for the one they missed.)

make up *v.* (stress on *up*) **1** To make by putting things or parts together. *A car is made up of many different parts.* (It has wheels, tires, seats and other parts.) **2** To invent; think and say something that is new or not true. *Jean makes up stories to amuse her little brother.* (She invents stories to please him.) **3a** To do or provide (something lacking or needed); do or supply (something not done, lost, or missed); get back; regain; give back; repay. *I have to make up the test I missed last week.* (I have to take the test I missed.) *I want to go to bed early to make up the sleep I lost last night.* (I want to gain back the sleep I lost.) *We have to drive fast to make up the hour we lost in Boston.* (We are an hour late and have to drive fast to get it back.) *Vitamin pills make up what you lack in your diet.* (The pills supply the vitamins you need.) *The toy cost a dollar and Ted only had fifty cents, so Father made up the difference.* (Father gave Ted the money he still needed to buy the toy.)—Often used in the phrase *make it up to*. *Uncle Fred forgot my birthday present, but he made it up to me by taking me to the circus.* (Uncle Fred took me to the circus instead of giving me a present.) *Mrs. Rich spent so much time away from her children that she tried to make it up to them by giving them things.* (Mrs. Rich was away often and tried to give her children things instead.) Compare MAKE GOOD. **3b** To do what is lacking or needed; do or give what should be done or given; get or give back what has been lost, missed, or not done; get or give instead; pay back.—Used with *for*. *We made up for lost time by taking an airplane instead of a train.* (We were late but we gained some time by going faster on an airplane.) *Saying you are sorry won't make up for the damage of breaking the window.* (Saying you are sorry will not pay for the window.) *Mary had to make up for the time she missed in school when she was sick, by studying very hard.* (Mary had to do the studying that she missed and also her regular lessons.) *The beautiful view at the top of the mountain makes up for the hard climb to get there.* (The view makes the hard climb worth it.) **4** To put on lip-

stick and face paint powder. *Clowns always make up before a circus show.* (They paint their faces and put on funny clothes for the show.) *Tom watched his sister make up her face for her date.* (He watched her put on lipstick for a date.) **5** To become friends again after a quarrel. *Mary and Joan quarreled, but made up after a while.* (The two girls quarreled but soon became friends again.) Compare BURY THE HATCHET. **6** To try to make friends with someone; to win favor. Followed by *to*. *The new boy made up to the teacher by sharpening her pencils.* (The new boy sharpened the teacher's pencils to make her like him.)

make up one's mind *v. phr.* To choose what to do; decide. *They made up their minds to sell the house.* (They decided to sell it.) *Tom couldn't decide whether he should tell Mother about the broken window, or let her find it herself.* (Tom could not decide what to do.) Contrast ON THE FENCE.

make waves *v. phr., informal* Make one's influence felt; create a disturbance, a sensation. *Joe Catwallender is the wrong man for the job; he is always trying to make waves.* (He is always trying to be overbearing and make his influence felt too strongly.)

make way *v. phr.* To move from in front so someone can go through; stand aside. *The people made way for the king.* (They moved aside so the king could go through.) *When older men retire they make way for younger men to take their places.* (When older workers retire, their places are filled by younger men who need work.)

mama's boy *n. phr., informal* A boy who depends too much on his mother; a sissy. *The other boys called Tommy a mama's boy because he wouldn't come out to play unless his mother stayed near him.* (Tommy was so dependent on his mother that he would not play with the other boys without her.)

man See COMPANY MAN, EVERY LAST MAN *also* EVERY MAN JACK, FRONT MAN, HIRED MAN, LADY'S MAN, NEW MAN, SEPARATE THE MEN FROM THE BOYS, TO A MAN, YES-MAN.

man *or* **the man** *n., slang* **1** The police, a policeman. *I am gonna turn you in to the man.* (I will turn you into the police.) **2** The boss, the leader, the most important figure in an organization or outfit. *The man will decide.* (The boss will decide.)

manger See DOG IN THE MANGER.

man in the street *n. phr.* The man who is just like most other men; the average man; the ordinary man.—A cliché. *The newspaper took a poll of the man in the street.* (The newspaper asked a large number of ordinary people what they thought about a problem.) Compare JOE DOAKES, JOHN Q. PUBLIC.

manner See ALL MANNER OF, TO THE MANNER BORN.

man of few words *n. phr.* A man who

doesn't talk very much; a man who says only what is needed.—A cliché. *The principal is a man of few words, but the pupils know what he wants.* (The principal makes clear what the pupils must do without saying much.)

man of his word *n. phr.* A man who keeps his promises and does the things he agrees to do; a man who can be trusted. *My uncle is a man of his word.* (He does what he promises; I trust him.)

man of parts *n. phr. literary* A man who has several different skills, talents, or qualities. *The pianist is a man of parts. He wrote the piece he played, and he also plays the organ and paints well.* (He does many different things. He plays the piano and the organ, he writes music, and he paints.)

man-to-man *adj.* Honest and full in the telling; not hiding anything embarrassing. *Tom and his father had a man-to-man talk about his playing hooky.* (Tom and his father talked over all of the reasons why Tom did not go to school.) Compare HEART-TO-HEART.

many See GOOD MANY or GREAT MANY, IN SO MANY WORDS, SO MANY.

many a *adj.* Many (persons or things)— Used with a singular noun. *Many a boy learns to swim before he can read.* (Many boys learn to swim before they can read.) *I have spent many a day in his home.* (I have visited often in his home.)

many hands make light work If many people work together, even a hard job becomes easier.—A proverb. *Come on boys, many hands make light work. If we work together, we can finish painting the barn.* (If we all work together, the painting will be done sooner.)

many is the There are a great number of (persons or things); many are the (persons or things)—Used at the beginning of a sentence with a singular noun. *Many is the man I have lent money to.* (I have lent money to many men.) *Many was the time I ate at that restaurant.* (I often ate at that restaurant.) Compare MANY A.

map See PUT ON THE MAP.

marble See HAVE ALL ONE'S BUTTONS or HAVE ALL ONE'S MARBLES.

March See MAD AS A HATTER or MAD AS A MARCH HARE.

march See STEAL A MARCH ON.

marine See TELL IT TO THE MARINES.

mark See MAKE ONE'S MARK, TOE THE LINE or TOE THE MARK, UP TO THE MARK at UP TO PAR 2, WALK THE CHALK or WALK THE CHALK LINE or WALK THE CHALK MARK, WIDE OF THE MARK.

market See FLEA MARKET, IN THE MARKET FOR, ON THE MARKET, PLAY THE MARKET.

mark time *v. phr.* **1** To move the feet up and down as in marching, but not going forward. *The officer made the soldiers mark time as a punishment.* (He told them to keep lifting their feet up and down.) **2** To be idle;

waiting for something to happen. *The teacher marked time until all the children were ready for the test.* (She did nothing, but waited for them.) **3** To seem to be working or doing something, but really not doing it. *It was so hot that the workmen just marked time.* (They moved around and pretended to work.)

masking tape *n.* A paper tape that is stuck around the edges of a surface being painted to keep the paint off the surface next to it. *The painters put masking tape around the window frames to keep the paint off the glass.* (The painters stuck the tape on the glass so the paint would go on the tape and not on the glass.)

masse See EN MASSE.

mast See NAIL ONE'S COLORS TO THE MAST.

master copy *n.* **1** A perfect text to which all copies are made to conform; a corrected version used as a standard by printers. *The master copy must be right, because if it isn't, the mistakes in it will be repeated all through the edition.* (It is important to have one copy right to use as a standard.) **2** A stencil from which other copies are made. *Mr. Brown told his secretary to save the master copy so that they could run off more copies whenever they needed them.* (Mr. Brown told his secretary not to throw the stencil away.) *The master copy was too light, so many of the copies didn't come out clear.* (The stencil was not good enough.)

mat See WELCOME MAT IS OUT.

matter See FOR THAT MATTER, LAUGHING MATTER, NO MATTER, THE MATTER.

matter of course *n. phr.* Something always done; the usual way; habit; rule. *It was a matter of course for John to dress carefully when he was meeting his wife.* (He always wore nice clothes to meet her.) *Bank officers ask questions as a matter of course when someone wants to borrow money.* (Bank officers always ask questions of anyone who wants to borrow money.)

matter of fact *n. phr.* Something that is really true; something that can be proved. *The town records showed that it was a matter of fact that the two boys were brothers.* (The town books showed that it was true that they were brothers.) *It is a matter of fact that the American war against England was successful.* (It is true that the war was successful.)—Often used for emphasis in the phrase *as a matter of fact. I didn't go yesterday, and as a matter of fact, I didn't go all week.* (I didn't go all week either.) *Mary wasn't wearing a blue dress. As a matter of fact, she hasn't got a blue dress.* (She hasn't got a blue dress, so how could she wear one?) Compare FOR THAT MATTER, IN FACT. Contrast MATTER OF OPINION.

matter-of-fact *adj.* **1** Simply telling or showing the truth; not explaining or telling more. *The newspaper gave a matter-of-fact account of the murder trial.* (The newspaper told about the court trial in a plain way.) **2** Showing little feeling or excitement or trouble; seeming not to care much. *When Mary's father died she acted in a very matter-of-fact way.* (She did not cry much and seemed not very troubled.) *He was a very matter-of-fact person.* (He never was very excited and never joked much.)

matter of opinion *n. phr.* Something that may or may not be true; something that people do not all agree on. *Whether or not he was a good general is a matter of opinion.* (Some people think he was good; others do not think so.) Compare MATTER OF FACT.

matter of record *n. phr.* A fact or event that is kept officially as a legal record. *If you are convicted of speeding, it becomes a matter of record.* (If you are convicted of speeding, the conviction is recorded for the future.) *A birth certificate or a marriage license is a matter of record.* (A copy of a birth certificate or marriage license is kept among the official records.)

may See BE THAT AS IT MAY, COME WHAT MAY, LET THE CHIPS FALL WHERE THEY MAY.

me See DEAR ME, PICK-ME-UP, SO HELP ME.

mean business *v. phr., informal* To decide strongly to do what you plan to do; really mean it; be serious. *The boss said he would fire us if we didn't work harder and he means business.* (The boss said he would fire us if we didn't work harder and he really will.) *When she went to college to study, she meant business.* (When she went to college to study, she really studied hard and didn't fool around or play.) *He just liked the company of the other girls he dated; but this time he seems to mean business.* (He seems to be serious about this girl.)

means See BY ALL MEANS, BY MEANS OF, BY NO MEANS, WAYS AND MEANS.

measure See BEYOND MEASURE, FOR GOOD MEASURE, MADE-TO-MEASURE, TAKE ONE'S MEASURE or TAKE THE MEASURE OF.

measure up *v.* To be equal; be of fully high quality; come up. *John didn't measure up to the best catchers, but he was a good one.* (John wasn't equal in ability to the best catchers.) *Lois' school work didn't measure up to her ability.* (Lois didn't do as good work as she should have when she was so smart.) Compare UP TO PAR. Contrast FALL SHORT.

meatball *n., slang* A dull, boring, slow-witted, or uninteresting person. *You'll never get an interesting story out of that meatball—stop inviting him.* (He is a dull person.)

medicine See TAKE ONE'S MEDICINE.

medium See STRIKE A HAPPY MEDIUM.

meet See MAKE ENDS MEET.

meet halfway See GO HALFWAY.

meeting See BEST BIB AND TUCKER or SUNDAY-GO-TO-MEETING CLOTHES.

meet one's eye *v. phr.* To be in plain view or come into plain view; appear clearly or obviously. *When John rounded the bend, a clear blue lake met his eye.* (When John rounded the bend, he saw a clear blue lake directly in front of him.) *On a first reading the plan looked good, but there was more to it than met the eye.* (On the surface the plan looked good, but there were hidden parts of it that would keep it from working well.)

meet one's Waterloo *v. phr.* To be defeated; lose an important contest.—A cliché. *After seven straight victories the team met its Waterloo.* (The team lost a game after winning seven.) *John fought instead of running, and the bully met his Waterloo.* (John fought the bully and beat him.)

meet up with *v. phr.* To meet by accident; come upon without planning or expecting to. *When he ran around the tree, Bob suddenly met up with a large bear.* (Bob came upon a large bear by surprise.) *The family would have arrived on time, but they met up with a flat tire.* (The family would have arrived on time, but their car had a flat tire on the way.)

meet with *v.* **1** To meet (someone), usually by accident. *In the woods, he met with two strangers.* (In the woods he happened to meet two strangers.) Syn. COME UPON. **2** To meet together, usually by plan; join; have a meeting with. *The two scouts met with the officers to talk about plans for the march.* (The two scouts met the officers by agreement to make plans.) **3** To experience (as unhappiness); suffer (as bad luck); have (as an accident or mishap). *The farmer met with misfortune; his crops were destroyed by a storm.* (The farmer suffered very bad luck; a storm destroyed his crops. *The traveler met with an accident on the road.* (The traveler had an accident on the road.)

melt See BUTTER WOULDN'T MELT IN ONE'S MOUTH.

melt in one's mouth *v. phr.* **1** To be so tender as to seem to need no chewing. *The chicken was so tender that it melted in your mouth.* (The chicken was so tender you didn't need to chew it.) **2** To taste very good; be delicious. *Mother's apple pie really melts in your mouth.* (Mother's apple pie tastes very good.)

memory See IN MEMORY OF.

mend See ON THE MEND.

mend one's fences *v. phr., informal* To do something to make people like or follow you again; strengthen your friendships or influence. *The Senator went home from Washington to mend his fences.* (He went home and talked with everybody to get them to vote for him.) *John saw that his friends did not like him, so he decided to mend his fences.* (John was nicer to them and got them to like him again.)

mental telepathy *n. phr.* The passing of one person's thoughts to another without any discoverable talking or carrying of signals between them. *Mrs. Smith knew the moment her husband's ship sank on the other side of the world. It seems like a case of mental telepathy.* (Mrs. Smith had no apparent way of knowing her husband's ship sank unless the news was carried from her husband's mind to hers.) *Most or all men who practice mental telepathy on stage have really trained themselves to detect tiny clues from the audience.* (These men use clues and hints from the audience rather than actually reading minds.)

mention See NOT TO MENTION.

meow See CAT'S MEOW.

mercy See AT THE MERCY OF.

merrier See MORE THE MERRIER.

merry See LEAD A MERRY CHASE, MAKE MERRY.

message See GET THE MESSAGE.

mess around *v. phr.* **1** To engage in idle or purposeless activity. *Come on, you guys,— start doing some work, don't just mess around all day!* (Don't just waste your day by doing idle and purposeless things.) **2** *vulgar* To be promiscuous, to indulge in sex with little discrimination as to who the partner is. *Allen needs straightening out; he's been messing around with the whole female population of his class.* (He has been sexually promiscuous with his female classmates.) Compare FOOL AROUND.

mess up *v. phr., slang, informal* **1** To cause trouble, to spoil something. *What did you have to mess up my accounts for?* (Why did you have to cause trouble with the accounts?) **2** To cause someone emotional trauma. *Sue will never get married; she got messed up when she was a teen-ager.* (She was traumatized emotionally as a teen-ager.) **3** To beat up someone physically. *When Joe came in after the fight with the boys, he was all messed up.* (He was beaten up badly enough to leave visible marks on him.)

met See HAIL FELLOW WELL MET.

mickey mouse[1] *adj., slang* Inferior, second rate, chicken, easy, gimmicky. *Watch out for Catwallender, he's full of mickey mouse ideas.* (He is full of second rate, inferior thoughts.)

mickey mouse[2] *n. (derogatory)* A stupid person, a policeman, a white man (as used by blacks).

midair See UP IN THE AIR 2 *also* IN MIDAIR.

middle See CHANGE HORSES IN THE MIDDLE OF THE STREAM, IN THE MIDDLE.

middle ground *n.* A place halfway between the two sides of an argument; a compromise. *John wanted to go running. Bill said it was too hot. Tom took the middle ground, and suggested a hike.* (John wanted to run, but Bill didn't want to do anything. They decided on a long walk instead.) *The committee found a middle ground between the two proposals.* (The committee took part of each of the proposals, and made a decision.)

middle of the road *n. phr.* A way of thinking which does not favor one idea or thing too much; being half-way between two different ideas. *The teacher did not support the boys or the girls in the debate, but stayed in the middle of the road.* (The teacher did not help or favor either side.)

middle-of-the-road *adj.* Favoring action halfway between two opposite movements or ideas; with ideas halfway between two opposite sides; seeing good on both sides. *The men who wrote the Constitution followed a middle-of-the-road plan on whether greater power belonged to the United States government or to the separate states.* (The men divided the power fairly and did not give all of it to either side.) *Senator Jones favors a middle-of-the-road policy in the labor-management dispute.* (Senator Jones tries to stay halfway between.)

midfield stripe *n.* The line across the center of a football field; the 50 yard line. *The visitors were able to cross the midfield stripe once during the whole game.* (They played most of the game in their own territory.)

midnight oil See BURN THE MIDNIGHT OIL.

midstream See CHANGE HORSES IN THE MIDDLE OF THE STREAM *or* CHANGE HORSES IN MIDSTREAM.

might See WITH MIGHT AND MAIN.

mighty See HIGH-AND-MIGHTY.

mile See GIVE ONE AN INCH AND HE WILL TAKE A MILE, JAW DROP *or* JAW DROP A MILE, MISS BY A MILE, MISS IS AS GOOD AS A MILE.

mile markers *n., slang, citizen's band radio jargon* Small signs along interstate highways usually bearing a number. *The Smokey is located at 131 mile marker.* (The police car is at marker number 131.)

milk See CRY OVER SPILLED MILK.

mill See RUN-OF-THE-MILL, THROUGH THE MILL.

million See FEEL LIKE A MILLION, LOOK LIKE A MILLION DOLLARS.

millstone around one's neck *n. phr.* An intolerable burden. *Max said that his old car was a millstone around his neck.* (The old car is more trouble than it is worth.) Compare MONKEY ON ONE'S BACK.

mind See CROSS ONE'S MIND *or* PASS THROUGH ONE'S MIND, GIVE A PIECE OF ONE'S MIND, HALF A MIND, IN MIND, IN ONE'S MIND'S EYE, MAKE UP ONE'S MIND, NEVER MIND, ON ONE'S MIND, OUT OF ONE'S HEAD *or* OUT OF ONE'S MIND, PUT IN MIND OF, READ ONE'S MIND.

mind like a steel trap *n. phr.* A very quick and understanding mind, which is quick to catch an idea.—An overworked simile. *Henry is not fond of sports, but he has a mind like a steel trap.* (He is very smart and quick in school.) *A successful lawyer must have a mind like a steel trap.* (He must understand very quickly and see how he can beat the other lawyers.)

mind one's p's and q's *v. phr.* To be very careful what you do or say; not make mistakes. —A cliché. *When the principal of the school visited the class, the students all minded their p's and q's.* (When the principal visited the school, the students were very careful to act politely and right.) *If you wish to succeed, you must mind your p's and q's.* (If you wish to succeed, you must be sure to do and say the right things.) Syn. WATCH ONE'S STEP.

mind-reader See READ ONE'S MIND.

mind you *v. phr., informal* I want you to notice and understand. *Mind you, I am not blaming him.* (Understand that I am not blaming him.)

mine See BACK TO THE SALT MINES, RUN OF THE MILL *or* RUN OF THE MINE.

minority leader *n. phr.* The leader of the political party that has fewer votes in a legislative house. *The minority leader of the Senate supported the bill.* (He tried to get the members belonging to his party to vote for the bill.) *The minority leader in the House of Representatives held a caucus.* (He called a meeting of the members of the house who belonged to his party.) Compare MAJORITY LEADER.

mint money See COIN MONEY.

miss See HEART SKIP A BEAT *or* HEART MISS A BEAT.

miss by a mile *v. phr., informal* **1** To shoot at something and be far from hitting it; not hit near. *Jack's first shot missed the target by a mile.* (It hit a long way from the target.) **2** To be very wrong, be far from right. *Lee tried to guess on the examination, but his answers missed by a mile.* (He guessed the answers, but they were all wrong.) **3** To fail badly, not succeed at all. *John Brown wanted to be governor, but in the election he missed by a mile.* (Very few people voted for him and he lost the election.)

missing link *n.* **1** Something needed to complete a group; a missing part of a chain of things. *A 1936 penny was the missing link in John's collection of pennies.* (The 1936 penny gave John a complete collection.) *The detective hunted for the fact that was the missing link in the case.* (The detective hunted for the fact that would fit in with the other facts and explain them.) **2** An unknown extinct animal that was supposed to be a connection between man and lower animals. *The missing link would be half man and half ape.* (Scientists looked for the bones of an animal that was partly like a man and partly like an ape.)

miss is as good as a mile It is the same if one fails or misses something by much or by little. —A proverb. *We thought Tom had a home run, but the ball went foul by inches. A miss is as good as a mile.* (It did not matter that the ball Tom hit came close to being a home run; it was still only a foul ball.)

Missouri See FROM MISSOURI.

miss out *v., informal* To fail; lose or not take a good chance; miss something good. *Jim's mother told him he missed out on a chance to go fishing with his father because he came home late.* (Jim lost the chance by coming home late.) *You missed out by not coming with us; we had a great time.* (You missed something good by not coming.) Compare LOSE OUT.

miss the boat, *also* **miss the bus** *v. phr., informal* To fail through slowness; to put something off until too late; do the wrong thing and lose the chance. —A cliché. *Mr. Brown missed the boat when he decided not to buy the house.* (If he had bought it he could sell it for a profit now.) *In college he didn't study enough so he missed the boat and failed to pass.* (He could have passed but did not use his time wisely.) *Ted could have married Lena but he put off asking her and missed the boat.* (She liked him but he waited too long and she married another man.)

mistake See BY MISTAKE.

misty-eyed *or* **dewey-eyed** *adj. phr.* **1** Having eyes damp with tears; emotional. *The teacher was misty-eyed when the school gave her a retirement gift.* (The teacher almost cried from pleasure when the school gave her a present.) **2** Of the kind who cries easily; sentimental. *The movie appealed to dewey-eyed girls.* (The movie was the kind that sentimental girls like.)

mixed blessing *n.* Something good that has bad features. —A hackneyed phrase. *John's new bicycle was a mixed blessing. The other boys were always asking John to ride it.* (It was nice to have a new bicycle, but it was not nice to be asked to ride it all the time.)

mixed up *adj. phr.* **1** *informal* Confused in mind; puzzled. *Bob was all mixed up after the accident.* (Bob was confused and didn't remember what had happened.) Compare BALL UP 1. **2** Disordered; disarranged; not neat. *The papers on his desk were mixed up.* (They were not neatly in order.) **3** *informal* Joined or connected (with someone or something bad.) *Harry was mixed up in a fight after the game.* (He took part in the fight.) *Mary's father told her not to get mixed up with the students that always break school rules.* (Mary's father told her not to join the students who break school rules; she should stay away from them.)

mix up *v.* To confuse; make a mistake about. *Jimmy doesn't know colors yet; he mixes up purple with blue.* (He thinks that purple is blue, or blue is purple.) *Even the twins' mother mixes them up.* (Even the twins' mother doesn't know which is which.) Compare MIXED UP.

molehill See MAKE A MOUNTAIN OUT OF A MOLEHILL.

moment See ON THE SPUR OF THE MOMENT.

Monday See BLUE MONDAY.

money See COIN MONEY or MINT MONEY, EASY MONEY, FOOL AND HIS MONEY ARE SOON PARTED, FOR LOVE OR MONEY, IN THE CHIPS or IN THE MONEY, MADE OF MONEY, PUT ONE'S MONEY ON A SCRATCHED HORSE, RUN FOR ONE'S MONEY, SEE THE COLOR OF ONE'S MONEY, SPENDING MONEY or POCKET MONEY.

money burns a hole in one's pocket See BURN A HOLE IN ONE'S POCKET.

money to burn *n. phr., informal* Very much money, more than is needed.--A cliché. *Dick's uncle died and left him money to burn.* (Now he is so rich he can buy anything.) *When Joe is twenty-one he will have money to burn.* (He will have lots of money.) *Jean is looking for a husband with money to burn.* (She wants to marry a very rich man.) Compare MADE OF MONEY.

monkey See GREASE MONKEY, MAKE A FOOL OF or MAKE A MONKEY OF.

monkey around See FOOL AROUND.

monkey business *n., slang, informal* **1** Any unethical, illegitimate or objectionable activity that is furtive or deceitful, e.g., undercover sexual advances, cheating, misuse of public funds, etc. *There is a lot of monkey business going on in that firm, you better watch out who you deal with!* (There is a lot of suspicious activity going on, better be careful.) **2** Comical or silly actions, goofing off. *Come on boys, let's cut out the monkey business and get down to work!* (Stop acting silly and start working!)

monkey on one's back *n. phr., informal* An unsolved or nagging problem. *"My math course is a real monkey on my back,"* Jack complained. (He says he can't deal with his course in math.) Compare ALBATROSS AROUND ONE'S NECK, MILLSTONE AROUND ONE'S NECK.

monkey wrench See THROW A MONKEY WRENCH.

monster See GREEN-EYED MONSTER.

month in, month out See DAY IN AND DAY OUT.

month of Sundays *n. phr., informal* A very long time.--A cliché. Used for emphasis after *for* or *in* and usually with a negative verb. *I have not had devil's food cake in a month of Sundays.* (I haven't had any for a long time.) *When he got her first letter, he felt that he had not heard from her for a month of Sundays.* (He felt he had waited a very long time for her letter.) Syn. DOG'S AGE.

moon See ASK FOR THE MOON or CRY FOR THE MOON, DARK OF THE MOON, FULL OF THE MOON, ONCE IN A BLUE MOON, PROMISE THE MOON.

mop the floor with or **mop up the floor with** or **wipe the floor with** or **wipe up the floor with** *v. phr., slang* To defeat very clearly or quickly; to beat badly. *The bully threatened to mop up the floor with Billy.* (The bully told Billy he would hit him and beat him up.) *Our team wiped the floor with the visiting team.* (Our team won by a very large score.)

mop up the floor with See MOP THE FLOOR WITH.

more See BITE OFF MORE THAN ONE CAN CHEW.

more often than not *adv. phr.* More than half the time; fifty-one or more times out of a hundred; not quite usually, but fairly regularly. *Nancy comes over on Saturday more often than not.* (Nancy comes over on more Saturdays than she stays away.) *Ben is a fairly good runner. He wins more often than not.* (Ben wins more races than he loses.)

more or less *adv. phr.* **1** Somewhat; rather; mostly; fairly. *Earl made some mistakes on the test, but his answers were more or less right.* (He did rather well, not poorly.) *Ed is more or less intelligent.* (He is more smart than dull.) *Betty believes more or less in fairies.* (She does not believe fully, but more than a little.) Compare IN A WAY, **2** About, nearly, not exactly, but almost. *The new building cost more or less what the builder figured.* (It cost very nearly what he thought.) *It is a mile, more or less, from his home to the school.* (It is about a mile, not exactly.) *He has wanted to date her more or less since he first saw her.* (It was about the first time he saw her.) Compare OR SO.

more than *adv.* Over what you might expect; very. *They were more than glad to help.* (They were very glad to help.) *He was more than upset by the accident.* (He was very much upset by the accident.) Contrast LESS THAN.

more than one can chew See BITE OFF MORE THAN ONE CAN CHEW.

more than one could shake a stick at *adj. phr., informal* Very many; a great many; more than you can count.--A cliché. *There were more people at the game than you could shake a stick at.* (There were very many people at the game.) *I had more assignments for homework than I could shake a stick at.* (I had a great many assignments for homework.)

more the merrier *n. phr.* The more people who join in the fun, the better it will be.--A cliché used in welcoming more people to join others in some pleasant activity. *Come with us on the boat ride; the more the merrier.* (We are glad to have you join us on the boat ride.)

morning after *n., slang* The effects of drinking liquor or staying up late as felt the next morning; a hangover. *One of the troubles of drinking too much liquor is the morning after.* (The hangover the next day is very unpleasant.) *Mr. Smith woke up with a big headache and knew it was the morning after.* (Mr. Smith woke up with a big headache and knew it was the result of too much beer the night before.)

Morpheus See IN THE ARMS OF MORPHEUS.

Moses See HOLY CATS or HOLY MOSES.

moss See ROLLING STONE GATHERS NO MOSS.

most See AT MOST, MAKE THE MOST OF.

mother See TIED TO ONE'S MOTHER'S APRON STRINGS.

motion See GO THROUGH THE MOTIONS.

mountain See MAKE A MOUNTAIN OUT OF A MOLEHILL.

mouse See PLAY CAT AND MOUSE WITH.

mouth See BORN WITH A SILVER SPOON IN ONE'S MOUTH, BUTTER WOULDN'T MELT IN ONE'S MOUTH, BY WORD OF MOUTH, DOWN IN THE DUMPS *or* DOWN IN THE MOUTH, FOAM AT THE MOUTH, HEART IN ONE'S MOUTH, KEEP ONE'S MOUTH SHUT, LAUGH ON THE WRONG SIDE OF ONE'S MOUTH, LEAVE A BAD TASTE IN ONE'S MOUTH, LIVE FROM HAND TO MOUTH, LOOK A GIFT HORSE IN THE MOUTH, MAKE ONE'S MOUTH WATER, MELT IN ONE'S MOUTH, PUT ONE'S FOOT IN IT *or* PUT ONE'S FOOT IN ONE'S MOUTH, PUT WORDS INTO ONE'S MOUTH, SHOOT OFF ONE'S MOUTH, STRAIGHT FROM THE HORSE'S MOUTH, TAKE THE BIT IN ONE'S MOUTH, TAKE THE BREAD OUT OF ONE'S MOUTH.

mouthful See SAY A MOUTHFUL.

move See GET A MOVE ON, ON THE MOVE.

move a muscle *v. phr.* To move even a very little.—Used in negative sentences and questions and with *if. The deer stood without moving a muscle until the hunter was gone.* (It stood very quietly.) *The girls were so startled that they did not move a muscle.* (They stood very quietly, not moving at all.) *You're sitting right where you were when I left! Have you moved a muscle?* (Have you moved even a little?) *The robber said he would shoot the bank worker if he moved a muscle.* (The robber warned the man to stand perfectly still.)

move heaven and earth *v. phr.* To try every way; do everything you can.—A hackneyed phrase. *Joe moved heaven and earth to be sent to Washington.* (He tried every possible way to get his boss to send him to work in Washington.)

move in on *v. phr., slang, colloquial* To take over something that belongs to another. *He moved in on my girl friend and now we're not talking to each other.* (He stole my girl friend from me, and that's the end of our friendship.)

movement See LABOR MOVEMENT.

much See AS MUCH AS, FOR AS MUCH AS, MAKE MUCH OF, SO MUCH, SO MUCH FOR, THINK A GREAT DEAL OF *or* THINK MUCH OF.

much as See AS MUCH AS 1.

much less *conj.* And also not; and even less able or likely to.—Used after a negative clause. *I never even spoke to the man, much less insulted him.* (I never even spoke to the man, and I was even less likely to insult him.) *John couldn't even pick up the box, much less carry it upstairs.* (John couldn't pick up the box, and he was even less able to carry it upstairs.) *George can hardly understand arithmetic, much less algebra.* (George can't understand arithmetic; he certainly can't understand algebra.) Compare LET ALONE, NOT TO MENTION.

mud See NAME IS MUD, STICK-IN-THE-MUD.

mum is the word You must keep the secret; keep silent; don't tell anyone.—Often used as an interjection. *We are planning a surprise party for John and mum is the word.* (Don't tell John about the party.) *"Mum is the word!" the robber captain told his men.* (He told them to say nothing and keep what they did a secret.)

murder See SCREAM BLOODY MURDER.

muscle See MOVE A MUSCLE.

muscle-bound *adj.* Having your muscles large, hard, and tight from too much exercising; having muscles so developed that you can hardly move. *Bob was big and strong, but he was muscle-bound, and Bill could beat him.* (Bob could not move as fast as Bill, so Bill could beat him.) *An athlete must train properly so as not to become muscle-bound.* (An athlete must train properly to keep his muscles firm and strong, but not too tight.)

music See FACE THE MUSIC.

musical chairs *n. phr.* (Originally the name of a children's game.) The transfer of a number of officers in an organization into different jobs, especially each other's jobs. *The boss regularly played musical chairs with department heads to keep them fresh on the job.* (He moved them frequently from one department to another so they would keep seeing ways to improve their work.)

music to one's ears *n. phr.* Something one likes to hear. *When the manager phoned to say I got the job, it was music to my ears.* (That was delightful news.)

mustard See CUT THE MUSTARD.

muster See PASS MUSTER.

my God *or* **my goodness** *interj.* Used to express surprise, shock, or dismay. *My God! What happened to the car?* (This is shocking! What caused the damage?)

N

nail See HARD AS NAILS, HIT THE NAIL ON THE HEAD, TOOTH AND NAIL.

nail down *v. phr., informal* To make certain; make sure; settle. *Joe had a hard time selling his car, but he finally nailed the sale down when he got his friend Sam to give him $300.* (Joe made sure Sam would buy the car by getting $300 from Sam.) *The New York Yankees nailed down the American League Championship when they beat the Red Sox 3 to 0 on September 15.* (They made sure that they would be the champions.)

nail one's colors to the mast *literary* To let everyone know what you think is right and refuse to change. *During the election campaign the candidate nailed his colors to the mast on the question of civil rights.* (He let everybody know what he believed about civil rights.)

name See CALL NAMES, HANDLE TO ONE'S NAME, IN NAME, TAKE ONE'S NAME IN VAIN, TO ONE'S NAME.

name calling See CALL NAMES.

name day *n.* The day of the saint for whom a person is named. *Lawrence's name day is August 10, the feast of St. Lawrence.* (Lawrence always observed August 10, because it is the day of St. Lawrence, for whom he was named.)

name is mud *informal* (You) are in trouble; a person is blamed or no longer liked.—Used in the possessive. *If you tell your mother I spilled ink on her rug, my name will be mud.* (If you tell your mother I spilled ink on her rug, I will be in trouble.) *Your name will be mud if you tell the teacher about the bad thing we did.* (We won't like you if you tell the teacher.) Compare IN THE DOG HOUSE.

name of the game *n., informal* The crux of the matter; that which actually occurs under the disguise of something else. *Getting medium income families to support the rest of society—that's the name of the game!* (That's what's really happening.)

napkin ring *n.* A large ring of wood or metal through which you put your rolled up napkin when you are not using it. *Some families use napkin rings to hold each person's napkin between meals so that each one gets his own napkin.*

nary a *informal* Not a single; not one; never a. *One afternoon a large dark cloud came in the sky. John thought it would rain, so he took his raincoat—but nary a drop fell.* (It did not rain a single drop.) *John went fishing, but he caught nary a one.* (He didn't catch any fish.)

nasty-nice *adj.* Unkind in a polite way; disagreeable while pretending to be gracious. *The bus driver has a nasty-nice way of showing his dislike.* (He can act disagreeable and polite at the same time to anyone he dislikes. He treats you nicely or says something nice to you in a way that lets you know that he doesn't really like you.)

natural See BIG AS LIFE *or* BIG AS LIFE AND TWICE AS NATURAL.

natural-born *adj.* **1** Being a (citizen) because you were born in the country. *Mr. and Mrs. Schmidt came to the U.S.A. from Germany and are naturalized citizens, but their children are natural-born citizens.* (Their children were born in the U.S.A. and are citizens by birth.) **2** Born with great ability to become (something); having great ability (as in a sport or art) almost from the start. *Joe has never played baseball before trying out for the team, but he showed that he was a natural-born pitcher, and he became the best in the League.* (Joe learned pitching so quickly and well that it seemed he had been born able to pitch.) *Mozart was a natural-born musician. He could play the piano well when he was only six years old.* (Mozart learned to play the piano very quickly when he was only six. He was born with great musical ability.)

nature See SECOND NATURE.

naught See GO FOR NOTHING *also* GO FOR NAUGHT.

near See FAR AND NEAR.

near at hand See AT HAND.

necessity See MAKE A VIRTUE OF NECESSITY, OF NECESSITY.

neck See BREATHE DOWN ONE'S NECK, BREAK ONE'S NECK, CATCH IT IN THE NECK *or* GET IT IN THE NECK, PAIN IN THE NECK, SAVE ONE'S NECK, STICK ONE'S NECK OUT.

neck and neck *adj. or adv., informal* Equal or nearly equal in a race or contest; abreast; tied. *At the end of the race the two horses were neck and neck.* (The two horses were in a tie at the end of the race.) *For months John and Harry seemed to be neck and neck in Alice's favor.* (For months John and Harry competed equally for Alice's liking.) Compare NIP AND TUCK.

neck of the woods *n. phr., informal* Part of the country; place; neighborhood; vicinity. *We visited Illinois and Iowa last summer; in that neck of the woods the corn really grows tall.* (In that part of the country the corn really grows tall.) *We were down in your neck of the woods last week.* (Last week we were in the part of the country where you live.)

necktie party *n., slang* A hanging by a mob; lynching. *Cattle thieves were stealing the rancher's cattle, but the cowboys caught them and had a necktie party.* (The cowboys caught the thieves and hanged them, without waiting for a court trial.) Compare STRING UP.

ned See RAISE THE DEVIL.

needle See ON PINS AND NEEDLES.

needle in a haystack *n. phr., informal* Something that will be very hard to find.—A cliché. *"I lost my class ring somewhere in the front yard," said June. Jim answered, "Too* *bad. That will be like finding a needle in a haystack."* (That will be very hard to find.)

neither fish nor fowl *also* **neither fish, flesh, nor fowl** Something or someone that does not belong to a definite group or known class; a strange person or thing; someone or something odd or hard to understand.—A cliché. *The man is neither fish nor fowl; he votes Democrat or Republican according to which will do him the most good.* (He is not a Democrat or a Republican.) *Mrs. Harris bought a piece of furniture that was both a table and a chair. Mr. Harris said it was neither fish nor fowl.* (Mr. Harris said it was something strange—not a table, and not a chair.) *The movie is neither fish nor fowl; it is a funny love story.* (The new movie is not just a funny story and not just a love story, but mixes up both fun and love.)

neither here nor there *adj. phr.* Not important to the thing being discussed; off the subject; not mattering. *Perhaps you did stay up late finishing your homework. That's neither here nor there. You still must come to school on time.* (Staying up late to finish your homework should not make any difference in the time you come to school.) *The boys all like the coach, but that's neither here nor there; the question is, "Does he know how to teach football?"* (The important question is, "Can he teach football?" Being liked by the boys does not make him know football; that is another matter.) Compare BESIDE THE POINT. Contrast HAVE TO DO WITH, COME TO THE POINT.

neither hide nor hair See HIDE OR HAIR.

Nellie See NICE NELLY *or* NICE NELLIE, NERVOUS NELLIE.

Nelly See NICE NELLY *or* NICE NELLIE, NERVOUS NELLIE.

nerve See GET ON ONE'S NERVES, GET UP THE NERVE.

nervous breakdown *n.* A mild or severe attack of mental illness; a collapse of a person's ability to make decisions and solve problems because of overwork, great mental strain, or the like. *When the mother saw her baby run over, she suffered a nervous breakdown.* (When she saw her baby run over she became mentally ill.)

Nervous Nellie *n., informal* A timid person who lacks determination and courage. *I say we will never win if we don't stop being Nervous Nellies!* (I say we will never win unless we stop being cowards.)

nervous prostration *n.* An illness of the mind that makes you feel very tired, worried, and bored, and that often causes headaches, upset stomach, and other sickness. *Aunt Jane said that taking care of us children all day was enough to give any woman nervous prostration.* (Aunt Jane said that a woman's mind would not work any more after she took care of us all day.)

nest See FEATHER ONE'S NEST, STIR UP A HORNET'S NEST.

never See BETTER LATE THAN NEVER, IT NEVER RAINS BUT IT POURS, LIGHTNING NEVER STRIKES TWICE IN THE SAME PLACE.

never mind *v. phr.* Don't trouble about it; don't worry about it; forget it; skip it.—Usually used in speaking or when writing dialogue. *Never mind preparing a picnic lunch: we'll find a lunchstand when we get to the beach.* (Don't bother making a picnic lunch.) *"What did you say?" "Oh, never mind."* ("What did you say?" "Let's just forget it.") *"What about money?" "Never mind that. I'll take care of it."* ("What shall we do about money?" "Don't worry about that. I'll take care of it.")

never say die *v. phr.* Don't quit; don't be discouraged.—A cliché. *"Never say die!" John said, as he got on his feet and tried to ice skate again.* (John fell down many times but he refused to quit and tried again and again.)

new See TURN OVER A NEW LEAF.

new blood *n.* Something or someone that gives new life or vigor, fresh energy or power. *New blood was brought into the company through appointment of younger men to important positions.* (Hiring several young executives gave the company new vigor.)

new broom sweeps clean A new person makes many changes.—A proverb. *The new superintendent has changed many of the school rules. A new broom sweeps clean.* (A new man changes many things.)

Newcastle See CARRY COALS TO NEWCASTLE.

new deal *n., informal* **1** A complete change; a fresh start. *People had been on the job too long; a new deal was needed to get things out of the old bad habits.* (There were too many people who had become bored and lazy and it took a complete change to get things moving right again.) **2** Another chance. *The boy asked for a new deal after he had been punished for fighting in school.* (He asked for another chance and promised never to fight again.)

new leaf See TURN OVER A NEW LEAF.

new man *n.* A person who has become very much better. *Diet and exercise made a new man of him.* (His health and appearance were greatly improved by diet and exercise. He looked like a different person.)

next door *adv. or adj.* **1** In or to the next house or apartment. *He lived next door to me.* (He was my closest neighbor.) *She telephoned next door to ask about John.* (She telephoned her closest neighbor to ask about John.) *The house next door caught fire.* (The house beside theirs caught fire.) **2** Very close.—Used with *to. The sick man was next door to death.* (He was nearly dead.) *Printing secrets about our country's missiles is next door to treason.* (It is almost the same as treason.)

next to *adv.* Almost; nearly. *It was next to impossible to believe that in a month the grass would be green and flowers would be blooming.* (It was almost impossible to imagine that in a month it would be spring.) *It was next to unthinkable that the boy would steal.* (It was nearly unbelievable that the boy would steal.) *When he first started to work, Mr. Black earned next to nothing.* (He earned very little money.)

next to *prep.* Just after; second to. *Next to his family, baseball was his greatest love.* (Second to his home, baseball was his greatest love.) *Next to pizza, Bob liked hamburger best.* (He liked hamburger better than anything but pizza.)

nice Nelly[1] *or* **nice Nellie** *n.,* *informal* Someone who acts too good to be true; a prude; a prig. *We took him for a nice Nelly when he wouldn't fight.* (We thought he was a prig when he refused to fight.)

nice Nelly[2] *or* **nice Nellie** *adj.,* *informal* Too careful not to say or do anything wrong or improper; too proper; prudish. *Her nice Nelly behavior made her unpopular at school.* (Her prudish ways made the other pupils at school dislike her.)

Nick See FULL OF THE OLD NICK.

nick See IN THE NICK OF TIME.

nigger in the woodpile *n. phr., slang.* Something unexpected that changes a situation; a hidden factor or trick.—A cliché that is offensive and now considered to be in poor taste. *I knew there had to be a nigger in the woodpile, because the man was being much too generous.* (I knew there had to be something I didn't know about, because the man was being much too generous.) *When the salesman gave him an extra tire for his bike, the boy suspected a nigger in the woodpile.* (The boy suspected a trick when the salesman gave him an extra tire for his bike.)

night See FLY-BY-NIGHT, MAKE A NIGHT OF IT.

night and day See DAY AND NIGHT.

night letter *n.* A telegram sent at night at a cheaper rate and delivered in the morning. *I waited until after six o'clock in the evening before sending the telegram home because I can say more for the same price in a night letter.* (A telegram sent at night is cheaper.)

night life *n. phr.* Entertainment at night. *People in the city are able to find more night life than those who live in the country.* (The city has many places to go for entertainment at night.)

nine See CAT HAS NINE LIVES, ON CLOUD NINE.

ninety See GAY NINETIES.

nip and tuck *adj. or adv., informal* Evenly matched; hard fought to the finish. *The game was nip and tuck until the last minute.* (The two teams played equally well and no one knew which team would win till the game ended.) *It was a nip and tuck race right to the finish line.* (The race was hard fought right to the end.) *The two salesmen fought nip and tuck for the contract all the way.* (Each of the two salesmen did all he could to get the contract as long as there was any chance.) Compare NECK AND NECK.

nip in the bud *v. phr.* To check at the outset; prevent at the start; block or destroy in the beginning.—A cliché. *The police nipped the plot in the bud.* (The police stopped the plot before it could get fully organized.) *The teacher nipped the disorder in the bud.* (The teacher quieted the disorder at the beginning.)

nobody See IT'S AN ILL WIND THAT BLOWS NOBODY GOOD.

nobody home *slang* 1 Your attention is somewhere else, not on what is being said or done here; you are absent-minded. *The teacher asked him a question three times, but he still looked out the window. She gave up, saying, "Nobody home."* (The teacher could not get the boy to answer. She said, "His attention is on something else.") 2 You are feeble-minded or insane. *He pointed to the woman, tapped his head, and said, "Nobody home."* (He meant that the woman's mind was not normal; she was not able to think and act normally.)

nobody's fool *n. phr.* A smart person; a person who knows what he is doing; a person who can take care of himself. *In the classroom and on the football field, Henry was nobody's fool.* (He did good work in the classroom and on the football field. He was one of the best students and players.) Contrast BORN YESTERDAY.

nod See LAND OF NOD.

no deal *or* **no dice** *or* **no go** *or* **no sale** *or* **no soap** *slang* Not agreed to; refused or useless; without success or result; no; certainly not.—Used in the predicate or to refuse something. *Billy wanted to let Bob join the team but I said that it was no deal because Bob was too young.* (I said that Bob couldn't join the team.) *"Let me have a dollar." "No dice!" answered Joe.* ("Certainly not!" answered Joe.) *I tried to get Mary on the telephone but it was no go.* (I didn't succeed in telephoning Mary.) *"Let's go to the beach tomorrow." "No sale, I have my music lesson tomorrow."* (I can't go tomorrow.) *I asked Dad for a new bicycle but it was no soap.* (Dad didn't agree.) Compare NOTHING DOING, NO USE.

no doubt *adv.* 1 Without doubt; doubtless; surely; certainly. *No doubt Susan was the smartest girl in her class.* (Susan was certainly the smartest girl in her class.) 2 Probably. *John will no doubt telephone us if he comes to town.* (It seems likely that John will call us if he comes to town.)

no end *adv., informal* 1 Very much; exceedingly. *Jim was no end upset because he couldn't go swimming.* (Jim was very much upset because he couldn't go swimming.) **2** Almost without stopping; continually. *The baby cried no end.* (The baby cried without stopping.)

no end to *or informal* **no end of** So many, or so much of, as to seem almost endless; very many or very much. *There was no end to the letters pouring into the post office.* (So many letters were coming into the post office that they seemed to be without end.) *Bob and Dick became close friends, and had no end of fun together.* (Bob and Dick had much fun together.)

noggin See USE ONE'S HEAD *or* USE ONE'S NOG- GIN.

no go See NO DEAL.

no good *adj. phr.* Not satisfactory; not adequate; not approved. *"That's no good,"* I told *him when he began to cry.* (I told him I didn't think much of crying from a boy his size.) *He was no good at arithmetic.* (He didn't do satisfactory work in arithmetic.) *He tried appealing to the man's pride, but it did no good.* (He tried appealing to the man's pride, but it didn't work.)

no great shakes *adj., informal* Mediocre, unimportant. *Joe Catwallender is no great shakes.* (He is unimportant, mediocre.)

no longer *adv.* Not any more; not at the present time. *He could no longer be trusted, and they had to let him go.* (He could not be trusted any more, so they had to discharge him.) *The shore was no longer in sight.* (They could not see the shore any more.)

no love lost *n. phr.* Bad feeling; ill will. *Bob and Dick both wanted to be elected captain of the team, and there was no love lost between them.* (They did not like each other; they treated each other badly.) *There was no love lost between the sales and the accounting departments.* (There was bad feeling between the sales and the accounting departments.)

no matter **1** Not anything important. *I wanted to see him before he left, but it's no matter.* (It's not important.) **2** It makes no difference; regardless of. *She was going to be a singer no matter what difficulties she met.* (She meant to be a singer regardless of what difficulties she met.) *He had to get the car fixed no matter how much it cost.* (He had to get the car fixed regardless of the amount of money it would cost.) *No matter what you try to do, it is important to be able to speak well.* (It makes no difference what you try to do: skill with words helps in any field.) *You can't go in no matter who you are.* (You can't go in, even if you are a very important person; it makes no difference.) *Charles had decided to go to the football game, and he felt he must go, no matter what.* (He felt that he must go even if it was very difficult.) *Mary wanted to get to school on time, no matter if she went without breakfast.* (She wanted to get to school on time, and she was willing to go without breakfast.)

nonce See FOR THE TIME BEING *also* FOR THE NONCE.

none See HALF A LOAF IS BETTER THAN NONE, HAVE NONE OF.

nonsense See STUFF AND NONSENSE.

noodle See USE ONE'S HEAD *or* USE ONE'S NOODLE.

nor See NEITHER . . . NOR.

no sale See NO DEAL.

nose See COUNT HEADS *or* COUNT NOSES, CUT OFF ONE'S NOSE TO SPITE ONE'S FACE, FOLLOW ONE'S NOSE, GO INTO A TAIL SPIN *or* GO INTO A NOSE DIVE, HARD-NOSED, KEEP ONE'S NOSE CLEAN, KEEP ONE'S NOSE TO THE GRINDSTONE, LEAD BY THE NOSE, LOOK DOWN ONE'S NOSE AT, ON THE NOSE, PAY THROUGH THE NOSE, PUT ONE'S NOSE OUT OF JOINT, SEE BEYOND ONE'S NOSE, SKIN OFF ONE'S NOSE, THUMB ONE'S NOSE, TURN UP ONE'S NOSE AT, UNDER ONE'S NOSE.

nose about *or* **nose around** *v. phr., informal* To look for something kept private or secret; poke about; explore; inquire; pry. *In Grandmother's attic, Sally spent a while nosing about in the old family pictures.* (Sally looked among the old family pictures for a while.) *The detective was nosing around in the crowd, looking for pickpockets.* (He moved about in the crowd, looking for pickpockets.)

nose down *v., of an aircraft* To head down; bring down the nose of. *The big airliner began to nose down for a landing.* (The airliner began to head down for a landing.) *The pilot nosed the plane down toward the runway.* (The pilot headed the plane down toward the runway.)

nose in[1] *informal* Prying or pestering interest in; unwelcome interest in; impolite curiosity. *He always had his nose in other people's business.* (He showed impolite curiosity in other people's business.) Contrast NOSE OUT OF.

nose in[2] *v.* To move in close; move slowly in with the front first. *The ship nosed in to the pier.* (The ship moved in close to the pier.) *The car nosed in to the curb.* (The car pulled in close to the curb.)

nose in a book *n. phr.* Busy interest in reading.—Used with a possessive. *Mother can't get Mary to help do the housework; she always has her nose in a book.* (Mary spends all her free time reading and does not help Mother do the housework.)

nose into[1] *informal* Impolite curiosity into; unwanted attention into.—Usually used with *poke* or *stick. He was forever sticking his nose into things that didn't concern him.* (He was always meddling in things that were not his business.)

nose into[2] *v.* **1** To head into; move head first into. *He nosed the canoe into the cove.* (He steered the canoe's bow into the cove.) *The ship nosed into its berth.* (The ship moved prow first into the landing place.) **2** *informal* To pry into (something private or secret); meddle in; poke into. *Mother told Laura* *not to nose into her drawers again.* (Mother told Laura not to look curiously through her dresser drawers.) *When Carol asked her big sister where she went on her date and how late she stayed out, her sister told Carol she was always nosing into her private life.* (Carol's sister thought Carol should not ask about personal things like that.)

nose is out of joint See PUT ONE'S NOSE OUT OF JOINT.

nose out *v., informal* **1** To learn by effort (something private or secret); uncover. *The principal nosed out the truth about the stolen examination.* (He learned who stole the examination by asking many questions of many people.) **2** To defeat by a nose length; come in a little ahead of in a race or contest. *The horse we liked nosed out the second horse in a very close finish.* (He won the horse race by inches.) *The Democratic candidate nosed out his rival for Congress by a few hundred votes.* (He defeated his opponent for the House seat by a few hundred votes.)

nose out of *informal* Curious attention; bothering.—Usually used with a possessive and usually used with *keep. When Billy asked his sister where she was going, she told him to keep his nose out of her business.* (Billy's sister told him not to ask about things that were not his business.) Contrast NOSE IN.

nose over *v.* To turn over on the nose so as to land upside down. *The airplane made a faulty landing approach and nosed over.* (The airplane came in wrong and turned over.)

nose up *v.* To head up; incline the forward end upwards; move up. *The airplane nosed up through the cloud bank.* (The airplane headed up through the clouds.) *The pilot nosed the plane up from the field.* (The pilot headed the plane up from the field.)

no-show *n., informal* A person who makes a reservation, e.g., at a hotel or at an airline, and then neither claims nor cancels it. *The airlines were messed up because of a great number of no-show passengers.* (They had a large number of people who made reservations but never claimed nor canceled them.)

no sooner ——— than As soon as; at once when; immediately when. *No sooner did he signal to turn than the other car turned in front of him.* (As soon as he signalled to turn, the other car cut in front of him.) *No sooner were the picnic baskets unpacked than it began to rain.* (Just when they were ready to eat, it began to rain.)

no sweat[1] *adj., slang, informal* Easily accomplished, uncomplicated. *That job was no sweat.* (That was an easy job.)

no sweat[2] *adv.* Easily. *We did it, no sweat.* (We did it easily.)

not a few See QUITE A FEW.

not a leg to stand on *n. phr., informal* No good proof or excuse; no good evidence or defense to offer. *The man with a gun and $300 in his pocket was accused of robbing an* oil station. *He did not have a leg to stand on.* (The man could not explain why he had a gun and so much money in his pocket.)

not a little See QUITE A LITTLE.

not at all See AT ALL.

not bad *or* **not so bad** *or* **not half bad** *adj., informal* Pretty good; all right; good enough. *The party last night was not bad.* (The party last night was good.) *It was not so bad, as inexpensive vacations go.* (It was good enough, considering how little it cost.) *The show was not half bad.* (It was a very good show.)

not by a long shot See BY A LONG SHOT.

not by any means See BY NO MEANS.

notch See TIGHTEN ONE'S BELT.

note See COMPARE NOTES, TAKE NOTE OF.

not for the world *or* **not for worlds** *adv. phr.* Not at any price; not for anything. *I wouldn't hurt his feelings for the world.* (I wouldn't hurt his feelings for any reason.) *Not for worlds would he let his children go hungry.* (Nothing could make him let his children go hungry.)

not half bad See NOT BAD.

not have anything on See HAVE NOTHING ON.

nothing See GO FOR NOTHING, HAVE NOTHING ON, HERE GOES NOTHING, IN NO TIME *or* IN NOTHING FLAT, NOT TO MENTION *or* TO SAY NOTHING OF.

nothing doing *adv. phr., informal* I will not do it; certainly not; no indeed; no. *"Will you lend me a dollar?" "Nothing doing!"* ("Will you lend me a dollar?" "Certainly not.") *"Let's go for a boat ride!" "Nothing doing!"* (No, I don't want to go.) Compare NO DEAL.

nothing if not *adv. phr.* Without doubt; certainly. *With its bright furnishings, flowers, and sunny windows the new hospital dayroom is nothing if not cheerful.* (It is a very cheerful room.)

nothing like See ANYTHING LIKE.

nothing succeeds like success Success in one thing makes success in other things easier; people like a successful person.—A proverb. *The girls all like Bob because he is football captain. Nothing succeeds like success.* (The girls like Bob because he is a good player.)

nothing to sneeze at See SNEEZE AT.

notice See SIT UP AND TAKE NOTICE, TAKE NOTE OF *or* TAKE NOTICE OF.

notion See HALF A MIND *also* HALF A NOTION, TAKE INTO ONE'S HEAD *or* TAKE A NOTION.

not know which way to turn *or* **not know which way to jump** *v. phr.* To be puzzled about getting out of a difficulty; not know what to do to get out of trouble. *When Jane missed the last bus home, she didn't know which way to turn.* (Jane did not know how she could get home.) *After Mr. Brown died, Mrs. Brown had no money to pay the bills. When the landlord told her to pay the rent or move out, she didn't know which way to jump.* (Mrs. Brown didn't know what she would do.)

not let any grass grow under one's feet See

LET GRASS GROW UNDER ONE'S FEET.

not on your life *adv. phr., informal* Certainly not; not ever; not for any reason.— Used for emphasis. *I wouldn't drive a car with brakes like that—not on your life.* (I would never drive that car, for any reason.) *Did he thank me for my advice? Not on your life.* (He certainly did not thank me.)

not see beyond one's nose See SEE BEYOND ONE'S NOSE.

not so bad See NOT BAD.

not the only fish in the sea *n. phr.* One of many; not the only one of the kind; not the only one available.—An overused phrase. *He said he could find other girls—she was not the only fish in the sea.* (He said he could find other girls—she was not the only one.) Compare NOT THE ONLY PEBBLE ON THE BEACH.

not the only pebble on the beach *n. phr.* Not the only person to be considered; one of many —An overused phrase. *George was acting pretty self-important, and we finally had to tell him that he wasn't the only pebble on the beach.* (George was acting conceited, and we had to tell him he was not the only person to be considered.) Compare NOT THE ONLY FISH IN THE SEA.

not to give one the time of day *v. phr., slang, informal* To dislike someone strongly enough so as to totally ignore him. *Sue wouldn't give Helen the time of day.* (She dislikes her so strongly that she would totally ignore her.)

not to mention *or* **not to speak of** *or* **to say nothing of** Without ever needing to speak of; in addition to; besides.—Used to add something to what you have already said or explained. *Dave is handsome and smart, not to mention being a good athlete.* (Dave has good looks and brains and is good in sports besides.) *They have three fine sons, not to speak of their two lovely daughters.* (They have three sons in addition to two daughters.) *Sally takes singing and dancing lessons, to say nothing of swimming and tennis lessons.* (Sally takes singing and dancing lessons besides swimming and tennis lessons.) Compare LET ALONE, TO SPEAK OF.

not to speak of See NOT TO MENTION.

not to touch (something) with a ten-foot pole *v. phr.* To consider something completely undesirable or uninteresting. *Some people won't touch spinach with a ten-foot pole.* (Some people thoroughly dislike spinach.) *Kids who wouldn't touch an encyclopedia with a ten-foot pole love to find information with this computer program.* (They think the book is dull, but the computer is fun.)

not worth a tinker's damn *or* **not worth a tinker's dam** *adj. phr., informal* Not worth anything; valueless.—A cliché. *As a bricklayer he was not worth a tinker's damn.* (He was no good as a bricklayer.) *I am not familiar with the subject, so my opinion would*

not be worth a tinker's dam. (I know nothing about it, so my opinion would have no value.)

no use *n.* **1** No purpose; no object; no gain. *There's no use in crying about your broken bicycle.* (Crying about it will not help.) *Bob said, "Let's try again." Dick answered "It's no use."* ("Let's try again." "It won't do any good.") **2** Bad opinion; no respect; no liking.—Usually used after *have. He had no use for dogs after a dog bit him.* (He didn't like dogs at all.) *Jimmy had no use for arithmetic because it was hard for him.* (He didn't want to study it and thought he didn't need to.)

no use crying over spilled milk *or* **no use crying over spilt milk** See CRY OVER SPILLED MILK.

now See EVERY NOW AND THEN *or* EVERY NOW AND AGAIN, HERE AND NOW, JUST NOW.

now and then *or* **now and again** *adv. phr.* Not often; not regularly; occasionally; sometimes. *Now and then he goes to a ball game.* (Occasionally he goes to a ball game.) *The maid broke a dish now and then.* (Occasionally the maid broke a dish.) Syn. AT TIMES, FROM TIME TO TIME, ONCE IN A WHILE. Compare EVERY NOW AND THEN, OFF AND ON.

nowhere See OUT OF NOWHERE.

nowhere near See ANYTHING LIKE.

now —— now *coord. adv.* Sometimes . . . sometimes; by turns; at one time . . . then at another.—Often used with adjectives that are very different or opposite, especially to show change. *The weather changed every day; it was now hot now cool.* (It was hot and then soon afterward was cool.) *The band played different songs, now fast, now slow; now soft, now loud.* (The songs were all different.) *Billy ran so quickly he seemed to be all over the field; he was now here and now there.* (Billy ran quickly from one place to another.)

no wonder *also* **small wonder** *adj.* Not surprising; to be expected. *It is no wonder that the children love to visit the farm.* (It is not surprising that the children love to visit the farm.) *The Browns didn't go to the Fair. Small wonder—they dislike large, noisy crowds.* (It is to be expected that the Browns didn't go to the Fair, because they dislike crowds.)

now that *conj.* Since; because; now. *Now that dinner is ready, wash your hands.* (Because dinner is ready, you must wash your hands.) *You came early but now that you're here, take off your coat.* (Since you have come anyway, take your coat off.) Syn. INASMUCH AS.

nth See TO THE NTH DEGREE.

nuisance See PUBLIC NUISANCE.

number See A NUMBER, ANY NUMBER, DAYS ARE NUMBERED, GET ONE'S NUMBER, HOT NUMBER, QUITE A FEW *or* QUITE A NUMBER.

number one *or* **Number One** *n. phr., informal* Yourself; your own interests; your private or selfish advantage. Usually used in the phrase *look out for number one*. *He was well known for his habit of always looking out for number one*. (He had a habit of thinking of himself first.)

number one *adj. phr.* **1** Of first rank or importance; foremost; principal. *He is easily America's number one golfer*. (He is the foremost American golfer.) **2** Of first grade; of top quality; best. *That is number one western steer beef*. (That is the best western steer beef.)

nurse See VISITING NURSE.

nurse a drink *v. phr., informal* To hold a drink in one's hand at a party, pretending to be drinking it or taking extremely small sips only. *John's been nursing that drink all evening*. (He has hardly touched it all evening. He has decided to drink less.)

nurse a grudge *v. phr.* To keep a feeling of envy or dislike towards some person; re-member something bad that a person said or did to you, and dislike the person because of that.—A cliché. *Tom nursed a grudge against John because John took his place on the basketball team*. (Tom felt disappointed because John took his place, and he disliked and envied John.) *Mary nursed a grudge against her teacher because she thought she deserved a better grade in English*. (Mary felt angry at her teacher because of her poor grade in English.)

nursing home See CONVALESCENT HOME.

nut See HARD NUT TO CRACK *or* TOUGH NUT TO CRACK.

nutshell See IN A NUTSHELL.

nutty as a fruitcake *adj. phr., slang* Very crazy; entirely mad.—A trite phrase. *He looked all right, as we watched him approach, but when he began to talk, we saw that he was as nutty as a fruitcake*. (He seemed normal until he spoke; then we could tell that he was crazy.)

O

oak See GREAT OAKS FROM LITTLE ACORNS GROW.

oars See REST ON ONE'S OARS.

oath See TAKE OATH.

oats See FEEL ONE'S OATS, SOW ONE'S WILD OATS.

occasion See ON OCCASION.

oddball *n., slang, informal* An eccentric person; one who doesn't act like everyone else. *John is an oddball—he never invites anyone.* (He acts strangely—he is a loner.)

odds See BY ALL ODDS.

odds-on *adj., informal* Almost certain; almost sure; probable. *Ed is the odds-on choice for class president, because he has good sense and good humor.* (Because of his good sense and good humor, Ed is almost certain to win the election.)

of age *adj. phr.* **1a** Old enough to be allowed to do or manage something. *Mary will be of driving age on her next birthday.* (She will be 16, old enough to be allowed to drive a car.) Contrast OVER AGE, UNDER AGE. **1b** Old enough to vote; having the privileges of adulthood. *The age at which one is considered of age to vote, or of age to buy alcoholic drinks, or of age to be prosecuted as an adult, varies within the United States.* (Statutes about these limits vary.) **2** Fully developed; mature. *Education for the handicapped came of age when special schools were accepted as a necessary part of the public school system.* (Schools for the blind, deaf, and other handicapped people developed when the public accepted responsibility for them.)

of a piece *adj. phr.* Of the same kind; in line. Usually used with *with*. *His quitting the job is of a piece with his dropping out of school.* (Leaving the job is the same kind of conduct as leaving school.)

of course *adv. phr.* **1** As you would expect; naturally. *Bob hit Herman, and Herman hit him back, of course.* (As you would expect, Herman hit him back and the fight began.) *The rain came pouring down, and of course the track meet was canceled.* (Because of the rain, the field was muddy, and naturally the meet could not be held.) **2** Without a doubt; certainly, surely. *Of course you know that girl; she's in your class.* (Surely you know that girl.)

off a duck's back See LIKE WATER OFF A DUCK'S BACK.

off again, on again *or* **on again, off again** *adj. phr., informal* Not settled; changeable; uncertain. *John and Susan had an off again, on again romance.* (Sometimes they thought they were in love, and sometimes not.) *I don't like this off-again, on-again business. Are we going to have the party or not?* (I don't like not being sure if the party will be held or not.)

off and on *also* **on and off** *adv.* Not regularly; occasionally; sometimes. *Joan wrote to a pen pal in England off and on for several years.* (Joan wrote to her friend in England occasionally.) *It rained off and on all day.* (Rain fell for a while, then stopped, then started, again and again.)—Sometimes used with hyphens like an adjective. *A worn-out cord may make a hearing aid work in an off-and-on way.* (A bad cord makes a hearing aid go off and then on instead of working all the time.) Compare BY FITS AND STARTS, FROM TIME TO TIME, NOW AND THEN.

off balance *adj. phr.* **1** Not in balance; not able to stand up straight and not fall; not able to keep from turning over or falling; unsteady. *Never stand up in a canoe; it will get off balance and turn over.* (If you stand up in a canoe, it is almost sure to turn over.) *Paul was speeding along on his bicycle, when an unexpected hole in the road caught him off balance and he fell over.* (The hole in the road caused Paul's bicycle to become unsteady and fall over.) **2** Not prepared; not ready; unable to meet something unexpected. *Our quarterback kept the other team off balance by changing often from line plays to passes and tricky end runs.* (Our quarterback changed plays so unexpectedly that the other team wasn't ready to stop them.) *The teacher's surprise test caught the class off balance, and nearly everyone got a poor mark.* (The surprise test caught the class unprepared.)

off base *adj. phr., informal* Not agreeing with fact; wrong. *The idea that touching a toad causes warts is off base.* (It is an old superstition that does not agree with fact.) *When Tom said that the teacher's explanation did not agree with the book, the teacher was embarrassed at being caught off base.* (The teacher was embarrassed when Tom said her explanation did not agree with facts given in the book.)

offbeat *adj., informal* Nonconventional, different from the usual, odd. *Linguistics used to be an offbeat field, but nowadays every self-respecting University has a linguistics department.* (It used to be an odd, unusual field, now that is no longer the case.)

off center *adv. phr.* Not exactly in the middle. *Mary hung the picture off center, because it was more interesting that way.* (Mary did not hang the picture in the middle of the wall.)

off-center *adj., informal* Different from the usual pattern; not quite like most others; odd. *Roger's sense of humor was a bit off-center.* (It was a little odd. He didn't laugh at the things most people thought were funny.) Compare OFF-KEY.

off-color *or* **off-colored** *adj.* **1** Not of the proper hue or shade; not matching a standard color sample. *The librarian complained that the painter had used an off-color green on the* *walls.* (She said he had used a green not matching the sample she had selected.) **2** *informal* Not of the proper kind for polite society; in bad taste; dirty. *When Joe finished his off-color story, no one was pleased.* (He told an impolite joke, and nobody laughed. The girls blushed.)

off duty *adj.* Not supposed to be at work; having free time; not working. *Sailors like to go sight-seeing, when they are off duty in a foreign port.* (When sailors are not supposed to be at work on the ship, they go ashore and visit around town.) *It seems that all the taxis in New York are off duty whenever it rains.* (Many taxi drivers are not working and will not take passengers.)—Often used with hyphens, before a noun. *The bank robber was captured by an off-duty policeman.* (The robber ·was caught by a policeman who was not working, but who happened to be passing the bank.) Contrast ON DUTY.

off feed *or* **off one's feed** *adj. phr., informal* Not feeling well; lacking in vitality; droopy; moody. *Mary was worried; her canary was off feed.* (It was not feeling well and would not eat.) *Jerry seemed to be off his feed; he did not joke and laugh with the others.* (He seemed to be feeling moody. He was acting strangely.)

off guard *adj.* In a careless attitude; not alert to coming danger; not watching. *In the second that the boxer was off guard, his opponent landed a knockout punch.* (As soon as the boxer was careless, his opponent knocked him out.) *Timmy's question caught Jean off guard, and she told him the secret before she knew it.* (Jean was so surprised by Timmy's question that she told him something that she wanted to keep secret.) Contrast ON GUARD.

off in a flash See IN A FLASH.

off-key *adj., informal* Not proper; queer. *When George told jokes at the funeral, everyone thought his action was off-key.* (Everyone thought that jokes were not proper at a funeral.) Compare OUT OF LINE.

off one's back *adj. phr.* **1** *informal* Stopped from bothering one; removed as an annoyance or pest. *"Having a kid brother always following me is a nuisance,"* Mary told her Mother. *"Can't you get him off my back?"* ("Can't you stop him from bothering me?") *The singer was so popular with teenagers that he took a secret vacation, to keep them off his back.* (He had to keep his travels secret so that they could not bother him for autographs or souvenirs.) Contrast ON ONE'S BACK. **2** See GIVE THE SHIRT OFF ONE'S BACK.

off one's chest *adj. phr., informal* Told to someone and so not bothering you any more; not making you feel worried or upset, because you have talked about it. *After Dave told the principal that he had cheated on the test, he was glad because it was off his chest.* (He knew he had done wrong and it was bothering him. He wanted to tell someone.) *Father felt that Tom wasn't helping enough around the house, so he got it off his chest by giving Tom a list of things to do.* (Father decided to say what he thought, and make Tom help more.) Compare MAKE A CLEAN BREAST OF. Contrast ON ONE'S CHEST.

off one's feet See KNOCK OFF ONE'S FEET, SWEEP OFF ONE'S FEET.

off one's hands *adv. phr.* No longer in your care or possession. *Ginny was glad to have the sick dog taken off her hands by the doctor.* (She was glad to have the doctor take it out of her care.) Contrast ON ONE'S HANDS.

off one's high horse *adj. phr., informal* **1** Not acting proud and scornful; humble and agreeable.—A cliché. *The girls were so kind to Nancy after her mother died that she came down off her high horse and made friends with them.* (She stopped being proud and acting important and became a good friend.) **2** Acting friendly again; not angry and unpleasant any more; agreeable.—A cliché. *Sally wouldn't speak to anyone all afternoon because she couldn't go to the movies, but she's off her high horse now.* (Sally was angry, but she is pleasant again now.) Contrast ON ONE'S HIGH HORSE.

off one's rocker *or* **off one's trolley** *adj. phr., informal* Not thinking correctly; crazy; silly; foolish. *Tom is off his rocker if he thinks he can run faster than Bob can.* (He is not thinking correctly; he is silly to think he is faster than Bob.) *If you think you can learn to figure skate in one lesson, you're off your trolley.* (Figure skating looks easy but it takes a lot of skill and practice, and if you think you can learn to do it in one lesson, you're crazy.) Syn. OUT OF ONE'S HEAD.

off one's trolley See OFF ONE'S ROCKER.

off the bat See RIGHT AWAY *or* RIGHT OFF THE BAT.

off the beam *adv. or adj. phr.* **1** (*Of an airplane*) Not in the radio beam that marks the path to follow between airports; flying in the wrong direction. *A radio signal tells the pilot of an airplane when his plane is off the beam.* **2** *slang* Wrong; mistaken. *Maud was off the beam when she said that the girls didn't like her.* (Maud was wrong. The girls did like her.) Contrast ON THE BEAM.

off the beaten track *adv. phr.* Not well known or often used; not gone to or seen by many people; unusual. *This theatre is off the beaten track.* (This theatre is not well known. Not many people go to it.) *We are looking for a vacation spot that is off the beaten track.* (We are looking for a quiet vacation spot that is not well known or popular.) Compare OUT OF THE WAY.

off the cuff *adv. phr., informal* Without preparing ahead of time what you will say; without preparation. *Some presidents like to speak off the cuff to newspaper reporters, but others prefer to think questions over and write their* *answers.* (Some presidents like to answer questions without carefully preparing what they say, but others like to prepare their answers so there will be no misunderstanding.)

off-the-cuff *adj., informal* Not prepared ahead of time.—Used of a speech or remarks. *Jack was made master of ceremonies because he was a good off-the-cuff speaker.* (He did not prepare his speeches before he gave them, but they were good.)

off the ground See GET OFF THE GROUND.

off the handle See FLY OFF THE HANDLE.

off the hog See LIVE HIGH OFF THE HOG.

off the hook *adv. phr.* Out of trouble; out of an awkward or embarrassing situation. *Thelma found she had made two dates for the same night; she asked Sally to get her off the hook by going out with one of the boys.* (Thelma asked Sally to get her out of an embarrassing situation by keeping one of the dates for her.)

off the record *adj. phr.* Not to be published or told; secret; confidential. *The President told the reporters his remarks were strictly off the record.* (He didn't want the reporters to tell people what he said.)—Sometimes used with hyphens, before the noun. *The governor was angry when a newspaper printed his off-the-record comments.* (The newspaper printed the things the governor asked to be kept secret.)

off the top of one's head *adv. or adj. phr., informal* Without thinking hard; quickly. *Vin answered the teacher's question off the top of his head.* (Vin answered the teacher's question without really thinking hard.) *When Lorraine was asked to recite, she talked off the top of her head.* (Lorraine talked without really thinking about what she was saying.)

off the wagon *adj. phr., slang* No longer refusing to drink whiskey or other alcoholic beverages; drinking liquor again, after stopping for a while. *When a heavy drinker quits, he must really quit. One little drink of whiskey is enough to drive him off the wagon.* (One drink can make a heavy drinker who has quit start drinking too much again.) Contrast ON THE WAGON.

of it See WHAT OF IT.

of late *adv. phr., formal* In the recent past; not long ago; a short time ago; lately; recently. *There have been too many high school dropouts of late.* (Too many young people have quit high school lately.)

of necessity *adv. phr.* Because there is no other way; because it must be; necessarily. *Being a professional actor of necessity means working nights and Sundays.* (A professional actor must work nights and Sundays, because that is the time when people want entertainment.)

of no avail See TO NO AVAIL.

of old[1] *adj. phr.* Of ancient times; of long ago. *Knights of old had to wear armor in battle.* (Knights of ancient times often wore armor to fight.)

of old[2] *adv. phr.* From earlier experience. *You won't get any money from Freddie. I know him of old.* (I know from earlier experience with Freddie that he will refuse to give any money.)

of oneself See GIVE OF ONESELF.

of one's life *adj. phr.* The best or worst; greatest.—Usually describing a time or effort. *At Disneyland, Tommy had the time of his life.* (Tommy had the best time he could.) *His race for the presidency was the political fight of his life.* (To be elected president took a greater effort than he had ever made before.)

of one's own accord *or* **of one's own free will** *adv. phr.* Without suggestion or help from anyone else; without being told; voluntarily. *On her Mother's birthday, Betsy did the dishes of her own accord.* (As a birthday present to her Mother, Betsy did the dishes. Nobody told her to; it was her own idea.) *But Johnny hates baths. I can't believe he would take one of his own free will.* (I can't believe he would take a bath unless someone made him do it.)

of one's own free will See OF ONE'S OWN ACCORD.

of service *adj. phr.* Valuable as a source of aid; helpful; useful. *When a visitor seems lost or confused, the courteous student will ask "May I be of service?"* (He will step up to the visitor and ask if he can help in answering questions or giving directions.) *A good jackknife is often of service to a camper.* (It is useful to him.)

of sorts *or* **of a sort** *adj. phr.* Not especially good; not very good; of common quality. *Joel was a magician of sorts, and popular at parties.* (He was not an especially good magician, but he was fun to watch.)

often See EVERY NOW AND THEN *or* EVERY SO OFTEN, MORE OFTEN THAN NOT.

of the devil See SPEAK OF THE DEVIL AND HE APPEARS.

of the first water *adj. phr., informal* Of the finest quality; superior; very good; best.—A cliché. *The jeweler chose diamonds of the first water for the queen's crown.* (He chose the best diamonds to put into it.) *The dance program at graduation was of the first water.* (It was very good.) Compare FIRST-CLASS.

oil See POUR OIL ON TROUBLED WATERS.

ointment See FLY IN THE OINTMENT.

old See CHIP OFF THE OLD BLOCK, COMFORTABLE AS AN OLD SHOE, COMMON AS AN OLD SHOE, OF OLD.

old boy *or* **old chap** *n., chiefly British* One of the men educated at the same institution and bound by strong ties of loyalty to each other. *He got the job because the boss was another old boy.* (He was hired because he had attended the same school as the boss.)

old hat *adj., informal* Old-fashioned; not new or different. *By now, putting satellites in orbit is old hat to space scientists.* (They are used to it now because they have practiced often.) *Andrea thought her Mother's ideas about dating were old hat.* (She thought her Mother's ideas were old-fashioned.)

Old Nick See FULL OF THE OLD NICK.

old story *n.* An everyday occurrence; something that often happens. *Jane's temper tantrums were an old story.* (She had had many tantrums before.) *It's an old story when a woman divorces her husband for too much drinking.* (It often happens that a woman divorces her husband for too much drinking.)

on account *adv. phr.* As part payment of a debt; to lessen the amount owed. *John paid $10 down and $5 on account each month for his bicycle.* (He paid the salesman $10 when he bought the bike, and sent the store $5 a month until he had finally paid the full price.)

on account of *prep.* As a result of; because of. *The picnic was held in the gym on account of the rain.* (The picnic was supposed to be held on the playing field but was moved indoors because of rain.) Compare ON ONE'S ACCOUNT, OF ONE'S OWN ACCORD.

on a dime *adv. phr., informal* In a very small space. *Bob can turn that car on a dime.* (Bob can turn his car in a very small space.) *Tom says his new sports car will stop on a dime.* (The new car will stop in a very short distance.)

on again, off again See OFF AGAIN, ON AGAIN.

on air See WALK ON AIR.

on a limb See OUT ON A LIMB.

on all four See HIT OR ALL FOUR.

on all fours *adv. phr.* **1** On all four legs; on hands and knees. *Fido sat up to "beg" but dropped down on all fours to eat the dog biscuit Sam gave him.* (The dog sat on his back legs to "beg" but dropped down on all four legs to eat his prize.) *Billy's father got down on all fours and gave the baby a ride.* (He got down on his hands and knees and let the baby ride on his back.) **2** *informal* On a level of equality; of the same value. *Wigs may be widely used, but they are still not on all fours with beautiful natural hair.* (Wigs are not equal to real hair.)

on an average *or* **on the average** *adv. phr.* In most cases; usually. *On an average Dan's mother has to ask him three times before he helps with the dishes.* (It usually takes her three tries to get him to help.) *On the average, Mr. Blank trades in his car for a new one every three years.* (Usually Mr. Blank gets a new car every three years.)

on and off See OFF AND ON.

on an even keel *adv. phr., informal* In a well-ordered way or condition; orderly. *When the football rally seemed almost ready to become a riot, the principal stepped to the platform and got things back on an even keel.* (He calmed the crowd and made things orderly again.)

on a pedestal *adv. phr.* Lovingly honored and cared for. *Mrs. Raymond's children served her breakfast in bed on Mother's Day and later took her out to dinner. She felt on a pedestal.* (Mrs. Raymond's children served her breakfast in bed and took her out to dinner on Mother's Day. It made her feel lovingly honored.) *Bill is always waiting on his fiancee and bringing her flowers and candy. He has certainly put her on a pedestal.* (Bill waits on his fiancee and gives her flowers and candy often. He is really making her feel lovingly honored and cared for.)

on approval *adv. phr.* With the understanding that the thing may be refused. *Mr. Grey bought his camera on approval.* (Mr. Grey bought his camera with the understanding that he could return it to the store if he was not satisfied.) *The company offered to send a package of stamps on approval.* (The company offered to send a package of stamps with the understanding that they could be returned if not purchased.)

on a scratched horse See PUT ONE'S MONEY ON A SCRATCHED HORSE.

on a shoestring *adv. phr.* With little money to spend; on a very low budget. *The couple was seeing Europe on a shoestring.* (They were spending very little money.)

on a volcano See SIT ON A VOLCANO.

on behalf of See IN BEHALF OF.

on board *prep.* On (a ship). *Joan was not on board the ship when it sailed.* (Joan was not on the ship when it sailed.)

on board *adv. or adj. phr.* On a ship. *The Captain was not on board when the S.S. Flandre sailed.* (The Captain was not on the ship when it sailed.) *A ship was leaving the harbor, and we saw the people on board waving.* (We saw the people on the ship waving their hands to say goodbye.)

on borrowed time See LIVE ON BORROWED TIME.

on call *adj. phr.* **1** Having to be paid on demand. *Jim didn't have the money ready even though he knew the bill was on call.* (Jim didn't have the money ready even though he knew the bill had to be paid on demand.) **2** Ready and available. *This is Dr. Kent's day to be on call at the hospital.* (This is Dr. Kent's day to be ready and available to work at the hospital.) *The nurse is on call for emergency cases.* (The hospital can call her when she is needed.)

once See AT ONCE, EVERY NOW AND THEN *or* EVERY ONCE IN A WHILE.

once and for all *adv. phr.* **1** One time and never again; without any doubt; surely, certainly, definitely. *Let me say, for once and for all, you may not go to the party Saturday.* (Let me say, one time and never again, that you may not go to the party Saturday.) *For once and for all, I will not go swimming with you.* (I certainly will not go swimming with you.) **2** Permanently. *Bill and Tom asked the teacher to settle the argument once and for* *all.* (Bill and Tom asked their teacher to settle the argument permanently.) *The General decided that two bombs would destroy the enemy and end the war once and for all.* (The General decided that two bombs would destroy the enemy and end the war permanently.)

once bitten, twice shy See BURNT CHILD DREADS THE FIRE.

once for all See ONCE AND FOR ALL.

once in a blue moon *adv. phr.* Very rarely; very seldom; almost never.—A cliché. *Coin collecting is interesting, but you find a valuable coin only once in a blue moon.* (Coin collecting is interesting, but you find a valuable coin only very rarely.) *Once in a blue moon someone grows a very pale marigold, but no truly white marigolds have been raised.* (On very rare occasions, someone grows a very pale marigold.)

once in a while *adv. phr.* Not often; not regularly; sometimes; occasionally. *We go for a picnic in the park once in a while.* (We go for a picnic in the park sometimes, but not very often.) *Once in a while the puppy would run away, but usually he stayed in the yard.* (Sometimes the puppy ran away.) Syn. AT TIMES, FROM TIME TO TIME, NOW AND THEN.

once-over *n., slang* **1** A quick look; a swift examination of someone or something.—Usually used with *give* or *get*. *The new boy got the once-over from the rest of the class when he came in.* (The class looked at the new boy to see what he was like.) *Bob gave his paper the once-over before handing it in.* (Bob looked his paper over for mistakes.) **2** or **once-over-lightly** A quick or careless job, especially of cleaning or straightening; work done hastily for now. *Ann gave her room a quick once-over-lightly with the broom and dust cloth.* (She cleaned and dusted in a hurry.) *"Just give my hair the once-over,"* Al said to the barber. (Just give my hair a quick cutting.) Compare LICK AND A PROMISE.

once upon a time *adv. phr.* Sometime before now; long ago.—A cliché. *Once upon a time she was thought to be the most talented actress in the country.* (Some time before now she was thought to be the most wonderful actress in the country.)—Often used at the beginning of fairy stories. *Once upon a time there lived a King who had an ugly daughter.* (Long ago there lived a King who had an ugly daughter.)

on cloud nine *adj. phr., slang* Too happy to think of anything else; very happy. *Ada has been on cloud nine since the magazine printed the story she wrote.* (Ada has been very happy since her story was printed in the magazine. She thinks of nothing but that.) *We were on cloud nine when our team won the state championship.* (We were as happy as we could be when our team won the state championship.) Compare ON TOP OF THE WORLD, WALK ON AIR.

on condition that *conj.* Providing that; if. *I will lend you the money on condition that you pay it back in one month.* (I will lend you the money if you will pay it back in one month.) *She agreed to act in the play on condition that she could keep her costumes.* (She agreed to act in the play if she could keep her costumes.)

on deck *adv. or adj. phr.* **1** On a floor of a ship open to the outdoors. *The passengers were playing shuffleboard on deck.* (The passengers were playing a game on the open floor of the ship.) *The sailors kept busy cleaning and painting on deck.* (The sailors kept busy cleaning and painting on the exposed floor of the ship.) **2** *informal* Ready to do something; present. *The scout leader told the boys to be on deck at 8:00 Saturday morning for the hike.* (The leader told the scouts to come to the meeting place at eight o'clock.) *Dick was at bat, and Bob was on deck.* (Bob was next in line to bat.)

on deposit *adv. phr.* In a bank. *I have almost $500 on deposit in my account.* (I have almost $500 in my bank account.) *The children save their pennies and each month place them on deposit.* (The children save their pennies and each month put them in the bank.)

on duty *adj. phr.* Doing one's job; supervising. *Two soldiers are on duty guarding the gates.* (Two soldiers are doing their job, guarding the gates.) *There is always one teacher on duty during study hour.* (There is always one teacher supervising during study hour.) Contrast OFF DUTY.

one See AT ONE, FOR ONE, GO IN ONE EAR AND OUT THE OTHER, HANG ONE ON, HOLE IN ONE, KILL TWO BIRDS WITH ONE STONE, NUMBER ONE, SIX OF ONE AND HALF-A-DOZEN OF THE OTHER, SLIP ONE OVER ON, TEN TO ONE, TWO TO ONE, WORDS OF ONE SYLLABLE.

one and the same *adj. phr.* The same; identical.—A hackneyed expression. *Erle Stanley Gardiner and A. A. Fair are one and the same person.* (Erle Stanley Gardiner and A. A. Fair are pen names for the same person.) *The spider lily and the Peruvian Daffodil are one and the same.* (The spider lily and the Peruvian Daffodil are identical. They are different names for the same flower.)

one-armed bandit *n., slang* A slot machine, like those used in Las Vegas and other Nevada gambling places. *Joe was playing the one-armed bandit all day—and he lost everything he had.* (He played the slot machines all day and he lost.)

on earth See IN THE WORLD.

on easy street *adj. phr., informal* Having enough money to live very comfortably; rather rich.—A cliché. *After years of hard work, the Grants found themselves on easy street.* (After years of hard work, the Grants found that they had plenty of money.) *Jim's novel was a success and put him on easy* *street.* (Jim's successful novel made him rather rich.) Compare IN CLOVER, IN THE CHIPS, WELL-TO-DO.

on edge *adj. phr.* Excited or nervous; impatient. *The magician kept the children on edge all through his show.* (He kept the children excited and interested.) *We were all on edge as we listened to the TV for news of the election results.* (We were all impatient to hear who had won the elections.) *Father was on edge after driving home through the heavy holiday traffic.* (Father was nervous after driving through the heavy traffic; little things annoyed him.) Contrast AT EASE 2.

on edge See SET ONE'S TEETH ON EDGE.

one eye on *informal* Watching or minding (a person or thing) while doing something else; part of your attention on.—Used after *have, keep,* or *with. Mother had one eye on the baby as she ironed.* (Mother ironed and minded the baby at the same time.) *Bill kept one eye on his books and the other on the clock.* (Bill read the book and kept looking to see what time it was.) *Chris tried to study with one eye on the TV set.* (Chris tried to study and look at the TV at the same time.) Compare KEEP AN EYE ON.

one foot in the grave *n. phr.* Near to death.—A cliché. *The dog is fourteen years old, blind, and feeble. He has one foot in the grave.* (The dog is old and weak. He will die soon.) *Grandfather has never been sick a day in his life, but mother cares for him as if he had one foot in the grave.* (Grandfather is very healthy, but mother acts as if he were near death.)

one for the books *n. phr., informal* Very unusual; a remarkable something. *The newspaper reporter turned in a story that was one for the books.* (The reporter wrote a story that was very unusual.) *Their trip through the Rocky Mountains was one for the books.* (Their trip through the Rockies was remarkable. Unusual things happened to them on their trip.)

on end *adj. phr.* Seemingly endless.—Used with plural nouns of time. *Judy spent hours on end writing and re-writing her essay.* (Judy spent seemingly endless hours writing and re-writing her essay.) *During July and August there was no rain for weeks on end.* (During July and August it did not rain for many weeks.)

one of these days *or* **some of these days** *adv. phr.* Someday; sometime soon. *One of these days Herbert will be famous.* (Someday Herbert will be famous.) *I'm going to do that sewing some of these days.* (I'm going to do that sewing some time soon.)

one on the city *n., slang* A glass of water (which is provided free of charge, as a free gift from the city.) *What will you have?—Oh, just give me one on the city.* (All I want is a glass of water.)

one's own row See HOE ONE'S OWN ROW.

one-two *n.* 1 A succession of two punches, the first a short left, followed by a hard right punch, usually in the jaw. *Ali gave Fraser the one-two.* (He gave him the two classical punches.) 2 Any quick or decisive action which takes the opposition by surprise, thereby ensuring victory. *He gave us the old one-two and won the game.* (He took quick, decisive action and won.)

one up *adj. phr.* Having an advantage; being one step ahead. *John graduated from high school; he is one up on Bob, who dropped out.* (John graduated from high school; he has an advantage over Bob, who quit.) *The Platters are one up on their neighbors. They own the only color television set in their neighborhood.* (The Platters are one step ahead of their neighbors because they have the only color television set where they live.)—**one-upmanship** *v., informal* Always keeping ahead of others; trying to keep an advantage. *No matter what I do, I find that Jim has already done it better. He's an expert at one-upmanship.* (Jim does everything before I do it, and does it better. He keeps one step ahead of me.) *Jack took the news to the principal while we were still talking about it. He's very quick to practice one-upmanship.* (Jim told the principal the news. He tried to keep an advantage over us by being first with the news.) Compare ONE-UP. [The word *one-upmanship* was made up by a British humorist, Stephen Potter, on the pattern of such words as *sportsmanship* and *workmanship.*]

on faith *adv. phr.* Without question or proof. *He said he was twenty-one years old and the employment agency took him on faith.* (He said he was twenty-one years old and the employment agency accepted his word without question.) *He looked so honest that we accepted his story on faith.* (He looked so honest that we believe his story without having proof that it was true.)

on fire See SET THE WORLD ON FIRE.

on foot *adv. or adj. phr.* 1 By walking. *Sally's bicycle broke and she had to return home on foot.* (Sally's bicycle broke and she had to return home by walking.) 2 Being planned. *The reporter said that a civil rights demonstration was on foot.* (The reporter said that a civil rights demonstration was being planned.) *Plans have been set on foot for a party for Miss Jackson, because she is retiring.* (Plans are being made for a party.)

on guard *adj. phr.* Watchful; watching. *The police warned people to be on guard for pickpockets during the Christmas rush.* (The police warned people to be watchful for people stealing pocketbooks during the Christmas rush.) *Two men are on guard at the door.* (Two men are watching at the door.) Contrast OFF GUARD.

on hand *adv. phr.* **1a** Nearby; within reach. *Always have your dictionary on hand when* *you study.* (Always have your dictionary nearby when you study. Always have it within reach.) **1b** Here. *Soon school will end and vacation will be on hand.* (Vacation will be here.) **2** Present. *Mr. Blake's secretary is always on hand when he appears in public.* (Mr. Blake's secretary is always present when he appears in public.) **3** In your possession; ready. *The Girl Scouts have plenty of cookies on hand.* (The Girl Scouts have plenty of cookies in their possession.) *Jim had no cash on hand to pay for the gas.* (Jim had no money ready to pay for the gas.) Compare IN STORE.

on high cotton See ON TOP OF THE WORLD *also* SITTING ON HIGH COTTON.

on ice *adv. or adj. phr., slang* **1** The same as won; sure to be won. *The score was 20–10 in the last inning, and our team had the game on ice.* (Our team was almost sure to win.) **2** Away for safekeeping or later use; aside. *You will have to put your vacation plans on ice until your debts are paid.* (You will have to suspend your vacation plans until you pay your debts.) *The Senator was voted out of office. He is on ice until the next election.* (The Senator was voted out of office. He is keeping quiet so that he will be free to campaign in the next election.)

on in years See ALONG IN YEARS.

onion See KNOW ONE'S WAY AROUND 2.

only See HAVE EYES ONLY FOR, IF ONLY.

on occasion *adv. phr.* Sometimes; occasionally. *We go to New York on occasion.* (We go to New York sometimes.) *On occasion we feel like celebrating and have a party.* (Sometimes we feel like celebrating and we have a party.) Compare ONCE IN A WHILE, FROM TIME TO TIME.

on one hand *adv. phr.* Looking at a thing in one of two possible ways; from one point of view.—Usually used with *on the other hand. John wants to be a printer or a teacher; on one hand, printing pays better; on the other hand, schools need good teachers.* (John can think of a good reason to become a printer and a good reason to become a teacher.)

on one's account *adv. phr.* For your good; because you want to help or please someone. *Barry studied hard on his mother's account.* (Barry studied hard because he wanted to please his mother.) *I hope you didn't bring tea to the picnic just on my account.* (I hope you didn't bring tea only to please me.) *The teacher stayed in school a little late on Tom's account.* (The teacher stayed past the usual time because he was helping Tom.) Compare OF ONE'S OWN ACCORD, ON ACCOUNT OF.

on one's back *adj. phr., informal* Making insistent demands of you; being an annoyance or bother. *My wife has been on my back for weeks to fix the front door screen.* (She has been making insistent demands of me for weeks to fix it. She bothers me about it.) *I*

can't get any work done with the children on my back from morning until night. (I can't get any work done with the children bothering me from morning until night.) *Jim could do a better job if his boss weren't on his back so often.* (Jim could do a better job if his boss didn't worry him so much.) Contrast OFF ONE'S BACK.

on one's bad side *or* **on the bad side of one** *adj. phr., informal* Not liked by someone; not friendly with a person. *Sally's boy friend got on Father's bad side by keeping Sally out too late after the dance.* (Father does not feel friendly toward Sally's boy friend, because he kept her out too late.) Contrast ON ONE'S GOOD SIDE.

on one's behalf See ON BEHALF OF.

on one's chest *adj. phr., informal* Hidden in your thoughts or feelings and bothering you; making you feel worried or upset; that is something you want to talk to someone about. *Jane looks unhappy because she has the quarrel with Susan on her chest.* (She feels worried and upset about the argument.) *"Well, Dave," said the coach, "You look sad —what's on your chest?"* (The coach asked Dave what was making him feel disturbed. Did he want to talk it over?) Compare ON ONE'S MIND. Contrast OFF ONE'S CHEST.

on one's coattails *adv. phr.* Because of another's merits, success, or popularity.—A cliché. *Bob and Jim are best friends. When Jim was invited to join a fraternity, Bob rode in on his coattails.* (Bob was invited mostly because he was Jim's close friend. Bob was invited because of Jim's popularity.) *Many people vote straight for all the candidates in the same political party. Most people voted for President K., so Governor B. rode in on K.'s coattails.* (Governor B. won because he was in the same political party as the popular President K.)

on oneself See TAKE ON ONESELF.

on one's feet *adv. phr.* **1** Standing or walking; not sitting or lying down; up. *Before the teacher finished asking the question, George was on his feet ready to answer it.* (George stood up to answer the question before the teacher finished asking it.) *In a busy gasoline station, the attendant is on his feet all day.* (The attendant is standing or walking all day.) Compare ON ONE'S FEET. Contrast OFF ONE'S FEET. **2** Recovering; getting better from sickness or trouble. *Jack is back on his feet after a long illness.* (Jack is recovering after a long illness.) *Susan was on her feet soon after the operation.* (Susan was recovering soon after her illness.) *The bank loaned the store money to get it back on its feet after the fire.* (The bank helped the store recover from its loss by lending it money.) **3** See LAND ON ONE'S FEET, STAND ON ONE'S OWN FEET, THINK ON ONE'S FEET.

on one's good behavior *adv. phr.* Behaving right to make a good impression. *While his* *father was around the boy was on his good behavior, but when the father left the boy soon got into mischief.* (The boy behaved right to make a good impression while his father was around, but when the father went away the boy soon got into mischief.) *The minister is coming to dinner, and Mother wants us to be on our good behavior.* (The minister is coming to dinner, and Mother wants us to behave politely to make a good impression.)

on one's good side *or* **on the good side of one** *adj. phr., informal* Friendly with someone; liked by a person. *John thought that he would get a good grade if he got on the good side of the teacher.* (John thought he would get a good grade if he could make the teacher like him.) *Successful workers stay on the good side of their bosses.* (Many workers succeed because they do not get in trouble with the boss.) Contrast ON ONE'S BAD SIDE.

on one's hands *adv. or adj. phr.* In your care or responsibility; that you must do something about. *Mrs. Blake left her five children with me while she shopped. I could not get anything done with the children on my hands.* (I could not do anything with the five children in my care.) *After everyone bought tickets to the dance, the club treasurer had over $100 on his hands.* (He had more than $100 to take care of.) *The electricity went off while Mother was cooking supper, and she had a problem on her hands.* (Mother had to do something about getting supper for the family.) *I had time on my hands before the bus came, so I bought a newspaper to read.* (I had time to spend before the bus came.) Contrast OFF ONE'S HANDS. See SIT ON ONE'S HANDS. Compare HANG HEAVY *or* HANG HEAVY ON ONE'S HANDS.

on one's head *or* **upon one's head** *adv. phr.* On one's self. *When the school board fired the superintendent of schools, they brought the anger of the parents upon their heads.* (When the school board fired the superintendent of schools, they made the parents angry with them.) *Billy had been naughty all day, but he really brought his parents' anger down on his head by pushing his little sister into a mud puddle.* (His mischief was bad enough, but he really brought punishment on himself by pushing his sister.) Compare ABOUT ONE'S EARS.

on one's heel See TURN ON ONE'S HEEL.

on one's high horse *adj. phr., informal* **1** Acting as if you are better than others; being very proud and scornful.—A cliché. *Martha was chairman of the picnic committee, and at the picnic she was on her high horse, telling everyone what to do.* (Martha thought she was important and was bossy at the picnic.) *Mrs. Jones asked to see a less expensive hat. The salesgirl got up on her high horse and said the shop did not sell cheap merchandise.* (Mrs. Jones asked to see a less costly hat.

The salesgirl, in a disdainful manner, said the shop did not sell cheap merchandise.) **2** Refusing to be friendly because you are angry; in a bad temper.—A cliché. *Joe was on his high horse because he felt Mary wasn't giving him enough attention.* (Joe was unpleasant because he wanted Mary to pay him more attention.) Contrast OFF ONE'S HIGH HORSE.

on one's honor *adj. phr.* Bound by one's honesty; trusted. *The students were not supervised during the examination. They were on their honor not to cheat.* (The students were trusted not to cheat on the examination because they were bound by their honesty not to do so.) *The housefather put the boys on their honor not to smoke in the dormitory.* (The boys are trusted not to smoke in the dormitory.)

on one's knees *adj. phr.* **1** Pleading; begging very hard. *The boys were on their knees for hours before their parents agreed to their camping plans.* (The boys pleaded for hours before their parents agreed to their camping plans.) *The Jacksons won't contribute to the Red Cross unless you get on your knees.* (The Jacksons won't contribute to the Red Cross unless you beg them.) **2** In a very weak condition; near failure. *When the graduates of the school heard that it was on its knees, they gave money generously so that it would not close.* (The school was badly in need of money so its alumni gave it help.)

on one's last legs *adj. phr.* Failing; near the end.—A cliché. *The blacksmith's business is on its last legs.* (The blacksmith's business is failing.) *The dog is old and sick. He is on his last legs.* (The dog is old and sick. He is near the end of life.) Compare ONE FOOT IN THE GRAVE, ON ONE'S KNEES 2.

on one's mind *adv. phr.* In one's thoughts. *I'm glad you want to talk about this. It's been on my mind for weeks.* (I'm glad you want to talk about that. It's been in my thoughts for weeks.) *What's on your mind?* (What are you thinking about?) Compare IN MIND.

on one's nerves See GET ON ONE'S NERVES.

on one's own *adj. phr.* With no help from others. *It is a happy day when you're allowed to drive a car on your own.* (To be allowed to drive a car with no help from others is a happy event.) *Being on your own may be a frightening experience.* (It may be frightening to do something with no help from others.) Compare GO IT 2.

on one's own account *or informal* **on one's own hook** *adv. phr.* **1** For yourself; as a free agent; independently. *After they had picked out the class gift, members of the committee did some shopping on their own account.* (As long as they were in the store, they did some shopping for themselves.) **2** See OF ONE'S OWN ACCORD.

on one's own feet See STAND ON ONE'S OWN FEET.

on one's own hook See ON ONE'S OWN AC-
COUNT.

on one's own time *adv. phr.* During one's
free time; not during working or school hours.
*If you want to play football, you'll have to do
it on your own time.* (You can't do it during
school hours.)

on one's part *or* **on the part of one** *adj. phr.*
1 Of or by you; of someone's. *When Miss
Brown said I was a good student, that was
pure kindness on her part.* (Miss Brown was
being kind, because I was not a very good
student.) *The other team blamed their defeat
on unfairness on the part of the referee.* (The
other team said they were beaten because
the referee was unfair.) **2** See FOR ONE'S PART.

on one's shoulders *adv. or adj. phr.* In your
care; as your responsibility. *The success of
the program rests on your shoulders.* (The
success of the program is your responsibility.
You are responsible for making the program
a success.) *He acts as if he had the cares of
the world on his shoulders.* (He acts as if the
troubles of the world were his responsibility.)

on one's toes *adj. phr., informal* Alert;
ready to act. *The successful ball player is always on his toes.* (A good ball player is
alert.) Compare HEADS-UP, ON THE BALL.

on one's uppers *adj. phr., informal* Very
poor.—A cliché. *Mr. White had been out of
work for several months and was on his uppers.* (He had almost nothing left to live on.)
Compare DOWN ON ONE'S LUCK.

on one's way See ON THE WAY.

on pain of *also* **under pain of** *prep., formal* At
the risk of; under penalty of. *The workers went
on strike on pain of losing their jobs.* (The
workers risked losing their jobs by going on
strike.)

on paper *adv. or adj. phr.* Judging by appearances only and not by past performance;
in theory; theoretically. *On paper, the American colonies should have lost the Revolutionary War.* (Because the British had a bigger
and more experienced army than the Americans, people thought the British would win.)
*The football team lost many games, even
though they looked good on paper.* (The football players were big boys and had much
experience; but they still lost many games.)

on pins and needles *adj. phr., informal*
Worried; nervous.—A cliché. *Jane's mother
was on pins and needles because Jane was
very late getting home from school.* (Jane's
mother was worried because Jane was so late.)
*Many famous actors are on pins and needles
before the curtain opens for a play.* (Many
actors are nervous about being in a play.)

on purpose *adv. phr.* For a reason; because
you want to; not accidentally. *Jane did not
forget her coat; she left it in the locker on
purpose.* (Jane left her coat in the locker for
a reason; she knew it was there.) *The clown
fell down on purpose.* (The clown did not
fall down by accident; he planned to fall
down.)

on record *adj. phr.* **1** Written down in a
record; said for everyone to know. *We do
not know when the famous writer was born,
but the date of his death is on record.* (The
date when the writer died is written down in
a book.) *The two candidates went on television to put their ideas on record.* (The candidates appeared on TV to let people know
their ideas.) **2** Known to have said or done
a certain thing.—Usually used with *as.* *The
mayor went on record as opposing a tax
raise.* (The mayor said publicly that he was
against raising taxes.) *The governor is on
record as favoring the new highway.* (The
governor has announced publicly that he
thinks the new highway is a good idea.) *That
congressman is on record as an enemy of
waste in government.* (That congressman is
known to fight against unnecessary government spending.)

on sale *adj. phr.* Selling for a special low
price. *Tomato soup that is usually sold for
twelve cents a can is now on sale for ten cents.*
(For today only soup is selling at a special
low price.) *John and Mary couldn't sell all of
the lemonade at five cents a cup so they have
it on sale for three cents a cup.* (The children
put a special price of three cents a cup on
their lemonade.)

on schedule *adv. phr.* As planned or expected; at the right time. *The school bus
arrived at school on schedule.* (The bus arrived at the right time.) *The four seasons
arrive on schedule each year.* (Spring, summer, fall and winter. arrive at the expected
time each year.) Compare ON TIME.

on second thought See SECOND THOUGHT.

on sight See AT SIGHT.

on table See WAIT AT TABLE *or* WAIT ON
TABLE.

on the air *adj. or adv. phr.* Broadcasting
or being broadcast on radio or T.V. *His
show is on the air at six o'clock.* (The show
starts at six.) *The ballgame is on the air now.*
(The game can be heard now.)

on the alert *adj. phr.* Alert; watchful; careful. *Campers must be on the alert for poison
ivy and poison oak.* (Campers should watch
out for poisonous plants.) *Drivers must be
on the alert for traffic signals.* (Drivers must
be especially careful to see signals when driving a car.) Compare ON ONE'S TOES.

on the average See ON AN AVERAGE.

on the back See PAT ON THE BACK.

on the ball *adj. phr., informal* **1** Paying
attention and doing things well.—A cliché.
Used after *is* or *get.* *Ben is really on the ball
in school.* (Ben pays attention and does well
in school.) *The coach told Jim he must get on
the ball or he cannot stay on the team.* (The
coach told Jim he must watch more closely
and play better.) Compare GET WITH IT,
HEADS-UP, KEEP ONE'S EYE ON THE BALL. **2**
That is a skill or ability; making you good at

things.—A cliché. Used after *have*. *John will succeed in life; he has a lot on the ball.* (John has a lot of ability; he is good at many things.) *The coach was eager to try out his new team and see what they had on the ball.* (The coach wanted to see what the new team could do.)

on the bandwagon *adj. phr., informal* In or into the newest popular group or activity; in or into something you join just because many others are joining it.—A cliché. Often used after *climb, get, or jump. When all George's friends decided to vote for Bill, George climbed on the bandwagon too.* (George decided to join his friends and do the same thing.)

on the band wagon See JUMP ON THE BAND WAGON.

on the barrelhead See CASH ON THE BARREL-HEAD.

on the beam *adv. or adj. phr.* **1** (Of an airplane) In the radio beam that marks the path to follow between airports; flying in the right direction. *A radio signal tells the pilot of an airplane when he is flying on the beam.* (A radio signal tells the pilot that he is going the right way.) **2** *slang* Doing well; just right; good or correct. *Kenneth's answer was right on the beam.* (Kenneth answered the teacher's question correctly.) Contrast OFF THE BEAM.

on the bench **1** Sitting in a law court as a judge. *Judge Wyzanski is on the bench this morning.* (Judge Wyzanski is the judge of this court this morning.) **2** Sitting among the substitute players. *The coach had to keep his star player on the bench with a sprained ankle.* (The coach couldn't let the star player play.) Compare BENCH WARMER.

on the blink *adj. phr., informal* Not working well; needing repair. *Bob's car went on the blink, so he rode to school with John.* (John gave Bob a ride because Bob's car was not working well.) *Mother called the repairman because her washing machine was on the blink.* (Mother's washing machine needs repairing.)

on the block *adj. phr.* To be sold; for sale. —A cliché. *The vacant house was on the block.* (The house was to be sold.) *Young cattle are grown and sent to market to be placed on the block.* (Cattle are sent to market to be sold.)

on the brain *adj. phr., slang* Filling your thoughts; too much thought about; almost always in mind.—A cliché. *Mary Ann has boys on the brain.* (Mary Ann thinks of boys often.) *Joe's hobby is ham radio and he has radio on the brain most of the time.* (Joe's hobby is radio and he spends a lot of time thinking about it.)

on the button *adv., adj., slang* At the right place; at the heart of the matter. *John's remark was right on the button.* (His remark was timely and accurate.) Compare ON THE DOT.

on the cards See IN THE CARDS.

on the carpet See CALL ON THE CARPET.

on the chin See TAKE IT ON THE CHIN.

on the contrary *adv. phr.* Exactly the opposite; rather; instead. *The principal thought that the children went to the zoo; on the contrary, they went to the bakery.* (Instead of going to the zoo, the class went to the bakery.) *"You don't like football, do you?" "On the contrary, I like it very much."* (You are wrong—I like it a lot.) Compare TO THE CONTRARY.

on the cuff *adj. or adv. phr., informal* Agreeing to pay later; to be paid for later; on credit. *Peter lost the money that Mother gave him to buy meat, and the store would not let him have meat on the cuff.* (The man who sold meat would not let Peter take it and pay later.) *Many people buy cars and television sets on the cuff.* (Many people get cars and television sets and pay a little each month until they are all paid for.)

on the dot *also* **on the button** *adv. phr., informal* Exactly on time; not early and not late. *Susan arrived at the party at 2:00 p.m. on the dot.* (Susan got to the party at exactly 2:00 P.M., just as she had planned.) *Ben's plane arrived on the dot.* (The plane came in right on time.)

on the eve of *prep.* Just before (an event). *On the eve of the election, the president proposed a plan to cut taxes.* (Just before the election, the president said he wanted to reduce people's taxes.)

on the face of it *adv. phr.* Apparently; as it seems. *On the face of it, Joe's claim that he can swim five miles is true.* (Apparently, Joe is telling the truth. It seems that his claim is true.) *His statement that he is a millionaire is, on the face of it, false.* (His statement that he is a millionaire seems not true. He does not look like a millionaire.)

on the fence *adj. or adv. phr.* Not able, or not wanting to choose; in doubt; undecided. —A cliché. Often used with *sit. Jack sat on the fence for a week last spring before he finally joined the track team instead of the baseball team.* (He didn't decide which he wanted to join until a week passed.) *Mrs. Jones has decided to vote for the Democrats, but Mr. Jones is still on the fence.* (Mr. Jones is still in doubt or unable to choose whether he will vote for the Democrats or Republicans.)—**fence-sitter** *n.* A person unable to pick between two sides; a person who does not want to choose. *Daddy says he is a fence-sitter because he doesn't know which man he wants for President.* (He has not made up his mind which man to vote for.)—**fence-sitting** *n. or adj.* Choosing neither side. *You have been fence-sitting for too long. It is time you made up your mind.* (You have not picked one side or the other. It's time you did.) Contrast MAKE UP ONE'S MIND, TAKE SIDES.

on the fly[1] *adv. phr.* **1** While in the air; in flight. *The bird caught a bug on the fly.* (The bird caught a bug while flying in the air.) *Joe was called out because the catcher caught the ball on the fly.* (The catcher caught the ball before it touched the ground.) **2** *informal* Between other activities; while busy with many things. *The President was so busy that he had to dictate letters on the fly.* (The President had to dictate letters while he was going places in his car.) *John is very busy, and people who want to talk to him have to catch him on the fly.* (People who want to talk to John must stop him while he is hurrying to go somewhere.) Compare ON THE GO, ON THE WING 2.

on the fly[2] *adj. phr., informal* Busy; going somewhere in a hurry; going about doing things. *Getting the house ready for the visitors kept Mother on the fly all day.* (Getting ready for visitors kept Mother very busy all day.) *The housekeeper of our school is always on the fly.* (The housekeeper is always hurrying around doing things.)

on the go *adj. phr., informal* Active and busy. *Successful business men are on the go most of the time.* (Very often businessmen take trips and move about in tending to their business.) *Healthy, happy people are usually on the go.* (People who are healthy and happy are usually active and busy.) Compare ON THE MOVE.

on the heels of *prep.* Just after; following (something, especially an event).—Often used with *hard* for emphasis. *Hard on the heels of the women's liberation parade, homosexuals declared a "gay pride week."* (The "gay pride week" came only a short time after the women's parade.)

on the hog See LIVE HIGH OFF THE HOG OR EAT HIGH ON THE HOG.

on the hour *adv. phr.* Each time the big hand of the clock points to 12. *The uptown bus goes past the school on the hour.* (The bus passes the school when the big hand of the clock points to 12.) *The woman must take her pill on the hour.* (The woman must take a pill at seven o'clock, eight o'clock, nine o'clock etc.)

on the house *adj. phr., informal* Paid for by the owner. *At the opening of the new hotel, the champagne was on the house.* (The owners of the hotel paid for the drinks served at the opening of the hotel.) *Oscar was the first customer at the diner, so his lunch was on the house.* (Since he was the first customer to come into the diner, the owner paid for Oscar's lunch.)

on the job *adj. phr., informal* Working hard; not wasting time. *Joe was on the job all of the time that he was at work.* (Joe worked hard all of the time that he was supposed to be working.) *The school paper came out on time because the editors were on the job.* (The editors of the school paper did their work and did not waste time.)

on the knees of the gods See IN THE LAP OF THE GODS.

on the lam *adj. or adv. phr., slang* Running away, especially from the law; in flight. *The bank robber was on the lam for ten months before the police caught him.* (He spent ten months trying to escape arrest.)—Sometimes used in the phrase *take it on the lam. After a big quarrel with her father, the girl took it on the lam.* (She ran away from home.)

on the level *adj. phr., informal* Honest and fair; telling the whole truth. *Our teacher respects the students who are on the level with her.* (The students who are honest gain the respect of our teacher.) *Joyce wondered if the fortune-teller was on the level.* (Joyce was not sure that the fortune-teller was honest.)

on the line See LAY ON THE LINE or PUT ON THE LINE.

on the lips See HANG ON THE WORDS OF or HANG ON THE LIPS OF.

on the lookout *adj. phr.* Watching closely. *The little boy was on the lookout for his father.* (The little boy stood at the window and watched closely for his father.) *Forest rangers are always on the lookout for forest fires.* (A part of the forest ranger's job is to watch for forest fires.) *The doctor is on the lookout for a new secretary.* (The doctor is trying to find a new secretary.)

on the loose *adj. phr., informal* Free to go; not shut in or stopped by anything. *The zoo keeper forgot to close the gate to the monkey cage and the monkeys were on the loose.* (Because the zoo keeper forgot to close the gate, the monkeys were free to go all over the zoo.) *All of the seniors were on the loose on "Senior Skip Day."* (There was a special day for all Seniors to go where ever they wanted.)

on the make *adj., slang* **1** Promiscuous or aggressive in one's sexual advances. *I can't stand Murray; he's always on the make.* (He is always making aggressive sexual advances.) **2** Pushing to get ahead in one's career; doing anything to succeed. *The new department head is a young man on the make, who expects to be company president in ten years.* (The young man will do anything to be promoted.)

on the map See PUT ON THE MAP.

on the market *adj. phr.* For sale. *In the summer many fresh vegetables are on the market.* (In the summer, many fresh vegetables are for sale in stores.) *The Goodwins put their house on the market in January, but they did not sell it till August.* (The Goodwins told people in January that they wanted to sell their house.)

on the mend *adj. phr.* Healing; becoming better. *John's broken leg is on the mend.* (John's broken leg is healing and will soon be well.) *Mary's relationship with Joan is on the mend.* (Mary and Joan had a disagreement, but their feelings toward each other are becoming better.)

on the move *adj. or adv. phr.* **1** Moving around from place to place; in motion. *It was a very cold day, and the teacher watching the playground kept on the move to stay warm.* (The teacher kept walking around to make himself warm.) *It was vacation time, and the highways were full of families on the move.* (The roads were full of families in cars and trailers going on their vacations.) **2** Moving forward; going somewhere. *The candidate promised that if people would make him President, he would get the country on the move.* (The man promised to make the country begin to do better; it would progress.)

on the nose *adv. phr., informal* Just right; exactly. *Stanley hit the ball on the nose.* (Stanley hit the ball just right.) *The airplane pilot found the small landing field on the nose.* (The pilot brought his plane into the airport just as planned; he did not need to look around for it.)

on the other foot See SHOE ON THE OTHER FOOT.

on the other hand *adv. phr.* Looking at the other side; from another point of view.— Used to introduce an opposite or different fact or idea. *Father and Mother wanted to go for a ride; the children, on the other hand, wanted to stay home and play with their friends.* (Father and Mother wanted to go riding, but the children wanted to stay home.) *Mr. Harris may still want a boy to mow his lawn; on the other hand, he may have found someone to do it.* (Mr. Harris may be still looking for help, or he may have found it.) Compare ON ONE HAND.

on the outs *adj. phr., informal* Not friendly; having a quarrel. *Mary and Sue were on the outs.* (Mary and Sue quarreled and were not friends for a time.) *Being on the outs with a classmate is very upsetting.* (We are upset when we are not friendly with our classmates.) Syn. AT ODDS.

on the point of *prep.* Ready to begin; very near to.—Usually used with a verbal noun. *The coach was on the point of giving up the game when our team scored two points.* (Just as the coach was ready to give up the game, we scored.) *The baby was on the point of crying when her Mother finally came home.* (The baby's Mother came home just as the baby was ready to cry.) Compare ABOUT TO, AT THE POINT OF.

on the Q.T. *adv. phr., informal* Secretly, without anyone's knowing.—A cliché. *George and Paul formed a club on the Q.T.* (George and Paul formed a club, but they told no one.) *The teachers got the principal a present strictly on the Q.T.* (Secretly, the teachers got a present for the principal.)

on the road *adv. or adj. phr.* **1** Traveling; moving from one place to another. *When we go on vacation, we take a lunch to eat while on the road.* (When we are travelling, we

take a lunch in the car with us.) *Mr. Smith is on the road for his insurance company.* (Mr. Smith does a lot of travelling on his work.) **2** Changing; going from one condition to another. *Mary was very sick for several weeks, but now she is on the road to recovery.* (Now Mary is getting well.) *Hard study in school put John on the road to success.* (Studying hard in school made John likely to succeed in life.)

on the rocks *adj. phr.* **1** *informal* Wrecked or ruined.—A cliché. *Mr. Jones' business was on the rocks.* (Mr. Jones' business was losing money and almost ruined.) **2** With ice only. *At the restaurant, Sally ordered orange juice on the rocks.* (Sally ordered orange juice with ice cubes.)

on the ropes *adv. or adj. phr.* **1** Against the ropes of a boxing ring and almost not able to stand up. *The fighter was on the ropes, and could hardly lift his gloves.* (The fighter was very weak and he was leaning on the ropes so that he would not fall down.) **2** Almost defeated; helpless; near failure.—A cliché. *The new supermarket took most of the business from Mr. Thomas's grocery, and the little store was soon on the ropes.* (Mr. Thomas's grocery store was soon failing.)

on the run *adv. or adj. phr.* **1** In a hurry; hurrying. *Mother called "Help!" and Father came on the run.* (Father ran to help Mother.) *Modern mothers are usually on the run.* (Mothers are hurrying to take children to school and to do their shopping.) **2** Going away from a fight; in retreat; retreating. *The enemy soldiers were on the run.* (They were retreating.)

on the shelf *adv. or adj. phr., informal* Laid aside, not useful anymore.—A cliché. *When a girl grows up, she puts childish habits on the shelf.* (When a girl lays her childish things aside, we know that she is growing up.) *Mr. Myron's company put him on the shelf when he reached the age of 65.* (When Myron was 65 years old, he was retired by the company.)

on the side *adv. phr., informal* **1** In addition to a main thing, amount or quantity; extra. *He ordered a hamburger with onions and French fries on the side.* (He ordered a hamburger with onions and French fries extra.) *His job at the hospital did not pay much, so he found another on the side.* (He had an extra, part-time job to get more money.) *The cowboys in the rodeo competed for prize money and also made bets on the side.* (The winner got the prize money and also got more by betting.) **2** *or on the —— side* Tending toward; rather. *Grandmother thought Jane's new skirt was on the short side.* (Grandmother thought the skirt was shorter than it should be.)

on the sly *adv. phr.* So that other people won't know; secretly. *The boys smoked on the sly.* (The boys smoked when no one was looking.) *Mary's mother did not approve of* *lipstick, but Mary used it on the sly.* (She used lipstick but her Mother didn't know.)

on the spot *adv. or adj. phr.* **1** *or* **upon the spot** At that exact time and at the same time or place; without waiting or leaving. *The news of important events is often broadcast on the spot over television.* (We see and hear what happens then and there.) *When Tom ruined an expensive machine, his boss fired him on the spot.* (His boss fired him without waiting or going to the office.) Compare AT ONCE, IN ONE'S TRACKS, THEN AND THERE. **2** *informal* also in a spot. In trouble, difficulty, or embarrassment. *Mr. Jones is on the spot because he cannot pay back the money he borrowed.* (Mr. Jones is in trouble because he cannot repay the money.) *Bill is on the spot; he invited George to visit him, but Bill's parents said no.* (Bill is embarrassed because he will have to take back his invitation.) Compare BACK TO THE WALL. **3** *slang* In danger of murder; named or listed for death. *After he talked to the police, the gangsters put him on the spot.* (They decided to murder him.)

on the spur of the moment *adv. phr.* On a sudden wish or decision; suddenly; without thought or preparation. *John had not planned to take the trip; he just left on the spur of the moment.* (John had not planned the trip before; he just suddenly decided to go.) *Mary saw a help-wanted advertisement and applied for the job on the spur of the moment.* (She suddenly decided to try for the job.)

on the stage *adv. or adj. phr.* In or into the work of being an actor or actress. *John's brother is on the stage.* (John's brother is an actor.) *Mary went on the stage.* (Mary became an actress.)

on the strength of *prep.* With faith or trust in; depending upon; with the support of. *On the strength of Jim's promise to guide us, we decided to climb the mountain.* (Because we trusted Jim's promise, we decided to climb the mountain.) *Bill started a restaurant on the strength of his experience as a cook in the army.* (Bill thought he could succeed with a restaurant because he had been a cook in the army.)

on the string *or* **on a string** *adv. phr., informal* Under your influence or control; obedient to every wish.—A cliché. *The baby had his mother on a string.* (The baby's mother was so obedient to his every wish that she ran to him whenever he cried.) *She was pretty and popular, with two or three boys on the string all the time.* (She always had two or three boys in love with her.)

on the tip of one's tongue See AT THE TIP OF ONE'S TONGUE.

on the town *adv. or adj. phr.* **1** Very poor and depending on charity; supported by the town or city.—No longer in common usage. *The father died, so the family has been on the town for years.* (The family receives money and help especially from the town or city government.) **2** *informal* In or into a town to celebrate; having a good time or enjoying the amusements in a town.—A hackneyed phrase. *When the sailors got off their ship they went out on the town.* (The sailors went to have a good time in the town.) Compare PAINT THE TOWN RED.

on the track of *or* **on the trail of** Hunting or looking for; trying to find; following. *The hunter is on the track of a deer.* (The hunter is following a deer in order to shoot him.) *The lawyer is on the trail of new proof in the case.* (The lawyer is looking for new proof to win his case in court.) *Jim collects old stamps; he is on the track of one in Midville this afternoon.* (Jim has gone to Midville to try to buy an old stamp.)

on the trail of See ON THE TRACK OF.

on the trigger See QUICK ON THE TRIGGER.

on the up and up *adj. phr., informal* Honest; trustworthy; sincere. *We felt that he was honest and could be trusted. This information is on the up and up.* (This information can be believed.) Compare ON THE LEVEL.

on the vine See DIE ON THE VINE *or* WITHER ON THE VINE.

on the warpath *adj. phr., informal* **1** Very angry.—A cliché. *When Mother saw the mess in the kitchen she went on the warpath.* (Mother was very angry.) *Betty has been on the warpath ever since she found out she was not invited to the party.* (Betty has been very angry.) **2** Making an attack; fighting.—A cliché. *The government is on the warpath against narcotics.* (The government is fighting against illegal drugs.) *The police are on the warpath against speeders.* (The police are trying to stop drivers from going too fast.)

on the watch *adj. phr.* Alert; watchful. *The customs inspector was on the watch for diamond smugglers.* (He watched carefully for people who bring diamonds into the countries secretly, without paying a tax.) *Mary was on the watch for bargains at the auction.* (Mary was alert to find a bargain.) Compare EYE OUT, LOOK OUT 2.

on the way *or* **on one's way** *adv. or adj. phr.* Coming; going toward a place or goal; started. *Help was on the way.* (Help was coming.) *The train left and Bill was on his way to New York.* (Bill started his trip to New York.) *He is well on the way to becoming a fine mechanic.* (He has started to become a good mechanic.)

on the whole *adv. phr.* **1** In the most important things; in most ways. *On the whole, Billy did very well in school this year.* (Considering everything, Billy did well.) *Everybody agreed that on the whole it was a good show.* (Everybody thought the show was pretty good.) Syn. IN ALL 2, FOR THE MOST PART. **2** In most cases; usually. *On the whole, men are stronger than women.* (Most men are stronger than women.) *On the whole,* *children begin walking when they are about one year old.* (Usually children learn to walk at one.) Syn. BY AND LARGE, IN GENERAL.

on the wing *adv. or adj. phr.* **1** In the air; while flying. *The duck flew away, but John shot it on the wing.* (John shot the duck while it was flying.) **2** *informal* In constant motion; always very busy. *Susan was on the wing doing things to get ready for her trip.* (Susan was very busy getting ready for her trip.) *Mr. Jones had a busy schedule and his secretary had to catch him on the wing to sign the letters.* (Mr. Jones signed the letters while he was rushing about.) Syn. ON THE FLY. **3** *informal* Moving from one place to another; traveling; going somewhere. *Mary's husband is a traveling salesman and he's always on the wing a lot.* (He travels about a lot.) *They stayed in France for a week and then they were on the wing again.* (After spending a week in France they moved on.) Syn. ON THE GO, ON THE MOVE.

on the words See HANG ON THE WORDS OF.

on the wrong foot See GET OFF ON THE WRONG FOOT.

on the wrong side of the bed See GET UP ON THE WRONG SIDE OF THE BED.

on time *adv. or adj. phr.* **1** At the time arranged; not late; promptly. *The train left on time.* (The train left at the time scheduled.) *Mary is always on time for an appointment.* (Mary is never late.) Contrast AHEAD OF TIME, BEHIND TIME. **2** On the installment plan; on credit; paying a little at a time. *John bought a car on time.* (John is paying for his new car on the installment plan.) *You can buy things at the department store on time.* (You can pay for what you buy a little at a time.)

on top *adv. or adj. phr., informal* In the lead; with success; with victory. *The horse that everyone had expected would be on top actually came in third.* (The horse that was expected to win, didn't.) *Although John had been afraid that he was not prepared for the exam, he came out on top.* (John was successful on the exam.)

on top of *prep.* **1** On the top of; standing or lying on; on. *When the player on the other team dropped the ball, Bill fell on top of it.* (Bill fell so that his body covered the ball.) *That high hill has a tower on top of it.* (That hill has a tower standing at its top.) **2** *informal* Very close to. *The elevator was so crowded that everybody was on top of each other.* (People were crowded close together in the elevator.) *I couldn't find my umbrella and then I realized I was almost on top of it.* (I was right next to it.) **3** *informal* In addition to; along with. *Mrs. Lane had many expenses and on top of everything else, her baby became ill.* (In addition to all her other expenses Mrs. Lane now needed a doctor for her baby.) *Mary worked at the store all day and on top of that she had to baby-sit with*

her brother. (In addition to working in the store, Mary had to be a baby-sitter.) **4** *informal* Managing very well; in control of. *Although his new job was very complicated, John was on top of it within a few weeks.* (John was managing his new job very well.) *No matter what goes wrong, Mary always stays on top of it.* (Mary keeps in control.) **4** Knowing all about; not falling behind in information about; up-to-date on. *Mary stays on top of the news by reading newspapers and magazines.* (Mary keeps up with the news.) *When he was in California, Mr. Jones kept on top of things in his office by telephoning every day.* (Mr. Jones kept up-to-date about his office affairs.)

on top of the world *or* **sitting on top of the world** *also* (*Southern*) **sitting on high cotton** *adj. phr., informal* Feeling pleased and happy; feeling successful.—A cliché. *John was on top of the world when he found out that he got into college.* (John was pleased and happy.) *When Ruth won first prize in the contest, she felt as though she was sitting on top of the world.* (Ruth felt very successful.) *The girls were sitting on high cotton because their basketball team had won the trophy.* (They were very happy.) Compare FLYING HIGH, WALK ON AIR.

on trial *adv. or adj. phr.* **1** For testing or trying out for a time before making a decision. *I was lucky that I had bought the machine on trial because I didn't like it and was able to return it.* (I bought the machine with the agreement that I could try it out and return it if I didn't like it.) *Mother bought a new dishwasher on trial and was trying it out before deciding whether to keep it.* (Mother had a certain amount of time to test the dishwasher.) **2** In a court being tried for a crime before a judge or jury. *John White was on trial for murder.* (He was accused of murder and was being judged in court.) *Mary was on trial before the Student Committee for spoiling school property.* (The Student Committee was judging Mary.)

on words See PLAY ON WORDS.

on your life See NOT ON YOUR LIFE.

open See EYES OPEN, THROW OPEN.

open arms See RECEIVE WITH OPEN ARMS.

open fire *v. phr.* To begin shooting. *The big warship turned its guns toward the enemy ship and opened fire.* (The warship began to shoot its guns at the other ship.) *When the policeman called to the robber to stop, he turned and suddenly opened fire.* (The robber began to shoot at the policeman.)

open heart *n.* **1** No hiding of your feelings; frankness, freedom.—A trite expression. *She spoke with an open heart of her warm feelings for her pupils.* (She did not hide her feelings.) *She told her troubles with an open heart.* (She told her troubles frankly.) Compare HEART ON ONE'S SLEEVE. **2** Kindness, generosity.—A trite expression. *She contributed* *to the fund with an open heart.* (She was very generous.) *Mr. Jones has an open heart for underprivileged children.* (Mr. Jones is very kind to poor children.) Compare OPEN ONE'S HEART.

open its doors *v. phr.* **1** To allow someone or something to enter or join; become open. *That college was started for women only, but a few years ago it opened its doors to men.* (The college now also takes men as students.) **2** To begin doing business; open. *Proffitts Department Store is having a birthday sale; it first opened its doors fifty years ago this month.* (The store first began selling things fifty years ago.) Contrast CLOSE ITS DOORS.

open one's eyes *or* **open up one's eyes** *v. phr.* To make a person see or understand the truth; make a person realize; tell a person what is really happening or what really exists. *Mary didn't believe that her cousin could be mean until the cousin opened Mary's eyes by scratching and biting her.* (Mary found out the truth about her cousin when her cousin scratched and bit her.) *John's eyes were opened up to the world of nature when he visited his grandfather's farm.* Compare EYES OPEN, WISE UP.—**eye opener** *n.* Something that makes you understand the truth. *Pam's first visit to school was a real eye-opener.* (When Pam first visited the school, she saw many things she had never seen before.)

open one's heart *v. phr.* **1** To talk about your feelings honestly; confide in someone. —A cliché. *After going around worrying, Mary opened her heart to her mother.* (Mary told her mother all about her worries.) *John felt much better after he opened his heart to Betty.* (John talked frankly to Betty.) **2** To be sympathetic to; give love or help generously.—A cliché. *Mrs. Smith opened her heart to the poor little boy.* (She loved him and was kind to him.) *After the moving speech by the UN official, the people opened their hearts to the poor people of India.* (The people gave generously.) Compare OPEN HEART, WEAR ONE'S HEART ON ONE'S SLEEVE.

open secret *n.* Something that is supposed to be a secret but that everyone knows. *It is an open secret that Mary and John are engaged.* (Mary and John's engagement is supposed to be a secret but everyone knows about it.) *Who will be appointed as the next president of the college is an open secret.* (Everyone knows who will be the next president even though it has not yet been announced.)

open the door *v. phr.* To allow more action or discussion; give a chance. *Learning to read and write opens the door to a better job and better living conditions.* (People who can read and write can get better jobs and more money than people who cannot read or write.) *Raising the tax rates will open the door to more help for older people.* (With more tax money,

more help can be given the older people.) Contrast CLOSE THE DOOR. Compare OPEN ITS DOORS.

open up *v.* **1** To show for the first time; make clear; reveal. *The story of Helen Keller's life opened up a whole new world to Mary.* (When Mary read about Helen Keller, she began to think about many new things.) *Einstein's theories opened up a whole new area for study.* (Einstein's theories started a new scientific search for facts.) **2** To make available; present an opportunity; offer. *The building of the railroad opened up new lands to the pioneers.* (Pioneers could go to land people could not live on before.) *John opened up a whole new section of the Scrabble board.* (John's word started a new section.) **3** *informal* To go faster. *When they got out on the highway John opened up and drove at 65 miles per hour.* (John drove faster out on the highway.) **4** *informal* To begin to shoot. *When they got close to the enemy lines, they opened up with all they had.* (They fired all their guns.) **5** *informal* To begin to talk frankly. *After John learned to trust Mr. Jones, he opened up and told him how he felt.* (John talked frankly when he trusted Mr. Jones.) **6** To spread out. *After a while the road opened up and they traveled more quickly.* (The road became wider.) **7** To become available. *When she got her college diploma, many new jobs opened up.* (Many jobs were possible for her.)

open up one's eyes See OPEN ONE'S EYES.

opinion See MATTER OF OPINION.

optional origin *n.* Stipulation in international commodities contract whereby the seller may ship from either his foreign or his domestic resources. *Be sure to enter that in the books as an optional origin order.* (Indicate that we can ship either from abroad or from the U.S.)

orbit See GO INTO ORBIT.

order See APPLE-PIE-ORDER, CALL TO ORDER, IN ORDER, IN ORDER TO, IN SHORT ORDER, JUST WHAT THE DOCTOR ORDERED, MADE TO ORDER, OUT OF ORDER, PUT ONE'S HOUSE IN ORDER *or* SET ONE'S HOUSE IN ORDER, SHORT ORDER COOK, TO ORDER, WALKING PAPERS *or* WALKING ORDERS.

ordinary See OUT OF THE ORDINARY.

or other *adv.* —Used to emphasize indefinite words or phrases beginning with *some* (as *someone, something, somewhere, somehow, sometime*). *Somehow or other, Linda managed to get to the show on time.* (Even though it was difficult Linda found a way to get there on time.) *I'll think of something or other for the program.* (I'll get some idea for the program.) *She found a beautiful cup and saucer somewhere or other.* (She found it someplace.) *I'll get around to cleaning the closets sometime or other.* (I'll do it someday.) *Someone or other will take the letters to the post office.* (They will be taken to the post office by someone.)

or so *adv.* About; or a little more. *Mr. Brown will be back in a day or so.* (He will be back in about a day.) *The book cost $5 or so.* (It cost about $5.) *There will be twenty or so people at the party.* (There will be about 20 people.) Compare MORE OR LESS.

other See EACH OTHER, EVERY OTHER, GRASS IS ALWAYS GREENER ON THE OTHER SIDE OF THE FENCE *or* GRASS IS ALWAYS GREENER ON THE OTHER SIDE OF THE HILL, GO IN ONE EAR AND OUT THE OTHER, LAUGH ON THE WRONG SIDE OF ONE'S MOUTH *or* LAUGH ON THE OTHER SIDE OF ONE'S MOUTH, ON THE OTHER HAND, OR OTHER, SHOE ON THE OTHER FOOT, SIX OF ONE AND HALF-A-DOZEN OF THE OTHER, THIS AND THAT *also* THIS, THAT, AND THE OTHER, TURN THE OTHER CHEEK.

other fish to fry *n. phr., informal* Other things to do; other plans.—A cliché. *They wanted John to be the secretary, but he had other fish to fry.* (John had other plans.) *Mary was invited to the party but she refused because she had other fish to fry.* (Mary had something else to do.)

other side of the tracks See WRONG SIDE OF THE TRACKS.

out-and-out *adj.* Extreme; complete; thorough. *The candidate was an out-and-out conservative.* (The candidate was extremely conservative.) *It was out-and-out robbery to charge twice the usual price for eggs just because they were scarce.* (To charge so much is complete robbery.) Compare THROUGH AND THROUGH.

out cold *adv.* or *adj., informal* Unconscious; in a faint. *The ball hit Dick in the head and knocked him out cold for ten minutes.* (Dick was unconscious for ten minutes.) *They tried to lift Mary when she fell down, but she was out cold.* (Mary fainted after her fall.) Syn. OUT LIKE A LIGHT 2. Compare PASS OUT.

outer space *n.* What is outside of the earth's air. *An astronaut cannot live without oxygen when he goes into outer space.* (An astronaut carries oxygen to breathe in the space outside the earth's air.)

out for *prep.* Joining, or planning to join; taking part in; competing for a place in. *John is out for the basketball team.* (John is trying to get on the basketball team.) *Mary is going out for the school newspaper.* (Mary wants to work on the school newspaper.) Compare TRY OUT.

out from under *adj. phr., informal* Free from something that worries you; seeing the end; finished.—Usually used with *be* or *get*. *Mary had so much to do in the new house, she felt as though she would never be out from under.* (Mary felt as though she would never finish her work.) *John had so many debts, he couldn't get out from under.* (John couldn't get rid of his debts.)

out in left field *adj. phr., informal* Far from the right answer; wrong; astray.—A cliché.

Johnny tried to answer the teacher's question, but he was way out in left field. (Johnny's answer was all wrong.) *Susan tried to guess what the surprise was but she was way out in left field.* (Susan was nowhere near the right answer.) **2** Speaking or acting very queerly; crazy. *The girl next door was always queer, but after her father died, she was really out in left field and had to go to a hospital.* (The girl became insane.) Compare OUT OF ONE'S HEAD.

out in the cold *adj. phr., informal* Alone; not included.—A cliché. *All the other children were chosen for parts in the play, but Johnny was left out in the cold.* (Johnny was not invited to take part in the play.) *Everybody made plans for Christmas Day and Mary found herself out in the cold.* (Mary was all alone on Christmas Day.) Compare HIGH AND DRY.

out like a light *adj. phr., informal* **1** Fast asleep; to sleep very quickly. *Tom got so much fresh air and exercise that he went out like a light as soon as he lay down.* (He fell fast asleep right away.) *As soon as the lights were turned off, Johnny was out like a light.* (Johnny fell asleep very quickly.) **2** In a faint; unconscious.—A cliché. *Johnny was hit by a ball and went out like a light.* (Johnny fainted when he was hit by a ball.) *After she read that Tom had married another girl, Jean was out like a light for several minutes.* (Jean was in a faint for several minutes.) Compare OUT COLD.

out loud *adv. phr.* In an ordinary speaking voice and not whispering or talking quietly; so everybody can hear; aloud. *The teacher read the final grades out loud.* (The teacher told the grades so that the whole class could hear.) *Mary spoke out loud so the people standing nearby would hear.* (Mary purposely spoke in a loud voice.) *Sometimes I find it helpful to think out loud.* (Sometimes I say my thoughts aloud.)

out of *prep.* **1a** From the inside to the outside of. *John took the apple out of the bag.* (He removed it from the bag.) *Get out of the car!* (Leave the inside of the car.) *The teacher has gone out of town.* (He left town for some other place.) **1b** In a place away from. *No, you can't see Mr. Jones; he is out of the office today.* (Mr. Jones is not in the office today.) *Our house is ten miles out of town.* (Our house is ten miles away from town.) **2** From a particular condition or situation; not in; from; in a way changed from being in. *The drugstore is going out of business.* (It will not be a store any more.) *The sick man is out of danger at last.* (He is no longer dangerously ill.) *Bob is never out of trouble.* (He is always in trouble with someone.) **3** Beyond the range of. *The plane is out of sight now.* (We can no longer see it.) *If you can't swim, don't go out of your depth.* (Don't go beyond the depth at which your head is above water.) **4** From (a source). *Mothe asked Billy who started the fight, but she couldn't get anything out of him.* (Mother learned nothing from Billy.) *The teacher gave a test to see what the students got out of the lesson.* (The teacher wanted to find out what the students learned from the lesson.) *Mr. Jones made a fortune out of cotton.* (He made much money through work with cotton.) **5** Because of; as a result of. *Mary scolded Joan out of jealousy.* (Mary scolded Joan because she was jealous of Joan.) *The cat ran away out of fear of the dog.* (The cat ran away because she was afraid.) **6** Without; not having. *The store is out of coffee.* (The store has no coffee.) *John's father is out of work.* (He is without work.) **7** From (a material). *The house is built out of stone.* (It is made from stone.) *His suit is made out of cotton and is cool.* (The suit is made from cotton.) **8** From among. *The man picked Joe out of the crowd.* (He chose Joe from among the crowd.) *Our team won eight out of ten games last season.* (The team played ten games and won eight of them.)

out of a bandbox See LOOK AS IF ONE HAS COME OUT OF A BANDBOX.

out of account See LEAVE OUT OF ACCOUNT.

out of a clear sky *or* **out of a clear blue sky** See OUT OF THE BLUE.

out of bounds *adv. or adj. phr.* **1** Outside of the boundary lines in a game; not on or inside the playing field. *Bill thought he had scored a touchdown, but he had stepped out of bounds before he reached the goal line.* (Bill stepped outside of the field and his touchdown was not allowed.) **2** Outside of the place where you may go; in or to a forbidden place. *The principal told the students that the new gymnasium being built on the school grounds was out of bounds.* (Students were not allowed to go into or near the gymnasium that was being built.) *The captain's cabin is out of bounds to the passengers on the ship.* (Passengers are forbidden to go into the captain's cabin.) Contrast WITHIN BOUNDS. **3** Outside of safe or proper limits; not doing what is proper; breaking the rules of good behavior. *John was out of bounds when he called Tom a liar in the meeting.* (He broke the rules of debate and went too far.)

out of breath *adj. or adv. phr.* Not breathing easily or regularly; gasping; panting. *The fat man was out of breath after climbing the stairs.* (The fat man was gasping for breath after the hard exercise.) *The mile run left Bill out of breath.* (He was breathing hard and fast at the end of the run.)

out of character *adv. or adj. phr.* **1** Not in agreement with a person's character or personality; not in the way that a person usually behaves or is expected to behave; not usual; unsuitable; uncharacteristic. *Mary is a nice*

girl. Her fit of temper was out of character. (Mary is really a nice girl and doesn't get angry.) **2** Not in character; unsuitable for a part or character. *It isn't always out of character for a young actor to play an old man, if he is a good actor.* (Sometimes a young actor can act the part of an old man if he acts well.) Contrast IN CHARACTER.

out of circulation *adj. phr., informal* Not out in the company of friends, other people, and groups; not active; not joining in what others are doing. *John has a job after school and is out of circulation with his friends.* (He can't be with his friends so much.) Contrast IN CIRCULATION.

out of commission *adj. phr.* **1** Retired from active military service; no longer on active duty. *When the war was over, many warships were placed out of commission.* (The ships were stored away or sold for scrap iron after the war because they were no longer needed.) Contrast IN COMMISSION 1. **2** Not in use or not working; so that it cannot work or be used. *The strike put the airline out of commission for a week.* (The airline could not do business for a week.) *John will have to walk to the store. His bicycle is out of commission.* (John's bicycle is broken, and he can't use it.) Compare OUT OF ORDER. Contrast IN COMMISSION 2.

out of condition See OUT OF SHAPE *or* OUT OF CONDITION.

out of date *adj. phr.* Too old to be used. *Father's suit is out of date; he needs a new one.* (His suit is in a style men are not wearing now.) *The news magazines in the doctor's office were all out of date.* (The magazines told about events that happened too long ago to be of interest.)

out of gear See THROW OUT OF GEAR.

out of hand *adv. phr.* **1** Out of control. *Bobby's birthday party got out of hand and the children were naughty.* (The children were naughty and out of control at the party.) *Small puppies often get out of hand.* (Puppies often do bad things and do not obey their master.) **2** Suddenly, quickly without examination of possible truth or merit; without any consideration.—Often used after *dismiss* or *reject*. *The senator rejected out of hand the critics' call for his resignation.* (He did not for a moment consider resigning.) Compare OUT OF LINE. Contrast IN HAND.

out of hot water See HOT WATER.

out of keeping *adj. phr.* Not going well together; not agreeing; not proper. *Loud talk was out of keeping in the library.* (Talking out loud was usually against the rules in the library.) *It was out of keeping for the kind man to kick the dog.* (Men who are kind do not hurt animals.) Contrast IN KEEPING.

out of kilter *adj. phr., informal* **1** Not balanced right; not in a straight line or lined up right. *The scale must be out of kilter because* *when I weighed myself on it, it said 300 pounds.* (The scale doesn't balance properly and doesn't weigh correctly.) *The wheels of my bicycle were out of kilter after it hit the tree.* (The wheels were crooked and wouldn't roll straight.) Contrast IN BALANCE. **2** Needing repair; not working right. *My watch runs too slowly; it must be out of kilter.* (My watch must need to be fixed.) Syn. OUT OF ORDER 2.

out of line[1] *adv. phr.* Not in a straight line; away from a true line. *The two edges were out of line and there was a space between them.* (The two edges did not fit snugly together.) *The sergeant ordered the soldier who was out of line to get properly lined up.* (The sergeant ordered the soldier to get into the same line with the other men.)

out of line[2] *adj. phr.* Not obeying or agreeing with what is right or usual; doing or being what people do not expect or accept; outside ordinary or proper limits; not usual, right, or proper. *Little Mary got out of line and was rude to Aunt Elizabeth.* (Mary broke the rules of politeness; she was naughty.) *The teacher asked Charlie not to tell one of the jokes because it was out of line.* (The teacher said the joke was not proper.) *Mrs. Green thought the repair man's charge was out of line.* (She thought he asked for too much money.) Compare OUT OF HAND, OUT OF ORDER. Contrast IN LINE 2.

out of line with *prep.* Not in agreement with. *The price of the bicycle was out of line with what Bill could afford.* (The price was higher than Bill could afford.)

out of luck *adj. phr.* Being unlucky; having bad luck; having something bad happen to you. *Mr. Jones missed his train and was out of luck in getting to the ball game on time.* (Mr. Jones missed his train and couldn't get to the ball game on time as he wanted.) *All of the girls had dates so Ben was out of luck.* (Ben could not get a partner because all the girls had dates.)

out of mind See OUT OF SIGHT, OUT OF MIND.

out of nowhere *adv. phr.* Without having been seen before; suddenly and unexpectedly. *Mr. Jones was driving too fast on the express highway when a police patrol car appeared out of nowhere and stopped him.* (Mr. Jones did not see the police car coming; suddenly it was there.) Syn. OUT OF THE BLUE.

out of one's blood *adv. phr.* Separate from one's feelings, interests, or desires.—A cliché. *When Tom moved to the city, he couldn't get the country out of his blood.* (When Tom moved to the city, he wished that he still lived in the country.) *Mary is having a hard job getting summer laziness out of her blood.* (Mary is having trouble getting to work again after being lazy all summer.) Contrast IN ONE'S BLOOD.

out of one's element *adv. phr.* Outside of your natural surroundings; where you do not belong or fit in. *Wild animals are out of their element in cages.* (Wild animals are not happy in cages. They like to run free.) *Chris is out of his element in singing class.* (Chris can't sing and does not like to sing.) Compare OUT OF PLACE, BEYOND ONE'S DEPTH. Contrast IN ONE'S ELEMENT.

out of one's hair *adj. phr., informal* Rid of as a nuisance; relieved of as an annoyance. *Harry got the boys out of his hair so he could study.* (Harry sent the boys away so they wouldn't bother him.) Compare OUT OF ONE'S WAY. Contrast IN ONE'S HAIR.

out of one's hand See EAT OUT OF ONE'S HAND.

out of one's head *or* **out of one's mind** *or* **out of one's senses** *also* **off one's head** *adj. phr., informal* Acting in a crazy way; especially; wildly crazy. *The patient was feverish and out of his head and had to be watched.* (The patient was wild and did not know what he was doing.) *Her friends thought she was out of her mind to marry that man.* (Her friends thought she was crazy to marry him, because he was not a good match.) Compare OFF ONE'S ROCKER. Contrast COME TO ONE'S SENSES.

out of one's mind See OUT OF ONE'S HEAD.

out of one's mouth See TAKE THE BREAD OUT OF ONE'S MOUTH, TAKE THE WORDS OUT OF ONE'S MOUTH.

out of one's sails See TAKE THE WIND OUT OF ONE'S SAILS.

out of one's senses See OUT OF ONE'S HEAD.

out of one's shell *adv. phr., informal* Out of one's bashfulness or silence; into friendly conversation.—Usually used after *come*. *John wouldn't come out of his shell and talk to the boys and girls at the party.* (John was very bashful at the party.) *The other girls tried to draw Ella out of her shell, but without success.* (They tried to get her to join in the talk and fun.) Contrast IN ONE'S SHELL.

out of one's skin See JUMP OUT OF ONE'S SKIN.

out of one's way See OUT OF THE WAY 3.

out of one's wits See SCARE OUT OF ONE'S WITS.

out of order *adv. or adj. phr.* **1** In the wrong order; not coming after one another in the right way. *Peter wrote the words of the sentence out of order.* (Peter wrote the words in the wrong places; he wrote "Like children cream ice," but he should have written "Children like ice cream.") *Don't get out of order, children. Stay in your places in line.* (Stay where you are in line and follow one another properly.) Contrast IN ORDER. **2** In poor condition; not working properly. *Our television set is out of order.* (Our television set is not working properly.) **3** Against the rules; not suitable. *The judge told the people in the courtroom that they were out of order because they were so noisy.* (The people were not obeying the rules of the court to be quiet.)

The children's whispering was out of order in the church. (The children's behavior was not suitable for church.) Compare OUT OF LINE, OUT OF PLACE, OUT OF THE WAY, OUT OF TURN, OUT OF COMMISSION 2. Contrast IN ORDER.

out of place[1] *adv. phr.* Not in the right or usual place or position. *Harry fell and knocked one of his teeth out of place.* (Harry's tooth was moved from its right place; it was knocked crooked.) *The teacher lined up the class and told them not to get out of place.* (The teacher told the students to stay in their right places in line.) Compare OUT OF ORDER. Contrast IN PLACE.

out of place[2] *adj. phr.* In the wrong place or at the wrong time; not suitable; improper. *Joan was the only girl who wore a formal at the party, and she felt out of place.* (She felt embarrassed because her dress was not suitable for the party.) *It was out of place for Russell to laugh at the old lady.* (It was not proper; he should not have done it.) Compare OUT OF ONE'S ELEMENT, OUT OF ORDER, OUT OF THE WAY. Contrast IN PLACE.

out of practice *adj. phr.* Not in proper condition; unable to do something well because of lack of practice. *The basketball team got out of practice during the Christmas holidays.* (The basketball team did not practice during the holidays so they cannot play as well as usual.) Compare OUT OF SHAPE. Contrast IN PRACTICE.

out of print *adj. phr.* No longer obtainable from the publisher because the printed copies have been sold out; no longer printed. *The book is out of print. An edition of one thousand copies was sold and no more copies were printed.* (The book is not being printed any longer and all the copies have been sold.) Compare OUT OF STOCK. Contrast IN PRINT.

out of school See TELL TALES OUT OF SCHOOL.

out of season *adv. phr.* 1 Not at the right or lawful time for hunting or catching. *The boys were caught fishing out of season.* (The boys were caught fishing at a time when it was not allowed.) 2 Not at the usual time for growing and selling. *The corn we get out of season is different from the kind we grow here.* (The corn we buy after corn is no longer grown and sold in our section of the country tastes and looks different.) Contrast IN SEASON.

out of shape *or* **out of condition** *adj. phr.* 1 Not in good condition; not able to perform well. *Father was out of shape when he took a long hike with the boys, and he was stiff and sore the next day.* (Father had not walked enough before the hike, and his muscles were not ready for so much use.) *Jack's pitching arm got out of condition during the winter, when he wasn't using it.* (After Jack had not pitched all winter, he could not pitch as well.) Compare OUT OF PRACTICE. 2 Not look the same; changed. *Someone sat on father's*

new hat and mashed it. It is now out of shape. (Father's hat is flat. Sitting on it changed its shape.) Contrast IN SHAPE.

out of sight *adj., slang, informal* 1 Extraordinarily expensive; beyond one's means. *The houses in this neighborhood are just out of sight.* (The houses are so expensive that no one can afford to buy one.) 2 Unbelievable; fantastic; incredible (both in the positive and the negative sense; an exaggeration.) *Roxanne is such a stunning beauty, it's simply out of sight.* (Roxanne is so beautiful that it seems incredible.) *Mr. Gargoyle is so repulsive, it's out of sight.* (It's unbelievable anyone can look so ugly.) 3 Unreachable, unrealizable, belonging to the world of fiction and fantasy. *Max's dreams about winning the Senatorial election are really out of sight; he admits it himself.* (Max's dreams cannot be realized, and he knows it.) Compare PIPE DREAM.

out of sorts *adj. phr.* In an angry or unhappy mood; in a bad temper; grouchy. *Mary was out of sorts and wouldn't say good morning.* (Mary was grouchy and wouldn't talk to anyone.) *Bob was out of sorts because he didn't get a bicycle for his birthday.* (Bob was mad because he didn't get a bicycle for his birthday.)

out of step *adv. or adj. phr.* 1 Not in step; not matching strides or keeping pace with another or others. *George always marches out of step with the music.* (George doesn't march evenly with the others marching or in time to the music.) 2 Out of harmony; not keeping up.—Often followed by *with*. *Just because you don't smoke, it doesn't mean you are out of step with other boys and girls your age.* (Even if you don't smoke, it doesn't mean you are not keeping up with other boys and girls.) Contrast IN STEP.

out of stock *adj. phr.* Having none for sale or use; no longer in supply; sold out. *When Father tried to get tires for an old car, the man in the store said that size was out of stock and were not sold anymore.* (The tires were of an old kind and the store did not sell them anymore.) *So many children have bought balloons that the store is now out of stock.* (The store has sold all its balloons but will get more to sell.) Compare OUT OF PRINT. Contrast IN STOCK.

out of the blue *or* **out of a clear sky** *or* **out of a clear blue sky** *adv. phr., informal* Without any warning; by surprise; unexpectedly. —A cliché. *At the last minute Johnny came out of the blue to catch the pass and score a touchdown.* (No one expected him to catch the pass.) *The cowboy thought he was alone but suddenly out of a clear sky there were Indians all around him.* (The Indians were so quiet that they surprised the cowboy.) Syn. OUT OF NOWHERE. Compare BOLT FROM THE BLUE.

out of the corner of one's eye *adv. phr.*

Without looking at a person or thing directly or openly; secretly; without being noticed.— A cliché. *The cat looked at the mouse out of the corner of his eye.* (The cat did not seem to be looking at the mouse, but he was.) *Mike watched the boys across the street out of the corner of his eye as he mowed the lawn.* (Mike didn't look right at the boys, but he was watching them.)

out of the frying pan into the fire Out of one trouble into worse trouble; from something bad to something worse.—A proverb. *The movie cowboy was out of the frying pan into the fire. After he escaped from the robbers, he was captured by Indians.* (The cowboy got out of one danger into another.)

out of the hole *adv. or adj. phr., informal* **1a** With a score better than zero in a game, especially a card game, to a score above zero. *It took us a long time to get out of the hole in the card game.* (We had lost more points than we had earned, so we had a score below zero, and it took us a long time to earn enough points to raise our score above zero again.) **1b** Even with an opponent after being behind; out of trouble in a sport or game. *The team played very hard, but could not get out of the hole.* (The other team still had a higher score.) **2** Out of debt; ahead financially. *It was a small business, but it was wisely managed, and it kept out of the hole.* (It kept out of debt.) *The first year was bad, but after that Fred got out of the hole.* (He got out of debt.) Contrast IN THE HOLE.

out of the ordinary *adj. phr.* Outside or beyond common experience; unusual; wonderful; extraordinary. *The parade will be something out of the ordinary because a real king will be there.* (The parade will not be like usual parades because a king will be there.) *This juggler was out of the ordinary because he could juggle with his feet as well as his hands.* (The juggler was unusually good.)

out of the question *adj. phr.* Not worth considering; unthinkable; impossible. *It sometimes snows as late as June in the mountains, but the summer campers thought that snow was out of the question.* (They did not even consider that it might snow and didn't prepare for it.) *The boys had no money, so it was out of the question for them to go to the movies.* (It was not possible to go to the movies without money.)

out of the rain See KNOW ENOUGH TO COME IN OUT OF THE RAIN.

out of the running · *adj. or adv. phr.* Having no chance to win; not among the real contenders; not among those to be considered. *John had been out of the running since his first date with Mary, but he didn't realize it.* (Mary hadn't taken him seriously from the beginning.) *Jones's horse was put out of the running early in the race.* (He was left too far behind to catch up.) Contrast IN THE

RUNNING.

out of the swim *adj. phr.* Not doing what others are doing; not active in business or social affairs. *Mary had to stay home and take care of Mother while she was sick, and soon felt out of the swim.* (Mary felt left out of her usual good times with her friends.) *The toy manufacturer who is out of the swim will lose money.* (The toy maker who does not follow the fashions will not sell his toys.) Contrast IN THE SWIM.

out of the way *adv. phr.* **1** Not where people usually go; difficult to reach. *When little Tommy comes to visit her, Aunt Sally puts her lamps and vases out of the way.* (Aunt Sally puts the things that Tommy might break in a place where he can't get at them.)— Often used with hyphens before a noun. *Gold was found in an out-of-the-way village in the mountains, and soon a good road and airfield were built.* (Gold was found in a mountain village that was hard to get to.) *Jack and Fred found an old gun in an out-of-the-way corner of the empty house.* (Jack and Fred found a gun in a place where people do not usually go.) Compare OFF THE BEATEN TRACK. **2** Not what is usual or proper, strange. *To leave before the guest of honor would be out of the way.* (That would be impolite.) *I'm sorry if I said something out of the way.* (I'm sorry if I said something wrong.) *The night watchman looked around the building, but he saw nothing out of the way.* (He saw nothing strange.) Compare OUT OF PLACE. **3** *or* **out of one's way** Not able to stop or bother you. *Tommy wished the visitors were out of the way so that he could have the candy for himself.* (Tommy wished the visitors would go home.) Compare OUT OF ONE'S HAIR, PUT OUT OF THE WAY.

out of the woods See CROW BEFORE ONE IS OUT OF THE WOODS.

out of thin air *adv. phr.* Out of nothing or from nowhere.—A cliché. *The teacher scolded Dick because his story was made out of thin air.* (Dick's story was not based on facts or knowledge.) *On the way home from town, Tom saw a house standing on the lot that had been empty that morning; it seemed to have appeared out of thin air.* (The house seemed to have come suddenly from nowhere, because it was built so quickly.) Compare INTO THIN AIR.

out of this world *adj. phr., slang* Wonderfully good or satisfying; terrific; super.—A cliché. *The dress in the store window was out of this world!* (The dress was very beautiful.) *Mother was on TV last night. Isn't that out of this world?* (Isn't that thrilling?)

out of touch *adj., phr.* Not writing or talking with each other; not getting news any more. *Fred had got out of touch with people in his home town.* (He no longer visited them or wrote them letters, or got letters from them.) *On his island Robinson Crusoe was* *out of touch with world news.* (He didn't know any news.) Compare LOSE TOUCH, LOSE TRACK. Contrast IN TOUCH.

out of tune   *adv. or adj. phr.*   **1** Out of proper musical pitch; too low or high in sound. *The band sounded terrible, because the instruments were out of tune.* (The band didn't sound right because they didn't play in the same key.) **2** Not in agreement; in disagreement; not going well together.—Often used with *with.* *What Jack said was out of tune with how he looked; he said he was happy, but he looked unhappy.* (His looks didn't agree with his words.) Compare OFF-KEY. Contrast IN TUNE.

out of turn   *adv. phr.*   **1** Not in regular order; at the wrong time. *John played out of turn.* (He played when it was time for someone else.) *By taking a day off out of turn, Bob got the schedule mixed up.* (He upset the time arrangements for others when he didn't come to work on his day.) **2** Too hastily or wrongly; at the wrong time or place; so as to annoy others. *Dick loses friends by speaking out of turn.* (He is too quick to blame or boast.)

out of wedlock   See BORN OUT OF WEDLOCK.

out of whack   *adj. phr., slang*   **1** Needing repair; not working right. *Ben was glad the lawn mower got out of whack, because he didn't have to mow the lawn.* (Ben was glad the lawn mower did not work.) Syn. OUT OF ORDER. **2** Not going together well; not in agreement.—Used with *with* or with two subjects. *The things Mr. Black does are out of whack with what he says.* (The things Mr. Black does do not agree with the things that he says.) *George's earnings and his spending were out of whack.* (George spent more than he earned.) Compare OUT OF LINE.

out on a limb   *adv. phr.*   With your beliefs and opinions openly stated; in a dangerous position that can't be changed.—A cliché. *The President went out on a limb and supported a foreign aid bill that many people were against.* (The President came out openly for the foreign aid bill even though many people were against it.) *Grandfather went out on a limb before the summer was over and said that the next winter would be long and cold with many snowstorms.* (Grandfather took a chance and told just what he thought the winter would be like.)

outside of   *prep.*   **1** Not in; outside. *I would not want to meet a lion outside of a zoo.* (I would not want to meet a lion that was not shut in a zoo.) Contrast INSIDE OF. **2** Except for; not including. *Outside of Johnny, all the boys on the basketball team are over six feet tall.* (Johnny is the only boy on the basketball team who is not six feet tall.) *Mrs. Cox had no jewelry outside of her wedding ring.* (The only jewelry she had was her wedding ring.) Syn. APART FROM.

out to lunch   *adj., slang, informal*   **1** Gone for the midday meal. **2** Inattentive, daydreaming, inefficient, stupid. *Neil Bender is just out to lunch today.* (He is very absent-minded.)

over a barrel *also* **over the barrel**   *adv. phr., informal*   In the power of your enemies; not able to do anything about what happens to you; in a helpless condition; trapped.—A cliché. *Bill had Tom over a barrel because Tom owed him money.* (Tom was in Bill's power.) *Ralph has me over a barrel; I need five dollars, and he won't lend it to me unless I let him use my bicycle.* (I don't want to lend Ralph my bicycle, but I must, because I need the five dollars.) Compare ON THE ROPES.

over age   *adj. phr.*   Too old; not young enough; above the legal age. *Grandfather wanted to fight in World War II, but he could not because he was over age.* (Grandfather was above the age that could enter the army, according to the law.) Contrast UNDER AGE.

overboard   See GO OFF THE DEEP END *or* GO OVERBOARD.

over one's head   *adv. or adj. phr.*   **1** Not understandable; beyond your ability to understand; too hard or strange for you to understand. *Mary laughed just to be polite, but the joke was really over her head.* (Mary didn't understand the joke.) *The lesson today was hard; it went over my head.* (I did not understand the lesson.) Compare BEYOND ONE'S DEPTH. **2** To a more important person in charge; to a higher official. *When Mary's supervisor said no, Mary went over her head to the person in charge of the whole department.* (Mary went to a bigger boss.) *If Johnny can't get what he wants from his big sister, he goes over her head and asks his mother.* (Johnny goes to his mother for what he wants without his sister's permission.) **3** See HANG OVER ONE'S HEAD.

over spilled milk   See CRY OVER SPILLED MILK.

over the coals   See HAUL OVER THE COALS *or* RAKE OVER THE COALS.

over the hill   *adj., informal*   Past one's prime, unable to function as one used to, senile. *Poor Mr. Catwallender is sure not like he used to be; well, he's over the hill.* (He is getting old and weak.)

over the hump   *adj. phr., informal*   Past the most difficult part; past the crisis; out of danger. *Mary was failing math, but she is over the hump now.* (Mary is doing all right in math now.) *John was very sick after his accident, but he's over the hump.* (John is out of danger.) *When Mr. Smith was out of work it looked as if his family would have to go on relief, but they got over the hump.* (They got past the difficult time.)

over the top   *adv. phr.*   **1** Out of the trenches and against the enemy. *The plan was to spend the night in the trenches and go over the top at dawn.* (The plan was to attack at dawn.)

Johnny found that he was braver than he thought he would be when his company went over the top. (Johnny was brave when he started to attack.) **2** Over the goal. *Our goal was to collect a half a million dollars for the new school building, but we went over the top.* (We collected more than our goal of half a million dollars.) *Mary was asked to sell twenty tickets, and she went over the top.* (Mary sold more than twenty tickets.)

over the traces See KICK OVER THE TRACES.

over with¹ *prep.* At the end of; finished with; through with. *They were over with the meeting by ten o'clock.* (They were finished by ten.) *By Saturday Mary will be over with the measles.* (Mary will be finished having the measles by Saturday; she will be well by then.)

over with² *adj., informal* At an end; finished. *John knew his mother would scold him for losing the money, and he wanted to get it over with.* (John wanted to be through with the scolding.) *After the hard test, Jerry said,* *"I'm glad that's over with!"* (Jerry felt glad that it was finished.)

own See OF ONE'S OWN ACCORD *or* OF ONE'S OWN FREE WILL, COME INTO ONE'S OWN, DOSE OF ONE'S OWN MEDICINE, HOLD ONE'S OWN, IN A WORLD OF ONE'S OWN, KEEP ONE'S OWN COUNSEL, ON ONE'S OWN ACCOUNT *or* ON ONE'S OWN HOOK, ON ONE'S OWN TIME, SIGN ONE'S OWN DEATH WARRANT, TAKE THE LAW INTO ONE'S OWN HANDS, UNDER ONE'S OWN STEAM.

own up *v., informal* To take the blame; admit your guilt; confess. *When Mr. Jones asked who broke the window, Johnny owned up.* (Johnny admitted that he broke the window.) *Mary owned up to having borrowed her sister's sweater.* (Mary confessed that she borrowed the sweater.) *When Mother saw that someone had broken the vase, Billy owned up to it.* (Billy took the blame for breaking the vase.)

oyster See WORLD IS ONE'S OYSTER.

P

p. See MIND ONE'S P'S AND Q'S.

pace See CHANGE OF PACE, KEEP PACE, PUT THROUGH ONE'S PACES, SNAIL'S PACE.

pace off See STEP OFF 2.

pace-setter, pace-setting See SET THE PACE.

pack a punch or **pack a wallop** v. phr. slang **1** To be able to give a powerful blow; have a dangerous fist. *He packed a mean punch.* (He could hit a very hard, painful blow.) **2** To have a violent effect; be powerful. *It was vodka, and it packed quite a wallop.* (It was vodka, and it was very strong liquor.)

pack off v., informal To send away; dismiss abruptly. *When an Englishman got in trouble long ago, his family would pack him off to Australia or some other distant land.* (His family would send him to some distant country.) *Mother couldn't really get started on the housework until she had packed the children off to school.* (Mother couldn't begin her housework until she had sent the children to school.)

pack rat n., informal A person who cannot part with old, useless objects; an avid collector of useless things; a junk hoarder. *"Why are there so many things in this room?" John asked. "It is my brother's room, and he is a pack rat; he is unable to throw stuff away."* (He is unable to get rid of useless objects accumulated over the years.)

paddle See UP THE CREEK or UP THE CREEK WITHOUT A PADDLE.

paddle one's own canoe v. phr., informal To work without help; earn your own living; support yourself.—A cliché. *After his father died, John had to paddle his own canoe.* (After his father died, John had to earn his own living.) Syn. HOE ONE'S OWN ROW. Compare MAKE ONE'S WAY.

paddy wagon n., informal A police van used for transporting prisoners to jail or the police station. *The police threw the demonstrators into the paddy wagon.* (They were thrown into the police van.)

pad the bill v. phr. To add false expenses to a bill; make a bill larger than it really was. *The salesman padded the bill for his traveling expenses by exaggerating his food expenses.* (He claimed that he spent more for food than he really had.)

pain See AT PAINS, FEEL NO PAIN, GIVE A PAIN, GROWING PAINS, ON PAIN OF, TAKE PAINS.

pain in the ass or **pain in the neck** n., slang, vulgar with ass An obnoxious or bothersome person or event. *Phoebe Hochreichter is a regular pain in the neck/ass.* (She is a bothersome and obnoxious person.) (This expression is not vulgar when used with "neck.")

paint oneself into a corner v. phr. To get oneself into a bad situation that is difficult or im-

possible to get out of. *By promising to both lower taxes and raise the defense budget, the president has painted himself into a corner.* (He has put himself into an impossible position.)

paint the lily See GILD THE LILY.

paint the town red or **paint the town** v. phr., slang To go out to drink and have a good time; celebrate wildly; carouse.—A cliché. *It was the sailors' first night ashore; they painted the town red.* (On their first night off the boat, the sailors went on a wild drinking celebration.) Compare ON THE TOWN 2.

pair See TAKE TO ONE'S HEELS also SHOW A CLEAN PAIR OF HEELS.

pair off v. **1** To make a pair of; put two together; associate; match. *Mrs. Smith paired off her guests by age and tastes.* (She arranged for couples of the same age and likes to sit together.) **2** To belong to a pair; become one of a pair. *Jane paired off with Alice in a tennis doubles match.* (Jane chose Alice as a partner for a game of tennis.) **3** To divide or join into pairs. *Later in the day the picnic crowd paired off for walks and boat rides.* (Later in the day, the crowd separated into couples to walk or go boating.)

pair up v. **1** To make a pair of; match. *When she finished the mending, she paired up the socks.* (After she finished mending the holes in the socks, she put the pairs together.) **2** To form a pair; to be or become one of a pair. *Not all the socks would pair up.* (Not all the socks matched; some were odd-colored socks; their mates had been lost or thrown away.) *Joe paired up with Charlie to work on the lesson.* (They agreed to work together as a team.)

pajamas See CAT'S MEOW or CAT'S PAJAMAS.

pal See PEN PAL.

pale See BEYOND THE PALE.

pale around the gills See GREEN AROUND THE GILLS.

palm See CARRY OFF THE PALM, GREASE ONE'S PALM, ITCHING PALM.

palm off v., informal **1** To sell or give (something) by pretending it is something more valuable; to sell or give by trickery. *He palmed off his own painting as a Rembrandt.* (He sold his own painting by telling the customer that it was a real Rembrandt.) *The salesman palmed off pine wood floors as oak.* (The salesman told the buyer that the wood floors were oak, but they were really only pine.) Syn. FOB OFF, PASS OFF. **2** To deceive (someone) by a trick or lie. *He palmed his creditors off with a great show of prosperity.* (He fooled the people to whom he owed money by pretending that he had plenty of money.) Syn. PUT OFF. **3** To introduce someone as a person he isn't; present in a false pretense. *He palmed the girl off as a real Broadway actress.* (He got the girl the job by saying that she had acted on Broadway.)

pan See FLASH IN THE PAN, OUT OF THE FRYING PAN INTO THE FIRE.

pan gravy *n.* Gravy made with meat drippings with seasoning and often a little water. *His wife liked cream gravy, but he preferred pan gravy.* (He didn't like milk, cream or flour in his gravy.) *Pan gravy from country ham is often called red-eye gravy.* (Red-eye gravy does not have any milk or flour in it.)

panic See PUSH THE PANIC BUTTON.

pan out *v., informal* To have a result, especially a good result; result favorably; succeed. *Suppose the class tried to make money by selling candy. How would that pan out?* (How would that succeed? Would it make money?) *Edison's efforts to invent an electric light bulb did not pan out until he used tungsten wires.* (He failed until he used tungsten wires.)

pants See ANTS IN ONE'S PANTS, CATCH ONE WITH ONE'S PANTS DOWN, FANCY PANTS, FLY BY THE SEAT OF ONE'S PANTS, GET THE LEAD OUT OF ONE'S PANTS, KICK IN THE PANTS, WEAR THE TROUSERS *or* WEAR THE PANTS.

paper See ON PAPER, WALKING PAPERS.

par See UP TO PAR.

parade See HIT PARADE.

parade rest *n.* A position in which soldiers stand still, with feet apart and hands behind their backs. *The Marines were at parade rest in front of the officials' platform.* (The Marines stood very still in front of the platform.) Compare AT EASE 3.

parallel bars *n.* Two horizontal bars the same distance apart, that are a few feet above the floor of a gymnasium. *The boys exercised on the parallel bars in the gym.* (The boys exercised with their hands on the horizontal bars at the gym.)

parcel See PART AND PARCEL.

parcel out *v.* To give out in parts or shares; divide. *He parcelled out the remaining food to the workers.* (He divided the food that was left among the workers.)

par for the course *n. phr., informal* Just what was expected; nothing unusual; a typical happening.—A cliché. Usually refers to things going wrong. *Mary is very clumsy so it was par for the course when she bumped into the table and broke the vase.* (It was typical of Mary to break something.) *When John came late again, Mary said, "That's par for the course."* (John was late, as usual.) Compare ALL IN A DAY'S WORK, RUNNING TRUE TO FORM.

parliamentary law *n.* The rules for legislative or other meetings. *The club followed parliamentary law at the business meeting.* (The rules of correct action were followed at the business meeting.)

partake of *v., formal* **1** To take some of; receive a share of; eat. *He partook of ordinary country fare as he traveled.* (He ate the usual everyday food of the country people, as he traveled.) **2** To have the same qualities as

show the characteristics of. *Her way of cooking partook of both Italian and American habits.* (Her cooking showed both Italian and American likes and customs.)

part See DISCRETION IS THE BETTER PART OF VALOR, FOOL AND HIS MONEY ARE SOON PARTED, FOR MY PART, FOR ONE'S PART *also* ON ONE'S PART, FOR THE MOST PART, IN PART, MAN OF PARTS, TAKE PART.

part and parcel *n. phr.* A necessary or important part; something necessary to a larger thing.—Usually followed by *of. Freedom of speech is part and parcel of the liberty of a free man.* (Freedom of speech is a necessary part of the liberty of a free man.)

part company *v. phr.* **1** To part with someone; leave each other; separate. *The boys parted company as they came from the park.* (They separated as they left the park.) *George parted company with the others at his front door.* (He left the others when he reached his front door.) **2** To be different from someone in opinion or action; follow your own way; disagree; differ. *They parted company on where the new highway should be built.* (They disagreed about where the new highway should be built.) *The mayor parted company with the newspapers on raising taxes.* (The mayor had a different opinion from the newspapers about raising taxes.)

particular See IN PARTICULAR.

parting of the ways *n. phr.* **1** The point where a road or path divides; a fork. *They stood undecided at a parting of the ways, where a forest path forked.* (They stopped for a while where the path divided into the woods.) **2** A time or place where a choice must be made; a deciding point.—An overused metaphor. *He had come to a parting of the ways: he had to choose the high school courses that would prepare him for college, or the courses that would prepare him for business.* (He had reached a point where he had to choose either college preparatory or business courses.)

part with *v.* **1** To separate from; leave. *He parted with us at the end of the trip.* (He separated from us at the end of the trip.) Compare PART COMPANY. **2** To let go. *They were sorry to part with the old house.* (They were sorry to sell the old house.) *He had to part with his secretary when she got married.* (He had to let his secretary go when she got married.) Compare GIVE UP.

party See HEN PARTY, LIFE OF THE PARTY, NECK-TIE PARTY, THROW A PARTY.

pass See BRING TO PASS, COME TO PASS, FORWARD PASS, JUMP PASS, SCREEN PASS.

pass away *v.* **1** To slip by; go by; pass. *We had so much fun that the weekend passed away before we realized it.* (We had so much fun that the weekend seemed very short.) *Forty years had passed away since they had met.* (Forty years had gone by since they had met.) **2** To cease to exist; end; disappear;

vanish. *When automobiles became popular, the use of the horse and buggy passed away.* (When automobiles were used by everyone, we all stopped using a horse and buggy; they disappeared.) **3** To have your life story; die. *He passed away at eighty.* (He died when he was eighty years old.)

pass by See PASS OVER.

pass by the board See GO BY THE BOARD.

passed ball *n.* A pitched baseball missed by the catcher when he should have been able to catch it. *The batter singled and went to second on a passed ball.* (The batter went to first with a single and then to second when the catcher missed a pitch.)

passing See IN PASSING.

pass muster *v. phr., informal* To pass a test or check-up; be good enough. *After a practice period, Sam found that he was able to pass muster as a lathe operator.* (After training on the new job, he became a satisfactory lathe operator.) *His work was done carefully, so it always passed muster.* (He worked carefully, so everyone was satisfied with the work.) Compare MEASURE UP.

pass off *v.* **1** To sell or give (something) by false claims; offer (something fake) as genuine. *The dishonest builder passed off a poorly-built house by pretending it was well constructed.* (He sold the badly built house by saying it was good.) Syn. FOB OFF, PALM OFF. **2** To claim to be someone you are not; pretend to be someone else. *He passed himself off as a doctor until someone checked his record.* (He claimed to be a doctor until someone checked up.) **3** To go away gradually; disappear. *Mrs. White's morning headache had passed off by that night.* Her morning's headache had disappeared by evening. **4** To reach an end; run its course from beginning to end. *The party passed off well.* (The party went well from beginning to end.) Syn. GO OFF.

pass on *v.* **1** To give an opinion about; judge; settle. *The college passed on his application and found him acceptable.* (The college examined his application and decided it was all right.) *The committee recommended three people for the job and the president passed on them.* (The president judged which one was best for the job.) **2** To give away (something that has been outgrown.) *As he grew up, he passed on his clothes to his younger brother.* (His clothes were given to his younger brother.) Compare HAND DOWN. **3** To die. *Mary was very sorry to hear that her first grade teacher had passed on.* (Mary's teacher died.)

pass out *v., informal* **1** To lose consciousness; faint. *She went back to work while she was still sick, and finally she just passed out.* (She was still weak, and finally she fainted.) Compare GIVE OUT 3. **2** *or slang* **pass out cold.** To drop into a drunken stupor; become unconscious from drink. *After three drinks, the man passed out.* (After having three drinks he went into a drunken sleep.) **3** To die. *Life came and went weakly in him for hours after surgery; then he passed out.* (He barely lived for several hours after the operation, and then died.) Syn. PASS AWAY.

pass over *or* **pass by** *v.* To give no attention to; not notice; ignore. *I can pass over the disorderliness of the troops, but their disobedience is serious.* (I can overlook the soldiers' poor housekeeping but their disobedience is serious.) *In choosing men to be given a salary raise, the foreman passed Mr. Hart by.* (In choosing men to be given a pay raise, the foreman paid no attention to Mr. Hart and did not raise his pay.) *She was unattractive, the kind of a girl that everybody would pass by.* (No one would notice her because she was not pretty.)

pass the buck *v. phr., informal* To make another person decide something or accept a responsibility or give orders instead of doing it yourself; shift or escape responsibility or blame; put the duty or blame on someone else.—A cliché. *Mrs. Brown complained to the man who sold her the bad meat, but he only passed the buck and told her to see the manager.* (The man who sold the meat would not take the blame for the bad meat.) *If you break a window, do not pass the buck; admit that you did it.* (If you break a window, do not say someone else did it. Accept the blame.) Compare LET GEORGE DO IT.—**buck-passer** *n. phr.* A person who passes the buck. *Mr. Jones was a buck-passer even at home, and tried to make his wife make all the decisions.* (Mr. Jones would not take responsibility.)—**buck-passing** *n. or adj.* *Buck passing clerks in stores make customers angry.* (Customers do not like to be sent from one person to another when they complain about something.)

pass the time of day *v. phr.* To exchange greetings; stop for a chat. *They met at the corner and paused to pass the time of day.* (They met at the corner and stopped to say a few words to each other.)

pass through one's mind See CROSS ONE'S MIND.

pass up *v.* To let (something) go by; refuse. *Mary passed up the dessert because she was on a diet.* (Mary didn't eat dessert.) *John was offered a good job in California, but he passed it up because he didn't want to move.* (John refused the job in California.) Compare TURN DOWN.

pass with flying colors See WITH FLYING COLORS.

pat See PIT-A-PAT, STAND PAT.

pat-a-cake *n.* A clapping game that keeps time to a nursery rhyme. *Mother played pat-a-cake with baby.* (Mother and baby clapped as Mother recited the nursery rhyme.)

patch up *v.* **1** To mend a hole or break; repair; fix. *He patched up a couple of old tires.*

(He mended the punctures in a couple of old tires.) *The lovers patched up their quarrel.* (The boy and girl became lovers again after their quarrel.) **2** To put together in a hurried or shaky way. *They patched up a hasty peace.* (They were able to make a hurried agreement.)

pat on the back[1] *v. phr.* **1** To clap lightly on the back in support, encouragement, or praise. *The coach patted the player on the back and said a few encouraging words.* (The coach struck the player lightly on the back and talked encouragingly to him.) **2** To make your support or encouragement for (someone) felt; praise.—An overused phrase. *After he won the game, everyone patted him on the back for days.* (Everyone praised him for days after the game.)

pat on the back[2] *n. phr.* **1** An encouraging tap of the hand on someone's back; a show of sympathy or support. *I gave her a pat on the back and told her she had done fine work.* (I gave her an encouraging tap and praised her for the good work she had done.) **2** A word or gesture of praise or other encouragement; applause.—A cliché. *Pats on the back weren't enough; he wanted hard cash.* (Kind words weren't enough; he wanted money, too.)

patrol   See SHORE PATROL.

Paul   See ROB PETER TO PAY PAUL.

pause   See GIVE PAUSE.

pavement   See POUND THE PAVEMENT.

pave the way   *v. phr.* To make preparation; make easy. *Aviation paved the way for space travel.* (Aviation opened up the way to space travel.) *A good education paves the way to success.* (A good education makes the way to success easier. It prepares you to become successful.)

pay   See DEVIL TO PAY.

pay as one goes   *v. phr.* To pay cash; to pay at once; to avoid charging anything bought; to avoid debt entirely by paying cash.—Usually used with *you*. *It is best to pay as you go; then you will not have to worry about paying debts later.* (It is best to pay cash, so you won't worry about owing people money later.)

pay dirt   *n., slang* **1** The dirt in which much gold is found. *The man searched for gold many years before he found pay dirt.* (After many years the man found much gold.) **2** *informal* A valuable discovery.—Often used in the phrase *strike pay dirt*. *When Bill joined the team, the coach struck pay dirt.* (When Bill joined the team, it became very strong because he was big and a good player.) *Jean looked in many books for facts about her home town, and finally she struck pay dirt.* (Jean looked for a long time, and finally she found good, useful material. Compare STRIKE IT RICH.

pay for   *v.* To have trouble because of (something you did wrong or did not do); be punished or suffer because of. *When Bob could not get a good job, he realized he had to pay for all the years of fooling around instead of working in school.* (He finally suffered because he had not worked hard in school.) *Mary was very mean to John because she wanted to make him pay for all the years in which he had ignored her.* (Mary made John suffer for paying no attention to her.) Compare MAKE UP 3b, PAY OFF.

pay off   *v.* **1** To pay the wages of. *The men were paid off just before quitting time, the last day before the holiday.* (The men got their pay just before going home on the day before the holiday.) **2** To pay and discharge from a job. *When the building was completed, he paid off the laborers.* (When the building was finished he handed the workmen their wages and let them go.) **3** To hurt (someone) who has done wrong to you; get revenge on. *When Bob tripped Dick, Dick paid Bob off by punching him in the nose.* (Dick punished Bob by hitting him in the nose.) Syn. PAY BACK. **4** *informal* To bring a return; make profit. *At first Mr. Harrison lost money on his investments, but finally one paid off.* (The investment made a profit.) **5** *informal* To prove successful, rewarding, or worth while. *Ben's friendship with the old man who lived beside him paid off in pleasant hours and broadened interests.* (The friendship gave him pleasure and widened his outlook.) *John studied hard before the examination, and it paid off. He made an A.* (John's studying was rewarded with a grade of A. It was worthwhile.)

pay one's way   *v. phr.* **1** To pay in cash or labor for your expenses. *He paid his way by acting as a guide.* (He earned his expenses by helping as a guide.) **2** To be profitable; earn as much as you cost someone; be valuable to an employer; to yield a return above expenses. *The bigger truck paid its way from the start.* (The bigger truck always saved more money than it cost to run it.) *We had to offer our new manager a large salary, but he was a capable man, and paid his way.* (We had to offer our new manager a large salary, but he was worth it.) Compare WORTH ONE'S SALT.

pay out   See PAY OFF.

pay the piper *or* **pay the fiddler**   *v. phr.* To suffer the results of being foolish; pay or suffer because of your foolish acts or wasting money.—A hackneyed phrase. *Bob had spent all his money and got into debt, so now he must pay the piper.* (Now he must work and suffer to pay his debts because he was careless and foolish before.) *Fred had a fight, broke a window, and quarreled with his counselor, so now he must pay the fiddler.* (Now he must be punished as a result of his acts.) Compare FACE THE MUSIC 2. [From the proverb "He who dances must pay the piper (or the fiddler)."]

pay through the nose   *v. phr., informal* To pay at a very high rate; pay too much.—A cliché. *He had wanted experience, but this job seemed like paying through the nose for it.* (This job seemed too hard for what experience he was getting.) *There was a shortage of cars; if you found one for sale, you had to pay through the nose.* (If you found a car for sale during the shortage, you had to pay too much for it.)

pay up *v.* To pay in full; pay the amount of; pay what is owed. *The monthly installments on the car were paid up.* (He had finished making all the monthly payments on the car.) *He pays his dues up promptly.* (He pays his membership dues in full and on time.) *He gets behind when he is out of work but always pays up when he is working again.* (He can't pay and is late when he is out of work but pays his bills when he starts work again.)

peace See HOLD ONE'S PEACE.

pearl See CAST PEARLS BEFORE SWINE *or* CAST ONE'S PEARLS BEFORE SWINE.

pebble See NOT THE ONLY PEBBLE ON THE BEACH.

peck See HUNT AND PECK.

pecking order *n.* The way people are ranked in relation to each other (for honor, privilege, or power); status classification, hierarchy. *After the president was in office several months, his staff developed a pecking order.* (There was a chain of command, the aides had influence according to the order of their authority.)

pedestal See ON A PEDESTAL.

peel See KEEP ONE'S EYES PEELED.

peel off *v.* To dive away from a group of airplanes in a flight formation; bring one plane down from a group. *As the group neared the home base, pilot after pilot peeled off for a landing.* (As the group came near the home base, one plane after another left the group to land.)

peeping Tom *n.* A man or boy who likes sly peeping. *He was picked up by the police as a peeping Tom.* (The police found him staring in a woman's window and arrested him.)

peg See SQUARE PEG IN A ROUND HOLE, TAKE DOWN A PEG.

peg away *v.* To work methodically, industriously, or steadily. *Thomson pegged away for years at a shoe repair business.* (He was a shoe repairman for years.) *Jones kept pegging away, and finally recognition came.* (He worked busily and finally the boss noticed his good work.)

pen See POISON-PEN, SLIP OF THE PEN.

penalty box *n.* A place where penalized hockey players are required to go to wait until the penalty is over. *Two players got into a fight and were sent to the penalty box for two minutes.* (They had to leave the game for two minutes.)

penny for one's thoughts Please tell me what you are thinking about; what's your daydream?—A cliché. *"A penny for your thoughts!" he exclaimed.* (He asked me to tell him what I was thinking about.)

penny pincher, penny pinching See PINCH PENNIES.

penny wise and pound foolish Wise or careful in small things but not careful enough in important things.—A proverb. *Mr. Smith's fence is rotting and falling down because he wouldn't spend money to paint it. He is penny wise and pound foolish.* (Mr. Smith would not spend money to buy paint, so he may have to spend more money to build a new fence.)

pen pal *n.* A friend who is known to someone through an exchange of letters. *John's pen pal writes him letters about school in Alaska.* (John writes letters to a boy in Alaska and the boy writes to John about school there.)

people who live in glass houses should not throw stones Do not complain about other people if you are as bad as they are.—A proverb. *Mary says that Betty is jealous, but Mary is more jealous herself. People who live in glass houses should not throw stones.* (Mary should not criticize Betty if she is just as bad.)

pep talk *n., informal* A speech that makes people feel good so they will try harder and not give up. *The football coach gave the team a pep talk.* (He encouraged them to keep trying.) *Mary was worried about her exams, but felt better after the teacher's pep talk.* (The teacher cheered Mary up.)

period of grace See GRACE PERIOD.

perish the thought *v. phr.* Let us not even think of it; may it never come true.—Used as an exclamation. *If John fails the college entrance exam—perish the thought—he will go back to high school for one more year.* (I hope that John will not fail, but if he does, he will go back to high school.) *Perish the thought that Mary should have cancer.* (I hope that it is not true that Mary has cancer.) Compare GOD FORBID.

perk up *v.* To get or give back pep, vigor, health, or spirit; become or make more lively, liven up. *He perked up quickly after his illness.* (He got back his strength and pep quickly after his illness.) *The rain perked up the flowers wonderfully.* (The rain freshened up the flowers wonderfully.)

person See IN PERSON.

petard See HOIST WITH ONE'S OWN PETARD.

Peter See ROB PETER TO PAY PAUL.

peter out *v., informal* To fail or die down gradually; grow less; become exhausted. *After the factory closed, the town pretty well petered out.* (After the factory shut down, the jobs were fewer and people began to move away from town.) *The mine once had a rich vein of silver, but it petered out.* (The mine once had a rich vein of silver, but it had all been dug out.) *But as he thought of her, his* *anger slowly petered out.* (But as he thought of her, his anger died down gradually.) Compare GIVE OUT.

pick See BONE TO PICK *or* CROW TO PICK.

pick a bone See BONE TO PICK.

pick a hole in *or* **pick holes in** *v. phr., informal* To find a mistake in or things wrong with; criticize; blame. *The witness said he had been walking in the moonlight last Sunday, but the lawyer picked a hole in what he said by proving that there was no moon and that it rained Sunday night.* (The lawyer found something wrong with what the witness said.) *Mary is always picking holes in what the other girls do.* (Mary always criticizes the other girls.) Compare FIND FAULT.

pick and choose *v.* To select with much care; choose in a fussy way; take a long time before choosing. *He was never one to pick and choose.* (He was easily satisfied; he was not hard to please.) *Some people pick and choose to get something perfect, and some just because they can't make up their minds.* (Some people take a long time to choose because they are not satisfied with imperfect things, and some just because they can't make up their minds.)

pick apart *or* **pick to pieces** *v. phr.* To criticize harshly; find things wrong with; find fault with. *After the dance, the girls picked Susan apart.* (After the dance, the girls talked about Susan; they criticized her cruelly.) *They picked the play to pieces.* (They discussed the play in detail and criticized all its faults.)

pick at *v.* 1 To reach or grasp for repeatedly. *The baby kept picking at the coverlet.* (He pulled again and again at the bed cover.) 2 To eat without appetite; choose a small piece every little while to eat. *He picked at his food.* (He ate only a few bites during the meal.) 3 To annoy or bother continually; find fault with. *They showed their displeasure by continually picking at her.* (They showed that they disliked what she had done by constantly doing little things to bother her and make her angry.) Syn. PICK ON.

pick-me-up *n. phr.* Something you take when you feel tired or weak. *John stopped at a drugstore for a pick-me-up after working three hours overtime.* (John was tired so he stopped and had a drink.) *Mary always carried a bar of chocolate in her pocketbook for a pick-me-up.* (Mary has a chocolate bar in case she feels tired.)

pick off *v.* 1 To pull off; remove with the fingers. *He picked off the burs that had stuck to his overcoat.* (He pulled the burs from his overcoat.) 2 To shoot, one at a time; knock down one by one. *The sniper picked off the slower soldiers as they came out into the road.* (The sharpshooter shot the soldiers one at a time.) 3 To catch a base runner off base by throwing the ball quickly to a fielder who tags him out. *The pitcher turned around sud-*

denly and threw to the second baseman to pick the runner off second base. (The pitcher caught the runner by surprise and he was tagged with the ball.) Compare OFF BASE. 4 To catch and especially, in football, to intercept. *Alert defenders picked off three of Jack's passes.* (Alert defenders intercepted three passes.)

pick on *v.* 1 *informal* To make a habit of annoying or bothering (someone); do or say bad things to (someone). *Other boys picked on him until he decided to fight them.* (Other boys teased him until he began to defend himself.) Syn. PICK AT 3. 2 To single out; choose; select. *He visited a lot of colleges, and finally picked on Stanford.* (He visited a lot of colleges, and finally decided to go to Stanford.)

pick one's way *v. phr.* To go ahead carefully in difficult or unfamiliar places; advance with care. *After nightfall we drove slowly along, picking our way until we found the right turn.* (When it got dark, we drove slowly, making sure of our way until we found the turn in the road that we wanted.) *He picked his way across the rough and rocky hillside.* (He walked carefully across the hillside to avoid rocks and holes.)

pick out *v.* 1 To choose. *It took Mary a long time to pick out a new dress at the store.* (It took her a long time to make up her mind and buy the one she wanted.) 2 To see among others; recognize; tell from others. *We could pick out different places in the city from the airplane.* (We could recognize places from high in the air.) *We could not pick Bob out in the big crowd.* (We couldn't see Bob among so many people.) Syn. MAKE OUT 2. 3 To find by examining or trying; tell the meaning. *The box was so dirty we couldn't pick out the directions on the label.* (We couldn't see what the directions were by looking very carefully at them.) Compare FIND OUT.

pick over *v.* To select the best of; look at and take what is good from; choose from. *She picked the apples over and threw out the bad ones.* (She examined the apples one by one and threw away those that were spoiled.) *We hurried to the big sale, but we were late and everything had already been picked over.* (People arriving before us at the store had already picked out all the best things and left what wasn't so good.)

pick the brains of *v. phr.* To get ideas or information about a particular subject by asking an expert. *If you have time, I'd like to pick your brains about home computers.* (I'd like to get some facts and ideas from you.)

pick to pieces See PICK APART.

pickup *n.,* (stress on *pick*) 1 A rugged, small truck. *When he got into the lumber business, Max traded in his comfortable two-door sedan for a pickup.* (He traded his personal automobile for a small truck to transport merchandise.) **2** Scheduled meeting in order to transfer merchandise or stolen goods. *The pickup goes down at 7 A.M. everyday by the loading dock.* (The scheduled delivery takes place behind the building early in the morning.) *The dope pushers usually make their pickup on Rush Street.* (They usually make their illegal deliveries on Rush Street.) **3** A person who is easy to persuade to go home with the suitor. *Sue is said to be an easy pickup.* (It is said that she goes with men on first encounter quite willingly.)

pick up *v.* **1** To take up; lift. *During the morning Mrs. Carter picked up sticks in the yard.* (She gathered sticks in the morning.) **2** *informal* To pay for someone else. *After lunch, in the restaurant, Uncle Bob picked up the check.* (He took the bill and paid for all the lunches.) **3** To take on or away; receive; get. *At the next corner the bus stopped and picked up three people.* (The bus stopped at the next corner and took on three people.) **4** To get from different places at different times; a little at a time; collect. *He had picked up rare corins in seaports all other the world.* (He had collected rare coins in seaports all over the world.) **5** To get without trying; get accidentally. *He picked up knowledge of radio just by staying around the radio station.* (He learned a little about radio by listening to people at the radio station.) *Billy picked up a cold at school.* (Billy caught a cold somehow.) **6a** To gather together; collect. *When the carpenter finished making the cabinet, he began picking up his tools.* (He began to get them together to take away with him.) **6b** To make neat and tidy; tidy up, put in order. *Pick up your room before Mother sees it.* (Make your room neater.) **6c** To gather things together; tidy a place up. *It's almost dinner time, children. Time to pick up and get ready.* (It's time to get your things together before dinner.) **7** To catch the sound of. *He picked up Chicago on the radio.* (He was able to hear a Chicago station on his radio.) **8** To get acquainted with (someone) without an introduction; make friends with (a person of the other sex). *Mother told Mary not to walk home by herself from the party because some stranger might try to pick her up.* (Some stranger might try to make friends with her.) **9** *informal* To take to the police station or jail; arrest. *Police picked the man up for burglary.* (Police arrested him for stealing.) **10** To recognize the trail of a hunted person or animal; find. *State police picked up the bandit's trail.* (State police found the way the robber had gone.) *The dogs picked up the fox's smell.* (The dogs found the smell and were able to follow the fox by it.) **11** To make (someone) feel better; refresh. *A little food will pick you up.* (Something to eat will make you feel better.) **12a** To increase (the speed); make (the speed) faster. *The teacher told her singing class to pick up the tempo.* (The teacher urged her class to sing faster.) *The car picked up speed.* (The car gathered speed.) **12b** To become faster; become livelier. *The speed of the train began to pick up.* (It began to go faster.) *After the band practiced for a while, the music began to pick up.* (The music got faster and more lively.) **13** To start again after interruption; go on with. *The class picked up the story where they had left it before the holiday.* (The class went on with the story from the place where they had stopped reading it before the holiday.) *They met after five years, and picked up their friendship as if there had been no interruption.* (After five years apart, they started their friendship again.) **14** *informal* To become better; recover; gain. *She picked up in her schoolwork.* (She began to do better in her schoolwork.) *He picked up gradually after a long illness.* (He regained his health slowly after a long illness.) *His spirits picked up as he came near home.* (He began to feel more cheerful.)

pie See EAT HUMBLE PIE, FINGER IN THE PIE, PIE IN THE SKY, SWEETIE PIE.

piece See BY THE PIECE, CONVERSATION PIECE, GIVE A PIECE OF ONE'S MIND, GO TO PIECES, OF A PIECE, PIECE OF CAKE, SAY ONE'S PIECE or SPEAK ONE'S PIECE, TO PIECES.

piece of cake *adj., slang* Easy. *The final exam was a piece of cake.* (It was very easy.)

piece out *v.* **1** To put together from many different pieces; put together from odd parts; patch. *They pieced out a meal from leftovers.* (They made up a meal from leftovers.) *He pieced out the machine with scrap parts.* (He fixed the machine with parts from the junkyard.) *The detective pieced out the story from a stray fact here, a clue there, and a hint somewhere else.* (The detective made up a connected story by putting together many separate parts that he heard.) **2** To make larger or longer by adding one or more pieces. *The girl grew so fast that her mother had to piece out her dresses.* (The mother had to add pieces of cloth to the dresses so they would fit.)

pie in the sky *n. phr., informal* An unrealistic wish or hope. *Our trip to Hawaii is still only a pie in the sky.* (It is an unrealistic dream.) Compare PIPE DREAM.

piggy-back *adj. or adv.* Sitting or being carried on the shoulders. *Little John loved to go for a piggy-back ride on his father's shoulders.* (Father carried little John on his shoulders.) *When Mary sprained her ankles, John carried her piggy-back to the doctor.* (John carried Mary on his shoulders.)

piggy bank *n.* A small bank, sometimes in the shape of a pig, for saving coins. *John's father gave him a piggy bank.* (John's father gave him a little bank in the shape of a pig.)

pig in a poke *n. phr.* An unseen bargain; something accepted or bought without looking at it carefully.—A cliché. *Buying land by mail is buying a pig in a poke: sometimes the land turns out to be under water.* (Buying land by mail is buying carelessly; sometimes agents may sell you part of the ocean bottom.)

pile up *v.* **1** To grow into a big heap. *He didn't go into his office for three days and his work kept piling up.* (He had a big pile of work that he hadn't done.) **2** To run aground. *Boats often pile up on the rocks in the shallow water.* (Boats run aground on the rocks.) **3** To crash. *One car made a sudden stop and the two cars behind it piled up.* (The cars crashed because of the sudden stop.)

pill See BITTER PILL.

pillar to post See FROM PILLAR TO POST.

pimple See GOOSE BUMPS *or* GOOSE PIMPLES.

pin See ON PINS AND NEEDLES.

pinch See TAKE WITH A GRAIN OF SALT *also* TAKE WITH A PINCH OF SALT, WHERE THE SHOE PINCHES.

pinch-hit *v.* **1** To substitute for another player at bat in a baseball game. *Smith was sent in to pinch-hit for Jones.* (Smith took Jones's turn at bat.) **2** *informal* To act for a while, or in an emergency, for another person; take someone's place for a while. *I asked him to pinch-hit for me while I was away.* (I asked him to take my place while I was away.) *The president of the City Council pinch-hits for the mayor when the mayor is out of town.* (The president of the City Council acts as Mayor when the mayor is out of town.)—**pinch hitter** *n. Jones was hit by a pitched ball and Smith came in as a pinch-hitter.* (Smith took Jones's turn at bat.) *When our teacher was sick, Mrs. Harris was called as a pinch hitter.* (Mrs. Harris was asked to come and teach for our teacher.)—**pinch hitting** *adj. or n. Pinch-hitting for another teacher is a hard job.* (Taking the place of another teacher is a hard job.)

pinch pennies *v.phr., informal* Not spend a penny more than necessary; be very saving or thrifty. *When Tom and Mary were saving money to buy a house, they had to pinch pennies.* (They had to spend money only for the most necessary things.)—**penny pincher** *n. informal* A stingy or selfish person; miser. *He spent so little money that he began to get the name of a penny pincher.* (He spent so little that people began to call him a selfish miser.)—**penny-pinching** *adj. or n., informal Bob saved enough money by penny-pinching to buy a bicycle.* (Bob got money for a bicycle by saving all he could.)

pin curl *n.* A curl made with a hair clip or bobby pin. *Mary washed her hair and put it up in pin curls.* (Mary set her hair.) *All the girls had their hair in pin curls to get ready for the party.* (All the girls had their hair set for the party.)

pin down *v.* **1a** To keep (someone) from moving; make stay in a place or position; trap. *Mr. Jones' leg was pinned down under the car after the accident.* (His leg was under the car so that he couldn't move it.) *The soldier was pinned down in the hole because rifle bullets were flying over his head.* (The bullets wouldn't let him move from the hole.) **1b** To keep (someone) from changing what (he) says or means; make (someone) admit the truth; make (someone) agree to something. *Mary didn't like the book but I couldn't pin her down to say what she didn't like about it.* (Mary wouldn't say or admit exactly what she didn't like about the book.) *I tried to pin Bob down to fix my bicycle tomorrow, but he wouldn't say that he could.* (He wouldn't agree to fix it tomorrow.) **2** To tell clearly and exactly; explain so that there is no doubt. *The police tried to pin down the blame for the fire in the school.* (They tried to find exactly who should be blamed for the fire.)

pink See IN THE PINK, TICKLE PINK.

pink around the gills See GREEN AROUND THE GILLS.

pin one's ears back *v. phr., slang* **1** To beat; defeat. *After winning three games in a row, the Reds had their ears pinned back by the Blues.* (The Blues beat the Reds.) **2** To scold. *Mrs. Smith pinned Mary's ears back for not doing her homework.* (Mrs. Smith scolded Mary.)

pin one's heart on one's sleeve See WEAR ONE'S HEART ON ONE'S SLEEVE.

pint-size *adj., informal* Very small. *The new pint-size, portable TV sets have a very clear picture.* (The new TV sets are small, but have a good picture.) *It was funny to hear a pint-size voice coming out of a great big man.* (The big man had a very small voice.)

pipe See PUT THAT IN YOUR PIPE AND SMOKE IT.

pipe down *v.* **1** To call (sailors) away from work with a whistle. *He piped the men down after boat drill.* (He dismissed the men from boat drill by blowing a whistle.) **2** *slang* To stop talking; shut up; be quiet. *"Oh, pipe down,"* *he called.* (He told the man to shut up.)—Often considered rude.

pipe dream *n., informal* An unrealizable, financially unsound, wishful way of thinking; an unrealistic plan. *Max went through the motions of pretending that he wanted to buy that $250,000 house, but his wife candidly told the real estate lady that it was just a pipe dream.* (Max's wife told the saleslady that they couldn't really buy the house and were just wishfully toying with the idea.) Compare PIE IN THE SKY.

piper See PAY THE PIPER.

pipe up *v., informal* To speak up; to be heard. *Mary is so shy, everyone was surprised when she piped up with a complaint at the club meeting.* (Mary spoke up about what she didn't like.) *Everyone was afraid to talk to the police, but a small child piped up.* (A small child began to speak.)

pip-squeak *n.. informal* A small, unimportant person. *If the club is really democratic, then every little pip-squeak has the right to say what he thinks.* (Everybody can talk, whether he is important or not.) *When the smallest boy was chosen to be the monitor, the class bully said he would not obey a little pip-squeak.* (The big bully refused to obey the small monitor.)

piss off *v., slang, vulgar, avoidable* To bother, annoy, irritate. *You really piss me off when you talk like that.* (What you say really irritates me.)—**pissed off** *adj. Why act so pissed off just because I made a pass at you?* (Why are you acting so irritated just because I expressed a romantic interest in you?)

pit against *v.* To match against; oppose to; put in opposition to; place in competition or rivalry with. *The game pits two of the best pro football teams in the East against each other.* (The game puts two very strong football teams against each other.) *He pitted his endurance against the other man's speed.* (He matched his endurance against the other man's speed.) *He was pitted against an opponent just as smart as he was.* (He was competing with an opponent who was fully as smart as he was.)

pit-a-pat *adv.* With a series of quick pats. *When John asked Mary to marry him, her heart went pit-a-pat.* (Mary's heart beat rapidly.) *The little boy ran pit-a-pat down the hall.* (The boy ran with small, fast steps.)

pitch See WILD PITCH.

pitcher See LITTLE PITCHERS HAVE BIG EARS, RELIEF PITCHER, STARTING PITCHER.

pitchfork See RAIN CATS AND DOGS *or* RAIN PITCHFORKS.

pitch in *v., informal* **1** To begin something with much energy; start work eagerly. *Pitch in and we will finish the job as soon as possible.* (Get to work and we will soon finish.) **2** To give help or money for something; contribute. *Everyone must pitch in and work together.* (Everyone must join together to work.) *We all pitched in a quarter to buy Nancy a present.* (We all gave a quarter.) Syn. CHIP IN. Compare FALL TO.

pitch into *v., informal* **1** To attack with blows or words. *He pitched into me with his fists.* (He struck me fast and hard with his fists.) *He pitched into the idea of raising taxes.* (He attacked suggestions for raising taxes.) Syn. LAY INTO 1, 2, RIP INTO. **2** To get to work at; work hard at. *She pitched into the work and had the house cleaned up by noon.* (She got to work busily and had the house cleaned up by noon.) *He pitched into his homework right after dinner.* (He attacked his homework busily right after dinner.) Compare LAY INTO, SAIL INTO.

pitch out *v.* **1** To deliberately throw a pitch outside of the home plate in baseball so that the batter cannot hit the ball and the catcher can make a quick throw. *The catcher*

wanted the pitcher to pitch out and see if they could catch the runner stealing.* (He wanted the pitcher to throw the ball wide so he could throw quickly to second and catch the man stealing.) **2** To toss the ball easily to a football back. *The quarterback faked to the fullback and pitched out to the halfback going wide.* (He pretended to give the ball to the fullback and then tossed it to the halfback.)

pitch woo *v. phr., slang* To kiss and hug; make love. *Mary and John pitched woo in the movies.* (Mary and John necked in the movies.) *While Bob drove, Betty and Jim sat in the back pitching woo.* (Jim and Betty were hugging and kissing in the back seat of the car.)

pity See TAKE PITY ON *or* TAKE PITY UPON.

place See HEART IN THE RIGHT PLACE, HIGH PLACE, IN PLACE, INSTEAD OF *or* IN PLACE OF, IN THE FIRST PLACE, JUMPING-OFF PLACE, LIGHTNING NEVER STRIKES TWICE IN THE SAME PLACE, OUT OF PLACE, PUT IN ONE'S PLACE, PUT ONESELF IN ANOTHER'S PLACE, TAKE PLACE.

plague on both your houses *or* **plague o' both your houses** Bad luck to both of you!— Used to show disgust at those who won't stop quarreling. *The bus drivers went on strike because the bus company would not raise their pay. After several weeks, the people who needed to ride the bus to work said, "A plague on both your houses."* (The bus riders were angry at both the drivers and the company because they could not agree and run the busses again.)

plain white wrapper *n., slang, citizen's band radio jargon* Unmarked police car. *There's a plain white wrapper at your rear door!* (There is an unmarked police care following you closely. Watch your speed!) See BROWN PAPER BAG.

plan See LAY AWAY PLAN.

plank See WALK THE PLANK.

plan on *v.* **1** To have the plan of; have in mind.—Used with a verbal noun. *I plan on going to the movies after I finish my homework.* (I expect to go to the movies.) *Mary was planning on seeing John at the baseball game.* (Mary was expecting to see John at the game.) Syn. FIGURE ON. **2** To think you will do or have; be sure about; expect. *I'm hoping to go away for the weekend, but I'm not planning on it.* (Maybe I can go away, but I'm not sure.) *We can't order the food for the party until we know how many people to plan on.* (We can't order the food until we know the number of people we can expect to come.) *We planned on Mary for the decorations, but she is sick.* (We thought that Mary would decorate the room, but she is sick.)

plate See HOME PLATE.

platter See HAND —— TO —— ON A SILVER PLATTER.

play See ALL WORK AND NO PLAY MAKES JACK A DULL BOY, DOUBLE PLAY, FAIR PLAY, FORCE PLAY, GAME AT WHICH TWO CAN PLAY, MAKE A PLAY FOR, TURN ABOUT IS FAIR PLAY.

play along (with) *v.* Cooperate; make no trouble. *The honest jockey refused to play along with the bookmaker's illegal plan.* (The jockey did not do what the bookmaker wanted.)

play around See FOOL AROUND.

play ball *v. phr.* **1** To begin play in a ball game. *When the umpire calls "Play ball," the game begins.* (When the umpire gives the command, the game begins.) **2** *informal* To join in an effort with others; cooperate. *To get along during Prohibition, many men felt that they had to play ball with gangsters.* (To get along during Prohibition, many men felt that they had to cooperate with gangsters.) *It is often good business to play ball with a political machine.* (In business it often helps to be friends with the local political powers.)

play by ear *v. phr.* **1** To play a musical instrument by remembering the tune, not by reading music. *Mary does not know how to read music. She plays the piano by ear.* (Mary plays music on the piano by remembering how she heard it played before.) *Joe doesn't need any music sheets when he plays his guitar; he knows many songs well and can play them by ear.* (Joe remembers many songs, and does not need the written music.) **2** *informal* To decide what to do as you go along, to fit the situation.—Used with *it*. *John decided to play it by ear when he went for his interview.* (John didn't plan in advance what to say but made it up as he was asked questions.) *It was her first job and she didn't know what to expect, so she had to play it by ear.* (She had to get along without planning in advance what to do or say.)

play cat and mouse with *v. phr.* To tease or fool (someone) by pretending to let him go free and then catching him again. *Joe's uncle had fun playing cat and mouse with him.* (Joe's uncle had fun pretending to let him go but not really letting him go.) *The policeman decided to play cat and mouse when he saw the woman steal the dress in the store.* (The policeman pretended to let the woman go, but he did not really let her go when he saw her steal the dress in the store.)

play down *v.* To give less emphasis to; make (something) seem less important; divert attention from; draw notice away from. *The newspaper stories played down the actor's unattractive past.* (The newspaper stories said little about the bad things in his past.) *A salesman's job is to emphasize the good points of his merchandise; he must play down any faults it has.* (A salesman should impress on people the good points of his mer-

chandise and say little or nothing of its weaknesses.)

played out *adj. phr.* Tired out; worn out; finished; exhausted. *It had been a hard day, and by night he was played out.* (It had been a tiring day, and by night he was worn out.) *For a while, at least, it seemed the interest in great speed was played out.* (People's interest in fast travel had gone: they only wanted comfort.) Compare ALL IN.

play fair *v. phr.* To do what is right to others; act in a fair and truthful way. *The boys like the Principal because he always plays fair.* (The Principal does what is fair; he keeps his promises and respects the boys' rights.) *Mary would not date any other boys while Jim, her favorite boy friend, was away; she said that would not be playing fair.* (Mary said it would not be fair to Jim if she dated other boys while Jim was gone.)

play ——— false *v. phr., literary* To act disloyally toward (a person); betray; cheat; deceive. *Good faith was not in him: he played anyone false who trusted him.* (He would deceive anyone who trusted him.) *His hopes had played him false.* (His hopes had failed to come true.)

play fast and loose *v. phr.* To do as you please without caring what will happen to other people; act so carelessly or unfairly that people cannot depend on you; be very unreliable.—A cliché. *He played fast and loose with the girl's affections.* (He encouraged affection from the girl but really did not care much for her.) *He played fast and loose with the company's good name.* (He failed to guard the company's reputation carefully.)

play footsie *v. phr., slang, informal* **1** Touch the feet of a member of the opposite sex under the table as an act of flirtation. *Have you at least played footsie with her?* (Have you at least engaged in mild flirtation with her?) **2** To engage in any sort of flirtation or collaboration, especially in a political situation. *The mayor was suspected of playing footsie with the Syndicate.* (They suspected the mayor of having underworld connections.)

play ——— for *v., informal* To treat (someone) as; act toward (someone) as, handle (someone) as; handle as. *He played the man for a sucker.* (He treated the man as easy to fool.)

play havoc with *or* **raise havoc with** *v. phr.* To cause destruction; ruin; injure badly. *The storm played havoc with the apple orchard.* (The storm destroyed the young apples and branches in the orchard.) *When Ralph was arrested for stealing the car, it played havoc with his plans for going to college.* (Ralph's plans for going to college were ruined when he was arrested.) *When Mr. White poisoned the cat it played havoc with his reputation in the neighborhood.* (Poisoning the cat injured Mr. White's reputation in the neighborhood.)

play hooky *v. phr., informal* To stay out of school to play. *Carl is failing in school because he has played hooky so many times during the year.* (He stayed out of school doing nothing often during the year.)

play into one's hands *v. phr.* To be or do something that another person can use against you; help an opponent against yourself. *In the basketball game, Jerry's foul played into the opponents' hands.* (Jerry's foul gave the other team a free throw.) *Mary and Bobby both wanted the last piece of cake, but Bobby played into Mary's hands by trying to grab it.* (Father gave the cake to Mary because Bobby tried to grab it.)

play off *v.* **1** To match opposing persons, forces, or interests so that they balance each other. *The girl played off her admirers against each other.* (She encouraged one man and then another so that they would do more to make her like them.) *Britain tried to play off European nations against each other so that she would have a balance of power.* (Britain tried to get the nations of Europe in a balance so that by adding British power to one side she would be in the winning group.) **2** To finish the playing of (an interrupted contest.) *The visitors came back the next Saturday to play off the game stopped by rain.* (They came back to finish the game stopped by rain.) **3** To settle (a tie score) between contestants by more play. *When each player had won two matches, the championship was decided by playing off the tie.* (They played another match to settle the tie; the winner of the extra match would be the champion.)

play on *or* **play upon** *v.* **1** To cause an effect on; influence. *A heavy diet of television drama played on his feelings.* (Much watching of TV kept him excited and anxious.) **2** To work upon for a planned effect; excite to a desired action by cunning plans; manage. *The makeup salesman played on the woman's wish to look beautiful.* (He got her to buy his makeup by making her want very much to be beautiful.) *In some places, leaders play upon people's superstitious fears.* (They frighten people into obedience through their belief in spirits, luck, and magic.) *He played on the man's ambition and love of honor.* (He caused the man to act by promising a future of power, wealth, and honor.)

play one's cards right *or* **play one's cards well** *v. phr., informal* To use abilities and opportunities so as to be successful; act cleverly; make the best use of your place or skills.—A cliché. *That millionaire started with very little but showed a skill in playing his cards right.* (He began with little but always did what got him the most money.) *People liked Harold, and he played his cards well—and soon he began to get ahead rapidly.* (He was likeable and had good sense and quickly succeeded.)

play on words *v. phr.* To use words so as to suggest a different meaning; bring out a joking connection between words; use words playfully; pun. *"Sue for damages," the lawyer told the man hurt in an accident. "I don't need any more damages," the man replied, "I need repairs." The man was playing on words.* (The man joked with two meanings of the word "damages.") *The boy asked his teacher what leather was and she said, "Hide." He asked why she told him to hide. This story plays on words.* (Hide has two meanings, "a cow's skin" and "to go where one cannot be seen.")

play politics *v. phr.* To make secret agreements for your own gain; handle different groups for your own advantage. *In order to get elected, he had to play politics with both the unions and the bosses.* (He had to arrange deals and make promises to the workers and the bosses.) *Mary always gets what she wants by playing office politics.* (Mary turns one person against another to get her own way.)

play possum *v. phr., informal* **1** To pretend to be asleep.—A cliché. *Johnny seemed to be fully asleep, but his mother knew that he was playing possum.* (Johnny seemed to be asleep, but his mother knew that he was only pretending.) **2** To stay quiet for self-protection; try to escape attention by inactivity. *The rabbit played possum under the bushes, hoping the hunter would not see him.* (The rabbit stayed quiet, not moving.) *Bob played possum when the teacher looked around.* (Bob did not say or do anything.)

play safe *or* **play it safe** *v. phr., informal* To be very careful; accept small gains or none to avoid loss; avoid danger for the sake of safety. *He got tired as the game went on, and began to play safe.* (He got tired after a while and stopped trying for points; he just tried to keep his opponent from scoring.) *Tom didn't know what the other driver would do, so he played it safe and stopped his own car.* (Tom was very careful and stopped his car to see what the other driver would do.)

play second fiddle *v. phr., informal* To act a smaller part; follow another's lead; be less noticed.—A cliché. *His wife had the stronger mind and he played second fiddle to her.* (His wife was more decisive and he let her lead.) *During the tournament, lessons played second fiddle to basketball.* (The students thought more about basketball than lessons.)

play the devil with *or* **play hob with** *v. phr., informal* To cause confusion in; upset. *Uncle Bob's unexpected visit played the devil with our own plans to travel.* (We were confused about dates because we did not know how long he would stay.) *Mother's illness played hob with our party.* (We were so worried about mother's illness we gave up our plans for a party.)

play the field *v. phr., informal* To date many different people; not always have dates with the same person. *Al had a steady girl* *friend, but John was playing the field.* (John dated many girls.) *Jim was crazy about Mary, but she was still playing the field.* (Mary did not want to go out only with Jim.) Contrast GO STEADY.

play the game *v. phr., informal* To obey the rules; do right; act fairly. *"That's not playing the game,"* we told him when he wanted to desert his wife. (That's not doing right.) *"Oh, let's play the game,"* he said, when his partner suggested a way to keep from paying some of their debts. ("Let's be honest," he said, when his partner suggested not paying some debts.) *Your parents want you to play the game in life.* (They want you to be honest and do what is right.)

play the market *v. phr.* To try to make money on the stock market by buying and selling stocks. *John lost all his savings playing the market.* (John lost his money because he took it out of the bank and used it to buy and sell stocks.) *Sometimes Mr. Smith makes a lot of money when he plays the market, and sometimes he loses.*

play to the gallery *v. phr.* To try to get the approval of the audience.—A cliché. *Whenever John recites in class he seems to be playing to the gallery.* (John shows off when he recites.) *The lawyer for the defense was more interested in playing to the gallery than in winning the case.* (He was interested in making an impression on the audience.) Compare SHOW OFF.

play up *v.* To call attention to; talk more about; emphasize. *The coach played up the possibilities, and kept our minds off our weaknesses.* (The coach talked more about what could be done, and kept us from thinking about what we could not do.) *The director played up the woman's glamor to conceal her lack of acting ability.* (The director called attention to the woman's beauty to make people forget her poor acting ability.)

play upon See PLAY ON.

play up to *v. phr., slang* 1 To try to gain the favor of, especially for selfish reasons; act to win the approval of; try to please. *He played up to the boss.* (He tried to make the boss like him so that he would get more pay.) 2 To use (something) to gain an end; to attend to (a weakness). *He played up to the old lady's vanity to get her support.* (He flattered the old lady so she would support his plan.)

play with fire *v. phr.* To put oneself in danger; to take risks.—A cliché. *Leaving your door unlocked in New York City is playing with fire.* (It's dangerous not to lock your door in New York.) *The doctor told Mr. Smith that he must watch his diet if he doesn't want to play with fire.* (If Mr. Smith doesn't watch his diet, he will be in danger.) Compare SKATE ON THIN ICE.

plow See PUT ONE'S HAND TO THE PLOW.

plow into *v.* 1 To attack vigorously. *He plowed into his work and finished it in a few hours.* (He attacked his work with great energy.) 2 To crash into with force. *A truck plowed into my car and smashed the fender.* (A truck crashed into my car.)

pluck up *v.* 1 To have (courage) by your own effort; make yourself have (courage). *In spite of failure, he plucked up heart to continue.* (Though he failed at first, he made himself brave enough to keep on.) *He plucked up courage when he saw a glimmer of hope.* (He was encouraged when he saw a little hope.) 2 To become happier; feel better; cheer up. *He plucked up when his wife recovered.* (He cheered up when his wife got well.)

pluck up one's courage See SCREW UP ONE'S COURAGE.

plug in *v. phr.* To connect (an electrical appliance) to a power wire by putting its plug into a receptacle or hole. *The transistor has multiplied the number of small radios that need not be plugged in.* (Small transistor radios usually need not be connected to a wire.)

plug into *v.* To connect (an electrical appliance) to a power wire by inserting its plug into a receptacle or hole. *He thought he had left the lamp plugged into the wall, and so was puzzled when it wouldn't light that night.* (He thought his lamp was connected, and was puzzled when it would not light.)

plume oneself *v. phr., literary* To be proud of yourself; boast. *He plumed himself on having the belle of the ball as his date.* (He was proud that his date was the prettiest and most popular girl at the dance.) *He plumed himself on his successful planning in the election.* (He was proud of himself for having planned actions that resulted in an election victory.) *She plumed herself on the grace with which she sat a horse.* (She was proud of her graceful riding.) Compare PRIDE ONESELF.

plunk down *v., informal* 1 To drop down; fall. *After walking a mile we plunked down on a bench to rest.* (We dropped on a bench.) 2 To drop something noisily or firmly. *He plunked the heavy suitcase down at the station.* (He dropped it noisily.) 3 To pay out. *He plunked a dollar down at the bar and ordered a beer.* (He paid out a dollar for a drink.)

please See AS YOU PLEASE.

pocket See BURN A HOLE IN ONE'S POCKET, LINE ONE'S POCKETS.

pocket money See SPENDING MONEY.

point See AT SWORDS' POINTS, AT THE POINT OF, BESIDE THE POINT, BOILING POINT, CASE IN POINT, COME TO THE POINT, EXTRA POINT, MAKE A POINT, ON THE POINT OF, SORE SPOT *or* SORE POINT, STRETCH A POINT *or* STRAIN A POINT, TALKING POINT.

point out *v.* 1 To show by pointing with the finger; point to; make clear the location of. *The guide pointed out the principal sights of the city.* (The guide showed us the chief things to see in the city.) **2** To bring to notice; call to attention; explain. *The policeman pointed out that the law forbids public sale of firecrackers.* (He explained that the law forbids public sale of firecrackers.) *The school secretary pointed out that the closing date for making applications had passed.* (She called it to their attention that the closing date for applying had passed.)

point up *v.* To show clearly; emphasize. *The increase in crime points up the need for greater police protection.* (The rise in crime shows that more police are needed.) *Johnny's report card points up his talent for math.* (Johnny got very high marks in mathematics. That shows clearly that he is good in that subject.)

poison-pen *adj.* Containing threats or false accusations; written in spite or to get revenge, and usually unsigned. *Mrs. Smith received a poison-pen letter telling her that her husband was untrue.* (Someone wrote Mrs. Smith a nasty letter falsely accusing her husband.) *To get revenge on Mary, Alice wrote a poison-pen letter to the teacher and signed Mary's name to it.* (Alice wrote a nasty letter to the teacher and made it look as though Mary wrote it.)

poke See PIG IN A POKE, TAKE A PUNCH AT *or* TAKE A POKE AT.

poke around *or* **poke about** *v.* **1** To search about; look into and under things. *The detective poked around in the missing man's office.* (He searched for any kind of evidence in the missing man's office.) **2** To move slowly or aimlessly; do little things. *He didn't feel well, and poked around the house.* (He felt ill, and worked at little things about the house.)

poke fun at See MAKE FUN OF.

poles apart *adj.* Completely different. *The two brothers were poles apart in personality.* (They had very different personalities.) *It was hard for the members to make any decisions because their ideas were poles apart.* (They could not agree on anything.)

polish See APPLE POLISHING.

polish off *v., informal* **1** To defeat easily. *The Dodgers polished off the Yankees in four straight games in the 1963 World Series.* (The Dodgers won the Series easily in four straight games.) **2** To finish completely; finish doing quickly, often in order to do something else. *The boys were hungry and polished off a big steak.* (They ate up the steak hungrily.) *Mary polished off her homework early so that she could watch TV.* (She did all her homework early.)

polish the apple *v. phr., slang* To try to make someone like you; to try to win favor by flattery.—A cliché. *Mary polished the apple at work because she wanted a day off.* (Mary tried to please her boss so he would give her a day off.) *Susan is the teacher's pet because she always polishes the apple.* (Susan does things to make the teacher like her.)—

apple polisher *n., slang* A person who is nice to the one in charge in order to be liked or treated better; a person who does favors for a superior. *Jane is an apple polisher. She is always helping the teacher and talking to him.* (Jane wants the teacher to like her better than he likes the other boys and girls.) *Joe is an apple-polisher. He will do anything for the boss.* (Joe never complains no matter what the boss tells him to do.) Compare EAGER BEAVER, YES-MAN.—**apple polishing** *n., slang* Trying to win someone's good-will by small acts; currying favor; the behavior of an apple polisher. *When John brought his teacher flowers, everyone thought he was apple polishing.* (Everyone thought John was trying to make the teacher like him.)

politics See PLAY POLITICS.

pond See LITTLE FROG IN A BIG POND.

pool See CAR POOL.

pooped out *adj., slang* Worn out; exhausted. *Everyone was pooped out after the hike.* (Everyone was exhausted.) *The heat made them feel pooped out.* (They were worn out from the heat.)

pop See EYES POP OUT.

pop fly *n.* A baseball batted high into the air but not very far from the plate. *The batter hit a pop fly to the shortstop.* (He hit the ball high in the air but only a short distance from the plate so that the shortstop could catch it.)

pop the question *v. phr., slang* To ask someone to marry you.—A cliché. *After the dance he popped the question.* (After the dance, he asked her to marry him.) *A man is often too bashful to pop the question.* (A man is often too bashful to ask a girl to marry him.)

pop up *v.* **1** *or* **bob up** To appear suddenly or unexpectedly; show up; come out. *Just when the coach thought he had everything under control, a new problem bobbed up.* (Just when things seemed to be going smoothly, the coach ran into more trouble.) *After no one had heard from him for years, John popped up in town again.* (After being away for years, John appeared in town again.) **2** To hit a pop fly in baseball. *Jim popped the pitch up.* (He hit a pop fly.)

pork See SALT PORK.

port of call *n. phr.* **1** Any of the ports that a ship visits after the start of a voyage and before the end; a port where passengers or cargo may be taken on or put off; an in-between port. *Savannah is a port of call for many Atlantic coasting vessels.* (Savannah is one of the regular stops made by ships plying between New York and New Orleans.) **2** A place you visit regularly or often; a stop included on your usual way of going. *It was an obscure little restaurant which I had made something of a port of call.* (It was a small eating place which I had formed the habit of patronizing.) *His home had become one of my regular ports of call in Boston.* (I visited his home regularly whenever I was in Boston.)

port of entry *n. phr.* **1** A port where things brought into the country to sell may pass through customs. *Other ports of entry have been taking business from New York.* (The ports of other cities have been getting some of the import trade that used to go through New York.) **2** A port where a citizen of another country may legally enter a country; a port having passport and immigration facilities. *Airports have joined seaports as ports of entry for the visiting foreigner.* (Many major airports now have passport and immigration offices, as only seaports once had.)

position See SCORING POSITION.

possessed of *adj. phr., formal* In possession of; having; owning. *He was possessed of great wealth.* (He had great wealth.) *He was possessed of great self-confidence.* (He had great self-confidence.)

possum See PLAY POSSUM.

post See FROM PILLAR TO POST.

pot See GO TO POT.

potato See HOT POTATO.

pot call the kettle black *informal* The person who is criticizing someone else is as guilty as the person he accuses; the charge is as true of the person who makes it as of the one he makes it against.—A cliché. *When the commissioner accused the road builder of bribery, the contractor said the pot was calling the kettle black.* (When the commissioner accused the road contractor of bribery, the contractor said the commissioner was equally guilty.) *Bill said John was cheating at a game but John replied that the pot was calling the kettle black.* (John meant that Bill was cheating too.)

potluck See TAKE POTLUCK.

potluck supper See COVERED-DISH SUPPER.

pound See PENNY WISE AND POUND FOOLISH.

pound the pavement *v. phr., informal* To walk up and down the streets; tramp about. *John pounded the pavement looking for a job.* (John walked everywhere looking for work.) *Mary and Bill pounded the pavement to find an apartment.* (They walked up and down looking for an apartment.)

pour See IT NEVER RAINS BUT IT POURS.

pour cold water on See THROW COLD WATER ON.

pour oil on troubled waters *v. phr.* To quiet a quarrel; say something to lessen anger and bring peace.—A cliché. *The groups were nearing a bitter quarrel until the leader poured oil on the troubled waters.* (A bad quarrel seemed certain until the leader quieted the opposing groups.)

pour out *v.* **1** To tell everything about; talk all about. *Mary poured out her troubles to her pal.* (Mary told her friend all about her troubles.) **2** To come out in great quantity;

stream out. *The people poured out of the building when they heard the fire alarm.* (All the people came out in a stream.)

powder See TAKE A POWDER.

powder room *n.* The ladies' rest room. *When they got to the restaurant, Mary went to the powder room to wash up.* (Mary went to the ladies' room.)

practice See IN PRACTICE *also* INTO PRACTICE, MAKE A PRACTICE OF, OUT OF PRACTICE.

present See AT PRESENT.

press box *n.* The place or room high in a sports stadium that is for newspaper men and radio and television announcers. *In baseball the official scorer sits in the press box.* (In baseball the man who keeps the official score stays in the high part of the stadium with the newspaper men.)

press conference *n. phr.* A meeting with news reporters. *The reporters questioned the President about foreign affairs at the press conference.* (The reporters interviewed the President about foreign affairs.) *The press conference with the Senator was broadcast on television.* (The Senator's interview with the reporters was shown on TV.)

press one's luck *or* **push one's luck** *v. phr.* To depend too much on luck; expect to continue to be lucky. *When John won his first two bets at the race track, he pressed his luck and increased his bets.* (John expected to go on winning.) *If you're lucky at first, don't press your luck.* (Don't depend on being lucky all the time.)

press the flesh *v., slang* To shake hands with total strangers by the hundreds, keeping an artificial smile all the way, in order to raise one's popularity during political elections. *Incumbent Governor Maxwell was pressing the flesh all day long at six different hotels.* (He kept shaking hands all day long to befriend the voters.) Compare BABY KISSER.

pretty See SITTING PRETTY.

pretty kettle of fish See KETTLE OF FISH.

prevail upon *or* **prevail on** *v.* To bring to an act or belief; cause a change in; persuade. *He prevailed upon the musician to entertain instead of the absent speaker.* (He persuaded the musician to entertain instead of the speaker who didn't come.) *He prevailed upon me to believe in his innocence.* (He made me believe he was innocent.)

prey on *or* **prey upon** *v.* **1** To habitually kill and eat; catch for food. *Cats prey on mice.* (Cats catch and eat mice.) **2** To capture or take in spoils of war or robbery. *Pirates preyed on American ships in the years just after the Revolutionary War.* (Pirates captured or robbed American ships for a while after the Revolutionary war.) **3** To cheat; rob. *Gangsters preyed on businesses of many kinds while the sale of liquor was prohibited.* (Gangsters robbed businesses of many kinds during the time when liquor could not be sold in America.) **4** To have a tiring and weakening effect on; weaken. *Ill health had preyed on him for years.* (Sickness had weakened his body for years.) *Business worries preyed on his mind.* (Business troubles tired and worried him.)

price on one's head *n. phr.* Reward offered to anyone who catches a thief or a murderer. *The hotel manager learned that the quiet man taken from his room by the police was a murderer with a price on his head.* (The hotel manager learned that there was a reward for the capture of the man who had stayed at the hotel because he had murdered someone.)

prick See KICK AGAINST THE PRICKS.

prick up one's ears *v. phr., informal* To come to interested attention; begin to listen closely; try to hear.—A cliché. *The woman pricked up her ears when she heard them talking about her.* (She heard her name spoken and listened closely.)

pride See SWALLOW ONE'S PRIDE.

pride oneself on *v. phr.* To be proud of; take satisfaction in; be much pleased by. *She prided herself on her beauty.* (She was proud of her beauty.) *He prided himself on his strength and toughness.* (He was proud of his strength and toughness.) Compare PLUME ONESELF.

print See FINE PRINT, IN PRINT, OUT OF PRINT.

private See IN PRIVATE.

private eye *n., colloquial* A private investigator; a detective. *Buddy Epsen plays a private eye on "Barnaby Jones."* (He portrays the role of a private investigator.)

progress See IN PROGRESS.

promise See AS GOOD AS ONE'S WORD, LICK AND A PROMISE.

promise the moon *v. phr.* To promise something impossible. *A politician who promises the moon during a campaign loses the voters' respect.* (A politician who promises something impossible during a campaign loses the voters' respect.) *I can't promise you the moon, but I'll do the best job I can.* (I can't promise to do a perfect job, but I'll do my best.) Compare ASK FOR THE MOON.

prune See FULL OF BEANS or FULL OF PRUNES.

psyched up *adj., informal* Mentally alert, ready to do something. *The students were all psyched up for their final exams.* (They were all mentally alert and ready to take the exams.)

psych out *v. phr., slang, informal* **1** To find out the real motives of (someone). *Sue sure's got Joe psyched out.* (Sue has figured out what Joe's real motives are.) **2** To go berserk, to lose one's nerve. *Joe says he doesn't ride his motorcycle on the highway anymore because he's psyched out.* (He lost his courage.) *Jim psyched out and robbed a liquor store, when he has all he needs and wants!* (He went berserk and committed a robbery when he had no need to do so.)

Public See JOHN Q. PUBLIC.

public See AIR ONE'S DIRTY LINEN IN PUBLIC or WASH ONE'S DIRTY LINEN IN PUBLIC, IN PUBLIC, IN THE PUBLIC EYE.

public-address system *n.* A set of devices for making a speaker's voice louder so that he can be heard by everyone within range. *The public-address system broke down during the Senator's speech.* (The set of devices that make a voice loud broke down and people could not hear the Senator's voice.) *The news was announced over the public-address system.* (The news was announced to everyone within range of the amplifying system.)

public speaker *n.* A person who speaks to the public. *A public speaker must appeal to all kinds of people.* (A person who speaks to the public must appeal to all kinds of people.)

pull See LONG HAUL or LONG PULL.

pull date *n., informal* The date stamped on baked goods, dairy products, or other perishable foods indicating the last day on which they may be sold before they must be removed from the shelves in a retail store. *This pie is way past the pull date—small wonder it's rotten.* (It is past the date to be removed from the shelf.)

pull down *v., informal* **1** To catch (a ball) after a hard run. *The outfielder pulled down a long drive to center-field.* (The outfielder ran hard and caught the baseball.) **2** To earn. *Mr. Blake pulls down $500 a week.* (Mr. Blake earns $500 a week.) *John pulled down an A in algebra by studying hard.* (John's hard studying earned him an A in algebra.) Compare HAUL DOWN.

pull down about one's ears or **pull down around one's ears** See ABOUT ONE'S EARS.

pull hitter *n.* A baseball batter who regularly hits the ball to the same side of the field as the side of the plate on which he stands. *The short left field fence favored right-handed pull hitters.* (Right-handed batters who regularly hit to left field like the short left field fence.)

pull in See HAUL IN.

pull in one's horns or **draw in one's horns** *v. phr., informal* **1** To reduce your boasts; calm down from a quarrel; back down on a promise.—A cliché. *He said he could beat any man there single-handed, but he pulled in his horns when Jack came forward.* (He said he could beat any man there alone, but he gave up when Jack offered to fight.) **2** To cut back from one's usual way of living; reduce spending or activities; save. *After the business failed, Father had to pull in his horns.* (After the business failed, Father had to reduce his spending.) *As one advances in years, it is prudent to pull in one's horns more and more as to physical activity.* (As one grows older, it is wise to exercise and work less.)

pull off *v., informal* To succeed in (something thought difficult or impossible); do. *Ben Hogan pulled off the impossible by winning* *three golf tournaments in one year.* (Ben Hogan succeeded in winning three golf tournaments in one year although that seemed impossible.) *The bandits pulled off a daring bank robbery.* (The bandits succeeded in robbing a bank, although that seems very difficult.) Compare PUT ACROSS 2.

pull oneself together *v. phr.* To become calm after being excited or disturbed; recover self-command; control yourself. *It had been a disturbing moment, but he was able to pull himself together.* (He had been badly upset, but got control of himself.)

pull oneself up by the boostraps *or* **pull oneself up by one's own bootstraps** *adv. phr.* To succeed without help; succeed by your own efforts. *He had to pull himself up by the bootstraps.* (He got no help but succeeded in life by himself.)

pull one's leg *v. phr., informal* To get someone to accept a ridiculous story as true; fool someone with a humorous account of something; trick.—A cliché. *For a moment, I actually believed that his wife had royal blood. Then I realized he was pulling my leg.* (For a moment. Then I really thought his wife was a princess. Then I knew he was fooling me.) *Western cowboys loved to pull a stranger's leg.* (They loved to tell big stories which were not true.) Compare STRING ALONG.—**leg-pulling** *n.* *Strangers were often fooled by the cowboys' leg-pulling.* (The cowboys' big stories often fooled strangers.)

pull one's punches *v. phr., informal* **1** Not to hit as hard as you can. *Jimmy pulled his punches and let Paul win the boxing match.* (Jimmy did not hit Paul as hard as he could.) **2** To hide unpleasant facts or make them seem good.—Usually used in the negative. *The mayor spoke bluntly; he didn't pull any punches.* (The mayor frankly told the unpleasant facts.) Contrast STRAIGHT FROM THE SHOULDER.

pull one's teeth *v. phr.* To take power away from; make powerless.—A hackneyed phrase. *The General pulled the teeth of the rebel army by blocking its ammunition supply line.* (The General made the rebel army powerless by blocking its supply of ammunition.) *The student government council was so irresponsible that the principal pulled its teeth.* (The student government council acted foolishly, so the principal took away its power.)

pull one's weight *v. phr.* To do your full share of work; do your part. *In a small shop, it is important that each man pull his weight.* (In a small shop, it is important for each man to do his full share.) *When Mother was sick in the hospital, Father said each child must pull his own weight.* (Father said each child must do his share of the housework.) Compare WORTH ONE'S SALT.

pull out of a hat *v. phr., informal* To get as if by magic; invent; imagine.—A cliché. *When the introduction to a dictionary tells you how many hours went into its making, these figures were not pulled out of a hat.* (These figures were not invented or imagined.) *Let's see you pull an excuse out of your hat.* (Let's see you make up an excuse.)

pull over *v.* To drive to the side of the road and stop. *The policeman told the speeder to pull over.* (The policeman told the speeder to drive to the side of the road and stop.) *Everyone pulled over to let the ambulance pass.* (Everyone drove to the side of the road to let the ambulance go by.)

pull rank *v. phr., slang, informal* To assert one's superior position or authority on a person of lower rank as in exacting a privilege or a favor. *How come you always get the night duty?—Phineas Leman pulled rank on me.* (He asserted his superiority and I got the worse end of the job.)

pull strings *or* **pull wires** *v. phr., informal* To secretly use influence and power, especially with people in charge or in important jobs to do or get something; make use of friends to gain your wishes. *If you want to see the Governor, Mr. Root can pull strings for you.* (Mr. Root can help you because he knows the Governor himself or he knows people who do.) *Jack pulled wires and got us a room at the crowded hotel.* (Jack arranged for us to get a room.)—**wire-puller** *n.* *Bill got a ticket for speeding, but his father is a wire-puller and got it fixed.* (Bill's father has power and important friends who arranged to have the ticket cancelled.)—**wire-pulling** *n.* *It took some wire-pulling to get the mayor to come to the party.* (It took some arranging and persuading to get the mayor to come.)

pull the plug on *v. phr., slang* To expose (someone's) secret activities *The citizens' committee pulled the plug on the mayor, and he lost his election.* (The committee exposed the mayor's secret activities and this caused the mayor to lose the election.)

pull the rug out from under *v. phr., informal* To withdraw support unexpectedly from; to spoil the plans of.—A cliché. *Bill thought he would be elected, but his friends pulled the rug out from under him and voted for Vin.* (Bill's friends withdrew their support of him without warning.) *We were planning a vacation, but the baby's illness pulled the rug out from under us.* (The baby's illness spoiled our vacation plans.)

pull the wool over one's eyes *v. phr., informal* To fool someone into thinking well of you; deceive.—A cliché. *The business man had pulled the wool over his partner's eyes about their financial position.* (He had fooled his partner about money matters.) *Bob tried to pull the wool over his teacher's eyes, but she was too smart for him.* (Bob tried to make her think he was a good student but she knew he wasn't.)

pull through *v.* **1** To help through; bring

safely through a difficulty or sudden trouble; save. *A generous loan showed the bank's faith in Father and pulled him through the business trouble.* (The bank had faith in Father and lent him money which saved his business.) **2** To recover from an illness or misfortune; conquer a disaster; escape death or failure. *By a near-miracle, he pulled through after the smashup.* (He recovered after the car accident, although at first he wasn't expected to live.)

pull together *v.* To join your efforts with those of others; work on a task together; cooperate. *Many men must pull together if a large business is to succeed.* (The success of large businesses depends on getting many men to work in agreement.) *Tim was a good football captain because he always got his teammates to pull together.* (Tim got his team to cooperate well; he was a good captain.)

pull up *v.* **1** To check the forward motion of; halt; stop. *He pulled up his horse at the gate.* (He made his horse stop at the gate.) **2** To tell (someone) to stop doing something; say (someone) is doing wrong and must stop; scold. *Jim talked rudely to Mother, and Father pulled him up.* (Father told Jim that was wrong and he must stop.) *Ann said in her report that America was discovered in 1634, and the teacher pulled her up.* (The teacher stopped Ann and told her that was wrong.) **3** To stop moving forward; halt. *The car slowed down and pulled up at the curb.* (The car stopped at the curb.) **4** To come even with; move up beside. *The other boat pulled up alongside us.* (The other boat moved up beside us.)

pull up stakes *v. phr., informal* To leave the place where you have been living. *We are going to pull up stakes and move to California.* (We are going to leave this place and move to California.) *The Jones family pulled up stakes three times in two years.* (The Jones family moved to different homes three times in two years.)

pull wires See PULL STRINGS.

punch See BEAT TO THE PUNCH, PACK A PUNCH, PULL ONE'S PUNCHES, TAKE A PUNCH AT.

punch-drunk *adj.* **1** Dazed or become dulled in the mind from being hit in the head. *He was a punch-drunk boxer who made his living shining shoes.* (He had become stupid from a blow on the head, and could not make a living at a real job.) **2** In a foggy state of mind; groggy. *Mary was so thrilled at winning the contest she acted punch-drunk.* (Mary was so thrilled she hardly knew where she was.) *Mark was punch-drunk for a few minutes after he fell off his bicycle.* (Mark was dazed for a few minutes after he fell off his bicycle.)

puppy love *also* **calf love** *n., informal* The first love of very young people. *When John and Mary began going around together in* junior high school, their parents said it was just puppy love. (Their parents said it was not real or lasting love.)

pure and simple *adj.* Simply stated; basic. —Follows the noun it modifies and is used for emphasis. *The problem, pure and simple, is finding a baby-sitter.* (The basic problem is finding a baby-sitter.) *The question, pure and simple, is whether you will support me.* (The question is basically whether you will support me.) Compare BOIL DOWN 3.

purpose See AT CROSS PURPOSES, ON PURPOSE, TO ALL INTENTS AND PURPOSES.

purse See LINE ONE'S POCKETS *also* LINE ONE'S PURSE.

purse strings *n.* Care or control of money. *Dad holds the purse strings in our family.* (Dad controls the money in our family.) *The Treasurer refused to let go of the club's purse strings.* (The Treasurer refused to give up control of the club's money.)

push around *v., informal* To be bossy with; bully. *Don't try to push me around!* (Don't try to be bossy with me.) *Paul is always pushing the smaller children around.* (Paul is always making the smaller children do what he wants.)

push off *or* **shove off** *v.* **1** To push a boat away from the shore. *Before Tom could reach the boat, Jake had shoved off.* (Jake pushed the boat away from the shore before Tom could reach it.) **2** *slang* To start; leave. *We were ready to push off at ten o'clock, but had to wait for Jill.* (We were ready to start at ten o'clock, but had to wait for Jill.) *Jim was planning to stay at the beach all day, but when the crowds arrived he shoved off.* (Jim left the beach when the crowds arrived.)

push one's luck See PRESS ONE'S LUCK.

push the panic button *v. phr., slang* To become very much frightened; nervous, or excited especially at a time of danger or worry. *John thought he saw a ghost and pushed the panic button.* (John imagined he saw a ghost and was greatly scared.) *Keep cool; don't hit the panic button!* (Keep cool; don't get scared!) Syn. LOSE ONE'S HEAD.

push-up *n.* An exercise to build strong arms and shoulders, in which you lie on your stomach and push your body up on your hands and toes. *At the age of seventy, Grandpa still does twenty push-ups every day.* (Grandpa still does an exercise to build strong arms and shoulders every day.) *The football team does push-ups every day.* (The members of the football team do an exercise to strengthen their arms and shoulders every day.)

push up daisies *v. phr., slang* To be dead and buried.—A cliché. *I'll be around when you're pushing up daisies.* (I'll be alive when you are dead and buried.) *Don't play with guns or you may push up the daisies.* (You may be killed.)

put See HARD PUT *or* HARD PUT TO IT, STAY PUT.

put a bee in one's bonnet See BEE IN ONE'S BONNET.

put a bug in one's ear *or* **put a flea in one's ear** See BUG IN ONE'S EAR.

put across *v.* **1** To explain clearly; make yourself understood; communicate. *He knew how to put his ideas across.* (He knew how to get his ideas understood.) Compare GET ACROSS. **2** *informal* To get (something) done successfully; bring to success; make real. *He put across a big sales campaign.* (He succeeded in a big selling plan.) *The new librarian put across a fine new library building.* (The new librarian persuaded people to raise the money and build a library building.) Syn. PUT OVER **2.** Compare PULL OFF.

put all one's eggs in one basket *v. phr.* To place all your efforts, interests, or hopes in a single person or thing.—A cliché. *Going steady in high school is putting all your eggs in one basket too soon.* (A person who goes steady when he is young puts too much hope in one boy, or girl, too soon.) *To buy stock in a single company is to put all your eggs in one basket.* (Investing in only one company limits a person's chances of making money in the stock market to those of the one company only.) *He has decided to specialize in lathe work, although he knows it is risky to put all his eggs in one basket.* (He has decided to learn only lathe work, although he knows that having only one skill may make it difficult to find a job.)

put an end to *or* **put a stop to** *v. phr.* **1** To make (something) end; stop; end. *The farmer built an electric fence around his field to put an end to trespassing.* (The farmer put up a fence to stop people who came onto his land without permission.) *The principal said that running in the halls was dangerous, and told the teachers to put a stop to it.* (He told the teachers to make students stop running in the halls.) **2** To destroy or kill. *The new highway took most of the traffic from the old road and put an end to Mr. Hanson's motel business.* (The new highway destroyed Mr. Hanson's business by taking travelers far from his motel.) *When the horse broke his leg, the farmer put an end to him.* (The farmer killed the horse.)

put away *v.* **1** To put in the right place or out of sight. *She put away the towels.* (She put them in the closet where they belonged.) **2** To lay aside; stop thinking about. *He put his worries away for the weekend.* (He stopped thinking about his worries.) **3** *archaic* To divorce. *Whosoever putteth away his wife, and marrieth another, committeth adultery.—St. Luke 16:18* (Any man who divorces his wife, and marries another woman, is guilty of adultery.) **4** *informal* To eat or drink. *He put away a big supper and three cups of coffee.* (He ate a big supper and drank three cups of coffee.) Compare STOW AWAY. **5** *informal* To put in a mental hospital. *He had to put his wife away when she became mentally ill.* (He had to put her in a mental hospital.) **6** To put to death for a reason; kill. *He had his dog put away when it became too old and unhappy.* (He had someone kill it because it was sick and weak.)

put back the clock *or* **turn back the clock** *v. phr.* To go back in time; relive the past. *If I could put back the clock, I'd give more thought to preparing for a career.* (If I could live the past over again, I would think more seriously about preparing for a career.) *Richard wishes that he had lived in frontier days, but he can't turn back the clock.* (Richard wishes that he had lived in frontier days, but he can't go back in time.)

put by *v.* To save for the future; lay aside. *He had put by a good sum during a working lifetime.* (He had saved much money during his earning years.)

put down *v.* **1** To stop by force; crush. *In 24 hours the General had entirely put down the rebellion.* (He stopped the fighting in a day's time.) **2** To put a stop to; check. *She had patiently put down unkind talk by living a good life.* (She had ended unkind gossip by living a good life.) **3** To write a record of; write down. *He put down the story while it was fresh in his mind.* (He wrote down his account while he remembered the happenings.) **4** To write a name in a list as agreeing to do something. *The banker put himself down for $1000.* (He agreed to give $1000.) *Sheila put Barbara down for the decorations.* (Sheila made a list of helpers for the class party, and she wrote Barbara's name on the list as the person who would decorate the room.) **5** To decide the kind or class of; characterize. *He put the man down as a bum.* (He decided that the man was a bum.) *He put it down as a piece of bad luck.* (He blamed it on bad luck.) **6** To name as a cause; attribute. *He put the odd weather down to nuclear explosions.* (He blamed the odd weather on nuclear explosions.) **7** To dig; drill; sink. *He put down a new well.* (He dug a new well.)

put in *v.* **1** To add to what has been said; say (something) in addition to what others say. *While the boys were discussing the car accident, Ben put in that the road was icy.* (Ben said that the road had been icy.) *My father put in a word for me and I got the job.* (My father said I was a good worker.) **2** To buy and keep in a store to sell. *He put in a full stock of drugs.* (He got all kinds of drugs to sell in his store.) **3** To spend (time). *He put in many years as a printer.* (He worked as a printer for years.) *He put in an hour a day reading.* (He read about an hour every day.) **4** To plant. *He put in a row of radishes.*

(He planted a row of radish seed.) **5** To stop at a port on a journey by water. *After the fire, the ship put in for repairs.* (It stopped at the next port.) **6** To apply; ask.—Used with *for*. *When a better job was open, he put in for it.* (When there was a better job, he asked for it.) *The sailor put in for time to visit his family before the ship went to sea.* (He asked permission to visit his family.)

put in an appearance *also* **make an appearance** *v. phr.* To be present, esp. for a short time; visit; appear. *He put in an appearance at work, but he was too ill to stay.* (He came to work, but he was too ill to stay.) *The President put in an appearance at several dances the evening after he was sworn in.* (The President appeared and stayed briefly at several dances on the night after the ceremony making him President.)

put in mind of *v. phr., nonstandard* To remind of; suggest to; call up the memory of. *She puts me in mind of my sister.* (She reminds me of my sister.) *That puts me in mind of a story.* (That makes me think of a story.)

put in one's place *v. phr., informal* To criticize someone for impolite boldness; remind someone of low rank or position; reduce someone's unsuitable pride; deflate. *The superintendent was taking command when the president put him in his place by saying, "No, I'm the boss here."* (The superintendent was going to settle things without talking to anyone, when the president reminded him that he wasn't the boss.) *She was a teacher who could put an impolitely bold boy in his place with just a glance.* (She could quiet a saucy boy with a look.) Syn. CUT DOWN TO SIZE.

put in one's two cents worth See TWO CENTS 2.

put in one's way See PUT IN THE WAY OF.

put in the way of *or* **put in one's way** *v. phr.* To set before (someone); give to (someone); show the way to; help towards. *After Joe graduated, the coach put him in the way of a good job.* (The coach helped him get a good job.) *The librarian put me in the way of a lot of new material on the subject of my report.* (She showed me where to find a lot of new facts on the subject.) *My uncle put a fine opportunity in my way when he asked me to tour Europe with him.* (He gave me a good chance to learn something.)

put it on thick See LAY IT ON.

put off *v.* **1** *informal* To cause confusion in; embarrass; displease. *I was rather put off by the shamelessness of his proposal.* (His suggestion was so boldly improper that I did not know what to say or do.) *The man's slovenliness put me off.* (The man's dirty condition displeased me.) **2** To wait and have (something) at a later time; postpone. *They put off the picnic because of the rain.* (They postponed the picnic because of the rain.) **3** To make (someone) wait; turn aside. *When*

he asked her to name a day for their wedding, she put him off. (When he asked her to name a day for their wedding, she made him wait for a decision.) *When the bill collector called, Mrs. Smith managed to put him off.* (When the man came to collect the bill, Mrs. Smith succeeded in getting him to wait.) **4** To draw away the attention; turn aside; distract. *Little Jeannie began to tell the guests some family secrets, but Father was able to put her off.* (Father was able to make her think and talk of something different.) **5** To move out to sea; leave shore. *They put off in small boats to meet the coming ship.* (They rowed out in small boats to meet the coming ship.) Syn. PUT OUT.

put on *v.* **1** To dress in. *The boy took off his clothes and put on his pajamas.* (He dressed in his pajamas.) *Mother put a coat on the baby.* (She dressed the baby in a coat.) **2a** To pretend, assume, show. *Mary isn't really sick; she's only putting on.* (She's only pretending to be sick.) *He put on a smile.* (He pretended to smile.) *The child was putting on airs.* (The child showed a proud manner.) **2b** To exaggerate; make too much of. *That's rather putting it on.* (That's claiming more than is true.) Compare LAY IT ON. **3** To begin to have more (body weight); gain (weight). *Mary was thin from sickness, and the doctor said she must put on ten pounds.* (She must gain ten pounds.) *Too many sweets and not enough exercise will make you put on weight.* (They will make you get fat.) **4a** To plan and prepare; produce; arrange; give; stage. *The senior class put on a dance.* (They held a dance.) *The actor put on a fine performance.* (He gave a fine show.) **4b** To make (an effort). *The runner put on an extra burst of speed and won the race.* (He made a last big effort.) **5** To choose to send; employ on a job. *The school put on extra men to get the new building ready.* (It employed more men to get the place ready.)

put one's back to it *v. phr.* To make a real effort; to try.—A cliché. *You can finish the job by noon if you put your back to it.* (You can finish the work by noon if you make a real effort.) *I'm sure you can make the football team if you put your back to it.* (I'm sure you can get on the football team if you try.)

put one's best foot forward *v. phr., informal* To try to make a good impression; try to make a good appearance; do one's best.—A hackneyed phrase. *During courtship, it is natural to put your best foot forward.* (During courtship, people usually try to make a good impression.) *When Ted applied for the job, he put his best foot forward.* (He acted politely and told what he could do for the employer.)

put one's cards on the table See LAY ONE'S CARDS ON THE TABLE.

put oneself in another's place *or* **put oneself in another's shoes** *v. phr.* To understand another person's feeling imaginatively; try to know his feelings and reasons with understanding; enter into his trouble. *It seemed like a dreadful thing for Bob to do, but I tried to put myself in his place.* (It seemed like a dreadful thing for Bob to do, but I tried to understand his thinking and why he had done it.) *If you will put yourself in the customer's shoes, you may realize why the thing isn't selling.* (If you will try to imagine how the customer thinks and feels, you may understand why the thing doesn't sell.)

put one's finger on *also* **lay one's finger on** *v. phr.* To find exactly. *The engineers couldn't put their fingers on the reason for the rocket's failure to orbit.* (The engineers could not find the exact reason for the failure.) *We called in an electrician hoping he could put a finger on the cause of the short circuit.* (We hired an electrician to find exactly what caused the short circuit.)

put one's foot down *v. phr., informal* To take a decided stand; be stubborn in decision. —A trite expression. *John didn't want to practice his piano lesson, but Father put his foot down.* (John didn't want to practice his piano lesson, but his father made him.) *When it came to liquor at parties, our parents put their foot down.* (Our parents refused to let us have liquor at our parties.) *When I tried to argue that lots of colleges were as good as Harvard, Father put his foot down.* (Father decided firmly I must go to Harvard.)

put one's foot in it *or* **put one's foot in one's mouth** *v. phr., informal* To speak carelessly and rudely; hurt another's feelings without intending to; make a rude mistake.—A cliché. *He put his foot in it with his remark about self-made men, because Jones was one of them.* (He made a bad mistake when he criticized men who become rich by their own efforts, because Jones was himself one of those men.) *She put her foot in her mouth with her joke about that church, not knowing that one of the guests belonged to it.* (She hurt one guest's feelings with her joke, because he was a member of the church she made fun of.)

put one's hand on See LAY ONE'S HANDS ON 3.

put one's hand to *or* **set one's hand to** *or* **turn one's hand to** *v. phr.* To start working at; try to do. *Hal does a good job at everything that he turns his hand to.* (Hal does a good job at everything he tries to do.) *After Mr. Sullivan found farming unprofitable, he moved to town and turned his hand to carpentry.* (Mr. Sullivan began to work as a carpenter.)

put one's hand to the plow *or* **set one's hand to the plow** *v. phr.* To start doing something of importance; give yourself to a big job.—A cliché. *We felt that he had put his hand to the plow, and we didn't like it when he quit.* (We felt that he had promised to do the job, and we didn't think he was right to quit.)

put one's head in the sand See HIDE ONE'S HEAD IN THE SAND.

put one's heart on one's sleeve See HEART ON ONE'S SLEEVE.

put one's money on a scratched horse *v. phr., informal* To bet on a certain failure; to gamble without a chance of winning.—A cliché. *You bet on the New York Mets to win the World Series? Why put your money on a scratched horse?* (Why were you so foolish as to bet on the Mets when they will certainly fail to win the Series?) Compare STACK THE CARDS.

put one's nose out of joint *v. phr., informal* **1** To make you jealous; leave you out of favor.—A cliché. *When Jane accepted Tom's invitation, it put Jack's nose out of joint.* (Jane made Jack jealous by going with Tom.) **2** To ruin your plans; cause you disappointment.—A cliché. *Joe's mother put his nose out of joint by not letting him go to the movie.* (Joe was disappointed when his mother did not let him go.)

put one's house in order *or* **set one's house in order** *v. phr.* To arrange your affairs in good order.—A cliché. *Grandfather knew he would not live long, and set his house in order.* (Grandfather knew he had not long to live, so he arranged his affairs in good order.) *When Mr. Black died, his lawyer helped the widow put her house in order.* (Mr. Black's lawyer helped the widow to get her business right.)

put one's shoulder to the wheel *v. phr.* To make a great effort yourself or with others; try hard; cooperate.—A cliché. *The effort to get a new high school succeeded because everyone put his shoulder to the wheel.* (The town got a new high school because everybody helped and voted for it.) *The company was failing in business until a new manager put his shoulder to the wheel.* (The new manager worked hard and made the company more successful.)

put on one's thinking cap *v. phr.* To think hard and long about some problem or question.—A cliché. *Miss Stone told her pupils to put on their thinking caps before answering the question.* (She wanted them to take time to think hard before answering.)

put on the line See LAY ON THE LINE.

put on the map *v. phr.* To make (a place) well known.—A hackneyed phrase. *The first successful climb of Mount Matterhorn put Zermatt, Switzerland on the map.* (The first successful climb of Mt. Matterhorn made Zermatt very well known.) *Shakespeare put his hometown of Stratford-on-Avon on the map.* (People all over the world have heard of Stratford-on-Avon because it was Shakespeare's home.)

put out *v.* **1** To make a flame or light stop burning; extinguish; turn off. *Please put the light out when you leave the room.* (Please turn off the light when you leave the room.)

The firemen put out the blaze. (The firemen extinguished the fire.) **2** To prepare for the public; produce; make. *For years he had put out a weekly newspaper.* (He had published a weekly newspaper for years.) *It is a small restaurant, which puts out an excellent dinner.* (It is a small cafe, which provides an excellent dinner.) **3** To invest or loan money. *He put out all his spare money at 4 per cent or better.* (He got 4 per cent or more on all the money he had for lending.) **4** To make angry; irritate; annoy. *It puts the teacher out to be lied to.* (It angers him to be lied to.) *Father was put out when Jane spilled grape juice on his new suit.* (Father was angry.) **5** *informal* To cause inconvenience to; bother. *He put himself out to make things pleasant for us.* (He went to much trouble to make things pleasant for us.) *Will it put you out if I borrow you pen?* (Will it be difficult for you if I borrow your pen?) Compare GO OUT OF ONE'S WAY. **6** To retire from play in baseball. *The runner was put out at first base.* (The runner was retired at first base.) **7** To go from shore; leave. *A Coast Guard boat put out through the waves.* (A small Coast Guard boat went out from shore through the waves.) **8** *vulgar, avoidable* Said of women easy and ready to engage in sexual intercourse. *It is rumored that Hermione gets her promotions as fast as she does because she puts out.* (It is rumored that she pays for her promotions with sex.)

put out of the way *v. phr.* To kill. *When people spoke against the dictator, he had them put out of the way.* (He had them killed.) *The old dog was very sick, and Father had the animal doctor put him out of the way.* (Father asked the doctor to take the dog's life without pain.)

put over *v.* **1** To wait to a later time; postpone. *They put over the meeting to the following Tuesday.* (They postponed the meeting to the next Tuesday.) Syn. PUT OFF. **2** *informal* To make a success of; complete. *He put over a complex and difficult business deal.* (He made a success of a many-sided, difficult deal.) Syn. BRING OFF, PUT ACROSS, SLIP OVER. **3** *informal* To practice deception; trick; fool.—Used with *on*. *George thought he was putting something over on the teacher when he said he was absent the day before because his mother was sick and needed him.* (He thought he was fooling the teacher.) *Tom really slipped one over on us when he came to the Halloween party dressed as a witch.* (He fooled us; no one recognized him.)

put someone on *v.* To play a joke on someone by saying or doing things that are only pretense; kid. *When the voice on the phone told Mrs. Jones she had won a $10,000 prize, she thought someone was putting her on.* (She thought someone was teasing her.)

put that in your pipe and smoke it *v. phr.,* *informal* To understand something told you; accept something as fact or reality; not try to change it.—Usually used as a command, normally only in speech, and often considered rude. *People don't vote against Santa Claus, and you might as well put that in your pipe and smoke it.* (People don't vote against anyone who provides them with things, and you might as well accept that as a fact.) *I am not going to do that and you can put that in your pipe and smoke it.* (I refuse to do it, and you can't change me.)

put the bite on *v. phr., slang* To ask (for money, favors, etc.) *John put the bite on his friend for several tickets to the dance.* (John asked his friend to buy several tickets to the dance for him.) *Willie Mays put the bite on the Giants for a large raise.* (Willie Mays asked the Giants for a large increase in pay.)

put the cart before the horse See CART BEFORE THE HORSE.

put their heads together *or* **lay their heads together** *v. phr., informal* To plan or consider things together; discuss something as a group; talk it over. *They put their heads together and decided on a gift.* (They chose a gift after talking it over.) *We laid our heads together and decided to have a picnic.* (We talked it over and decided to have a picnic.)

put through one's paces *v. phr., informal* To test the different abilities and skills of a person or a thing; call for a show of what one can do. *He put his new car through its paces.* (He tried out the car at different speeds and in different places.) *Many different problems put the new mayor through his paces in the first months of his term.* (Problems made the new mayor show what he could do.)

put to bed *v. phr.* **1** To put to rest for the night. *Father put the three children to bed.* (Father put the three children to rest for the night.) *The boy seemed ill, so the nurse put him to bed.* (The boy seemed ill, so the nurse helped him get into bed.) **2** *informal* To complete preparations and print. *The newspaper was put to bed at 1:15 A.M.* (The newspaper was ready to go to press at 1:15 A.M.) *The pressroom was late in putting the sports section to bed.* (The pressmen were late in printing the sports section of the newspaper.)

put to it *adj. phr.* Hard pressed; having trouble; in difficulty; puzzled. *When he lost his job, he was rather put to it for a while to provide for his family.* (When he lost his job, he had trouble for a while supporting his family.) *The boy was put to it to answer the teacher's question.* (He didn't know how to answer the question and had to think.)

put to rights *or* **set to rights** *v. phr., informal* To put in good order; clean up. *It took the company a long time to put the office to rights after the fire.* (It took the company a long time to put the office in good order after the fire.) *It took Mrs. Smith an hour to set* *the room to rights after the party.* (It took Mrs. Smith an hour to clean up the room after the party.)

put to sea *v. phr.* To start a voyage. *The Captain said the ship would put to sea at six in the morning.* (The Captain said the ship would start its voyage at six in the morning.) *In the days of sailing ships, putting to sea depended on the tides.* (In the days of sailing ships, the time of beginning a voyage depended upon the rise and fall of the sea.)

put to shame *v. phr.* **1** To disgrace. *The cleanliness of European cities puts our cities to shame.* (European cities are so clean that they make American cities look dirty.) *That filthy dump puts our town to shame.* (That filthy dump is a disgrace to our town.) **2** To do much better than surpass. *Roger Maris put other players to shame when he hit 61 home runs in 1961.* (Roger Maris did much better than other players when he hit 61 home runs in 1961.)

put to the sword *v. phr., literary* To kill (people) in war, especially with a sword. *The Romans put their enemies to the sword.* (The Romans killed their enemies with their swords.) *In some wars captives have been put to the sword.* (They have all been killed.)

put to use *v. phr.* To use. *During the early part of the Korean war the cooks and office workers of the U.S. Army were put to use in battle.* (The cooks and office workers were used as regular soldiers in battle.) *Henry decided to put his dictionary to use.* (Henry decided to use his dictionary.) *I wish you'd put the lawn mower to use!* (I wish you'd mow the lawn!)

put two and two together *v. phr.* To make decisions from the seeming proofs; reason from the known facts; conclude; decide.—A cliché. *He had put two and two together and decided where they had probably gone.* (After weighing the various bits of evidence, he decided where they had probably gone.) *It was just a matter of putting two and two together: the facts seemed to permit only one decision.* (It seemed from the evidence that only one conclusion was possible.) *Some people can put two and two together and get three.* (They see some evidence and guess other things.)

put up *v.* **1a** To make and pack (especially a lunch or medicine); get ready; prepare. *Every morning Mother puts up lunches for the three children.* (Every morning Mother makes sandwiches and packs lunches for the three children.) *The druggist put up the medicine that the doctor had prescribed.* (The druggist prepared the medicine that the doctor had advised.) Compare MAKE UP 1. **1b** To put food into jars or cans to save; can. *Mother is putting up peaches in jars.* (She is putting peaches in jars to save them.) **1c** To store away for later use. *The farmer put up three tons of hay for the winter.* (The farmer stored three tons of hay to feed to his ani-

mals.) **2** To put in place; put (something) where it belongs. *After he unpacked the car, Father put it up.* (Father put the car in the garage, where he kept it when he was not using it.) *After the hard ride, the doctor gave the horse to the stable boy to put up.* (The doctor gave the horse to the stable boy to put in the stable.) *After the battle, the knight put up his sword.* (The knight put his sword in its holder.) Syn. PUT AWAY. **3** To suggest that (someone) be chosen a member, officer, or official. *The club decided to take in another member, and Bill put up Charles.* (Bill suggested that Charles be chosen as a member of the club.)—Often used with *for. The Republicans put Mr. Williams up for mayor.* (The Republicans named Mr. Williams to try to be elected mayor.) **4** To put (hair) a special way; arrange. *Aunt May puts up her hair in curlers every night.* (Aunt May winds her hair around curlers every night so that it will have a special wave.) *Sue put her hair up in a twist for the dance.* (Sue arranged her hair in a twist for the dance.) Compare DO UP 3a. **5** To place on sale; offer for sale. *She put the house up for sale.* (She offered the house for sale.) **6a** To provide lodging for; furnish a room to. *The visitor was put up in the home of Mr. Wilson.* (The visitor was given a room in Mr. Wilson's home.) *They put Frank up at a good hotel.* (They got him a room at a good hotel.) **6b** To rent or get shelter take lodging; stay in a place to sleep. *The traveler put up at a motel.* (He rented a room at a motel.) *We put up with friends on our trip to Canada.* (We stayed in the home of friends in Canada.) **7** To make; engage in. *He put up a good fight against his sickness.* (He fought bravely to get well.) Compare CARRY ON. **8** To furnish (money) or something needed; pay for. *He put up the money to build a hotel.* (He provided the money to build a hotel.) *He put up money to start making the movie.* (He provided the money to start making the movie.)

put up *or* **shut up** *v. phr., informal* **1** To bet your money on what you say or stop saying it. —Often used as a command; often considered rude. *The man from out of town kept saying their team would beat ours, and finally Father told him, "Put up or shut up."* (Father told the man to make a bet on it with money, or else to be quiet.) **2** To prove something or stop saying it.—Often used as a command; often considered rude. *George told Al that he could run faster than the school champion, and Al told George to put up or shut up.* (Al told George to prove it.)

put upon *v.* To use (someone) unfairly; expect too much from.—Used in the passive or in the past participle. *Martha was put upon by the bigger girls.* (The bigger girls made Martha do things for them.) *Arthur was a much put-upon person.* (Arthur was expected to do too much.)

put up to *v. phr., informal* To talk to and make do; persuade to; get to do. *Older boys put us up to painting the statue red on Halloween.* (Older boys told us we should do it.) Compare EGG ON. •

put up with *v.* To accept patiently; bear. *We had to put up with Jim's poor table manners because he refused to change.* (We had to accept Jim's poor table manners patiently, because he refused to change.) *The mother told her children, "I refuse to put up with your tracking in mud!"* (The mother said she refused to let her children track mud into the house any more.) Compare STAND FOR.

put wise *v., slang* To tell (someone) facts that will give him an advantage over others or make him alert to opportunity or danger. *The new boy did not know that Jim was playing a trick on him, so I put him wise.* (I told him that Jim was playing a trick on him.)— Often used with *to. Someone put the police wise to the plan of the bank robbers, and when the robbers went into the bank, the police were waiting to catch them.* (Someone told the police about the plan to rob the bank.) Compare TIP OFF.

put words into one's mouth *v. phr.* To say without proof that another person has certain feelings or opinions; claim a stand or an idea is another's without asking; speak for another without right.—A cliché. *When he said "John here is in favor of the idea," I told him not to put words in my mouth.* (I told him not to speak for me without asking me.)

Q

q See MIND ONE'S P'S AND Q'S.
Q.T. See ON THE Q.T.
quantity See UNKNOWN QUANTITY.
quarterback sneak *n.* A football play in which the quarterback takes the ball from the center and dives straight ahead in an attempt to gain a very short distance. *Johnson took the ball over on a quarterback sneak for a touchdown.* (He took the ball and dived over quickly for the touchdown.)
quest See IN SEARCH OF *also* IN QUEST OF.
question See BEG THE QUESTION, BESIDE THE POINT *or* BESIDE THE QUESTION, BEYOND QUESTION *also* WITHOUT QUESTION, CALL IN QUESTION, IN QUESTION, INTO QUESTION, OUT OF THE QUESTION, POP THE QUESTION.
quick buck See FAST BUCK.
quick on the trigger *or* **trigger happy** *adj. phr.* Ready to shoot without warning; fast with a gun. *He's a dangerous criminal quick on the trigger.* (Be careful in going near him because he has a gun and is ready to shoot without warning.) **2** *informal* Fast at answering questions or solving problems.—A cliché. *In class discussions John is always quick on the trigger.* (John is fast at answering the teacher's questions.)
quit See CALL IT QUITS.
quite a few *or* **quite a number** *also formal*

not a few *n. or adj. phr.* Rather a large number; more than a few. *Quite a few went to the game.* (A rather large number of people went to the game. There was a good crowd.) *The basket had quite a few rotten apples in it.* (There were more than a few rotten apples in the basket.)—The phrase *quite a number* is used like an adjective only before *less, more. Few people saw the play on the first night, but quite a number more came on the second night.* (Many more people came on the second night.)—Sometimes used like an adverb. *We still have quite a few more miles to go before we reach New York.* (We must drive many more miles.) Syn. GOOD MANY; NOT A FEW. Compare A FEW; A NUMBER.
quite a little *or informal* **quite a bit** *also formal* **not a little** *n. or adj. phr.* Rather a large amount; rather much; more than a little. *We are not finished; quite a little is left to do.* (Much work is left to do.) *Cleaning the back yard needed quite a little work.* (The yard needed much work.)—The phrase *quite a bit* is used like an adjective only before *less, more. Six inches of snow fell today, and quite a bit more is coming tonight.* (Much more will fall tonight.)—Sometimes used like an adverb. *Harry was sick quite a little last winter.* (Harry was often sick.) Compare A LITTLE, A LOT, QUITE A FEW.
quite a number See QUITE A FEW.

R

rabbit See JACK-RABBIT START.

race See DRAG RACE, RAT RACE.

rack one's brain v. phr. To try your best to think; make a great mental effort; especially: to try to remember something you have known. *Bob racked his brain trying to remember where he left the book.* (He tried his best to think what he did with it.) *Susan racked her brain trying to guess whom the valentine came from.* (She made a great mental effort to guess who sent it.) *John racked his brain during the test trying to solve the problem.* (John tried hard to remember how to solve the problem during the test.)

rag See CHEW THE FAT *or* CHEW THE RAG, GLAD RAGS.

rag doll n. A doll made of cloth and filled with soft stuffing. *My baby brother won't go to bed without his rag doll.* (He has to have his cloth doll with soft stuffing to hold or he can't get to sleep.)

ragged See RUN RAGGED.

rain See IT NEVER RAINS BUT IT POURS, KNOW ENOUGH TO COME IN OUT OF THE RAIN.

rain cats and dogs *or* **rain buckets** *or* **rain pitchforks** v. phr., informal To rain very hard; come down in torrents.—A cliché. *In the middle of the picnic it started to rain cats and dogs, and everybody got soaked.* (While people were busy eating, a storm cloud suddenly appeared and they got caught in a hard rain.) *Terry looked out of the window and said, "It's raining pitchforks, so we can't go out to play right now."* (Terry said, "It's raining very hard, so we can't go out to play.")

rain check n. 1 A special free ticket to another game or show which will be given in place of one canceled because of rain. *When the drizzle turned into a heavy rain the manager announced that the baseball game would be replayed the next day. He told the crowd that they would be given rain checks for tomorrow's game as they went out through the gates.* (He said the special cards would be their free tickets for tomorrow's game.) 2 informal A promise to repeat an invitation at a later time. *Bob said, "I'm sorry you can't come to dinner this evening, Dave. I'll give you a rain check."* (Dave had other plans for the evening, so Bob promised to invite him to dinner some other time when he could come.)

rained out adj. Stopped by rain. *The ball game was rained out in the seventh inning.* (It rained so hard that the players could not finish the game.) *The Friday night rally in the stadium was rained out.* (Because of rain, the students decided not to hold the rally.)

rain on v. phr., slang To bring misfortune to (someone); to complain to (someone) about one's bad luck. *Don't rain on me.* (Stop complaining.)

rain or shine adv. phr. 1 If the weather is stormy or if it is fair.—A cliché. *The parade will start promptly, rain or shine.* (The parade will begin on time if the weather is stormy or if it is fair.) 2 No matter, if your luck is good or bad.—A cliché. *Sam knows he can depend on his family, rain or shine.* (He knows they will continue to love and trust him, if his luck is good or bad.)

rainy day n. A time of need; especially: a time when you really need money.—A trite expression. *Squirrels gather acorns for a rainy day.* (They do not eat every nut they see, but store some where they can find them in a time of scarcity.) *Each week Mrs. Carlson saved a little money for a rainy day.* (Each week Mrs. Carlson saved a little money for a sudden need.)

raise a hand See LIFT A FINGER.

raise Cain v. phr., slang To be noisy; cause trouble. *When John couldn't go on the basketball trip with the team he raised Cain.* (John was so angry he threw things, and was loud and noisy.) *The children raised Cain in the living room.* (The children played roughly, broke a lamp, and made much trouble in the living room.) Compare KICK UP A FUSS, RAISE THE DEVIL.

raise eyebrows v. phr. To shock people; cause surprise or disapproval. *The news that the princess was engaged to a commoner raised eyebrows all over the kingdom.* (Members of the royal family usually marry titled nobility so people were shocked to learn that the princess was going to marry a commoner.)

raise hackles *or* **raise one's hackles** v. phr. To make (someone) upset or annoyed; arouse hostility. *Attempts to add new ingredients to the beer raised hackles among all the old brew masters.* (They didn't like the idea at all.)

raise havoc See PLAY HAVOC WITH.

raise heck See RAISE THE DEVIL.

raise hob See RAISE THE DEVIL.

raise the devil *or* **raise heck** *or* **raise hob** *or* **raise ned** v. phr., informal To make trouble; start a fight or an argument. *Mr. Black raised heck when he saw the dented fender. He blamed the other driver.* (He was very angry about the damage and started an argument about whose fault it was.) *Some teen age boys raised the devil in town on Halloween night and damaged a lot of property.* (The teen age boys broke windows, wrote on cars with soap, and tore down signs. They made a lot of trouble.) Compare KICK UP A FUSS.

raise the roof v. phr., informal 1 To make a lot of noise, be happy and noisy. *The gang raised the roof with their singing.* (They made so much noise it seemed as if their singing would blow the roof off the house.) 2 To scold loudly. *Mother raised the roof when she saw the dog's muddy footprints on her new bedspread.* (She was very angry and scolded the dog loudly.) Compare KICK UP A FUSS, RAISE CAIN.

rake over . the coals See HAUL OVER THE COALS.

ram down one's throat See SHOVE DOWN ONE'S THROAT.

random See AT RANDOM.

rank See CLOSE RANKS, PULL RANK.

rap See TAKE THE RAP.

rap one's knuckles *v. phr.* To scold or punish. *The principal rapped our knuckles for cheating on the test.* (The principal punished us.) *If you talk back to Dad, you'll get your knuckles rapped.* (If you talk back, he will punish you.) *The club got its knuckles rapped by the principal for hazing new members.* (The principal told the club that it should not have hazed new members.) *Why rap my knuckles? It wasn't my fault.* (Why scold me for something I didn't do?) Compare DRESSING DOWN, GIVE IT TO 2.

rat See SMELL A RAT.

rate See AT ANY RATE, FIRST RATE.

rather See HAD RATHER.

rat out *or* **rat out on** *v. phr., slang* To desert, to leave at a critical time. *Joe ratted out on Sue when she was 7 months pregnant.* (He deserted her.)

rat race *n., slang* A very confusing, crowded, or disorderly rush; a confusing scramble, struggle, or way of living that does not seem to have a purpose. *The dance last night was a rat race. It was too noisy and crowded.* (The dance was noisy and there wasn't enough room to dance.) *School can be a rat race if you don't keep up with your studies.* (If you are always behind in your work and hurrying to catch up, school can be a confusing struggle.) *This job is a rat race. The faster you work, the faster the boss wants you to work.* (More and more work is expected and not enough time is given to do it.)

rattle See SABRE RATTLING.

rattle off *or* **reel off** *v.* To say quickly without having to stop to think; recite easily and rapidly. *When Roger was seven he could rattle off the names of all the states in alphabetical order.* (When Roger was only seven he could say quickly and easily the names of all the states.) *Joan memorized the "Gettysburg Address" so well that she could reel it off.* (Joan memorized the "Gettysburg Address" so well she could say it quickly and easily.) *We asked the waitress what flavors of ice cream she had, and she rattled them off.* (The waitress quickly named the flavors of ice cream.)

raw See IN THE RAW.

razzle-dazzle *n., slang* Fancy display; showing off. *He is such a good player that he doesn't have to add razzle-dazzle to his game.* (He is such a good player that he doesn't need to show off.) *Do we need all this razzle-dazzle to advertise our fair?* (Do we need all this fancy showing off to advertise our fair?)

reach See BOARDING HOUSE REACH.

reach first base See GET TO FIRST BASE.

reach for the sky *v. phr., slang* To put your hands high above your head or be shot.—A cliché; usually used as a command. *A holdup man walked into a gas station last night and told the attendant "Reach for the sky!"* (He pointed a gun at the attendant and told him to put his hands high above his head.) Syn. HANDS UP.

read between the lines *v. phr.* To understand all of a writer's meaning by guessing at what he has left unsaid.—A cliché. *Some kinds of poetry make you read between the lines.* (Some poets make a comparison in only a word or two and they leave their readers to guess at what they have left unsaid.) *A clever foreign correspondent can often avoid censorship by careful wording, leaving his audience to read between the lines.* (Experienced readers guess at all of a foreign correspondents' meaning by noticing what he has not said.)

read one like a book *v. phr., informal* To understand someone completely; know what he will think or do at any time. *John's girl friend could read him like a book.* (She knew right away what he would think or do at any time.) Compare READ ONE'S MIND.

read one's mind *v. phr.* To know what someone else is thinking. *I have known John so long that I can read his mind.* (I have known him so long that I can tell what he is thinking about.)—**mind reader** *n. That's exactly what I was going to say. You must be a mind reader!* (I was going to say that. You must be able to know what I am thinking.) Compare READ LIKE A BOOK.

read the riot act *v. phr.* To give someone a strong warning or scolding. *Three boys were late to class and the teacher read the riot act to them.* (He reminded them of the rules of the school and told them not to be late again or there would be serious trouble.)

ready See AT THE READY, ROUGH-AND-READY.

real See FOR REAL, IT'S BEEN REAL.

rear See BRING UP THE REAR.

rear end *n.* 1 The back part (usually of a vehicle). *The rear end of our car was smashed when we stopped suddenly and the car behind us hit us.* (The back of our car was damaged.)—Often used like an adjective, with a hyphen. *A head-on crash is more likely to kill the passengers than a rear-end crash.* (When cars going opposite directions crash, more people are killed than when one car hits another from behind.) Contrast HEAD-ON. 2 Rump; backside. *Bobby's mother was so annoyed with his teasing that she swatted his rear end.* (Bobby's mother spanked him on the rump.)

reason See IN REASON, LISTEN TO REASON, RHYME OR REASON, STAND TO REASON, WITHIN REASON.

receive with open arms See WITH OPEN ARMS.

reckon with *v.* To consider as one of the things which may change a situation; consider (something) that will make a difference in the results. *The coach said the opposing pitcher had a fast ball to be reckoned with.* (He said the players should consider it as one of the things which might make a difference in the game.) Syn. TAKE INTO ACCOUNT.

reckon without *v.* To fail to consider as one of the things which might change a situation; not think about. *The committee for the class picnic party made careful plans for a beach party but they reckoned without a sudden change in the weather.* (They thought of everything else but failed to consider that there might be a sudden change in the weather. It turned cold and everybody shivered.)

record See MATTER OF RECORD, OFF THE RECORD, ON RECORD.

red See IN THE RED, PAINT THE TOWN RED, SEE RED.

red carpet See ROLL OUT THE RED CARPET.

reel off See RATTLE OFF.

reference See IN REFERENCE TO *or* WITH REFERENCE TO.

refine on *or* **refine upon** *v.* **1** To make better; improve. *Mary was asked to refine on her first outline to make it clearer and more exact.* (Mary was asked to improve her outline by putting it into a better order and adding good examples.) **2** To be better than; surpass. *Modern medical techniques refine on those of the past.* (They are better than the methods used by doctors many years ago because medical knowledge is improving every day.)

regain one's feet *v. phr.* To get back up again after falling down. *Tom fell while he skied down the hill but he regained his feet quickly.* (Tom got back up after he fell.) Compare TO ONE'S FEET.

regard See IN REFERENCE TO *or* IN REGARD TO *or* WITH REGARD TO.

regular guy *or* **regular fellow** *n., informal* A friendly person who is easy to get along with; a good sport. *You'll like Tom. He's a regular guy.* (He's a good sport, friendly and agreeable.) Syn. GOOD EGG.

rein See FREE REIN, GIVE REIN TO *or* GIVE FREE REIN TO.

relation See IN RELATION TO *or* WITH RELATION TO.

relative to **1** On the subject of; about. *Relative to school athletics, the principal said the students should not allow athletics to interfere with homework.* (On the subject of athletics, the principal said he was in favor of them if students did not let athletics interfere with studies.) **2** In comparison with; in proportion to. *Relative to the size of an ant, a blade of grass is as tall as a tree.* (In comparison with his own size, a blade of grass looks as tall to an ant as a tree does to a human being.)

relief pitcher *n.* A baseball pitcher who replaces another during a game. *Radatz, a right-handed relief pitcher, came into the game in the seventh inning.* (Radatz replaced another pitcher in the seventh inning.)

repeat oneself *v. phr.* To say the same thing over again, often in the same words; repeat ideas because you forget what you said or because you want to stress their importance. *Grandfather is forgetful and often repeats himself when he tells a story.* (Grandfather often says the same thing two or three times when he tells a story, because he is forgetful.) *A teacher often has to repeat herself several times before her pupils remember what she tells them.* (The teacher has to say the same thing again and again so pupils can understand and remember the facts.)

resign oneself *v. phr.* To stop arguing; accept something which cannot be changed. *When Jane's father explained that he could not afford to buy her a new bicycle, she finally resigned herself to riding the old one.* (She finally stopped arguing and accepted her father's explanation.) Compare GIVE UP.

resistance See LINE OF LEAST RESISTANCE.

rest See LAY TO REST, PARADE REST.

rest home See CONVALESCENT HOME.

rest on one's laurels *v. phr.* To be satisfied with the success you have already won; stop trying to win new honors.—A cliché. *Getting an A in chemistry almost caused Mike to rest on his laurels.* (He was almost satisfied with this one success in chemistry, but he wanted to do as well in other subjects.)

rest on one's oars *v. phr.* To stop trying; stop working for a while; rest.—A cliché. *The man who wants to become a millionaire can never rest on his oars.* (The man who wants to be a millionaire can never rest; he has to work all the time at getting more money.) *A high school student who wants to go to college cannot rest on his oars.* (He must work all the time.)

rest room *n.* A room or series of rooms in a public building which has things for personal comfort and grooming, such as toilets, washbowls, mirrors, and often chairs or couches. *Sally went to the rest room to powder her nose.* (She used the things for comfort and personal grooming given by the restaurant.) Compare POWDER ROOM.

retreat See BEAT A RETREAT.

return See IN RETURN.

return the compliment *v. phr.* To say or do the same to someone that he has said or done to you; pay someone back. *Mary said, "I love your new hairdo" and Suzy returned the compliment with "What a pretty dress you're wearing, Mary."* (When Mary complimented Suzy on her hairdo, Suzy replied by complimenting Mary on her dress.) *John punched Jerry in the nose, and Jerry returned the compliment.* (John was punched back by Jerry.)

reverse See DOUBLE REVERSE, IN REVERSE.

rev up *v. phr., informal, slang* **1** To press down sharply several times on the accelerator of an idling car in order to get maximum acceleration. *The race driver revved up his car by pumping his accelerator.* (The race driver made it speed up by pumping the gas pedal.) **2** To get oneself ready in order to accomplish a demanding or difficult task. *The boys were getting all revved up for the football game.* (The boys were getting into the fighting spirit in order to win.) See PSYCHED UP.

rhyme or reason *n. phr.* A good plan or reason; a reasonable purpose or explanation. —A cliché; used in negative, interrogative, or conditional sentences. *Don could see no rhyme or reason to the plot of the play.* (He saw no well-organized plot in the play.) *It seemed to Ruth that her little brother had temper tantrums without rhyme or reason.* (He seemed to have tantrums without causes.)

rib See STICK TO ONE'S RIBS *or* STICK TO THE RIBS.

rich See STRIKE IT RICH.

ride See ALONG FOR THE RIDE, LET RIDE, TAKE FOR A RIDE, RUN WITH HARE AND HUNT (RIDE) WITH THE HOUNDS, THUMB A RIDE.

ride herd on *v. phr.* **1** To patrol on horseback around a herd of animals to see that none of them wanders away. *Two cowboys rode herd on the cattle being driven to market.* (Two men on horseback rode around to watch the herd to see that none of the cattle got lost on the way.) **2** *informal* To watch closely and control; take care of. *A special legislative assistant rides herd on the bills the President is anxious to have Congress pass.* (The assistant watches their progress closely, and if necessary urges Congress to act promptly on these bills.) *Mary rode herd on the small children walking home from school to keep them from running into the street.* (She made them walk together and behave so they wouldn't be hurt.)

ride out *v.* To survive safely; endure. *The captain ordered all sails lowered so the ship could ride out the storm.* (He ordered the sails taken down so that the ship could stand the storm and not sink.) *Jack decided to ride out his troubles by saying that he had made a mistake but that he had learned his lesson.* (Jack decided to endure his troubles by saying he had been wrong.)

ride roughshod over *v. phr.* To do as you wish without considering the wishes of (another person); treat with scorn or lack of courtesy; show no sympathy for. *The city officials rode roughshod over the people who did not want their homes torn down for a new school.* (The officials had the homes torn down for the new school, and showed no sympathy for the people.) *The boss rode roughshod over the men when they asked for higher wages.* (The boss did not consider their wish and treated them with scorn.)

ride the brake *or* **ride the clutch** *v. phr., informal* To keep your foot on the pedal. *Riding the brake is a bad habit for a driver to form.* (Keeping your foot constantly on the brake pedal is not a good idea. It wears out the brake linings.)

ride up *or* **crawl up** *v.* To slip gradually upward on the body. *Shorts that ride up can be very uncomfortable.* (Shorts that slip gradually upward on the body make the wearer uncomfortable and self-conscious.)

riding for a fall *adj. phr.* Behaving in an over confident way that is likely to lead to trouble; being too sure of yourself; doing something dangerous. *The student who does not study for exams is riding for a fall.* (A student who doesn't study because he thinks he knows it all may fail.) *Mr. Smith has borrowed too much money on his home He is riding for a fall.* (He is doing something dangerous. He may lose his home. Compare COME A CROPPER 2.

riding high *adj.* Attracting attention; enjoying great popularity. *After scoring the winning touchdown, John is riding high with his classmates.* (He is enjoying great popularity with them because of his winning play.)

rid of Free of; away from; without the care or trouble. *The puppy is finally rid of worms.* (The puppy is finally free of worms.) *If I could be rid of the children for the day, I would go.* (If I could be away from the children for the day, I would go.) *I wish you'd get rid of that cat!* (I wish you'd give away or kill that cat!) Compare DO AWAY WITH, THROW AWAY 1, THROW OFF 1.

right See ALL RIGHT, ALL RIGHT FOR YOU, GIVE ONE'S RIGHT ARM, HEART IN THE RIGHT PLACE, IN THE RIGHT, PLAY ONE'S CARDS RIGHT, PUT TO RIGHTS *or* SET TO RIGHTS, SERVE RIGHT, TO RIGHTS, DEAD TO RIGHTS.

right along *adv. phr., informal* **1a** On your way satisfactorily or without trouble. *They fixed the engine and the train ran right along.* (It went on its way without trouble.) **1b** On your way without delay. *Don't wait for me. Go right along.* (Continue on your way without delay.) **2** See ALL ALONG.

right and left *adv. phr.* In or from every direction; all around; on all sides. *The knight rode into battle striking at the enemy right and left with his broadsword.* (He struck at them all around.) *When the talk ended, questions were thrown at the speaker right and left.* (Questions came at him from every direction.)

right away *or informal* **right off** *also informal* **right off the bat** *adv. phr.* Immediately; as the next thing in order; without delay.—A cliché. *Phil's mother told him to do his homework right away so that he could enjoy the weekend.* (She told him to do it the next thing so that he wouldn't have to be worrying about it from Friday to Sunday night.) *The Red Cross aids disaster victims right away.* (It gets help to them without delay.) *Jill knew the answer right off.* (She knew it the next minutes.) *The teacher said he could not think of the title of the book right off the bat.* (He said he couldn't remember it immediately. He needed a little time to think of it). Syn. AT ONCE 2. Compare HERE AND NOW, ON THE SPOT. Contrast AFTER A WHILE.

right field *n.* The part of a baseball outfield to the batter's right. *Left-handed batters usually hit to right field.* (Left-handed batters usually hit toward the right.) Compare CENTER FIELD, LEFT FIELD.—**right fielder** *n.* The outfielder in baseball who plays in right field. *The batter hit a high fly ball and the right fielder caught it easily.* (The batter hit the ball in the air to his right and the fielder who was playing there caught it.)

right on *adj., interj., slang, informal* **1** Exclamation of animated approval "Yes," "That's correct," "You're telling the truth," "we believe you," etc. *Orator: And we shall see the promised land! Crowd: Right on!* (That's true, that's what we want to hear!) **2** Correct, to the point, accurate. *The reverend's remark was right on!* (It was correct.)

right out *or* **straight out** *adv.* Plainly; in a way that hides nothing; without waiting or keeping back anything. *When Mother asked who broke the window, Jimmie told her right out that he did it.* (Jimmie told Mother that he broke the window; he did not try to hide the truth.) *When Ann entered the beauty contest, her little brother told her straight out that she was crazy.* (Ann's little brother was not polite; he told her she was crazy to think she could win a beauty contest.)

right side of the tracks See THE TRACKS.

right-wing *adj.* Being or belonging to a political group which opposes any important change in the way the country is run. *Some countries with right-wing governments have dictators.* (In some countries, the people who are against change control the government through a dictator, who does not allow any changes.) Contrast LEFT-WING.

Riley See LIFE OF RILEY.

ring See GIVE A RING, NAPKIN RING, RUN CIRCLES AROUND *or* RUN RINGS AROUND, THREE-RING CIRCUS, THROW ONE'S HAT IN THE RING.

ring a bell *v. phr.* To make you remember something; sound familiar.—A cliché. *Not even the cat's miaowing seemed to ring a bell with Judy. She still forgot to feed him.* (Even the miaowing of the cat did not make Judy remember that it was time to feed him.) *When Ann told Father the name of the new teacher, it rang a bell, and Father said, "James Carson! I went to school with a James Carson."* (The name James Carson made Father remember that he went to school with someone named James Carson.)

ring in *v. phr., informal* **1** To bring in (someone or something) from the outside dishonestly or without telling; often: hire and introduce under a false name. *Bob offered to ring Jim in on the party by pretending he was a cousin from out of town.* (He offered to get him in to the party dishonestly by telling the hostess that Jim was a cousin from out of town.) *No wonder their team beat us; they rang in a professional to pitch for them under the name of Dan Smith.* (The reason they won the game was because they had a professional pitcher called by another name.) **2** To ring a special clock that records the time you work. *We have to ring in at the shop before eight o'clock in the morning.* (We have to punch a card on a time clock which tells the time we get to work in the morning.)

ring out *v.* To ring a special clock that records the time you leave work. *Charles can't leave early in his new job; he has to ring out.* (In his new job, Charles has to punch a card on a special clock that records the time he leaves.)

ring the changes *v. phr.* To say or do the same thing in different ways; repeat the same idea in many ways.—A cliché. *David wanted a new bicycle and he kept ringing the changes on it all day until his parents got angry at him.* (David kept hinting and saying in different ways that he wanted the bicycle.) *A smart girl saves money on clothes by learning to ring the changes on a few dresses and clothes.* (She learns to make the best use of a few clothes by changing the things she wears together.)

ring up *v.* **1** To add and record on a cash register. *The supermarket clerk rang up Mrs. Smith's purchases and told her she owed $33.* (The clerk added up the prices of the things Mrs. Smith had bought and told her the total.) *Business was bad Tuesday; we didn't ring up a sale all morning.* (No one bought anything Tuesday morning, so we didn't use the cash register.) **2** *informal* To telephone. *Sally rang up Sue and told her the news.* (Sally telephoned Sue.)

riot See READ THE RIOT ACT, RUN RIOT.

ripe See TIME IS RIPE.

rip into *or* **tear into** *v., informal* **1** To start a fight with; attack. *The puppy is tearing into the big dog.* (The puppy is not afraid of the big dog and is even starting a fight with him.) Syn. PITCH INTO. **2** To quarrel with; scold. *Mrs. Brown ripped into her daughter for coming home late.* (Mrs. Brown gave her daughter a hard scolding for coming home late.) Syn. BAWL OUT, LACE INTO, LAY OUT, LET HAVE IT.

rip off *v., slang* (Accent on *off*) Steal. *The hippies ripped off the grocery store.* (They burglarized the grocery store; they stole from it.)

rip-off *n., slang* (Accent on *rip*) An act of stealing or burglary. *Those food prices are so high, it's almost a rip-off.* (The prices are so high, it is almost like burglary.)

rise See GET A RISE OUT OF, GIVE RISE TO.

rise in the world See COME UP IN THE WORLD.
rise to *v.* To succeed in doing what is expected by trying especially hard in or on; show that you are able to do or say what is needed or proper in or on. *Jane was surprised when the principal handed her the prize, but she rose to the occasion with a speech of thanks.* (Jane succeeded in saying what was proper.) *When Michael became sick on the day before the program, Paul rose to the need and learned Michael's part.* (Paul showed that he could do what was needed.)
risk See CALCULATED RISK, RUN A RISK.
road See ALL ROADS LEAD TO ROME, BURN UP THE ROAD, END OF THE ROAD, GET THE SHOW ON THE ROAD, HIT THE ROAD, HUG THE ROAD, MIDDLE OF THE ROAD, ON THE ROAD.
road gang *n.* A group of men who work at road construction. *Football players often work with road gangs during summer vacations.* (Football players often take jobs as construction workers on roads during the summer.)
road hog *n., informal* A car driver who takes more than his share of the road. *A road hog forced John's car into the ditch.* (A selfish driver crowded John's car off the road.)
road show *n.* A theatrical play that is performed for a few days in one town and then moves to other towns. *Many actors get their start in road shows.* (Many actors begin by acting in plays that travel from place to place.) *The road show is often not as good as the original play on Broadway.* (Plays that are performed for a few days in many different towns usually are not as good as the original shows in New York.)
road sign *n.* A sign on which there is information about a road or places; a sign with directions to drivers. *The road sign read, "25 MPH LIMIT" but Jack drove along at fifty miles an hour.* (The sign giving information about the road said the speed limit was 25 miles an hour.) *The road sign said Westwood was four miles away.* (The sign giving information about the road said Westwood was four miles from it.)
road test *n.* **1** A test to see if you can drive a car. *Jim took the road test and got his driver's license last week.* (Jim passed the test of his driving ability.) **2** A test to see if a car works all right on the road. *Most new cars are given road tests before they are put on the market.* (Most new cars are tested to find out if they work all right on the road before they are sold.) *After he repaired the car, the mechanic gave it a road test.* (He drove it on the road to be sure it worked right.)
roast See WEINER ROAST *or* HOT DOG ROAST.
roasting ear *n.* An ear of corn young and tender enough to be cooked and eaten; *also;* corn cooked on the cob. *The Scouts buried the roasting ears in the coals of their campfire.* (The Scouts put unhusked ears of corn that they had prepared for roasting in the

embers of their campfire.) *At the Fourth of July picnic we had fried chicken and roasting ears.* (We had corn on the cob.)
robbery See HIGHWAY ROBBERY.
robin See ROUND ROBIN.
rob Peter to pay Paul *v. phr.* To change one duty or need for another; take from one person or thing to pay another.—A cliché. *Bill owed Sam a dollar, so he borrowed another from Joe to pay Sam back. He robbed Peter to pay Paul.* (Bill still owes a dollar; he paid one debt by making another.) *Trying to study a lesson for one class during another class is like robbing Peter to pay Paul.* (You neglect one class when you are studying for another.)
rob the cradle *v. phr., informal* To have dates with or marry a person much younger than yourself.—A cliché. *When the old woman married a young man, everyone said she was robbing the cradle.* (The woman was criticized for marrying a man much younger than herself.)—**cradle-robber** *n.* The *Judge died when he was seventy. He was a real cradle-robber because he left a thirty-year-old widow.* (The Judge had been married to a woman forty years younger than himself.)—**cradle-robbing** *adj. or n.* Bob is *seventeen and I just saw him with a girl about twelve years old. Has he started cradle-robbing? No, that girl was his sister, not his date!* (Bob wasn't dating the young girl. She was his sister.)
rob the till *or* **have one's hand in the till** *v. phr., informal* To steal money in your trust or for which you are responsible. *The supermarket manager suspected that one of the clerks was robbing the till.* (The manager suspected that one of the clerks was stealing money from the cash register.) *Mr. Jones deposited one thousand dollars in their joint savings account and told his wife not to rob the till.* (He told his wife not to withdraw money from their savings account.) *The store owner thought his business was failing until he discovered that the treasurer had his hand in the till.* (The owner found out that the treasurer was stealing money that he should have put in the bank.)
rock See HAVE ROCKS IN ONE'S HEAD, ON THE ROCKS.
rock and roll See ROCK 'N' ROLL.
rock bottom *n.* The lowest possible point. *The nation's morale hit rock bottom in the hours following the President's assassination.* (The spirits of the people reached their lowest possible level during the hours after the President was murdered.)—Often used like an adjective, with a hyphen. *The rock-bottom price of this radio is $25.* (The lowest possible price of this radio is $25.)
rocker See OFF ONE'S ROCKER.
rock hound *n., slang* A person who studies and collects rocks for a hobby. *Many young rock hounds grow up to be geologists.* (Many

young people who make a hobby of studying and collecting rocks grow up to be scientists who study the materials of which the earth is made.) *Tony is an eager rock hound, and we have rocks all through our house.* (Tony is so enthusiastic about studying and collecting rocks that our house is full of his collections.)

rock 'n' roll *or* **rock and roll** *n.* A style of popular music with heavily accented rhythm. *Rock 'n' roll appeals mostly to youngsters nine to sixteen years old.* (Music with heavily accented rhythm is most enjoyed by young people.) *Rock and roll became popular for dances about 1954.* (Dance music with a strong beat became popular about 1954.)

rock the boat *v. phr., informal* To make trouble and risk losing or upsetting something; cause a disturbance that may spoil a plan.—A cliché. *The other boys said that Henry was rocking the boat by wanting to let girls into their club.* (The boys thought that girls might break up their club.) *Politicians don't like to rock the boat around election time.* (Politicians don't like to say or do anything that may make people not like them or elect them.) Compare UPSET THE APPLE CART. Contrast LET WELL ENOUGH ALONE.

rod See HOT ROD.

roll See GET THE BALL ROLLING, KEEP THE BALL ROLLING, ROCK 'N' ROLL *or* ROCK AND ROLL.

roll around *v., informal* To return at a regular or usual time; come back. *When winter rolls around, out come the skis and skates.* (When winter returns at its regular point in the cycle of the year, people get out their skis and skates.)

rolling stone gathers no moss A person who changes jobs or where he loves often will not be able to save money or things of his own. —A proverb. *Uncle Willie was a rolling stone that gathered no moss. He worked in different jobs all over the country.* (Uncle Willie didn't stay in one place long enough to save money or buy property.)

roll out *v.* To take the football from the center and run toward the side, either to run for a gain or to throw a pass. *The quarterback rolled out to the left, faked a pass, and ran for an eight-yard gain.* (He moved to the left side, pretended to pass, and ran around the left end for eight yards.)

roll out the red carpet *v. phr.* **1** To welcome an important guest by putting a red carpet down for him to walk on. *They rolled out the red carpet for the Queen when she arrived in Australia.* (They unrolled a red carpet on which she walked from her airplane.) **2** To greet a person with great respect and honor; give a hearty welcome.—A cliché. *Margaret's family rolled out the red carpet for her teacher when she came to dinner.* (They greeted her with great respect. They wore their best clothes and set the table with

their best silver and china.) Compare WELCOME MAT.—**red-carpet** *adj.* *When the President visited the foreign country, he was given the red-carpet treatment and welcomed by a great crowd.* (The President was treated with great respect and politeness.) *We gave Uncle Willie the red-carpet treatment when he returned from Hong Kong.* (We gave him a hearty welcome.)

roll up one's sleeves To get ready for a hard job; prepare to work hard or seriously.—A cliché. *When Paul took his science examination, he saw how little he knew about science. He rolled up his sleeves and went to work.* (He sat down and began to study hard.)

Roman collar *n.* The high, plain, white collar worn by priests and clergymen. *The man with the Roman collar is the new Episcopalian preacher.* (The man wearing the high, white collar is the new preacher.) *Many Protestant churches do not require their ministers to wear Roman collars.* (Many Protestant churches do not insist that their ministers wear the high, white collar traditionally used by clergymen.)

Rome See ALL ROADS LEAD TO ROME.

roof See HIT THE CEILING *or* HIT THE ROOF, RAISE THE ROOF.

rooftop See SHOUT FROM THE HOUSETOPS *or* SHOUT FROM THE ROOFTOPS.

room See CONTROL ROOM, POWDER ROOM, UTILITY ROOM.

room clerk *or* **desk clerk** *n.* A person who is responsible for assigning rooms and providing service to guests in hotels, motels, inns, etc. *At first-class hotels, room clerks are trained to be at the service of every guest.* (At the best hotels, persons who are responsible for room rentals and service are trained to help the guests in every way.) *Sometimes resort hotels in the mountains hire college students as room clerks during the summer.* (Sometimes resort hotels hire college students to look after their guests' wishes during the summer months.)

room in See LIVE IN.

room service *n.* Service provided to hotel guests in their rooms. *Also:* The hotel workers who give this service. *We called for room service when we wanted ice.* (We telephoned the person responsible for providing service to guests and asked that ice be sent to our hotel room.) *Room service will install a TV set in your room upon demand.* (The hotel workers who take care of the rooms will put a TV set in your room if you ask for one.)

roost See CHICKENS COME HOME TO ROOST, RULE THE ROOST.

root See TAKE ROOT.

root-bound *adj.* **1** Having a limited amount of space for root growth. *After seven or eight years day lilies become root-bound and will not bloom well unless they are divided.* (After seven or eight years of growing in one place, the roots of day lily plants become so crowded that they will not bloom well unless they are dug up and separated.) **2** Liking the familiar place where you live and not wanting to go away from it; having a sentimental attachment to one place. *Mr. Jones has lived in Connecticut all his life. He is too root-bound to consider moving to another state.* (Mr. Jones has a sentimental attachment to Connecticut and would never dream of moving to another state.)

rope See END OF ONE'S ROPE, GIVE ONE ENOUGH ROPE AND HE WILL HANG HIMSELF, ON THE ROPES, THE ROPES.

rope in *v., informal* **1** To use a trick to make (someone) do something; deceive; fool. *The company ropes in high school students to sell magazine subscriptions by telling them big stories of how much money they can earn.* (It talks them into believing they will make a lot of money if they join in selling subscriptions.) Syn. TAKE UP 5a. **2** To get (someone to join or help); persuade to do something. *Martha roped in Charles to help her decorate the gym for the party.* (Martha talked to Charles until he agreed to help.) *I didn't want the job of selling tickets for the dance, but I was roped in because everyone else was too busy to do it.* (I was persuaded to do the job, even though I didn't want to!)

rope into *v., informal* **1** To trick into; persuade dishonestly. *Jerry let the big boys rope him into stealing some apples.* (The big boys tricked Jerry and made him steal apples.) **2** To get (someone) to join in; persuade to work at. *It was Sue's job to bathe the dog, but she roped Sam into helping her.* (She got Sam to help her.) *Mother did not go to the first meeting of the club because she was afraid she would be roped into something.* (Mother was afraid the other women would give her a big job to do.) Compare TALK INTO.

rose See BED OF ROSES, LOOK AT THE WORLD THROUGH ROSE-COLORED GLASSES.

rose-colored glasses See LOOK AT THE WORLD THROUGH ROSE-COLORED GLASSES.

rotten egg *n., informal* A person whose character or way of acting is not good. *His friends have all learned he is a rotten egg.* (He is just no good, a bad man.) Often used by children in fun, as of someone who is slow in doing something. *The boys ran to the river to go swimming and Dick cried, "Last one in is a rotten egg!"* (Just for fun, they would name the late one a rotten egg.)

rough See DIAMOND IN THE ROUGH.

rough-and-ready *adj.* **1** Not finished in detail; not perfected; rough but ready for use now. *We asked Mr. Brown how long it would take to drive to Chicago and his rough-and-ready answer was two days.* (Mr. Brown didn't know exactly but gave us an answer that was good enough.) **2** Not having nice manners but full of energy and ability. *Jim is a rough-and-ready character; he'd rather fight than talk things over.* (Jim is always

ready to act; He would rather fight than argue.)

rough-and-tumble **1** *n.* Very rough, hard fighting or arguing that does not follow any rules. *There was a rough-and-tumble on the street last night between some soldiers and sailors.* (The soldiers and sailors had a very rough fight.) *Many people don't like the rough-and-tumble of politics.* (Many people don't like the arguing and name-calling in politics.) **2** *adj.* Fighting or arguing in a very rough and reckless way; struggling hard; not following rules or laws. *It took strong men to stay alive in the rough-and-tumble life of the western frontier.* (The men had to be tough and strong to live where there was a struggle to stay alive.)

rough diamond See DIAMOND IN THE ROUGH.

rough it *v. phr.* To live like primitive people; live with little of the comfort and equipment of civilization. *Scouts like to rough it in the woods on weekend hikes.* (They like to live like primitive people in the woods, cooking over campfires and sleeping outdoors.)

rough-shod See RIDE ROUGH-SHOD OVER.

rough sledding See HARD SLEDDING.

rough up *v.* To attack or hurt physically; treat roughly; beat. *Three boys were sent home for a week because they roughed up a player on the visiting team.* (The boys beat a visiting player.) *While Pete was walking in a strange part of town, some boys roughed him up and told him to stay out of their territory.* (The boys pushed and hit Pete.)

roulette See RUSSIAN ROULETTE.

round See BRING AROUND *or* BRING ROUND, COME ROUND, GO THE ROUNDS, MAKE ROUNDS, SQUARE PEG IN A ROUND HOLE, YEAR-ROUND.

round-eyed *or* **wide-eyed** *also* **large-eyed** *adj.* Very much surprised; astonished; awed. *The people were round-eyed when they learned what the computer could do.* (The people were astonished to know what the computer could do.) *The children were wide-eyed at the sight of the Christmas tree and didn't make a sound.* (The children were so awed at the sight of the Christmas tree that they couldn't speak.)

round off *v.* **1** To make round or curved. *John decided to round off the corners of the table he was making so that no one would be hurt by bumping them.* (He decided to make the edges curved instead of straight.) **2** To change to the nearest whole number. *The teacher said to round off the averages.* (She said to eliminate fractions from the averages by changing them into the nearest whole number.) **3** To end in a satisfactory way; put a finishing touch on; finish nicely. *We rounded off the dinner with mixed nuts.* (Mixed nuts were a pleasant end to our dinner.) *A boat ride in the moonlight rounded off the day at the lake.* (A moonlight ride in a boat was just the right thing to end the day.) Compare TOP OFF.

round robin *n. phr.* **1** Something written, especially a request or protest that is signed by a group of people.—Often used like an adjective. *The people in our neighborhood are sending a round robin to the Air Force to protest the noise the jet planes make flying over our houses.* (The people in the neighborhood are sending a letter which many of the neighbors have signed, to complain to the Air Force.) **2** A letter written by a group of people each writing one or two paragraphs and then sending the letter to another person, who adds a paragraph, and so on. *The class sent a round-robin letter to Bill in the hospital.* (The class sent a letter in which each member wrote something in the letter to Bill.) **3** A meeting in which each one in a group of people takes part; a talk between various members of a group.—Often used like an adjective. *There is a round robin meeting of expert fishermen on the radio, giving advice on how to catch fish.* (Each one of the group of experts takes part in the talk and gives advice.) **4** A contest or games in which each player or team plays every other player or team in turn.—Often used like an adjective. *The tournament will be a round robin for all the high school teams in the city.* (Each team will play every other team.)

rounds See GO THE ROUNDS.

round the clock See AROUND THE CLOCK.

round up *v.* **1** To bring together (cattle or horses). *Cowboys round up their cattle in the springtime to brand the new calves.* (The cowboys bring the cattle together in one place.) **2** *informal* To collect; gather. *Dave rounded up many names for his petition.* (Dave got many people who were for his idea to sign their names on the paper.)

row See HARD ROW TO HOE *or* TOUGH ROW TO HOE, HOE ONE'S OWN ROW, SKID ROW.

rub-a-dub *n.* The sound made by beating a drum. *We heard a great rub-a-dub as the parade marched into view.* (We heard a loud sound of drum beating as the parade marched into view.)

rubber check *n., informal* A check written without enough money in the bank to make it good. *Bill got into trouble when he paid his bills with rubber checks.* (He paid his bills by writing checks when he did not have enough money in the bank to cover them.) *By the time we knew he had paid us with a rubber check, the man had left the state.* (By the time we found out that he had paid us with a worthless check, the man had left the state.) *The rubber check bounced.* (The bank refused to honor the worthless check.)

rub down *v.* **1** To dry the body of (an animal or person) by rubbing. *Stablemen rub down a horse after a race.* (Stablemen clean the sweat and mud off the horse by rubbing

it with a rubber or some straw.) **2** To rub and press with the fingers on the body of (a person) to loosen muscles or prevent stiffness; massage. *Trainers rub down an athlete after hard exercise.* (Trainers rub and press the athlete's body to keep his muscles from getting stiff.)

rub elbows *also* **rub shoulders** *v. phr.* To be in the same place (with others); meet and mix.—A cliché. *City people and country people, old and young, rub elbows at the horse show.* (People from different places and of different ages mix together at the horse show.) *On a visit to the United Nations Building in New York, you may rub elbows with people from faraway lands.* (You may be in the same place with people from the other side of the world.)

rub it in *v. phr., slang* To remind a person again and again of an error or short-coming; tease; nag. *Jerry was already unhappy because he fumbled the ball, but his teammates kept rubbing it in.* (Jerry's teammates were unkind; they reminded Jerry again and again of his error.) *I know my black eye looks funny. You don't need to rub it in.* (You don't need to tease me about my black eye.)

rub off *v.* **1** To remove or be removed by rubbing; erase. *The teacher rubs the problem off the chalkboard.* (The teacher erases the problem.) *After Ann shook hands with the President, she would not shake hands with anyone else, because she thought that the good luck would rub off.* (Pam thought that the President's touch would bring her good luck and that if anyone else touched that hand, it would take away the good luck.) **2** To stick to something touched; come off. *Don't touch that charcoal; it will rub off.* (The black powder from the charcoal will stick to your hand.) *Mary's dress touched the door that Father was painting, and some paint rubbed off on her dress.* (Some paint stuck to her dress.) **3** To pass to someone near as if by touching. *Jimmy is very lucky; I wish some of his luck would rub off on me.* (I hope some of Jimmy's luck comes to me if I'm near him.)

rub out *v. slang* To destroy completely; kill; eliminate. *The gangsters rubbed out four policemen before they were caught.* (The gangsters killed four police officers before they were caught.) *The gangsters told the storekeeper that if he did not pay them to protect him, someone would rub him out.* (Someone would kill him.) Compare WIPE OUT, RID OF.

rub shoulders See RUB ELBOWS.

rub the wrong way *v. phr., informal* To make (someone) a little angry; do something not liked by (someone); annoy; bother.—A cliché. *John's bragging rubbed the other boys the wrong way.* (John talked about the big things he did, and the other boys did not like it.) *Mother's friend called Harold a little boy, and that rubbed Harold the wrong way.* (Being called a little boy made Harold rather angry.) Compare AGAINST THE GRAIN 2.

ruffle feathers *or* **ruffle one's feathers** *v. phr.* Insult or disturb slightly; offend. *The author ruffled some feathers by his portrait of his hometown.* (Townspeople were offended by the way he wrote about the town.)

rug See PULL THE RUG OUT FROM UNDER, SWEEP UNDER THE RUG.

rule See EXCEPTION PROVES THE RULE, GROUND RULE.

rule out *v.* **1** To say that (something) must not be done; not allow; *also:* decide against. *The principal ruled out dances on school nights.* (The principal said there could be no dances on school nights.) *The play was ruled out by the referee.* (The play was not allowed by the referee.) *Jean probably will not go to college, but she has not ruled that out.* (Jean has not surely decided against going to college.) **2** To show that (someone or something) is not a possibility; make it unnecessary to think about; remove (a chance). *We have to find a baby-sitter for tonight; Betsy has a date, so that rules her out.* (We need not think of Betsy as a possibility.) *The doctor took X-rays to rule out the chance of broken bones.* (The doctor took X-rays to be sure there were no broken bones.) **3** To make impossible; prevent. *Father's death seems to rule out college for Jean.* (Father's death seems to make it impossible for Jean to go to college.) *Betsy's date for the dance ruled out any baby-sitting that evening.* (Betsy's date made it impossible for her to baby-sit that night.)

rule the roost *v. phr., informal* To be leader or boss; be in charge.—A cliché. *Jim is very bossy; he always wants to rule the roost.* (He wants people to do what he says.) *Who rules the roost in the Smith's house?* (Who is boss?) Compare WEAR THE TROUSERS.

run See BLOOD RUNS COLD, END RUN, CUT AND RUN, FIRST-RUN, HOME RUN, IN THE LONG RUN, IN THE RUNNING, ON THE RUN, OUT OF THE RUNNING, SECOND-RUN.

run across See COME ACROSS 1.

run after *or* **chase after** *v.* **1** To try to find; look for; hunt. *The Dramatic Club has to run all over town after things for setting the stage when it puts on a play.* (The members must look everywhere for furnishings.) **2** *informal* To seek the company of; chase. *Some boys spend a lot of time and money running after girls.* (They spend a lot of time and money doing things with girls.)

run along *v.* To go away; leave. *Joan said she had errands to do and must run along.* (She couldn't stay longer because she had to go and do her errands.)

run a risk *or* **take a risk** *v. phr.* To be open to danger or loss; put yourself in danger; be

unprotected. *A baseball umpire wears a mask and chest protector so he won't run the risk of being hit by the ball.* (The umpire protects himself from being hit by wearing the mask and chest protector.) *Billy takes a risk of being hit by a car when he runs into the street without looking.* (Billy puts himself in danger by running without looking.) *I was afraid to run the risk of betting on the game.* (I was afraid I might lose.) Compare TAKE A CHANCE.

run around *or* **chase around** *v., informal* To go to different places for company and pleasure; be friends. *Tim hasn't been to a dance all year; with school work and his job, he hasn't time to run around.* (Tim is too busy to go different places for company and pleasure.) *Chuck and Jim chase around a lot together.* (They often go places together; they are friends.)—Often used with *with. Ruth runs around with girls who like to go dancing.* (Ruth's friends are girls who like to dance.) Compare GO AROUND, HANG AROUND.

run a temperature *v. phr.* To have a body temperature that is above normal; have a fever. *Jimmy didn't look ill, although he was running a temperature.* (Jimmy didn't seem sick, although his temperature was unusually high.) *We took the baby to the doctor because he was running a temperature.* (We took the baby to the doctor because he had a fever.)

run away *or* **run off** *v.* To leave and not plan to come back; go without permission; escape. *Many times Tommy said he would run away from home, but he never did.* (Tommy often said he was going to leave home and never come back, but he didn't mean it.) *The guards in jail make sure that none of the prisoners run away.* (The guards stop any prisoner from escaping.) Compare GET AWAY.

run away with *v.* **1a** To take quickly and secretly, especially without permission; steal. *A thief ran away with grandma's silver teapot.* (He stole it.) Syn. MAKE OFF. **1b** To go away with; elope. *Mary said that if her parents wouldn't let her marry Phil, she would run away with him.* (She said if they wouldn't let her marry she would elope.) **1c** To take hold of; seize. *The boys thought they saw a ghost in the old house last night; they let their imagination run away with them.* (The boys became afraid and imagined they saw a ghost.) Compare GET THE BETTER OF. **2** To be much better or more noticeable than others in; win easily. *Our team ran away with the game in the last half.* (Our team beat the other team badly in the second half of the game.) *The fat comedian ran away with the TV show.* (The funny fat man was so good that he was noticed more than anyone else in the show.) Compare STEAL THE SHOW.

run circles around *also* **run rings around** *v.*

phr. To show that you can do a task much better than; do better than (someone) very easily. *In spelling, Ruth could run circles around Barbara any day.* (She could do better than Barbara without trying.) *Frank ran rings around the other boys on the basketball team.* (Frank was much faster and better.)

run down *v.* **1** To crash against and knock down or sink. *Jack rode his bicycle too fast and almost ran down his little brother.* (Jack went too fast and almost hit his brother with the bicycle.) *It was so foggy that the steamship almost ran down a small boat leaving port.* (The big ship almost hit the boat and sank it.) Compare RUN INTO 3a. **2a** To chase until exhausted or caught. *The dogs ran down the wounded deer.* (They chased him until he was tired out.) **2b** To find by hard and thorough search; *also:* trace to its cause or beginning. *The policeman ran down proof that the burglar had robbed the store.* (He searched until he found proof that the burglar had robbed the store. Compare HUNT DOWN. **2c** To catch (a base runner) between bases and tag out in baseball. *The pitcher saw that the base runner was not on base, so he surprised him by throwing the ball to the first baseman. who ran him down before he reached second base.* (The runner was caught between first and second bases and the first baseman ran after him and tagged him with the ball.) **3** *informal* To say bad things about; criticize. *Suzy ran down the club because the girls wouldn't let her join.* (Suzy criticized the girls and their club because she couldn't be a member herself.) Compare FIND FAULT. **4** To stop working; not run or go. *The battery in Father's car ran down this morning.* (The battery wouldn't work so the car wouldn't go.) *The kitchen clock ran down because we forgot to wind it.* (The clock stopped.) **5** To get into poor condition; look bad. *A neighborhood runs down when the people don't take care of their houses.* (The houses need paint and repairs; the whole street looks bad.)

run-down *adj.* In poor health or condition; weak or needing much work. *Father caught a cold because he was very run-down from loss of sleep.* (Father was weak and caught a cold.) *The houses near the center of the city get more run-down every year.* (The condition of the houses in the center of the city becomes worse every year.)

run for it *or* **make a run for it** *v. phr.* To dash for safety; make a speedy escape. *The bridge the soldiers were on started to fall down and they had to run for it.* (They had to dash for safety to the end of the bridge.) *The policeman shouted for the robber to stop but the robber made a run for it.* (The robber tried to escape by running away.)

run for one's money *n. phr.* **1** A good fight; a hard struggle.—A cliché. Usually used with *give* or *get*. *Our team didn't win the game,* but *they gave the other team a run for their money.* (Our team played a very close game with the other team.) **2** Satisfaction; interest; excitement.—A cliché. Usually used with *give* or *get*. *People like to watch the champion fight because they get a good run for their money from him.* (The champion is an exciting fighter and satisfies the customers who pay to see him.) *A good student gives a teacher more than a run for his money.* (A good student makes the teacher's job more interesting.)

run in *v.* **1** *informal* To take to jail; arrest. *The policeman ran the man in for peddling without a license.* (He arrested the peddlar for not having a license.) **2** To make a brief visit. *The neighbor boy ran in for a minute to see Bob's newest model rocket.* (He made a brief visit to inspect it.) Syn. DROP IN. Compare STOP OFF.

run in the blood *or* **run in the family** *v. phr.* To be a common family characteristic; be learned or inherited from your family.—A cliché. *A great interest in gardening runs in his family.* (Gardening is an interest many members of his family have had.) *Red hair runs in the family.* (It is a common family trait. Many members of the family have red hair.)

run into *v.* **1** To mix with; join with. *If the paint brush is too wet, the red paint will run into the white on the house.* (The red and the white colors will be mixed together on the house.) *This small brook runs into a big river in the valley below.* (The brook joins the big river.) **2** To add up to; reach; total. *Car repairs can run into a lot of money.* (Car repairs may cost many dollars.) *The number of people killed on the highways during holidays runs into hundreds.* (The total number of deaths reaches several hundred.) *A good dictionary may run into several editions.* (A good dictionary may be revised and printed again and again.) **3a** Bump; crash into; hit. *Joe lost control of his bike and ran into a tree.* (Joe hit a tree.) Compare RUN DOWN. **3b** To meet by chance. *I ran into Joe yesterday on Main Street.* (I met Joe accidentally; I was not expecting to meet him.) Compare BUMP INTO, CHANCE ON, COME ACROSS 2. **3c** Be affected by; get into. *I ran into trouble on the last problem on the test.* (I had trouble with the last problem.) *When I ran into a problem while making my model airplane, I asked Uncle Mark for help.* (When I was stopped by a problem, I got help.)

run into a brick wall *or* **run into a stone wall** See STONE WALL.

run into the ground *v. phr., informal* **1** To do or use (something) more than is wanted or needed.—A cliché. *It's all right to borrow my hammer once in a while, but don't run it into the ground.* (Don't try to borrow my hammer so much that you are a nuisance.) **2** To win over or defeat (someone) completely. *We lost the game today, but tomor-*

row we'll run them into the ground. (We'll beat them badly tomorrow.)

run off *v.* **1** To produce with a printing press or duplicating machine. *The print shop ran off a thousand copies of the newspaper.* (The print shop printed 1,000 copies of the newspaper.) **2** To drive away. *The boys saw a dog digging in mother's flower bed, and they ran him off.* (The boys chased the dog away.) *When the salesman tried to cheat the farmer, the farmer ran him off the farm with a shot gun.* (The farmer said he would shoot the salesman, and the man left.) **3** See RUN AWAY.

run-of-the-mill *or* **run-of-the-mine** *adj.* Of a common kind; ordinary; usual. *Frank is a very good bowler, but Joe is just run-of-the-mill.* (Joe is no better than most bowlers.) *It was just a run-of-the-mine movie.* (There was nothing unusual about the movie. It was an average movie.)

runner-up *n.* The person who finishes second in a race or contest; the one next after the winner. *Tom won the race and Jack was runner-up.* (Tom came in first and Jack came in second in the race.) *Joan was runner-up in the contest for class secretary.* (Joan got the second highest number of votes for class secretary.) Compare SECOND-BEST.

running start *n. phr.* Good progress at the beginning. *The team was off to a running start, having won the first two games.* (The team had made good progress at the beginning of the season by winning the first two games.) *Contributions of $5000 before the drive began gave the charity fund a running start.* (The charity fund made good progress at the beginning because $5000 was given before the drive began.) Compare HEAD START.

run out *v.* **1a** To come to an end; be used up. *Jerry almost got across the brook on the slippery stones but his luck ran out and he slipped and fell.* (His luck ended and he fell into the brook.) *We'd better do our Christmas shopping; time is running out.* (There isn't much time left.) Syn. GIVE OUT 5. **1b** To use all of the supply; be troubled by not having enough. *The car ran out of gas three miles from town.* (It used all its gas and stopped.) *Millie never runs out of ideas for clever party decorations.* (She is never troubled by a lack of ideas. She has lots of them.) Compare RUN SHORT. **2** *informal* To force to leave; expel. *Federal agents ran the spies out of the country.* (They made them leave.) Syn. KICK OUT, RUN OFF.

run over *v.* **1** To be too full and flow over the edge; spill over. *Billy forgot he had left the water on, and the tub ran over.* (Water filled up the tub and flowed over onto the floor.) **2** To try or go over (something) quickly; practise briefly. *During the lunch hour, Mary ran over her history facts so she would remember them for the test.* (Mary quickly looked again at her notes before the test.) *The coach ran over the signals for the trick play with the team just before game time.* (The coach reviewed the signals briefly.) **3** To drive on top of; ride over. *At night cars often run over small animals that are blinded by the headlights.* (Cars often crush small animals under their wheels.) Syn. RUN DOWN.

run ragged *v. phr.* To tire out; make nervous by too much worry or work.—A hackneyed phrase. *Trying to keep up with too many clubs, sports, and activities in addition to his homework ran Tom ragged.* (It exhausted him physically. He found he couldn't do it.) *On a rainy day the children sometimes ran Mother ragged.* (They were noisy and bothered her, and she got tired and nervous.) Compare WEAR OUT.

run rings around See RUN CIRCLES AROUND.

run riot *v. phr.* **1** To act freely or wildly; not control yourself. *The monkey got out of his cage and ran riot in the pet shop.* (The monkey made a lot of trouble and mixed everything up.) *John let his imagination run riot, thinking he was hunting lions in Africa.* (John did not try to control his imagination.) **2** To be or grow in great numbers or large amounts. *Daisies ran riot in the meadow.* (They grew thickly there. You saw them everywhere you looked.) Compare RUN WILD.

run scared *v. phr.* To expect defeat, as in a political campaign. *The one-vote defeat caused him to run scared in every race thereafter.* (Since the close defeat, he has always been afraid it might happen again.)

run short *v. phr.* **1** To not have enough. *Bob asked Jack to lend him five dollars because he was running short.* (Bob asked Jack to lend him five dollars because he did not have enough money.) *We are running short of sugar.* (We do not have very much sugar left.) Compare RUN OUT. **2** To be not enough in quantity. *We are out of potatoes and the flour is running short.* (We don't have enough flour to last us long.)

run the gauntlet *also* **gantlet** *v. phr.* **1** To be made to run between two lines of people facing each other and be hit by them with clubs or other weapons. *Joe had to run the gauntlet as part of his initiation into the club.* (He had to run between a double line of the members, who tried to hit him with ping-pong paddles as he passed them.) *When the Indians caught an enemy hunting in their forest, they lined up in their village and made him run the gauntlet.* (The hunter was the Indians' enemy and they caught and punished him.) **2** To face a hard test; bear a painful experience.—A cliché. *Ginny had to run the gauntlet of her mother's questions about how the ink spot got on the dining room rug.* (She had to bear the hard experience of her mother's questioning.)

run through *v.* **1** To make a hole through, especially with a sword; pierce. *The pirate was a good swordsman, but the hero finally ran him through.* (The hero finally pierced him with his sword and won the fight.) **2** To spend recklessly; use up wastefully. *The rich man's son quickly ran through his money.* (He spent it recklessly and was soon poor.) Syn. GO THROUGH 4. **3** To read or practice from beginning to end without stopping. *The visiting singer ran through his numbers with the orchestra just before the program.* (He sang them from beginning to end without a pause.)

run to seed See GO TO SEED.

run true to form *v. phr.* To follow a usual way; act as expected; agree with how a person usually acts.—A cliché. *The little boy's actions ran true to form. He bothered his mother until she gave him his way.* (The boy's behavior followed his usual way of bothering his mother until she let him do as he wanted.) Compare PAR FOR THE COURSE.

run up *v.* **1** To add to the amount of; increase. *Karl ran up a big bill at the bookstore.* (He increased it by purchases from time to time until it was quite large.) **2** To put together or make hastily; sew quickly together. *Jill ran up a costume for the party on her sewing machine.* (She made it in a hurry.) **3** To pull (something) upward on a rope; put (something) up quickly. *The pirates ran up the black flag.* (They pulled it upward on a rope to the top of the mast.)

run wild *v. phr.* To be or go out of control. *The students ran wild during spring vacation.* (The students went out of control during spring vacation.) *The new supervisor lets the children run wild.* (The new supervisor lets the children do as they please. He cannot control them.) *The violets are running wild in the flower bed.* (The violet plants are spreading out of control.) Compare RUN RIOT.

run with the hare and hunt (ride) with the hounds *v. phr.* To appear to support both parties in a conflict; to conduct things in ambiguous ways. *Critics accused the king of running with the hare and hunting with the hounds.* (They said he tried to make each opposing political party think that he supported it.)

rush See BUM'S RUSH.

Russian roulette *n.* A game of chance in which one bullet is placed in a revolver, the cartridge cylinder is spun, and the player aims the gun at his own head and pulls the trigger. *Only a fool would risk playing Russian roulette.* (Only a fool would play a game in which he risks killing himself.)

S

saber rattling *or* **sword rattling** *n.* A show of military strength usually to frighten; a threat of military force. *The dictator marched his troops and tanks along the border of our country and did some sabre rattling.* (The dictator showed off his troops and tanks along the border to frighten us.)

sack See GET THE SACK *at* GET THE BOUNCE 2, GIVE THE SACK *at* GIVE THE BOUNCE 2, HIT THE HAY *or* HIT THE SACK, LEAVE HOLDING THE BAG *or* LEAVE HOLDING THE SACK.

sack in/out *v., slang* To go to sleep for a prolonged period (as in from night to morning). *Where are you guys going to sack in/ sack out?* (Where are you going to sleep?)

sacred cow *n.* A person or thing that is never criticized, laughed at, or insulted even if it deserves such treatment. *Motherhood is a sacred cow to most politicians.* (Most politicians never criticize, laugh at, or insult the idea of Motherhood.) *The bold young governor had no respect for the state's sacred cows.* (He had no respect for the things the state had always honored.) *Television respects too many sacred cows.* (Television is afraid to hurt many people's feelings.)

sacrifice fly *n.* A baseball hit high in the air that helps a runner score after it is caught. *Mantle drove in two runs with a single and a sacrifice fly.* (He enabled two runners to score, once when he singled, and once when he hit a long fly.)

saddle See IN THE SADDLE.

saddle shoe *n.* A white shoe with a black or brown piece of leather shaped like a saddle across the top of the shoe. *Mary wore bobby socks and saddle shoes.* (Mary wore bobby socks and shoes with a brown piece of leather shaped like a saddle across the top of the shoe.)

safe See PLAY SAFE.

safe and sound *adj. phr.* Not harmed; not hurt; safe and not damaged. *The package arrived safe and sound.* (The package arrived undamaged.) *The children returned from their trip safe and sound.* (The children returned from their trip unharmed.) Compare WITH A WHOLE SKIN.

safety blitz *n.* A defensive play in football in which the defensive safety man makes a quick run to tackle the offensive quarterback. *Bob's safety blitz kept Tom from making a touchdown.* (Bob tackled the opposing quarterback thus preventing him from scoring.)

safety glass *n.* Two panes of glass with a sheet of plastic between them so that the glass will not break into pieces. *Safety glass is used in cars because it does not break into pieces.* (It is safer for the people who are riding in the car.)

safety island *or* **safety zone** *n.* A raised area in a highway or road to be used only by people walking. *John was half-way across the street when the light changed. He stayed on the safety island until it changed again.* (John stayed on the raised part of the street until it was safe to finish crossing.)

sail See SET SAIL, RAKE THE WIND OUT OF ONE'S SAILS.

sail into *v., informal* **1** To attack with great strength; begin hitting hard. *George grabbed a stick and sailed into the dog.* (George began to hit the dog as hard and as fast as he could.) Compare LAY INTO, PITCH INTO. **2** To scold or criticize very hard. *The coach really sailed into Bob for dropping the pass.* (The coach scolded him hard for dropping the ball.) Syn. BAWL OUT, LAY INTO.

sailor collar *n.* A large square collar like those worn by sailors. *Little Timmy's suit has a sailor collar.* (Timmy's coat has a square collar in the back.) *Mary's blouse has a sailor collar.* (Mary's blouse has a square collar with a wide loose tie.)

sail under false colors *v. phr.* **1** To sail a ship, often pirate, under the flag of another country. *The pirate ship flew the American flag until it got near, then raised the black flag.* (The pirates wanted us to think that it was an honest American ship.) **2** To pretend to be what you are not; masquerade.—A cliché. *The garage hired Jones as a mechanic, but fired him when they found he was sailing under false colors.* (Jones pretended to be a mechanic, but proved to know little about cars.) *They found out that Smith was an escaped convict who had been sailing under false colors as a lawyer.* (Smith was an escaped convict and had been pretending to be a lawyer.)

sake See FOR ——— SAKE.

sale See NO DEAL *or* NO SALE, ON SALE, WHITE SALE.

sales check *or* **sales slip** *n.* A paper which the clerk gives the person who bought something; a paper that shows what you bought in a store and how much you paid for it. *Mrs. Smith checked the sales slip with what she bought.* (She checked to see that she got everything she paid for.) *Mary brought the sales check when she returned the dress so she could get her money back.* (She brought back the sales check because it showed how much she paid for the dress.)

sales talk *n.* A speech made to point out all the good reasons why the sale would help someone who might buy the product. *Mrs. Goldsmith gave the man a good sales talk about the new house.* (She made a speech in which she pointed out all the good things which would make the house a good home.) *The coach gave a sales talk on exercise in the school assembly.* (The coach told the students they should get more exercise.)

salisbury steak *n.* A broiled or fried hamburg patty sometimes containing eggs, milk, bread crumbs, and seasoning. *James ordered* *a salisbury steak for lunch.* (James ordered a patty of chopped beef mixed with other things.)

salt See BACK TO THE SALT MINES, TAKE WITH A GRAIN OF SALT *also* TAKE WITH A PINCH OF SALT, WORTH ONE'S SALT.

salt away *v., informal* To save (money) for the future. *Every week Joe salts away half of his pay.* (He puts half of his earnings in the bank every week.)

salt pork *n.* Very fat pork that has been packed in salt or dipped in brine for curing. *Mother cooked beans with salt pork for supper.* (Mother cooked beans with salt-cured pork added for seasoning.)

same See AT THE SAME TIME, ALL THE SAME, *or* JUST THE SAME, IN THE SAME BREATH, LIGHTNING NEVER STRIKES TWICE IN THE SAME PLACE, ONE AND THE SAME.

same here *informal* And it is the same with me; and the same for me.—Used only in speech. *Mary ordered an ice cream soda, and Jill said, "Same here."* (Mary ordered a soda, and Jill ordered one, too.) *Tom said he was too tired to run any further, and Bill said, "Same here."* (Tom said he was too tired to run any further, and Bill said he was too.)

sand See HIDE ONE'S HEAD IN THE SAND.

sand lot *n.* A field, vacant lot, or other open place used as a sports playing field, usually by younger teams or by amateurs who can't afford to use anything better. *Rogers Hornsby, who was National League baseball batting champion six times, first started playing on Texas sand lots.* (Hornsby learned to play on open fields or vacant lots when he was a boy.)

sand-lot *adj.* Of the kind seen on sand lots; not professional. *The professional football team was so confused by their opponents' fast play that they acted like a bunch of sand-lot amateurs.* (They were so confused that they acted as if they didn't know much about football.)

sand trap *n.* A low place on a golf course that is filled with sand to stop the ball. *The golfer lost four strokes trying to get the ball out of the sand trap.* (The golfer had to hit the ball four times before it would go back onto the grass.)

sandwich board *n.* Two advertising signs worn by a man, one on his chest and the other on his back. *The man walking along Main Street wore a sandwich board saying "Eat at Joe's."* (The man carried a sign over his shoulders advertising Joe's restaurant.)

sauce See HIT THE SAUCE.

save face *v. phr.* To save your good reputation, popularity, or dignity when something has happened or may happen to hurt you; hide something that may cause you shame. *The policeman was caught accepting a bribe; he tried to save face by claiming it was money owed to him.* (He tried to hide his shame by saying it was the payment of a debt.) *Bill would not play in the game because he knew he could not do well and he wanted to save face.* (He didn't want to be shamed by losing.) *The colonel who lost the battle saved face by showing his orders from the general.* (His orders showed that the general had made a mistake, not the colonel.) Contrast LOSE FACE.—

face-saver *n.* The shop teacher's note was a face-saver when another teacher thought John and Bill were playing hookey in town. (The note, which gave them permission to go to town for something, saved the boys from trouble and shame.)—**face-saving** *adj.* The note was a face-saving idea. (The note was an idea that saved the boys from embarrassment.)—**face-saving** *n.* Face-saving is not helped by too many invented excuses. (Preventing embarrassment is not successful if too many excuses are used.)

save for a rainy day See RAINY DAY.

save one's breath *v. phr., informal* To keep silent because talking will not help; not talk because it will do no good. *Save your breath; the boss will never give you the day off.* (Don't ask the boss for a day off; he won't give it to you.)

save one's neck *or* **save one's skin** *v. phr., slang* To save from danger or trouble. *The fighter planes saved our skins while the army was landing from the ships.* (The air force kept us alive during that battle.) *Betty saved Tim's neck by typing his report for him; without her help he could not have finished on time.* (Betty saved Tim from getting in trouble with the teacher and making a bad grade.)

save the day *v. phr.* To bring about victory or success, especially when defeat is likely. *The forest fire was nearly out of control when suddenly it rained heavily and saved the day.* (The forest fire was nearly out of control when suddenly it rained heavily and brought us success in controlling the fire.) *The team was behind, but at the last minute Sam saved the day with a touchdown.* (Sam scored the winning points with a touchdown.)

save up *v. phr.* To put away for future use; keep as savings; save. *John was saving up for a new bicycle.* (John was saving money to buy a new bicycle.) *Mary saved up pieces of cloth to make a quilt.* (Mary put away pieces of cloth until she had enough to make a quilt.)

savings account *n.* An account in a bank, where people put money to save it, and the bank uses the money and pays interest every year. *If you leave your money in your savings account for six months or a year, the bank will pay interest on it.* (The bank will pay you interest if you leave your money in the bank so they can lend it or use it in other ways.) Compare CHECKING ACCOUNT.

savings bond *n.* A government certificate given for money and saved for a number of years so that the government will pay back the money with interest. *Mary bought a $25 savings bond for $18.75.* (Mary lent the government $18.75, and the government promised to pay back $25 after several years.) *John's father gave him a savings bond for graduation.* (John's father bought a bond and put John's name on it. He gave it to John.)

sawed-off *adj., informal* Shorter than usual; small of its kind. *The riot police carried sawed-off shotguns* (The riot police carried shotguns with very short barrels.) *Jimmy was a sawed-off, skinny runt.* (Jimmy was a very short thin boy.)

saw wood *also Southern* **saw gourds** *v. phr., slang* To breathe loudly through the nose while sleeping; snore. *John was sawing wood.* (John was snoring loudly.) *In Alabama a boy who snores saws gourds.* (In Alabama snoring is called sawing gourds.)

say See DARE SAY, GO WITHOUT SAYING, I'LL SAY, NEVER SAY DIE, NOT TO MENTION *or* TO SAY NOTHING OF, STRANGE TO SAY, THAT IS *or* THAT IS TO SAY, YOU DON'T SAY, YOU SAID IT *or* YOU CAN SAY THAT AGAIN.

say a mouthful *v. phr., slang* To say something of great importance or meaning; say more by a sentence than the words usually mean.—Usually in past tense. *Tom said a mouthful when he guessed that company was coming to visit. A dozen people came.* (Tom thought that only a few people would come, but twelve people were there.)—Often used for emphasis. *"Bob is a good pitcher, Bill." "You said a mouthful, Joe. He has a 7–0 record."* (Bob is not just a good pitcher, but one of the best pitchers. He has won seven games and lost none.) Compare YOU SAID IT.

say one's piece *or* **speak one's piece** *v. phr.* To say openly what you think; say, especially in public, what you usually say or are expected to say. *John told the boss that he thought he was wrong and the boss got angry. He said, "You've said your little piece, so go on home."* (The boss said, "You've said that you think I'm wrong, if that is what you think, leave me alone." *Every politician got up and said his piece about how good the mayor was and then sat down.* (Every one said what he was expected to say: that the mayor was a good mayor.)

says who *or* **says you** *v. phr., slang* I don't believe or accept that.—A rude expression often used to make fun of someone or oppose him. *"I am the strongest boy on the block." "Says you."* ("I am the strongest boy on the block." "You're the only one that thinks so, and you'll have to prove it to me.") *"That brook is full of trout." "Says who. I never saw anybody catch trout there."* (I don't believe there are any trout in that brook.) *"You can't take Mary to the party—she's my girl." "Says who?"* (I don't accept the idea that she is your girl.)

say the word *v. phr., informal* To say or show that you want something or agree to something; show a wish, willingness, or readiness; give a sign; say yes; say so. *Just say the word and I will lend you the money.* (If you want me to lend you the money, you need only tell me.) *I will do anything you want; just say the word.* (Tell me if you want anything and I will do it.) *If you get tired of those pictures, say the word.* (If these pictures bore you, let me know.)

say uncle *also* **cry uncle** *v. phr., informal* To say that you surrender; admit that you have lost; admit a defeat; give up. *Bob fought for five minutes, but he had to say uncle.* (Bob fought for five minutes, but he had to give up.) *The bully twisted Jerry's arm and said, "Cry uncle."* (The bully hurt Jerry's arm and commanded him to surrender.) *The other team was beating us, but we wouldn't say uncle.* (We wouldn't quit.) Compare GIVE IN.

scale See TO SCALE.

scale down *v.* To make smaller or less; decrease. *John scaled down each boy's share of food after a bear robbed the camp.* (After a bear robbed the camp there was less food for all so each boy was given a smaller share.) *Tom built a scaled down model of the plane.* (Tom built a small model of the plane with each part of the model smaller in proportion to the same part of the plane.) Compare CUT DOWN.

scalp lock *n.* A small patch of long hair left on the shaved scalp of an American Indian brave. *The trapper grabbed the Indian by his scalp lock.* (The trapper grabbed the Indian's long hair.)

scandal sheet *n.* A newspaper that prints much shocking news and scandal. *Bob wanted to find out who won the election, but he could find only a scandal sheet.* (Bob couldn't find out who won the election because the paper left out important news and printed a lot of scandals.) *The scandal sheet carried big headlines about the murder.* (The paper exaggerated the importance of the murder because many people like to read such news.)

scarcely any See HARDLY ANY.

scarcely ever See HARDLY EVER.

scaredy-cat *or* **scared-cat** See FRAIDY-CAT.

scare out of one's wits *or* **scare stiff** *or* **scare the daylights out of** *v. phr., informal* To frighten very much. *The owl's hooting scared him out of his wits.* (The owl's cry frightened him very much.) *The child was scared stiff in the dentist's chair.* (The child was frightened at the thought of pain.) *Pete's ghost story scared the daylights out of the smaller boys.* (The ghost story frightened the smaller boys.)

scare to death See TO DEATH.

scare up *or* **scrape up** *v., informal* To find, collect, or get together with some effort when needed. *The boy scared up enough money to* *go to college.* (By an effort the boy collected enough money to go to college although he didn't seem to have that much to begin with.) *"Will you stay for supper?" she asked. "I can scare up enough for us all."* (She said she could find and prepare enough food for them all.) *He managed to scrape up the money for his speeding fine.* (It wasn't easy, but he got the money.)

scene See BEHIND THE SCENES.

scent See THROW OFF THE SCENT.

schedule See ON SCHEDULE.

scheme See COLOR SCHEME.

school See TELL TALES OUT OF SCHOOL.

school of hard knocks *n. phr.* Life outside of school or college; life out in the world; the ordinary experience of learning from work and troubles.—A cliché. *He never went to high school; he was educated in the school of hard knocks.* (He never went to high school; he learned by life experience, working his way up to the position he now has.)

score See SETTLE A SCORE *also* WIPE OUT AN OLD SCORE, THE SCORE.

scoring position *n.* A place (such as second or third base in baseball) from which it is rather easy to score. *The Cubs were in trouble as the Giants had Willie coming to bat and two men in scoring position.* (The Giants had a good chance to score against the Cubs when Willie came to bat with runners on second and third base.)

scotch broth *n.* A thick barley soup with vegetables and mutton or beef. *Mother cooked a hearty scotch broth for dinner.* (Mother cooked mutton and vegetables in a barley broth.)

Scott See GREAT GODFREY *or* GREAT SCOTT.

scout See GOOD EGG *or* GOOD SCOUT.

scrape See BOW AND SCRAPE.

scrape the bottom of the barrel *v. phr., informal* To use or take whatever is left after the best has been taken; accept the poor ones. —A cliché. *At first the best men were picked for military service, but the war lasted so long that they had to scrape the bottom of the barrel and take those men that were left.* (All the best men had been taken, so the poorer men were called.) *The garage owner had to scrape the bottom of the barrel to get a mechanic to work for him.* (He had to hire a mechanic who was not very good because the best men had been taken.)

scrape up See SCARE UP.

scratch See FROM SCRATCH, PUT ONE'S MONEY ON A SCRATCHED HORSE, UP TO PAR *or* UP TO SCRATCH.

scratch one's back *v. phr., informal* To do something kind and helpful for someone or to flatter him in the hope that he will do something for you.—A cliché. Usually used in the expression *"You scratch my back and I'll scratch yours." Mary asked Jean to introduce her to her brother. Jean said, "You scratch*

my back and I'll scratch yours." (Jean said that if Mary would help her she would help Mary.)

scratch the surface *v. phr.* To learn or understand very little about something.—Usually used with a limiting adverb (as *only, hardly*). *We thought we understood Africa but when we made a trip there we found we had only scratched the surface.* (We thought we understood Africa, but when we visited there we found we knew very little about it.) *High school students have only scratched the surface of their subjects, and even after college graduation, they still find there is much more to learn.* (It takes years of hard study to learn more than a little about anything.)

scream bloody murder *v. phr., informal* To yell or protest as strongly as one can. *When the thief grabbed her purse, the woman screamed bloody murder.* (She yelled as loudly as she could.) *When the city doubled property taxes, home owners screamed bloody murder.* (People who owned houses protested strongly.)

screen pass *n.* A short pass in football thrown over the heads of the onrushing defenders to a back who has a screen or line of blockers in front of him. *The screen pass completely fooled the defensive linemen who were expecting a long pass.* (Because they expected the long pass, the linemen rushed in to catch the passer, and left the line of scrimmage open.)

screen test *n.* A short movie made to see if an actor or actress is good enough or the right one to play a part. *Ellen acted well on the stage, but she failed her screen test.* (Ellen acted well on the stage, but the film showed that she did not have the right talents to be a movie star.)

screw See HAVE A SCREW LOOSE, PUT ON THE SCREWS.

screw around *v. phr., vulgar, avoidable* To hang around idly without accomplishing anything, to loaf about, to beat or hack around. *You guys are no longer welcome here; all you do is screw around all day.* (All you do is hang around idly without accomplishing anything.)

screws See TIGHTEN THE SCREWS.

screw up *v. phr., slang, semi-vulgar, best avoided* **1** To make a mess of, to make an error which causes confusion. *The treasurer screwed up the accounts of the Society so badly that he had to be fired.* (He made such a mess of the accounts that he had to be fired.) **2** To cause someone to be neurotic or maladjusted. *Her divorce screwed her up so badly that she had to go to a shrink.* (Her divorce caused her to be so maladjusted that she had to go to a psychiatrist.)

screw up one's courage *or* **pluck up one's courage** *v. phr.* To force yourself to be brave. *The small boy screwed up his courage and* *went upstairs in the dark.* (The small boy forced himself to be brave and went upstairs in the dark.) *When his father came home in a bad mood, it took Pete some time to screw up his courage and ask him for a dollar.* (Pete was afraid for a while but then he got brave.) Compare WHISTLE IN THE DARK.

scrimmage See LINE OF SCRIMMAGE.

scrounge around *v. phr., slang* **1** To search for an object aimlessly without having one clearly in mind. *I don't know what's the matter with him, he is just scrounging around all day long.* (He is just looking around aimlessly.) **2** To look around for a way to get a free drink or a free meal. *Sue and her husband are so broke they never eat properly; they just scrounge around from one place to the next until someone offers them something.* (They just wander from one place to the next until someone offers them some food and drink.)

Scylla See BETWEEN THE DEVIL AND THE DEEP BLUE SEA *or* BETWEEN SCYLLA AND CHARYBDIS.

sea See AT SEA, BETWEEN THE DEVIL AND THE DEEP BLUE SEA, HIGH SEAS, NOT THE ONLY FISH IN THE SEA, PUT TO SEA.

seam See BURST AT THE SEAMS.

search See IN SEARCH OF.

search me *informal* I don't know; how should I know?—May be considered rude. *When I asked her what time it was, she said, "Search me, I have no watch."* (When I asked her what time it was, she said, "I don't know.")

search one's heart *or* **search one's soul** *v. phr. formal* To study your reasons and acts; try to discover if you have been fair and honest. *The teacher searched his heart trying to decide if he had been unfair in failing Tom.* (After the teacher failed Tom, the teacher thought he might have been unfair and asked himself if he had done the right thing.)— **heart-searching** *or* **soul-searching** *n. or adj. After much heart-searching, Jean told Beth she was sorry for the unkind things she had said.* (Jean thought hard about the things she had said and decided she should say she was sorry.) *The minister preached a soul-searching sermon about the thoughtless ways people hurt each other.* (The sermon made people look hard at the hurtful things they had done.)

search out *v.* To search for and discover; find or learn by hunting. *The police were trying to search out the real murderer.* (The police were trying to find the real murderer.)

search with a fine-tooth comb See FINE-TOOTH COMB.

season See IN SEASON, OUT OF SEASON.

seat See BACK SEAT DRIVER, FLY BY THE SEAT OF ONE'S PANTS, HOT SEAT, JUDGMENT SEAT, TAKE A BACK SEAT.

seat belt *n.* A strong strap used to protect a person in a moving car or other vehicle by holding him in his seat. *When the plane began to land, Billy and his mother fastened their seat belts.* (They fastened the straps right around themselves for protection.) *Passengers in automobiles should wear seat belts for safety.* (Automobile passengers should fasten seat belts around themselves while they are riding.)

second See PLAY SECOND FIDDLE, SPLIT SECOND.

second base *n.* The base to be touched second in baseball. *Charlie slid into second base with a double.* (His hit helped him to reach the second of the four bases.)

second best *n.* Something that is lower than or not quite as good as the best. *Tom liked the deluxe model bicycle; but he could afford only a second best.* (Tom could not buy the best bicycle.) *Joan chose the best and Mary had to take the second best.* (Mary had to take what was left after Joan chose the best.) *There were ten boys in the race. Jack won and Fred was a close second best.* (Fred beat everyone else except Jack.) Compare RUNNER UP.

second best *adv.* Second; in second place. *The team came off second best in the game.* (The team lost the game.)

second-best *adj.* Next to best; second in rank. *Mary wore her second-best dress.* (Mary did not wear her best dress, but she wore the one that was almost as good.) *Bob was the second-best player on the team.* (There was only one player better than Bob on the team.)

second class *n.* **1** The second best or highest group; the class next after the first. *Joe was good enough in arithmetic to be put in the second class but was not good enough for the first.* (He was good enough in arithmetic to be put in the class next to the highest but not good enough for the highest.) Compare FIRST CLASS. **2** The place or quarters, especially on a ship, train, or airplane which people travel who pay the next to the highest fare. *Aunt May bought a ticket to travel in the second class on the boat trip.* (Aunt May paid the fare to travel in the place that was next to the highest.) Compare FIRST CLASS, THIRD CLASS. **3** A class of mail that includes magazines and newspapers published at least four times a year and costs less for mailing than first class mail. Compare FIRST CLASS.

second-class[1] *adj.* **1** Belonging in the class that is next to the highest or next best. *He was only a second-class math student.* (He was in the second class in math.) *His parents traveled as second-class passengers on the boat.* (His parents traveled in the second class on the boat.) *The periodical came as second-class mail.* (The periodical came in mail that belonged to the second-class.) Compare FIRST-CLASS, THIRD-CLASS. **2** Not so good as others;

second-rate. *They were never given full dem-ocratic rights but were always treated as second-class citizens.* (They were never given all of the rights that others had; they were not allowed to be real citizens.)

second-class *adv.* By second class. *We went second-class on the train to New York.* (We went on the second-class coach.) *I mailed the newspaper second-class.* (I mailed it the next best way to first class.)

second cousin *n.* A child of your father's or mother's first cousin. *Mary and Jane are second cousins.* (Mary's father or mother is a first cousin of Jane's father or mother.)

second-guess *v. phr.* 1 To criticize another's decision with advantage of hindsight. *The losing team's coach is always second-guessed.* (The losing team's coach is always criticized after the game.) 2 To guess what someone else intends or would think or do. *Television planners try to second-guess the public.* (They guess what people will like.)

second nature *n.* Something done without any special effort, as if by natural instinct. *Cutting tall trees has become second nature to the experienced lumberjack.* (The lumberjack cuts down trees as if the feat is an ordinary thing to be doing.)

second-run *adj.* Of a movie: Shown in many movie theaters before, and allowed to be shown later in other movie theaters. *Tickets to second-run movies cost much less.* (You pay less to see a movie the second time it comes to town than you pay the first time.)

second thought *n.* A change of ideas or opinions resulting from more thought or study. *Your second thoughts are very often wiser than your first ideas.* (Longer thought often shows the way to better judgment.) *We decided to climb the mountain, but on second thought realized that it was too dangerous.* (We thought it over and wisely decided not to risk the climb.) Compare THINK BETTER OF.

second wind *also* **second breath** *n.* 1 The easier breathing that follows difficult breathing when one makes a severe physical effort, as in running or swimming. *After the first quarter mile, a mile runner usually gets his second wind and can breathe better.* (He gets used to running and his heart works harder.) *We climbed with labored breathing for half an hour, but then got our second wind and went up more easily.* (Our hearts beat faster and we breathed easier.) 2 *informal* The refreshed feeling you get after first becoming tired while doing something and then becoming used to it. *Tom became very tired of working at his algebra, but after a while he got his second wind and began to enjoy it.* (Tom became tired of algebra, but after a while he got used to it and liked it.)

secret See IN SECRET, OPEN SECRET.

section gang *or* **section crew** *n.* A group of railroad workers who watch and repair a number of miles of track. *The section crew was called out to fix the broken bridge.* (The crew was called to fix the bridge.)

section hand *n.* A worker who repairs railway track; one of the men in a section gang. *The section hands moved off the track while the train went by.* (The workers stopped working and moved off the track while the train went by.)

security blanket, *n., slang, colloquial* An idea, person, or object that one holds on to for psychological reassurance or comfort as infants usually hang on to the edge of a pillow, a towel, or a blanket. *Sue has gone to Aunt Mathilda for a chat; she is her security blanket.* (Aunt Mathilda is the person Sue confides in when she has a problem.)

see See CAN'T SEE THE WOODS FOR THE TREES, LET ME SEE *or* LET'S SEE.

see about *v.* 1 To find out about; attend to. *If you are too busy, I'll see about the train tickets.* (If you are too busy, I'll take care of getting the train tickets.) 2 *informal* To consider; study. *I cannot take time now but I'll see about your plan when I have time.* (I cannot take time now, but I'll think over your plan when I have time.) Compare SEE TO, LOOK INTO, THINK OVER.

see after See LOOK AFTER.

see better days *v. phr.* 1 To enjoy a better or happier life.—A cliché. *Mr. Smith is poor now, but he will see better days.* (Mr. Smith will not always be poor.) 2 To become old, damaged, or useless.—A cliché. Used in the perfect tense. *My blue coat is ten years old. It has seen better days.* (It is getting too old to wear.) *Our car wasn't old, but it had seen better days.* (It had been used very much and was worn out.)

see beyond one's nose *or* **see beyond the end of one's nose** *v. phr.* To make wise judgments about questions of importance to yourself and others; act with farseeing understanding.—A cliché. Used in negative, conditional, and interrogative sentences. *He couldn't save money or make plans for the future; he just never saw behond the end of his nose.* (All he thought about was the present time.) *People who always complain about school taxes would stop it if they could see beyond their noses and understand the importance of first-class schools.* (They think more about their own interests, not the education of future citizens.)

seed See GO TO SEED *or* RUN TO SEED.

see daylight *v. phr., informal* To know that an end or success is near. *We thought we would never finish building the house, but now we can see daylight.* (Building the house took a long time, but now it is almost done.) *Sarah thought it would take forever to read the book for her report, but finally she saw daylight.* (Finally Sarah saw that she had only a little left to read.)

see eye to eye *v. phr.* To agree fully; hold

exactly the same opinion. *Though we did not usually agree, we saw eye to eye in the matter of reducing taxes.* (Though we did not usually agree we were in full agreement in the matter of reducing taxes.) *Mother did not see eye to eye with Father on where we would go for our vacation.* (Father and Mother did not agree; they had different ideas.)

see fit *or* **think fit** *v. phr.* To decide that an action is necessary, wise, or advisable; choose. *Margaret asked, "Mother, what time must I come home after the dance?" Mother answered, "You may do as you see fit."* (Mother told Margaret to decide what would be a reasonable time.)—Often used with an infinitive. *After much thought, we did not see fit to join in the fight against the dictator.* (We decided not to join the fight.) *The boys were angry because Ed thought fit to report the fight to the principal.* (Ed reported the fight to the principal because he thought he should.)

seeing is believing Seeing something is good proof.—A cliché. *Bill told Joe he had passed his test, but Joe said, "Seeing is believing."* (He meant that he would not believe it until he saw his grade.)

see into *v.* To know or understand the real nature or meaning of. *Suddenly the teacher saw into Linda's strange actions.* (The teacher suddenly understood why Linda was acting strangely.)

see off *v.* To go to say or wave goodbye to. *His brother went to the train with him to see him off.* (His brother went to the train with him to say goodbye to him when he left.) *When Marsha flew to Cleveland, Flo saw her off at the airport.* (Flo went to the airport with Martha and told her goodbye there.)

see one's way clear *v. phr.* To know no reason for not doing something; feel that you are free. *John finally saw his way clear to help his friends.* (John wanted to help his friends so he finally found ways of solving the problems which stood in the way.) *Mary had to do her homework and help her mother before she could see her way clear to go to the movies with Jane.* (Mary had to do her work before she could go to the movies.)

see out *v.* **1** To go with to an outer door. *A polite man sees his company out after a party.* (A gentleman goes to the door with his guests as they leave.) **2** To stay with and finish; not quit. *Pete's assignment was hard but he saw it out to the end.* (His lesson was hard but he kept on and finished it.)

see red *v. phr., informal* To become very angry. *Whenever anyone teased John about his weight, he saw red.* (Whenever anyone teased John about being fat, he became very angry.)

see stars *v. phr., informal* To imagine you are seeing stars as a result of being hit on the head. *When Ted was hit on the head by the ball, he saw stars.* (He thought for a minute that he was seeing stars.) *The boxer's head hit the floor, making him see stars.* (He imagined he saw stars.)

see the beat See HEAR THE BEAT.

see the color of one's money *v. phr., informal* To know that you have money to spend.—A cliché. *The realtor would not show us a house until he saw the color of our money.* (He would not show us a house until he knew that we had money to spend for one.) *Before I show you the diamond, let me see the color of your money.* (First, prove to me that you can afford it.)

see the light *v. phr., informal* To understand or agree, often suddenly; accept another's explanation or decision. *I did not approve of his action, but he explained his reason and then I saw the light.* (Then I understood and agreed with him.) *Bill wanted Harry to help him, but Harry wasn't in the mood until Bill offered to pay him. Then Harry saw the light.* (Harry changed his mind and agreed to help.) *Mary thought it was fun to date older boys but when they started drinking, she saw the light.* (She understood why she should not date them.)

see the light of day *v. phr.* To be born or begun.—A cliché. *The children visited the old house where their great-grandfather first saw the light of day.* (They visited the house where their great-grandfather was born.) *The party was a failure, and Jean wished her plan had never seen the light of day.* (Jean wished that her plan for the party had never been made.)

see things *v. phr., informal* To imagine sights which are not real; think you see what is not there. *I had not seen him for twenty years and when we met on the street I thought I was seeing things.* (I thought he was a ghost.) *She woke her husband to tell him she had seen a face at the window, but he told her she was seeing things.* (He told her she was dreaming.)

see through *v.* **1** To understand the real meaning of or reason for; realize the falseness of. *Mother saw through Johnny's excuses not to go to bed on Christmas Eve. She knew he wanted to stay up to see Santa Claus.* (She knew that Santa Claus was the real reason he wanted to stay up.) *The teacher saw through the boy's story of having to help at home.* (She knew his story was not true; it was just an excuse.) **2** To do (something) until finished; stay with until the end. *Once Charles started a job, he saw it through till it was finished.* (He didn't quit before it was done.) **3** To help and encourage (a person) through trouble or difficulty. *Mrs. Miller saw Jane through her sickness.* (She stayed and helped her.) *When Mr. and Mrs. Brown lost their little girl, their friends saw them through with help and sympathy.* (They comforted Mr. and Mrs. Brown and did things for them.) *His* *business was about to fail, but his banker saw him through.* (His banker lent him money and gave advice until his business was saved.) **4** To be enough for; last. *This money will see us through the week.* (This money will be enough for the week; we will not need more.) *Here is a long report to type. Do you have enough paper to see you through?* (Do you have enough paper to last till the report is all typed?) Compare TIDE OVER.

see to *also* **look to** *v.* To attend to; take care of; do whatever needs to be done about. *While Donna bought the theatre tickets, I saw to the parking of the car.* (While Donna bought the theatre tickets, I took care of the parking of the car.) Compare SEE ABOUT.

see to it *v. phr.* To take care; take the responsibility; make sure.—Usually used with a noun clause. *We saw to it that the child was fed and bathed.* (We took care that the child was fed and bathed.)

see with rose-colored glasses See LOOK AT THE WORLD THROUGH ROSE-COLORED GLASSES.

seize on *v.* To make use of (a happening or idea.) *Bob seized on the rain as an excuse for missing school.* (He didn't want to go to school and the rain gave him a reason for staying home.)

sell down the river *v. phr.* To give harmful information about someone or something to one's enemies; betray. *The traitor sold his country down the river to the enemy army.* (The traitor gave the enemy army information about his country's plans.) *The criminal told the hiding place of his companions and sold them down the river.* (The criminal told the police where his companions were hiding.) Compare SELL OUT 2.

sell out *v.* **1a** To sell all of a certain thing which a store has in stock. *In the store's January white sale the sheets and pillowcases were sold out in two days.* (The store sold all its sheets and pillowcases in two days.) **1b** To sell all the stock and close the store; go out of business. *The local hardware store sold out last month and was replaced by a cafe.* (The hardware store went out of business and a cafe took its place.) **2** *informal* To be unfaithful to your country for money or other reward; be disloyal; sell a secret; accept a bribe. *In the Revolutionary War, Benedict Arnold sold out to the British.* (He left the American army to help the British for a reward.) *The dishonest wrestler sold out to his opponent for a hundred dollars.* (He agreed to lose for $100.)

sell short *v.* To think (a person or thing) less good or valuable than is true; underestimate. *Don't sell the team short; the players are better than you think.* (Don't think the team is poor; you will be wrong.) *Some teachers sold John short.* (They thought he was not smart, but he fooled them.)

send up *v. phr., colloquial* To sentence (someone) to prison. *Did you know that*

Milton Shaeffer was sent up for fifteen years? (Did you know he was sentenced to jail for 15 years?)

senior citizen *n.* An older person, often one who has retired from active work or employment. *Mrs. North, the history teacher, is a senior citizen.* (Mrs. North is old enough to retire from teaching.)

sense See COME TO ONE'S SENSES, HORSE SENSE, MAKE SENSE, OUT OF ONE'S HEAD *or* OUT OF ONE'S SENSES.

separate the men from the boys *v. phr., informal* To show who has strength, courage, and loyalty and find who do not.—A cliché. *When the ship hit an iceberg and sank, it separated the men from the boys.* (It showed who were brave and strong like men.) *The mile run separates the men from the boys.* (Those who can run the mile are strong and tough; the others are not.)

serve See FIRST COME, FIRST SERVED.

serve one right *v. phr.* To be what (someone) really deserves as a punishment; be a fair exchange for what (someone) has done or said or failed to do or say. *He failed his exam; it served him right because he had not studied.* (He failed his exam; he really deserved to fail because he had not studied.) *Bob said it served Sally right when she cut her finger; she had taken his knife without asking him.* (Bob said that was a fair punishment for taking his knife without asking.) Compare ASK FOR, HAVE IT COMING.

serve up *v.* To prepare and serve (as a food). *Father caught a trout and Mother served it up at dinner.* (The trout was caught, cooked, and served at dinner.)

service See AT ONE'S SERVICE, CURB SERVICE, LIP SERVICE, OF SERVICE, ROOM SERVICE.

session See BULL SESSION.

set See GET SET.

set about *v.* To begin; start. *Benjamin Franklin set about learning the printer's trade at an early age.* (He began learning the printer's trade while young.) *After breakfast, Mother set about her household duties.* (She began to do her housework.)

set aside *v.* **1** To separate from the others in a group or collection. *She set aside the things in the old trunk which she wanted to keep.* (She separated the things she wanted from the things she didn't want.) **2** To select or choose from others for some purpose. *The governor set aside a day for thanksgiving.* (He named a certain day for all to observe as a day for thanks.) **3** To pay no attention to (something); leave out. *The complaint was set aside as of no importance.* (The complaint was not attended to.) **4** *formal* To refuse to accept; annul; cancel as worthless or wrong. *The Supreme Court set aside the decision of the lower courts.* (The Supreme Court disagreed with the lower courts.)

set back **1** To cause to put off or get behind

schedule; slow up; check. *The cold weather set back the planting by two weeks.* (The cold weather put off the planting by two weeks.) **2** *informal* To cause to pay out or to lose (a sum of money); cost. *His new car set him back over $3000.* (His new car cost him over $3000.)

set back on one's heels *or* **knock back on one's heels** *v. phr., informal* To give an unpleasant surprise; upset suddenly; stop or turn back (someone's) progress. *Jack brags too much and it set him back on his heels when the coach told him he wasn't as good a player as he thought he was.* (The coach told Jack something unpleasant that surprised him.) *Jean was doing very well in school until sickness knocked her back on her heels.* (Jean's work in school was good until she became sick.) Compare KNOCK FOR A LOOP, THROW FOR A LOSS.

set down *v.* **1** To write; record. *He set down all his important thoughts in his diary.* (He wrote all his important thoughts there.) *At the beginning of his letter Dan set down the date.* (He wrote the date.) Syn. PUT DOWN. **2** To stop a bus or other vehicle and let (someone) get off. *The bus driver set her down at the corner.* (He stopped and let her get off at the corner.) **3** To put into some group; classify; consider. *When he heard the man speak, he set him down as a fool.* **4** (After hearing him talk, he decided he was foolish.) To explain; think a reason for. *The teacher set down the boy's poor English to his foreign birth.* (The teacher said that the boy spoke poor English because he was born in another country.)

set eyes on See LAY EYES ON.

set fire to *v. phr.* To cause to burn; start a fire in. *The sparks set fire to the oily rags.* (The sparks caused the oily rags to burn.) Compare CATCH FIRE.

set foot *v. phr.* To step; walk; go.—Used with a negative. *She would not let him set foot across her threshold.* (She would not let him step through her door.) *She told the boy not to set foot out of the house until he had finished supper.* (She told the boy not to go out of the house until he had finished supper.)

set forth *v., formal* To explain exactly or clearly. *The President set forth his plans in a television talk.* (The president explained his plans in a talk on television.) **2** To start to go somewhere; begin a trip. *The troop set forth on their ten-mile hike early.* (The troop started on their ten-mile hike early.) Compare SET OUT.

set great store by See SET STORE BY.

set in *v.* To begin; start; develop. *Before the boat could reach shore, a storm had set in.* (The storm began before the boat reached shore.) *He did not keep the cut clean and infection set in.* (Infection started because he did not keep the cut clean.) *The wind set in from the east.* (The wind began to blow from the east.)

set loose See LET LOOSE 1a.

set off *v.* **1** To decorate through contrast; balance by difference. *The bright colors of the birds were set off by the white snow.* (The whiteness made the colors seem brighter.) *A small gold pin set off her plain dark dress.* (The gold pin contrasted with her dark dress.) **2** To balance; make somewhat equal. *Her great wealth, as he thought, set off her plain face.* (He thought her wealth made up for her plain face so he decided to marry her.) **3a** To begin to go. *They set off for the West in a covered wagon.* (They started West.) Compare SET OUT. **3b** To cause to begin. *A letter from home set off an attack of homesickness.* (The letter started him feeling homesick.) *An atomic explosion is created by setting off a chain reaction in the atom.* (A series of reactions are caused to begin in the atom and finally there is an explosion.) Compare TOUCH OFF. **3c** To cause to explode. *On July 4 we set off firecrackers in many places.* (We explode firecrackers on July 4.)

set on *also* **set upon** *v.* **1** To begin suddenly to fight against; attack fiercely. *Tom was walking through the park when a gang of boys set on him.* (The boys attacked him in the park.) **2** To cause to attack. *Some boys went to steal melons but the farmer set his dog on them.* (The farmer told his dog to bite the boys.)

set one's cap for *v. phr., informal* To attempt to win the love of or to marry.—A cliché. Usually used of a girl or woman. *The young girl set her cap for the new town doctor, who was a bachelor.* (The girl determined to win the love of the new doctor and marry him.)

set one's face against *v. phr., literary* To be very much against; strongly disapprove. *The banker's daughter wanted to marry a poor boy, but her father set his face against it.* (He was against the marriage; he opposed it.)

set one's hand to See PUT ONE'S HAND TO.

set one's hand to the plow See PUT ONE'S HAND TO THE PLOW.

set one's heart on *v. phr.* To want very much. *He set his heart on that bike.* (He hoped very much to get that bike.) *also:* To be very desirous of; hope very much to succeed in.—Used with a verbal noun. *He set his heart on winning the race.* (He really wanted to win the race.)

set one's house in order See PUT ONE'S HOUSE IN ORDER.

set one's sights *v. phr.* **1** To want to reach; aim for. *John has set his sights higher than the job he has now.* (John wants something better than his present job.) **2** To wish to get or win. *Owen set his sights on the championship.* (He wanted to win the championship.)

set one's teeth on edge *v. phr.* **1** To have a sharp sour taste that makes you rub your teeth together. *The lemon juice set my teeth on edge.* (The sour lemon made my teeth rub together.) **2** To make one feel nervous or annoyed. *She looks so mean that her face sets my teeth on edge.* (I don't like to see her; her face makes me nervous.)

set on foot See ON FOOT.

set out *v.* **1** To leave on a journey or voyage. *The Pilgrims set out for the New World.* (The Pilgrims began their voyage to the New World.) Compare SET FORTH 2, SET OFF 4, START OUT. **2** To decide and begin to try, attempt. *George set out to improve his pitching.* (George decided to improve his pitching and began to try.) **3** To plant in the ground. *The gardener set out some tomato seedlings.* (He put some young tomato plants in the ground.)

set sail *v. phr.* To begin a sea voyage; start sailing. *The ship set sail for Europe.* (The ship began the voyage to Europe.)

set store by *v. phr., informal* To like or value; want to keep. Used with a qualifying word between *set* and *store*. *George sets great store by that old tennis racket.* (George really likes that old tennis racket.) *Pat doesn't set much store by Mike's advice.* (Pat doesn't think Mike's advice is right and wise.)

set the ball rolling See GET THE BALL ROLLING.

set the pace *v. phr.* To decide on a rate of speed of travel or rules that are followed by others. *The scoutmaster set the pace so that the shorter boys would not get tired trying to keep up.* (The scoutmaster hiked at a speed of march that was not too fast for the shorter boys.) *Louise set the pace in selling tickets for the school play.* (Louise sold the most tickets, but the other girls tried to sell as many as she sold.)—**pace-setter** *n. John is the pace-setter of the class.* (The other members of the class try hard to learn as fast as John learns.)—**pace-setting** *adj. Bob's time in the cross-country race was pace-setting.* (Bob ran the race faster than anyone before him, and now everyone who runs the race in the future will have to try to beat Bob's record.) *The country is growing at a pace-setting rate.* (The country is growing faster than ever, and other countries are trying to keep up.)

set the stage for *v. phr.* To prepare the way or situation for (an event); to make a situation ready for something to happen. *The country's economic problems set the stage for a depression.* (The country's economic problems prepared the way for a depression.)

set the world on fire *v. phr., informal* To do something outstanding; act in a way that attracts much attention or makes you famous. —A cliché. *John works hard, but he will never set the world on fire.* (John works hard, but he will never be an outstanding success in his work.) *Mary could set the world on fire with her piano playing.* (Mary could become a very famous pianist.)

setting-up *adj.* Done early in the morning to make you fresh and feel strong for the day. *Tom jumped out of bed and did his setting-up exercises.* (Tom did his early morning exercises.) Compare DAILY DOZEN.

settle a score *also* **wipe out an old score** To hurt (someone) in return for a wrong or loss. *John settled an old score with Bob by beating him.* (Bob made trouble for John and at last John beat him in a fight.) Compare GET BACK AT, GET EVEN.

settle down *v.* **1** To live more quietly and sensibly; have a regular place to live and a regular job; stop acting wildly or carelessly, especially by growing up. *John will settle down after he gets a job and gets married.* (His conduct will improve.) **2** To become quiet, calm, or comfortable. *Father settled down with the newspaper.* (He made himself comfortable as he read the paper.) *The house settled down for the night after the children were put to bed.* (The house became quiet.) *The teacher told the students to settle down and study the lesson.* (The teacher told the students to stop talking and playing, and study.)

settle for *v.* To be satisfied with (less) agree to; accept. *Jim wanted $200 for his old car, but he settled for $100.* (He wanted to sell it for $200 but at last agreed to a price of only $100.)

settle one's hash *v. phr., informal* To give a full punishment or defeat to. *Jim tried to sneak out of study hall but the teacher saw him and settled his hash.* (He boxed Jim's ears and sat him down again.)

set to *v.* **1** To make a serious beginning. *Charlie took a helping of turkey, grabbed his knife and fork, and set to.* (He began eating hungrily.) **2** To start to fight. *One man called the other a liar and they set to.* (They fought.)

set to rights See PUT TO RIGHTS.

set up *v.* **1** To provide the money for the necessities for. *When he was twenty-one, his father set him up in the clothing business.* (His father helped him with the money to start a clothing store.) **2** To establish; start. *The government has set up many hospitals for veterans of the armed forces.* (The government built many hospitals for soldiers and sailors.) **3** To make ready for use by putting the parts together or into their right place. *The men set up the new printing press.* (They put the parts together so it would work.) **4** To bring into being; cause. *Ocean tides are set up by the pull between earth and the moon.* (The pull of the moon causes the tides.) **5** To claim; pretend. *He set himself up to be a graduate of a medical school, but he was not.* (He pretended to be a medical school graduate.) **6** To harm someone by entrapment or some other ruse. *Joe was actually innocent of the* robbery, but his "trusted friends" set him up, so the police found the gun in his car. (The "friends" arranged it so that Joe seemed guilty when in fact he wasn't.)

setup *n.* (stress on *set*) **1** Arrangement, management, circumstances. *Boy, you really have a wonderful setup in your office!* (Your circumstances are enviably good.) *I just can't do my work in such a messy setup!* (I can't work under such disorderly circumstances.) **2** Financial arrangement. *It is a fairly generous setup sending your uncle $1,000 a month.* (It is a generous arrangement on your part.)

set upon See SET ON.

seven See AT SIXES AND SEVENS.

sewed up *adj. phr., informal* Won or arranged as you wish; decided. *They thought they had the game sewed up, but the other team won it with a touchdown in the last quarter.* (They were sure they had the victory, but the other team won with a last-minute score.) *Dick thought he had the job sewed up, but another boy got it.* (Dick felt sure he would get the job, but the man hired another boy.) Compare IN THE BAG.

shack up with *v. phr., slang* To move in with (someone) of the opposite sex without marrying the person. *Did you know that Ollie and Sue aren't married? They just decided to shack up for a while.* (They just decided to move in with each other.) See LIGHT HOUSEKEEPING.

shadow See AFRAID OF ONE'S SHADOW, EYE SHADOW.

shake See MORE THAN ONE COULD SHAKE A STICK AT.

shake a leg *v. phr., slang* To go fast; hurry. *Shake a leg! The bus won't wait.* (Hurry— the bus is leaving!) Compare STEP ON IT.

shake down *v.* **1** To cause to fall by shaking. *He shook some pears down from the tree.* (He made them fall by shaking the tree.) **2** *informal* To test, practice, get running smoothly (a ship or ship's crew). *The captain shook down his new ship on a voyage to the Mediterranean Sea.* (He sailed it there to test it and get everything working right.) **3** *slang* To get money from by threats. *The gangsters shook the store owner down every month.* (They got money from the owner by telling him they would harm him.)

shake in one's shoes *or* **shake in one's boots** *v. phr., informal* To be very much afraid. *The robber shook in his boots when the police knocked on his door.* (He was very much afraid because the police were after him.)

shake off *v., informal* To get away from when followed; get rid of; escape from. *A convict escaped from prison and shook off the officers trying to follow him.* (He got away and the officers didn't catch him.) *Tom could not shake off his cold.* (Tom had a cold and could not get well.)

shake up *v., informal* To bother; worry; disturb. *The notice about a cut in pay shook up everybody in the office.* (They were all worried by the news that they would be paid less.)

shame See FOR SHAME, PUT TO SHAME.

shape See IN SHAPE, OUT OF SHAPE, TAKE SHAPE.

shape up *v., informal* **1** To begin to act or work right; get along satisfactorily. *If the new boy doesn't begin to shape up soon, he'll have to leave school.* (He will be expelled if he doesn't behave and do his work.) *"How is the building of the new gym coming along?" "Fine. It's shaping up very well."* (The building is getting along very well with no trouble.) **2** To show promise. *Plans for our picnic are shaping up very well.* (The plans look favorable for our picnic.)

sharp See LOOK SHARP.

sharp as a tack *adj. phr.* **1** Very neatly and stylishly dressed—A trite expression. *That new boy always looks sharp as a tack in class.* (He is very well-dressed.) **2** Very intelligent; smart; quick-witted.—A trite expression. *Tom is sharp as a tack; he got 100 on every test.* (Tom is very bright.)

sheep See WOLF IN SHEEP'S CLOTHING.

sheet See SCANDAL SHEET, THREE SHEETS IN THE WIND *or* THREE SHEETS TO THE WIND.

shelf See ON THE SHELF.

shell See IN ONE'S SHELL *or* INTO ONE'S SHELL, OUT OF ONE'S SHELL.

shell out *v., informal* To pay or spend. *Dick had to shell out a lot of money for his new car.* (He spent a large amount of money.)

shift for oneself *v. phr.* To live or act independently with no help, guidance or protection from others; take care of yourself. *Mrs. McCarthy was forced to shift for herself after her husband died.* (No one helped her; she was responsible for her own living.)

shine See RAIN OR SHINE, TAKE A SHINE TO.

shine up to *v., slang* To try to please; try to make friends with. *Smedley shines up to all the pretty girls.* (He likes them and tries to get them to like him.)

shingle See HANG OUT ONE'S SHINGLE.

ship See GIVE UP THE SHIP, LANDING SHIP.

ship come in All the money a person has wished for is received; wealth comes to a person. *Used with a possessive.—A cliché. When my ship comes in, I will take a trip to Norway.* (I will go there when I am rich.) *Mr. Brown is just waiting for his ship to come in.* (He hopes to be rich some day.)

ship out *v.* To begin a journey; leave. *The army group shipped out for the Far East today.* (They began their voyage to Korea.)

shirt See GIVE THE SHIRT OFF ONE'S BACK, KEEP ONE'S SHIRT ON, LOSE ONE'S SHIRT.

shoe See COMFORTABLE AS AN OLD SHOE. COMMON AS AN OLD SHOE, FILL ONE'S SHOES, IF THE SHOE FITS, WEAR IT, IN ONE'S SHOES,

SHAKE IN ONE'S SHOES, SADDLE SHOE, STEP INTO ONE'S SHOES, WHERE THE SHOE PINCHES.

shoe on the other foot The opposite is true; places are changed. *He was my captain in the army but now the shoe is on the other foot.* (Now I am his boss here in the factory.)

shoestring See ON A SHOESTRING.

shoestring catch *n.* A catch of a hit baseball just before it hits the ground. *The left fielder made a shoe-string catch of a line drive to end the inning.* (He caught the hard-hit ball just before it touched the ground.)

shoo-in *n., informal* Someone or something that is expected to win; a favorite; sure winner. *Chris is a shoo-in to win a scholarship.* (Chris is sure to be a winner of a merit scholarship.) *Do you think he will win the election? He's a shoo-in.* (He is a certain victor; he will certainly win the election.) *This horse is a shoo-in. He can't miss winning.* (He is certain to win.) Syn. SURE THING 1.

shoot off one's mouth *or* **shoot off one's face** *v. phr., slang* To give opinions without knowing all the facts; talk as if you know everything.—A cliché. *Tom has never been to Florida, but he's always shooting his mouth off about how superior Florida is to California.* (Tom says Florida is better than California even though he doesn't know much about the state.) *I want to study the problem before I shoot off my face.* (I want to know more about the problem before I say what I think.) *The editor of the newspaper is always shooting his mouth off about the trouble in Africa.* (The editor of the newspaper talks as if he knows everything about the trouble in Africa.)

shoot one's wad *v. phr., slang, colloquial* **1** To spend all of one's money. *We've shot our wad for the summer and can't buy any new garden furniture.* (We have spent all our money and cannot afford to buy anything new, such as garden furniture.) **2** To say everything that is on one's mind. (Also said as to shoot one's load.) *Joe feels a lot better now that he's shot his wad at the meeting.* (He feels much better now that he said everything that was on his mind.)

shoot out *v.* **1** To fight with guns until one person or side is wounded or killed; settle a fight by shooting.—Used with *it. The cornered bank robbers decided to shoot it out with the police.* (The trapped robbers and the police shot guns at each other.) **2** To go through or past suddenly. *The moment she opened the door, the cat shot out and ran around the house.* (The cat went out of the door quickly and suddenly.) *During the last half-minute of the race, Dick shot out in front of the other runners.* (Dick suddenly passed the other runners.)

shoot straight *or* **shoot square** *v., informal* To act fairly; deal honestly. *You can trust that salesman; he shoots straight with his customers.* (That salesman deals honestly with his customers.) *We get along well because we always shoot square with each other.* (We always act honestly with each other.)—**straight shooter** *or* **square shooter** *n., informal* *Bill is a square-shooter.* (Bill is completely honest.)—**straight-shooting** *adj. The boys all liked the straight-shooting coach.* (The boys liked the coach because he was fair.)

shoot the breeze *or* **bat the breeze** *or* **fan the breeze** *or* **shoot the bull** *v. phr., slang* To talk.—A cliché. *Father shot the breeze with his neighbor while the children were playing.* (They talked to each other while the children were playing.) *Come into the kitchen and we'll bat the breeze over a cup of coffee.* (Come into the kitchen and we'll talk while we drink coffee.) *The women were shooting the breeze about Jim's latest trouble with the police.* (The women were gossiping about Jim's trouble with the police.) *The fishermen were shooting the bull about the school of sailfish they had seen.* (The fishermen were discussing the school of sailfish they had seen.)

shoot the works *v. phr., slang* **1** To spare no expense or effort; get or give everything. —A cliché. *Billy shot the works when he bought his bicycle; he got a bell, a light, a basket, and chrome trimmings on it, too.* (Billy got everything that could go on a bicycle.) *The Greens shot the works on their daughter's wedding reception.* (The Greens spent a lot of money and worked hard to give their daughter an impressive wedding reception.) **2** To go to the limit; take a risk.—A cliché. *The motor of Tom's boat was dangerously hot, but he decided to shoot the works and try to win the race.* (Tom decided to risk burning out his boat's motor in his attempt to win the race.)

shoot up *v.* **1** To grow quickly. *Billy had always been a small boy, but when he was thirteen years old he began to shoot up.* (When he became thirteen years old he began to grow quickly.) **2** To arise suddenly. *As we watched, flames shot up from the roof of the barn.* (Flames arose suddenly from the roof of the barn.) **3** *informal* To shoot or shoot at recklessly; shoot and hurt badly. *The cowboys got drunk and shot up the bar room.* (They fired their guns wildly and damaged the bar room.) *The soldier was shot up very badly.* (He was badly wounded.) **4** To take drugs by injection. *A heroin addict will shoot up as often as he can.* (A heroin addict will inject himself with the drug as often as he can.)

shop See CLOSE UP SHOP, TALK SHOP.

shopping center *n.* A place usually for neighborhood shopping, where there is a group of stores and shops inside of a large parking lot. *There is a bowling alley at the* nearest *shopping center.* (The nearest place where several stores are grouped together with parking space for customers has a place for people to bowl.) *All the stores in our shopping center stay open until nine o'clock on Friday evenings.* (The super markets and other stores are open Friday evenings.)

shore leave *n.* Permission given to a man in the Navy to leave his ship and go where he wants for a certain length of time. *Jim went to visit New York when he was given three days' shore leave.* (He went to visit New York when he was given permission to stay ashore for three days.) *The ship did not dock long enough for the sailors to get shore leave.* (There was not enough time for the sailors to be given time to go ashore.)

shore patrol *n.* The police of a navy. *The sailors who were fighting in town were arrested by the shore patrol.* (They were arrested by naval policemen.) *The shore patrol was ordered to search every sailor who went on board the ship.* (The police of the navy were ordered to search each sailor who went onto the ship.)

shore up *v.* To add support to (something) where weakness is shown; make (something) stronger where support is needed; support. *When the flood waters weakened the bridge, it was shored up with steel beams and sandbags until it could be rebuilt.* (The weakened bridge was made stronger for a while by putting steel beams and sandbags under it.) *The coach sent in a substitute guard to shore up the line when Fitchburg began to break through.* (The coach put a fresh player in the line to try to stop the Fitchburg team from breaking through.)

shorn See GOD TEMPERS THE WIND TO THE SHORN LAMB.

short See CAUGHT SHORT, FALL SHORT, FOR SHORT, IN BRIEF *or* IN SHORT, IN SHORT ORDER, IN SHORT SUPPLY, MAKE SHORT WORK OF, RUN SHORT, SELL SHORT, THE LONG AND THE SHORT.

short and sweet *adj.* Brief and to the point. —A cliché. *Henry's note to his father was short and sweet. He wrote, "Dear Dad, please send me $5. Love, Henry."* (Henry wrote a brief note to his father asking for money.)

short end *n.* The worst or most unpleasant part. *The new boy got the short end of it because all the comfortable beds in the dormitory had been taken before he arrived.* (The new boy got the worst part of it, because the best beds had been taken.) *The girls who served refreshments at the party got the short end of it. When everybody had been served, there was no cake left for them.* (The girls who served refreshments got the worst share of the party because there was no cake left for them.)

short haul *n.* A short distance; a short trip. *The Scoutmaster said that it was just a short* haul *to the lake.* (He said that it was only a short trip to the lake.) *The man from the moving company said they did not make short hauls, so we hired a truck to move our furniture three blocks to our new house.* (The man said that his company did not accept short distance jobs.) Contrast LONG HAUL.

short of [1] *adj. phr.* **1** Less or worse than. *Don't do anything short of your best.* (Do your best, nothing else.) **2** Not having enough. *We did not buy anything because we were short of money.* (We did not buy anything because we did not have enough money.) *The girls were asked to wait on table because the kitchen was short of help.* (The kitchen did not have enough workers.)

short of [2] *adv. phr.* Away from; at a distance from. *The day's drive still left us a hundred miles short of the ocean.* (We drove all day, but we were still a hundred miles from the ocean.) *The golfer's shot fell far short of the hole.* (The ball wasn't close to the hole.)

short-order cook *n.* A person who prepares food that cooks quickly. *Bruce found a summer job as a short-order cook in a drive-in restaurant.* (Bruce found a job as a person who prepares food that cooks quickly.) *The new diner needs another short-order cook.* (The new diner needs another person to prepare quick-cooking food.) Compare SLING HASH.

short shrift *n.* Little or no attention. —Usually used with *get* or *give. In books about jobs, women's work is consistently given short shrift.* (The books say little about jobs usually held by women.)

short-spoken *adj.* Using so few words that you seem impatient or angry; speaking in a short impatient way; saying as little as possible in an unfriendly way. *Jim is always short-spoken when he is tired.* (Jim always speaks impatiently when he is tired.) *We were hoping to borrow Dad's car, but he was so short-spoken when he came home that we were afraid to ask.* (Dad seemed angry when he came home—he would hardly talk.)

shot See BIG CHEESE *or* BIG SHOT, BY A LONG SHOT, CALL ONE'S SHOT, CALL THE SHOTS, FOUL SHOT, LONG SHOT.

shot in the arm *n. phr., informal* Something inspiring or encouraging. —A cliché. *The General's appearance was a shot in the arm for the weary soldiers.* (Seeing the General encouraged the tired soldiers.) *We were ready to quit, but the coach's talk was a shot in the arm.* (We were ready to quit, but the coach's talk inspired us.)

shot in the dark *n. phr.* An attempt without much hope or chance of succeeding; a wild guess. —A cliché. *It was just a shot in the dark, but I got the right answer to the teacher's question.* (I answered correctly with a lucky guess.)

shot through with Full of. *His speech was shot through with praise for the president.* (He praised the president many times in his speech.) *Jane's letter was shot through with hints for a pony.* (Jane's letter was full of hints that she wanted a pony.)

shoulder See CHIP ON ONE'S SHOULDER, COLD SHOULDER, GOOD HEAD ON ONE'S SHOULDERS, HEAD AND SHOULDERS, PUT ONE'S SHOULDER TO THE WHEEL, ON ONE'S SHOULDERS, RUB ELBOWS *or* RUB SHOULDERS, SQUARE ONE'S SHOULDERS, WEIGHT OF THE WORLD ON ONE'S SHOULDERS.

shoulder to shoulder *adv. phr.* **1** One beside the other; together. *The three boys were shoulder to shoulder all during the working hours.* (The three boys were together throughout the time they were working.) Compare SIDE BY SIDE. **2** Each helping the other; in agreement; together.—Often used with *stand. We can win the fight if we all stand shoulder to shoulder.* (We can win if we each help the others work together.) Compare SEE EYE TO EYE.

shoulder to the wheel See PUT ONE'S SHOULDER TO THE WHEEL.

shout down *v.* To object loudly to; defeat by shouting. *Grace suggested that we give our club money to charity, but she was shouted down.* (We objected loudly to Grace's idea, and it was beaten.) *The crowd shouted down the Mayor's suggestions.* (The people yelled loud disagreement to the Mayor's suggestions.)

shout from the housetops *or* **shout from the rooftops** *v. phr., informal* To tell everyone; broadcast, especially one's own personal business. *Mr. Clark was so happy when his son was born that he shouted the news from the housetops.* (Mr. Clark was so happy that he had told everybody that his son had been born.) *When Mary bleached her hair, her neighbors shouted it from the housetops.* (Mary's neighbors told everyone that she had bleached her hair.)

shouting See ALL OVER BUT THE SHOUTING.

shove down one's throat *or* **ram down one's throat** *v. phr., informal* To force you to do or agree to (something not wanted or liked.)—A cliché. *We don't want Mr. Bly to speak at our banquet, but the planning committee shoved him down our throats.* (The committee forced us to accept having Mr. Bly speak even though we did not want him.) *The president was against the idea, but the club members rammed it down his throat.* (The members forced the president to accept the idea to which he was opposed.)

shove off See PUSH OFF.

show See GET THE SHOW ON THE ROAD, GO TO SHOW *or* GO TO PROVE, ROAD SHOW, STEAL THE SHOW, TALENT SHOW, VARIETY SHOW, WHOLE CHEESE *or* WHOLE SHOW.

show a clean pair of heels See TAKE TO ONE'S HEELS.

show off *v.* **1** To put out nicely for people to see; display; exhibit. *The Science Fair gave Julia a chance to show off her shell collection.* (The Fair gave Julia an opportunity to display her shell collection.) *The girls couldn't wait to show off their fine needlework to our visitors.* (The girls were proud of their needlework and were eager to exhibit it to our visitors.) **2** *informal* To try to attract attention; *also,* try to attract attention to. *The children always show off when we have company.* (The children try to get the attention of our company.) *Joe hasn't missed a chance to show off his muscles since that pretty girl moved in next door.* (Joe tries to attract the pretty girl's attention to his muscles.)

show one's colors *v. phr.* **1** To show what you are really like.—A cliché. *We thought Toby was timid, but he showed his colors when he rescued the ponies from the burning barn.* (Toby showed us that he was really brave by rescuing the ponies from the fire.) **2** To make known what you think or plan to do.—A cliché. *Mr. Ryder is afraid that he will lose the election if he shows his colors on civil rights.* (Mr. Ryder is afraid people won't elect him if he tells what he thinks about civil rights.) *We would not help Jim until he showed his colors.* (We would not help Jim until we knew his plans.)

show one's face *v. phr.* To be seen; appear.—A cliché. *Bill is afraid to show his face since Tom threatened to beat him up.* (Bill is afraid to let Tom see him.) *Judy is a wonderful mimic but she is too shy to show her face on stage.* (Judy can act but she is so bashful she won't appear on stage.) *After cheating on the test, Chris was ashamed to show his face.* (After he cheated on the test, Chris was ashamed to be seen.)

show the door *v. phr.* To ask (someone) to go away. *Ruth was upsetting the other children, so I showed her the door.* (Ruth was disturbing the other children, so I asked her to go away.) *Our neighbors invited themselves to the party and stayed until Harry showed them the door.* (The neighbors came to the party without being invited and stayed until Harry asked them to leave.)

show up *v.* **1** To make known the real truth about (someone). *The man said he was a mind reader, but he was shown up as a fake.* (The man claimed to be a mind reader, but the truth that he was a fake was made known.) **2** To come or bring out; become or make easy to see. *The detective put a chemical on the paper, and the fingertips showed up.* (They became easy to see.) *This test shows up your weaknesses in arithmetic.* (This test makes your weaknesses in arithmetic stand out; the test shows plainly what your weaknesses are.) **3** *informal* To come; appear. *We had agreed to meet at the gym, but Larry didn't show up.* (Larry didn't come to the gym to meet me.) *Only five stu-*

dents showed up for the class meeting. (Only five came.) Compare TURN UP 2.

shrift See SHORT SHRIFT.

shrink See HEAD SHRINKER.

shrug off *or* **shrug away** *v.* To act as if you are not interested and do not care about something; not mind; not let yourself be bothered or hurt by. *Adam shrugged off our questions; he would not tell us what had happened.* (Adam acted as if he was not interested and did not care about our questions.) *Muriel shrugged away every attempt to comfort her.* (Muriel seemed indifferent to everyone who tried to comfort her.) *The ballplayer shrugged off the booing of the fans.* (He didn't mind or pretended not to mind.) *Father cut his hand but he tied a cloth around it and shrugged it away.* (He paid no more attention to the cut.)

shut See KEEP ONE'S MOUTH SHUT, PUT UP *or* SHUT UP, CLOSE ONE'S EYES.

shut down See CLOSE DOWN.

shut-eye *n., slang* Sleep. *It's very late. We'd better get some shut-eye.* (It's very late, and we had ought to get some sleep.) *I'm going to get some shut-eye before the game.* (I'm going to sleep for a while before the game.) Compare FORTY WINKS.

shut off *v.* **1** To make (something like water or electricity) stop coming. *Please shut off the hose before the grass gets too wet.* (Please turn off the hose before the grass gets too wet.) Compare TURN OFF 1. **2** To be apart; be separated from; *also* to separate from. *Our camp is so far from the highway we feel shut off from the world when we are there.* (Our camp is so far from the road that we feel apart from the world when we are there.) *The sow is so bad tempered we had to shut it off from its piglets.* (We had to separate the sow from its piglets.)

shut one's eyes See CLOSE ONE'S EYES.

shut out *v.* **1** To prevent from coming in; block. *During World War II Malta managed to shut out most of the Italian and German bombers by throwing up an effective antiaircraft screen.* (Malta managed to prevent most of the Italian and German bombers from coming in.) *The boys were annoyed by Tom's telling club secrets and shut him out of their meeting.* (The boys were cross with Tom and would not let him come to their meeting.) **2** To prevent (an opposing team) from scoring throughout an entire game. *The Dodgers shut out the Reds, 5–0.* (The Dodgers didn't let the Reds score and won the game 5–0.) *Our team hasn't been shut out once this season.* (Our team hasn't failed to score once this season.)

shut the door See CLOSE THE DOOR.

shut up *v.* **1** *informal* To stop talking. *Little Ruthie told Father about his birthday surprise before Mother could make shut her up.* (Before Mother could make Ruthie stop talking, Ruthie had told the secret.)—Often used as a command; usually considered rude. *Shut up and let Joe say something.* (Stop talking and let Joe say what he thinks.) *If you'll shut up for a minute, I'll tell you our plan.* (Stop talking for a minute and I'll tell you our plan.) Syn. BUTTON YOUR LIP, DRY UP 3, KEEP ONE'S MOUTH SHUT. **2** To close the doors and windows of. *We got the house shut up only minutes before the storm hit.* (We got the doors and windows of the house closed just before the storm hit.) **3** To close and lock for a definite period of time. *The Smiths always spend Labor Day shutting up their summer home for the year.* (The Smiths always close and lock their summer home on Labor Day.) *We got to the store only to find that the owner had shut up shop for the weekend.* (When we got to the store we found that the owner had closed and locked it for the weekend.) **4** To confine. *That dog bites. It should be shut up.* (That dog should be confined because it bites.) *John has been shut up with a cold all week.* (John had a cold and had to stay indoors all week.)

shy See ONCE BITTEN, TWICE SHY *at* BURNT CHILD DREADS THE FIRE.

shy away *or* **shy off** *v.* To avoid; seem frightened or nervous. *The boys shied away from our questions.* (The boys avoided answering our questions.) *The horse shied off when Johnny tried to mount it.* (The horse seemed frightened and avoided Johnny's attempt to mount it.)

sick See TAKE ILL *or* TAKE SICK.

sick and tired *adj.* **1** Feeling strong dislike for something repeated or continued too long; exasperated; annoyed. *Jane was sick and tired of always having to wait for Bill, so when he didn't arrive on time she left without him.* (Jane was annoyed at always being kept waiting, so when Bill was late again she left without him.) *John is sick and tired of having his studies interrupted.* (John is angry at being bothered while he is studying.) *I've been studying all day, and I'm sick and tired of it.* (I hate it; I don't want to study any more.) Compare FED UP.

side See CHOOSE UP SIDES, FROM SIDE TO SIDE, GET UP ON THE WRONG SIDE OF THE BED, GRASS IS ALWAYS GREENER ON THE OTHER SIDE OF THE FENCE *or* GRASS IS ALWAYS GREENER ON THE OTHER SIDE OF THE HILL, LAUGH ON THE WRONG SIDE OF ONE'S MOUTH, ON ONE'S BAD SIDE, ON ONE'S GOOD SIDE, ON THE SIDE, SUNNY-SIDE UP, TAKE SIDES, THORN IN THE FLESH *or* THORN IN THE SIDE.

side against *v.* To join or be on the side that is against; disagree with; oppose. *Bill and Joe sided against me in the argument.* (They were on the same side against me.) *We sided against the plan to go by plane.* (We were on the side that didn't want to go by airplane.) Contrast SIDE WITH.

side by side *adv.* **1** One beside the other in a

row. *Alice's dolls were lined up side by side on the window seat.* (Alice's dolls were arranged in a row on the window seat.) *Charles and John are neighbors; they live side by side on Elm Street.* (Charles lives beside John.) Compare SHOULDER TO SHOULDER. **2** Close together. *The two boys played side by side all afternoon.* (They played together all afternoon.)

side of the tracks See THE TRACKS.

side street *n.* A street that runs into and ends at a main street. *The store is on a side street just off Main Street.* (The store is on a smaller street near Main Street.) *The Spellmans bought a house on a side street that runs off Broad Street.* (The Spellmans bought a house on a small street that ends at Broad Street.) Compare BACK STREET, CROSS STREET.

side with *v.* To agree with; help. *Adam always sides with Johnny in an argument.* (Adam always agrees with Johnny in an argument.) *Gerald sided with the plan to move the club.* (Gerald supported the plan to move the club.) Contrast SIDE AGAINST.

sight See AT FIRST GLANCE *or* AT FIRST SIGHT, AT SIGHT *or* ON SIGHT, CATCH SIGHT OF, HEAVE IN SIGHT, LOSE SIGHT OF, ON SIGHT, SET ONE'S SIGHTS.

sight for sore eyes *n. phr., informal* A welcome sight.—A cliché. *After our long, dusty hike, the pond was a sight for sore eyes.* (We were glad to see the pond after our long, dusty hike.) *"Jack! You're a sight for sore eyes!"* (Jack, it's good to see you!)

sight unseen *adv. phr.* Before seeing it; before seeing her, him, or them. *Tom read an ad about a car and sent the money for it sight unseen.* (He paid the money for the car before he ever saw it.)

sign See HIGH SIGN, INDIAN SIGN, ROAD SIGN.

sign in *v.* To write your name on a special list or in a record book to show that you are present. *Every girl must sign in when she comes back to the dormitory.* (Every girl must write her name on a record to show that she has come back to the dormitory.) *Teachers go to the office and sign in each morning before going to their classrooms.* (Teachers write their names on a list to show that they have arrived at school.) Contrast SIGN OUT.

sign off *v.* **1** To end a program on radio or television. *That TV newscaster always signs off by saluting.* (He always salutes at the end of his program.) **2** To stop broadcasting for the day. *That TV station always signs off after the late movie.* (The late movie is its last program of the evening.)

sign one's own death warrant *v. phr.* To cause your own death or the loss of something you want very much.—A cliché. *Mr. Carter had lung trouble, and the doctor told him he would sign his own death warrant if he didn't stop smoking.* (The doctor said Mr.

Carter must stop smoking or he would die.) *when Jim's fiancée saw him on a date with another girl, he signed his own death warrant.* (Jim lost his chance to marry the girl he loved, because she was angry and broke the engagement.)

sign out *v.* To write your name on a special list or in a record book to show that you are leaving a place. *Most of the students sign out on Friday.* (Most of the students write their names on a list to show that they are leaving the school on Friday.) Contrast SIGN IN.

sign over *v.* To give legally by signing your name. *He signed his house over to his wife.* (He gave his wife the house by signing a document prepared by his lawyer.)

sign up *v.* **1** To promise to do something by signing your name; join; sign an agreement. *We will not have the picnic unless more people sign up.* (More people must sign their names on the paper promising to come to the picnic.) *John wants to sign up for the contest.* (John wants to sign his name to promise to be in the contest.) *Miss Carter has signed up to be the chaperone at the dance.* (Miss Carter has promised to be the chaperone at the dance.) **2** To write the name of (a person or thing) to be in an activity; also, to persuade (someone) to do something. *Betty decided to sign up her dog for obedience training.* (Betty decided to put her dog's name on the list for obedience school.) *The superintendent has signed up three new teachers for next year.* (The superintendent has found three new teachers who agree to teach next year.)

silence gives consent If you say nothing or do not say no to something, it means that you agree.—A proverb. *Don't be afraid to say, if you don't like something. Silence gives consent.* (People will think that you like something if you don't say what you do not.)

silent majority *n., informal* The large majority of people who, unlike the militants, do not make their political and social views known by marching and demonstrating and who, presumably, can swing an election one way or the other. *Sidney Miltner is a member of the silent majority.* (He is a person who does not indulge himself in demonstrating and marching.)

silver See BORN WITH A SILVER SPOON IN ONE'S MOUTH, EVERY CLOUD HAS A SILVER LINING, HAND —— TO —— ON A SILVER PLATTER.

simmer down *v., informal* To become less angry or excited; become calmer. *Tom got mad, but soon simmered down.* (He became angry, but soon grew calmer.)

Simon Legree *n., informal* A strict person, especially a boss, who makes others work very hard. *Don't talk on the job; the boss is a real Simon Legree.* (Don't talk while you are working because the boss is a strict man who makes the employees work very hard.) *Everybody avoids the foreman. He acts like a Simon Legree.* (He seems to be a person who forces others to work very hard.)

simple See PURE AND SIMPLE.

sing a different tune *or* **whistle a different tune** *also* **sing a new tune** *v. phr., informal* To talk or act in the opposite way; contradict something said before. *Charles said that all smokers should be expelled from the team, but he sang a different tune after the coach caught him smoking.* (After the coach saw him smoking, Charles said that no players should be expelled from the team for smoking.) Syn. CHANGE ONE'S TUNE, DANCE TO ANOTHER TUNE. Compare LAUGH OUT OF THE OTHER SIDE OF ONE'S MOUTH.

single See EVERY SINGLE.

sink See HEART SINKS.

sinker See HOOK, LINE AND SINKER.

sink in *or* **soak in** *v., informal* To be completely understood; be fully realized or felt. *Everybody laughed at the joke but Joe; it took a moment for it to sink in before he laughed too.* (Joe didn't understand the meaning of the joke at first.) *When Frank heard that war had started, it didn't sink in for a long time until his father was drafted into the army.* (He didn't understand what the war meant until his father went to the army.) Compare BRING HOME.

sink one's teeth into See GET ONE'S TEETH INTO.

sink or swim *v. phr.* To succeed or fail by your own efforts, without help or interference from anyone else; fail if you don't work hard to succeed. *When Joe was fourteen, his parents died, and he was left by himself to sink or swim.* (He had to earn his own living after his parents died.) *Tom's new job was confusing and no one had time to help him learn, so he had to sink or swim.* (Tom had to learn how to do his work without help, or lose his job.)

sit See GO SIT ON A TACK, ON THE FENCE *also* FENCE-SITTING.

sit back *v.* **1** To be built a distance away; stand away (as from a street). *Our house sits back from the road.* (Our house is not on the road.) **2** To relax; rest, often while others are working; take time out. *Sit back for a minute and think about what you have done.* (Relax for a minute and think about what you have done.)

sit by *v.* **1** To stay near; watch and care for. *The nurse was told to sit by the patient until he woke up.* (The nurse was told to stay near the patient until he woke up.) *Mother sat by her sick baby all night.* (Mother watched and cared for her sick baby all through the night.) **2** To sit and watch or wait especially while others work. *Don't just sit idly by while the other children are all busy.* (Don't sit and do nothing.)

sit down *v.* To sit on a seat or resting place. *After gym class Jim was tired and was glad to sit down and rest.* (He gladly sat and rested after so much running and jumping.)

sit in *v.* **1** To be a member; participate. *We're having a conference and we'd like you to sit in.* (We want you to be there and to talk and vote.) *also* **sit in on:** To be a member of; participate in. *We want you to sit in on the meeting.* (They want him to participate in the meeting.) **2** To attend but not participate. Often used with *on. Our teacher was invited to sit in on the conference.* (He could not talk or vote because he was not a member.) Compare LOOK ON.

sit on *v.* **1** To be a member of (a jury, board, commission), etc. *Mr. Brown sat on the jury at the trial.* (He was a member of the jury at the trial.) **2** *informal* To prevent from starting or doing something; squelch. *The teacher sat on Fred before he could get started with the long story.* (Fred was stopped as soon as he began his long story.) *The teacher sat on Joe as soon as he began showing off.* (The teacher made Joe stop.)

sit on a volcano *v., informal* **1** To be in a place where trouble may start or danger may come suddenly.—A cliché. *Bob was in that part of South America before the revolution began. He knew he was sitting on a volcano.* (He was very nervous being in a place where trouble might start at any time.) *The policemen who patrolled the big city slum area that summer were sitting on a volcano.* (They knew that trouble might start at any time.)

sit on one's hands *v. phr., informal* To do nothing; fail or refuse to do anything. *We asked Bill for help with our project, but he sat on his hands.* (He did not help us.)

sit on the fence See ON THE FENCE.

sit out *v.* To not take part in. *The next dance is a polka. Let's sit it out.* (Let's not dance the polka.) *Toby had to sit out the last half of the game because his knee hurt.* (Toby didn't take part in the last half of the game because his knee hurt.)

sit through *v.* To watch or listen until (something) is finished. *The show was so boring that we could hardly sit through the first act.* (The show was so dull that it was hard for us to stay in our seats until the first act was finished.) *Elaine liked the movie so much that she sat through three showings.* (Elaine liked the movie so much that she stayed in her seat and watched until three showings were over.)

sitter See ON THE FENCE *also* FENCE-SITTER.

six See AT SIXES AND SEVENS.

sit tight *v. phr., informal* To make no move or change; stay where you are.—Often used as a command. *Sit tight; I'll be ready to go in a few minutes.* (Wait while I get ready to go.) *The doctor said to sit tight until he ar-*

rived. (The doctor said to do nothing but wait until he arrived.) *The gangsters sat tight in the mountains while the police looked for them.* (The gangsters stayed hidden.) Compare STAND PAT.

sitting on top of the world See ON TOP OF THE WORLD.

sitting pretty *adj., slang* To be in a lucky position. *The new library is sitting pretty because a wealthy woman gave it $10,000 worth of reference books.* (The new library is in a lucky position because it was given books worth $10,000.) *Mr. Jones was sitting pretty until his $25,000-a-year job was dropped by the company.* (Mr. Jones was in a lucky position until his job was dropped by the company.)

sit up *v.* **1** To move into a sitting position. *Joe sat up when he heard the knock on his bedroom door.* (Joe moved into a sitting position when he heard the knock.) **2** To stay awake instead of going to bed. *Mrs. Jones will sit up until both of her daughters get home from the dance.* (Mrs. Jones won't go to bed until her daughters come home.) *We sat up until two A.M. hoping for news from Alaska.* (We kept ourselves awake until two A.M. hoping for news from Alaska.) **3** *informal* To be surprised. *Janice really sat up when I told her the gossip about Tom.* (Janice was surprised by the gossip.)

sit up and take notice *v. phr., informal* To be surprised into noticing something.—A trite phrase. *Grace had never impressed her teachers. Hearing that she had won the essay contest made them sit up and take notice.* (When Grace won the essay contest, her teachers were surprised and impressed.) *George's sudden success made the town sit up and take notice.* (George's sudden success made the town notice and talk about him.)

sit well (with) *v.* Find favor with; please. *The reduced school budget did not sit well with the teachers.* (They did not like it.)

sit with *v., informal* To be accepted by; affect.—Used in interrogative sentences and in negative sentences modified by *well. How did your story sit with your mother?* (How did your mother accept your story?) *Bob's poor sportsmanship doesn't sit well with the coach.* (The coach does not accept or approve of Bob's poor sportsmanship.)

six See DEEP-SIX.

six bits *n., slang* Seventy-five cents. *"Lend me six bits till Friday, Sam," said Jim. "I've spent all my allowance."* (Jim asked Sam to lend him 75¢ until Friday.) Compare TWO BITS.

six of one and half-a-dozen of the other *n. phr.* Two things the same; not a real choice; no difference.—A cliché. *Which coat do you like better, the brown or the blue? It's six of one and half-a-dozen of the other.* (The two coats are the same.) *Johnny says it's six of one and half-a-dozen of the other whether he*

does the job tonight or tomorrow night. (Johnny doesn't care which night he works.)

size See CUT DOWN TO SIZE, PINT-SIZE.

size up *v., informal* To decide what one thinks about (something); to form an opinion about (something). *Give Joe an hour to size up the situation and he'll tell you what to do next.* (Let Joe have an hour to decide what he thinks and then he will tell you what to do.) *Our coach went to New York to size up the team we'll face in our homecoming game.* (Our coach went to New York to watch and form an opinion of the team we will face in our home-coming game.) Compare TAKE STOCK 2.

skate See CHEAP SKATE.

skate on thin ice *v. phr.* To take a chance; risk danger, disapproval or anger. *You'll be skating on thin ice if you ask Dad to increase your allowance again.* (You'll be taking a chance if you ask Dad for more money.) *John knew he was skating on thin ice, but he could not resist teasing his sister about her boy friend.* (John knew he was risking his sister's anger, but he could not resist teasing her.)

skating rink *n., slang, citizen's band radio jargon* Slippery road. *Attention all units— there's a skating rink ahead!* (The road ahead is slippery.)

skeleton in the closet *n. phr.* A shameful secret; someone or something kept hidden, especially by a family.—A cliché. *The skeleton in our family closet was Uncle Willie. No one mentioned him because he drank too much.* (No one in the family talked about Uncle Willie or his drinking.)

skid lid *n., slang* A crash helmet worn by motorcyclists and race drivers. *How much did you pay for that handsome skid lid?* (How much did your crash helmet cost?)

skid row *n.* The poor part of a city where men live who have no jobs and drink too much liquor. *That man was once rich, but he drank and gambled too much, and ended his life living on skid row.* (The man became a heavy drinker, lost everything, and died in the poorest part of the city.) *The Bowery is New York City's skid row.* (Drunks and other men without jobs live in the Bowery.)

skin See BY THE SKIN OF ONE'S TEETH, GET UNDER ONE'S SKIN, JUMP OUT OF ONE'S SKIN, KEEP ONE'S EYES PEELED *or* KEEP ONE'S EYES SKINNED, SAVE ONE'S NECK *or* SAVE ONE'S SKIN, WITH A WHOLE SKIN *or* IN A WHOLE SKIN.

skin alive *v. phr.* **1** *informal* To scold angrily. *Mother will skin you alive when she sees your torn pants.* (Mother will scold you angrily when she sees your torn pants.) **2** *informal* To spank or beat. *Dad was ready to skin us alive when he found we had ruined his saw.* (Dad was ready to spank us when he discovered we had ruined his saw.) **3** *slang* To defeat. *We all did our best, but the* *visiting gymnastic team skinned us alive.* (We all tried to win, but the visiting team defeated us.)

skin and bones *n.* A person or animal that is very thin; someone very skinny.—A cliché. *The puppy is healthy now, but when we found him he was just skin and bones.* (When we found the puppy, he was very thin.) *Have you been dieting? You're nothing but skin and bones!* (Have you been trying to lose weight? You are very skinny!)

skin-deep *adj.* Only on the surface; not having any deep or honest meaning; not really or closely connected with what it seems to belong to. *Mary's friendliness with Joan is only skin-deep.* (Mary pretends to be Joan's friend, but she really is not.) *Ralph crammed for the test and got a good grade, but his knowledge of the lesson is only skin-deep.* (Ralph has only a surface knowledge of the lesson that he will soon forget.) Contrast BRED IN THE BONE.

skin off one's nose *n. phr., slang* Matter of interest, concern, or trouble to you.—A trite expression; normally used in the negative. *Go to Jake's party if you wish. It's no skin off my nose.* (Go to Jake's party if you want to; it doesn't concern me.) *Grace didn't pay any attention to our argument. It wasn't any skin off her nose.* (Grace didn't listen to our argument because it didn't interest her.) *You could at least say hello to our visitor. It's no skin off your nose.* (It wouldn't put you to any trouble to say hello to our visitor.)

skip See HEART SKIP A BEAT.

skip bail See JUMP BAIL.

skip it *v. phr., informal* To forget all about it. *When Jack tried to reward him for returning his lost dog, the man said to skip it.* (The man told Jack to forget all about the reward.) *I asked what the fight was about, but the boys said to skip it.* (I asked what the fight was about, but the boys said to forget all about it.)

skip out *v., informal* To leave in a hurry; especially after cheating or taking money dishonestly; sneak away; leave without permission. *The man skipped out of the hotel without paying his bill.* (The man left the hotel without notice and did not pay his bill.) *"How did you get out of the house after supper, Harry?" "I skipped out!"* (I left without permission.)

sky See OUT OF THE BLUE *or* OUT OF A CLEAR SKY *or* OUT OF A CLEAR BLUE SKY, REACH FOR THE SKY.

slam See GRAND SLAM.

slap down *v., slang* **1** To stop (someone, usually in a lower position or job) from doing or saying something, in a rough way or with a scolding; silence. *When Billy talked back, the teacher slapped him down.* (The teacher stopped Billy from arguing and scolded him.) **2** To put a quick stop to; refuse roughly. *The boss slapped down our idea of taking a nap*

on the job every afternoon. (The boss didn't like our idea at all and quickly refused to do it.)

slap in the face[1] *n.* An insult; a disappointment. *We felt that it was a slap in the face when our gift was returned unopened.* (We felt that it was an insult when our gift was sent back to us unopened.) *Doris thought it was a slap in the face when her boy friend invited another girl to the dance.* (Doris felt insulted and disappointed when her boy friend invited another girl to the dance.) Compare KICK IN THE PANTS.

slap in the face[2] *v. phr.* To insult; embarrass; make feel bad. *John slapped our club in the face by saying that everyone in it was stupid.* (John called everyone in the club stupid.) *I don't want to slap her in the face by not coming to her party.* (I don't want to make her feel bad.)

slap together See THROW TOGETHER 1.

slate See CLEAN SLATE.

slated for *or* **slated to be** Going to be; planned or intended for. *People think the governor is slated to be president.* (People think that the governor is going to be president one day.) *That subject is slated for debate at the next meeting.* (That subject is intended for discussion at the next meeting. We plan to argue about it.)

sledding See HARD SLEDDING *or* ROUGH SLEDDING *or* TOUGH SLEDDING.

sleep See BEAUTY SLEEP, LET SLEEPING DOGS LIE, SLEEP A WINK.

sleep around *v. phr., slang, vulgar, avoidable* To be free with one's sexual favors, to behave promiscuously. *Sue Catwallender is a nice girl but she sleeps around an awful lot with all sorts of guys.* (She is nice but too promiscuous.)

sleep a wink *v. phr.* To get a moment's sleep; enjoy a bit of sleep.—A trite phrase; used in negative and conditional statements and in questions. *I didn't sleep a wink all night.* (I went without sleep the whole night.)

sleep on *v.* To postpone a decision about. *We asked Judy if she would join our club and she answered that she would sleep on it.* (Judy said she would think about joining our club and decide later.) *We will have to sleep on your invitation until we know whether we will be free Monday night.* (We will have to postpone deciding whether we can accept your invitation for Monday night.)

sleep out *v.* **1** To sleep outdoors. *The Scouts plan to sleep out next Saturday.* (The Scouts plan to sleep outdoors next Saturday.) **2** To go home at night instead of sleeping at the place where you work. *Mrs. Jones' maid sleeps in, but her cook sleeps out.* (Mrs. Jones' maid sleeps in Mrs. Jones' house, but the cook goes to her own home at night.)

sleeve See CARD UP ONE'S SLEEVE, LAUGH UP ONE'S SLEEVE *or* LAUGH IN ONE'S SLEEVE,

ROLL UP ONE'S SLEEVES, UP ONE'S SLEEVE *or* IN ONE'S SLEEVE, WEAR ONE'S HEART ON ONE'S SLEEVE *also* PIN ONE'S HEART ON ONE'S SLEEVE.

sling hash *v., slang* To serve food, especially in a cheap, small diner, a drive-in, or short-order restaurant. *Jake got a job slinging hash at the new drive-in restaurant.* (Jake got a job at the new restaurant serving people food.) *Jody earned money for college by slinging hash in a restaurant during the summer.* (Jody earned money for college by waiting on tables in a diner during the summer. Compare SHORT-ORDER COOK.

slip See GIVE THE SLIP, SALES CHECK *or* SALES SLIP.

slip a cog *or* **slip a gear** *v. phr., slang* To make a mistake. *I must have been slipping a cog when I said that I would run for mayor.* (I must have been making a mistake when I said that I would run for mayor.) *Jim hates to sleep outdoors. He's slipping his gears if he's promised to take the boys camping.* (Jim is making a mistake if he's promised to take the boys camping.) Compare SLIP UP.

slip of the lip See SLIP OF THE TONGUE.

slip of the pen *n. phr.* The mistake of writing something different from what you should or what you planned.—A cliché. *That was a slip of the pen. I meant to write September, not November.* (That was a mistake. I meant to write "September" and wrote "November" by mistake.) *I wish you would forget it. That was a slip of the pen.* (I wish you would ignore it. It was a mistake for me to write that.)

slip of the tongue *also* **slip of the lip** *n. phr.* The mistake of saying something you had not wanted or planned to say; an error of speech.—A cliché. *No one would have known our plans if Kay hadn't made a slip of the tongue.* (No one would have known if Kay had not made the mistake of saying something she had not planned to say.) *She didn't mean to tell our secret; it was a slip of the lip.* (She didn't mean to tell our secret; it was an error she made when she was talking.)

slip over See PUT OVER 2.

slip through one's fingers *v. phr.* To escape without someone's knowing how.—A cliché. *Policemen surrounded the building, but the thief managed to slip through their fingers.* (The thief managed to evade the policemen and to escape.) *Mike earns a good wage, but he doesn't save a penny. Money just slips through his fingers.* (Mike earns enough, but he doesn't save anything because he spends his money foolishly.)

slip up *v.* To make a mistake. *Someone at the bank slipped up. There are only 48 pennies in this 50¢ roll of coins.* (Someone at the bank made a mistake and put only 48 pennies in the roll.) *If he hadn't slipped up on the last questions, his score on the test would have been perfect.* (If he hadn't made a mistake on the last question, he would have gotten a perfect score on the test.)

slow burn *n., informal* A slowly increasing feeling of anger. *The boys kept teasing John, and watched him do a slow burn.* (The boys watched John get angrier and angrier from their teasing.) *Barbara's slow burn ended only when Mary explained the misunderstanding.* (Barbara stopped getting angry when she found that the reason she got mad was all a mistake.)

slow down *v.* To go more slowly than usual. *The road was slippery, so Mr. Jones slowed down the car.* (Mr. Jones drove his car more slowly than usual because the road was slippery.) *Pat once could run a mile in five minutes, but now that he's older he's slowing down.* (Pat runs more slowly now than he did when he was younger.) Compare LET UP 2. STEP DOWN. Contrast SPEED UP.

slow time See STANDARD TIME.

slow up *v.* 1 To go more slowly. *The truck slowed up as it approached the toll gate.* (The truck went more slowly as it drew near the toll gate.) *Construction on the road slows up traffic.* (Construction on the road makes traffic go more slowly.) 2 To become less busy. *Business slows up at the stores after Christmas.* (The stores become less busy after Christmas.)

sly See ON THE SLY.

smack-dab *also Southern* **smack-to-dab** *adv., informal* Exactly; squarely. *The ball landed smack-dab at our feet.* (The ball stopped on the ground exactly at our feet.) *The plane landed smack-to-dab in the middle of the hayfield.* (The plane landed exactly in the middle of the hayfield.)

small See BIG FROG IN A SMALL POND.

small frog in a big pond See LITTLE FROG IN A BIG POND.

small fry *n.* 1 Young children. *In the park, a sandbox is provided for the small fry.* (There is a sandbox for the little children.) 2 Something or someone of little importance. *Large dairies ignore the competition from the small fry who make only a few hundred pounds of cheese a year.* (The activities of the small producers are of no concern to the big businesses.)

small-time *adj., informal* Unimportant; minor; with little power or importance. *He has a job as a drummer with a small-time band.* (He has a job as a drummer with an unimportant band.) *It is a small-time business, but it may grow.* (It's not a big and rich business, but it may become important.) Contrast BIG-TIME.

small wonder See NO WONDER.

smash hit *n., informal* A very successful play, movie or opera. *The school play was a smash hit.* (The school play was a great success.)

smell a rat *v. phr., informal* To be suspicious; feel that something is wrong.—A cliché. *Every time Tom visits me, one of my ash trays disappears. I'm beginning to smell a rat.* (I'm starting to suspect that Tom is stealing my ash trays.) *When the policeman saw a light go on in the store at midnight, he smelled a rat.* (When the policeman saw a light go on in the store at midnight, he felt that something was wrong.)

smell out See FERRET OUT.

smell up *v., informal* To make a bad smell. *A skunk smelled up our yard last night.* (A skunk made a bad smell in our yard last night.) *Mr. Brodsky's cigar smelled up the living room.* (Mr. Brodsky's cigar made the living room smell bad.)

smile See CRACK A SMILE.

smoke See CHAIN-SMOKE, GO UP IN FLAMES *or* GO UP IN SMOKE, PUT THAT IN YOUR PIPE AND SMOKE IT, WATCH ONE'S DUST *or* WATCH ONE'S SMOKE.

smoke out *v.* **1** To force out with smoke. *The boys smoked a squirrel out of a hollow tree.* (The boys made a fire and sent smoke into the hollow tree, forcing the squirrel out.) *The farmer tried to smoke some gophers out of their burrows.* (The farmer tried to force the gophers out by sending smoke into their burrows.) **2** *informal* To find out the facts about. *It took the reporter three weeks to smoke out the whole story.* (It took the reporter three weeks to find out the facts of the story.)

Smokey Bear *or* **Smokey-the-Bear** *or* **the Smokies** *n., slang, citizen's band radio jargon* A policeman; a patrol car; frequently abbreviated as *Smokey. Slow down, Smokey's ahead*! (Observe the speed limit as there are police ahead.) *A Smokey is on the move, heading east.* There is a police car heading east.)

smooth away *v.* To remove; (unpleasant feelings) take away. *Mr. Jones' new job smoothed away his worry about money.* (He didn't have to worry about money any more.)

smooth down *v.* To make calm; calm down. *Mrs. Smith's feelings were hurt and we couldn't smooth her down.* (We couldn't make her calm.)

smooth over *v.* To make something seem better or more pleasant; try to excuse. *Bill tried to smooth over his argument with Mary by making her laugh.* (He tried to make her forget the argument.) Syn. GLOSS OVER. Compare PATCH UP.

snail's pace *n.* A very slow movement forward. *Time moved at a snail's pace before the holidays.* (Time passed very slowly just before the holidays.) *The donkey on which he was riding moved at a snail's pace.* (The donkey walked very slowly.)

snake in the grass *n. phr., informal* A person who cannot be trusted; an unfaithful traitor; rascal.—A cliché. *Did Harry tell you*

that? He's .a snake in the grass! (If Harry told you that, he is a bad person who tells his friends' secrets.) *Some snake in the grass told the teacher our plans.* (Someone we trusted told our secret plans to the teacher. Someone betrayed us.)

snap See COLD SNAP.

snap it off See MAKE IT SNAPPY.

snap one's fingers at *v. phr.* To show contempt for; show no respect for; pay no attention to; scorn; disregard.—A cliché. *John snapped his fingers at the sign that said "Do not enter," and he went in the door.* (John read the sign but he paid no attention to it.) *The highway sign said "Speed limit, 35 miles per hour," but when a driver snapped his fingers at it by going 55 miles an hour, a motorcycle policeman arrested him.* (When the driver showed no respect for the speed law, he was arrested.)

snap out of *v., informal* To change quickly from a bad habit, mood, or feeling to a better one.—Often used with *it. Mary was unhappy when her doll was broken, but she snapped out of it when she got a new one.* (Mary's unhappiness quickly changed to joy when she got a new doll.) *The coach told the lazy player to snap out of it.* (The coach told the lazy player to do better and work harder.)

snappy See MAKE IT SNAPPY.

snap up *v., informal* To take or accept eagerly. *Eggs were on sale cheap, and the shoppers snapped up the bargain.* (The shoppers quickly bought all of the cheap eggs.) *Mr. Hayes told Bob that he would take him skiing, and Bob snapped up the offer.* (Bob quickly said he would go.)

sneak See QUARTERBACK SNEAK.

sneak up on See CREEP UP ON.

sneeze at *v., informal* To think of as not important; not take seriously.—Used with negative or limiting words and in questions. —A cliché. *Mr. Jones was chosen by his party to run for President. He was not elected, but to be chosen to run is not to be sneezed at.* (Being a candidate is not to be thought a small thing. It is an honor to be thought worthy of being President.) *If you think Mrs. Green's tests are things to be sneezed at, you have a surprise coming.* (If you do not take Mrs. Green's tests seriously you will be surprised when you have one.) *Is a thousand dollars anything to sneeze at?* (Is a thousand dollars something to take lightly?) *John finished third in a race with twenty other runners. That is nothing to sneeze at.* (John did not win the race, but he ran faster than most of the runners. That is no a small thing. He deserves praise for that.)

sniff out See FERRET OUT.

snow in *v.* To block up or trap by much snow; keep inside. *After the storm the farmer and his family were snowed in for three days.* (They had to stay in the house for three days.) *The train went off the track and the* *passengers were snowed in for several days.* (They could not leave the train because the snow was so heavy.)

snow job *n., slang, informal* **1** Insincere or exaggerated talk designed to gain the favors of someone. *Joe gave Sue a snow job and she believed every word of it.* (He flattered her in exaggerated terms, but she believed it.) **2** The skillful display of technical vocabulary and prestige terminology in order to pass oneself off as an expert in a specialized field without really being a knowledgeable worker in that area. *That talk by Nielsen on pharmaceuticals sounded very impressive, but I will not hire him because it was essentially a snow job.* (It was essentially an artificial display of prestige terminology covering up a gap in actual knowledge.)

snow under *v.* **1** To cover over with snow. *The doghouse was snowed under during the blizzard.* (Enough snow fell during the storm to cover the top of the doghouse.) **2** *informal* To give so much of something that it cannot be taken care of; to weigh down by so much of something that you cannot do anything about it.—Usually used in the passive. *The factory received so many orders that it was snowed under with work.* (The factory got so many orders that they could not fill all of them quickly.) *The crippled girl was snowed under with Christmas letters.* (She received so many letters that she could not read all of them the day they came.)

snuff See UP TO PAR *or* UP TO SNUFF.

so See AND SO FORTH *or* AND SO ON, EVEN SO, EVERY NOW AND THEN *or* EVERY SO OFTEN, HOW SO, IN SO MANY WORDS, IS THAT SO, OR SO, THUS AND SO.

soak in See SINK IN.

soak up *v.* **1** To take up water or other liquid as a sponge does. *The rag soaked up the water that I spilled.* (The rag took the water up into itself.) **2** To use a sponge or something like a sponge to take up liquid. *John soaked up the water with the rag.* (John put the rag in the water, and the rag took up the water into itself.) **3** *informal* To take up into yourself in the way a sponge takes up water. *Mary was lying on the beach soaking up the sun.* (Mary was taking the hot rays of the sun into her skin in the form of a tan.) *Charles soaks up facts as fast as the teacher gives them.* (Charles understands and remembers facts quickly.)

so-and-so[1] *pronoun, informal* Someone whose name is not given. *Don't tell me what so-and-so thinks. Tell me what you think.* (Don't tell me what this person or that person thinks. I don't care about what anybody else thinks. I want to know what you think.)

so-and-so[2] *n., informal* A person of a special kind and usually of a very bad kind.—This word is used in place of a more unac-

ceptable word or swear word. *I wish that old so-and-so who thinks digging is easy work was right here digging now.* (I wish that annoying person who thinks digging is easy work was right here with me now, helping.) *He called me a dirty so-and-so and I hit him in the mouth.* (He called me a dirty name and I hit him in the mouth.)—Sometimes used in a joking way. *Peter met his friend John and said, "Hello there, you old so-and-so."* (Peter met John and called him a bad name as a friendly joke.)

so ———— as to—Used with an adjective or adverb before an infinitive to show a result. *Who could be so mean as to do a thing like that?* (Who would do something that mean?) *Ruth wouldn't be so careless as to forget her pen.* (Ruth is not a careless girl, she probably would not forget her pen.) Compare SO ———— THAT.

so as to See IN ORDER TO.

so bad See NOT BAD.

so be it *also* **be it so** *adv. phr., formal* **1** Let it be that way; may it be so. *So be it. We shall smoke the pipe of peace.* (It will be done, then. We shall smoke the pipe of peace.) **2** Very well; all right. *Will the company lose money by doing this? So be it, then.* (Even if the company loses money by this action, we shall do it anyway.)

sob story *n.* A story that makes you feel pity or sorrow; a tale that makes you tearful.—A trite phrase. *The beggar told us a long sob story before he asked for money.* (The beggar told us a long story that made us feel sorry for him before he asked for money.) *The movie is based on a sob story, but people love it.* (The movie is about a sad story that makes you feel tearful, but people love it.)

social climber *n.* A person who tries to mix with rich or well-known people and be accepted by them as friends and equals. *People do not like Mrs. Brown very well; she is known as a social climber.* (She prefers rich or well-known people and is not sincere.) *Social climbers are usually soon known and they are not accepted by those they run after.* (Persons who run after well-known people are usually not accepted.)

sock See TAKE A PUNCH AT *or* TAKE A SOCK AT.

sock it *v. phr., also interj., slang, informal* To give one's utmost; everything one is capable of; to give all one is capable of. *Right on, Joe, sock it to 'em!* (We agree with you, Joe, you are correct, let them have it; do your best in convincing them.) *I was watching the debate on television and more than once Bill Buckley really socked it to them.* (He, more than once, really let them have it, as a clever debater.)

soda jerk *or* **soda jerker** *n., informal* A person who serves soda and ice cream to customers, usually in a drug store or ice cream parlor.

Bob worked as a soda jerk at the drug store all summer. (Bob worked as a person who serves soda and ice cream at the drug store.) *He is just a soda jerker with no future.* (He is just a person who serves soft drinks and ice cream, and he has no career ahead of him.)

so far *also* **thus far** *adv.* Until this time or to this place. *The weather has been hot so far this summer.* (The weather has been hot until now.) *This is a lonely road. We have not met another car so far.* (We have not seen another car up to this place.)

so far as See AS FAR AS.

so far, so good *informal* Until now things have gone well. *So far, so good; I hope we keep on with such good luck.* (Up until now, we have done well. I hope we keep on doing well.)

so help me *interj., informal* I promise; I swear; may I be punished if I lie. *I've told you the truth, so help me.* (I swear that I have told you the truth.) *So help me, there was nothing else I could do.* (I swear that there was nothing else I could do.)

soil one's hands See DIRTY ONE'S HANDS.

so long *interj., informal* Good-bye.—Used when you are leaving someone or he is leaving you. *So long, I will be back tomorrow.* (Good-bye. I am leaving now, but I will be back tomorrow.)

so long as See AS LONG AS.

so many[1] *adj.* **1** A limited number of; some. *Our school auditorium will hold only so many people.* (Our school auditorium will hold only a limited number of people; it cannot hold everyone in town.) **2** A group of.—Often used for emphasis. *The children were all sitting very quietly in their chairs, like so many dolls.* (The children sat so still, they looked like dolls.) Compare so MUCH. (*adj.*) *Bob is always bragging; his stories are just so many lies.* (Bob's stories are a bunch of lies.)

so many[2] *pron.* A limited number; some. *Many people want to come to the prom; but the gymnasium will hold only so many.* (The gymnasium will not hold all of the people who want to come to the dance.) *Don't give the boys all the cookies they want; give so many to Tom, so many to Dick, and so many to Bob.* (Give a few to one boy, a few to another, and so on.) Compare SO MUCH.

some See AND THEN SOME.

somebody up there loves/hates me *slang* An expression intimating that an unseen power in heaven, such as God, has been favorable or unfavorable to the one making the exclamation. *Look at all the money I won! I say somebody up there sure loves me!* (I am so fortunate that it must be because of divine help.) *Look at all the money I've lost! I say somebody up there sure hates me!* (I am so unfortunate that it must be that I am under divine punishment.)

some of these days See ONE OF THESE DAYS.

something See HAVE SOMETHING GOING FOR ONE, HAVE SOMETHING ON, MAKE SOMETHING OF, START SOMETHING

something else *adj., slang, informal* So good as to be beyond description; the ultimate; stupendous. *Janet Hopper is really something else.* (She is indescribably beautiful and striking.)

something else again *n. phr.* A different kind of thing; something different. *I don't care if you borrow my dictionary sometimes, but taking it without asking and keeping it is something else again.* (Taking and keeping my dictionary is different from borrowing and returning it; I don't like that.) *"But I don't want a new car," Charles said to the car dealer. "I want a used car." "Oh," said the car dealer, "that's something else again."* (The car dealer realized that Charles was looking for something different from what he first thought.)

so much[1] *adj.* **1** A limited amount of; some. *Sometimes students wonder if the teacher knows they have only so much time to do their lessons.* (Students have only a limited time to study; they do not have an endless amount.) *If you can't give everyone a full glass of milk, just put so much milk in each glass.* (Put enough milk in each glass so that everyone gets some.) **2** Equally or amounting to; only amounting to.—Often used for emphasis. *Charley spends money as if it were so much paper.* (Charley spends money as if it is paper.) *What Mary said was so much nonsense; there wasn't a word of truth in it.* (What Mary said was only foolish talk and bragging. Don't believe any of it.) Compare SO MANY.[1]

so much[2] *pron.* A limited amount; some; a price or amount that is agreed or will be agreed on. *You can do only so much in a day.* (There is a limit to how much you can do in one day.) *Milk costs so much a quart but cream costs so much a pint.* (Milk costs a certain price for a quart and cream costs a certain price for a pint.) Compare SO MANY.[2]

so much[3] *adv.* By that much; by the amount shown; even.—Used with the comparative and usually followed by *the*. *I can't go tomorrow. So much the better; we'll go today.* (It's even better than going tomorrow because we'll go sooner.) *John isn't coming to the picnic. So much the more for us to eat!* (If John doesn't come, we can eat his share too!) *So much the worse for you if you break the rules.* (It will be even worse for you if you break rules than it is now.) Syn. ALL THE.[2]

so much as *adv. phr.* **1** Even.—Usually used in negative sentences and questions. *He didn't so much as thank me for returning his money that I found.* (He didn't even thank me for giving his money back.) *Would you so much as get me a glass of water? No, you* *wouldn't.* (You wouldn't even help me that much.) **2** See AS MUCH AS 2.

so much for Enough has been said or done about.—Used to point out that you have finished with one thing or are going to take up something else. *So much for the geography of Ireland. We will now talk about the people who live there.* (That is all we will say about the geography of Ireland.) *"I have nothing more to say to you, Tommy, and so much for that," Mary said angrily.* (Mary said that she would say no more.)

son See FAVORITE SON, LIKE FATHER, LIKE SON.

song See FOR A SONG.

song and dance *n., informal* **1** Foolish or uninteresting talk; dull nonsense.—A cliché. Usually used with *give. I met Nancy today and she gave me a long song and dance about her family.* (She talked for a long time foolishly about her family and it was very uninteresting.) **2** A long lie or excuse, often meant to get pity.—A cliché. Usually used with *give. Billy gave the teacher a song and dance about his mother being sick as an excuse for being late.* (He told the teacher a long lie.) *The tramp asked us for money and tried to give us a big song and dance about having to buy a bus ticket to Chicago.* (The tramp gave a long excuse for trying to borrow money and get pity.)

sonic boom *n.* A loud noise and vibration in the air, made when a jet plane passes the speed of sound (1087 feet per second). *Fast jet planes sometimes cause a sonic boom, which can break windows and crack the plaster in houses below them.* (Fast jet planes can cause a noise and vibration in the air which can break windows and plaster below.) *We thought there was an explosion or earthquake, but it was only a sonic boom that shook the house.* (It was only the noise and vibration from a jet plane above us, passing the speed of sound.)

son of a bitch *or* **sunuvabitch** *also* **S.O.B.** *n. phr., vulgar, avoidable (but becoming more and more acceptable, especially if said with a positive or loving intonation)* Fellow, character, guy, individual. Negatively: *Get out of here you filthy, miserable sunuvabitch!* (You're most unpleasant; remove yourself!) Positively: *So you won ten million dollars at the lottery, you lucky son of a bitch (or sunuvabitch)!* (I admire and envy you for having won the lottery.) Compare SON OF A GUN.

son of a gun *n. phr., slang* **1** A bad person; a person not liked. *I don't like Charley; keep that son of a gun out of here.* (Keep that fellow Charley away from me.) Syn. BAD ACTOR. **2** A mischievous rascal; a lively guy. —Often used in a joking way. *The farmer said he would catch the son of a gun who let the cows out of the barn.* (The farmer said he would catch the mischief maker.)

Hello Bill, you old son of a gun! (Hello, you old rascal!) Compare SO AND SO. **3** Something troublesome; a hard job. *The test today was a son of a gun.* (It was very hard.) **4**— Used as an exclamation, usually to show surprise or disappointment. *Son of a gun! I lost my car keys.* (I'm surprised to have lost my keys.) Compare SON OF A BITCH.

soon See AS SOON, FOOL AND HIS MONEY ARE SOON PARTED.

sooner See HAD RATHER *or* HAD SOONER, NO SOONER —— THAN.

sooner or later *adv. phr.* At some unknown time in the future; sometime. *John will come back sooner or later.* (John will come home sometime, but we don't know when.) *Father is very slow about fixing things around the house, but he always does it sooner or later.* (Father always fixes the broken thing sometime.) Compare OR OTHER.

sore See SIGHT FOR SORE EYES.

sore spot *or* **sore point** *n.* A weak or sensitive part; a subject or thing about which someone becomes angry or upset easily. *Don't ask Uncle John why his business failed; it's a sore spot with him.* (Uncle John gets upset and doesn't like to talk about his business failure.) Compare WHERE THE SHOE PINCHES.

sorrow See DROWN ONE'S SORROWS.

sort See OF SORTS, IN A WAY *also* IN A SORT OF WAY.

sort of See KIND OF.

so-so *adj.* Fair; neither good nor bad. *The children's grades were just so-so on the test.* (The children got fair marks on the test.) *How is the fishing today? So-so.* (The fishing is neither good nor bad.)

so that *conj.* **1** *or* in order that; for the purpose that; so.—"So that" is usually followed by *can* or *could;* "in order that" is usually followed by *may* or *might. Let's get ready now so that we can leave when Father comes.* (Let us get ready so that we can leave without delay.) *Betty saved her money in order that she might buy a doll.* (Betty saved her money for the purpose of buying the doll.) Compare IN ORDER TO. **2** With the result that; so. *My pencil fell under my desk, so that I couldn't see it.* (Because my pencil had fallen under my desk, I couldn't see it.) *George often told stories that weren't true, so that no one believed him when he told about a deer in the school yard.* (No one believed George because he often told stories that were not true.)

so —— **that**—Used with an adjective or adverb before a clause of result. *The bus was so full that I could hardly turn around.* (Because the bus was so crowded, I could hardly turn or move.) *Billy pitched so well that everyone cheered him at the end of the game.* (Everyone cheered Billy because of his good pitching.)

so to speak *adv. phr.* To say it in this way. *John was, so to speak, the leader of the club,* *but he was officially only the club's secretary.* (John was the real leader of the club, but he was not its elected leader.) *The horse, so to speak, danced on his hind legs.* (The horse did not really dance but seemed to do so.) Compare AS IT WERE.

sought after *adj.* Wanted by many buyers; searched for. *Antiques are much sought after nowadays.* (People look everywhere for very old things nowadays.) Syn. IN DEMAND.

soul See HEART AND SOUL, KEEP BODY AND SOUL TOGETHER.

soul-searching See SEARCH ONE'S HEART *or* SEARCH ONE'S SOUL.

sound See HIGH-SOUNDING, SAFE AND SOUND.

sound effects *n.* The noises made to imitate real sounds in a play, movie, or program. *Greg agreed to plan the sound effects for the class play.* (Greg promised to plan the noises that would make the class play sound more real.) *The movie was good but the sound effects were not very true to life.* (The movie was good, but the noises in it did not sound natural.)

sound off *v.* **1** To say your name or count "One! Two! Three! Four!" as you march.— Used as orders in U.S. military service. *"Sound off!" said the sergeant, and the soldiers shouted, "One! Two! Three! Four!" with each step as they marched.* (They said a number with each step they took until the sergeant said to stop.) **2** *informal* To tell what you know or think in a loud clear voice, especially to brag or complain. *If you don't like the way we're doing the job, sound off!* (Say what you think!) *George sounded off about how the game should have been played.* (George talked about how the game should have been played, as if he knew everything about it.) *The teacher is always sounding off about the students not doing their homework.* (The teacher is always talking about the students not doing their homework.) Compare SPEAK ONE'S PIECE, SPEAK OUT.

sound out *v.* To try to find out how a person feels about something usually by careful questions. *Alfred sounded out his boss about a day off from his job.* (Alfred tried to find out how his boss felt about giving him a day off from work.) *When you see the coach, sound him out about my chances of getting on the basketball team.* (Try to find out what the coach thinks of my chances for getting on the basketball team.) Syn. FEEL OUT.

sound sheet *n., slang, informal* A thin, low-quality phonograph recording frequently bound into books and magazines for use as promotional or advertising material; it may have either a spoken or a musical message. *Don't throw that away; Sue is collecting sound sheets for her market research course.* (Sue collects sound [verbal or musical] advertisements for her course in marketing.)

soup See IN THE SOUP.

souped-up *adj., informal* More powerful or faster because of changes and additions. *Many teen-aged boys like to drive souped-up cars.* (Many teen-aged boys like to drive cars that have been made more powerful by adding or making changes to the motor.) *The basketball team won the last five games with souped-up plays.* (The basketball team won the last five games with plays that were changed to make them more powerful.)

so what *informal* Used as an impolite reply showing that you don't care about what another has said. *Roy boasted that he was in the sixth grade, but Ted said, "So what? I am in Junior High."* (Ted didn't care about Roy's being in the sixth grade because Ted himself was in a higher grade.) Syn. WHAT OF IT.

sow one's wild oats *v. phr.* To do bad or foolish things, especially while you are young. —A cliché. *Mr. Jones sowed his wild oats while he was in college, but now he is a wiser and better man.* (Mr. Jones acted unwisely when he was a young man, but now he is older and has stopped living foolishly.)

space See OUTER SPACE.

spaced out *adj., slang, informal* Having gaps in one's train of thought, confused, incoherent; resembling the behavior of someone who is under the influence of drugs. *Joe's been acting funny lately—spaced out, you might say.* (He has been incoherent and his thoughts and sentences were gappy as if under the influence of drugs.)

space probe *n., Space English* An unmanned spacecraft other than an Earth satellite fitted with instruments which gather and transmit information about other planets in the solar system (e.g., Venus, Mars, and Jupiter) on what are called fly-by missions, i.e., without the craft landing on any of these bodies. *Both the U.S.A. and the U.S.S.R. have sent up many a space probe in the past decade.* (Both countries have sent up many unmanned spacecraft which gather and transmit planetary information without landing.)

spade See CALL A SPADE A SPADE.

Spain See BUILD CASTLES IN THE AIR *or* BUILD CASTLES IN SPAIN.

spar with See FENCE WITH.

speak See ACTIONS SPEAK LOUDER THAN WORDS, CHILDREN AND FOOLS SPEAK THE TRUTH, NOT TO MENTION *or* NOT TO SPEAK OF, SHORT-SPOKEN, SO TO SPEAK, TO SPEAK OF.

speaker See PUBLIC SPEAKER.

speak for *v.* **1** To speak in favor of or in support of. *At the meeting John spoke for the change in the rules.* (John told the meeting why he thought the rules should be changed.) *The other girls made jokes about Jane, but Mary spoke for her.* (When the other girls made jokes, Mary defended Jane.) **2** To make a request for; to ask for. *The teacher was giving away some books. Fred and Charlie spoke for the same one.* (Fred and Charlie asked for the same book.) **3** To give an impression of; be evidence that (something) is or will be said.—Used with the words *well* or *ill*. *It seems that it will rain today. That speaks ill for the picnic this afternoon.* (It may rain. If it rains we cannot have the picnic.) *Who robbed the cookie jar? The crumbs on your shirt speak ill for you, Billy.* (The crumbs on Billy's shirt make us think he robbed the cookie jar.) *John wore a clean shirt and a tie when he went to ask for a job, and that spoke well for him.* (He dressed neatly, and that made a good impression.) *It speaks well for Mary that she always does her homework.* (It is proof of Mary's good study habits that she always does her homework.)

speak of the devil and he appears A person comes just when you are talking about him.—A proverb. *We were just talking about Bill when he came in the door. Speak of the devil and he appears.* (Bill came when we were talking about him and did not expect him.)

speak one's mind *v. phr.* To say openly what you think; give advice that may not be liked.—A cliché. *John thought it was wrong to keep George out of the club and he spoke his mind about it.* (John told the other boys they were wrong.) Compare SOUND OFF.

speak one's piece See SAY ONE'S PIECE.

speak out *or* **speak up** *v.* **1** To speak in a loud or clear voice. *The trucker told the shy boy to speak up.* (The trucker told him to speak loudly and clearly. He was afraid to speak.) **2** To speak in support of or against someone or something. *Willie spoke up for Dan as club president.* (Willie said Dan would make a good president for the club.) *Ed spoke up against letting girls join the club.* (Ed said he didn't want girls in the club.)

speak volumes *v. phr.* To tell or show much in a way other than speaking; be full of meaning. *The nice present she gave you spoke volumes for what she thinks of you.* (The present shows she likes you.) *A child's choice of hobbies speaks volumes.* (A child's choice of hobbies is full of meaning. His interests tell much about him.) Compare READ BETWEEN THE LINES.

speed trap *n.* A place where police hide and wait to catch drivers who are going even a little faster than the speed limit. *Mr. Jones was caught in a speed trap.* (Mr. Jones was driving at a speed of only 30 miles per hour, but he was arrested by a traffic policeman waiting beside the road. The policeman showed him a small sign that said "Speed Limit: 25 M.P.H.")

speed up *v.* To go faster than before; *also,* to make go faster. *The car speeded up when it reached the country.* (The car went faster when it reached the country.) *Push in the throttle to speed up the engine.* (Push in the throttle to make the engine go faster.) Compare PICK UP 12. Contrast SLOW DOWN.

spell out *v.* **1** To say or read aloud the letters of a word, one by one; spell. *John could not understand the word the teacher was saying, so she spelled it out on the blackboard.* (John did not understand the word she said, so she wrote it on the blackboard and said the letters one by one.) **2** To read slowly, have trouble in understanding. *The little boy spelled out the printed words.* (He read slowly, "t-h-e b-o-y.") **3** *informal* To explain something in very simple words; explain very clearly. *The class could not understand the problem, so the teacher spelled it out for them.* (The teacher explained the problem again slowly and in simple words.) *Before the game the coach spelled out to the players what he wanted them to do.* (The coach explained exactly how he wanted them to play.) Compare WORDS OF ONE SYLLABLE.

spending money *or* **pocket money** *n.* Money that is given to a person to spend. *When the seniors went to New York City on a trip, each was given $10 in spending money.* (Each of the seniors was given ten dollars to spend for anything he wished.) *Father gave John a nickel in pocket money when he went to the store with Mother.* (Father gave John 5¢ to spend as he chose when he went to the store with Mother.)

spill See CRY OVER SPILLED MILK.

spill the beans *v. phr., informal* To tell a secret to someone who is not supposed to know about it. *John's friends were going to have a surprise party for him, but Tom spilled the beans.* (Tom told John about the party, so he was not surprised.) Compare GIVE AWAY 3, LET THE CAT OUT OF THE BAG, TELL TALES OUT OF SCHOOL.

spine-chilling *adj.* Terrifying; causing great fear. *Many children find the movie, "Frankenstein," spine-chilling.* (Many children are terrified by the movie.) *It was spine-chilling to learn that a murderer was in our neighborhood.* (It frightened us to learn that a murderer was in our neighborhood.) Compare HAIR STAND ON END.

spine-tingling *adj.* Very exciting; thrilling. *Our ride up the mountain in a chair lift was spine-tingling.* (Our ride up the mountain in a chair lift was exciting.) *The children's plane ride was a spine-tingling adventure to them.* (The children's plane ride was a thrilling adventure to them.)

spite See CUT OFF ONE'S NOSE TO SPITE ONE'S FACE.

spitting image *n.* **spit and image** *informal* An exact likeness; a duplicate. *John is the spitting image of his grandfather.* (John is an exact likeness of his grandfather. He looks exactly like his grandfather.) *That vase is the spitting image of one I wanted to buy in Boston.* (That vase looks exactly like one I wanted to buy.) Compare LIKE FATHER, LIKE SON.

spit up *v.* To vomit a little. *The baby always spits up when he is burped.* (The baby always vomits a little when his back is patted to make him burp.) *Put a bib on the baby. I don't want him to spit up on his clean clothes.* (I don't want him to vomit on his clean clothes.)

split end *n.* An end in football who plays five to ten yards out from the tackle in the line. *The split end is one of the quarterback's most important targets for passes.* (The quarterback throws many passes to the end who plays a wide position.) Contrast TIGHT END.

split hairs *v. phr.* To find and argue about small and unimportant differences as if the differences are important. *John is always splitting hairs; he often starts an argument about something small and unimportant.* (John is always arguing about differences that do not really matter.) *Don't split hairs about whose turn it is to wash the dishes and make the beds; let's work together and finish sooner.* (Don't waste time arguing about something unimportant, like whose turn it is; let's work together and finish sooner.)

split second *n.* A very short time; less than a second. *The lightning flash lasted a split second, and then disappeared.* (The flash lasted only a moment, and then it was gone.)

split the difference *v. phr., informal* To settle a money disagreement by dividing the difference, each person giving up half. *Bob offered $25 for Bill's bicycle and Bill wanted $35; they split the difference.* (They agreed on $30, which is half-way between $25 and $35.)

split ticket *n.* A vote for candidates from more than one party. *Mr. Jones voted a split ticket.* (He voted for candidates from more than one party.) *An independent voter likes a split ticket.* (He likes voting for some candidates from one party and some from another party.) Contrast STRAIGHT TICKET.

sponge See THROW IN THE SPONGE.

sponge bath *n.* A bath with a cloth or sponge and a little water. *During the drouth the family had only sponge baths.* (During the drouth they had only baths with a rag and a little water.) *The family took sponge baths because they had no bathtub.* (They took baths with a rag and a little water because they had no bathtub.)

spoon See BORN WITH A SILVER SPOON IN ONE'S MOUTH.

spoon-feed *v.* **1** To feed with a spoon. *Mothers spoon-feed their babies.* (They feed them with a spoon.) **2a** To make something too easy for (a person). *Bill's mother spoonfed him and never let him think for himself.* (She treated him like a baby.) *Alice depended on her mother for all decisions because she had been spoon-fed.* (Alice's mother always told her what to say and think.) **2b** To make (something) too easy for someone. *Some students want the teacher to spoon-feed the lessons.* (Some students want the teacher to make the lesson very easy and do all their thinking for them.)

sporting blood *n.* Willingness to take risks; spirit of adventure. *The cowboy's sporting blood tempted him to try to ride the wild horse.* (His willingness to take risks made him try to ride it.) *The boy's sporting blood caused him to run away with a circus.* (His spirit of adventure caused him to run away with a circus.)

spot See HIT THE HIGH SPOTS, HIT THE SPOT, JOHNNY-ON-THE-SPOT, ON THE SPOT *or* UPON THE SPOT *also* IN A SPOT, SORE SPOT.

spotlight See STEAL THE SPOTLIGHT.

spread it on thick See LAY IT ON *or* LAY IT ON THICK.

spread oneself too thin *v. phr.* To try to do too many things at one time. *As the owner, chef, waiter, and dishwasher of his restaurant, Pierre was spreading himself too thin.* (He could not manage so many jobs.)

spring chicken *n., slang* A young person. —Usually used with *no. Mr. Brown is no spring chicken, but he can still play tennis well.* (He is not a young person, but he can still play tennis well.) *The coach is no spring chicken, but he can show the players what to do.* (He is no young person, but he can show the players what to do.)

spruce up *v., informal* To make clean or neat. *Mary spruced up the house before her company came.* (Mary cleaned the house and set things in order before her company came.) *John spruced himself up before he went out on his date.* (John washed, combed his hair, and put on his best clothes before he went out on his date.)

spur See ON THE SPUR OF THE MOMENT, WIN ONE'S SPURS.

squad See FIRING SQUAD.

square See FAIR AND SQUARE, SHOOT STRAIGHT *or* SHOOT SQUARE.

square away *v. phr.* **1** To arrange the sails of a ship so that the wind blows from behind. *The captain ordered the crew to square away and sail before the wind.* (The captain ordered the crew to set the sails to have the wind push the ship from directly behind.) **2** *informal* To put right for use or action.— Often used in the passive or participle. *The living room was squared away for the guests.* (The living room was arranged for the comfort of the visitors.) *Harry got into trouble, but his scoutmaster talked with him and got him squared away.* (His scoutmaster helped him to do better.) Syn. STRAIGHTEN OUT. **3** *informal* To stand ready to fight; put up your fists. *Jack and Lee squared away.* (They got ready to fight with each other.) Syn. SQUARE OFF.

square off *v. phr., informal* To stand ready for fighting with the fists. *The two boxers squared off when the bell rang.* (The boxers put their fists up and stood ready to fight or defend themselves.)

square one's shoulders *v. phr.* To stand strong and ready to give battle; be brave.—A hackneyed phrase. *Jack squared his shoulders and entered the game.* (He stood strong and ready to give battle and entered the game.) *Graduates must square their shoulders and face the world.* (They must be brave and face the world.)

square peg in a round hole *n., informal* A person who does not fit into a job or position; someone who does not belong where he is.—A cliché. *Arthur is a square peg in a round hole when he is playing ball.* (Arthur isn't good at playing ball.) *George likes to work with his hands. When it comes to books, he's a square peg in a round hole.* (George does not enjoy books or studies; he likes to work with his hands.)—Sometimes used in a short form, **square peg.**

square shooter See SHOOT STRAIGHT.

squeak See PIP-SQUEAK.

squeak through *v., informal* To be successful but almost fail; win by a small score. *Susan squeaked through the history examination.* (She passed but almost failed the history examination.) *The football team squeaked through 7–6.* (The football team won by a small score.) Compare BY THE SKIN OF ONE'S TEETH.

stab in the back[1] *v. phr., slang* To say or do something unfair that harms (a friend or someone who trusts you). *Owen stabbed his friend Max in the back by telling lies about him.* (Max and Owen were friends but Owen lied about Max and hurt him unfairly.)

stab in the back[2] *n. phr., slang* An act or a lie that hurts a friend or trusting person; a promise not kept, especially to a friend. *John stabbed his own friend in the back by stealing from his store.* (He stole from his friend.) *My friend stabbed me in the back by telling the teacher I was playing hooky when I was home sick.* (My friend told a bad lie about me.)

stack See BLOW A FUSE *or* BLOW ONE'S STACK.

stack the cards *v. phr.* **1** To arrange cards secretly and dishonestly for the purpose of cheating. *The gambler had stacked the cards against Bill.* (He had secretly arranged the cards so that Bill would lose.) **2** To arrange things unfairly for or against a person; make things so that a person has an unfair advantage or disadvantage; make sure in an unfair way that things will happen.—Usually used in the passive with "in one's favor" or "against one." *A tall basketball player has the cards stacked in his favor.* (If a basketball player is tall, he can do better than a shorter player.) *The cards are stacked against a poor boy who wants to go to college.* (It is hard for a poor boy to go to college without help.)

stage See AT —— STAGE OF THE GAME, HOLD THE STAGE, ON THE STAGE, SET THE STAGE.

stake See AT STAKE, PULL UP STAKES.

stake a claim *v. phr.* **1** To claim ownership of land by driving stakes to show boundaries.

The gold hunters staked claims in the West. (They claimed ownership by driving stakes to show boundaries.) **2** *informal* To claim a person or thing as your own by some sign. —A cliché; usually used with *on. George staked a claim on Dianne by giving her his class ring.* (He claimed her as his own by giving her his class ring to wear.)

stamp See SAVINGS STAMP, TRADING STAMP.

stamping ground *n., informal* A place where a person spends much of his time. *Pete's soda fountain is an after-school stamping ground.* (They usually go to Pete's soda fountain after school.) *When John returned to his home town many years later, he visited all of his old stamping grounds.* (When John came back to his home town, he visited the places he used to go to often.)

stamp out *v.* To destroy completely and make disappear. *In the last few years, we have nearly stamped out polio by using vaccine.* (In recent years, we have given people polio shots, and now almost nobody catches polio.) *The police and judges are trying to stamp out crime.* (They try to stop murder, robbery, and other bad things.) Compare WIPE OUT.

stand See GOAL LINE STAND, HAIR STAND ON END, HEART STAND STILL, LEG TO STAND ON.

stand a chance *or* **stand a show** *n. phr.* To have a possibility or opportunity; be likely to do or get something.—A cliché. *Fred doesn't stand a chance of being elected.* (Fred cannot possibly win the election.) *We stand a good chance of seeing Mary at the party.* (Mary will probably go to the party and we will see her there.)

standard time *also* **slow time** *n.* Clock time that is set by law or agreement in a country or in part of a country; *especially, in the United States:* the clock time used between fall and spring, which is an hour slower than the time used in the summer.—Abbreviation ST. *When we go to bed Saturday night, we will set our clocks back an hour, because Sunday we will be on standard time again.* (In the fall we set our clocks back an hour to the clock time that is one hour slower than the time we use in summer.) *Next week it will get dark an hour earlier, because we will be on standard time.* (Darkness will come an hour earlier because the clocks are an hour earlier by the time we use in winter.) Contrast DAYLIGHT SAVING TIME.

stand by *v.* **1** To be close beside or near. *Mary could not tell Jane the secret with her little brother standing by.* (Mary could not tell Jane the secret because her little brother was near.) *Would you just stand by and watch the big boys beat your little brother?* (Would you stay near and do nothing while big boys hurt your little brother?) **2** To be near, waiting to do something when needed. *The policeman in the patrol car radioed the station about the robbery, and then stood by* *for orders.* (He stayed where he was and waited.) *Lee stood by with a fire extinguisher while the trash was burning.* (He set fire to the trash and stood near, ready to put out the fire.) **3** To follow or keep (one's promise). *He is a boy who always stands by his promises.* (He does what he promises to do.) **4** To be loyal to; support; help. *When three big boys attacked Bill, Ed stood by him.* (Ed helped Bill fight the big boys.) *Some people blamed Harry when he got into trouble, but Joe stood by him.* (Joe was loyal and said Harry was all right.) Compare BACK UP, HANG TOGETHER, STAND UP FOR.

stand by one's guns See STICK TO ONE'S GUNS.

stand for *v.* **1** To be a sign of; make you think of; mean. *The letters "U.S.A." stand for "United States of America."* ("U.S.A." means "United States of America.") *The written sign "=" in an arithmetic problem stands for "equals."* ("=" means "equals.") *Our flag stands for our country.* (It makes us think of our country.) *The owl stands for wisdom.* (The owl is a sign of wisdom.) **2** To speak in favor of something, or show that you support it. *The new President stood for honest government.* (The new President made speeches saying he was in favor of honest government.) *John always stands for what is right.* (John always tries to do what is right.) **3** *Chiefly British* To try to be elected for. *Three men from London are standing for parliament.* (These are three London men who want to be members of parliament.) *The governor did not stand for reelection.* (The governor did not want to be elected again.) **4** *informal* To allow to happen or to be done; permit.—Usually used in the negative. *The teacher will not stand for fooling in the classroom.* (The teacher will not allow foolishness in the classroom.) Compare HAVE IT 4, PUT UP WITH.

stand in awe of *v. phr.* To look upon with wonder; feel very respectful to. *Janet always stands in awe of the superintendent.* (She always looks upon him with wonder.) *The soldier stood in awe of his officers.* (He was very respectful to them.)

stand ⸺ in good stead *v. phr.* To be helpful or useful to. *A boy scout knife will stand you in good stead when you do not have other tools.* (A boy scout knife is very useful. It can be used instead of several different tools.) *Julia knew how to typewrite, and that stood her in good stead when she looked for a job.* (Knowing how to type helped Julia find a job.)

stand in one's way See IN ONE'S WAY.

stand in with *v. phr., informal* To be liked by or friendly with.—Usually used with *well*. *John stands in well with the teacher.* (John is well-liked by the teacher.)

stand off *v.* **1** To stay at a distance; stay apart. *At parties, Mr. Jones goes around talk-*

ing to everyone, but Mrs. Jones is shy and stands off. (Mrs. Jones is not friendly.) **2** To keep (someone or something) from coming near or winning. *The soldiers defending the fort stood off a large band of Indians.* (The soldiers kept the Indians from coming into the fort.) *The other schools wanted to beat our team and win the championship, but our boys stood them all off.* (Our team kept the other teams from taking the championship away from us.) Contrast GIVE GROUND.

stand on ceremony *v. phr.* To follow strict rules of politeness; be very formal with other people.—Usually used with a helping verb in the negative. *Grandmother does not stand on ceremony when her grandchildren call.* (Grandmother does not follow strict rules of politeness when her grandchildren visit her. She is very informal with them.)

stand one's ground *also* **hold one's ground** *v. phr.* **1** To stay and fight instead of running away. *The enemy attacked in great numbers but our men stood their ground.* (Many enemy soldiers attacked, but our men fought and did not run away.) Compare GAIN GROUND. Contrast GIVE GROUND, LOSE GROUND. **2** To defend a belief or statement; refuse to weaken when opposed; insist you are right. *John's friends said he was mistaken, but he stood his ground.* (John believed he was right and did not change his ideas.) Compare STICK TO ONE'S GUNS.

stand on one's own feet *or* **stand on one's own two feet** *v. phr.* To depend on yourself; do things yourself; earn your own living; be independent.—A cliché. *After his father died, John had to stand on his own feet and earn his own living.* (John's father died and John then supported himself.) *You should learn to stand on your own two feet.* (You should decide things and act yourself, not depend on others.)

stand out *v.* **1** To go farther out than a near by surface; project. *A mole stood out on her cheek.* (The mole was higher than the skin around it.) Compare STICK OUT 1b. **2** To be more noticeable in some way than those around you; be higher, bigger, or better. *Fred was very tall and stood out in the crowd.* (He was so tall that it was easy to see him in the crowd.) *John stood out as a track star.* (John was a track star and better than others.)

stand over *v.* **1** To watch closely; keep checking all the time. *Ted's mother had to stand over him to get him to do his homework.* (She had to watch him closely to make sure that he did it.) **2** To be held over for later action; be postponed; wait. *The committee decided to let the proposal stand over until its next meeting.* (They decided to delay action on it until their next meeting.)

stand pat *v., informal* To be satisfied with things and be against a change. *Bill had made up his mind on the question and when his* *friends tried to change his mind, he stood pat.* (Bill liked things as they were, and was against any change.) Compare STAND ONE'S GROUND 2.

stand the gaff *v. phr., informal* To stand rough treatment; do well in spite of great physical or mental hardship.—A cliché. *An athlete must learn to stand the gaff.* (He must learn to do well in spite of the great physical hardship of sports.) *No person running for office gets far unless he can stand the gaff.* (He can't succeed unless he is able to stand rough treatment without letting it upset him.) Compare HOLD OUT 2, STICK OUT 2.

stand to reason *v. phr.* To seem very likely from the known facts. *If you have a driver's license, it stands to reason you can drive.* (If you have a driver's license, you are almost sure to know how to drive.) *Joe is intelligent and studies hard; it stands to reason that he will pass the examination.* (Being smart and a good student, Joe is almost sure to pass the examination.)

stand up *v.* **1** To rise to a standing position; get up on your feet. *A gentleman stands up when a lady enters a room.* (A gentleman rises from his seat and stands when a lady enters a room.) **2** To be strong enough to use hard or for a long time. *A rocket must be built strongly to stand up under the blast-off.* (A rocket must be built strongly so that it does not break under the force of the blast-off.) *The old car has already stood up for twenty years.* (The old car has lasted in use for twenty years.) Compare WEAR WELL. **3** *informal* To make a date and then fail to keep it. *June cried when Bill stood her up on their first date.* (June cried when Bill did not meet her after he had invited her on a date.)

stand up and be counted *v. phr.* To be willing to say what you think in public; let people know that you are for or against something.—A cliché. *The equal rights movement needs people who are willing to stand up and be counted.* (The equal rights movement needs people who are willing to publicly support it.) *If you disagree with the group, you should be ready to stand up and be counted.* (If you do not agree with the group, you should be ready to tell why you disagree. You should be willing to let your opinion be known.)

stand up for *or informal* **stick up for** *v.* To defend against attack; fight for. *John always stands up for his rights.* (John always claims what he has a right to do or have.) *When Mary was being criticized, Jane stuck up for her.* (When Mary was being criticized, Jane spoke for her against the criticism.) Compare BACK UP, GO TO BAT FOR, STAND BY, STAND ONE'S GROUND, STICK TO ONE'S GUNS, GO TO BAT FOR.

stand up to *v.* To meet with courage. *Mary stood up to the snarling dog that leaped to-*

ward her. (Mary bravely faced the dog.) *A soldier must stand up to danger.* (A soldier must be brave in a dangerous situation.)

stand up with *v., informal* To be best man or maid of honor at a wedding. *A groom often chooses his brother to stand up with him.* (He often asks his brother to be best man when he gets married.)

star See FIVE-STAR, SEE STARS, HITCH ONE'S WAGON TO A STAR, LUCKY STAR, THANK ONE'S LUCKY STARS.

starch See TAKE THE STARCH OUT OF.

stare in the face *n. phr.* **1** To be about to meet or to happen to (you.)—A cliché. *Grandmother became very sick and death was staring her in the face.* (Grandmother was very sick and about to die.) *Defeat stared them in the face, but the soldiers fought on bravely.* (The soldiers were about to lose the battle, but they fought on bravely.) **2** To be easy to see; be plain. *Are you looking for your pencil? It's on your desk, staring you in the face.* (Your pencil is on your desk in a place easy to see.) *Their friends all knew that Mary loved John, but John did not see it even though it was staring him in the face.* (It was plain to see that Mary loved John, but John did not notice it.)

stars in one's eyes *n. phr.* **1** An appearance or feeling of very great happiness or expectation of happiness.—A cliché. *Mary gets stars in her eyes when she thinks of her boy friend.* (Mary feels and looks very happy; her eyes sparkle.) **2** A belief in the possibility of quick and lasting reforms in people and life and an eagerness to make such changes. —A cliché. *Some inexperienced people get stars in their eyes when they think of improving the world.* (They are sure they can improve the world and are eager to try.)—**starry-eyed** *adj.* Very happy and excited, perhaps with little reason; eager and self-confident about improving human nature and general conditions of life. *Young people are often starry-eyed and eager to improve the world; they do not know how hard it is.* (They are eager to change the world and think they can make it better quickly.)

start See BY FITS AND STARTS, HEAD START, JACK-RABBIT START, RUNNING START.

start from scratch See FROM SCRATCH.

start in *v., informal* **1** To begin to do something; start. *Fred started in weeding the garden.* (Fred began to weed the garden.) *The family started in eating supper.* (The family began eating supper.) Compare GO AT. **2** To begin a career. *Bob started in as an office boy and became president.* (Bob first worked as an office boy, but at last he became president.) **3** To give a first job to. *The bank started him in as a clerk.* (The bank gave him a job as clerk first.)

starting pitcher *n.* The baseball pitcher who begins the game. *The coach did not announce the name of his starting pitcher until the day* *of the game.* (He did not say which pitcher would begin the game until the day the game was to be played.)

start out *v.* **1** To begin to go somewhere. *Bill started out for school on his bicycle.* (He began to go to school.) *Art started out on a voyage around the world.* (He began a trip around the world.) Compare SET OUT. **2** To begin a career or life. *Harry started out as an errand boy in a business office.* (He began working as an errand boy.) *We all start out in life as helpless infants.* (We begin life as dependent babies.) Syn. START IN. **3** *informal* To give one a first job. *The garage man started Pete out as a grease rack man.* (He first gave Pete the job of greasing cars.) Syn. START IN 3.

start something *v. phr., informal* To make trouble; cause a quarrel or fight. *John is always starting something.* (He is always starting trouble.) *Jack likes to play tricks on the other boys to start something.* (He likes to play tricks on them to cause fights.) Compare MAKE SOMETHING OF.

start the ball rolling See GET THE BALL ROLLING.

start up *v.* **1** To begin operating. *The driver started up the motor of the car.* (The driver started the motor running.) *The engine started up with a roar.* (The engine started running with a roar.) **2** To begin to play (music). *The conductor waved his baton, and the band started up.* (The conductor waved his baton, and the band started playing.) *The orchestra started up a waltz.* (The orchestra started to play a waltz.) Compare STRIKE UP. **3** To rise or stand suddenly. *When he heard the bell, he started up from his chair.* (He stood up suddenly.)

stash bag *or* **stuff bag** *n., slang, informal* **1** A small bag containing marijuana cigarettes or the ingredients for making them. *The police are holding John because they found a stash bag full of the stuff on him.* (John was found in possession of marijuana kept in a pouch.) **2** Any small bag resembling a stash bag used for small personal items such as lipstick, driver's license, etc. *Do you have any room for my keys in your stash bag?* (Can you put my keys in your purse?)

state See LIE IN STATE.

stead See STAND IN GOOD STEAD.

stave off *v., literary* To keep from touching or hurting you. Syn. WARD OFF. *The white knight struck with his sword. The black knight staved it off with his own sword.* (The black knight kept away the white knight's sword with his own.) *Bill's warm new coat staved off the cold.* (Bill's warm new coat kept him from being cold.) *They staved off starvation by eating two of the sled dogs.* (They ate two of the sled dogs to keep from starving.)

stay put *v. phr.* To stay in place; not leave. *Harry's father told him to stay put until he came back.* (His father told him not to leave

until he came back.) *The rocks can be glued to the bulletin board to make them stay put.* (They can be glued to the bulletin board so they will stay in place.) *After Gradmother came home from her trip to visit Aunt May, she said she wanted to stay put for a while.* (Grandmother says she has had enough traveling; she wants to stay home and go nowhere.)

stay with See STICK WITH.

steady See GO STEADY.

steak See SALISBURY STEAK, T-BONE STEAK.

steal See LOCK THE BARN DOOR AFTER THE HORSE IS STOLEN.

steal a march on *v. phr.* To get ahead of someone by doing a thing unnoticed; get an advantage over. *The army stole a march on the enemy by marching at night and attacking them in the morning.* (The army marched at night and surprised the enemy.) *Jack got the job by getting up earlier than Bill. He stole a march on him.* (Jack got up early without Bill's knowing it.) Compare GET THE JUMP ON, GET THE BETTER OF, TAKE BY SURPRISE.

steal one's thunder *v. phr.* To do or say something, intentionally or not, that another person has planned to say or do.—A cliché. *Fred intended to nominate Bill for president, but John got up first and stole Fred's thunder.* (John nominated Bill himself, so Fred had nothing to say.) *Mary was going to sing "Oh! Susanna," but Ellen did it first and Mary said Ellen had stolen her thunder.* (Ellen did what Mary had meant to do.) *Smith heard that Jones was going to offer a new law which people wanted, so he himself proposed the law first, stealing Jones' thunder.* (Smith offered the new law first and got the praise which Jones deserved.)

steal the show *v. phr.* To act or do so well in a performance that you get most of the attention and the other performers are unnoticed. *Mary was in only one scene of the play, but she stole the show from the stars.* (Mary's acting was so good that the audience paid more attention to her than to the stars.)

steal the spotlight *v. phr.* To attract attention away from a person or thing that people should be watching. *When the maid walked on the stage and tripped over a rug, she stole the spotlight from the leading players.* (When the maid tripped, the audience paid attention to her, and forgot the leading players.) *Just as the speaker began, a little dog ran up the aisle, and stole the spotlight from him.* (When the dog ran up the aisle, the people looked at him, and did not listen to the speaker.)

steam See LET OFF STEAM *or* BLOW OFF STEAM, UNDER ONE'S OWN STEAM.

steamed up *adj., informal* Excited or angry about or eager to do something. *The coach gave the team a pep talk before the game, and he got them all steamed up to win the game.* (The coach gave the team a pep talk, and he made them very eager to win the game.) *When Mary found out that Jane had not kept their secret, she became all steamed up.* (When Mary heard that Jane had told their secret, she became very angry.) *Bill was all steamed up about the movie he had just seen.* (Bill was very excited about the movie he had just seen.)

steel See MIND LIKE A STEEL TRAP.

steer clear of *v.* **1** To steer a safe distance from; go around without touching. *A ship steers clear of a rocky shore in stormy weather.* (A ship stays away from a rocky shore when the weather is stormy.) **2** *informal* To stay away from; keep from going near. *Fred was angry at Bill, and Bill was steering clear of him.* (Because Fred was angry, Bill was trying not to meet him.) *Some words Martha always spells wrong. She tries to steer clear of them.* (Martha always spells some words wrong. She tries not to have to write these words and uses others instead.)

step See IN STEP, OUT OF STEP, TAKE STEPS.

step all over See WALK OVER.

step down *v.* **1** To come down in one move from a higher position to a lower. *As soon as the train stopped, the conductor stepped down to help the passengers off.* (When the train stopped, the conductor got off to help the passengers off.) **2** To make go slower little by little. *The train was approaching the station, so the engineer stepped it down.* (The engineer decreased the speed of the train because it was nearing the station.) Compare SLOW DOWN, STEP UP. **3** To leave a job as an official or some other important position. *When the judge became ill, he had to step down.* (When the judge became ill, he had to resign.)

step in *v.* **1** To go inside for a quick visit. *It was a cold night, and when the policeman passed, we invited him to step in for a cup of coffee.* (We invited the policeman to come inside the house for a cup of coffee.) **2** To begin to take part in a continuing action or discussion, especially without being asked. *When the dogs began to fight, John stepped in to stop it before they were hurt.* (John tried to stop the fight and drive the dogs away.) *When Bill had done as much as he was able to on his model plane, his father stepped in to help him.* (Bill's father helped him after Bill had done as much as he could himself.)

step inside *v.* To come or go inside. *Mother invited the callers to step inside.* (Mother invited the callers to come into the house.)

step into *v.* **1** To come or go into. *The taxi stopped, and we stepped into it.* (The taxi stopped, and we got in.) *Mr. Jones called to his secretary to step into his office.* (Mr. Jones called his secretary to come into his office.) **2** To begin to do, undertake. *When the star became sick, his understudy stepped into his part.* (When the star became sick, the understudy acted his part.) *When Bill grad-*

uates from college, he will step into a job in his father's bank. (Bill will go directly from college into a job in his father's bank.)

step into one's shoes *v. phr.* To do what someone else usually does after he has stopped doing it.—A cliché. *When Bill's father died, Bill had to step into his father's shoes to support his mother.* (Bill's father worked to support his mother. When his father died, Bill had to take a job to support her.) *A coach trains the junior varsity to step into the shoes of the members of the varsity team when they graduate.* (The junior varsity is trained to take the place of the graduating varsity players.) *When the boss retires, his son will step into his shoes.* (When the boss retires, his son will move into his job and become boss.) Compare IN ONE'S SHOES.

step off *v.* **1** To walk or march quickly. *The drum major lowered his baton and the band stepped off.* (The drum major signalled, and the band began to march.) **2** *or* **pace off.** To measure by taking a series of steps in a line. *The farmer stepped off the edge of the field to see how much fencing he would need.* (The farmer counted the number of steps along the edge of the field, and decided how much fencing he would need.) *The referee stepped off a five-yard penalty against our team.* (The referee made a series of steps until he had gone five yards and set the football down.)

step on it *or* **step on the gas** *v. phr.* **1** To push down on the gas pedal to make a car go faster. *Be very careful when you step on the gas. Don't go too fast.* (Be careful that you do not make the car go too fast.) Compare GIVE IT THE GUN. **2** *informal* To go faster; hurry. *Step on it, or we'll be late for school.* (Move faster or we will be late for school.) *John is a slow starter, but he can step on the gas when it looks as if he might lose the race.* (John can run faster when he must win.) *Lee was wasting time at breakfast and his father told him to step on it or they would miss the bus.* (His father told him to hurry up and eat.)

step on one's toes *or* **tread on one's toes** *v. phr.* To do something that embarrasses or offends someone else. *If you break in when other people are talking, you may step on their toes.* (If you interrupt other people, you may embarrass them or make them angry.) *Mary is pretty, and she often treads on the toes of the girls by stealing their boyfriend.* (Mary makes the other girls angry by stealing their boyfriends.)

step on the gas See STEP ON IT.

stepped up *adj.* Carried on at a faster or more active rate; increased. *To fill the increase in orders, the factory had to operate at a stepped-up rate.* (To fill the orders, the factory had to work faster.)

step up *v.* **1** To go from a lower to a higher place. *John stepped up onto the platform and began to speak.* (John went up onto the platform and began to speak.) **2** To come towards or near; approach. *The sergeant called for volunteers and Private Jones stepped up to volunteer.* (The sergeant called for men who would do a job, and Private Jones came forward and offered himself.) *John waited until the teacher had finished speaking to Mary, and then he stepped up.* (John waited until the teacher was through speaking, and then he approached her.) **3** To go or to make (something) go faster or more actively. *When John found he was going to be late, he stepped up his pace.* (When John found he was going to be late, he walked faster.) *After we had reached the outskirts of town, we stepped up the engine.* (When we reached the outskirts, we ran the car faster.) *The enemy was near, and the army stepped up its patrols to find them before they got too close.* (The enemy was near and the army sent out more patrols than usual so that they would be more likely to find the enemy.) **4** To rise to a higher or more important position; be promoted. *This year Mary is secretary of the club, but I am sure she will step up to president next year.* (Mary is secretary this year, but I am sure she will be promoted to president next year.) Contrast STEP DOWN 3.

stew in one's own juice *v. phr., informal* To suffer from something that you have caused to happen yourself.—A cliché. *John lied to Tom, but Tom found out. Now Tom is making John stew in his own juice.* (Since Tom found that John had lied to him, he has been making John suffer. If John had not lied in the first place, he would not be suffering.) *I warned you not to steal those apples. You got caught, and you can stew in your own juice.* (I won't help you. I warned you not to steal, but you did it anyway. Now you must suffer the results.)

stick See CARROT AND STICK, MORE THAN ONE COULD SHAKE A STICK AT.

stick around *v., informal* To stay or wait nearby. *John's father told him to stick around and they would go fishing.* (John's father told him to wait nearby and they would go fishing.) *After work Mr. Harris stuck around to ride home with his friend.* (He stayed to ride home with his friend.)

stick in one's craw *or* **stick in one's crop** *v. phr.* To make you angry; bother you; annoy you.—A cliché. *His parents' praise of his brother stuck in Jerry's craw.* (Their praise of his brother made Jerry angry.) *Sue's failure to get a better grade than Ann stuck in her crop.* (Sue's failure to get a better grade than Ann bothered her.)

stick in one's throat *v. phr.* To be something you do not want to say; be hard to say. *Jean wanted to ask the teacher's pardon, but the words stuck in her throat.* (Jean wanted to say she was sorry, but the words were hard to say.)

stick-in-the-mud *n., informal* An over-careful person; someone who is old-fashioned and fights change. *Mabel said her mother was a real stick-in-the-mud to make a rule that she must be home by 10 o'clock on week nights and 11:30 Saturdays.* (She said her mother was very old-fashioned to make such rules.) *Mr. Thomas is a stick-in-the-mud who plows with mules; he won't buy a tractor.* (He is old-fashioned; he won't change his way of farming.)

stick one's neck out *or* **stick one's chin out** *v. phr., informal* To do something dangerous or risky.—A cliché. *When I was in trouble, Paul was the only one who would stick his neck out to help me.* (When I was in trouble, Paul was the only one who would put himself in danger to help me.) *John is always sticking his chin out by saying something he shouldn't.* (John is always getting himself into trouble by saying something that he shouldn't say.)

stick one's nose into See NOSE INTO.

stick out *v.* **1a** To stand out from a wall or other surface; project; extend. *The limb stuck out from the trunk of the tree.* (The limb projected out of the trunk.) **1b** To be seen or noticed more easily or quickly than others; be noticeable. *My house is the only brick one on the street. It sticks out and you can't miss it.* (My house is different from the others on the street. You will notice it at once.) *Mary plays basketball very well. The others on the team are good, but she really sticks out.* (The others on the team are good, but Mary is much better.) **1c**—Often used in the informal phrase *stick out like a sore thumb. John is so shy and awkward that he sticks out like a sore thumb.* (John is so shy and awkward that everyone notices him.) Syn. STAND OUT. **2** *informal* To keep on doing something until it is done, no matter how long, hard, or unpleasant. *Bill is not a fast runner and he doesn't have a chance of winning the marathon, but he will stick out the race even if he finishes last.* (Bill can't win the race, but he will run all the way.)—Often used in the phrase *stick it out. Mathematics is hard, but if you stick it out you will understand it.* (Mathematics is hard, but if you keep on working hard at it you will learn it.) Compare HANG ON 2, STICK WITH 1.

stick together *v.* To remain close together in a situation. *Stick together in the cave so that no one gets lost.* (Stay in a group in the cave so that no one gets lost.) *The gang stuck together after the game.* (The gang stayed together after the game.) *Bill and Bob stick together in a game or in a fight.* (Bill and Bob always are on the same side with each other.) Syn. HANG TOGETHER 1.

stick to one's guns *or* **stand by one's guns** *v. phr.* To hold to an aim or an opinion even though people try to stop you or say you are wrong.—An overworked phrase. *People laughed at Columbus when he said the world was round. He stuck to his guns and proved* *he was right.* (Columbus did not change his mind when others said he was wrong.) *At first the boss would not give Jane the raise in pay she wanted, but she stood by her guns and he gave it to her.* (Jane insisted that he raise her pay and he did.) Compare STAND ONE'S GROUND.

stick to one's knitting *or* **tend to one's knitting** *v. phr., informal* To do your own job and not bother other people.—A cliché. *The trouble with Henry is that he is always telling other people what to do; he can't stick to his knitting.* (Henry doesn't pay enough attention to his own work; he bothers other people.)

stick to one's ribs *or* **stick to the ribs** *v. phr., informal* To keep you from getting hungry again too quickly.—A cliché. *Doctors say you should eat a good breakfast that sticks to your ribs.* (You should eat a good breakfast that gives you lots of energy and keeps you from getting hungry again too quickly.) *Farmers eat food that sticks to the ribs.* (They eat food that keeps them from getting hungry again too quickly.)

stick up *v., informal* To rob with a gun. *When the messenger left the bank, a man jumped out of an alley and stuck him up.* (A man jumped out of the alley and pointed a gun at the messenger to rob him.) Syn. HOLD UP. *In the old West, outlaws sometimes stuck up the stage coaches.* (Outlaws sometimes robbed the coaches with guns.)

stick-up *n., informal* A robbery by a man with a gun. *Mr. Smith was the victim of a stick-up last night.* (Mr. Smith was robbed by a man with a gun last night.)

stick up for See STAND UP FOR.

stick with *v., informal* **1** *or* **stay with** To continue doing; not quit. *Fred stayed with his homework until it was done.* (Fred spent a long time on his homework, but he finished it.) *Practicing is tiresome, but stick with it and some day you will be a good pianist.* (Practice constantly, and some day you will be a good pianist.) Compare STICK TO. **2** To stay with; not leave. *Stick with me until we get out of the crowd.* (Stay with me. Do not leave me.) *For two months Bill's boss could not pay his salary, but Bill stuck with him, because he thought the company would soon succeed.* (Bill did not quit his job; he stayed with his boss.) **3** To sell (someone) something poor or worthless; cheat. *Father said that the man in the store tried to stick him with a bad TV set.* (The man tried to sell Father a set that was no good.) **4** To leave (someone) with (something unpleasant); force to do or keep something because others cannot or will not.—Usually used in the passive. *When Harry and I went to the store to buy ice cream cones, Harry ran out with his cone without paying and I was stuck with paying for it.* (I was left to pay because Harry was gone.) *Mary didn't wash the dishes before*

she left so I'm stuck with it. (I have to do Mary's job.) *Mr. Jones bought a house that is too big and expensive, but now he's stuck with it.* (He has it and can't get rid of it.)

sticky fingers *n. phr., slang* **1** The habit of stealing things you see and want. *Don't leave money in your locker; some of the boys have sticky fingers.* (Don't leave money in your locker because some of the boys are easily tempted to steal.) *Don't leave that girl alone in the room with so many valuable objects around, because she has sticky fingers.* (Don't leave her alone with valuable things because she is very likely to steal something.) **2** Ability to catch a ball, especially football forward passes. *Jack is very tall and has sticky fingers. He is an end on the football team.* (He catches passes well.)

stiff See KEEP A STIFF UPPER LIP, SCARE OUT OF ONE'S WITS *or* SCARE STIFF.

still See HEART STAND STILL.

stir up *v.* **1** To bring (something) into being, often by great exertion or activity; cause. *It was a quiet afternoon, and John tried to stir up some excitement.* (John tried to bring about something exciting that would get rid of his boredom.) *Bob stirred up a fight between Tom and Bill.* (Bob caused a fight between Tom and Bill.) Compare WHIP UP 2. **2** To cause (someone) to act; incite to action or movement; rouse. *The coach's pep talk stirred up the team to win.* (The coach's talk incited the team to win.) *When Mary heard what Betty said about her, she became stirred up.* (When Mary heard what Betty said, she became very angry.)

stir up a hornet's nest *v. phr.* To make many people angry; do something that many people don't like. *The principal stirred up a hornet's nest by changing the rules at school.* (He changed the rules and many pupils and teachers got angry.)

stitch See IN STITCHES.

stock See IN STOCK, OUT OF STOCK, TAKE STOCK, TAKE STOCK IN.

stolen base *n.* A gaining of a base in baseball by running without a hit or an error to help. *Aparicio leads the American League in stolen bases.* (He took more bases by running alone than anybody else in the league did.)

stomach See EYES BIGGER THAN ONE'S STOMACH, BUTTER-FLIES IN YOUR STOMACH, TURN ONE'S STOMACH.

stone See CAST THE FIRST STONE, HAVE A HEART OF STONE, KILL TWO BIRDS WITH ONE STONE, LEAVE NO STONE UNTURNED, PEOPLE WHO LIVE IN GLASS HOUSES SHOULD NOT THROW STONES, ROLLING STONE GATHERS NO MOSS.

stone-broke *or* **dead broke** *or* **flat broke** *adj., informal* having no money; penniless. *Jill wanted to go to the movies but she was stone-broke.* (She had no money with which to buy a ticket.) *The man gambled and was soon* *flat broke.* (He gambled and was soon penniless.)

stone-cold *adj.* Having no warmth; completely cold.—Used to describe things that are better when warm. *The boys who got up late found their breakfast stone-cold.* (The boys who got up late found their breakfast was completely cold.) *The furnace went off and the radiators were stone-cold.* (They had no warmth in them. They were completely cold to the touch.)

stone-dead *adj., informal* Showing no signs of life; completely dead. *Barry tried to revive the frozen robin but it was stone-dead.* (He brought it in and tried to warm it up but it showed absolutely no signs of life.)

stone wall *or* **brick wall** *adj.* Something hard to overcome; an idea or belief that is hard to change. *The students ran into a brick wall when they asked the principal to put off the examination.* (They ran into something hard to overcome when they asked the principal to put off the examination.) *Dick tried to change Father's mind about letting him use the car Saturday night, but he was up against a stone wall.* (Dick found that Father would not change his mind.)

stop See PUT AN END TO 1, *or* PUT A STOP TO.

stop by See DROP BY.

stop cold *or* **stop dead** *or* **stop in one's tracks** *v. phr., informal* To stop very quickly or with great force. *The hunter pulled the trigger and stopped the deer cold.* (The hunter shot the deer and the deer dropped right there.) *When I saw Mary on the street, I was so surprised I stopped dead.* (When I saw Mary, I was so surprised I stopped right there.) *The deer heard a noise and he stopped in his tracks.* (The deer stopped where he was to listen to the noise.)

stop off *v.* To stop at a place for a short time while going somewhere. *We stopped off after school at the soda fountain before going home.* (We stopped at the soda fountain and then went home.) *On our trip to California we stopped off in Las Vegas for two days.* (We stayed in Las Vegas and then went on to California.)

stop over *v.* To stay at a place overnight or for some other short time while on a trip elsewhere. *When we came back from California, we stopped over one night near the Grand Canyon.* (We stayed one night near the Grand Canyon.)

stop street *n.* A street where cars must come to a full stop before crossing another street. *Johnny was late because he traveled on a stop street.* (Johnny had to stop at every corner because there were stop signs at each one.) Contrast THROUGH STREET.

store See DIME STORE, IN STORE, SET STORE BY, VARIETY STORE.

storm See TAKE BY STORM.

story See OLD STORY, SOB STORY, UPPER STORY

stow away *v.* **1** *informal* To pack or store away. *After New Year's Day the Christmas decorations were stowed away until another season.* (The Christmas decorations were stored for the next season.) **2** To hide on a ship or another kind of transportation to get a free ride. *John ran away from home and stowed away on a freighter going to Jamaica.* (John hid on the freighter to get a trip to Jamaica on it.)

straight See GO STRAIGHT, SHOOT STRAIGHT.

straighten out *v.* To correct a mistake; make you realize you are wrong. *The teacher saw Jim's awkward sentence on the board and asked for volunteers to straighten it out.* (She asked for volunteers to correct the mistakes in it.) *Sometimes only a good spanking will straighten out a naughty child.* (Sometimes only a good spanking will make him understand that he is wrong.) Syn. SQUARE AWAY 2.

straighten up *v.* To put in order; make neat. *Vic had to straighten up his room before he could go swimming.* (He had to put his room in order before he could go swimming.) *Mrs. Johnson straightened up the house before company came.* (She made the house neat before company came.) Compare PICK UP 6b, SQUARE AWAY.

straight face *n.* A face that is not laughing or smiling. *Mary told all the funny stories she knew to try to make Joan laugh, but Joan kept a straight face.* (Joan didn't laugh or smile at Mary's stories.) *It is hard to tell when Jim is teasing you. He can tell a fib with a straight face.* (Jim can tell a fib without showing it by smiling or laughing.) *When Bob fell into the water, he looked funny and I could hardly keep a straight face.* (I wanted to laugh but did not.)

straight from the horse's mouth *slang* Directly from the person or place where it began; from a reliable source or a person that cannot be doubted. *They are going to be married. I got the news straight from the horse's mouth—their minister.* (I heard it from a person who can't be doubted—their minister.) *John found out about the painting straight from the horse's mouth, from the painter himself.* (John was told about the painting by the man who painted it.)

straight from the shoulder *adv. phr., informal* In an open and honest way of speaking; without holding back anything because of fear or politeness or respect for someone's feelings; frankly.—An overused phrase. *John asked what he had done wrong. Bob told him straight from the shoulder.* (Bob told John what he had done wrong.) *The candidate for Congress spoke out against his opponent's dishonesty straight from the shoulder.* (The candidate spoke out frankly and bravely against dishonesty.) Contrast PULL ONE'S PUNCHES.

straight off *adv. phr.* At once; immediately.

After school is over, you come home straight off, and don't waste time. (After school is over, come home the shortest, quickest way.) *He asked his father for the car, but his father said straight off that he couldn't have it.* (His father told him quickly that he could not.)

straight out See RIGHT OUT.

straight shooters See SHOOT STRAIGHT.

straight ticket *n.* A vote for all the candidates of a single party. *Uncle Fred was a loyal member of his party. He always voted the straight ticket.* (He always voted for all the candidates of his party.) Contrast SPLIT TICKET.

strain a point See STRETCH A POINT.

strange to say *adv. phr.* Not what you might think; surprisingly.—Used for emphasis. *Strange to say, Jerry doesn't like candy.* (Surprisingly, he doesn't like candy.) *Strange to say, the Indians didn't kill Daniel Boone.* (They didn't kill him as you might think.)

straw See GIVE A HANG, GRASP AT A STRAW, GRASP AT STRAWS, LAST STRAW *or* STRAW THAT BREAKS THE CAMEL'S BACK, MAKE BRICKS WITHOUT STRAW.

straw boss *n.* **1** The boss of a few workers who is himself under another boss or foreman. *The straw boss told Jim he would have to see the foreman about a job.* (The less important boss could not hire anyone.) **2** A man who works himself and also bosses a few other workers. *Smith worked better than the other men, so the foreman made him straw boss, too.* (Smith's foreman made him a boss but he still worked himself, too.)

straw in the wind *n. phr.* A small sign of what may happen.—A cliché. *The doctor's worried face was a straw in the wind.* (His worried face was a sign that something serious might happen.) *The quickly-called meeting of the President and his cabinet was a straw in the wind.* (It was a sign that something might happen.)

straw that breaks the camel's back See LAST STRAW.

streak See WINNING STREAK.

stream See CHANGE HORSES IN THE MIDDLE OF THE STREAM, SWIM AGAINST THE CURRENT *or* SWIM AGAINST THE STREAM.

street See BACK STREET, CROSS STREET, MAN IN THE STREET, ON EASY STREET, SIDE STREET, STOP STREET, THROUGH STREET.

strength See ON THE STRENGTH OF.

stretch a point *or* **strain a point** *v. phr.* To permit something different or more than usual; not tell the exact truth or make an exception. *Mother stretched a point because it was Christmas time and let the children stay up later than usual.* (Mother broke the rule of going to bed early because it was Christmas.) *It's straining a point to call Joe a hero just because he saved the kitten from drowning in the bath tub.* (It is not exactly the truth to call Joe a hero because anybody could have saved the kitten.)

stride See HIT ONE'S STRIDE, TAKE IN STRIDE.

strike See CALLED STRIKE, HAVE TWO STRIKES AGAINST ONE, LIGHTNING NEVER STRIKES TWICE IN THE SAME PLACE, TWO STRIKES AGAINST ONE.

strike a happy medium *v. phr.* To find an answer to a problem that is half-way between two unsatisfactory answers. *Mary said the dress was blue. Jane said it was green. They finally struck a happy medium and decided it was blue-green. Two teaspoons of sugar made the cup of coffee too sweet, and one not sweet enough. One heaping teaspoon struck a happy medium.*

strike all of a heap See ALL OF A HEAP.

strike it rich *v. phr., informal* **1** To discover oil, or a large vein of minerals to be mined, or a buried treasure. *The old prospector panned gold for years before he struck it rich.* (The old prospector mined gold for years before he found a large gold mine and became rich from it.) **2** To become rich or successful suddenly or without expecting to. *Everyone wanted to buy one of the new gadgets, and their inventor struck it rich.* (The inventor sold very many gadgets and became rich from the sales.) *John did not know that he had a rich Uncle John in Australia. John struck it rich when his uncle left his money to John.* (John became rich when his uncle died and left his money to John.) Compare PAY DIRT 2.

strike one's colors See HAUL DOWN ONE'S COLORS.

strike out *v.* **1** To destroy something that has been written or drawn by drawing a line or cross through it or by erasing it. *John misspelled "corollary." He struck it out and wrote it correctly.* (John drew a line through the word that was misspelled, and wrote it again.) **2** To begin to follow a new path or a course of action that you have never tried. *The boy scouts struck out at daybreak over the mountain pass.* (The boy scouts started to hike over the pass.) *John quit his job and struck out on his own as a traveling salesman.* (John began a new career as a traveling salesman.) **3** To put (a batter) out of play by making him miss the ball three times; *also:* To be put out of play by missing the ball three times. *The pitcher struck out three men in the game.* (The pitcher got three men out on three strikes each.) *The batter struck out twice.* (The batter was out on three strikes two different times.) **4** To push out an arm suddenly in a hitting motion. *The boxer saw his chance and struck out at his opponent's jaw.* (The boxer hit his opponent on the jaw.)

strike up *v.* **1a** To start to sing or play. *We were sitting around the campfire. Someone struck up a song, and we all joined in.* (Someone began to sing and everyone started to sing with him.) *The President took his place* *on the platform, and the band struck up the national anthem.* (The band began to play the national anthem.) **1b** To give a signal to start (a band) playing. *When the team ran on the field, the band director struck up the band.* (When the team ran on, the band director made the band start playing.) **2** To bring about; begin; start. *The policeman struck up a conversation with John while they were waiting for the bus.* (The policeman said something to John, and started a conversation with him.) *It did not take Mary long to strike up acquaintances in her new school.* (Mary made new friends quickly at the new school.)

strike zone *n.* The space above home base in baseball through which a pitched ball must go to be called a strike by the umpire. *The batter did not swing at the pitch but it was in the strike zone so the umpire called it a strike.* (The pitch was over the home plate and not too high or too low so that the umpire called it a strike even though the batter did not swing at it.)

string See FIRST STRING, LATCH STRING, ON THE STRING *or* ON A STRING, PULL STRINGS, PURSE STRINGS, SHOE-STRING CATCH, TIED TO ONE'S MOTHER'S APRON STRINGS.

string along *v., informal* **1** To deceive; fool; lead on dishonestly. *Mary was stringing John along for years but she didn't mean to marry him.* (She fooled him for years but didn't mean to marry him.) *George told the new boy that he must always call the teacher "Sir," but the new boy soon saw that George was stringing him along.* (The new boy found that George was fooling him.) Compare ON A STRING. **2** To follow someone's leadership; join his group. *Those of you who want to learn about wild-flowers, string along with Jake.* (Follow Jake's leadership. He will show you where they grow and tell you what they are.)

string out *v.* To make (something) extend over a great distance or a long stretch of time. *The telephone poles were strung out along the road as far as we could see.* (The telephone poles were set one after another as far as we could see.) *Mary and Ann did not have much to say but they did not want to go home. They strung out their gossip for a long time.* (Mary and Ann took a long time to say very little because they did not want to go home.)

string up *v., slang* To put a rope around the neck of a person and choke him to death; hang. *The posse strung up the rustler without a trial.* (The posse hanged the rustler before he could be tried. Compare NECKTIE PARTY.

strip See DRAG STRIP.

stripe See MIDFIELD STRIPE.

stroke See AT A STROKE *or* AT ONE STROKE.

strung out *adj., slang, colloquial* **1** Nervous, jittery, jumpy; generally ill because of drug use or withdrawal symptoms. *The only explanation I can think of for Max's behavior is that he must be strung out.* (Max must be on drugs, or suffering from withdrawal symptoms.) **2** To suffer because of a lack of something previously accustomed to, such as the love and affection of someone. *Sue is all strung out for Jim; they've just split up.* (Sue misses Jim very badly.) Compare SPACED OUT.

stuck on *slang* Very much in love with; crazy about. *Judy thinks she is very pretty and very smart. She is stuck on herself.* (Judy is very vain. She is proud of her good looks and her intelligence.) *Lucy is stuck on the football captain.* (Lucy is very fond of the football captain.)

stuck-up *adj., informal* Acting as if other people are not as good as you are; conceited; snobbish. *Mary is very stuck-up, and will not speak to the poor children in her class.* (Mary feels that she is better than the poor children, so she will not speak to them.)

study See BROWN STUDY.

stuff See KNOW ONE'S WAY AROUND 2.

stuff and nonsense *n.* Foolish or empty writing or talk; nonsense. *Fred told a long story about his adventures in Africa, but it was all stuff and nonsense.* (Fred's story was nothing but silly lies he invented. He had never been to Africa.) Often used as an interjection. *When Jane said she was too sick to go to school, her mother answered, "Stuff and nonsense! I know there's a test today."* (Jane's mother said, "That's not your real reason; you don't want to go because there's a test.")

stuff the ballot box *v. phr.* To give more votes to a candidate in an election than there are people who actually voted for him. *It is a crime to stuff the ballot box.* (It is a crime to give a candidate extra votes.)—**ballot-stuffing** *adj. phr.*

stump See TAKE THE STUMP *or* TAKE TO THE STUMP, UP A STUMP.

style See CRAMP ONE'S STYLE, HIGH STYLE.

subject to *adj. phr.* **1** Under the government or control of; in the power of. *The English colonies in America were subject to the English king.* (The colonies were ruled by the English king.) *The principal and the teachers of a school are subject to the school board.* (They are under the control of the board.) **2** Likely to get or have; liable. *John is in rather poor health and is subject to colds.* (He often has a cold.) *The western plains are subject to tornadoes.* (The western plains often have tornadoes.) **3** Depending on some change, happening, or need. *The company and the union agreed that the workers' wages should be subject to changes in the cost of living.* (The wages would go up or down as the cost of living changed.) *Agreements made by the President with other countries are subject to the approval of the Senate.* (The Senate can approve or disapprove of the agreements.)

substance See IN SUBSTANCE.

succeed See HOWLING SUCCESS, NOTHING SUCCEEDS LIKE SUCCESS.

such and such *pron.* Something whose name is not mentioned because it does not need to be mentioned. *George's argument tries to prove such and such to be true, but it does not convince me.* (George's argument tries to prove something—it doesn't matter exactly what—but his argument doesn't convince me.)

such-and-such *adj. phr.* Being one whose name has been forgotten or whose name does not need to be mentioned. *She told me to go to such-and-such a street and turn right.* (She told me to go to a street whose name I don't remember and turn right.) *Suppose, now, that we have such-and-such a group coming to the school, and we don't have enough chairs. What do we do then?* (Now suppose we have a group of people, and it doesn't matter just who these people are, and they are coming to the school but we don't have enough chairs. What can we do in this case?)

such as *conj.* **1** Of a kind or amount shown or named; of a kind like. *The explorer took only such men and things as he really needed into the jungle with him.* (The explorer took no more men and things than he needed in the jungle.) *They felt such heat in the jungle as they had never felt before.* (They had hot weather that they never knew about before.) *Many different pies were in the bakery such as apple, cherry, and blueberry pies.* (Pies like those named were in the bakery.) **2** Of the average or ordinary kind; poor; humble. *Such as the food was, there was plenty of it.* (The food was not of the best kind, but at least there was enough of it.) *The room is not very nice, but such as it is, you may stay there for the night.* (You may stay in the room although it isn't really nice.)

such as it is Just as it appears or is presented, not being any better or worse than most others of its kind: being average or mediocre. *This pie, such as it is, is the best I can make.* (I know this pie is not very good. But it is not bad and I can't make a better one.) *Jane told her grandmother her grades, such as they were.* (Jane's grades were not as good as she wished.)

such that *conj.* Of a kind or amount that; so great or so little that; enough that. *There was such a big line at the movie that we had to wait before we could get in.* (The line was so long that we had to wait.) *Jimmy made such noise that his sister told him to be quiet.* (The noise that Jimmy made was so loud that his sister told him to be quiet.) *Mother's answer was such that she didn't say yes and she didn't say no.* (Mother's answer was the kind that didn't say yes or no.)

sucker list *n., slang* A list of easily-fooled people, especially people who are easily persuaded to buy things or give money. *The crook got hold of a sucker list and started out to sell his worthless stock.* (He got a list of easily fooled people.) *Mr. Smith gets so many advertisements in his mail that he says he is on every sucker list in the country.* (Mr. Smith gets so many offers to sell things in the mail that he says people believe he is easily fooled.)

suck in *v.* **1** *informal* To pull in by taking a deep breath and tightening the muscles; flatten. *"Suck in those stomachs," the gym teacher said.* ("Pull in your stomachs by taking a deep breath and tightening the muscles," he told them.) **2** *slang* To make a fool of; cheat. *The uneducated farmer was sucked in by a clever crook.* (The farmer was cheated by a clever crook.)

sugar daddy *n., slang, semi-vulgar, avoidable* An older, well-to-do man, who gives money and gifts to a younger woman or girls usually in exchange for sexual favors. *Betty Morgan got a mink coat from her sugar daddy.* (The older man who keeps her bought her a mink coat.)

suit See BIRTHDAY SUIT, FOLLOW SUIT.

suit to a T See TO A T.

sum total *n.* The final amount; everything taken together; total. *The sum total of expenses for the trip was $450.* (We added together all the expenses for the trip and the total was $450.) *Ten years was the sum total of John's education.* (Ten years was all of his education.)

sum up *v.* To put something into a few words; shorten into a brief summary; summarize. *The teacher summed up the lesson in three rules.* (The teacher gave all of the important material from her lesson again in three rules.) *The mailman's job, in all kinds of weather, is summed up in the phrase "Deliver the mail."* (All of the many different things a mailman has to do are told quickly in the words "Deliver the mail.")

sun See UNDER THE SUN.

sunbelt *n., informal* A portion of the southern United States where the winter is very mild in comparison to other states. *The Simpsons left Chicago for the sunbelt because of Jeff's rheumatism.* (They left the harsh climate of Chicago for the warmer places.)

Sunday See MONTH OF SUNDAYS.

Sunday best *or* **Sunday-go-to-meeting clothes** See BEST BIB AND TUCKER.

sunny-side up *adj.* Fried on one side only. *Barbara likes her eggs sunny-side up.* (She likes them fried on one side only, so that the yolk is not flattened by being turned over.)

supper See COVERED-DISH SUPPER *or* POTLUCK SUPPER.

supply See IN SHORT SUPPLY.

sure See FOR SURE, MAKE SURE, TO BE SURE.

sure enough *adv.* As expected. *Charles was afraid he had done badly on the test, and sure enough, his grade was failing.* (As Charles expected, he failed the test.) *The children saw a familiar shape coming up the street and* hoped it was their lost dog. When it came near, sure enough, it was Spot. (Spot had come home, just as they had hoped he would.) Compare SURE THING 2.

sure-enough *adj.* Real; genuine. *Rick found a sure-enough nickel.* (It was a real nickel, not a piece of iron or lead.) *Martha's uncle gave her a sure-enough pearl on a little gold chain.* (He gave her a genuine pearl.) *Jane's uncle is a sure-enough cowboy.* (He is a real cowboy.)

sure thing 1 *n., informal* Something sure to happen; something about which there is no doubt. *It's no fun betting on a sure thing.* (It's no fun to bet on something about which there is no doubt.)—**sure thing 2** *adv.* Of course; certainly. *Sure thing, I'll be glad to do it for you.* (Of course, I'll be glad to do it for you.) Compare FOR SURE 2, SURE ENOUGH.

surface See SCRATCH THE SURFACE.

surprise See TAKE BY SURPRISE.

survival of the fittest *n. phr.* The staying alive or in action of the best prepared; often: idea that those living things best able to adjust to life survive and those unable to adjust die out. *Life in the old West was often a case of survival of the fittest.* (It was a life suitable only for the strongest and best prepared.) *With changes in the world's climate, dinosaurs died but many smaller animals lived on. It was survival of the fittest.* (When the climate changed, dinosaurs died but many smaller animals lived on because they were smarter and could change their habits to agree with other changes.) *On the 50-mile hike it was survival of the fittest; only 12 out of 25 Scouts finished.* (Only the 12 stronger and more careful Scouts finished; the others had to give up.)

suspicion See ABOVE SUSPICION.

swallow See LOOK LIKE THE CAT THAT ATE THE CANARY.

swallow hook, line, and sinker See HOOK, LINE, AND SINKER.

swallow one's pride *v. phr.* To bring your pride under control; humble yourself.—A cliché. *After Bill lost the race, he swallowed his pride and shook hands with the winner.* (After Bill lost the race he brought his pride under control and shook hands with the winner.) Compare EAT ONE'S WORDS.

swallow one's words 1 To speak unclearly; fail to put enough breath into your words. *Phyllis was hard to understand because she swallowed her words.* (She was hard to understand because she didn't speak clearly.) **2** See EAT ONE'S WORDS.

swat team *n., informal* Police unit trained for especially hazardous or sensitive law-enforcement assignments; short for Special Weapons and Tactics. *Joe made the SWAT team of the NYPD due to his athletic skills.* (He was chosen to serve in the team using special weapons and tactics.)

swathe See CUT A SWATHE.

swear by *v.* **1** To use as the support or authority that what you are saying is truthful; take an oath upon. *A witness swears by the Bible that he will tell the truth.* (A witness promises to tell the truth with his hand on the Bible.) *In ancient Greece a doctor swore by Apollo, the god of healing, that he would be a good doctor.* (A doctor said that Apollo could punish him if he were not a good doctor.) *John swore by his honor he would return the bike.* (If John did not return the bike, then he would lose his honor. John would not expect anyone to trust him after that.) **2** To have complete confidence in; be sure of; trust completely. *When John has to go somewhere fast, he swears by his bike to get there.* (John knows that his bike will get him where he has to go.) *We can be sure that Fred will come on time, since his friend Tom swears by him.* (We can be sure that Fred will come, since Tom tells us he is sure Fred will come.)

swear in *or* **swear into** *v.* To have a person swear or promise to do his duty as a member or an officer of an organization, government department, or similar group.—*Swear into is* used when the name of the group is given. *Mary and Ann will be sworn into the club tonight.* (They will promise to be faithful members.) *Fred was sworn in as class president.* (He promised to do his duty as class president.) *Many new men were sworn into the army last month.* (They promised to do their duty as soldiers.) *At the inauguration, the Chief Justice of the Supreme Court swore in the new President.* (The Chief Justice asked the new President if he would faithfully do his duty.)

swear off *v., informal* To give up something you like or you have got in the habit of using by making a promise. *Mary swore off candy until she lost ten pounds.* (Mary promised herself she would not eat candy until she lost ten pounds.) *John has sworn off dessert for Lent.* (John promised not to eat dessert during Lent.)

swear out *v.* To get (a written order to do something) by swearing that a person has broken the law. *The policeman swore out a warrant for the suspect's arrest.* (The policeman swore that, as far as he knew, the suspect had committed the crime; so that the judge would give him a legal order to arrest the suspect.) *The detectives swore out a search warrant.* (The detectives got a legal order to search a house by swearing that in the house there was evidence of a crime.)

sweat See BY THE SWEAT OF ONE'S BROW.

sweat blood *v. phr., slang* **1** To be very much worried. *The engine of the airplane stopped, and the pilot sweated blood as he glided to a safe landing.* (The pilot was badly worried until he landed the plane.) **2** To work very hard. *Jim sweated blood to finish his* *composition on time.* (Jim worked very hard to finish his composition on time.)

sweat out *v., informal* To wait anxiously; worry while waiting. *Karl was sweating out the results of the college exams.* (He was waiting anxiously to hear how well he did on them.) *The search plane signalled that help was on the way. The men in the lifeboat just had to sweat it out.* (They had to worry while waiting for the rescue ship to come.)

Sweeney See TELL IT TO THE MARINES *or* TELL IT TO SWEENEY.

sweep See NEW BROOM SWEEPS CLEAN.

sweep off one's feet *v. phr.* To make (someone) have feelings (as love or happiness) too strong to control; overcome with strong feeling; win sudden and complete acceptance by (someone) through the feelings.—A cliché. *The handsome football captain swept Joan off her feet when he said so many things to her at the dance.* (The football captain quickly won her love.) *Joan was swept off her feet when the football captain started flirting with her.* (Joan almost fell in love with the football captain when he started to flirt with her.) *Mary is swept off her feet whenever she hears a band start playing.* (Mary feels great pleasure when a band starts playing.) *John was swept off his feet when he won the contest.* (John felt very proud when he won.) Compare BOWL OVER 2, CARRY AWAY.

sweep under the rug *v. phr.* To hide or dismiss casually (something one is ashamed of or does not know what to do about). *In many places, drug abuse by school children is swept under the rug.* (People refuse to admit that their students abuse drugs.)

sweet See SHORT AND SWEET.

sweetie pie *n., informal* A person who is loved; darling; sweetheart. *Arnold blushed with pleasure when Annie called him her sweetie pie.* (He blushed when she called him her darling.) *Nancy is Bill's sweetie pie.* (She is his sweetheart.)

sweet on *adj. phr., informal* In love with; very fond of. *John is sweet on Alice.* (John is in love with Alice.)

sweet talk 1 *n., informal* Too much praise; flattery. *Sometimes a girl's better judgment is overcome by sweet talk.* (Her better judgment is overcome by flattery.) **2** *v., informal* To get what you want by great praise; flatter. *Polly could sweet talk her father into any-*

thing. (She could get him to do anything she wanted to by flattering him.)

swelled head *n., informal* A feeling that you are very important or more important than you really are. *When John won the race, he got a swelled head.* (When John won the race, he became very conceited.) *Pretty girls shouldn't get a swelled head about it.* (Pretty girls shouldn't feel too proud of their prettiness.)—**swell-headed** *adj. phr.* *After he was elected captain of the team, Bob became swell-headed.* (Bob acted as if he were more important than he really was.) Compare BIG HEAD.

swell-headed See SWELLED HEAD.

swim See IN THE SWIM, SINK OR SWIM.

swim against the current *or* **swim against the stream** *v. phr.* To do the opposite of what most people want to do; go against the way things are happening; struggle upstream. *The boy who tries to succeed today without an education is swimming against the stream.* (Today you need an education for most jobs, and without education you will have a hard struggle.)

swine See CAST PEARLS BEFORE SWINE *or* CAST ONE'S PEARLS BEFORE SWINE.

swing See IN FULL SWING.

swing one's weight *v. phr.* To use your personal power to get something done. *The President swings his weight to get laws passed.* (He uses his personal power to get laws passed.) *Mr. Thomas swung his weight to get his son a job with the company.* (He used his personal power to get his son a job with the company.)

switch See ASLEEP AT THE SWITCH.

switched on *adj., slang* **1** In tune with the latest fads, ideas, and fashions. *I dig Sarah, she is really switched on.* (I like her because she knows the current fads and fashions.) **2** Stimulated; as if under the influence of alcohol or drugs. *How come you're talking so fast? Are you switched on or something?* (Why do you speak so rapidly? Are you under the influence of alcohol or some drug?)

swoop See AT ONE FELL SWOOP.

sword See AT SWORDS' POINTS, PUT TO THE SWORD.

sword rattling See SABRE RATTLING.

syllable See WORDS OF ONE SYLLABLE.

system See PUBLIC-ADDRESS SYSTEM.

T

T See TO A T.

tab See KEEP TAB ON *or* KEEP TABS ON.

table See AT THE TABLE *or* AT TABLE, COFFEE TABLE, PUT ONE'S CARDS ON THE TABLE *at* LAY ONE'S CARDS ON THE TABLE, TURN THE TABLES, WAIT AT TABLE *or* WAIT ON TABLE.

tack See GET DOWN TO BRASS TACKS, GO SIT ON A TACK, SHARP AS A TACK.

tackle See FLYING TACKLE.

tag end *or* **tail end** *n., informal* The end, farthest to the rear, last in line, nearest the bottom, or least important. *John was at the tail end of his class.* (John made the lowest grades in his class.) *Mary's part in the play came at the tag end, and she got bored waiting.* (Mary got tired waiting until near the end of the play to do her part.) *Bill waited at the crossing for the tag end of a freight to go by.* (Bill waited for the last cars of a freight train to go by.)

tail See COW'S TAIL, HEADS I WIN, TAILS YOU LOSE, MAKE HEAD OR TAIL OF, TURN TAIL.

tail between one's legs *n. phr.* State of feeling beaten, ashamed, or very obedient, as after a scolding or a whipping.—A cliché. *The army sent the enemy home with their tails between their legs.* (The army beat the enemy very badly and they went home ashamed.) *The boys on the team had boasted they would win the tournament, but they went home with their tails between their legs.* (They lost the tournament and were disappointed and ashamed.) [So called because a beaten dog usually puts his tail down between his legs and slinks away.]

tail end See TAG END.

tailor-made See MADE-TO-MEASURE.

tailspin See GO INTO A TAILSPIN.

take See CAN TAKE IT WITH ONE, GIVE-AND-TAKE, GIVE ONE AN INCH AND HE WILL TAKE A MILE, GIVE OR TAKE, SIT UP AND TAKE NOTICE.

take aback See TAKEN ABACK.

take a back seat *v. phr., informal* To accept a poorer or lower position; be second to something or someone else. *During the war all manufacturing had to take a back seat to military needs.* (During the war all manufacturing was secondary in importance to filling army needs.) *She does not have to take a back seat to any singer alive.* (No other singer is any better than she.) Compare PLAY SECOND FIDDLE.

take a bath *v. phr., informal* To come to financial ruin. *Boy, did we ever take a bath on that merger with Brown & Brown, Inc.* (Speaker says that the merger with the firm named caused them financial ruin.)

take a bow *v. phr.* To stand up or come on a stage to be clapped for or praised for success. *The audience shouted for the author of the play to take a bow.* (The crowd called to the author of the play to stand up and be praised with handclapping.) *The basketball team should take a bow for fine work this season.* (The players on the basketball team should stand up and let people clap for them.)

take a chance *v. phr.* To accept the risk of failure or loss (as in planning or starting something.) *We will take a chance on the weather and have the party outdoors.* (We will have the party outdoors though rain may possibly spoil it.)

take a dim view of *v. phr.* **1** To have doubts about; feel unsure or anxious about.—A cliché. *Tom took a dim view of his chances of passing the exam.* (Tom was afraid he would not pass the exam.) *Betty hoped to go on a picnic, but she took a dim view of the weather.* (Betty thought it might rain; then she would not be able to go on the picnic.) **2** To be against; disapprove. *John's father took a dim view of his wanting to borrow the car.* (John's father didn't want him to use the car.) *The teacher took a dim view of the class's behavior.* (The teacher didn't like the class's behavior.)

take advantage of *v. phr.* **1** To make good use of. *The cat took advantage of the high grass to creep up on the bird.* (The cat made use of the high grass to hide while she crept up on the bird.) *Jean took advantage of the lunch hour to finish her homework.* (She made use of the time.) **2** To treat (someone) unfairly for your own gain or help; make unfair use of. *He took advantage of his friend's kindness.* (He took more help from his friend than he should have because his friend was very kind.) *The little children did not know how much to pay for the candy, and Ralph took advantage of them.* (He made them pay more than was right.) Syn. IMPOSE ON.

take after *v.* To be like because of family relationship; to have the same looks or ways as (a parent or ancestor). *He takes after his father in mathematical ability.* (He is like his father in mathematical skill.) *She takes after her father's side of the family in looks.* (She looks like her father's people.) Compare LIKE FATHER, LIKE SON; RUN IN THE FAMILY.

take aim *v. phr.* To get ready to hit, throw at, or shoot at by sighting carefully. *When the captain orders "Take aim," raise your gun to your shoulder and sight along the barrel at the target.* (Be ready to shoot when the captain orders "Take aim.") *Before the hunter could take aim, the deer jumped out of sight* (The deer disappeared before the hunter could get ready to shoot.)

take a long breath See DRAW A LONG BREATH.

take a notion See TAKE INTO ONE'S HEAD.

take a poke at See TAKE A PUNCH AT *or* TAKE A POKE AT.

take a powder *v. phr., slang* To leave hurriedly; run out or away; desert, flee. *All the gang except one had taken a powder when* *the cops arrived.* (All the boys had run away except one when the police came.)

take a punch at *or* **take a poke at** *or* **take a sock at** *v. phr.* To try to hit (someone) with the fist; swing or strike at; attack with the fists. *Bob was very angry and suddenly he took a punch at Fred.* (Bob was so angry that he tried to hit Fred.) *Johnny knocked my hat off, so I took a poke at him.* (Johnny made me angry and I swung at him with my fist.) *I felt like taking a sock at Joe, but I kept my temper.* (I felt angry enough to hit him, but I didn't.)

take a risk See RUN A RISK.

take a shine to *v. phr., slang* To have or show a quick liking for.—A trite expression. *He took a shine to his new teacher the very first day.* (He liked his teacher the very first day.) Compare TAKE A FANCY TO.

take a sock at See TAKE A PUNCH AT *or* TAKE A SOCK AT.

take at one's word *v. phr.* To believe everything (someone) says; to act on what is said. *If you say you don't want this coat, I'll take you at your word and throw it away.* (I will believe you, and will throw it away.) *When the king said he wished to be rid of his advisor, a friend took him at his word and murdered the councillor.* (A friend fully believed him and murdered the advisor.)

take a turn *v. phr.* To become different; change. *Mary's fever suddenly took a bad turn.* (Mary's fever became very high.) *The story took an odd turn.* (The story changed in an unexpected way.)—Often used with *for the better* or *for the worse. In the afternoon the weather took a turn for the better.* (The weather improved in the afternoon.) *Suddenly the battle took a turn for the worse.* (They were winning the battle until suddenly they began to lose to the enemy.)

take a turn for the worse See FOR THE WORSE.

take back *v.* To change or deny something offered, promised, or stated; admit to making a wrong statement. *I take back my offer to buy the house now that I've had a good look at it.* (I will change my offer and refuse to buy the house.) *I want you to take back the unkind things you said about Kenneth.* (I want you to say you were wrong, or don't mean now the unkind things you said about Kenneth.)

take by storm *v. phr.* 1 To capture by a sudden or very bold attack.—A cliché. *The army did not hesitate. They took the town by storm.* (They marched right in and captured it.) 2 To win the favor or liking of; make (a group of people) like or believe you.—A cliché. *The comic took the audience by storm.* (He made everyone laugh and like him.) *John gave Jane so much attention that he took her by storm, and she said she would marry him.* (He made her love him by doing many nice things for her.) Compare MAKE A HIT.

take by surprise *v. phr.* 1 To appear in front of someone suddenly or to suddenly discover him before he discovers you; come before (someone) is ready; appear before (someone) unexpectedly. *The policeman took the burglar by surprise as he opened the window.* (The policeman caught the burglar breaking in through the window.) *When Mrs. Green's dinner guests came half an hour early, they took her by surprise.* (She did not expect them early, and was not ready.) 2 To fill with surprise or amazement; astonish. *Ellen was taken by surprise when the birthday cake was brought in.* (Ellen was surprised by the birthday cake.) *When our teacher quit in the middle of the year to work for the government, it took us all by surprise.* (We were surprised because we did not expect him to do that.)

take care *v. phr.* To be careful; use wisdom or caution. *Take care that you don't spill that coffee!* (Try not to spill that coffee.) *We must take care to let nobody hear about this.* (We must be careful not to let anybody hear about this.)

take care of *v. phr.* 1 To attend to; supply the needs of. *She stayed home to take care of the baby.* (She stayed home to keep the baby safe, clean, warm, and fed.) Syn. KEEP AN EYE ON 2, LOOK AFTER. Compare IN CHARGE 2. 2 *informal* To deal with; do what is needed with. *I will take care of that letter.* (I will write an answer to that letter and mail the answer.) *The coach told Jim to take care of the opposing player.* (He told Jim to keep the opposing player away from the ball carrier.) Compare SEE TO.

take charge *v. phr.* To begin to lead or control; take control or responsibility; undertake the care or management (of persons or things). *When Mrs. Jackson was in the hospital, her sister took charge of the Jackson children until Mrs. Jackson could care for them.* (The aunt cared for the children till Mrs. Jackson was well again.) *The child care class gave a party for the nursery children, and Mary took charge of the games.* (Mary led the games.) *John was elected the new president of the club and took charge at the next meeting.* (John took control as leader of the club at the next meeting.) *Bob is a natural leader, and can take charge in an emergency.* (Bob knows how to tell people what to do when an accident happens.) Compare IN CHARGE 2.

take cold See CATCH COLD.

take down *v.* 1 To write or record (what is said). *I will tell you how to get to the place; you had better take it down.* (I will give you directions to reach the place; you should write them now.) 2 To pull to pieces; take apart. *It will be a big job to take that tree down.* (It will take much time and work to cut and pull the tree down.) *In the evening the campers* put up a tent, and the next morning they took it down. (The next morning they took it apart and folded it up again.) **3** *informal* To reduce the pride or spirit of; humble. *Bob thought he was a good wrestler, but Henry took him down.* (Bob was proud of his wrestling but Henry humbled him by beating him.) Syn. TAKE DOWN A NOTCH.

take down a notch *or* **take down a peg** *v. phr., informal* To make (someone) less proud or sure of himself.—A cliché. *The team was feeling proud of its record, but last week the boys were taken down a peg by a bad defeat.* (Losing the game last week made the boys feel less proud.)

take effect *v. phr.* **1** To have an unexpected or intended result; cause a change. *It was nearly an hour before the sleeping pill took effect.* (It was nearly an hour before the sleeping pill caused the sick person to go to sleep.) **2** To become lawfully right, or operative. *The new tax law will not take effect until January.* (The new law will not be enforced until January 1.)

take exception to *v. phr.* To speak against; find fault with; be displeased or angered by; criticize. *There was nothing in the speech that you could take exception to.* (There was nothing in the speech for you to criticize or oppose.) *Did she take exception to my remarks about her cooking?* (Was she hurt and angry because I said her cooking was not good?)

take for *v.* To suppose to be; mistake for. *Do you take me for a fool?* (Do you suppose I am a fool?) *At first sight you would take him for a football player, not a poet.* (At first sight you would mistakenly think he was a football player, not a poet.)

take for a ride *v. phr., slang* **1** To take out in a car intending to murder.—A cliché. *The gang leader decided that the informer must be taken for a ride.* (The gang leader decided to have the man killed who told the police.) **2** To play a trick on; fool. *The girls told Linda that a movie star was visiting the school, but she did not believe them; she thought they were taking her for a ride.* (She thought they were trying to fool her.) Compare STRING ALONG. **3** To take unfair advantage of; fool for your own gain. *His girl friend really took him for a ride before he stopped dating her.* (She was interested in him only for the entertainment and gifts he gave her.)

take for granted *v. phr.* **1** To suppose or understand to be true. *Mr. Harper took for granted that the invitation included his wife.* (He supposed that the invitation was for both him and his wife.) *A teacher cannot take it for granted that students always do their homework.* (A teacher cannot suppose that students always do their homework.) Compare BEG THE QUESTION. **2** To accept or become used to (something) without noticing

especially or saying anything. *George took for granted all that his parents did for him.* (George accepted their help and care without really noticing it or thanking them.) *No girl likes to have her boy friend take her for granted; instead, he should always try to make her like him better.* (No girl wants her boy friend to suppose that he is the only boy she could be interested in.)

take heart *v. phr.* To be encouraged; feel braver and want to try. *The men took heart from their leader's words and went on to win the battle.* (They felt braver and won the battle.) *When we are in trouble we can take heart from the fact that things often seem worse than they are.* (We will feel better if we remember that things often look bad but are not very.) Contrast LOSE HEART.

take heed *v. phr., literary* To pay attention; watch or listen carefully; notice. *Take heed not to spill coffee on the rug.* (Be careful not to spill coffee on the rug.)

take ill *or* **take sick** *v.* To become sick. *Father took sick just before his birthday.* (He became sick just before his birthday.)—Used in the passive with the same meaning. *The man was taken ill on the train.* (The man became sick on the train.)

take in *v.* **1** To include. *The country's boundaries were changed to take in a piece of land beyond the river.* (The lines of the country were changed to include some land across the river.) *The class of mammals takes in nearly all warm-blooded animals except the birds.* (The class of mammals includes most animals but not birds.) **2** To go and see; visit. *The students decided to take in a movie while they were in town.* (They decided to go to see a movie while they were in town.) *We planned to take in Niagara Falls and Yellowstone Park on our trip.* (We planned to see Niagara Falls and Yellowstone Park on our trip.) **3** To make smaller. *This waist band is too big; it must be taken in about an inch.* (The waist must be made smaller.) *They had to take in some sail to keep the ship from turning over in the storm.* (They had to take down some of the sail to keep the boat from turning over.) **4** To grasp with the mind; understand. *He didn't take in what he read because his mind was on something else.* (He didn't understand what he read because he was thinking of something else.) *He took in the situation at a glance.* (He understood what was going on the minute he saw it.) **5a** To deceive; cheat; fool. *The teacher was taken in by the boy's innocent manner.* (The teacher was fooled by the boy's acting as if he had done nothing.) Compare PUT OVER, ROPE IN. **5b** To accept without question; believe. *The magician did many tricks, and the children took it all in.* (They believed that the magician really made things disappear.) **6a** To receive; get. *The senior class held a* dance to make money and took in over a hundred dollars. (The class earned more than a hundred dollars.) **6b** Let come in; admit; *The farmer took in the lost travelers for the night.* (He let the lost travelers stay in his house for the night.) *When her husband died, Mrs. Smith took in boarders.* (She let people eat meals in her house to make money.) **7** To see or hear with interest; pay close attention to. *When Bill told about his adventures, the other boys took it all in.* (They listened with great interest.)

take in stride *v. phr.* To meet happenings without too much surprise; accept good or bad luck and go on. *He learned to take disappointments in stride.* (He learned to meet disappointments without being greatly upset or discouraged by them.)

take into account *v. phr.* To remember and understand while judging someone or something; consider. *How much time will we need to get to the lake? You have to take the bad road into account.* (You must remember that the road to the lake is bad, and you must drive slowly.) *His acting in the play was remarkable, taking into account his youth and inexperience.* (His acting was wonderful, remembering his youth and inexperience.) Syn. RECKON WITH. Contrast LEAVE OUT OF ACCOUNT.

take issue with *v. phr.* To be openly against; speak against; disagree with. *He thought his boss was wrong but was afraid to take issue with him on the matter.* (He thought the boss was wrong but was afraid to disagree with him.)

take it *v. phr.* **1** To get an idea or impression; understand from what is said or done.—Usually used with *I. I take it from your silence that you don't want to go.* (Your silence makes me think you don't want to go.) **2** *informal* To bear trouble, hard work, criticism; not give up or weaken. *Henry could criticize and tease other boys, but he couldn't take it himself.* (Henry teased other boys, but could not accept teasing himself.) *Bob lost his job and his girl in the same week, and we all admired the way he took it.* (We all admired Bob's ability to bear trouble.)

take it easy *v. phr., informal* **1** *or* **go easy** *or* **take things easy** To go or act slowly, carefully, and gently.—Often used with *on. Take it easy. The roads are icy.* (Drive slowly and carefully.) *"Go easy," said Billy to the other boys carrying the table down the stairs.* (Go carefully down the stairs and don't fall.) *"Take it easy on John and don't scold him too much," said Mrs. Jones to Mr. Jones.* (Don't be too strict with John.) *Go easy on the cake. There isn't much left.* (Don't eat all of the cake too quickly.) **2** *or* **take things easy** To avoid hard work or worry; have an easy time; live in comfort. *The doctor said that Bob would have to take things easy for*

awhile after he had his tonsils out. He would have to rest and not work or play.) *Barbara likes to take it easy.* (She doesn't like to work hard and is lazy.) *Grandfather will retire from his job next year and take things easy.* (He will not work any more.) *Mr. Wilson has just made a lot of money and can take things easy now.* (He won't have to work hard any more because he has enough money.)

take it into one's head *or informal* **take a notion** *v. phr.* To get a sudden idea; decide without thinking. *The boy suddenly took it into his head to leave school and get a job.* (The boy suddenly decided, without much thinking, to leave school and get a job.) *Grandmother keeps a bag packed so that she can go visiting whenever she takes a notion.* (She can leave for a visit when she gets the idea to go.)

take it on the chin *v. phr., informal* **1** To be badly beaten or hurt. *Our football team really took it on the chin today. They are all bumps and bruises.* (They are all sore from the beating they got on the football field.) *Mother and I took it on the chin in the card game.* (We lost the card game by a very great amount.) **2** To accept without complaint something bad that happens to you; accept trouble or defeat calmly. *A good football player can take it on the chin when his team loses.* (A good player will not be discouraged or upset or angry when his team loses.)

take it or leave it *v. phr., informal* To accept something without change or refuse it; decide yes or no.—Often used like a command. *He said the price of the house was $10,000, take it or leave it.* (He would not change anything; he would not sell for less than $10,000.)

take it out on *v. phr., informal* To be unpleasant or unkind to (someone) because you are angry or upset; get rid of upset feelings by being mean to.—Often used with the name of the feeling instead of "it." *The teacher was angry and took it out on the class.* (He was angry but didn't know whom to blame, so he punished the whole class.) *Bob was angry because Father would not let him use the car, and he took it out on his little brother.* (He was cross and spoke roughly to his brother.)

take its toll *v. phr.* To cause loss or damage. *The bombs had taken their toll on the little town.* (The bombs had ruined much of the little town.) *The budget cut took its toll of teachers.* (The cut in funds caused some teachers to be discharged.)

take kindly to *v.* To be pleased by; like. —Usually used in negative, interrogative, and conditional sentences. *He doesn't take kindly to any suggestions about running his business.* (He doesn't like to be advised about managing his business.) *Will your father take* *kindly to the idea of your leaving college?* (Will your father like the idea of your leaving college?)

take leave of *v. phr.* **1** To abandon, go away from, or become separated from.—Usually used in the phrase *take leave of one's senses. Come down from the roof, Billy! Have you taken leave of your senses?* (Come down or you'll fall. Have you become crazy?) **2** See TAKE ONE'S LEAVE.

take liberties *v. phr.* To act toward in too close or friendly a manner; use as you would use a close friend or something of your own. *Mary would not let any boy take liberties with her.* (Mary would not let any boy become too friendly with her.) *Bill took liberties with Tom's bicycle.* (Bill took Tom's bicycle without asking.) Compare MAKE FREE WITH.

taken aback *also* **taken back** *adj.* Unpleasantly surprised; suddenly puzzled or shocked. *When he came to pay for his dinner he was taken aback to find that he had left his wallet at home.* (He was confused and embarrassed.)

take no stock in See TAKE STOCK IN.

take note of *or* **take notice of** *v. phr.* **1** To look carefully at; pay close attention to; observe well. *A detective is trained to take note of people and things.* (A detective has learned to look carefully at and remember people and things.) **2** To notice and act in response; pay attention. *Two boys were talking together in the back of the room but the teacher took no notice of them.* (The teacher did not do anything to show that he heard or saw them.) *The principal thanked everyone who helped in the program, and took note of the decorations made by the art class.* (In his thank-you speech, the principal said something about the decorations made by the art class.)

take oath *v. phr.* To promise to tell the truth or to do some task honestly, calling on God or some person or thing as a witness. *Mary took her oath that she did not steal the watch.* (Mary swore that she did not steal the watch.) *John took oath that he would fill the office of president faithfully.* (John promised that he would be a faithful president by appealing to God.)

take off *v.* **1a** To leave fast; depart suddenly; run away. *The dog took off after a rabbit.* (The dog ran after a rabbit.) Compare LIGHT OUT. **1b** *informal* To go away; leave. *The six boys got into the car and took off for the drug store.* (They left to go to the drug store.) **2** To leave on a flight, begin going up. *A helicopter is able to take off and land straight up or down.* (A helicopter can go straight up and come straight down.) **3** *informal* To imitate amusingly; copy another person's habitual actions or speech. *He made a career of taking off famous people for night club audiences.* (He made a living by copying famous people for night club crowds.) *At the*

party, *Charlie took off the principal and some of the teachers.* (He imitated them.) **4** To take (time) to be absent from work. *When his wife was sick he took off from work.* (When his wife was sick, he did not go to his job.) *Bill was tired out so he took the day off.* (He was very tired and didn't go to work that day.)

take off one's hat to *v. phr.* To give honor, praise, and respect to.—A cliché. *He is my enemy, but I take off my hat to him for his courage.* (I honor and respect his bravery.) Compare HAND IT TO.

take off the edge See TAKE THE EDGE OFF.

take on *v.* **1** To receive for carrying; be loaded with. *A big ship was at the dock taking on automobiles in crates to carry overseas for sale.* (A ship was being loaded with automobiles.) *The bus driver stopped at the curb to take the woman on.* (The bus stopped to let the woman get into the bus.) **2** To begin to have (the look of); take (the appearance of). *Others joined the fist fight until it took on the look of a riot.* (Others got into the fight and it began to look like a riot.) *After the students put up Christmas decorations, the classroom took on a holiday appearance.* (The room began to look pretty for the Christmas season.) **3a** To give a job to; hire, employ. *The factory has opened and is beginning to take on new workers.* (The factory is open and is beginning to hire new workers.) Contrast LET GO 4, LET OFF, LET OUT 6. **3b** To accept in business or a contest. *The big man took on two opponents at once.* (He fought with two men at one time.) *After his father died, Bill took on the management of the factory.* (After his father died, Bill became the manager of the factory.) *We knew their football team was bigger and stronger, but we took them on anyway and beat them.* (We agreed to play them even though they were bigger.) **4** *informal* To show great excitement, grief, or anger. *At the news of her husband's death she took on like a madwoman.* (At the news of her husband's death she began to scream and cry as if she were crazy.) Compare CARRY-ON.

take one's breath away *v. phr.* To surprise greatly; impress very much; leave speechless with surprise or wonder or delight; astonish.—A cliché. *The sunset is so beautiful it takes our breath away.* (The beautiful sight impresses us and makes us quiet.) *His refusal was so unexpected it took my breath away.* (I was very much surprised when he refused, and I could not say anything.) Compare CATCH ONE'S BREATH 1.

take one's death of See CATCH ONE'S DEATH OF.

take one's leave *or* **take leave of** *v. phr., formal* To say good-bye and leave. *He stayed on after most of the guests had taken their leave.* (He stayed after most of the guests had said good-bye and had gone.) *The messenger bowed and took leave of the queen.* (The messenger bowed and went away from the queen.)—**leave-taking** *n.* *The end of school in June is a time of leave-taking.* (In June school ends, and the students say good-bye to each other and leave.)

take one's life in one's hands *v. phr.* To face great danger or take great risk. *Driving that car with those worn tires would be taking your life in your hands.* (It would be putting your life in danger.) *He took his life in his hands when he tried to capture the wild horse.* (He risked his life to capture the horse.)

take one's measure *or* **take the measure of** *v. phr.* To judge the character, quality, or nature of; try to guess about something—how hard or easy, dangerous or safe, good or bad, etc. *The boxers sparred for a while taking each other's measure.* (Each boxer fought carefully to find out how good a boxer the other was.) *John took the measure of the cliff before he climbed it.* (John guessed how hard the climb would be before he started to climb the cliff.) Compare SIZE UP.

take one's medicine *v. phr.* To accept punishment without complaining. *The boy said he was sorry he broke the window and was ready to take his medicine.* (He was ready to accept punishment without complaining or excusing himself.) Compare FACE THE MUSIC 2.

take one's name in vain *v. phr.* **1** To call upon (God) as a witness to your truth or honesty when you are lying; swear by (God) untruthfully. *You shall not take the name of the Lord your God in vain.* (Do not swear by God unless you are telling the truth and the situation is very solemn.) **2** *informal* To talk about a person or mention his name. *"Did I hear someone taking my name in vain?" asked Bill as he joined his friends.* (Did I hear someone mention my name?)

take one's time *v. phr.* To avoid haste; act in an unhurried way. *He liked to take his time over breakfast.* (He liked to eat breakfast without hurrying.) *It is better to take your time at this job than to hurry and make mistakes.* (It is better to work slowly and carefully at this job.)

take on oneself *or* **take upon oneself** *v. phr.* **1** To accept as a duty or responsibility. *He took it on himself to see that the packages were delivered.* (He promised to make sure they were delivered.) **2** To assume wrongfully or without permission as a right or privilege. *You should not have taken it upon yourself to accept the invitation for the whole family.* (It was not right for you to do it.)

take out *v. phr.* **1** To ask for and fill in. *Mary and John took out a marriage license.* (Mary and John filled out a paper at the town hall which will let them get married.) **2** To

begin to run. *When the window broke, the boys took out in all directions.* (They ran away in different directions.) *When the wind blew the man's hat off, Charlie took out after it.* (Charlie ran after the man's hat.) See TAKE IT OUT ON.

take over *v.* **1a** To take control or possession of. *He expects to take over the business when his father retires.* (He expects to own and run the business.) **1b** To take charge or responsibility. *The airplane pilot fainted and his co-pilot had to take over.* (His copilot had to become the pilot and commander of the airplane.) **2** To borrow, imitate, or adopt. *The Japanese have taken over many European ways of life.* (The Japanese have begun to do things the way Europeans do them.)

take pains *v. phr.* To do something very carefully and thoroughly. *She had taken pains to see that her guests had everything that they could possibly want.* (She had been careful and thorough in preparing for her guests.) *She always takes pains with her appearance.* (She always dresses neatly and looks nice.)

take part *v. phr.* To have a part or share; join. *Jim saw the new boy watching the game and asked him to take part.* (He asked the new boy to become a player in the game.) *The Swiss did not take part in the two World Wars.* (The Swiss did not fight or declare war.)

take pity on *also* **take pity upon** *v. phr.* To feel sympathy or pity and do something for. *Mary took pity on the orphan kittens.* (Mary felt sorry for the kittens and gave them a home.) *The farmer took pity upon the campers, and let them stay in his barn during the rain.* (The farmer did not want the boys to get wet.)

take place *v. phr.* To happen; occur. *The accident took place only a block from his home.* (The accident happened only a block from his home.) *The action of the play takes place in ancient Rome.* (The action occurs in ancient Rome.) *The dance will take place after the graduation exercises.* (The dance will follow the graduation exercises.) Compare GO ON 3.

take pot luck *v. phr.* To share as a guest an everyday meal without special preparation. *You are welcome to stay to dinner if you will take potluck.* (You are welcome to stay to dinner if you are willing to share whatever we happen to have.) *They were about to have lunch when he phoned, and they asked him to take potluck with them.* (They invited him to lunch without any special or extra food.)

take root *v. phr.* **1** To form roots so as to be able to live and grow. *We hope the transplanted apple trees will take root.* (We hope they will live and grow.) **2** To be accepted; to be adopted; to live and succeed in a new place. *Many European customs failed to take* *root in the New World.* (Many European customs were not accepted in the New World.) *The immigrants to our country took root and began to think of themselves as native Americans.* (The immigrants were accepted as Americans and forgot their old ways.)

take shape *v. phr.* To grow or develop into a certain fixed form. *Plans for our vacation are beginning to take shape.* (They are becoming exact and certain.) *Their new home took shape as the weeks went by.* (As the men worked on it, it became more and more what they wanted.) Compare SHAPE UP.

take sick See TAKE ILL.

take sides *v. phr.* To join one group against another in a debate or quarrel. *Switzerland refused to take sides in the two World Wars.* (Switzerland stayed out of the wars.) *Tom wanted to go fishing. Dick wanted to take a hike. Bob took sides with Tom, so they all went fishing.* (Bob agreed with Tom that they should go fishing.) Compare LINE UP 4b. Contrast ON THE FENCE.

take someone for a ride *v. phr., informal* **1** To cheat or swindle someone. *Poor Joe Catwallender was taken for a ride.* (He was cheated and swindled.) **2** To kill someone after kidnapping. *The criminals took the man for a ride.* (They kidnapped him and then killed him.)

take steps *v. phr.* To begin to make plans or arrangements; make preparations; give orders.—Usually used with *to* and an infinitive. *The city is taking steps to replace its street cars with busses.* (The city is making arrangements to change street cars for busses.)

take stock *v. phr.* **1** To count exactly the items of merchandise or supplies in stock; take inventory. *The grocery store took stock every week on Monday mornings.* (They counted up all the things they had in the store.) **2** To study carefully a situation, or a number of possibilities or opportunities. *During the battle the commander paused to take stock of the situation.* (He stopped to consider how everything was, how the battle was going, what needed to be done.) Compare SIZE UP.

take stock in *v. phr., informal* To have faith in; trust; believe.—Usually used in the negative. *He took no stock in the idea that women were better cooks than men.* (He did not believe that women were better cooks than men.) *They took little or no stock in the boy's story that he had lost the money.* (They didn't believe he had lost the money.) *Do you take any stock in the gossip about Joan?* (Do you think the gossip is true at all?)

take the bit in one's mouth *also* **take the bit in one's teeth** *adv. phr.* To have your own way; take charge of things; take control of something. *When Mary wanted something, she was likely to take the bit in her teeth and her parents could do nothing with her.* (She

went ahead without restraint.) Compare TAKE THE BULL BY THE HORNS, TAKE THE LAW INTO ONE'S OWN HANDS.

take the bread out of one's mouth *v. phr.* To take away or not give your rightful support, especially through selfish pleasure.—A cliché. *She accused her husband of drinking and gambling—taking bread out of his children's mouths.* (His drinking and gambling left him no money with which to feed his children.)

take the bull by the horns *v. phr., informal* To take definite action and not care about risks; act bravely in a difficulty.—A cliché. *He decided to take the bull by the horns and demand a raise in salary even though it might cost him his job.* (He decided to act directly and decisively in spite of the risk.) Compare TAKE THE BIT IN ONE'S MOUTH, TAKE THE LAW INTO ONE'S OWN HANDS.

take the cake *v. phr., slang* **1** To take the first prize; be the best; rank first. *Mr. Jones takes the cake as a storyteller.* (No one can beat him at telling stories.) **2** To be the limit; to be the worst; have a lot of nerve; be a very rude, bold, or surprising action. *I let Jack borrow my baseball and he never gave it back. Doesn't that take the cake?* (Doesn't Jack have a lot of nerve to keep the ball?) *For being absent-minded, Mr. Smith takes the cake.* (He is the most absent-minded man I know.) Compare BEAT ALL.

take the edge off *also* **take off the edge** *v. phr.* To lessen, weaken, soften, or make dull. *Eating a candy bar before dinner has taken the edge off Becky's appetite.* (She had eaten a candy bar before dinner so that she was not very hungry for dinner.) *Bob was sorry for hurting Tom and that took the edge off Tom's anger.* (Bob was sorry and Tom was less angry.) *A headache took the edge off Dick's pleasure in the movie.* (Dick did not fully enjoy the movie because he had a headache.)

take the fifth *v. phr., informal* **1** Taking refuge behind the Fifth Amendment of the Constitution of the United States which guarantees any witness the right not to incriminate himself while testifying at a trial. *Alger Hiss took the Fifth when asked whether he was a member of the Communist Party.* (He declined to answer the question as guaranteed him by the Constitution on grounds of possible self-incrimination.) **2** Not to answer any question in an informal setting. *Have you been married before? — I take the Fifth.* (I am not telling you—it's none of your business.)

take the law into one's own hands *v. phr.* To protect one's supposed rights or punish a suspected wrongdoer without reference to a court.—An overused expression. *When the men of the settlement caught the suspected murderer, they took the law into their own hands and hanged him to a tree.* (They didn't wait for a trial, but just hanged him at once.) *His farm was going to be sold for taxes, but he took the law into his own hands and drove the sheriff away with a shotgun.* (He decided he was right and the sheriff wrong and refused to let him sell his farm.) Compare LAW UNTO ONESELF, TAKE THE BIT IN ONE'S MOUTH.

take the measure of See TAKE ONE'S MEASURE.

take the rap *v. phr., slang* To receive punishment; to be accused and punished. *All of the boys took apples, but only John took the rap.* (John was the only boy punished for taking apples.) *Joe took the burglary rap for his brother and went to prison for two years.* (Joe did not want his brother to go to prison so he pretended that he was the thief and went to prison instead.)

take the starch out of *v. phr., informal* **1** To make (someone) feel weak or tired. *The hot weather took the starch out of Mrs. Jones, and she didn't feel like doing a thing.* (The hot weather made Mrs. Jones too tired to do anything.) *The cross-country run took all the starch out of the boys.* (The cross-country run tired the boys out.) **2** See TAKE THE WIND OUT OF ONE'S SAILS.

take the stump *or* **take to the stump** *v. phr.* To travel around to different places making political speeches. *The men running for president took to the stump to attract votes.* (The candidates made speeches to get the voters in different places to vote for them.)

take the trouble See GO TO THE TROUBLE.

take the wind out of one's sails *v. phr.* To surprise someone by doing better or by catching him in an error.—A cliché. *John came home boasting about the fish he had caught; it took the wind out of his sails when he found his little sister had caught a bigger one.* (John could not say anything when his sister beat him.) *Dick took the wind out of Bob's sails by showing him where he was wrong.* (Dick caught Bob in an error and stopped his boasting.) Compare TAKE THE STARCH OUT OF 2.

take the words out of one's mouth *v. phr.* To say what another is just going to say; to put another's thought into words.—A cliché. *"Let's go to the beach tomorrow." "You took the words right out of my mouth; I was thinking of that."* ("You said what I was going to say.") *I was going to suggest a movie, but she took the words out of my mouth and said she would like to see one.* (She suggested what I was thinking of myself.)

take things easy See TAKE IT EASY 2.

take to *v.* **1** To go to or into; get yourself quickly to.—Often used in the imperative. *Take to the hills! The Indians are coming!* (Get into the hills and hide as fast as you can!) *We took to the woods during the day so no one would see us.* (We went to the woods.) *Take to the boats! The ship is sinking.* (Get into the lifeboats quickly.) *We*

stopped at a hotel for the night but took to the road again the next morning. (We began to travel again the next morning.) **2** *To begin* the work or job of; make a habit of. *He took to repairing watches in his spare time.* (He did the job of repairing watches when he wasn't on his regular job.) *She took to knitting when she got older.* (She learned knitting to have something to do.) *Grandfather took to smoking cigars when he was young and he still smokes them.* (He began his habit of smoking cigars.) *Uncle Willie took to drink while he was a sailor.* (He began to drink too much liquor too often.) *The cat took to jumping on the table at mealtime.* (He got into the habit of jumping on the table.) **3** To learn easily; do well at. *Father tried to teach John to swim, but John didn't take to it.* (John didn't learn easily; swimming was hard for him.) *Mary takes to mathematics like a duck takes to water.* (Mary has a great talent for mathematics.) **4** To like at first meeting; be pleased by or attracted to; accept quickly. *Our dog always takes to children quickly.* (He always likes children.) *Mary didn't take kindly to the new rule that her mother made of being home at 6 o'clock.* (Mary did not like the new rule.)

take to heart *also* **lay to heart** *v. phr.* To be seriously affected by; to feel deeply. *He took his brother's death very much to heart.* (He felt his brother's death deeply.) *He took his friend's advice to heart.* (He remembered and acted on his friend's advice.)

take to one's heels *also* **show a clean pair of heels** *v. phr.* To begin to run or run away. *When he heard the police coming, the thief took to his heels.* (The thief ran away.)

take to task *v. phr.* To reprove or scold for a fault or error. *He took his wife to task for her foolish wastefulness.* (He scolded his wife.) *The principal took Bill to task for breaking the window.* (He scolded Bill.)

take to the cleaners *v. phr., slang* **1** To win all the money another person has (as in poker). *Watch out if you play poker with Joe; he'll take you to the cleaners.* (He will win all your money.) **2** To cheat a person out of his money and possessions by means of a crooked business transaction or other means of dishonest conduct. *I'll never forgive myself for becoming associated with Joe; he took me to the cleaners.* (I lost all I had because of working with him.)

take to the woods *v. phr., informal* To run away and hide.—A cliché. *When John saw the girls coming, he took to the woods.* (When John saw the girls, he hid from them.) *Bob took to the woods so he would not have to mow the grass.* (John ran away to avoid mowing the grass.) Compare HEAD FOR THE HILLS.

take turns *v. phr.* To do something one after another instead of doing it all at the same time. *In class we should not talk all at* *the same time; we should take turns.* (First one should talk, then another, then a third, and so on.) *Jean and Beth took turns on the swing.* (First Jean swung, then Beth, then Jean, then Beth, and so on.) *The two boys took turns at digging the hole.* (One boy dug, then the other dug, then the first, and so on.) *The three men took turns driving so one would not be too tired.* (They drove the car one after another.)

take under one's wing See UNDER ONE'S WING.

take up *v.* **1** To remove by taking in. *Use a blotter to take up the spilled ink.* (Use a blotter to remove the ink that spilled.) *When the vacuum cleaner bag is full, it will not take up dirt from the rug.* (The vacuum cleaner will not lift dirt out of the rug when the bag is full of dirt.) **2** To fill; (a place or tir occupy. *All his evenings were taken up with study.* (He was busy every evening studying.) *The oceans take up the greater part of the earth's surface.* (The oceans cover most of the earth's surface.) *The mayor has taken up residence on State Street.* ⟨He has begun to live there.) **3** To gather together; collect. *We are taking up a collection to buy flowers for John because he is in the hospital.* (We are collecting money from people who will give it for flowers.) **4** To take away. *John had his driver's license taken up for speeding.* (He lost his license because he was speeding. It was taken away.) **5a** To begin; start. *The teacher took up the lesson where she left off yesterday.* (She started where she stopped yesterday.) **5b** To begin to do or learn; go into as a job or hobby. *He recently took up gardening.* (He started to learn about gardening.) *He took up the carpenter's trade as a boy.* (He learned to be a carpenter.) Compare GO INTO 3, GO IN FOR, TAKE TO. **6** To pull and make tight or shorter; shorten. *The tailor took up the legs of the trousers.* (He shortened the legs.) *Take up the slack on the rope!* (Pull the rope tighter so it won't be so loose.) Compare TAKE IN 3. **7** To take or accept something that is offered. *The boss offered me a $5 raise and I took him up.* (I accepted it.) *I took John up on his bet.* (I accepted the bet that John offered.) Compare JUMP AT.

take up arms *v. phr., literary* To get ready to fight; fight or make war. *The people were quick to take up arms to defend their freedom.* (They were quick to fight.) *The President called on people to take up arms against poverty.* (He called them to fight for poor people.) Contrast LAY DOWN ONE'S ARMS.

take upon oneself See TAKE ON ONESELF.

take up the cudgels for *v. phr., literary* To come to the defense of; to support or fight for. *He was the first to take up the cudgels for his friend.* (He was the first to speak in favor of his friend.) Compare STAND UP FOR.

take up with *v.* To begin to go around with (someone); see a lot of. *Frank has taken up with Lucy lately.* (Frank likes Lucy and is with her often.)

take with a grain of salt *also* **take with a pinch of salt** *v. phr.* To accept or believe only in part; not accept too much.—A cliché. *A man who says he is not a candidate for President should usually have his statement taken with a grain of salt.* (A man who says he is not a candidate should not be believed completely.) *We took Uncle George's stories of the war with a pinch of salt.* (We believed them in part, but not all.)

take with a pinch of salt See TAKE WITH A GRAIN OF SALT.

taking pictures *v. phr., slang, citizen's band radio jargon* To use a radar-operated speed indicator in order to enforce the 55 MPH speed limit. *The Smokeys are taking pictures!* (The police are tracking the drivers' speed with their radar devices, so slow down!)

tale See TELL TALES OUT OF SCHOOL.

talent show *n.* An entertainment in which new entertainers try to win a prize. *Mary won the talent show by her dancing.* (Mary's dancing was the best of all.) *The people liked Bill's singing in the talent show.* (The people thought Bill sang better than the others in the show.)

talk See DOUBLE-TALK, PEP TALK, SALES TALK, SWEET TALK.

talk back *also* **answer back** *v., informal* To answer rudely; reply in a disrespectful way; be fresh. *When the teacher told the boy to sit down, he talked back to her and said she couldn't make him.* (The teacher told the boy to sit down, but he was fresh.) *Mary talked back when her mother told her to stop watching television; she said, "I don't have to if I don't want to."* (She spoke disrespectfully, instead of saying "All right, Mother.") *Russell was going somewhere with some bad boys; when his father told him it was wrong, Russell answered him back, "Mind your own business."* (When Russell's father told him that was bad, he acted rude.)

talk big *v., informal* To talk boastfully; brag. *He talks big about his pitching, but he hasn't won a game.* (He tries to make people believe that he is a very good pitcher.)

talk down *v.* **1** To make (someone) silent by talking louder or longer. *Sue tried to give her ideas, but the other girls talked her down.* (Sue stopped talking because the other girls spoke so loud and long.) Compare SHOUT DOWN. **2** To use words or ideas that are too easy. *The speaker talked down to the students, and they were bored.* (He used words that were too easy, and told them things they knew before.)

talking book *n.* A book recorded by voice on phonograph records for blind people.

Billy, who was blind, learned history from a talking book. (Billy listened to history lessons which were recorded on a phonograph record.)

talking point *n.* Something good about a person or thing that can be talked about in selling it. *The streamlined shape of the car was one of its talking points.* (The streamlined shape was pointed out by the salesman as a good feature of the car.) *John tried to get Mary to date Bill. One of his talking points was that Bill was captain of the football team.* (Mary would probably want to date the captain of the football team because he is so important.)

talk into *v.* 1 To get (someone) to agree to; make (someone) decide on (doing something) by talking; persuade to.—Used with a verbal noun. *Bob talked us into walking home with him.* (Bob made us agree to go home with him.) Compare TALK OVER 2. Contrast TALK OUT OF. 2 To cause to be in or to get into by talking. *You talked us into this mess. Now get us out!* (Your talking got us into this trouble.) *Mr. Jones lost the customer in his store by arguing with him. "You'll talk us into the poor house yet!" said Mrs. Jones.* (Your talking will make us poor!) Contrast TALK OUT OF.

talk out *v.* To talk all about and leave nothing out; discuss until everything is agreed on; settle. *After their quarrel, Jill and John talked things out and reached full agreement.* (They talked about things until everything was understood.)

talk out of *v.* 1 To persuade not to; make agree or decide not to.—Used with a verbal noun. *Mary's mother talked her out of quitting school.* (Mary's mother talked to her and persuaded her not to quit.) Contrast TALK INTO. 2 To allow to go or get out by talking; let escape by talking. *Johnny is good at talking his way out of trouble.* (Johnny is a good talker and people believe him.) Contrast TALK INTO.

talk over *v.* 1 To talk together about; try to agree about or decide by talking; discuss. *Tom talked his plan over with his father before he bought the car.* (Tom talked with his father and got his advice.) *The boys settled their argument by talking it over.* (The boys reached an agreement by talking together.) 2 To persuade; make agree or willing; talk and change the mind of. *Fred is trying to talk Bill over to our side.* (Fred is trying to make Bill agree with us.) Compare TALK INTO.

talk shop *v. phr., informal* To talk about things in your work or trade. *Two chemists were talking shop, and I hardly understood a word they said.* (The chemists were talking about their work and they used many words I did not know.)

talk through one's hat *v. phr., informal* To say something without knowing or understanding the facts; talk foolishly or ignorantly. —A hackneyed phrase. *John said that the earth is nearer the sun in summer, but the teacher said he was talking through his hat.* (The teacher meant that John didn't know the truth; he was wrong.)

talk turkey *v. phr., informal* To talk about something in a really businesslike way; talk with the aim of getting things done. *Charles said. "Now, let's talk turkey about the bus trip. The fact is, it will cost each student $1.50."* (Everyone thought it would be nice to take a bus trip, but Charles reminded them that it would cost money.) *The father always spoke gently to his son, but when the son broke the windshield of the car, the father talked turkey to him.* (He told his son that he must pay for it or not use the car again.)

talk up *v.* 1 To speak in favor or support of. *Let's talk up the game and get a big crowd.* (Let's tell people the game is important so that they will come.) 2 To speak plainly or clearly. *The teacher asked the student to talk up.* (The teacher asked the student to speak more loudly and clearly.) Syn. SPEAK UP. 3 *informal* To say what you want or think; say what someone may not like. *Talk up if you want more pie.* (If you want pie, say so; don't be shy.) *George isn't afraid to talk up when he disagrees with the teacher.* (George says what he thinks even when the teacher may not like it.) Syn. SPEAK UP. Compare SPEAK OUT.

tamper with *v.* 1 To meddle with (something); handle ignorantly or foolishly. *He tampered with the insides of his watch and ruined it.* (He handled the works of the watch without knowing what he was doing and ruined it.) 2 To secretly get someone to do or say wrong things, especially by giving him money, or by threatening to hurt him. *A friend of the man being tried in court tampered with a witness.* (He tried to get a witness to change his story and say something not true.)

tank See THINK TANK.

tan one's hide *v. phr., informal* To give a beating to; spank hard. *Bob's father tanned his hide for staying out too late.* (Bob's father gave him a beating because he stayed out too late.)

tape See FRICTION TAPE, MASKING TAPE.

taper off *v.* 1 To come to an end little by little; become smaller toward the end. *The river tapers off here and becomes a brook.* (The river becomes smaller and smaller and at last is a brook.) 2 To stop a habit gradually; do something less and less often. *Robert gave up smoking all at once instead of tapering off.* (He did not smoke less every day, but broke his habit and never smoked any more.) Contrast COLD TURKEY.

tar See BEAT THE ——— OUT OF.

tar and feather *v.* To pour heated tar on and cover with feathers as a punishment. *In* *the Old West bad men were sometimes tarred and feathered and driven out of town.* (In the Old West men sometimes put warm tar and feathers on bad men and ran them out of town.)

task See TAKE TO TASK.

taste See LEAVE A BAD TASTE IN ONE'S MOUTH.

tat See TIT FOR TAT.

tax trap *n., informal* Predicament in which taxpayers in middle-income brackets are required to pay steeply progressive rates of taxation as their earnings rise with inflation but their personal exemptions remain fixed, resulting in a loss of real disposable income. *Everybody in my neighborhood has been caught in a tax trap.* (We all pay higher taxes as we get raises but have less to spend as prices go up.)

T-bone steak *n.* A steak with a bone in it which looks like a "T". *On Father's birthday we had T-bone steak for supper.* (We had steak with the T-shaped bone.)

tea See CUP OF TEA *also* DISH OF TEA.

teach a lesson *v. phr.* To show that bad behavior can be harmful. *When Johnny pulled Mary's hair, she taught him a lesson by breaking his toy boat.* (Johnny found out that it was not nice to tease Mary, when she broke his boat.) *The burns Tommy got from playing with matches taught him a lesson.* (Tommy learned that playing with matches can be bad for him.)

teach the ropes See THE ROPES.

teapot See TEMPEST IN A TEAPOT.

tear down *v.* **1** To take all down in pieces; destroy. *The workmen tore down the old house and built a new house in its place.* (The old house was destroyed and the parts were taken away to make a place for the new house.) **2** To take to pieces or parts. *The mechanics had to tear down the engine, and fix it, and put it together again.* (They took the engine apart to repair it.) **3** To say bad things about; criticize. *Why do you always tear people down. Why don't you try to say nice things about them?* (Why do you always say bad things about people? Why not praise them instead?) *Dorothy doesn't like Sandra, and at the class meeting she tore down every idea Sandra suggested.* (Dorothy criticized Sandra's ideas.)

tear into See RIP INTO.

tear one's hair *v. phr.* To show sorrow, anger, or defeat.—A cliché. *Ben tore his hair when he saw the wrecked car.* (Ben was angry because his car was wrecked.) *The teacher tore his hair at the boy's stupid answer.* (The boy's answer was so very wrong that the teacher felt defeated.) *It was time to go to class, but Mary had not finished the report she had to give, and she began tearing her hair.* (She felt wild because she did not have her report ready.)

tears See BORE TO TEARS, CROCODILE TEARS.

tear up *v.* **1** To dig a hole in; remove the surface of; remove from the surface. *The city tore up the street to lay a new water pipe.* (The city dug a trench in the street to put in a new pipe.) *Mother tore up the carpeting in the living room and had a new rug put in.* (Mother removed the old rug and had a new one put in its place.) **2** To tear into pieces. *Mary tore up the old sheets and made costumes for the play out of the pieces.* (Mary tore the sheets into pieces and used the pieces to make costumes.) *John tore up his test paper so that his mother wouldn't see his low grade.* (John destroyed his test paper so his mother wouldn't see it.)

tee off *v.* **1** To hit the golf ball from a small wooden peg or tee to begin play for each hole. *We got to the golf course just in time to see the champion tee off.* (We got there just in time to see the champion begin.) **2** *slang* To hit a ball, especially a baseball, very hard or far. *He teed off on the first pitch.* (He hit the first pitch very hard.) **3** *slang* To attack vigorously. *The governor teed off on his opponent's speech.* (The governor attacked his opponent's speech very strongly.) **4** *slang* To make (someone) angry or disgusted. *It teed me off when Billy stole my candy.* (It made me angry.) *Joe was teed off because he had to wait so long.* (Joe was disgusted because he had to wait.)

teeth See TOOTH.

tee up *v.* To set the golf ball on the tee in preparation for hitting it toward the green. *Arnold Palmer teed the ball up for the final hole.* (He put the ball on the tee and got ready to hit it.)

telepathy See MENTAL TELEPATHY.

tell See DO TELL, I'LL SAY *or* I TELL YOU, I'LL TELL YOU WHAT, I'M TELLING YOU, YOU'RE TELLING ME, YOU TELL 'EM.

tell apart *v. phr.* To see the difference between; know each of. *The teacher could not tell the twins apart.* (The teacher could not see the difference between the twins.)

tell a thing or two *v. phr., informal* To tell in plain or angry words; scold.—A cliché. *When John complained about the hard work, his father told him a thing or two.* (John's father scolded him for complaining that the work was hard.) *If Bert thinks he would like to join the army, I'll tell him a thing or two that will make him change his mind.* (I'll explain how things really are.) Compare BAWL OUT, GIVE A PIECE OF ONE'S MIND, TELL OFF, THING OR TWO.

tell it like it is *v. phr., slang, informal* To be honest, sincere; to tell the truth. *Joe is the leader of our commune; he tells it like is.* (He tells the truth and makes no subterfuges about it.)

tell it to the marines *or* **tell it to Sweeney**

slang I don't believe you; stop trying to fool me. John said, "My father knows the President of the United States." Dick answered, "Tell it to the marines." (Dick did not believe John; Dick thought John was trying to fool him.)

tell off v. 1 To name or count one by one and give some special duty to; give a share to. Five boy scouts were told off to clean the camp. (They were named or counted off and were told to clean the camp.) 2 informal To speak to angrily or sharply; attack with words; scold. Mr. Black got angry and told off the boss. (Mr. Black angrily told his boss that he was wrong.) Bobby kept pulling Sally's hair; finally she got angry and told him where to get off. (Sally angrily told Bobby to stop.) Syn. TELL —— WHERE TO GET OFF. Compare GIVE A PIECE OF ONE'S MIND, LAY DOWN THE LAW, TELL A THING OR TWO.

tell on v. 1 To tire; wear out; make weak. The ten-mile hike told on Bill. (Walking ten miles made Bill tired.) 2 informal To tell someone about another's wrong or naughty acts.—Used mainly by children. Andy hit a little girl and John told the teacher on Andy. (John told the teacher that Andy hit a little girl.) If you hit me, I'll tell Mother on you. (If you hit me, I will tell Mother that you did it.)

tell tales out of school v. phr. To tell something that is secret; tell others something that is not meant to be known.—A hackneyed phrase. Don't tell Jane anything. She is always telling tales out of school. (She tells other people things that they should not know.) Compare LET THE CAT OUT OF THE BAG, SPILL THE BEANS.

tell —— where to get off or **tell —— where to head in** v. phr., informal To talk angrily to; speak to or answer with rough language; scold.—A cliché. Bob told Ted to get out of his way. Ted told Bob where to get off. (Ted answered Bob angrily and refused to move.) Mary laughed at Barbara's hairdo. Barbara told Mary where to head in. (Barbara scolded Mary with angry words.) Compare TELL A THING OR TWO, TELL OFF.

tell you what See I'LL TELL YOU WHAT.

temper See GOD TEMPERS THE WIND TO THE SHORN LAMB, HOLD ONE'S TEMPER or KEEP ONE'S TEMPER, LOSE ONE'S TEMPER.

temperature See RUN A TEMPERATURE.

tempest in a teapot n. phr. Great excitement about something not important.—A cliché. Bess tore her skirt a little and made a tempest in a teapot. (She was greatly excited and upset about a little tear in her skirt.)

tempt fate or **tempt the fates** v. phr. To take a chance; run a risk; gamble. You're tempting fate every time you drive that old wreck of a car. (The car is old and may break down any time.)

ten See DIME STORE or FIVE-AND-TEN, COUNT TO TEN.

ten-four? v. phr. interrog., slang, citizen's band radio jargon Do you understand? Is that a ten-four? (Do you understand me?)

ten gallon hat n., informal A tall felt hat with a wide, rolled brim worn by men in the western part of the U.S. Men from the southwest usually wear ten gallon hats. (Men from the southwest usually wear large hats like the cowboys.)

ten roger v. phr., slang, citizen's band radio jargon I acknowledge. That's a ten roger. (I acknowledge what you said.)

ten to one or **two to one** adv. or adj. phr., informal Almost certainly, nearly sure to be true; very likely to happen. Ten to one it will rain tomorrow. (It is sure to rain tomorrow.) It is ten to one that Bill will be late. (It is almost certain that Bill will be late.)

term See BRING TO TERMS, COME TO TERMS, IN SO MANY WORDS 2 or IN NO UNCERTAIN TERMS, IN TERMS OF.

terror See HOLY TERROR.

test See ROAD TEST, SCREEN TEST.

tether See END OF ONE'S ROPE or END OF ONE'S TETHER.

Texas leaguer n. A short fly ball in baseball that goes just back of the infield. Frank hit a Texas leaguer behind first base for a double. (Frank hit a short fly ball just past the first baseman and he went to second base.)

than See LESS THAN, LESS THAN NO TIME, MORE THAN.

thank one's lucky stars v. phr., informal To be thankful for good luck; think oneself lucky. —An overused expression. You can thank your lucky stars you didn't fall in the hole. (You were lucky not to fall in the hole.)

thanks to prep. With the help of. Thanks to a good teacher, John passed the examination. (John's teacher helped him pass by her good teaching.) I finally finished washing the dishes, no thanks to you. (I finally finished washing the dishes, without any help from you.) 2 Owing to; because of. Thanks to a sudden rain, the children came home with wet clothes. (Because of a sudden rain, the children came home wet.)

that is or **that is to say** I mean; that means; in other words. John is a New Yorker; that is, he lives in New York. Susan is a good student; that is to say, she gets good grades in school.

that is that or **that's that** informal The matter is decided; there is nothing more to be said; it is done. Jim, you will go to school this morning, and that is that. (Jim must go to school, and it is useless for him to complain.)

that'll be the day informal That will never happen. Joe wanted me to lend him money to take my girl to the movies. That'll be the day! (I will never do that.) "Wouldn't it be nice if we had to go to school only one day a week?" "That'll be the day!" (That will never happen.)

that's ——— for you That's the way (someone or something) is; (someone or something) is like that. *John tried hard, but he lost the game. That's life for you.* (John tried, but he lost. That's the way life is. Trying isn't enough to win.) *Mary changed her mind about going. That's a girl for you.* (Mary changed her mind. Girls are always changing their minds.)

theater See LITTLE THEATER.

the business *n., slang* —Usually used with *give* or *get.* **1** All that you are able to do; greatest effort. *Johnny gave the tryouts the business but he failed to make the team.* (Johnny did his best, but failed.) **2** The most harm possible; the greatest damage or hurt. *Fred got the business when Tom caught him with his bicycle.* (Tom gave Fred a terrible beating for taking his bicycle.) **3** A harsh scolding. *The teacher gave Walter the business when he came to school late again.* (The teacher gave Walter a harsh scolding.) *Mike thought he was the star of the team until he got the business from the coach.* (Mike did not feel so important after the coach scolded him.) Compare THE WORKS.

the creeps *n., informal* **1** An uncomfortable tightening of the skin caused by fear or shock. *Reading the story of a ghost gave Joe the creeps.* (Joe felt uncomfortable while reading the story.) *The queer noises in the old house gave Mary the creeps.* (Mary's skin began to tighten up when she heard the queer noises.) **2** A strong feeling of fear or disgust. *The cold, damp, lonely swamp gave John the creeps.* (The swamp made John full of horror and fear.) *The dog was so ugly it gave Mary the creeps.* (The dog filled Mary with fright and disgust.)

the edge *n., informal* The advantage.—Usually used in the phrases *get the edge on, have the edge on. In the last quarter of the game, our team got the edge on the other team and kept it.* (Our team got a higher score and kept it.) *Mary has the edge on Jane in the beauty contest.* (Mary is more likely to win the beauty contest than Jane is.)

the idea *or* **the very idea** *n. phr.*—Used in exclamations to show that you do not like something. *The idea! Thinking Mother was my sister!* (Someone thought my mother was my sister, and that made me angry.) *The very idea of Tom bringing that dirty dog into my clean house!* (I think it was a very bad thing for Tom to do.)

the lid *n., slang* Something that holds back or holds out of sight. *The police blew the lid off the gambling operations.* (The police discovered and made public the gambling operations.) *John kept the lid on his plans until he was ready to run for class president.* (John kept his plans secret until he was ready to run for president.) *The chief of police placed the lid on gambling in the town.* (The chief drove all the gamblers away so that there was no more gambling in the town.)

the likes of *informal* Something like or similar to; something of the same kind as. *I have never seen the likes of John.* (I have never seen a boy like John.) *It was a chocolate sundae the likes of which Mary would never see again.* (Mary would never see such a wonderful sundae again.)

the long and the short *or* **the long and short** *n. phr.* All that needs to be said; the basic fact; point.—A hackneyed phrase. *The long and the short of the matter is that the man is no actor.* (When everything has been said, the fact is that the man is not a good actor.) *The money isn't there, and that's the long and short of it.* (We haven't the money for what you want, and that is all to say.)

the matter *adj.* Not as it should be; wrong. —Used in questions or with negatives or *if. Why don't you answer me? What's the matter?* (What is wrong?) *John may be slow in arithmetic, but nothing's the matter with his pitching arm.* (John is a good pitcher.) *If anything is the matter, please tell me.* (Tell me if something is wrong.)

the more ——— the more ——— *or* **the ——— er the ——— er**—*Used in two halves of a sentence to show that when there is more of the first, there is more of the second too. The more you eat, the fatter you will get.* (If you eat more, you will become fatter; if you eat twice as much, you may get twice as fat.) *Get your report in when you can; the sooner, the better.* (If you can give your report to the teacher very soon, that will be very good.) *The bigger they are, the harder they fall.* (An important person has bad luck in a big way.) *The more Bill worked on the arithmetic problem, the more confused he became.* (Bill could not understand the problem; when he worked more, he became more confused.)

then See AND THEN SOME, EVERY NOW AND THEN, NOW AND THEN.

then again *adv.* As an opposite possibility; another thing. *He may be here tomorrow. Then again, he may not come until next week.* (But the opposite may be true—he may not come till next week.) *I thought you told me about the fire, but then again it could have been Bill.* (Maybe it was Bill who told me.)

then and there *adv. phr.* At that very time and place in the past; right then. *He said he wanted his dime back then and there, so I had to give it to him.* (He said he wanted his dime back right then, so I had to give it to him.) Compare IN ONE'S TRACKS, ON THE SPOT, HERE AND NOW.

the picture *n.* The way things are or were; the facts about something; the situation; what happened or happens. *Where does Susan come into the picture.* (What part does Susan have in what is going on?) *When you are looking for a job your education enters into the picture.* (Your education makes a difference whether you get a job and what you get.) *Old Mr. Brown is out of the picture now and his son runs the store.* (Mr. Brown's son runs the store now and not Mr. Brown.) *After the fight on the playground, the principal talked to the boys who were watching, until he got the whole picture.* (The principal talked to the boys until he understood what had happened and why it happened.) Compare GET THE MESSAGE.

the pits *n., slang* **1** A low class, blighted and ill-maintained place, motel room or apartment. *Max, this motel is the pits, I will not sleep here!* (She considers the motel too run down to sleep in.) **2** The end of the road, the point of no return, the point of total ruin of one's health (*from the drug anticulture referring to the arm-pits as the only place that had veins for injections*). *John flunked high school this year for the third time; he will never get to college; it's the pits for him.* (He is at the end of his chances to make good in society; it is the end of the road for him.) **3** A very depressed state of mind. *Poor Marcy is down in the pits over her recent divorce.* (She is extremely depressed because of the divorce.)

there See ALL THERE, HERE AND THERE, NEITHER HERE NOR THERE, THEN AND THERE.

the ropes *n. plural, informal* Thorough or special knowledge of a job; how to do something; the ways of people or the world. *On a newspaper a cub reporter learns his job from an older reporter who knows the ropes.* (The older reporter knows people and he knows his job very well.) *When you go to a new school it takes a while to learn the ropes.* (It takes a while to learn what to do, and to learn the people and places.) *Betty showed Jane the ropes when she was learning to make a dress.* (Betty showed Jane how to make dresses.) *Mr. Jones was an orphan and he had to learn the ropes when he was young to make his way in the world.* (He was alone and had to support himself and learn many things about people and places.) Compare BE AROUND, INS AND OUTS, TRICK OF THE TRADE.

the score *n., slang* The truth; the real story or information; what is really happening; the way people and the world really are. *Very few people know the score in politics.* (Few people know what goes on in politics.) *You are too young to know the score yet.* (You are not experienced yet. You haven't lived long enough.) *What's the score anyhow? When will the program begin?* (What's going on to make the program late?) Compare KNOW ONE'S STUFF, KNOW ONE'S WAY AROUND, THE ROPES.

these See ONE OF THESE DAYS *or* SOME OF THESE DAYS.

the ticket *n.* Exactly what is needed.—Often used with *just*. *This airtight locker is just the ticket for storing your winter clothes.* (It does the job perfectly.)

the tracks *n.* The line between the rich or fashionable part of town and the poor or unfashionable part of town.—A cliché. *The poor children knew they would not be welcome on the other side of the tracks.* (The poor children knew that the rich people did not want them to come to their neighborhood.) *Mary's mother did not want her to date Jack, because he came from across the tracks.* (Mary's family was rich, and her mother did not want her to be too friendly with a poor boy.)—Often used in the expression *the wrong side of the tracks. The mayor was born on the wrong side of the tracks, but he worked hard and became successful.* (The mayor was born in a poor family, but became successful by hard work.)

the whole way See ALL THE WAY.

the wiser *adj.* Knowing about something which might be embarrassing of knowing.—Usually used with *nobody* or *no one. Mary took the teacher's book home by mistake, but early the next morning she returned it with nobody the wiser.* (Mary put the teacher's book back before the teacher noticed it was missing.)

the works *n., plural, slang* **1** Everything that can be had or that you have; everything of this kind, all that goes with it. *When the tramp found $100, he went into a fine restaurant and ordered the works with a steak dinner.* (He wanted everything he could possibly eat.) **1b** See SHOOT THE WORKS. **2** Rough handling or treatment; a bad beating or scolding; killing; murder.—Usually used with *get* or *give. The boy said that Joe was going to get the works if he ever came back to that neighborhood again.* (He said that Joe would get a beating.) *The newspaper gave the police department the works when they let the burglars get away.* (The paper said bad things because the police let the robbers escape.) *The gangster told his friend he would give him the works if he double-crossed him.* (The gangster said he would kill him.) Compare THE BUSINESS.

they See LET THE CHIPS FALL WHERE THEY MAY.

thick See BLOOD IS THICKER THAN WATER, LAY IT ON *or* LAY IT ON THICK, THROUGH THICK AND THIN.

thicker See BLOOD IS THICKER THAN WATER.

thin See INTO THIN AIR, OUT OF THIN AIR, SIT ON THIN ICE, SPREAD ONESELF TOO THIN, THROUGH THICK AND THIN, WEAR THIN.

thing See A LITTLE KNOWLEDGE IS A DANGEROUS THING, DO ONE'S THING *or* DO ONE'S OWN THING, FIRST THINGS COME FIRST, FOR ONE THING, SEE THINGS, SURE THING, TAKE IT EASY *or* TAKE THINGS EASY, TELL A THING OR TWO.

thing or two *n. phr., informal* **1** Facts not generally known, or not known to the hearer or reader; unusual or important information. *Mary told Joan a thing or two about Betty's real feelings.* (Mary told Joan things about Betty that Betty kept hidden from other people.) **2** A lot; much. *Bob knows a thing or two about sailing.* (Bob knows much more than most people about sailing; he is quite a good sailor.) Compare TELL A THING OR TWO.

think See COME TO THINK OF IT.

think a great deal of *or* **think a lot of** *also* **think much of** *v. phr.* To consider to be very worthy, valuable, or important; to esteem highly. *Mary thinks a great deal of Tim.* (Mary likes Tim very much.) *The teacher thought a lot of Joe's project.* (The teacher thought Joe's project was very good work.) —The phrase *think much of* is usually used in negative sentences. *Father didn't think much of Paul's idea of buying a goat to save lawn mowing.* (Father did not think Paul's plan was good.) Contrast THINK LITTLE OF.

think a lot of See THINK A GREAT DEAL OF.

think aloud *or* **think out loud** *v.* To say what you are thinking. *"I wish I had more money for Christmas presents," Father thought aloud. "What did you say?" said Mother. Father answered, "I'm sorry. I wasn't talking to you. I was thinking out loud."* (I was saying the things I was thinking, instead of thinking silently.)

think better of *v.* To change your mind about; to consider again and make a better decision about. *John told his mother he wanted to leave school, but later he thought better of it.* (John changed his mind.) Compare SECOND THOUGHT, THINK TWICE.

think fit See SEE FIT.

thinking cap See PUT ON ONE'S THINKING CAP.

think little of *v. phr.* Think that (something or someone) is not important or valuable. *John thought little of Ted's plan for the party.* (John didn't like Ted's plan.) *Joan thought little of walking two miles to school.* (Joan liked school so much she didn't mind walking two miles to get there.) Contrast THINK A GREAT DEAL OF.

think much of See THINK A GREAT DEAL OF.

think nothing of *v. phr.* To think or consider easy, simple, or usual. *Jim thinks nothing of hiking ten miles in one day.* (Jim thinks it is easy to hike ten miles in one day.)

think nothing of it *v. phr., informal* —Used as a courteous phrase in replying to thanks. *"Thank you very much for your help." "Think nothing of it."* (What I did was very little.) Compare YOU'RE WELCOME.

think on one's feet *v. phr.* To think quickly; answer or act without waiting; know what to do or say right away. *A good basketball player can think on his feet.* (A good basketball player knows right away what he should

do; he does not have to wait till he thinks about it.) *Our teacher can think on his feet; he always has an answer ready when we ask him questions.* (Our teacher thinks very quickly.)

think out *v.* **1** To find out or discover by thinking; study and understand. *Andy thought out a way of climbing to the top of the pole.* (He studied it and found out how to do it.) Compare FIGURE OUT, WORK OUT. **2** To think through to the end; to understand what would come at last. *Bill wanted to quit school, but he thought out the matter and decided not to.* (Bill thought about the future and felt he would have trouble without a good education.)

think out loud See THINK ALOUD.

think over *v.* To think carefully about; consider; study. *When Charles asked Betty to marry him, she asked him for time to think it over.* (Betty wanted time to think carefully about marrying Charles before she said yes or no.) *Think over what we studied in history this year and write a lesson on the thing that interested you most.* (Remember all the things we studied in history, and write about the most interesting thing.) Compare MAKE UP ONE'S MIND, SEE ABOUT.

think piece *n., slang* **1** The human brain. *Lou's got one powerful think piece, man.* (Lou is really smart.) **2** Any provocative essay or article that, by stating a strong opinion, arouses the reader to think about it and react to it by agreeing or disagreeing. *That article by Charles Fenyvesi on Vietnamese refugees in the Washington Post sure was a think piece!* (It certainly was an article that challenged the readers intellectually.)

think tank *n.* A company of researchers who spend their time developing ideas and concepts. *The government hired a think tank to study the country's need for coins, and was advised to stop making pennies.* (The researchers' study produced the idea that pennies were no longer needed.)

think twice *v.* To think again carefully; reconsider; hesitate. *The teacher advised Lou to think twice before deciding to quit school.* (Lou should not make a quick decision.) Compare THINK BETTER OF.

think up *v.* To invent or discover by thinking; have a new idea of. *Mary thought up a funny game for the children to play.* (She had never seen or heard of the game; she invented it.)

third base *n.* The base to be touched third in baseball. *He reached third base standing up on a long triple.* (His hit let him go to the third of the four bases without having to run very fast.)

third class *n.* **1** The third best or highest group; the class next after the second class. *Mary won the pie-making contest in the third class, for the youngest girls.* (Mary's pie got the prize as the best in the class for youngest girls.) **2** Mail that is printed, other than magazines and newspapers that are published regularly, and packages that are not sealed and weigh less than a pound. *The company uses third class to mail free samples of soap.* (The class of mail for sending the samples is third class.) **3** *The least expensive class of travel. I couldn't afford anything better than the third class on the ship coming home from France.* (I had to buy the cheapest place to eat and sleep coming home.) Compare FIRST CLASS, SECOND CLASS.

third-class[1] *adj.* Belonging to the third class; of the third highest or best class. *Much advertising is sent by third-class mail.* (Companies send papers to advertise by third-class mail.) *I bought a third-class airline ticket to Hawaii.* (I bought the least expensive ticket.)

third-class[2] *adv.* By third class. *How did you send the package? Third class.* (The way I sent it was by third-class mail.) *We travelled third-class on the train.* (We went the cheapest way.)

third sex *n., euphemism, slang, informal* Homosexual individuals who are either men or women. *Billy is rumored to belong to the third sex.* (The gossip about Billy is that he may be a homosexual.)

third world *n.* **1** The countries not aligned with either the U.S.S.R.-dominated Communist bloc or the U.S.A.-dominated capitalist countries. *New Zealand made a move toward third country status when it disallowed American nuclear submaries in its harbors.* (By refusing to harbor U.S. nuclear submarines, the New Zealanders moved toward neutrality.) **2** The developing nations of the world where the industrial revolution has not yet been completed. *Africa and the rest of the third world must be freed from starvation and illiteracy.* (We must see to it that there is no starvation and illiteracy in the developing countries.

this See OUT OF THIS WORLD.

this and that *also* **this, that, and the other** *n. phr.* Various things; different things; miscellaneous things. *When the old friends met they would talk about this and that.* (When the old friends met they would talk about many different things.) *The quilt was made of this, that, and the other.* (The quilt was made of many different scraps of material.)

this, that, and the other See THIS AND THAT.

this is how the cookie crumbles *or* **that's how the cookie crumbles** *or* **this is how it crumbles cookie-wise** *v. phr., informal, trite* *It's too bad about John and Mary getting divorced, but then that's how the cookie crumbles.* (It's a pity John and Mary got divorced, but then, that's life.)

thither See HITHER AND THITHER.

thorn in the flesh *or* **thorn in one's side** *n.*

phr. Something that causes stubborn trouble; a constant bother; a vexation. *The new voter organization soon became the biggest thorn in the senator's side.* (The new group became the senator's biggest trouble.) *The guerrilla band was a thorn in the flesh of the invaders.* (The guerrillas were a bother to the army that came into the country.)

though See AS IF *or* AS THOUGH.

thought See FOOD FOR THOUGHT, PENNY FOR ONE'S THOUGHTS, PERISH THE THOUGHT, SECOND THOUGHT.

thousand See BY THE DOZEN *or* BY THE THOUSAND.

thread See HANG BY A THREAD.

threat See TRIPLE THREAT.

three-ring circus *n.* A scene of much confusion or activity.—A cliché. *The street was a three-ring circus of cars, people, noise, and lights.* (The street was crowded with cars and people and full of confused activity, sights, and sounds.) *It is a three-ring circus to watch that silly dog play.* (The dog is constantly running and jumping from one place to another.)

three sheets in the wind *or* **three sheets to the wind** *adj. phr., informal* Unsteady from too much liquor, drunk.—A cliché. *The sailor came down the street, three sheets in the wind.* (The drunken sailor staggered down the street.)

throat See CUT ONE'S THROAT, FLY AT ONE'S THROAT, JUMP DOWN ONE'S THROAT, LUMP IN ONE'S THROAT, RAM DOWN ONE'S THROAT *at* SHOVE DOWN ONE'S THROAT.

through a hoop See JUMP THROUGH A HOOP.

through and through *adv.* Completely; entirely; whole-heartedly. *Bob was a ball player through and through.* (Bob was completely devoted to playing ball.) *Mary was hurt through and through by Betty's remarks.* (Mary was deeply hurt by Betty's remarks.) Compare OUT-AND-OUT.

through hell and high water See HELL AND HIGH WATER.

through one's hat See TALK THROUGH ONE'S HAT.

through one's head See GET THROUGH ONE'S HEAD.

through one's mind See CROSS ONE'S MIND *or* PASS THROUGH ONE'S MIND.

through one's paces See PUT THROUGH ONE'S PACES.

through street *n.* **1** A street on which cars can move without stopping at intersections, but cars on streets crossing it have to stop at the intersection. *You have to be especially careful crossing a through street.* (When you walk across a street where the cars don't have to stop, you must be sure no cars are coming before you cross.) *Mr. Jones stopped his car when he came to the through street. He waited until there were no cars on it, and drove across it.* (Mr. Jones waited until all the cars that did not have to stop had gone by, and then drove across.) Contrast STOP STREET. **2** A street that is open to other streets at both ends; a street that has a passage through it, so that it is not necessary to come back to get out of it. *We thought we could get through to Main St. by going up a side street but there was a sign that said "Not a through street."* (The side street did not go through to the Main St.)

through the mill *adv. phr., informal* Through real experience of the difficulties of a certain way of life.—A cliché. *He won't be surprised by anything on the new job. He's been through the mill.* (He has had enough experience in that line not to be surprised by anything on the new job.) *Jones is a good teacher of printing because he has gone through the mill as a printer himself.* (Jones used to be a printer and knows what one must learn and do.) *Poor Jerry has had three operations in one year, and now he's back in the hospital. He's really gone through the mill.* (Jerry has really had a hard time.) Compare GO THROUGH HELL AND HIGH WATER, COME HELL OR HIGH WATER.

through the motions See GO THROUGH THE MOTIONS.

through the nose See PAY THROUGH THE NOSE.

through thick and thin *adv. phr.* Through all difficulties and troubles; through good times and bad times.—A cliché. *The friends were faithful through thick and thin.* (The friends were faithful in good times and bad.) *George stayed in college through thick and thin, because he wanted an education.* (George had many troubles in college, but he did not quit.)

throw See FREE THROW, PEOPLE WHO LIVE IN GLASS HOUSES SHOULD NOT THROW STONES.

throw a curve *v. phr., slang, informal* **1** To mislead or deceive someone, to lie. *John threw me a curve about the hiring.* (John lied to me about the hiring.) **2** To take someone by surprise in an unpleasant way. *Mr. Weiner's announcement threw the whole company a curve.* (It took the whole company by surprise in an unpleasant manner.)

throw a fit See HAVE A FIT.

throw a monkey wrench *or* **throw a wrench** *v. phr., informal* To cause something that is going smoothly to stop. *The game was going smoothly until you threw a monkey wrench into the works by fussing about the rules.* (We were having fun playing the game until you spoiled it by fussing about the rules.) *The Michigan tacklers threw a wrench into the Wisconsin team's offense.* (The Michigan tacklers upset the Wisconsin team's offensive plays.) *He hoped to see the class plan fail and looked for a chance to throw a wrench in the machinery.* (He was looking for a chance to do something to spoil the plan.)

throw a party *v. phr., informal* To hold a party; have a party. *The club is throwing a party in the high school gym Saturday night.* (The club will give a party in the high school gym Saturday night.) *The Seniors threw a masquerade party on Halloween.* (The Seniors had a masquerade party.)

throw a punch *v. phr.* To strike at someone with your fist; hit; punch. *Bob became so mad at Fred that he threw a punch at him.* (Bob got so made he hit Fred.) *The bell rang and the boxers started throwing punches.* (The boxers began to hit each other.) Compare TAKE A PUNCH AT.

throw away *v.* **1** To get rid of as unwanted or not needed; junk. *Before they moved they threw away everything they didn't want to take with them.* (They junked everything they didn't want when they moved.) *I never save those coupons; I just throw them away.* (I just drop the coupons in the waste basket.) Syn. THROW OUT. **2** To waste. *The senator criticized the government for throwing away billions on the space program.* (The senator claimed the government wasted billions of dollars on the space program.) **3** To fail to make use of. *She threw away a good chance for a better job.* (She had a chance for a better job, but didn't take it.)

throw a wet blanket See WET BLANKET.

throw caution to the winds *also* **throw discretion to the winds** *v. phr.* To be daring; make a bold or risky move. *Hearing that Indians were planning to start a war, the white settlers decided to throw caution to the winds and attack the Indians first.* (The settlers decided to make a bold and risky move by attacking the Indians before they were ready.)

throw cold water on *also* **dash cold water on** *or* **pour cold water on** *v. phr.* To discourage; say or do something to discourage. *We had high hopes of victory but our opponents soon threw cold water on them.* (We had high hopes of victory, but the other team played so well that we were soon discouraged.) *Henry's father threw cold water on his plans to go to college by saying he could not afford it.* (His father told him he could not pay for a college education, so the boy was discouraged.)

throw a loop See KNOCK FOR A LOOP.

throw down the gauntlet *v. phr.* To challenge, especially to a fight. *Another candidate for the presidency has thrown down the gauntlet.* (Another person has entered the fight to become president.)

throw for a loss *v. phr.* **1** To tackle a member of the opposing football team behind the place where his team had the ball at the beginning of the play; push the other team back so that they lose yardage in football. *The Blues' quarterback ran back and tried to pass, but before he could, the Reds' end threw him for a loss.* (The quarterback was tackled so that the Blues' team was thrown backwards on the play.) Compare LOSE GROUND. **2** *informal.* To surprise or shock (someone); upset; make worry greatly; cause trouble. *It threw Jim for a loss when he failed the test.* (Jim was very surprised and disturbed.) *Mr. Simpson was thrown for a loss when he lost his job.* (Mr. Simpson was very worried.) Compare KNOCK FOR A LOOP, SET BACK ON ONE'S HEELS.

throw in *v.* **1** To give or put in as an addition; to give to or with something else. *John threw in a couple of tires when he sold Bill his bicycle.* (John gave Bill a couple of tires with the bicycle he sold him.) *Mary and Tess were talking about the prom, and Joan threw in that she was going with Fred.* (Mary and Tess were talking about the prom, and Joan added a remark to the conversation about who she was going with.) Compare FOR GOOD MEASURE. **2** To push into operating position. *Mr. Jones threw in the clutch and shifted gears.* (Mr. Jones pushed the clutch pedal to the floor so that he could shift gears.)

throw ——— in one's face *or* **throw ——— in one's teeth** *v. phr.* To blame a person for (something wrong); not allow someone to forget (a mistake or failure).—Often used with *back. Bob came home late for dinner last week, and his mother keeps throwing it back in his face.* (She won't let him forget he was late.) *I made a mistake in the ball game and the boys keep throwing it back in my teeth.* (They still blame me because I made the mistake.) Compare IN ONE'S FACE.

throw in one's lot with *or literary* **cast in one's lot with** *v. phr.* To decide to share or take part in anything that happens to; join. *The thief decided to throw in his lot with the gang when he heard their plans.* (The thief decided to join the gang when he heard their plans.) *Washington was rich, but he decided to cast in his lot with the colonies against Britain.* (He joined those who fought for independence.) *When Carl was old enough to vote, he threw in his lot with the Democrats.* (Carl voted for Democratic candidates.) Syn. JOIN FORCES.

throw in the sponge *or* **throw up the sponge** *or* **throw in the towel** *v. phr., informal* To admit defeat; accept loss.—A cliché. *After taking a beating for five rounds, the fighter's seconds threw in the sponge.* (After the fighter had been badly beaten for five rounds, his attendants had him stop fighting.) *When Harold saw his arguments were not being accepted, he threw in the towel and left.* (He quit and left when he saw his arguments were not successful.) Syn GIVE UP.

throw off *v.* **1** To get free from. *He was healthy enough to throw off his cold easily.* (He was healthy enough to free himself of the cold easily.) Compare RID OF. **2** To mislead; confuse, fool. *They went by a different route to throw the hostile Indians off their track.* (They went a different way to fool the enemy Indians.) **3** *To produce easily or as if without effort. She could throw off a dozen poems in a night.* (She could produce a dozen poems in one night with no trouble at all.)

throw off the scent *v. phr.* To mislead; confuse.—A cliché. *The robbers went different ways hoping to throw the sheriff's men off the scent.* (The robbers hoped to fool the sheriff's men by going different ways.) Syn. THROW OFF 2.

throw oneself at someone's feet *v. phr.* To make a public display of serving, loving, or worshiping someone.—A cliché. *When Arthur became king, almost all of the nobles threw themselves at his feet and promised to obey and serve him.* (They promised publicly that they would obey and serve him.) *When the new girl entered school, several boys threw themselves at her feet.* (Several boys showed that they were very much in love with her.)

throw oneself at someone's head *or* **fling oneself at someone's head** *v. phr., informal* To try hard and openly to make a person love you.—A cliché. *She threw herself at his head, but he was interested in another girl.* (She tried hard and openly to get him interested in her and love her.) Compare AT ONE'S FEET.

throw one's hat in the ring *or* **toss one's hat in the ring** *v. phr., informal* To announce that you are going to try to be elected to an official position; become a candidate for office.—A cliché. *Bill tossed his hat in the ring for class president.* (Bill announced that he wanted to be elected class president.) *The senator threw his hat in the ring for re-election.* (The senator became a candidate to be elected again.)

throw one's weight around *v. phr., informal* To use one's influence or position in a showy or noisy manner.—A cliché. *John was the star of the class play, and he was throwing his weight around telling the director how the scene should be played.* (John was using his position as the star to tell the director what to do.) *Bob was stronger than the other boys, and he threw his weight around.* (Bob used his strength to get what he wanted.)

throw open **1** To open wide with a sudden or strong movement. *He dashed in and threw open the windows.* (He ran in and opened the windows with a rush.) **2** To remove limits from. *The Homestead Act threw open the West.* (The Homestead Act made it possible for the people to move to the West.) *When a hurricane and flood left many people homeless, public buildings were thrown open to shelter them.* (When the hurricane destroyed many homes, the owners were allowed to stay in public buildings until they could find places to live.)

throw out *or* **toss out** *v.* **1** To put somewhere to be destroyed because not wanted.

He didn't need the brush any more so he threw it out. (He junked the brush when it was no longer useful.) Syn. THROW AWAY 1. **2** To refuse to accept. *The inspector tossed out all the parts that didn't work.* (The inspector refused to accept any parts that were no good.) **3** To force to leave; dismiss. *When the baseball manager complained too loudly, the umpires threw him out.* (The umpires ordered the manager to leave the game when he complained too loudly.) Syn. KICK OUT, TURN OUT 1. **4** To cause to be out in baseball by throwing the ball. *The shortstop tossed the runner out.* (The shortstop threw the ball to the first baseman, and the first baseman tagged the runner, putting him out.)

throw out of gear *v. phr.* **1** To separate the gears of (a car or some other machine) when you want to stop it. *When John wanted to stop, he threw the car out of gear and braked sharply.* (John moved the gearshift to neutral and stepped hard on the brake.) **2** To stop or bother (what someone is doing or planning); confuse; upset. *The whole country was thrown out of gear by the assassination of the President.* (Everything was upset.) *My mother's illness threw my plans for the summer out of gear.* (My plans were interrupted.)

throw over *v.* To give up for another; break your loyalty or attachment to. *Bob threw Mary over for a new girl friend.* (Bob left Mary for a new girl friend.) *Tom threw over those who helped him run for class president after he was elected.* (Tom stopped being friendly with his supporters when he no longer needed them.)

throw the baby out with the bath (bathwater) *v. phr.* To reject all of something because part is faulty. *There are weaknesses in the program, but if they act too hastily they may cause the baby to be thrown out with the bathwater.* (They may reject a good program just because part of it hasn't worked.)

throw the book at *v. phr., informal* To give the most severe penalty to (someone) for breaking the law or rules. *Because it was the third time he had been caught speeding that month, the judge threw the book at him.* (Because it was his third speeding arrest that month, the judge gave him the greatest penalty.)

throw together *v.* **1** *also* **slap together** To make in a hurry and without care. *Bill and Bob threw together a cabin out of old lumber.* (Bill and Bob built a cabin without paying attention to the way a strong building should be built.) *The party was planned suddenly, and Mary threw together a meal out of leftovers.* (Mary made a meal quickly out of whatever she could find in the house.) **2** To put in with other people by chance. *The group of strangers was thrown together when the storm trapped them on the highway.* (The

strangers became grouped together by accident when the storm caught them.) *Bill and Tom became friends when they were thrown together in the same cabin at camp.* (Bill and Tom became friends when they were put in the same cabin.)

throw to the wolves *v. phr.* To send into danger without protection.—A cliché. *Mary was very shy. Her friends did not come to speak before the club in her place. They threw her to the wolves.* (Her friends left Mary to do what she was afraid to do.) *The boys on the football team were so small that when they played a good team they were thrown to the wolves.* (The boys were too small to defend themselves against a good team.)

throw up *v.* **1** *informal or slang* **heave up.** To vomit. *The heat made him feel sick and he thought he would throw up.* (The heat made him sick and he thought he would vomit.) *He took the medicine but threw it up a minute later.* (He took the medicine but vomited it a minute later.) **2** *informal* To quit; leave; let go; give up. *When she broke their engagement he threw up his job and left town.* (When their engagement was broken he left his job and went elsewhere.) **3** To build in a hurry. *The contractor threw up some temporary sheds to hold the new equipment.* (The contractor hurriedly built sheds for the new equipment to be kept in for a while.) **4** To mention often as an insult. *His father threw up John's wastefulness to him.* (John's father often mentioned his wastefulness.)

throw up one's hands *v. phr.* To give up trying; admit that you cannot succeed. *Mrs. Jones threw up her hands when the children messed up the living room for the third time.* (Mrs. Jones stopped trying to keep the living room clean after the children had ruined her cleaning three times.) *When Mary saw the number of dishes to be washed, she threw up her hands in dismay.* (When Mary saw the dishes, she almost thought she couldn't do them.)

throw up one's hands in horror *v. phr.* To be horrified; feel alarmed; give up hope of straightening things out; be shocked by something terrible.—A cliché. *When Mrs. Brown saw the mess the children were making in her living room, she threw up her hands in horror.* (Mrs. Brown thought she would never be able to clean up the mess in her living room.) *Everybody threw up their hands in horror at the destruction caused by the hurricane.* (People were horrified.)

throw up the sponge See THROW IN THE SPONGE.

thumb See ALL THUMBS, GREEN THUMB, TURN THUMBS DOWN, TWIDDLE ONE'S THUMBS, UNDER ONE'S THUMB *or* UNDER THE THUMB OF.

thumb a ride *v. phr., informal* To get a ride

by hitchhiking; hitchhike. *Not having much money, Carl decided to thumb a ride to New York.* (Since Carl was low on money he decided to hitchhike to New York.)

thumb one's nose *v. phr.* **1** To hold one's open hand in front of one's face with one's thumb pointed at one's nose as a sign of scorn or dislike. *After Bob ran into the house he thumbed his nose at Tom through the window.* (Bob made an impolite gesture at Tom when he knew he was safe.) **2** *informal* To look with disfavor or dislike; regard with scorn; refuse to obey.—Used with *at*. *Betty thumbed her nose at her mother's command to stay home.* (Betty went out although her mother ordered her to stay home.) Compare LOOK DOWN ON. *Mary thumbed her nose at convention by wearing odd clothes.* (Mary wore odd clothes to show she didn't care about what other people thought was proper.)

thunder See BLOOD AND THUNDER, STEAL ONE'S THUNDER.

thus and so *also* **thus and thus** *adv. phr.* In a particular way; according to directions that have been given. *The teacher is very fussy about the way you write your report. If you don't do it thus and so, she gives you a lower mark.* (If you don't write your report just the way the teacher tells you, she gives you a lower mark.)

thus far See SO FAR.

ticket See SPLIT TICKET, STRAIGHT TICKET, THE TICKET, WALKING PAPERS *also* WALKING TICKET.

tickle pink *v. phr., informal* To please very much; thrill; delight.—A trite expression, usually used in the passive participle. *Nancy was tickled pink with her new dress.* (Nancy was delighted with her new dress.)

tickle to death See TO DEATH.

tick off *v.* **1** To mention one after the other; list. *The teacher ticked off the assignments that Jane had to do.* (The teacher listed one assignment after the other.) **2** To scold; rebuke. *The boss ticked off the waitress for dropping her tray.* (He criticized her harshly.) **3** To anger or upset. Usually used as *ticked off*. *She was ticked off at him for breaking their dinner date again.* (She was angry at him because he again cancelled their date to go to dinner.)

tide See TURN THE TIDE.

tide over *v.* To carry past a difficulty or danger; help in bad times or in trouble. *He was out of work last winter but he had saved enough money to tide him over until spring.* (He had enough money to live on until spring although he didn't work all winter.) *An ice cream cone in the afternoon tided her over until supper.* (The ice cream cone satisfied her hunger until it was time for supper.) Compare SEE THROUGH.

tide turn See TURN THE TIDE.

tie See FIT TO BE TIED.

tie down *v.* To keep (someone) from going somewhere or doing something; prevent from leaving; keep in. *Mrs. Brown can't come to the party. She's tied down at home with the children sick.* (Mrs. Brown can't leave her sick children and come to the party.) *The navy tied the enemy down with big gun fire while the marines landed on the beach.* (The navy used big guns to keep the enemy from attacking the marines who were landing.) *I can't help you with history now! I'm tied down with these algebra problems.* (I can't help you now with your history because I must do my algebra problems.)

tied to one's mother's apron strings Not independent of your mother; not able to do anything without asking your mother.—A cliché. *Even after he grew up he was still tied to his mother's apron strings.* (Even after he grew up he was unable to make any decisions without asking his mother what to do.)

tie in *v.* To connect with something else; make a connection for.—Often used with *with*. *The teacher tied in what she said with last week's lesson.* (The teacher showed the connection between what she said today and last week's lesson.) *The English teacher sometimes gives compositions that tie in with things we are studying in other classes.* (The English assignment is sometimes about the same subject as the history or science assignment.) *The detectives tied in the fingerprints on the man's gun with those found on the safe, so they knew that he was the thief.* (The detectives connected the fingerprints on the gun with those found on the safe.)

tie in knots *v. phr.* To make (someone) very nervous or worried. *The thought of having her tooth pulled tied Joan in knots.* (Joan was made very nervous by the thought of having her tooth pulled.) *The little boy's experience with the kidnapper tied him in knots and it was hard for him to sleep well for a long time.* (His memories of the kidnapping made him nervous for a long time.)

tie into See LACE INTO.

tie one's hands *v. phr.* To make (a person) unable to do anything.—Usually used in the passive. *Since Mary would not tell her mother what was bothering her, her mother's hands were tied.* (Since Mary would not tell what her trouble was, her mother could do nothing to help her with it.) *Charles wanted to help John get elected president of the class, but his promise to another boy tied his hands.* (Charles could not help John, because his help was promised to another boy.) *Father hoped Jim would not quit school, but his hands were tied; Jim was old enough to quit if he wanted to.* (Father could not make Jim stay in school because the law did not make a son obey at his age.)

tie the knot *v. phr., informal* To get married; *also* to perform a wedding ceremony.— A cliché. *Diane and Bill tied the knot yesterday.* (Diane and Bill were married yesterday.) *The minister tied the knot for Diane and Bill yesterday.* (The minister married Diane and Bill yesterday.)

tie up *v.* **1** To show or stop the movement or action of; hinder; tangle. *The crash of the two trucks tied up all traffic in the center of town.* (The accident stopped traffic in the center of town.) *The strike tied up the factory.* (The strike slowed down—sometimes even stopped—the work done in the factory.) **2** To take all the time of. *The meeting will tie the president up until noon.* (The meeting will take all of the president's time until noon.) *The Senate didn't vote because a debate on a small point kept it tied up all week.* (A debate on a small point kept the Senate from voting.) *He can't see you now. He's tied up on the telephone.* (He can't see you now because he can't leave the telephone call he is making.) **3** To limit or prevent the use of. *His money is tied up in a trust fund and he can't take it out.* (His money has been put in a trust fund so he can't take it out all at once.) *Susan tied up the bathroom for an hour.* (She used it for an hour and nobody else could use it.) **4** To enter into an association or partnership; join. *Our company has tied up with another firm to support the show.* (Our company has joined with another to put the show on.) **5** To dock. *The ships tied up at New York.* (The ships docked at New York.) **6** *slang* To finish; complete. *We've talked long enough; let's tie up these plans and start doing things.* (Let's finish making these plans.)

tight See SIT TIGHT.

tight end *n.* An end in football who plays close to the tackle in the line. *The tight end is used to catch passes but most often to block.* (The end that plays close to the tackle is used mostly as a blocker although he does catch passes.) Contrast SPLIT END.

tighten one's belt *v. phr.* To live on less money than usual; use less food and other things.—A trite phrase. *When father lost his job we had to tighten our belts.* (When father lost his job we had to do without many things.) Often used in the expression tighten one's belt another notch. *Father lost his job and we had to do without many things, but when our savings were all spent, we had to tighten our belts another notch.* (We learned to use even less food and other things than before.)

tighten the screws *v. phr.* To try to make someone do something by making it more and more difficult not to do it; apply pressure. *When many students still missed class after he began giving daily quizzes, the teacher tightened the screws by failing anyone absent four times.* (The teacher put more pressure on students to come to class by adding a more severe punishment.)

Tijuana taxi *n., slang, citizen's band radio jargon* A police car. *I've got a Tijuana taxi in sight.* (I have spotted a police car.)

till See ROB THE TILL *or* HAVE ONE'S HAND IN THE TILL.

till the last gun is fired *or* **until the last gun is fired** *adv. phr.* Until the end; until everything is finished or decided.—A cliché. *Fred always liked to stay at parties until the last gun was fired.* (He wanted to stay until the very end.) *The candidate didn't give up hope of being elected until the last gun was fired.* (He didn't give up until it was clearly over.)

tilt See FULL TILT.

time See ABOUT TIME, AGAINST TIME, AT A TIME, AT ONE TIME, AT THE SAME TIME, AT TIMES, BEHIND THE TIMES, BEHIND TIME, BIDE ONE'S TIME, BIG TIME, EVERY TIME ONE TURNS AROUND, FOR THE TIME BEING, FROM TIME TO TIME, GIVE A HARD TIME, HAVE A TIME, HIGH TIME, IN GOOD TIME, IN NO TIME, IN THE NICK OF TIME, IN TIME, KEEP TIME, LESS THAN NO TIME, LIVE ON BORROWED TIME, MAKE TIME, MARK TIME, ONCE UPON A TIME, ON ONE'S OWN TIME, ON TIME, PASS THE TIME OF DAY, SMALL-TIME, TAKE ONE'S TIME, TWO-TIME.

time and again *or* **time and time again** *adv.* Many times; repeatedly; very often. *I've told you time and again not to touch the vase!* (I've told you many many times not to touch the vase!) *Children are forgetful and must be told time and time again how to behave.* (Children must be told many times before they will remember.)

time and a half *n. phr.* Pay given to a worker at a rate half again as much as he usually gets. *John got time and a half when he worked beyond his usual quitting time.* (John got paid his usual rate plus half of it besides for working late.) *Tom gets one dollar for regular pay and a dollar and a half for time and a half.* (Tom gets a dollar plus half of a dollar when he works late.)

time is ripe The best time has come for doing something. *The Prime Minister will hold elections when the time is ripe.* (The Prime Minister will call for elections when he thinks he will win.) *Lee saw his mother was upset, so he decided the time was not ripe to tell her about the broken window.* (Lee decided that it was not a good time to tell his mother that he had broken the window.)

time of day See NOT TO GIVE ONE THE TIME OF DAY.

time of one's life *n. phr.* A very gay or wonderful time.—A cliché. *John had the time of his life at the party.* (John had a wonderful time at the party.) *I could see that she was having the time of her life.* (It was plain that she was enjoying herself greatly.)

time out *n. phr.* Time during which a game or other activity is stopped for a while for some reason. *He took a time out from studying to go to a movie.* (He interrupted his studying to go to a movie.) *The player called time out so he could tie his shoe.* (The player stopped the game so he could tie his shoe.)

tingle See SPINE-TINGLING.

tinker's damn See NOT WORTH A TINKER'S DAMN.

tip See AT THE TIP OF ONE'S TONGUE, FROM TIP TO TIP.

tip off *v., informal* To tell something not generally known; tell secret facts to; warn. *The class president tipped off the class that it was the superintendent's birthday.* (The class president informed the class in private that it was the superintendent's birthday. *The thieves did not rob the bank as planned because someone tipped them off that it was being watched by the police.* (Someone warned them that the bank was being watched.) Compare PUT WISE.

tip the balance See TIP THE SCALES 2.

tip the scales *v. phr., informal* **1** To weigh. *Martin tips the scales at 180 pounds.* (Martin weighs 180 pounds.) **2** *or* **tip the balance** To have important or decisive influence; make a decision go for or against you; decide. *John's vote tipped the scales in our favor, and we won the election.* (John's vote gave us the most votes, and we won.) Compare TURN THE TIDE.

tired See DEAD TIRED, SICK AND TIRED.

tire out See WEAR OUT 2.

tit for tat *n. phr.* Equal treatment in return; a fair exchange. *Billy hit me, so I gave him tit for tat.* (Billy hit me, so I hit him back.) *I told him if he did me any harm I would return tit for tat.* (I said I would return harm for harm.) *They had a warm debate and the two boys gave each other tit for tat.* (Each boy answered the other with good points.) Compare GET BACK AT, EYE FOR AN EYE AND A TOOTH FOR A TOOTH.

to a conclusion See JUMP TO A CONCLUSION.

to a crisp See BURN TO A CRISP.

to a degree *adv. phr.* **1** *Chiefly British* Very; to a large extent. *In some things I am ignorant to a degree.* (In some things I am very ignorant.) **2** Somewhat; slightly; in a small way; rather. *His anger was, to a degree, a confession of defeat.* (His anger gave a hint that he was defeated.) *To a degree, Mary was to blame for Bob's failing mathematics, because he spent much time with her when he should have been studying.* (Mary was a little to blame for John's failure.)

to advantage *adv. phr.* So as to bring out the good qualities of; favorably; in a flattering way. *The jeweler's window showed the diamonds to advantage.* (The jeweler's window brought out the beauty in the diamonds.) *The green dress showed up to advantage with her red hair.* (The green dress and her red hair went well together.)

to a fault *adv. phr.* So very well that it is in a way bad; to the point of being rather foolish; too well; too much. *Aunt May wants everything in her house to be exactly right; she is neat to a fault.* (Aunt May is really too

neat; she makes other people uncomfortable.) *Mary acts her part to a fault.* (Mary acts her part very well, but she acts so realistically that she draws attention to herself.) *John carries thoroughness to a fault; he spends many hours writing his reports.* (John is too thorough; he spends more time than is helpful in writing his reports.)

to a halt See GRIND TO A HALT.

to all intents and purposes *adv. phr.* In most ways; in fact. *The president is called the head of state, but the prime minister, to all intents and purposes, is the chief executive.* (The prime minister is the one who really does most of the administrative work.)

to a man *adv. phr.* Without exception; with all agreeing. *The workers voted to a man to go on strike.* (Every single worker voted to go on strike.) *To a man John's friends stood by him in his trouble.* (They all were loyal to him.) Compare EVERY LAST MAN.

to and fro *adv. phr.* Forward and back again and again. *Father pushed Judy in the swing, and she went to and fro.* (Judy swung forward and back, again and again.) *Busses go to and fro between the center of the city and the city limits.* (Busses go from the center of the city to the city limits and back, again and again.) *The man walked to and fro while he waited for his phone call.* (The man walked away and came back many times while he was waiting for his phone call.) Compare BACK AND FORTH.

to another tune See DANCE TO ANOTHER TUNE.

to a T *or* **to a turn** *adv. phr.* Just right; to perfection; exactly. *The roast was done to a turn.* (The roast was done just right.) *His nickname, Tiny, suited him to a T.* (He was so small that "Tiny" fitted him.) Compare TO THE LETTER.

to bat See GO TO BAT FOR.

to bay See BRING TO BAY.

to-be *adj.* That is going to be; about to become.—Used after the noun it modifies. *Bob kissed his bride-to-be.* (Bob kissed the girl who is going to marry him.) *The principal of the high school greeted the high school students-to-be on their last day in junior high.* (The principal spoke to the junior high students who will be in high school next year.)

to bed See PUT TO BED, PUT TO BED WITH A SHOVEL.

to be sure *adv. phr.* Without a doubt; certainly; surely. *"Didn't you say Mr. Smith would take us home?" "Oh, yes. To be sure, I did."* (That's right. I did say that.)—Often used before a clause beginning with *but.* *He works slowly, to be sure, but he does a good job.* (No doubt he works slowly, but he does a good job.) *To be sure, Jim is a fast skater, but he is not good at doing figures.* (It is true that Jim is a good skater, but he is not good at figure-skating.) Syn. OF COURSE.

to blame *adj. phr.* Having done something wrong; to be blamed; responsible. *John was to blame for the broken window.* (John broke the window.) *The teacher tried to find out who was to blame in the fight.* (The teacher tried to find out who started the fight.)

to boot *adv. phr.* In addition; besides; as something extra. *He not only got fifty dollars, but they bought him dinner to boot.* (He was given the fifty dollars and in addition they paid for his dinner.) Compare FOR GOOD MEASURE, IN THE BARGAIN, THROW IN.

to date *adv. or adj. phr.* Up to the present time; until now. *To date twenty students have been accepted into the school.* (Up to now, twenty students have been accepted into the school.) *The police have not found the runaway to date.* (The police have not found the runaway yet.) *Jim is shoveling snow to earn money, but his earnings to date are small.* (Jim has earned only a little money up to the present time.) Syn. SO FAR.

to death *adv. phr., informal* To the limit; to the greatest degree possible.—A trite phrase used for emphasis with verbs such as *scare, frighten, bore. Cowboy stories bore me to death, but I like mysteries.* (I don't like cowboy stories because I find them dull.) *Sara is scared to death of snakes.* (Sara is very much afraid of snakes.) *John is tickled to death with his new bike.* (John likes his new bike very much.)

to do See HAVE TO DO WITH.

toe See CURL ONE'S HAIR *or* CURL ONE'S TOES, ON ONE'S TOES, STEP ON THE TOES OF.

toe the line *or* **toe the mark** *v. phr.* To be very careful to do just what you are supposed to do; obey the rules and do your duties. *The new teacher will make Joe toe the line.* (The new teacher will make Joe behave and do his work.) *Bill's father is strict with him and he has to toe the mark.* (Bill's father expects him to obey him and do right.) Compare WALK THE CHALK.

to first base See GET TO FIRST BASE.

together See GET IT ALL TOGETHER.

together with *prep.* In addition to; in the company of; along with. *John, together with his brother, has gone to the party.* (John has gone to the party with his brother.) *The police found a knife, together with the stolen money, hidden in a hollow tree.* (The police found a knife, besides the stolen money, in a hollow tree.)

to grips See COME TO GRIPS WITH.

to heart See TAKE TO HEART *also* LAY TO HEART.

to heel *adj. phr.* **1** Close behind. *The dog ran after a rabbit, but Jack brought him to heel.* (Jack made the dog stay just behind him.) **2** Under control; to obedience. *When Peter was sixteen, he thought he could do as he pleased, but his father cut off his allowance, and Peter soon came to heel.* (Peter soon began to obey his father again.)

to hell with *or* **the hell with** *prep. phr., informal*—Used to express disgusted rejection of something. *It's slop; the hell with what the cook calls it.* (I don't care what the cook calls it.) Compare FED UP, GIVE A HANG.

to it See PUT ONE'S BACK TO IT.

to light See BRING TO LIGHT, COME TO LIGHT.

toll See TAKE ITS TOLL.

Tom See PEEPING TOM.

Tom, Dick, and Harry *n. phr.* People in general; anyone; everyone.—Usually preceded by *every* and used to show scorn or disrespect. *The drunk told his troubles to every Tom, Dick and Harry who passed by.* (The drunk told his troubles to anyone who happened to pass by.)

tone down *v.* To make softer or quieter; make less harsh or strong; moderate. *He toned down the sound of the TV.* (He made the sound softer and quieter.) *She wanted the bright colors in her house toned down.* (She wanted softer colors, not too bright.) *When the ladies arrived, he toned down his language.* (He talked more quietly and politely.) *The strikers were asked to tone down their demands for higher pay so that there might be a quicker agreement and an end to the strike.* (The strikers were asked to reduce their demands so the company would accept them.)

tong See GO AT IT HAMMER AND TONGS.

tongue See AT THE TIP OF ONE'S TONGUE, CAT GET ONE'S TONGUE, HOLD ONE'S TONGUE, KEEP A CIVIL TONGUE IN ONE'S HEAD, SLIP OF THE TONGUE.

tongue-lashing *n.* A sharp scolding or criticism. *Jim's mother gave him a tongue-lashing for telling family secrets.* (Jim's mother scolded him very much for telling secrets.) Syn. PIECE OF ONE'S MIND.

tongues wag *informal* People speak in an excited or gossipy manner; people spread rumors. *If married women go out with other men, tongues will wag.* (People will talk about them.) *When the bank clerk showed up in an expensive new car, tongues wagged.* (They began to wonder where the clerk got the money to buy such an expensive car.)

to no avail *or* **of no avail**[1] *adj. phr., formal* Having no effect; useless, unsuccessful. *Tom's practicing was of no avail. He was sick on the day of the game.* (Tom's practicing for the game was useless because he couldn't play.) *Mary's attempts to learn embroidering were to no avail.* (Mary couldn't learn embroidering.)

to no avail[2] *adv. phr., formal* Without result; unsuccessfully. *John tried to pull the heavy cart, but to no avail.* (John tried to pull the cart but he couldn't.) *Mary studied hard for the test but to no avail.* (Mary studied hard, but she failed the test.) Compare IN VAIN.

too See EAT ONE'S CAKE AND HAVE IT TOO.

too bad *adj.* To be regretted; worthy of sorrow or regret; regrettable.—Used as a predicate. *It is too bad that we are so often lazy.* (It is to be regretted that we are so often lazy.) *It was too bad Bill had measles when the circus came to town.* (It was bad luck for Bill to have measles so he missed the circus.)

too big for one's breeches *or* **too big for one's boots** *adj. phr.* Too sure of your own importance; feeling more important than you really are.—A cliché. *That boy had grown too big for his breeches. I'll have to put him back in his place.* (That boy is acting much more important than he is. I'll have to make him less proud.) *When the teacher made Bob a monitor, he got too big for his boots and she had to warn him.* (He got too proud of himself and too rough with the other pupils.)

too —— by half *adj. (princ. British)* Much too; excessively. *The heroine of the story is too nice by half; she is not believable.* (The reader cannot believe anyone would be that nice.)

too many irons in the fire See IRONS IN THE FIRE.

to one See TEN TO ONE, TWO TO ONE.

to oneself[1] *adv. phr.* **1** Silently; in the thoughts; without making a sign that others can see; secretly. *Tom thought to himself that he could win.* (Tom thought he could win, but he told no one so.) *Mary said to herself that Joan was prettier than Ann.* (Mary judged that Joan was prettier, but she didn't tell Joan.) *Bill laughed to himself when John fell down.* (Bill laughed silently and did not let John see he was laughing.) **2** Without telling others; in private; as a secret.—Used after *keep. Mary keeps her affairs to herself.* (Mary doesn't tell others about what she is doing.) *John knew the answer to the problem, but he kept it to himself.* (John didn't tell anyone the answer to the problem.)

to oneself[2] *adj. phr.* **1** Without company; away from others; alone; deserted. *The boys went home and John was left to himself.* (The boys went home and left John alone.) *When Mary first moved to her new neighborhood she was very shy and kept to herself.* (Mary did not mix with other people; she stayed alone.) **2** Following one's own beliefs or wishes; not stopped by others. *When John insisted on going, Fred left him to himself.* (When John insisted, Fred gave up trying to stop him from going.) *The teacher left Mary to herself to solve the problem.* (The teacher didn't help Mary, but let her solve the problem in her own way.)

to one's face *adv. phr.* Directly to you; in your presence. *I told him to his face that I didn't like the idea.* (I told him directly that I didn't like the idea.) *I called him a coward to his face.* (I told him plainly that he was a coward.) Compare IN ONE'S FACE. Contrast BEHIND ONE'S BACK.

to one's feet *adv. phr.* To a standing position; up. *After Henry had been tackled hard by four big players, he got to his feet slowly and painfully.* (Henry stood up slowly and painfully.) *When Sally saw the bus coming, she jumped to her feet and ran out.* (Sally stood up quickly.) Compare ON ONE'S FEET.

to one's guns See STICK TO ONE'S GUNS.

to one's heart's content *adv. phr.* As much as you want.—A cliché. *She told them they could eat cake to their heart's content.* (She told them they could eat all the cake they wanted.) *There was even a place where he could dig to his heart's content.* (There was a place where he could dig as much as he wanted.)

to one's heels See TAKE TO ONE'S HEELS.

to one's name *adv. phr.* In your ownership; of your own; as part of your belongings. *David did not have a book to his name.* (David owned no books.) *Ed had only one suit to his name.* (He owned only one suit.)

to one's ribs See STICK TO ONE'S RIBS.

to one's senses See COME TO ONE'S SENSES.

to order *adv. phr.* According to directions given in an order in the way and size wanted. *The manufacturer built the machine to order.* (The manufacturer made the machine in the style and size asked for in the customer's order.) *A very big man often has his suits made to order.* (He orders suits made in his size and as he wants them.) **2** See CALL TO ORDER.

tooth See BY THE SKIN OF ONE'S TEETH, CUT TEETH *or* CUT EYETEETH, EYE FOR AN EYE AND A TOOTH FOR A TOOTH, FED TO THE GILLS *or* FED TO THE TEETH, GET ONE'S TEETH INTO *or* SINK ONE'S TEETH INTO, KICK IN THE PANTS *or* KICK IN THE TEETH, PULL ONE'S TEETH, SET ONE'S TEETH ON EDGE, TAKE THE BIT IN ONE'S TEETH, THROW —— IN YOUR FACE *or* THROW —— IN YOUR TEETH.

tooth and nail *adv. phr.* With all weapons or ways of fighting as hard as possible; fiercely.—Used after *fight* or a similar word. *When the Indian girl was captured, she fought tooth and nail to get away.* (She scratched and bit to get away.) *The farmers fought tooth and nail to save their crops from the grasshoppers.* (They did everything they could to kill and drive off the grasshoppers and save their crops.) *His friends fought tooth and nail to elect him to Congress.* (They tried very hard to help him win.)

toot one's own horn See BLOW ONE'S OWN HORN.

top See AT THE TOP OF ONE'S VOICE, BIG TOP, BLOW A FUSE *or* BLOW ONE'S TOP, HARD-TOP, OFF THE TOP OF ONE'S HEAD, ON TOP, ON TOP OF, ON TOP OF THE WORLD, OVER THE TOP.

top banana *or* **top dog** *n., slang, informal* The head of any business or organization; the most influential or most prestigious person in an establishment. *Who's the top banana/dog* *in this outfit?* (Who is the boss in the place?) See MAIN SQUEEZE.

to pass See COME TO PASS.

top-drawer *adj., informal* Of the best; or most important kind. *Mary's art work was top-drawer material.* (Her work was the best among the artists.) *Mr. Rogers is a top-drawer executive and gets a very high salary.* (Mr. Rogers is an important boss in his company.)

to pieces *adv. phr.* **1** Into broken pieces or fragments; destroyed. *The cannon shot the town to pieces.* (The cannon destroyed the town.) *The vase fell to pieces in Mary's hand.* (The vase broke in Mary's hand.) **2** *informal* So as not to work; into a state of not operating. *After 100,000 miles the car went to pieces.* (After 100,000 miles the car wouldn't run any more.) *When Mary heard of her mother's death, she went to pieces.* (When Mary heard the news, she became so upset she could do nothing.) **3** *informal* Very much; greatly; exceedingly.—A hackneyed phrase. *Joan was thrilled to pieces to see Mary.* (Joan was very glad to see Mary.) *The noise scared Bob to pieces.* (The noise scared Bob very much.) **4** See PICK APART.

top off *v.* To come or bring to a special or unexpected ending; climax. *John batted three runs and topped off the game with a home run.* (John completed his good day by hitting a home run.) *Mary hadn't finished her home work, she was late to school, and to top it all off she missed a surprise test.* (Mary had a lot of trouble, but missing the test was the worst trouble of all.) *George had steak for dinner and topped it off with a fudge sundae.* (George brought a good dinner to a special ending with a hot fudge sundae.)

torch See CARRY A TORCH.

to reason See STAND TO REASON.

to rest See LAY TO REST.

to rights See PUT TO RIGHTS *or* SET TO RIGHTS.

to Rome See ALL ROADS LEAD TO ROME.

to say nothing of See NOT TO MENTION.

to scale *adv. phr.* In the same proportions as in the true size; in the same shape, but not the same size. *The statue was made to scale, one inch to a foot.* (The statue was one-twelfth full size.) *He drew the map to scale, making one inch represent fifty miles.* (One inch on the map was fifty miles in real length.

to sea See PUT TO SEA.

to shame See PUT TO SHAME.

to size See CUT DOWN TO SIZE.

to speak of *adj. phr., informal* Important; worth talking about; worth noticing.—Usually used in negative sentences. *Did it rain yesterday? Not to speak of.* (Did it rain? Very little.) *What happened at the meeting? Nothing to speak of.* (Nothing very important happened.) *Judy's injuries were nothing to speak of; just a few scratches.* (Judy was not hurt much.) Compare NOT TO MENTION.

to spite one's face See CUT OFF ONE'S NOSE TO SPITE ONE'S FACE.

toss off *v.* **1** To drink rapidly; drain. *He tossed off two drinks and left.* (He quickly drank two drinks and left.) **2** To make or say easily without trying or thinking hard. *She tossed off smart remarks all during dinner.* (She made many witty remarks all through dinner.) *He thinks a reporter should be able to toss off an article every few hours.* (He thinks a news writer should be able to write many articles quickly and without any trouble.)

toss out See THROW OUT.

total See SUM TOTAL.

to task See TAKE TO TASK.

to terms See BRING TO TERMS, COME TO TERMS.

to that effect *adj. or adv. phr.* With that meaning. *She said she hated spinach, or words to that effect.* (She said she hated spinach, or said something that meant she hated spinach.) *When I leave, I will write you to that effect so you will know.* (When I leave, I will write and tell you that I have left.)

to the best of one's knowledge As far as you know; to the extent of your knowledge. *He has never won a game, to the best of my knowledge.* (If he has won a game, I don't know about it.) *To the best of my knowledge he is a college man, but I may be mistaken.* (I think he is a college man.)

to the bitter end *adv. phr.* To the point of completion or conclusion.—A cliché used especially of a very painful or unpleasant task or experience. *Although Mrs. Smith was bored by the lecture, she stayed to the bitter end.* (Although bored by the lecture, Mrs. Smith stayed until it was over.) *They knew the war would be lost, but the men fought to the bitter end.* (They kept on fighting though they knew it was no use.)

to the bone *adv., slang, informal* Thoroughly, entirely, to the core, through all layers. *I am dreadfully tired; I've worked my fingers to the bone.* (I've worked so hard that it almost eroded the flesh off my hands—an obvious exaggeration.) See ALSO WORK ONE'S FINGERS TO THE BONE.

to the bottom See GET TO THE BOTTOM OF.

to the contrary *adv. or adj. phr.* With an opposite result or effect; just the opposite; in disagreement; saying the opposite. *Although Bill was going to the movies, he told Joe to the contrary.* (Bill was going but he said he was not.) *We will expect you for dinner unless we get word to the contrary.* (We will expect you for dinner unless you send us a message saying you cannot come.) *School gossip to the contrary, Mary is not engaged to be married.* (Mary isn't engaged, but the gossip say she is.) Compare ON THE CONTRARY.

to the effect that *adj. phr.* With the meaning or purpose; to say that. *He made a speech to the effect that we would all keep our jobs even if the factory were sold.* (He made a speech to say that we would all keep our jobs even if the factory were sold.) *The new governor would do his best in the office to which he had been elected.* (He made a few remarks with the meaning that he would do his best.)

to the eye *adv. phr.* As it is seen; as a person or thing first seems; apparently. *That girl looks to the eye like a nice girl to know, but she is really rather mean.* (That girl appears at first to be a nice girl, but she isn't.) *That suit appears to the eye to be a good buy, but it may not be.* (The suit may not be as it appears.) Compare AT FIRST GLANCE.

to the fore *adv. or adj. phr.* Into leadership; out into notice or view; forward. *The hidden skill of the lawyer came to the fore during the trial.* (The lawyer's abilities had not been noticed before, but everyone saw them during the trial.) *In the progress of the war some new leaders came to the fore.* (Men who were not known before were noticed and promoted to leadership.)

to the full *adv. phr.* Very much; fully. *The campers enjoyed their trip to the full.* (The campers enjoyed their trip very much.) *We appreciated to the full the teacher's help.* (We were very grateful for the teacher's help.) Compare TO THE HILT.

to the gallery See PLAY TO THE GALLERY.

to the good *adv. phr.* On the side of profit or advantage; in one's favor; to one's benefit; ahead. *After I sold my stamp collection, I was ten dollars to the good.* (I made ten dollars profit when I sold my stamp collection.) *The teacher did not see him come in late, which was all to the good.* (Luckily, the teacher did not see him come in late.)

to the grindsone See KEEP ONE'S NOSE TO THE GRINDSTONE.

to the heart See GET TO THE HEART OF.

to the hilt *or* **up to the hilt** *adv. phr.* To the limit; as far as possible; completely.—An overused phrase. *The other boys on the team told Tom he couldn't quit. They said, "You're in this to the hilt."* (The boys told Tom that he had promised his complete loyalty to the team.) *The Smith's house is mortgaged up to the hilt.* (The Smith's house is mortgaged as much as it can be mortgaged; they can not borrow any more money on it.) Compare HEART AND SOUL, TO THE FULL, UP TO THE —— IN.

to the king's taste *or* **to the queen's taste** *adv. phr.* Perfectly; just as anyone could want it; very satisfactorily.—A trite phrase. *The rooms in their new home were painted and decorated to the queen's taste.* (The rooms could not be more perfectly decorated.) *The soldiers dressed and marched to the king's taste.* (Even a king couldn't expect better dressed or trained soldiers.)

to the letter *adv. phr.* With nothing done wrong or left undone; exactly; precisely. *He carried out his orders to the letter.* (He did everything exactly as he was told.) *When writing a test you should follow the instructions to the letter.* (You should follow them exactly.) Compare TO A T.

to the manner born *adj. phr.* At ease with something because of lifelong familiarity with it. *She says her English is the best because she is to the manner born.* (She claims that hers is the most correct English because she grew up among people who spoke only correct English, so it comes naturally.)

to the nth degree *adv. phr.* To the greatest degree possible; extremely; very much so. *Scales must be accurate to the nth degree.* (Scales must be as exact as possible.) *His choice of words was exactly to the nth degree.* (He always used his words in exactly the right way and place.)

to the point See COME TO THE POINT.

to the punch See BEAT TO THE PUNCH.

to the ribs See STICK TO ONE'S RIBS *or* STICK TO THE RIBS.

to the salt mines See BACK TO THE SALT MINES.

to the stump See TAKE THE STUMP *or* TAKE TO THE STUMP.

to the sword See PUT TO THE SWORD.

to the tune of *adv. phr., informal* To the amount or extent of; in the amount of.—A trite phrase. *He had to pay to the tune of fifty dollars for seeing how fast the car would go.* (It cost him fifty dollars for speeding because he wanted to see how fast his car would go.) *When she left the race track she had profited to the tune of ten dollars.* (She won ten dollars.)

to the wall *adv. phr.* Into a place from which there is no escape; into a trap or corner.—A hackneyed phrase; usually used after *drive* or a similar word. *John's failing the last test drove him to the wall.* (By failing the last test, John no longer had a chance of passing the course.) *The score was 12–12 in the last minute of play, but a touchdown forced the visitors to the wall.* (Our side won the game in the last minute of play.) *Bill had to sell his five Great Danes. The high cost of feeding them was driving him to the wall.* (He had to sell the dogs because he could not afford to keep on feeding them.)

to the wolves See THROW TO THE WOLVES.

to the woods See TAKE TO THE WOODS.

to the world See DEAD TO THE WORLD.

to think of it See COME TO THINK OF IT.

toto See IN TOTO.

touch See COMMON TOUCH, IN TOUCH, LOSE TOUCH, OUT OF TOUCH.

touch and go *adj. phr.* Very dangerous or uncertain in situation. *Our team won the game, all right, but it was touch and go for a while.* (Our team won, but for a while it looked like we wouldn't win.) *At one time while they were climbing the cliff it was touch and go whether they could do it.* (They were in a dangerous place and might have fallen.)

touch bottom See HIT BOTTOM.

touch off *v.* **1** To cause to fire or explode by lighting the priming or the fuse. *The boy touched off a firecracker.* (The boy lit the fuse of a firecracker, and it exploded.) Compare SET OFF. **2** To start something as if by lighting a fuse. *The coach's resignation touched off a quarrel.* (The coach's resignation started a quarrel.) Compare SET OFF.

touch on *or* **touch upon** *v.* To speak of or write of briefly. *The speaker touched on several other subjects in the course of his talk but mostly kept himself to the main topic.* (The speaker kept mostly to his topic although he did mention briefly several other topics.) Contrast DWELL ON.

touch up *v.* **1** To paint over (small imperfections.) *I want to touch up that scratch on the fender.* (I want to paint over the scratch on the fender.) *The woodwork is done, but there are a few places he has to touch up.* (The woodwork has been done but there are still a few places that need a little more paint.) **2** To improve with small additions or changes. *He touched up the photographic negative to make a sharper print.* (He made small improvements in the negative so that the picture would be sharper.) *It's a good speech, but it needs a little touching up.* (It's a good speech, but it needs a few small improvements.) **3** *slang* To talk into lending; wheedle from. *He touched George up for five bucks.* (He talked George into lending him five dollars.)

tough cat *n., slang* A man who is very individualistic and, as a result, highly successful with women. *Joe is a real tough cat, man.* (He is highly individualistic and succeeds easily with women.)

tough nut to crack See HARD NUT TO CRACK.

tough row to hoe See HARD ROW TO HOE.

tough sledding See HARD SLEDDING.

to use See PUT TO USE.

tow See IN TOW.

towel See THROW IN THE SPONGE *or* THROW IN THE TOWEL.

town See GO TO TOWN, ON THE TOWN, PAINT THE TOWN RED.

town and gown *n.* The residents of a college town and the students and teachers of the college. *The senator made a speech attended by both town and gown.* (Both the people of the town and the college students and teachers heard the speech.) *There were fights between town and gown.* (The boys of the town fought with the college boys.)

to your hat See HANG ON TO YOUR HAT *or* HOLD ON TO YOUR HAT.

trace See KICK OVER THE TRACES *also* JUMP THE TRACES.

track See COVER ONE'S TRACKS, IN ONE'S TRACKS, INSIDE TRACK, JUMP THE TRACK, KEEP TRACK, LOSE TRACK, MAKE TRACKS, OFF THE BEATEN TRACK, ON THE TRACK OF, THE TRACKS.

track down *v.* To find by or as if by following tracks or a trail. *The hunters tracked down game in the forest.* (The hunters found animals in the forest by following the animals' trails.) *She spent weeks in the library tracking the reference down in all their books on the subject.* (She spent weeks in the library hunting through books to find the reference.) Compare HUNT DOWN.

trade See CARRIAGE TRADE, HORSE TRADE, TRICKS OF THE TRADE.

trade in *v.* To give something to a seller as part payment for another thing of greater value. *The Browns traded their old car in on a new one.* (The Browns gave their old car to the dealer as part payment for the new one.) Syn. TURN IN 3.

trade-in *n.* Something given as part payment on something better. *The dealer took our old car as a trade-in.* (The dealer took our old car as part payment on a new one.) —Often used like an adjective. *We cleaned up the car at trade-in time.* (We cleaned up the car when it was time to trade it in.)

trade on *v.* To use as a way of helping yourself. *The coach traded on the pitcher's weakness for left-handed batters by using all his southpaws.* (The coach used his own left-handers because in that way he could best take advantage of the other side's weakness.) *The senator's son traded on his father's name when he ran for mayor.* (The son was unknown, but his father was famous. So the son made sure that everyone knew whose son he was.)

trading stamp *n.* One of the stamps that you get (as from a store or gas station) because you buy something there; a stamp you get with a purchase and save in special books until you have enough to take to a special store and trade for something you want. *Mother always buys things in stores where they give trading stamps.* (Mother always buys from stores that give stamps to exchange later for things.)

trail See BLAZE A TRAIL, ON THE TRACK OF *or* ON THE TRAIL OF.

trail-blazer See BLAZE A TRAIL.

trap See MIND LIKE A STEEL TRAP, SAND TRAP, SPEED TRAP.

travel light *v. phr.* To travel with very little luggage or with very little to carry. *Plane passengers must travel light.* (Plane passengers cannot take very much baggage.) *Tom and Fred traveled light on their camping trip.* (Tom and Fred carried small packs and no tents.)

tread on the toes of *or* **tread on one's toes** See STEP ON THE TOES OF *or* STEP ON ONE'S TOES.

tread water *v. phr.* To keep the head above water with the body in an upright position by moving the feet as if walking. *He kept afloat by treading water.* (He kept his head above water by moving his feet up and down.)

treat See TRICK OR TREAT.

tree See BARK UP THE WRONG TREE, CAN'T SEE THE WOOD FOR THE TREES, UP A TREE.

trembling See FEAR AND TREMBLING.

trial See ON TRIAL.

trial and error *n.* A way of solving problems by trying different possible solutions until you find one that works. *John found the short circuit by trial and error.* (John kept testing different wires until he found the one that was causing the short circuit.) *The only way Tom could solve the algebra problem was by the method of trial and error.* (Tom had to solve the problem by guessing at possible answers and then seeing if they would satisfy the problem.)

trial balloon *n.* A hint about a plan of action that is given out to find out what people will say. *John mentioned the class presidency to Bill as a trial balloon to see if Bill might be interested in running.* (John mentioned the presidency to see if Bill might make some remarks about the job.) *The editorial was a trial balloon to test the public's reaction to a change in the school day.* (The editorial was designed to get the public to write letters in support of, or against changing the school day.)

trice See IN A FLASH *also* IN A TRICE.

trick See DO THE TRICK, TURN THE TRICK.

trick of the trade *n. phr.; usually in plural, informal* **1** A piece of expert knowledge; a smart, quick, or skillful way of working at a trade or job.—A cliché. *Mr. Olson spent years learning the tricks of the trade as a carpenter.* (He spent years learning to do the work quickly and well.) *Anyone can learn how to hang wallpaper, but only an expert can show you the tricks of the trade.* (An expert can show you the quickest way to do it.) **2** A smart and sometimes tricky or dishonest way of doing something in order to succeed or win. *The champion knows all the tricks of the boxing trade; he knows many ways to hurt his opponent and to get him mixed up.* (The champion knows many tricks and unfair ways to beat his opponents.)

trick or treat *n.* The custom of going from house to house on Halloween asking for small gifts and playing tricks on people who refuse to give. *When Mrs. Jones answered the doorbell, the children yelled "Trick or treat." Mrs. Jones gave them all some candy.* (Mrs. Jones gave the children candy so they would not play a trick on her.) *On Halloween Bill and Tom went out playing trick or treat.* (Bill and Tom went out begging food and threatening to play tricks if they were refused.)

trigger See QUICK ON THE TRIGGER.

trigger happy See QUICK ON THE TRIGGER 1.

triple threat *n.* A football player who is able to pass, kick, and run all very well. *The triple threat halfback was the star of the team.* (Because he could do all these things well, he was the most valuable offensive player on the team.)

tripped out *adj., slang, informal* Incoherent, confused, faulty of speech, illogical; as if under the influence of drugs or alcohol. *It was hard to make sense of anything Max said yesterday; he sounded so tripped out.* (People had difficulty understanding Max, for he was so confused and illogical.) See SPACED OUT.

trip up *v.* **1** To make (someone) unsteady on the feet; cause to miss a step, stumble, or fall. *A root tripped Billy up while he was running in the woods, and he fell and hurt his ankle.* (The root of a tree caught Billy's foot while he was running.) **2** To cause (someone) to make a mistake. *The teacher asked tricky questions in the test to trip up students who were not alert.* (The teacher put tricky quesions in the test to catch those students who were not giving careful attention.)

trolley See OFF ONE'S ROCKER *or* OFF ONE'S TROLLEY.

trouble See BORROW TROUBLE, GO TO THE TROUBLE *or* TAKE THE TROUBLE.

troubled waters See POUR OIL ON TROUBLED WATERS.

trousers See WEAR THE TROUSERS.

trowel See LAY IT ON.

truck See PANEL TRUCK.

true See COME TRUE, HOLD TRUE, RUN TRUE TO FORM.

trump See HOLD ALL THE TRUMPS.

trump card *n.* Something kept back to be used to win success if nothing else works. *The coach saved his star pitcher for a trump card.* (The coach kept his star pitcher in reserve in case he was needed later in the game to stop the other team.) *Mary had several ways to get Joan to come to her party. Her trump card was that the football captain would be there.* (Mary would use all her other reasons before she told Joan about the football captain, but then Joan would be sure to come.)

trump up *v.* To make up (something untrue); invent in the mind. *Every time Tom is late getting home he trumps up some new excuse.* (He makes up an untrue story to explain his being late.) *The Russians were afraid he was a spy, so they arrested him on a trumped-up charge and made him leave the country.* (The Russians arrested him on false accusations and made him leave the country.)

trust See IN TRUST.

truth See CHILDREN AND FOOLS SPEAK THE TRUTH.

try on *v.* To put (clothing) on to see if it fits. *She tried on several pairs of shoes before she found one she liked.* (She put on several pairs of shoes before she found a comfortable pair.) *The clerk told him to try the coat on.* (The clerk told him to put on the coat and see how he liked it.)

try one's hand   *v. phr.*   To make an inexperienced attempt (at something unfamiliar.) *I thought I would try my hand at bowling, although I had never bowled before.* (I thought I would give bowling a try although I had never bowled before.)

try out   *v.*   **1** To test by trial or by experimenting. *He tried golf out to see if he would like it.* (To see if he would life golf, he tried playing the game.) *The scientists tried out thousands of chemicals before they found the right one.* (The chemists tested thousands of chemicals before they found the one they needed.) *The coach wants to try the new play out in the first game.* (The coach wants to see if the new play will work.) **2** To try for a place on a team or in a group. *Tom tried out for the basketball team.* (Tom went to basketball practice and tried to be chosen as a member of the team.) *Shirley will try out for the lead in the play.* (Shirley will practice the leading part in the play and hopes she will be selected to play it.) Compare OUT FOR.

tuck   See NIP AND TUCK.

tucker   See BEST BIB AND TUCKER.

tug-of-war   *n.*   **1** A game in which two teams pull on opposite ends of a rope, trying to pull the other team over a line marked on the ground. *The tug-of-war ended when both teams tumbled in a heap.* (Both teams fell down together and neither side won.) **2** A contest in which two sides try to defeat each other; struggle. *A tug-of-war developed between the boys who wanted to go fishing and those who wanted to go hiking.* (The boys who wanted to go fishing started arguing with those who wanted to go hiking.) *Betty felt a tug-of-war between her wish to go to the movies and her realizing she had to do her homework.* (Betty felt pulled to one side by her wishes and to the other side by her duty.) *The tug of war between the union men and management ended in a long strike.* (The meetings between the Union and the company failed to settle the problem.)

tune   See CALL THE TUNE, CHANGE ONE'S TUNE, IN TUNE, SING A DIFFERENT TUNE *or* WHISTLE A DIFFERENT TUNE *also* SING A NEW TUNE, TO THE TUNE OF.

tune in   To adjust a radio or television set to pick up a certain station. *Bob tuned in his portable radio to a record show.* (Bob set his radio to a station playing records.) *Tom tuned in to Channel 11 to hear the news.* (Tom got Channel 11 on the television so that he could hear the news.)

tune up   *v.*   **1a** To adjust (a musical instrument) to make the right sound. *Before he began to play, Harry tuned up his banjo.* (Harry put his banjo in tune by tightening the

strings to the proper sound.) **1b** To adjust a musical instrument or a group of musical instruments to the right sound. *The orchestra came in and began to tune up for the concert.* (The members of the orchestra adjusted their instruments so they could play together.) **2** To adjust many parts of (car engine) which must work together so that it will run properly. *He took his car to the garage to have the engine tuned up.* (He took the car to the garage so that the mechanics could adjust parts of the engine to run properly.)

tune-up   *n.*   **1** The adjusting or fixing of something (as a motor) to make it work safely and well. *Father says the car needs a tune-up before winter begins.* (Things wrong with the car's motor must be fixed or corrected before winter starts.) **2** Exercise or practicing for the purpose of getting ready; a trial before something. *The team went to the practice field for their last tune-up before the game tomorrow.* (The team will have exercise and practice for the last time before their game.) Syn. WARM UP.

turkey   See TALK TURKEY.

turn   See AT EVERY TURN, BLOOD RUN COLD *or* BLOOD TURNS TO ICE, BY TURNS, CALL THE TURN *at* CALL ONE'S SHOTS 2, EVERY TIME ONE TURNS AROUND, IN TURN, NOT KNOW WHICH WAY TO TURN, OUT OF TURN, TAKE A TURN, TAKE TURNS, TO A T *or* TO A TURN.

turn a blind eye   *v. phr.*   To pretend not to see; not pay attention. *The corrupt police chief turned a blind eye to the open gambling in the town.*—A trite expression. (The police chief pretended not to know there was gambling in the town.) *Bob turned a blind eye to the "No Fishing" sign.* (Bob pretended not to see the "No Fishing" sign.) Compare CLOSE ONE'S EYES.

turn a cold shoulder   See COLD SHOULDER.

turn a deaf ear to   *v. phr.*   To pretend not to hear; refuse to hear; not pay attention.—A trite expression. *Mary turned a deaf ear to Lois's asking to ride her bicycle.* (Mary paid no attention when Lois asked to ride her bicycle.) *The teacher turned a deaf ear to Bob's excuse.* (The teacher would not listen to Bob's excuse.) Compare COLD SHOULDER.

turn a hand   *v. phr.*   To do anything to help. —Usually used in the negative. *When we were all hurrying to get the house ready for company, Mary sat reading and wouldn't turn a hand.* (Mary refused to help.) Syn. LIFT A FINGER.

turn ———— around one's little finger   See TWIST ———— AROUND ONE'S LITTLE FINGER.

turn back the clock   See PUT BACK THE CLOCK.

turn color   *v. phr.*   To become a different color. *In the fall the leaves turn color.* (In the fall the leaves turn from green to red and brown.) *When the dye was added the solution turned color.* (The dye changed the color of the solution.)

turn down v. **1** To reduce the loudness, brightness, or force of. *The theater lights were turned down.* (The lights were dimmed.) *Turn down that radio, will you?* (Please make the radio play more quietly.) *The hose was throwing too much water so I turned down the water a little bit.* (I reduced the pressure of the water in the hose.) **2** To refuse to accept; reject. *His request for a raise was turned down.* (He asked for a raise but it was refused.) *If she offers to help, I'll turn her down.* (I won't accept any help from her.) *Many boys courted Lynn, but she turned them all down.* (Many boys courted Lynn, but she wouldn't marry any of them.)

turn for the worse See FOR THE WORSE.

turn in v. **1** or **hand in** To give to someone; deliver to someone. *I want you to turn in a good history paper.* (I want you to give me a good history paper.) *When the football season was over, we turned in our uniforms.* (At the end of the season we returned our uniforms.) **2** To inform on; report. *She turned them in to the police for breaking the street light.* (She reported them to the police for breaking the street light.) **3** To give in return for something. *They turned in their old money for new.* (They gave their old money in exchange for new.) *We turned our car in on a new model.* (We gave our old car as part payment for a new one.) Syn. TRADE IN. **4** *informal* To go to bed. *We were tired, so we turned in about nine o'clock.* (We went to bed at about nine o'clock.) Contrast TURN OUT 4.

turn in one's grave or **turn over in one's grave** v. phr. To be so grieved or angry that you would not rest quietly in your grave.—A cliché. *If your grandfather could see what you're doing now, he would turn over in his grave.* (Your grandfather would be so angry with what you're doing he wouldn't be able to lie still in his grave.)

turn loose See LET LOOSE 1a.

turn off v. **1** To stop by turning a knob or handle or by working a switch; to cause to be off. *He turned the water off.* (He stopped the water by turning the handle.) *He turned off the light.* (He made the light go off by working the switch.) **2** To leave by turning right or left onto another way. *Turn off the highway at exit 5.* (Leave the highway at exit 5.) *The car turned off on Bridge Street.* (The car went off the street it was on and turned and went along Bridge Street.) *slang* **3** To disgust, bore, or repel (someone) by being intellectually, emotionally, socially, or sexually unattractive. *I won't date Linda Bell anymore—she just turns me off.* (I am repelled by her.) Contrast TURN ON.

turn of the century n. phr. The time at the end of one century and the beginning of the next century; *especially:* The time when the 1800's became the 1900's; the early 1900's.

Automobiles were strange things to see at the turn of the century. (About the year 1900 people were surprised to see automobiles.)

turn on v. **1** To start by turning a knob or handle or working a switch; cause to be on. *Jack turned on the water.* (Jack started the water running by turning the handle.) *Who turned the lights on?* (Who switched the lights on?) **2** *informal* To put forth or succeed with as easily as turning on water. *She really turns on the charm when that new boy is around.* (She makes herself charming when the new boy is around.) **3** To attack. *The lion tamer was afraid the lions would turn on him.* (The lion tamer was afraid the lions would attack him.) *After Joe fumbled the ball and lost the big game, his friends turned on him.* (Even his friends said bad things about him because he lost the game.) **4** *slang* The opposite of turning someone off; to become greatly interested in an idea, person, or undertaking; to arouse the senses pleasantly. *Mozart's music always turns me on.* (I always derive a pleasant sensation by listening to Mozart.) **5** Introducing someone to a new experience, or set of values. *Benjamin turned me on to transcendental meditation, and ever since I've been feeling great!* (He introduced me to meditation.) Contrast TURN OFF.

turn one's back on v. phr. To refuse to help (someone in trouble or need.)—A cliché. *He turned his back on his own family when they needed help.* (He would not help his family when they needed it.) *The poorer nations are often not grateful for our help, but still we can not turn our back on them.* (We cannot refuse to help them.) Compare GO BACK ON 1.

turn one's hand to See PUT ONE'S HAND TO.

turn one's head v. phr., informal To make you lose your good judgment.—A trite expression. *The first pretty girl he saw turned his head.* (The first pretty girl he saw made him act foolishly.) *Winning the class election turned his head.* (Winning the class election made him too proud of himself.)

turn one's stomach v. phr., informal To make you feel sick. *The smell of that cigar was enough to turn your stomach.* (The smell of that cigar was enough to make you sick.) *The sight of blood turns my stomach.* (I feel sick when I see blood.)

turn on one's heel v. phr. To turn around suddenly. *When John saw Fred approaching him, he turned on his heel.* (When John saw Fred, he turned around quickly so as not to have to speak to him.) *When little Tommy's big brother showed up, the bully turned on his heel.* (When the bully saw Tommy's brother, he ran away.)

turn out v. **1** To make leave or go away. *His father turned him out of the house.* (His father made him leave the house.) *If you* *don't behave, you will be turned out.* (If you don't behave, you will have to leave.) Compare THROW OUT. **2** To turn inside out; empty. *He turned out his pockets looking for the money.* (He turned his pockets inside out looking for the money.) *Robbers turned out all the drawers in the house in a search for jewels.* (Robbers emptied all the drawers in the house looking for jewels.) **3** to make; produce. *The printing press turns out a thousand books an hour.* (The printing press prints a thousand books an hour.) *Sally can turn out a cake in no time.* (Sally can make a cake with no trouble and in little time.) *Martin turns out a poem each week for the school paper.* (Martin writes a poem each week for the school paper.) **4** *informal* To get out of bed. *At camp the boys had to turn out early and go to bed early too.* (At camp they got up early.) Contrast TURN IN 4. **5** *informal* To come or go out to see or do something. *Everybody turned out for the big parade.* (Everybody came to watch the big parade.) *Many boys turned out for football practice.* (Many boys went to football practice.) Compare FALL OUT. **6** To prove to be; be in the end; be found to be. *The noise turned out to be just the dog scratching at the door.* (The noise proved to be just the dog scratching at the door.) *Her guess turned out to be right.* (Her guess was found right in the end.) *Everything turned out all right.* (Everything ended up by being all right.) **7** To make (a light) go out. *Please turn out the lights.* (Please switch the lights off.) Syn. TURN OFF 1.

turn over *v.* **1** To roll, tip, or turn from one side to the other; overturn; upset. *He's going to turn over the page.* (He's going to turn the page from one side to the next.) *The bike hit a rock and turned over.* (The bike hit a rock and fell onto its side.) **2** To think about carefully; to consider. *He turned the problem over in his mind for three days before he did anything about it.* (He thought about the problem three days before he did anything.) **3** To give to someone for use or care. *I turned my library books over to the librarian.* (I gave my library books to the librarian.) *Mrs. Jackson brought her boy to the school and turned him over to the house father.* (Mrs. Jackson brought her boy to the school and put him in the care of the house father.) *Bob turns over most of the money he earns to his mother.* (He gives most of his money to his mother to use.) **4** Of an engine or motor; to start. *The battery is dead and the motor won't turn over.* (The battery is dead and the motor won't start.) **5a** To buy and then sell to customers. *The store turned over $5,000 worth of skiing equipment in January.* (The store sold $5,000 worth of things for skiing to customers after buying them from the makers.) **5b** To be bought in large enough

amounts; sell. *In a shoe store, shoes of medium width turn over quickly, because many people wear that size, but a pair of narrow shoes may not be sold for years.* (A shoe store may buy and sell several pairs of shoes of medium width before it sells a pair of narrow width.)

turn over a new leaf *v. phr.* To make a sudden change for the better in conduct.—A cliché. *George turned over a new leaf and stopped disturbing the class.* (George suddenly began behaving much better in class.) *Julie decided to turn over a new leaf and study harder.* (Julie suddenly decided to be a better student.) Compare CLEAN SLATE.

turn over in one's grave See TURN IN ONE'S GRAVE.

turn tail *v. phr., informal* To run away from trouble or danger. *When the bully saw my big brother, he turned tail and ran.* (The bully was scared and ran away from my big brother.)

turn the clock back *v. phr.* To return to an earlier period. *Mother wished she could turn the clock back to the days before the children grew up and left home.* (Mother wished to live again in the time when the children were living at home.) *Will repealing the minimum wage for workers under age eighteen turn the clock back to the abuses of the last century?* (Will the unfair practices of a hundred years ago come again?)

turn the other cheek *v. phr.* To let someone do something to you and not to do it in return; not hit back when hit; be patient when injured or insulted by someone; not try to get even.—A cliché. *Joe turned the other cheek when he was hit with a snowball.* (He did not throw a snowball back at the person who hit him with one.)

turn the tables *v. phr.* To make something happen just the opposite of how it is supposed to happen. *The boys turned the tables on John when they took his squirt gun away and squirted him.* John was going to squirt the boys, but they got his squirt gun and squirted him instead.)

turn the tide *v. phr.* To change what looks like defeat into victory. *We were losing the game until Jack got there. His coming turned the tide for us, and we won.* (We were losing the game until Jack came. He helped us turn the defeat into victory.) Compare TIP THE SCALES.

turn the trick *v. phr., informal* To bring about the result you want; succeed in what you plan to do. *Jerry wanted to win both the swimming and diving contests, but he couldn't quite turn the trick.* (Jerry wanted to win both contests but he could only win one of them.) Compare DO THE TRICK.

turn thumbs down *v. phr.* To disapprove or reject; say no.—Usually used with *on. The company turned thumbs down on Mr. Smith's* *sales plan.* (The company refused to accept his sales plans.) *The men turned thumbs down on a strike at that time.* (They didn't approve of a strike at that time.)

turn to *v.* To begin working with much energy. *All the boys turned to and cleaned the cabin in a few minutes.* (All the boys worked hard and they cleaned the cabin very fast.) *Mary turned to and studied for the test.* (Mary concentrated on studying for the test.) Syn. FALL TO.

turn turtle *v. phr.* To turn upside down. *The car skidded on the ice and turned turtle.* (The car skidded on the ice and turned upside down.)

turn up *v.* **1** To find; discover. *The police searched the house hoping to turn up more clues.* (The police searched the house hoping to find more things that would help explain what happened.) **2** To appear or be found suddenly or unexpectedly. *The missing boy turned up an hour later.* (The boy was found an hour later.) *A man without training works at whatever jobs turn up.* (He works at whatever jobs happen to come along.) Compare SHOW UP 3.

turn up one's nose at *v. phr.* To refuse as not being good enough for you.—A trite expression. *He thinks he should only get steak, and he turns up his nose at hamburger.* (He thinks hamburger isn't good enough for him.)

turn up one's toes *v. phr., slang* To die. *One morning the children found that their pet mouse had turned up his toes, so they had a funeral for him.* (The mouse died.) Compare PUSH UP THE DAISIES.

turtle See TURN TURTLE.

tut-tut *interj., informal* —Used to express mild disapproval. *"Tut-tut," said the teacher. "You shouldn't cross the street without looking."* (The teacher said that it is not right to cross the street without looking.) *Tut-tut, put that piece of candy back. You've already had three pieces.* (You can't have another piece of candy now.)

twice See BIG AS LIFE 2, LIGHTNING NEVER STRIKES TWICE IN THE SAME PLACE, THINK TWICE, ONCE BITTEN, TWICE SHY *at* BURNT CHILD DREADS THE FIRE.

twice as natural See BIG AS LIFE *or* BIG AS LIFE AND TWICE AS NATURAL.

twiddle one's thumbs *v. phr.* To do nothing; be idle. *I'd rather work than stand around here twiddling my thumbs.* (I'd rather work than stand around doing nothing.)

twist ——— around one's little finger *also* **turn ——— around one's little finger** *or* **wrap**

——— around one's finger *v. phr.* To have complete control over; to be able to make (someone) do anything you want.—A cliché. *Sue can twist any of the boys around her little finger.* (Sue can get any of the boys to do what she wants them to.) Compare JUMP THROUGH A HOOP.

twist one's arm *v. phr., informal* To force someone; threaten someone to make him do something.—Usually used jokingly. *Will you dance with the prettiest girl in school? Stop, you're twisting my arm!* (Don't worry, I don't have to be forced to dance with the pretty girl!) *I had to twist Tom's arm to make him eat the candy!* (Tom had to be forced to eat candy!)

two See BETWEEN THE DEVIL AND THE DEEP BLUE SEA *or* BETWEEN TWO FIRES, TWO CENTS, BIRD IN THE HAND IS WORTH TWO IN THE BUSH, CUT BOTH WAYS *or* CUT TWO WAYS, HAVE TWO STRIKES AGAINST ONE, IN TWO, KILL TWO BIRDS WITH ONE STONE, NO TWO WAYS ABOUT IT, PUT TWO AND TWO TOGETHER, STAND ON ONE'S OWN FEET *or* STAND ON ONE'S OWN TWO FEET, TELL A THING OR TWO, THING OR TWO.

two bits *n., slang* Twenty-five cents; a quarter of a dollar. *A haircut only cost two bits when Grandfather was young.* (You paid the barber only twenty-five cents for a haircut then.) Compare FOUR BITS, SIX BITS.

two cents *n., informal* **1** Something not important or very small; almost nothing. *Paul was so angry that he said for two cents he would quit the team.* (It would not take much to make Paul quit.) *When John saw that the girl he was scolding was lame, he felt like two cents.* (He was ashamed to be scolding a lame girl and felt very small.) **2** *or* **two cents worth** Something you want to say; opinion.—Used with a possessive. *The boys were talking about baseball, and Harry put in his two cents worth, even though he didn't know much about baseball.* (Harry said what he thought about it.) *If we want your two cents, we'll ask for it.* (If we want your opinion, we ask for it.)

two-time *v., slang* To go out with a second boy or girl friend and keep it a secret from the first. *Joan was two-timing Jim with Fred.* (Joan was Jim's girl, but she was going out with Fred without telling Jim.) *Mary cried when she found that Joe was two-timing her.* (Mary cried when she found out that Joe was dating another girl.) Compare DOUBLE-CROSS.

two to one See TEN TO ONE.

two ways about it See NO TWO WAYS ABOUT IT.

U

ugly duckling *n.* An ugly or plain child who grows up to be pretty and attractive. *Mary was the ugly duckling in her family, until she grew up.* (Mary is pretty now but she was not a pretty child.)

uh-huh *or* um-hum *adv., informal* Yes.— Used only in speech or when recording dialogue. *Are you going to the Fair? Uh-huh.* (Are you going to the Fair? Yes.) *We were in Alaska, um-hum, but that was long before the earthquakes.* (We were in Alaska, yes, but that was long before the earthquakes.) *When I asked for an appointment, the nurse said, "Um-hum, I have an opening at four o'clock on Friday."* (When I asked for an appointment, the nurse said, "Yes, you can come at four o'clock on Friday.") Contrast HUH-UH.

um-hum See UH-HUH.

uncertain See IN SO MANY WORDS 2 *or* IN NO UNCERTAIN TERMS.

uncle See SAY UNCLE *also* CRY UNCLE.

under See CUT THE GROUND FROM UNDER, GO UNDER, OUT FROM UNDER, SNOW UNDER.

under a bushel See HIDE ONE'S LIGHT UNDER A BUSHEL.

under a cloud *adj. phr.* **1** Under suspicion; not trusted.—A cliché. *Joyce has been under a cloud since her roommate's bracelet disappeared.* (Joyce has been under suspicion of stealing her roommate's bracelet.) *The butcher is under a cloud because the inspectors found his scales were not honest.* (The butcher is not trusted because the inspectors found his scales did not weigh correctly.) **2** Depressed, sad, discouraged.—A cliché. *Joe has been under a cloud since his dog died.* (Joe has been very sad since his dog died.)

under age *adj. phr.* Too young; not old enough; below legal age. *He could not enlist in the army because he was under age.* (He could not enlist in the army because he was below age 18.) *Rose was not allowed to enroll in the Life Saving Course because she was under age.* (Rose was not permitted to take the Life Saving Course because she was not old enough.) Contrast OF AGE 1.

under arrest *adj. phr.* Held by the police. *The man believed to have robbed the bank was placed under arrest.* (The man was held by the police.) *The three boys were seen breaking into the school building and soon found themselves under arrest.* (The boys were seen breaking into the school building and soon found themselves held by the police.)

under cover *adv. or adj. phr.* Hidden; concealed. *The prisoners escaped under cover of darkness.* (The prisoners escaped, hidden by the darkness.) *He kept his invention under cover until it was patented.* (He concealed his invention until it was patented.) Compare UNDER WRAPS.

under false colors See SAIL UNDER FALSE COLORS.

under fire *adv. phr.* Being shot at or being attacked; hit by attacks or accusations; under attack. *The soldiers stood firm under fire of the enemy.* (The soldiers did not retreat when the enemy shot at them.) *The principal was under fire for not sending the boys home who stole the car.* (The principal was accused of being too easy.)

under one's belt *adv. phr., informal* **1** In your stomach; eaten; or absorbed. *Once he had a good meal under his belt, the man loosened his tie and fell asleep.* (When he had eaten a good meal, the man loosened his tie and fell asleep.) *Jones is talkative when he has a few drinks under his belt.* (Jones talks a lot when he has absorbed a few drinks.) **2** In your experience, memory or possession; learned or gotten successfully; gained by effort and skill. *Jim has to get a lot of algebra under his belt before the examination.* (Jim has to learn a lot of algebra before the examination.) *With three straight victories under their belts, the team went on to win the championship.* (After they won three games, the team kept winning until they were champions.)

under one's breath *adv. phr.* In a whisper; with a low voice. *The teacher heard the boy say something under his breath and she asked him to repeat it aloud.* (The teacher heard the boy whisper something and she asked him to say it aloud.) *I told Lucy the news under my breath, but Joyce overheard me.* (I told Lucy the news with a low voice, but Joyce heard what I said.)

under one's hat See KEEP UNDER ONE'S HAT.

under one's nose *or* **under the nose of** *adv. phr., informal* In sight of; in an easily seen or noticeable place. *The thief walked out of the museum with the painting, right under the nose of the guards.* (The thief walked out of the museum with the painting in sight of the guards.) *When Jim gave up trying to find a pen, he saw three right under his nose on the desk.* (When Jim gave up trying to find a pen, he saw three very close and in plain sight on the desk.)

under one's own steam *adv. phr., informal* By one's own efforts; without help. *The boys got to Boston under their own steam and took a bus the rest of the way.* (The boys got to Boston by their own efforts and took a bus the rest of the way.) *We didn't think he could do it, but Bobby finished his homework under his own steam.* (We didn't think he could do it, but Bobby finished his homework without help.)

under one's skin See GET UNDER ONE'S SKIN.

under one's thumb *or* **under the thumb** *adj. or adv. phr.* Obedient to you; controlled by you; under your power. *The Jones family is under the thumb of the mother.* (Mrs. Jones makes her family obey her.) *Jack is a bully. He keeps all the younger children under his thumb.* (Jack is a bully. He controls all the younger children.) *The mayor is so popular that he has the whole town under his thumb.* (The mayor is so well-liked that he has the town under his influence.) Compare JUMP THROUGH THE HOOP.

under one's wing *adv. phr.* Under the care or protection of. *Helen took the new puppy under her wing.* (Helen took care of the new puppy.) *The boys stopped teasing the new student when Bill took him under his wing.* (The boys stopped teasing the new student when Bill took him under protection.) Compare IN TOW.

under pain of See ON PAIN OF *also* UNDER PAIN OF.

understand See GIVE ONE TO UNDERSTAND.

under the circumstances *also* **in the circumstances** *adv. phr.* In the existing situation; in the present condition; as things are. *In the circumstances, Father couldn't risk giving up his job.* (He couldn't take a chance on getting along without steady income because we needed the money.) *Under the circumstances, the stagecoach passengers had to give the robbers their money.* (The robbers had them at gunpoint and they could not refuse.)

under the collar See HOT UNDER THE COLLAR.

under the counter *adv. phr., informal* Secretly (bought or sold). *That book has been banned, but there is one place you can get it under the counter.* (That book has been forbidden, but there is one place where you can buy it secretly.) *The liquor dealer was arrested for selling beer under the counter to teenagers.* (The liquor dealer was arrested for unlawfully selling beer to teenagers.)— Also used like an adjective, with hyphens. *During World War II, some stores kept scarce things hidden for under-the-counter-sales to good customers.* (Stores sold scarce things secretly only to good customers.)

under the hammer *adv. phr.* Up for sale at auction. *The Brights auctioned off the entire contents of their home. Mrs. Bright cried when her pewter collection went under the hammer.* (Mrs. Bright cried when her pewter collection was sold at auction.) *The picture I wanted to bid on came under the hammer soon after I arrived.* (The picture I wanted to bid on was sold at auction soon after I arrived.)

under the nose of See UNDER ONE'S NOSE.

under the sun *adj. or adv. phr.* On earth; in the world.—Used for emphasis. *The President's assassination shocked everyone under the sun.* (The President's murder shocked everyone on earth.) *Where under the sun could I have put my purse?* (Where in the world could I have put my purse?)

under the thumb of See UNDER ONE'S THUMB.

under wraps *adv. or adj. phr.* Not allowed to be seen until the right time; not allowed to act or speak freely; in secrecy; hidden.—A cliché; usually used with *keep. We have a new player, but we are keeping him under wraps until the game.* (We won't let him be seen or known before.) *What the President is planning will be kept under wraps until tomorrow. The spy was kept under wraps and not allowed to talk to newspapermen.* (The police did not let the spy tell anything he knew.) Compare UNDER COVER.

unknown quantity *n.* Someone or something whose value and importance are not known, especially in a certain situation, time or place; a new and untested person or thing. *What we would find if we could fly to the moon is an unknown quantity.* (No one knows what is on the moon.) *The new player is still an unknown quantity. We'll find out how good he is in the game.* (The player hasn't been tried out yet. He will be tested in the game.)

unseen See SIGHT UNSEEN.

until hell freezes over *Adv. phr., slang* Forever, for an eternity. *He can argue until hell freezes over; nobody will believe him.* (He can talk forever, nobody will be convinced.) Contrast WHEN HELL FREEZES OVER.

until the last gun is fired See TILL THE LAST GUN IS FIRED.

unturned See LEAVE NO STONE UNTURNED.

up against *prep. phr.* Blocked or threatened by. *When she applied to medical school, the black woman wondered whether she was up against barriers of sex and race prejudice.* (She wondered whether she had to overcome prejudice in the admissions committee in order to be accepted.)

up against it *adj. phr., informal* Faced with a great difficulty or problem; badly in need. *The Smith family is up against it because Mr. Smith cannot find a job.* (The Smith family does not have enough money to buy what they need to live.) *You will be up against it if you don't pass the test. You will probably fail arithmetic.* (You will be almost sure to fail arithmetic if you don't pass the test.) Compare HARD UP, END OF ONE'S ROPE, BACK TO THE WALL 2.

up a stump *adj. phr., slang* Stumped; blocked; mixed up or confused in what you are trying to do. *Jimmy knows how to add and subtract but fractions have him up a stump.* (Fractions have Jimmy puzzled.)

up a tree *adv. or adj. phr.* 1 Hunted or chased into a tree; treed. *The dog drove the coon up a tree so the hunter could shoot him.* (The coon was caught in the tree and couldn't get away.) 2 *informal* in trouble; having problems; in a difficulty that it is hard to escape or think of a way out of. *John's father has him up a tree in the checker game.* (John is trapped and it will be hard for him to win the game.) Compare UP THE CREEK.

up for grabs *adj. phr., informal* Available for anyone to try to get; ready to be competed for; there for the taking. *When the captain of the football team moved out of town, his place was up for grabs.* (The other players could compete to become captain.)

up front[1] *n., slang, informal* The managerial section of a corporation or firm. *Joe Catwallender finally made it (with the) up front.* (He became a member of the managerial section of the firm.)

up front[2] *adj., slang, informal* Open, sincere, hiding nothing. *Sue was completely up front about why she didn't want to see him anymore.* (She told the truth about why she doesn't want to date him any longer.)

up in arms *adj. phr.* **1** Equipped with guns or weapons and ready to fight. *All of the colonies were up in arms against the Redcoats.* (All of the people had their guns ready to fight against the Redcoats.) Syn. IN ARMS. **2** Very angry and wanting to fight. *Robert is up in arms because John said he was stupid.* (Robert is insulted and wants to fight.) *The students were up in arms over the new rule against food in the dormitory.* (The students were angry and ready to fight against the new rule.)

up in the air *adj. or adv. phr.* **1** *informal* In great anger or excitement. *My father went straight up in the air when he heard I damaged the car.* (He was very angry at me.) *The Jones family are all up in the air because they are taking a trip around the world.* (They are very excited and mixed up.) Compare HIT THE CEILING, BLOW A FUSE. **2** *also* **in midair** Not settled; uncertain; undecided. *Plans for the next meeting have been left up in the air until Jane gets better.* (It isn't sure when or where the meeting will be, or even if it will be held until Jane is better.) *The result of the game was left hanging in midair because it rained before the finish.* (The game was not finished, and will have to be continued before we know who won.) Compare LEAVE HANGING.

up one's alley See DOWN ONE'S ALLEY.

up one's sleeve *or* **in one's sleeve** *adv. phr.* **1** Hidden in the sleeve of one's shirt or coat and ready for secret or wrongful use. *The crooked gambler hid aces up his sleeve during the card game so that he would win.* (He hid the cards to use secretly during the game.) **2** *informal* Kept secretly ready for the right time or for a time when needed.—A cliché. *Jimmy knew that his father had some trick up his sleeve because he was smiling to himself during the checker game.* (His father had some secret trick planned and would use it at the right time.) Compare CARD UP ONE'S SLEEVE. **3** See LAUGH UP ONE'S SLEEVE.

upon oneself See TAKE ON ONESELF *also* TAKE UPON ONESELF.

upon one's head See ON ONE'S HEAD.

upon the spot See ON THE SPOT 1.

upper See KEEP A STIFF UPPER LIP, ON ONE'S UPPERS.

upper crust *n., informal* The richest, most famous, or important people in a certain place; the highest class. *It is a school that only the children of the upper crust can afford.* (The school is expensive and only rich people can afford to send their children there.)

upper hand *or* **whip hand** *n.* Controlling power; advantage. *In the third round the champion got the upper hand over his opponent and knocked him out.* (The champion began to win the fight in the third round.) *The cowboy trained the wild horse so that he finally got the whip hand and tamed the horse.* (The cowboy could finally control the horse.)

upper story *n.* **1** A floor or level of a building above the first floor. *The apartment house where Gene lives is five stories high and he lives in one of the upper stories.* (Gene lives in one of the floors above the ground.) **2** *slang* A person's head or brain. *Lulu has nobody home in the upper story.* (She is crazy or very silly.) *Bill's sister says he is weak in the upper story.* (Bill's brain is weak; he is not smart.)

upset the applecart *or* **upset one's applecart** *v. phr., informal* To ruin a plan or what is being done, often by surprise or accident; change how things are or are being done, often unexpectedly; ruin or mix up another person's success or plan for success.—A cliché. *John upset the other team's applecart by hitting a home run in the last inning and we won the game.* (John ruined the other team's hope that they would win.) *We are planning a surprise party for Bill, so don't let Mary upset the applecart by telling him before the party.* (Don't let her spoil our plan.) *Frank thinks he is going to be the boss, but I'll upset his applecart the first chance I get.* (I won't let him be boss.) Compare ROCK THE BOAT.

upstairs See NOBODY HOME UPSTAIRS.

up the creek *or* **up the creek without a paddle** *adj. phr., informal* In trouble or difficulty and unable to do anything about it; stuck.—A cliché. *Father said that if the car ran out of gas in the middle of the desert, we would be up the creek without a paddle.* (We would be in serious trouble because we couldn't get any gas there.) *I'll be up the creek if I don't pass this history test.* (I may not pass the course in history.) Compare DEEP WATER, IN THE SOUP, UP A TREE, OUT OF LUCK.

up tight *or* **uptight** *adj., slang, informal* Worried, irritated, excessively eager or anxious. *Why are you so uptight about getting that job? The more you worry, the less you'll succeed.* (Why are you so excessively concerned about it?)

up to *prep.* **1** As far, as deep, or as high as. *The water in the pond was only up to John's knees.* (The water was as high as his knees.) *Mary is small and just comes up to Bill's* *chest.* (She measures as high as Bill's chest.) *The shovel sank in the soft mud all the way up to the handle.* (It sank deep in the soft mud.) **2** Close to; approaching. *The team did not play up to its best today.* (They didn't play nearly as well as they could.) *Because of the rain, the number of people at the party didn't come up to the number we expected.* (The number of people didn't come near being as many as we expected to come.) **3** As high as; not more than; as much or as many as. *Pick any number up to ten.* (Pick a number lower than ten.) *There were up to eight fire engines at the fire.* (There were at least eight of them.) **4** *or* **up till** *or* **up until**—Until; till. *Up to her fourth birthday, the baby slept in a crib.* (She slept in the crib till she was four years old.) *Up to now I always thought John was honest.* (Until now, I thought so, but not any more.) *We went swimming up till breakfast time.* (When it was breakfast time, we stopped.) *Up until last summer we always went to the beach for our vacation.* (We went to the beach until last summer, but now we don't go there any more.) **5** Capable of; fit for; equal to; strong or well enough for. *We chose Harry to be captain because we thought he was up to the job.* (We thought Harry was able to be a good captain.) *Mother is sick and not up to going out to the store.* (Mother is not strong or well enough to go there.) **6** Doing or planning secretly; ready for mischief. *What are you up to with the matches, John?* (You are going to start a fire with the matches?) *Mrs. Watson was sure that the boys were up to no good, because they ran when they saw her coming.* (She knew they were doing something naughty.) **7** Facing as a duty; to be chosen or decided by; depending on. *It's up to you to get to school on time.* (You're responsible. It's your duty.) *I don't care when you cut the grass. When you do it is up to you.* (You may decide when you do it.)

up to par *or informal* **up to scratch** *or informal* **up to snuff 1** In good or normal health or physical condition. *I have a cold and don't feel up to par.* (I don't feel well.) *The boxer is training for the fight but he isn't up to scratch yet.* (He still is not in his best and strongest condition to fight.) **2** *or* **up to the mark** As good as usual; up to the usual level or quality. *The TV program was not up to par tonight.* (The program wasn't as good as usual.) *John will have to work hard to bring his grades up to snuff.* (He will have to work to raise his marks so that he will pass.) Compare MEASURE UP.

up to scratch See UP TO PAR.

up to snuff See UP TO PAR.

up to the chin in *or* **in ——— up to the chin** *adj. phr., informal* —A trite expression used also with *ears, elbows, eyes* or *knees* instead of *chin,* and with a possessive instead of *the.*

1 Having a big or important part in; guilty of; not innocent of; deeply in. *Was Tom mixed up in that trouble last night? He was up to his ears in it.* (He was very much mixed up in it.) *Mr. Johnson is up to the eyes in debt.* (He is deeply in debt.) *Mrs. Smith is in debt up to her chin.* (She is heavily in debt.) Compare TO THE HILT. **2** Very busy with; working hard at. *Bob is up to his neck in homework.* (He is very busy.) *He is up to their elbows in business before Christmas.* (They are extremely busy.) **3** Having very much or many of; flooded with. *Mary was up to her knees in invitations to go to parties.* (She had very many invitations.) Compare KNEE-DEEP.

up to the hilt See TO THE HILT.

up to the mark See UP TO PAR 2.

urban homesteading *n., informal* Renovation and occupation through cooperative ownership by tenants of previously abandoned city apartment buildings. *Urban homesteading is on the rise in many big American cities these days.* (People get settled in previously abandoned city apartment buildings more and more.)

use See NO USE, PUT TO USE.

used to[1] *adj phr.* In the habit of or familiar with. *People get used to smoking and it is hard for them to stop.* (They get the habit of smoking.) *Farmers are used to working outdoors in the winter.* (Farmers often work outdoors in the winter cold and are not bothered by it as much as people who don't work outdoors.) *After my eyes became used to the dim light in the cave, I saw an old shovel on the ground.* (After I was able to see in the poor light. I saw a shovel.) *On the hike Bob soon got tired, but Dick did not because he was used to walking.* (Dick was in the habit of walking, so it did not bother him.)

used to[2] *or* **did use to** *v. phr.* Did formerly; did in the past.—Usually used with an infinitive to tell about something past. *Uncle Henry used to have a beard, but he shaved it off.* (Uncle Henry once had a beard.) *Did your father use to work at the bank?* (Did your father work at the bank for a while?) *People used to say that tomatoes were poison.* (Years ago people said tomatoes were poison.)—Sometimes used without the infinitive. *I don't go to that school any more, but I used to.* (Now I don't go to that school, but before, I did.) *We don't visit Helen as much as we used to.* (We don't visit Helen as much as we did before.) *I used to go to the movies often. Did you use to?* (Did you go often, too?)

used to be *or* **did use to be** *v. phr.* Formerly or once was. *Mary used to be small; but she has grown up.* (Mary was small but she is bigger now.) *Dick used to be the best pitcher on the team last year; now two other pitchers are better than he is.* (Last year Dick was the best pitcher.)

use one's head *or slang* **use one's bean** *or slang*

use one's noodle *or slang* **use one's noggin** *v. phr.* To use your brain or mind; think; have common sense.—Often used as a command. *If you used your bean you wouldn't be in trouble now.* (If you acted with good sense, you would not be in trouble.) *Never point a gun at anybody, John. Use your head!* (Don't be so stupid as to point a gun at anybody!)

use up *v.* **1** To use until nothing is left; spend or consume completely. *Don't use up all the soap. Leave me some to wash with.* (Don't use all of the soap.) *Jack used up his last dollar to see the movies.* (Jack spent his last dollar.) Compare GIVE OUT 5. **2** *informal* To tire completely; make very tired; exhaust; leave no strength or force in.—Usually used in the passive. *After rowing the boat across the lake, Robert was used up.* (Robert's strength was all gone because he was very tired.) Compare GIVE OUT 4, WEAR OUT.

utility room *n.* A room in a house or building for machinery and other things important in the daily use of the building and the work of the people in it. *There is a utility room upstairs where Mother does the laundry.* (The machines for washing clothes are in the room.) *The oil burner is kept in the utility room in the basement.* (The oil furnace for heat is there.)

V

vain See IN VAIN, TAKE ONE'S NAME IN VAIN.

valor See DISCRETION IS THE BETTER PART OF VALOR.

value See FACE VALUE.

vanishing cream *n.* A cosmetic cream for the skin that is used chiefly before face powder. *Mrs. Jones spread vanishing cream on her face before applying her face powder.* (She used a cosmetic cream before face powder.)

vanity case *n.* **1** A small case containing face powder, lipstick, and other things and usually carried in a woman's handbag; a compact. *She took out her vanity case and put lipstick on.* (She took out her small case which had cosmetics in it and used the lipstick.) **2** A handbag or a small bag carried by a woman and holding various toilet articles. *She had the porter carry her big bags and she herself carried her vanity case.* (The porter carried her heavy bags, but she kept her small one.)

variety show *n.* A program that includes several different kinds of entertainment (as songs, dances, comic skits and little dramas). *Jane's father was the master of ceremonies of a variety show on TV.* (Jane's father introduced people who did different things to entertain on TV.)

variety store *n.* A store that sells many different kinds of things, especially items that are fairly small and in everyday use. *I went into a variety store and bought some paint.* (The store sold many different small things.) *Five-and-ten cent stores are a kind of variety store.* (Five-and-ten cent stores sell many kinds of things.)

vein See FREEZE ONE'S BLOOD *or* FREEZE THE BLOOD IN ONE'S VEINS, FREEZE ONE'S VEINS.

very See ALL VERY WELL.

very well *interj., formal* Agreed; all right. —Used to show agreement or approval. *Very well. You may go.* (All right, I approve. You may go.) *Very well, I will do as you say.* (All right, I agree to do as you say.) Compare ALL RIGHT 2.

vibrations *or* **vibes** *n.* Psychic emanations radiating from an object, situation, or person.

I don't think this relationship will work out— this guy has given me bad vibes. (I have the sensation that we will not get along well.)

Vietnam syndrome *n., informal* An attitude in government circles that diplomacy may be more effective in solving local political problems in other countries than the use of military force, stemming from the failure of the U.S. military intervention in Vietnam. *The pundits of Foggy Bottom display the Vietnam syndrome these days when it comes to Iran.* (State Department experts advocate diplomacy rather than military intervention when discussing the Iran crisis.)

view See IN VIEW, IN VIEW OF, TAKE A DIM VIEW OF.

vine See DIE ON THE VINE *or* WITHER ON THE VINE, CLINGING VINE.

virtue See BY VIRTUE OF, MAKE A VIRTUE OF NECESSITY.

visiting nurse *n.* A nurse who goes from home to home taking care of sick people or giving help with other health problems. *After John returned home from the hospital, the visiting nurse came each day to change his bandages.* (She stopped at his home every day on her way to different homes.)

voice See AT THE TOP OF ONE'S VOICE, GIVE VOICE.

voice box *n.* The part of the throat where the sound of your voice is made; the larynx. *Mr. Smith's voice box was taken out in an operation, and he could not talk after that.* (The doctor cut out the part of Mr. Smith's throat that made noise when he talked.)

voiceprint *n., technological, colloquial* The graphic pattern derived from converting an individual's voice into a visible graph used by the police for identification purposes, much as fingerprints. *They have succeeded in identifying the murderer by using a voiceprint.* (They identified the murderer by studying a visible graphic pattern of his voice.)

volcano See SIT ON A VOLCANO.

volume See SPEAK VOLUMES.

vote down *v.* To defeat in a vote. *Congress voted the bill down.* (Congress defeated the proposed law when a majority of its members voted against it.)

W

wade in *or* **wade into** *v., informal* **1** To go busily to work. *The house was a mess after the party, but Mother waded in and soon had it clean again.* (The house was a mess after the party, but Mother went busily to work and soon had it clean again.) **2** To attack. *When Bill had heard Jim's argument, he waded in and took it apart.* (When Bill had heard Jim's argument, he attacked and showed it was wrong.) *Jack waded into the boys with his fists flying.* (Jack attacked the boys ·with his fists.)

wag See TONGUES TO WAG *or* TONGUES WAG.

wagon See FIX SOMEONE'S WAGON, HITCH ONE'S WAGON TO A STAR, JUMP ON THE BAND WAGON, OFF THE WAGON, ON THE WAGON.

wait See LIE IN WAIT.

wait at table *or* **wait on table** *or* **wait table** *v. phr.* To serve food. *Mrs. Lake had to teach her new maid to wait on table properly.* (Mrs. Lake had to teach her new maid to serve food properly.) *The girls earn spending money by waiting at table in the school ·dining rooms.* (The girls earn money by serving food in the school dining rooms.)

waiting list *n.* A list of persons waiting to get into something (as a school). *The nursery school enrollment was complete, so the director put our child's name on the waiting list.* (The nursery school was full, so the director put our child's name on the list of persons waiting to get in. If another child does not come, our child will take his place.) *The landlord said there were no vacant apartments available, but that he would put the Rogers' name on the waiting list.* (The landlord said he would put the Rogers' name on the list of persons waiting for apartments.)

wait on *or* **wait upon** *v.* **1** To serve. *Sue has a summer job waiting on an invalid.* (She has a summer job serving a sick person.) *The clerk in the store asked if we had been waited upon.* (The clerk asked if we had been served.) **2** *formal* To visit as a courtesy or for business. *We waited upon the widow out of respect for her husband.* (We visited the widow as a courtesy, to show our respect for her husband.) *John waited upon the President with a letter of introduction.* (John visited the President to give him a letter introducing John.) **3** To follow. *Success waits on hard work.* (Success follows hard work.)

wait on hand and foot *v. phr.* To serve in every possible way; do everything for (someone). *Sally is spoiled because her mother waits on her hand and foot.* (Sally is spoiled because her mother serves her in every possible way.) *The gentlemen had a valet to wait on him hand and foot.* (The gentlemen had a servant to do everything for him.) Compare HAND AND FOOT.

wait on table See WAIT AT TABLE.

wait upon See WAIT ON.

wake See IN THE WAKE OF.

walk See WIN IN A WALK.

walk all over See WALK OVER.

walk away with *or* **walk off with** *v.* **1** To take and go away with; take away; steal.—A cliché. *When Father went to work, he. accidentally walked off with Mother's umbrella.* (Father was not paying attention and took Mother's umbrella.) *How can a thief walk off with a safe in broad daylight?* (How can a thief steal a safe in the daytime?) **2** To take, get, or win easily.—A cliché. *Jim walked away with all the honors on Class Night.* (Jim got all the honors on Class Night.) *Our team walked off with the championship.* (Our team easily won the championship.)

walking papers *or* **walking orders** *also* **walking ticket** *n., informal* A statement that you are fired from your job; dismissal. *The boss was not satisfied with Paul's work and gave him his walking papers.* (The boss was not satisfied with Paul's work and dismissed him from the job.) *George is out of work. He picked up his walking ticket last Friday.* (George is out of work. He was told last Friday that he was fired from his job.)

walk off with See WALK AWAY WITH.

walk of life *n. phr.* Way of living; manner in which people live. *Many rich people have yachts; people in their walk of life can afford them.* (People of their kind who have wealth, can own yachts.) *The banker did not want his son to marry a girl in a different walk of life.* (The banker was wealthy and did not want his son to marry a poor girl.) *People from every walk of life enjoy television.* (All kinds of people enjoy television.) Compare THE TRACKS.

walk on air *v. phr., informal* To feel happy and excited.—A cliché. *Sue has been walking on air since she won the prize.* (Sue has felt happy and excited since she won the prize.) *His father's compliment left Jed walking on air.* (His father's praise left Jed feeling happy and excited.) Compare ON CLOUD NINE, ON TOP OF THE WORLD.

walk out *v.* **1** To go on strike. *When the company would not give them higher pay, the workers walked out.* (When the company refused to raise their pay, the workers went on strike.) **2** To leave suddenly; especially to desert. *He didn't say he wasn't coming back; he just walked out.* (He didn't say he wasn't coming back; he just left suddenly.)—Often used informally with *on*. *The man walked out on his wife and children.* (The man deserted his family.) Compare LEAVE FLAT; LEAVE IN THE LURCH.

walk over *or* **walk all over** *or* **step all over** *v. phr., informal* To make (someone) do whatever you wish; make selfish use of; treat like a slave; impose upon.—A cliché. *Jill is so friendly and helpful that people walk all over her.* (Jill is so friendly and helpful that people make her help them too much.) *We wanted the man's business, so we let him step all over us.* (We wanted the man's business, so we let him treat us like slaves.) Compare TAKE ADVANTAGE OF.

walk the chalk *or* **walk the chalk line** *or* **walk the chalk mark** To act exactly as you are supposed to; behave properly; obey.—A cliché. *That new teacher really makes the students walk the chalk.* (That new teacher makes the students behave in class.) *In some classes the students play and talk, but Mr. Parker makes them walk the chalk.* (He makes them behave properly in class.) *That theater owner wants his place to be orderly, and if boys and girls don't walk the chalk, he puts them out.* (They must act right or get out.) [From the fact that sailors used to be asked to walk a chalk line along the deck of the ship to prove they were not drunk.] Compare TOE THE MARK.

walk the floor *v. phr.* To walk one direction and then the other across the floor, again and again; pace. *Mr. Black walked the floor, trying to reach a decision.* (Mr. Black walked across the floor and back many times, trying to decide what to do.) *The sick baby had his mother walking the floor all night.* (The baby's mother walked back and forth carrying him and trying to make him sleep.) *Mrs. Black's toothache hurt so much that she got up and walked the floor.* (She couldn't sleep or read, and walking one way and then the other again and again, seemed to help.)

walk the plank *v. phr.* **1** To walk off a board extended over the side of a ship and be drowned. *The pirates captured the ship and forced the crew to walk the plank.* (The pirates captured the ship and forced the crew to walk over the side of the ship and be drowned.) **2** *informal* To resign from a job because someone makes you do it.—A cliché. *When a new owner bought the store, the manager had to walk the plank.* (When a new owner took control of the store, the manager was forced to resign from his job.)

wall See BACK TO THE WALL, BEAT ONE'S HEAD AGAINST A WALL, CLIMB THE WALL, FORWARD WALL, HANDWRITING ON THE WALL, HOLE-IN-THE-WALL, STONE WALL *or* BRICK WALL, TO THE WALL.

wallop See PACK A PUNCH *or* PACK A WALLOP.

war See COLD WAR, TUG OF WAR.

war baby *n., informal* A person born during a war. *War babies began to increase college enrollments early in the 1960s.* (Persons born during World War II began to enlarge college enrollments early in the sixties.) *The war babies forced many towns to build new schools.* (The large number of children born during World War II forced many towns to build more schools.)

warmer See BENCH WARMER.

warm one's blood *v. phr.* To make you feel warm or excited. *When the Bakers came to visit on a cold night, Mr. Harmon offered them a drink to warm their blood.* (He offered them a drink to make them feel warm.)

warm the bench *v. phr., informal* To act as a substitute on an athletic team.—A cliché. *Bill has been warming the bench for three football seasons; he hopes that the coach will let him play this year.* (Bill has been acting as a substitute for three seasons.)—**bench warmer** *n., informal* A substitute player. *Last year Ted was only a bench warmer, but this year he is the team's star pitcher.* (Last year Ted was only a substitute, pitching when the regular pitchers were out of the game.)

warm up *v.* **1** To reheat cooked food. *Mr. Jones was so late that his dinner got cold; his wife had to warm it up.* (Mr. Jones was so late that his wife had to heat his dinner again.) *When the children had left for school, their mother warmed up the breakfast coffee.* (When the children had left, their mother reheated the breakfast coffee.) **2** To become friendly or interested. *It takes an hour or so for some children to warm up to strangers.* (It takes an hour or so for some children to become friendly with strangers.) *As he warmed up to his subject, Tom forgot his bashfulness.* (As he became more interested in his subject, Tom forgot his shyness.) **3** To get ready for a game or other event by exercising or practicing. *The dancers began to warm up fifteen minutes before the performance.* (The dancers exercised for fifteen minutes before the performance to loosen their muscles.) *The coach told us to warm up before entering the pool.* (The coach told us to exercise briefly before entering the pool.

warm-up *n.* A period of exercise or practice in preparation for a game or other event. *During the warm-up the baseball players were throwing the ball around and running up and down the side of the field.* (During the period of getting ready to play, the players were practicing and exercising.) *Before the television quiz program, there was a warm-up to prepare the contestants.* (Before the program, the people in the quiz practised what they would do.)

warpath See ON THE WARPATH.

warrant See SIGN ONE'S OWN DEATH WARRANT.

wash and wear *adj.* Not needing to be ironed.—Refers especially to snythetic and synthetic blend fabrics. *Dick bought three wash and wear shirts to take on his trip.* (Dick bought three shirts that do not need ironing to take on his trip.) *Sally's dress is made of a wash and wear fabric.* (Sally's dress is made of a fabric that can be laundered and worn without ironing.)

wash one's dirty linen in public See AIR ONE'S DIRTY LINEN IN PUBLIC.

wash one's hands of *v. phr.* To withdraw from or refuse to be responsible for.—A cliché. *We washed our hands of politics long ago.* (We quit politics a long time ago.) *The school washed its hands of the students' behavior during spring recess.* (The school refused to be responsible for things that the students did during spring vacation.)

waste See GO TO WASTE, LAY WASTE.

waste away *v.* To become more thin and weak every day. *Jane is wasting away with tuberculosis.* (Jane is becoming thin and weak from tuberculosis.) *After Mrs. Barnes died, her husband wasted away with grief.* (Her husband lost interest in life and became more and more thin and weak.)

waste one's breath *v. phr.* To speak or to argue with no result; do nothing by talking.— A hackneyed phrase. *The teacher saw that she was wasting her breath; the children refused to believe her.* (The teacher realized that she was talking in vain; the children could not accept what she said.) *I know what I want. You're wasting your breath.* (I will not change my ideas. You are gaining nothing by talking to me.)

watch See BIRD WATCHER, BEAR WATCHING, ON THE WATCH.

watcher See CLOCK WATCHER.

watch it *v. phr., informal* To be careful. —Usually used as a command. *You'd better watch it. If you get into trouble again, you'll be expelled.* (You'd better be careful not to get into trouble again.) *Watch it—the bottom stair is loose!* (Be careful where you step—the bottom stair is loose.)

watch one's dust *or* **watch one's smoke** *v. phr., slang* To notice your quick action; watch you do something quickly.—A cliché. *Offer Bill a dollar to shovel your sidewalk, and watch his smoke!* (Offer to pay Bill a dollar to shovel your sidewalk and see how quickly he will do it.) *"We'll have your yard cleaned in a jiffy," the Boy Scouts told Mr. Truitt." "Watch our smoke!"* (The Boy Scouts told Mr. Truitt that they would have his yard cleaned up quickly.) *"I can go to the store and be back in five minutes," bragged Tom. "Just watch my dust."* (Tom said to see how quickly he could go to the store and return.)

watch out See LOOK OUT.

water See BLOOD IS THICKER THAN WATER, COME HELL OR HIGH WATER, DEEP WATER, FISH OUT OF WATER, GO THROUGH HELL AND HIGH WATER, HEAD ABOVE WATER, HOLD WATER, HELL AND HIGH WATER, HOT WATER, LIKE WATER, LIKE WATER OFF A DUCK'S BACK, MAKE ONE'S MOUTH WATER, OF THE FIRST WATER, POUR OIL ON TROUBLED WATERS, THROW COLD WATER ON, TREAD WATER.

water down *v.* To change and make weaker; weaken. *The Senator argued that the House should water down the bill before passing it.* (The senator argued that the bill was too strong and that the House should weaken it before making it a law.) *The American Negro will not tolerate watered down Civil Rights legislation.* (The American Negro will not accept weakened Civil Rights legislation.) *After talking with the management about their demands, the workers agreed to water them down.* (After talking with the management, the workers agreed to ask for less.) *The teacher had to water down the course for a slow-learning class.* (The teacher had to simplify the lessons for a slow-learning class.)

waterfront See COVER THE WATERFRONT.

Waterloo See MEET ONE'S WATERLOO.

water over the dam *or* **water under the bridge** *n. phr.* Something that happened in the past and cannot be changed.—A cliché. *Since the sweater is too small already, don't worry about its shrinking; that's water over the dam.* (Since the sweater is too small already, don't worry about its shrinking because it can't be changed back into the right size.) Compare CRY OVER SPILLED MILK.

water under the bridge See WATER OVER THE DAM.

way See ALL THE WAY *or* THE WHOLE WAY, BY THE WAY, BY WAY OF, COME A LONG WAY, CUT BOTH WAYS *or* CUT TWO WAYS, EVERY WHICH WAY, FROM WAY BACK, GO OUT OF ONE'S WAY, HARD WAY, HAVE A WAY WITH, IN A BAD WAY, IN A BIG WAY, IN A FAMILY WAY, IN A WAY, IN ONE'S WAY *or* IN THE WAY, KNOW ONE'S WAY AROUND *or* KNOW ONE'S WAY ABOUT, LEAD THE WAY, MAKE ONE'S WAY, MAKE WAY, NOT KNOW WHICH WAY TO TURN, NO TWO WAYS ABOUT IT, ON THE WAY, *or* ON ONE'S WAY, PARTING OF THE WAYS, PUT IN THE WAY OF *or* PUT IN ONE'S WAY, PUT OUT OF THE WAY, RUB THE WRONG WAY, SEE ONE'S WAY CLEAR.

wayside See FALL BY THE WAYSIDE.

way the wind blows *or* **how the wind blows** *n. phr.* The direction or course something may go; how things are; what may happen. *Most senators find out which way the wind blows in their home state before voting on bills in Congress.* (The senators find out if the people want the bill or not before voting.)

ways and means *n. plural* Methods of getting something done or getting money; how something can be done and paid for. *The boys were trying to think of ways and means to go camping for the weekend.* (They were thinking how to go camping and pay for it.) *The United States Senate has a committee on ways and means.* (The Senate has a committee which studies how to raise money through taxes.)

wear See IF THE SHOE FITS—WEAR IT, WASH AND WEAR, WORSE FOR WEAR.

wear away See WEAR OFF.

wear down *v.* **1** To make or become smaller, weaker, or less by use or wear; make or become useless or less useful by wearing or aging. *My pencil is so worn down, it is too small to write with.* (The pencil has become too short from writing and sharpening.) *The heels of my shoes are wearing down.* (The shoes are becoming damaged from so much wear.) **2** To exhaust; tire out, win over or persuade by making tired. *Mary wore her mother down by begging so that she let Mary go to the movies.* (Mary tired her mother out by asking her over and over.) **wear off** *or* **wear away** *v.* **1** To remove or disappear little by little through use, time, or the action of weather. *Time and weather have worn off the name on the gravestone.* (Long exposure to weather has removed the letters of the name.) *The eraser has worn off my pencil.* (Much use has removed the eraser.) *The grass has worn away from the path near the house.* (People have walked on the path so much that there is now no grass on it.) **2** To lessen; become less little by little. *The people went home as the excitement of the fire wore off.* (They went home as the excitement passed.) *John could feel the pain again as the dentist's medicine wore away.* (John felt the pain as the effect of the medicine lessened.) Compare DIE OUT, WEAR DOWN.

wear on *v.* **1** To anger or annoy; tire. *Having to stay indoors all day long is tiresome for the children and wears on their mother's nerves.* (It makes their mother tired and nervous.) **2** To drag on; pass gradually or slowly; continue in the same old way. *Johnny tried to wait up for Santa Claus, but as the night wore on, he couldn't keep his eyes open.* (Time went by very slowly because it was Christmas Eve.) *As the years wore on, the man in prison grew old.* (The time in prison passed very slowly.) *The boys' quarrel wore on all afternoon.* (The boys continued to quarrel all afternoon in the same old way.)

wear one's heart on one's sleeve *also* **pin one's heart on one's sleeve** *v. phr.* To show your feelings openly; show everyone how you feel; not hide your feelings.—A cliché. *She wears her heart on her sleeve. It's easy to see if she is sad or happy.* (Everyone can see if she feels sad or happy.) *Sometimes it is better not to pin your heart on your sleeve.* (Sometimes it is better to hide how you feel.) Compare OPEN ONE'S HEART.

wear out *v.* **1a** To use or wear until useless. *Bobby got a toy truck that would run on a battery, and he used it so much that he soon wore it out.* (Bobby ran the new truck until the parts became worn and broken, and the truck would not go any more.) *The stockings are so worn out that they can't be mended any more.* (The stockings have been worn to pieces.) Compare GIVE OUT 4, USE UP. **1b** To become useless from use or wear. *The old clock finally wore out.* (The clock was so old it wouldn't run any more.) *One shoe wore out before the other.* (One shoe got a hole in the sole, but the other was still good.) **2** *or* **tire out** To make very tired; weaken. *The children played inside when it rained, and they soon wore out their mother.* (The children made their mother very tired.) *When Dick got home from the long walk, he was all worn out.* (He was weak; he felt that he could not walk any more.)—Often used with oneself. *Don't wear yourself out by playing too hard.* (Don't make yourself too tired.) Compare GIVE OUT 4. **3** To make by rubbing, scraping, or washing. *The waterfall has worn out a hole in the stone beneath it.* (The water falling on the stone has made a hole in it.)

wear out one's welcome *v. phr., informal* To visit somewhere too long or come back too often so that you are not welcome any more. *The Smith children have worn out their welcome at our house because they never want to go home.* (The Smith children always stay too long and are a nuisance.) *This hot weather has worn out its welcome with us.* (We are tired of its lasting so long.)

wear the trousers *or* **wear the pants** *v. phr., informal* To have a man's authority; be the boss of a family or household.—A cliché. *Mr. Wilson is henpecked by his wife; she wears the trousers in that family.* (Mrs. Wilson tells Mr. Wilson and their family what to do.) *Mrs. Jones talks a lot but Mr. Jones wears the pants in their house.* (Mr. Jones is the real boss in their house.) Compare RULE THE ROOST.

wear thin *v.* **1** To become thin from use, wearing, or the passing of time. *My old pair of pants has worn thin at the knees.* (The cloth is thin from wear.) *This old dime has worn very thin.* (It has become thin from being handled so much.) **2** To grow less, or less interesting; decrease. *The joke began to wear thin when you heard it too many times.* (The joke was not so funny when you heard it too often.) *The teacher's patience began to wear thin when he saw that no one knew the lesson.* (His patience was less and he became angry.)

wear well *v.* **1** To continue to be satisfactory, useful, or liked for a long time. *My old overcoat has worn very well.* (It has lasted a long time and is still useful.) *Their marriage has worn well.* (Their marriage has continued to be satisfactory and successful.) *That author wears well.* (His books are still liked and widely read.) Compare STAND UP 2. **2** To carry, accept, or treat properly or well. *Grandfather wears his years well.* (He does not act like an old man but still acts much the same.) *Tommy has won many honors, but he wears them well.* (Tommy accepts his honors in the right way, modestly and pleasantly.)

weasel word *n., informal* A word which has more than one meaning and may be used to deceive others. *When the thief was being questioned by the police, he tried to fool them with weasel words.* (He would not give plain answers.)

weather See FAIR-WEATHER FRIEND.

weather eye *n.* **1** Eyes that can tell what the weather will be. *Grandfather's weather eye always tells him when it will rain.* (Grandfather knows when it will rain.) **2** Eyes ready or quick to see; careful watch.—Usually used in phrases like *keep a weather eye on, open,* or *out for. Mrs. Brown kept a weather eye on the children so they wouldn't hurt each other.* (She watched them carefully.) *Keep a weather eye out for Uncle George at the store.* (Try to see him at the store among the other people.) *Keep a weather eye open for deer.* (Be ready to see them if they are near.) *The police have a weather eye out for the robbers.* (They are watching carefully.) Compare LOOK OUT.

wedge See FLYING WEDGE.

wedlock See BORN OUT OF WEDLOCK.

weeper See FINDERS KEEPERS *or* FINDERS KEEPERS LOSERS WEEPERS.

weed out *v.* **1** To remove what is unwanted, harmful, or not good enough from. *Mother weeded out the library because there were too many books.* (She removed the unwanted books from the library.) *Many colleges and universities weed out their freshman classes to make room for better students.* (The colleges drop the poorer students to make room for better ones.) **2** To take (what is not wanted) from a collection or group; remove (a part) for the purpose of improving a collection or group; get rid of. *The coach is weeding out the weak players this week.* (The coach is letting the poor players go and keeping the good ones.) *The teacher told Elizabeth to read over her English composition and weed out every sentence that was not about the subject.* (The teacher told her to take out every part of the composition that was not needed, to make it better.)

wee folk *or* **little folk** *or* **little people** *n. pl.* Fairy people; brownies; elves; fairies; or goblins. *Mother read me a story about the wee folk who lived in the forest and came out at night.* (Mother read me a fairy story.) *There are many stories about little people dancing in the moonlight.* (There are many stories about fairies and elves who dance in the moonlight.)

week in, week out See DAY IN, AND DAY OUT.

weigh down *also* **weight down** **1** To make heavy; cause to go down or bend with weight; overload. *The evergreens are weighed down by the deep snow.* (The evergreen trees' branches are pushed down by the snow.)—Often used with *with* or *by. There are so many children in the back seat that they are weighing down the back of the car.* (The weight of the children is making the back of the car sink down.) **2a** To overload with care or worry; make sad or low in spirits.—Usually used in the passive. *The family is weighed down by sorrow.* (The hearts of the family are heavy. They are very sad.) *The company is weighed down by debt.* (The company is having trouble because it owes much money.) **2b** To make heavy, hard, or slow; make dull or uninteresting.—Often in the passive used with *by* or *with. The book is weighted down with footnotes.* (Too many notes at the bottom of the pages make the book hard to read.) *The TV program is weighed down by commercials.* (The program is made slow and boring by too many commercials.)

weigh in *v.* **1a** To take the weight of; weigh. *The man at the airport counter weighed in our bags and took our plane tickets.* (Before we got on the plane the man weighed our bags.) *A doctor weighed in the wrestlers.* (The doctor found out their weights.) **1b** To have yourself or something that you own weighed.—Often used with *at. I weighed in at 100 pounds on the scale today.* (I weighed 100 pounds on the scale.) *We took our bags to the airport counter to weigh in.* (We had our bags weighed.) **1c** To have yourself weighed as a boxer or wrestler by a doctor before a match.—Often used with *at. The champion didn't want to weigh in at more than 160 pounds.* (He wanted to weigh under 160 pounds.) **2** *slang* To join or interfere in a fight, argument, or discussion. *We told Jack that if we wanted him to weigh in with his opinion, we would ask him.* (We told Jack to mind his own business and not give his opinion until we asked for it.) Compare TAKE PART.

weigh on *or* **weigh upon** *v.* **1** To be a weight or pressure on; be heavy on. *The pack weighed heavily on the soldier's back.* (The load of the pack was heavy.) **2** To make sad or worried; trouble; disturb; upset. *Sadness weighed on Mary's heart when her kitten died.* (Mary felt very sad.) *John's wrongdoing weighed upon his conscience.* (John was sorry he had done wrong.) *The teacher's advice weighed upon Tom's mind.* (The teacher's advice troubled him.)

weigh on one's mind See WEIGH ON 2.

weigh one's words *v. phr.* To choose your words carefully; be careful to use the right words. *When a teacher explains about religion, he must weigh his words because his pupils may be of several different faiths.* (The teacher must choose his words carefully so that no student will misunderstand or be offended.) *When old Mr. Jones talked to the students about becoming teachers, he spoke* *slowly, weighing his words.* (He chose strong words to make some students want to become teachers.) *In a debate, a political candidate has little time to weigh his words, and may say something foolish.* (He hasn't time to think about his words before he speaks.)

weight See PULL ONE'S WEIGHT, SWING ONE'S WEIGHT, THROW ONE'S WEIGHT AROUND.

weight down See WEIGH DOWN.

weight of the world on one's shoulders *or* **world on one's shoulders** *or* **world on one's back** *n. phr.* A very heavy load of worry or responsibility; very tired or worried behavior, as if carrying the world; behavior as if you are very important.—A cliché. *Don't look as if you had the weight of the world on your shoulders, Henry, just because you have to mow the lawn.* (Don't act as if you had to carry the world.) *John acts as if he were carrying the world on his back because he has a paper route.* (John tries to act very important.)

weigh upon See WEIGH ON.

welcome See WEAR OUT ONE'S WELCOME.

welcome mat *n.* **1** A mat for wiping your shoes on, often with the word *welcome* on it, that is placed in front of a door. *Mother bought a welcome mat for our new house.* (Mother bought a mat to put in front of our front door.) **2** *informal* A warm welcome; a friendly greeting.—Used in such phrases as *the welcome mat is out* and *put out the welcome mat. Our welcome mat is always out to our friends.* (We are always ready to welcome friends who come to visit us.) *Spread out the welcome mat, children, because Uncle Bill is visiting us tonight.* (Get ready to welcome Uncle Bill.) Syn. LATCH STRING 2. Compare ROLL OUT THE RED CARPET, WITH OPEN ARMS.

welcome with open arms See WITH OPEN ARMS.

well See ALL VERY WELL, AS WELL, AS WELL AS, HAIL FELLOW WELL MET, LET WELL ENOUGH ALONE, PLAY ONE'S CARDS RIGHT *or* PLAY ONE'S CARDS WELL, VERY WELL, WEAR WELL.

well and good *adj. phr.* Good; satisfactory. *If my daughter finishes high school, I will call that well and good.* (I will be satisfied if she finishes high school.)—Often used without a verb to show agreement or understanding. *Well and good; I will come to your house tomorrow.* (The plans are satisfactory; I will come to your house.) Compare ALL RIGHT, ALL VERY WELL, VERY WELL.

well-heeled *adj., slang* Wealthy; having plenty of money. *Bob's father, who is well-heeled, gave him a sports car.* (Bob's father is rich. He gave Bob a sports car.) Compare IN CLOVER, ON EASY STREET.

well-to-do *adj.* Having or making enough money to live comfortably; prosperous. *John's father owns a company and his family is*

well-to-do. (The family has enough money and lives well.)—Often used with *the* like a plural noun. *This is the part of town where the well-to-do live.* (People with money live here.) Compare IN THE LAP OF LUXURY, IN THE CHIPS, ON EASY STREET.

wet See ALL WET, GET ONE'S FEET WET, MAD AS A WET HEN, WRINGING WET.

wet behind the ears *adj. phr., informal* Not experienced; not knowing how to do something; new in a job or place.—A cliché. *The new student is still wet behind the ears; he has not yet learned the tricks that the boys play on each other.* (The new boy does not know what to expect.) Compare DRY BEHIND THE EARS.

wet blanket *n., informal* A person or thing that keeps others from enjoying life. *The teenagers don't invite Bob to their parties because he is a wet blanket.* (Bob just sits in a corner when he comes to a party, so he is never invited.) *The weatherman throws a wet blanket on picnic plans when he forecasts rain.* (The weatherman discourages picnic plans when he says it will rain.) Compare CREPE HANGER.

wet one's whistle *v. phr., slang* To have a drink, especially of liquor.—A cliché. *Uncle Willie told John to wait outside for a minute while he went in to the cafe to wet his whistle.* (He had a drink in the cafe.)

whack See OUT OF WHACK.

whale away *v., informal* **1** To beat or hit hard; strike again and again.—Often used with *at. The boxer is whaling away at his opponent with both fists.* (He is hitting him hard and often.) **2** To attack severely or again and again; go on without stopping or with great force; pound away. *Mary has been whaling away on the typewriter for an hour.* (Mary has been working hard on the typewriter.)—Often used with *at. During the election the Mayor whaled away at the other party in his speeches.* (He attacked and criticized the other party.)

whale the ——— out of See BEAT THE ——— OUT OF.

what See COME WHAT MAY, GET WHAT'S COMING TO ONE, I'LL TELL YOU WHAT, JUST WHAT THE DOCTOR ORDERED, SO WHAT.

what about *interrog.* **1** About *or* concerning what; in connection with what.—Often used alone as a question. *"I want to talk to you." "What about?"* (Why? What do you want to talk to me about?) Compare WHAT FOR. **2** See WHAT OF IT. **3** See HOW ABOUT.

what about that See HOW ABOUT THAT.

what for[1] *interrog.* For what reason; why? *I told Mary what I was going to town for.* (I told her the reason.) *What are you running for?* (What is the purpose of your running?)—Often used alone as a question. *Billy's mother told him to wear his hat. "What for?" he asked.* (Why should I wear a hat?) Compare HOW COME.

what for[2] *n. phr., informal* A scolding, or other punishment.—Usually used with *get* or *give. Tom got what for from his father for answering him rudely, and I heard him crying in the house.* (Tom got a spanking.) *The teacher gave me what for because I was late.* (The teacher gave me a strong scolding.)

what have you *or* **what not** *n. phr., informal* Whatever you like or want; anything else like that. *The store sells big ones, small ones, medium ones, or what have you.* (The store sells any size you want.) *We found suits, coats, hats and what not in the closet.* (We found suits, coats, hats, and other clothing in the closet.) Syn. AND SO FORTH.

what if What would, or will, happen if, what is the difference if, suppose that. *What if you go instead of me?* (What would happen if you went in my place?) *What if we paint it red. How will it look?* (If we paint it red, how will it look?) *"You can't go now,"* said mother. *"What if I do?" Dick asked.* (What's the difference, or what do you care, if I do?) *What if Jack scores a touchdown?* (Just suppose that Jack scores a touchdown.)

what is what See WHAT'S WHAT.

what of it *or* **what about it** *interj., informal* What is wrong with it; what do you care. *Martha said, "That boy is wearing a green coat." Jan answered, "What of it?"* (What is wrong with a green coat?) *"John missed the bus." "What of it?"* (What do you care?) Syn. SO WHAT.

what not See WHAT HAVE YOU.

what's cooking See WHAT'S UP.

what's doing See WHAT'S UP *also* WHAT'S DOING.

what's the big idea *or* **what's the idea** *informal* What is the purpose; what do you have in mind; why did you do that; what are you doing; how dare you.—Often used to question someone or something that is not welcome. *The Smith family painted their house red, white, and blue. What's the big idea?* (What was the reason for doing that?) *What's the idea of coming in here after I told you not to?* (How dare you come in here again?) *I heard you are spreading false rumors about me, what's the big idea?* (Why are you spreading rumors about me?)

what's the idea See WHAT'S THE BIG IDEA.

what's up *or* **what's cooking** *also* **what's doing** *slang* What is happening or planned; what is wrong.—Often used as a greeting. *"What's up?" asked Bob as he joined his friends. "Are you going to the movies?"* (What are you going to do?) *What's cooking? Why is the crowd in the street?* (What is happening that so many people are in the street?) *What's doing tonight at the club?* (What is planned?) *Hello Bob, what's up?* (How are you and what are you doing?) Compare WHAT'S WITH.

what's what *or* **what is what** *n. phr., informal* **1** What each thing is in a group; one thing from another. *The weeds and the flowers are coming up together, and we can't tell what is what.* (We can't tell what plants are weeds and what plants are flowers.) **2** All that needs to be known about something; the important facts or skills. *Richard did the wrong thing, because he is new here and doesn't yet know what's what.* (Richard doesn't yet know what we do and how we do it and who is in charge.) *When Bob started his new job, it took him several weeks to learn what was what.* (He was new on the job and it took him a few weeks to learn about it.) *When it comes to cooking, Jenny knows what's what.* (Jenny knows all about cooking.) *Harold began to tell the teacher how to teach the class, and the teacher told him what was what.* (The teacher told Harold the important factors about who was boss in the classroom.) Compare WHICH IS, WHICH, WHO'S WHO.

what's with *or* **what's up with** *also* **what's by** *slang* What is happening to; what is wrong; how is everything; what can you tell me about. *Mary looks worried. What's with her?* (What's wrong with her?) *What's with our old friends?* (What are our old friends doing?) *I'm fine. What's with you?* (I'm fine. How are you?)

what with *prep.* Because; as a result of. *I couldn't visit you, what with the snowstorm and the cold I had.* (I couldn't visit you because there was a snowstorm and I had a cold.) *What with dishes to wash and children to put to bed, mother was late to the meeting.* (Because she had much to do, mother was late.) Compare ON ACCOUNT OF.

wheel See BIG CHEESE *or* BIG WHEEL, GREASE THE WHEELS, PUT ONE'S SHOULDER TO THE WHEEL.

wheel and deal *v. phr., slang* To make many big plans or schemes; especially with important people in government and business; in matters of money and influence; handle money or power for your own advantage; plan important matters in a smart or skillful way and sometimes in a tricky, or not strictly honest way.—A cliché. *Mr. Smith made a fortune by wheeling and dealing on the stock market.* (Mr. Smith invested his money cleverly on the stock market and became rich.) *The senator got this law passed by wheeling and dealing in Congress.* (He made plans and arrangements with other people to pass the law in Congress.)—**wheeler-dealer** *n. phr., slang* A person with power and control. *The biggest wheeler-dealer in the state has many friends in high places in business and government and is a rich man himself.* (The man has much money and power, and can influence much that happens in the business and government of the state.)

when hell freezes over *adv. phr., slang* Never. *I'll believe you when hell freezes over.* (I will never believe you.) Contrast UNTIL HELL FREEZES OVER.

when it comes to See COME TO 4.

when one's ship comes in See SHIP COME IN.

when the chips are down *adv. cl., informal* When the winner and loser of a bet or a game are decided; at the most important or dangerous time.—A cliché. *Tom hit a home run in the last inning of the game when the chips were down.* (Tom hit a home run at the most important time and decided the game.) *When the chips were down, the two countries decided not to have war.* (When there was the greatest danger of war, the countries decided not to start a war.) [From the facts that in gambling games, a person puts chips or money down in front of him to show that he is willing to risk an amount in a bet.]

where See TELL ——— WHERE TO GET OFF *or* TELL ——— WHERE TO HEAD IN.

wherefore See WHY AND WHEREFORE.

where it's at *adv. phr., informal* That which is important; that which is at the forefront of on-going social, personal, or scientific undertakings. *Young, talented and black, that's where it's at.* (The future and the 'action' belong to those who are young, talented and black.) *We send sophisticated machines to Mars instead of people; that's where it's at.* (The important thing is to send sophisticated machinery rather than people to Mars.)

where the shoe pinches *n. phr., informal* Where or what the discomfort or trouble is. —A cliché. *Johnny thinks the job is easy, but he will find out where the shoe pinches when he tries it.* (He will learn by experience that the job isn't easy.) *The coach said he wasn't worried about any position except quarterback; that was where the shoe pinched.* (His trouble was that he didn't have an experienced quarterback.)

whether one is coming or going See KNOW IF ONE IS COMING OR GOING.

whether ——— or *or* **whether ——— or whether 1** *coord. conj.* Used to introduce an indirect question. *You must decide whether you should go or stay.* (You must answer the question: Shall I go or stay?) *I don't know whether Jack or Bill is a better player.* (I don't know which boy is a better player.) Compare EITHER ——— OR **2**—Used to show a choice of things, or that different things are possible. *Whether the bicycle was blue or red, it didn't matter to Frank.* (Frank didn't care if it was a blue or a red bicycle.)

which See GAME AT WHICH TWO CAN PLAY.

which is which *n. phr.* Which is one person or thing and which is the other; one from another; what the difference is between different ones; what the name of each one is. *Joe's coat and mine are so nearly alike that I can't tell which is which.* (Our coats are so nearly alike that I can't tell which one is mine and which one is Joe's.) *Mr. Hadley hadn't seen his friend's daughters in such a long time that he couldn't remember which was which.* (He hadn't seen the girls in a long time, and he couldn't remember which one was Sally and which one was Jane.) Compare WHAT'S WHAT, WHO'S WHO.

which was which See WHICH IS WHICH.

while See AFTER A WHILE *or* IN A WHILE, ALL THE TIME 1, EVERY NOW AND THEN *or* EVERY ONCE IN A WHILE, ONCE IN A WHILE.

while ago *adv.* At a time several minutes in the past; a few minutes ago; a short time ago.—Used with *a*. *I laid my glasses on this table a while ago, and now they're gone.* (I put my glasses on this table only a short time ago, and they have already been taken away.) *A while ago, Mary was tired and wanted to go home; now she's dancing with Bob as if she could dance all, night.* (A few minutes ago, Mary felt very tired; now she feels like dancing.) Compare JUST NOW 2.

while away *v.* To make time go by pleasantly or without being bored; pass or spend. *We whiled away the time that we were waiting by talking and playing cards.* (We spent the time pleasantly.) *We whiled away the summer swimming and fishing.* (We used our time this summer for swimming and fishing.)

while back *adv.* At a time several weeks or months in the past.—Used with *a*. *We had a good rain a while back, but we need more now.* (We had rain several weeks ago.) *Grandfather is well now, but a while back he was in the hospital for three weeks.* (Several months ago Grandfather was sick for three weeks.)

whip See CRACK THE WHIP.

whip hand See UPPER HAND.

whip up *v., informal* **1** To make or do quickly or easily. *Mary whipped up a lunch for the picnic.* (She prepared the lunch quickly.) *The reporter whipped up a story about the fire for his paper.* (He wrote the story fast and easily.) **2** To make active; stir to action; excite. *The girls are trying to whip up interest for a dance Saturday night.* (The girls are trying to interest the boys in having a dance.) Compare STIR UP, WHOOP IT UP 2.

whispering campaign *n.* The spreading of false rumors, or saying bad things, about a person or group, especially in politics or public life. *A bad man has started a whispering campaign against the mayor, saying that he isn't honest.* (The bad man has told lies about the mayor because he doesn't like him or because he wants a new mayor.)

whistle See BLOW THE WHISTLE ON, WET ONE'S WHISTLE.

whistle a different tune See SING A DIFFERENT TUNE.

whistle for *v., informal* To try to get (something) but fail; look for (something) that will not come.—A cliché. *Mary didn't even thank us for helping her, so the next time she needs help she can whistle for it.* (The next time, she can ask us but we won't help.)

389 wild pitch

whistle in the dark *v. phr., informal* —A cliché. To try to stay brave and forget your fear. *Tom said he could fight the bully with one hand, but we knew that he was just whistling in the dark.* (We knew that he was really scared, and trying to keep up his courage by bragging.) [From the fact that people sometimes whistle when walking in a dark, scary place to keep up their courage.]

white See BLACK AND WHITE, IN BLACK AND WHITE.

white around the gills See GREEN AROUND THE GILLS.

white sale *n.* The selling, especially at lower prices, of goods or clothing usually made of white cloth. *Mother always buys many things at the January white sale to save money.* (By buying sheets, towels, and other white goods at a sale, she doesn't have to buy them at higher prices later.)

whitewash *n., informal* A soothing official report that attempts to tranquilize the public. *Some people believe that the Warren Commission's report on the Kennedy assassination was a whitewash.* (Some people think that the Warren Commission's report is a document meant to soothe the masses.)

whitewash something *v., informal* To explain a major, national scandal in soothing official terms so as to assure the public that things are under control and there is no need to panic. *Many people in the United States believe that President Kennedy's assassination was whitewashed by the Warren Commission.* (Many people believe that the true facts weren't told and that the Commission's long report was meant to tranquilize the public.) See WHITEWASH, *n.*

whiz See GEE WHIZ.

who See SAYS WHO.

who is who See WHO'S WHO.

who laughs last laughs best See HE LAUGHS BEST WHO LAUGHS LAST.

whole See ALL THE WAY *or* THE WHOLE WAY, GO THE WHOLE HOG, ON THE WHOLE, WITH A WHOLE SKIN *or* IN A WHOLE SKIN.

whole cheese *slang or informal* **whole show** *n., informal* The only important person; big boss. *Joe thought he was the whole cheese in the game because he owned the ball.* (Joe owned the ball so he thought he could tell everyone else what to do.) *You're not the whole show just because you got all A's.* (You're not the only one who is important in school.) Compare BIG CHEESE.

whole hog See GO THE WHOLE HOG.

whole lot See A LOT.

whole show See WHOLE CHEESE.

whoop it up *v. phr., slang* **1** To make a loud noise; have a noisy celebration; enjoy yourself noisily. *The team whooped it up after winning the game.* (The team cheered and shouted happily.) **2** To praise something enthusiastically; encourage enthusiasm or support.—Often used with *for*. *Father wanted to go to the country, but the children whooped it up for the beach.* (The children enthusiastically tried to make Father go to the beach instead of the country.)

who's who *or* **who is who** *informal* **1** Who this one is and who that one is; who the different ones in a group of people are or what their names or positions are. *It is hard to tell who is who in the parade because everyone in the band looks alike.* (It is hard to tell if you know any of them.) *It took the new teacher a few days to remember who was who in the class.* (She could not remember the names and faces of everyone right away.) Compare WHICH IS WHICH. **2** Who the important people are. *John didn't recognize the champion on television. He doesn't know who is who in boxing.* (He doesn't know who the important people in boxing are.) *After about a year, Mr. Thompson had lived in this town long enough to know who was who.* (He had lived there long enough to know who the important people were.) Compare WHAT'S WHAT.

why and wherefore *n.* The answer to a question or problem;—A cliché; usually used in the plural. *Father told him not to always ask the whys and wherefores when he was told to do something.* (His father told him not to always ask why he had to do something, but to do it.)

wide See FAR AND WIDE, GIVE A WIDE BERTH.

wide-eyed See ROUND-EYED.

wide of the mark *adv. or adj. phr.* **1** Far from the target or the thing aimed at. *James threw a stone at the cat but it went wide of the mark.* (The stone didn't come near to hitting the cat.) **2** Far from the truth; incorrect. *You were wide of the mark when you said I did it, because Bill did it.* (You were not right at all.) Contrast HIT THE BULL'S-EYE, HIT THE NAIL ON THE HEAD.

widow See GOLF WIDOW.

wiener roast *or* **hot dog roast** *n.* A party where frankfurthers are cooked and eaten over an outdoor fire. *For his birthday party, John had a wiener roast in his back yard.* (John had a hot dog party for his birthday.) *Mary's Girl Scout troop had a hot dog roast on their overnight hike.* (The girls cooked frankfurthers outdoors.)

wig See BIG CHEESE *or* BIG WIG.

wild See RUN WILD, SOW ONE'S WILD OATS.

wild cat strike *n., informal* A strike not ordered by a labor union; a strike spontaneously arranged by a group of workers. *The garbage collectors have gone on a wild cat strike, but the union is going to stop it.* (They started a spontaneous strike, but the union will make them go back to work.)

wild pitch *n.* A pitch in baseball that is so high, so low, or so far from the plate that the catcher cannot catch it and a base runner can move to the next base. *The runner went to* *second base on a wild pitch.* (The runner went to second base when the pitcher threw the ball over the catcher's head.)

will See AT WILL, OF ONE'S OWN ACCORD *or* OF ONE'S OWN FREE WILL.

will not hear of *v. phr.* Will not allow or consider; refuse attention to or permission for. *I want to go to the show tonight, but I know my mother will not hear of it.* (I want to go to the show, but I know she will not let me.) *Mary needs another day to finish her book report, but the teacher won't hear of any delay.* (The teacher will not allow any delay.) *John's father told him he would not hear of his having a car.* (His father told John he wouldn't let him have a car.)

win See HEADS I WIN, TAILS YOU LOSE.

wind See GET WIND OF, GOD TEMPERS THE WIND TO THE SHORN LAMB, GONE WITH THE WIND, IN THE WIND, IT'S AN ILL WIND THAT BLOWS NOBODY GOOD, SECOND WIND, STRAW IN THE WIND, TAKE THE WIND OUT OF ONE'S SAILS, THREE SHEETS IN THE WIND *or* THREE SHEETS TO THE WIND, THROW CAUTION TO THE WIND, WAY THE WIND BLOWS *or* HOW THE WIND BLOWS.

window See GO OUT THE WINDOW.

wind up *v.* **1** To tighten the spring of a machine; to make it work or run. *Mary wound up the toy car and let it run across the room.* (She tightened the spring so the toy would run.) *He doesn't have to wind up his watch because it is run by a battery.* (He doesn't have to tighten the spring in his watch; it has no mainspring.) **2** To make very excited, nervous, upset.—Usually used in the past participle. *The excitement of her birthday party got Jane all wound up so she could not sleep.* (The party made her feel excited.) **3** *informal* To bring or come to an end; finish; stop. *John got two hits and wound his afternoon up with a home run.* (He made two base-hits and finished the game with a home run.) *Before Jim knew it, he had spent all his money and he wound up broke.* (He ended his trip to the big city with no money.) *The boys followed the path to the left and wound up where they started.* (The boys followed the path to the left, and ended where they started.) Syn. END UP. Compare FINISH OFF, TURN OUT 6. **4** To put (your business or personal affairs) in order; arrange; settle. *Fred wound up his business and personal affairs before joining the Navy.* (He got everything in order before going into the Navy.) **5** To swing your arm with the ball just before pitching to a batter. *The pitcher wound up quickly and then threw a curve.* (He swung his arm to throw the ball harder and faster.)

wing See CLIP ONE'S WINGS, LEFT-WING, ON THE WING, RIGHT-WING, UNDER ONE'S WING.

win in a walk *or* **win in a breeze** *v. phr., informal* To win very easily; win without having to try hard.—A cliché. *Joe ran for class president and won in a walk.* (No one else

was close to winning.) *Our team won the game in a breeze.* (They won very easily.) Compare HANDS DOWN.

wink See FORTY WINKS, SLEEP A WINK.

wink at *v.* To allow and pretend not to know about (a rule or law being broken). *John was not allowed to stay out late at night, but his parents winked at his being five minutes late.* (They kept quiet about his coming in only a little late.) *A judge should never wink at any law-breaking.* (A judge should never allow the law to be broken if he knows about it.)

winning streak *n.* A series of several wins one after the other. *The team extended their winning streak to ten.* (They won ten games one right after the other.)

win one's spurs *v. phr.* **1** In old times, to be named a knight with the right to wear little sharp spikes on your heels. *A young squire won his spurs in battle.* (He fought bravely and the king made him a knight.) **2** To win fame or honor.—A cliché. *The young lieutenant won his spurs by leading an attack on enemy machine guns.* (He won notice and honor by leading his men bravely.) *Edison won his spurs as an inventor while rather young.* (Edison was young when he first won fame and honor as an inventor.) *He has yet to win his spurs as a big league ball player.* (He is not famous yet.)

win out *v.* To be victorious or successful after hard work or difficulty; win or succeed; in the end. *Half way through the race Tom was last, but in the end he won out.* (Tom was far behind, but he ran hard and won the race.) *Jack won out over the giant because he was smarter than the giant.* (He finally beat the huge giant.) *Frank was a poor boy but he won out and became rich by hard work.* (He succeeded and made money.)

wipe out *v.* **1** To remove or erase by wiping or rubbing. *The teacher wiped out with an eraser what she had written on the board.* (The teacher erased what she had written.) Compare RUB OUT. **2** *informal* To remove, kill, or destroy completely. *The earthquake wiped out the town.* (The earthquake destroyed all of the town.) *Doctors are searching for a cure that will wipe out cancer.* (Doctors are hunting for a cure that will end all cancer.) *The Indians wiped out the soldiers who were sent to stop their attacks.* (The Indians killed all the soldiers.) Compare RUB OUT, STAMP OUT.

wipe out an old score See SETTLE A SCORE.

wipe the floor with *or* **wipe up the floor with** See MOP THE FLOOR WITH.

wire See ACROSS THE WIRE, DOWN TO THE WIRE, PULL STRINGS *or* PULL WIRES.

wise See GET WISE, PENNY WISE AND POUND FOOLISH, PUT WISE, THE WISER.

wise guy *n. phr., informal* A person who acts as if he were smarter than other people; a person who jokes or shows off too much.

Bill is a wise guy and displeases others by what he says. (Bill thinks he is very smart and says things he shouldn't.)

wise up to *v. phr., slang* To finally understand what is really going on after a period of ignorance. *Joe immediately quit his job when he wised up to what was really going on.* (As soon as he realized what was happening, he quit his job.)

wish on *v.* **1** To use as a lucky charm while making a wish. *Mary wished on a star that she could go to the dance.* (Mary wished that she could go to the dance and called on a star to make her wish come true.) *Bob wished on his lucky rabbit's foot that he could pass the test.* (Bob held his rabbit foot and wished.) **2** *or* **wish off on** *informal* To get rid of (something unwanted) by passing it on to someone else. *Martha did not like to do the dishes and wished the job on to her little sister.* (Martha got her little sister to wash the dishes so she didn't have to.) *Tom got a very ugly tie for his birthday and when Billy's birthday came, Tom wished the tie off on Billy.* (Tom gave the ugly tie to Billy as a birthday present because he did not want it.)

wit See AT ONE'S WITS' END, KEEP ONE'S HEAD *or* KEEP ONE'S WITS ABOUT ONE, SCARE OUT OF ONE'S WITS.

with a free hand See FREE HAND.

with a grain of salt *or* **with a pinch of salt** See TAKE WITH A GRAIN OF SALT.

with all one's heart See FROM THE BOTTOM OF ONE'S HEART.

with an eye to See EYE TO.

with a silver spoon in one's mouth See BORN WITH A SILVER SPOON IN ONE'S MOUTH.

with a whole skin *also* **in a whole skin** *adv. phr.* With no injury; unhurt; safely.—A trite expression. *The boy was lucky to escape with a whole skin when the car went off the road.* (He was not hurt in the accident.) *Jack came through the game with a whole skin.* (He was not hurt in the game.) *The horse threw him off, but he got away in a whole skin.* (He was not hurt when the horse threw him off.) Syn. SAFE AND SOUND.

with bad grace *or* **with a bad grace** *adv. phr.* In an unpleasant or discourteous way; unwillingly. *Fred takes defeat with bad grace.* (When Fred is beaten he accepts it angrily; he is not a good sport.) *Tom shouted "Hello" to Bill. Bill was in a sour mood and replied with a bad grace.* (Tom shouted "Hello," and Bill answered crossly.) Contrast WITH GOOD GRACE.

with bells on *adv. phr., informal* With enthusiasm; eager or ready and in the best of spirits for an event. *"Will you come to the farewell party I'm giving for Billy?" asked Jerry. "I'll be there with bells on," replied Ed.* (Ed said he would be there and all ready to enjoy it.)

with child *adv. phr., literary* Going to have a baby; pregnant. *The angel told Mary she was with child.* (The angel told Mary she was going to have a baby.) Compare IN A FAMILY WAY *or* IN THE FAMILY WAY.

wither on the vine See DIE ON THE VINE.

with fire See PLAY WITH FIRE.

with flying colors *adv. phr.* With great or total success; victoriously. *Tom finished the race with flying colors.* (Tom won the race way in front of the other runners.) *Mary came through the examination with flying colors.* (Mary did well in the examination.)

with good grace *adv. phr.* With pleasant and courteous behavior; politely; willingly; without complaining. *The boys had been well-coached; they took the loss of the game with good grace.* (They were not cross or impolite about the loss.) *The principal scolded Nora, who accepted his criticism with good grace.* (Nora did not talk back or get angry; she was polite about it.) Contrast WITH BAD GRACE.

with heart and soul See HEART AND SOUL.

within an ace of *informal or* **within an inch of** *adv. phr.* Almost but not quite; very close to; nearly. *Tim came within an ace of losing the election.* (Tim almost lost the election, but he did win.) *John was within an inch of drowning before he was pulled out of the water.* (John nearly drowned before he was rescued from the water.) Compare BY THE SKIN OF ONE'S TEETH.

within an inch of one's life *adv. phr.* Until you are almost dead; near to dying. *The bear clawed the hunter within an inch of his life.* (The bear clawed the hunter almost to death.)—Often used after *to*. *The prize fighter was beaten to within an inch of his life.* (The fighter was in danger of death.)

within bounds *adv. or adj. phr.* **1** Inside of the boundary lines in a game; on or inside of the playing field. *You must hit the ball inside the lines of the tennis court or it will not be within bounds.* (If the ball goes outside of the lines of the court, you will lose the point.) *If you kick the football over a sideline, it will not be in bounds.* (The ball will be off the playing field.) **2** Inside of a place where one is allowed to go or be. *The soldiers are within bounds on one side of the city, but are out of bounds on the other side.* (The soldiers are allowed to go into one side of the city, but not the other.) **3** Inside of safe or proper limits; allowable. *If you ask Father for a quarter, he might give it to you, but a dollar would not be within bounds.* (A dollar would be too much, and Father wouldn't allow you to have it.) *He succeeded in keeping his temper within bounds.* (He was angry but controlled himself.) Contrast OUT OF BOUNDS.

within call *adv. phr.* **1** *or* **within hail** Near enough to hear each other's voices. *When the two ships were within hail, their officers exchanged messages.* (When the ships were near enough, their officers talked to each other.) *Billy's mother told him to stay within call because supper was nearly ready.* (She told Billy to stay near enough to hear her when she called him to supper.) **2** In a place where you can be reached by phone, radio, or TV and be called. *The sick man was very low and the doctor stayed within call.* (He stayed where he could be called on the phone or by a messenger.) *The soldiers were allowed to leave the base by day, but had to stay within call.* (They had to stay in places where they could be called over the phone, radio, or TV if needed.)

within hail   See WITHIN CALL.

within reason   *adv. or adj. phr.* Within the limits of good sense; in reasonable control or check; moderate. *I want you to have a good time tonight, within reason.* (I want you to have a good time, but not to do anything foolish.) *If Tom wants to go to the fair, he must keep his expenses within reason.* (If Tom wants to go to the fair, he must spend only a reasonable amount of money.) *Jean's plans are quite within reason.* (Jean's plans are very sensible.)

with it   See GET WITH IT.

with might and main   *adv. phr.* With full strength or complete effort.—A cliché. *The sailors pulled the rope with might and main.* (The sailors pulled the rope with their full strength.) *John tried with all his might and main to solve the problem.* (John tried as hard as he could to solve the problem.)

with one's boots on   See DIE IN ONE'S BOOTS *or* DIE WITH ONE'S BOOTS ON.

with one's pants down   See CATCH ONE WITH ONE'S PANTS DOWN.

with open arms   *adv. phr.* **1** With the arms spread wide for hugging or catching. *When Father came home from work, little Sally ran out to meet him with open arms.* (Sally ran out ready to hug her father.) *Dick stood under the window with open arms, and Jean dropped the bag of laundry down to him.* (Dick stretched out his arms to catch the bag of laundry.) **2** With words or actions showing that you are glad to see someone; gladly, warmly, eagerly.—A cliché. *When Grandmother came to visit us at Christmas, we welcomed her with open arms.* (We were very happy that Grandmother had come and greeted her warmly.) *After his pioneering flight in the Friendship VII, Col. John Glenn was welcomed with open arms by the people of his home town.* (Col. Glenn's friends and neighbors turned out to welcome him warmly after his historic flight.)

without   See DO WITHOUT *or* GO WITHOUT, MAKE BRICKS WITHOUT STRAW, RECKON WITHOUT.

without a paddle   See UP THE CREEK *or* UP THE CREEK WITHOUT A PADDLE.

without batting an eye *or* **without batting an eyelash**   See BAT AN EYE.

without fail   *adv. phr.* Without failing to do it or failing in the doing of it; certainly, surely. *Be here at 8 o'clock sharp, without fail.* (Be sure to be here at exactly 8 o'clock. You must be here by then.) *Ben promised to return the bike at a certain time without fail.* (Ben promised to return the bike on time no matter what might happen.)

without number   See BEYOND NUMBER.

without rhyme or reason   See RHYME OR REASON.

with reference to   See IN REFERENCE TO.

with regard to   See IN REFERENCE TO.

with relation to   See IN RELATION TO.

with respect to   See IN RESPECT TO.

with the best *or* **with the best of them**   *adv. phr.* As well as anyone. *Bob could horseback ride with the best of them, but he never boasted about it.* (Bob never bragged about being a good horseback rider.) *John can bowl with the best of them.* (John is an excellent bowler.)

with the Joneses   See KEEP UP WITH THE JONESES.

wolf   See CRY WOLF, KEEP THE WOLF FROM THE DOOR, LONE WOLF, THROW TO THE WOLVES.

wolf in sheep's clothing   *n. phr.* A person who pretends to be good but really is bad.—A cliché. *Mrs. Martin trusted the lawyer until she realized that he was a wolf in sheep's clothing.* (She realized that he was really dangerous.) *Mr. Black was fooled by the salesman's manners until he showed that he was really a wolf in sheep's clothing, by selling Mr. Black a car that was falling apart.* (When the salesman cheated him, Mr. Black knew that his nice ways were just hiding his mean character.)

wonder   See NO WONDER *also* SMALL WONDER.

woo   See PITCH WOO.

wood   See CAN'T SEE THE WOOD FOR THE TREES, KNOCK ON WOOD, SAW WOOD.

woodpile   See NIGGER IN THE WOODPILE.

woods   See BABE IN THE WOODS, CROW BEFORE ONE IS OUT OF THE WOODS, NECK OF THE WOODS, TAKE TO THE WOODS.

wool   See ALL WOOL AND A YARD WIDE, PULL THE WOOL OVER ONE'S EYES.

word   See ACTIONS SPEAK LOUDER THAN WORDS, AS GOOD AS ONE'S WORD, BY WORD OF MOUTH, EAT ONE'S WORDS, FROM THE WORD "GO", GET A WORD IN, GET THE MESSAGE *or* GET THE WORD, HANG ON THE WORDS OF, IN BRIEF *or* IN A WORD, IN SO MANY WORDS, LAST WORD, MAN OF FEW WORDS, MAN OF HIS WORD, MUM IS THE WORD, PLAY ON WORDS, PUT WORDS INTO ONE'S MOUTH, SAY THE WORD, SWALLOW ONE'S WORDS, TAKE AT ONE'S WORD, TAKE THE WORDS OUT OF ONE'S MOUTH, WEASEL WORD, WEIGH ONE'S WORDS.

word for word   *adv. phr.* In exactly the same words. *Mary copied Sally's composition word for word.* (Mary and Sally's compositions were exactly the same. *Mary copied every word of Sally's story.) Joan repeated the conversation word for word.* (Joan told exactly what everyone had said.) *She learned the poem many years ago but she recited it word for word.* (She remembered every word of the poem.)

words of one syllable *n. phr.* Language that makes the meaning very clear; simple, or frank language.—Usually used after *in. Mary explained the job to Ann in words of one syllable so that she would be sure to understand.* (Mary spoke in very simple language.) *Some people say that John is cute and mischievous, but in words of one syllable, he's just a brat.* (If you want to be honest, you have to call John a brat.) Compare IN SO MANY WORDS, SPELL OUT.

work See. ALL IN A DAY'S WORK, ALL WORK AND NO PLAY MAKES JACK A DULL BOY, AT WORK, BUSY WORK, IN THE WORKS, MAKE SHORT WORK OF, MANY HANDS MAKE LIGHT WORK, SHOOT THE WORKS, THE WORKS, IN THE WORKS.

work cut out See CUT OUT² *adj.* 1.

worked up *also* **wrought up** *adj., literary* Feeling strongly; excited; angry; worried. *Mary was all worked up about the exam.* (Mary was worried and nervous.) *John got worked up when they blamed him for losing the game.* (John was angry and troubled.) Compare ON EDGE.

work in *v.* **1** To rub in. *The nurse told Mary to put some cream on her skin and to work it in gently with her fingers.* (The nurse told Mary to rub some cream on her skin.) **2** To slip in; mix in; put in. *When Mary was planning the show, she worked a part in for her friend Susan.* (Mary included Susan in the show.)

working girl *n., slang* **1** (*vulgar, avoidable*) A prostitute. *I didn't know Roxanne was a working girl.* (I didn't know Roxanne was a prostitute.) **2** A girl, usually single, who supports herself by working in an honest job, such as in an office, etc. *The average working girl can't afford such a fancy car.* (A self-supporting young woman earning an office salary cannot pay for such an expensive car.)

work into *v.* **1** Force into little by little. *John worked his foot into the boot by pushing and pulling.* (John forced his foot into the boot.) **2** Put into; mix into. *Mary worked some blue into the rug she was weaving.* (Mary mixed blue into the color pattern of the rug.)

work off *v.* To make (something) go away, especially by working. *John worked off the fat around his waist by doing exercise every morning.* (John got rid of some extra weight.) *Mr. Smith worked off his anger by chopping wood.* (Mr. Smith made his angry feelings go away by keeping himself busy with hard physical work.)

work on *also* **work upon** *v.* **1** Have an effect on; influence. *Some pills work on the*

nerves and make people feel more relaxed. (Some pills cause the nerves to relax.) **2** To try to influence or convince. *Senator Smith worked on the other committee members to vote for the bill.* (Senator Smith tried to convince the others to vote for the bill.)

work one's fingers to the bone *v. phr.* To work very hard.—A cliché. *Mary and John worked their fingers to the bone to get the house ready for the party.* (They worked very hard so that the house would be ready on time.) *Mr. Brown worked his fingers to the bone to make enough money to buy a new car.* (He worked very hard.)

work out *v.* **1** To find an answer to. *John worked out his math problems all by himself.* (John solved his problems without help.) *Mary had trouble getting along with her room mate, but they worked it out.* (Mary and her room mate found a way to live together without fighting.) Compare FIGURE OUT. **2** To plan; develop. *Mary worked out a beautiful design for a sweater.* (Mary designed a plan for making a sweater.) *Alice worked out a new hair-do.* (Alice developed a new hairstyle.) **3** To accomplish; arrange. *The engineers worked out a system for getting electricity to the factory.* (They arranged it so that the factory would have electricity.) **4** To be efficient; get results. *If the traffic plan works out, it will be used in other cities too.* (If the plan does what it is supposed to, other people will use it too.) **5** To exercise. *John works out in the gym two hours every day.* (John does exercises.)

work over *v. phr., slang* To beat someone up very roughly in order to intimidate him or extort payment, etc. *Matthew was worked over by the hoodlums in the park right after midnight.* (He was beaten up very badly.)

work up *v.* **1** To stir up; arouse; excite. *I can't work up any interest in this book.* (I can't make myself be interested in this book.) *He worked up a sweat weeding the garden.* (The work in the garden made him sweat.) **2** To develop; originate. *He worked up an interesting plot for a play.* (He made up a good story.)

work upon See WORK ON.

world See COME UP IN THE WORLD *or* RISE IN THE WORLD, DEAD TO THE WORLD, FOR ALL THE WORLD, IN A WORLD OF ONE'S OWN *or* IN A WORLD BY ONESELF, IN THE WORLD, LOOK AT THE WORLD THROUGH ROSE-COLORED GLASSES, NOT FOR THE WORLD, ON TOP OF THE WORLD *or* SITTING ON TOP OF THE WORLD, OUT OF THIS WORLD, SET THE WORLD ON FIRE, THIRD WORLD.

world is one's oyster Everything is possible for you; the world belongs to you; you can get anything you want.—A cliché. *When John won the scholarship, he felt as though the world was his oyster.* (John felt as though he had won the whole world for himself.)

The rich girl acts as though the world is her oyster. (She acts as though she could have anything she wanted.)

world on one's shoulders See WEIGHT OF THE WORLD ON ONE'S SHOULDERS.

world on one's back See WEIGHT OF THE WORLD ON ONE'S SHOULDERS.

world without end *adv. phr., literary* Endlessly; forever; eternally. *Each human being has to die, but mankind goes on world without end.* (Life goes on forever.)

worm See EARLY BIRD CATCHES THE WORM *or* EARLY BIRD GETS THE WORM.

worse See BARK WORSE THAN ONE'S BITE, FOR BETTER OR WORSE *or* FOR BETTER OR FOR WORSE, FOR THE WORSE, GO FROM BAD TO WORSE.

worse for wear *adj. phr.* Not as good as new; worn out; damaged by use.—Used with *the. Her favorite tablecloth was beginning to look the worse for wear.* (It was getting worn out.)—Often used with *none* to mean: as good as new. *The doll was Mary's favorite toy but it was none the worse for wear.* (Mary played with the doll often but it was not worn out.)

worst See GET THE WORST OF *also* HAVE THE WORST OF, IF WORST COMES TO WORST.

worth See BIRD IN THE HAND IS WORTH TWO IN THE BUSH, FOR ALL ONE IS WORTH, GAME IS NOT WORTH THE CANDLE, NOT WORTH A TINKER'S DAMN, WORTH A CENT.

worth a cent *adj. phr.* Worth anything; of any value.—Used in negative, interrogative, and conditional sentences. *The book was old and it was not worth a cent.* (The book was old and hadn't any value.)

worth one's salt *adj. phr.* Being a good worker, or a productive person; worth what you cost.—A cliché. *Mr. Brown showed that he was worth his salt as a salesman when he got the highest sales record for the year.* (Mr. Brown earned his salary by getting more sales than any other salesman.)—Often used with *not* or *hardly. When the basketball team did so poorly, people felt that the coach was hardly worth his salt.* (The coach did not do a good job with the team.) Compare PAY ONE'S WAY 2.

would that *or* **I would that** *or* **would God** *or* **would heaven** *literary* I wish that.—Used at the beginning of a sentence expressing a wish; followed by a verb in the subjunctive; found mostly in poetry and older literature. *Would that I could only drop everything and join you.* (I wish that I were free to go with you.) *Would that my mother were alive to see me married.* (I wish that my mother were still living so that she could come to my wedding.) Syn. IF ONLY.

wrack See GO TO WRACK AND RUIN.

wrap See UNDER WRAPS.

wrap ——— around one's finger See TWIST ——— AROUND ONE'S LITTLE FINGER.

wrapped up in *adj. phr.* Thinking only of; interested only in. *John has no time for sports because he is all wrapped up in his work.* (John is so busy in his work that he has no time for play.) *Mary was so wrapped up in her book, she didn't hear her mother calling her.* (Mary was very much interested in her book.) *Jean is so wrapped up in herself, she never thinks of helping others.* (Jean thinks only of herself.) *Mrs. Brown gave up her career because her life was all wrapped up in her children.* (Everything Mrs. Brown did was for her children.) Compare IN A WORLD OF ONE'S OWN 2b.

wrap up *or* **bundle up** *v. phr.* **1** To put on warm clothes; dress warmly. *Mother told Mary to wrap up before going out into the cold.* (Mother told Mary to put on warm clothing.) **2** *informal* To finish (a job). *Let's wrap up the job and go home.* (Let's finish.) **3** *informal* To win a game. *The Mets wrapped up the baseball game in the seventh inning.* (They really won the game in the seventh inning.)

wrench See THROW A MONKEY WRENCH.

wringing wet *adj.* Wet through and through; soaked; dripping. *He was wringing wet because he was caught in the rain without an umbrella.* (His clothes were all wet from the rain.) *He was wringing wet after working in the fields in the hot sun.* (He was wet with perspiration.)

write home about *v. phr.* To become especially enthusiastic or excited about; boast about.—A cliché; often used after *to. Mary's trip to the World's Fair was something to write home about.* (She had a very exciting time and saw many new and interesting things.) *Joe did a good enough job of painting but it was nothing to write home about.* (Joe's painting was fair but nothing to boast about.) *"That was a dinner worth writing home about!" said Bill, coming out of the restaurant.* (That was really a good dinner!)

write off *v. phr.* **1** To remove (an amount) from a business record; cancel (a debt); accept as a loss. *If a customer dies when he owes the store money, the store must often write it off.* (The store must cancel the debt since the man is dead and can't pay what he owes.) Compare CHARGE OFF. **2** To accept (a loss or trouble) and not worry any more about it; forget. *Mr. Brown had so much trouble with the new TV set that he finally wrote it off and bought a new one.* (Mr. Brown realized that the TV set was no good and that he had lost the money he paid for it.) *Jim's mistake cost him time and money, but he wrote it off to experience.* (He accepted losing the time and money as an experience that taught him something.) Compare CHARGE OFF 2. Contrast CHALK UP 2. To say that (something) will fail or not be good; believe worthless. *Just because the boys on the team are young, don't write the team off.* (Don't think the team is not good, or too young to play well.) Compare COUNT OUT.

writer's cramp *n.* Pain in the fingers or hand caused by too much writing. *Holding your pencil too tightly for too long often gives you writer's cramp.* (If you write a great deal and hold the pencil too hard, your hand may ache.)—Often used humorously to stress the idea that you have been doing a lot of writing. *By the time Mary finished her Christmas cards she complained of writer's cramp.* (Mary pretended that she had so many cards to write that her hand ached from doing it.)

write-up *n.* A report or story in a newspaper or magazine. *There was a write-up of the accident in the newspaper.* (The accident was reported in the newspaper.) *I read an interesting write-up about the President in a new magazine.* (I read an interesting article.)

write up *v.* **1** To write the story of; describe in writing; give a full account of. *Reporters from many newspapers are here to write up the game.* (Reporters will write all about the game for their newspapers.) *The magazine is writing up the life of the President.* (The magazine is telling the story of the President's life.) **2** To put something thought or talked about into writing; finish writing (something). *John took notes of what the teacher said in class and he wrote them up when he got home.* (John wrote short notes so he could remember what the teacher said and write it all down later.) *The author had an idea for a story when he saw the old house, and he wrote it up later.* (He wrote a whole story from the idea he had when he saw the house.)

wrong See BARK UP THE WRONG TREE, BET ON THE WRONG HORSE, GET OFF ON THE WRONG FOOT, GET UP ON THE WRONG SIDE OF THE BED, IN THE WRONG, LAUGH ON THE WRONG SIDE OF ONE'S MOUTH, RUB THE WRONG WAY.

wrong side of the tracks See THE TRACKS.

wrought up See WORKED UP.

X

x-double minus *adj., slang, informal* Extremely poorly done, bad, inferior (said mostly about theatrical or musical performances). *Patsy gave an x-double minus performance at the audition and lost her chance for the lead role.* (Patsy gave an unusually bad performance and will not be selected for a role in the play.)

x-rated *adj., slang, informal* Pertaining to movies, magazines, and literature judged pornographic and therefore off limits for minors. *My son celebrated his 21st birthday by going to an x-rated movie.* (My son celebrated his birthday by going to a pornographic movie reserved for those over 21.)

x-raying machine *n., slang, citizen's band radio jargon* Speed detection device by radar used by the police. *The smokies are using the x-raying machine under the bridge!* (There is a police radar unit under the bridge.)

Y

yak-yak or **yakety-yak** or **yakity-yak** *n., slang* Much talk about little things; talking all the time about unimportant things. *Tom sat behind two girls on the bus, and he got tired of their silly yak-yak.* (The two girls talked all the time about silly things and Tom got tired of it.)

year See ALONG IN YEARS or ON IN YEARS.

year in, year out See DAY IN AND DAY OUT.

year-round or **year-around** *adj.* Usable, effective, or operating all the year. *In New England an outdoor pool can be used only in the summer but an indoor pool makes swimming a year-round sport.* (An indoor swimming pool can be used all year.) *Colorado is a year-around resort; there is fishing in the summer and skiing in the winter.* (People visit Colorado both in summer and in winter.)

yellow around the gills See GREEN AROUND THE GILLS.

yellow-bellied *adj., slang* Extremely timid, cowardly. *Joe Bennett is a yellow-bellied guy, don't send him on such a tough assignment!* (He is too timid and cowardly to handle such a difficult job.)

yes-man *n., informal* A person who tries to be liked by agreeing with everything said; especially, someone who always agrees with a boss or the one in charge. *John tries to get ahead on his job by being a yes-man.* (He agrees with everyone because he wants everyone to like him.) *Nobody respects the boss's helper because he is just a yes-man.* (He always agrees with his boss and never says what he really thinks.)

yesterday See BORN YESTERDAY.

yon See HITHER AND THITHER or HITHER AND YON.

yoo-hoo *interj.* —Used as an informal call or shout to a person to attract his attention. *Louise opened the door and called, "Yoo-hoo, Mother—are you home?"*

you See ALL RIGHT FOR YOU, I'M TELLING YOU, SAYS WHO or SAYS YOU, THAT'S ——— FOR YOU, WHAT HAVE YOU.

you bet or **you bet your boots** or **you bet your life** *informal* Most certainly; yes, indeed; without any doubt.—Used to declare with emphasis that a thing is really so. *Do I like to ski? You bet your life I do.* (I like to ski very much.) *You bet I will be at the party.* (I will surely be there.) *You can bet your boots that Johnny will come home when his money is gone.* (You can be sure.) Compare BET ONE'S BOTTOM DOLLAR.

you can say that again See YOU SAID IT.

you don't say *interj., informal* —Used to show surprise at what is said. *Your ring is a real diamond? You don't say!* (Although I know you are telling the truth, I am surprised.) *"Bill and Jean are going to get married." "You don't say!"* (I am surprised to hear it.) Syn. DO TELL.

your See HANG ON TO YOUR HAT or HOLD ON TO YOUR HAT or HOLD YOUR HAT, YOU BET YOUR BOOTS or YOU BET YOUR LIFE.

you're telling me *interj., informal* —Used to show that a thing is so clear that it need not be said, or just to show strong agreement. *"You're late." "You're telling me!"* (I know very well that I'm late. You don't have to tell me.) Compare YOU BET, YOU SAID IT.

you said it or (a cliché) **you can say that again** *interj., slang* —Used to show strong agreement with what another person has said. *"That sure was a good show." "You said it!"* (I agree with you wholeheartedly when you say that was a good show.) *"It sure is hot!" "You can say that again!"* (I agree perfectly that it is really hot!) Compare SAY A MOUTHFUL.

you tell 'em *interj., slang* —Used to agree with or encourage someone in what he is saying.—A cliché. *The drunk was arguing with the bartenders and a man cried, "You tell 'em!"* (He wanted the drunk to keep on arguing.) *The speaker said his party would win the election and the crowd shouted, "You tell 'em!"* (The crowd agreed with the speaker.)

yum-yum *interj., informal* —Used usually by or to children, to express great delight, especially in the taste of food. *"Yum-Yum! That pie is good!"* (That pie tastes very good.)

Z

zero hour *n.* **1** The exact time when an attack or other military action is supposed to start. *Zero hour for the bombers to take off was midnight.* (The air force planned to have the bombers leave exactly at midnight.) **2** The time when an important decision or change is supposed to come; the time for a dangerous action. *It was zero hour and the doctor began the operation on the man.* (It was the dangerous time for the man.) *On the day of the championship game, as the zero hour came near, the players grew nervous.* (As the time for the important game came near, the players were nervous.)

zero in on *v.* **1** To adjust a gun so that it will exactly hit (a target); aim at. *Big guns were zeroed in on the enemy fort.* (The big guns were aimed exactly to hit the fort.) *American missiles have been zeroed in on certain targets, to be fired if necessary.* (American missiles have aimed at and are ready to hit certain marks.) **2** *slang* To give your full attention to. *The Senate zeroed in on the Latin-American problems.* (The Senate gave its full attention to matters connected with South and Central America.) *Let's zero in on grammar tonight.* (Let's really study our grammar lessons tonight.)

zip one's lip See BUTTON ONE'S LIP.

zone defense *n.* A defense in a sport (as basketball or football) in which each player has to defend a certain area. *The coach taught his team a zone defense because he thought his players weren't fast enough to defend against individual opponents.* (Instead of telling each of his players to defend against one particular player on the other team, the coach taught his players to defend a certain part of the basketball floor.)

zonk out *v. phr., slang* **1** To fall asleep very quickly. *Can I talk to Joe?—Call back tomorrow, he zonked out.* (He fell asleep.) **2** To pass out from fatigue, or alcohol. *You won't get a coherent word out of Joe, he has zonked out.* (He has collapsed and is unconscious.)

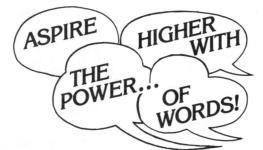